BMDP Statistical Software

1983 Printing with Additions

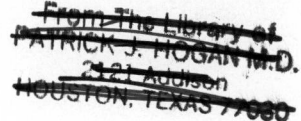

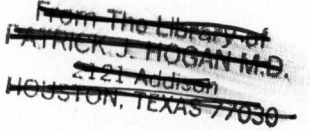

```
┌──────────── SUGGESTIONS FOR USING THIS MANUAL ────────────┐
│                                                            │
│          CHAPTER 1 (Section 1.1) contains a guide to the   │
│          entire manual.                                    │
│                                                            │
│                                                            │
│   If you                                                   │
│                                                            │
│     ● have not used computers before, start with Chapters 1 and 3. │
│                                                            │
│     ● are unfamiliar with the BMDP programs, read Chapters 1 and 2. │
│                                                            │
│     ● know the type of analysis you want to do, read Chapters 1 and 4, │
│       and then turn to the appropriate chapter (see Table of Contents). │
│                                                            │
│     ● have used BMDP programs before, read Chapter 4 and then turn to │
│       the appropriate analysis (see list of programs on the inside of │
│       the front cover).                                    │
│                                                            │
└────────────────────────────────────────────────────────────┘
```

```
┌──────────── CHANGES IN THIS REVISED REPRINT ────────────┐
│                                                          │
│   ● P3M -- Block Clustering has been entirely replaced with new │
│     documentation and output to reflect major program changes. │
│                                                          │
│   ● P1T -- Univariate and Bivariate Spectral Analysis has been │
│     substantially revised, with the addition of new output. │
│                                                          │
│   ● Chapters 4 and 6 contain several new sections documenting new │
│     common program options and abilities, such as extended trans- │
│     formation capabilities and the FOR % notation, which generates │
│     a number of similar instructions, paragraphs, or problems from │
│     a single one.                                        │
│                                                          │
│   ● Appendix F presents new features in P2R -- Stepwise Regression, │
│     the SAVE paragraph, P4V -- General Univariate and Multivariate │
│     Analysis of Variance and Covariance, and further examples of │
│     the features outlined in Chapters 4 and 6.           │
│                                                          │
│   ● Typographical corrections have been made throughout. │
│                                                          │
└──────────────────────────────────────────────────────────┘
```

BMDP Statistical Software

1983 Printing with Additions

W. J. Dixon, chief editor

M. B. Brown
L. Engelman
J. W. Frane
M. A. Hill
R. I. Jennrich
J. D. Toporek

UNIVERSITY OF CALIFORNIA PRESS

BERKELEY · LOS ANGELES · LONDON · 1983

This publication reports work sponsored in part under grant RR-3 and continuation contract number N01-RR-8-2107 of the Biotechnology Resources Branch of the National Institutes of Health. Reproduction in whole or in part is permitted for any purpose of the United States Government

The time series programs, 1T and 2T, were supported in part by National Science Foundation grant number CDP 80-20837.

Orders for this publication should be directed to

UNIVERSITY OF CALIFORNIA PRESS

2223 Fulton Street
Berkeley, California 94720
Telephone: (415) 642-6682
Telex: 33-5347

UNIVERSITY OF CALIFORNIA PRESS, LTD.

Ely House
37 Dover Street
London WIX 4HQ
ENGLAND
Telephone: 01-499-4688
Telex: 24224 Ref: 3545

Comments on programs or orders for copies of the
program should be addressed to
BMDP Statistical Software
as described in Appendix D.

Manufactured in the United States of America

Contents

Tables

Preface

This manual describes the capabilities and usage of the BMDP computer programs. These programs provide a wide variety of analytic capabilities that range from plots and simple data description to advanced statistical techniques. The first chapter outlines the organization of the manual and suggests how to use it.

This edition differs in many respects from earlier editions; therefore we recommend that you read Chapter One even if you are familiar with the previous editions.

The first BMD Biomedical Computer Programs manual appeared in 1961, and was followed by numerous editions. Each new edition included new programs with improved features, novel statistical techniques and more robust statistical algorithms. In 1968 we began to develop the English-based Control Language used with the BMDP programs described in this manual. This method of specifying instructions is more flexible than the fixed format used in the BMD programs. In addition, repeated analyses of the same data, or similar analyses of multiple sets of data, can be done by stating a minimum number of Control Language instructions.

In this edition we attempt to integrate an extensive discussion of most program features with examples of how they are used. There are numerous input/output examples, many of which are annotated. Our emphasis is on the use of the statistical techniques and not on the numerical results obtained -- therefore we explain the terms used in the results, but do not repeat the numerical answers in the discussion of the results.

The manual is written for new users of computer programs as well as for experienced statisticians. Chapter One gives an outline of the entire manual and a guide to its use. Chapter Two describes the scope of analytical techniques available, basic terminology and a short description of each program. In chapters four through seven we discuss the specifications common to many programs and explain how they are specified in Control Language. Chapters eight through twenty are devoted to the individual programs. The programs are discussed in relation to the analyses they perform. Each program is extensively illustrated by annotated input/output examples. Difficult formulas and computational algorithms are provided in an appendix.

New chapters are written by the designated authors. Revisions of material appearing in previous editions were done primarily by James Frane, MaryAnn Hill and W.J. Dixon. This process was simplified by the expert editing provided by Morton Brown who edited the previous edition.

This revision could not have been completed without the support of many BMDP staff members. In addition to those mentioned elsewhere, we wish to acknowledge the assistance of Noel Wheeler, Linda Moody, and Peter Mundle.

Ellen Sommers tested and retested the programs to document how the options work and prepared the examples in this manual.

Throughout Janice Gammell provided expert technical editing, improved phrasing, organization and attention to detail. Ching Liu and Avis Williams expertly typed the many drafts of the manuscript and prepared the camera-ready copy. The text in this manual was produced with the aid of a text-editing program produced by the Clinical Evaluation Unit of the Brentwood Veterans Administration Medical Center under the direction of Michael Beyer. Layout was done by Barbara Widawski. The revised reprint was supervised by Pat Britt, and edited by Melonia Musser-Brauner, assisted by Darlene Hescox.

Appendix D contains information on ordering the programs and the computers on which they are available. Although the programs have been under test and development for some time we know difficulties may arise in their use; these difficulties should be reported to us as described in Appendix D. Your comments and criticisms about the programs and this manual will also be appreciated.

In the first edition of the manual, 26 programs were described. The 1979 edition contained 36. This edition contains 42 programs. The development of new programs and revision of those previously released is an ongoing project, with new options continually being added. New programs in this manual are:

BMDP4F – Two-way and Multiway Frequency Table Analysis - includes all essential features of the older BMDP1F, BMDP2F, & BMDP3F programs and adds new features for screening log-log-linear models. Models can be selected in a stepwise manner. Structural zeros are permitted for both two-way and multiway tables. Cells or strata whose frequencies deviate from the expected frequencies under a proposed model can be identified in a stepwise manner.

BMDP2L - Cox Models for Survival Analysis - analyzes Cox style proportional hazards survival analysis models with covariates. There can be both time-independent and time-dependent covariates. Models can be selected in a stepwise manner by either exact maximum likelihood or by an efficient approximation using partial derivatives. Several plots can be selected to accompany the results.

BMDP1T - Spectral Analysis - performs spectral analysis. Control Language is a series of brief commands to allow easy interactive use. Features include estimation of spectral densities, coherences, variable vs. time plots, lagged scatter plots, and complex demodulation plots. Attention is given to missing values, removal of seasonal means and linear trends and the use of several kinds of filters.

BMDP2T - Interactive Box-Jenkins Analysis, Including Transfer Functions - deals with a general class of time series models that includes ARIMA, intervention, and transfer function components. For the ARIMA component, it allows any number of autoregressive and moving-average factors and each factor may have any number of parameters of any order of lags. Intervention and transfer function components also have dynamic structure similar to the ARIMA components. Plots include individual and multiple time series, autocorrelation, partial autocorrelation and cross correlation functions. Control Language is designed for interactive and batch use. Output is adjusted to the width of a computer terminal and can be performed in a series of steps guided by the user.

BMDP4V - Univariate and Multivariate Analysis of Variance and Covariance, Including Repeated Measures and Cell Weights - expands the analysis of variance capabilities of the older BMDP2V. (It was originally developed as URWAS, the University of Rochester Weighted ANOVA System.) Some of its new features include Greenhouse-Geisser and Huynh-Feldt adjustments to the univariate approach to repeated measures; univariate and multivariate approaches to repeated measures; covariates for both fixed effects and repeated measures; user defined cell weights (cell importance) for hypotheses tested; interactive analysis of submodels; and orthogonalization of effects under user control in order to yield various types of sums of squares for unbalanced designs.

BMDP8M - Boolean (Binary Data) Factor Analysis - performs a factor analysis of dichotomous (binary) data. The analysis in this program differs from that of classical factor analysis (see P4M) based on binary data even though the goal and model (symbolically) appear similar. The goal is to express p variables by m factors where m is considerably smaller than p.

The arithmetic used in the matrix multiplication is Boolean, so the scores and loadings are binary.

A case has a score of one if it has a positive response for any of the variables dominant in the factor (those not having zero loadings) and zero otherwise. The program has been found useful in serological and other studies.

BMDP9M - Linear Scores from Preference Pairs - constructs for each case a score that is a linear combination of the variables where the coefficients are based on the judgments (preferences) of experts. The expert compares cases two at a time, stating which of the pair he prefers. The analysis weights the observed variables to best replicate the preference of the judge (whatever subjective or objective information he may use). The expert need not judge all possible pairs of cases.

The score is determined in a stepwise manner weighting the variables by their importance to the expert. Preferences from more than one expert can be analyzed.

Other New Features

Other modules added since the 1977 edition are:

BMDPKM - K-means Cluster Analysis
BMDPLR - Stepwise Logistic Regression
BMDP8V - Mixed-model Anova, Equal Cell Sizes

Important modifications have been made to several programs:

BMDP1D - Option for file sorting
BMDP2D - Option for stem and leaf display
BMDP3D - Robust option for t statistics
BMDP6D - Multiple pairs of variables in bivariate plots permitted
BMDP7D - Capacity to handle more groups in side-by-side histograms, plot of cell means vs. standard deviations
BMDP8D - Completely rewritten with a much more efficient algorithm for computing correlations from incomplete data
BMDP2M - Option for single linkage and related case clustering
BMDPAM - Maximum likelihood estimation of covariance matrices from incomplete data, display of pattern of occurrence of missing values after clustering pattern of missingness by rows and columns
BMDP3R - Specification of function and derivatives for nonlinear regression through BMDP Control Language rather than FORTRAN
BMDPAR - Specification of function for derivative-free nonlinear regression through BMDP Control Language rather than FORTRAN, modifications to permit pharmacokinetic models defined by differential equations
BMDP2V - Cell mean vs. cell standard deviation plot, Greenhouse-Geisser and Huynh-Feldt adjustments to degrees of freedom for repeated measures

Features added to all BMDP modules include:

- Character handling through the transformation processor, e.g., conversion of alphabetic codes to numeric codes
- Easier specification of category codes and names
- Free-format data reader
- Fortran variable format data reading replaced by conversion within BMDP of card images to numbers for enhanced diagnostics and permitting blanks as missing value codes for all computer systems
- Codebook interpretation of input format
- Dynamic storage mechanism to allow easy specification of very large analyses
- CPU usage report, date and time report
- Increased control over output, e.g., for interactive execution
- Output of data files in binary, F, and G format
- Printing of problem title at top of each page
- Improved data printing
- Specification of certain special characters in variable names without the need for enclosing them in apostrophes, e.g., the use of underscore allows easier interface with SAS
- Enhanced portability, especially for CDC and 16 bit machines

ACKNOWLEDGEMENTS

It is impossible to properly credit all who have contributed to the development of these programs. Each program goes through many stages from the initial planning to the final release for distribution. In this manual we list as author(s), where possible, the person(s) who was most instrumental in the development of the program. Generally this person showed originality in the design of the program and also contributed to the statistical methodology required for the analytic technique. At the end of each program we name the designer and programmer. But these credits do not, and cannot, fully cover the contributions of our staff.

Laszlo Engelman designed the basic framework of the BMDP programs, such as the Control Language used to specify instructions, the methods used for transformations and the method of saving data and results between analyses (the BMDP (Save) File). He also programmed many of the subroutines common to all programs and several of the BMDP analyses. For many years he was supervisor of applications programming and supervised the development of many of the programs.

Robert Jennrich proposed and designed many of the programs in regression analysis, analysis of variance and discriminant analysis. He made significant contributions in nonlinear regression (P3R), factor analysis (P4M) and the analysis of variance (P2V and P3V). He supervised Mary Ralston's Ph.D. thesis, which provides the algorithm for the derivative-free nonlinear regression. He is currently involved in planning other programs.

Jim Frane made significant contributions in the area of multivariate analysis. He designed and programmed several of the analyses at a level that makes the programs more accessible to the user.

Alan Hopkins developed BMDP2L and substantially enhanced BMDP1L.

Morton Brown developed the frequency table programs, and John Hartigan (of Yale University) contributed greatly in the area of cluster analysis.

Other staff members, such as Al Forsythe, Ray Mickey, Peter Mundle, Paul Sampson, and Jerry Toporek made significant contributions to many of the programs.

Many statisticians have made contributions and suggestions for developing the programs: R.L. Anderson in regression and analysis of variance, Virginia Clark and Robert Elashoff in survival analysis, Robert Ling in the method of pictorially representing a matrix, and John Tukey in data analysis. Valuable comments have been received from David Andrews, Peter Claringbold, Cuthbert Daniel, Michael Davidson, Charles Dunnett, Janet Elashoff Ivor Francis, George Furnival, Don Guthrie, Henry Kaiser, Sir Maurice Kendall, H. L. Lucas, John Nelder, Shayle Searle, Frank Stitt, Max Woodbury, Karen Yuen, and Coralee Yale. This list is incomplete. Many statisticians have visited the Department of Biomathematics, and/or have discussed the programs with us at conferences. Even the list of references, is, of necessity, incomplete.

Tony Thrall, Lon-Mu Liu, and Laszlo Engelman developed the time series programs, receiving helpful comments from John Tukey, David Brillinger, Peter Bloomfield, George Box and George Tiao.

In recent years, NIH provided us with an Advisory Committee that considered directions for our research, making suggestions for improvements in numerical methods, program design and standards, statistical techniques, exchange of information with statisticians and the statistical computing community.

BMDP has benefited from the work of many conversion centers that have customized BMDP for use on a variety of computer systems. For a complete list of systems, contact BMDP at (213) 475-5700. Some of the many who have been responsible for conversions include Rachel Countryman and Iain Liddell (Burroughs), Eli Cohen (CDC 6000, Cyber), Michael Matzek (DEC 10/20), Gary Anderson (HP 3000), M.M. Barritt (ICL 2900), James Krupp (PDP-11), Mitch Modeleski and Jody Ames (Prime), Malte Sund (Siemens), Robert Byers (Univac 70/90), Kevin Rushforth and Byron Davis (Univac 1100), Bernie Ryan (VAX), Randal Leavitt (Xerox), Lois Secrist (Perkin-Elmer), Aenea Reid (Honeywell 66), H. Koll (Telefunken), W. Haase (MODCOMP Classic), Tony Wexler (Data General MV-8000), and Fred Learman (IBM DOS).

W. J. Dixon

1

INTRODUCTION

The BMDP computer programs are designed to aid data analysis by providing methods ranging from simple data display and description to advanced statistical techniques. Data are usually analyzed by an iterative "examine and modify" series of steps. First the data are examined for unreasonable values, graphically and numerically. If unreasonable values are found they are checked and, if possible, corrected. An analysis is then performed. This analysis may identify other inconsistent observations or indicate that further analyses are needed. The BMDP programs are designed to handle all steps in an analysis, from the simple to the sophisticated.

The BMDP programs are organized so the problem to be analyzed, the variables to be used in the analysis, and the layout of the data are specified in a uniform manner for all programs. This permits different analyses of the same data with only minor changes in the instructions.

This manual is arranged by the type of analysis appropriate to the data. Included are chapters on data description and screening, plotting, frequency tables, regression, analysis of variance, multivariate analysis, etc. Each chapter describes the programs that are available to do a specific type of analysis. In the introduction to each chapter the programs are described and contrasted with each other to indicate which is preferred for a specific analysis. Programs in other chapters are cross-referenced if they provide a similar function.

The programs are loosely classified into series:

D: data description
F: frequency tables
R: regression analysis
V: analysis of variance
M: multivariate analysis
L: life tables and survival analysis
S: special (miscellaneous)
T: time series

Many programs cross boundaries between two series. For example, multivariate regression belongs to both the multivariate (M) and regression (R) series.

Each program is identified by a three-character code; the first is P (from BMDP) and the last is the series classification. The middle character is assigned when the programming begins; it can be 1-9 or a letter. The order does not indicate increasing complexity, and some numbers do not appear.

For example, the program "Simple Data Description" is labelled P1D, since it is the first program in the Descriptive series, and "Nonlinear Regression" is labelled P3R as the third program in the Regression series. Since programs in this manual are described by content, "Multivariate Regression" (P6R) is explained in the chapter on Multivariate Analysis with programs from the M-series.

New programs are continually being developed and released. The first edition of the BMDP manual (Dixon, 1975) contained 26 programs, the 1979 edition, thirty-six. New in this manual are:

P4F -- Frequency Tables -- Two-way and Multiway
   This program replaces P1F, P2F and P3F and
   expands the capability for analyzing
   contingency tables
P2L -- Survival Analysis with Covariates --
   Cox models
P8M -- Boolean Factor Analysis
P9M -- Linear Scores for Preference Pairs
P1T -- Univariate and Bivariate Spectral Analysis
P2T -- Box-Jenkins Time Series Analysis
P4V -- General Univariate and Multivariate
   Analysis of Variance, Including Cell
   Weights and Repeated Measures

In addition, all programs are reviewed and revised in response to suggestions from users, to improve efficiency or to correct errors. For example:

- P3D (t tests) has been expanded to give trimmed t statistics and Levene's test for equality of variances
- P7D now plots an estimate of the cell standard deviation vs. the cell mean and also plots the logs of each cell statistic. The slope of the regression line for the second plot is used to determine a transformation for stabilizing variances
- P8D (Missing Value Correlation) has been rewritten to include a much more efficient algorithm
- PAM (Description and Estimation of Missing Values) has been expanded to include the maximum likelihood method of estimating covariance and correlation matrices from incomplete data
- P2V (Repeated Measures ANOVA) now includes the Greenhouse-Geisser and Huynh-Feldt adjustments to degrees of freedom.

In addition, diagnostic messages for data reading have been enhanced and free-formatted data reading is now available.

Major changes in the programs and novel ways to use them are documented in the newsletter, BMDP Communications. Articles from BMDP Communications that describe ways to use the programs are reprinted in Appendix C.

This manual describes the current status of the programs. Since your facility may have an earlier version of the programs, we have included notes in the manual regarding changes since our November 1978 release. Note that each BMDP program prints a date in the upper left corner of the first page of the output.

An abbreviated manual, the BMDP User's Digest and a BMDP Control Language Pocket Guide are available. See Appendix D.

1.1 A GUIDE TO THIS MANUAL

Introductory Material (Chapters 1 through 3)

The scope of the statistical analyses provided by the BMDP programs is discussed in Chapter 2. Section 2.1 introduces terms used throughout this manual and describes analytical features available in more than one program. The scope of the possible analyses with the BMDP programs is outlined in Section 2.2.

For readers who are using a computer for the first time, Chapter 3 gives annotated examples of simple analyses, describes how to organize your data sheets (research forms), and describes the layout (format) of your data.

Features Common to All BMDP Programs (Chapters 4 through 7)

Chapter 4 describes the English-based BMDP instruction language used to describe the data and specify the analysis. The terminology and notation used throughout this manual are defined here. We recommend that you read the definitions in Section 4.1 even if you are familiar with the BMDP programs. The BMDP instructions used to describe the data and variables are presented in Chapter 5. The free-format data reader described in Chapter 5 is available in all programs except P4D. Methods of transforming and editing data are treated in Chapter 6. Since an analysis often requires multiple steps, the data or results from one program can be saved in a BMDP (Save) File (Chapter 7) and then used in other programs. The use of a BMDP File eliminates having to repeat the description of your data.

Program Descriptions (Chapters 8 through 20)

Chapters 8 through 20 describe methods of analysis and the programs available to perform them. Each chapter begins with an introduction describing alternate methods and programs. This is followed by detailed descriptions of each program. (The features described in Chapters 4 through 7 are not repeated).

Each program description begins with a short abstract and a list of the examples and other options & features. This is followed by one or more examples that illustrate the simplest or most common usage of the program. Each example consists of the BMDP instructions that are required by the program and the results produced by the program. The

instructions and results are labelled Example and Output respectively and are identified by the last two characters of the program name and a sequence number within the program, e.g., 2R.3 denotes the third example for BMDP2R. Numbers in circles (e.g., ①, ②, ...) are used to annotate the results; the numbers on the output correspond to circled numbers in the legend or the text.

A list of program options follows the example(s) with page references to where they are discussed. Each option is described; examples are provided for many of them.

The BMDP programs can analyze large amounts of data. Near the end of each program description a statement is made of the largest problem the program can analyze without modification. A more detailed formula for determining the size of problem the program can analyze is given in Appendix B. If your problem exceeds the limit, Appendix B also contains a description of the changes needed to analyze larger problems.

The last section in the program description states the formulas and algorithms that are described in greater detail in Appendix A. The more difficult formulas and computational procedures are collected in the appendix.

Each program concludes with a summary. The summary consists of a table that describes the BMDP instructions used in the program, and provides short definitions and page references to explanations of the program options. These tables can be used as indexes to the program descriptions.

Useful Aids

An index to the manual is included in the last few pages.

On the inside front cover the programs are listed by their three-character identification codes; page references are given to program descriptions and summaries.

On the inside back cover the Control Language common to all programs (and described in Chapters 4-7) is presented in summary form. Opposite the inside back cover, space is left for you to fill in the instructions necessary to begin an analysis on your computer (see Chapters 4-7).

Where to Start Reading

If you are using computers for the first time, we recommend that you start with Chapter 3. Then read Chapters 4 and 5 for a description of the Control Language. And finally, try one of the programs in Chapters 8, 9 or 10.

If you are not familiar with the BMDP programs, but have previously used a computer, we recommend that you read Chapter 2 (Section 2.1 and 2.2) for an overview of the programs and Chapters 4 and 5 for a description of the Control Language before turning to the specific analysis you want to do.

If you are already familiar with the BMDP programs, but not with this manual, we recommend that you skim Chapter 4. If you are already familiar with the program to be used, turn to the summary for the program (see the list of programs inside the front cover); otherwise you can either turn to the chapter describing the type of analysis that you want to do, or to Chapter 2 for an overview of all the programs.

2
DATA ANALYSIS
Using the BMDP Programs

INTRODUCTION

The meaning of "data analysis" is different for each of us, depending on our level of statistical training. Techniques used in data analysis vary from the simplest display of data in a histogram or a plot and the calculation of statistics (such as the mean and standard deviation) to advanced methods of multivariate analysis. To some, data analysis involves a single display or set of computations; to others it involves a sequence of steps, detecting the presence of outliers and inconsistencies, ensuring that assumptions necessary to the analysis are met, etc. Each step may suggest further analyses.

The BMDP programs provide many analytical capabilities -- from elementary to advanced. In this chapter we describe features that are available in more than one program and outline the scope of available analytical techniques.

WHERE TO FIND IT

2.1 BASIC TERMINOLOGY FOR COMMON FEATURES AND STATISTICS

Each BMDP program is designed to provide a certain analytical capability, such as data description, plots, or regression analysis. Some statistics, plots, or other results are provided by several programs.

In this section we describe some of the common features and introduce terminology that is used throughout this manual. Table 2.1 (p. 7) lists the features and identifies the programs that contain each feature.

3

Data and Acceptable Values

Data are codes representing characteristics (e.g., sex, eye color), values of measurements (e.g., height, weight) or responses to questions. Each characteristic, measurement or response is called a variable. Each case contains values for all the variables for one subject, animal, or sampling unit. A case may represent such things as responses to questions, outcomes of tests or measurements made on a subject or test animal.

Some values in a case may not be recorded. A value that is not recorded may be left blank or may be recorded with a special code; the blank or special code, whichever is used, is called a missing value code and the unrecorded value is called a missing value. Missing values are excluded from all computations.

In any program you can restrict the analysis of a variable to a specified range by assigning an upper limit (maximum) and a lower limit (minimum) for values of the variables. A value that is greater than the upper limit or less than the lower limit is out of range and is excluded from all computations.

An acceptable value is one that is not equal to a missing value code and is not out of range. A complete case is a case in which the values of all the variables are acceptable (there are no values missing or out of range).

Cases Used When Some Values are Unacceptable (Missing)

All BMDP programs (except P4D) check for values missing and out of range. The treatment of cases depends on the primary purpose of the analysis. For example, P1D -- Simple Data Description -- computes statistics for each variable from all acceptable values for the variable; but P2R -- Stepwise Regression -- uses only complete cases to estimate the linear regression equation.

The BMDP programs include cases in an analysis according to one of three criteria:

A All cases are included (all acceptable values for each variable are used)
B Cases are included only if they have acceptable values for all variables specified in the analysis
C Only complete cases are included (cases that have acceptable values for all variables)

The difference between the above criteria can be explained in terms of an example. Suppose we have three variables, each of which has some unacceptable values. The data for five cases are:

	height	weight	age
1)	67	130	-
2)	64	106	21
3)	65	117	27
4)	67	-	24
5)	-	121	29

We request means for the first two variables only. Using Method A, the mean of each variable is computed from all its acceptable values, whether or not either of the other variables have acceptable values (i.e., four values for each variable). By Method B the means of the first two variables are computed from data in only those cases that have acceptable values for both variables (cases 1, 2 and 3). Method C allows the means to be computed from cases that have acceptable values for all three variables (only cases 2 and 3).

Method C may use fewer cases than either of the other methods. You can specify a list of variables to be checked by Method C with the USE list in the VARIABLE paragraph. Variables that are excluded from the list are not used in any of the computations (not even their means are computed). In Chapter 5 we describe how this list is specified.

The method used by each program is shown in Table 2.1. Three programs, P3D, P8D and PAM allow you to choose explicitly between methods. P8D computes estimates of correlation matrices using all observed values instead of only those values from complete cases. PAM does the same and, in addition, provides estimates to fill in where observations are missing. PAM also has features useful for describing the pattern of where values are missing.

Transformations and Selecting Subpopulations for Analysis

Transformations can be used to replace the value of a variable by its transformed value; e.g., weight by the logarithm of weight. Also, new variables can be created from the observed variables by transformations. For example, if pulse rate is measured before and after exercise, the difference between the two measurements can be a meaningful quantity. This difference can be specified as a new variable and can be used in the analysis. Any number of new variables can be treated as functions of the observed variables. These functions, called transformations, can involve arithmetical operations (e.g., +, -, *, /), powers, trigonometric functions, and complex conditional statements (IF(A/B-C LT 0) THEN D=0.).

You can also select cases to be used in an analysis (e.g., data for males and for respondents in their twenties -- USE = SEX EQ 1 AND AGE GE 20 AND AGE LT 30.).

Methods of specifying transformations and case selection are described in detail in Chapter 6.

How to Define Subpopulations or Groups

Some analyses, such as a t test between two groups or a one-way analysis of variance, require that the cases be classified into groups. The variable whose values are used to classify the cases into groups is called a grouping variable. Groups can be identified as codes (such as sex codes 1 and 2 for males and females) or as intervals (such as age 10-19, 20-29, etc.).

In all programs you can select cases belonging to specific groups (fulfilling certain criteria) by case selection (Chapter 6). The purpose of some analyses is to compare groups, such as in a plot or by a t test or by an analysis of variance. In some programs you can explicitly specify groups to be analyzed (or plotted).

Univariate Statistics

Most programs compute the mean, standard deviation and frequency for each variable. In addition, other univariate statistics are computed in several BMDP programs. We review the definitions of these statistics below.

Let x_1, x_2, ..., x_N be the observed (acceptable) values for a variable in the cases used in an analysis. Then N is the sample size, frequency or count for the variable. The mean, $\bar{x}$, is defined as

$$\bar{x} = \Sigma x_j/N$$

(Other estimates of location, such as the median and more robust estimates, are available in P2D and P7D.) The standard deviation, s, is

$$s = [\Sigma(x_j - \bar{x})^2/(N - 1)]^{\frac{1}{2}}.$$

The variance is s^2 and the standard error of the mean is $s/\sqrt{N}$. The coefficient of variation is the ratio of the standard deviation to the mean, $s/\bar{x}$. If a variable has a very small coefficient of variation, loss of computational accuracy can result due to the limited accuracy with which a number can be represented internally in the computer.

Many analyses require that the distribution of the data be normal, or at least symmetric. A measure of symmetry is skewness, and a measure of long-tailedness is kurtosis. The BMDP programs compute skewness, g_1, as

$$g_1 = \Sigma(x_j - \bar{x})^3/(Ns^3)$$

and kurtosis, g_2, as

$$g_2 = \Sigma(x_j - \bar{x})^4/(Ns^4) - 3$$

If the data are from a normal distribution, the standard error of g_1 is $(6/N)^{\frac{1}{2}}$ and of g_2 is $(24/N)^{\frac{1}{2}}$. A significant nonzero value of skewness is an indication of asymmetry -- a positive value indicating a long right tail, a negative value a long left tail. A value of g_2 significantly greater than zero indicates a distribution that is longer-tailed than the normal. We recommend that you also examine histograms when using these statistics for they are sensitive to a few extreme values.

The smallest observed (acceptable) value, x_{min}, and the largest, x_{max}, are printed by several programs. The range is $(x_{max} - x_{min})$. The smallest and largest standard scores (z-scores, z_{min} and z_{max} respectively) are also printed by some programs. We define z_{min} and z_{max} as

$$z_{min} = (x_{min} - \bar{x})/s \quad \text{and} \quad z_{max} = (x_{max} - \bar{x})/s .$$

Covariances and Correlations

Covariances and correlations are used in many statistical analyses. The covariance between two variables, x and y, is

$$cov(x,y) = \Sigma(x_j - \bar{x})(y_j - \bar{y})/(N - 1) .$$

The correlation, r, between two variables is

$$r = \frac{cov(x,y)}{s_x s_y} = \frac{\Sigma(x_j - \bar{x})(y_j - \bar{y})}{[\Sigma(x_j - \bar{x})^2\Sigma(y_j - \bar{y})^2]^{\frac{1}{2}}}$$

This is also called the product-moment correlation coefficient.

The correlation can also be computed after adjusting for the linear effect of one or more other variables. For example, we may want the correlation between x and y adjusted for z and w (sometimes referred to as correlation at a fixed value of z and w). This is called the partial correlation coefficient between x and y given z and w. It is equivalent to fitting separate regression equations in z and w to x and to y, and computing the correlation between the residuals from the two regression lines.

A multiple correlation coefficient (R) is the maximum correlation that can be attained between one variable and a linear combination of other variables. This is the correlation between the first variable and the predicted value from the multiple regression of that variable on the other variables. R^2 is the proportion of variance of the first variable explained by the multiple regression relating it to the other variables.

Plots and Histograms

An assumption of normality is required by many analyses. The assumption can be assessed by a normal probability plot. The assumption of normality is not usually with respect to the data, but with respect to the residuals, the differences between the observed value and the value predicted by the statistical model. Many programs plot the residuals in a normal probability plot.

Scatter plots of one variable against another are useful in examining the relationships between the two variables; they are also useful in assessing the fit of a statistical model (such as regression). Scatter plots of the data and results are provided in many BMDP programs.

Histograms, or bar graphs, are a basic tool in data screening. They can be used to screen for extreme values or for the shape of the distribution of data. Several BMDP programs plot histograms as part of their analyses.

Table 2.1 indicates which programs produce plots and histograms as part of their analyses. Chapter 10 describes two programs whose primary purpose is to provide plots and histograms in final form.

Printing the Data and Results for Each Case

Many programs can list the data for each case. Some programs print results for each case, such as predicted values and residuals from a regression or scores from a factor analysis. Several programs have special capabilities for listing the data:

- P4D can print the data in a compact card image form
- P4D can also print only cases that contain nonnumeric symbols
- P1D can list all the data so that each column contains all the values of one variable or so that all variables for one case are printed before those for the next case
- P1D can print only cases with missing values or only cases that have values out of range
- P1D can also print the data after sorting the cases according to one or more variables
- PAM can print, in a compressed list, the positions of the missing values and values out of range
- P2M and P4M can print standard scores

The BMDP File

A set of data is usually analyzed many times by BMDP programs. For example, the data may first be examined for extreme values (outliers) and for distributional assumptions; then necessary transformations can be performed, meaningful hypotheses tested, or relationships between the variables studied. The results of an analysis may suggest that further analyses are needed.

All programs can read a data matrix as input. All programs (except P4D) can copy the data into a BMDP File. The BMDP File is a means of storing your data or results from an analysis so you can reuse them more efficiently in other BMDP programs; the File can be created or read by any BMDP program (except P4D). There are several advantages to using a BMDP File:

- data are read efficiently from a BMDP File; the cost of reading a large amount of data from a BMDP File is substantially less than when a format statement is used
- many of the Control Language instructions, specified when the BMDP File is created, need not be respecified for each additional analysis. For example, the variable names, the indicators for missing values and values out of range, codes and names for categories, etc., are stored with the File
- data are stored in the BMDP File after transformations and case selection are performed
- the BMDP File is the only way to store results (such as factor scores, residuals from a regression analysis or a covariance matrix) so they can be analyzed further by other BMDP programs

Table 2.1 shows that all programs (except P4D) can save the data in a BMDP File. Many programs save results, such as predicted values or residuals. Some programs can also save a covariance or correlation matrix or some other matrix of results.

All programs but P4D accept data from a BMDP File (a BMDP File can be created by one program and read by a different program). Several regression and multivariate analysis programs accept the covariance or correlation matrix from a BMDP File, thus saving computer time and cost. P4F accepts multiway tables as input.

Case Weights

Most statistical analyses assume that the error of each observation has a constant variance. When the variance is not constant, the computations of the mean, standard deviation and other statistics are best done by weighting each case by the inverse of the variance. For example, the researcher knows the variance from previous work and includes its inverse as an additional variable for each case.

Case weights can also be used to represent the frequency of an observation when the same observation is made more than once but is recorded in only one case; however, except for the frequency table programs, the sample size will be the number of cases and not the sum of weights.

You can specify case weights in many BMDP programs. The effect of the case weight on the computation of the univariate statistics, covariance and correlation is described below.

Let w be the case weight for the jth case. Then

$$\bar{x} = \Sigma w_j x_j / \Sigma w_j$$

$$s = \{\Sigma w_j (x_j - \bar{x})^2 / [(N - 1)\Sigma w_j/N]\}^{\frac{1}{2}}$$

$$cov(x,y) = \Sigma w_j (x_j - \bar{x})(y_j - \bar{y}) / [(N -1)\Sigma w_j/N]$$

$$r = \frac{\Sigma w_j (x_j - \bar{x})(y_j - \bar{y})}{\{\Sigma w_j (x_j - \bar{x})^2 \Sigma w_j (y_j - \bar{y})^2\}^{\frac{1}{2}}}$$

where N is the number of acceptable observations used in the analysis with positive (nonzero) weights.

When case weights are not specified, w_j is set to one for all cases and the formulas are identical to the formulas given on p. 5.

Computational Accuracy

The computer represents each number by a binary sequence of limited accuracy. As a result there can be a loss of accuracy in certain types of computation, such as matrix inversion. Loss of accuracy is especially pronounced if a variable has a small coefficient of variation ($s/\bar{x}$) or if a variable has a very high multiple correlation with other variables.

All programs represent data values in single precision. Some programs do computations in single precision. Others do computations in double precision; these programs are the ones whose computations are most likely to be affected by a loss of accuracy if the computations are done in single precision.

2.2 OVERVIEW OF DATA ANALYSIS WITH BMDP

The breadth of techniques available in the BMDP programs is indicated by the chapter titles:

8. Data Description
9. Data in Groups -- Description, t Tests and One-Way Analysis of Variance
10. Plots and Histograms
11. Frequency Tables
12. Missing Values -- Patterns, Estimation and Correlation
13. Regression
14. Nonlinear Regression and Maximum Likelihood Estimation
15. Analysis of Variance and Covariance
16. Nonparametric Analysis
17. Cluster Analysis
18. Multivariate Analysis
19. Survival Analysis
20. Time Series Analysis

In this section we describe some of these techniques in general terms, and explain when the techniques are useful (see also "First Steps",

Table 2.1 Features common to BMDP programs

Chapter → Program	8 124 DDD	9 379 DDD	10 56 DD	11 4 F	12 8A DM	13 12945 RRRRR	14 3AL RRR	15 12348 VVVVV	16 3 S	17 123K MMMM	18 466789 MMRMMM	19 12 LL	6 1 S	20 12 TT
Cases used														
A all cases (all acceptable values)	AAA	AAA	AA	A	AA					AA	A		A	A
B cases with acceptable values for all vars. specified in analysis (see p. 4)		B				B B		BBBB			BB	BB		
C complete cases only					CC	CC C	CCC	C	C	CC	C C			C
Analytic capabilities														
T transformations and case selection	TTT	TTT	TT	T	TT	TTTTT	TTT	TTTTT	T	TTTT	TTTTTT	TT	T	TT
W case weights				W	WW	WWW W		WW		W W	WWWW W			
D double precision				D		D D	DDD	DDDD			DDDD	D		D
Univariate statistics														
$\bar{x}$ mean	$\bar{x}\bar{x}$	$\bar{x}\bar{x}\bar{x}$	$\bar{x}\bar{x}$	$\bar{x}$	$\bar{x}\bar{x}$	$\bar{x}\bar{x}\bar{x}\bar{x}$	$\bar{x}\bar{x}\bar{x}$	$\bar{x}\bar{x}$ $\bar{x}\bar{x}$	$\bar{x}$ $\bar{x}$	$\bar{x}$	$\bar{x}\bar{x}\bar{x}\bar{x}$	$\bar{x}$	$\bar{x}$	$\bar{x}\bar{x}$
$\tilde{x}$ other estimates of location	$\tilde{x}$	$\tilde{x}$												
s standard deviation	ss	sss	ss	s	ss	ssss	sss	ss s	s s	s	ssss	s	s	ss
v coefficient of variation	v				vv	vvvv					vvv			
g skewness and kurtosis	g				g	gg	g				ggg	g		
m min. and max. of the acceptable value	mm	mm		m	m	mmm	mmm	m m	m	m	mmm	m	m	m
z z-score for min. and max. values	z				z	zz				z	zzz			
N number of cases (sample size)	NNN	NNN	NN	N	NN	NNNNN	NNN	NNNN	N	NNNN	NNNNNN	NN		NN
G above statistics computed for each group	G	GGG	GG	G	G			GG GG		G	G	G		
Other statistics														
r covariances and/or correlations		rr	r		rr	rrrr	r		r	r	rrr			r
p partial correlations						p					p p			p
R squared multiple correlation (R² or SMC)					R	RRR					R R R			R
f frequency counts, for each value or category	fff		f	f			f			f		f		
% frequency counts, in %	%		%	%										
λ eigenvalues and/or eigenvectors						λ	λ				$\lambda\lambda$ λ			
G above statistics computed for each group		GG	GG	G	G	G		G			G			
Test statistics														
F comparison of group means (t,F)		FFF						FFFFF	F	F	F			
V comparison of group variances		VVV												
χ comparison of group or cell frequencies		χ		χ										
D multivariate comparison of group means (T², D², λ, U)		D							D		D			
Plots and graphical displays														
H histograms	H	HH	H											
N normal probability plots			N			NNNNN	NN				N			
S scatter plots of data			S		S	S				S	SSS S			
R scatter plots of results					R	RRRRR	RRR	R			RRRR R	R		
O other (see program description)	O	O								OOOO		OO		OO
Prints for each case														
D data (after transformations, if any)	D D	D			D	DDD D	DDD	D		D D	DDDDD	D	D	DD
S cases with special values	S S				S									
z standardized scores										z	z			
R residuals and/or predicted values				R		RRR R	RRR	RR R			RR	R		R
F factor, princ. comp. or canon. var. scores						F					FF FF			
M Mahalanobis distances					M	M		M		M	M M			
O other (see program description)		O			O		O			OOO	OO	OO		O
BMDP File output														
D data (after transformations, if any)	DD	DDD	DD	D	DD	DDDDD	DDD	DDDDD	D	DDDD	DDDDDD	DD	D	DD
R results for each case as part of data					R	RRR R	RRR	R			RRRRR			R
G codes/cutpoints saved with data	G	GGG	GG	G	G	G		GGG			G			
C correlation and/or covariance matrix					CC	CCC				CCC				
O other (see program description)				O	O			O			O O O			O
Input from BMDP File														
D data	DD	DDD	DD	D	DD	DDDDD	DDD	DDDDD	D	DDDD	DDDDDD	DD	D	DD
C correlation or covariance matrix						CCC					CCC			
O other (see program description)											O O			O
Input not from BMDP File														
D data	DDD	DDD	DD	D	DD	DDDDD	DDD	DDDDD	D	DDDD	DDDDDD	DD	D	DD
O other (see program description)				O		O		O			O			O

Appendix C.11). Specific program options are presented in the program descriptions. Some of the more advanced techniques, such as maximum likelihood estimation, are discussed only in the program descriptions.

Data Screening and Description

The first step in an analysis is to examine the data for errors and for the appropriateness of assumptions to be used in the analysis (such as normality). If errors remain in the data they can cause a "garbage-in, garbage-out" analysis. Blunders or extreme outliers in the data may need to be removed to achieve a meaningful analysis. The data may need to be transformed to fit the various assumptions (constant variance, normality, etc.) required by the statistical model.

After the original data have been recorded, various descriptive characteristics of the data can be used to detect gross errors in the observations, in coding the data, in including inappropriate cases, etc. A good place to begin screening is to check for

- symbols or characters, such as letters where numbers should be (P4D counts all distinct characters for each column of data, one column at a time); many programs will not run if nonnumeric symbols are in the data used for analysis - error messages are reported, however, by all programs when illegal characters are found.
- outliers or blunders (P2D can be used to obtain a small histogram and frequency counts for all distinct values of each variable)

Listing the cases by one of the methods described on p. 5 may also locate problems in the data.

Outliers can be identified by multivariate screening. For each case P4M prints the Mahalanobis distance squared from the case to the center of all cases. Within group multivariate outliers can be identified by using P7M, which prints the Mahalanobis distance squared from the case to the center of each group. P9R also prints distance measures helpful for identifying unusual cases.

Univariate descriptive statistics are found in most programs, but especially in P2D and P1D. For example, from the cumulative percentiles printed in P2D for each distinct value, you can make summary statements such as, "sixty percent of the patients are in the 50-60 age group, while only seven percent are in their twenties", etc. A stem and leaf histogram is also available in this program.

Data in Groups

In screening, you often need to examine groups (strata or subpopulations) of the data. Unusual data values that are masked in a total population may stand out when the data are separated into groups or strata. Some variables are easily coded into groups, such as sex (males=1, females=2). Continuous variables can be categorized by a grouping variable.

P7D is especially powerful for examining groups; it prints histograms (side-by-side for each group) and statistics for each group; it also provides a choice of one-way or two-way analysis of variance to check group differences. From this output you can identify extreme outliers, obtain an idea of the distribution of data within groups, and examine whether the assumption of normality is reasonable. Heteroscedasticity (lack of constant variance over groups) can also be observed and tested, and may indicate that the input data should be transformed.

An analysis of variance using P7D can indicate whether group differences are large enough to suggest that future analyses should be stratified. P7D also computes ANOVA tests that do not assume equal group variances, plots cell standard deviations vs. cell means and reports Bonferroni probabilities for pairwise tests of cell means. More information on group differences (both univariate and multivariate) can be obtained by using P3D. It yields t statistics, Hotelling's T^2 and Mahalanobis D^2 for each pair of groups; t statistics, based on both pooled and separate variance estimates, are printed in the output. A trimmed t test is available in the 1979 version. The Levene test for equality of variances is in both P3D and P7D.

When the cases are classified by more than one grouping variable or factor, P9D (Multiway Description of Groups) can be used to compute cell frequencies, means and standard deviations. Grouping variables can be suppressed to obtain information about marginal cells. The program tests for the equality of cell frequencies and cell means and for homogeneity of cell variances. These tests are performed on all cells or on specified marginals. Cell means are plotted four variables per page in a compact graphical display scaled by the overall mean and standard deviation. This display is helpful for understanding interactions in more complex ANOVA designs.

Transformations

After screening and describing your data, you should be ready to make decisions regarding transformations. The transformed data can be put directly on a BMDP File ready for easy input into any other BMDP program. Although all programs can perform data transformations, you may need to use P1S, the multipass transformation program, for getting the data transformed and ready for further analyses. P1S can be used when your transformation requires more than one pass through the data.

Plots and Histograms

Many research workers like to see their data in graphical form; scatter plots, for example, are a good way to present information concisely and clearly in final reports. Scatter plots that take advantage of known information can be designed to display unusual cases or outliers -- for example, to show whether or not an individual's systolic blood pressure level is higher than his diastolic level. A scatter plot of these two variables will show if the data coding is mistakenly reversed for some cases. Or in a plot of height versus weight, a case that has a height of 72 inches and 225 lbs. will clearly stand out if the height is mispunched as 52 inches.

A grouping variable can be used in the P6D scatter plot program to provide information about a variable not used as the plot axes. If age, for example, is divided into groups -- less than or equal to 15, 16-35, 36-55 and over 55 -- the letters A, B, C and D are used to represent cases from each age group. When two other measurements for the subjects are plotted, the children may appear in a separate area of the plot, indicating that they should be analyzed separately in later analyses. P6D can also perform a simple regression analysis for the data in a scatter plot. This analysis may indicate whether or not an analysis of covariance should be used later. Variables can be plotted against time of entry into a study to see if observations are independent, or if a drift over time is occurring.

P5D can print a histogram for all the data or for one or more groups, each identified by a different letter. You can specify the scales of the histogram to produce a histogram suitable for a final report.

Normality can be roughly checked by looking at histograms in P7D or P5D. P5D can also print a normal probability plot that provides a better assessment of normality and helps to identify outliers.

Frequency Tables

Cross tabulations are frequently used as a form of final reporting to give a picture of the number of cases in specified categories (or cross-classifications). Tables can be formed from data or from cell frequencies. Tables can also be formed for each level of a third variable (such as separately for males and females). Twenty-three statistics appropriate for the analysis of contingency tables are available in P4F (which includes all the features formerly contained in programs P1F, P2F and P3F).

P4F can test whether rows are independent of columns using the frequencies in all cells. P4F can also test the same hypothesis using any subset of the cells; for example, are rows independent of the columns for all cells, excluding the cells on the diagonal? P4F can also identify cells that contribute heavily to a significant chi-square test of independence.

Multiway frequency tables are formed and analyzed by P4F. A log-linear model can be fitted to the cell frequencies and the fit tested. P4F can be used to select an appropriate model for the data and to estimate the parameters of the model.

Missing Values

All too often the data recorded are not complete and some values are missing. These missing values are usually left blank or coded by a special code called the "missing value code". Missing values, and unusually extreme values that appear to be wrong, are excluded from an analysis.

PAM lists cases containing missing values or data to be excluded from the analysis, computes the percentage of missing data for each variable, and reports special patterns in the data. PAM can also estimate values to replace the missing value code (or excluded values) based upon the data present in the case.

Most regression and multivariate analyses require complete cases; i.e., no missing or excluded values in any case. Many of these analyses can begin from a correlation or covariance matrix. Both PAM and P8D can estimate correlations using cases with some data missing; the correlation matrix can then be stored in a BMDP File and used as input to other programs, including those that require complete data. PAM insures that the resulting correlation matrix is numerically appropriate (positive semidefinite) for a regression or factor analysis; P8D allows you to choose between four methods to compute the correlations.

Regression

A regression analysis studies the relationship between a dependent variable, y, and one or more independent variables, x_i. The linear least squares model with parameters or regression coefficients, β_i, can be written

$$y = \beta_0 + \beta_1 x_1 + \ldots + \beta_p x_p + e .$$

For simple linear regression (x_1 is the only independent variable in the model), P6D, P1R and P2R can be used. If there are several independent variables, P1R, P2R or P9R can be used to perform multiple linear regression analyses.

P1R, P2R and P9R differ in three important respects:

- the criterion for including independent variables in the multiple linear regression
- the ability to repeat the analysis on subgroups of the cases and to compare the subgroups
- the residual analysis available

P1R includes all the specified independent variables in the multiple regression equation. It computes a multiple linear regression on all the data and on groups or subpopulations. If grouping is requested, P1R first analyzes all cases combined and then analyzes each group separately. After all groups have been analyzed, the regression equations are tested for equality between groups.

P2R computes the multiple linear regression in a stepwise manner. At each step it enters into the regression equation the variable that best helps to predict y or removes the least helpful variable. Several criteria are available for entering or removing variables from the equation (see P2R program description). A stepwise procedure is useful for identifying a good set of predictor variables (separating the most important variables from those that may not be necessary at all), and when sufficient preliminary information regarding the effectiveness of the independent variables is not available. In practical applications the stepwise procedure is often a satisfactory solution.

P9R identifies "best" subsets of independent variables in terms of a criterion such as R^2, adjusted R^2 or Mallows' C_p (described in P9R program description). It also identifies alternative good subsets of the independent variables. P9R computes only a small fraction of all possible regressions to find the numerically best subset.

All three programs print and plot residuals and predicted values. The plots are useful in detecting lack of linearity, heteroscedasticity (lack of constant variance), unusual outliers, gross errors, an unusual subpopulation that should be separated from the analysis, etc. The plots may also indicate that transformations of the data are necessary or that an inappropriate model was chosen.

The residual analysis in P9R is the most extensive of the three. P9R also allows easy cross-validation of the regression model by testing it on a subset of the cases excluded from the analysis.

P4R creates new independent variables, called principal components, that are linear combinations of the original independent variables. These principal components are determined in a way that provides a parsimonious summary of the original variables; a subset of the principal components explains most of the total variance of the original set of independent variables. The program then regresses the dependent variable in a stepwise manner on the principal components; not all the principal components may be used, but useful information is based on all the variables. The regression equations at each step are expressed in terms of the principal components and the original variables.

The relation between an independent and a dependent variable may require terms with higher powers. The model for polynomial regression in P5R is

$$y = \beta_0 + \beta_1 x + \beta_2 x^2 + \ldots + \beta_k x^k + e \; .$$

P5R reports polynomials of degree one through a specified degree; this helps to determine the highest-order equation necessary for an adequate fit of the data. As higher-order terms are introduced into the model, the fitted regression curve and the original data can be plotted at each step for a visual check on how the fit is proceeding.

Nonlinear Regression

To fit a model where the equation is not linear in the parameters you can use the nonlinear regression programs, P3R and PAR. These are least squares programs appropriate for a wide variety of problems that are not well-represented by equations with linear parameters. Several different functions are available in P3R by simply stating a number, including such functions as sums of exponentials

$$p_1 e^{p_2 t} + p_3 e^{p_4 t} \; ,$$

ratios of polynomials, a combination of sine and exponential functions, etc. If you want a function different from those described in the P3R program description, you can request it by FORTRAN statements in P3R or PAR. In P3R you must also specify the function's partial derivatives.

A special nonlinear model is the logistic function. PLR computes the maximum likelihood estimates of the parameters of

$$E\left(\frac{s}{n}\right) = \frac{e^{\beta x}}{1 + e^{\beta x}}$$

where s is the sum of the binary (0,1) dependent variable y ($\sum_n y = s$) and x represents the independent variables. The dependent (outcome) variable records events such as success or failure, response or no response, etc. The independent (explanatory or covariate) variables can be categorical (e.g., sex, treatment, hospital) and continuous (e.g., age, height, blood pressure). The program generates design variables for the categorical variables and their interactions.

Analysis of Variance and Covariance

Analysis of variance is used to test for differences between the means of two or more groups or subpopulations. In a simple one-way analysis of variance each individual (or subject) is classified into one category or group -- for example, in a medical problem patients could be assigned to treatment A, B or C. The patients are grouped by the type of treatment. The model for this one-way design is

$$Y_{ik} = \mu + \alpha_i + e_{ik}$$

where α_1, α_2 and α_3 might represent the effect of treatments A, B and C, respectively, on the dependent variable, Y_{ik}, a blood pressure reading for case k in group i. Programs P7D, P9D, P1V and P2V can be used to test the hypothesis

$$H_o: \text{ all } \alpha_i = 0$$

that there is no difference between treatments. Group sizes may be unequal in all four of these programs. For each dependent variable analyzed, P7D presents side-by-side histograms that give an excellent visual picture of how the groups differ.

In the medical treatment example above, if the covariate x (age) also affects the dependent variable (blood pressure), the one-way model becomes

$$Y_{ik} = \mu + \alpha_i + \beta(x_{ik} - \bar{x}) + e_{ik} \; .$$

P1V could be used to examine treatment effects after adjusting for the linear effect of age. P1V also allows multiple covariates. It prints an analysis of variance table with F tests for equality of slopes, zero slopes and equality of adjusted group means (which adjusts for the effect of the covariate) and a number of residual plots.

Several factors (or characteristics) may be involved in an analysis of variance model. In a two-way factorial analysis of variance, the individuals in each group are classified by two characteristics, such as sex and treatment. The model can be written

$$Y_{ijk} = \mu + \alpha_i + \eta_j + (\alpha\eta)_{ij} + e_{ijk} \; .$$

Here the α_i's could be treatment effect, the η_j's sex effect and $(\alpha\eta)_{ij}$ a possible interaction between sex and treatment. P7D can be used to analyze these data. The accompanying histograms give additional information.

P2V handles general fixed effects analysis of variance and covariance models. This program can analyze repeated responses, such as the measurements of a subject's blood pressure every day for a week. The repeated responses are called trial factors or repeated measures factors and need not be statistically independent. In the blood pressure example above, time could be a seven-level trial factor (e.g., a subject's blood pressure could be recorded every day of the week). In P2V the usual analysis of variance factors, such as sex and treatment, are called grouping factors to distinguish them from trial factors. The models may have only trial factors, only grouping factors, or both. The groups can contain an unequal number of subjects, but data for each subject must include all observations over the trial factor (a blood pressure reading must be given for each day).

Mixed models are treated by P8V (which requires equal cell sizes) and by P3V (which allows unequal cell sizes and covariates). P4V is a very general program that handles multivariate models, including those with repeated measures and covariates. The user may specify cell weights for use in the definition of model components such as main effects and lower order interactions in factorial models or specify unequal intervals for orthogonal polynomials in response surface analysis.

Nonparametric Statistics

If your data grossly violate the usual analysis of variance normality assumptions, you could try two nonparametric tests in P3S -- the Kruskal-Wallis one-way analysis of variance test, or the Friedman two-way analysis of variance test. Nonparametric tests such as the Mann-Whitney U test, the sign test and the Wilcoxon signed rank test can also be computed with P3S. These tests can be used when the researcher wants to avoid a t test assumption of normality.

Cluster Analysis

Although many research studies involve multivariate observations (many variables observed for each case), sometimes little is known about the inter-relations between variables, between cases, or between variables and cases. In discussing screening and data description, we emphasized that groups or subpopulations should be examined; however, problems often arise when groups are not clearly defined or when it is difficult to see if the data are structured. Clustering is a good technique to use in exploratory or early data analysis when you suspect that the data may not be homogeneous and you want to classify or reduce the data into groups. Clustering performs a display function for multivariate data similar to graphs or histograms for univariate data; it provides a multivariate summary -- a description of characteristics of clusters instead of individual cases.

Three different types of clustering can be performed by BMDP programs: clusters of variables (P1M), clusters of cases (P2M and PKM), and clusters of both cases and variables (P3M). After deciding which program is applicable to your problem, other questions must be answered: How will you measure distances between objects (variables in P1M, cases P2M and PKM)? How will you use the distances to amalgamate or group the objects into clusters? How will you display the resulting clusters? The best answers to these questions are still being developed; investigators have their own preferences as to which distance measure or which amalgamation procedure is best. You may want to try several options given in the program descriptions to see which one provides the best results for your problem.

In both P1M and P2M the clustering begins by finding the closest pair of objects (in P1M, columns, or variables; in P2M, rows, or cases) according to the distance matrix and combining them to form a cluster. The algorithm continues, joining pairs of objects, pairs of clusters, or an object with a cluster, until all the data are in one cluster. These clustering steps are shown in the output cluster diagram, or tree. The correlation or distance matrix can also be printed in shaded form to display pictorially the clusters.

The clustering method in P2M is hierarchical. The procedure in PKM is called k-means and begins with user-specified clusters or with all the data in one cluster: at each step one cluster is split into two. This procedure is useful when you have a large number of cases or when your goal is to divide the cases into homogeneous subsets. PKM provides several ways to standardize the data in order to avoid problems caused by scale differences.

The programs discussed above look for variables to be clustered across all cases or for cases to be clustered (by similarity) across all variables. However, your data may include differences between cases that do not extend across all the variables, or your variables may not cluster across all cases. P3M allows some of the variables (columns) to be clustered as a subset of the cases (rows) and vice versa. This clustering by both cases and variables is represented by a data matrix in the form of a block diagram; rows and columns are permuted and smaller blocks (submatrices) of similar values within the larger block are outlined. This gives a good visual representation of patterns of like values in the data matrix and can be used as a multivariate histogram. P3M is best suited to treat categorical variables that take on a small number of values.

Multivariate Analysis

Cluster analysis is not appropriate for expressing complex functional relationships. For example, if you are interested in describing the inter-relations among your variables, factor analysis may be better suited to your needs, and discriminant analysis provides functions of the variables that best separate cases into predefined groups.

Factor analysis. Factor analysis is useful in exploratory data analysis. It has three general objectives: to study the correlations of a large number of variables by clustering the variables into factors, such that variables within each factor are highly correlated; to interpret each factor according to the variables belonging to it; and to summarize many variables by a few factors. The usual factor analysis model expresses each variable as a function of factors common to several variables and a factor unique to the variable:

$$z_j = a_{j1}f_1 + a_{j2}f_2 + \cdots + a_{jm}f_m + U_j$$

where

z_j = the jth standardized variable
m = the number of factors common to all the variables
U_j = the factor unique to variable z_j
a_{ji} = factor loadings
f_i = common factors

The number of factors, m, should be small and the contributions of the unique factors should also be small. The individual factor loadings, a_{ji}, for each variable should be either very large or very small so each variable is associated with a minimum number of factors.

To the extent that this factor model is appropriate for your data, the objectives stated above can be achieved. Variables with high loadings on a factor tend to be highly correlated with each other, and variables that do not have the same loading patterns tend to be less highly correlated. Each factor is interpreted according to the magnitudes of the loadings associated with it. The original variables may be replaced by the factors with little loss of information. Each case receives a score for each factor; these <u>factor scores</u> are computed as:

$$f_i = b_{i1}z_1 + b_{i2}z_2 + \cdots + b_{ip}z_p$$

where b_{ij} are the factor score coefficients. Factor scores can be used in later analyses, replacing the values of the original variables. Under certain circumstances these few factor scores are freer from measurement error than the original variables, and are therefore more reliable measures. The scores express the degree to which each case possesses the quality or property that the factor describes. The factor scores have mean zero and standard deviation one.

There are four main steps in factor analysis: first, the correlation or covariance matrix is computed; second, the factor loadings are estimated (initial factor extraction); third, the factors are rotated to obtain a simple interpretation (making the loadings for each factor either large or small, not in-between); and fourth, the factor scores are computed. P4M provides several methods for initial factor extraction and rotation. You can specify the methods to be used or P4M will use preassigned options. The results can be presented in a variety of plots.

P8M, <u>Boolean Factor Analysis</u>, is an alternate technique when the variables are binary or dichotomous.

<u>Canonical correlation analysis</u>. Canonical correlation analysis (P6M) examines the relationship between two sets of variables, and can be viewed as an extension of multiple regression analysis or of multiple correlation. Multiple regression deals with one dependent variable, Y, and p independent variables, x_i. The regression problem is to find a linear combination of the X variables that has maximum correlation with Y. In canonical correlation there is more than one dependent Y variable -- there is a set of them. The problem is to find a linear combination of the X variables that has maximum correlation with a linear combination of the Y variables. This correlation is called the canonical correlation coefficient. Then a second pair of linear combinations, with maximum correlation between this pair and zero correlations with the first pair of linear combinations is found. The number of pairs of linear combinations of the X and Y sets is equal to the number of variables in the smaller set (X or Y). The technique can be used to test the independence of two sets of variables, or to predict information about a hard-to-measure set of variables from a set that is easier to measure. It can also be used to relate a combination of outcome measures to a combination of history or baseline measures. The original and canonical variables can be plotted one against the other in scatter plots.

<u>Partial correlations and multivariate regression</u>. Partial correlations can be computed in P6R; the correlation between each pair of dependent variables is computed after taking out the linear effect of the set of independent variables. For example, if you want to do a factor analysis on several variables (systolic blood pressure, diastolic blood pressure, blood chemistry measurements, income, etc.) but want to remove the linear effect of two variables (age and weight) from the measurements, you can state that the two variables (age and weight) are independent variables and the rest are dependent variables. The resulting partial correlation matrix (of the dependent variables with the effects of age and weight removed) can be stored as a matrix in a BMDP File, and can be used as input in P4M, the factor analysis program.

P6R can be used to regress a number of dependent variables on one set of independent variables. This <u>multivariate regression</u> program gives you a separate regression equation for each dependent variable, squared multiple correlation (R^2) of each independent variable with all other independent variables, R^2 of each dependent variable with the set of independent variables, and tests of significance of multiple regression.

<u>Discriminant analysis</u>. In discriminant analysis, the cases or subjects are divided into groups and the analysis is used to find classification functions (linear combinations of the variables) that best characterize the differences between the groups. These functions are also useful for classifying new cases.

P7M, the stepwise discriminant analysis program, is used to find the subset of variables that maximizes group differences. Variables are entered into the classification function one at a time until the group separation ceases to improve notably (this is similar to the stepwise regression program, P2R, used to find a good subset of variables for prediction). P7M is also used as a multivariate test for group differences (or multivariate analysis of variance); Wilks' lambda (U statistic) and the F approximation to lambda are printed at each step of the output for testing group differences.

A geometrical interpretation of discriminant analysis can be given by plotting each case as a point in a space where each variable is a dimension (has an axis). The points are projected onto a plane or hyperplane selected so the groups are farthest apart, giving a good visual representation of how distinct the groups are (for two groups, the points (cases) are projected onto a line where the groups are farthest apart). P7M presents plots that show such a plane. The X axis is the direction where the groups have the maximum spread; the Y axis shows the maximum spread of the groups in a direction orthogonal to the X axis - this is a plot of the canonical variables.

The canonical variables are related to canonical correlation analysis, which finds the linear combinations of the two sets of variables that are most highly correlated. The first set contains the variables in the classification function; the second set can be viewed as dummy variables used to indicate group membership. The value of the first canonical variable of the classification function set is plotted on the X axis; the value of the second on the Y axis. The coefficients for these canonical variables appear in the output. The coefficients for the second set (dummy variables) do not appear in the output. The eigenvalues and canonical correlations for all canonical variables and the canonical variable scores associated with the first and second canonical variables are also reported.

At each step, P7M uses a one-way analysis of variance F statistic (F-to-enter) to determine which variable should join the function next. At step zero, the standard univariate analysis of variance test is made for each of the variables. The variable for which the means differ most is entered first into the classification function. After step zero, the computed F-to-enter values are conditioned on the variables already present in the function. This is like an analysis of covariance, where the previously entered variables can be viewed as covariates and the nonentered variables are considered as dependent variables.

At each step after a variable is entered, the classification functions are recomputed including the newly entered variable. The number of classification functions is equal to the number of groups. If you have six groups, the values of all six functions are computed for each case and the values are used to compute the posterior probability; each case is assigned to the group in which the value of the posterior probability is maximum. In multiple group discriminant analysis, one function is sometimes stated in the literature for separating each pair of groups. To get this function from P7M, you subtract the classification function coefficients of the the first member from those of the second. At each step, F statistics (the F matrix) that test the equality of means between each pair of groups are given. These F statistics are proportional to Hotelling's T^2 and the Mahalanobis D^2 and give an indication of which group means are closest together and which are farthest apart. After all variables have been entered, the program lists the Mahalanobis D^2 from each case to the center of each group, and the posterior probability of the case assigned to each group. These two bits of information present a good picture of how well (or how poorly) each case has been classified.

The discriminant analysis procedure is successful if few cases are classified into the wrong groups. If a large percentage of the cases are classified correctly (if the posterior probability assigns them to their original group) you know that group differences do exist and that you have selected a set of variables that exhibit the differences. The P7M output presents this classification information in a table of counts indicating how many cases from each original group are assigned to each of the possible groups. A pseudo-jackknife classification table is also printed: for each case a classification function is computed with the case omitted from the computations. The function is then used to classify the omitted case. This results in a classification with less bias. (A classification function can produce optimistic results when it is used to classify the same cases that were used to compute it.)

PLR, Stepwise Logistic Regression, provides an alternative to the multivariate normal model of P7M. When there are only two groups, the all possible

subset regression program, P9R, prints alternative functions for each subset which may classify the cases equally as well.

Preference Pairs. P9M, Linear Scores from Preference Pairs, is used to obtain a linear function of one set of variables that reproduces the ordering of cases as established by recorded preferences (stated by expert judges) between selected pairs of cases.

Survival Analysis

The techniques described in Chapter 19 are appropriate when outcome measurements represent the time to occurrence of some event or response (e.g., survival time, or time to disease recurrence). What distinguishes the techniques of this chapter from other statistical methodology is the ability to handle censored (incomplete) data; that is, there are cases for which the response is not observed but the data (time in study) are included in the analysis. This could occur in a study of survival, where an individual may remain alive at the close of the observation period or may drop out before the end.

P1L estimates the survival (time-to-response) distribution of individuals observed over varying time periods. These estimates can be obtained separately for different groups of patients; the equality of the distributions for these groups can be tested by two nonparametric rank tests. Plots of the survival, hazard and related functions can be printed.

P2L provides Cox model survival analysis when there are covariates. Covariates can be selected in a stepwise manner.

Time Series Analysis

The primary distinguishing feature of time series analysis, as opposed to other types of statistical analysis, is the assumption that cases of data represent measurements or observations made at equispaced points along some linear dimension. Usually the underlying linear dimension is time, as in the record of a subject's blood pressure taken every second over a period of time. However time is occasionally replaced by some other dimension. For example, the thickness of thread from a certain manufacturing process might be measured each millimeter along the length of the thread. This would constitute a 'time' series in which length replaces time as the underlying linear dimension. Nevertheless, we follow conventional terminology and use the word 'time'.

A basic goal of time series analysis is to characterize the way in which the data vary over time. The a priori assumption, common in most other types of statistical analysis, that cases are statistically independent, is here relaxed. We allow that cases may be correlated, assuming that the correlation between cases depends on the time interval separating them. In addition, we allow for the presence of a trend in the data. Thus the trend of increasing commodity prices over the last decade might be represented by a straight line, or by an exponential curve. So the estimated trend and autocorrelation function are one possible characterization of a time series. Other characterizations and more elaborate models are also possible.

The BMDP package includes two programs for time series analysis: BMDP1T employs the frequency domain approach, while BMDP2T uses the time domain approach. We may describe the frequency domain approach as representing the data by a superposition of sinusoidal waves at different frequencies. A central function of BMDP1T is to enable the user, by means of printer plots and accompanying printout, to identify the groups of frequencies contributing most of the overall variability of the data. In the time domain approach, we seek a model from a family of parametric time domain models that is simple and yet captures the variability of the data. BMDP2T uses the iterative model building procedure of Box and Jenkins, consisting of tentative model identification, parametric estimation, and diagnostic checking or residual analysis. Once a satisfactory model has been reached, the user may request BMDP2T to forecast future values of the time series. Both programs have further capabilities which are described in Chapter 20.

3
USING BMDP PROGRAMS

INTRODUCTION

This manual should be regarded as a reference book for the BMDP programs; it contains much more information than you need to analyze a set of data. The programs cover a wide range of statistical techniques; they are designed to be used by research workers who may not be experienced in using a computer.

The three examples presented here are elementary. After reading through them we recommend that you try to use one of the programs in Chapters 8, 9 or 10. To do so you will first want to read or skim through Chapters 4 and 5, which describe the language used to state instructions to the program. The more advanced programs differ from the elementary ones in the level of their statistical analyses and not in the method of stating instructions. Once you have used any program, you will be ready for all the programs.

WHERE TO FIND IT

3.1 EXAMPLES WITH INPUT AND OUTPUT

Example 3a Counting the Frequency of Digits and Characters Using P4D

As our first example we keypunched the following five cards to submit as data to program P4D:

```
BMDP PROGRAMS ARE
EASY TO USE IF YOU
IGNORE WHAT YOU
DON'T NEED TO KNOW
1234567890$.,
```

The statement is true. BMDP programs use preassigned values for most options. The preassigned values are appropriate for a wide variety of problems. Therefore you can ignore the options that are not important to you.

BMDP program P4D (Section 8.3) reports the frequency of each symbol in each column of your data cards. All other programs require that all data be numeric (numbers). In our first example we use P4D to report the frequency of each symbol in the above data cards. The following cards are submitted to the computer:

```
------------------------------------
// (job card)                ┐
// EXEC BIMED,PROG=BMDP4D     │ IBM OS System Cards
//SYSIN DD *                  ┘
/ PROBLEM                     ┐ BMDP
/ END                         ┘ instructions
BMDP PROGRAMS ARE             ┐
EASY TO USE IF YOU            │
IGNORE WHAT YOU               │ data
DON'T NEED TO KNOW            │
1234567890$.,                 ┘
//                            ┐ IBM OS System Card
------------------------------------
```

15

The first three cards are System Cards that are required to start an analysis by P4D; they are the cards used at the Hospital Computing Facility at UCLA and may differ for your computing center. Our System Cards always begin with two slashes. The first card is an accounting card that shows that you are a legal user of the computer. The second card names the BMDP program (BMDP4D) to be used. The third card specifies that instructions for the program will follow immediately. Each System Card must begin in the first column of the computer card. One or more blanks must be used where each blank space is shown; blanks cannot be used where no blank is shown. For the examples in this chapter we list the required system cards; in later chapters we omit them.

The next two cards contain the minimum BMDP instructions necessary to use P4D. No program options are specified; therefore the preassigned options are used.

The next five cards contain the data for this analysis.

The last card is a System Card that indicates the end of the instructions and data.

The computer output from the above cards is shown in Output 3a. It correctly shows, for example, that column 1 of the data cards contains one each of the characters B, E, I, D and 1. The printed results are explained in footnotes to the output.

Key:

① In this example, the variable numbers are column numbers.

② The card code column indicates which holes the keypunch machine punches to represent each

Output 3a   Results produced by program P4D from Example 3a

FREQUENCY COUNT OF CHARACTERS PER VARIABLES

CHAR	CARD CODE	1	2	3	4	5	6	7	8	9	10	11	12	13	14	15	16	17	18	19	20
	BLANK	0	0	0	0	2	1	1	1	0	0	1	2	0	3	2	2	2	3	5	5
0	0	0	0	0	0	0	0	0	0	0	1	0	0	0	0	0	0	0	0	0	0
1	1	1	0	0	0	0	0	0	0	0	0	0	0	0	0	0	0	0	0	0	0
2	2	0	1	0	0	0	0	0	0	0	0	0	0	0	0	0	0	0	0	0	0
3	3	0	0	1	0	0	0	0	0	0	0	0	0	0	0	0	0	0	0	0	0
4	4	0	0	0	1	0	0	0	0	0	0	0	0	0	0	0	0	0	0	0	0
5	5	0	0	0	0	1	0	0	0	0	0	0	0	0	0	0	0	0	0	0	0
6	6	0	0	0	0	0	0	1	0	0	0	0	0	0	0	0	0	0	0	0	0
7	7	0	0	0	0	0	0	0	1	0	0	0	0	0	0	0	0	0	0	0	0
8	8	0	0	0	0	0	0	0	1	0	0	0	0	0	0	0	0	0	0	0	0
9	9	0	0	0	0	0	0	0	0	1	0	0	0	0	0	0	0	0	0	0	0
A	12-1	0	1	0	0	0	0	0	0	0	1	1	0	0	1	0	0	0	0	0	0
B	12-2	1	0	0	0	0	0	0	0	0	0	0	0	0	0	0	0	0	0	0	0
D	12-4	1	0	1	0	0	0	0	0	0	1	0	0	0	0	0	0	0	0	0	0
E	12-5	1	0	0	0	0	1	0	1	1	0	1	0	0	0	0	0	1	0	0	0
F	12-6	0	0	0	0	0	0	0	0	0	0	0	0	0	1	0	0	0	0	0	0
G	12-7	0	1	0	0	0	0	0	0	1	0	0	0	0	0	0	0	0	0	0	0
H	12-8	0	0	0	0	0	0	0	0	1	0	0	0	0	0	0	0	0	0	0	0
I	12-9	1	0	0	0	0	0	0	0	0	0	0	0	1	0	0	0	0	0	0	0
K	11-2	0	0	0	0	0	0	0	0	0	0	0	0	0	1	0	0	0	0	0	0
M	11-4	0	1	0	0	0	0	0	0	0	0	1	0	0	0	0	0	0	0	0	0
N	11-5	0	0	2	0	0	1	0	0	0	0	0	0	0	0	1	0	0	0	0	0
O	11-6	0	1	0	1	0	0	1	1	0	0	0	0	1	1	0	0	2	0	0	0
P	11-7	0	0	0	1	0	1	0	0	0	0	0	0	0	0	0	0	0	0	0	0
R	11-9	0	0	0	0	1	0	1	0	0	1	0	0	0	0	1	0	0	0	0	0
S	0-2	0	0	1	0	0	0	0	0	0	1	0	0	1	0	0	0	0	0	0	0
T	0-3	0	0	0	0	1	1	0	0	0	0	1	1	0	0	0	0	0	0	0	0
U	0-4	0	0	0	0	0	0	0	0	1	0	0	0	0	1	0	1	0	0	0	0
W	0-6	0	0	0	0	0	0	0	1	0	0	0	0	0	0	0	0	1	0	0	0
Y	0-8	0	0	0	1	0	0	0	0	0	0	0	0	1	0	1	0	0	0	0	0
$	11-3-8	0	0	0	0	0	0	0	0	0	0	1	0	0	0	0	0	0	0	0	0
,	0-3-8	0	0	0	0	0	0	0	0	0	0	0	0	1	0	0	0	0	0	0	0
'	5-8	0	0	0	1	0	0	0	0	0	0	0	0	0	0	0	0	0	0	0	0
.	12-3-8	0	0	0	0	0	0	0	0	0	0	0	1	0	0	0	0	0	0	0	0

TOTALS --

		1	2	3	4	5	6	7	8	9	10	11	12	13	14	15	16	17	18	19	20
NUMERIC	④	1	1	1	1	1	1	1	1	1	1	0	0	0	0	0	0	0	0	0	0
ALPHABETIC		4	4	4	3	2	3	3	3	4	4	3	2	4	2	3	3	3	2	0	0
SPECIAL		0	0	0	1	0	0	0	0	0	0	1	0	1	0	0	0	0	0	0	0
PERIOD		0	0	0	0	0	0	0	0	0	0	0	1	0	0	0	0	0	0	0	0

--⑤--

----

character; e.g., a 12 and a 1 are punched to represent A.

③ The 1's in the first column (variable) indicate that a 1, B, D, E and I were found in the first column of the 5 records.

④ The total frequency for the first column is one numeric symbol (1) and four alphabetic symbols (B, D, E and I).

⑤ The program output continues by reporting five blanks in each of the remaining columns (21-80, not shown in the above output).

Example 3b Descriptive Statistics for Age and Cholesterol Using P1D

As our second example we use P1D -- Simple Data Description. P1D is described in Chapter 8; the BMDP instructions to describe the data are explained in Chapter 5. To illustrate the results of P1D we use part of the data from a study of blood chemistries. (A more complete set is shown in Table 5.1 and is used in the examples throughout this manual.) We use only the values of age and cholesterol for 188 women. Each woman's values are punched on a separate card, with age first then cholesterol. The entire card deck submitted to the computer is

```
// (job card)                              ⎤  IBM OS
// EXEC BIMED,PROG=BMDP1D                   ⎬  System Cards
//SYSIN  DD  *                             ⎦
/ PROBLEM    TITLE IS 'DESCRIPTIVE         ⎤
               STATISTICS FOR AGE
               AND CHOLESTEROL'.            ⎬  BMDP
/ INPUT      VARIABLES ARE 2.                  instructions
             FORMAT IS '(F2.0, F4.0)'.
/ VARIABLE   NAMES ARE AGE, CHOLSTRL.
/ END                                      ⎦
```

22 200	22 192	27 195	39 198	
22 600	22 247	27 185	39 260	
25 243	22 175	27 168	39 180	
25 50	22 155	27 200	39 210	
19 158	22 215	27 250	39 235	
19 255	22 200	27 280	40 196	
20 210	22 247	28 260	40 305	
20 192	23 220	28 250	40 170	
21 246	23 207	28 175	40 276	
21 245	23 266	28 305	40 272	
21 208	23 240	28 200	40 315	
21 260	24 195	28 235	40 300	
21 204	24 250	29 177	40 290	
21 192	24 225	29 235	41 320	
21 280	24 200	29 226	41 255	
21 230	24 180	29 230	41 306	
21 215	24 240	30 198	41 324	
21 225	25 330	30 295	42 240	
21 165	25 175	30 230	42 210	
21 200	25 205	30 200	43 210	
21 220	25 235	30 230	43 250	
21 255	25 295	30 262	43 335	
22 263	25 230	30 174	43 230	
22 173	26 240	30 250	43 285	
22 170	26 238	30 217	43 200	
22 290	26 198	30 212	43 280	
22 263	26 196	31 250	43 276	
22 220	27 172	31 237	44 253	
22 200	27 317	31 270	44 242	
cont'd	cont'd	31 280	45 160	
		31 238	45 263	
		31 218	46 250	
		32 185	46 320	
		32 235	46 257	
		32 262	46 190	
		32 160	46 230	
		32 189	46 265	
		32 205	47 297	
		32 260	47 255	
		32 240	47 257	
		32 197	47 257	
		32 180	48 300	
		33 205	48 225	
		33 260	48 216	
		33 243	48 248	
		33 195	48 306	
		33 203	48 235	
		33 222	48 195	
		34 197	48 338	
		34 245	49 255	
		35 180	49 217	
		35 223	50 295	
		35 254	50 390	
		35 245	52 250	
		36 247	52 265	
		36 175	53 227	
		36 215	53 220	
		36 270	54 305	
		37 237	54 220	
		37 200	54 227	
		37 270	54 260	
		37 230	54 320	
		38 255	54 245	
		38 275	55 275	
		39 210	55 298	
		cont'd	//	⎤ IBM OS System Card

The first three System Cards are similar to those in Example a except that BMDP1D replaces BMDP4D. The BMDP instructions specify a <u>title</u> for the analysis, the number of <u>variables</u> in the data, the layout (<u>format</u>) of the data for each case, and <u>names</u> for the two variables. The format is described in detail below. The remaining instructions are explained in Chapter 5.

The results are presented in Output 3b.

Output 3b   Analysis of the data in Example 3b by P1D

---

①

BMDP1D - SIMPLE DATA DESCRIPTION AND DATA MANAGEMENT
DEPARTMENT OF BIOMATHEMATICS
UNIVERSITY OF CALIFORNIA, LOS ANGELES 90024
(213)-825-5940
PROGRAM REVISED JANUARY 1981
MANUAL REVISED -- 1981
COPYRIGHT (C) 1981 REGENTS OF UNIVERSITY OF CALIFORNIA

PROGRAM CONTROL INFORMATION   ②

/ PROBLEM   TITLE IS 'DESCRIPTIVE
                    STATISTICS FOR AGE
                    AND CHOLESTEROL'.
/ INPUT   VARIABLES ARE 2.
                    FORMAT IS '(F2.0, F4.0)'.
/ VARIABLE   NAMES ARE AGE, CHOLSTRL.
/ END

③
    PROBLEM TITLE . . . . . .
DESCRIPTIVE STATISTICS FOR AGE AND CHOLESTEROL

    NUMBER OF VARIABLES TO READ IN.   2
    NUMBER OF VARIABLES ADDED BY TRANSFORMATIONS. .   0
    TOTAL NUMBER OF VARIABLES   2
    NUMBER OF CASES TO READ IN. . . . . TO END
    CASE LABELING VARIABLES . . . .
    LIMITS AND MISSING VALUE CHECKED BEFORE TRANSFORMATIONS
    BLANKS ARE. . . . . MISSING
    INPUT UNIT NUMBER   5
    REWIND INPUT UNIT PRIOR TO READING. . DATA. . .   NO
    NUMBER OF WORDS OF DYNAMIC STORAGE. 18430
    NUMBER OF CASES DESCRIBED BY INPUT FORMAT . . .   1

VARIABLES TO BE USED
    1 AGE   2 CHOLSTRL

    INPUT FORMAT. . . . .
    (F2.0, F4.0)   ④

MAXIMUM LENGTH DATA RECORD IS   6 CHARACTERS.

I N P U T   V A R I A B L E S . . . . .

VARIABLE INDEX	NAME	RECORD NO.	COLUMNS BEGIN	END	FIELD WIDTH	TYPE		VARIABLE INDEX	NAME	RECORD NO.	COLUMNS BEGIN	END	FIELD WIDTH	TYPE
1	AGE	1	1	2	2	F	+	2	CHOLSTRL	1	3	6	4	F

BASED ON INPUT FORMAT SUPPLIED   1 RECORDS READ PER CASE.

    NUMBER OF CASES READ.   188

VARIABLE NO. NAME	TOTAL FREQUENCY	MEAN	STANDARD DEVIATION	ST.ERR. OF MEAN	COEFF. OF VARIATION	SMALLEST VALUE	Z-SCORE	LARGEST VALUE	Z-SCORE	RANGE
1 AGE	188	33.818	10.113	0.7376	0.29904	19.000	-1.47	55.000	2.09	36.000
2 CHOLSTRL	188	237.095	51.807	3.7784	0.21851	50.000	-3.61	600.000	7.00	550.000

⑤ (at VARIABLE NO. NAME)

NUMBER OF WORDS OF STORAGE USED   214

Key:

① When the computer system finds the program you specify (P1D) this heading is printed before your instructions are interpreted or the data are read. Check the program revision date and manual date to see if they coincide with the documentation that you are using.

② The Control Language instructions are printed: We are interested in the two variables punched on the data cards -- age and cholesterol count. The FORMAT statement in the INPUT paragraph describes where these variables are found on the card.
    'F2.0' says to read two columns (1-2) as the value of the first variable.
    'F4.0' says to read the next four columns (3-6) as the value of the second variable.
F-format is for numbers; letters and special characters are not allowed. The two variables are named AGE and CHOLSTRL in the VARIABLE paragraph. The names are listed in the same order as the variables in the FORMAT statement.

③ Interpretation of the BMDP instructions and reporting of preassigned values. Since the number of cases is not specified, it is reported as "TO END" and all the data are read. The other preassigned values are explained in Chapter 5.

④ The input format is reported and a description is given of the data layout: The values for CHOLSTRL are in a field 4 characters wide beginning in column 3 and ending in column 6. The number of cases read is also reported.

⑤ Univariate statistics are printed for each variable. Note that the largest cholesterol value (600) has a z-score of 7.0.

Example 3c A First Look at Group Differences Using P7D

As our third example we use P7D -- Description of Groups (Strata) with Histograms and Analysis of Variance. P7D is described in Section 9.2. We want to see whether the distributions of cholesterol are similar across the age groups (25 OR LESS, 26 TO 35, 36 TO 45, and OVER 45) and whether there are any unusual values or features in the data.

We submit the same card deck illustrated in Example b. with one modification (BMDP1D is changed to BMDP7D on the second systems card) and two additions: a BMDP instruction about the HISTOGRAM and GROUP information about AGE. (We also changed the TITLE of the analysis.)

The card deck submitted to the computer for this example is

```
    -------------------------------------
// (job card)
// EXEC BIMED,PROG=BMDP7D
//SYSIN DD *
/ PROBLEM   TITLE IS 'COMPARE FEMALE CHOLESTEROL
                      LEVELS FOR FOUR AGE GROUPS'.
/ INPUT     VARIABLES ARE 2.
            FORMAT IS '(F2.0, F4.0)'.
/ VARIABLE  NAMES ARE AGE, CHOLSTRL.
/ HISTOGRAM GROUPING IS AGE.
/ GROUP     CUTPOINTS(1) ARE 25, 35, 45.
            NAMES(1) ARE '25ORLESS', '26 TO 35',
                         '36 TO 45', 'OVER 45'.
/ END
     .
     .
     .
     .
//
    -------------------------------------
```

The BMDP instructions specify a title for the analysis, the number of variables in the data, the layout (format) of the data, the names of the variables, the grouping variable (the variable used to classify cases into groups), three endpoints (cutpoints) that define four intervals for age, and names for the four intervals.

The results are presented in Output 3c.

Key:

① The BMDP instructions are printed. The grouping variable is age. Histograms of cholesterol values will be made for each age group. The age groups are defined by CUTPOINTS in the GROUP paragraph -- four age groups are defined as 25 or less, 26 to 35, 36 to 45, and over 45. In the GROUP paragraph, the '(1)' following CUTPOINTS and NAMES identifies the first variable (age) as the grouping variable. The group names are in apostrophes because they begin with a number or contain a special character (blank).

② The BMDP instructions are interpreted.

③ This output shows histograms turned on their sides. The midpoint cholesterol level for each interval in the histograms is given at the left. In the histogram for women 25 years of age or less, the asterisk by 600 represents one woman's cholesterol reading. One woman has a reading around 330, two near 300, etc. The 'M' represents the mean for the group. The actual value of the mean can be found below the histogram (226.1). Univariate statistics for each group are displayed below its histogram. Statistics for all 188 women are displayed at the lower left. Note that the mean increases for older women: 226.1 for women 25 or less; 224.6 for those 26-35; 248.3 for those 36-45; and 262.1 for those over 45. The mean for all 188 women is 237.1. The standard deviation is largest for the 25 or less group (68.6) due to the unusual cholesterol reading of 600. There is also a very low value (50) in this group. The investigator should verify these two values. We removed these cases and reran the analysis; the new mean for women 25 or less was 222.1 and the standard deviation dropped to 37.4.

④ Explanation of other portions of the output, including the results for the test of equality of group means are explained in the program description for P7D (Section 9.2).

Output 3c   Annotated results from P7D in Example 3c
----

①
```
/ PROBLEM   TITLE IS 'COMPARE FEMALE CHOLESTEROL
                      LEVELS FOR FOUR AGE GROUPS'.
/ INPUT     VARIABLES ARE 2.
            FORMAT IS '(F2.0, F4.0)'.
/ VARIABLE  NAMES ARE AGE, CHOLSTRL.
/ HISTOGRAM GROUPING IS AGE.
/ GROUP     CUTPOINTS(1) ARE 25, 35, 45.
            NAMES(1) ARE '25ORLESS', '26 TO 35',
                         '36 TO 45', 'OVER 45'.
/ END
```

②
```
PROBLEM TITLE . . . . . .
COMPARE FEMALE CHOLESTEROL LEVELS FOR FOUR AGE GROUPS

   NUMBER OF VARIABLES TO READ IN. . . . . . . .       2
   NUMBER OF VARIABLES ADDED BY TRANSFORMATIONS. .     0
   TOTAL NUMBER OF VARIABLES . . . . . . . . . .       2
   NUMBER OF CASES TO READ IN. . . . . . . . . . TO END
   CASE LABELING VARIABLES . . . . . . . . . . .
   LIMITS AND MISSING VALUE CHECKED BEFORE TRANSFORMATIONS
   BLANKS ARE. . . . . . . . . . . . . . . . . MISSING
   INPUT UNIT NUMBER . . . . . . . . . . . . . .       5
   REWIND INPUT UNIT PRIOR TO READING. . DATA. . .    NO
   NUMBER OF WORDS OF DYNAMIC STORAGE. . . . . . 15358
   NUMBER OF CASES DESCRIBED BY INPUT FORMAT . . .     1


VARIABLES TO BE USED
  1 AGE          2 CHOLSTRL


   INPUT FORMAT. . . . .
(F2.0, F4.0)
```

(output continued)

Output 3c (continued)

```
MAXIMUM LENGTH DATA RECORD IS    6 CHARACTERS.

I N P U T   V A R I A B L E S . . . . .
    VARIABLE      RECORD   COLUMNS    FIELD  TYPE            VARIABLE      RECORD   COLUMNS    FIELD  TYPE
  INDEX  NAME      NO.   BEGIN  END   WIDTH               INDEX  NAME      NO.   BEGIN  END   WIDTH
  -----  -------   ----  -----  ---   -----  ----         -----  -------   ----  -----  ---   -----  ----
    1 AGE           1      1     2      2     F     +        2 CHOLSTRL     1      3     6      4     F

BASED ON INPUT FORMAT SUPPLIED    1 RECORDS READ PER CASE.




    NUMBER OF CASES READ. . . . . . . . . . . . .      188
    PRINT DATA MATRIX . . . . . . . . . . . . . .       NO
    PRINT DATA MATRIX AFTER ORDERING. . . . . . . .      NO
    PRINT WINSORIZING TABLE . . . . . . . . . . .       NO
    PRINT CORRELATION TABLE . . . . . . . . . . .       NO
```

```
PAGE   3    COMPARE FEMALE CHOLESTEROL LEVELS FOR FOUR AGE GROUPS

              ************                                                    ************
HISTOGRAM OF * CHOLSTRL *  (VARIABLE     2). CASES DIVIDED INTO GROUPS BASED ON VALUES OF * AGE     * (VARIABLE     1)
              ************                                                    ************

            25ORLESS              26 TO 35              36 TO 45              OVER45
          .........................+........................+........................+.....................+
MIDPOINTS
  630.000)
  600.000)*        ③
  570.000)
  540.000)
  510.000)
  480.000)
  450.000)
  420.000)
  390.000)                                                      *
  360.000)
  330.000)*                *                  ***                ***
  300.000)**               **                 *****              ******
  270.000)*****            ********            *********          M******
  240.000)M***********     *******************  M**********       **********
  210.000)*****************  M***************    *********         *****
  180.000)*********         ************         ***              **
  150.000)***              *                    *
  120.000)
   90.000)
   60.000)*
   30.000)
    0.0  )
GROUP MEANS ARE DENOTED BY M'S IF THEY COINCIDE WITH *'S, N'S OTHERWISE

MEAN         226.077          224.633          248.333          262.059
STD.DEV.      68.643           35.742           44.809           43.267
R.E.S.D.      50.442           37.427           46.613           42.448
S. E. M.       9.519            4.614            6.914            7.420
MAXIMUM      600.000          317.000          335.000          390.000
MINIMUM       50.000          160.000          160.000          190.000
SAMPLE SIZE       52               60               42               34
```

```
          ALL GROUPS COMBINED       ***************************** ANALYSIS OF VARIANCE TABLE *****************************
        (EXCEPT CASES WITH UNUSED VALUES  *
          FOR AGE        )              *   SOURCE              SUM OF SQUARES   DF     MEAN SQUARE    F VALUE   TAIL PROBABILITY
                                        *
MEAN         237.096                    *   BETWEEN GROUPS        42123.4180      3    14041.1367       5.62        0.0010
STD.DEV.      51.807                    *   WITHIN   GROUPS      459776.8413    184     2498.7872
R.E.S.D.      43.629                    *                                                               ④
S. E. M.       3.778                    *   TOTAL               501900.2500    187
MAXIMUM      600.000                    ***************************************************************************************
MINIMUM       50.000                    *   LEVENE'S TEST FOR EQUAL VARIANCES    3, 184                 0.85        0.4703
SAMPLE SIZE      188                    ***************************************************************************************
                                        *   ONE-WAY ANALYSIS OF VARIANCE
                                        *   TEST STATISTICS FOR WITHIN-GROUP
                                        *   VARIANCES NOT ASSUMED TO BE EQUAL
                                        *      WELCH                           3,  91                 7.42        0.0002
                                        *      BROWN-FORSYTHE                  3, 146                 5.71        0.0010
```

3.2 RESEARCH FORMS, CODING SHEETS AND KEYPUNCHING CARDS

The data must be recorded before an analysis can be performed. The method that you choose to record the data will depend on its quantity and source. When the data collection is not automated, the data are usually recorded on either a research form designed for the study or a coding sheet.

Design of research forms. A proper research form can save both time and money. A form designed with foresight can mean the difference between a smoothly run study and one that becomes a disaster.

The following rules should be considered when designing a research form:

- Make an outline of all data to be collected.
- Make a rough draft of the form. Include a space for indicating the card columns used for specific data on the form, preferably on the right-hand margin; this will simplify coding and keypunching, and the correct transfer of data to the assigned fields will be insured. Consult the keypunch supervisor and statistician for suggestions. Revise the form and check with them again. When the form is completed and approved, have it printed for use.
- Include a subject or case number on each form and each card that identifies each subject individually; this number is used to identify all data pertaining to one subject. Examples are hospital patient numbers, social security numbers or sequence numbers. If you question the data on a card, the identification number allows you to refer back to the form to check for errors. A sequence number on each card allows for the cards to be ordered by machine if they are dropped or otherwise disordered.
- Assign a number to each card if more than one form is involved or if there is more than one card per case. This number identifies the data on the card.
- Include explicit instructions at the beginning of each form specifying how it should be filled out. If the form is misunderstood the data may not be entered properly and the study may be useless. Forms that are filled out by subjects must be simple, easily understood and ordered conveniently.

A sample of one research form is given in Figure 3.1.

Coding sheets. The research form in Figure 3.1 gives one example of a coding sheet -- the data to be keypunched are organized in a column to the right of the form. Below or beside each line appears the card columns into which the numbers are keypunched. If weight is recorded and can be either two digits (< 100 lbs.) or three digits (> 100 lbs.), three columns must be allowed for the number. Values less than 100 should be written with a leading zero (e.g., 095) or right-justified (a blank followed by 95). Do not try to conserve space by simply recording "1" low, "2" average and "3" heavy, for you may limit the type of analyses available - a full range of weights can easily be collapsed later into three categories but the reverse is not true. A second type of coding sheet is one that contains lines divided into 80 columns; each column on the form represents one card column. Actually ruled graph paper serves very well. The values for

each variable are recorded in a fixed position (set of columns) on the sheet. Each line is keypunched as a computer card.

Coding sheets should be prepared with care to avoid common keypunch errors. If the decimal point location is the same for every case, they need not be punched; and plus signs need not be punched. Care should be taken to avoid ambiguity in the use of letters, numbers and symbols. For example, the letter O may be written with a slash through it ($\emptyset$) to distinguish it from the number zero. Other number-letter pairs that may be confused are 1 and I, 2 and Z, 6 and G, and 7 and T.

Always use numbers when coding information (assigning numbers to represent race, age, sex, etc.), so they can be included in computations (e.g., to represent groups or categories). For example, sex can be coded 1 for male and 2 for female. One column should be used for each digit in the number: 1-9, one column; 10-99, two columns; 100-999, three columns, etc. Additional columns are needed if decimal points or signs are used with the numbers.

Keypunching cards. In large studies data are often entered directly into the computer through a terminal entry system. However, for the beginner it is easy to conceptualize each row of data as a separate card. Data information is punched on a card as small rectangular holes in specific locations. The standard IBM card has 80 vertical columns and 12 horizontal rows. This gives 12 punching positions in each column. One or more punches in a single column represent a character. There are two kinds of keypunch machines: the 026 character set has 47 acceptable characters, and the 029 character set has 62 acceptable characters. The BMDP programs accept instructions and data from both kinds of keypunch machines. However, System Cards must be punched on an 029 keypunch machine. To see how the keypunch works, insert a card in the machine and type every key on the keyboard: each letter, symbol or number is represented on the card by a specific combination of holes in one column.

3.3 SPECIFYING THE DATA FORMAT

Each BMDP program reads the data one case at a time. In this section we first describe fixed format entry. Each variable must be located in the same columns on the data card or in the data record for all cases. The layout of the data card or record is described by a format statement. The word "format" refers to the arrangement of information on a data card or record. The format specifications tell the program which columns of the record to skip, which columns to group together as one number, and which columns to treat as numbers in a row. For example, the format statement tells the program whether "345890021" is to be read as

"34.5, 890.0, 0.21"
"34., 9002.1"
"589.002"
or "3, 4, 58, 90, 0, 2, 1"

A format specification indicates the size of a field (the number of columns) and the method of handling that field (skipping, entering it into the computer as a whole number, entering it into the

Figure 3.1   Example of a research form

MULTIPLE CHOICE FORM

UCLA Operation _____   Name of Coder: *Ariel Meyerbeer*   Col.

Patient Name *Henrietta Smithson*   Patient I.D. _____ *653* _____   *653*
                                                                              ――――
                                                                              1-3

Operation Date *11 / 06 / 81* _____   *110681*
                                                                              ――――――
                                                                              4-9

Type of Operation (Check One):

    1) Hemiarthroplasty – AM .... [ ]   8) THR – McKee .... [ ]   *65*
    2) Hemiarthroplasty – FR Thompson ..... [ ]   9) THR – Zimmer .... [ ]   ―――――
    3) Hemiarthroplasty – Zimmer .... [ ]   10) THR – Other .... [ ]   10-11
    4) Cup Arthroplasty .... [ ]   11) Girdlestone .... [ ]
    5) Trochanteric Arthroplasty .... [✓]   12) Osteotomy .... [ ]
    6) Hemiarthroplasty – Other .... [ ]
    7) Total Hip Replacement – Charnley ... [ ]

Surgeon:

    1) Resident _____ [ ]   4) *Berlioz* _____ [✓]   *4*
    2) HCA _____ [ ]   5) _____ [ ]   ―――
    3) AC _____ [ ]   6) _____ [ ]   12

Position:

    1) Supine [ ]   3) Prone   [ ]   *2*
    2) Lateral [✓]   4) Other (Specify) _____   [ ]   ―――
                                                                   13

Type of Anesthesia:

    1) Halothane [ ]   3) Nitrous & Pentothal   [✓]   *3*
    2) Pentothane [ ]   4) Other (Specify) _____ [ ]   ―――
                                                                  14

Greater Trochanter:

    1) No Osteotomy   [ ]   3) Mod. Secure Reattachment [ ]   *4*
    2) Secure Reattachment [ ]   4) Insecure Reattachment   [✓]   ―――
                                                                         15

Fixation Method:

    2-Criss-crossed Superior Wire through Bone   2-Parallel   *1*
                                                                               ―――
                                                                                16
    1) Stainless #18 .... [✓]   4) Stainless #18 .... [ ]
    2) Stainless #17 .... [ ]   5) Stainless #17 .... [ ]
    3) Vitallium .040 .... [ ]   6) Vitallium .040 .... [ ]
                        7) Other (Specify) _____ [ ]

Transverse Fasciotomy:
                                        1) Yes   2) No
    Iliotibal Band   [✓]   [ ]   (17)   *1*
                                                                    ―――
    Section Iliopsoas   [ ]   [✓]   (18)   *2*
                                                                    ―――
    Resuture Iliopsoas   [ ]   [✓]   (19)   *2*
                                                                    ―――
    Adductor Subcutaneous Tenotomy   [✓]   [ ]   (20)   *1*
                                                                    ―――

computer as a number with two decimal digits, etc.). Each case is assumed to have the same format as other cases in the same analysis.

The BMDP programs are written to allow you to vary the format according to the requirements of the data -- this is called "variable format." It allows considerable freedom in how to read the data. A complete description of formats can be found in FORTRAN programming manuals. The features required for the BMDP programs are described below.

F-type format. The F-type format is used when all data input values are signed (+ or -) or unsigned <u>numbers</u> with or without a decimal point punched. Letters and special characters are not allowed. The following examples illustrate F-type format:

F2.0 specifies that the number is a whole number (zero digits after the decimal point) and has at most two digits (e.g., 21,99,02, 2)

F5.1 specifies that the number has at most five digits and the decimal point precedes the last digit (e.g., 12345 is read as 1234.5, 1234 is read as 123.4)

2F5.1 describes two numbers, each with the format F5.1, and that one number follows the other in the data record

That is,
- a number before the F specifies how many consecutive variables are described by this format specification
- the first number after the F specifies the maximum number of columns in which the number can appear (be written)
- the last number specifies the number of digits after the decimal point.

When a data value being <u>read</u> contains a decimal point, it overrides the position for the decimal point stated in the F-type format. When a data value is being <u>written</u> by an F-type format, the decimal point is always printed and the number of digits printed is determined by the format (e.g., the number 12.345 printed under the format F5.1 will appear as 12.3 -- only one digit is printed after the decimal point); the number of columns specified for printing must allow for the decimal point and the minus sign if the number is negative.

Skipping columns and records. Columns in the record can be skipped (ignored) by specifying the number to be skipped followed by an "X" (alphabetic X). For example, 20X specifies that 20 columns are to be skipped.

A slash (/) instructs the program to skip the remainder of the card and begin the next card. Any number of slashes can be used. Slashes are used if the data for a case are recorded on more than one card.

A-type format. The A-type format is required when alphabetical, numerical or special characters (or a combination of the three) are in the data, and is usually used for labeling cases (names, for example). Data using the A-type format specification <u>cannot</u> be used in computations. The following examples illustrate certain rules:

Punched Data	Format Specification	Stored Data
AGE	A3	AGEƀ
$	A1	$ƀƀƀ
GERTRUDE	2A4	GERTRUDE

Each specification of a field results in a computer word consisting of exactly 4 characters. When the specified width is less than 4, the characters are positioned in the left of the field and the remaining characters are filled in with blanks (indicated by ƀ). In the third example GERTRUDE is stored in two consecutive variables (GERT in the first, RUDE in the second).

The A-type format is used only for variables that contain case identification, such as patient name, and are <u>not</u> used in computations. P4D -- Single Column Frequencies - Numeric and Nonnumeric -- is the only program that uses the A-type format for purposes other than case identification.

The format statement. The format statement begins with a left parenthesis followed by a sequence of specifications, and closes with a right parenthesis. Each specification is followed by a comma. Blank columns in the format statement are allowed, since they are ignored.

In the BMDP instructions, the format is specified as a sentence starting with FORMAT IS, continuing with the format statement enclosed in apostrophes and terminating with a period.

- FORMAT IS '(12F3.0, F4.0, 11F2.0)'.
describes twenty-four variables recorded in twelve three-column numbers, followed by one four-column number, and followed by eleven two-column numbers. Each data card will be read according to this format, beginning in column one of each card.

- FORMAT IS '(5X, 2F6.0, F1.0, 3X, F5.0/5X,F6.0)'.
describes five variables recorded on a pair of cards as follows:
1. Skip five columns in the first card.
2. Pick up two six-digit numbers in columns 6-11 and 12-17.
3. Pick up a one-digit number in column 18.
4. Skip three columns (columns 19-21).
5. Pick up a five-digit number in columns 22-26.
6. Go to the second card.
7. Skip the first five columns of the second card.
8. Pick up a six-digit number in columns 6-11 of the second card.

- FORMAT IS '(12F3.0, F4.0, 11F2.0/)'.

describes the same twenty-four variables as in the first example but the program will read the data in one card and then skip the next card (because of the slash). The next case will then begin on the third card, etc.

Format statements are frequent sources of clerical errors. They should be checked very carefully.

In versions of BMDP dated 1981 or after, the ".0" part of an F-type format can be dropped. For example, the last format above can be simply stated as (12F3, F4, 11F2/).

23

Free-format data reading. Although the above fixed format is convenient when using punched cards, other formats may be more desirable when using a computer terminal, e.g., separating data items with a space or a comma rather than entering them in fixed colummns. In Chapter 5 we give details of free format data reading. There are three types available

FORMAT IS FREE.

Each case starts on a new record. More than one record can be used for each case provided each case has the same number of records. No excess data are allowed on any record. After all variables for a case are read the remainder of the record must be blank.

FORMAT IS STREAM.

Cases need have no record boundaries; one record can contain more than one case. The only error checks that are made are bad data (e.g., illegal characters) and END-OF-DATA before all variables are read for the last case.

FORMAT IS SLASH.

Cases need have no record boundaries; one record can contain more than one case. Either the end of a record or a slash must follow the last variable for each case.

Common rules for all free-format read modes of reading data are given in Section 5.6. These formats can greatly simplify data entry from a terminal.

4

REQUIREMENTS FOR AN ANALYSIS

BMDP and System Instructions

INTRODUCTION

BMDP instructions are used to specify an analysis to the programs. The instructions called Control Language, form an English-based language that uses statements and commands organized as sentences and paragraphs. For example,

        PLOT   YVARIABLES ARE HEIGHT, WEIGHT.
                XVARIABLES ARE   AGE, HEIGHT.

specifies that HEIGHT is to be plotted against AGE, and WEIGHT against HEIGHT. The Control Language rules and terms used throughout this manual are described in Section 4.1.

The operating system (computer) also needs instructions: you must indicate the BMDP program you want to use and verify that you are a legitimate user of the computer. These instructions are given on System Cards and are discussed in Section 4.2. Common errors and how to deal with them are described in Section 4.3. Special options of the CONTROL, PRINT, and PROBLEM paragraphs are found in Section 4.4. Information on running the programs from a terminal is given in Section 4.5. Options useful for program development and debugging are also described in this section.

WHERE TO FIND IT

4.1 THE BMDP INSTRUCTION LANGUAGE

BMDP instructions are used to describe the analysis to be performed. These English-based instructions are read and interpreted by all BMDP programs, and are used to

- describe the data input
- name the variables, and state missing value codes and upper and lower limits for the variables
- specify the analysis, such as regression
- request optional results to be printed
- specify variables to be plotted

The following example from P6D -- Bivariate (Scatter) Plots -- demonstrates the BMDP instruction language.

```
/ PROBLEM    TITLE IS 'WERNER BLOOD CHEMISTRY DATA'.
/ INPUT      VARIABLES ARE 9.
             FORMAT IS '(A4, 5F4.0, 3F4.1)'.
/ VARIABLE   NAMES ARE ID, AGE, HEIGHT, WEIGHT,
                 BRTHPILL, CHOLSTRL, ALBUMIN,
                 CALCIUM, URICACID.
             LABEL IS ID.
/ PLOT       YVARIABLES ARE CHOLSTRL, WEIGHT.
             XVARIABLES ARE     AGE, HEIGHT.

/ END
```

The instructions specify a title (Werner blood chemistry data) for the analysis; the number of variables in the data (9); the format (layout) of the data in a case; names for the 9 variables (ID is the name of the first variable, AGE the second, etc.); that the variable containing case labels is ID; that blanks are missing value codes; and the pairs of variables to be plotted (CHOLSTRL against AGE and WEIGHT against HEIGHT).

Syntax and punctuation. The BMDP instructions are written in sentences that are grouped into paragraphs. In the above example PROBLEM, INPUT, VARIABLE, PLOT and END are paragraph names.

Sentences end with a period. Paragraphs are separated by a slash (/); we prefer to put the slash before the paragraph name so it is not forgotten.

Values or names in a list are separated by commas. Each word or value must be separated from the following word or value either by one or more blanks or by the appropriate punctuation (slash, period, comma or equal sign).

The instructions can be typed in columns 1 through 80 on each card (record). They can be typed continuously, or an arbitrary number of blanks can be used between words, sentences or paragraphs to make them easier to read as in the above example.

Paragraphs. Several paragraphs are common to all BMDP programs and are described in Chapters 5, 6 and 7 (e.g., PROBLEM, INPUT and VARIABLE). Paragraphs specific to a program are described in the individual program descriptions (e.g., PLOT).

The paragraph name must be the first word in the paragraph. We will be dropping this feature when the Control Language processor is rewritten to allow better diagnostics. Paragraphs must be separated by a slash (/). We usually recommend that the slash be placed immediately before the paragraph name at the beginning of the paragraph, as shown in the example above. Paragraphs can be typed continuously; they do not need to begin on separate cards (lines) as in our example.

A given paragraph can be used only once in each problem unless otherwise stated in the program description. Some paragraphs can be repeated to allow additional analyses of the same data. Except where noted, paragraphs can be stated in any order in the BMDP instructions.

The END paragraph has a special function; it terminates the BMDP instructions for a problem. It consists only of the paragraph name; i.e., / END. No other instructions should be typed after END on the same card. END should not appear in columns 78-80.

For interactive use of BMDP, the FINISH paragraph is used when you have finished using a program; i.e., after your last analysis, type a line containing / FINISH. See Section 4.4.

Sentences. Paragraphs are composed of sentences that are commands (e.g., CORRELATION) or make assignments (e.g., VARIABLES ARE 9). The sentences can be typed in any order within the paragraph. Each sentence is terminated by a period.

A command is given either as

          command.
     or
          NO command.

depending on whether or not the command is to be executed. Each command must be followed by a period. The command must be specified as described in the program description. For example, the command

          CORRELATION.

is specified in the PRINT paragraph of many regression programs. It requests that the correlation matrix be printed. The command

          NO CORRELATION.

states that the correlation matrix is not to be printed. You may also be asked to choose between mutually exclusive commands, such as

          BEFORE. or AFTER.

Then you need only specify the command that you want, the other command is automatically negated.

A sentence is used to assign a list of numbers, variable names, variable subscripts, etc. to a BMDP word or parameter. The general form of an assignment sentence is

$$\text{BMDP word} \left\{ \begin{array}{c} = \\ \text{IS} \\ \text{ARE} \end{array} \right\} \begin{array}{l} \text{value(s) assigned to the} \\ \text{specified word.} \end{array}$$

The BMDP words (or parameters or options) are defined in the program descriptions. Examples are TITLE, FORMAT, NAMES and XVARIABLES. Note that in the chapters below, the definitions of the BMDP words are enclosed within boxes. Each assignment statement must end with a period. IS and ARE are special words that are interchangeable with the equal sign (=). They can be used only in this context unless they are enclosed in apostrophes. The values can be numbers, names, titles, etc., according to the definition of the particular word. In our definitions that assign values to BMDP words (options) we use one of the following forms (examples follow):

     BMDP word =

a) specific names or values
b) #.   one number
    # list.   one or more numbers
```
```

c) v.   one variable name or subscript
    v list.   one or more variable names or
                subscripts
d) c.   one name, not exceeding 8
                characters.
    c list.   one or more names, not exceeding
                8 characters each
e) 'c'.   format, title or label often
                requiring apostrophes (see rule
                below).

a) When the assignment to a BMDP word is limited to
<u>specific BMDP words</u>, we write

        BMDP word = (one only) list of BMDP words.

        BMDP word = (one or more) list of BMDP words.

depending on whether <u>only one</u> or <u>more than one</u>
option can be selected. The option for handling
blank values in the data input is an example of the
first:

        BLANK = (one only) ZERO, MISSING.

That is, blanks can be treated as numeric zeros <u>or</u>
as missing value codes.

b) Examples of assignment statements that require
one or more <u>numbers</u> (but not names) are

        VARIABLES ARE 9.
        CASES = 188.
        CONTRAST = -1, 1, 1, -1.

In our program descriptions we write the definition
of VARIABLE as

        VARIABLE = #.

to indicate that only one value (a number) is
permissible. In the definition of CONTRAST we write

        CONTRAST = # list.

to indicate that more than one number can be
assigned.

c) Examples of assignment statements that require
one or more values that can be either a <u>variable
name</u> or a <u>variable subscript</u> are

        GROUPING IS AGE.
        LABEL IS ID.
        XVARIABLES ARE AGE, WEIGHT.
        XVARIABLES ARE   2,   4.
        XVARIABLES ARE AGE,   4.

A variable <u>subscript</u> is the sequence number of the
variable: 1 is the subscript for the first variable,
2 the second, etc. Variable names and subscripts are
interchangeable and may be mixed in the same
statement. In the above example all XVARIABLE
statements mean the same thing when the variables
are ordered as in the example on p. 26. In the
definition of GROUPING we specify

        GROUPING = v.

to show that only one grouping variable is possible.
For XVARIABLES we specify

        XVARIABLES = v list.

to indicate that more than one variable can be
specified.

d) Examples of statements that require one or more
<u>names</u> (but not numbers) are

        CODE IS MYDATA.
        NAMES ARE ID, AGE, HEIGHT, WEIGHT.

When only one name is possible as for CODE, the
definition is written as

        CODE = c.

When one or more names are possible, we specify

        NAMES = c list.

Each name is limited to a maximum of eight
characters. The name may need to be enclosed in
apostrophes. See the rule about apostrophes below.

    For some options the BMDP word requires a
<u>subscript</u>. For example, codes can be specified for a
grouping variable that classifies cases into groups.
Names can be assigned to the codes. An example is

        CODES(5) ARE   1,   2.
        NAMES(5) ARE NOPILL, PILL.

In this example the fifth variable can take on two
codes. These codes define two groups that are named
NOPILL and PILL. These statements have the general
form

        CODES(#) = # list.
        NAMES(#) = c list.

where # is the subscript of a variable or is a
number specified in the definition of the item.
Beginning with the 1981 BMDP release, # may be a
variable name.

27

e) Examples of statements that contain a <u>title</u>, <u>lengthy label</u> or <u>format</u> are.

```
TITLE IS 'WERNER BLOOD CHEMISTRY DATA'.
FORMAT IS '(A4, 5F4.0, 3F4.1)'.
```

Formats must always be enclosed in apostrophes since they contain parentheses and other characters that are not letters or numbers; therefore we write

```
FORMAT = 'c'.
```

in our definitions. Titles and labels that are longer than eight characters are likely to contain one or more blanks (to separate words); therefore they require apostrophes. To remind you that apostrophes are probably needed, we write the definition as

```
TITLE = 'c'.
```

The maximum length of the title, label or format is specified in the program description. We use c in definitions when apostrophes are probably not needed, and 'c' when they are likely to be required. However, it is not an error to use apostrophes to enclose a name even when they are not required.

<u>Apostrophe rule</u>. Names, labels and titles <u>must</u> be enclosed in apostrophes (') when

- they do not begin with a letter
- they contain a character (symbol) that is not a letter or a number (i.e., a blank, parenthesis, comma, etc.)

Apostrophes can be used around names even when they are not required. Apostrophes must <u>not</u> be used when the value is a number except when the numbers are used as names.

<u>Preassigned Values</u>. Does the user need to assign values to all BMDP words? No. Very few specifications are necessary to run a program. Many programs only require that you specify the number of variables and their format. In addition, others require that you specify which variable contains codes for separating the subjects (or cases) into groups or, say, which variable is the dependent variable for a regression analysis. If not specified, many items are given <u>preassigned values</u> that are appropriate for most problems (e.g., the SIZE of a plot has a fixed size unless you change it). The <u>preassigned value</u> is the value used for an option when you do not specify its value. The definition of each BMDP word includes a statement to describe the preassigned value.

Experienced users sometimes repeat one analysis with modifications during a single computer run. When you use a program for more than one analysis (problem) or subanalysis (subproblem), many options do not need to be respecified; once specified, the same value is reused until respecified. In definitions we write

```
value(s)/prev.
```

if the value once specified remains unchanged until respecified (i.e., the value specified in the previous problem(s) is used); and we write

```
value(s)
```

if each time an item is not specified, the pre-assigned values are used (rather than the values specified in the previous problem).

<u>Reserved words and symbols</u>. IS, ARE, TO, BY, FOR, INCLUDE, and MACUNIT are special words in the BMDP instruction language explained below. Therefore they should not be used except in their special context. If they are used in any other way, they must be enclosed in apostrophes ('). The apostrophe ('), percent sign (%), and vertical bar (|) are reserved symbols and should not be otherwise used. Unfortunately, on some keypunches the @ symbol is keypunched on a card in an identical manner to an apostrophe on other keypunches. Therefore, the @ symbol should not be used in Control Language statements.

<u>Number notation</u>. Numbers can be either integers or real numbers (numbers with a decimal point). In addition, numbers can be in E-notation (scientific notation). That is, .000218 can also be written as 21.8E-5, or as .218E-3. And 218000 can be written as 218000.0 or as 2.18E5.

<u>Blanks</u>. Blanks can be used freely to space sentences and lists, but cannot be used in the middle of numbers or names (unless the name is enclosed in apostrophes). We use blanks to space sentences and paragraphs so they are easy to read.

```
/ INPUT    VARIABLES ARE 2.
           CASES ARE 10.
           FORMAT IS '(2F5.0)'.
```

is easier to read than

```
/INPUT VARIABLES ARE 2.CASES ARE 10.FORMAT IS
  '(2F5.0)'.
```

but both are correct.

<u>Manual format for definitions and summary of instructions</u>. In this manual the following format is used to define a new BMDP word or option:

```
Paragraph name ────────────────────────
  Statement         restriction,        preassigned
  or Command        if any              value(s)
   .... (definition)
```

For example, in the definition of the missing value code,

```
VARiable ───────────────────────────
  MISSing = # list.   one per var.      none/prev.
    The first number is the missing value code for
    the first variable, the second number for the
    second variable, ...
```

MISSING is a BMDP word in the VARIABLE paragraph. Its abbreviated form is MISS. 'none/prev.' indicates that there are <u>no</u> codes for missing values unless stated. Once stated, the specified codes are used until changed. The restriction "one per variable" means that only one code can be specified for each variable. Therefore if we specify

                    MISSING = 9, 99, 9.

the missing value code for the first variable is 9, for the second 99, and for the third 9.
    Another example of a definition is

VARiable ──────────────────────────────
 │ BLANK = (one only)   MISSING/prev.
 │   ZERO, MISSING.
 │ Definition of BLANK.
 ╰────────────

There are only two correct forms.

                    BLANK = ZERO.
          or
                    BLANK = MISSING.

The name on the right side of the equal sign must be spelled exactly as shown. No abbreviation is possible. BLANKS are MISSING unless otherwise specified. An assignment for BLANK remains unchanged until a new assignment is made.
    Our last example is

VARiable ──────────────────────────────
 │ USE = v list.   all variables
 │ Definition of USE.
 ╰────────────

USE selects a subset of the original variables to be used in the analysis. The preassigned value specifies that all variables are used unless otherwise specified. Each time a new problem begins, USE is reset to the preassigned value (since /prev. is not stated).
    There is a <u>summary table</u> at the end of each program description where we review the definitions of paragraphs, assignment statements and commands. The form used is

/ Paragraph name
    Statement   preassigned value   Comment and
    or Command   Manual
                                          Reference
                                          (page number)

    Statements and commands common to all BMDP programs are summarized on one page inside the back cover. Statements and commands specific to each program are summarized separately following each description.

Convenience Features for the BMDP Instructions

    <u>Abbreviated BMDP words</u>. Longer words have a greater chance of being misspelled. To minimize errors, many long words need not be typed completely. For example, the following abbreviations can be used:

        VAR   (VARIABLES)
        PROB   (PROBLEM)
        CASE   (CASES)
        MAX   (MAXIMUMS), etc.

When the instructions are defined in later chapters (in boxes), we use capital letters to indicate the required portion of each word. Since the program checks only the part of the word we show in CAPITALS, any suffix can be added to make the word more understandable, such as completing the word or writing it in the plural rather than singular.

    <u>Tab feature</u>. To avoid specifying all items in a list (such as names or maximums for all variables), you can tab directly to the selected item. Tabbing is necessary to specify MAXIMUMS (upper limits) or NAMES for some variables but not for all. A number k in parentheses followed by a name or value indicates that the following name or number is the kth in a list. For example,

NAMES = AGE, SEX, (15)WEIGHT, (20)PULSE, PRESSURE.

states that the 1st, 2nd, 15th, 20th and 21st names are AGE, SEX, WEIGHT, PULSE, PRESSURE respectively. The names for the other variables remain unchanged (either their preassigned names or names specified previously).

    <u>Repeating numbers in a list</u>. Repetition of the same numerical values (but not names) in a list can be specified by the notation: number*value.

        1, 2, 3, 3, 3, 3, 5, 5, 5, 5, 11.

            can be written

        1, 2, 4*3, 4*5, 11.

This notation is often useful, e.g., when the same missing value code is used for many variables.

    <u>Reassigning values in a list</u>. To specify that the maximums for 20 variables are 99, except for the 7th and 16th whose maximums are 9, the statement can be

        MAXIMUM = 6*99, 9, 8*99, 9, 4*99.

and also

        MAXIMUM = 20*99, (7)9, (16)9.

That is, by using the tab feature a value can be reassigned; the last value assigned in a statement is the value that is used.

   Repeated sentences. If two sentences in the same paragraph refer to the same BMDP word, only the first is interpreted as specifying the item unless the program description explicitly states otherwise. (e.g., GROUP IS BOYS. GROUP IS GIRLS. in the P6D plotting program.)

   The TO and BY feature for shortening lists of equally spaced values. When cutpoints or codes are used to partition a variable into groups or categories, the values are often equally spaced. To facilitate the specification of such a list, you can state

$$\#_1 \text{ TO } \#_2 \text{ BY } \#_3 .$$

For example, the list of values

$$1, 2, 3, 4, 6, 8, 10, 15, 20, 25.$$

can also be written

$$1 \text{ TO } 4 \text{ BY } 1, 6, 8, 10 \text{ TO } 25 \text{ BY } 5.$$

or as

$$1 \text{ TO } 4, 6, 8, 10 \text{ TO } 25 \text{ BY } 5.$$

If BY is not specified, the difference between values is assumed to be 1. Any of the numbers can be negative or zero. As shown in the example, implied list(s) can be used interchangeably with values. An implied list can be used in any list of numbers. Because TO and BY are given a special meaning in the implied list they cannot be used as names or in any other context unless they are enclosed in apostrophes.

   The TO feature to shorten lists of NAMES (new in 1981). Implied lists can now be used with NAMES. For example, if AGE is the second variable in the file and CHOLSTRL is the sixth and for a particular analysis you want to use only variables 2,3,4,5 and 6, you may state

   USE = AGE TO CHOLSTRL.

To be used in this manner the names AGE and CHOLSTRL must be specified in the NAME list in the VARIABLE paragraph.

   The FOR% notation, for generating a number of similar instructions, names, paragraphs, or problems from a single one (new in 1983). Multiple versions of an instruction, a name, a paragraph, or a problem can be generated easily, using the notation:

   FOR a=b. % c %

where c is the instruction, name, paragraph, or problem to be repeated (the % signs define its beginning and end); a is the name to be replaced in c; and b is the list of names or numbers to replace a in c. For example, if you want to repeat the same transformations for many variables,

$$X(5) = LOG(X(5)).$$
$$X(6) = LOG(X(6)).$$
$$\cdot$$
$$\cdot$$
$$\cdot$$
$$X(20) = LOG(X(20)).$$

You can generate these 16 statements by specifying:

   FOR K = 5 TO 20.
   % X(K) = LOG(X(K)). %

The text between the % signs is repeated for each value of K.
   Several replacements may be made concurrently, as in

   FOR K = 1, 2, 3.
       L = 5, 9, 13.
   % X(K) = X(K) + X(L). %

FOR% instructions may also be nested, and the notation can be used to generate names, such as SCORE1, SCORE2,..., SCORE30.
   Examples of some common applications of this feature and rules for using it are given in Appendix F.

   The INCLUDE file feature, for incorporating BMDP instructions stored in a file into BMDP instructions. Lengthy sequences of instructions that you use frequently or that will be used several times in the course of an analysis can be written once on a file and included, where needed, as you run BMDP programs. For example, suppose you want to perform the same transformations in several analyses. The first step is to establish an INCLUDE file containing the transformations, specify the FORTRAN unit of the INCLUDE file in a CONTROL paragraph before the problem in which you want them to apply, and use the INCLUDE file instruction to select the transformations. For example, imagine that an INCLUDE file on Fortran unit 23 contains 60 records of the following form:

```
T1              /TRANSFORM
T1                  USE=AGE GE 20 AND SEX EQ 2.
T1                  IF (X(3) GT .06) THEN...
 .                      .
 .                      .
 .                      .
T1                  IF (X(305) EQ XMIS AND...
```

where T1 is the name you have given to this set of transformation instructions. To use the transformations in a regression, specify:

```
/ CONTROL MACUNIT IS 23. / END
/ INPUT  UNIT IS 9.  CODE IS MYDATA.

    FOR  %  INCLUDE T1  %

/ REGRESS...
/ END
```

The data are read from a BMDP file on unit 9, the INCLUDE file from unit 23. The first eight character positions of each record on the unit 23 file must contain the characters associated with the INCLUDE instruction (T1, in our example). One to eight characters may be used; they should be left-justified. The transformation statements begin after the eighth character position.

A different set of transformations or other instructions can also be included in the unit 23 file; they should be prefixed with different characters -- T2, TRANS, or GROUP, for example. In our example the program will scan all records in the file and use only those prefixed with T1.

The INCLUDE feature may be used in combination with the FOR% instruction-generating feature, enabling the user to incorporate stored instructions in each version of the generated text (see example in Appendix F).

The basic form of the INCLUDE feature is:

FOR a=b. % INCLUDE d %

where:

- a and b are the same as for instruction generation, except that "a=b." may be omitted when no changes to the included text are necessary.

- d is the name identifying the text to be included from the INCLUDE file.

The INCLUDE file is a card image file; its unit number (#) is specified with

/CONTROL MACUNIT=#. /END

and it precedes the instructions for the problem being executed (see CONTROL paragraph, Section 4.4). The first eight characters of each record in the INCLUDE file contain the name, d, that identifies the text. If fewer than eight characters are used, they should be left-justified. There may be several different identifiers in the same INCLUDE file.

The INCLUDE feature may be nested to any desirable depth; i.e., it may contain other instruction-generating or INCLUDE statements. When nested, all instruction-generating statements are resolved before another level of INCLUDE is performed. In effect, the outermost INCLUDE is resolved first.

Matched lists. Lists of two or more elements in the same paragraph can be stated in a form that matches and tabulates elements. For example,

```
VARIABLE    NAMES    = AGE, WEIGHT, SEX, CHANGE.
            MINIMUMS =  0,      0,    1,    -10.
            MAXIMUMS = 20,    275,    2,     10.
```

can be stated as

```
VARIABLE    NAMES,      MINIMUMS,      MAXIMUMS =
            AGE,            0,             20,
            WEIGHT,         0,            275,
            SEX,            1,              2,
            CHANGE,       -10,             10.
```

BMDP words (NAMES, MINIMUMS, MAXIMUMS) must be separated by commas. The matching element form cannot be used with the repetition, implied list and tab features described above, nor when the BMDP word has a subscript.

Extraneous instructions. When instructions from one program are used in another, BMDP words that are not required in the second program do not need to be removed. They are automatically ignored. For example, the same set of control cards can be used for running both P6D and P3D. If P6D uses the PLOT paragraph it does not need to be removed to run P3D (which does not include a PLOT paragraph). PLOT is simply ignored in P3D.

Misspelled BMDP words may not be recognized as valid instructions. Unrecognized language will be reported.

Remarks and comments to document the output. Comments can be used freely in the BMDP instruction language if they do not interfere with the sentences and paragraphs required by the program. A safe procedure is to place them after a slash (/) to keep them out of other paragraphs. Since COMMENT is not a valid paragraph name, the COMMENT paragraph will be ignored in the analysis.

```
/ COMMENT 'THIS IS A COMMENT OF ANY KIND.  IT IS
ENCLOSED IN SINGLE APOSTROPHES BECAUSE IT
INCLUDES BLANKS.  IT COULD ALSO INCLUDE SPECIAL
CHARACTERS ("$+-...ETC.)'.
```

A comment must not be used in or at the end of a TRANSFORMATION paragraph.

4.2 SYSTEM CARDS

In order to run a BMDP program you must supply information to the computer system. This information is communicated using system control statements ("system cards"). To run a BMDP program, the system needs to know:

- your user identification (to establish that you are a legitimate user) and accounting information
- the name of the BMDP program to be run.

The format for supplying this information is specific to your particular computer system. Check at your installation for their documentation on using BMDP or talk with a consultant.

In our examples in the following chapters we show Systems Cards for an IBM OS system (these are the instructions that begin with two slashes). We now describe the JOB statement and EXEC statement for some IBM compatible systems (OS, VS1, SVS, MVS).

The JOB card. Accounting information is provided on the JOB statement. It has the general form:

```
//jobname   JOB    accounting information
```

The exact form required is specific to each installation. The JOB card may resemble the following:

```
//HSX391    JOB   HSX391,USER=HS#CML,PASSWORD=GOODUS
```

When entering system information you should not add extra blanks - the only blanks in the above statement are before and after the word JOB.

The EXEC Card. The EXEC statement informs the system which BMDP program will be run. It has the form

```
//   EXEC   BIMED,PROG=BMDPxx
```

where "xx" is the last two characters of the program name.

REGION and WRKSPCE are additional parameters that may be required on the EXEC card. When a BMDP program is executed, all available memory space is obtained for use by the program (the REGION). A specified amount of this memory space is freed by the computer system for input/output buffers (this space is called WRKSPCE). Individual computer installations set the default (preassigned) specifications for REGION and WRKSPCE. For unusual problems, you may need to adjust these space requests by specifying one or both on the EXEC card using the form

```
// EXEC BIMED,PROG=BMDPxx,REGION=nnnK,WRKSPCE=mmm
```

(See Appendix B for further discussion of program size requirements.)

A general example incorporating the three types of information necessary to run an analysis is

```
//P123      JOB   P123,EASY
//          EXEC  BIMED,PROG=BMDP6D
/ PROBLEM   TITLE IS 'PLOT CHOLESTEROL VERSUS AGE'.
/ INPUT     VARIABLES ARE 2.
            FORMAT IS FREE.
/ VARIABLE  NAMES ARE AGE, CHOLSTRL.
/ PLOT      XVARIABLE IS AGE.
            YVARIABLE IS CHOLSTRL.
/ END
   21    203 ⎫
   34    452 ⎪
   59    316 ⎬ data
    .     .  ⎪
    .     .  ⎭
//          ⎭
```

The three types of information shown above are:

- BMDP instructions (also called Control Language). These statements are the PROBLEM through END paragraphs that are preceded by a single slash.
- system statements include a JOB and an EXEC statement. These statements begin with a double slash. Note that the last "//" (null) statement is always the final entry in any run. The BMDP programs check for this end-of-file (//) indicator to know when the reading of your BMDP instructions or data (if on cards) is completed.
- data. These are the values of age and cholesterol that P6D will plot.

Data on disk or tape and BMDP Files. If your input data are on a disk or tape file, or if you request that results or data be written to a BMDP File for permanent storage, system statements describing the location of the file and its name are required. See Chapter 7 for further details.

4.3 COMMON ERRORS IN SPECIFYING BMDP INSTRUCTIONS

Several kinds of errors may cause your program to run improperly or fail to finish; these may be errors in the System Cards, in the BMDP instructions, or possibly in the program itself (called a bug). An error message is often written in the output to locate where an error occurs. Since one error may trigger others, it is always wise to look for the first error message and try to correct the indicated error.

If the BMDP heading (the program number and name -- e.g., BMDP4D SINGLE COLUMN FREQUENCIES - NUMERIC AND NONNUMERIC) is not printed in the output, your error is probably in the System Cards; if the system finds the program you specify, the heading is always printed before anything else is done. Check the program revision date in the BMDP heading to see if the program you are using was distributed long before the current 1981 documentation.

When the mistake is in the syntax (punctuation) of your BMDP instructions, an error message will usually point to the place in the instructions where the error was sensed; the error will be at, or before, that place. Check the statement where the error is indicated and the previous statements (if necessary) to see if you specified the instructions correctly. Have you

- included periods at the end of each sentence?
- included a slash between paragraphs?
- used matching pairs of apostrophes and parentheses?
- put commas between all items in lists of numbers or names?
- put apostrophes around names that do not begin with a letter or that contain a character that is not a letter or a number (i.e., blank, parenthesis, comma, etc.)?
- used a reserved name (IS, ARE, TO, BY, FOR, INCLUDE, MACUNIT) or symbol (', $, %, |) in the wrong context?

Remember that misspelled or misplaced words, sentences or paragraphs may keep the program from operating.

If you are submitting your job from a computer terminal, see Section 4.5.

In addition to error messages printed by the BMDP programs, the computing system may generate its own messages. If the system is one of the IBM 360 or 370 series, the following messages are typical, but may vary in different facilities. (The IBM code for the error is given in parentheses.)

- Computer operator cancelled your job; see the operator. (122 or 222)
- The amount of time for your job has been exceeded; check to see if you misspecified some option; if not, find out how to increase the time on your System Cards. (322)

32

- The program you are calling for was not found; is the program name spelled correctly? Is the program that you are requesting available at your installation? (806)
- More region or memory space in the computer is required for your job; you may need to specify a larger region size on your System Cards. (804)
- Sufficient memory was available to start running your job, but not enough space was available for file buffers. Increase the WRKSPCE request on the EXEC statement as described in Section 4.2. (80A)
- The amount of computer disk space required for your data is too large or the allotted space that the program needs for temporary storage must be increased. (B37 or D37)
- The program stopped because of a program error; if you added any FORTRAN statements (Chapters 6 and 14) you should check them carefully. (0C4)

The following FORTRAN error messages may also be encountered, but only rarely because the new data input reader released in the 1981 version of the programs prints its own helpful error messages:

- Error in your FORMAT statement when input TYPE is not data. (IHC 211 I)
- Your FORMAT tried to read more data than you have on a card or in a record. (IHC 212 I)
- Illegal character in input when input TYPE is not data; e.g., nonnumeric character found instead of a number; use P4D to identify the case(s) containing the nonnumeric data. (IHC 215 I)
- The computer grumbles because the argument of a function is incorrect; e.g., calculating the logarithm of zero or the square root of a negative number, or a result has an exponent that is too large, etc. This is a rare error since the BMDP programs are designed to avoid it. (IHC 25n).

If you cannot locate your error after checking for all the errors described above, ask a consultant at the computing facility to help you.

What to do if you find a program bug. If you suspect that there is an error in a BMDP program, we would appreciate receiving a report from you. Please include the following with your report:

1. Your name, address and telephone number.
2. The program revision date from the top of the first page of your output.
3. Address of the computing facility you use if different from your address.
4. Sufficient computer output to describe the difficulty you are having. If the complete setup is reasonably small, please include it.
5. Send the above to

> BMDP Statistical Software
> 1964 Westwood Blvd., Suite 202
> Los Angeles, CA 90025

In addition, you may want to try the DEBUG option described at the end of this chapter.

4.4 SPECIAL OPTIONS OF THE CONTROL, PRINT, AND PROBLEM PARAGRAPHS

The options of the CONTROL, PRINT, and PROBLEM paragraphs described below are useful for many fre-

quent users of BMDP, and for anyone who uses it from a computer terminal. (See Section 4.5 for additional tips on using BMDP from a computer terminal.)

The BMDP instruction File. The BMDP instruction File is assumed to have 80 columns of relevant information. If a text editor has been used to create the file, there may be some form of sequence numbers in columns 73 through 80. Unless these sequence numbers are all digits, they can interfere with the interpretation of the instructions. You can avoid this problem by specifying the number of columns (characters) in each line that are to be read and interpreted. For example, if the sequence numbers begin in column 73, state

> / CONTROL   COLUMN = 72.   / END

Both the CONTROL and END paragraphs are stated in the first line of the instructions before any other BMDP instructions. Your other paragraphs (INPUT, VARIABLE, etc.) begin on the next line.

BMDP instructions are usually read from the same unit as the system cards -- unit 5 in most implementations. However, two options of the CONTROL paragraph permit reading BMDP instructions from a different unit, which is useful if you use the same or a similar set of instructions frequently. The first option, the UNIT parameter, tells BMDP to read its instructions from the unit specified. For example, when running a program interactively, it may be convenient to have a BMDP instruction file containing the PROBLEM, INPUT, VARIABLE, etc. paragraphs in a standard configuration. The program first reads these from the file, then returns to the terminal for the user to input specific paragraphs necessary for a particular analysis, e.g., a REGRESSION or PLOT paragraph. Assume that a file on UNIT 9 contains instructions for the PROBLEM, INPUT, and VARIABLE paragraphs. On the current run the user enters

> / CONTROL   UNIT IS 9.   /END

The program then reads the instructions from the file on UNIT 9, and when the end-of-file is reached on UNIT 9, the program returns to the terminal for the remainder of the BMDP instructions.

The second feature permits including a stored set of instructions in one or more places in the instruction file. Modifications may be made to the stored instructions on each inclusion. The MACUNIT parameter of the CONTROL paragraph specifies the unit on which it is stored. See Section 4.1 for a description of the use of this feature.

The INTERACTIVE parameter in the CONTROL paragraph is a signal to the program that the user is able to respond to queries. This parameter is used in the BMDP programs that have specialized interactive capabilities. When both INTERACTIVE and an alternate CONTROL UNIT are specified, the program expects to find responses from queries at the terminal. INTERACTIVE also changes the defaults for several options of the PRINT paragraph (see below). This parameter is also available in the PROBLEM paragraph (the effect is the same).

```
CONTrol ─────────────────────────────────────────
  COLumn = #.          80 (72 if INTERACTIVE)/prev.
    Maximum  number  of  characters  per  line  that
    contain  BMDP  instructions.  Required  only  if the
    system  automatically  inserts  a  sequence  number
    or  other  identification  at  the  end  of  each
    line.  If  only  digits  (no  blanks)  are  found  in
    columns  73  through  80  of  the  first  BMDP
    instruction  record,  COL = 72.  is  assumed.
  UNIT = #.                                       none
    Input  unit  for  BMDP  instruction  File.  The
    instructions  are  read  from  the  specified  unit
    and  at  the  end-of-file,  reading  reverts  to  the
    primary  control  unit  (terminal,  if  interac-
    tive).
  INTeractive.                          not INT/prev.
    Specifies  that  the  user  will  respond  (at  the
    terminal)  if  queried  by  the  program.
  MACUNIT = #.  /END                              none
    Specifies  the  unit  number  of  the  INCLUDE  file
    (see  Section  4.1).
```

Printing cases. A new feature has been implemented for all programs that print data. When
printing each case, the default for variables with
grouping information is to print category names instead of values. If a value does not fall into any
of the categories defined, then the value itself is
printed. The VALUes option in the PRINt paragraph
changes the default, causing values to be printed
for all variables.

Viewing the output. The PRINT paragraph can be
used to limit the width of the output (the LINESIZE
option), to suppress page skips (the PAGESIZE option), and to suppress certain portions of the output (VNAME, GNAME, VUSE, AND LEVEL). The NEWS
option permits the user to request printing information on new BMDP features, etc. Note that the width
of many output panels can be controlled with the
LINESIZE option, but this capability is not yet uni-
versal for all output.

Finding BMDP program bugs. This feature is not
of interest to most users. However, if you suspect
that you have uncovered a bug in a distributed BMDP
program, it is helpful if

           / PRINT   DEBUG IS ALL.

is specified when preparing a run to demonstrate the
program problem for the BMDP staff.

```
PRINT ──────────────────────────────────────────
  LINEsize = #.       132(80 if INTERACTIVE)/prev.
    Maximum  number  of  characters  printed  per  line.
  PAGEsize = #.                              60/prev.
    Maximum  number  of  printed  lines  per  page.  Spec-
    ify  PAGE = 0.  to  suppress  all  page  skips  in-
    duced  by  line  counting.
  NEWS.                                   NO NEWS/prev.
    Requests  printing  of  news  and  notes  at  the  be-
    ginning  of  the  output.  Information  is  given
    about  new  features  and  program  changes  made
    after  the  manual  date  printed  in  the  output
    banner.
  VALUes                               no values/prev.
    Specifies  that  values  instead  of  category  names
```

```
    will  be  printed  for  variables  with  grouping
    information  when  printing  each  case.
  VNAME.        VNAME(NO VNAME if INTERACTIVE)/prev.
    State  NO  VNAME.  to  suppress  the  printing  of  the
    code  book  of  variable  names,  location,  and
    input  format  (for  formatted  files)  or  the  list
    of  variable  names  and  index  (BMDP  File).
  GNAME.        GNAME(NO GNAME if INTERACTIVE)/prev.
    State  NO  GNAME.  to  suppress  the  codebook  of
    category  information  (grouping  variable  names,
    missing  value  codes,  range  limits  (MIN and MAX),
    category  CODES,  CUTPOINTS,  and  NAMES).
  VUSE.            VUSE(NO VUSE if INTERACTIVE)/prev.
    State  NO  VUSE.  to  suppress  the  printing  of
    variable  names  in  the  /VARIABLE  USE  list.
  LEVEL = (one only)        NORMAL (MINIMAL if
    MINimal, BRIEF, NORMAL.     INTERACTIVE)/prev.
    Amount  of  output.  MINimal  suppresses  page
    skips  and  PROBLEM  TITLE,  and  implies  NO  VNAME,
    NO  GNAME,  and  NO  VUSE  (see  above).  BRIEF  im-
    plies  NO  VNAME,  NO  GNAME,  and  NO  VUSE.  NORMAL
    permits  printing  of  all  these  outputs.
  DEBUG = (one only)                        NONE/prev.
         NONE, TEST, INFO, ALL.
    Level  of  debugging  diagnostics  in  output.  TEST
    turns  on  internal  storage  checking,  but  pro-
    duces  no  results  unless  a  problem  is  detected.
    INFO  also  prints  storage  management  messages.
    ALL  produces  program-specific  debugging  infor-
    mation  as  well.  If  INTERACTIVE  (see  above)  is
    also  invoked,  the  DEBUG  procedure  will  ask
    questions  of  the  user  at  the  terminal.
```

4.5 RUNNING BMDP FROM A TERMINAL

There are two ways in which a BMDP program can be
run from a computer terminal. In one, you run the
programs interactively (i.e., the program responds
immediately to an instruction or small subset of
instructions); in the other, you submit a "batch"
job, which the computer system handles like jobs
submitted through a card reader. For the second
method you use a text editor to create a file of
BMDP instructions and cause the editor to modify
the instructions for subsequent runs. (Check with
you computer facility on using a text editor.) All
programs can be run interactively, but only P2R,
P7M, PLR, P1T P2T, and P4V have portions that respond to small subsets of instructions. Check with
your computer facility for documentation or consul-
tants to help you run BMDP from a terminal.

Users who run BMDP programs from a terminal
should check the options of the CONTROL and PRINT
paragraphs described in Section 4.4. Note that the
defaults for INTERACTIVE are usually the options you
would prefer when using a terminal. The INTERACTIVE
option of the CONTROL paragraph specifies that the
user will respond from the terminal if queried by
the program. The programs employing stepwise techniques (P2R, P7M, and PLR) have a feature for interactive execution. At each step the programs an-
nounce which variable they are about to move and
then give the user the opportunity to intercede and
select a different one. Users trying this feature
will find it to be self-explanatory.

5

DESCRIBING DATA AND VARIABLES

with BMDP Instructions

The BMDP programs allow great flexibility in the form and source of the data and in labeling the variables and the cases. This flexibility is achieved by allowing you to specify (or not specify) many options, depending on the analysis desired.

The BMDP instructions used to describe the data and variables are common to all BMDP programs. In this chapter we describe the following paragraphs and how they are used:

- the PROBLEM paragraph to give a title to the analysis
- the INPUT paragraph to describe the input data (number of cases, number of variables and format), to tell where the data are located (cards, terminal, tape or disk) and whether or not the data are in a BMDP File
- the VARIABLE paragraph to name the variables, state upper and lower limits for each variable, specify missing value codes, select variables to be used in an analysis, and identify the variables that contain case labels
- the GROUP or CATEGORY paragraph to stratify or classify the cases into groups or categories (this paragraph is used primarily in BMDP programs that compare groups or form frequency tables)

Data editing and case selection (e.g., selecting a subpopulation based on attributes of the data like age, sex, treatment, location, etc.) are available in all BMDP programs. The data can be modified and new variables can be formed by transforming the data (e.g., the analysis may require the logarithm of height when the height is recorded). Methods for case selection and transformation are described in Chapter 6.

Data and results (such as covariance matrix) can be transferred from one BMDP program to another by using a BMDP File. The BMDP File is a means of storing data or results from a BMDP program on disk or magnetic tape. The data or results can then be used as input to other BMDP programs. The advantages of using a BMDP File are

- it greatly reduces the BMDP instructions needed to describe the data and the variables because all variable and group names, flags for values exceeding

range limits, missing value information, and group codes and cutpoints are stored with the data
- it is more efficient to read than data read with a format specification and can reduce the costs of reading a large amount of data
- it is the best method of transferring results from one BMDP program to another

The creation and use of a BMDP File is described in detail in Chapter 7.

5.1 INPUT AND OUTPUT EXAMPLES ILLUSTRATING INSTRUCTIONS COMMON TO ALL BMDP PROGRAMS

In these examples we execute two computer runs for the same problem:

- in the first run (A), we use the minimum set of instructions required to produce output
- in the second run (B), we add several options that are commonly used to improve the analysis and to make the output more readable.

We first show the input instructions and the resulting output; a detailed discussion of the instructions follows the output.

Our statistical problem is to investigate differences between women using contraceptive pills and women who do not. We use program P3D, Comparison of Two Groups with t Tests, to analyze the Werner Blood Chemistry data shown in Table 5.1. The data include physical measurements (age, weight, height) and blood chemistry measurements (cholesterol, albumin, calcium, uric acid) on 188 women: 94 women take birth control pills and 94 do not. The fifth variable listed for each woman contains a code designating her as being in a 'pill' or 'no pill' group. The data are organized as 94 pairs (one on,

one off the pill in each pair) of age-matched women. The age matching is used in an example in a later chapter.

The minimal set of instructions for Run A is:

```
-----------------------------------------
/ INPUT       VARIABLES ARE 9.
             FORMAT IS '(A4, 5F4.0, 3F4.1)'.
/ VARIABLE    GROUPING IS 5.
             LABEL IS 1.

/ END
-----------------------------------------
```

These instructions tell the program to read nine observations (variables) for each woman: the first is a label (A4 format), the next five observations have at most four digits (with no digits assumed following the decimal) and the last three observations have at most four digits with the decimal assumed to precede the last digit. The GROUPING statement in the VARIABLE paragraph specifies that the fifth variable on each record contains CODES for sorting the women (cases) into the two groups. (This instruction is only used by the programs that require the cases be separated into cells or groups.) The program will operate without the LABEL instruction.

For Run B we use the required instructions listed above and add VARIABLE and GROUP NAMES and a TITLE to label the output. We also specify that extreme cholesterol values be excluded from the calculations. The program will automatically treat blanks in the data file as missing observations.

```
-----------------------------------------
/ PROBLEM    TITLE IS 'HOW TO LABEL THE OUTPUT AND
                      HOW TO EXCLUDE EXTREME VALUES'.

/ INPUT      VARIABLES ARE 9.
            FORMAT IS '(A4, 5F4.0, 3F4.1)'.

/ VARIABLE   NAMES ARE ID, AGE, HEIGHT, WEIGHT,
                      BRTHPILL, CHOLSTRL, ALBUMIN,
                      CALCIUM, URICACID.
            MAXIMUM IS (6)400.
            MINIMUM IS (6)150.
            LABEL IS ID.
            GROUPING IS BRTHPILL.
/ GROUP      CODES(5) ARE      1,    2.
            NAMES(5) ARE NOPILL, PILL.

/ END
-----------------------------------------
```

(In these two examples we assume that the BMDP instructions and data are on cards (or in the same input stream). See end of this chapter for organization of systems information, BMDP instructions and data.)

Using either of the above instruction sets, P3D will automatically compute two-sample t tests for AGE, HEIGHT, WEIGHT, CHOLSTRL, ALBUMIN, CALCIUM and URICACID. The results for CHOLSTRL (variable 6) are shown in Output Run A and Output Run B. The circled numbers below correspond to those in the output.

① This panel presents the analysis for CHOLSTRL (X(6)). Note that CHOLSTRL appears on the first panel of Output Run B. (Also note that the TITLE from the Run B PROBLEM paragraph is printed at the top of the t test results.) See Chapter 9 for definitions of the statistics and other output features.

② Descriptive statistics are given in a vertical column for the women in the group with code '1'. In Output Run B you see the name NOPILL in the same position. The results for the group coded '2' (PILL) are given in the next column.

③ The PILL group has one unusually large cholesterol value and one that is considerably smaller than the others. Note that both histograms are scaled using the minimum and maximum values of all the data. By reading the descriptive statistics in the panel to the left of the histogram, we see the MINIMUM value for group 2 is 50, the MAXIMUM value is 600. (We insert these extreme values in the data file for demonstration purposes.) We delete them from the computations in Run B.

④ The instructions

MIN IS (6)150.
MAX IS (6)400.

for Run B cause values outside the limits of 150 and 400 for the sixth variable, CHOLSTRL, to be excluded from the computations. Note that the sample size for the PILL group is now 92.

5.2 THE PROBLEM PARAGRAPH

The analysis of a single set of data is called a <u>problem</u>. A second analysis of the <u>same</u> data is called a <u>subproblem</u>. When you want to do the same analysis for subsets of the data (e.g., the same analysis for each hospital), many instructions need not be repeated because after they are stated they remain unchanged until restated. The summary at the end of each program description provides information on how to use the program for repeated analyses during one computer run (some allow paragraphs like REGRESSION to be repeated, others do not).

The PROBLEM paragraph may be omitted if an INPUT paragraph is present in any problem. In any case, it need not be followed by instructions (e.g., TITLE). That is,

/ PROBLEM   or   / PROB

is sufficient. We do not use a PROBLEM paragraph in Run A, and include it in Run B, where the TITLE specified is printed at the top of the page with the results from the t tests.

<u>TITLE</u>: a label for the output. A title can be specified in the PROBLEM paragraph to label the output. In some programs the title appears at the top of each page of output. For example, in Run B we use

TITLE IS 'HOW TO LABEL THE OUTPUT AND
          HOW TO EXCLUDE EXTREME VALUES'.

Output Run A   Results from P3D using the minimum BMDP instructions
----

DIFFERENCES ON SINGLE VARIABLES

```
***********
*  X(6)   *   VARIABLE NUMBER   6      GROUP     1 * 1.0000  2 * 2.0000    1 * 1.0000(N=  94)         2 * 2.0000(N=  94)
***********                            MEAN          232.9678    241.2231                                    X
         ① STATISTICS   P VALUE   DF    STD DEV        43.4914     58.9134     H H                            XX
                                        S.E.M.          4.4858      6.0765     H H                            XXX      ③
T (SEPARATE)  -1.09   0.276  171.2     SAMPLE SIZE         94          94     HHHH                            XXX
T (POOLED)    -1.09   0.276  186       MAXIMUM       335.0000    600.0000     HHHHHH                          XXXXXXX
                                       MINIMUM       155.0000     50.0000     HHHHHHHH           X XXXXXXXX X        X
F(FOR VARIANCES)                                                             MIN-----------------MAX   MIN-----------------MAX
   LEVENE      0.02   0.878   1, 186                                          AN H =    5 CASES            AN X =    5 CASES
```

Output Run B   Results from P3D after useful options are added to the BMDP instructions.

HOW TO LABEL THE OUTPUT AND HOW TO EXCLUDE EXTREME VALUES.

DIFFERENCES ON SINGLE VARIABLES

```
***********
* CHOLSTRL *  VARIABLE NUMBER   6      GROUP     1 NOPILL  2 PILL       1 NOPILL  (N=  94)         2 PILL    (N=  92)
***********                            MEAN          232.9678    239.4019
         ① STATISTICS   P VALUE   DF    STD DEV        43.4914     41.5620          H
                                        S.E.M.          4.4858      4.3331     H   H                       X XXXX      ④
T (SEPARATE)  -1.03   0.304  183.9     SAMPLE SIZE         94          92     H HHHHHHH                     X XXXX
T (POOLED)    -1.03   0.304  184       MAXIMUM       335.0000    390.0000     HHHHHHHHH  H                  XXXXXXXXX
                                       MINIMUM       155.0000    160.0000     HHHHHHHHHHHHH HH              XXXXXXXXXXXXX   X
F(FOR VARIANCES)                                                             MIN-----------------MAX   MIN-----------------MAX
   LEVENE      1.49   0.223   1, 184                                          AN H =    3 CASES            AN X =    3 CASES
```

Table 5.1 Werner et al. (1970) Blood Chemistry Data[1]

ID Number	Age	Height	Weight	Birthpill[2]	Cholesterol	Albumin[3]	Calcium[3]	Uric Acid[3]
2381	22	67	144	1	200	43	98	54
1946	22	64	160	2	600	35		72
1610	25	62	128	1	243	41	104	33
1797	25	68	150	2	50	38	96	30
561	19	64	125	1	158	41	99	47
2519	19	67	130	2	255	45	105	83
225	20	64	118	1	210	39	95	40
2420	20	65	119	2	192	38	93	50
1649	21	60	107	1	246	42	101	52
3108	21	65	135	2	245	34	106	48
1375	21	63	100	1	208	38	98	54
2936	21	64	120	2	260	47	106	38
988	21	67	134	1	204	40	108	34
408	21	67	145	2	192	39	95	49
913	21	63	138	1	280	41	102	41
2373	21	64	113	2	230	39	99	38
736	21	63	160	1	215	39	96	39
2334	21	64	115	2	225	44	105	44
3035	21	68	125	1	165	48	105	28
1883	21	62	106	2	200	38	95	40
2729	21	68	150	1	220	47	102	75
1848	21	64	130	2	255	34	102	40
1890	22	62	135	1	263	43	98	47
266	22	62	110	2	173	42	97	37
2125	22	57	105	1	170	46	98	45
2092	22	64	120	2	290	37	98	59
1291	22	64	115	1	263	42	102	47
1922	22	59	94	2	220	47	105	46
307	22	67	125	1	200	43	100	44
1790	22	62	97	2	192	38	95	43
239	22	58	100	1	247	42	104	52
3096	22	66	130	2	175	44	106	58
1068	22	60	100	1	155	41	96	45
2730	22	65	135	2	215	40	93	43
51	22	60	95	1	200	47	99	34
2648	22	67	124	2	247	44	102	45
906	23	63	125	1	220	32	92	42
97	23	64	105	2	207	42	100	40
649	23	63	125	1	266	42	103	47
3014	23	63	120	2	240	43	101	39
962	24	68	125	1	195	49	106	52
1912	24	64	130	2	250	39	103	46
957	24	65	130	1	225	50	108	39
338	24	65	148	2	200	37	104	49
1819	24	64	135	1	180	37	96	49
420	24	71	156	2	240	42	102	51
494	25	62	107	1	330	48	101	53
2779	25	67	175	2	175		93	51
477	25	66	112	1	205	46	101	33
2870	25	63	120	2	235	44	103	40
3	54	62	120	1	227		86	25
2077	54	67	127	2	260	44	106	57
3095	25	67	135	1	295	46	106	47
2363	25	67	141	2	230	38	101	52
2698	26	66	135	1	240	48	103	51
3006	26	64	118	2	238	40	99	46
796	26	65	125	1	198	44	96	43
2351	26	65	120	2	196	38	95	43
1627	27	64	120	1	172	43	98	60
152	27	64	180	2	317	37	98	84
2305	27	69	137	1	195	46	101	42
2121	27	64	125	2	185	36	94	54
883	27	63	125	1	168	42	97	41
1882	27	64	124	2	200	40	96	52
416	27	60	140	1	250	36	98	68
16	27	65	155	2	280	42	103	52
1637	28	65	108	1	260	48	106	51
3138	28	62	110	2	250	44	105	38
457	28	65	120	1	175	48	100	47
2830	28	66	113	2	305	41	93	24
1083	28	62	135	1	200	43	97	37
3359	28	65	160	2	235	42	101	41
1255	29	61	142	1	177	39	99	46
3256	29	61	115	2	235	45	98	47
1207	29	68	155	1	226	38	94	43
3210	29	65	118	2	230	44	99	44
2871	30	66	143	1	198	45	107	65
1775	30	63	110	2	295	45	98	46
1274	30	61	99	1	230	43	99	39
2365	30	63	132	2	200	37	96	34
949	30	62	125	1	230	46	104	48
3519	30	63	110	2	262	33	99	41
609	30	64	135	1	174	40	95	35
3021	30	66	112	2	250	44	100	35
1668	30	64	160	1	217	35	95	31
2877	30	68		2	212	38	100	66
3349	31	65	125	1	250	43	98	39
2454	31	66	120	2	237	34	91	49
2098	31	65	115	1	270	41	111	64
1916	31	63	110	2	280	44	99	49
782	31	66	123	1	238	37	96	33
2947	31	67	136	2	218	38	95	42
2996	32	67	132	1	185	39	103	37
441	32	68	203	2	235	38	99	37
3506	32	62	155	1	262	37	99	43
2617	32	65	126	2	160	41	97	40
2522	32	63	125	1	189	40	94	40
2400	32	71	170	2	205	37	90	60
1249	32	62	120	1	260	43	107	38
2367	32	62	145	2	240	45	108	42
57	32	66	140	1	197	44	106	58
2267	32	68	133	2	180	32	95	40
63	54	67	145	1	320	39		
234	54	67	140	2	245	39	104	56
3334	33	64	115	1	205	47	100	54
480	33	60	118	2	260	38	99	38
828	33	67	137	1	243	41	106	55
3019	33	68	130	2	195	40	95	58
61	33	65	130	1	203	44	101	48
2062	33	69	138	2	222	40	104	42
1770	34	62	112	1	197	37	93	44
3208	34	63	125	2	245	38	95	41
1140	35	62	115	1	180	40	91	59
3194	35	67	125	2	223	40	100	37
216	35	66	138	1	254	39	107	41
2501	35	66	140	2	245	39	105	56
1309	36	62	135	1	247	34	90	44
2942	36	67	120	2	175	46	103	39
819	36	66	112	1	215	43	104	42
3277	36	65	121	2	270	43	98	35
2456	37		141	1	237		105	45
2254	37	67	125	2	200	45	99	66
46	37	65	116	1	270	42	100	48
1803	37	63	129	2	230	36	91	22
2811	38	64	165	1	255	44	102	62
2341	38	65	151	2	275	38	94	46
2349	39	64	135	1	210	40	95	46
523	39	64	108	2	198	44	90	38
2675	39	63	195	1	260	40	108	42
2153	39	69	132	2	180	39	94	30
1111	39	62	100	1	210	45	91	27
1959	39	62	110	2	235	41	99	35
1701	40	63	110	1	196	39	97	42
1910	40	64	151	2	305	39	99	48
1571	40	65	145	1	170	45	100	43
2818	40	66	140	2	276	46	100	55
544	40	65	140	1	272	41	91	44
3312	40	65	137	2	315	37	96	99
383	40	67	130	1	300	40	106	52
48	40	62	117	2	290	42	99	42
263	41	62	116	1	320	44	111	61
77	41	68	215	2	255	43	105	45
564	41	64	125	1	306	45	98	62
2709	41	69	170	2	324	40	99	55
1715	42	60	105	1	240	41	101	51
1896	42	63	129	2	210	40	100	46
1326	43	66	167	1	210	40	100	52
1965	43	68	145	2	250	36	98	42
1317	43	66	138	1	335	44	105	58
1837	43	66	132	2	230	42	98	48
2220	43	64	125	1	285	45	105	50
2437	43	62	113	2	200	40	93	36
221	43	64	126	1	280	45	106	38
3286	43	65	148	2	276	41	105	50
520	55	64	124	1	275	40	98	53
22	55	64	165	2	298	36	100	63
59	44	62	118	1	253	43	94	44
2497	44	63	133	2	242	47	104	49
56	45	67	180	1	160	38	97	59
15	45	65	140	2	263	45	107	52
5	46	66		1	250	41	101	73
850	46	67	145	2	320	40	101	37
1218	46	63	138	1	257	40	90	61
132	46	62	118	2	190	38	95	43
695	46	62	103	1	230	43	102	33
541	46	65	190	2	265	41	108	85
473	47	67	135	1	297	42	100	45
2657	47	67	143	2	255	41	100	44
164	47	61	132	1	257	39	96	38
2865	47	59	94	2	257	41	103	53
554	48	62	120	1	300	39	94	51
644	48	66	143	2	225	40	100	62
852	48	67	143	1	216	40	96	47
629	48	65	134	2	248	42	102	42
1241	48	65	164	1	306	44	100	78
156	48	66	120	2	235	36	97	35
1251	48	60	125	1	195	41	95	53
64	48	64	138	2	338	37	100	58
2102	49	64	126	1	255	41	102	48
1932	49	69	158	2	217	36	106	65
44	50	69	135	1	295	43	105	63
3134	50	66	140	2	390	46	97	55
1250	52	68	150	1	250	42	97	59
1789	52	62	107	2	265	46	104	64
1149	53		178	1	227	39		50
575	53	65	140	2	220	40	107	46
2271	54	66	158	1	305	42	103	48
39	54	60	170	2	220	35	88	63

continued

1 Two values of cholesterol (cases 2 and 4) have been deliberately modified to represent extreme values to be excluded from the analysis. Eight other values were left blank to represent missing data. Each case is recorded in columns 1 to 36 of a card; each variable uses 4 columns. The appropriate format to read the data is (A4, 5F4.0, 3F4.1).

2 Birth control pill user: 1 no pill; 2 pill.

3 Albumin, calcium and uric acid are recorded to the nearest 1/10 of a unit. Other measurements are to the nearest unit.

The title cannot exceed 160 characters (two cards) in length. If omitted, the title on the output is left blank. Using the form for definitions described in Section 4.1, we write the definition of TITLE as

PROBlem ───
  TITLE = 'c'.   blank
     c is a title for the output not exceeding 160 characters in length. The title must be enclosed in apostrophes if it does not begin with a letter or if it contains a symbol that is neither a letter nor a number, e.g., blank, comma, period, etc.

5.3 READING THE DATA: THE INPUT PARAGRAPH

You must specify how many observations (variables) are to be read for each subject (case), how the observations are organized (their format), where the data are located (cards, terminal, tape or disk) and whether or not the data are in a BMDP File. The instructions for reading and writing BMDP Files are given in Chapter 7.

The INPUT paragraph is required for the first problem (analysis). When raw data are read, the INPUT paragraph must contain the number of VARIABLES and the FORMAT. If the data are read from a file different from that containing the BMDP instructions, the UNIT where the data are located must also be specified.

VARIABLES: the number of variables. The Werner blood chemistry data contain nine variables -- a variable containing a case label (ID), three physical measurements, a variable indicating whether the woman is taking the pill, and four blood chemistry variables. Therefore we specify

VARIABLES ARE 9.

in the INPUT paragraph.

Although the meaning of "variable" is usually clear, at times it is worth dividing a variable into parts so you can refer to each part separately. For example, dates are commonly written with six digits, such as 010276 or 081277. These observations can be read as a six-digit number called DATE or as three variables called MONTH, DAY and YEAR, each two digits long. It is easier to compute time differences between dates if they are read as three separate variables.

Data need not be read as input. You may want to generate data using random numbers within a BMDP program or you may want to read data that is in nonstandard form (cannot be read in the same manner for each case). You will then want to specify that there are zero variables to be read as input and use one of the methods described in Chapter 6 to generate or read your data. When

VARIABLE = 0.

is specified, you must state the number of CASES and you can omit the FORMAT.

FORMAT: the layout of the data. The FORMAT statement in the example above reads observations located in fixed fields on the data card or record. There are several other ways that data can be read into BMDP programs:

- from a BMDP File (see Chapter 7)
- in a free format where each observation is not restricted to a fixed position on the card (or record). The observations are simply separated by a blank or a comma. BMDP provides three methods for free format data reading; they are described in Section 5.6
- from a disk or tape file in binary (unformatted) (described in this section)
- by using the subroutine TRANSF with the BIMEDT procedure (described in Chapter 6)
- by the SAS or P-STAT software systems which places the data in BMDP Files.

The FORMAT statement describes the layout of the data for each subject (case). If you are not familiar with the format statement used in FORTRAN or in the BMDP programs, we recommend that you read Section 3.3.

The format must describe all variables (except those containing case labels) using F or I format. The variables to be identified as case labels must be described in A-format. The format statement for the Werner data is

FORMAT IS '(A4, 5F4.0, 3F4.1)'.

Equally acceptable FORMATS are

'(A4, 5F4, 3F4.1)'   or   '(A4, 5I4, 3F4.1)'.

The first variable contains the case identification and is used as a case label; it is read using an A4 specification. The format must begin with an open parenthesis and end with a closed parenthesis. Therefore, to conform to BMDP instruction rules it must be enclosed in apostrophes.

The user can also specify certain options to be used in connection with the fixed format statement. These are discussed in Section 5.7. For example, data for several subjects may be entered on one card (record). The instruction MULT allows you to read several cases from one record (see Section 5.7 and the example at the end of Section 9.3).

The option BINARY is used instead of the format specification if your data are on a tape or disk file in binary form (not on a BMDP File).

UNIT: the unit number. When the data are not on the same file as the BMDP instructions you must specify where they can be found. In the INPUT paragraph the UNIT number specifies where the data are stored. (The same UNIT number is also specified on a System Card that describes to the computer where the data are stored.) There are some restrictions in the choice of a unit number: 5 is used for the BMDP instruction input file (often the data follow the BMDP instructions), 6 is the printed file of output, 1 and 2 are used by the programs for temporary storage, 3 and 4 are reserved for the user to pass temporary BMDP Files from one program step to another, 26-30 are also reserved for use by the programs.

CASE: the number of cases. The number of cases need not be specified unless only a portion of the file is to be read (e.g., if a file contains 1000 cases and you want to analyze the first 50). Each BMDP program stops reading the data when an end-of-file indicator (e.g., /*) or a /END paragraph is found. Any System Card immediately following the data cards serves the purpose. Data from BMDP Files are terminated by an end-of-file indicator that is recognized by the BMDP program. (This is true of most system files.)

When multiple problems are analyzed during one computer run (that is, more BMDP instructions follow the data for an additional problem or subproblem) then the number of cases must be specified or an END must follow the last data record.

In our example we have 188 cases. This is specified as

CASES ARE 188.

REWIND: reading data from the middle of the file. When the data are on a disk or magnetic tape, the data to be used in an analysis need not start with the first data record; they may start at some other record. The BMDP programs assume that the data begin with the first record and position the disk or tape accordingly (REWIND). But sometimes the data may be in sequential subsets; the first subset is used in the first analysis, the second in the second analysis, etc. In this situation you would not want to reposition to the beginning of the data after completing the first analysis -- you would want the disk or tape to remain positioned exactly where it is left by the previous problem (NO REWIND). This is a rarely used option.

The common options for the INPUT paragraph are listed below.

INPut ————
VARiable = #.   none/prev.
   The number of VARIABLES in each case. This is required for the first problem unless the data are from a BMDP File. The value assigned in the first problem is used in subsequent problems unless the number of VARIABLES is respecified.
FORMat = 'c'   'c' cannot exceed   none/prev.
or (one only)   800 characters
FREE, STREAM,
SLASH, BINARY.
   The format c specifies the layout (in fixed fields) of the data in a single case. Up to two variables may be read in A-format and used as case labels but not as data. The usual FORTRAN rules (as amended in Section 5.7) for the format are applicable. FREE, STREAM and SLASH are defined in Section 5.6. If your data are on a tape or disk file in binary (unformatted) form (not on a BMDP File), state FORMAT = BINARY. The format must be stated unless the data are from a BMDP File.

Note: If you are using the fixed format specification and need to read more than one case per card see the instruction MULT in Section 5.7.
UNIT = #.   # (use 5, 7 to 25)   5/prev.
   The unit number from which the data are to be read by the program. Not required if data are on cards or are in the same file, or input stream, as the BMDP instructions.
Note: When a UNIT number other than 5 is specified, an extra System Card must be included to describe the location of the data to the computer.
CASE = #.   end-of-file/prev.
   The number of cases or observations to be read. Not required when the data are from a BMDP File or are terminated by an end-of-file indicator or when an END follows the data.
REWIND.   use only when data   REWIND/prev.
           are from disk or tape
   REWIND positions UNIT at the beginning (first case) of the data. NO REWIND leaves the UNIT positioned where it is.

Note: See additional INPUT options in Section 5.7, including how to specify the disposition of blanks in the input data.

5.4 DESCRIBING THE VARIABLES: THE VARIABLE PARAGRAPH

In the VARIABLE paragraph

- variables can be NAMED
- upper and lower limits (MAXIMUM and MINIMUM) can be specified for the data in each variable
- MISSING value codes can be specified
- variables containing case LABELS can be identified
- variables can be selected (to be USED) for the analysis

In addition, the VARIABLE paragraph is used to indicate whether new variables are created by transformations. This is described in Chapter 6 where transformations are treated in depth. The VARIABLE paragraph is optional and can be omitted if the above features are not needed.

NAME: naming the variables. Variables often have short names that are easy to remember such as SEX, AGE, HEIGHT, WEIGHT, ID, etc. Your results can be interpreted more easily if these names are printed in the output. For the Werner data in Table 5.1, we specify variable names as

NAMES ARE ID, AGE, HEIGHT, WEIGHT,
        BRTHPILL, CHOLSTRL, ALBUMIN,
        CALCIUM, URICACID.

The first name is that of the first variable, the second that of the second variable, etc.

Variable names are restricted to eight characters. Therefore we omit several vowels to shorten names in our example:

> BRTHPILL is used in place of birthpill

and

> CHOLSTRL is used in place of cholesterol.

Variable names, like all names in the BMDP instructions, must be enclosed in apostrophes if they do not begin with a letter or if they contain a symbol (blank, comma, etc.) that is neither a letter nor a number.

Names do not need to be specified for all of the variables. Tabbing (p. 29) can be used to skip when naming variables. Variables can always be referred to by their sequence numbers, as in

> DEPENDENT = 5.

stating that the 5th variable is the dependent variable. In TRANSFORM and FUNCTION paragraphs, they can be referred to by the notation X (sequence number), as in

> $X(5) = X(1) + X(2).$

MAXIMUM and MINIMUM. Upper and lower limits can be specified to eliminate extreme values or errors and to restrict the range of data used in an analysis. In Table 5.1 two erroneous values were deliberately entered into the data (600 for cholesterol in the second case and 50 for cholesterol in the fourth case.) In the Run B example, we eliminate both from the analysis by specifying

> MAXIMUM IS (6)400.
> MINIMUM IS (6)150.

Since cholesterol is the sixth variable, we tabbed to (6) (p. 29) and set limits only for cholesterol. Either limit can be specified without the other. If we also want to restrict our analysis to those over 19 years old and 60" or taller, we write

> MINIMUM IS (2)20, 60, (6)150.

That is, we tab to the second variable, AGE, allowing 20 as the minimum acceptable value, next set a lower limit for the third variable, HEIGHT (positioned next to the second variable so no tabbing is necessary), and then tab to the sixth variable, CHOLSTRL. Thus the MIN and MAX statements can be helpful for selecting subpopulations. For more power in case selection see the transformation section in Chapter 6.

MISSING values and BLANKS. In many experiments some of the data values are not recorded for various reasons. The unrecorded values are called missing values. When the data are coded, we recommend that a special code be assigned to indicate a missing value; the missing value code can then be identified and missing values eliminated from the analysis. Alternatively, missing observations can be left blank in the data file: the program will automatically assume they are missing unless you state otherwise.

We deliberately left several data values blank in Table 5.1 to illustrate how missing values are handled. Note that in Example P1D.1 (Chapter 8), the number of observations (frequency count) for AGE and BRTHPILL is 188: the frequency for HEIGHT, however, is 186, because two values were left blank. To specify whether blank fields denote missing values or zeros, either

> BLANKS ARE MISSING.

or

> BLANKS ARE ZERO.

can be specified. The former is the preassigned method of treating blank fields if neither is specified, and is appropriate for the Werner data in Table 5.1. If you want to use blanks to denote missing values for some of your variables and to denote zeros for other variables, use the NONB transformation (p. 51).

Numbers can also be used as missing value codes for the variables. If you use a number as your missing value code, it should be an integer since computers do not represent fractions exactly and so the missing value code may not be recognized.

For the Werner data, we could have placed missing value codes in the data file instead of leaving the field blank. For example, for a record with two missing observations (they are blank),

> 1149 53   178 1 227 39   50,

we could have used 99 and 999 to fill in the blank values

> 1149 53 99 178 1 227 39 999 50.

For each variable we select a code outside the range of possible values, (i.e., the code for sex could be 9, the code for body weight 999). The statement to identify these numbers as missing value codes would be

> MISS = (3)99, 999, 9, 999, 99, 999, 99.

The code for the third variable (3) is 99, the fourth variable, WEIGHT, is 999, the fifth variable, SEX, is 9, etc.

LABEL: case labels for data listings. Many BMDP programs print the data or results like factor scores for each case. When each case contains identifying information (a case label), such as a patient ID or name, the case label can be printed to identify the data. One or two variables (not exceeding four characters each) can be specified as a case label. These variables must be read using A-format (p. 23) and cannot be used as data in the analysis.

In the Werner data (Table 5.1) the first variable (ID) is an identification number. Therefore we specify

> LABEL IS ID.

The effects of this instruction are not shown in our example above -- we do not print out the data or results for each case. See Example 1D.2 in Chapter 8 where data for some cases from the Werner file are listed. The ID for each case is printed at the left along with a sequence number indicating the order of the case in the data file.

USE: selecting variables for analyses. All programs allow you to select the variables to be analyzed. In many programs variables can be selected by a USE statement in the VARIABLE paragraph. The selection can also be done by specifying the variables in a manner specific to the program; e.g., by specifying the XVARIABLES and YVARIABLES for scatter plots in P6D or by specifying the ROW and COLUMN variables for two-way frequency tables in P1F.

The USE option is convenient when you have a large data file with complicated format, many range limits and missing value code specifications, but require an analysis for only a few of the variables. With the USE specification you simply list the subscripts for the variables you want and do not need to rewrite your format and other specifications.

The USE list is an important option for many multivariate analysis programs that require data to be present for all variables analyzed. If you include extra variables that have missing values or values outside acceptable range limits, they may cause cases to be excluded from the analysis that were complete for the variables of interest (see method C below). Cases that contain values equal to the missing value code or values out of range (above a specified upper limit or below a specified lower limit) are handled in three different ways by the BMDP programs:

A. all cases are used (all acceptable values are included in the computations)
B. cases used in the analysis must have acceptable values for all variables specified in the analysis; other cases are not used
C. cases used in the analysis must have acceptable values for all variables selected by the USE statement (or all variables when there is no USE statement)

Programs using method C are P1R, P2R, P3R, P4R, PAR, P1V, P3S, P1M, P2M, P4M and P7M. For these programs you may want to exclude irrelevant variables by a USE statement even if the variables to be analyzed are explicitly specified by other instructions.

For example, if we want to include only the blood chemistry measurements from Table 5.1 in an analysis and not exclude cases because their height and weight observations are missing, we specify

        USE = CHOLSTRL, ALBUMIN, CALCIUM, URICACID.

or

        USE = 6 TO 9.

The common options for the VARIABLE paragraph are listed below.

VARiable

NAME = c list. one per variable   X(1), X(2), .../prev.

Names for the variables. Each name is restricted to eight characters. Variable names are used to label the output. They (or the variable subscripts) are used in the BMDP instructions to identify the variable.

MAXimum = # list. one per variable   none/prev.

The first number is the upper limit for the first variable, the second for the second variable, etc. Limits for any or all variables can be specified. Values of a variable greater than its upper limit are excluded from all computations.

MINimum = # list. one per variable   none/prev.

The first number is the lower limit for the first variable, the second for the second variable, etc. Limits for any or all variables can be specified. Values of a variable less than its lower limit are excluded from all computations.

BLANK = (one only)   MISSING/prev.
    ZERO, MISSING.

Unless ZERO is specified, all blank fields are treated as missing value codes and are eliminated from all analyses. When ZERO is specified, all blank fields are treated as numeric ZEROS (0.0). If your version of the BMDP programs is dated prior to 1981, check with your computing facility to make sure that the BLANKS ARE MISSING option is operative on your system.

Note: ZERO is the preassigned value for BLANK in all versions of BMDP dated before 1981.

MISSing = # list. one per variable   none/prev.

The first number is the missing value code for the first variable, the second for the second, etc. Missing value codes are not used in the analyses. Tabbing (p. 29) can be used to skip variables. Repetition of the same number (p. 29) is useful when the same code is used for many variables.

LABEL = v list. one or two variables, each   none/prev.
    not exceeding 4 chars.

Names or subscripts of one or two variables that are used to label the cases in the output. They must be read using A-format and are excluded from all computations. No LABEL statement, or LABEL = 0. specifies that there are no case labels.

USE = v list.   all variables

Names or subscripts of variables to be used in the analysis. This should include all variables needed, such as the variable containing case weights (if any) or a variable used to classify the cases into groups (if any). Variables omitted from a USE statement can be used in transformations; they are not used in any computations and no results are printed for the omitted variables. Case label variables can be, but need not be, included in the USE statement; they are used automatically when appropriate for labeling output.

5.5 THE GROUP OR CATEGORY PARAGRAPH

Two paragraph names, GROUP and CATEGORY, can be used interchangeably. We use GROUP when the purpose of the paragraph is to sort (group) the cases so that each case is in the correct group or cell for two-sample t tests, for analysis of variance, etc. We also want to put the cases into groups when we study subpopulations separately; for example, one plot of height versus weight for pill users, another plot for the 'no pill' group. We use CATEGORY when the paragraph defines categories (intervals) for contingency (frequency) tables.

The GROUP (CATEGORY) paragraph is used to

- specify values of a discrete variable that are used as codes to define group membership for each case
- define intervals for a continuous variable that are used in the same manner as codes to identify group membership
- assign names to the groups
- combine codes or intervals to define a single group

The GROUP (or CATEGORY) paragraph is not used in BMDP programs that do not group cases or form frequency tables. The paragraph can be omitted in other programs if the preassigned method of assigning codes provides the desired grouping. The usual method of assigning codes is to use up to ten values for the variable. If the variable used to identify groups takes on no more than ten values (such as sex or the answer to a multiple choice question) there may be no need for a GROUP paragraph unless you want to name the groups. If the variable used to identify groups is continuous, the GROUP paragraph is required.

CODE and NAME: using discrete codes to group cases. A variable that takes on only a few values (such as SEX) is often used to identify groups in an analysis. The values of the variable are codes that identify the groups. For example, BRTHPILL in the Werner data takes on two values: 1 if the woman is not on the pill (NOPILL) and 2 if the woman is on the pill (PILL). Cases can be classified into two groups according to the value of BRTHPILL by specifying

          CODES(BRTHPILL) ARE 1, 2.
or
          CODES(5) ARE 1,2.

where (BRTHPILL) indicates that the CODES are associated with the variable BRTHPILL. Alternatively, the variable index could be supplied, as in

          CODES(5)

The two groups can then be named by specifying

          NAMES(BRTHPILL) ARE NOPILL, PILL.

The first name (NOPILL) is the name of the group formed by the first code (1) and the second name

(PILL) is the name of the group formed by the second code (2). When NAMES are specified, CODES or CUTPOINTS must also be stated.

CODES can be stated in any order and can be any number (positive, zero or negative). If you specify NAMES, the number of CODES and NAMES should agree. Groups with the same NAME are combined into one group. For example, the following CODE and NAME specifications

          CODE(GRADE) = 1 TO 5.
          NAMES(GRADE) = LOW, MEDIUM, MEDIUM, MEDIUM, HIGH.

form three groups - the cases with codes 2, 3 and 4 are combined into one group labeled MEDIUM.

Using CUTPOINTS to separate a variable into intervals. A variable that is continuous (such as AGE) can also be used to define groups in an analysis. Suppose we want to classify the cases into four groups according to the AGES of the women. We can specify

          CUTPOINTS(2) ARE 25, 35, 45.

where 2 is the subscript for the variable AGE in the Werner data. The four intervals formed are

- up to and including 25
- above 25 but less than or equal to 35
- above 35 but less than or equal to 45
- above 45

The CUTPOINTS are the upper limits for each interval. The first interval is from the specified lower limit (MINIMUM in the VARIABLE paragraph), if any, up to and including the first cutpoint. The last interval is from above the last cutpoint to the specified upper limit (MAXIMUM), if any. That is, k cutpoints define (k+1) intervals since the endpoints are not stated as cutpoints.

The groups formed by using these groupings for AGE can be NAMED. The number of NAMES must be one greater than the number of CUTPOINTS. For example,

          NAMES(2) ARE '25ORLESS', '26 TO 35',
                       '36 TO 45', 'OVER 45'.

(Apostrophes are required because each name either starts with a number or includes a blank or both.)

Extended convenience for grouping specification (new in 1981). Often several variables may have the same NAMES, CODES and/or CUTPOINT specification. Instead of using separate statements for each variable, you may combine information in one statement. For example, if variables 10 through 25 all contain codes 1 and 2 and names YES and NO, the specification may be written

          CODES(10 TO 25) = 1, 2.
          NAMES(10 TO 25) = YES, NO.

In the example above, if variable 10 is named Q1 (in the VARIABLE paragraph) and variable 25, Q16, the code specification can be written as

CODES(Q1 TO Q16) = 1, 2.

Additional GROUP specifications in the VARIABLE paragraph. Nine of the BMDP programs (1D, 3D, 5D, 6D, 7M, AM, 1R, 3S and 1V) require that, in addition to specifying the group NAMES, CODES or CUTPOINTS in the GROUP paragraph, you identify the variable containing the grouping information in the VARIABLE paragraph. The instruction,

/ VARIABLE   GROUPING IS 5.

in the input for Run A and Run B above states that the fifth variable contains information for separating the cases into two samples. (See individual program descriptions.)

RESET: cancelling previous CODE and CUTPOINT assignments. Any CODE or CUTPOINT assignment remains until changed in a subsequent GROUP or CATEGORY paragraph. At times you may want to cancel all previous assignments and respecify only what is necessary. For example, if CODE and CUTPOINT values are stored with the data on a BMDP File and you now want to do an analysis with different categories, this can be done by specifying

RESET.

The common options for the GROUP paragraph are listed below.

GROUP ──────────────────────────────────────

CODE(v list) = # list.   up to 10 observed values/prev.

The numbers in the list are values of the variable that has subscript (v list). The values are used as codes to identify group (or category) membership. Cases containing values for the specified variable that are not equal to any of the numbers specified will not be included in the groups (or categories) formed. CODE(v list) can be repeated in the same GROUP paragraph for different variables. (v list) must be a variable subscript or a variable name.
Note: Some programs may require that grouping information be explicitly stated.

CUTPoint(v list) = # list.   none/prev.

The numbers in the list are the upper limits of intervals for variable (v list). Each interval contains its upper limit. k cutpoints define (k+1) intervals, i.e., the endpoints should not be stated. Each interval is treated as a code to identify group (or category) membership. Do not specify both a CODE and a CUTPOINT statement for the same variable. CUTPOINT(v list) can be repeated in the same GROUP paragraph for different variables. (v list) must be a variable subscript or name.

NAME(v list) = c list.   one per code   CODE or
                          or interval   CUTPoint
                                          values/prev.

The first name in the list is the name of the first code or interval specified by a CODE(v list) or CUTPOINT(v list) statement, the second the name of the second, etc. A CODE or CUTPOINT statement must also be specified for the variable (v list). Groups or categories with the same NAME are combined into the same group or category. This has the same effect as recoding the values of the variable. If the user does not specify names, the program creates names from the CODES or CUTPOINTS; these preassigned names for groups or intervals cannot be used in BMDP instructions and are reset in each problem.

RESET   no

When RESET is specified, all assignments read from a BMDP File or made in previous GROUP or CATEGORY paragraphs are cancelled.

5.6 FREE FORMAT DATA READING (NEW IN 1981)

In Section 5.3 and Chapter 3 we discuss how to read data when they are positioned in a fixed location on each record (e.g., AGE is in columns 7 and 8 for each of the 188 records). BMDP now allows three methods for free format data reading where the observations are simply separated by blanks and/or a comma. Missing data can be indicated by a symbol, multiple commas or a user-specified code.

The free format data reading methods FREE, STREAM and SLASH. The instructions for the three methods of free-format data reading are FREE, STREAM and SLASH. For the FREE method, the data for each case start on a new record. More than one record can be used for each case provided each case has the same number of records. No excess data are allowed on any record. After all variables for a case are read, the remainder of the record must be blank. This allows BMDP to check that you have specified the correct number of variables for each case. Below is an example of a minimal set of instructions for reading the data for three cases with method FREE.

```
/ INPUT   VARIABLES = 5. FORMAT IS FREE.
/ END
  1.2  3.4    5.4 2.3 1.2
 4.3 2.1  3.4 3  1.
        4 * 6 5 4
/END
```

The data for the first case are 1.2, 3.4, 5.4, 2.3 and 1.2; for the second case, 4.3, 2.1, 3.4, 3.0 and 1.0; and for the last case, 4.0, missing, 6.0, 5.0 and 4.0. Note that the missing observation is indicated by an asterisk, the observations are separated by varying numbers of blanks and decimal points are omitted from some numbers. The last data record is followed by /END.

For the STREAM method, each case does not need to start on a new record, e.g., data for five subjects could be on one card. The only error checks that are made are for illegal data and for an end-of-data before all variables are read for the last case. We illustrate how to read three variables per case using STREAM format

```
/ INPUT    VARIABLES ARE 3.  FORMAT IS STREAM.
/ END
1 2 3 4 3 2 2 3 4 5 4 3 2 5 4   /END
```

The data for five cases are read: the values for the first case are 1.0, 2.0 and 3.0; the values for the last case are 2.0, 5.0 and 4.0.

As with the STREAM method, the SLASH method allows more than one case per record. Either a slash or the end of a record must occur after the last variable for each case. We show how to read data similar to that in the STREAM method.

```
/ INPUT    VARIABLES ARE 3.  FORMAT IS SLASH.
/ END
1 2 3/ 4 3 2/ 4 3 2/ 4 3 2/ 2 3 4
/END
```

Note that the /END may be on a separate record for STREAM or SLASH.

Missing data are indicated by a missing value symbol (e.g., an asterisk), multiple commas or by missing value codes (the same as those described above in the VARIABLE paragraph). The missing value symbol is assumed to be an asterisk, but may be user-defined by the MCHAR sentence in the INPUT paragraph. The data field length for indicating a missing value may be more than one character long, but all characters must be the same missing value symbol, e.g., one or more consecutive asterisks can indicate a single missing value. For example, if your instructions and data look like

```
/ INPUT    VARIABLES ARE 3.
           MCHAR = '$'.
           FORMAT IS FREE.
/ END
 1.5  4.3  $$$
 2, 3, 4
 $  $  5.44
 4.4, , 1.0
/END
```

the data are read as

X(1)	X(2)	X(3)
1.5	4.3	missing
2.0	3.0	4.00
missing	missing	5.44
4.4	missing	1.00

Numbers may be signed, and may contain either an 'E' or 'D' type exponent specification (e.g., .123E5

is equivalent to 12300). Note that both E and D will be treated as single precision, since data in BMDP are always single precision, even in programs where computations are performed in double precision.

Case LABELING variables are stored as characters. The maximum length is four characters for each case labeling variable. If two consecutive case labeling variables are specified, then it is assumed that they are contiguous (with no separating blanks). If the instructions are

```
/ INPUT    VAR = 5.   FORMAT = FREE.
/ VAR      LABEL = 1, 2.
/ END
```

and your data are

```
JOHN    5   9   6
PETER   7   1   9
JOANNE  4   8   8
SAM A   1   2   3
```

then the first three cases will be read correctly, but the fourth case is in error because the characters in 'SAM A' contain a blank.

Illegal data found in a data field will cause that value to be set to missing. Errors of this type are counted along with the other errors associated with the specific free-format input methods. The count is incremented only once for each case, regardless of the number of data errors for that case. If this count exceeds the maximum limit for the error count, then the program is stopped. The user may change the preassigned error limit of 10 by using the ERRMAX instruction in the INPUT paragraph.

Record length for data input records is ordinarily the same as the record length for the BMDP instructions (80, or 72 if card sequence numbers are found in columns 73–80). If the data are from a different unit than the BMDP instructions, the assumed record length will be 80. The record length may also be specified by the RECLEN sentence in the INPUT paragraph when reading data records from a tape or disk file. If you have a large number of records, but only part of each record contains data, then it is recommended that you specify RECLEN = number of columns that must be scanned. For example, if your data are in columns 1 to 20, then specify RECLEN = 20.

End-of-Data is indicated by either an END-OF-FILE condition when reading the data, or by the presence of /END. The examples above demonstrate the use of /END for the three methods. Note that when End-of-Data is indicated by /END, another set of Control Language may follow the data.

I/O errors. I/O errors will cause the program to stop and write an error message which contains the case index.

INPUT ─────────────────────────────

> FORMAT = (one only)   none/prev.
>   FREE, STREAM, SLASH.
> The free format input type desired. See
> definitions and examples above.
> RECLEN = #.   80 or 72/prev.
> The record length can be changed if your data
> records are not 80 columns or if you want to
> limit the number of columns scanned.
> MCHAR = 'c'.   */prev.
> A symbol inserted in the data file to indicate
> that the observation is missing.
> ERRMAX = #.   10/prev.
> Limit for the maximum number of cases with
> errors. Errors encountered in the free format
> input reading are counted. The program stops
> when this limit is exceeded.

5.7 ADDITIONAL OPTIONS AND FEATURES FOR FORMATTED DATA READING (NEW IN 1981)

Formatted data reading allows you to specify a FORTRAN-like format to describe the column and record locations of the data fields that are to be read for a case. Formats are interpreted by the new data reader in basically the same manner as FORTRAN processed variable formats. There are a number of new features provided by the new data reader. A summary of the new features and differences in the use of formatted input between FORTRAN and the BMDP data reader follows:

- Names of the variables being read are printed in a list that details the location of the data fields.
- Illegal data characters in a data field cause the variable to be set to missing, and a detailed description of the error is printed.
- Multiple cases may be described by the format. This allows you to read several cases from a single record. (See MULT.)
- The missing value symbol (MCHAR) described above for free formatted reading can also be used.
- The number of cases with data errors (ERRMAX) that can occur before the program is to be terminated can be specified (as described above for free formatted reading).
- End-of-Data can be indicated by /END. If the data are being read from the same unit as the BMDP instructions, and /END is used to signal the end of the data, then more BMDP instructions may be entered after the data without having to specify the number of cases.
- If record length is specified in the RECLEN sentence in the INPUT paragraph, then a check will be made to verify that your format does not require a longer record length.
- Five methods are available for treating blanks in input fields (see instruction summary below).

New options associated with formatted data reading are summarized below.

INPUT ─────────────────────────────

> MULTiple = #.   1/prev.
> The number of cases described by the format
> specification. This allows you to read several
> cases from a single record.
> RECLEN = #.   none/prev.
> When the record length (the number of columns)
> is specified a check is made to verify that
> your format specification does not need a
> longer record length.
> ERRMAX = #.   10/prev.
> Limit for the maximum number of cases with
> errors in the input reading. The program stops
> when this limit is exceeded.
> MCHAR = 'c'.   */prev.
> A symbol that is inserted in the data file to
> indicate that the observation is missing.
> BLEVEL = #.   2/prev.
> Treatment of blanks in input fields where
>
> # = {
>   1 - all embedded and trailing blanks are illegal. (An embedded blank is a blank in the middle of a number, e.g., weight is recorded as 1 3 instead of 153.)
>   2 - embedded blanks and trailing blanks are illegal, except that trailing blanks in a field with a decimal point are null or zero.
>   3 - trailing blanks in a field without a decimal point are ignored (i.e., an integer number need not be right-justified).
>   4 - all trailing blanks are converted to zero.
>   5 - all trailing blanks and embedded blanks are converted to zero (corresponds to standard FORTRAN input reading).

Summary of Differences Between IBM FORTRAN Input and the BMDP Data Reader

- For repeats (e.g., 17F3.0), the FORTRAN limit is 255, for the BMDP data reader the limit is 2**31.
- For nested parentheses, FORTRAN allows two levels; the data reader 5 levels.
- For illegal data, FORTRAN prints an IHC215I error message and changes the character to zero. The data reader prints an error message giving the case number, the index and name of the variable(s) in error, the record position within the case, the position within the record, the contents of the field, and the character in error. It then sets the value of the variable to missing.
- For blank fields, FORTRAN reads them as either zero or missing. The data reader operates similarly and is available on all machine types.
- For trailing or embedded blanks, FORTRAN reads zeros. The BMDP reader has five methods for dealing with blanks. (See summary above.)
- For record length, FORTRAN prints an IHC212I message if the logical record length is not long enough. The data reader computes the required record

length from the format. If RECLEN is included in the INPUT paragraph, the number must be equal to or greater than the computed length, or the program will stop. An IHC212I message may be printed if you have an error both in your format and in RECLEN.

 - Format notation such as F4.0 in FORTRAN may be written as F4 or I4 for the BMDP data reader (in either case the data are stored as floating point numbers in BMDP). Some FORTRANs use T10; the data reader can accept either T10 or C10 to indicate that reading should proceed in column 10. Some FORTRANs use P3F4.1; the data reader works the same way.

5.8 MULTIPLE PROBLEMS AND SUBPROBLEMS

Every BMDP program can analyze multiple problems. A problem consists of a collection of paragraphs such as INPUT, VARIABLE, and END together with a set of data that may be included with the Control Language or may be on a disk or tape file. For multiple problems, with data on tape or disk, you merely include consecutive complete sets of Control Language. If your data are included with the Control Language, then the basic setup for multiple problems is as follows:

```
/ INPUT  ...
   ...
/ END
   (data)
/END
/ INPUT  ...
   ...
/ END
   (data)
/END
```

Note that /END follows the data for each problem unless you state the number of cases for each problem.

If the data for each problem are the same and if your data are included with your Control Language (say on computer cards), then it may be inconvenient for you to repeat the data as in the above example. In this case, you should consider temporary BMDP Files (Section 7.5).

Several BMDP programs permit multiple analyses within a single problem. These multiple analyses are called subproblems. There are three methods of specifying subproblems. The first method is usually used when only a single paragraph is needed to specify a new analysis, e.g., the REGRESSION paragraph in stepwise regression, P2R. To specify subproblems in P2R, you merely include multiple REGRESSION paragraphs, e.g.,

```
/ INPUT  ...
   ...
/ REGR    DEPEND = ....
/ REGR    DEPEND = ....
/ END
```

This could be done, for example, to obtain separate analyses for different dependent variables. BMDP programs that allow subproblems by repeating the same paragraph (with different options) within the same set of BMDP Control Language are P3D, P5D, P6D, P7D, (P1F, P2F, P3F older releases), P4F, P1L, P1R, P2R, P4R, P1V and P3V.

Other BMDP programs allow subproblems by repeating a subset of Control Language paragraphs (after the data if other data are included with the Control Language rather than being read from a tape or disk file). The setup for use of the nonlinear regression program, P3R, would be

```
/ INPUT  ...
   ...
/ REGRession ...
/ PARAMeter  ...
/ END
   (data if not in a tape or disk file)
/ REGR  ...
/ PARAM ...
/ END
```

where the subset of paragraphs REGRESSION, PARAMETER and END may be repeated as many times as you like. Note that if data are not on a tape or disk file, /END should also follow the data unless you have specified the number of cases in the INPUT paragraph. Programs that allow subproblems in this manner include P9D, P1M, P3R, P5R, PAR, P1S, and P3S.

Repeated analyses are also allowed in P1T, P2T, and P4V, which are oriented toward possible interactive use. See the descriptions of these programs for details.

Paragraph Statement	Preassigned	Comment and Manual Reference
/ PROBlem		
TITLE = 'c'.	blank	Title for the output not exceeding 160 characters in length. 39
LENGTH = #.	none	Maximum length of storage array (in integer words). Use only to decrease storage. (Some older programs run more efficiently when excessive storage is not used.) 33
INTeractive.	NO INT.	Specifies that the user will respond (at the terminal) if queried by the program. If omitted, NO INTERACTIVE is assumed. 33
ERRlev = (one only) STRICT, NORMAL.	NORMAL.	Controls how the program checks the BMDP Instructions for errors. If STRICT is specified, the program stops when it finds extra information (e.g., the instructions contain a paragraph from another program). If NORMAL is specified, the program scans the instructions for instructions specific to the program and ignores extra information. If omitted, NORMAL is assumed.
/ INPut		
VARiable = #.	none	Number of variables in each case. * 40
FORMat = 'c' or (one only) FREE, STREAM, SLASH, BINARY.	none	Required unless data are in BMDP File. Format 'c' specifies the layout (in fixed fields) of the data in a single case (_ 800 char.). FREE, STREAM and SLASH are free format parameters with observations separated with a blank and/or a comma. BINARY is for data on tape or disk in binary (unformatted) form. * 40, 44
UNIT = #.	5	Input unit if data are not on cards (use 5, 7 to 25. * 40
CASE = #.	end-of-file	Number of cases in data. * 40
REWIND.	REWIND.	Rewind input unit. * 40
RECLEN = #.	80 or 72	Record length. * 46
MCHAR = 'c'.	*	Symbol indicating missing observation. * 46
ERRMAX = #.	10	Program stops if this number of errors is exceeded. * 46
MULTiple = #.	1	Number of cases per read. * 46
BLEVEL = #.	2	Treatment of blanks in input fields. See p. 46 for codes. *
/ VARiable		
NAME = c list.	X(1),X(2),...	Variable names (one per variable). * 42
MAXIMUM = # list. MINimum = # list.	none	Upper and lower limits (one per variable). * 42
BLANK = (one only) ZERO, MISSING.	MISSING.	Blanks treated as missing value codes or zeros. * 42
MISSing = # list.	none	Missing value codes (one per variable). * 42
LABEL = v list.	none	Variables used to label cases. Read under A format. * 42
USE = v list.	all	Variables to be used in analysis.
/ GROUP		
CODE (v list) = # list.	see comment	Codes for variable designated, may be repeated. Up to ten distinct values of the variable. * 44
CUTPoint (v list) = # list.	none	Cutpoints to define intervals of variable designated. May be repeated. * 44
NAME (v list) = c list.	CODE or CUTPoint. values	Code or interval names for the variable designated. May be repeated. * 44
RESET.	no	All assignments in previous GROUP or CATEGORY paragraph are cancelled. 44

Key:

/	–indicates paragraph
.	–period ends a sentence
●	–required
v	–variable (name or subscript)
g	–group (name or subscript)
#	–number
'c'	–characters (name or parameter) may omit apostrophes if contiguous letters only

*	–assigned value remains the same for additional problems or subproblems
VT	–number of variables after transformations
list	–more than one item, often one per var.
Capitalized letters	–paragraph or sentence names recognized by BMDP
Page numbers following refer to this Manual	

6

DATA EDITING

Variable Transformation and Case Selection

Laszlo Engelman
Jerry Johnson

INTRODUCTION

This chapter describes three basic capabilities:

1) the BMDP TRANSFORM paragraph, which provides a powerful set of options available in all BMDP programs for computing new variables, replacing a data value by a corrected value, selecting a subpopulation for analysis (case selection), changing the scale of the data (e.g., taking the log or square root of each observation), recoding the values of a variable, handling dates, and generating random numbers for random subsamples or simulation studies

2) the BIMEDT procedure, which allows you to write FORTRAN code for complicated transformations. Your code can read other files, write to files or call non-BMDP subroutines. Your statements are processed by the FORTRAN compiler and temporarily become part of the BMDP program

3) P1S, the Multipass Transformation program, which allows statistics computed at one pass of the data file to be used in computing transformations for the next pass of the data

The simplest form of data editing is to exclude data values from an analysis because they are either equal to a missing value code or outside specified upper and lower limits. Section 5.4 describes how to specify missing value codes (BLANK and MISSING) and upper and lower limits (MAXIMUM and MINIMUM). If additional editing is unnecessary for your data, this chapter can be skipped. However, you may find that some data editing will be required as a result of your initial data screening. In this chapter we describe methods of variable transformation and case selection that are common to all BMDP programs.

Variable transformation may be necessary, for example, to combine two or more variables into a single variable (for example, if height is recorded as FEET and INCHES, then either FEET can be replaced by FEET + INCHES/12 or INCHES can be replaced by 12*FEET + INCHES; time differences and meaningful ratios are often formed from two or more separate measurements).

Case selection may be necessary to omit cases because only a subgroup of the cases is needed in the analysis (such as women under 30), or to exclude a random subsample of cases against which the results of the analysis can be verified.

Variable transformations and case selection are described by BMDP statements in the TRANSFORM paragraph or by FORTRAN statements in a FORTRAN subroutine. These features are available in all BMDP programs. Variable transformations and case selection use data from one case at a time. It is possible to compute differences between data in successive cases (lagged differences, Appendix C.14). However, more complicated functions that require data from several cases (such as a mean) are difficult if not impossible to perform by the above transformations. A special program, P1S -- Multipass Transformation -- is available to help with more complicated functions. P1S reads the data as often as specified and additional transformations can be performed at each reading.

WHERE TO FIND IT

6.1 DATA EDITING AND TRANSFORMATIONS — THE BMDP TRANSFORM PARAGRAPH

The TRANSFORM paragraph can contain statements to transform, modify, or recode your data. This paragraph can include BMDP instructions for selecting subpopulations and deleting cases. There are also random number generators that are used to choose random subsamples or are used in simulation studies.

Computing New Variables that are Functions of the Variables in the File

The BMDP programs execute the statements in the TRANSFORM paragraph for one case at a time. Simple as well as complex statements can be used, such as

```
A = B + C.
A = SQRT(B + C).
A = -LOG(RNDU(1794371)).
IF(A GT B) THEN C = D.
A = SUM(A,B,C)
```

The variables are identified by single letters to illustrate the form of the transformations: examples using named variables are:

```
LOGAGE = LOG(AGE).
TOTAL = SCORE1 + SCORE2.
HYPOTNSE = SQRT(BASE**2 + HEIGHT**2).
WEIGHT = MEAN(WEIGHT1,WEIGHT2,WEIGHT3).
```

(The permissible operations and functions are summarized in Table 6.1.) For example, if you need to compute a subject's age from his birth year (recorded with only two digits) the statement

```
AGE = YEARNOW - YEARBORN.
```

will not give the correct answer for those people born before 1900. You can use the IF-THEN type statement to compute their correct age:

```
IF(YEARBORN GT YEARNOW)
    THEN (AGE = YEARNOW + 100 - YEARBORN).
```

Thus, if a subject's birth year is 98 (1898) and it is now 82 (1982), the program will compute

```
AGE = 82 + 100 - 98     or 84.
```

The transformations' result (e.g., 84 above) can be stored as a <u>new</u> variable added (inside the computer) to your data file or it can <u>replace</u> the value of a variable read as input (e.g., the log of body weight can replace weight). The ADD instruction (below) must be used when adding variables; no special instructions are needed when a transformation replaces the value of an existing variable.

The multiple-argument functions provide a variety of statistics and are used primarily for creating summary variables. For example, suppose you have recorded weights each week for the participants in a six-week weight loss program. The MIN function can be used to obtain the minimum weight recorded for each participant:

```
MINWT = MIN(WT1,WT2,WT3,WT4,WT5,WT6).
```
while
```
VISITS = N(WT1,WT2,WT3,WT4,WT5,WT6).
```
will store the number of times a weight was recorded in the new variable VISITS (some participants may have missed appointments).

These functions, like other BMDP transformation functions, are available in all BMDP programs and operate on <u>one case</u> of the data matrix at a time -- <u>not</u> on one <u>variable</u> across cases. The functions may be nested within one another and they may be executed conditionally, e.g.,

```
IF (VISITS GT 3) THEN
    CHANGE = WT1 - LVAL(WT1,WT2,WT3,WT4,WT5,WT6).
```

The FOR % notation (see p. 30) may also be used with the new functions, as in

```
MINWT = MIN (FOR K = 1 TO 6.  % WT|K,  %).
```

Date functions make it easier to calculate the number of days between two dates or to convert dates from one standard form to another. For example, the DAYS function can be used to compute the number of days between June 17, 1980 and March 5, 1982:

```
NUMDAYS = DAYS(3,5,82) - DAYS(6,17,80).
```

The "commands" listed in Table 6.1 differ from the usual transformations in that they do not yield a single value as a result. REPL and FILL use linear interpolation to fill in missing values and TEXT and SHOW are print requests.

Other examples of multiple argument functions, date functions, and commands appear in Appendix F.

Conventions and Rules for Specifying Transformations

All variables can be used in BMDP transformations, even variables omitted from the USE list in the VARIABLE paragraph.

<u>Variable notation or identification, temporary variables, and punctuation.</u> In the TRANSFORM paragraph, refer to variables by their NAME (assigned in the VARIABLE paragraph) or by the form X(sub-

Table 6.1 BMDP transformations available in the TRANSFORM paragraph

Kind of Transformation	Usage[1]	Result	Example	Result is missing[2]
Assignment	y = a.	a	X(7)=X(1)+X(2)/5. X(7)=5.0.	
Arithmetic	a + b	a+b (addition)	X(1)+X(2)	
	a − b	a−b (subtraction)	WEIGHT−X(3)	
	a * b	a·b (multiplication)	RATE*TIME	
	a/b	a/b (division)	1/TIME	b = 0
	a ** b	a^b (exponentiation)	HEIGHT**3	a < 0 and b ≠ integer
	a MOD b	a MOD b = a − [a/b]·b The remainder of (a divided by b). For example 14 MOD 4 yields 2 as result.	AGE MOD 12	b = 0
Function	LOG(a)	$\log_{10}(a)$ (base 10 log)	LOG (WEIGHT)	a ≤ 0
	LN(a)	$\log_e(a)$	LN(WEIGHT)	a ≤ 0
	SQRT(a)	$\sqrt{a}$ (square root)	SQRT(INCOME)	a < 0
	EXP(a)	e^a (exponential)	EXP(X(2))	|a| > 174
	ABS(a)	|a|: absolute value for a	ABS(X(17))	
	SIN(a)	sin(a) (trigonometric sine, a in radians)	SIN(X(1))	
	COS(a)	cos(a) (trigonometric cosine, a in radians)	COS(X(2))	
	TAN(a)	tan(a) (trigonometric tangent, a in radians)	TAN(ANGLE)	
	ATAN(a)	arctan(a) (trigonometric arc tangent	ATAN(X(3))	
	ASIN(a)	arc sine, result in redians	ASIN(B)	
	ACOS(a)	arc cosine	ACOS(B)	
	INT(a)	[a]: integer part of a	INT(AGE)	
	SIGN(a)	−1 if a < 0; 0 if a = 0; 1 if a > 0	SIGN(X(1))	
	NONB(a)	Blank field detection; a is recoded to missing if it was read as a blank. Blank field detection is computer dependent. Check with your computer center for the availability of this option.	NONB(X(7))	a was read as blank
	CHAR(c)	The characters c are available for comparison (EQ) with data read in A format (see p. 55)	USE=SEX EQ CHAR(MALE).	

Logical operation. (The result of any logical operation is either one if true, zero if false, or missing (XMIS).
Logical operations that require true and false arguments, e.g., AND, OR and IF, treat zero as false; "not equal zero"
as true and XMIS as missing.)

	a LE b	true if a ≤ b, false if a > b	WT72 LE WT73	
	a LT b	true if a < b, false if a ≥ b	X(2) LT X(3)	
	a GE b	true if a ≥ b, false if a < b	WEIGHT GE 50	
	a GT b	true if a > b, false if a ≤ b	WEIGHT GT 50	
	a NE b	true if a ≠ b, false if a = b	X(2) NE X(3)	
	a EQ b	true if a = b, false if a ≠ b	X(2) EQ X(3)	
	a AND b	true if a = 1 (true) and b = 1 (true)	TEMPA AND TEMPB	
	a OR b	true if a = 1 (true) or b = 1 (true)	TEMPA OR TEMPB	
	IF(...)THEN...	The THEN expression is executed if, and only if, the IF expression is true.	IF (A GT B) THEN C=D.	

<u>Note:</u> A blank must precede and follow LE, LT, GE, GT, NE, EQ, AND, and OR.

Case selection	USE = #.	(See p. 55)	IF(KASE LT 10)THEN USE=0.	
	OMIT=# list.	(See p. 55)	OMIT=17,18,37.	
	DELETE=# list.	(See p. 55)	DELETE=32,40 TO 50.	
Random number Functions	RNDU(i)	uniform (0,1) random number	RNDU(76347)	
	RNDG(i)	normal (0,1) random number	RNDG(46791)	

<u>Key:</u> [1] y may be a variable name or X(#), or USE.
a and b may be a variable name or X(#), a constant, KASE, USE, XMIS, an arithmetic expression or a function.

[2] If a or b is flagged as missing, the result is missing except for the logical operations NE, EQ, AND, OR,
IF (see p. 53)

(continued)

Kind of Transformation	Usage[3]	Result	Result is missing[2]
Summary Statistic (multiple argument functions)	N (a1,a2,...,an)	Number of usable values; i.e., the number of values in the list a1,a2,...,an that are not missing and are within usable range.	15
	MIN (a1,a2,...,an)	Smallest usable value.	5
	MAX (a1,a2,...,an)	Largest usable value.	5
	SUM (a1,a2,...,an)	Sum of usable values.	5
	SUMC(a1,a2,...,an)	Sum of values; if any value is missing, the result is missing.	8
	MEAN(a1,a2,...,an)	Mean of usable values.	5
	MED (a1,a2,...,an)	Median of usable values; central value or the average of the two central values.	5
	SD (a1,a2,...,an)	Standard deviation of usable values.	6
	SEM (a1,a2,...,an)	Standard error of the mean of usable values.	6
	T (a1,a2,...,an)	t-value of the mean; i.e., mean/(sd/sqrt(n)).	6
	TRIM(i,a1,a2,...,an)	Trimmed mean; mean after trimming the i largest and i smallest values, where i is an integer.	7
	TT (i,a1,a2,...,an)	Trimmed t; the t-value of the i level trimmed mean. This is a t-value with (n-1-2*i) df.	7
	IQR (a1,a2,...,an)	Interquartile range of usable values; Q3-Q1.	6
	RHO (y1,y2,...,yn)	Correlation of (1,2,...,n) and (y1,y2...yn).	6
	B (x1,y1,...,xn,yn)	Coefficient b of the regression line y=a+bx.	9
	A (x1,y1,...,xn,yn)	Constant a of the regression line y=a+bx.	9
	R (x1,y1,...,xn,yn)	Correlation coefficient r(x,y).	9
	TRND(y1,y2,...,yn)	Trend of the (y1,y2...yn) over (1,2,...,n).	6
	TCON(y1,y2,...,yn)	Intercept of the trend line; i.e., constant of regression line through (1,y1),...,(n,yn).	6
	AREA(y1,y2,...,yn)	Area under y: $(y_1+2*y_2 +...+2*y_{n-1}+y_n)/2$.	10
	TRAP(x1,y1,...,xn,yn)	Area under y via the trapezoidal rule: $sum((x_{i-1}-x_i)*(y_i+y_{i-1})/2)$.	11
	LINT(x0,x1,y1,x2,y2)	Linear interpolation: $y_1+(x_0-x_1)*(y_2-y_1)/(x_2-x_1)$.	8 or 12
	LIND(a1,a2,...,an)	Index of last usable value (1, 2,..., or n).	5
	LVAL(a1,a2,...,an)	Last usable value (a1, a2, ... , or an).	5
	INDX(a,b1,b2,...,bn)	Index of first b that is equal to a.	15
	REC(a,b1,c1,...,bn,cn)	A recode function, cj is stored as the result when bj is equal to a.	13
Dates[4]	DAYS (mm,dd,yy)	The number of days since January 1, 1960.	8
	DAYS (mmddyy)	The number of days since January 1, 1960.	8
	MDY (# of days)	mmddyy - six digit date as one variable.	8
	MM (# of days)	mm - two digits for the month within the year.	8
	DD (# of days)	dd - two digits for the day within the month.	8
	YY (# of days)	yy - two digits for the year.	8
	JULN (# of days)	Julian date form in five digits.	8
	DAYJ (Julian)	The number of days since January 1, 1960.	8
Commands	REPL(y1,y2,...,yn)	Replace missing values using linear interpolation of surrounding usable values. Arguments are variable names or X(i).	7
	FILL(x1,y1,...,xn,yn)	Replace missing y values using linear interpolation of surrounding usable value pairs (x,y). The y arguments are variable names.	8
	TEXT('message')	Print case number and label with message.	
	SHOW(a1,a2,...,an)	Print case number and label with the values of a1,a2,...,an.	

Key: [3] a_i, b_i, c_i, x_i, y_i, are arguments, which may be variable names, explicit values, functions, or algebraic expressions

[4] The values of the variables used as date function arguments have specific values - the following notation is used:

mmddyy   - the date is recorded as one variable with six digits
            (Sept. 17, 1981 is 091781)
mm,dd,yy - three variables, two digits each, record the date
            (for Sept.17, 1981, the variable mm has the value 09,
            dd is 17, and yy is 81)
# of days - the number of days since Janaury 1, 1960
Julian   - the date is recorded as one variable with five digits (Feb. 15, 1981 is 81046,
            where the date is the 46th day of the year 1981)
The variables may have any name (e.g., DATE1, X(5), NUMDAYS, etc.). We use "mm," for example, as a convenience for these definitions.

(continued)

<u>Key for missing values</u>

The result is a missing value code (or values are not replaced) if:

 5 - there are no usable values.
 6 - there are fewer than two usable values
 7 - there are fewer than (2*i + 1) usable values.
 8 - any value is missing.
 9 - the variance of x over usable (x,y) pairs is zero
10 - y1 or yn is missing.

11 - x1, y1, xn, or yn is missing.
12 - x1 = x2.
13 - no b is equal to a.
14 - "mm" is less than 1 or greater than 12 or
     "dd" is less than 1 or greater than 31.
15 - there is never a missing value code.

----

script). That is, to compute the log of the fourth variable, WEIGHT, write:

$$X(4) = LOG(X(4)).$$

or

$$X(4) = LOG(WEIGHT).$$

Note that this differs from other paragraphs, where the subscript alone is used.

If a name that is not listed in the VARIABLE paragraph is used in the TRANSFORM paragraph, it is considered a <u>temporary variable</u> and may be referred to again in the TRANSFORM paragraph, but not used in the analysis (e.g., it would not be available for a plot). You can refer to a temporary variable by any name that is not assigned in the VARIABLE paragraph.

BMDP transformations follow somewhat different syntax rules than other paragraphs. Each statement must be terminated by a period. A variable name must be stated on the left side of the equal sign (=, IS, or ARE). One or more variable names or numbers and the name of functions or operators must be stated on the right side. A blank must precede and follow MOD, LE, LT, GE, GT, NE, EQ, AND, OR, IS, ARE, and THEN.

Any arithmetically correct statement is permitted in BMDP transformations, except that the arguments for the random number generators must be integer constants, e.g.,

RNDU(1579431)

rather than variables or expressions such as

RNDU(AGE)

The BMDP transformation processor checks for syntax errors and other usage errors such as A = B. where the variable B is an undefined temporary variable.

<u>The IF-THEN conditional statement</u>. The IF clause of a conditional statement can contain arithmetic operations and functions, e.g.,

IF(A/B+C GT 15 AND AGE GT 50) THEN GROUP = 2.

Logical operators (EQ, GT, AND, etc.) are used in the IF clause. Note that if you have two conditions that must be met, then the form

IF(A NE B AND A NE C) ...

must be used rather than

IF(A NE B OR C) ...

The THEN clause of a conditional statement can contain several statements, e.g.,

IF(A GT B) THEN (C = D. E = F. USE = 0.).

When values are assigned in the THEN clause, an equal sign (=) is used, and <u>not</u> the logical operator EQ. Note that if the THEN clause contains only one statement, the statement need not be enclosed in parentheses, but if the THEN clause contains several statements, the entire list should be enclosed in parentheses. The THEN clause can also contain conditional statements, e.g.,

IF(A GT B) THEN (C = D. IF(E LT F) THEN G = H.).

The transformation(s) stated after THEN are executed only if the IF expression is true; e.g., if you state

IF(A) THEN C = B.

and A is false or missing, C is unchanged.

<u>BMDP words in the TRANSFORM paragraph</u>. The following words are reserved names that have a special meaning in the TRANSFORM paragraph:

<u>KASE</u> - the sequence number of the case in data read by the BMDP program; e.g., A = KASE creates a variable, A, which equals the sequential case number.
<u>XMIS</u> - the name assigned to the value used internally by the BMDP program as a code for values that are excluded because they are equal to a missing value code. <u>TOOBIG</u> and <u>TOOSMALL</u> are the names assigned to values above and below limits (MIN and MAX limits specified in the VARIABLE paragraph). These words can be used in the IF clause of conditional expressions, such as

IF(INCOME GT TOOBIG) THEN INCOME = 30000.

XMIS can be used on the right side of an equal sign, but in BMDP versions prior to 1981, TOOBIG and TOOSMALL cannot.

- <u>USE</u> indicates whether or not a case should be included in an analysis.
- <u>OMIT</u> and <u>DELETE</u> indicate that specified cases should not be used in the analysis.
- <u>END</u> terminates Control Language instructions.
- All function names listed in Table 6.1.

USE, OMIT, and DELETE are discussed in the next section. The reserved words cannot be names of variables unless they are enclosed in apostrophes. KASE, XMIS, TOOBIG, and TOOSMALL cannot be used on the left side of the equal sign. (They can be used on the left side of a logical operator: "IF (KASE EQ 20) THEN ...".)

<u>Missing values in transformations</u>. Appropriate action is taken when variables used in transformations are missing or out of range. If you state

$$A = SIN(B).$$

and B is missing, then A is set to missing. The rules about missing values are:

- Arithmetic: if the required arithmetic cannot be performed (e.g., $\sqrt{-1}$) or if any argument is missing or exceeds the upper or lower bounds for the variable, the result is missing.
- Logical: if any argument is missing, the result is set equal to the missing value code except in the following cases:

false AND missing	yields false
true OR missing	yields true

- If one of the arguments for EQ or NE is XMIS the result is true or false depending on the value of the other arguments; e.g., in the statement X(1) = X(2) EQ XMIS, if X(2) is missing, X(1) is true; otherwise X(1) is false.
- The result in an expression involving IF is unchanged unless the condition is true. For example,

IF(STATUS EQ 7) THEN X(1) = 3.

leaves X(1) unaltered if either STATUS is missing or STATUS is not equal to 7.

- If USE (see next section) is equal to the missing value code after all the Control Language transformations have been performed, USE is set equal to zero, e.g., if USE = X(7) and X(7) is missing, USE is set equal to zero.

Blank fields on data cards are assumed to be missing values (when data are read with an F-type fixed FORMAT). In versions dated before 1981, blanks are assumed to be zero unless BLANKS ARE MISSING. is specified. If you want blanks to denote zeros for all variables, specify BLANK = ZERO in the VARIABLE paragraph (Section 5.4). If you want blanks to denote missing values for some variables and zero for other variables, specify BLANKS ARE ZEROS and use the NONB transformation, e.g.,

AGE = NONB(AGE).

That is, AGE is missing whenever it is recorded as a blank; blanks for other variables are treated as zeros. In versions of BMDP dated before 1981, the detection of blanks is computer-dependent; check with your computer center to see whether this feature is available.

Recoding a value to missing. You can set the value of a variable to XMIS (the missing value code) by using BMDP transformations, e.g., if the variable (say STATUS) has more than one code for missing values (say 7 and 8), both can be recoded to missing by using this statement in the TRANSFORM paragraph.

IF (STATUS EQ 7 OR STATUS EQ 8) THEN STATUS = XMIS.

You can recode one data value to another value in a similar manner by specifying the recoded value in place of XMIS in the above example.

Creating new variables. You can create new variables by transformation and use them in addition to the original variables; the BMDP program must be told that new variables are created. For example, to create a new variable RATIO that is the ratio of WEIGHT to HEIGHT in the Werner blood chemistry data (Table 5.1), you specify

RATIO = WEIGHT/HEIGHT.

To use RATIO in an analysis, RATIO must be added to the list of VARIABLE NAMES and the number of variables must be increased by an ADD statement in the VARIABLE paragraph. Therefore, in the VARIABLE paragraph you specify the NAMES of the nine original variables plus the NAME(S) of added variable(s).

```
/ VARIABLE   NAMES = ID, AGE, HEIGHT, WEIGHT,
                     BRTHPILL, CHOLSTRL, ALBUMIN,
                     CALCIUM, URACID, RATIO.
             ADD   = 1.
```

Note that variables added by transformations are initialized as missing values for each case, unless you ask that their values be retained from case to case via a RETAIN. statement in the VARiable paragraph (see Appendix C.14). If a variable is added through transformations and never defined, it will be missing for all cases. If RETAIN is requested, then before transformations are performed for any given case past case 1, a variable added through transformations is equal to the value it had for the previous case.

```
VARiable ─────────────────────────────────────────────
  ADD = #.                                    0/prev.
     The number of variables added by transformation
     (created in the TRANSFORM paragraph or in the
     FORTRAN subroutine). If ADD is negative, vari-
     ables are deleted. The total number of var-
     iables (largest subscript of any variable) used
     in an analysis is the sum of ADD and the number
     of VARIABLES specified in the INPUT paragraph.
     If ADD is positive, the new variables are added
     to the variables read in as data; the sub-
     scripts of the new variables are integers be-
     ginning at one greater than the number of
     VARIABLES specified in the INPUT paragraph. If
     ADD is negative, the last variable(s) in the
     INPUT paragraph are eliminated.
     If ADD is positive, the number of NAMES that
     can be specified in the VARIABLE paragraph is
     the sum of ADD and the number of VARIABLES in
     the INPUT paragraph. Thus, NAMES can be speci-
     fied for variables added by transformation.
  RETAIN. or NO RETAIN.                            no
     Variables added through transformations are re-
     initialized to missing value for each case. If
     RETAIN is requested, however, added variables
     retain the value set at the previous case. This
     can be used to create lagged variables.
```

Data checking -- before or after transformations. As the data are read, they can be checked for values equal to the missing value codes (MISS) or outside the upper and lower limits (MIN and MAX) if the user specifies MISS, MIN, or MAX in the VARIABLE paragraph. The values that are missing or out of range are recoded. In the Control Language transformations the recoded values are called XMIS, TOOBIG, and

TOOSMALL. If you want these values recoded after transformations are performed, you must specify

AFTER.

in the VARIABLE paragraph. When AFTER is specified, the data values are recoded after the BMDP Control Language (and the FORTRAN subroutine) transformations are processed. (This does not affect the automatic recoding of blanks to missing values.) If you do not want any checking either before or after transformations, state NO CHECK.

In summary, as each case is read, its values are checked in the following order:

- blanks are replaced by the internal code for missing values (unless BLANKS ARE ZERO is specified)
- if BEFORE (the preassigned option for data checking) is in effect, appropriate internal codes replace the user-specified missing value codes (MISS) or values outside the MIN and MAX limits.
- FORTRAN transformations are executed. The user must include his or her own checks for extreme or missing values (see examples in Section 6.2)
- transformations in the BMDP TRANSFORM paragraph are executed. The BMDP program incorporates information from the user's MISS, MIN, and MAX statements in the transformations, e.g.,

LOGAGE = LOG(AGE).

LOGAGE is set to XMIS if AGE is missing. Some operations may also produce missing values (e.g., $\sqrt{-1}$, $\ln(0)$, or $1/0$)
- if the user specifies AFTER, variables for which MISS, MAX, or MIN are stated are now checked. Appropriate internal codes are inserted when necessary. Note: For any checking to occur, you must state missing value codes (MISS) or range limits (MIN or MAX) in the VARIABLE paragraph.

VARiable ─────────────────────────
BEFore. or AFTer. or NO CHECK.   BEFORE/prev.
The data are recoded to internal codes for missing data or data out of range BEFORE or AFTER processing the transformations in both the TRANSFORM paragraph and the FORTRAN subroutine. AFTER is a rarely used option.

Transformation defaults for multiple problems. If in one computer run, you want to apply the same transformations to the data in subsequent problems, specify only

/ TRAN

without repeating the entire previous TRANSFORM paragraph. However, if any instructions are specified in the TRANSFORM paragraph, only these new instructions are performed; those in the previous TRANSFORM paragraph are ignored. If you do not include a TRANSFORM paragraph in a subsequent problem, no transformations are performed in that problem.

Selecting Subpopulations and Deleting Cases

The BMDP transformation word USE plus the functions and logical operators listed in Table 6.1

provide powerful case selection capabilities. (Note that the BMDP word USE in the TRANSFORM paragraph specifies case selection; USE in the VARIABLE paragraph specifies the variables to be used.)

For example, if you want to restrict your analysis to 20- to 40-year-old women who come from the third treatment center, state

USE = AGE GE 20 AND AGE LE 40 AND SEX EQ 2
AND CENTER EQ 3.

USE is stored internally as an additional variable for each case. The value of USE is positive (true) for each case unless you reset it. If the value of USE is

- positive (or true)   the data for the case are used in the analysis and included in the BMDP File, if one is being created (Chapter 7).
- zero (or false or missing)   the data for the case are not used in the analysis, but if a BMDP File is being created, the data for the case will be included in it; the fact that USE is specified as zero is recorded in the file.
- negative   the data for the case are not used in the analysis and are not included in a BMDP File, if one is being created.

In the example above, a +1 will be stored in USE for a particular case if all statements to the right of the equal sign are true. If one or more are false (e.g., the sex code is 1, not 2), a zero is stored in the variable USE and the case is not used in the analysis. Note the difference between the logical operators AND and OR: when AND connects statements, both segments must be true for the combined statement to be true (to have the value 1 assigned); when OR connects statements, only one need be true for the combined statement to be considered true. For example, the value assigned to USE in the statement

USE = DISEASE EQ 2 OR TREATMNT EQ 3.

will be zero if DISEASE does not equal 2 and if treatment does not equal 3. But if either statement or both statements are true, the value of USE will be 1 and the case will be used. If a BMDP File is being created (Chapter 7) the value of USE for the case is also included in the BMDP File. The value of USE can be reset by subsequent statements; only the last setting of USE is followed; e.g., if you state

/ TRAN   USE = KASE NE 1.   USE = KASE NE 13.

it excludes only the 13th case because the value of USE after the first statement is reset by the second statement. To exclude cases 1 and 13, specify

IF(KASE EQ 1 OR KASE EQ 13) THEN USE = 0.

If the value of USE is set equal to -100 for a particular case, then data reading will terminate at that case as if an end-of-file had been encountered. This option is handy if you want to read a subset of cases from a sorted file. If your file was sorted in P1D by sex, then the statement

IF (SEX EQ 2) THEN USE = -100.

causes cases with SEX code 1 to have the value 1 stored in USE. Reading stops for the first case with SEX code 2 because the value -100 is assigned to USE.

Deleting a list of cases. Two statements, OMIT and DELETE, can be used to simplify case selections when the sequence numbers of cases not being analyzed are known.

OMIT = list of case numbers.

has the same effect as setting USE = 0 for each case in the list.

DELETE = list of case numbers.

has the same effect as setting USE = -1 (a negative value) for each case in the list. Implied lists using TO and BY (p. 30) make it easy to list the case numbers. For example,

DELETE = 1 TO 10, 61, 63.

deletes the first ten, and the 61st and 63rd cases.
To omit odd numbered cases from an analysis that contains 20 cases, you can state

OMIT = 1 TO 19 BY 2.

Note: OMIT and DELETE cannot be used in a conditional statement. To omit or delete many cases, the USE statement is more efficient than OMIT or DELETE.

```
TRANsform ─────────────────────────────
  USE = #.                                    1
    If USE = 1 (positive or true), the case is used
    in the analysis and copied into a BMDP File if
    one is created.  If USE is 0 (false), the case
    is not used in the analysis but is copied into
    a BMDP File.  If USE is -1 (negative), the case
    is not used and not copied into a BMDP File.
    If USE = -100, data reading is terminated as if
    an end-of-file had occurred on the input file.
  OMIT = # list.                           none
    Sequence numbers of cases that are to be omit-
    ted from the analysis but included in a BMDP
    File if one is created.  OMIT sets USE to zero
    for each case specified.
  DELETE = # list.                         none
    Sequence numbers of cases that are to be
    omitted from the analysis and not copied into a
    BMDP File if one is created. DELETE sets USE to
    -1 for each case specified.
```

Random Numbers for Random Subsamples or for Simulations

Two random number functions can be specified in the TRANSFORM paragraph.

- RNDU(i) generates uniform random numbers on the interval from zero to one
- RNDG(i) generates random numbers from a normal distribution with mean zero and variance one

In both functions i is a large positive odd integer constant that is used to start the random number se-

quence (it is not used as a random number). If RNDU or RNDG are specified more than once, the value of i should be different each time. The random number generators are described in Appendix A.1. Suppose you want a random sample of the cases -- deleting about 25% from the analysis. You can use the uniform generator to specify

IF (RNDU(7864521) LT .25) THEN USE = 0.

Data can be generated using two random number generators. This is useful if you want to see the effect of violating an assumption of a test. For example, suppose you want to generate data for two groups from a normal distribution with mean zero: the first group has standard deviation 1.0 and comprises about 70% of the cases; the second group has standard deviation 3.0. You can do it this way:

```
GROUP = 1.
IF (RNDU(762381) LT .3) THEN GROUP = 2.
RANDOM = RNDG(24573).
IF (GROUP EQ 2) THEN RANDOM = RANDOM * 3.
```

In the TRANSFORM paragraph, GROUP is set equal to 1. If the value of a uniform random number is less than 0.3 (approximately 30% of the cases), GROUP is set to 2. RANDOM is first set to a random number generated from a normal distribution with mean zero and standard deviation 1. If GROUP is 2, RANDOM is multiplied by 3, i.e., it will be from a normal distribution with mean zero and standard deviation three.
Note that if the number of input variables is zero (all variables are generated by transformation), the number of cases must be stated. In the above example you generate your own variables; therefore you must specify zero variables and the number of cases in the INPUT paragraph. In the VARIABLE paragraph specify that two variables named GROUP and RANDOM are added by transformation.
Data appropriate to a regression model with a normal (or uniform) error distribution can be generated in a similar manner. Quick and dirty Monte Carlo is described in Appendix C.10 and random case selection in Appendix C.6.

The CHAR Function and Recoding Nonnumeric Data

Nonnumeric data can be recoded in the TRANSFORM paragraph of any BMDP program by using the CHAR function, provided that the variable has been read with an A-type format. For example, if the variable SEX has been read with an A1 format and the letter M is used as a code to indicate males, you can change M to the number "1" by stating

IF(SEX EQ CHAR(M)) THEN SEX = 1.

Similarly, if the data file contains the word MALE, and SEX is read with an A4 format, we can recode MALE to 1 by stating:

IF (SEX EQ CHAR(MALE)) THEN SEX = 1.

The CHAR function also provides a way to do case selection on one or both alphabetic case labeling variables.
Note that the CHAR function compares a string of as many as four characters (or the number of charac-

ters in a floating point word on your machine). The CHAR function takes the characters between the two parentheses and inserts enough blanks on the right side to complete a word on your machine. For machines with four character words (b means blank)

CHAR(M)	becomes	Mbbb
CHAR( )	becomes	bbbb
CHAR(FEMALE)	becomes	FEMA

Therefore, in the example above we could not use CHAR(M) to make a comparison with the data MALE (read in A4 format) because Mbbb would be compared with MALE. Also note that leading blanks are counted: CHAR(bbM) is not the same as CHAR(bM).

Note: Data checking specified in the VARIABLE paragraph for missing (MISS) or extreme values (MIN and MAX) applies to values read as numbers (not characters). So, if checks for range limits or missing values are necessary for variables read in A format, request them after the characters are transformed to numbers by specifying AFTER in the VARIABLE paragraph. Because of this restriction, it may be necessary to use two problems to perform all your transformations.

The CHAR function is new in the 1981 release. It is somewhat machine-dependent and may not be available in the 1981 release of some non-IBM versions.

Also note the REC function, which is new in the 1983 release (see Table 6.1 and Appendix F).

6.2 FORTRAN TRANSFORMATIONS USING THE BIMEDT PROCEDURE

FORTRAN transformations are sometimes more economical than the BMDP instruction transformations when you have large quantities of data or the same transformation is applied to many variables. FORTRAN statements are processed by the FORTRAN compiler and temporarily become part of the BMDP program. Transformations specified in FORTRAN are processed before those specified in the TRANSFORM paragraph, if both types are used. The BEFORE and AFTER statements in the VARIABLE paragraph regarding checks for values missing and out of range apply both to FORTRAN and the BMDP statements in the TRANSFORM paragraph.

Any legitimate FORTRAN statements, such as READ, WRITE, DATA, DIMENSION, FUNCTION and SUBROUTINE, can be used. The FORTRAN subroutine in which the transformations are included starts with the following two statements:

```
SUBROUTINE TRANSF(X, KASE, NPROB, USE, NVAR, XMIS)
DIMENSION X(NVAR)
```

where the following values should not be changed:

KASE — sequence number of case being processed.
NPROB — sequence number of the problem (PROBLEM paragraph) being processed.
NVAR — the greater of the number of variables read or the number of variables after transformation (i.e., the number of variables read plus the number of variables ADDED by transformation, p. 54).
XMIS — missing value code used internally by the BMDP program. Values less than the lower limit or greater than the upper limit specified

for a variable are recoded to values ($-2 *$ XMIS and $2 *$ XMIS, respectively) greater in absolute value than XMIS. The values are recoded BEFORE the transformations are processed unless AFTER is specified in the VARIABLE paragraph (p. 54).

You can change the values of X and USE.
X — vector containing the data for the case being processed. The values for all variables read in the data are present. X(1) is the value of the first variable, X(2) the second, etc. The values of X can be modified to contain the transformed values.
USE — flag for case selection. Its interpretation is identical to that of USE in the TRANSFORM paragraph (p. 55). If USE is positive(1), the case is used in the analysis; if zero(0), the case is not used, but is included in a BMDP File if one is created; if negative(−1), the case is not used or copied into a BMDP File. USE = −100 indicates that data reading should terminate as if an end-of-file had occurred.

Any transformation possible using the TRANSFORM paragraph can also be performed using FORTRAN transformations. Examples comparing FORTRAN transformations with simple BMDP transformations are in Appendix F. FORTRAN transformations can also be used when it is difficult or impossible to achieve the same result with BMDP transformations. Examples showing FORTRAN transformations for case selection and deletion and for reading data with a nonstandard format follow. Use of FORTRAN transformations for recoding nonnumeric data is illustrated in Appendix F.

Conventions and rules for specifying FORTRAN transformations. FORTRAN transformations follow FORTRAN rules, not the rules for BMDP instructions. (For example, there are no periods at the end of statements.) Variable names are not recognized in the FORTRAN subroutine and cannot be used in place of X(subscript). You must check for missing values; they are not automatically excluded from the transformation computations.

FORTRAN statements must begin in column 7 (except for numbered statements where the number is in columns 1 − 5). Note also that logical operators (LT, GT, EQ, etc.) are separated by periods, not blanks.

If new variables are added by the transformation, ADD must be stated in the VARIABLE paragraph. (See p. 54 for definition of ADD.) The data can be checked for missing value codes BEFORE or AFTER the transformations are processed. The programs are preset to BEFORE; AFTER must be specified when needed (p.54).

BMDP functions are not available in FORTRAN, although some functions are available in both BMDP and FORTRAN. In some cases, their names differ (e.g, the BMDP functions LOG and LN correspond to the FORTRAN functions ALOG10 and ALOG.)

Case Selection and Deletion with FORTRAN Transformations

You can select cases by setting the value of USE. Since AGE is the second variable, we can select the cases of subjects aged 20 to 30 by stating

```
USE = 0.
IF(X(2).GE.20.0 .AND. X(2).LE.30.0) USE = 1.
```

USE can be set equal to -100 to signal that you do not want to read more data. The statements OMIT and DELETE cannot be used in the FORTRAN subroutine.

Random Subsamples and Simulation for FORTRAN Transformations

To randomly select cases or generate data you can call the FORTRAN functions that generate uniform or normal random numbers (Appendix A.1).

System Cards for FORTRAN Transformations

When you specify transformations in the FORTRAN subroutine, the System Cards must be altered. The subroutine containing the FORTRAN statements must be compiled and integrated with the previously compiled BMDP program to form a modified program that will transform the data and perform the analysis.

For IBM OS systems, we have a simple procedure to compile the subroutine and execute the BMDP program.

- First you must specify three System Cards

```
//job card
//   EXEC   BIMEDT,PROG=BMDPxx
//TRANSF DD  *
```

(Note the T in BIME<u>DT</u>; xx must be replaced by the two character identification of the BMDP program.)
- This is followed by the <u>FORTRAN statements</u> defining the transformations. The SUBROUTINE and DIMENSION cards at the beginning and the RETURN and END cards at the end must be omitted; they are ordinarily automatically supplied by the BIMEDT procedure for IBM OS and similar systems. Check at your facility to see whether these cards are required.
- This is followed by a <u>System Card</u>

```
//GO.SYSIN  DD  *
```

- This is followed by the BMDP instructions for the BMDP program and the data, if on cards.
- This is terminated by a final System Card.

```
//
```

If data are read from a disk or magnetic tape, or if a BMDP File is created, the System Cards describ-ing the data location are placed immediately before //GO.SYSIN DD * (see page opposite back cover).

Variations exist for the System Cards; check with your facility consultant for those required. Space is provided opposite the inside back cover for you to record the System Cards used at your facility.

Reading Data with a Nonstandard Format

The data are usually read by the program according to the specifications in the INPUT paragraph. Unfortunately, not all data can be read by a single format statement in the cases-by-variable form that the BMDP programs expect. Data in nonstandard format can be read by the FORTRAN subroutine. To do it, set

```
/ INPUT     VARIABLE = 0.
            CASE     = number of cases.
/ VARIABLE  ADD      = number of variables to be
                       read by FORTRAN subroutine.
```

The data are not read in the usual manner by the BMDP program, so the number of cases must be stated.

The data are read in the FORTRAN subroutine and passed to the program as the vector X. For example, if the data (5 variables) were keypunched in 2 different formats [the first 10 cases as (5F5.0) and the last 15 cases as (1X,5F5.0)] the data can be read by

```
      IF(KASE.GT.10) GO TO 2
      READ(5,10) (X(I),I=1,5)
   10 FORMAT(5F5.0)
      RETURN
    2 READ(5,11) (X(I),I=1,5)
   11 FORMAT(1X,5F5.0)
```

The data records may have been collected from different sources, e.g., clinics where each clinic used its own format. However, if the clinic ID was uniformly recorded in the same place in each data record, the record can be read in A-format except for the clinic ID; it could then be written to a temporary unit and reread under the appropriate format for a specific clinic.

Another use of this feature is when each subject's data have a common first record, but vary in other regards, such as number of followup records or type of record. The first record can be read for each subject, then each of the followup records can be read by an appropriate format. This feature can be used to merge data from two different locations.

P1S

6.3 Multipass Transformations

ABSTRACT

P1S passes (reads) the data one or more times. At each pass, P1S can compute univariate statistics, perform variable transformations, or edit the data using statistics computed in a previous pass. Z-scores can be computed and saved in a BMDP File. P1S computes means, standard deviations, geometric means, harmonic means and largest and smallest values for the variables in one pass and uses them in the next pass. The program computes the transformed data and requested statistics for each pass.

Transformations in P1S are frequently specified in FORTRAN or specified by a word specific to P1S, e.g., ZSCORE. The transformation statements described in Section 6.1 for the BMDP TRANSFORM paragraph are also available in P1S (beginning with the 1981 version). Note that unlike other BMDP programs the BMDP TRANSFORM paragraph transformations are performed before the FORTRAN transformations rather than after.

Note that the transformation capabilities described in Section 6.1 and 6.2 are available in all programs, and are adequate for the great majority of problems. They are designed to compute values for each case individually and require only one reading of the data. Use P1S only if your transformation requires information from an earlier reading of the complete data file (e.g., it uses the mean or the minimum and maximum of all the data values).

WHERE TO FIND IT

Example 1S.1 Basic Setup for Z-Scores

One of the most common uses of program P1S is to change data to standard scores (z-scores, i.e., each value of a variable is transformed by subtracting the mean of the variable and then dividing by the standard deviation). In this example we use the BMDP word ZSCORE to request the scores. In Example 1S.2 we use FORTRAN statements to specify the calculations. The output is the same for both examples: we present it after Example 1S.2.

The Werner data (Table 5.1) are used to illustrate how blood chemistry measurements can be transformed to z-scores. The BMDP instructions for this example include the PROBLEM, INPUT and VARIABLE paragraphs that are explained in Chapter 5. Note that we specify the number of cases, because more instructions follow the data. Our instructions are

```
------------------------------------------
/ PROBLEM    TITLE IS 'WERNER BLOOD CHEMISTRY DATA'.
/ INPUT      VARIABLES ARE 9.
            FORMAT IS '(A4, 5F4.0, 3F4.1)'.
            CASES ARE 188.
/ VARIABLE   NAMES ARE ID, AGE, HEIGHT, WEIGHT,
                BRTHPILL, CHOLSTRL, ALBUMIN,
                CALCIUM, URICACID.
            MAXIMUM IS (6)400.
            MINIMUM IS (6)150.
            LABEL IS ID.
/ PASS       TITLE IS 'COMPUTE MEANS AND STANDARD
                DEVIATIONS'.

/ END

    (--- the data go here ---)

/ PASS       TITLE IS 'COMPUTE Z-SCORES'.
/ COMPUTE    ZSCORE.
            VARIABLES ARE 6 TO 9.
/ PRINT      DATA.
            VARIABLES ARE 2 TO 9.
/ END
------------------------------------------
```

(See end of this P1S program section for organization of systems information, BMDP instructions and data. This run uses the BIMED procedure; Example 15.2 uses the BIMEDT procedures.)

A PASS paragraph is required for each reading of the data. If the data are on cards all PASS paragraphs but the first are placed after the data. The ZSCORE statement in the COMPUTE paragraph in the second pass requests that z-scores be computed for the variables specified. We specify that the data be printed to demonstrate how the transformed data look in the output (Output 1S.2). If we omit the VARIABLE statement in the PRINT paragraph, the program would print only those variables specified in the COMPUTE paragraph (6 TO 9).

Passing the data: the PASS paragraph. During the first pass the data are read one case at a time, specified transformations are performed, and the transformed data are copied onto a temporary unit. At each subsequent pass the data are read from the last temporary unit onto which they were copied, specified transformations are performed and the transformed data are copied onto the other temporary unit (two temporary units are used alternately to store the data). If the BIMED procedure has been installed in the recommended way at your computer facility, you do not need to specify additional systems information about these units.

A PASS paragraph is required for each pass of the data. If the data are on cards, all but the first PASS paragraph must follow the data (see order of input in the summary at the end of this section). A TITLE can be specified to identify each pass. However, it is sufficient to specify only

/ PASS

without a title.

```
PASS ─────────────────────────────────────────
    TITLE = 'c'.    ≤ 160 char.              blank
       c is a title for this pass of the data.
```

The COMPUTE paragraph. The COMPUTE paragraph specifies the statistics to be computed at each pass and used in the transformations of the next pass. The COMPUTE paragraph can be repeated for each PASS paragraph.

The statistics are

- mean: $\bar{x} = \Sigma x_j / N$
  where x_1, x_2, ... are acceptable values for a variable and N the frequency of the acceptable values
- standard deviation: $s = [\Sigma(x_j - \bar{x})^2 / (N-1)]^{\frac{1}{2}}$
- z-scores: $z_j = \dfrac{x_j - \bar{x}}{s}$
- harmonic mean: $\bar{x}_h = (\Sigma^+ \dfrac{1}{x_j} / N^+)^{-1}$

where Σ^+ is the sum over positive values only and N^+ is the frequency of the positive values

- geometric mean: $\bar{x}_g = (\Pi^+ x_j)^{1/N^+}$
  where Π^+ is the product of the positive values only
- minimum: $\min_j x_j$
- maximum: $\max_j x_j$
- K1 and K2 in the FORTRAN subroutine are N and N^+ respectively (see Example 1S.2)

The means and standard deviations are computed unless

NO MEANS.

is specified in the COMPUTE paragraph. The z-scores are computed if

ZSCORE.

is specified in the second or subsequent pass using means and standard deviations defined in the previous pass. The HARMONIC mean is computed if

HARMONIC.

is specified and the GEOMETRIC mean if

GEOMETRIC.

is specified. Both the minimum and maximum are computed if

EXTREMES.

is specified.

If you want to select the VARIABLES to be used in the computations you can specify which ones to use. If not specified, all variables are used.

```
COMPute ─────────────────────────────────────────
    MEAN.                                  MEAN/prev.
       The means and standard deviations are computed
       and can be used in transformations in the next
       pass of the data. To negate, specify NO MEAN.
    ZSCORE.                                   no/prev.
       z-scores are computed in the second and
       subsequent passes of the data using means and
       standard deviations computed in the previous
       pass.
    HARMonic.                                 no/prev.
       The harmonic means are computed and can be used
       in transformations in the next pass of the
       data.
    GEOMetric.                                no/prev.
       The geometric means are computed and can be
       used in transformations in the next pass of the
       data.
    EXTRemes.                                 no/prev.
       The minimums and maximums are computed and can
       be used in transformations in the next pass of
       the data.
    VARiable = v list.                all variables/prev.
       Names or subscripts of variables for which
       statistics are to be computed.
```

The PRINT paragraph. In the PRINT paragraph you can request a listing of the transformed data. The PRINT paragraph can be repeated for each PASS paragraph. The preassigned value for the PRINT VAR statement is to print only those variables requested in the COMPUTE paragraph. If there is no VARIABLE list in the COMPUTE paragraph, data for all variables (or all variables in the VARIABLE USE list, if specified) are printed. Our request to PRINT DATA after the ZSCORE statement in the COMPUTE paragraph causes the transformed variables (6 - 9), the z-scores, to be printed in ④ in Output 1S.1. The untransformed variables (2 - 5) are also included because of the VARIABLE statement in the PRINT paragraph.

```
PRINT ─────────────────────────────────────────
    DATA.                                     no/prev.
       The transformed data are printed.
    VARiable = v list.            (those in the
                                      COMPUTE
                                      paragraph)
       Names or subscripts of variables for which the
       data are printed.
```

Output 1S.1 and Output 1S.2   z-scores computed by P1S.

NUMBER OF CASES READ.   188   ①

PASS TITLE. . . . .
COMPUTE MEANS AND STANDARD DEVIATIONS

		2 AGE	3 HEIGHT	4 WEIGHT	5 BRTHPILL	6 CHOLSTRL	7 ALBUMIN	8 CALCIUM	9 URICACID
②	SAMPLE SIZE	188	186	186	188	186	186	185	187
	MEAN	33.82	64.51	131.7	1.500	236.1	4.111	9.962	4.771
	STAN.DEV	10.11	2.485	20.66	0.5013	42.56	0.3580	0.4796	1.157

PROGRAM CONTROL INFORMATION   ③

/ PASS   TITLE IS 'COMPUTE Z-SCORES'.

/ COMPUTE   ZSCORE.
             VAR = 6 TO 9.

/ PRINT   DATA.
             VAR = 2 TO 9.

/ END

① Number of cases read. All acceptable values are used in the computations. An acceptable value is one that is not equal to the missing value code or outside the specified lower or upper limits for the variable.

② Means and standard deviations computed at the first pass of the data.

③ The second PASS paragraph from Example 1S.1 is printed.

④ The data matrix, after computing all transformations specified in the first (none) and second (z-scores for variables 6 to 9) pass of the data. The second column is the case LABEL: it is the ID variable that was read in A4 format.

⑤ Mean and standard deviations computed at the second pass of the data. The means for variables 6 to 9 are zero, except for rounding error, and the standard deviations are one.

PASS TITLE. . . . .
COMPUTE Z-SCORES

DATA AFTER TRANSFORMATIONS

C A S E NO. LABEL ④	2 AGE	3 HEIGHT	4 WEIGHT	5 BRTHPILL	6 CHOLSTRL	7 ALBUMIN	8 CALCIUM	9 URICACID
1 2381	22	67	144	1	-.849	.527	-.338	.544
2 1946	22	64	160	2	MISSING	-1.708	MISSING	2.099
3 1610	25	62	128	1	.161	-.0314	.913	-1.271
4 1797	25	68	150	2	MISSING	-.869	-.755	-1.530
5 561	19	64	125	1	-1.836	-.0314	-.130	-.0610

----cases 6 to 183----

184 1789	52	62	107	2	.678	1.365	.913	1.408
185 1149	53	MISSING	178	1	-.215	-.590	MISSING	.198
186 575	53	65	140	2	-.380	-.311	1.539	-.147
187 2271	54	66	158	1	1.618	.248	.705	.0255
188 39	54	60	170	2	-.380	-1.708	-2.423	1.322

	2 AGE	3 HEIGHT	4 WEIGHT	5 BRTHPILL	6 CHOLSTRL	7 ALBUMIN	8 CALCIUM	9 URICACID
SAMPLE SIZE ⑤	188	186	186	188	186	186	185	187
MEAN	33.82	64.51	131.7	1.500	0.1729E-04	0.1192E-03	0.8674E-04	0.3992E-04
STAN.DEV	10.11	2.485	20.66	0.5013	1.000	1.000	1.000	1.000

Example 1S.2 Using FORTRAN Transformations to Compute z-Scores

In this example we show how to specify a FORTRAN subroutine to transform the Werner data to z-scores. (The instructions in Example 1S.1 produce the same output.) We omit the COMPUTE paragraph after the second PASS paragraph in Example 1S.1 and add FORTRAN statements ahead of the BMDP instructions. The rules for the FORTRAN statements follow Output 1S.2. Lines of instructions are explained below.

```
      -------------------------------------
(a)  [ //job card
     [ // EXEC  BIMEDT,PROG=BMDP1S
     [ //TRANSF  DD  *
     [         IF(NPS.EQ.1) RETURN
     [ C
(b)  [         DO 2 I=6,9
     [         IF(ABS(X(I)).GE.XMIS) GO TO 2
     [         X(I) = (X(I)-XB(I))/SD(I)
     [       2 CONTINUE
(c)  [ //GO.SYSIN  DD  *
     [ / PROBLEM    TITLE IS 'WERNER BLOOD CHEMISTRY
     [                           DATA'.
     [ / INPUT      VARIABLES ARE 9.
     [              FORMAT IS '(A4, 5F4.0, 3F4.1)'.
     [              CASES ARE 188.
     [ / VARIABLE   NAMES ARE ID, AGE, HEIGHT, WEIGHT,
     [                        BRTHPILL, CHOLSTRL, ALBUMIN,
(d)  [                        CALCIUM, URICACID.
     [              MAXIMUM IS (6)400.
     [              MINIMUM IS (6)150.
     [              LABEL IS ID.
     [
     [ / PASS       TITLE IS 'COMPUTE MEANS AND
     [                        STANDARD DEVIATIONS'.
     [ / END
(e)  [      --- the data (Table 5.1) go here ---
     [ / PASS       TITLE IS 'COMPUTE Z-SCORES'.
(f)  [ / PRINT      DATA.
     [ / END
(g)  [ //
      -------------------------------------
```

(a) System cards for an IBM OS system

(b) FORTRAN statements describing the transformation at the second pass (NPS = 2)

(c) System Card

(d) BMDP instructions to describe the data and the first pass

(e) The data

(f) BMDP instructions to describe the second pass

(g) System Card

Note: We do not use the BIMED procedure; we use the BIMEDT procedure (second System Card) when FORTRAN statements are used. If the data were read from a file the System Card describing the unit should precede

```
                //GO.SYSIN  DD  *
```

FORTRAN transformation subroutine. The rules for using the FORTRAN transformations in P1S are the same as those described in Section 6.2 for all BMDP programs. The major difference is in the first two records of the subroutine. Transformations in P1S <u>must</u> be specified by FORTRAN statements in a subroutine that is called once for each case. The first two records of the subroutine for P1S are

```
SUBROUTINE P1STRN(X,KASE,NPROB,USE,NPS,NV,NVAR,XB,
*                 SD,HM,GM,XMIN,XMAX,K1,K2,XMIS)
DIMENSION  X(NVAR),XB(NVAR),SD(NVAR),HM(NVAR)
*          GM(NVAR),XMIN(NVAR),XMAX(NVAR),
*          K1(NVAR),K2(NVAR)
```

where the following values should not be changed:

KASE   is the sequence number of the case being processed

NPROB   is the sequence number of the problem (PROBLEM paragraph) being processed

NPS   is the sequence number of the PASS paragraph being processed (each pass involves one reading of the data)

NV   is the number of variables read as input

NVAR   is the larger of NV and the number of variables after transformation

XB   contains the means of the variables from the previous pass

SD   contains the standard deviations of the variables from the previous pass

HM   contains the harmonic means of the variables from the previous pass

GM   contains the geometric means of the variables from the previous pass

XMIN   contains the minimums of the variables from the previous pass

XMAX   contains the maximums of the variables from the previous pass

K1   contains the numbers of acceptable values for the variables from the previous pass

K2   contains the numbers of <u>positive</u> (acceptable) values for the variables from the previous pass

XB, SD, HM, GM, XMIN, XMAX, K1 and K2 are vectors. The first value (e.g., XB(1), SD(1), ...) refers to the first variable; the second value (e.g., XB(2), SD(2), ...) refers to the second variable, etc. XB and SD are computed unless NO MEAN is specified in the COMPUTE paragraph. HM, GM, XMIN and XMAX are computed only if specified in the COMPUTE paragraph. K1 and K2 are always computed.

XMIS   is the value of the missing value code used internally by the BMDP program. Values that are less than the lower limit or greater than the upper limit specified for a variable are recoded to values greater in <u>absolute value</u> than XMIS. The values are recoded BEFORE the transformations unless AFTER is specified in the VARIABLE paragraph (p.54). It is necessary to compare the absolute values of the variables against XMIS since values out of range are set to internal codes more extreme than XMIS that can be positive (if greater than the upper limit) or negative (if less than the lower limit).

You may change the values of X and USE.

X is the vector containing the data for the case being processed. X(1) is the value of the first variable, X(2) the second, etc. The values of X can be modified to contain the transformed values.

USE is a flag for case selection. Its interpretation is identical to that of USE in the TRANSFORM paragraph (p. 55). If USE is positive (1), the case is used in the analysis; if zero (0), the case is <u>not</u> used but is included in a BMDP File if one is created; if negative (-1) the case is <u>not</u> used and is <u>not</u> copied into a BMDP File. When USE is negative, the case is discarded but the sequence numbers (KASE) of the remaining cases are not changed.

Example 1S.3 Saving the Transformed Data

P1S performs complex transformations that are not possible in other BMDP programs. The transformed data matrix is usually saved in a BMDP File, and can then be analyzed by other BMDP programs. The BMDP File is discussed in detail in Chapter 7; you need to read Chapter 7 before using a BMDP File.

You must specify the sequence number of the PASS at which a BMDP File is to be created. In Examples 1S.1 and 1S.2 the transformed z-scores are created in the second pass of the data (PASS = 2). Therefore to create a BMDP File we use the following SAVE paragraph inserted in the BMDP instructions before the <u>first</u> PASS paragraph in the instructions of either Example 1S.1 or Example 1S.2.

```
------------------------------------------
/ SAVE    UNIT IS 9.
         NEW.
         CODE IS WERNER.
         PASS IS 2.
------------------------------------------
```

The System Cards for this example are identical to those for Example 1S.1 or 1S.2 except that a System Card to describe where to store the BMDP File must be inserted after the EXEC card in Example 1S.1 or

before the

```
        //GO.SYSIN  DD  *
```

in Example 1S.2. This card is described in Chapter 7.

The creation of a BMDP File produces the messages shown in Output 1S.3. The values of variables 6 - 9 in the file are z-scores as shown in ④ in Output 1S.2. The first five variables were not transformed.

```
SAVE ─────────────────────────────────────
  PASS = #.                        none/prev.
     Sequence number of the pass at which the BMDP
     File is created. The data at this pass are
     copied into a BMDP File. If PASS is not stated,
     or this pass is not reached, a BMDP File is not
     created.
```

SIZE OF PROBLEM

P1S can read and transform data for at least 350 variables at one time on large computer systems. Appendix B describes how to increase the capacity of the program.

COMPUTATIONAL METHOD

In the first pass the data are read, transformed, and written onto a temporary unit. At each subsequent pass the data are read from one temporary unit, transformed, and written onto a second temporary unit. Means and standard deviations at each pass are computed by the method of provisional means (Appendix A.2).

ACKNOWLEDGEMENT

P1S was programmed by Caroline Ho. Later revisions were made by James Frane.

Output 1S.3 z-scores computed by P1S are saved. The other printed results are those in Outputs 1S.1 and 1S.2.

```
      PASS TITLE.................
COMPUTE Z-SCORES


BMDP FILE IS BEING WRITTEN ON UNIT        9
CODE. . . IS      WERNER
CONTENT . IS      DATA
LABEL . . IS
VARIABLES ARE
      1 ID          2 AGE        3 HEIGHT      4 WEIGHT      5 BRTHPILL
      6 CHOLSTRL    7 ALBUMIN    8 CALCIUM     9 URICACID


BMDP FILE ON UNIT  9 HAS BEEN COMPLETED.
```

SUMMARY

A. Order of Input Cards for BIMED procedure (The user does not supply FORTRAN statements, e.g., see Example 1S.1 for z-scores)

```
// (job card)
// EXEC BIMED,PROG=BMDP1S
//SYSIN  DD  *
/ PROBLEM
/ INPUT
/ VARIABLE
/ SAVE
/ PASS
/ COMPUTE
/ PRINT
/ END
   (data, if on cards)
/ PASS        ┐
/ COMPUTE     │  Repeat for
/ PRINT       │  subproblems
/ END         ┘
// (system card)
```

B. Order of Input Cards for BIMEDT procedure (the user specifies transformations using statements in FORTRAN)

```
// (job card)
// EXEC BIMEDT,PROG=BMDP1S       (see Appendix E)
//TRANSF  DD  *
   (user's FORTRAN statements)
//GO.SYSIN  DD  *
/ PROBLEM
/ INPUT
/ VARIABLE
/ SAVE
/ PASS
/ COMPUTE
/ PRINT
/ END
   (data, if on cards)
/ PASS        ┐
/ COMPUTE     │  Repeat for
/ PRINT       │  subproblems.
/ END         ┘
// (system card)
```

Full sets of BMDP paragraphs (and data, if on cards) can be repeated for additional problems; see Section 5.8.

instructions specific to P1S

Paragraph Statement	Preassigned	Comment and Manual Reference
/●PASS		Required for each pass of the data. / PASS is sufficient without a TITLE. During the first pass, for example, means are computed and are then available for computations specified in the second pass. 60
TITLE = 'c'.		Title, up to 160 characters, is printed on the output for this pass of the data.
/ COMPute		Optional to specify statistics to be computed at each / PASS and used in the transformations of the next / PASS. Can be repeated for each / PASS. 60
MEAN.	yes	Means and standard deviations. *
HARM.	no	Harmonic means. *
GEOM.	no	Geometric means. *
EXTR.	no	Minimums and maximums. *
VARiables = v list.	all	Names or subscripts for which statistics and data are to be printed. * computed. *
ZSCORE.	no	Standard scores replace the data, using means and standard deviations from the previous pass. *
/ PRINT		Optional to request printed output. Can be repeated with each / PASS to display data and statistics transformed or computed at that pass. 60
VARiables = v list.	those in COMPUTE	Names or subscripts for which statistics are to be printed. *
DATA.	no	Transformed data. *
/ SAVE		Additional option required only if a BMDP File is to be created. 63
PASS = #.	none	Sequence number of the pass at which the BMDP File is created. The data at this pass are copied into the File.

Key:

/	-indicates paragraph		*	-assigned value remains the same for additional problems
.	-period ends a sentence		VT	-number of variables after transformations
●	-required		list	-more than one item, often one per var.
v	-variable (name or subscript)			
g	-group (name or subscript)			
#	-number		Capitalized letters-paragraph or sentence names recognized by BMDP	
'c'	-characters (name or parameter) may omit apostrophes if contiguous letters only		Page numbers following refer to this Manual	

7

THE BMDP FILE

Saving Data and Statistics for Further Analysis

A set of data is usually analyzed many times by BMDP programs. For example, the data may first be examined for extreme values (outliers) and for distributional assumptions; then necessary transformations can be performed, meaningful hypotheses tested, or relationships between the variables studied. The results of an analysis may suggest that further analyses are needed.

The BMDP (Save) File is a means of storing your data or results from an analysis so you can reuse them in other BMDP programs; the File can be created or read by any BMDP program (except P4D). There are several advantages to storing data in a BMDP File:

- The BMDP File contains the number of variables, the variable names, flags for values missing or out of range, and group (or category) names, codes, and cutpoints. Therefore, when you use a BMDP File as input, you do not specify this information unless you want to change it.
- Data are read efficiently from a BMDP File; the cost of reading a large amount of data from a BMDP File is substantially less than when a FORMAT statement is used (the BMDP File is unformatted).
- Data are stored in the BMDP File after transformation and case selection are performed.
- The BMDP File is the only way to store results (such as factor scores or residuals from a regression analysis or a covariance matrix) so they can be analyzed further by other BMDP programs.

Using a BMDP File shortens and simplifies the Control Language instructions needed for subsequent analyses. Note that the eleven lines of instructions used in Example 7a (the INPUT, VARIABLE and GROUP paragraphs) to describe the data are replaced by one single paragraph in Example 7b when the file is read:

```
/ INPUT     UNIT IS 9.
            CODE IS WERNER.
```

Interfaces with files of other computer packages have been built (see Section 7.5). It is also easy to read and write a BMDP File for use in programs outside BMDP.

7.1 EXAMPLES OF WRITING AND USING A BMDP FILE

BMDP File is a term used to describe a set of data, variable names, limits for extreme values, category codes and names, results, e.g., residuals from regression analysis, etc., that are stored either on a disk or magnetic tape in a manner recognizable to BMDP programs. A BMDP File is generated when you specify in a SAVE paragraph what is to be stored in the File. In addition to the information in the SAVE paragraph, you must specify to the computer on a System Card where the BMDP File is to be stored.

Example 7a Writing a BMDP File

In this example we illustrate the writing of a BMDP File by saving the Werner blood chemistry data during the execution of the two-sample t test program, P3D. In the second example we use this new file as input to the same program and repeat the analysis from the file (note that our file can be read by any program except P4D). We discuss BMDP Files and the necessary instructions in detail after the second example.

We now use the BMDP instructions from Example 5.1 and add a SAVE paragraph. The instructions for the INPUT, VARIABLE and GROUP paragraphs are explained in Chapter 5. When writing a BMDP File, the instructions in the VARIABLE and GROUP paragraphs are not required: we use them here to illustrate how additional information is stored with the data in the file. We also add a card to the system information with a name for the system file in which the BMDP File is stored (HSX391.WERNER) and the number of the unit where the file is stored (the 09 in FT09F001). The full information supplied for an IBM OS system is as follows (check with a consultant at your facility for differences in the system information - the cards beginning with two slashes). Use spaces only as indicated for systems information:

IBM OS System Cards:

```
//job card
// EXEC BIMED,PROG=BMDP3D
//FT09F001 DD DSNAME=HSX391.WERNER,DISP=OLD
//SYSIN DD *
```

Control Language instructions:

```
/ PROBLEM   TITLE IS 'WERNER BLOOD CHEMISTRY DATA'.
/ INPUT     VARIABLES ARE 9.
           FORMAT IS '(A4, 5F4.0, 3F4.1)'.
/ VARIABLE  NAMES ARE ID, AGE, HEIGHT, WEIGHT,
             BRTHPILL, CHOLSTRL, ALBUMIN,
             CALCIUM, URICACID.
           MAXIMUM IS (6)400.
           MINIMUM IS (6)150.
           LABEL IS ID.
           GROUPING IS BRTHPILL.
/ GROUP     CODES(5)          1,   2.
           NAMES(5) ARE NOPILL, PILL.
/ SAVE      CODE IS WERNER.
           UNIT IS 9.
           NEW.
/ END
```

Data:

```
     ---- the data (Table 5.1) go here ----
```

IBM OS System Card:

```
//
```

Output 7a shows the message printed by all BMDP programs when a BMDP File is written (the two-sample t test output is the same as that shown in Output 5.1). In Output 7a, all lines but the last are

printed when the program begins to write the BMDP File. The last line is written when the BMDP File is completed. The last message may be separated from the first part by some program results. If a BMDP program terminates with an error, you should check if the last line has been printed to be sure the BMDP File is complete.

The BMDP File named WERNER now contains the data, the NAMES of the nine variables and CODES and NAMES for the GROUPING variable BRTHPILL. Values below 150 and above 400 for the sixth variable CHOLSTRL are recoded as too small and too large (the recoded values are recognized by any BMDP program). Blanks in the data file are automatically replaced by a special code to indicate that the observation is missing. The variable ID is identified as containing a LABEL for each case.

Output 7a   Messages printed by the BMDP program when a BMDP File is created.

```
① BMDP FILE IS BEING WRITTEN ON UNIT        9
   CODE. . . IS        WERNER
   CONTENT . IS        DATA
   LABEL . . IS
   VARIABLES ARE
     1 ID         2 AGE        3 HEIGHT     4 WEIGHT     5 BRTHPILL
     6 CHOLSTRL   7 ALBUMIN    8 CALCIUM    9 URICACID

        ----some results may appear here----

② BMDP FILE ON UNIT  9 HAS BEEN COMPLETED.
```

① is printed when the program begins to write the BMDP File.

② is printed when the program completes the BMDP File.

Example 7b Using a BMDP File as Input

We now use the BMDP instructions from Example 5.1 and add a SAVE paragraph. The instructions for the INPUT, VARIABLE and GROUP paragraphs are explained in Chapter 5. When writing a BMDP File, the instructions in the VARIABLE and GROUP paragraphs are not required: we use them here to illustrate how additional information is stored with the data in the file. We also add a card to the system information with a name for the system file in which the BMDP File is stored (HSX391.WERNER) and the number of the unit where the file is stored (the 09 in FT09F001). The full information supplied for an IBM OS system is as follows (check with a consultant at your facility for differences in the system information - the cards beginning with two slashes). Use spaces only as indicated for systems information:

IBM OS System Cards:

```
//job card
// EXEC BIMED,PROG=BMDP3D
//FT09F001 DD DSNAME=HSX391.WERNER,DISP=OLD
//SYSIN DD *
```

Control Language instructions:

```
/ PROBLEM    TITLE IS 'WERNER BLOOD CHEMISTRY DATA'.
/ INPUT      UNIT IS 9.
            CODE IS WERNER.
/ VARIABLE GROUPING IS BRTHPILL.
/ END
```

IBM OS System Card:

```
//
```

Compare these instructions with those in Example 7a. The information in the INPUT, VARIABLE and GROUP paragraphs was stored in the file with the data, except for the GROUPING statement in the VARIABLE paragraph. GROUPING IS BRTHPILL is specific to program P3D and is used to separate the cases into the two samples for the t test.

In Output 7b we reproduce the message that the BMDP File is used as input.

Output 7b   The message ① printed when a BMDP File is read as input.

```
     PROBLEM TITLE . . . . . .
WERNER BLOOD CHEMISTRY DATA

     NUMBER OF VARIABLES TO READ IN. . . . . . . .      9
     NUMBER OF VARIABLES ADDED BY TRANSFORMATIONS. .     0
     TOTAL NUMBER OF VARIABLES . . . . . . . . . .      9
     NUMBER OF CASES TO READ IN. . . . . . . . . . 1000000
     CASE LABELING VARIABLES . . . . . . . . . . .      ID
     LIMITS AND MISSING VALUE CHECKED BEFORE TRANSFORMATIONS
     BLANKS ARE. . . . . . . . . . . . . . . . . MISSING
     INPUT UNIT NUMBER . . . . . . . . . . . . . .      9
     REWIND INPUT UNIT PRIOR TO READING. . DATA. . .   YES
     NUMBER OF WORDS OF DYNAMIC STORAGE. . . . . . 16384


     INPUT BMDP FILE
     CODE. . . IS     WERNER     ①
     CONTENT . IS     DATA
     LABEL . . IS
     VARIABLES
       1 ID          2 AGE        3 HEIGHT    4 WEIGHT     5 BRTHPILL
       6 CHOLSTRL    7 ALBUMIN    8 CALCIUM   9 URICACID
```

7.2 WHAT IS STORED IN A BMDP FILE

Data. When you create a BMDP File to save your data, the data are written into a File _after_

- all transformations are performed, if any are specified (i.e., the transformed data are saved)
- values of any variable equal to its missing value code are recoded to a unique missing value code (called XMIS) that is automatically recognized by all BMDP programs (blanks are recoded as missing unless you state BLANKS ARE ZERO in the VARIABLE paragraph)
- values of any variable outside the upper (MAXIMUM) and lower (MINIMUM) limits are recoded to codes (called TOOBIG and TOOSMALL) recognized by all BMDP programs
- cases for which USE in the TRANSF paragraph have been set to a negative value are deleted

When the BMDP File is being created, the NAMES of the variables and the identity of the case LABEL variables are written in the File. As described above, missing values and values out of range are recoded to special values that are recognized by

every BMDP program. The number of VARIABLES (after transformations, if any) is also recorded. If the BMDP program that creates the File adds results (such as residuals) to each case, the number of variables recorded in the File is increased to include all additional variables. When data are stored in a BMDP File, the USE statement in the VARIABLE paragraph, if specified, does not affect the BMDP File. All variables are copied into the File. To save a subset of variables use the KEEP instruction, available only in P1D.

Cases for which USE is set (in the TRANSFORMATION paragraph) to a negative value by case selection or transformation (Section 6.1) are _not_ copied into the File; otherwise, the value of USE (zero or one) is recorded for each case written into the BMDP File.

The data in the BMDP File are _not_ written with a FORMAT statement; they are written as binary records. (If you want to output a file with only the binary records and no variable names or descriptive information, say, to be read by a non-BMDP program, see the BINARY instruction below.) A record is written at the end of each File that is recognized by each program as the end of the data.

Therefore, when reading a BMDP File the FORMAT must not be stated, and the number of VARIABLES and the number of CASES need not be stated. The absence of FORMAT and presence of CODE signal to the program that a BMDP File is read as input.

If a GROUP or CATEGORY paragraph is specified when a BMDP File is created, the CODES, CUTPOINTS and NAMES are included in the File. If your input is from a BMDP File and you are creating a new BMDP File, the CODES, CUTPOINTS and NAMES from the first File are copied into the new File unless you update the GROUP or CATEGORY paragraph.

Covariance or correlation matrix. Several BMDP programs allow you to save a covariance or correlation matrix that can then be used as input for subsequent analyses by other BMDP programs. Since a covariance matrix can be converted to a correlation matrix, and conversely, the two matrices are equivalent for the purpose of analysis.

When a covariance or correlation matrix is saved in a BMDP File, each row is written as a separate record. Although each record has the same length, only the lower triangular part of the matrix is filled with values. That is, the first record contains one value, the second two values, ..., and the last contains all values. The remainder of each record is padded. After the covariance or correlation matrix, the variance, mean, frequency and sum of case weights for each variable are recorded in the File. When the correlations or covariances are computed by a missing value formula, as in P8D or PAM, this fact is also recorded in the File.

The covariance or correlation matrix saved is the one being used in the analysis when the file is written. Therefore only variables used in the analysis are saved. The number of VARIABLES saved is recorded, and the NAMES of the variables and their original subscripts are saved.

A correlation or covariance matrix can be punched onto cards from a BMDP File. To do so, you must read the BMDP File into a program such as P1D that only accepts data as input. (The CONTENT must be correctly specified as it is in the BMDP File.) Then you can use the method described in Section 7.5 to copy the data (the covariance or correlation matrix) into your own data file or onto the punch unit. Remember that the lower triangular matrix contains the covariances and correlations.

<u>Other results from the analysis</u>. Other results that can be saved in a BMDP File are described in the individual program descriptions. To highlight a few,

- P4F saves data in table form
- P4M saves factor scores
- P7M saves a code for the predicted group assignment and scores for canonical variables
- PAM saves a data matrix where estimates are inserted for missing values
- PKM saves a code indicating final group membership
- P9R saves four types of residuals, Cook's distance and the Mahalanobis distance for each case
- P1S saves standardized scores

<u>Printing a description of BMDP File contents</u>. When several BMDP data sets have been written on the same disk or tape file, you may want a directory of the contents for each data set. To get a directory and perform no analysis, simply state

/ INPUT   UNIT IS #.   DIRECTORY.   / END

(Be sure to include the proper system card - see Section 7.3 below.) The program will terminate after producing a directory. However, if you also state a BMDP File CODE, the file named in the CODE will be analyzed after printing the directory information.

```
INPUT ─────────────────────────────────
  DIRectory.                                no
     Request to print the BMDP File CODE, CONTENT,
  LABEL, variable names and number of cases for
  each data set in the BMDP File. Before 1981
  this option was requested by specifying CODE IS
  ALL. in the INPUT paragraph.
```

7.3 CREATING A BMDP FILE: THE SAVE PARAGRAPH

In the discussions below it will be helpful for you to distinguish between a BMDP File and a system file. Several BMDP Files may be stored in one system file. If you are new to computers plan to have a consultant help you with the system information.

The SAVE paragraph is used to create a BMDP file and to specify what to store in it, how to label it, and where to write it. You can create a BMDP File to store your data in all BMDP programs (Except P4D). Each case in the File contains the data, or transformed data when transformations are specified; several programs also store results for each case computed in the analysis, such as residuals and predicted values from the regression programs.

If you need to write only one data file, restrict your reading to the discussion about CODE, UNIT and NEW. Each BMDP File should be uniquely identified. It must be assigned a name using <u>CODE</u> in the SAVE paragraph. This CODE must be specified each time the BMDP File is used as input. When more than one BMDP File is created in the same analysis, each File is assigned the same CODE: the instructions CONTENT and/or LABEL are also specified in order to uniquely identify the File.

The <u>CONTENT</u> statement is used to specify what to save in a BMDP File. It is preset to DATA (that is,

data are saved after transformations are performed). The program descriptions specify whether any matrices, in addition to DATA, can be saved in a BMDP File; when only DATA can be saved, CONTENT is not specified. Note that the instruction DATA includes results computed for each case that are appended on the data matrix (see writeups for programs of interest).

In addition to CODE and CONTENT a BMDP File can be further identified with a <u>LABEL</u>. This label is printed each time the File is read. Two BMDP Files with the same CODE and CONTENT can be differentiated by specifying a LABEL. This instruction is not necessary when you are writing one file.

When creating the File you must specify in the SAVE paragraph a number for the <u>UNIT</u> to which the File is written. The BMDP File is stored in a system file on a disk or magnetic tape. A <u>system file</u> is any block of information that is uniquely identified by the computer on disk or tape. The computer identifies system files by a <u>filename</u> specified on a System Card; the computer <u>cannot</u> use BMDP instructions to identify a system file (except on some systems such as VAX, PDP-11, DEC-10 and DEC-20 which use a FILE statement in place of the UNIT statement). The number of the UNIT specified in the SAVE paragraph is also specified on the System Card; in this way the computer connects the BMDP File with the system file. A detailed example of this System Card for an IBM OS system is given below. Documentation is distributed by our BMDP non-IBM redistribution centers for other computer types.

You must also indicate when the BMDP File created in an analysis is to be placed in a <u>NEW</u> system file. A NEW system file is one in which BMDP Files have not been written previously. You can also specify that the system file is NEW in order to write over existing BMDP Files. When NEW is specified, the BMDP File created is placed at the beginning of the system file; <u>all</u> BMDP Files previously written in this system file are deleted.

Several BMDP Files can be written into one system file. For example, all the BMDP Files (one or more) created in a single analysis are written in the same system file -- one BMDP File after another. You can also write BMDP Files from different analyses into the same system file; new BMDP Files are placed last.

```
SAVE ─────────────────────────────────
  CODE = c.    required, ≤ 8 char.            none
     A CODE used to name the BMDP File. The name
  assigned to CODE in this paragraph must be
  specified each time the BMDP File is used as
  input.
  UNIT = #.   required, not 1,2,5,6 or 26-30 none
     The number of the UNIT on which the BMDP File
  is written. This number must also appear on the
  System Card describing the location of the
  File.
  NEW.   required for first file          not NEW
     NEW is stated when the BMDP File being created
  is written into a system file that contains no
  previous BMDP Files or to erase all previous
  BMDP Files in the system file. If the BMDP File
  is added to previous Files in the system file,
  NEW must not be specified. If FORMAT = BINARY,
  the assumption is that the output file is NEW:
  i.e., the tape is rewound before writing on it.
  CONTent = c list.                          DATA
     CONTENT is required only in programs that save
```

results (such as a covariance or correlation matrix) in a BMDP File in addition to the DATA. When CONTENT is necessary, the program description states which matrices can be saved.
LABEL = 'c'. optional, $\leq$ 40 char. blank
A lengthier label for the BMDP File. It is printed in the output each time the BMDP File is used. When two BMDP Files have the same CODE and CONTENT but differ in their LABELS, the LABEL can be used to uniquely identify the File to be read.
FORMAT = (one only) BMDP, BINARY,   BMDP
         F, G, or '(c)'.
Format of output BMDP file. If BMDP, a file with complete header information (p. 68) will be written. Otherwise, only the data (or other information as requested by CONTENT) will be written. This allows generation of a file easily read by a non-BMDP program. If BINARY is requested, the data are written in binary form using standard FORTRAN unformatted output statements. If any of the remaining forms are used, a formatted file is written (i.e., one that is easily inspected visually or modified by a text editor). If F is requested, the data are written using 10F8.3 format. The G format used will be 5G16.6. Alternatively, a complete format can be specified.

Allocating space for a BMDP File. To obtain a permanent BMDP file (one that remains in the computer system after your job has finished), space must be allocated for the file. Otherwise, if you are simply passing results from one program to another during one computer run, you can use one of the built-in files as described in the Additional File Features section below.

Before a NEW permanent system file can be written, space on a disk or a magnetic tape must be reserved for it. The method of reserving the space depends on your computing facility. Check with your facility for the method required.

Some file allocating procedures require you to estimate the amount of space needed. If a data matrix is saved, the amount of space is approximately the number of variables times the number of cases times the space for one single precision word (four bytes for IBM systems). If a covariance matrix is being saved, space should be allocated for the square of the number of variables. If more than one BMDP File is to be saved in the same system file, the space required is approximately the sum of the space needed for the individual files.

The following are general properties of BMDP Files:

- BMDP Files are written as sequential files
- BMDP Files are written with binary FORTRAN WRITE statements (RECFM=VBS)
- to increase efficiency for very large files, BMDP File records should be blocked as large as possible; if you have a large blocksize you may need to increase the region size in your program (see Appendix B.1)
- if the system file is to contain more than one BMDP File, sufficient space should be allocated to accommodate all Files
- the BMDP File should not be deleted when the job that created it is completed; it should be retained
- the record length (LRECL) should be 4 bytes shorter than the block size (BLKSIZE).

The preferred way to allocate and maintain a BMDP File differs from system to system. Consult your facility for exact instructions.

System Card describing the File. The UNIT stated in the SAVE paragraph tells the BMDP program where to write the BMDP File. A System Card must also describe the system file into which the BMDP File is written.

The form of the System Card depends on your facility. For IBM OS this card has the form

    //FTyyF001 DD DSNAME=prefix.filename,DISP=OLD

where
- yy   is the number of the UNIT in the SAVE paragraph, and
- prefix   is a data set prefix that conforms to local convention
- filename is the filename (name of the system file) that appears in the ALLOCATE procedure

For example, the SAVE paragraph used with the Werner blood chemistry data was specified as

        / SAVE   CODE IS WERNER.
                  UNIT IS 9.
                  NEW.

the System Card is

    //FT09F001 DD DSNAME=HSX391.WERNER,DISP=OLD

The system filename and the BMDP File CODE need not be the same. The System Card should immediately precede

        //SYSIN DD *

(For transformations specified in FORTRAN, the System Card order is described in the summary, p. 72.)

Writing a binary file without descriptive information. BMDP Files contain the names of variables and other information. To write a file without the descriptive information, say to be read by a program outside BMDP, then specify FORMAT = BINARY in the SAVE paragraph. Missing values will be indicated in your output file as 16.**31, values above range as 2.*16**31, and values below range as -2.*16**31.

7.4 READING THE BMDP FILE: THE INPUT PARAGRAPH

In Example 7b we use the instructions CODE and UNIT in the INPUT paragraph to specify that the BMDP File be read as input. In addition, a System Card is necessary to describe the location of the system file to the computer.

The CODE name must be the same as that specified when the file was created. If you specify CODE = 'b'. where b is a blank, the first BMDP File is read as input and the CODE is reported in the output. When the file contents are not DATA, the instruction CONTENT must also be stated.

You must retrieve a BMDP File from the system file into which it was written to use it for input. The System Card to identify the system file must be similar to the System Card used when the File was created. The System Card we use to identify the system file is

    //FTyyF001 DD DSNAME=prefix.filename,DISP=OLD

where

        yy   is the UNIT specified in the INPUT paragraph

        prefix.filename   is identical to that on the System Card when the BMDP File was created

For Example, if the INPUT paragraph is

    / INPUT   UNIT IS 7.
                   CODE IS WERNER.

the appropriate IBM OS System Card is

   //FT07F001 DD DSNAME=HSX391.WERNER,DISP=OLD

The System Card should immediately precede

             //SYSIN DD *

You can use a BMDP File as input and also create another BMDP File in the same problem. The two BMDP Files must have the same UNITS (in the SAVE and INPUT paragraphs) if they are in the same system file, and different UNITS if they are in different system files. When creating a BMDP File to store DATA and the BMDP program you are using does not add additional statistics to the File (such as residuals or predicted values), the BMDP File being created cannot be in the same system file as the BMDP File read as input.

When using input and output in BMDP Files that are in two system files, two System Cards are necessary. The System Card with the smaller UNIT number must precede that with the larger UNIT number and both must be placed before the

             //SYSIN DD *

System Card.

To see a list of CODES, CONTENTS, LABELS and/or variable NAMES stored on all BMDP Files in your system file, specify the UNIT number and DIRECTORY. in the INPUT paragraph. No analysis is performed.

INPut (The FORMAT must not be specified.) ─────
   CODE = c. required   none
   The CODE name assigned to the BMDP File when the File was created.
   <u>Note</u>: If you specify CODE = 'b'. where b is a blank, the first BMDP File is read as input and the CODE is reported in the output.
   UNIT = #. not 1,2,5,6 or 26-30 required to read
                         a BMDP File/prev.
   The UNIT from which to read the BMDP File. A System Card is also necessary to describe the location of the system file containing the BMDP File to the computer. See order of input in the summary (p. 72).
   CONTent = c.   DATA
   Required only if the CONTENT of the BMDP File to be read is not DATA. If specified, it must be identical to the CONTENT specified in the SAVE paragraph when the File was created.
   LABEL = 'c'. optional   blank
   The LABEL is required only if two BMDP Files in the same system file have identical CODES and CONTENTS. If specified it must be identical to the LABEL specified when the File was created.

7.5 ADDITIONAL BMDP FILE FEATURES

<u>Respecifying information: changing BMDP Files</u>. In Section 7.2 we described the Control Language information that is stored in the BMDP File. It is possible to modify that information for a particular analysis, or to copy the BMDP File into a second File with slightly different specifications. When data are from a BMDP File, the FORMAT must not be specified. The number of CASES and number of VARIABLES need not be specified.

You can specify a smaller number of CASES than there are in the BMDP File; only the number of cases specified will be read.

You can RENAME the variables, but you cannot respecify the case LABEL variable(s). You can reduce the upper limit (MAXIMUM) or increase the lower limit (MINIMUM) for any variable; increasing the upper limit or lowering the lower limit does not affect the data since values out of range have been recoded and are not used in the analysis. You can specify additional MISSING value codes; the missing values already recoded will still be treated as missing. A USE statement in the VARIABLE paragraph can be specified to select variables for individual analysis.

You can perform additional transformations and add new variables to the data. You can respecify which cases are to be used by case selection.

You can add to or change the GROUP or CATEGORY information contained in the BMDP File by specifying another GROUP or CATEGORY paragraph.

You can create a smaller file (eliminate variables) from a larger file using the KEEP instruction in all BMDP programs. Range limits, missing value codes, and variable names will automatically be specified for the smaller file. The user does not specify a format for the smaller file; he lists only the numbers of the variables he wants.

<u>Temporary BMDP Files</u>. If you need to create a BMDP File within a computer run (say passing values from one program to another), and do not need the file at the end of the computer run, then you can write a temporary BMDP File. For IBM OS systems the temporary file can be on unit 3 and/or 4. For example, if you want to perform a number of different analyses with the same data in the same program (multiple problems) your setup could be:

```
/ PROB
/ INPUT ...
        .
        .
        .
/ SAVE   NEW.  UNIT=3.  CODE=TEMP.
/ END
   (data if on cards)
/ PROB
/ INPUT  UNIT=3.   CODE= TEMP.
   ...
/ END
```

You can also use a temporary BMDP File to pass data from one program to the next within one computer run. For example, you might have:

```
//   EXEC   BIMED,PROG=BMDP1D
//SYSIN DD  *
```

```
/ PROB
/ INPUT     ...
           .
           .
           .
/ SAVE     NEW.   UNIT = 3.   CODE = TEMP.
/ END
    (data if on cards)
//   EXEC   BIMED,PROG=BMDP6D
/ PROB
/ INPUT    UNIT = 3.   CODE = TEMP.
/ PLOT     ...
/ END
//
```

<u>Copying data from a BMDP File</u>. There are two ways to save data and results for use in non BMDP programs. The first is to specify FORMAT = BINARY in the SAVE paragraph (explained in Section 7.3 above). The second is to use either of two ways to read and copy data from a BMDP File.

If the data are in a BMDP File and you want to use them in your own program or in a program that does not accept the BMDP file as input, the data can be copied or punched by inserting a WRITE statement in the FORTRAN transformation subroutine (Section 6.2). This WRITE statement follows all the rules of FORTRAN. For example:

```
        WRITE(7,1000)   (X(I),I=1,NVAR)
   1000 FORMAT(5F6.0)
```

where 7 is the UNIT to which the data are copied using the format statement 1000.

<u>Note</u>: System Cards are required to describe the BMDP File and the file to which the data are copied. See the order of input when FORTRAN transformations are specified.

This feature can also be used to subdivide your data file into several subfiles according to any condition you want to specify (in FORTRAN). Depending upon the condition, each subfile can be written to a different FORTRAN unit using your own format. Remember that System Cards are needed to describe the FORTRAN units if the data on each unit are to be saved.

When copying the data into your own file, you may recode any missing values and values out of range to other codes. You can recode these values as follows:

```
   DO 1 I=1, NVAR
   IF(X(I).EQ.XMIS) X(I)  = your code for missing
                             values
   IF(X(I).GT.XMIS) X(I)  = your code for values
                             greater than the upper
                             limit
   IF(X(I).LT.(-XMIS))X(I)= your code for values
                             less than the lower
                             limit
 1 CONTINUE
```

If you have any case LABEL variables, they should not be included in the above recoding loop; they should be skipped. The FORTRAN statements to check for XMIS and values out of range should be placed before the WRITE statement above.

Note that this method recovers the data and not the BMDP information in the File (such as variable names).

You can also read a BMDP File directly. Note that typically, a single BMDP File is written in a single tape or disk file. The following example illustrates the basic method for reading 100 cases of 20 variables from a BMDP File on unit seven that is the first BMDP File in a disk or tape file. (This code skips over the variable names and descriptive information stored at the beginning of the file.)

```
        DIMENSION X(20,100)
        READ(7) IDUMMY
        READ(7) IDUMMY
        READ(7) IDUMMY
        IF(IDUMMY .EQ. 1) GO TO 5
          READ(7) IDUMMY
          READ(7) IDUMMY
      5 CONTINUE
        DO 10 I=1, 100
          READ(7) IDUMMY, DUMMY, (X(J,I), J=1, 20)
     10 CONTINUE
```

<u>Interface with other systems</u>. BMDP Files can be read into or written by the SAS (SAS Institute, 1978) and P-STAT (Buhler and Buhler, 1978) systems, and can be written by the STR (Robinson et al., 1978) data management system. As this manual is being prepared, an interface is also being established with MINITAB.

<u>New features: KEEP, DELETE, COMPLETE, MISSING and APPEND</u>. New features have been added to the SAVE paragraph, allowing structural changes to the data, and replacement and elimination of missing values. These features are included in the table of instructions on p. 72, and are explained in Appendix F.5.

SUMMARY

A) Order of Input to Read or **Create**[1] a BMDP File (standard procedure)

System Cards, for IBM OS:

```
// (job card)
// EXEC   BIMED,PROG=BMDPxx
//FTyyF001  DD   DSNAME=HSXnnn.filename,DISP=OLD
//SYSIN DD *
```

Control Language instructions and data, if on cards (include SAVE UNIT IS yy. for creating the file and INPUT UNIT IS yy. when reading it):

see program description

System Card, for IBM OS this is:

```
//
```

B) Order of Input to Read or **Create**[1] a BMDP File (when transformations are specified in FORTRAN)

System Cards, for IBM OS:

```
// (job card)
// EXEC   BIMEDT,PROG=BMDPxx
//TRANSF  DD  *
```

FORTRAN statements:

FORTRAN transformations

System Cards, for IBM OS:

```
//GO.FTyyF001  DD   DSNAME=HSXnnn.filename,DISP=OLD
//GO.SYSIN  DD   *
```

Control Language instructions and data, if on cards (include SAVE UNIT IS yy. for creating the file and INPUT UNIT IS yy. when reading the file):

see program description

System Card, for IBM OS this is:

```
//
```

Footnote: [1] Be sure that space has been allocated for the file before creating it.

instructions specific to BMDP files

Paragraph Statement	Preassigned	Comment and Manual Reference
/ SAVE		Required to create a BMDP File.
CODE = c.	none	Code to identify BMDP File, required. 68
LABEL = 'c'.	blank	Label for BMDP File, ≤ 40 characters. 69
UNIT = #.	none	Unit on which to write BMDP File; not 1, 2, 5, 6 or 26 through 30. 68
NEW.	not NEW	NEW if this is first BMDP File in system file. 68
FORMAT = (one only) BMDP, BINARY.	BMDP	BINARY writes file in binary without variable names and descriptive information. 69
KEEP = v list.	all	Names or subscripts of variables to be saved. 77,78
/ INPut		Required to read BMDP File as input.
CONTent = c.	DATA	Data or matrix in BMDP File. 70
CODE = c.	none	Code to identify BMDP File, required. 70
LABEL = 'c'.	blank	Label for BMDP File. 70
UNIT = #.	none/prev.	Unit from which to read BMDP File; not 1, 2, 5, 6 or 26 through 30. 70
DIRectory.	no	Request to print a description of the file (CODE, CONTENT, variable names, etc.). 70

Note: CONTENT, CODE and LABEL, if specified, must be identical to that when BMDP File was created. FORMAT must not be specified.

Key:

/	–indicates paragraph	*	–assigned value remains the same for additional problems
.	–period ends a sentence		
●	–required	VT	–number of variables after transformations
v	–variable (name or subscript)	list	–more than one item, often one per var.
g	–group (name or subscript)		
#	–number		Capitalized letters–paragraph or sentence names recognized by BMDP
'c'	–characters (name or parameter) may omit apostrophes if contiguous letters only		Page numbers following refer to this Manual

8
DATA DESCRIPTION

INTRODUCTION

The first step in an analysis is to examine the data for recording, transcribing or keypunching errors and for outliers or extreme values. Many powerful statistical techniques can be severely affected by errors or extreme values in the data and do not provide a warning that the data fail to fulfill the assumptions of the analysis. Pitfalls caused by faulty data can often be avoided by examining the data closely, either one variable at a time or one variable in relation to another.

The three BMDP programs discussed in this chapter provide descriptions of the data one variable at a time.

Computations in P1D and P2D use all acceptable values for each variable; i.e., values that are not equal to the missing value code and are not outside specified upper and lower limits. The data that are not used are called excluded values.

P1D provides a compact summary of the data. For each variable, P1D computes the mean, standard deviation, coefficient of variation and the largest and smallest standard scores (z-scores). These statistics can be reported separately for each level of a grouping variable (e.g., the mean body weight for males and the mean for females). It reports the number of acceptable values, and can also list all the cases, or only the cases that contain one or more values excluded from the computations. PAM, described in Section 12.2, prints the position of each excluded value in a compressed list.

P2D plots a histogram of the values for each variable, counts the frequency of each distinct value, and computes the relative frequency distribution (percent of cases less than or equal to each value). When you have many cases, the values

for each continuous variable can be rounded or truncated to provide fewer distinct values in the analysis. P2D computes the mean, standard deviation, skewness and kurtosis for each variable. It calculates the median and can estimate several new robust measures of location. The mean, mode, quartiles and measures of location are plotted on a line graph. A stem and leaf display is also available.

P4D is the only BMDP program that analyzes nonnumeric data (although other BMDP programs can convert nonnumeric data to numeric data by transformations). It counts the frequency of each distinct character (letter, number, symbol) found in each column of the data records (cards). It can list all the cases, or only the cases that contain specified kinds of characters (such as numbers, letters, or symbols). This feature can be used to identify cases that contain nonnumeric data due to a recording or keypunching error.

The three programs (P1D, P2D, P4D) complement each other in data screening and description. P4D is especially useful when there is a possibility that nonnumeric characters are in the data. (When the nonnumeric characters represent codes for a variable, such as M and F for SEX, they can be recoded to numeric codes in any BMDP program, see Section 6.1.) When many of the variables are coded into single columns; i.e., have values from 1 to 9, P4D is useful and inexpensive. P1D can be used before P2D to find the range of values for each continuous variable. You can then specify values to round or truncate the data to produce fewer distinct values for an analysis by P2D. P3D can also be used (without specifying a grouping variable). It gives greater detail than P1D but less than P2D.

Histograms are a valuable method of examining the data for extreme values and distributional assumptions (e.g., symmetry or normality). P2D plots a small histogram for each variable. Larger and better labelled histograms are printed by P5D (Section 10.1). When the cases are grouped, as by SEX, side-by-side histograms (one for each group) give you a better picture of the data; these histograms are available in P7D (Section 9.2).

P1D

8.1 Simple Data Description and Data Management

Jerome Toporek

ABSTRACT

P1D provides descriptive statistics for each variable for all cases, and separately for each level of all grouping variables specified in the VARIABLE paragraph. Data can be sorted on one or more variables, and can be listed for all the cases or for only cases with invalid entries. A File merge capability is planned for late 1981. Descriptive statistics include mean, standard deviation, standard error, coefficient of variation, standardized and unstandardized extreme values, and frequencies. P1D is useful for data screening.

WHERE TO FIND IT

Example 1D.1 Basic Setup for Simple Data Description

We analyze the Werner blood chemistry data (Table 5.1). For this example, <u>no</u> instructions specific to P1D are needed: we use only those instructions common to all BMDP programs for describing the data and naming the variables. An explanation of the PROBLEM, INPUT and VARIABLE paragraphs is given in Chapter 5. If data editing or transformations are necessary, the methods described in Chapter 6 can be used. If the data are in a BMDP File, see Chapter 7. Our BMDP instructions are

```
/ PROBLEM    TITLE IS 'WERNER BLOOD CHEMISTRY DATA'.
/ INPUT      VARIABLES ARE 9.
             FORMAT IS '(A4, 5F4.0, 3F4.1)'.
/ VARIABLE   NAMES ARE ID, AGE, HEIGHT, WEIGHT,
                BRTHPILL, CHOLSTRL, ALBUMIN,
                CALCIUM, URICACID.
             MAXIMUM IS (6)400.
             MINIMUM IS (6)150.
             LABEL IS ID.

/ END
```

(See end of this P1D section for organization of systems information, BMDP instructions and data.) In the VARIABLE paragraph we request that values of the sixth variable, cholesterol, greater than 400 or less than 150 be omitted from the analysis. In this example blanks are treated as missing values and are omitted.

The results of the analysis by P1D are presented in Output 1D.1. Circled numbers below correspond to those in the output.

(1) The number of cases read is 188. The number of cases is not specified in the BMDP instructions, so all cases are read. All computations by P1D use all acceptable values for each variable -- i.e., all values that are not missing and not out of range.

Output 1D.1   Univariate statistics computed by P1D. Circled numbers correspond to those in the text
----

--- the BMDP instructions are printed and interpreted ---

NUMBER OF CASES READ. 188 (1)

VARIABLE NO. NAME	(2) TOTAL FREQUENCY	(3) MEAN	(4) STANDARD DEVIATION	(5) ST.ERR. OF MEAN	(6) COEFF. OF VARIATION	(7) S M A L L E S T VALUE	Z-SCORE	(8) L A R G E S T VALUE	Z-SCORE	(9) RANGE
2 AGE	188	33.818	10.113	0.7376	0.29904	19.000	-1.47	55.000	2.09	36.000
3 HEIGHT	186	64.510	2.485	0.1822	0.03852	57.000	-3.02	71.000	2.61	14.000
4 WEIGHT	186	131.671	20.661	1.5149	0.15691	94.000	-1.82	215.000	4.03	121.000
5 BRTHPILL	188	1.500	0.501	0.0366	0.33423	1.000	-1.00	2.000	1.00	1.000
6 CHOLSTRL	186	236.150	42.555	3.1203	0.18020	155.000	-1.91	390.000	3.62	235.000
7 ALBUMIN	186	4.111	0.358	0.0262	0.08707	3.200	-2.55	5.000	2.48	1.800
8 CALCIUM	185	9.962	0.480	0.0353	0.04814	8.600	-2.84	11.100	2.37	2.500
9 URICACID	187	4.771	1.157	0.0846	0.24258	2.200	-2.22	9.900	4.43	7.700

For each variable P1D prints the

② total frequency of the acceptable values

③ mean

④ standard deviation

⑤ standard error of the mean

⑥ coefficient of variation

⑦ smallest acceptable value observed in the data and its standard score (z-score)

⑧ largest acceptable value observed in the data and its standard score (z-score)

⑨ range

These statistics are defined in Chapter 2.

There are several very large standard scores, such as 4.0 computed for a weight of 215 pounds and 4.4 computed for a uric acid reading of 9.9. All variables except AGE and BRTHPILL have total frequencies less than 188; i.e., each variable has one or more excluded values.

Example 1D.2 Statistics for Subpopulations

The statistics reported in Example 1D.1 can be obtained for subpopulations (groups or subsets of the cases). In this example we request separate

summary statistics for women using birth control pills and for women not using pills. We also request descriptive statistics for each of four age groups. Note that we use one variable at a time to split the cases into groups and are not using subpopulations defined by combinations of grouping variables. For groups defined by the combination of levels of two variables, see P7D; when more than two variables are needed to define a group, see P9D.

We use the GROUPING statement in the VARIABLE paragraph to identify those variables containing grouping information. The NAMES, CODES or CUTPOINTS for these variables are specified in the GROUP paragraph. We insert the following BMDP instructions before the END paragraph of the Control Language of Example 1D.1 (the first statement is part of the VARIABLE paragraph).

```
         ------------------------------------
         GROUPING IS BRTHPILL, AGE.
/ GROUP  CODES(5) ARE       1,    2.
         NAMES(5) ARE NOPILL, PILL.
         CUTPOINTS(2) ARE 25, 35, 45.
         NAMES(2) ARE '25ORLESS', '26 TO 35',
                      '36 TO 45', 'OVER 45'.
         ------------------------------------
```

Note that three cutpoints divide the interval variable, AGE, into four groups.

The results are shown in Output 1D.2. We have deleted the results for BRTHPILL, CHOLESTRL, ALBUMIN, CALCIUM and URICACID.

⑩ The average height for all 186 women is 64.5 inches: the average height for 92 women in the

Output 1D.2   P1D prints descriptive statistics for subpopulations and counts the frequencies of codes or intervals specified in the GROUP paragraph

VARIABLE NO. NAME	GROUPING VARIABLE	LEVEL	TOTAL FREQUENCY	MEAN	STANDARD DEVIATION	ST.ERR. OF MEAN	COEFF. OF VARIATION	SMALLEST VALUE	SMALLEST Z-SCORE	LARGEST VALUE	LARGEST Z-SCORE	RANGE
2 AGE			188	33.818	10.113	0.7376	0.29904	19.000	-1.47	55.000	2.09	36.000
	BRTHPILL	NOPILL	94	33.819	10.140	1.0459	0.29983	19.000	-1.46	55.000	2.09	36.000
		PILL	94	33.819	10.140	1.0459	0.29983	19.000	-1.46	55.000	2.09	36.000
	AGE	25ORLESS	52	22.308	1.628	0.2257	0.07296	19.000	-2.03	25.000	1.65	6.000
		26 TO 35	60	30.266	2.577	0.3327	0.08514	26.000	-1.66	35.000	1.84	9.000
		36 TO 45	42	40.286	2.597	0.4008	0.06447	36.000	-1.65	45.000	1.82	9.000
		OVER 45	34	49.706	3.186	0.5465	0.06411	46.000	-1.16	55.000	1.66	9.000
3 HEIGHT			186	64.510	2.485	0.1822	0.03852	57.000	-3.02	71.000	2.61	14.000
	BRTHPILL	NOPILL ⑩	92	64.087	2.492	0.2599	0.03889	57.000	-2.84	69.000	1.97	12.000
		PILL	94	64.925	2.420	0.2496	0.03727	59.000	-2.45	71.000	2.51	12.000
	AGE	25ORLESS	52	64.192	2.780	0.3855	0.04330	57.000	-2.59	71.000	2.45	14.000
		26 TO 35	60	64.633	2.386	0.3081	0.03692	60.000	-1.94	71.000	2.67	11.000
		36 TO 45	41	64.610	2.120	0.3311	0.03281	60.000	-2.17	69.000	2.07	9.000
		OVER 45	33	64.667	2.654	0.4619	0.04104	59.000	-2.14	69.000	1.63	10.000
4 WEIGHT			186	131.671	20.661	1.5149	0.15691	94.000	-1.82	215.000	4.03	121.000
	BRTHPILL	NOPILL	93	130.150	18.887	1.9585	0.14512	95.000	-1.86	195.000	3.43	100.000
		PILL	93	133.193	22.293	2.3116	0.16737	94.000	-1.76	215.000	3.67	121.000
	AGE	25ORLESS	52	125.500	18.166	2.5192	0.14475	94.000	-1.73	175.000	2.72	81.000
		26 TO 35	59	130.627	18.749	2.4409	0.14353	99.000	-1.69	203.000	3.86	104.000
		36 TO 45	42	135.476	23.963	3.6975	0.17688	100.000	-1.48	215.000	3.32	115.000
		OVER 45	33	138.424	20.954	3.6476	0.15137	94.000	-2.12	190.000	2.46	96.000

VARIABLE NO. NAME	CATEGORY NAME	CATEGORY NUMBER	CATEGORY FREQUENCY	NO. OF VALUES MISSING OR OUTSIDE THE RANGE	TOTAL FREQUENCY
2 AGE				0	188
	25ORLESS	1	52		
	26 TO 35	2 ⑪	60		
	36 TO 45	3	42		
	OVER 45	4	34		
5 BRTHPILL				0	188
	NOPILL	1	94		
	PILL	2	94		

NOPILL group is 64.1 inches. The average for the women over 45 is 64.7 inches.

⑪ P1D provides a separate report of the frequencies of codes or intervals specified in the GROUP paragraph. If we omit the GROUPING IS BRTHPILL, AGE statement (and keep the GROUP paragraph) this panel is still printed. Any number of variables can be assigned codes or cutpoints in the GROUP paragraph.

VARiable —————————————
| GROUPing = v list.   none
| The values of the variables in the list are
| used to identify subpopulations (groups).
| Statistics are reported for each group formed
| for each variable.

Example 1D.3 Printing All the Data or Only Those Cases with Unusual Values

Any one or all of the following can be printed:

- all cases
- cases in which a value is equal to a missing value code specified in the VARIABLE paragraph
- cases in which the value for any variable is less than its specified lower limit (MINIMUM in the VARIABLE paragraph)
- cases in which the value for any variable is greater than its specified upper limit (MAXIMUM in the VARIABLE paragraph)

In any listing of the cases, missing values are replaced by the word MISSING, values less than the lower limit are replaced by TOOSMALL, and values greater than the upper limit are replaced by TOOBIG. The data are printed only if a PRINT paragraph is specified with one or more of the commands DATA, MISSING, MINIMUM, or MAXIMUM, which correspond to the four options described above.

To illustrate the PRINT paragraph, we add

```
-----------------------------------------
      / PRINT   MISSING.
              MINIMUM.
              MAXIMUM.
-----------------------------------------
```

to the BMDP instructions of Example 1D.1 before the END paragraph.

The cases listed in Output 1D.3 are obtained by this analysis in addition to the results shown in Output 1D.1. Each of the eight cases listed contains one or more values replaced by MISSING, TOOSMALL or TOOBIG. The criteria used to select the cases are printed above the list. Note that the second number listed for each case is the subject's ID number. (The ID is the first variable on each record and is read in A-Format allowing, for example, the use of the subject's name.)

You can save residuals (or other results like factor scores) from a BMDP program in a BMDP File and use P1D to select and print cases with extreme values.

Before printing, the cases may be sorted (ordered) using the values of one or more variables (see SORT below).

Controlling how the data are printed. There are two styles in which data are printed: by case and by variable. For the by case method, all the data for one case are printed before any data for the next case. For the by variable method, P1D prints for each case only as many variables as fill the print line and begins the next line with the same variables for the next case. Thus the data for each variable are in an easy-to-scan column. When the program finishes printing the first subset of variables for all cases, it continues with another subset.

The user may also control the number of columns (character positions, not the number of variables)

Output 1D.3   P1D lists cases containing values excluded from the computations
----

PRINT CASES CONTAINING MISSING VALUES.

PRINT CASES CONTAINING VALUES GREATER THAN THE STATED MAXIMA.

PRINT CASES CONTAINING VALUES LESS THAN THE STATED MINIMA.

C A S E NO. LABEL	2 AGE	3 HEIGHT	4 WEIGHT	5 BRTHPILL	6 CHOLSTRL	7 ALBUMIN	8 CALCIUM	9 URICACID
2 1946	22	64	160	2	TOO BIG	3.500	MISSING	7.200
4 1797	25	68	150	2	TOOSMAL	3.800	9.600	3
51 3	54	62	120	1	227	MISSING	8.600	2.500
86 2877	30	68	MISSING	2	212	3.800	10	6.600
103 63	54	67	145	1	320	3.900	MISSING	MISSING
121 2456	37	MISSING	141	1	237	MISSING	10.500	4.500
161 5	46	66	MISSING	1	250	4.100	10.100	7.300
185 1149	53	MISSING	178	1	227	3.900	MISSING	5

NUMBER OF CASES READ.   188

--- statistics printed in Output 1D.1 appear here ---

----

that are printed across the page in order to have a narrower page size. P1D assumes that the length of a line is 132 characters unless you specify a smaller number using LINESIZE. The number of printed lines per page is controlled using PAGESIZE.

```
PRINT ─────────────────────────────────
  DATA.                                no/prev.
    List all cases.
  MISSing.                             no/prev.
    List cases in which at least one variable has a
    value equal to a missing value code.
  MINimum.                             no/prev.
    List cases in which at least one variable has a
    value less than its specified lower limit.
  MAXimum.                             no/prev.
    List cases in which at least one variable has a
    value greater than its specified upper limit.
  METHod = (one   only)               VAR/prev.
        VARiables, CASes.
    The data are printed one column per VARIABLE,
    unless CASE is specified, then all data for one
    case are printed (possibly filling several
    print lines) before any data for the next case
    are printed.
  LINEsize = #.                        132/prev.
    Number of columns to print data for a narrower
    page size.
  PAGEsize = #.                         60/prev.
    Number of printed lines per page.
```

Example 1D.4 Storing Data in a BMDP File

A BMDP File is an efficient way to save the data on a disk or magnetic tape so it can be used as input to other BMDP programs. The creation and use of a BMDP File is described fully in Chapter 7. When a BMDP File is used as input to a program, much of the information specified in the INPUT, VARIABLE and GROUP paragraphs need not be repeated (Chapter 7).

P1D is often the first program used to analyze a set of data. In this example we illustrate how to create a BMDP File that contains the data, the NAMES of the nine variables, the NAMES, CODES and

CUTPOINTS for the variables BRTHPILL and AGE. Values below 150 and above 400 for the sixth variable CHOLSTRL are recoded as TOOSMALL and TOOBIG. Blanks are automatically replaced by a special value to indicate that the observation is missing. When the data in the BMDP File are used in an analysis, the above information need not be respecified. We add the following SAVE paragraph to the instructions of Example 1D.2 before the END paragraph.

```
-------------------------------------
  / SAVE   UNIT IS 9.
           NEW.
           CODE IS WERNER.
-------------------------------------
```

The system cards that precede the BMDP instructions must contain a card describing where to store the BMDP File (see Chapter 7). In addition, space must be allocated for the system file.

The messages printed by P1D are shown in Output 1D.4; they tell you that a BMDP File has been created and the data are saved. The message about the code, content, label and variables is printed before the BMDP File is written. Always be sure there is also a message that says the BMDP File has been completed. The output will also include the output as shown in Example 1D.2.

Saving subsets of variables and cases. A subset of variables can be saved in a BMDP File by using the KEEP statement in the SAVE paragraph. Variable NAMES and codes for missing values and extreme values are saved; GROUP CODES, CUTPOINTS, and NAMES are not saved. The KEEP instruction is useful when you have many variables in a BMDP File and want to make another file containing a small subset of variables - you do not have to write a new format statement and lists of names, missing value codes, and range limits. As of 1983, the KEEP option is available in all BMDP programs.

To save a subset of cases, specify

$$USE = -1.$$

in the TRANSFORM paragraph for each case not to be saved (see Chapter 6). For example, to create a file

Output 1D.4 Messages printed by P1D to indicate that a BMDP File is created

```
-------------------------------------------------------------------------------
        BMDP FILE IS BEING WRITTEN ON UNIT        9
        CODE. . . IS        WERNER
        CONTENT . IS        DATA
        LABEL . . IS

        VARIABLES ARE
            1 ID        2 AGE        3 HEIGHT       4 WEIGHT      5 BRTHPILL
            6 CHOLSTRL  7 ALBUMIN    8 CALCIUM      9 URICACID


        BMDP FILE ON UNIT  9 HAS BEEN COMPLETED.
        NUMBER OF CASES WRITTEN TO FILE        188


        --- statistics printed in Output 1D.2 appear here ---

-------------------------------------------------------------------------------
```

with subjects who are older than 20 years state

```
/ TRANSFORM
      IF (AGE LE 20.) THEN USE = -1.
```

```
SAVE
   KEEP = v list.                              all
      Variables in the list (plus names, missing
      value codes and range limits, if specified) are
      saved when a BMDP File is made. Variables
      omitted from the list are not included in the
      file.
```

Sorting the data for printing or for a BMDP File.
The data may be sorted using the values of the
variables in the SORT list in the INPUT paragraph.
For example, the instruction

SORTS ARE BRTHPILL, AGE.

separates the cases into women not using birth
control pills (CODE 1) and women using them (CODE
2); within each group the cases are ordered by age
beginning with the youngest. You may also indicate
if the cases should be sorted in an ascending (A) or
descending (D) order. If the instruction ORDER IS D,
A. were placed after the SORT statement, the data
for the PILL group would be placed before that of
the NOPILL group. If a SAVE paragraph is included,
the sorted data are saved. The sorted data are
printed when a PRINT paragraph is present.

```
INPUT
   SORT = v list.
      Variables used to sort the data. The sorted
      data are used if PRINT commands are given or if
      a BMDP File is created. Levels of the first
      variable change the slowest, the levels of the
      last change the fastest. When sorting, unit 26
      (on IBM and similar systems) is used as a
      scratch unit and cannot be used as your input
      or output unit number.
   ORDER = (one for each variable              A
           in the SORT list)
           D or A.
      Use a 'D' or an 'A' for each variable in the
      SORT list to indicate ascending (A) or a
      descending (D) order. The default value for
      each variable is 'A'.
```

SIZE OF PROBLEM

On medium-sized computer systems P1D can
simultaneously analyze over 300 variables. Appendix
B describes how to increase the capacity of the
program.

COMPUTATIONAL METHOD

P1D computes the the means and standard
deviations in single precision by a provisional
means algorithm described in Appendix A.2.

ACKNOWLEDGEMENT

P1D was designed and written by Jerome Toporek.
An earlier version was programmed by Koji Yamasaki.

SUMMARY

Order of Input Cards

```
// (job card)
// EXEC BIMED,PROG=BMDP1D        (see Appendix E)
//SYSIN DD *
/ PROBLEM
/ INPUT
/ VARIABLE
/ TRANSFORM
/ SAVE
/ GROUP
/ PRINT
/ END
    (data, if on cards)
// (system card)
```

Full sets of BMDP paragraphs (and data, if on cards)
can be repeated for additional problems; see Section
5.8.

instructions specific to P1D

Paragraph Statement	Preassigned	Comment and Manual Reference
/ INPut		Additional input options relevant for / PRINT or / SAVE.
SORT = v list.	none	Names or subscripts of variables used to sort data. 78
ORDER = c list.	all A's	Ascending (A) or descending (D) order of sort for each variable in the SORT list. 78
/ VARiable		Additional option to classify cases into groups.
GROUPing = v list.	none	Names or subscripts of variables used to define group membership. Statistics for other variables are reported for each level of each grouping variable. Also include / GROUP (group names may not be repeated). 76
/ PRINT		Optional to direct printing of cases.
MISSing.		
MINimum.	no	All variables are printed only for cases with invalid MISS, MAX, or MIN. * 77
MAXimum.		
DATA.	no	Print all the data. * 77
METHod = c.	VAR.	VAR or CASE: VAR prints data in blocks of variables based on LINESIZE; all cases for the first block variables are printed, then the second block, etc. CASE prints data for all the variables of the first case, then the second case, etc. * 77
LINEsize = #.	132.	Number of columns to print data for a narrower page size. *
PAGEsize = #.	60.	Number of printed lines per page. * 77
/ SAVE		Additional option to save variables.
KEEP = v list.	all	Names or subscripts of variables to be saved. 78

Key:

/	-indicates paragraph	*	-assigned value remains the same for additional problems
.	-period ends a sentence		
●	-required	VT	-number of variables after transformations
v	-variable (name or subscript)	list	-more than one item, often one per var.
g	-group (name or subscript)		
#	-number		Capitalized letters-paragraph or sentence names recognized by BMDP
'c'	-characters (name or parameter) may omit apostrophes if contiguous letters only		Page numbers following refer to this Manual

P2D

8.2 Detailed Data Description, Including Frequencies

Laszlo Engelman

ABSTRACT

P2D computes the frequency, percent and cumulative percent for each distinct value in the analysis. It calculates the mean, median, mode, standard deviation, standard errors for mean and median, skewness and kurtosis, extreme values and half the interquartile range. A histogram and line plot are displayed. Data may be rounded or truncated before counting and calculations. Three robust alternatives to the mean are available. Stem and leaf displays can be requested.

Example 2D.1 Basic Setup for Detailed Variable Description

We analyze the Werner blood chemistry data (Table 5.1). For this example, no instructions specific to P2D are needed: we use instructions that are common to all BMDP programs for describing the data and variables (see summary p. 48). The explanation of the PROBLEM, INPUT and VARIABLE paragraphs is given in Chapter 5. If data editing or transformations are necessary, the methods described in Chapter 6 can be used. If the data are in a BMDP File see Chapter 7. Our BMDP instructions are

```
-------------------------------------
/ PROBLEM    TITLE IS 'WERNER BLOOD CHEMISTRY DATA'.
/ INPUT      VARIABLES ARE 9.
            FORMAT IS '(A4, 5F4.0, 3F4.1)'.
/ VARIABLE   NAMES ARE ID, AGE, HEIGHT, WEIGHT,
                      BRTHPILL, CHOLSTRL, ALBUMIN,
                      CALCIUM, URICACID.
            MAXIMUM IS (6)400.
            MINIMUM IS (6)150.
            LABEL IS ID.
/ END
-------------------------------------
```

(see end of this P2D section for organization of systems information, BMDP instructions and data.) In the VARIABLE paragraph we request that values of the sixth variable, cholesterol, greater than 400 and less than 150 be omitted from the analysis. Values that are blank are also omitted.

The results of the analysis by P2D are presented in Output 2D.1. Circled numbers below correspond to those in the output.

(1) Number of cases read is 188. The number of cases is not specified in the BMDP instructions, so all the cases are read. The computations use all acceptable values for each variable, i.e., values not equal to a missing value code and not outside specified upper and lower limits.

(2) Each variable is analyzed in a separate panel. We present only the results for CHOLSTRL in Output 2D.1.

(3) There are 188 cases in the Werner data. Two values for CHOLSTRL are excluded from the analysis by the MINIMUM and MAXIMUM specification in the VARIABLE paragraph. Therefore 186 cases are counted (N). Since CHOLSTRL is continuous, there are many distinct values (80).

(4) Univariate statistics contain
- the maximum and minimum observed values (not out of range)
- the range
- the variance (s^2) and standard deviation
- the interquartile range: $(Q_3-Q_1)/2$
where Q_1 and Q_3 correspond to the 25th and 75th percentiles respectively (first and third quartiles)
- the maximum and minimum standardized scores for cases within range.

(5) Location estimates and their standard errors include
- the mean ($\bar{x}$) and the standard error of the mean ($s/\sqrt{N}$)
- the median: the 50th percentile (when there is an even number of observations, the two observations nearest the 50th percentile are averaged). The standard error for the median is computed as $(x_{(i)}-x_{(j)})/(2\sqrt{3})$ (pseudostandard error formula proposed by J.W. Tukey in a personal communication) where $x_{(i)}$ and $x_{(j)}$ are the ith and jth order statistics (values of rank i and j), i is defined as the integer part of $\frac{1}{2}(N+\sqrt{3N})+1$ and j is defined as the integer part of $\frac{1}{2}(N-\sqrt{3N})+1$.
- mode: the value with the maximum frequency

(6) Skewness, g_1, and kurtosis, g_2. The expected value of the skewness, g_1, is zero for a symmetric distribution. The standard error of g_1 is $(6/N)^{1/2}$ under the assumption of normality. The ratio of skewness to its standard error (labelled VALUE/S.E. in Output 2D.1) is a test of normality. (For CHOLSTRL this ratio is 2.6, which indicates that the distribution is skewed to the right.) The expected value of the kurtosis, g_2, is zero for a normal distribution, positive for a distribution with heavier tails than the normal and negative for a distribution with lighter tails. The standard error of g_2 is $(24/N)^{1/2}$. The ratio of kurtosis to its standard error (labelled DIV. BY S.E. in Output 2D.1) is a test of normality. The formulas for the standard errors of g_1 and g_2 are from Cramer (1946, p. 375).

⑦ Quartiles and mean ± standard deviation include
- Q_1: the 25th percentile
- Q_3: the 75th percentile
- S–: $\bar{x} - s$
- S+: $\bar{x} + s$

All four are plotted in a line plot (⑨ below).
Q_1 is defined as (a+b)/2 where a is the largest value such that at most 25 percent of the values for the cases are less than or equal to a, and b is the smallest value such that at least 25 percent of the values of the cases are less than or equal to b. Q_3 is defined similarly.

⑧ The data are plotted in a histogram that is limited to a maximum height of 10 lines and a

Output 2D.1 Detailed description of a variable printed by P2D. Circled numbers correspond to those in the text

----

--- the BMDP instructions are printed and interpreted ---

NUMBER OF CASES READ.   188   ①

--- analysis of variables 2 to 5 ---


```
***********
* CHOLSTRL *   ②                 MAXIMUM  ④   390.0000000
***********                      MINIMUM      155.0000000                    H  H
                                 RANGE        235.0000000                    H  HH
VARIABLE NUMBER . . . . . .    6     VARIANCE   1810.9609375                  H  HH
NUMBER OF DISTINCT VALUES . .  80    ST.DEV.      42.5553894                  H  HHH   ⑧    EACH 'H'
NUMBER OF VALUES COUNTED. .   186    (Q3-Q1)/2    30.0000000                  HHHHH          REPRESENTS
NUMBER OF VALUES NOT COUNTED  ③  2   MX.ST.SC.     3.62                      H HHHHH            3
                                     MN.ST.SC.    -1.91                      HHHHHHHH        COUNT(S)
                                                                            HHHHHHHHH
LOCATION ESTIMATES                              ST.ERROR                    HHHHHHHHHHHH
           MEAN         236.1505280             3.1203117                   HHHHHHHHHHHHH  H
           MEDIAN  ⑤    235.0000000             3.4641027                   L-------------------U
           MODE         200.0000000

                                                                    EACH '-' ABOVE =    15.0000
                                                                             L=       105.0000
                                                                             U=       435.0000
                                                          CASE NO. OF MIN. VAL. =   33
                                                          CASE NO. OF MAX. VAL. =  182      ⑦

                                                                            Q1=  200.0000000
                                          VALUE   VALUE/S.E.                Q3=  260.0000000
                              SKEWNESS  ⑥  0.47      2.60                   S-=  193.5951385
                              KURTOSIS     0.09      0.24                   S+=  278.7058105

                                                          EACH '.' BELOW =     2.0000
```

```
           ⑨      S Q                              Q      S
  M               - M              M               3      +                                    M
  I...............O.............E...............................................................A
  N               D              A                                                              X
                  E              N
  ⑩        PERCENTS              PERCENTS                PERCENTS                PERCENTS
  VALUE  COUNT CELL  CUM   VALUE COUNT CELL CUM   VALUE COUNT CELL CUM   VALUE COUNT CELL CUM
   155.    1   0.5   0.5    200.  10  5.4  25.8    237.   2  1.1  52.2    272.   1   0.5  82.3
   158.    1   0.5   1.1    203.   1  0.5  26.3    238.   2  1.1  53.2    275.   2   1.1  83.3
   160.    2   1.1   2.2    204.   1  0.5  26.9    240.   5  2.7  55.9    276.   2   1.1  84.4
   165.    1   0.5   2.7    205.   3  1.6  28.5    242.   1  0.5  56.5    280.   4   2.2  86.6
   168.    1   0.5   3.2    207.   1  0.5  29.0    243.   2  1.1  57.5    285.   1   0.5  87.1
   170.    2   1.1   4.3    208.   1  0.5  29.6    245.   4  2.2  59.7    290.   2   1.1  88.2
   172.    1   0.5   4.8    210.   5  2.7  32.3    246.   1  0.5  60.2    295.   3   1.6  89.8
   173.    1   0.5   5.4    212.   1  0.5  32.8    247.   3  1.6  61.8    297.   1   0.5  90.3
   174.    1   0.5   5.9    215.   3  1.6  34.4    248.   1  0.5  62.4    298.   1   0.5  90.9
   175.    4   2.2   8.1    216.   1  0.5  34.9    250.   8  4.3  66.7    300.   2   1.1  91.9
   177.    1   0.5   8.6    217.   2  1.1  36.0    253.   1  0.5  67.2    305.   3   1.6  93.5
   180.    4   2.2  10.8    218.   1  0.5  36.6    254.   1  0.5  67.7    306.   2   1.1  94.6
   185.    2   1.1  11.8    220.   5  2.7  39.2    255.   6  3.2  71.0    315.   1   0.5  95.2
   189.    1   0.5  12.4    222.   1  0.5  39.8    257.   3  1.6  72.6    317.   1   0.5  95.7
   190.    1   0.5  12.9    223.   1  0.5  40.3    260.   6  3.2  75.8    320.   3   1.6  97.3
   192.    3   1.6  14.5    225.   3  1.6  41.9    262.   2  1.1  76.9    324.   1   0.5  97.8
   195.    4   2.2  16.7    226.   1  0.5  42.5    263.   3  1.6  78.5    330.   1   0.5  98.4
   196.    2   1.1  17.7    227.   2  1.1  43.5    265.   2  1.1  79.6    335.   1   0.5  98.9
   197.    2   1.1  18.8    230.   8  4.3  47.8    266.   1  0.5  80.1    338.   1   0.5  99.5
   198.    3   1.6  20.4    235.   6  3.2  51.1    270.   3  1.6  81.7    390.   1   0.5 100.0
```

--- analysis of variables 7 to 9 ---

----

maximum width of 40 characters. The width is the minimum of 40 and $10 \log_{10} N$. As a result it may be necessary for an "H" in the histogram to represent more than one observation. This is indicated in a note to the right of the histogram. The width of each histogram interval is printed (15) along with the case numbers for the records containing the smallest and largest cholesterol values.

⑨ The location estimates (such as the mean, median, mode, quartiles and S+ and S-) are plotted on a line 130 characters wide. If two measures coincide in their plotting positions, the one listed first in the statistics is plotted. In Output 2D.1 the measures are plotted from left to right in the following order: minimum, S-, Q_1 and the mode, median, mean, Q_3, S+ and maximum.

⑩ A table is printed in which each distinct observed value is listed with its frequency, the percent of observations with this distinct value, and the cumulative percent of observations less than or equal to this distinct value. For example, 10.8 percent of the women have a CHOLSTRL value less than or equal to 180. This table may be of limited value if there are too many distinct values -- which also makes it costly to compute. Fewer distinct values can be obtained by rounding or truncating the values before the analysis. (See Example 2D.3.) This table can be omitted by specifying NO COUNT in the PRINT paragraph (Example 2D.2).

Example 2D.2 Robust Measures of Location

We add the following PRINT paragraph (before the END paragraph) to the instructions in Example 2D.1 to obtain three robust measures of location and to delete the table of frequencies and percents.

```
------------------------------------------
      / PRINT       ESTIMATES.
                    NO COUNT.

------------------------------------------
```

Note: BMDP programs dated before 1980 require ESTIMATE to be specified in the COUNT paragraph.

The three robust measures of location are the trimmed mean, Hampel and biweight (Andrews et al., 1972). These measures estimate with less variability the location (mean) of a symmetric distribution than does the mean or median when the data come from a long-tailed symmetric distribution, or when the data have outliers or extreme values. The mean is an estimate of location in which each observation is given the same weight. These three new measures do not weight observations equally: extreme values receive less weight.

The trimmed mean omits the largest 15 percent of the acceptable values and the smallest 15 percent and computes the mean using the remaining observations (the central 70 percent). That is, each observation in the central 70 percent has weight one and the extreme observations (large or small) have weight zero. If the number of cases is not a multiple of 20, the number of cases trimmed from each tail is the smallest number such that at least 15 percent of the cases are dropped.

Both the Hampel and biweight estimates assign higher weights to the observations near the estimate than to those far from the estimate. The two diagrams below show the weights used as a function of

$$u = \frac{\text{observed value} - \text{estimate of location}}{\text{estimate of dispersion}}$$

Output 2D.2   Three robust estimates of location are printed and plotted by P2D

```
     ************
     * CHOLSTRL *                   MAXIMUM      390.0000000
     ************                   MINIMUM      155.0000000
                                    RANGE        235.0000000                    H  H
     VARIABLE NUMBER . . . . . .   6  VARIANCE   1810.9609375                   H HH
     NUMBER OF DISTINCT VALUES .  80  ST.DEV.      42.5553894                   H HH
     NUMBER OF VALUES COUNTED. .  186 (Q3-Q1)/2    30.0000000                   H HHH          EACH 'H'
     NUMBER OF VALUES NOT COUNTED  2  MX.ST.SC.     3.62                        HHHHH         REPRESENTS
                                      MN.ST.SC.    -1.91                      H HHHHH            3
                                                                              HHHHHHHH          COUNT(S)
     LOCATION ESTIMATES                           ST.ERROR                    HHHHHHHHH
                   MEAN      236.1505280          3.1203117                  HHHHHHHHHHH
                   MEDIAN    235.0000000          3.4641027                  HHHHHHHHHHHH  H
                   MODE      200.0000000                                    L-------------------U

                                                                            EACH '-' ABOVE =    15.0000
                                                                                           L=   105.0000
                                                                                           U=   435.0000
                                                                            CASE NO. OF MIN. VAL. =  33
                                                                            CASE NO. OF MAX. VAL. = 182

           SOME NEW LOCATION ESTIMATES                                                              Q1=  200.0000000
                   HAMPEL     233.6554759                      VALUE    VALUE/S.E.                   Q3=  260.0000000
        ⑪         TRIM(.15)  233.5522273                                                           S-=  193.5951385
                   BIWEIGHT   233.7855072          SKEWNESS    0.47       2.60                       S+=  278.7058105
                                                   KURTOSIS    0.09       0.24
                                                                               EACH '.' BELOW =     2.0000

                    S   Q                          Q      S
     M              -   M        ⑫   HM            3      +                                                       M
     I............................O..............AE....................................................................A
     N                  D              MA                                                                          X
                        E              PN
```

where the estimate of dispersion is MAD, the median of the absolute deviations from the sample median:

$$MAD = median \left| observation - median \right| .$$

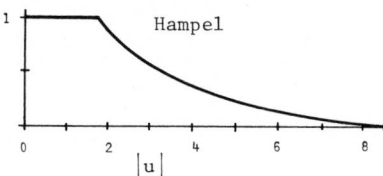

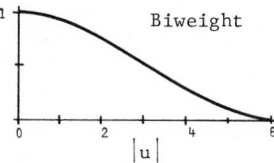

Since the estimate of location is used in the formula for u, the estimate of location must be found by iteration. The biweight estimator is parameterized here to perform well for distributions with extremely long tails. We feel the 15 percent trimmed mean and this Hampel estimator are satisfactory for many data analysis problems when the tails of the distributions are longer than those for a normal distribution.

The three measures are printed in Output 2D.2.

(11) The Hampel, trimmed mean and biweight estimates of location are printed.

(12) The three estimates can also be plotted along the line. Only the Hampel estimate is plotted since it coincides with the other two estimates in their plotting positions. The statistic listed first in the results takes precedence in the line plot when two or more values coincide.

```
PRINT ─────────────────────────────────────
   │ ESTIMate.                       no/prev.
   │   If ESTIMATE is specified, the trimmed mean,
   │   Hampel and biweight estimates of location are
   │   computed and plotted on a line plot. In program
   │   releases before 1980, ESTIMATE is specified in
   │   the COUNT paragraph.
   │ COUNT.                          yes/prev.
   │   The table of frequencies, percents and
   │   cumulative percents is printed unless NO COUNT.
   │   is stated. This option is not available in
   │   versions dated before 1980.
```

Example 2D.3 Rounding the Data Values before Analysis

When a variable is continuous and there are many cases in the data, the table of distinct values and frequencies may have too many entries. P2D produces a large table that is time-consuming (costly) to build. Rounding or truncating values to fewer digits produces fewer distinct values and, hence, a smaller table that is easier to interpret and much faster to construct. If either rounding or truncation is requested all computations use the rounded or truncated values. Rounding and truncating are specified by ROUND and TRUNCATE assignments in the COUNT paragraph.

If you examine the distinct values of CHOLSTRL in Example 2D.1, you see that 98 of the 186 values end with the last digit 0 or 5. Therefore it is reasonable to round the values to the nearest 5 or 10 units. In the following example we round CHOLSTRL to the nearest 10 units by adding a COUNT paragraph (before the END paragraph) to the instructions in Example 2D.1.

```
------------------------------------------
      / COUNT      ROUND = (6)10.
------------------------------------------
```

specifies that the values for CHOLSTRL (the sixth variable in the Werner data) are to be rounded to the nearest number divisible by 10. Tabbing (p. 29) to the sixth variable is necessary when it is desired to round only certain variables. If both ROUND and TRUNCATE are specified for the same variable, the ROUND specification takes precedence.

The rounded results for CHOLSTRL are shown in Output 2D.3. Compare these results with those in Output 2D.1. There are 20 distinct values instead of 80, and each distinct value is divisible by 10. All computations in Output 2D.3 are performed using the rounded data. The mean is now 237.8 instead of 236.2; the median is 240 instead of 235.

```
COUNT ─────────────────────────────────────
   │ ROUND = # list.      one per       no rounding
   │                      variable
   │   The units to which the variables are to be
   │   rounded. For example, setting the second number
   │   to 10 specifies that the second variable is to
   │   be rounded to the nearest number divisible by
   │   10. Data can be rounded to any positive value,
   │   including values less than one, e.g., 0.1,
   │   0.05, etc. Tabbing (p. 29) can be used to skip
   │   variables.
   │ TRUNCate = # list.   one per       no truncation
   │                      variable
   │   The units to which the variables are to be
   │   truncated. For example, setting the second
   │   number to 10 requests that the second variable
   │   be truncated to the nearest lower number
   │   divisible by 10. Data can be truncated to any
   │   positive value including values less than one;
   │   e.g., 0.1, 0.05, etc. Tabbing (p. 29) can be
   │   used to skip variables. If both ROUND and
   │   TRUNCATE are specified for the same variable,
   │   the ROUND specification takes precedence.
```

Output 2D.3 Effect of rounding the values of CHOLSTRL to the nearest 10 units. Compare these results with those in 2D.1 using the original values

----

```
************
* CHOLSTRL *
************

VARIABLE NUMBER . . . . . .        6
NUMBER OF DISTINCT VALUES .        20
NUMBER OF VALUES COUNTED. .       186
NUMBER OF VALUES NOT COUNTED        2
***VALUES ARE ROUNDED TO. .   10.0000

LOCATION ESTIMATES
              MEAN      237.7956848
              MEDIAN    240.0000000
              MODE      200.0000000
```

```
MAXIMUM     390.0000000
MINIMUM     160.0000000
RANGE       230.0000000
VARIANCE   1825.9228516
ST.DEV.      42.7308197
(Q3-Q1)/2    30.0000000
MX.ST.SC.     3.56
MN.ST.SC.    -1.82

ST.ERROR
  3.1331749
  2.8867521
```

```
                                   H
                                   H  H
                                   H  H  H            EACH 'H'
                                   H  H  H            REPRESENTS
                                   H  HHH                 4
                                   H HHHHH             COUNT(S)
                                   H HHHHH  H
                                   HHHHHHHHHH
                                   HHHHHHHHHHHH  H
                                 L---------------------U

                           EACH '-' ABOVE =      15.0000
                                           L=    120.0000
                                           U=    450.0000
                        CASE NO. OF MIN. VAL. =    33
                        CASE NO. OF MAX. VAL. =   182

                                                 Q1=  200.0000000
                              VALUE   VALUE/S.E.  Q3=  260.0000000
                  SKEWNESS    0.46      2.58      S-=  195.0648651
                  KURTOSIS    0.05      0.13      S+=  280.5263672

                              EACH '.' BELOW =      2.0000
```

```
          S Q                        Q      S
M         - M             MM         3      +                                M
I.........O.........EE.....................................................A
N          D             AD                                                 X
           E             NI
```

VALUE	COUNT	PERCENTS CELL	PERCENTS CUM	VALUE	COUNT	PERCENTS CELL	PERCENTS CUM	VALUE	COUNT	PERCENTS CELL	PERCENTS CUM	VALUE	COUNT	PERCENTS CELL	PERCENTS CUM
160.	4	2.2	2.2	210.	11	5.9	32.8	260.	20	10.8	78.5	310.	5	2.7	94.6
170.	7	3.8	5.9	220.	14	7.5	40.3	270.	7	3.8	82.3	320.	6	3.2	97.8
180.	9	4.8	10.8	230.	14	7.5	47.8	280.	8	4.3	86.6	330.	1	0.5	98.4
190.	7	3.8	14.5	240.	18	9.7	57.5	290.	3	1.6	88.2	340.	2	1.1	99.5
200.	23	12.4	26.9	250.	19	10.2	67.7	300.	7	3.8	91.9	390.	1	0.5	100.0

Example 20.4 Stem and Leaf Display

In a stem and leaf histogram the data values are displayed in up to 20 rows (bars). For each number, the varying digits are separated into two pieces: the stem and the leaf. In Output 2D.4 for cholesterol, we see that the stem contains the digits from the hundreds position and that the leaves contain the digits from the tens position. The smallest two numbers have a stem of 1 (100) with leaves in the fifties. We do not recover the value from the units position. From Output 2D.1 we see these values are 155 and 158. The next bar contains four numbers with leaves in the sixties (6666) and 10 numbers with leaves in the seventies. The largest number displayed has a stem of 3 and a leaf of 9; it is 390 (the final zero is not printed on the leaf). In the display, 'M' marks the bar with the median, Q marks the first and third quartiles and E marks the lower and upper eighths. The column labelled DEPTH accumulates the number of cases beginning at the top and bottom of the display, moving in towards the median.

To specify the stem and leaf display shown in Output 2D.4, we add a PRINT paragraph (before the END paragraph) to the instructions of Example 2D.1.

```
------------------------------------
         / PRINT     STEM.
------------------------------------
```

Output 2D.4   Stem and leaf display printed by P2D

```
                    *
DEPTH   STEM  *  LEAVES
                    *
   0      1   *
   0          *
   2          *  55
  16          *  66667777777777
  38          E  888888899999999999999
  68      2   Q  00000000000000001111111111111
+ 31          M  2222222222222233333333333333333
  87          *  444444444444444455555555555555555555
  51          Q  666666666666666677777777
  29          E  888889999999
  17      3   *  000000011
   8          *  2222333
   1          *
   1          *
   1          *  9
                    *
DEPTH   STEM  *  LEAVES
                    *

MINIMUM  =   155.00000
MAXIMUM  =   390.00000
 COUNT   =   186
```

```
PRINT ──────────────────────────────────────────────
  STEM.                                    no/prev.
     If STEM. is specified, stem and leaf histograms
  are printed for each variable. This option is
  not available in programs released before 1980.
  If the sample size is very large an alternate
  display is provided. If there are too many
  leaves on a stem to print it in one printer
  line, then the program prints a "stem and leaf
  frequency count" table.
```

frequency of each distinct value. First the mean is computed, and then the variance, skewness and kurtosis are calculated using differences from the mean.

ACKNOWLEDGEMENT

P2D was designed and programmed by Laszlo Engelman. Contributions were made by Peter Mundle.

SUMMARY

Order of Input Cards

```
// (job card)
// EXEC BIMED,PROG=BMDP2D        (see Appendix E)
//SYSIN DD *
/ PROBLEM
/ INPUT
/ VARIABLE
/ TRANSFORM
/ COUNT
/ PRINT
/ SAVE
/ END
    (data if on cards)
// (system card)
```

Full sets of BMDP paragraphs (and data, if on cards) can be repeated for additional problems; see Section 5.8.

SIZE OF PROBLEM

On medium-sized computer systems, frequencies for approximately 200 variables can be counted at the same time if each requested variable has relatively few distinct values (less than 25). If frequencies for only one variable are counted, the variable can have approximately 6,800 distinct values. Appendix B describes how to increase the capacity of the program.

COMPUTATIONAL METHOD

The data for each variable are read and the frequency table of distinct values is constructed. All statistics are computed from the frequency table (not from the original data). Therefore, when the data are rounded or truncated, the statistics are affected. The formulas for the statistics use the

instructions specific to P2D

Paragraph Statement	Preassigned	Comment and Manual Reference

/ COUNT
ROUND = # list.
TRUNCate = # list.
	no	Optional.
		Round or truncate the data values of first variable by the first number, second variable by second number, etc. 83

/ PRINT ESTIMate. COUNT. STEM.	 no yes no	Optional (see note below for pre-1980 program). Calculate robust estimates: 15% trimmed mean, Hampel and Biweight. * 83 Printing of value-count-percent tables. * NO COUNT negates this request. 83 Printing of stem-and-leaf histograms. * 85

Key:

- / —indicates paragraph
- . —period ends a sentence
- ● —required
- v —variable (name or subscript)
- g —group (name or subscript)
- # —number
- 'c' —characters (name or parameter) may omit apostrophes if contiguous letters only

- * —assigned value remains the same for additional problems
- VT —number of variables after transformations
- list —more than one item, often one per var.

Capitalized letters-paragraph or sentence names recognized by BMDP
Page numbers following refer to this Manual

Note: In BMDP programs dated before 1980
  a) ESTIM. must be stated in the COUNT paragraph
  b) COUNT. and STEM. options were not available.

P4D

8.3 Single Column Frequencies — Numeric and Nonnumeric

W. J. Dixon
Laszlo Engelman

ABSTRACT

P4D counts the frequency of each number, letter or symbol in single column fields. The data can be listed to highlight nonnumerics. This program uses nonstandard simplified input information and does not interface with BMDP Files.

P4D is useful in preliminary data screening to verify the kinds of data present, to count frequencies of single column data, and to indicate extreme values and outliers. It summarizes each digit of a variable separately, e.g., for a measurement ranging from 0 to 99, the values in the units position are summarized separately from those in the tens position.

The CHAR function (implemented in 1981) makes it easy to do a first screening of large files by summarizing each card type or form type separately. P4D thus provides economy in data handling for non rectangular files (the subjects may have varying numbers of forms). This allows screening and correction of errors prior to structuring elaborate files.

WHERE TO FIND IT

Example 4D.1 Basic Setup for Column by Column Summaries

We use P4D to analyze the Werner blood chemistry data (Table 5.1). The Control Language instructions are as follows:

```
------------------------------------
/ PROBLEM   TITLE IS 'WERNER BLOOD CHEMISTRY DATA'.

/ END
                ------------------------------------
or
                ------------------------------------
/ PROB

/ END
                ------------------------------------
```

(See end of this P4D section for organization of systems information, BMDP instructions and data.) P4D is an exception. It is the only program not requiring an INPUT paragraph.

The results of the analysis by P4D are presented in Output 4D.1. The circled numbers below correspond to those in the output.

(1) Each variable represents the data in a single column. The term "variable" does not have the same meaning as variable in other BMDP programs. For example, AGE is coded in columns 7 and 8 of the data cards. Therefore P4D reads AGE as two variables (the 7th and 8th). The frequency of the tens digit is reported as variable 7 and the frequencies of the units digit are reported as variable 8. Fourteen women are aged 50-59 (5 in the tens position) and none are 60 or over.

(2) The Werner data is entirely numeric except for several blank codes inserted in the data. Therefore the characters printed are zero to nine and blank. When nonnumeric data are present, this list is expanded (see Example 4D.2).

(3) BRTHPILL is coded in column 20 of the data card. Here we see that variable (column) 20 has 94 ones and 94 twos.

(4) The data for CHOLSTRL are in columns 22 to 24 of the data card. Therefore variable 22 contains the distribution of the 100's digit of CHOLSTRL. This column contains one 6 (a value for CHOLSTRL of 600 or over) and one blank but the remaining values are between 1 and 3. This kind of examination can identify unusual values.

Common Control Language differences in P4D. P4D describes the data and variables in the PROBLEM, INPUT and VARIABLE paragraphs described in Chapter 5. However, most specifications are not necessary or relevant. Therefore we quickly review definitions of items that are most useful in P4D.

The PROBLEM paragraph is required. TITLE can be specified for the analysis.

The INPUT paragraph is optional. (It is not required as it is in all other BMDP programs.) VARIABLES refer to single columns of data (except for one or two case label variables that can be up to four characters each). Therefore the preassigned number of VARIABLES is 80 (the number of columns on a data card). FORMAT, if specified, must be in A1 format for each variable (column) that is to be summarized. Case labeling variables may be read in A4 format. Variables read in F format may be used in transformations but must be recoded to single characters via the CHAR function or eliminated from the column summary by using a USE statement in the VARIABLE paragraph. The preassigned FORMAT is (80A1), i.e., the whole data card is to be counted column by column. This is the only BMDP program with a preassigned format and the only program that uses A1 format; all other BMDP programs use F format or free format. The FORMAT need not be specified unless you wish to skip columns or use case LABELS. Data can be read from multiple cards, e.g., (60A1/40A1) for input from two cards. Format cannot be FREE or STREAM. CASES, UNIT and REWIND are the same as described in Section 5.3, and need not be used when the data are on cards.

The VARIABLE paragraph can be used to NAME variables (for use in the TRANSFORM paragraph) or to specify one or two variables that LABEL cases. The remainder of the VARIABLE paragraph is not relevant to P4D: there are no capabilities to check extreme values (MIN and MAX) or identify missing value codes (MISS).

The TRANSFORM paragraph is available with the 1981 version of BMDP. All transformations and special BMDP words described in Chapter 6 (USE,

Output 4D.1 Frequency counts of each column by P4D for the data in Table 5.1. Circled numbers correspond to those in the text

--- the BMDP instructions are printed and interpreted ---

FREQUENCY COUNT OF CHARACTERS PER VARIABLES

CHAR	CARD CODE	VARIABLES (1) 1	2	3	4	5	6	7	8	9	10	11	12	13	14	15	16	17	18	19	20
	BLANK	68	18	2	0	188	188	0	0	188	188	2	2	188	7	2	2	188	188	188	0
0	0	0	13	17	18	0	0	0	22	0	0	0	8	0	0	15	54	0	0	0	0
1	1	47	15	24	21	0	0	2	24	0	0	0	6	0	179	31	5	0	0	0	94 (3)
(2) 2	2	51	25	18	16	0	0	72	30	0	0	0	26	0	2	43	10	0	0	0	94
3	3	22	21	18	14	0	0	54	20	0	0	0	20	0	0	39	12	0	0	0	0
4	4	0	15	22	17	0	0	46	16	0	0	0	31	0	0	25	9	0	0	0	0
5	5	0	14	23	17	0	0	14	16	0	0	4	28	0	0	11	54	0	0	0	0
6	6	0	15	18	22	0	0	0	14	0	0	180	21	0	0	8	8	0	0	0	0
7	7	0	14	18	23	0	0	0	16	0	0	2	25	0	0	5	10	0	0	0	0
8	8	0	20	11	16	0	0	0	16	0	0	0	13	0	0	2	20	0	0	0	0
9	9	0	18	17	24	0	0	0	14	0	0	0	8	0	0	7	4	0	0	0	0
		ID				AGE				HEIGHT				WEIGHT				BRTHPILL			
TOTALS NUMERIC		120	170	186	188	0	0	188	188	0	0	186	186	0	181	186	186	0	0	0	188

FREQUENCY COUNT OF CHARACTERS PER VARIABLES

CHAR	CARD CODE	VARIABLES 21	22	23 (4)	24	25	26	27	28	29	30	31	32	33	34	35	36	37	38	39	40
	BLANK	188	1	0	0	188	188	2	2	188	95	3	3	188	188	1	1	188	188	188	188
0	0	0	0	25	74	0	0	0	24	0	0	91	22	0	0	0	17	0	0	0	0
1	1	0	38	15	0	0	0	0	18	0	93	2	18	0	0	0	15	0	0	0	0
2	2	0	131	17	10	0	0	0	19	0	0	0	11	0	0	5	25	0	0	0	0
3	3	0	17	21	9	0	0	62	16	0	0	0	15	0	0	36	21	0	0	0	0
4	4	0	0	17	4	0	0	123	21	0	0	0	16	0	0	78	18	0	0	0	0
5	5	0	0	22	50	0	0	1	15	0	0	0	26	0	0	43	20	0	0	0	0
6	6	0	1	18	10	0	0	0	16	0	0	0	24	0	0	17	14	0	0	0	0
7	7	0	0	18	18	0	0	0	17	0	0	0	14	0	0	4	16	0	0	0	0
8	8	0	0	12	12	0	0	0	21	0	0	2	22	0	0	3	24	0	0	0	0
9	9	0	0	23	1	0	0	0	19	0	0	90	17	0	0	1	17	0	0	0	0
		CHOLSTRL				ALBUMIN				CALCIUM					URICACID						
TOTALS NUMERIC		0	187	188	188	0	0	186	186	0	93	185	185	0	0	187	187	0	0	0	0

--- similar counts for variables (columns) 41-60 and 61-80, which reported all blanks ---

KASE, etc.) may be used except for XMIS, TOOBIG and TOOSMALL. Note that the new CHAR function can be used to make character comparisons (equal or not equal) with values read in A-type format. For example,

USE = X(4) EQ CHAR(2).

selects only those cases from the file that contain a "2" in the fourth column. It is also possible to use variables read in F format in the transformations provided that they are recoded to single characters or are eliminated from the P4D process. This can be done by including a USE statement in the VARIABLE paragraph, listing only the A1 format variables. For example, P4D can print and summarize the data in the first 20 columns for only the cases with subjects between 20 and 40 years of age (see Example 4D.3 -- columns 21 and 22 contain age).

```
/ PROB
/ INPUT      VARIABLES ARE 21.
            FORMAT IS '(20A1, F2.0)'.
/ VARIABLE   NAME = (21)AGE.
            USE = 1 TO 20.
/ TRANS
            USE = AGE GE 20
            AND AGE LE 40.
/ PRINT
/ END
```

Example 4D.2 Detecting Unwanted Characters and Symbols

We use the data in Table 8.1. To reduce the output we specify the number of variables (26 columns).

```
/ PROBLEM   TITLE IS 'DATA WITH NONNUMERIC SYMBOLS'.
/ INPUT     VARIABLES ARE 26.
/ END
```

Output 4D.2   Frequency counts by P4D for the data in Table 8.1

THERE WERE ONLY   19 CASES PRIOR TO END OF FILE.

FREQUENCY COUNT OF CHARACTERS PER VARIABLES

CHAR	CARD CODE	1	2	3	4	5	6	7	8	9	10	11	12	13	14	15	16	17	18	19	20
	BLANK	0	1	1	1	0	0	0	0	1	0	1	0	0	0	0	0	1	1	0	0
0	0	1	0	3	3	0	2	0	1	0	3	3	10	1	1	2	0	0	1	2	3
1	1	6	6	1	0	0	0	0	0	9	0	0	0	3	2	1	2	3	3	2	0
2	2	0	3	6	3	0	1	1	3	4	3	0	0	2	1	1	6	1	5	1	2
3	3	0	4	3	1	4	0	1	0	0	0	4	0	2	8	4	2	5	0	1	1
4	4	4	1	0	0	1	1	0	0	0	3	4	0	2	2	1	2	3	1	3	2
5	5	1	4	1	6	4	1	9	3	3	7	1	9	2	2	5	3	3	4	3	5
6	6	0	0	3	4	3	1	0	6	0	2	3	0	3	1	0	2	2	3	2	3
7	7	3	0	0	0	6	3	3	1	1	1	0	0	1	0	4	1	1	1	1	0
8	8	4	0	0	0	0	0	3	4	0	0	3	0	2	1	0	1	0	0	3	2
9	9	0	0	0	0	0	0	0	0	0	0	0	0	0	0	0	0	0	0	1	1
A	12-1	0	0	0	0	0	0	1	0	0	0	0	0	0	0	0	0	0	0	0	0
E	12-5	0	0	0	0	0	0	0	0	1	0	0	0	0	1	0	0	0	0	0	0
H	12-8	0	0	0	0	0	0	0	0	0	0	0	0	0	0	0	0	0	0	0	0
I	12-9	0	0	0	1	0	0	0	0	0	0	0	0	0	0	0	0	0	0	0	0
K	11-2	0	0	0	0	0	0	0	1	0	0	0	0	0	0	0	0	0	0	0	0
M	11-4	0	0	1	0	0	0	0	0	0	0	0	0	0	0	0	0	0	0	0	0
O	11-6	0	0	0	0	0	0	0	0	0	0	0	0	0	0	0	0	0	0	0	0
S	0-2	0	0	0	0	1	0	0	0	0	0	0	0	0	1	0	0	0	0	0	0
T	0-3	0	0	0	0	0	1	0	0	0	0	0	0	0	0	0	0	0	0	0	0
W	0-6	0	0	0	0	0	0	0	0	0	0	0	0	0	0	0	0	0	0	0	0
Y	0-8	0	0	0	0	0	0	0	0	0	0	0	0	1	0	0	0	0	0	0	0
'	5-8	0	0	0	0	0	0	0	0	0	0	0	0	0	0	0	0	0	0	0	0
.	12-3-8	0	0	0	0	0	9	1	0	0	0	0	0	0	0	0	0	0	0	0	0

M I S T A K E   Y E S

TOTALS																					
NUMERIC	19	18	17	17	18	9	17	18	17	19	18	19	18	18	18	19	18	18	19	19
ALPHABETIC	0	0	1	1	1	1	1	1	1	0	0	0	1	1	1	0	0	0	0	0
SPECIAL	0	0	0	0	0	0	0	0	0	0	0	0	0	0	0	0	0	0	0	0
PERIOD	0	0	0	0	0	9	1	0	0	0	0	0	0	0	0	0	0	0	0	0

--- similar analysis for variables (columns) 21-26 ---

The results are presented in Output 4D.2. The characters found in the data include letters (MISTAKE and YES), decimal points and an apostrophe symbol. (The apostrophe is in column 24 so it is not shown.) This example is described in greater detail in Section 3.1.

Table 8.1 Nineteen cases of data containing nonnumeric characters. The data are in columns 1-26 of each card

```
04563758254031753284.63754
13056785154063725170.65W19
81257056143523582640.32734
12365478250073156045.63245
5    452076 020713548.32540
45203752526505534283.65024
43MISTAKE6508351 65.65883
85135237 73066234598.60H53
71627056108588325100.65027
81257.56143534561756.40335
13056.851540YES63524.62755
71627.56108512573256.77215
12365.78250053027616.64'32
45203.52526544321565.98325
812576.6143545443212.96352
12365.78250053324132.537 6
13056.85154013725689.53408
45203.52526563041255.64325
71627.56108511356405.65310
```

Example 4D.3 Identifying Cases with Errors or Blanks

In the last example the existence of the apostrophe symbol and the letters MISTAKE and YES was identified. For large data files it is important to locate the cases in which any such error occurs. P4D has a print option that allows the listing of only those cases with problems.

Each type of character in the data file can be printed as is or replaced by a single character of your choice. For example, if we request that numbers be recoded to blanks and blanks in the input data be recoded to asterisks,

- the records with all numbers will become blank
- blanks in the data will appear as asterisks
- other characters and symbols will be highlighted because the surrounding numbers are now blank

In addition, all records that are completely blank after recoding are not printed; this results in a printout of only those cases with errors.

To specify the above recodes we insert a PRINT paragraph (before the END paragraph) in the Control Language of Example 4D.2:

```
---------------------------------------
/ PRINT    NUMERIC IS ' '.
          BLANK   IS '*'.
---------------------------------------
```

The results are shown in Output 4D.3. These results are in addition to the column frequencies printed in Output 4D.2. Note that no numbers appear. The asterisks show where blanks previously occurred.

Output 4D.3 P4D lists the cases after substituting blanks for numbers and asterisks for blanks

```
-----------------------------------------------------------------------------------------------------
```

LISTING OF FIRST CHARACTER OF EACH VARIABLE AFTER CHARACTER REPLACEMENT AS REQUESTED IN 'PRINT' PARAGRAPH.
CASES THAT BECOME ALL BLANK AFTER REPLACEMENT ARE NOT LISTED.

```
CASE    CASE    V A R I A B L E S
LABEL   NUMBER        1          2          3          4          5          6          7          8
                 1234567890 1234567890 1234567890 1234567890 1234567890 1234567890 1234567890 1234567890

          1                          .
          2                          . W
          3                          .
          4                          .
          5      ***        *        .
          6                          .
          7      MISTAKE         **  .
          8            *             . OH
          9                          .
         10       .                  .
         11       .        YES       .
         12       .                  .
         13       .                  .
         14       .                  .
         15        .                 .
         16       .                  .    *
         17       .                  .
         18       .                  .
         19       .                  .

                 1234567890 1234567890 1234567890 1234567890 1234567890 1234567890 1234567890 1234567890
                     1          2          3          4          5          6          7          8
```

THERE WERE ONLY   19 CASES PRIOR TO END OF FILE.

--- results in Output 4D.2 appear here ---

```
-----------------------------------------------------------------------------------------------------
```

One decimal point appears to be out of line. Letters and the apostrophe are quickly located. If decimal points were omitted from the data file, only records 2, 5, 7, 8, 11, 13, and 16 would be displayed in Output 4D.3.

<u>Listing the data with or without character recodes</u>. P4D can print all the data or parts of the data. If only

/ PRINT

is specified, all the data are printed in the order read with a space inserted after every 10th variable (column). Records that are completely blank are not printed.

<u>A subset of the data</u> can be printed by modifying types of characters (such as letters, numbers or symbols) into blanks. The characters are divided into seven types:

1. letters of the alphabet
2. numbers (numeric data)
3. period or decimal point
4. plus and minus sign
5. blanks
6. symbols; i.e., comma, slash and any nonnumeric and nonalphabetic characters not listed above
7. illegal characters; i.e., characters not read under A1 format

The possible assignments are explained below. Any symbol, number or letter can be used in place of each 'c' (character). Blanks may also be used; e.g., NUMERIC is ' '. in Example 4D.3. Any assignment that is not made leaves the data unchanged.

<u>Using the case labeling capability to print messages in the data listing</u>. The characters in the variables identified as case labels (Chapter 5) are displayed in the far left column of each data listing. The characters in the case label can be changed by using the CHAR function (in the TRANSFORM paragraph). We can flag cases in a printout that have a particular character in a given column. For example, we could use a label such as *NO* to identify all cases with a 9 in column 3.

We assume for this example that the case label is in column 77 through 80. Our instructions are

```
/ PROB
/ INPUT      VARIABLES ARE 77.
             FORMAT IS '(76A1, A4)'.
/ VARIABLE   LABEL IS 77.
/ TRANS
    IF(X(3) EQ CHAR(9)) THEN
        X(77) = CHAR(*NO*).
/ PRINT
/ END
```

These instructions result in the printing of the data file with the word *NO* printed at the left for each case containing a 9 in column 3. If we want to list the case numbers for <u>only</u> those cases with the value 9 (omitting all other cases and also the data values for the selected cases) we can state

```
/ PROB
/ TRANS
    IF (X(3) EQ CHAR(9)) THEN X(3) = CHAR(*).
/ PRINT
    NUMERIC IS ' '.
/ END
```

PRINT ─────

> Note: When a PRINT paragraph is specified, all data records are printed that are not entirely blank after any specified substitutions.
>
> NUMeric = 'c'.   1 char.   unchanged
>   All numeric data are replaced by a user supplied character.
> ALPhabetic = 'c'.   1 char.   unchanged
>   All letters are replaced by a user supplied character.
> PERIOD = 'c'.   1 char.   unchanged
>   All periods are replaced by the character c.
> SIGN = 'c'.   1 char.   unchanged
>   The plus (+) and minus (−) signs are replaced by the character c.
> BLANK = 'c'.   1 char.   unchanged
>   All blanks are replaced by the character c.
> SYMBol = 'c'.   1 char.   unchanged
>   All symbols are replaced by the character c. Symbols are those commonly available on a keypunch machine but not a number, letter, sign, period or blank. They include ()&/¢!$,=*<>%@'_:;|¬?." and several punches that have no associated printed characters. Since some punches cannot be printed, their position in the data can be identified by assigning a printable character to SYMBOL.
> ILLegal = 'c'.   1 char.   unchanged
>   All illegal characters are replaced by a user supplied symbol. Illegal characters are characters that occur when reading the data under a FORMAT other than A1, or by keypunching a card with more than one character in the same column.

SIZE OF PROBLEM

On medium-sized computer systems the frequencies of characters in approximately 200 variables (columns) can be counted at the same time. Appendix B describes how to increase the capacity of the program.

ACKNOWLEDGEMENT

P4D was designed by W.J. Dixon and Laszlo Engelman and programmed by Laszlo Engelman.

SUMMARY

Order of Input Cards

```
// (job card)
// EXEC BIMED,PROG=BMDP4D        (see Appendix E)
//SYSIN DD *
/ PROBLEM
/ INPUT
/ VARIABLE
/ TRANSFORM
/ PRINT
/ END
     (data, if on cards)
// (system card)
```

Full sets of BMDP paragraphs (and data, if on cards)
can be repeated for additional problems; see Section
5.8.

instructions specific to P4D

Paragraph Statement	Preassigned	Comment and Manual Reference
/ INPut		Nonstandard optional paragraph. Case label variables (if present) can use A4 format, all others must be A1. CASES, UNIT and REWIND may be used but are not needed for card data sets.
VARiable = #.	80	Number of single column variables plus label variables, if any (up to 200). * 40
FORMat = '(c)'.	'(80A1)'	Data must be read with A1 format. Column skip X, and record skip / are permitted. * 40
/ PRINT		Optional to control printing of cases.

NUMeric = 'c'.
    BLANK = 'c'.
    PERIOD = 'c'.
    ALPhabetic = 'c'.
    SIGN = 'c'.
    SYMBol = 'c'.
    ILLegal = 'c'.
	none	Each of the listed types of values can be replaced by blanks or any other character (can be different for each type). After replacement, completely blank cases are not printed. The unchanged value is printed if no replacement character is supplied. 90

Key:

```
/    -indicates paragraph
.    -period ends a sentence
●    -required
v    -variable (name or subscript)
g    -group (name or subscript)
#    -number
'c'  -characters (name or parameter) may omit
       apostrophes if contiguous letters only
```

```
*    -assigned value remains the same for
       additional problems
VT   -number of variables after transformations
list -more than one item, often one per var.

Capitalized letters-paragraph or sentence names
    recognized by BMDP
Page numbers following refer to this Manual
```

9

DATA IN GROUPS

Description, t Tests, One-Way and Two-Way Analysis of Variance

Data are often classified into groups -- such as by sex, by age or by treatment. Unusual data values may be recognized when the data are examined separately for each group. For example, if the data are classified by age, a height of six feet in the under-ten group is almost certainly an error, but six feet in an over-twenty group does not arouse suspicion. Examining histograms of the data in each group is a convenient way to screen the data for unusual values and for normality.

Group means can be compared by a t test when there are only two groups, or by a one-way analysis of variance (ANOVA) when there are more than two groups. The choice of t test or ANOVA statistic depends primarily on whether the variances in the groups are equal or unequal.

In this chapter we discuss three BMDP programs that summarize data in groups, and compare the groups.

P3D -- Comparison of Two Groups with t Tests p. 94
P7D -- Description of Groups (Strata) with
Histograms and Analysis of Variance p. 105
P9D -- Multiway Description of Groups p. 116

P3D analyzes data in one or two groups. If the cases are classified into more than two groups, pairs of groups can be compared -- or all possible pairings of the groups can be compared. Univariate statistics and a histogram are printed for each variable in each group. If there is only one group, the one-sample t test is computed to test if the mean is zero. If there are two groups, their means are compared by two two-sample t tests -- with and without the assumption of the equality of variances; the equality of variances is tested by Levene's (1960) test. The means of several variables can be simultaneously tested for equality between two groups by Hotelling's T and Mahalanobis D. The correlations between the variables in each group can be printed. Now in 1979 are the provision of trimmed t tests and the reporting of extreme values.

P7D analyzes data for each variable in any number of groups and plots side-by-side histograms of the data in each group. The intervals of the histograms are labelled. Values that are equal to a missing value code or are out of range are tallied separately. A one-way (or two-way) analysis of variance is performed to test the equality of variance, P7D also computes two statistics that do

not assume the equality of variance in each group. Levene's (1960) test is used to test equality of variances. The input data, including any transformations, can be listed in the original order or after sorting the cases according to the values of a variable. P7D can also compute Winsorized means for each group and confidence limits for the Winsorized means. The correlations between the variables for each group and for all groups combined can be printed.

P9D analyzes data for each variable in any number of groups; the groups can be defined as all combinations of the levels of several variables. Univariate statistics are provided for each group. A one-way ANOVA is computed to test the equality of the means of all the groups. To test for homogeneity (equality) of variances, Bartlett's statistic is evaluated. A plot that shows the shift in means from group to group is an option. P9D also tests for the equality of group frequencies. If tests of the frequencies are your primary interest, the frequency table program, Chapter 11, may be more appropriate.

Many other programs also present or analyze data in groups. For example, more than one group can be plotted in the same histogram in P5D (Section 10.1); more complex analysis of variance models, including the one-way ANOVA with covariates, are considered in Chapter 15; and nonparametric tests to compare groups are treated in Chapter 16.

Control Language

The Control Language instructions to describe the data and variables are common to all BMDP programs and are explained in Chapter 5: the PROBLEM, INPUT, VARIABLE and GROUP paragraphs are used in the programs discussed in this chapter.

If data editing or transformations are necessary, the methods described in Chapter 6 can be used. Data can be read using a FORMAT statement or from a BMDP File (Chapter 7). If a BMDP File is read as input and a new BMDP File is created in the same problem, the two Files must be in different system files and must have different UNIT numbers.

A summary of the Control Language instructions common to all BMDP programs is on the back cover; summaries of the Control Language instructions specific to each program described in this chapter follow each program. These summaries can be used as indexes to the program descriptions.

Example 3D.1 Basic Setup for Comparing Two Groups with t Tests

We use P3D to analyze the Werner blood chemistry data (Table 5.1). The analysis compares two groups of women -- those on the pill with those not on the pill. Except for GROUPING IS BRTHPILL the BMDP instructions in Example 3D.1 are described in Chapter 5.

```
    --------------------------------------------
/ PROBLEM    TITLE IS 'WERNER BLOOD CHEMISTRY DATA'.
/ INPUT      VARIABLES ARE 9.
            FORMAT IS '(A4, 5F4.0, 3F4.1)'.
/ VARIABLE   NAMES ARE ID, AGE, HEIGHT, WEIGHT,
                    BRTHPILL, CHOLSTRL, ALBUMIN,
                    CALCIUM, URICACID.
            MAXIMUM IS (6)400.
            MINIMUM IS (6)150.
            LABEL IS ID.
            GROUPING IS BRTHPILL.

/ GROUP      CODES(5) ARE      1,    2.
            NAMES(5) ARE NOPILL, PILL.

/ END
    --------------------------------------------
```

(See end of this P3D section for organization of systems information, BMDP Instructions and data.)

To classify the cases into groups you must specify a GROUPING variable in the VARIABLE paragraph. In this example we specify

GROUPING IS BRTHPILL.

and also include a GROUP paragraph to name the groups. The GROUP paragraph can be omitted when the values of the GROUPING variable contain ten or fewer distinct values (as in our example) and you do not want to name the groups.

When no grouping variable is specified, a one-sample t test is performed (Example 3D.7).

The results of the above analysis using P3D are shown in Output 3D.1. Circled numbers below correspond to those in the output.

(1) Interpretation of the TEST paragraph and items specific to P3D. No TEST paragraph is specified; therefore preassigned values are printed.

(2) Number of cases read. The number of cases is not specified in our example, so all cases are read. The computations use all acceptable data; i.e., values not equal to a missing value code and not outside specified upper and lower limits.

(3) Interpretation of the GROUP paragraph.

P3D

9.1 Comparison of Two Groups with t Tests

ABSTRACT

P3D analyzes data in one or two groups. If the cases are classified into more than two groups, pairs of groups or all possible pairings of the groups can be compared. Univariate statistics and a histogram are printed for each variable in each group. If there is only one group, the one-sample t test is computed to test if the mean is zero. If there are two groups, the group means are compared by two two-sample t tests -- with and without the assumption of the equality of variances. The equality of variances is tested by Levene's test. The means of several variables can be simultaneously tested for equality between two groups by Hotelling's T^2 and Mahalanobis D^2. The correlations between the variables in each group can be printed.

P3D can also be used in place of P1D or P2D for initial screening when a grouping variable is not specified. P3D provides more detail than P1D, and the output can be easily viewed from a computer terminal. P2D provides more detail than P3D.

WHERE TO FIND IT

Output 3D.1   Comparison of two groups. Circled numbers correspond to those in the text

----

--- the BMDP instructions read by P3D are printed and interpreted ---


```
TEST TITLE. . . . . . . .WERNER BLOOD CHEMISTRY DATA
INDEXES OF VARIABLES TO BE ANALYZED . . . . . .   2  3  4  6  7  8  9
USE COMPLETE CASES ONLY . . . . . . . . . . . .   NO
PRINT GROUP CORRELATION MATRICES. . . . . . . .   NO      ①
COMPUTE HOTELLINGS T SQUARE . . . . . . . . . .   NO
INDEX OF GROUPING VARIABLE. . . . . . . . . . .   5
```


```
NUMBER OF CASES READ. . . . . . . . . . . . .    188    ②
```

VARIABLE NO. NAME	BEFORE TRANSFORMATION MINIMUM LIMIT	MAXIMUM LIMIT	MISSING CODE	CATEGORY CODE	CATEGORY NAME	INTERVAL RANGE GREATER THAN	LESS THAN OR EQUAL TO
5 BRTHPILL			③	1.00000	NOPILL		
				2.00000	PILL		

```
GROUPS USED IN COMPUTATIONS . . . . . . . . . . .   1   2
```


DIFFERENCES ON SINGLE VARIABLES


```
************
* AGE      * VARIABLE NUMBER   2      GROUP    1 NOPILL  2 PILL          1 NOPILL   (N= 94)           2 PILL    (N= 94)
************                           MEAN       33.8188   33.8188
      ④  STATISTICS   P VALUE  DF     STD DEV    10.1400   10.1400       H                    ⑥    X
                                       S.E.M.      1.0459    1.0459       H                         X
T (SEPARATE)  0.0  1.000  186.0       SAMPLE SIZE      94        94       H     HH    H            X    XX   X
T (POOLED)  ⑦ 0.0  1.000  186         MAXIMUM    55.0000   55.0000       HHHHHHHH   H H HH  H      XXXXXX   X X XX   X
                                       MINIMUM  ⑤ 19.0000   19.0000       HHHHHHHHHHHHHHHHHHH      XXXXXXXXXXXXXXXXXX
F(FOR VARIANCES)                                                         MIN------------------MAX  MIN------------------MAX
     LEVENE    0.0  1.000   1, 186                                         AN H =     3 CASES         AN X =     3 CASES


************
* HEIGHT.  * VARIABLE NUMBER   3      GROUP    1 NOPILL  2 PILL          1 NOPILL   (N= 92)           2 PILL    (N= 94)
************                           MEAN       64.0866   64.9252                 H                          XX
          STATISTICS   P VALUE  DF    STD DEV     2.4924    2.4196                 H   H                        XX   X
                                       S.E.M.      0.2599    0.2496                HH  HHH  H                   XX XXX  X
T (SEPARATE) -2.33  0.021  183.5      SAMPLE SIZE      92        94                HH  HHH  H                   XX  XXX  XX
T (POOLED)   -2.33  0.021  184        MAXIMUM    69.0000   71.0000             H   HH HHH HH                    XX  XXX  XX X
                                       MINIMUM    57.0000   59.0000          HH  HH HH HHH HH H                 X XX XX XXX XX X X
F(FOR VARIANCES)                                                         MIN------------------MAX  MIN------------------MAX
     LEVENE    0.30  0.584   1, 184                                        AN H =     3 CASES         AN X =     3 CASES


************
* WEIGHT   * VARIABLE NUMBER   4      GROUP    1 NOPILL  2 PILL          1 NOPILL   (N= 93)           2 PILL    (N= 93)
************                           MEAN      130.1502  133.1932
          STATISTICS   P VALUE  DF    STD DEV    18.8869   22.2926              H
                                       S.E.M.      1.9585    2.3116              HH                            X
T (SEPARATE) -1.00  0.317  179.2      SAMPLE SIZE      93        93             HHH                          XXXXXX
T (POOLED)   -1.00  0.317  184        MAXIMUM   195.0000  215.0000          H HHHHHHH  H                     XXXXXXX X
                                       MINIMUM    95.0000   94.0000          HHHHHHHHHHHHHHHH H               XXXXXXXXXXXXXX  XX
F(FOR VARIANCES)                                                         MIN------------------MAX  MIN------------------MAX
     LEVENE    1.52  0.220   1, 184                                        AN H =     4 CASES         AN X =     4 CASES


************
* CHOLSTRL * VARIABLE NUMBER   6      GROUP    1 NOPILL  2 PILL          1 NOPILL   (N= 94)           2 PILL    (N= 92)
************                           MEAN      232.9678  239.4019
          STATISTICS   P VALUE  DF    STD DEV    43.4914   41.5620                H
                                       S.E.M.      4.4858    4.3331            H   H                         X XXXX
T (SEPARATE) -1.03  0.304  183.9      SAMPLE SIZE      94        92          H HHHHHHH                       X XXXX
T (POOLED)   -1.03  0.304  184        MAXIMUM   335.0000  390.0000          HHHHHHHHHH  H                    XXXXXXXXXX
                                       MINIMUM   155.0000  160.0000          HHHHHHHHHHHHH HH                XXXXXXXXXXXXXX   X
F(FOR VARIANCES)                                                         MIN------------------MAX  MIN------------------MAX
     LEVENE    1.49  0.223   1, 184                                        AN H =     3 CASES         AN X =     3 CASES
```


--- analysis for variables 7 to 9 ---

----

④ The names of the variables being analyzed. Each variable is analyzed in turn.

⑤ For each group (identified by the group subscript and group name) P3D prints
- mean: $\bar{x}$
- standard deviation: s
- S.E.M. (standard error of the mean): $s/\sqrt{N}$
- sample size (frequency): N
- maximum observed value (not out of range)
- minimum observed value (not out of range)

⑥ A histogram of the data for each group. The histogram is a maximum of six lines high and 20 characters wide. These histograms provides a quick look at the shape of the distribution. Both histograms are plotted on the same scale extending from the minimum value to the maximum value in all the groups analyzed in the subproblem. The label under the histogram specifies how many observations each H or X represents. (The number of H's or X's to be plotted is raised to the next highest integer. That is, when there is only one observation to be plotted, an H or X is printed.)

⑦ Three tests are computed to compare the two groups.
- t (separate variances). This is a two-sample t statistic in which the variance of each group is estimated separately. It is appropriate whenever the population variances are <u>not</u> assumed to be equal. The t statistic is

$$t = (\bar{x}_1 - \bar{x}_2) \Bigg/ \left(\frac{s_1^2}{N_1} + \frac{s_2^2}{N_2} \right)^{\frac{1}{2}}$$

where the subscripts 1 and 2 refer to the two groups. The degrees of freedom are approximated (Brownlee, 1965, p. 299) by

$$f = \left[\frac{c^2}{N_1 - 1} + \frac{(1 - c)^2}{N_2 - 1} \right]^{-1}$$

where

$$c = \frac{var(\bar{x}_1)}{var(\bar{x}_1 + \bar{x}_2)} = \frac{s_1^2/N_1}{s_1^2/N_1 + s_2^2/N_2}$$

- t (pooled variances). When the population variances in the two groups are assumed to be equal, the estimate of the variance can be obtained by pooling (averaging) the two estimates of the variance. This two-sample t statistic is

$$t = (\bar{x}_1 - \bar{x}_2) \Bigg/ \left[\left(\frac{(N_1 - 1)s_1^2 + (N_2 - 1)s_2^2}{N_1 + N_2 - 2} \right) \left(\frac{1}{N_1} + \frac{1}{N_2} \right) \right]^{\frac{1}{2}}$$

The degrees of freedom are $N_1 + N_2 - 2$. When N_1 and N_2 differ and the two population variances are not equal, the distribution of this t statistic can be strongly affected and may not resemble a t distribution. The separate variance t and pooled variance t statistics will not differ when the sample sizes are equal.

For the standard error for the difference of two means, divide the difference of the two means by

either the separate variance or pooled variance t statistic.
- F (for variances). Levene's test of equality of variances is computed. The Levene test is obtained by performing an analysis of variance on the absolute deviations of each case from its cell mean.

The p-values for the above three statistics correspond to two-sided tests of significance (i.e., test inequality in either direction) when the samples are drawn from normal distributions. For all but small sample sizes the p-values for the t tests are not greatly affected by moderate departures from normality (Armitage, 1971, p. 119). The distribution of the usual F statistic (Bartlett) to test the equality of variances is sensitive to departures from normality (Armitage, 1971, p. 143) so we use the Levene (1960) W test (Brown and Forsythe, 1974b), which is based on the average absolute deviation from the mean. (Note that the Levene test should be used with caution when sample sizes are small. See Church and Wike (1976).)

VARiable ───────
| GROUPing = v.   no grouping var./prev.
| Name or subscript of the variable used to classify the cases into groups. If GROUPING is not specified or is set to zero, there is no grouping variable. If a GROUPING variable has more than ten distinct values, CODES or CUTPOINTS must be specified for it in the GROUP paragraph (Section 5.5).

Example 3D.2 Specifying Groups and Variables to be Analyzed

When the GROUPING variable classifies the cases into more than two groups, all possible pairs of the groups are compared, unless you explicitly state which groups are to be compared in the TEST paragraph. In this example we form four groups based on AGE and compare all pairs of the first three groups (the first TEST paragraph) and then compare the youngest with the oldest groups (the second TEST paragraph).

In addition, you can select the variables to be compared.

To illustrate both group and variable selection we use the following BMDP instructions

```
  ----------------------------------------
/ PROBLEM    TITLE IS 'WERNER BLOOD CHEMISTRY DATA'.
/ INPUT      VARIABLES ARE 9.
            FORMAT IS '(A4, 5F4.0, 3F4.1)'.
/ VARIABLE   NAMES ARE ID, AGE, HEIGHT, WEIGHT,
                 BRTHPILL, CHOLSTRL, ALBUMIN,
                 CALCIUM, URICACID.
            MAXIMUM IS (6)400.
            MINIMUM IS (6)150.
            LABEL IS ID.
            GROUPING IS AGE.
/ GROUP      CUTPOINTS(2) ARE 25, 35, 45.
            NAMES(2) ARE '25ORLESS', '26 TO 35',
                 '36 TO 45', 'OVER 45'.

/ TEST       VARIABLE IS CHOLSTRL.
            GROUPS ARE 1 TO 3.
```

```
/ TEST      VARIABLES ARE CHOLSTRL, ALBUMIN,
                        CALCIUM, URICACID.
            GROUPS ARE 1, 4.

/ END      --------------------------------------
```

These instructions are similar to Example 1D.1 except we now use AGE as the GROUPING variable; AGE is used to classify the cases into four groups. The results are presented in Output 3D.2.

Two TEST paragraphs are used. The first paragraph specifies that only the variable CHOLSTRL is to be analyzed and that three groups (with subscripts 1, 2 and 3) are to be compared. These groups are named '25ORLESS', '26 TO 35' and '36 TO 45'. There are three possible pairings of three groups. therefore three analyses of CHOLSTRL are computed, each using a different pair of groups.

The second TEST paragraph specifies that two groups (with subscripts 1 and 4) are to be compared using the data from the four blood chemistry measurements. This analysis follows the interpretation of the second TEST paragraph. We omit

the results for CALCIUM and URICACID.

A title can be specified in each TEST paragraph to label the analysis.

```
TEST ──────────────────────────────────
 VARiable = v list.      all variables except the
                          GROUPING variable/prev.
   Names or subscripts of the VARIABLES to be
   analyzed. When USE is stated in the VARIABLE
   paragraph, VARIABLES in the TEST paragraph must
   be included in the USE list.
 GROUP = g list.              all groups/prev.
   The groups to be compared. Lists are the GROUP
   NAMES or group subscripts. A group subscript is
   the sequence number of the group in the list of
   CODES or CUTPOINTS specified in the GROUP
   paragraph, or, if not specified in a GROUP
   paragraph, the rank order of the group. If more
   than two GROUPS are specified, each possible
   pair of groups is compared.
 TITLE = 'c'.     ≤ 80 char.          blank
   A title for the analysis.
```

Output 3D.2   A subset of groups and variables are selected for analysis by P3D
```
TEST TITLE. . . . . . . .WERNER BLOOD CHEMISTRY DATA
INDEXES OF VARIABLES TO BE ANALYZED . . . . . .   6
USE COMPLETE CASES ONLY . . . . . . . . . .      NO
PRINT GROUP CORRELATION MATRICES. . . . . . . .  NO
COMPUTE HOTELLINGS T SQUARE . . . . . . . . .    NO
INDEX OF GROUPING VARIABLE. . . . . . . . . .     2

GROUPS USED IN COMPUTATIONS . . . . . . . . . .   1   2   3
```

DIFFERENCES ON SINGLE VARIABLES

```
************
* CHOLSTRL *  VARIABLE NUMBER    6    GROUP   1 25ORLESS  2 26 TO 35     1 25ORLESS(N= 50)      2 26 TO 35(N= 60)
************                          MEAN      222.1198   224.6331
     STATISTICS    P VALUE   DF       STD DEV    37.4441    35.7419       H                      X
                                      S.E.M.      5.2954     4.6143       H                      X     X
T (SEPARATE)  -0.36  0.721  102.6     SAMPLE SIZE     50         60       H  H  H               X X  XXXX
T (POOLED)    -0.36  0.720  108       MAXIMUM   330.0000   317.0000       HH HHHHHHHH           XXXXXXXXX
                                      MINIMUM   155.0000   160.0000       HHH HHHHHHHHHHHH  H   XXXXXXXXXXXXX XXX
F(FOR VARIANCES)                                                         MIN----------------MAX  MIN----------------MAX
   LEVENE     0.01  0.912   1, 108                                         AN H =    2 CASES       AN X =    2 CASES
```

DIFFERENCES ON SINGLE VARIABLES

```
************
* CHOLSTRL *  VARIABLE NUMBER    6    GROUP   1 25ORLESS  3 36 TO 45     1 25ORLESS(N= 50)      3 36 TO 45(N= 42)
************                          MEAN      222.1198   248.3332
     STATISTICS    P VALUE   DF       STD DEV    37.4441    44.8088       H
                                      S.E.M.      5.2954     6.9141       H
T (SEPARATE)  -3.01  0.003  80.1      SAMPLE SIZE     50         42       H  H  H                 X
T (POOLED)    -3.06  0.003  90        MAXIMUM   330.0000   335.0000       HH HHHHHHHH           X X XXXXXX X
                                      MINIMUM   155.0000   160.0000       HHH HHHHHHHHHHHH  H   XXX X X XXXXXXX XXXX
F(FOR VARIANCES)                                                         MIN----------------MAX  MIN----------------MAX
   LEVENE     1.87  0.174   1, 90                                          AN H =    2 CASES       AN X =    2 CASES
```

DIFFERENCES ON SINGLE VARIABLES

```
************
* CHOLSTRL *  VARIABLE NUMBER    6    GROUP   2 26 TO 35  3 36 TO 45     2 26 TO 35(N= 60)      3 36 TO 45(N= 42)
************                          MEAN      224.6331   248.3332
     STATISTICS    P VALUE   DF       STD DEV    35.7419    44.8088       H
                                      S.E.M.      4.6143     6.9141       H     H
T (SEPARATE)  -2.85  0.006  75.3      SAMPLE SIZE     60         42       H H   HHHH              X
T (POOLED)    -2.97  0.004  100       MAXIMUM   317.0000   335.0000       HHHHHHHHHH            X X XXXXXX X
                                      MINIMUM   160.0000   160.0000       HHHHHHHHHHHHHHH HHH   XXX X X XXXXXXX XXXX
F(FOR VARIANCES)                                                         MIN----------------MAX  MIN----------------MAX
   LEVENE     2.60  0.110   1, 100                                         AN H =    2 CASES       AN X =    2 CASES
```

(output continued)

Output 3D.2 (continued)

```
TEST TITLE. . . . . . . . .WERNER BLOOD CHEMISTRY DATA
INDEXES OF VARIABLES TO BE ANALYZED . . . . . .   6   7   8   9
USE COMPLETE CASES ONLY . . . . . . . . . . . .     NO
PRINT GROUP CORRELATION MATRICES. . . . . . . .     NO
COMPUTE HOTELLINGS T SQUARE . . . . . . . . . .     NO
INDEX OF GROUPING VARIABLE. . . . . . . . . . .      2

NUMBER OF CASES READ. . . . . . . . . . . . .      188

GROUPS USED IN COMPUTATIONS . . . . . . . . . . .    1   4
```

DIFFERENCES ON SINGLE VARIABLES

```
************
* CHOLSTRL *  VARIABLE NUMBER    6      GROUP    1 25ORLESS  4 OVER 45      1 25ORLESS(N=  50)         4 OVER 45 (N=  34)
************                            MEAN       222.1198   262.0566
           STATISTICS     P VALUE   DF  STD DEV     37.4441    43.2672
                                        S.E.M.       5.2954     7.4203      H
T (SEPARATE)  -4.38   0.000    64.0     SAMPLE SIZE       50         34      H  H  H                    X
T (POOLED)    -4.50   0.000    82       MAXIMUM    330.0000   390.0000      HHH H                      X   X   X
                                        MINIMUM    155.0000   190.0000      HH HHHHHHH                  XX X   X
F(FOR VARIANCES)                                                            HHHHHHHHHHHHH  H            XX XXXXXXX XX   X
    LEVENE    0.38   0.537    1,  82                                       MIN------------------MAX    MIN------------------MAX
                                                                              AN H =    2 CASES          AN X =    2 CASES

************
* ALBUMIN  *  VARIABLE NUMBER    7      GROUP    1 25ORLESS  4 OVER 45      1 25ORLESS(N=  52)         4 OVER 45 (N=  33)
************                            MEAN         4.1538     4.0394
           STATISTICS     P VALUE   DF  STD DEV      0.4118     0.2680
                                        S.E.M.       0.0571     0.0467                 H
T (SEPARATE)   1.55   0.124    82.9     SAMPLE SIZE       52         33       HH   H                     XX X
T (POOLED)     1.42   0.161    83       MAXIMUM      5.0000     4.6000       HHH  HHHH HH              X  XX XX
                                        MINIMUM      3.2000     3.5000     H HH HHHH HHHHHHHHHH         XXXXX XXXX X
F(FOR VARIANCES)                                                          MIN------------------MAX    MIN------------------MAX
    LEVENE    7.22   0.009    1,  83                                          AN H =    2 CASES          AN X =    2 CASES
```

--- similar analyses for variables 8 and 9 ---

Example 3D.3 Requesting Hotelling's T^2 and Mahalanobis D^2

The equality of group means of several variables can be tested simultaneously by the multivariate Hotelling's T^2 (Morrison, 1967, p. 120) and Mahalanobis D^2. The statistics are equivalent and can be transformed to an F statistic when there are one or two groups.

We add the following TEST paragraph to the Control Language of Example 3D.1 to request the Hotelling's T^2 for equality of four named variables in the two groups PILL and NOPILL.

```
----------------------------------------
/ TEST     VARIABLES ARE CHOLSTRL, ALBUMIN,
                       CALCIUM, URICACID.
          HOTELLING.
----------------------------------------
```

The results for the multivariate tests are displayed in Output 3D.3. The results for the univariate tests follow: we display only those for CHOLSTRL.

The definitions of Hotelling's T^2 and Mahalanobis D^2 are as follows.

In matrix notation let $\overline{X}_1$ be a column vector that contains the means of the variables in one group, $\overline{X}_2$ the corresponding means in a second group, and S a square matrix representing the pooled within-groups covariance matrix for the two groups being compared. Mahalanobis D^2 is a measure of the distance between the means of the two groups

$$D^2 = (\overline{X}_1 - \overline{X}_2)' S^{-1} (\overline{X}_1 - \overline{X}_2)$$

where the prime indicates the transpose of a matrix. Hotelling's T^2 is

$$T^2 = D^2 \bigg/ \left(\frac{1}{N_1} + \frac{1}{N_2} \right).$$

Both Mahalanobis D^2 and Hotelling's T^2 can be transformed to an F statistic.

$$F = \frac{T^2(N_1 + N_2 - v - 1)}{v(N_1 + N_2 - 2)}$$

where v is the number of variables in the analysis.

When there is only <u>one group</u>, the formulas are

$$D^2 = \overline{X}_1' S^{-1} \overline{X}_1, \quad T^2 = N_1 D^2 \quad \text{and } F = T^2 \frac{N_1 - v}{v(N_1 - 1)}$$

Output 3D.3   Hotelling's T^2 and Mahalanobis D^2 - using all acceptable values
----

```
        TEST TITLE. . . . . . . . .WERNER BLOOD CHEMISTRY DATA
        INDEXES OF VARIABLES TO BE ANALYZED . . . . . .   6   7   8   9
        USE COMPLETE CASES ONLY . . . . . . . . . . .        NO
        PRINT GROUP CORRELATION MATRICES. . . . . . . .      NO
        COMPUTE HOTELLINGS T SQUARE . . . . . . . . .        YES
        INDEX OF GROUPING VARIABLE. . . . . . . . . .         5

        GROUPS USED IN COMPUTATIONS . . . . . . . . . . .    1   2


    DIFFERENCES AMONG GROUP MEANS USING ALL VARIABLES
    FOR THE FOLLOWING GROUPS
    ************
    * NOPILL   *
    * PILL     *
    ************

        MAHALANOBIS D SQUARE              0.2819
        HOTELLING T SQUARE              13.0364
        F VALUE                          3.2057      P VALUE    0.014
           DEGREES OF FREEDOM        4,   180.0


    WARNING - SINCE SPECIAL MISSING VALUE FORMULAS ARE USED,
              THESE MULTIVARIATE STATISTICS ARE ONLY APPROXIMATE.

    DIFFERENCES ON SINGLE VARIABLES


    ************
    * CHOLSTRL * VARIABLE NUMBER   6   GROUP    1 NOPILL   2 PILL        1 NOPILL  (N=  94)        2 PILL    (N=  92)
    ************                       MEAN      232.9678  239.4019
              STATISTICS   P VALUE  DF  STD DEV    43.4914   41.5620                H
                                        S.E.M.      4.4858    4.3331          H     H                      X XXXX
    T (SEPARATE)  -1.03  0.304  183.9  SAMPLE SIZE    94        92        H  HHHHHHH                        X XXXX
    T (POOLED)    -1.03  0.304  184    MAXIMUM   335.0000  390.0000      HHHHHHHHHH  H                      XXXXXXXXXX
                                       MINIMUM   155.0000  160.0000      HHHHHHHHHHHHHH HH         XXXXXXXXXXXXXXX   X
    F(FOR VARIANCES)                                                MIN------------------MAX   MIN------------------MAX
       LEVENE      1.49  0.223   1, 184                               AN H =     3 CASES          AN X =     3 CASES

                    --- similar analyses for variables 7 to 9 ---
```

Output 3D.4   Hotelling's T^2 and Mahalanobis D^2 - using complete cases only
----

```
        TEST TITLE. . . . . . . . .WERNER BLOOD CHEMISTRY DATA
        INDEXES OF VARIABLES TO BE ANALYZED . . . . . .   6   7   8   9
        USE COMPLETE CASES ONLY . . . . . . . . . . .        YES
        PRINT GROUP CORRELATION MATRICES. . . . . . . .      NO
        COMPUTE HOTELLINGS T SQUARE . . . . . . . . .        YES
        INDEX OF GROUPING VARIABLE. . . . . . . . . .         5

        GROUPS USED IN COMPUTATIONS . . . . . . . . . . .    1   2


    DIFFERENCES AMONG GROUP MEANS USING ALL VARIABLES
    FOR THE FOLLOWING GROUPS
    ************
    * NOPILL   *
    * PILL     *
    ************

        MAHALANOBIS D SQUARE              0.2864
        HOTELLING T SQUARE              13.0284
        F VALUE                          3.2028      P VALUE    0.014
           DEGREES OF FREEDOM        4,   177.0


    DIFFERENCES ON SINGLE VARIABLES


    ************
    * CHOLSTRL * VARIABLE NUMBER   6   GROUP    1 NOPILL   2 PILL        1 NOPILL  (N=  90)        2 PILL    (N=  92)
    ************                       MEAN      232.0886  239.4019
              STATISTICS   P VALUE  DF  STD DEV    43.4700   41.5620                H
                                        S.E.M.      4.5821    4.3331          H     H                      X XXXX
    T (SEPARATE)  -1.16  0.248  179.2  SAMPLE SIZE    90        92        H  HHH HHH                        X XXXX
    T (POOLED)    -1.16  0.247  180    MAXIMUM   335.0000  390.0000      HHHHHHHHHH  H                      XXXXXXXXXX
                                       MINIMUM   155.0000  160.0000      HHHHHHHHHHHHHH HH         XXXXXXXXXXXXXXX   X
    F(FOR VARIANCES)                                                MIN------------------MAX   MIN------------------MAX
       LEVENE      1.79  0.182   1, 180                               AN H =     3 CASES          AN X =     3 CASES

                    --- similar analyses for variables 7 to 9 ---
```

When the group means are unequal both T^2 and F increase as N_1 (and N_2) increases, while D^2 does not. Therefore D^2 is a better description of the distance between groups when distances are compared.

The above formulas assume that the data are available in each case for all the variables compared. If some data values are equal to missing value codes or are out of range, observations for all variables may not be present in each case. Then N_1 and N_2 are replaced by the harmonic means of the frequencies of variables of the first and second groups respectively; this provides an approximate test of the equality of means. The formula is given in Appendix A.3.

TEST ─────────────────────────────
| HOTELling.   no/prev.
| When HOTELLING is specified, Hotelling's T^2 and Mahalanobis D^2 are computed.

Example 3D.4 Restricting Analysis to Complete Cases

Usually an analysis of a single variable uses all the acceptable values for the variable whether or not the value of any other variable is acceptable. Conversely, the usual definition of Hotelling's T^2 requires that the data values be acceptable for all the variables for any case that is included in the computations.

Cases containing acceptable data values for all variables that are included in the analysis are called complete cases.

In P3D you can specify whether all the computations are to be based on COMPLETE cases only, or on all acceptable values. If COMPLETE is specified, the univariate statistics and the t statistics are also computed using only complete cases.

To illustrate the effect COMPLETE has on the results, we add the command COMPLETE to the TEST paragraph of Example 3D.3 as follows

```
---------------------------------------
 / TEST     VARIABLES ARE CHOLSTRL, ALBUMIN,
                        CALCIUM, URICACID.
            HOTELLING.
            COMPLETE.
---------------------------------------
```

The results for modified analysis are presented in Output 3D.4 and can be compared with the analysis in Output 3D.3. We do not display the results for ALBUMIN, CALCIUM and URICACID. The small differences between the two results are due to the fact that there are only eight cases containing unacceptable data. Note the different frequencies (sample sizes) and degrees of freedom used in the two analyses.

A large difference between the two analyses would indicate that the results may be biased due to the pattern of missing values or values out of range. If your analyses show a large difference, you may want to examine the data by using PAM (Section 12.2) to study the pattern of values excluded from the analysis.

TEST ─────────────────────────────
| COMPlete.   no/prev.
| When COMPLETE is specified, only complete cases are used in all the computations. Complete cases are cases in which the data are acceptable (not missing or out of range) for all variables specified in the USE statement of the VARIABLE paragraph (all variables if USE is not specified). COMPLETE or NO COMPLETE can be specified in only the first TEST paragraph of any problem. It cannot be altered until a new problem begins.

Example 3D.5 Correlation of Variables in Each Group

The CORRELATIONS between the variables in each group are printed when CORRELATION is specified in the TEST paragraph. If we submit the Control Language of Example 3D.1 with the added TEST paragraph

```
---------------------------------------
 / TEST     VARIABLES ARE CHOLSTRL, ALBUMIN,
                        CALCIUM, URICACID.
            CORRELATIONS.
---------------------------------------
```

we obtain the results shown in Output 3D.5.

Output 3D.5   Correlation matrices for each group

```
TEST TITLE. . . . . . . . .WERNER BLOOD CHEMISTRY DATA
INDEXES OF VARIABLES TO BE ANALYZED . . . . . .  6  7  8  9
USE COMPLETE CASES ONLY . . . . . . . . . . . .      NO
PRINT GROUP CORRELATION MATRICES. . . . . . . .      YES
COMPUTE HOTELLINGS T SQUARE . . . . . . . . . .      NO
INDEX OF GROUPING VARIABLE. . . . . . . . . .         5

GROUPS USED IN COMPUTATIONS . . . . . . . . . . .    1   2
```

CORRELATION MATRIX FOR GROUP   1 NOPILL

		CHOLSTRL 6	ALBUMIN 7	CALCIUM 8	URICACID 9
CHOLSTRL	6	1.0000			
ALBUMIN	7	0.0296	1.0000		
CALCIUM	8	0.2874	0.4452	1.0000	
URICACID	9	0.2739	0.0858	0.2009	1.0000

CORRELATION MATRIX FOR GROUP   2 PILL

		CHOLSTRL 6	ALBUMIN 7	CALCIUM 8	URICACID 9
CHOLSTRL	6	1.0000			
ALBUMIN	7	0.1160	1.0000		
CALCIUM	8	0.2153	0.4258	1.0000	
URICACID	9	0.2473	-0.0485	0.1916	1.0000

--- analyses of variables 6 to 9 as in Output 3D.1 ---

The method of computing correlations depends on whether COMPLETE cases or all acceptable data are used. When COMPLETE cases are used, the correlation between two variables (i and k) is

$$r_{ik} = \frac{\Sigma_j (x_{ij} - \bar{x}_i)(x_{kj} - \bar{x}_k)}{\left[\Sigma_j (x_{ij} - \bar{x}_i)^2 \Sigma_j (x_{kj} - \bar{x}_k)^2\right]^{\frac{1}{2}}}$$

where the summations are over all complete cases in the group. When all available data are used, the covariance of variables i and k is computed using complete pairs of observations; i.e.,

$$cov_{ik} = \Sigma_j (x_{ij} - \bar{x}_{i(k)})(x_{kj} - \bar{x}_{k(i)})/(N_{ik} - 1)$$

where $\bar{x}_{i(k)}$ is the mean of variable i for cases that also contain variable k. The summation is over the cases in the group for which data for both variables are present (N_{ik} cases). The correlation is computed as

$$r_{ik} = cov_{ik}/(s_i s_k)$$

where s_i and s_k are the standard deviations for each variable (that is, they are each based on all acceptable data for the variable in the group). It is therefore possible that the correlation matrix will not be positive definite (for a definition of positive definite, see Scheffe, 1959, p. 398), and that a computed correlation will be greater than one.

TEST
CORRelation.	no/prev.
Print the correlation matrix for each group used.	

Example 3D.6 Trimmed t and Extreme Values.

When there are outliers or bad values in the data, the t test can be overly sensitive to these extreme scores. A trimmed t (removing the influence of the largest and smallest values in each group) can be obtained by specifying ROBUST. in the TEST paragraph.

We submit the following Control Language to show the use of trimmed t. We drop the maximum and minimum specification from the VARIABLE paragraph as submitted in Example 3D.2 and include ROBUST in the TEST paragraph

```
/ PROBLEM    TITLE IS 'WERNER BLOOD CHEMISTRY DATA'.
/ INPUT      VARIABLES ARE 9.
            FORMAT IS '(A4, 5F4.0, 3F4.1)'.
/ VARIABLE   NAMES ARE ID, AGE, HEIGHT, WEIGHT,
                        BRTHPILL, CHOLSTRL, ALBUMIN,
                        CALCIUM, URICACID.
            LABEL IS ID.
            GROUPING IS AGE.
/ GROUP      CUTPOINTS(2) ARE 25, 35, 45.
            NAMES(2) ARE '25ORLESS', '26 TO 35'
                        '36 TO 45', 'OVER 45'.

/ TEST       VARIABLE IS CHOLSTRL.
            GROUPS ARE 1, 4.
            ROBUST.

/ END
```

The results are in Output 3D.6.

The trimmed t is reported in both a pooled variance and separate variance version. (See Yuen and Dixon, 1973 and Yuen, 1974.) When the trimmed t is requested, additional statistics are reported: the case numbers for the largest and smallest values in each group (CS.NO.MX. and CS.NO.MN.), the standard score for the largest and smallest values in each group (MX.ST.SC. and MN.ST.SC.), and the second largest and second smallest values in each group MAX(2ND) and MIN(2ND).

TEST
ROBUST.	no/prev.
Print trimmed t and related statistics.	

Output 3D.6   Extreme values and the trimmed t test

DIFFERENCES ON SINGLE VARIABLES

```
************
* CHOLSTRL *   VARIABLE NUMBER   6      GROUP     1 25ORLESS  4 OVER 45      1 25ORLESS(N= 52)           4 OVER 45 (N=  34)
************                            MEAN         226.0767    262.0566    H
            STATISTICS   P VALUE   DF   STD DEV       68.6428     43.2672    H
                                        S.E.M.         9.5190      7.4203    HHH                             X
T (SEPARATE)   -2.98      0.004   83.9  SAMPLE SIZE        52          34    HHH                            XX
T (POOLED)     -2.72      0.008   84    MAXIMUM      600.0000    390.0000    HHH                            XX X
T (TRIM SEP.)  -4.09      0.000   67.7  MINIMUM       50.0000    190.0000  H HHHHHH H         H            XXXXXX X
T (TRIM POOLED)-4.06      0.000   80    MAX(2ND)     330.0000    338.0000   MIN-------------------MAX      MIN-------------------MAX
F(FOR VARIANCES)                        MIN(2ND)     155.0000    195.0000       AN H =    3 CASES              AN X =    3 CASES
    LEVENE      0.40      0.528   1, 84 MX.ST.SC.      5.4474      2.9571   CS.NO.MN.  4  CS.NO.MX.  2    CS.NO.MN. 164 CS.NO.MX. 182
                                        MN.ST.SC.     -2.5651     -1.6654
```

Example 3D.7 The One-Sample (or Matched Pairs) t Test

The Werner data (Table 5.1) consist of 94 pairs of age-matched women. In each <u>pair</u> the first woman is <u>not</u> on the pill and the second woman is. We perform a paired t test by reading each pair of data records as a single case. We then use BMDP transformations to form <u>four</u> new variables that represent differences in the blood measurement variables. The Control Language rules for the TRANSFORM paragraph are described in Chapter 6. Note that we state that we ADD four variables in the VARIABLE paragraph. We request a one-sample t test for each new variable (those representing differences) by <u>not</u> specifying a GROUPING variable. The Control Language is as follows

```
------------------------------------
/ PROBLEM    TITLE IS 'WERNER BLOOD CHEMISTRY DATA'.
/ INPUT      VARIABLES ARE 13.
            FORMAT IS '(A4, 5F4.0, 3F4.1/ 20X,
                F4.0, 3F4.1)'.
```

```
/ VARIABLE   NAMES ARE ID, AGE, HEIGHT, WEIGHT,
                BRTHPILL, CHOL1, ALB1, CAL1,
                URIC1, CHOL2, ALB2, CAL2,
                URIC2, CHOLDIFF, ALBDIFF,
                CALDIFF, URICDIFF.
            MAXIMUMS ARE (6)400, (10)400.
            MINIMUMS ARE (6)150, (10)150.
            LABEL IS ID.
            ADD IS 4.

/ TRANSFORM  CHOLDIFF = CHOL1 - CHOL2.
            ALBDIFF  = ALB1  - ALB2.
            CALDIFF  = CAL1  - CAL2.
            URICDIFF = URIC1 - URIC2.

/ TEST       VARIABLES ARE 14 TO 17.
            HOTELLING.

/ END
------------------------------------
```

Output 3D.7 shows the results for CHOLDIFF and ALBDIFF; the results for ALBDIFF (the difference in

Output 3D.7 Paired t test by P3D

```
--------------------------------------------------------------------------------------------------
```

```
            MAHALANOBIS D SQUARE        0.1303
            HOTELLING T SQUARE         11.8567
            F VALUE                     2.8654     P VALUE    0.028
                DEGREES OF FREEDOM    4,    87.0
```

```
            WARNING - SINCE SPECIAL MISSING VALUE FORMULAS ARE USED,
                    THESE MULTIVARIATE STATISTICS ARE ONLY APPROXIMATE.
```

```
            DIFFERENCES ON SINGLE VARIABLES


            ************
            * CHOLDIFF *  VARIABLE NUMBER  14
            ************
                                    MEAN        -6.1848
            T STATISTIC  P VALUE  DF  STD DEV     59.5390                  H
                                    S.E.M.       6.2074               H  H
                -1.00     0.322   91  SAMPLE SIZE      92           HHHHH H H
                                    MAXIMUM    155.0000             HHHHHHHH H
                                    MINIMUM   -145.0000      HHHHHHHHHHHHHHHHH  H
                                                             MIN------------------MAX
                                                             AN H =    3 CASES


            ************
            * ALBDIFF  *  VARIABLE NUMBER  15
            ************
                                    MEAN         0.1804                  H
            T STATISTIC  P VALUE  DF  STD DEV      0.5315                 HH
                                    S.E.M.       0.0554           H  HHH  H
                 3.26     0.002   91  SAMPLE SIZE      92          HHHHHHH HH
                                    MAXIMUM      1.3000        HHHHHHHHHHHHHH H
                                    MINIMUM     -1.2000      HHHHHHHHHHHHHHHHH H
                                                             MIN------------------MAX
                                                             AN H =    2 CASES
```

```
            --- similar analyses for CALDIFF and URICDIFF ---
```

ALBUMIN measurements) are significant. When there is only one group, the two t tests are identical and the F (for variances) is meaningless.

To test that a variable mean is equal to a constant, the constant can be subtracted from each value of the variable in the TRANSFORM paragraph. For example, to subtract 125 from a variable named XYZ, you can specify

        / TRANSFORM NEWXYZ = XYZ - 125.

The one-sample t test on NEWXYZ is equivalent to a test that the mean of XYZ is 125.

Output for Terminal (new in 1979)

To obtain narrow output on a computer terminal specify LINE = 72. in the PRINT paragraph. See also Section 4.4.

```
PRINT
   LINE = #.                              132/prev.
      The number of characters in a line for
      printing.
```

Printing Data (new in 1979)

If requested, data can be printed.

```
PRINT
   CASE = #.                              0/prev.
      The number of cases to be printed.
```

On medium-sized computer systems P3D can analyze very large problems; it is not limited by the number of cases in the data. The maximum number of variables V depends on the number of groups G. The following table can be used as a guide for large computer systems:

G	2	3	4	5	10
V without HOTEL and CORR	240	160	120	96	48
V with HOTEL or CORR	53	42	36	31	21

Appendix B describes how to increase the capacity of the program.

COMPUTATIONAL METHOD

Means, standard deviations and covariances are computed in single precision using the method of provisional means (Appendix A.2). The formulas for Hotelling's T^2 and Mahalanobis D^2 are given in Appendix A.3.

ACKNOWLEDGEMENT

P3D was programmed by Sandra Fu and Jerry Douglas. Later revisions were made by Lanaii Kline and Peter Mundle.

SUMMARY

Order of Input Cards

```
// (job card)
// EXEC BIMED,PROG=BMDP3D        (see Appendix E)
//SYSIN DD *
/ PROBLEM
/ INPUT
/ VARIABLE
/ GROUP
/ TRANSFORM
/ SAVE
/ TEST           repeat for subproblems
/ END
    (data,if on cards)
// (system card)
```

Full sets of BMDP paragraphs (and data, if on cards)
can be repeated for additional problems; see Section
5.8.

instructions specific to P3D

Paragraph Statement	Preassigned	Comment and Manual Reference
/ VARiable		Additional option to classify cases into groups.
GROUPing = v.	none	Variable used to define group membership (see also / GROUP). If GROUPING is not specified or GROUPING = 0 is stated, one-sample tests are performed. * 96
/ TEST		Optional to select groups and variables to be considered concurrently (may be repeated).
VARiables = v list.	all	Names or subscripts of variables to be analyzed. * 97
GROUPs = g list.	all	Names or subscripts of groups to be compared. If not specified, all possible pairs of groups are compared. * 97
TITLE = 'c'.	blank	A title for the analysis, up to 80 characters, to label the output. 97
HOTELling.	no	Calculate multivariate Hotelling's T^2 and Mahalanobis' D^2 simultaneously on all variables, in addition to the univariate tests. * 100
CORRelation.	no	Print correlations between variables for each group. * 101
COMPlete.	no	Use only complete cases in the computations. A complete case has valid data (not missing or out of range) for all variables in USE list. If not stated, all available cases for each variable are used. May be specified in the first TEST paragraph only, and cannot be altered until a new problem begins. Only cases selected by the first TEST paragraph can be used in following TEST paragraphs when COMPLETE is specified. * 100
ROBUST.	no	Request for robust t and related statistics. * 101

Note: For matched, paired or correlated group comparisons with t tests and T : (1) each pair should be within a case, (2) take the difference between values by transformation, and (3) do not specify GROUP = v in the / VARIABLE paragraph.

Paragraph Statement	Preassigned	Comment and Manual Reference
/ PRINT		Optional.
LINEsize = #.	132	Width for printed output. * 103
CASE = #.	0	Number of cases to be printed. * 103

Key:

/   -indicates paragraph
.   -period ends a sentence
●   -required
v   -variable (name or subscript)
g   -group (name or subscript)
-number
'c'   -characters (name or parameter) may omit apostrophes if contiguous letters only

*   -assigned value remains the same for additional problems
VT   -number of variables after transformations
list   -more than one item, often one per var.

Capitalized letters-paragraph or sentence names recognized by BMDP
Page numbers following refer to this Manual

P7D

9.2 Description of Groups (Strata) with Histograms and Analysis of Variance

W. J. Dixon

ABSTRACT

P7D analyzes data for each variable in any number of groups and plots side-by-side histograms for each group. The intervals of the histograms are labelled. Values that are missing or out of range are tallied separately. A one-way or two-way analysis of variance is performed to test the equality of means between groups. In addition to the classical one-way analysis of variance, P7D also computes two statistics that do not assume the equality of variances in each group. The input data, including any transformations, can be listed in the original order, or after sorting the cases, according to the values of a variable. P7D can also compute Winsorized means for each group and confidence limits for the Winsorized means. When Winsorized means are requested, the six largest and six smallest values in each group are reported together with their case numbers and case labels. A plot of the cell means versus cell standard deviations and their logarithms can be requested to help select possible data transformations. Pairwise t-tests and Bonferroni probabilities can also be printed. The correlations between the variables for each group and for all groups combined can be printed. Users can also define statistics in terms of cell means, standard deviations, and cell sizes by means of their own FORTRAN subroutines that can be interfaced with P7D by the BIMEDT procedure. For example, you can specify contrasts across the cell means.

WHERE TO FIND IT

Example 7D.1 Basic Setup for Histogram of Strata

We use P7D to analyze the Werner blood chemistry data (Table 5.1) comparing four groups of women, classified according to their ages (as in Example 3D.2). Except for the HISTOGRAM paragraph, the Control Language instructions are explained in Chapter 5.

```
-------------------------------------
/ PROBLEM    TITLE IS 'WERNER BLOOD CHEMISTRY DATA'.
/ INPUT      VARIABLES ARE 9.
            FORMAT IS '(A4, 5F4.0, 3F4.1)'.
/ VARIABLE   NAMES ARE ID, AGE, HEIGHT, WEIGHT,
                BRTHPILL, CHOLSTRL, ALBUMIN,
                CALCIUM, URICACID.
            MAXIMUM IS (6)400.
            MINIMUM IS (6)150.
            LABEL IS ID.

/ GROUP      CUTPOINTS(2) ARE 25, 35, 45.
            NAMES(2) ARE '25ORLESS', '26 TO 35',
                '36 TO 45', 'OVER 45'.

/ HISTOGRAM  GROUPING IS AGE.

/ END
-------------------------------------
```

(See end of this P7D section for organization of systems information, BMDP instructions and data.)

The results of the above analysis by P7D are shown in Output 7D.1. Circled numbers below correspond to those in the output.

① Side-by-side histograms of the data in each group. We present the histograms for the variable CHOLSTRL. (Histograms are also plotted for all the other variables.) The base of each histogram is the vertical axis. The frequencies are plotted horizontally with the groups offset from one another. Each asterisk represents an observation. All observations are plotted in this example. When there are too many observations to be plotted in the available space, the number of observations are printed at the right end of the line of asterisks. The M in the histogram represents the group mean; when the group mean does <u>not</u> coincide with an observation, an N is plotted instead of an M.

Values excluded from the computations are tallied above the histogram in the appropriate group or in the rightmost group if the grouping variable does not have an acceptable value. Two values are excluded from the first group in our example.

The midpoint for each interval is printed to the left of the histograms. Each interval includes its upper limit. For example, 210.0 and 225.0 are successive midpoints, so the value 217.5 would be classified into the interval with midpoint 210.0.

② For each group, P7D prints
- mean: $\bar{x}$
- standard deviation: s based on sample variance
- standard error of the mean (S.E.M.) based on sample variance
- robust estimate of standard deviation based on mean deviation from the mean

- maximum and minimum observed value (not out of range)
- sample size (frequency): N

③ For all groups combined, P7D prints the mean, standard deviation, standard error of the mean, maximum, minimum and frequency. The standard deviation is computed from the overall mean for the variable (not from the group means).

④ A one-way analysis of variance (ANOVA) that tests the equality of group means.

Let x_{ij} represent the jth observation in the ith group and $\bar{x}_i$ the mean and N_i the number of

Output 7D.1 Comparison of groups. Circled numbers correspond to those in the text.

--- the BMDP instructions read by P7D are printed and interpreted ---

```
                  ***********                                                    ************
HISTOGRAM OF * CHOLSTRL * (VARIABLE    6). CASES DIVIDED INTO GROUPS BASED ON VALUES OF * AGE      * (VARIABLE     2)
                  ***********                                                    ************

          250RLESS              26 TO 35              36 TO 45              OVER 45
          .........................+.........................+.........................+..................+
VAR 6
EXCLUDED
VALUES
          **
              TABULATIONS AND COMPUTATIONS WHICH FOLLOW EXCLUDE VALUES LISTED ABOVE
MIDPOINTS
 435.000)
 420.000)
 405.000)
 390.000)                                                                   *
 375.000)
 360.000)
 345.000)                                                                   *
 330.000)*          ①                         **
 315.000)                      *              **              **
 300.000)*                     **             ***             ******
 285.000)**                    **             ***
 270.000)***                   *              *******         ***
 255.000)****          *********         M****          M********
 240.000)********      ***********        *****          **
 225.000)M******       M******           **             ******
 210.000)*******       *****             *****           **
 195.000)*********     ***********       ****            **
 180.000)****          *******           **
 165.000)***           ***              **
 150.000)*
 135.000)
 120.000)
GROUP MEANS ARE DENOTED BY M'S IF THEY COINCIDE WITH *'S, N'S OTHERWISE

MEAN         222.120        224.633        248.333        262.059
STD.DEV.      37.444         35.742         44.809         43.267
R.E.S.D.      38.044         37.427         46.613         42.448
S. E. M.       5.295    ②     4.614          6.914          7.420
MAXIMUM      330.000        317.000        335.000        390.000
MINIMUM      155.000        160.000        160.000        190.000
SAMPLE SIZE       50             60             42             34
```

```
        ALL GROUPS COMBINED         ******************** ANALYSIS OF VARIANCE TABLE ********************
(EXCEPT CASES WITH UNUSED VALUES    *
       FOR AGE    )                 *   SOURCE              SUM OF SQUARES    DF    MEAN SQUARE    F VALUE   TAIL PROBABILITY
                                    *
MEAN        236.150                 *   BETWEEN GROUPS        46857.3398       3    15619.1133  ④  9.86        0.0000
STD.DEV.     42.556  ③              *   WITHIN   GROUPS      288172.4290     182     1583.3650
S. E. M.      3.120                 *
MAXIMUM     390.000                 *   TOTAL               335029.7500     185
MINIMUM     155.000                 ****************************************************************************
SAMPLE SIZE     186                 *   LEVENE'S TEST FOR EQUAL VARIANCES    3, 182        ⑤  0.98        0.4054
                                    ****************************************************************************
                                    *   ONE-WAY ANALYSIS OF VARIANCE
                                    *   TEST STATISTICS FOR WITHIN-GROUP
                                    *   VARIANCES NOT ASSUMED TO BE EQUAL
                                    *       WELCH                            3,  90        ⑥  9.11        0.0000
                                    *       BROWN-FORSYTHE                   3, 151           9.42        0.0000
```

--- the analyses for variables 2 to 5 precede that for CHOLSTRL, those for variables 7 to 9 follow ---

----

observations in the ith group. Then

- between sum of squares: $BSS = \Sigma_i N_i(\bar{x}_i - x)^2$
  where $\bar{x} = \Sigma_i N_i \bar{x}_i / \Sigma N_i$
- between degrees of freedom = g - 1
  where g is the number of groups
- between mean square = BSS/(g-1)
- within sum of squares: $WSS = \Sigma_i \Sigma_j (x_{ij} - \bar{x}_i)^2$
- within degrees of freedom = $\Sigma_i(N_i - 1)$
- within mean square = $WSS/\Sigma_i(N_i - 1)$
- F value
  = (between mean square)/(within mean square)
- tail probability is the probability of exceeding the F ratio when the group means are equal (the probability reported is appropriate when the data are sampled from normal populations with equal population variances; the distribution of the F ratio is sensitive to the assumption of equal population variances, Brown and Forsythe, 1974a)

The F value (analysis of variance) is a test of the equality of group means. When the groups are ordered (as in this example), you may want to test contrasts on the group means, such as a linear trend. (See Fortran Interface below.) Both contrasts and covariates can be used in P1V (Section 15.1).

⑤ A robust test of the equality of variances is provided by a one-way analysis of variance computed on the absolute values of the deviations from the group means (Brown and Forsythe, 1974b).

⑥ Two additional one-way analysis of variance statistics are computed. Neither statistic assumes the equality of variances in each group. The two are:

Welch statistic:

$$W = \frac{\Sigma_i w_i(\bar{x}_i - \tilde{x})^2/(g-1)}{\left[1 + \frac{2(g-2)}{g^2 - 1}\Sigma_i(1 - w_i/u)^2/(N_i - 1)\right]}$$

where

$$w_i = N_i/s_i^2 \ , \quad u = \Sigma_i w_i \ , \quad \text{and } \tilde{x} = \Sigma w_i \bar{x}_i/u$$

When all population means are equal (even if the variances are unequal), W is approximately distributed as an F statistic with g-1 and f degrees of freedom, where f is implicitly defined as

$$1/f = (3/(g^2 - 1))\Sigma_i(1 - w_i/u)^2/(N_i - 1) \ .$$

Brown-Forsythe statistic:

$$F^* = \Sigma_i N_i(\bar{x}_i - x)^2/\Sigma_i(1 - N_i/N)s_i^2 \ .$$

Critical values are obtained from the F distribution with g-1 and f degrees of freedom where f is implicitly defined by the Satterthwaite approximation

$$\frac{1}{f} = \Sigma_i c_i^2/(N_i - 1)$$

and

$$c_i = (1 - N_i/N)s_i^2/[\Sigma_i(1 - N_i/N)s_i^2] \ .$$

When there are only two groups both F* and W reduce to the separate variance t test computed by P3D (p. 96). W and F* weight the sums of squares in the numerator differently. The two statistics are described by Brown and Forsythe (1974a).

Specifying Groups. The HISTOGRAM paragraph is required and may be repeated before the END paragraph to specify additional analyses of the same data. In the HISTOGRAM paragraph you must specify a GROUPING variable to classify the cases into groups. You may also select variables to be analyzed.

Cases are classified into groups by a GROUPING variable as in Example 7D.1. If two GROUPING variables are specified, groups are formed for each combination of the two grouping variables and a two-way ANOVA is computed as described in detail on p. 109.

If the variables used to identify groups is continuous, the GROUP paragraph is required. If the variable takes on no more than ten values (e.g., sex), the GROUP paragraph may be omitted unless you want to name the groups. The inclusion of group names makes the output much more readable.

Selecting VARIABLES to be analyzed. When you do not want to analyze all the variables, you can select the variables required by a USE statement in the VARIABLE paragraph or by a VARIABLE statement in the HISTOGRAM paragraph. When a USE statement is specified, it remains effective for all analyses of the same set of data. A VARIABLE statement in the HISTOGRAM paragraph can be altered in any additional analysis of the same set of data.

HISTogram ─────────────────────
  GROUPing = v list.   required,   none/prev.
                         one or two variables
    Names or subscripts of one or two GROUPING variables. When one GROUPING variable is specified, the cases are classified according to the GROUPING variable and a one-way ANOVA is computed. When two GROUPING variables are specified, the cases are classified simultaneously by both GROUPING variables and a two-way ANOVA is computed.
    If a GROUPING variable has more than ten distinct values, CODES or CUTPOINTS must be specified for it in the GROUP paragraph (Section 5.5).
  VARiable = v list.   all variables/prev.
    Names or subscripts of the variables to be analyzed. That is, histograms, the ANOVA and all results are computed only on the specified variables.

Output 7D.2   Two-way analysis of variance. Only the results for CHOLSTRL are shown.

```
                      ***********                                              ***********
HISTOGRAM OF * CHOLSTRL * (VARIABLE    6). CASES DIVIDED INTO GROUPS BASED ON VALUES OF * BRTHPILL * (VARIABLE    5)
                      ***********                                              * AGE      * (VARIABLE    2)
                                                                               ***********

            NOPILL        NOPILL        NOPILL        NOPILL       PILL          PILL          PILL          PILL
            25ORLESS      26 TO 35      36 TO 45      OVER 45      25ORLESS      26 TO 35      36 TO 45      OVER 45
        ..........+..........+..........+..........+..........+..........+..........+..........+
  VAR  6
EXCLUDED
VALUES
                                                        **
          TABULATIONS AND COMPUTATIONS WHICH FOLLOW EXCLUDE VALUES LISTED ABOVE
MIDPOINTS
  435.000)
  420.000)
  405.000)
  390.000)                                                                                             *
  375.000)
  360.000)
  345.000)                                                                                             *
  330.000)*                     *                                          *
  315.000)                     *             *                 *           *           *
  300.000)*                     **            *****                        **           *           *
  285.000)*                     **                            *           **           *
  270.000)***          *         **            *                                       *****          **
  255.000)          ******  M**       M****          ****       ****       M*           M***
  240.000)***       ***       ***                    *****      M*******    **           **
  225.000)M**       ***                   ***         M***       ****        **           ***
  210.000)*****     M**        ****         *          **         **         *            *
  195.000)****      *******     *           *          *****      ****        ***          *
  180.000)*         *****                              ***        **          **
  165.000)***       **          **                                *     .
  150.000)*
  135.000)
  120.000)
GROUP MEANS ARE DENOTED BY M'S IF THEY COINCIDE WITH *'S, N'S OTHERWISE

MEAN         221.654    214.767    249.095    262.471    222.625    234.500    247.571    261.647
STD.DEV.      43.265     31.865     47.226     36.690     30.853     37.179     43.411     50.146
R.E.S.D.      43.404     35.970     48.429     39.624     32.847     35.905     45.954     46.526
S. E. M.       8.485      5.818     10.306      8.899      6.298      6.788      9.473     12.162
MAXIMUM      330.000    270.000    335.000    320.000    290.000    317.000    324.000    390.000
MINIMUM      155.000    168.000    160.000    195.000    173.000    160.000    175.000    190.000
SAMPLE SIZE       26         30         21         17         24         30         21         17
```

```
        ALL GROUPS COMBINED       ******************************* ANALYSIS OF VARIANCE TABLE *******************************
  (EXCEPT CASES WITH UNUSED VALUES  *
     FOR BRTHPILL AND AGE      )    *   SOURCE            SUM OF SQUARES    DF     MEAN SQUARE    F VALUE    TAIL PROBABILITY
                                    *
MEAN           236.150             *   BRTHPILL             936.8744        1       936.8744       0.59         0.4431
STD.DEV.        42.556             *   AGE                46814.3673        3     15604.7891       9.84         0.0000
S. E. M.         3.120             *   INTERACTION         4133.9575        3      1377.9858       0.87         0.4584
MAXIMUM        390.000             *   ERROR             282289.4463      178      1585.8958
MINIMUM        155.000             *********************************************************************************************
SAMPLE SIZE        186             *   LEVENE'S TEST FOR EQUAL VARIANCES     7, 178                 0.86         0.5381
                                    *********************************************************************************************
                                    *   ONE-WAY ANALYSIS OF VARIANCE
                                    *   TEST STATISTICS FOR WITHIN-GROUP
                                    *   VARIANCES NOT ASSUMED TO BE EQUAL
                                    *      WELCH                             7,  71                 4.82         0.0002
                                    *      BROWN-FORSYTHE                    7, 140                 4.54         0.0001
```

Example 7D.2 Specifying a Two-way Analysis

A two-way ANOVA is computed when two GROUPING variables are stated. For example, if

```
/ HISTOGRAM    GROUPING IS BRTHPILL, AGE.
```

is specified the cases are classified into eight groups (2 BRTHPILL codes x 4 AGE groupings). We replace the GROUP and HISTOGRAM paragraphs of Example 7D.1 by the following paragraphs to request the two-way ANOVA.

```
------------------------------------
/ GROUP       CODES(5) ARE  1,    2.
              NAMES(5) NOPILL, PILL.
              CUTPOINTS(2) ARE 25, 35, 45.
              NAMES(2) ARE '25ORLESS', '26 TO 35,
                      '36 TO 45', 'OVER 45'.

/ HISTOGRAM   GROUPING IS BRTHPILL, AGE.
------------------------------------
```

The results for CHOLSTRL are presented in Output 7D.2. Eight groups are formed and a two-way ANOVA is computed. The levels of the first grouping variable (BRTHPILL) represent the rows and those of the second grouping variable (AGE) represent columns in the analysis of variance calculations.

The sums of squares in the one-way ANOVA are well known. The sums of squares in the two-way ANOVA depend upon the hypothesis of interest unless there are the same number of observations in each group or the rows are independent of the columns in the two-way table of group (cell) frequencies. We test hypotheses that are not dependent on the group frequencies.

Let $\mu_{ij} = E(Y_{ij})$, where Y_{ij} is an observation of the group (i,j). The test of equality of row means is the test that

$$\sum_j \mu_{ij} = \sum_j \mu_{kj} \qquad \text{for all i, k.}$$

The test of equality of column means is the test that

$$\sum_i \mu_{ij} = \sum_i \mu_{i\ell} \qquad \text{for all j, } \ell.$$

The test of no interaction is the test that

$$\mu_{ij} + \mu_{k\ell} = \mu_{i\ell} + \mu_{jk} \qquad \text{for all } i{\neq}k \text{ and } j{\neq}\ell.$$

The model can also be expressed as

$$E(Y_{ij}) = \mu + \alpha_i + \beta_j + \gamma_{ij}$$

with constraints

$$\Sigma_i \alpha_i = 0; \quad \Sigma_j \beta_j = 0; \quad \text{and} \quad \Sigma_i \gamma_{ij} = \Sigma_j \gamma_{ij} = 0.$$

The hypotheses tested are

$$\alpha_i = 0, \quad \beta_j = 0, \quad \text{and} \quad \gamma_{ij} = 0.$$

This formulation of the model and hypotheses is equivalent to the one above.

There are many different hypotheses (besides those in P7D) that could be tested, especially when cell sizes are unequal.

The hypotheses tested here are the same for equal or unequal cell size problems. In particular, the hypotheses tested are not affected by the loss of some of the cases. It should be noted that although the hypotheses tested are orthogonal, the sums of squares for unequal cell size problems are not in general orthogonal. Orthogonal sums of squares methods (or "sequential" methods) test hypotheses that are functions of cell sizes, and are not given here but are available in P4V. For more detailed discussions see Kutner (1974) and Speed and Hocking (1976). The P7D analysis is the same as Yates' (1934) weighted squares of means.

Computationally, the sums of squares that test these hypotheses can be obtained as the difference in fitting two regression models. In one model the effects corresponding to the rows, columns and interaction are fitted. In the second model the effects corresponding to row or column or interaction (whichever is being tested) are set to zero.

Example 7D.3 Requesting Correlations within Each Group and for All Data Combined

The correlations between the variables are computed when CORRELATION is specified in the PRINT paragraph. The correlations are computed for all the data combined and for the cases in each group separately. Each correlation is computed using only cases containing acceptable values for both of the variables.

The correlations are requested by using the following PRINT paragraph with the Control Language of Example 7D.1

```
------------------------------------
        / PRINT    CORRELATION.
------------------------------------
```

The correlations in Output 7D.3 are printed immediately after the histograms for CHOLSTRL. Each correlation is between the variable specified in the left-hand column and CHOLSTRL. First the correlation based on data from all groups is printed and then the correlations within each group. The correlation for all groups uses the means for the variables, not the group means. The number of cases from which the correlations are computed is printed in parentheses under the correlations.

The correlations are not printed as the usual correlation matrix. Each panel of correlations contains all possible pairings of variables with the variable presented in the histograms above.

```
PRINT ─────────────────────────────────
│ CORRelation.                      no/prev.
│    Correlations are computed between the variables
│    specified in the VARIABLE statement of the
│    HISTOGRAM paragraph for each group and for all
│    groups combined by using the data in complete
│    pairs.
```

Output 7D.3 Panel of correlations. Only the results for CHOLSTRL are shown.

```
                                 ************
        CORRELATIONS WITH VARIABLE  6 * CHOLSTRL *
                                 ************
```

(COUNTS IN PARENTHESES)

VARIABLE	ALL GROUPS	25ORLESS	26 TO 35	36 TO 45	OVER 45
2	0.3678	0.1947	-0.0221	0.1312	0.0705
AGE	(186)	(50)	(60)	(42)	(34)
3	0.0199	-0.0282	-0.1342	-0.0352	0.2606
HEIGHT	(184)	(50)	(60)	(41)	(33)
4	0.1474	0.0195	0.0299	0.1065	0.1235
WEIGHT	(184)	(50)	(59)	(42)	(33)
5	0.0758	0.0131	0.2784	-0.0172	-0.0097
BRTHPILL	(186)	(50)	(60)	(42)	(34)
7	0.0533	0.0680	0.0227	0.0320	0.3170
ALBUMIN	(184)	(50)	(60)	(41)	(33)
8	0.2515	0.3431	0.2889	0.3426	0.1462
CALCIUM	(184)	(50)	(60)	(42)	(32)
9	0.2660	0.1804	0.0643	0.4202	0.1801
URICACID	(185)	(50)	(60)	(42)	(33)

Example 7D.4 Winsorized Means and Extreme Scores

The usual formula for the mean assigns an equal weight to each observation. This estimate is known to be sensitive to outliers. Therefore in more robust estimates of the mean, extreme observations are assigned less weight than observations nearer the center. The Winsorized mean is a robust estimate. Other robust estimates are provided in P2D (Section 8.2).

The following PRINT paragraph used with the Control Language instructions of Example 7D.1 requests the Winsorized means

```
/ PRINT    WINSORIZED.
```

The results for CHOLSTRL are presented in Output 7D.4.

The Winsorized mean is similar to the arithmetic mean except that an equal number of observations, say g, in each tail are set equal to the (g+1)st observation in the tail. This is known as g-level Winsorization. Dixon and Tukey (1968) studied the Winsorized mean and its approximate standard error. The zero-level Winsorized mean is the arithmetic mean. P7D computes the g-level Winsorized means for g = 0, 1, 2, 3, 4, 5 and half-length of the 95% confidence limit. The latter is defined as

$$c_j = t_{N-2g-1} \cdot \frac{N-1}{N-2g-1} \cdot \sqrt{\frac{S_g^2}{N(N-1)}}$$

where N is the number of observations for a variable in a group, S_g^2 is the sum of squares using the

Winsorized observations, and t_k is the 97.5 percentile of the Student t statistic with k degrees of freedom.

Whenever Winsorized means are requested, the six largest values and six smallest values in each group are reported together with their case numbers and case labels (new for 1981).

The leftmost column indicates the level of Winsorization. The remaining columns contain the results for each group (identified at the top of the column). Four horizontal panels are printed. The

Output 7D.4 Winsorized means. Only the results for CHOLSTRL are shown

---

--- histograms and analyses of CHOLSTRL ---

```
                                 ************
        WINSORIZATION OF VARIABLE  6 * CHOLSTRL *
                                 ************
```

	25ORLESS	26 TO 35	36 TO 45	OVER 45
MEAN	**INDICATES THE MEAN CORRESPONDING TO THE SHORTEST CONFIDENCE INTERVAL, * TO THE NEXT SHORTEST CONFIDENCE INTERVAL			
0	222.120	224.633**	248.333**	262.059
1	221.480 *	224.567	248.309 *	260.676 *
2	221.560	224.367	248.357	260.852**
3	221.260	223.717 *	248.357	260.940
4	220.380**	223.783	249.024	259.646
5	220.280	223.117	249.143	259.499

(LENGTH OF .95 CONFIDENCE INTERVAL)/2

0	10.6448	9.23635	13.9666	15.0969
1	10.5505	9.37228	14.3935	14.5522
2	10.7526	9.45549	14.9352	14.0431
3	10.7344	9.35583	15.3759	15.0855
4	10.5060	9.70064	14.8904	14.8998
5	10.7899	9.59370	15.6736	16.1549

LARGEST VALUES IN EACH GROUP

1	330.000	317.000	335.000	390.000
2	295.000	305.000	324.000	338.000
3	290.000	295.000	320.000	320.000
4	280.000	280.000	315.000	320.000
5	266.000	280.000	306.000	306.000
6	263.000	270.000	305.000	305.000

SMALLEST VALUES IN EACH GROUP

1	155.000	160.000	160.000	190.000
2	158.000	168.000	170.000	195.000
3	165.000	172.000	175.000	216.000
4	170.000	174.000	180.000	217.000
5	173.000	175.000	196.000	220.000
6	175.000	177.000	198.000	220.000

CASE NUMBERS AND LABELS FOR LARGEST VALUES

47	494	60	152	149	1317	182	3134
53	3095	70	2830	144	2709	178	64
26	2092	78	1775	141	263	162	850
15	913	66	16	138	3312	103	63
39	649	90	1916	143	564	175	1241
23	1890	89	2098	134	1910	187	2271

CASE NUMBERS AND LABELS FOR SMALLEST VALUES

33	1068	96	2617	159	56	164	132
5	561	63	883	135	1571	177	1251
19	3035	59	1627	118	2942	173	852
25	2125	83	609	130	2153	180	1932
24	266	69	457	133	1701	186	575
32	3096	73	1255	128	523	188	39

---

uppermost contains the Winsorized means, the second, the half-length of the 95% confidence interval, the third, the six largest values in the group, and the last, the six smallest values in the group. The mean corresponding to the shortest confidence interval in each group is indicated by ** and the mean corresponding to the next shortest is indicated by *.

```
 PRINT ─────────────────────────────────────
│ WINSORized.                        no/prev.
│   The g-level Winsorized means for g = 0, 1, ...,
│   5 are printed; also the half-lengths of the 95%
│   confidence  intervals  and  the  maximum  and
│   minimum observations after Winsorization.
 ──────────────────────────────────────────
```

Output 7D.5 Diagnostic plots. Only the results for CHOLSTRL are shown
----

```
              ************                           ************
HISTOGRAM OF * CHOLSTRL * (VARIABLE    6). CASES DIVIDED INTO GROUPS BASED ON VALUES OF * AGE     * (VARIABLE    2)
              ************                           ************
```

--- the results in Output 7D.1 are printed here ---

DIAGNOSTIC PLOTS TO DETERMINE WHETHER THERE IS A RELATIONSHIP BETWEEN CELL MEANS AND CELL STANDARD DEVIATIONS. FOR THE USE OF THE REGRESSION OF LOG CELL STANDARD DEVIATION ON LOG CELL MEAN WHEN SELECTING A TRANSFORMATION SEE BOX AND COX, 'AN ANALYSIS OF TRANSFORMATIONS,' J. ROYAL. STATIST. SOC. B 26 (1964), PP. 211-252.
THE VERTICAL AXES REPRESENT THE ESTIMATES OF THE STANDARD DEVIATION BASED ON THE MEAN DEVIATIONS FROM THE GROUP MEAN AND ITS NATURAL LOG. THE HORIZONTAL AXES REPRESENT THE GROUP MEAN AND ITS NATURAL LOG. THE LOGARITHMIC PLOT IS NOT MADE WHEN LOGARITHMS CANNOT BE EVALUATED.

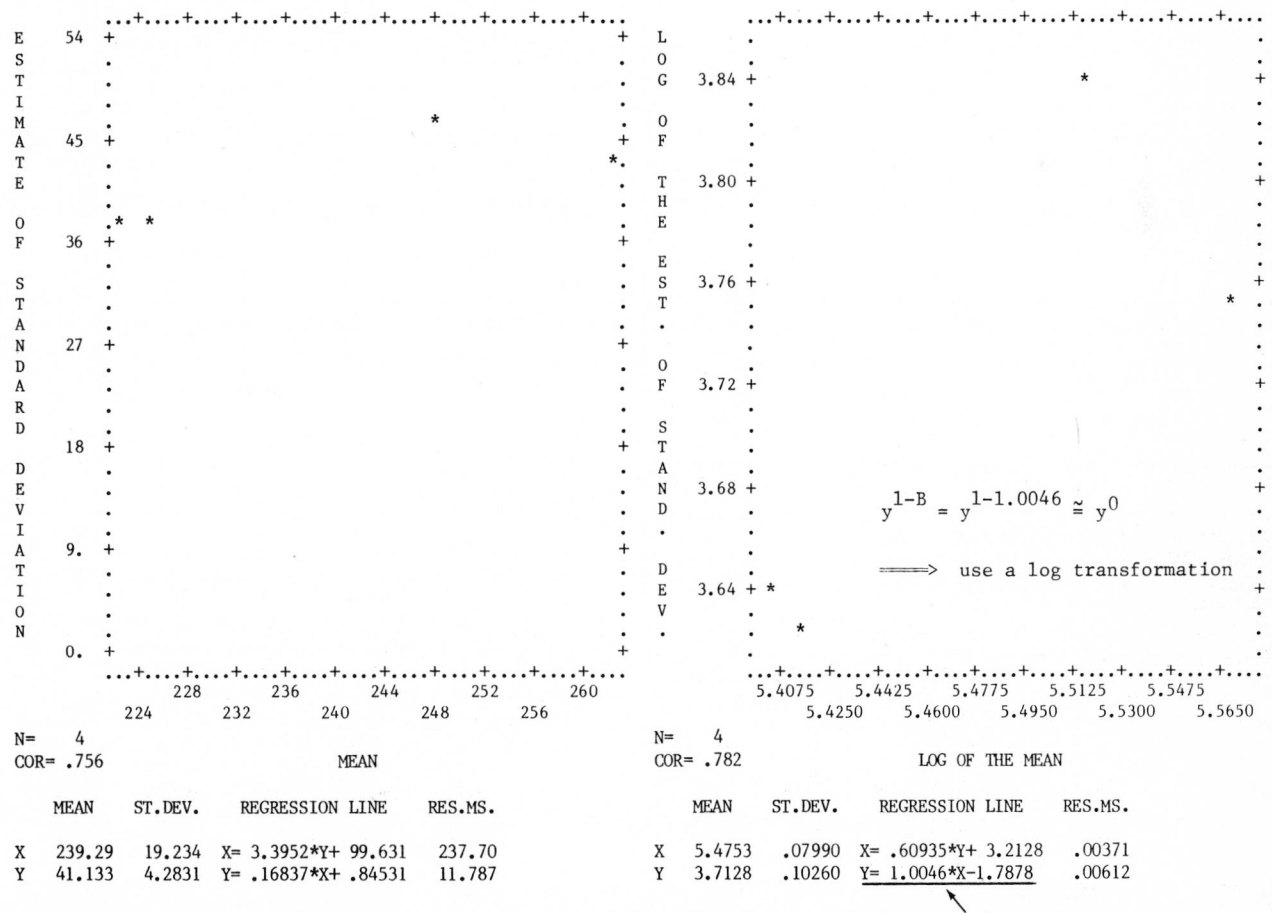

$$y^{1-B} = y^{1-1.0046} \cong y^0$$

$\implies$ use a log transformation

	MEAN	ST.DEV.	REGRESSION LINE	RES.MS.			MEAN	ST.DEV.	REGRESSION LINE	RES.MS.
X	239.29	19.234	X= 3.3952*Y+ 99.631	237.70		X	5.4753	.07990	X= .60935*Y+ 3.2128	.00371
Y	41.133	4.2831	Y= .16837*X+ .84531	11.787		Y	3.7128	.10260	Y= 1.0046*X-1.7878	.00612

N= 4 COR= .756 MEAN
N= 4 COR= .782 LOG OF THE MEAN

Example 7D.5 Plots of Means versus Standard Deviations (new in 1981)

To illustrate this option we add the following PRINT paragraph to the Control Language of Example 7D.1

```
-------------------------------------
          / PRINT     PLOT.
-------------------------------------
```

The output is shown in Output 7D.5.

One of the assumptions for the standard analysis of variance is that the variances in each cell are equal, procedures such as Brown-Forsythe and Welch can be used when the assumption is not met. However, unequal variances are often accompanied by skewness in the distribution within each cell. When this occurs, it may be desirable to transform the data; e.g., to analyze the logarithm, square root, or reciprocal of each observation. To assist in selecting an appropriate transformation, we can examine the histograms for skewness. We can also request a plot of the cell standard deviations (y-axis) versus the cell means (x-axis) and a second plot of the same quantities on a logarithmic scale. If there is a relationship between the means and the standard deviations a suggested transformation to obtain approximately equal variances can be obtained from the regression of the logarithm of cell standard deviations on the logarithm of the cell means. Let b denote the regression coefficient, then a suggested transformation is to raise the dependent variable to the power 1-b with zero representing the logarithm. Examples of the correspondence are:

b	transform
2	reciprocal
1	logarithm
$\frac{1}{2}$	square root
0	none

Note that the regression coefficient should only be used as an approximate indicator; e.g., if b = .45, use b = .5 . It would be better to consider that b = .5 and investigate the square root transformation.

Sometimes unequal variances indicate the presence of outliers. Ordinary sample variances and standard deviations are quite sensitive to outliers so in making these plots we use estimates of standard deviations that are based on the mean absolute deviations from cell means rather than the squared deviations. The estimated standard deviation is obtained by multiplying the mean deviation by the square root of $2(n-1)n$ where n is the sample size (Pearson and Hartley, p. 41).

```
PRINT ─────────────────────────────────
  PLOT.                              no/prev.
    Request to print plot of cell means versus
    standard deviations.
  SIZE = #, #.                       50,35/prev.
    Number of characters for plot width and height.
```

Pairwise t Tests (new in 1981)

t tests between every pair of groups can be requested. To adjust for the fact that a large number of tests is made, these tests are accompanied by Bonferroni probabilities. Both pooled (ordinary) t tests and separate variance (Welch) tests are reported.

```
PRINT ─────────────────────────────────
  TTEST.                             no/prev.
    Request for pairwise t-tests.
```

Scaling the Histograms

Unless otherwise specified, the histograms are scaled to an INCREMENT (step size) of

$$\frac{\text{maximum value} - \text{minimum value}}{\text{no. of intervals}}$$

where the number of INTERVALS is the smaller of 30 and $10 \log_{10}$ (number of cases read). If the data are single digit data (e.g., the integers 0 to 9), the scale of the histograms can be improved by setting the INCREMENTS for the single digit variables to one. Similarly, the scale of histograms for data with a few equally spaced values is improved by specifying the increment. The maximum number of intervals is 30.

```
HISTogram ─────────────────────────────
  INCRement = # list.   one per      max. - min.
                        variable     # of intervals
    The difference between the points on the base
    of the histogram is set to INCREMENT. The first
    number is the INCREMENT for the first variable,
    etc.
  INTERval =         one per variable     zero/prev.
    # list.
    The maximum number of intervals in each
    histogram. If zero, INTERVAL is the smaller of
    30 and $10 \log_{10}$ (no. of cases). If both
    INCREMENT and INTERVAL are specified for a
    variable, INCREMENT is used if it does not
    yield more intervals than specified by
    INTERVAL; otherwise INCREMENT is computed from
    INTERVAL.
```

Listing and Sorting the Data

The data for variables specified in the USE statement of the VARIABLE paragraph can be listed in the same order as read by specifying DATA in the PRINT paragraph. The data can also be listed after the cases are ordered (or sorted) according to the GROUPING variable by specifying ORDER in the PRINT paragraph. When there are two grouping variables, the primary sort is on the first grouping variable.

The Control Language instructions to specify both these options require the addition of the following PRINT paragraph to the Control Language of Example 7D.1.

```
/ PRINT    DATA.
           ORDER.
```

This will call for the data to be listed first in the order in which the data are read. The second listing will be ordered according to the GROUPING variable AGE. Program P1D has more extensive sorting and listing features.

```
PRINT ─────────────────────────────────────────
  DATA.                                      no/prev.
    Print the input data in the order they are read
    into the computer.
  ORDER.                                     no/prev.
    Print the input data after reordering according
    to the GROUPING variable.
```

FORTRAN Interface (new in 1981)

The capabilities in this section are for the more experienced user. You can define contrasts or your own statistic in terms of cell means, standard deviations, and sample sizes in a FORTRAN subroutine, P7DFUN. FORTRAN statements may be used to write cell descriptive information to a file for use in reports or analysis in other programs. The FORTRAN subroutine is interfaced with P7D by way of the BIMEDT procedure similar to the way your own FORTRAN statements can be used to define transformations.

As an illustration of the FORTRAN interface we evaluate a linear contrast across the means of the four age groups shown in Example 7D.1. The BMDP instructions and output are identical to Example 7D.1 except we use the BIMEDT procedure and add FORTRAN code that produces three extra lines of output containing the contrast results. The contrast coefficients are selected to test for linear trend across equally spaced groups: the vector V, of coefficients is

$$V(I) = (-3, -1, 1, 3).$$

Many text books describe the use of contrasts including Dixon and Massey (page 284).

The value of the contrast is $C = \Sigma V_i \bar{X}_i$ and the single degree of freedom sum of squares is

$$\text{sum of squares} = \frac{C^2}{\Sigma \dfrac{V_i^2}{n_i}}.$$

An F ratio results when this sum of squares is divided by the error mean square (EMS). We evaluate the significance of the F statistic by using the subroutine FTAIL to compute the p value. Alternatively we could print only the F statistic and check for significance in standard tables. The FORTRAN statements for this example are:

```
C=========================================================
C       CONTRAST EVALUATION FOR LINEAR TREND
C       V(I) = VECTOR OF CONTRAST COEFFICIENTS
C=========================================================
C
      V(1) = -3.
      V(2) = -1.
      V(3) =  1.
      V(4) =  3.
C     WRITE HEADING AND INITIALIZE VARIABLES
      WRITE (6, 100) INDV, DVNAME
100   FORMAT ('1 LINEAR TREND FOR VARIABLE ', I2,
     *          1X, A8)
      C  = 0.
      CS = 0.
      TSS= 0.
      T  = 0.
C     EVALUATE CONTRAST C, SQUARED WEIGHTS CS,
C          TOTAL N, AND WITHIN SUM OF SQUARES TSS
      DO 10 I=1, NGRP
        C = C + V(I) * GMEAN(I)
        CS = CS + V(I) + V(I)/SIZE(I)
        T = T + SIZE(I)
      TSS = TSS + SS(I)
10    CONTINUE
C     CALCULATE CONTRAST SUM OF SQUARES (SM),
C     DEGREES OF FREEDOM (NDF), MEAN SQUARE (EMS),
C     WITHIN GROUPS F RATIO (F) AND
C     THE TAIL PROBABILITY P
      SM = C * C/CS
      NDF = T - FLOAT(NGRP)
      EMS = TSS/FLOAT(NDF)
      F = SM / EMS
      P = FTAIL(F,1,NDF)
C     PRINT RESULTS
      WRITE (6, 200)
200   FORMAT (16HDCONTRAST VALUE, 10X, 7HF VALUE,
     *           10X, 6HTAIL D)
      WRITE (6, 300) C, F, P
300   FORMAT (F10.3, 14X, F10.3, 5X, F10.5)
C     THIS IS THE END OF THE FORTRAN CODE
```

The three lines of output that result from this subroutine are

```
LINEAR TREND FOR VARIABLE  6 CHOLSTRL
CONTRAST VALUE          F VALUE          TAIL P
   143.517              26.811          0.00000
```

This FORTRAN "handle" into P7D can be used for many other computations. The experienced user could graph confidence intervals for each group, print Bayesian estimates of group statistics one line per variable, perform isotonic regression, etc.

We now describe the arguments and parameters available in subroutine P7DFUN. The subroutine is called once for each variable in each HISTOGRAM paragraph; i.e., it is called once for each set of histograms. The calling sequence of P7DFUN is

```
SUBROUTINE P7DFUN(INDV,DVNAME,NGRP,GMEAN,SIZE,SS,
*    U, V, W, X, GNAME, VNAME, INDEX, GMEAN2,
*    SIZ2, SS2, GNAM1, GNAM2, VNAM1, VNAM2, INDX1,
*    INDX2, NR, NC)
DIMENSION GMEAN(NGRP),SIZE(NGRP),SS(NGRP),U(NGRP),
*    V(NGRP),W(NGRP),X(NGRP),GMEAN2(NR,NC),
```

```
*       SIZ2(NR,NC),SS2(NR,NC),GNAME(NGRP),
*       GNAM1(NR,NC), GNAM2(NR,NC)
 DOUBLE PRECISION GNAME,VNAME,GNAM1,GNAM2,VNAM1,
*       VNAM2,DVNAME
 DOUBLE PRECISION GMEAN,SS,U,V,W,X,GMEAN2,SS2
```

The arguments of P7DFUN are defined as follows:

```
   INDV    - index of the dependent variable
   DVNAME  - name of the dependent variable
   U       - Scratch vector
   V       - Scratch vector
   W       - Scratch vector
   X       - Scratch vector
```

Use the following parameters when a one-way ANOVA is requested

```
   NGRP    - Number of groups
   GMEAN   - Vector of group means
   SIZE    - Vector of sample sizes
   SS      - Vector of group sum of squares
   GNAME   - Vector of group names
   VNAME   - Name of the grouping variable
   INDEX   - Index of the grouping variable
```

If a two-way ANOVA is requested and no empty cells result the following parameters should be used

```
   NR      - Number of levels of the second
             variable
   NC      - Number of levels of the first grouping
             variable

   GMEAN2  - Matrix of group means
   SIZ2    - Matrix of sample sizes
   SS2     - Matrix of sums of squares

   GNAM1   - Matrix of group names of the first
             grouping variable
```

```
   GNAM2   - Group names of the second grouping
             variable
   VNAM1   - Name of the first grouping variable
   VNAM2   - Name of the second grouping variable
   INDX1   - Index of the first grouping variable
   INDX2   - Index of the second grouping variable
```

The SUBROUTINE, DIMENSION, and DOUBLE PRECISION statements above are automatically provided by the BIMEDT procedure. The BIMEDT procedure also automatically provides RETURN and END statements just as it provides RETURN and END statements after your FORTRAN transformations.

SIZE OF PROBLEM

Unlike most BMDP programs, P7D keeps the data in computer memory. The number of cases (C) that it can analyze depends on the number of variables (V). The following table provides a guide for large computer systems:

V	2	3	4	5	10	20	50
C	4700	3500	2800	2350	1250	670	275

Appendix B describes how the capacity of the program can be increased.

COMPUTATIONAL METHOD

Means, standard deviations and covariances are computed in single precision using the method of provisional means (Appendix A.2).

ACKNOWLEDGEMENT

P7D was programmed by Paul Sampson. Later revisions were made by Peter Mundle and James Frane. P7D supersedes BMD07D whose design was proposed by W.J. Dixon.

SUMMARY

A. Order of Input Cards for BIMED procedure

```
// (job card)
// EXEC BIMED,PROG=BMDP7D        (see Appendix E)
//SYSIN DD *
/ PROBLEM
/ INPUT
/ VARIABLE
/ GROUP
/ TRANSFORM
/ SAVE
/ HISTOGRAM      repeat for subproblems
/ PRINT
/ END
     (data, if on cards)
// (system card)
```

B. Order of Input Cards for BIMEDT procedure

```
// (job card)
// EXEC BIMEDT,PROG=BMDP7D        (see Appendix E)
//TRANSF  DD  *
     (user's FORTRAN statements)
//GO.SYSIN  DD  *
/ PROBLEM
/ INPUT
/ VARIABLE
/ GROUP
/ TRANSFORM
/ SAVE
/ HISTOGRAM      repeat for subproblems
/ PRINT
/ END
     (data, if on cards)
// (system card)
```

Full sets of BMDP paragraphs (and data, if on cards) can be repeated for additional problems; see Section 5.8.

instructions specific to P7D

Paragraph Statement	Preassigned	Comment and Manual Reference
/●HISTogram		Required. Specifies variables to group cases and variables to be analyzed (may be repeated).
●GROUPing = v. or v,v.	none	Name(s) or subscript(s) of variable(s) used to classify cases into groups. (See also / GROUP.) One grouping variable specifies a one-way ANOVA; two, a two-way ANOVA. **Cell sizes may be unequal.** * 107
VARiable = v list.	all	Names or subscripts of variables to be analyzed (histograms, ANOVA, etc.). * 107
INCRement = # list. ⎤ INTERvals = # list. ⎦	(see comment)	Two options to control the size and number of histogram intervals. If omitted, the program determines the distance between midpoints in the histogram (INCR) and the number of intervals (INTER) based on the number of cases and the data range for each variable. To override these values, specify a list of values corresponding to the VARIABLE statement above. * 112
/ PRINT		Optional to print additional summary statistics for each group and for all groups combined.
CORRelation.	no	Correlation between each variable in the VARIABLE statement and each ANOVA variable. These are product moment correlations on complete pairs. * 109
WINSORized.	no	Robust means and diagnostic information. * 111
DATA.	no	Data in the order they are read into the computer. * 113
ORDER.	no	Data after reordering according to the GROUPING variable. (See P1D) * 113
TTEST.	no	Pairwise t tests of group means and multiple comparison significance level. * 112
PLOT.	no	Diagnostic plot of standard deviations versus means. This is useful for the selection of transformations. * 112
SIZE = #, #.	50,35	Width of x-axis (characters); height of y-axis (lines) for plot. * 112

/ -indicates paragraph	* -assigned value remains the same for additional problems
. -period ends a sentence	
● -required	VT -number of variables after transformations
v -variable (name or subscript)	list -more than one item, often one per var.
g -group (name or subscript)	
# -number	Capitalized letters-paragraph or sentence names recognized by BMDP
'c' -characters (name or parameter) may omit apostrophes if contiguous letters only	Page numbers following refer to this Manual

P9D

9.3 Multiway Description of Groups

Laszlo Engelman

ABSTRACT

P9D analyzes data for each variable in any number of groups; the groups can be defined as all combinations of the levels of several variables. Univariate statistics are provided for each group. A one-way ANOVA is computed to test the equality of the means of all the groups. To test for homogeneity (equality) of variances, Bartlett's statistic is evaluated. P9D also tests for the equality of group frequencies. A plot that shows the shift in means from group to group is an option.

P9D is useful as a screening aid for analysis of variance factorial designs and repeated measures designs. Cell standard deviations are printed in vertical columns making it easy to scan for extreme values and the plots of cell means are useful for observing trends in main effects and interactions.

WHERE TO FIND IT

Example 9D.1 Basic Setup for Multiway Description of Groups

We analyze the Werner blood chemistry data (Table 5.1). We classify the cases both by the age of the woman and by whether or not she is on the pill. Except for the TABULATE paragraph, the BMDP instructions in Example 9D.1 are described in Chapter 5. Compare these BMDP instructions with those for Example 7D.2.

```
/ PROBLEM    TITLE IS 'WERNER BLOOD CHEMISTRY DATA'.
/ INPUT      VARIABLES ARE 9.
             FORMAT IS '(A4, 5F4.0, 3F4.1)'.
/ VARIABLE   NAMES ARE ID, AGE, HEIGHT, WEIGHT,
                       BRTHPILL, CHOLSTRL, ALBUMIN,
                       CALCIUM, URICACID.
             MAXIMUM IS (6)400.
             MINIMUM IS (6)150.
             LABEL IS ID.

/ GROUP      CODES(5) ARE       1,    2.
             NAMES(5) ARE NOPILL, PILL.
             CUTPOINTS(2) ARE 25, 35, 45.
             NAMES(2) ARE '25ORLESS', '26 TO 35',
                          '36 TO 45', 'OVER 45'.

/ TABULATE   GROUPING ARE AGE, BRTHPILL.
             VARIABLES ARE CHOLSTRL, URICACID.
             PLOTMEANS.

/ END
```

(See end of this P9D section for organization of systems information, BMDP instructions and data.)

The results of the above analysis are shown in Output 9D.1. Circled numbers below correspond to those in the output.

① P9D analyzes data in cells formed by all possible combinations of the GROUPING variables specified in the TABULATE paragraph. In our example AGE (4 intervals) and BRTHPILL (2 codes) are the GROUPING variables. The eight possible combinations of these two variables are listed. For example, cell 4 is OVER45 and NOPILL. The cell numbers are used to identify the eight combinations in the results.

② For each cell (identified in ①), P9D prints

- the frequency of acceptable data in the ith cell: N_i

- the mean: $\bar{x}_i = \Sigma_j x_{ij}/N_i$
  where x_{ij} is the jth observation in the ith cell

- the standard deviation: $s_i = \{\Sigma_j (x_{ij} - \bar{x}_i)^2/(N_i-1)\}^{\frac{1}{2}}$

P9D can print descriptive panels for four variables across each page. When more than four variables are requested, P9D completes the description of the first four before starting the next set of four variables.

③ The data in the cells are compared by

- a χ^2 test of the equality of cell frequencies; i.e.,

$$\text{CHI-SQUARE} = \Sigma_i (N_i - \bar{N})^2/\bar{N}$$

where $\bar{N} = \Sigma N_i/g$ and g is the number of groups

$$\text{D.F.} = g - 1$$

$$\text{PROB(CHI-SQ)} = \text{probability of exceeding this } \chi^2$$

- a test of the equality of group means; i.e., a one-way analysis of variance. The components are

Output 9D.1 An analysis by descriptive statistics and plot of cell means by P9D using cells formed from all combinations of two grouping variables. Circled numbers correspond to those in the text

---

CELL DEFINITIONS
FOR INDEXING VARIABLES WITH CUTPOINTS 'VALUE' IS THE INCLUSIVE UPPER LIMIT OF THE INTERVAL.

CELL NUMBER	AGE 2	BRTHPILL 5
1	25 OR LESS	NOPILL
2	26 TO 35	NOPILL
3	36 TO 45	NOPILL
4	OVER 45	NOPILL
5	25 OR LESS	PILL
6	26 TO 35	PILL
7	36 TO 45	PILL
8	OVER 45	PILL

①

DESCRIPTIVE STATISTICS FOR NON-EMPTY CELLS

CELL NUMBER	VARIABLE 6 CHOLSTRL FREQ.	MEAN	STD.DEV.	VARIABLE 9 URICACID FREQ.	MEAN	STD.DEV.
1	26.	221.65384	43.2647	26.	4.51153	0.9488
2	30.	214.76666	31.8647	30.	4.66666	0.9897
3	21.	249.09523	47.2259	21.	4.81904	0.8835
4	17.	262.47046	36.6898	16.	5.15624	1.3574
5	24.	222.62500	30.8528	26.	4.73461	1.1164
6	30.	234.50000	37.1787	30.	4.59333	1.1274
7	21.	247.57143	43.4115	21.	4.65714	1.5416
8	17.	261.64697	50.1460	17.	5.43529	1.2777

②

EQUALITY OF CELL FREQ.	CHI-SQUARE	8.06451	8.89305
	D.F.	7.	7.
	PROB.(CHI-SQ)	0.3269	0.2604

WITHIN	SUM OF SQUARES	282288.93750	235.83162
	D.F.	178.	179.
	MEAN SQUARE	1585.89282	1.31749

BETWEEN	SUM OF SQUARES	52740.32031	13.25559
	D.F.	7.	7.
	MEAN SQUARE	7534.32813	1.89365

③

EQUALITY OF MEANS	F-VALUE	4.75084	1.43731
	D.F.'S	7. 178.	7. 179.
	PROB.(F)	0.0001	0.1929

HOMOG. OF VARIANCE	BARTLETT TEST	9.48999	10.75478
	APPROX. F	1.33224	1.50981
	D.F.'S	7. 28708.	7. 28597.
	PROB.(F)	0.2301	0.1586

GROUPED DISTRIBUTIONS OF VARIABLES
IN THE GRAPHS BELOW POSITIONS ARE DETERMINED BY CELL MEAN VALUES, CHARACTERS INDICATE CELL FREQUENCIES.
WHEN POSITIONS COINCIDE FREQUENCIES ARE SUMMED.

	VARIABLE 6 CHOLSTRL	VARIABLE 9 URICACID
MEAN	236.1505	4.7706
ST.DV.	42.555	1.157

④

```
CELL  *-  S   S   M   S   S   +**-  S   S   M   S   S   +*
  1   * )         B              ( ** )         B              ( *
  2   * )           C            ( ** )           C            ( *     NOPILL
  3   * )             B          ( ** )             B          ( *
  4   * )               A        ( ** )               A        ( *
  5   * )         B              ( ** )         B              ( *
  6   * )           C            ( ** )           C            ( *     PILL
  7   * )             B          ( ** )             B          ( *
  8   * )               A        ( ** )               A        ( *
```

$$\text{WITHIN SUM OF SQUARES} = \Sigma_i \Sigma_j (x_{ij} - \bar{x}_i)^2$$

$$\text{D.F.} = \Sigma_i (N_i - 1)$$

$$\text{WITHIN MEAN SQUARE} = \text{within sum of squares/D.F.}$$

$$\text{BETWEEN SUM OF SQUARES} = \Sigma_i N_i (\bar{x}_i - \bar{x})^2$$

$$\text{where } \bar{x} = \Sigma N_i \bar{x}_i / \Sigma N_i$$

$$\text{D.F.} = g - 1, \quad \text{where g is the number of nonempty groups}$$

$$\text{MEAN SQUARE} = \text{between sum of squares/D.F.}$$

$$\text{F-VALUE} = \text{between mean square/ within mean square}$$

$$\text{D.F.'S} = (g - 1), \quad \Sigma(N_i - 1)$$

$$\text{PROB(F)} = \text{probability of exceeding this F}$$

The computation of PROB(F) assumes that the data are sampled from normal populations with equal variances. When the samples sizes (N_i) of the cells and the population variances are not equal, the distribution of F can be strongly affected and the PROB(F) may not be meaningful. In this case the Welch or Brown-Forsythe statistics in P7D (Section 9.2) or a transformation of the data should be considered.

The F value (analysis of variance) is a test of the equality of group means. When the groups are ordered (as in this example), you may want to test contrasts on the group means, such as a linear trend. Both contrasts and covariates can be used in P1V (Chapter 15).

- Barlett's test of equality (homogeneity) of variances for groups with nonzero variances. Its formula is in Appendix A.4. The significance of Bartlett's test, PROB(F), is evaluated using Box's approximation (Dixon and Massey, 1969, p. 308). The test is sensitive to the assumption of normality and may improperly reject the null hypothesis too often when the distribution of the data is nonnormal. P7D computes Levene's test, which is less sensitive to the assumption of normality.

④ The means of the cells are plotted relative to the overall mean in a compact plot when PLOTMEAN is specified in the TABULATE paragraph.

There are two plots (one for CHOLSTRL and one for URICACID). The vertical scale is the cell identification number. The horizontal axis contains an M for the overall mean and S's that represent differences in one standard deviation along the horizontal axis: the width of each display is scaled to represent ± 2.5 standard deviations from the overall mean. The letters in the graph are codes for the number of observations in the cell (see definition below). The letters are plotted at the position of the mean of the cell.

We have drawn a horizontal line between the means for cell 4 and cell 5 in Output 9D.1. The means (for the four age groups) of CHOLSTRL for the NOPILL women are above the line, those for the PILL women below the line. Within each pill group we see that the means for the younger groups (cells 1, 2, 5 and 6) tend to be average (the M at the top of the display) or below, while the means for the older groups (cells 3, 4, 7 and 8) are above average. The means tend to increase linearly with age especially in the pill group. We scan this display for effects to test later in a formal manner.

The <u>TABULATE paragraph</u> is required and can be repeated (together with an END paragraph) for additional analyses. If repeated, it must be placed <u>after</u> the data (if on cards). The order of input in the summary (p. 122) shows where to place the paragraph.

The TABULATE paragraph is used to specify the GROUPING variables used to classify the cases, the VARIABLES analyzed, MARGINAL subsets of the cells studied, and to state whether the means are plotted (PLOTMEAN).

TABULate ─────────────────────────────
GROUPing = v list.   required   non/prev.
Names or subscripts of the variables used to classify the cases into groups (cells) for the analysis. The cells are formed from all possible combinations of the levels of the v list; the levels for each variable are the intervals or codes assigned in the GROUP paragraph. The order in which the variables are listed is important: the levels of the first variable change the fastest, the levels of the last variable the slowest.
If a GROUPING variable has more than ten distinct values, CODES or CUTPOINTS must be specified for it in the GROUP paragraph (Section 5.5).
VARiable = v list.   all variables
Names or subscripts of the variables to be analyzed. If not specified, all variables except the GROUPING variables are analyzed.
PLOTmeans.   no/prev.
Plots of the means for each group. Each group is represented in a plot by its frequency plotted at its group mean. Blank indicates zero frequency. Single digit frequencies are read directly. The following symbols are used for other frequencies.

Symbol	Freq.	Symbol	Freq.
A	10–19	J	100–199
B	20–29	K	200–299
C	30–39	L	300–399
D	40–49	M	400–499
E	50–59	N	500–599
F	60–69	O	600–699
G	70–79	P	700–799
H	80–89	Q	800–899
I	90–99	R	900–999
		S	≥ 1000

Example 9D.2 Analysis of Marginal Data

We can request the same results as in Example 9D.1 for marginal subsets of the cells -- such as AGE groupings only, or BRTHPILL codes only.

We replace the TABULATE paragraph of Example 9D.1 by the following to demonstrate this option

```
-------------------------------------
/ TABULATE   GROUPING ARE AGE, BRTHPILL.
            VARIABLES ARE CHOLSTRL, URICACID.
            MARGINS ARE 'AB', 'A.', '.B', '..'.
            PLOTMEANS.
-------------------------------------
```

Output 9D.2 Analysis of marginal subsets of the cells

```
                         --- the results in Output 9D.1 appear here ---


     CELL DEFINITIONS FOR MARGINALS OVER INDICES INDICATED BY POINTS IN  'A.'
     FOR INDEXING VARIABLES WITH CUTPOINTS 'VALUE' IS THE INCLUSIVE UPPER LIMIT OF THE INTERVAL.

                              ALL
          CELL     AGE        BRTHPILL
          NUMBER    2          5
            1     25 ORLESS
            2     26 TO 35
            3     36 TO 45
            4     OVER 45


     DESCRIPTIVE STATISTICS FOR NON-EMPTY CELLS OF   'A.'


         CELL     VARIABLE   6 CHOLSTRL        VARIABLE   9 URICACID
         NUMBER  FREQ.    MEAN    STD.DEV.    FREQ.    MEAN    STD.DEV.

           1     50.   222.12000  37.4442    52.    4.62307   1.0320
           2     60.   224.63333  35.7420    60.    4.62999   1.0524
           3     42.   248.33333  44.8089    42.    4.73809   1.2437
           4     34.   262.05859  43.2673    33.    5.29999   1.3038


     EQUALITY    CHI-SQUARE     7.97849              8.87165
     OF CELL        D.F.        3.                   3.
     FREQ.     PROB.(CHI-SQ)    0.0465               0.0310


     WITHIN   SUM OF SQUARES  288172.06250          237.47621
                   D.F.        182.                 183.
                MEAN SQUARE   1583.36279              1.29768

     BETWEEN  SUM OF SQUARES   46857.34766           11.61095
                   D.F.        3.                    3.
                MEAN SQUARE   15619.11328             3.87031

     EQUALITY     F-VALUE        9.86452              2.98248
     OF MEANS     D.F.'S       3.  182.             3.   183.
                  PROB.(F)      0.0000               0.0327


     HOMOG.    BARTLETT TEST    3.35889              3.58682
       OF       APPROX. F       1.10897              1.18421
     VARIANCE    D.F.'S       3. 54058.            3. 53838.
                 PROB.(F)       0.3439               0.3140


     GROUPED DISTRIBUTIONS OF VARIABLES AT CELLS OF 'A.'
     IN THE GRAPHS BELOW POSITIONS ARE DETERMINED BY CELL MEAN VALUES, CHARACTERS INDICATE CELL FREQUENCIES.
     WHEN POSITIONS COINCIDE FREQUENCIES ARE SUMMED.

                     VARIABLE   6 CHOLSTRL        VARIABLE   9 URICACID
          MEAN            236.1505                   4.7706
          ST.DV.           42.555                    1.157

          CELL  *-  S   S   M   S   S  +**-  S   S   M   S   S  +*
            1   * )          E           ( ** )         BB         ( *
            2   * )        C  C          ( ** )         CC         ( *
            3   * )             BB       ( ** )         D          ( *
            4   * )            C         ( ** )          AA        ( *


                    --- results for '.B' and '..' appear here ---
```

The results are shown in Output 9D.2. The results corresponding to 'AB' are a repetition of Output 9D.1. Output 9D.2 shows results for 'A.'. The results for the other two marginals are omitted. The results for 'A.' classify the data <u>only</u> by AGE before doing the statistical analysis. However, the means for <u>all</u> eight AGE by BRTHPILL groups are used for the plots; for each age group, the means for the PILL and NOPILL women are plotted on the same line. If two cell means coincide in their plotting position, the letter printed corresponds to the total frequency of the two groups. (The plots for '.B' contain four cell means on each line.)

<u>How to specify marginal subsets.</u> Marginal subsets are specified as follows: when there are two GROUPING variables, the statement

MARGIN = 'AB', 'A.', '.B', '..'.

specifies

'AB'   two letters. <u>All</u> possible combinations of the two GROUPING variables are used (this is the preassigned value if MARGIN is not specified)

'A.'   a letter in the first position and a period in the second. A period is interpreted as "average over." Therefore classification is by the first GROUPING variable only

'.B'   a period in the first position and a letter in the second. Classification is by the <u>second</u> GROUPING variable only

'..'   two periods. There is no GROUPING variable by which to classify cases. Only one cell is formed

The number of letters and periods between the apostrophes must be the same as the number of GROUPING variables. The position of the letters and periods between the apostrophes instructs P9D to classify by GROUPING variable according to the positions. Therefore MARGIN IS 'X..Y.Z'. specifies that all three-way combinations (marginals) of the first, fourth and sixth GROUPING variables are to be used, that is, cells are formed by all combinations of the levels of variables X, Y and Z. A mean and a standard deviation is computed for each cell. In the plot of the cell means, one print line is used for each mean; the values of the means from the original six-way combinations are plotted on the lines for the combinations of X, Y and X. To obtain a plot of the means for only the combinations of X, Y and Z specify a new TABULATE paragraph with GROUPING IS X, Y, Z.

```
TABULate ─────────────────────────────
  MARGIN = 'c' list.      cells as defined by all
                          GROUPING variables
  Each 'c' represents a marginal subset of cells
  to be analyzed. The number of characters
  including periods in each 'c' must be equal to
  the number of variables in the GROUPING
  statement. A period in place of a character
  means "averaged over."
```

Organizing the Data for Screening a Repeated Measures ANOVA.

The plot of the cell means can be used to study changes across the levels of a repeated measures factor and also to highlight differences between grouping factors. If the data are organized for analysis in program P2V they may need to be reorganized for screening and plotting programs.

For this discussion we use data for weight (W), temperature (T) and blood pressure (BP) recorded for patients at two different hospitals. Each subject was measured on three different days. Program P2V uses data organized as in Figure 9a.

ID	HOSPITAL		DAY 1 W T BP	DAY 2 W T BP	DAY 3 W T BP
1	1		- - -	- - -	- - -
2	1		- - -	- - -	- - -
3	1		- - -	- - -	- - -
4	1		- - -	- - -	- - -
5	1		- - -	- - -	- - -
6	1		- - -	- - -	- - -
1	2		- - -	- - -	- - -
2	2		- - -	- - -	- - -
3	2		- - -	- - -	- - -
4	2		- - -	- - -	- - -
5	2		- - -	- - -	- - -
6	2		- - -	- - -	- - -

Figure 9a

Each line in Figure 9a is the record for one subject with a patient ID number and a code for hospital followed by the values of weight, temperature and blood pressure measured on each of three days.

Program P9D and other screening programs require that the data for each level of the repeated measures factor be placed in a different record as shown in Figure 9b. Note that one additional variable is added to indicate the day - i.e., the level of the factor with repeated measures. The first three lines in Figure 9b contain the same data

ID	HOSPITAL	DAY	WT T BP
1	1	1	- - -
2	1	1	- - -
2	1	2	- - -
2	1	3	- - -
.		.	
.		.	
.		.	
6	2	1	- - -
6	2	2	- - -
6	2	3	- - -

Figure 9b

as the first line in Figure 9a; the last three lines in Figure 9b correspond to the last line in Figure 9a.

The user can change data recorded like those in Figure 9a to the structure shown in Figure 9b by reading the raw data using a FORMAT statement and the MULT instruction in the INPUT paragraph (first available in the 1981 BMDP release). (MULT is not available for other forms of input.) In this example we read three cases from each record shown in Figure 9a (one case for each day). For each day we reread the grouping information (ID and HOSPITAL in columns 1 through 4) using "T" to indicate the column being read and add a new variable (in the TRANSFORM paragraph) to indicate the day of the measurements. The instructions are

```
/ INPUT      VARIABLES ARE 5.     MULT = 3.
             FORMAT IS '(2F2.0, 3F4.0,
                     T1, 2F2.0, T17, 3F4.0,
                     T1, 2F2.0, T29, 3F4.0)'.
/ VARIABLE   ADD = 1.
             NAMES = ID, HOSPITAL, WEIGHT, TEMP,
             BP, DAY.

/ TRANSFORM  DAY = ((KASE + 2) MOD 3) + 1.

/ TABULATE   PLOTMEANS.
             VARIABLES ARE WEIGHT, TEMP, BP.
             GROUPING IS DAY, ID, HOSPITAL.
             MARGINS ARE 'DIH',
                        'D.H',
                        '.IH'.

/ END
```

In the original record, weight, temperature and blood pressure for the first day are recorded in columns 5 through 16 in three fields four columns wide. The data for Day 2 are in columns 17 to 28 and those for Day 3 in columns 29 to 40.

The output produced from the MARGIN specification includes:

'DIH' A plot of the original data with the repeats for each subject grouped together on sequential lines. Cells are defined by all combinations of the levels of DAY, ID and HOSPITAL. There is only one record for each cell so the original data are plotted. The data on the first plot line (cell) are the day 1 values for the first patient in hospital 1; the second line contains his day 2 values, etc. These data have values for only three days: the

display is especially useful when subjects are measured many times and it is desirable to assess trends over time. The plots for WEIGHT, TEMP and BP appear side by side in three vertical panels for a comparison of variables.

'D.H' The levels of DAY and HOSPITAL are used to define six cells:

1.	day 1	hospital 1
2.	day 2	"
3.	day 3	"
4.	day 1	hospital 2
5.	day 2	"
6.	day 3	"

The first line of the table of printed means and standard deviations contains the day 1 average for all six hospital 1 patients; the first line of the plot of the means shows the values for all six subjects. Requesting GROUPING IS DAY, HOSPITAL in a new TABULATE paragraph will produce a plot showing the average.

'.IH' Twelve cells are formed by the combinations of the six ID codes and the two HOSPITAL codes. The first plot line contains the day 1, day 2 and day 3 values for the first patient at hospital 1.

SIZE OF PROBLEM

P9D can analyze very large amounts of data. Appendix B describes how the capacity of the program can be increased.

COMPUTATIONAL METHOD

P9D computes means and standard deviations in single precision by a provisional means algorithm (Appendix A.2). The formula for Bartlett's test is in Appendix A.4.

P9D copies the data to a temporary unit and determines how many variables (V = 1, 2, 3 or 4) to analyze at one time. It then rereads the data from the temporary unit as many times as necessary to analyze all the variables.

ACKNOWLEDGEMENT

P9D was designed and programmed by Laszlo Engelman. Later revisions were made by Peter Mundle.

SUMMARY

Order of Input Cards

```
// (job card)
// EXEC BIMED,PROG=BMDP9D        (see Appendix E)
//SYSIN DD *
/ PROBLEM
/ INPUT
/ VARIABLE
/ TRANSFORM
/ SAVE
/ TABULATE
/ GROUP
/ END
     (data, if on cards)

/ TABULATE  ⎤
/ GROUP     ⎬ repeat for subproblems
/ END       ⎦

// (system card)
```

Full sets of BMDP paragraphs (and data, if on cards)
can be repeated for additional problems; see Section
5.8.

instructions specific to P9D

Paragraph Statement	Preassigned	Comment and Manual Reference
/●TABULate		Required to specify the analysis (may be repeated).
●GROUPing = v list.	none	Names or subscripts of variables used to classify the cases into groups (cells) (see also / GROUP). * 118
VARiables = v list.	all vars.	Names or subscripts of variables to be analyzed. If not specified, all variables except GROUPING are analyzed. 118
PLOTmeans.	no	Plot cell means vs. cell identification number. The symbol used represents the cell frequency. * 118
MARGINal = 'c' list.	all subsets	Each 'c' represents a marginal subset of cells to be analyzed. The number of characters, including periods, in each 'c' must be equal to the number of variables in the GROUPING statement. A period in place of a character means "averaged over." 120

Key:

/	–indicates paragraph	*	–assigned value remains the same for additional problems
.	–period ends a sentence		
●	–required	VT	–number of variables after transformations
v	–variable (name or subscript)	list	–more than one item, often one per var.
g	–group (name or subscript)		
#	–number		Capitalized letters–paragraph or sentence names recognized by BMDP
'c'	–characters (name or parameter) may omit apostrophes if contiguous letters only		Page numbers following refer to this Manual

10
PLOTS AND HISTOGRAMS

A graphical display is a very useful way to describe data, reveal unusual values or discover relationships between variables. The data for a variable can be plotted as a histogram of the frequency distribution or of the cumulative distribution, or as a graph of the data values in a normal or half-normal probability plot. To demonstrate relationships between two variables the data for one variable can be plotted against the data for the other variable in a scatter plot.

In this chapter we describe two programs that produce graphical displays:

P5D -- Histograms and Univariate Plots
P6D -- Bivariate (Scatter) Plots

P5D prints histograms of the frequency distribution and of the cumulative distribution function. The cases can be classified into groups and plotted in a single figure using different symbols for each group. The frequency distribution and cumulative distribution are printed beside each histogram, both as frequencies and as percentages.

P5D prints normal or half-normal probability plots of the data. The linear trend can be removed from a normal probability plot before printing it; this produces a detrended normal probability plot. Normal probability plots can be used to screen data or residuals for nonnormality or for the presence of outliers. P5D also plots cumulative frequencies against the data values. When the cases are classified into groups, the data for several groups can be plotted in the same graph; each group is uniquely identified. The frequency, mean and standard deviation are printed for each group.

P6D plots one variable against another variable in a scatter plot. It computes and prints equations of the simple linear regressions relating each variable to the other, and indicates the intersections of the regression lines with the frame of the plot. The cases can be classified into groups; the data for one or more groups can be plotted in a single frame and the data points identified by group. More than one pair of variables can be plotted in a single plot. The size of the plots can be specified.

Histograms are plotted in three BMDP programs other than P5D:

- P2D (Section 8.2) produces a compact histogram (a maximum of 40 characters wide and 10 characters high) for each variable. P2D also prints a variation of a histogram called a stem and leaf display.
- P3D (Section 9.1) plots two side-by-side compact histograms (each a maximum of 20 characters wide and 6 characters high) for each variable when the cases are classified into two groups.
- P7D (Section 9.2) plots side-by-side histograms for each variable when the cases are classified into one or more groups. The bases of the histograms are plotted vertically and a scale is printed.

Normal probability plots of residuals are available in all regression programs (Chapters 13 and 14, and in P6R, Section 18.3).

Scatter plots are produced by many BMDP programs as an aid in interpreting the analysis. For example, the regression programs (Chapters 13 and 14) plot residuals and predicted values against the observed data. However, you may want to plot one variable against another variable (where variable may refer to a residual, predicted value, factor score or any function of the data) in a manner not permitted by the BMDP program you are using to perform an analysis. The data matrix, augmented by the residuals, predicted values or factor scores, can be saved in a BMDP File and then input to P6D to produce the desired plots.

Control Language

The Control Language instructions to describe the data and variables are common to all BMDP programs and are explained in Chapter 5: the PROBLEM, INPUT, VARIABLE and GROUP paragraph are used in the programs discussed in this chapter. If data editing or transformations are necessary, the methods described in Chapter 6 can be used. Data can be read using free format or a fixed format specification or from a BMDP File (Chapter 7). If a BMDP File is read as input and a new BMDP File is created in the same problem, the two Files must be in different system files and must have different UNIT numbers.

A summary of the Control Language instructions common to all BMDP programs is on the back cover; summaries of the Control Language instructions specific to each program described in this chapter follow each program. These summaries can be used as indexes to the program descriptions.

P5D

10.1 Histograms and Univariate Plots

Steve Chasen

ABSTRACT

P5D prints histograms or other plots for ungrouped or grouped data. When cases are classified into groups symbols can be used to identify each group; the groups can be graphed separately or combined in one plot.

Frequencies and percentages and cumulative frequencies and percentages are printed beside each histogram. A normal or half-normal probability plot of the data can be printed. The linear trend can be removed from a normal probability plot before printing it; this produces a detrended normal probability plot. Normal probability plots can be used to screen data or residuals for nonnormality or for the presence of outliers. P5D also plots cumulative frequencies against the data values.

You can control the size, scale, histogram interval, and number of observations represented by each plot symbol.

WHERE TO FIND IT

Example 5D.1 Basic Setup for Histograms

We use the Werner blood chemistry data (Table 5.1) to illustrate the plots produced by P5D. The PROBLEM, INPUT and VARIABLE paragraphs are common to all programs and are explained in Chapter 5. We use the preassigned options in the PLOT paragraph to produce a histogram for each variable. Note that the

PLOT paragraph is required in P5D. If all you want are histograms for each variable, you specify only

/ PLOT

Note that we specify CASES ARE 200. The program will operate without this instruction, but we suggest that the user guess a reasonable upper bound for the number of cases. This ensures that the number of histogram bins will be reasonable for the sample size.

The instructions for printing histograms are:

```
-------------------------------------
/ PROBLEM    TITLE IS 'WERNER BLOOD CHEMISTRY DATA'.
/ INPUT      VARIABLES ARE 9.
             FORMAT IS '(A4, 5F4.0, 3F4.1)'.
             CASES ARE 200.
/ VARIABLE   NAMES ARE ID, AGE, HEIGHT, WEIGHT,
                  BRTHPILL, CHOLSTRL, ALBUMIN,
                  CALCIUM, URICACID.
             MAXIMUM IS (6)400.
             MINIMUM IS (6)150.
             LABEL IS ID.

/ PLOT

/ END
-------------------------------------
```

(See end of this P5D section for organization of systems information, BMDP instructions and data.)

In Output 5D.1 only the histogram produced for CHOLSTRL is presented. The base of the histogram is the vertical axis. The number of X's printed in a line (horizontally) is the frequency of cases. Each value on the vertical axis represents the upper limit of the interval. Therefore there are four cases less than or equal to 162.5.

The frequency of observations in each interval and the cumulative frequency of observations up to and including the interval, as well as the percents of observations represented by the frequency and the cumulative frequency, are printed to the right of the histogram. When there are more observations than can be printed in a single line, the entire line is filled with X's terminated by an asterisk; the exact frequency is printed to the right of the line.

Example 5D.2 Normal Probability Plots

Three types of normal probability plots are produced by P5D. All three are requested in this example. If SIZE is not specified, each plot fills a computer page (80 characters wide and 50 lines high); we have reduced the size of the plots to 40 characters wide and 25 lines high. The PLOT

Output 5D.1   A histogram printed by P5D

--- the BMDP instructions read by P5D are printed and interpreted.
Then a table of contents to the histograms and plots is printed ---

```
HISTOGRAM OF VARIABLE    6 CHOLSTRL
                       SYMBOL   COUNT      MEAN      ST.DEV.
                         X       186     236.150     42.555
                  EACH SYMBOL REPRESENTS        1 OBSERVATIONS
INTERVAL                                                                  FREQUENCY PERCENTAGE
NAME       5   10  15  20  25  30  35  40  45  50  55  60  65  70  75  80  INT. CUM. INT. CUM.
           +---+---+---+---+---+---+---+---+---+---+---+---+---+---+---+---+
  *  162.5 +XXXX                                                            4    4   2.2   2.2
  *  175.0 +XXXXXXXXXXX                                                     11   15   5.9   8.1
  *  187.5 +XXXXXXX                                                         7   22   3.8  11.8
  *  200.0 +XXXXXXXXXXXXXXXXXXXXXXXXXX                                      26   48  14.0  25.8
  *  212.5 +XXXXXXXXXXXXX                                                   13   61   7.0  32.8
  *  225.0 +XXXXXXXXXXXXXXXXX                                               17   78   9.1  41.9
  *  237.5 +XXXXXXXXXXXXXXXXXXX                                            19   97  10.2  52.2
  *  250.0 +XXXXXXXXXXXXXXXXXXXXXXXXXXX                                     27  124  14.5  66.7
  *  262.5 +XXXXXXXXXXXXXXXXXXX                                            19  143  10.2  76.9
  *  275.0 +XXXXXXXXXXXX                                                   12  155   6.5  83.3
  *  287.5 +XXXXXXX                                                         7  162   3.8  87.1
  *  300.0 +XXXXXXXXX                                                       9  171   4.8  91.9
  *  312.5 +XXXXX                                                           5  176   2.7  94.6
  *  325.0 +XXXXXX                                                          6  182   3.2  97.8
  *  337.5 +XX                                                              2  184   1.1  98.9
  *  350.0 +X                                                               1  185   0.5  99.5
  *  362.5 +                                                                0  185   0.0  99.5
  *  375.0 +                                                                0  185   0.0  99.5
  *  387.5 +                                                                0  185   0.0  99.5
  *  400.0 +X                                                               1  186   0.5 100.0
           +---+---+---+---+---+---+---+---+---+---+---+---+---+---+---+---+
           5   10  15  20  25  30  35  40  45  50  55  60  65  70  75  80
```

--- histograms for variables 2 to 5 appear before that for
CHOLSTRL; histograms for variables 7 to 9 appear after ---

Output 5D.2   Normal probability plots printed by P5D. Only those for CHOLSTRL are shown

----

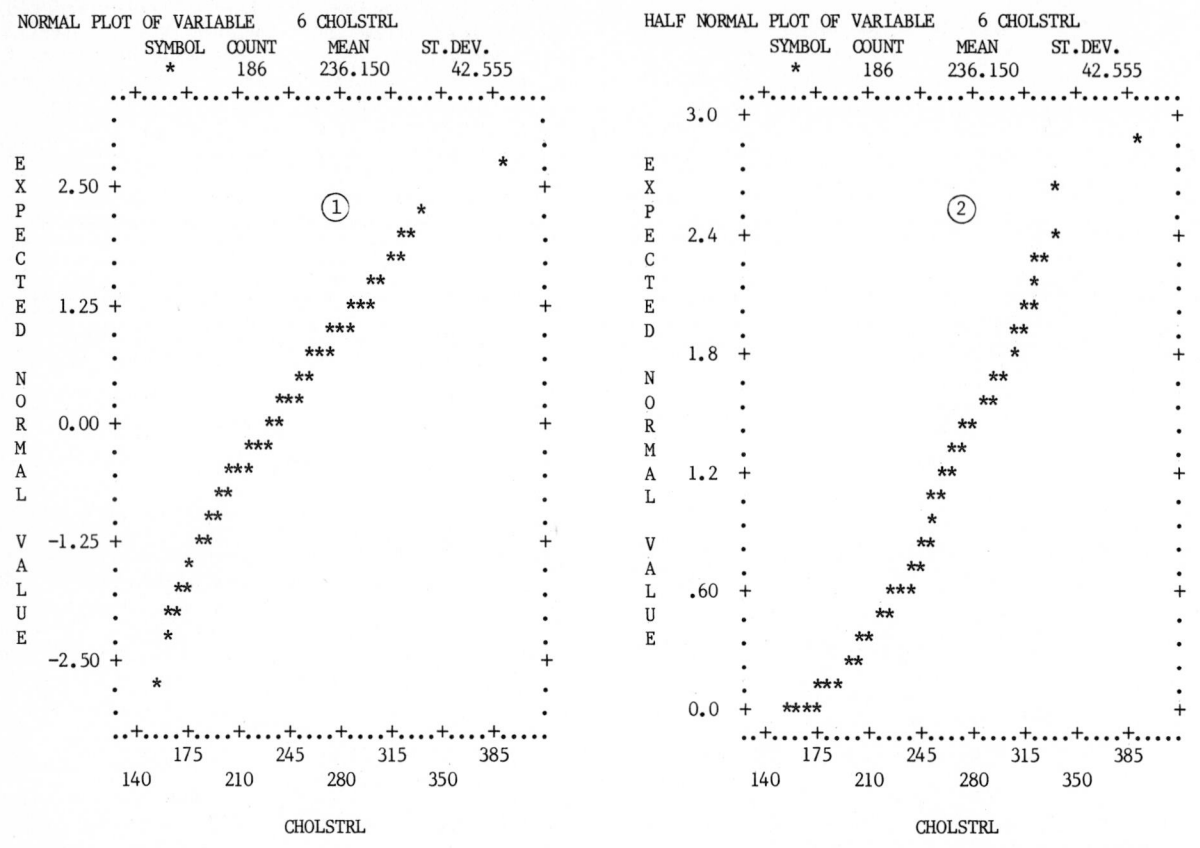

paragraph of Example 5D.1 is expanded as follows:

```
    ------------------------------------
 / PLOT     TYPES ARE NORM, HALFNORM, DNORM.
            SIZE IS 40, 25.

 / END
    ------------------------------------
```

The three probability plots are printed for each variable. In Output 5D.2 we present only the plots for CHOLSTRL.

① Normal probability plots. The observed values are plotted along the horizontal axis. The data values are ordered before plotting: the vertical axis corresponds to the expected normal value based on the rank of the observation. Let $x_{(1)}$, $x_{(2)}$, ... represent the data values after ordering from smallest to largest. The subscript (j) is the rank order of the observation. If N is the total frequency, the vertical plotting position corresponds to the expected normal value for the relative rank (j out of N) of the observation. The expected normal value is estimated as

$$\Phi^{-1}[(3j-1)/(3N+1)]\ ,$$

the standard normal value corresponding to the probability (3j-1)/(3N+1). If the data are from a normal distribution, this line will be straight, except for random fluctuations.

② Half-normal plot. This is also similar to the normal plot; however, the expected values are computed by using only the positive half of the normal distribution. The expected value of the jth observation (after ordering) is estimated by

$$\Phi^{-1}[(3N+3j-1)/(6N+1)]\ .$$

This plot is primarily used in residual plots when you want to ignore the sign of the residual; for example, when the residual is proportional to the square root of a chi-square variate with one degree of freedom (Daniel, 1959).

③ Detrended normal probability plot. This is similar to the normal probability plot except that the linear trend is removed before the plot is printed. The vertical scale represents the differences between the expected normal values and the standardized values of the observations. That is, each observation is transformed into a standardized value by subtracting the mean and dividing by the standard deviation; i.e., $z_{(j)} = (x_{(j)} - \bar{x})/s$. We then compute

$$\Phi^{-1}[(3j-1)/(3N+1)] - z_{(j)}\ .$$

```
------------------------------------------------------------

       DEVIATIONS FROM NORMAL PLOT OF VARIABLE    6 CHOLSTRL
              SYMBOL   COUNT      MEAN       ST.DEV.
                *       186      236.150     42.555
              ..+....+....+....+....+....+....+....+.....
              .                                         .
    D         .                                         .
    E     .4  +                                         +
    V         .                                         .
    I         .              ③                          .
    A         .                                         .
    T         .                                         .
    I     .2  +         *       *                       +
    O         .         ***     **                      .
    N         .         *****  ****                     .
              .       * ************                    .
    F         .       **************                 * .
    R     0.  +       ***** * **** **                   +
    O         .       *****   ****    *    *            .
    M         .       ** *    *      **                 .
              .       *             * * *               .
    E         .       *            ***** *              .
    X    -.2  +       **           ** *                 +
    P         .       *             **                  .
    E         .      **              * *                .
    C         .                                         .
    T         .       *                                 .
    E    -.4  +                                         +
              .      *                                  .
              .                                         .
              ..+.**.+....+....+....+....+....+**....
                  175       245       315       385
              140       210       280       350

                         CHOLSTRL
------------------------------------------------------------
```

The vertical scale ranges from −0.5 to 0.5. Deviations outside this range are plotted in the border, as shown on the bottom of plot number 3, Output 5D.2.

```
PLOT ─────────────────────────────────────────
  │  TYPE = (one or more)              HIST/prev.
  │        HIST, NORM, HALFNORM,
  │        DNORM, CUM, CHIST.
  │   The types of plots to be printed, where
  │    HIST   = histogram
  │    NORM   = normal probability plot
  │    HALFNORM = halfnormal plot
  │    DNORM  = detrended normal probability plot
  │    CUM    = cumulative frequency distribution
  │             plot (Example 5D.3)
  │    CHIST  = cumulative histogram (Example
  │             5D.4)
  │  These plots are illustrated in Output 5D.1 −
  │  5D.4. The desired types should be spelled
  │  correctly, separated by commas and terminated
  │  by a period.
  ────────────────────────────────────────────
```

Example 5D.3 Cumulative Frequency Plots

In a cumulative frequency plot the cumulative frequency distribution is plotted against the data values. We use the following PLOT paragraph (added to the Control Language of Example 5D.1) to specify a cumulative frequency plot. Again we request the size to be smaller than the preassigned width of 80 characters and height of 50 lines.

```
------------------------------------------
 / PLOT      TYPE IS CUM.
            SIZE IS 40, 25.
------------------------------------------
```

The cumulative frequency plot of CHOLSTRL is presented in Output 5D.3. The cumulative frequency distribution is plotted on the vertical axis and the data values on the horizontal axis. This plot is similar to a cumulative histogram (see Output 5D.4) except that the area under the curve is not filled with asterisks.

Output 5D.3   Cumulative frequency plot printed by P5D. Only the plot for CHOLSTRL is shown

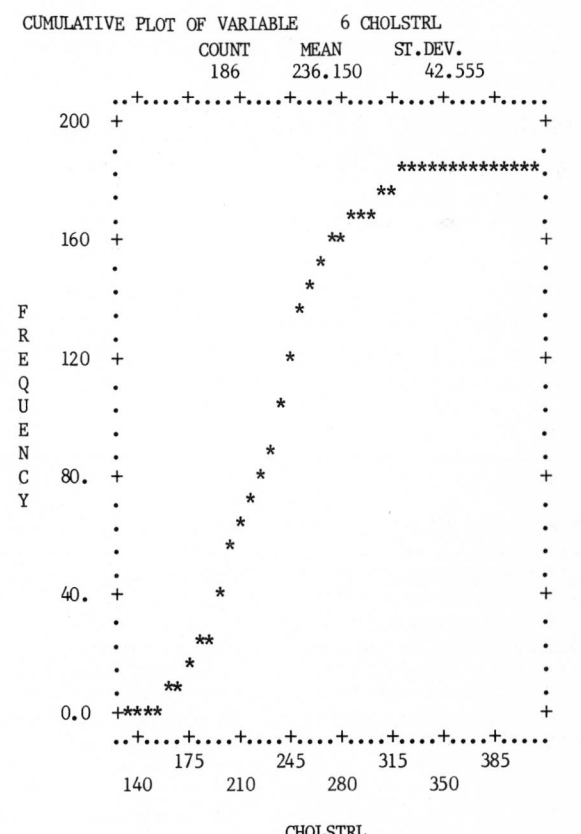

Example 5D.4 Cumulative Histograms

A cumulative histogram shows the frequencies accumulated over all data values less than or equal to the plotted frequency. P5D prints a cumulative histogram when

```
------------------------------------
                TYPE = CHIST.
------------------------------------
```

is specified in the PLOT paragraph of Example 5D.1.

The cumulative histogram for CHOLSTRL is presented in Output 5D.4 (and again in Output 5D.6 with a different, and improved, scale). The base is the vertical axis. The number of X's printed in a line corresponds to the cumulative frequency of cases up to and including the value printed on the vertical axis. Therefore, there are 22 cases less than or equal to 187.5. The same four columns of frequencies and percents as in the histogram shown in Output 5D.1 are printed to the right of the cumulative histogram.

When there are more observations than can be printed in a single line, the entire line is filled with X's terminated by an asterisk. The cumulative frequency can be read from the second column of frequencies to the right of the plot.

Example 5D.5 Subpopulation Identification in Plots

Each subpopulation (or group) can be printed in an individual plot or specified groups can be combined into a single plot where members of each group are identified by a different symbol (e.g., "A" for women who do not use contraceptive pills and "B" for women who do).

Cases are classified into groups by specifying a GROUPING variable in the VARIABLE paragraph. For example, when

```
                GROUPING IS BRTHPILL.
```

is specified in the VARIABLE paragraph, the user may request plots of one or more groups in the PLOT paragraph with symbols (A, B, ...) identifying group membership. We add GROUPING IS BRTHPILL to the VARIABLE paragraph and the following GROUP and PLOT paragraphs to the Control Language of Example 5D.1:

```
-------------------------------------
        ↗ GROUPING IS BRTHPILL.

/ GROUP      CODES(5) ARE       1,    2.
             NAMES(5) ARE NOPILL, PILL.

/ PLOT       VARIABLE IS CHOLSTRL.
             TYPES ARE HIST, NORM.
             GROUP IS NOPILL.
             GROUP IS PILL.
             GROUPS ARE NOPILL, PILL.
             SIZE IS 40, 25.
-------------------------------------
```

A GROUP paragraph is required when the GROUPING variable is continuous or takes on more than 10 distinct values. A GROUP paragraph is also used to

Output 5D.4   Cumulative histogram printed by P5D. Only the histogram for CHOLSTRL is shown
----

```
CUMULATIVE HISTOGRAM OF VARIABLE    6 CHOLSTRL
                    SYMBOL   COUNT       MEAN       ST.DEV.
                       X       186     236.150       42.555
               EACH SYMBOL REPRESENTS         1 OBSERVATIONS
```

INTERVAL NAME	plot	FREQUENCY INT.	CUM.	PERCENTAGE INT.	CUM.
* 162.5	+XXXX	4	4	2.2	2.2
* 175.0	+XXXXXXXXXXX	11	15	5.9	8.1
* 187.5	+XXXXXXXXXXXXXXXXXXX	7	22	3.8	11.8
* 200.0	+XXXXXXXXXXXXXXXXXXXXXXXXXXXXXXXXXXXXXXXXXXXXXX	26	48	14.0	25.8
* 212.5	+XXXXXXXXXXXXXXXXXXXXXXXXXXXXXXXXXXXXXXXXXXXXXXXXXXX	13	61	7.0	32.8
* 225.0	+XXXXXXXXXXXXXXXXXXXXXXXXXXXXXXXXXXXXXXXXXXXXXXXXXXXXXXXXXXX	17	78	9.1	41.9
* 237.5	+XXXXXXXXXXXXXXXXXXXXXXXXXXXXXXXXXXXXXXXXXXXXXXXXXXXXXXXXXXXXXXXX*	19	97	10.2	52.2
* 250.0	+XXXXXXXXXXXXXXXXXXXXXXXXXXXXXXXXXXXXXXXXXXXXXXXXXXXXXXXXXXXXXXXX*	27	124	14.5	66.7
* 262.5	+XXXXXXXXXXXXXXXXXXXXXXXXXXXXXXXXXXXXXXXXXXXXXXXXXXXXXXXXXXXXXXXX*	19	143	10.2	76.9
* 275.0	+XXXXXXXXXXXXXXXXXXXXXXXXXXXXXXXXXXXXXXXXXXXXXXXXXXXXXXXXXXXXXXXX*	12	155	6.5	83.3
* 287.5	+XXXXXXXXXXXXXXXXXXXXXXXXXXXXXXXXXXXXXXXXXXXXXXXXXXXXXXXXXXXXXXXX*	7	162	3.8	87.1
* 300.0	+XXXXXXXXXXXXXXXXXXXXXXXXXXXXXXXXXXXXXXXXXXXXXXXXXXXXXXXXXXXXXXXX*	9	171	4.8	91.9
* 312.5	+XXXXXXXXXXXXXXXXXXXXXXXXXXXXXXXXXXXXXXXXXXXXXXXXXXXXXXXXXXXXXXXX*	5	176	2.7	94.6
* 325.0	+XXXXXXXXXXXXXXXXXXXXXXXXXXXXXXXXXXXXXXXXXXXXXXXXXXXXXXXXXXXXXXXX*	6	182	3.2	97.8
* 337.5	+XXXXXXXXXXXXXXXXXXXXXXXXXXXXXXXXXXXXXXXXXXXXXXXXXXXXXXXXXXXXXXXX*	2	184	1.1	98.9
* 350.0	+XXXXXXXXXXXXXXXXXXXXXXXXXXXXXXXXXXXXXXXXXXXXXXXXXXXXXXXXXXXXXXXX*	1	185	0.5	99.5
* 362.5	+XXXXXXXXXXXXXXXXXXXXXXXXXXXXXXXXXXXXXXXXXXXXXXXXXXXXXXXXXXXXXXXX*	0	185	0.0	99.5
* 375.0	+XXXXXXXXXXXXXXXXXXXXXXXXXXXXXXXXXXXXXXXXXXXXXXXXXXXXXXXXXXXXXXXX*	0	185	0.0	99.5
* 387.5	+XXXXXXXXXXXXXXXXXXXXXXXXXXXXXXXXXXXXXXXXXXXXXXXXXXXXXXXXXXXXXXXX*	0	185	0.0	99.5
* 400.0	+XXXXXXXXXXXXXXXXXXXXXXXXXXXXXXXXXXXXXXXXXXXXXXXXXXXXXXXXXXXXXXXX*	1	186	0.5	100.0

```
          5    10   15   20   25   30   35   40   45   50   55   60   65   70   75   80
```

----

name the groups for labels in the output. In the PLOT paragraph we specify that HISTOGRAMS and NORMAL probability plots are to be printed for CHOLSTRL. Each GROUP statement describes a different plot. Therefore, first the group NOPILL is plotted by itself, then the group PILL by itself and finally the groups NOPILL and PILL are plotted together. If GROUPS are not specified in the PLOT paragraph, all groups defined by the GROUPING variable are plotted; each with a different symbol. For compact output, we request all plots to be printed smaller than the preassigned size.

The plots are shown in Output 5D.5. The first histogram and normal plot contain only A's, the symbol assigned to the first group (NOPILL). The second histogram and normal plot contain B's (PILL). Above each plot are the names of the groups printed,

their symbols, frequencies, mean and standard deviations. In the normal plots each group is plotted separately; an asterisk indicates group overlap (i.e., points from different groups fall in the same place).

```
VARiable ─────────────────────────────────
  GROUPing = v.                    no grouping/prev.
    Name or subscript of the variable used to
    classify the cases into groups. If not
    specified or if set to zero, the cases are not
    grouped. If the GROUPING variable takes on more
    than 10 distinct values or codes, CODES or
    CUTPOINTS for the variable must be specified in
    the GROUP paragraph (Section 5.5).
```

Output 5D.5 Histograms and normal probability plots for subpopulations and for the combined groups

----

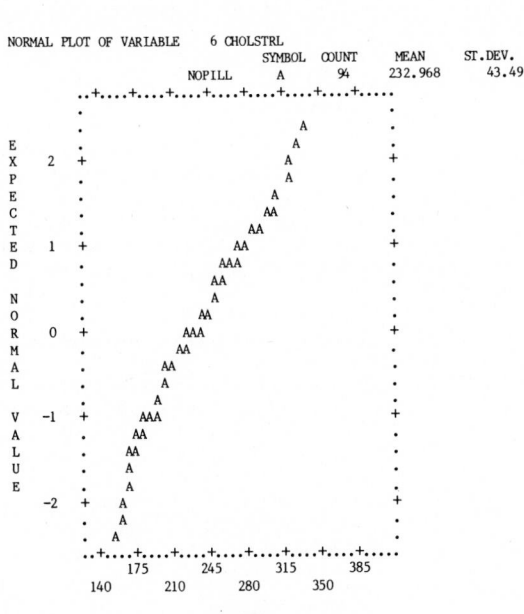

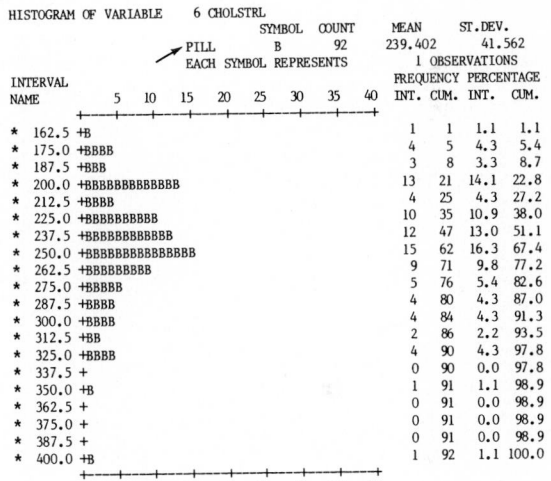

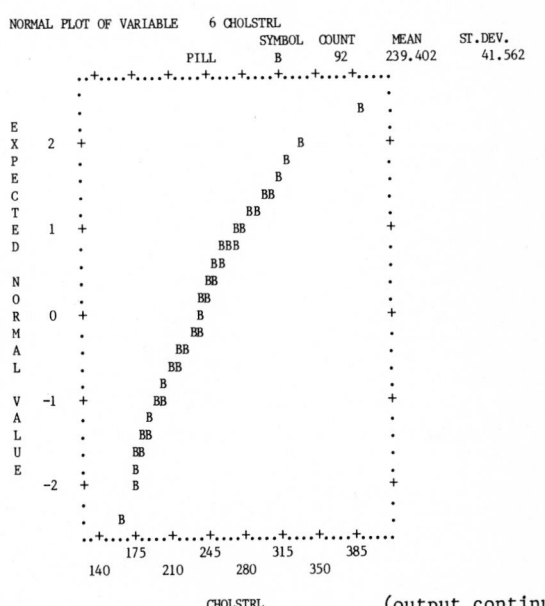

(output continued)

```
PLOT ─────────────────────────────────────
  │ GROUP = g list.  can  be  repeated      all  groups
  │   Group NAMES (from the GROUP paragraph) or group
  │   subscripts. The specified groups are plotted in
  │   the  same  graph.  A  group  subscript  is  the
  │   sequence  number  of  the  group  as  specified  in
  │   the  GROUP  paragraph.  The  GROUP  statement  can  be
  │   repeated  in  the  PLOT  paragraph.  Each  GROUP
  │   statement defines a separate plot.
  └─────────────────────────────────────────
```

Output 5D.5 (continued)

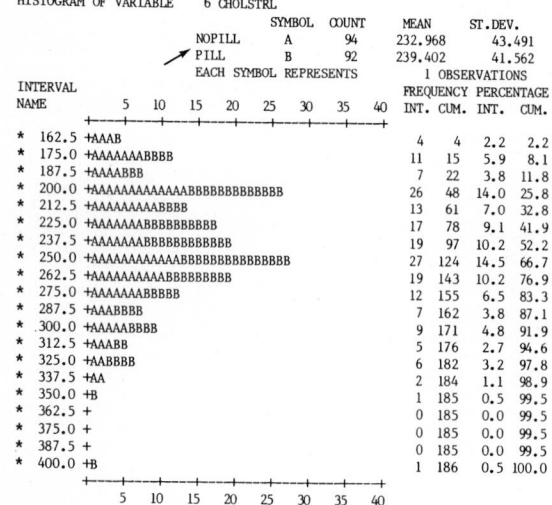

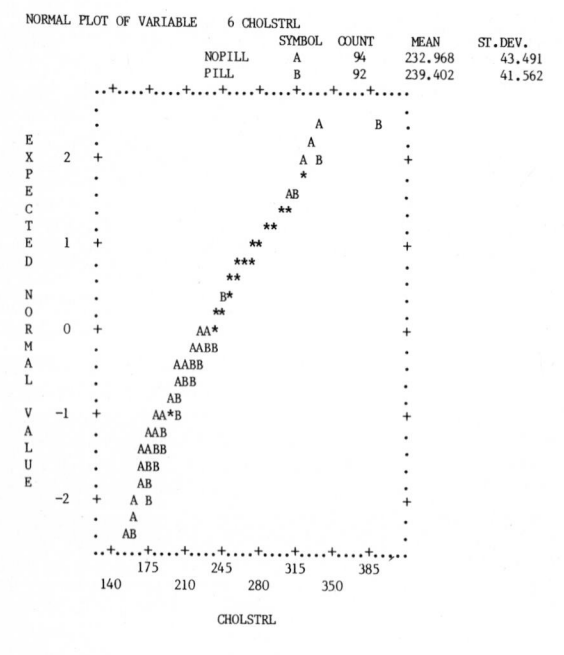

Example 5D.6 Adjusting Plot Size, Labeling and Scale

In Examples 5D.2, 5D.3 and 5D.5 we specify

$$SIZE = 40, 25.$$

in the PLOT paragraph. The first number (40) determines the number of characters for the horizontal axis (width) and the second the number of lines for the vertical axis (height) of the normal probability plots and the cumulative frequency plot. If not specified, SIZE is preassigned to 80 characters wide and 50 lines high.

The width of the histogram and of the cumulative histogram is also determined by the first number assigned to SIZE (40 in our example). The height of the histogram is the number of codes or intervals specified for the variable in the GROUP paragraph (each line represents a code or an interval); if neither is specified, the height (number of bins) is equal to $8 \log_{10}(N) + 2$, where N is the number of cases read.

Note that we are discussing a second use of the GROUP paragraph – in Example 5D.4 we use the GROUP paragraph to specify subpopulations. Here we use the GROUP paragraph to specify more precisely the number of bars displayed in the histograms. GROUP CUTPOINTS (or CODES) can define the bars of the histogram and GROUP NAMES can label the bars in the output. Remember that a CUTPOINT defines the maximum value of the interval. For the cholesterol intervals you might specify

```
CUTPOINTS(6) = 165 TO 390 BY 15.
NAMES(6)     = UPTO165, '166-180'. '181-195',
               ..., OVER390.
```

The scale for the horizontal axis of the histograms is composed of the integers 1, 2, ... up to the width of the plot. This scale can be reset by specifying the origin and the frequency represented by each symbol. For example

$$SCALE = 0, 3.$$

specifies that 0 is the frequency at the base of the histogram and each symbol represents three units. This is demonstrated by using the following PLOT paragraph with the Control Language of Example 5D.1. We also include cutpoints and names to define the histogram bins.

```
-------------------------------------
/ GROUP    CUTPOINTS(6) = 165 TO 390 BY 15.
           NAMES(6)     = UPTO165, '166-180',
                          '181-195', '196-210',
                          '211-225', '226-240',
                          '241-255', '256-270',
                          '271-285', '286-300',
                          '301-315', '316-330',
                          '331-345', '346-360',
                          '361-375', '376-390',
                          OVER390
```

```
/ PLOT    VARIABLE IS CHOLSTRL.
          TYPE IS CHIST.
          SCALE IS 0, 3.
          ------------------------------------
```

The cumulative histogram with a reset scale is printed in Output 5D.6. Compare this with the one in Output 5D.4, which uses the preassigned scale.

```
PLOT
   SIZE = #, #.  first number ≤ 100    80, 50/prev.
      The first number is the number of characters in
      the horizontal axis (width) of all six types of
      plots. The second number is the number of
      characters (lines) in the vertical axis
      (height) of the normal plots and cumulative
      frequency plot.
   SCALE = #,#.                          0, 1/prev.
      The first number is the value of the frequency
      at the base of the histograms. The second
      number is the number of units represented by
      each symbol plotted in the histogram.
```

Selecting Variables to be Plotted and Repeating the PLOT Paragraph

All variables are plotted unless a selection is specified. Specification can be made by either USE in the VARIABLE paragraph (Section 5.4) or by VARIABLE in the PLOT paragraph.

In Output 5D.1 to 5D.6 we present only the plots for CHOLSTRL although plots for all the variables are printed. If we add

```
                VARIABLE IS CHOLSTRL.
```

to the PLOT paragraph in each example, only the plot for CHOLSTRL is printed.

The PLOT paragraph can be repeated before END to specify more than one set of plots. Thus you can specify histograms for some variables in one PLOT paragraph, cumulative distributions for other variables in another paragraph or groups in one and not the other.

```
PLOT
   VARiable = v list.              all variables/prev.
      Names or subscripts of variables to be plotted.
```

SIZE OF PROBLEM

P5D copies the data to a temporary unit and rereads it as many times as necessary to form the specified plots. On most large systems each time the data are read P5D constructs as many plots as it can fit into memory (about 10 if the plots are the preassigned size, more if the plots are smaller). The largest single plot that can be printed is about 100 characters wide by 150 lines tall.

COMPUTATIONAL METHOD

Computations of the means and standard deviations are in single precision by the method of provisional means (Appendix A.2).

ACKNOWLEDGEMENT

P5D was designed and programmed by Steve Chasen. Later revisions were made by Lanaii Kline.

Output 5D.6 A cumulative histogram with user specified intervals and names. Each histogram symbol represents 3 observations.

```
CUMULATIVE HISTOGRAM OF VARIABLE    6 CHOLSTRL
                       SYMBOL  COUNT    MEAN      ST.DEV.
                         X      186    236.150     42.555
                  EACH SYMBOL REPRESENTS      3 OBSERVATIONS
INTERVAL                                                                     FREQUENCY PERCENTAGE
NAME       15   30   45   60   75   90  105  120  135  150  165  180  195  210  225  240  INT. CUM.  INT.   CUM.
           +----+----+----+----+----+----+----+----+----+----+----+----+----+----+----+----+
UPTO165   +XX                                                                   5    5    2.7    2.7
166-180   +XXXXXXX                                                             15   20    8.1   10.8
181-195   +XXXXXXXXXX                                                          11   31    5.9   16.7
196-210   +XXXXXXXXXXXXXXXXXXX                                                 29   60   15.6   32.3
211-225   +XXXXXXXXXXXXXXXXXXXXXXXXX                                           18   78    9.7   41.9
226-240   +XXXXXXXXXXXXXXXXXXXXXXXXXXXXXXXXXX                                  26  104   14.0   55.9
241-255   +XXXXXXXXXXXXXXXXXXXXXXXXXXXXXXXXXXXXXXXX                            28  132   15.1   71.0
256-270   +XXXXXXXXXXXXXXXXXXXXXXXXXXXXXXXXXXXXXXXXXXXXXXXX                    20  152   10.8   81.7
271-285   +XXXXXXXXXXXXXXXXXXXXXXXXXXXXXXXXXXXXXXXXXXXXXXXXXX                  10  162    5.4   87.1
286-300   +XXXXXXXXXXXXXXXXXXXXXXXXXXXXXXXXXXXXXXXXXXXXXXXXXXXX                 9  171    4.8   91.9
301-315   +XXXXXXXXXXXXXXXXXXXXXXXXXXXXXXXXXXXXXXXXXXXXXXXXXXXXX                6  177    3.2   95.2
316-330   +XXXXXXXXXXXXXXXXXXXXXXXXXXXXXXXXXXXXXXXXXXXXXXXXXXXXXX               6  183    3.2   98.4
331-345   +XXXXXXXXXXXXXXXXXXXXXXXXXXXXXXXXXXXXXXXXXXXXXXXXXXXXXX               2  185    1.1   99.5
346-360   +XXXXXXXXXXXXXXXXXXXXXXXXXXXXXXXXXXXXXXXXXXXXXXXXXXXXXX               0  185    0.0   99.5
361-375   +XXXXXXXXXXXXXXXXXXXXXXXXXXXXXXXXXXXXXXXXXXXXXXXXXXXXXX               0  185    0.0   99.5
376-390   +XXXXXXXXXXXXXXXXXXXXXXXXXXXXXXXXXXXXXXXXXXXXXXXXXXXXXX               1  186    0.5  100.0
OVER390   +XXXXXXXXXXXXXXXXXXXXXXXXXXXXXXXXXXXXXXXXXXXXXXXXXXXXXX               0  186    0.0  100.0
           +----+----+----+----+----+----+----+----+----+----+----+----+----+----+----+----+
             15   30   45   60   75   90  105  120  135  150  165  180  195  210  225  240
```

SUMMARY

Order of Input Cards

```
// (job card)
// EXEC BIMED,PROG=BMDP5D        (see Appendix E)
//SYSIN DD *
/ PROBLEM
/ INPUT
/ VARIABLE
/ GROUP
/ TRANSFORM
/ SAVE
/ PLOT          repeat for subproblems
/ END
     data if on cards
// (system card)
```

Full sets of BMDP paragraphs (and data if on cards)
can be repeated for additional problems; see Section
5.8.

instructions specific to P5D

Paragraph Statement	Preassigned	Comment and Manual Reference
/ VARiable		Additional option to classify cases into groups.
GROUPing = v.	no	Variable used to define group membership (see also / GROUP). * 129
/●PLOT		Required to specify histograms and plots (may be repeated).
TYPE = c list.	HIST.	Print selected output (one or more). * 127
		HIST – histogram
		NORM – normal probability plot
		HALFNORM – halfnormal plot
		DNORM – detrended normal probability plot
		CUM – cumulative frequency distribution plot
		CHIST – cumulative histogram
VARiables = v list.	all	Names or subscripts of variables to be plotted. * 131
GROUPs = g list.	all	Groups to be included on the same graph. May be repeated in same paragraph; each statement produces one graph. * 130
SIZE = #,#.	80, 50.	Width of x-axis (characters); height of y-axis (lines). * 131
SCALE = #,#.	0, 1.	The frequency at the base of the histogram; the number of observations (for each symbol). * 131

Key:

/	–indicates paragraph	*	–assigned value remains the same for additional problems
.	–period ends a sentence		
●	–required	VT	–number of variables after transformations
v	–variable (name or subscript)	list	–more than one item, often one per var.
g	–group (name or subscript)		
#	–number	Capitalized letters–paragraph or sentence names recognized by BMDP
'c'	–characters (name or parameter) may omit apostrophes if contiguous letters only	Page numbers following refer to this Manual

```
--------------------------------------
/ PROBLEM     TITLE IS 'WERNER BLOOD CHEMISTRY DATA'.
/ INPUT       VARIABLES ARE 9.
             FORMAT IS '(A4, 5F4.0, 3F4.1)'.
/ VARIABLE    NAMES ARE ID, AGE, HEIGHT, WEIGHT,
                   BRTHPILL, CHOLSTRL, ALBUMIN,
                   CALCIUM, URICACID.
             MAXIMUM IS (6)400.
             MINIMUM IS (6)150.
             LABEL IS ID.

/ PLOT        YVAR ARE CHOLSTRL, URICACID.
             XVAR ARE AGE     , WEIGHT.
             SIZE IS 40, 25.
/ END
--------------------------------------
```

(See end of this P6D section for organization of
systems information, BMDP instructions and data.)

Two plots are printed in Output 6D.1: CHOLSTRL
against AGE and URICACID against WEIGHT. Numbers in
the plots are the frequencies of points plotted at
the same positions. For counts greater than 9, A
denotes 10, B denotes 11, etc., and an asterisk
indicates a frequency of 36 or more. Asterisks (*)
plotted on the frame (e.g., the top and right
borders of the second plot) correspond to values
that are equal to the missing value code (the
program assumes that blanks in the data file are
missing values) or out of range (less than the
specified MINIMUM or greater than the specified
MAXIMUM).

The PLOT paragraph. The PLOT paragraph specifies
the variables to be plotted vertically (YVAR) and
horizontally (XVAR), the SIZE of the plot and the
GROUPS to be plotted if the cases are classified
into groups (see Example 6D.2). PLOT can be repeated
several times before the END paragraph to specify
different combinations of variables to be plotted or
to modify the size of the plots.

In our example the variables in the XVAR and YVAR
statements are assumed to be PAIRED: CHOLSTRL versus
AGE and URICACID versus WEIGHT. If we added the
CROSS instruction to the PLOT paragraph

```
/ PLOT     YVAR ARE CHOLSTRL, URICACID.
          XVAR ARE AGE     , WEIGHT.
          CROSS.
```

four plots would be printed: (1) CHOLSTRL versus
AGE, (2) CHOLSTRL vs. WEIGHT, (3) URICACID vs. AGE
and (4) URICACID vs. WEIGHT (i.e., CROSS requests
plots for every combination of X and Y variables).

```
PLOT ─────────────────────────────────────
  YVAR = v list.              last variable/prev.
    Names or subscripts of variables to be plotted
    vertically (along the Y-axes).
  XVAR = v list.              first variable/prev.
    Names or subscripts of variables to be plotted
    horizontally (along the X-axes).
  PAIR. or CROSS.                          PAIR
    The program is preset to PAIR the YVAR
    variables with the XVAR variables, the first
    YVAR against the first XVAR, etc., and plot
    each pair in a separate graph. If CROSS is
    specified, all possible pairings of the YVAR
    and XVAR variables are plotted, each in a
    separate graph.
```

P6D

10.2 Bivariate (Scatter) Plots

Steve Chasen

ABSTRACT

P6D plots one variable against another and
calculates correlation and simple linear regression
equations. Group membership can be identified and
several variables can appear on the same plot. The
use of MINIMUM and MAXIMUM allows zooming in on an
area of interest. The SIZE can be specified larger
than the printer page, so oversized plots can be
produced.

WHERE TO FIND IT

Example 6D.1 Basic Setup for Bivariate Plots

The Werner blood chemistry data (Table 5.1) are
used to illustrate the plots produced by P6D. We use
the PLOT paragraph to specify the variables to be
plotted along the vertical or Y-axis (YVAR) and the
horizontal or X-axis (XVAR). (We also request that
the SIZE of the plot be reduced. SIZE is explained
in Example 6D.2.) The other instructions are those
used by all BMDP programs to read the data and name
the variables: the instructions for the INPUT and
VARIABLE paragraphs are described in Chapter 5. Our
BMDP instructions are:

Output 6D.1 Scatter plots

--- the BMDP instructions read by P6D are printed and interpreted.
A table of contents to the plots is also printed ---

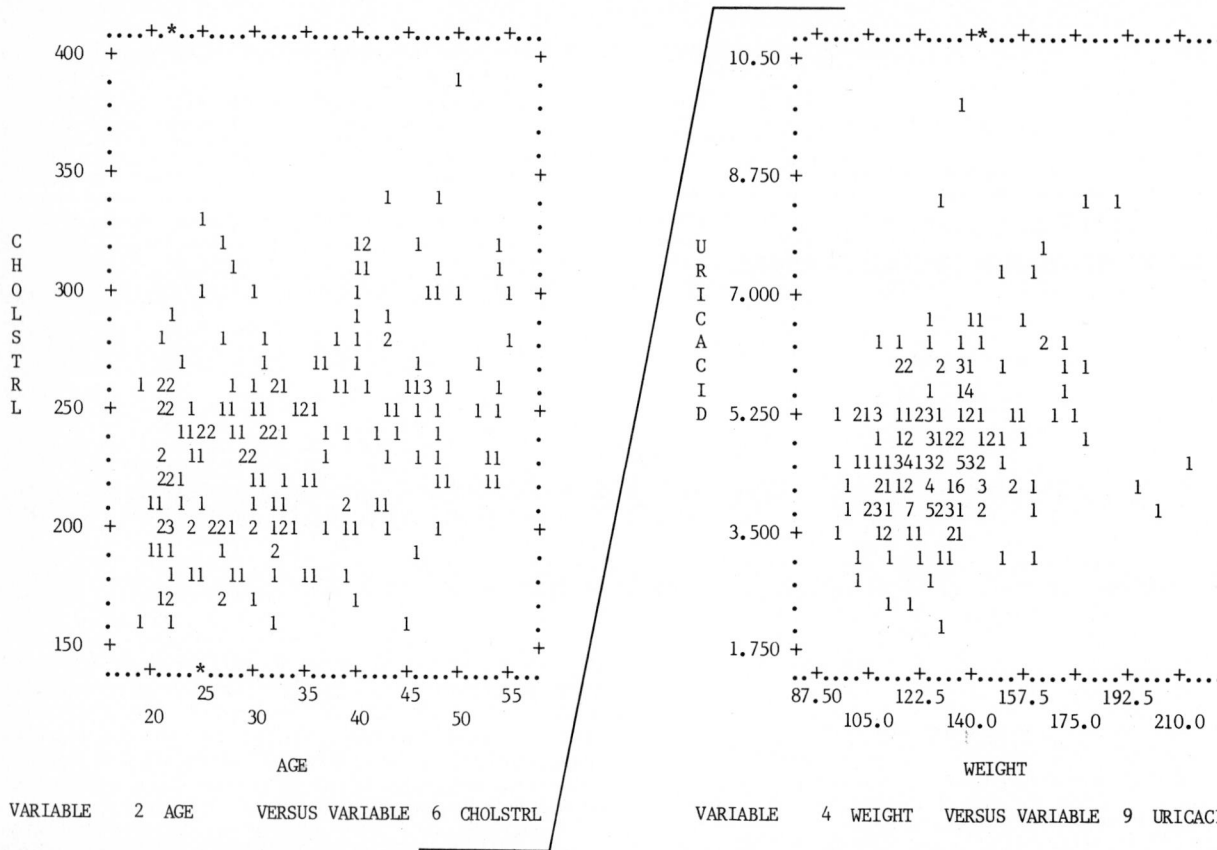

VARIABLE 2 AGE VERSUS VARIABLE 6 CHOLSTRL   VARIABLE 4 WEIGHT VERSUS VARIABLE 9 URICACID

Example 6D.2 Requesting Statistics and Regression Lines for Plots

We add the word STATISTICS to the PLOT paragraph of Example 6D.1 as follows

```
----------------------------------
/ PLOT    YVAR ARE CHOLSTRL, URICACID.
         XVAR ARE AGE       , WEIGHT.
         SIZE IS 40, 25.
         STATISTICS.
----------------------------------
```

The statistics and plots are printed in Output 6D.2. The STATISTICS instruction requests the following

- frequency (N) of points plotted. Points are plotted for all cases that contain acceptable values for both variables; i.e., values not missing or out of range.
- correlation (r) between the two variables computed using all pairs of acceptable values.
- mean for each variable: $\bar{x}$ and $\bar{y}$
- standard deviation for each variable: s_x and s_y
- the regression lines of X on Y (i.e., $X = b'Y + a'$) and of Y on X (i.e., $Y = bX + a$)

$$b' = rs_x/s_y ; \qquad a' = \bar{x} - b'\bar{y}$$
$$b = rs_y/s_x ; \qquad a = \bar{y} - b\bar{x}$$

- the residual mean square error (labelled RES.MS. in the results):

$$s^2_{x|y} = \Sigma(x_j - \hat{x}_j)^2/(N-2) \quad \text{where } \hat{x}_j = b'y_j + a'$$
$$s^2_{y|x} = \Sigma(y_j - \hat{y}_j)^2/(N-2) \quad \text{where } \hat{y}_j = bx_j + a$$

On the frame of each plot are two X's and two Y's. The X's show where the line $X = b'Y + a'$ intersects the frame of the plot, and the Y's show where the line $Y = bX + a$ intersects the frame. Asterisks (*) on the frame represent values that were excluded from the computations because one or both of the values for the two variables were missing or out of range.

Controlling the size and scale of plots. You can reduce the size of the plots as in the examples above or request plots that require several pages.

The size of the plot can be specified as the number of characters for the X-axis (the width) and the number of lines for the Y-axis (heights). The width is stated first; the program is preset to 70, 42 if SIZE is not specified. In the examples we reduced the figures to 40 characters wide and 25 lines high by specifying

SIZE = 40, 25.

The statement of width also affects the statistics printed under the plot. Therefore, if you request STATISTICS, the plot width must be at least 8 to have the means and standard deviations printed, at least 28 to have the regression equations printed, and at least 38 to have the residual mean squares printed. The statistics and the label for the X-axis use six lines plus one line per symbol defining characters used in the plot (e.g., for groups such as in Example 6D.3). You may want to

choose the number of lines for the Y-axis to allow the statistics and labels to appear on the same page as the plot.

You can specify the scale on each axis by setting a MINIMUM and MAXIMUM limit for the variable in the PLOT paragraph. The MINIMUM and MAXIMUM instructions in the VARIABLE paragraph apply to all PLOT paragraphs; the MINIMUM and MAXIMUM limits within a particular PLOT paragraph may restrict the limits further. If limits are not specified, the observed minimum and maximum are used. If groups are plotted in separate graphs (as in Example 6D.3) each group may have a different observed minimum and maximum. Therefore, if MINIMUM and MAXIMUM are not specified, the scales may differ from graph to graph.

The SIZE, MINIMUM and MAXIMUM parameters can be used to adjust plot scales, remembering that most printers print 6 or 8 lines per inch and 10 characters per inch horizontally. If you wish to have equal distances on the printed page for the two axes, the vertical size will need to be set as 8/10 or 6/10 of the size set for the horizontal axis.

Output 6D.2   Scatter plots with statistics and estimates of regression lines

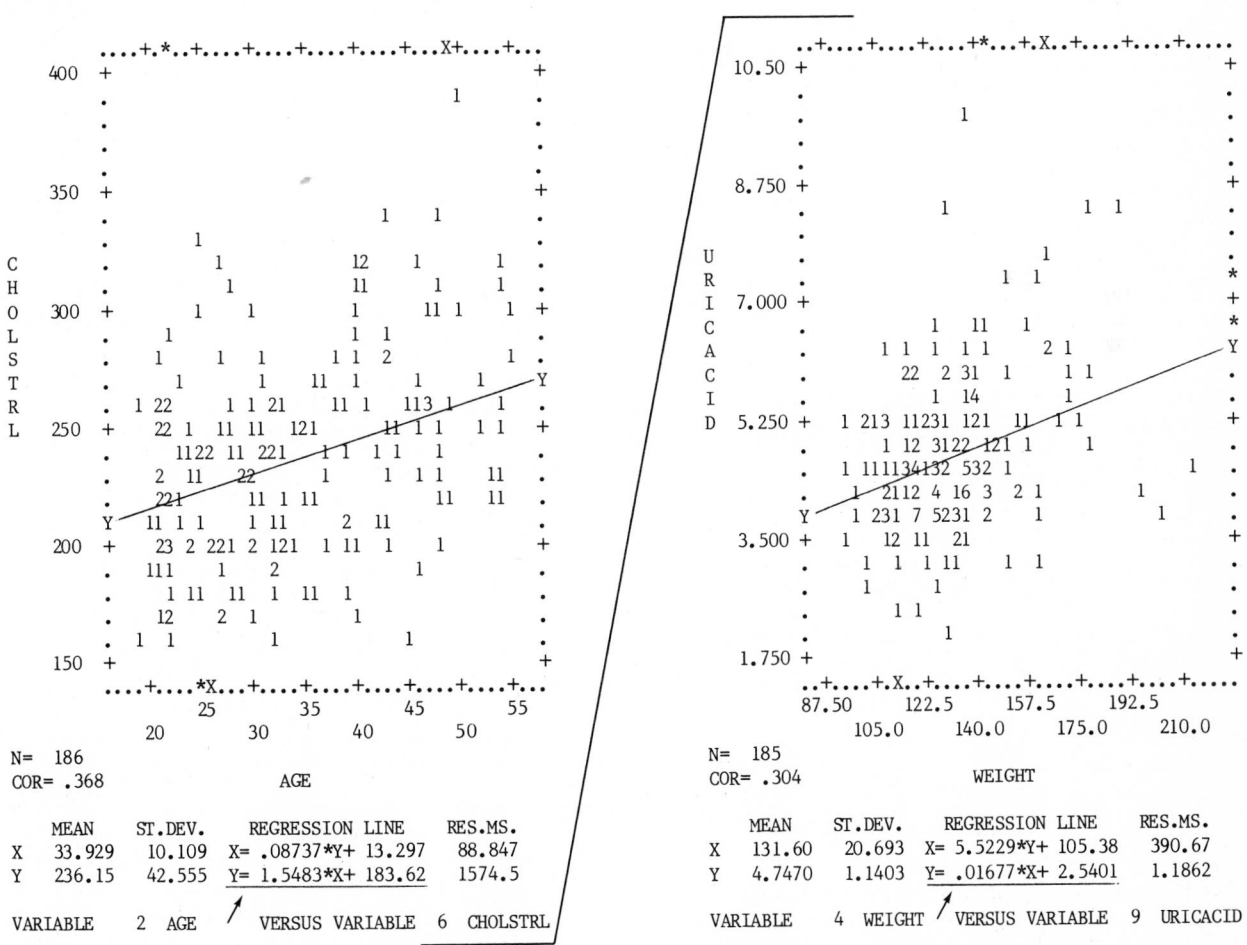

Note: In the above plots we have drawn a line between the two Y's on the frames of the plots. This shows the least squares regression line Y = bX + a. Similar lines can be drawn joining the two X's.

```
PLOT ─────────────────────────────────────────
  STATistics.                                    no/prev.
     If STATISTICS is specified, the following are
  computed: the mean and standard deviation for
  each variable, the correlation and the two
  regression lines

                   X = b'Y + a'
                   Y = bX  + a

  and the residual mean squares. In addition, the
  intersections of the two lines with the frame
  of the plot are indicated by X's and Y's
  respectively. All computations are based on
  data from the plotted cases.
  SIZE = #, #.                                   70, 42/prev.
     The first number is the number of characters
  for the X-axis (the width) and the second
  number is the number of lines for the Y-axis
  (the height). The width is stated first.
  MINimum = # list.     one per              none/prev.
                        variable
     Lower limits for the variables. The first
  number is the lower limit for the first
  variable, the second for the second, etc. If a
  lower limit is specified, it is used as the
  lower limit of the plot's scale and values less
  than the lower limit are omitted from the plot
  and from all computations.
  MAXimum = # list.     one per              none/prev.
                        variable
     Upper limits for the variables. The first
  number is the upper limit for the first
  variable, etc. If an upper limit is specified,
  it is used as the upper limit of the plot's
  scale and values greater than the upper limit
  are omitted from the plot and from all
  computations.
```

Example 6D.3 Plots for Subgroups of Data or Adding Information About a Third Variable to a Bivariate Plot

Separate plots may be printed for each subpopulation (group) and/or values for all groups may be combined in one plot with different plot symbols to identify group membership. In this example we request separate plots (of URICACID vs. WEIGHT) for the women using contraceptive pills and the no-pill women. The cases are classified into groups by specifying a GROUPING variable in the VARIABLE paragraph. For example,

                   GROUPING IS BRTHPILL.

in the VARIABLE paragraph specifies that cases are sorted into two groups according to the two values of the variable BRTHPILL (1 and 2).
   The values of a grouping variable are not restricted to a few codes: an interval scaled variable may be used as a grouping variable. For example, in the plot of URICACID vs. WEIGHT, we could use AGE as a grouping variable. By defining,

say, four CUTPOINTS on AGE, the program would sort the cases into five age groups and the symbol plotted for each case would indicate the age group of the woman. Thus the researcher could scan the plot to see if the values for younger women tend to cluster in a different region from that of the older women displaying information for three variables (URICACID, WEIGHT and AGE) in one plot.
   In this example we specify that the GROUPING variable is BRTHPILL in the VARIABLE paragraph. We define the CODES and NAMES for the grouping variable in the GROUP paragraph. A GROUP paragraph is required unless the variable has less than 10 distinct values. Although we have only two codes, we use the GROUP paragraph here because we want to NAME the groups so the output will be labelled appropriately. We insert the following instructions in those for Example 6D.1 omitting the PLOT paragraph shown there and adding a new PLOT paragraph. The GROUPING IS BRTHPILL instruction is the last one stated in the VARIABLE paragraph.

Output 6D.3   Scatter plots by P6D with symbols to represent group membership

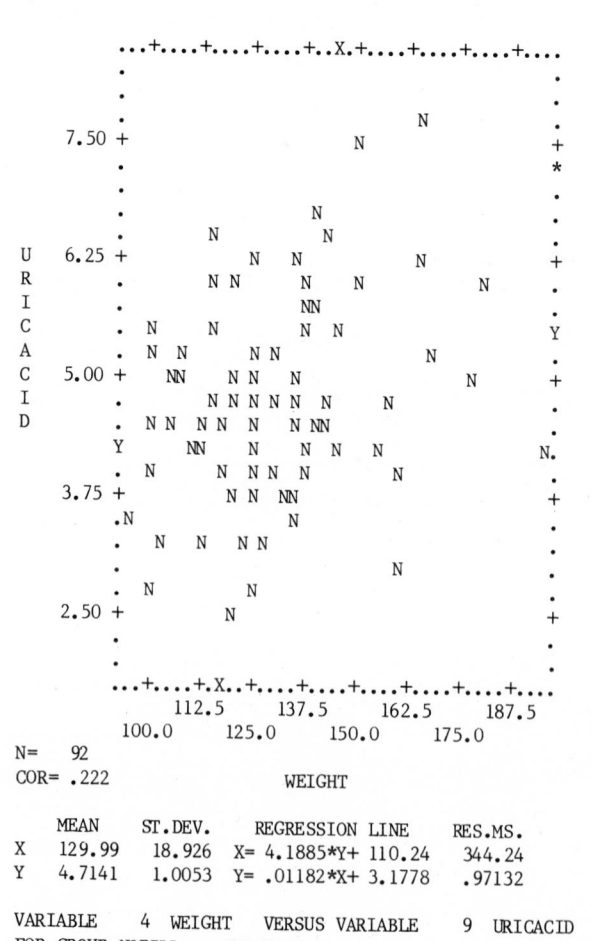

```
N=  92
COR= .222                         WEIGHT

       MEAN      ST.DEV.    REGRESSION LINE      RES.MS.
  X    129.99    18.926     X= 4.1885*Y+ 110.24  344.24
  Y    4.7141    1.0053     Y= .01182*X+ 3.1778   .97132

  VARIABLE    4  WEIGHT   VERSUS VARIABLE    9  URICACID
  FOR GROUP NOPILL    SYMBOL=N
```

```
------------------------------------
      ↗GROUPING IS BRTHPILL.

/ GROUP   CODES(5) ARE      1,   2.
          NAMES(5) ARE NOPILL, PILL.

/ PLOT    YVAR IS URICACID.
          XVAR IS WEIGHT.
          GROUP IS NOPILL.
          GROUP IS PILL.
          GROUPS ARE NOPILL, PILL.
          STATISTICS.
          SIZE IS 40, 25.
------------------------------------
```

Three GROUP statements are specified in the PLOT paragraph. In Output 6D.3 the symbol N represents the cases in the first group (NOPILL) and P the cases in the second group (PILL). Note that in requesting groups, we use the order in which their CODES are listed and not the codes themselves. If points from different groups fall in the same place

an asterisk is used, as in the third plot. Computations are performed using all data plotted in a plot frame without regard to group membership. Compare the last plot of NOPILL and PILL users with the plot in Example 6D.2 which contains the frequencies.

Since MINIMUM and MAXIMUM limits are not specified for WEIGHT, WEIGHT has a different scale in the first plot from the scale in the other plots.

```
VARiable ─────────────────────────────
 GROUPing = v.                no grouping/prev.
   Name or subscript of the variable used to
   classify the cases into groups. If GROUPING is
   not specified or is set to zero, the cases are
   not grouped. If the GROUPING variable takes on
   more than 10 distinct values or codes, CODES or
   CUTPOINTS for the variable must be specified in
   the GROUP paragraph (Section 5.5).
```

```
N= 93
COR= .357              WEIGHT

     MEAN    ST.DEV.   REGRESSION LINE    RES.MS.
X   133.19   22.293    X= 6.2988*Y+ 103.09   438.30
Y   4.7795   1.2644    Y= .02026*X+ 2.0808   1.4099

VARIABLE   4  WEIGHT  VERSUS VARIABLE    9  URICACID
FOR GROUP PILL     SYMBOL=P
```

```
N= 185
COR= .304              WEIGHT

     MEAN    ST.DEV.   REGRESSION LINE    RES.MS.
X   131.60   20.693    X= 5.5229*Y+ 105.38   390.67
Y   4.7470   1.1403    Y= .01677*X+ 2.5401   1.1862

VARIABLE   4  WEIGHT  VERSUS VARIABLE    9  URICACID
FOR GROUP NOPILL   SYMBOL=N
FOR GROUP PILL     SYMBOL=P
```

```
PLOT ─────────────────────────────────────────
    GROUP = g list.   can be repeated      all groups
      The group NAMES (from the GROUP paragraph) or
      group subscripts. The specified groups are
      plotted in the same graph. A group subscript is
      the sequence number of the group as specified
      in the GROUP paragraph. The GROUP statement can
      be repeated in the PLOT paragraph. Each GROUP
      statement defines a separate graph.
```

Example 6D.4 Multiple Plots in the Same Frame

More than one pair of variables can be plotted in the same frame. This is useful when several variables represent the same type of measurements or the same variable is measured at different times, and all are to be plotted against a common variable. To allow flexibility you can specify whether all the XVARIABLES are to be plotted in a common X-axis (XCOMMON), whether all the YVARIABLES are to be plotted on a common Y-axis(YCOMMON), or whether all plots are to be made in a common frame (COMMON). For any of these instructions each pair of variables can be plotted using a different symbol.

COMMON may be specified with PAIR or with CROSS. When XCOMMON or YCOMMON is specified, the default changes to CROSS; the PAIR specification is not allowed. We caution that the number of symbols may become too large to be useful if many variables are plotted in one frame. This problem is compounded when group identification is also requested.

As a simple example we plot both 'NET PAY' (in thousands of dollars) and GROSS earnings per year on the Y-axis versus the YEAR in which the money was earned. Note that the default is CROSS. Our BMDP instructions and data are

```
----------------------------------------
/ PROBLEM    TITLE IS 'TWO PLOTS IN ONE FRAME'.
/ INPUT      VARIABLES ARE 3.
            FORMAT IS FREE.
/ VARIABLE   NAMES ARE 'NET PAY', GROSS, YEAR.
/ PLOT       YVAR ARE 'NET PAY', GROSS.
            XVAR IS YEAR.
            YCOM.
            MIN = 0.
            SIZE IS 40, 25.
            CHAR IS VARIABLE.
/ END
    12.0    15.5       1
    12.1    13.7       2
    12.6    16.5       3
    14.3    17.5       4
    17.6    20.2       5
    19.8    22.4       6
    22.1    25.0       7
    23.8    27.9       8
----------------------------------------
```

The plot is printed in Output 6D.4. We specified a MINIMUM value of zero for 'NET PAY', the first variable, to make the plot scale on the Y-axis start at zero. If more than one variable is plotted on one plot, the lowest minimum of the variables determines the lower limit of the scale. For each variable, the first letter of the VARIABLE NAME is used as the plot symbol instead of the frequency. (The CHARACTER instruction is explained below.)

```
PLOT ─────────────────────────────────────────
  XCOMmon.                                      no
    All the XVARIABLES specified in this PLOT
    paragraph are plotted on a common X-axis.
  YCOMmon.                                      no
    All the YVARIABLES specified in this PLOT
    paragraph are plotted on a common Y-axis.
  COMmon.                                       no
    All plots specified in this PLOT paragraph are
    plotted in one frame. (COM means the same as
    XCOM and YCOM together.)

  Note: If your BMDP programs are dated before
  1980, only one pair of variables can be plotted
  in the same frame; XCOM, YCOM and COM are not
  available.
```

Selecting Plot Symbols: Identifying Groups and/or PAIRS of VARIABLES

The user has control over the symbols used in the plots. We first discuss the options available for plots with one variable on the x-axis and one on the y-axis (grouping information may also be given). We then discuss the more complex situation where three or more variables (plus groups) are displayed in one plot.

One x-variable and one y-variable. There are three choices when there is one variable on each axis:

1) The frequency of each point is plotted as in Example 6D.1. This is the preassigned symbol (when a GROUPING variable is not specified in the VARIABLE paragraph).

2) Group membership can be identified using the first letter (or character) of each group NAME listed in the GROUP paragraph (points for the PILL and NOPILL groups in Example 6D.3 are identified by the symbols P and N). If no names are specified or if the first letters are not unique, P6D uses A, B, C, ... For group identification, the user must specify the GROUPING variable in the VARIABLE paragraph. If the grouping variable has 10 or more distinct values, CODES or CUTPOINTS must also be specified in the GROUP paragraph.

3) User specified symbols can be requested with the SYMBOL instruction in the PLOT paragraph. You can specify a uniform symbol, such as an asterisk, be plotted for all points, by stating

$$SYMBOL = '*'.$$

You can also specify a symbol for each group. If a GROUPING variable is specified, the number of symbols listed must be equal to the total number of groups (i.e., the total number of groups defined by the GROUPING variable, not the number of groups in the PLOT paragraph GROUP statement).

Three or more variables per plot. If two or more variables are plotted on a common axis, or if a GROUP statement is specified, each group for each pair of variables may be identified. You can specify the degree of labeling you want by any combination of the following:

Output 6D.4   Gross income and net pay versus time in one scatter plot by P6D

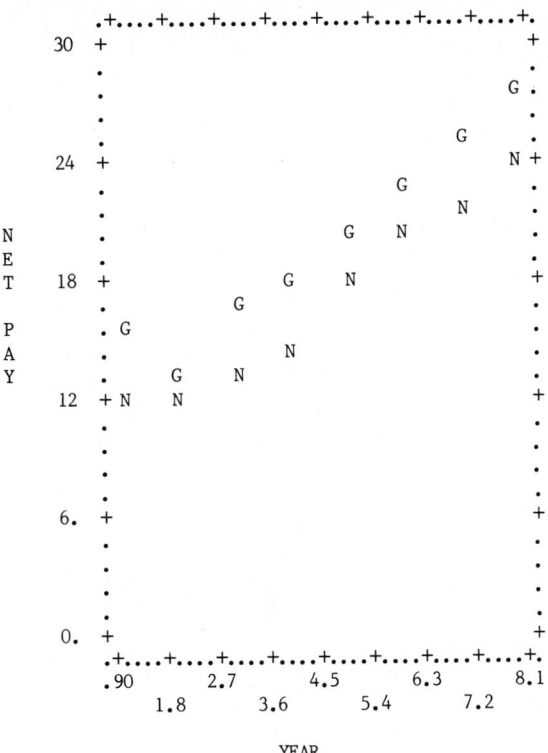

```
              .+....+....+....+....+....+....+....+.
        30  +                                    +
             .                                 G .
             .                                   .
             .                         G         .
        24  +                                N  +
             .                      G          .
      N      .                  G          N     .
      E      .              G       N           .
      T  18  +          G       N               +
             . .      G                         .
      P      . G                                .
      A      .          N                       .
      Y      .      G   N                        .
        12  + N   N                             +
             .                                   .
             .                                   .
             .                                   .
         6. +                                    +
             .                                   .
             .                                   .
             .                                   .
         0. +                                    +
              .+....+....+....+....+....+....+....+.
            .90    2.7    4.5    6.3    8.1
                1.8    3.6    5.4    7.2

                      YEAR
```

VARIABLE   3   YEAR   VERSUS VARIABLE   1   NET PAY   SYMBOL=N
VARIABLE   3   YEAR   VERSUS VARIABLE   2   GROSS   SYMBOL=G

CHARACTER = {
  FREQ.   frequency is plotted at each point
  GROUP.   groups only are uniquely identified
  VAR.   pairs of variables only are uniquely identified
  GROUP,VAR.   both groups and pairs of variables are uniquely identified
}

When x variables and/or y variables and groups are to be identified in one plot frame, (CHARACTER IS GROUP, VARIABLE.) the characters A, B, C, ... are preassigned in an order where the x variables move slowest and group index moves fastest, as in the following list, for example:

x_1 y_1 G_1 ——— A
x_1 y_1 G_2 ——— B
x_1 y_2 G_1 ——— C
x_1 y_2 G_2 ——— D
x_2 y_1 G_1 ——— E
x_2 y_1 G_2 ——— F
x_2 y_2 G_1 ——— G
x_2 y_2 G_2 ——— H

The SYMBOL instruction may be used to change the plot symbols from A, B, C, ... (the symbols should be ordered as shown in the list above). The number of symbols, if specified, must equal the product of the number of groups and the number of pairs of variables (here we have two groups times four pairs, or eight symbols).

For CHARACTER IS GROUP and CHARACTER IS VARIABLE, P6D uses as the preassigned symbol the first letter from user-specified GROUP or VARIABLE names. For GROUP the symbols plotted are the first letter of the group NAMES specified in the GROUP paragraph. If the first letters are not unique, A, B, C, ... are used. (The GROUPING variable must also be identified in the VARIABLE paragraph.) The SYMBOL instruction may be used to change the preassigned symbols.

The preassigned symbols for CHARACTER IS VARIABLE depend on other instructions specified in the PLOT paragraph. For PAIR, CROSS, YCOMMON or for both PAIR and COMMON, the first letters of the YVARIABLE names are plotted. For XCOMMON the first letters of the XVARIABLE names are used. The names of the plot variables must be stated in the NAME list in the VARIABLE paragraph. If the first letters of the names are not unique, the letters A, B, C, ... are used. If both CROSS and COMMON are specified, the characters A, B, C, ... are used as stated in the above list. The SYMBOL list may be used to change the preassigned symbol. The number of symbols, if specified, must equal the number of pairs of variables in the plot frame.

```
┌ PLOT ──────────────────────────────────────────────────────────┐
│  │ CHARacter = FREQ.                    FREQ if no GROUP         │
│  or CHARacter = (one or both)          statement; GROUP         │
│                 GROUP, VAR.            otherwise                 │
│     See explanation above.                                      │
│  SYMBol = 'c ', 'c ',    .             1, 2,... if              │
│                                        CHAR = FREQ;             │
│                                        otherwise, see           │
│                                        discussion above         │
│                                                                 │
│     See explanation above.                                      │
│                                                                 │
│  Note: If your BMDP programs are dated before                   │
│  1980, only FREQ or GROUP can be assigned to                    │
│  CHARACTER; SYMBOL is not available.                            │
└─────────────────────────────────────────────────────────────────┘
```

Multiple Data Points

If several subjects (several cases) have the same values for the variables of interest you can write one record (row of the data matrix) with the values and include an additional variable with the count — instead of a separate record for each case. The variable containing the counts is identified in the COUNT statement of the VARIABLE paragraph. The values for the correct sample size are used in the plot frequencies as well as in the computation of the statistics. For example,

```
/ PROBLEM    TITLE IS 'MULTIPLE DATA POINTS'.
/ INPUT      VARIABLES ARE 3.
             FORMAT IS FREE.
/ VARIABLE   NAMES ARE GROSS, YEAR, PEOPLE.
             COUNT IS PEOPLE.
/ PLOT       YVAR IS GROSS.
             XVAR IS YEAR.
             STATISTICS.
/ END
    10.0    1    3
    20.0    1    5
    30.0    1    6
    40.0    1    2
    10.0    2    7
    30.0    2    3
    40.0    2    5
    10.0    3    2
    20.0    3    2
    20.0    4    1
    30.0    4    5
    50.0    4    1
```

In this example, the variable named PEOPLE contains the number of people having a certain GROSS on a given YEAR. The frequency will be the symbol plotted for the plot of GROSS versus YEAR. The statistics will reflect the multiple data points. For example, five people grossed $40,000 during the second year. The plot symbol will be five, the frequency for this point. (No output is given for this example.)

```
┌ VARiable ──────────────────────────────────────────────────────┐
│  │ COUNT = v.                               none/prev.          │
│     The name or subscript of the variable                       │
│  containing the case counts. Only the integer                   │
│  part of the COUNT variable is used.                            │
└─────────────────────────────────────────────────────────────────┘
```

SIZE OF PROBLEM

P6D copies the data and rereads it as many times as necessary to form the specified plots. Each time the data are read, P6D constructs as many plots as it can fit into memory (about 10 if the plots are the preassigned size (70, 42), more if the plots are smaller). On a medium-sized computer system, the largest single plot can have approximately 24,000 plot positions (length of X-axis times the length of Y-axis).

COMPUTATIONAL METHOD

Computation of the means, standard deviations and covariances are in single precision by the method of provisional means (Appendix A.2).

When MINIMUMS and MAXIMUMS are not specified in the PLOT paragraph for any variable to be plotted, the data are first read to find the observed minimums and maximums and then reread to construct the scatter plots. Thus, stating the minimums and maximums improves the program's efficiency.

ACKNOWLEDGEMENT

P6D was designed and programmed by Steve Chasen. Later revisions were made by Laszlo Engelman and Lanaii Kline.

SUMMARY

Order of Input Cards

```
// (job card)
// EXEC BIMED,PROG=BMDP6D        (see Appendix E)
//SYSIN DD *
/ PROBLEM
/ INPUT
/ VARIABLE
/ GROUP
/ TRANSFORM
/ SAVE
/ PLOT            Repeat for subproblems
/ END
   (data, if on cards)
// (system card)
```

Full sets of BMDP paragraphs (and data, if on cards) can be repeated for additional problems; see Section 5.8.

Paragraph Statement	Preassigned	Comment and Manual Reference
/ VARiable		Additional option required to classify cases into groups.
GROUPing = v.	none	Variable used to define group membership (see also / GROUP). Zero implies cases are not grouped. * 137
COUNT = v.	none	Variable containing number of cases represented by each row of data. Statistics and plot frequencies are adjusted accordingly. * 140
/●PLOT		Required to specify printed plots (may be repeated).
●XVAR = v list.	first var.	Names or subscripts of variables plotted horizontally (along the X-axis). * 133
●YVAR = v list.	last var.	Names or subscripts of variables plotted vertically (along the Y-axis). *
PAIR. or CROSS.	PAIR.	The program PAIRS the YVAR variables with the XVAR variables unless CROSS is specified. * 133 PAIR: The first XVAR vs. the first YVAR; the second XVAR vs. the second YVAR; etc. CROSS: The first XVAR vs. the first YVAR; the first XVAR vs. the second YVAR, etc.; the second XVAR vs. the first YVAR; the second XVAR vs. the second YVAR, etc.
GROUPS = g list.	all groups in one plot	Groups to be included in graph. May be repeated in this paragraph: each group sentence requests a separate graph. 138
STATistics.	no	Compute the mean, standard deviation, correlation and the two regression lines equal to $bX + a$ and $b'Y + a'$ (the intersection of each line with the plot frame is indicated by Y's and X's respectively.) * 136

MINimums = # list.
MAXimums = # list.
	none	Lower and upper limits for the variables. The program forms pairs of corresponding numbers from both lists, one pair of numbers (MIN and MAX) for each variable. The first pair are the limits for including the first variable in plots and computations; the second, for the second variable, etc. Values outside limits are omitted from the plot and all computations. * 136

SIZE = #, #.	70, 42.	Width of x-axis (characters); height of y-axis (lines). * 136
XCOMmon.	no	All XVARS are plotted on a common X-axis. 138
YCOMmon.	no	All YVARS are plotted on a common Y-axis. 138
COMmon.	no	All plots are plotted in a common frame. 138
SYMBol = c list.	1,2,... if CHAR=FREQ; A,B,... otherwise	Symbols used for group or variable identification. 140
CHARacter = c.	(see comment)	FREQUENCY or one or both of GROUP and variable. Each point on the graph is a frequency count or a letter indicating group. The initial letters of the group names are used when they are unique, otherwise the program supplies letters. FREQ is preassigned unless GROUPING variable is specified - then GROUP is preassigned. 140

Key:

/	-indicates paragraph
.	-period ends a sentence
●	-required
v	-variable (name or subscript)
g	-group (name or subscript)
#	-number
'c'	-characters (name or parameter) may omit apostrophes if contiguous letters only

*	-assigned value remains the same for additional problems
VT	-number of variables after transformations
list	-more than one item, often one per var.

Capitalized letters-paragraph or sentence names recognized by BMDP

Page numbers following refer to this Manual

11

FREQUENCY TABLES

P4F

Two-Way and Multiway Frequency Tables —
Measures of Association and the Log-linear Model
(Complete and Incomplete Tables)

Morton B. Brown
Tel-Aviv University

ABSTRACT

Frequency tables (or cross-tabulations) are used to summarize results from surveys, clinical studies and experiments. These tables are appropriate when the data are qualitative or categorical (e.g., sex, treatment or outcome group, or an answer to a multiple choice question), discrete but ordered (e.g., number of pregnancies, level of education attained, or a judgement on an ordered scale) or continuous but grouped into intervals (e.g., intervals of age, weight or height).

In this chapter we discuss the formation of frequency tables, statistics appropriate to categorical data and tests of hypotheses about the data. The tables can be two-way, multiway, or cross sections of a multiway table. The tabulation of disease severity by drug treatment is an example of a two-way table. If the tabulation is performed for each sex separately, then each table (one for males and one for females) is a cross section of a three-way table (disease by drug by sex). Similarly a four-way table can be separated into cross sections that are three-way tables or two-way tables. Often it is useful to examine the multiway table as well as cross sections of it.

P4F combines features of earlier BMDP programs--P1F[1], P2F[1], and P3F[1] -- with new features not present in the earlier programs. The new features are indicated by *'s in the following descriptions:

The observed frequency tables are printed
- with row and column totals and the total frequency
* - followed by a table that summarizes the reasons that cases were not included in the observed frequency tables (such as an index with a value missing or out of range)

* <u>More than one index</u> can be printed horizontally by use of the stack option.

Two-way frequency tables can be printed as
- tables of percentages of row totals, of column totals or of the total frequency
- expected values under the model that the row index is independent of the column index ($e_{ij} = r_i c_j / N$ where r_i is the ith row total, c_j is the jth column total, N is the total frequency and e_{ij} is the expected values of cell (i,j))
- functions of the difference between the observed

****

[1] The Control Language of the earlier programs is described in Appendix A.8.

(a_{ij}) and expected (e_{ij}) cell frequencies, such as Freeman-Tukey deviates, standardized deviates (($a_{ij} - e_{ij}$)/e_{ij}^2), components of chi-square, etc.

Two-way and multiway frequency tables can be
- tabulated from data read as cases
- formed from data recorded as cell frequencies and indices resulting from a previous tabulation
- read as a multiway frequency table

Tests of independence and statistics available for two-way tables include
- the chi-square test of independence between rows and columns, the likelihood ratio test of independence
- Fisher's exact test of independence for the 2x2 table
- functions of the chi-square statistic, such as the contingency coefficient, phi and Cramer's V
* - statistics for a 2x2 table such as Yule's Q and Y, the cross-product ratio, Yates' corrected chi-square and the Mantel-Haenszel statistics
- measures of association when both indices of the table are ordered, such as Goodman and Kruskal's Γ, Kendall's τ_b, Stuart's τ_c, Somers' D and the correlation and rank correlation coefficients
- measures of prediction when both indices are unordered, such as Goodman and Kruskal's τ and λ and the uncertainty coefficient
- McNemar's test of symmetry for square tables
- a test of linear trend of the proportions when the table is 2xk or kx2.

For variables used as indices in frequency tables, P4F prints
- univariate statistics (means, standard deviations, frequencies, minimums and maximums)
* - number of values equal to the code for missing values, above specified MAXIMUM limits, below specified MINIMUM limits, or not equal to specified category CODES.

* Cases excluded from one or more tables can be crosstabulated against sequence numbers of the table from which they are excluded: this provides a terse representation of the presence of incomplete data.

Multiway frequency tables can be
* - printed as tables of percentages of row totals, column totals or of the total frequency
- summarized as marginal subtables (obtained by summing over one or more indices of the table).

The log-linear model is a primary tool in the analysis of relationships between variables crosstabulated into multiway frequency tables. The log-linear model represents the logarithm of the expected cell frequency as a linear combination of effects (similar to an analysis of variance model except that the logarithm of the expected cell frequency replaces the expected value in the ANOVA model). For example, in the two-way table the logarithm of the expected value under the model of independence can be written as

$$\ln e_{ij} = \alpha_i + \beta_j + k$$

where $\alpha_i = \ln r_i$, $\beta_j = \ln c_j$ and $k = -\ln N$; this is the simplest log-linear model. We recommend the texts by Bishop et al (1975), Fienberg (1977) and

Plackett (1974) for more detailed discussions of the log-linear model.

Selection of appropriate log-linear models is facilitated by several options available in P4F. P4F can fit and test
- all possible models (when the table is two-way or three-way)
- all models of full order (models that contain all interactions of a given order)
- tests of marginal and partial association for each interaction
- user-specified models
* - models formed in a stepwise manner by the addition or deletion of interactions from a user-specified model

For each user-specified log-linear model P4F provides
- a test-of-fit of the model
- expected cell frequencies estimated from the specified model
* - estimates of the log-linear parameters and their standard errors
- functions of the differences between the observed and expected cell frequencies, such as Freeman-Tukey deviates, standardized deviates and components of the chi-square statistic.

*   Interactions (marginal subtables) fixed by design can be included in all models by a single instruction.

A test of quasi-independence (Goodman, 1968) describes the test of independence using frequencies in a subset of the cells in a two-way table. For example, there may be zero probability that an observation will fall in some cells (called structural zeros) even if the experiment is repeated many times; the test of independence can only be applied to cells in which there are no zero probabilities of finding observed values. A second example is when the hypothesis of interest excludes one or more cells (such as cells on the diagonal). In both examples the hypothesis of independence is limited to a subset of the table. Similarly in a multiway table, it is possible to fit models that do not apply to all cells; i.e., apply only to a subset of the table.

*   Structural zeros or cells to be excluded from the model fitting can be specified. The model is fitted to the data in the remaining cells and the appropriate test-of-fit is computed.

The model of independence in a two-way table may be appropriate for most but not all of the cell frequencies. For example, the model may fit all cell frequencies except those on the diagonal; or the model may be appropriate for all but one of the cell frequencies when one cell frequency is incorrectly recorded. Similarly, in a multiway table a model may explain the frequencies in most cells of the table. P4F can identify, in a stepwise manner, cells whose frequencies deviate from the expected frequencies under the proposed model. This type of screening can help identify patterns or unusual features in the data.

*   P4F screens for divergent cells by identifying

the cell whose Freeman-Tukey deviate or standardized deviate is extreme with respect to the model fit; this cell is eliminated (treated as a structural zero) and the algorithm repeated for a number of steps. Unusual observed frequencies may be identified in this manner.

* The data in a frequency table may be fitted well by a model except for the data at one of the levels of a categorical variable. (P4F can refit the model to the data after eliminating in turn each one of the levels (strata) of an index.) For example; if the variable were 'marital status', the first analysis might exclude all those 'married', the second analysis all those 'single', etc.

WHERE TO FIND IT

P4F Instructions (see also Chapters 5, 6 and 7)

Paragraph structure and ordering

/ PROBLEM
/ INPUT   see Chapter 5
/ VARIABLE
/ TRANSFORMATION   see Chapter 6
/ CATEGORY (or GROUP)   see Chapter 5,
          the CATEGORY CODES or CUTPOINTS are
          required if there are more than 10
          values for any categorical variable
          or if you are forming multiway
          tables; otherwise 10 levels are
          allocated for each index. P4F
          initially allocates space for all
          tables requested using the number of
          levels specified for each index or
          ten (the default allocation). If
          one four-way table is requested and
          ten levels are assumed for each
          index, 10^4 = 10,000 cells will be
          required. This may exceed the space
          available to the program. Therefore
          we recommend that CODES or CUTPOINTS
          be specified when the tables are
          more than two-way.
/ SAVE   see Chapter 7

/ TABLE   - defines tables to be formed; may be repeated
/ PRINT   - specifies types of tables to be printed, applies to preceding TABLE paragraph, may appear once after each TABLE paragraph
/ STATISTICS - tests of independence and statistics for two-way table only, applies to preceding TABLE paragraph, may appear once after each TABLE paragraph
/ FIT   - describes log-linear models to be fit to data in a multiway table, may be repeated several times after each TABLE paragraph
/ END   - terminates Control Language

The above list of examples and options can be used as an index to the program description. The tests and statistics for the two-way table are summarized in Table 11.2. Additionally the summary table (p. 205) or the index at the back can be used to find topics in the program description.

TWO-WAY TABLES — DESCRIPTIVE

Example 4F.1 Basic Setup for Forming Tables

P4F can tabulate many two-way frequency tables at one time. Each table is formed from all cases with valid (acceptable) data values for the two indices of the table. When some data values are not included in the table (because they are out of range, missing or not equal to one of the category CODES), P4F also prints summaries of the values excluded from the table.

The Kasser coronary data presented in Table 11.1 (Kasser and Bruce, 1969; Kronmal and Tarter, 1973) are used to illustrate the ease of obtaining two-way tables. The Control Language instructions to describe the data and variables are common to all BMDP programs and are explained in Chapter 5: the PROBLEM, INPUT, VARIABLE and CATEGORY paragraphs are used in the frequency table programs discussed in this chapter. (For input already in table form see Examples 4F.10, 4F.11 and 4F.13.) If data editing or transformations are necessary, the methods described in Chapter 6 can be used.

In our first example we request (in the TABLE paragraph) the formation of three two-way frequency tables: the first is INFARCT classified against ANGINA, the second is FUNCTION classified against ACTIVE, and the third is AGE against INFARCT. The CATEGORY paragraph is used to specify intervals for the continuous variable AGE and to name the CODES: when there are 10 or fewer codes (distinct values) for each categorical variable and naming the codes is not desired, this paragraph can be omitted (Section 5.5). The BMDP instructions are:

```
     ----------------------------------------
/ PROBLEM    TITLE IS 'KASSER CORONARY DATA'.
/ INPUT      VARIABLES ARE 6.
             CASES ARE 117.
             FORMAT IS '(6F4.0)'.
/ VARIABLE   NAMES ARE AGE, FUNCTION, ACTIVE,
                       INFARCT, ANGINA, HIGHBP.

/ CATEGORY   CUTPOINTS(1) ARE 50, 60.
             NAMES(1) ARE 'UNDER 51', '51-60',
                         'OVER 60'.
             CODES(2) ARE 0, 1, 2, 3.
             NAMES(2) ARE NONE, MINIMAL, MODERATE,
                         SEVERE.
             CODES(3) ARE 1, 2, 3.
             NAMES(3) ARE VERY, NORMAL, LIMITED.
             CODES(4) ARE 0, 1.
             NAMES(4) ARE NONE, PRESENT.
             CODES(5) ARE 0, 1.
             NAMES(5) ARE NONE, PRESENT.
             CODES(6) ARE 0, 1.
             NAMES(6) ARE NONE, PRESENT.

/ TABLE      COLUMNS  ARE INFARCT, FUNCTION, AGE.
             ROWS     ARE ANGINA, ACTIVE, INFARCT.
/ END
     ----------------------------------------
```

(See end of this P4F section for organization of systems information, BMDP instructions and data.)

The frequency tables specified in the TABLE paragraph are printed in Output 4F.1. Circled numbers below correspond to those in the output.

① Interpretation of the options specific to P4F. P4F lists only the options that cause results to be

Table 11.1 Data on 117 male coronary patients from a study by Kasser and Bruce (1969) as presented in Kronmal and Tarter (1973)

```
42  2  2  1  1  0      51  3  0  0  1  0      53  2  2  1  0  0      55  3  3  1  0  0
66  2  2  1  1  0      50  0  0  0  1  0      58  1  2  1  0  1      52  0  0  1  1  0
56  2  0  1  1  0      72  3  3  0  1  1      38  1  2  0  1  0      61  2  2  0  0  0
55  2  2  1  1  0      56  3  3  1  1  0      35  2  2  1  1  0      45  2  2  0  1  0
41  2  2  1  1  1      56  3  3  1  1  0      34  2  3  1  1  0      51  2  0  1  1  0
62  0  0  1  0  1      63  2  2  1  1  0      68  3  2  1  1  0      55  3  3  1  1  1
46  2  2  1  1  1      53  1  2  1  1  0      49  3  2  0  1  0      51  1  0  1  0  0
44  2  1  0  1  1      53  0  1  1  0  0      55  2  2  0  1  1      46  1  0  1  1  0
50  1  2  0  1  1      57  3  2  0  1  0      58  0  2  1  1  0      69  1  2  0  1  0
73  3  3  0  1  0      57  1  2  0  1  1      43  2  2  1  1  0      51  3  3  1  1  1
48  2  2  1  1  0      62  2  2  1  1  0      39  2  1  0  1  0      49  1  1  0  1  1
53  2  2  1  1  0      73  2  2  0  1  0      66  3  3  0  1  1      58  3  3  1  1  0
51  3  1  1  1  1      44  2  0  0  1  0      50  2  2  1  1  0      38  3  3  1  1  0
59  0  0  0  1  1      63  3  2  1  1  0      45  3  3  0  1  0      50  1  1  1  0  0
54  3  3  1  1  1      59  1  0  1  0  0      53  0  0  1  0  0      38  1  3  1  1  0
41  2  2  1  1  1      51  1  0  1  0  0      56  3  3  1  1  1      58  1  0  1  0  0
56  2  2  1  0  1      52  3  0  1  1  0      49  2  2  1  1  1      69  0  0  0  1  0
38  0  2  0  1  1      64  0  0  1  0  0      49  0  0  1  0  0      66  0  0  0  1  0
40  3  3  1  1  0      53  2  2  1  0  0      56  2  2  1  1  0      49  2  2  0  1  0
42  1  2  1  1  0      58  1  2  0  1  0      38  0  0  1  1  0      62  0  0  1  1  0
51  1  2  0  1  0      53  0  2  1  1  1      39  0  0  1  1  0      44  0  0  1  1  1
52  1  0  1  1  0      58  2  2  1  0  0      62  2  2  1  1  0      58  3  0  1  1  0
37  0  1  0  1  0      45  1  2  1  1  1      70  3  2  1  1  1      45  2  2  1  1  0
48  1  2  1  0  0      42  3  2  0  1  0      53  2  0  1  1  1      58  3  3  1  1  1
35  0  0  1  1  0      60  2  2  0  1  1      68  2  2  1  1  0      54  2  2  1  1  0
35  1  1  1  0  0      34  1  0  1  0  1      50  2  0  0  0  1      55  2  2  1  1  1
48  3  3  0  1  1      64  2  2  1  1  0      46  2  2  1  1  0      58  2  2  1  1  0
52  2  2  0  1  1      35  1  2  1  0  1      58  3  2  1  1  0      68  2  2  1  1  0
46  2  3  0  1  1      42  2  2  0  1  0      57  2  2  0  0  0      47  1  2  1  1  1
                                                                    55  0  0  0  1  0
```

Key:

AGE (in years)

FUNCTION – functional class: 0 none, 1 minimal, 2 moderate, 3 more than moderate (3 is a combination of two groups)

ACTIVE: 0 unknown, 1 very, 2 normal, 3 limited (note: 0 is not specified as a valid code in the CATEGORY paragraph.)

INFARCT – history of past myocardial infarctions: 0 none, 1 present

ANGINA – history of angina pectoris: 0 none, 1 present

HIGHBP – history of high blood pressure: 0 none, 1 present

The variable AGE is recorded in columns 3 and 4; the other variables are recorded in columns 8, 12, 16, 20 and 24

Output 4F.1 Two-way frequency tables formed by P4F. Circled numbers correspond to those in the text

----

--- the BMDP instructions are printed and interpreted ---

***NOTE—REQUESTED OPTIONS ONLY ARE PRINTED BELOW.   ①

INTERPRETATION OF TABLE PARAGRAPH 1.
----
   3 TABLES ARE REQUESTED —
   TABLE 1   INFARCT   BY   ANGINA
   TABLE 2   FUNCTION   BY   ACTIVE
   TABLE 3   AGE   BY   INFARCT

INTERPRETATION OF PRINT PARAGRAPH — APPLIED TO TABLE PARAGRAPH   1 ABOVE

PRINT TABLE OF OBSERVED VALUES.
PRINT TABLE OF EXCLUDED VALUES.
LIST FIRST   5 CASES WITH UNACCEPTABLE VALUES.

INTERPRETATION OF THE STATISTICS PARAGRAPH — APPLIED TO TABLE PARAGRAPH   1 ABOVE

COMPUTE CHI-SQUARE STATISTICS.

(output continued)

147

Output 4F.1 (continued)

PRINT LIST OUTPUT— M'S INDICATE TABLES FOR WHICH THE CASE HAS INVALID DATA FOR AT LEAST ONE INDEX.

CASE NO.	TABLE NUMBER
	1 2 3
3	M
6	M (2)
14	M
22	M
25	M

NUMBER OF CASES READ.   117   (3)

						NUMBER OF VALUES			
VARIABLE	MEAN	STANDARD	SMALLEST	LARGEST	TOTAL	MISSING	BELOW	ABOVE	NOT EQUAL TO
NO. NAME		DEVIATION	VALUE	VALUE	FREQUENCY		MINIMUM	MAXIMUM	STATED CODES
1 AGE	52.32	9.47	34.00	73.00	117	0	0	0	0
2 FUNCTION	1.68	1.01	0.0	3.00	117	0	0	0	0 (4)
3 ACTIVE	1.59	1.04	0.0	3.00	117	0	0	0	29
4 INFARCT	0.63	0.48	0.0	1.00	117	0	0	0	0
5 ANGINA	0.84	0.37	0.0	1.00	117	0	0	0	0

--- CATEGORY paragraph is interpreted ---

```
************************
* TABLE PARAGRAPH   1  *
************************
```

***** OBSERVED FREQUENCY TABLE   1

| ANGINA | INFARCT | | |
| ------ | ----- | | |
| | NONE | PRESENT | TOTAL | (5)
NONE	3	16 I	19
PRESENT	40	58 I	98
------		I	
TOTAL	43	74 I	117

ALL CASES HAD COMPLETE DATA FOR THIS TABLE.

MINIMUM ESTIMATED EXPECTED VALUE IS   6.98   (6)

STATISTIC	VALUE	D.F.	PROB.
PEARSON CHISQUARE	4.288	1	0.0384
YATES CORRECTED CHISQ.	3.279	1	0.0702

(output continued)

Output 4F.1 (continued)

***** OBSERVED FREQUENCY TABLE 2

ACTIVE		FUNCTION			
	NONE	MINIMAL	MODERATE	SEVERE	TOTAL
VERY	2	4	2	1 I	9
NORMAL	3	13	37	7 I	60
LIMITED	0	1	2	16 I	19
TOTAL	5	18	41	24 I	88

29 CASES HAD INCOMPLETE DATA.

***** NUMBER OF EXCLUDED CASES — TABLE 2   ⑦

ACTIVE			FUNCTION			
	IN RANGE	MISSING	TOOSMALL	TOOLARGE	UNCOUNTD	TOTAL
IN RANGE	0	0	0	0	0 I	0
MISSING	0	0	0	0	0 I	0
TOOSMALL	0	0	0	0	0 I	0
TOOLARGE	0	0	0	0	0 I	0
UNCOUNTD	29	0	0	0	0 I	29
TOTAL	29	0	0	0	0 I	29

***** ANALYSIS OF OBSERVED FREQUENCY TABLE 2

MINIMUM ESTIMATED EXPECTED VALUE IS   0.51

STATISTIC	VALUE	D.F.	PROB.
PEARSON CHISQUARE	48.365	6	0.0000

***** OBSERVED FREQUENCY TABLE 3

INFARCT		AGE			
	UNDER 51	51-60	OVER 60		TOTAL
NONE	20	15	8 I		43
PRESENT	27	33	14 I		74
TOTAL	47	48	22 I		117

ALL CASES HAD COMPLETE DATA FOR THIS TABLE.

MINIMUM ESTIMATED EXPECTED VALUE IS   8.09

STATISTIC	VALUE	D.F.	PROB.
PEARSON CHISQUARE	1.307	2	0.5202

printed; other options are not listed. Since PRINT and STATISTICS paragraphs were not specified in this example, P4F describes the default options in effect that produce output. Each of the options is described in its appropriate section in this chapter.

② When data are excluded from one of the tables, P4F lists the cases for which the data were omitted and prints an M under the appropriate table number(s). In this problem the variable ACTIVE is assigned three CODES (1, 2 and 3) in the CATEGORY paragraph; however, the value zero (corresponding to unknown) also appears in the data (see Table 11.1). Cases containing the value zero for ACTIVE are omitted from the second table (FUNCTION by ACTIVE). In our example only the first five cases omitted are shown; this is the default for LIST in the PRINT paragraph. More cases would be shown if the value for LIST were increased.

Note: Each table is formed using all acceptable values for the categorical variables; that is, values that are not missing or out of range. When CODES are specified for a categorical variable, only values of the variable equal to one of the specified CODES are used in the analysis.

③ Number of cases read.

④ For each variable, P4F prints the following descriptive statistics. Some of these will not be useful for categorical data. If, however, the variable is ordered or continuous, the information can be useful.

- mean
- smallest observed value (not out of range)
- largest observed value (not out of range)
- frequency of acceptable values (values not out of range and not missing)
- standard deviation
- number of cases with missing values
- number of cases above upper limit (MAXIMUM)
- number of cases below lower limit (MINIMUM)
- number of cases not counted (not equal to a CODE that is specified).

Note: for ACTIVE three codes are specified (1, 2 and 3) but there are also values of zero recorded; the zero values are summarized in the column NOT COUNTED.

Note: only variables used as an index in at least one table are included in this list.

⑤ The two-way frequency table is printed. Around the border of the table P4F prints the row and column totals.

⑥ Under the hypothesis of independence between row and column variables, the expected value of cell (i,j) is $e_{ij} = r_i c_j / N$, where r_i is the row total, c_j the column total and N the total frequency in the table. The smallest expected value is printed (6.98 in the first table). A very small minimum expected value indicates that the chi-square test of independence may be poorly approximated by a chi-square distribution. The minimum expected value in the second table (FUNCTION by ACTIVE) is 0.51. With this small an expected value you may want to combine categories of one of the variables (see p. 159).

Note: Rows or columns that are entirely zero are excluded from the computations of all statistics in the two-way frequency table.

The (Pearson) chi-square test of independence between rows and columns is computed for every frequency table. It is defined as

$$\chi^2 = \Sigma\Sigma(a_{ij} - e_{ij})^2/e_{ij}$$

where a_{ij} is the observed frequency in cell (i,j). P4F prints the values of the chi-square statistic, its degrees of freedom (D.F.) and its probability (the probability of a more extreme result under the hypothesis of independence; i.e., its p-value). If you choose to test a hypothesis at a given level of significance (say .01), a probability less than this level is a significant result.

The table of INFARCT vs ANGINA is 2x2 (2 rows and 2 columns). In addition to the chi-square test, Yates' corrected chi-square and its probability are also printed (see p. 152).

(7) Data excluded from the table. Each table is compiled using all available data for the variables indexing the table. For example, in the Kasser data, the table FUNCTION by ACTIVE contains all cases for which both FUNCTION and ACTIVE have valid codes, whether or not there are valid data for the other variables. When some of the cases contain invalid data (missing, out of range or not equal to a specified code) for the indices of the table, P4F compiles a second table that summarizes the cases not included in the table. The row/column headings for this table are

IN RANGE	- valid for this categorical variable, but failed for one of the other indices in the table
MISSING	- equal to a missing value code
TOO SMALL	- below the specified minimum
TOO LARGE	- above the specified maximum
UNCOUNTD	- not equal to a specified code when category codes are given

The table of excluded values shows that 29 values are uncounted (not equal to a specified CODE) for ACTIVE; however the values of FUNCTION for these cases are in range (acceptable).

If the table is two-way, there will be a zero frequency in the cell (IN RANGE, IN RANGE). However, if the table is three-way or higher, only the two-way cross section (column index by row index) is printed. The frequency reported in the cell (IN RANGE, IN RANGE) is the number of cases that do not have valid data for the third index or higher but have valid data for the first two indices of the table. This table may be omitted from the output by specifying NO EXCLUDE in the PRINT paragraph.

How to create tables - the TABLE paragraph. Tables are specified in the TABLE paragraph. The TABLE paragraph can be repeated before the END paragraph to create additional tables. For two-way tables, the usual method to describe the tables is to specify the COLUMN variable(s) and ROW variable(s). In Example 4F.1,

```
/ TABLE    COLUMN IS INFARCT, FUNCTION, AGE.
           ROW    IS ANGINA, ACTIVE, INFARCT.
```

produces three two-way tables INFARCT by ANGINA, FUNCTION by ACTIVE and AGE by INFARCT. The first ROW variable is paired with the first COLUMN variable, the second ROW variable with the second COLUMN variable, etc. To form tables from all possible pairings of the ROW and COLUMN variables, specify

```
                CROSS.
```

in the TABLE paragraph. If CROSS were specified in Example 4F.1, nine tables would be requested:

```
    INFARCT   against ANGINA
    INFARCT   against ACTIVE
    INFARCT   against INFARCT
    FUNCTION  against ANGINA
    FUNCTION  against ACTIVE
    FUNCTION  against INFARCT
    AGE       against ANGINA
    AGE       against ACTIVE
    AGE       against INFARCT
```

Eight tables will be printed. One of the tables (INFARCT against INFARCT) has the same index for more than one dimension; therefore it will be omitted. However, the sequence numbers of the tables will be from one to nine (with the third skipped) to allow you to compute the sequence number assigned more easily. (This assigned number is of importance when frequency tables are saved in a BMDP File.)

Note: The first COLUMN variable is crossed with all ROW variables, then the second COLUMN variable is crossed, etc.

TABLE ─────────────────────────────────

COLumn = v list.   required   none
    Names or subscripts of variables that define the column categories (index). (If a COLUMN variable has more than 10 distinct values, you must specify its CODES or CUTPOINTS in the CATEGORY paragraph.)

ROW = v list.   required   none
    Names or subscripts of variables that define the row categories (index). (If a ROW variable has more than 10 distinct values, you must specify its CODES or CUTPOINTS in the CATEGORY paragraph.)

PAIR. or CROSS.   PAIR
    If CROSS is specified, tables are formed from all possible combinations of the ROW and COLUMN variables. The first COLUMN variable is crossed with all the ROW variables in turn, then the second COLUMN variable, etc. Otherwise, the first ROW variable and first COLUMN variable define the first table, the second ROW variable and second COLUMN variable the second table, etc.

Note 1: You may also use the form described for multiway tables (p. 162), where you would specify only two indices or two categorical variables for each table.

Note 2: P4F allocates space for each table to be formed based on the number of codes or intervals specified for each index in the

CATEGORY paragraph. If codes or cutpoints are not specified, 10 levels are allocated. When there are many tables specified, the latter method of allocation (using 10 levels) can cause P4F to be inefficient in its initial space allocation and to exceed the capacity of the program to set up all tables simultaneously. Therefore, we recommend using the CATEGORY paragraph both for neater labelling and for more efficient allocation.

PRINT

OBServed.   OBS/prev.
   Tables of observed frequencies are printed unless NO OBSERVED is specified.
EXClude.   EXCLUDE/prev.
   A two-way table of frequencies of the excluded cases is printed unless NO EXCLUDE. is specified. See ⑦ in Example 4F.1.
LIST = #.   5/prev.
   Maximum number of cases to be printed in a case-by-table display. Only cases that are excluded from one or more tables are printed. See ② in Example 4F.1.

Example 4F.2 Percentages

P4F can print the observed frequencies also as row percentages, column percentages or percentages of the total frequency. To request these percents, we insert the following paragraph into the instructions for Example 4F.1 after the TABLE paragraph. It must appear before the END paragraph.

```
/ PRINT     PERCENT = ROW, COL, TOT.
```

The tables are presented in Output 4F.2. Circled numbers below correspond to those in the output. The tables are:

⑧ Percentages of the total row marginal frequencies: $100\ a_{ij}/r_i$

⑨ Percentages of the total column frequencies: $100\ a_{ij}/c_j$

⑩ Percentages of the total frequency: $100\ a_{ij}/N$

PRINT

PERCent = (one or more)   none/prev.
          NO,ROW,COL,TOT.
   If ROW is specified, a table of percents of the row totals is printed; if COL is specified, a table of percents of the column totals is printed; if TOT is specified, a table of percents of the total frequency in the table is printed. See Example 4F.2.

Output 4F.2   Percentages in two-way tables printed by P4F

--- ① to ④ in Ouput 4F.1 appear here ---

```
************************
* TABLE PARAGRAPH   1  *
************************
```

***** OBSERVED FREQUENCY TABLE   1

ANGINA	INFARCT		
	NONE	PRESENT	TOTAL
NONE	3	16 I	19
PRESENT	40	58 I	98
TOTAL	43	74 I	117

ALL CASES HAD COMPLETE DATA FOR THIS TABLE.

***** PERCENTS OF ROW TOTALS — TABLE   1

ANGINA	INFARCT			⑧
	NONE	PRESENT	TOTAL	
NONE	15.8	84.2 I	100.0	
PRESENT	40.8	59.2 I	100.0	
TOTAL	36.8	63.2 I	100.0	

***** PERCENTS OF COLUMN TOTALS — TABLE   1

ANGINA	INFARCT			⑨
	NONE	PRESENT	TOTAL	
NONE	7.0	21.6 I	16.2	
PRESENT	93.0	78.4 I	83.8	
TOTAL	100.0	100.0 I	100.0	

***** PERCENTS OF THE TABLE TOTAL — TABLE   1

ANGINA	INFARCT			⑩
	NONE	PRESENT	TOTAL	
NONE	2.6	13.7 I	16.2	
PRESENT	34.2	49.6 I	83.8	
TOTAL	36.8	63.2 I	100.0	

MINIMUM ESTIMATED EXPECTED VALUE IS   6.98

STATISTIC	VALUE	D.F.	PROB.
PEARSON CHISQUARE	4.288	1	0.0384
YATES CORRECTED CHISQ.	3.279	1	0.0702

--- similar results for tables 2 and 3 ---

Table 11.2 Tests and Measures Computed by P4F

Test or measure	Indices ordered?	Table	Range of values	Formula	Test that measure is zero	Interpretation
χ^2 test	no	RxC	$0,\infty$	$\chi^2 = \Sigma\Sigma \dfrac{(a_{ij}-e_{ij})^2}{e_{ij}}$	Chisquare with $(R-1)(C-1)$ df	Tests of independence of rows and columns or equality of proportions between rows or columns
G^2 likelihood ratio test	no	RxC	$0,\infty$	$G^2 = 2\Sigma\Sigma \ a_{ij} ln\left(\dfrac{a_{ij}}{e_{ij}}\right)$	Chisquare with $(R-1)(C-1)$ df	
χ_y^2 (Yates corrected χ^2)	no	2x2	$0,\infty$	$\chi_y^2 = \dfrac{N(|ad-bc|-\frac{N}{2})^2}{r_1 r_2 c_1 c_2}$	Chisquare with 1 df	
Fisher's exact test	no	2x2	$0,1$	probability of more extreme configuration (1-tail or 2-tail)		
ϕ (phi)	no	RxC	$0,m$	$\phi = (\chi^2/N)^{\frac{1}{2}}$	use χ^2 test	Same as χ^2 but not dependent on N. Used to compare tables
		2x2	$-1,1$	$\phi = \dfrac{ad-bc}{(r_1 r_2 c_1 c_2)^{\frac{1}{2}}}$	use χ^2 test	
Contingency coefficient, C	no	RxC	$0,1$	$C = \left[\dfrac{\chi^2}{N+\chi^2}\right]^{\frac{1}{2}}$	use χ^2 test	
Cramer's V	no	RxC	$0,1$	$V = \left[\dfrac{\chi^2}{N(m-1)}\right]^{\frac{1}{2}}$	use χ^2 test	
Yule's Q		2x2	$-1,1$	$Q = \dfrac{ad-bc}{ad+bc}$	use χ^2 test	Probability of similar (dissimilar) ranking on two ordered indices among cases with different values for both indices
Yule's Y		2x2	$-1,1$	$Y = \dfrac{\sqrt{ad}-\sqrt{bc}}{\sqrt{ad}+\sqrt{bc}}$	use χ^2 test	Similar to Q but less weighting for similar and dissimilar rankings
Cross-product ratio α		2x2	$0,\infty$	$\alpha = \dfrac{ad}{bc}$	to test $\alpha=1$ use χ^2 test	odds-ratio · ratio of two proportions
Mantel-Haenszel		2x2		Appendix A.5		Combines and compares odds ratios between 2x2 tables
Tetrachoric correlation, r_t		2x2	$-1,1$	Appendix A.5	$r_t/s_o(r_t)$	Correlation of bivariate normal with the probabilities a/N, b/N, c/N, d/N in the four quadrants
Gamma, Γ	yes	RxC	$-1,1$	$\Gamma = \dfrac{P-Q}{P+Q}$	$\Gamma/s_o(\Gamma)$	Probability of similar (dissimilar) ranking on two indices among cases with different values for both indices
Kendall's τ_b	yes	RxC	$-1,1$	$\tau_b = \dfrac{P-Q}{[(N^2-\Sigma r_i^2)(N^2-\Sigma c_j^2)]^{\frac{1}{2}}}$	$t_b/s_o(t_b)$	Numerator as in Γ, denominator $\geq$ that of Γ
Stuart's τ_c	yes	RxC	$-1,1$	$\tau_c = \dfrac{P-Q}{N^2}\left[\dfrac{m}{m-1}\right]$	$t_c/s_o(t_c)$	Numerator as in Γ, τ_b. Denominator $\geq$ that of Γ, τ_b.
Product-moment correlation, r	yes	RxC	$-1,1$	$r = \dfrac{\Sigma a_{ij}(i-\bar{i})(j-\bar{j})}{[\Sigma r_i(i-\bar{i})^2 \Sigma c_j(j-\bar{j})^2]^{\frac{1}{2}}}$	$r/s_o(r)$	Correlation using values of the indices with frequencies as number of replicates
Spearman rank correlation, r_s	yes	RxC	$-1,1$	r_s = r applied to ranks	$r_s/s_o(r_s)$	As in r except ranks of the indices are the values
Somers' D	yes	RxC	$-1,1$	$D_{j|i} = \dfrac{P-Q}{N^2 - \Sigma r_i^2}$	$D/s_o(D)$	Probability of similar (dissimilar) ranking on two indices among cases with different values for row index. Note: $\tau_b^2 = D_{j|i} \cdot D_{i|j}$
Goodman and Kruskal τ	no	RxC	$0,1$	$\tau_{j|i} = \dfrac{N\Sigma\Sigma a_{ij}^2/r_i - \Sigma c_j^2}{N^2 - \Sigma c_j^2}$	use χ^2 test	Compares random proportional prediction of one index with conditional proportional prediction based upon knowledge of second index
Optimal prediction λ	no	RxC	$0,1$	$\lambda_{j|i} = \dfrac{\Sigma\limits_i \max\limits_j a_{ij} - \max\limits_j c_j}{N - \max\limits_j c_j}$		Measure of predictive association--relative degree of success with which one index can be used to predict second index
Optimal prediction λ^*	no	RxC	$0,1$	$\lambda_{j|i}^* = \dfrac{\Sigma\limits_i (\max\limits_j a_{ij})/r_i - \max\limits_j \Sigma(a_{ij}/r_i)}{R - \max\limits_j \Sigma(a_{ij}/r_i)}$		Similar to λ but adjusted to have common row marginals
Uncertainty coefficient, U	no	RxC	$0,1$	$U_{j|i} = \dfrac{\Sigma\Sigma a_{ij} ln[r_i c_j/(a_{ij}N)]}{\Sigma c_j \ ln \ [c_j/N]}$	use G^2 test	Relative reduction in uncertainty about one index when the second index is known
McNemar's test of symmetry	no	RxR (square)	$0,\infty$	$\chi_{MC}^2 = \Sigma\Sigma\limits_{i<j} \dfrac{(a_{ij}-a_{ji})^2}{a_{ij}+a_{ji}}$	chisquare with $R(R-1)/2$ df	Test of symmetry by comparing each pair of cells about diagonal
Kappa	no	RxR (square)	$0,\infty$	$\kappa = \dfrac{\sum\limits_{i=1}^{\kappa} x_{ii}/n_{..} - \sum\limits_{i=1}^{\kappa} n_{1i}n_{2i}/n_{..}^2}{1 - \sum\limits_{i=1}^{\kappa} n_{1i}n_{2i}/n_{..}^2}$	$t = \kappa/\sigma_\kappa$	A test of reliability computed for square two-way tables
Test of linear trend	yes	2xC or Rx2	$0,\infty$	Appendix A.5	chisquare with 1 df	Test of linear trend on the proportions of the first row or first column

Note: The notation is defined in Appendix A.5.

TWO-WAY TABLES — ANALYSIS

Example 4F.3 Tests of Independence and Measures of Association and Prediction

P4F computes tests of independence and a large number of measures of association and correlation and other statistics for the two-way table. These measures can be subdivided into six principal classes:

- tests of independence and related measures: chi-square test, likelihood ratio chi-square test G^2, ϕ, contingency coefficient and Cramer's V
- tests of independence appropriate only for 2x2 tables: Fisher's exact test and Yates' corrected chi-square
- measures of association appropriate for a 2x2 table: Yule's Q and Y, cross-product ratio and tetrachoric correlation r_t and Mantel-Haenszel statistics
- measures of association and correlation when the categories of both factors are ordered: Goodman and Kruskal Γ, Kendall's τ_b, Stuart's τ_c, product-moment correlation r and Spearman rank correlation r_s
- predictive measures when the categories of both factors are ordered: Somers' D
- predictive measures when either or both factors are qualitative: Goodman and Kruskal τ, λ and $\lambda*$ and the uncertainty coefficient.

Three additional tests treat special problems:

- McNemar's test of symmetry for square tables
- Kappa -- a test of reliability computed for square two-way tables
- a test of linear trend in the proportions when the table is 2xk or kx2

(The statistics and measures are discussed according to their use following Output 4F.3.) The columns in Table 11.2 are:
- the name of the test or measure
- an indication of whether the test or measure assumes that the levels of the categorical variables are ordered
- the size of the table (any size (RxC) or square (RxR) or 2x2)
- the range of possible values for the statistics
- the formula (the formulas for all statistics and their standard errors, if computed, are given in Appendix A.5)
- the test that the measure is zero (many tests are equivalent either to the chi-square or likelihood ratio G^2); for several measures, a t-like statistic is used (Brown and Benedetti, 1977a)
- an interpretation of the tests or measure's meaning or usage

In Example 4F.3, we request all the tests and measures in Table 11.2 by inserting

```
------------------------------------
/ STATISTICS CHISQUARE.   CONTINGENCY.   LRCHI.
            FISHER.       TETRACHORIC.   CORRELATION.
            SPEARMAN.     GAMMA.         LAMBDA.
            TAUS.         UNCERTAINTY.   MCNEMAR.
            LINEAR.
------------------------------------
```

into the instructions of Example 4F.1 after the TABLE paragraph and before the END paragraph. You

may request a subset of these. We caution that a request for all tests is not appropriate – we have done so to illustrate the mechanical operation of the program and the format of the output. The results are presented in two panels under the observed frequency table (see Output 4F.3).

⑪ Chi-square tests and related measures and Fisher's exact test appear in the top panel. For each chi-square test, its degrees of freedom (D.F.) and tail probability (PROB, p-value) are also printed.

⑫ The measures of association are printed in the second panel. An estimate of the asymptotic standard error is printed in column ASE1. This asymptotic standard error can be used in setting approximate 95% confidence interval for the parameter being estimated – the limits are value ± 2 ASE1. The t-value is the ratio of the statistic to its estimated asymptotic standard error under the null hypothesis that the parameter is zero. See Brown and Benedetti (1977a) for a derivation of these tests. Where no t-value is given, the test for the null hypothesis described in Table 11.2 should be used. When the statistic is asymmetric in its treatment of the two table indices, the dependent variable is indicated in the column DEP.

Note: The denominator used in the t-value is the estimated asymptotic standard error under the null hypothesis and not under the alternate hypothesis (ASE1). Therefore the t-value is not the ratio of the statistic to the value listed under ASE1.

Note: The first table is 2x2; therefore the tables of tests and statistics include Yates' corrected chi-square, Fisher's exact test, Yule's Q and Y, the cross-product ratio and the tetrachoric correlation in addition to the other statistics. The third table is 2x3; therefore the tests include the test for a linear trend over the ordered categories of AGE.

Note: If a 2x2 table is formed for each level of a third variable (by CONDITIONING on the third variable), the Mantel-Haenszel statistics are computed when CONTINGENCY is specified in the STATISTICS paragraph.

Usage of the Statistics and Measures

The statistics and measures are now discussed according to their use.

Note 1: Computation of the statistics does not include rows and columns that are entirely zero.
Note 2: If there are fewer observations than cells or if there is only one nonzero row or one nonzero column, no statistics are computed.

Tests of independence between rows and columns, or of the equality of proportions. The most familiar test for the independence of the rows and columns in a two-way table is the (Pearson) chi-square test. When the table has two rows or two columns, the chi-square test is also a test for equality of proportions. If this is the only statistic you want, the STATISTICS paragraph is not needed.

An alternative to the usual (Pearson) chi-square test is the likelihood ratio chi-square statistic G^2. This test is based on maximum likelihood

Output 4F.3   Measures and tests computed by P4F

--- ① to ④ in Output 4F.1 appear here ---

```
*************************
* TABLE PARAGRAPH   1  *
*************************
```

***** OBSERVED FREQUENCY TABLE 1

```
ANGINA      INFARCT
------      -------

            NONE  PRESENT   TOTAL
---------------------------------------
NONE           3      16 I     19
PRESENT       40      58 I     98
---------------------------I---------
TOTAL         43      74 I    117
```

ALL CASES HAD COMPLETE DATA FOR THIS TABLE.

> *Kappa, a test of reliability, appears between Yule's Y and tetrachoric correlation (see arrow) in releases dated 1982 and later.*

MINIMUM ESTIMATED EXPECTED VALUE IS   6.98   ⑪

STATISTIC	VALUE	D.F.	PROB.
PEARSON CHISQUARE	4.288	1	0.0384
FISHER EXACT TEST(1-TAIL)			0.0309
YATES CORRECTED CHISQ.	3.279	1	0.0702
PHI = CRAMER'S V	-0.191		
CONTINGENCY COEF. C	0.188		
MCNEMAR TEST OF SYMMETRY	10.286	1	0.0013

STATISTIC	VALUE	D.F.	PROB.
LIKELIHOOD-RATIO CHISQ.	4.778	1	0.0288
FISHER EXACT TEST(2-TAIL)			0.0413
MAXIMUM VALUE FOR PHI	-0.336		
MAX.VALUE FOR CONTINGEN.	0.318		

⑫

STATISTIC	VALUE	ASE1	T-VALUE	DEP.
YULE'S Q	-0.572	0.222	-2.202	
YULE'S Y	-0.315	0.149	-2.420	
TETRACHORIC CORRELATION	-0.396	0.166	-2.231	
GAMMA	-0.572	0.222	-2.359	
KENDALL TAU-B	-0.191	0.075	-2.359	
SOMERS D	-0.250	0.097	-2.359	4
CORRELATION COEFFICIENT	-0.191	0.075	-2.359	
LAMBDA SYMMETRIC	0.0	0.0		
LAMBDA ASYMMETRIC	0.0	0.0		4
LAMBDA-STAR ASYMMETRIC	0.0	0.0		4
UNCERTAINTY COEF NORMED	0.037	0.031		
UNCERTAINTY ASYMMETRIC	0.031	0.026		4
TAU ASYMMETRIC	0.037	0.028		4

STATISTIC	VALUE	ASE1	T-VALUE	DEP.
CROSS-PRODUCT RATIO	0.272			
LN(CROSS-PRODUCT RATIO)	-1.302	0.662	-2.505	
STUART TAU-C	-0.136	0.058	-2.359	
SOMERS D	-0.146	0.062	-2.359	5
SPEARMAN RANK CORR.	-0.191	0.075	-2.359	
LAMBDA ASYMMETRIC	0.0	0.0		5
LAMBDA-STAR ASYMMETRIC	0.0	0.0		5
UNCERTAINTY ASYMMETRIC	0.046	0.038		5
TAU ASYMMETRIC	0.037	0.029		5

--- similar results for table 2 except that the statistics for 2x2 tables are not printed ---

***** OBSERVED FREQUENCY TABLE 3

```
INFARCT            AGE
-------            ---

         UNDER 51  51-60  OVER 60   TOTAL
------------------------------------------------
NONE          20     15       8 I     43
PRESENT       27     33      14 I     74
--------------------------------I---------
TOTAL         47     48      22 I    117
```

ALL CASES HAD COMPLETE DATA FOR THIS TABLE.

MINIMUM ESTIMATED EXPECTED VALUE IS   8.09

STATISTIC	VALUE	D.F.	PROB.
PEARSON CHISQUARE	1.307	2	0.5202
TEST FOR LINEAR TREND	0.534	1	0.4648
PHI	0.106		
CONTINGENCY COEF. C	0.105		

STATISTIC	VALUE	D.F.	PROB.
LIKELIHOOD-RATIO CHISQ.	1.309	2	0.5197
CRAMER'S V	0.106		

STATISTIC	VALUE	ASE1	T-VALUE	DEP.
GAMMA	0.130	0.162	0.802	
KENDALL TAU-B	0.071	0.089	0.802	
SOMERS D	0.083	0.104	0.802	1
CORRELATION COEFFICIENT	0.068	0.093	0.723	
LAMBDA SYMMETRIC	0.045	0.051		
LAMBDA ASYMMETRIC	0.072	0.083		1
LAMBDA-STAR ASYMMETRIC	0.057	0.079		1
UNCERTAINTY COEF NORMED	0.007	0.011		
UNCERTAINTY ASYMMETRIC	0.005	0.009		1
TAU ASYMMETRIC	0.007	0.012		1

STATISTIC	VALUE	ASE1	T-VALUE	DEP.
STUART TAU-C	0.077	0.097	0.802	
SOMERS D	0.061	0.076	0.802	4
SPEARMAN RANK CORR.	0.075	0.094	0.802	
LAMBDA ASYMMETRIC	0.0	0.0		4
LAMBDA-STAR ASYMMETRIC	0.0	0.0		4
UNCERTAINTY ASYMMETRIC	0.009	0.015		4
TAU ASYMMETRIC	0.011	0.019		4

---

theory, and is used more than any other test statistic in the analysis of multiway frequency tables.

When the table is 2x2, two statistics are often used – the Yates' corrected chi-square (χ_y^2) and Fisher's exact test. Yates' correction is intended to improve the approximation to the chi-square distribution, and is automatically printed when the table is 2x2 (some studies indicate that Yates' test may be too conservative however).

P4F computes Fisher's exact test for a 2x2 table when the minimum expected value is less than 20. The two-tail probability is the sum over all configurations (e.g., patterns of cell frequencies) whose probability assuming independence is less than or equal to the probability of the observed configuration (each pattern must preserve the observed row and column totals). The one-tail probability is the sum over the configurations that have a probability less than or equal to that observed when the cell with minimum frequency is decremented to zero. If your hypothesis is one-sided, the configurations appropriate to test the hypothesis may differ from those used to compute the one-tail probability; if they differ from those used by P4F, the one-tail probability exceeds 0.5 and is therefore nonsignificant.

Note: Unless a one-sided hypothesis is being tested, the two-tail probability for Fisher's exact test should be used.

Other statistics, such as the contingency coefficient C, ϕ and Cramer's V, are functions of chi-square that do not increase with N. That is, when the model of independence is not appropriate (i.e., the row variable is related to the column variable), the expected value of the chi-square statistic is proportional to the sample size N. Measures not dependent on N are useful in comparing results between tables based on different sample sizes, and are of a descriptive nature only.

When the table is 2x2, ϕ corresponds to Cramer's V. Otherwise V is always less than or equal to unity, but ϕ can exceed unity. C is normalized differently from ϕ and V. All three measures are zero if (and only if) the chi-square test is zero. Therefore the hypothesis that they are equal to zero can be tested by the chi-square test for independence.

If the row and column totals are held fixed, the totals determine the maximum value that these measures can attain. In the 2x2 table ϕ_{max} and C_{max} are printed, where ϕ_{max} is the largest positive value of ϕ attainable when the observed ϕ is positive, and the largest negative value of ϕ attainable when the observed ϕ is negative. C_{max} is obtained from ϕ_{max}.

Measures of association and correlation. For a 2x2 table, the odds-ratio, Yule's Q and Y and the tetrachoric correlation are measures of association. The measures are zero if (and only if) the chi-square test for independence is zero. Therefore the hypothesis that a measure is zero can be tested by the chi-square test or by the ratio of the statistic to its estimated standard error.

The tetrachoric correlation is an estimate of the correlation of the bivariate normal distribution of the row and column variables when the 2x2 table is formed by splitting each of the two continuous variables into two parts, and counting the frequencies (number of cases) in the four quadrants formed by this division. If the frequency in one cell is zero, it is set to 1/2 and all other frequencies are altered to preserve row and column totals. This provides a lower limit on the correlation. See Brown and Benedetti (1977b) for a discussion of the tetrachoric correlation.

The measures Γ, τ_b and τ_c are appropriate for RxC tables when both indices of the table have ordered categories. They differ only in their denominator; that is, in how ties are treated ($|\tau_c| \leq |\tau_b| \leq |\Gamma|$). Tests that these measures, the correlation r and the Spearman rank correlation r_s are zero are discussed by Brown and Benedetti (1977a). They use the ratio of the estimate of the measure to its approximate asymptotic standard error (s_o) under the hypothesis that the measure is zero. For sufficiently large samples, this ratio is approximately a t statistic. Also for sufficiently large samples, confidence limits can be constructed for the measure by using the asymptotic standard error formula developed by Goodman and Kruskal (1972) (ASE1 in the printed output).

Somers' D is an asymmetric measure of association. Table 11.2 shows how it is related to τ_b.

Measures of prediction and uncertainty. Goodman and Kruskal's τ, λ, $\lambda*$ and the uncertainty coefficient U all measure the gain in predicting one categorical variable of the table when the value of the second categorical variable is known, relative to when it is not known. The conditions imposed on the frequencies differ between statistics. See Goodman and Kruskal (1954) for a discussion of the first three measures and Brown (1975) for the last one. These measures assume no ordering of the categories. They are inherently asymmetric. Each categorical variable can be predicted from the other one. P4F computes both asymmetric forms for each statistic. You must choose the one appropriate to your problem. Both λ and U also have a symmetric form created by summing the numerators and denominators of the two asymmetric forms and then calculating the ratio.

The cross-product (odds-ratio) and the Mantel-Haenszel statistics. In the 2x2 table the cross-product, also called the odds ratio, ($\alpha = a_{11}a_{22}/a_{12}a_{21}$) is an approximation to the relative risk when large samples are used to estimate the incidence of disease. The use of the cross-product in retrospective studies is discussed by Mantel and Haenszel (1959) and by Fleiss (1973, Chapter 5 and 6). Since the cross-product has a very skew distribution, it is usually transformed by taking its natural logarithm. P4F prints both the cross-product and ln(cross-product), as well as an estimate of the asymptotic standard error of the latter. This asymptotic standard error can be used to set approximate confidence limits for ln(cross-product); by taking antilogs of the limits, approximate confidence limits for the cross-product can be obtained.

P4F computes after the last of a series of 2x2 tables, the Mantel-Haenszel measure of relative risk and a one degree of freedom chi-square statistic that tests whether the relative risk is one; a significant chi-square indicates that the incidence differs between the two groups. P4F also prints the antilog of the weighted ln(cross-product ratio) and approximate 95% confidence limits for it. Finally P4F prints the chi-square test for homogeneity of the relative risk between the 2x2 tables; a significant result indicates that the relative risk varies between tables. For further discussion of these statistics, see Armitage (1971).

McNemar's test of symmetry. When the same subjects are measured at two different times, square frequency tables are produced; the two categorical variables represent the results. For such frequency tables it may be more appropriate to test for change around the diagonal rather than for independence. One diagonal test is McNemar's test of symmetry (Bowker, 1948), which tests the equality of frequencies in all pairs of cells that are symmetric about the diagonal. In the 2x2 table, this reduces to the test of equality of the two off-diagonal cells. For example, subjects could be asked a yes-no question before and after the occurrence of an event. The results are tabulated in a 2 by 2 table with BEFORE and AFTER the factors. The diagonal cells are not relevant.

Testing a linear trend on the proportions. When one categorical variable is dichotomous (i.e., the table is 2xC or Rx2), hypotheses can be specified about linear combinations of the proportions. Cochran (1954) proposed a test of the linear trend of the proportions on an arbitrary set of weights. This is equivalent to testing the slope of a simple linear regression where the dependent variable is the proportion. When CUTPOINTS are specified the independent variable is arbitrarily assigned the values 1, 2, 3,.... Otherwise the code values of the index with more than two categories are used as the independent variable.

STATistics ─────────

CHISQuare.   CHISQUARE/prev.
  The chi-square test and (if the table is 2x2) Yates' corrected chi-square (χ^2_y) are computed.
LRCHI.   no/prev.
  The likelihood ratio chi-square G^2 is computed.
FISHer.   2x2   table   only   no/prev.
  Fisher's exact probabilities, both 1-tail and 2-tail are computed. See above for a definition, and Appendix A.5 for the exact formula.
CONTingency.   no/prev.
  The contingency coefficient C, ϕ, Cramer's V and, if the table is 2x2, Yule's Q and Y, C_{max}, ϕ_{max} and the odds-ratio α are computed. C, V and ϕ are computed from the value of the chi-square test. The others are computed only if the observed table is 2x2.
  Note: When a series of 2x2 tables is formed by CONDITIONING the ROW and COLUMN variables on a third variable and CONTINGENCY is specified, P4F computes and prints the Mantel-Haenszel statistic and a test of homogeneity of the cross-product ratios across the 2x2 tables.
TETRAchoric.   no/prev.
  The tetrachoric correlation r_t is computed for a 2x2 table only. See Appendix A.5 for an exact definition.
GAMma.   no/prev.
  Γ, Kendall's τ_b, Stuart's τ_c and Somers' D are computed.
CORRelation.   no/prev.
  The product-moment correlation is computed.
SPEARman.   no/prev.
  The Spearman rank correlation is computed
TAUS.   no/prev.
  Goodman and Kruskal's τ is printed.
LAMBda.   no/prev.
  Goodman and Kruskal's λ and $\lambda*$, both asymmetric and symmetric, are printed.

UNCertainty.   no/prev.
    The uncertainty coefficients, both asymmetric
and symmetric, are printed.
MCNemar   RxR tables only   no/prev.
    McNemar's test of symmetry and kappa are
printed.
LINear.   2xC or Rx2 table only   no/prev.
    The codes of the variable with R or C catego-
ries are used in testing the probabilities in a
dichotomy for a linear trend. When CUTPOINTS
are specified for this variable, P4F assigns
values 1, 2, 3, ... See Appendix A.5 for the 1
degree of freedom chi-square test formula.
NO ALL.   NO ALL
    Do not print all statistics. NO ALL is over-
ridden by any other requests in the STATISTICS
paragraph. For example, NO ALL. LINEAR. requests that only LINEAR be computed.

Note 1: The computations of all statistics,
except Fisher's exact test, are affected by the
addition of a constant DELTA to each cell
frequency (p. 161).

Note 2: The computation of ϕ, the contingency
coefficient and Cramer's V are affected by
automatic collapsing (when MINIMUM is
specified, p. 160).

Note 3: Not all statistics are applicable to a
single table. For example, the categories are
either ordered or not ordered. The question may
be that of independence or of prediction. You
must select the statistics appropriate to your
specific problem.

Example 4F.4 Expected Values and Cell Deviations

In a two-way table the test most often performed
is the chi-square test of independence. Under the
hypothesis that rows are independent of columns, the
expected frequency in each cell is

$$\frac{(\text{row total}) \times (\text{column total})}{\text{total in table}} = \frac{r_i c_j}{N}$$

Expected frequencies are of interest:
    a) to decide whether the distribution of the
chi-square statistic is approximately chi-square. As
a guideline we use the rule: no cell may have an
expected value less than 1, and not more than 20% of
the cells have expected values less than 5. When
there are more cells that have small frequencies
than indicated by this rule, the distribution of the
chi-square statistic can differ widely from the
chi-square distribution; therefore the probability
printed in the output should be used only as a
guideline and not as an exact estimate. Many
investigators use a more conservative rule suggested
by Fisher; that is, no cell may have an expected
value less than 5. This latter rule should be
adhered to whenever the table is 2x2.
    P4F prints the minimum expected value in the
table above the panel of statistics. This value can
provide a warning that there are very small expected
values. If so, see p. 159.
    b) to examine patterns in the data that
contribute to a significant value for the chi-square
test. In addition to the expected values, various
cell deviates can be obtained.
    In this example the expected values for all cells
are requested, as well as three types of deviates
that measure the difference between the observed and
expected values. The following PRINT paragraph is
inserted into the Control Language of Example 4F.1
before the END paragraph.

```
/ PRINT     EXPECTED.        FREEMAN.
            STANDARDIZED.    ADJUSTED.
```

The results are presented in Output 4F.4

⑬ Table of expected values

Output 4F.4   Expected values and deviates for two-way tables

--- ① to ④ in Output 4F.1 appear here ---

```
************************
* TABLE PARAGRAPH   1  *
************************
```

***** OBSERVED FREQUENCY TABLE 1

```
ANGINA      INFARCT
------      -------
            NONE  PRESENT   TOTAL
---------------------------------
NONE           3    16 I       19
PRESENT       40    58 I       98
------------------------I--------
TOTAL         43    74 I      117
```

ALL CASES HAD COMPLETE DATA FOR THIS TABLE.

```
MINIMUM ESTIMATED EXPECTED VALUE IS     6.98

STATISTIC                VALUE   D.F.   PROB.
PEARSON CHISQUARE        4.288    1    0.0384
YATES CORRECTED CHISQ.   3.279    1    0.0702
```

***** EXPECTED VALUES — TABLE 1

```
ANGINA      INFARCT                    ⑬
------      -------
            NONE  PRESENT   TOTAL
---------------------------------
NONE         7.0    12.0 I    19.0
PRESENT     36.0    62.0 I    98.0
------------------------I--------
TOTAL       43.0    74.0 I   117.0
```

(output continued)

Output 4F.4 (continued)

```
*****  FREEMAN-TUKEY DEVIATES   — TABLE  1

ANGINA      INFARCT                    ⑭
──────      ──────
            NONE  PRESENT    TOTAL
───────────────────────────────────────
NONE        -1.6     1.1 I   -0.5
PRESENT      0.7    -0.5 I    0.2
─────────────────────────I─────────
TOTAL       -1.0     0.6 I   -0.3
```

```
*****  STANDARDIZED DEVIATES  = (OBS - EXP) / SQRT(EXP)

ANGINA      INFARCT                    ⑮
──────      ──────
            NONE  PRESENT    TOTAL
───────────────────────────────────────
NONE        -1.5     1.1 I   -0.4
PRESENT      0.7    -0.5 I    0.2
─────────────────────────I─────────
TOTAL       -0.8     0.6 I   -0.2
```

```
*****  ADJUSTED STANDARDIZED DEVIATES   — TABLE  1

ANGINA      INFARCT                    ⑯
──────      ──────
            NONE  PRESENT    TOTAL
───────────────────────────────────────
NONE        -2.1     2.1 I    0.0
PRESENT      2.1    -2.1 I    0.0
─────────────────────────I─────────
TOTAL        0.0     0.0 I    0.0
```

--- similar results for tables 2 and 3 ---

---

⑭ Table of Freeman-Tukey deviates

$$d_{ij}^{(1)} = \sqrt{a_{ij}} + \sqrt{a_{ij}+1} - \sqrt{4e_{ij}+1}$$

where a_{ij} and e_{ij} are the observed and expected frequencies respectively. These deviates are similar to z-scores when the data are from a Poisson distribution.

⑮ Table of standardized deviates

$$d_{ij}^{(2)} = (a_{ij} - e_{ij})/e_{ij}^{\frac{1}{2}} .$$

These are square-roots of the components used in computing the chi-square statistic.

⑯ Table of adjusted standardized deviates

$$d_{ij}^{(3)} = \frac{a_{ij} - e_{ij}}{\left[e_{ij}(1 - \frac{r_i}{N})(1 - \frac{c_j}{N}) \right]^{\frac{1}{2}}} .$$

These are standardized deviates normalized to have variance one when the data are from a multinomial distribution (Haberman, 1973).

PRINT ─
  EXPected.   no/prev.
    Print the expected values e_{ij} of all cells under the null hypothesis of independence. $e_{ij} = r_i c_j /N$ for all cells.
  DIFferences.   no/prev.
    Print the differences d_{ij} between the observed and expected values. $d_{ij} = a_{ij} - e_{ij}$ for all cells.
  FReeman.   no/prev.
    Print the Freeman-Tukey deviates

$$d_{ij}^{(1)} = \sqrt{a_{ij}} + \sqrt{a_{ij}+1} - \sqrt{4e_{ij}+1}$$

    for all cells.
  STANdardized.   no/prev.
    Print the standardized deviates
    $d_{ij}^{(2)} = (a_{ij} - e_{ij})/e_{ij}^{\frac{1}{2}}$ for all cells.
  ADJusted.   no/prev.
    Print the adjusted standardized deviates

$$d_{ij}^{(3)} = (a_{ij}-e_{ij}) / \left[e_{ij}(1- \frac{r_i}{N})(1 - \frac{c_j}{N}) \right]^{\frac{1}{2}}$$

    (Haberman, 1973) for all cells.
  CHISquare.   no/prev.
    Print components of the Pearson chi-square statistic = $(a_{ij} - e_{ij})^2/e_{ij}$.
  LRCHI.   no/prev.
    Print components of the likelihood ratio chi-square statistic $G^2 = 2 a_{ij} \ln (a_{ij}/e_{ij})$.

Example 4F.5 Combining Rows/Columns with Small Expected Values

When there are too many small expected values, it is preferable to collapse categories to form new categories with larger frequencies. This is best done by examining the table of observed frequencies and modifying the names of the CODES or CUTPOINTS -- CODES or CUTPOINTS with the same name are combined by P4F when forming the table.

A poorer alternative is to add a constant DELTA to the frequency in each cell. Often the constant 1/2 (DELTA=0.5) is added.

Alternatively, P4F can automatically collapse adjacent categories until the minimum expected value exceeds a specified MINIMUM value. Such a method can combine categories that are neighboring but dissimilar. Therefore, this option should be used with caution, especially when the categories are not ordered. Depending on the problem at hand, it may be more reasonable to run the program twice -- once to

determine the expected cell values, and a second time to collapse by modifying cutpoints or names in the CATEGORY paragraph.

This example illustrates how rows and columns are collapsed by the addition of a MINIMUM statement in the STATISTICS paragraph. We also request that the expected values be printed. The STATISTICS and PRINT paragraphs are placed after the TABLE paragraph in Example 4F.1.

```
/ STATISTICS    MINIMUM IS 1.
/ PRINT         EXPECTED.
```

The results are presented in Output 4F.5.

The first table is 2x2. Therefore it will not be collapsed even if the minimum expected value is less than 1.

(17) The minimum expected value in the second table is 0.51. This is less than the MINIMUM value

Output 4F.5 Automatic collapsing of a two-way table by P4F

--- (1) to (4) in Output 4F.1 appear here ---

```
***********************
* TABLE PARAGRAPH   1  *
***********************
```

***** OBSERVED FREQUENCY TABLE 1

ANGINA	INFARCT		
	NONE	PRESENT	TOTAL
NONE	3	16 I	19
PRESENT	40	58 I	98
TOTAL	43	74 I	117

ALL CASES HAD COMPLETE DATA FOR THIS TABLE.

MINIMUM ESTIMATED EXPECTED VALUE IS   6.98

STATISTIC	VALUE	D.F.	PROB.
PEARSON CHISQUARE	4.288	1	0.0384
YATES CORRECTED CHISQ.	3.279	1	0.0702

***** EXPECTED VALUES — TABLE 1

ANGINA	INFARCT		
	NONE	PRESENT	TOTAL
NONE	7.0	12.0 I	19.0
PRESENT	36.0	62.0 I	98.0
TOTAL	43.0	74.0 I	117.0

***** OBSERVED FREQUENCY TABLE 2

ACTIVE	FUNCTION				
	NONE	MINIMAL	MODERATE	SEVERE	TOTAL
VERY	2	4	2	1 I	9
NORMAL	3	13	37	7 I	60
LIMITED	0	1	2	16 I	19
TOTAL	5	18	41	24 I	88

29 CASES HAD INCOMPLETE DATA.

***** NUMBER OF EXCLUDED CASES — TABLE 2

ACTIVE	FUNCTION					
	IN RANGE	MISSING	TOOSMALL	TOOLARGE	UNCOUNTD	TOTAL
IN RANGE	0	0	0	0	0 I	0
MISSING	0	0	0	0	0 I	0
TOOSMALL	0	0	0	0	0 I	0
TOOLARGE	0	0	0	0	0 I	0
UNCOUNTD	29	0	0	0	0 I	29
TOTAL	29	0	0	0	0 I	29

***** ANALYSIS OF OBSERVED FREQUENCY TABLE 2

(17)

MINIMUM ESTIMATED EXPECTED VALUE IS   0.51

STATISTIC	VALUE	D.F.	PROB.
PEARSON CHISQUARE	48.365	6	0.0000
CHISQ COLLAPSED TABLE	47.014	4	0.0000

(output continued)

Output 4F.5 (continued)

```
*****  EXPECTED VALUES — TABLE  2        (18)
```

ACTIVE		FUNCTION			
------		------			
	NONE	MINIMAL	MODERATE	SEVERE	TOTAL
VERY	0.5	1.8	4.2	2.5 I	9.0
NORMAL	3.4	12.3	28.0	16.4 I	60.0
LIMITED	1.1	3.9	8.9	5.2 I	19.0
				I	
TOTAL	5.0	18.0	41.0	24.0 I	88.0

```
*****  OBSERVED FREQUENCY TABLE  3
```

INFARCT		AGE			
------		------		
	UNDER 51	51-60	OVER 60	TOTAL
NONE	20	15	8 I	43
PRESENT	27	33	14 I	74
			I	
TOTAL	47	48	22 I	117

ALL CASES HAD COMPLETE DATA FOR THIS TABLE.

```
MINIMUM ESTIMATED EXPECTED VALUE IS      8.09

STATISTIC                   VALUE     D.F.   PROB.
PEARSON CHISQUARE           1.307      2    0.5202
```

```
*****  EXPECTED VALUES  — TABLE  3
```

INFARCT		AGE			
------		------		
	UNDER 51	51-60	OVER 60	TOTAL
NONE	17.3	17.6	8.1 I	43.0
PRESENT	29.7	30.4	13.9 I	74.0
			I	
TOTAL	47.0	48.0	22.0 I	117.0

---

specified (1.00) and therefore automatic collapsing will be performed. First P4F prints the chi-square test based on the original table (48.365 with 6 D.F.). The program then collapses the table by combining adjacent rows and columns until the minimum expected value is greater than the MINIMUM specified. The method by which rows or columns are chosen is as follows: scan the table for the minimum expected value. Test if the row total is smaller than the column total. If so, combine rows; if not, combine columns. Combine this row (or column) with the adjacent row (or column) having the lower total. Scan the modified table for the minimum expected value. If less than MINIMUM, stop; otherwise, repeat the algorithm.

(18) If we examine the table of expected values for Table 2, we see that the minimum expected value (0.51) is in cell (1,1). Since the column total is less than the row total, the first and second columns are combined. In effect, the modified expected values for the combined column are the sums of the expected values in the first two columns; the expected values of the remaining cells are unchanged. The modified table has its minimum expected value equal to 2.3 (= 0.5 + 1.8) again in cell (1,1). Since this value is greater than the specified MINIMUM, automatic collapsing stops. The resultant table is 3x3 (i.e., there are 4 D.F.) and the chi-square is 47.014.

If the minimum expected value 2.3 were less than MINIMUM, the algorithm would continue by combining rows 1 and 2 since the total in row 1 (9) is less than the total in column 1 of the modified table (23 = 5 + 18).

Note: If collapsing is performed, the statistics ϕ, the contingency coefficient C and Cramer's V are computed from the collapsed chi-square statistic. All other statistics are computed from the original observed table.

Note: the appropriate test of independence for the collapsed table is Fisher's exact test.

The minimum expected value for the third table is greater than MINIMUM. Therefore, no collapsing is performed.

STATISTICS
MINimum = #.   0/prev.
  If the minimum expected frequency in the table is less than MINIMUM, adjacent rows or columns are combined (see below for method) before the "collapsed" chi-square test, ϕ, contingency coefficient C and Cramer's V are computed; the other statistics and all tables are not affected.
  Method of collapsing: If the minimum expected frequency is less than a specified constant (1.0 or 5.0 is often used), the row or column (whichever has a smaller total frequency--the row is used if both have the same total) containing the cell is combined with a neighboring row or column (the neighbor with the smaller total frequency--if they both have the same total, the neighbor with the higher index is used). The minimum expected frequencies are computed for the collapsed tables and additional rows or columns are combined until all expected frequency values exceed the specified constant.
  Note: Automatic collapsing can combine incompatible categories especially when categories are not ordered.

160

Adding a Constant to Each Cell

When the cell frequencies are small, some investigators prefer to add a constant to each cell frequency prior to analysis. Adding such a constant (0.5 is often used) generally reduces the chi-square test since the constant increases the expected cell frequencies (which appear in the denominator of the chi-square statistic). Therefore, it tends to make the test more conservative and, as such, to compensate for the inflation of the chi-square due to the small expected values. However, it is a better procedure to combine categories to increase the minimum expected frequencies than to rely on the above argument.

You can add a constant to each cell by specifying

DELTA = value to be added.

in the TABLE paragraph.

TABLE
DELTA = #.   0.0/prev.
A constant added to the frequency in each cell of the table. The following results are printed before DELTA is added -- the observed frequency table, marginal subtables and tables of percents. In the two-way frequency table Fisher's exact probabilities are computed without DELTA. All other statistics and tables are computed after DELTA is added. In the two-way table DELTA is not added to rows or columns that are entirely zero.

MULTIWAY TABLES — DESCRIPTIVE

In many problems the investigator needs to present his data as frequencies classified by three or more categorical variables; for example, a frequency table of survival (live, dead) by treatment by age by sex. At times forming and presenting the table is sufficient; at other times it may be necessary to fit a model to the frequencies in the cells to better understand the relationships between the factors (indices). In this section we describe how to form multiway tables using P4F. Model-fitting is described on p. 176.

The four-way frequency table described above can also be thought of as two three-way tables - one for males and the other for females. This type of division is useful when separate analyses are desired for each sex. In this case we describe the two tables as survival by treatment by age given (or conditioned on) sex; the two three-way tables are cross sections of the original four-way table. Similarly two-way tables can be defined as cross sections of a three-way table; then P4F performs the requested analysis for each of the two-way cross sections as described in Example 4F.3.

Example 4F.6 Forming Multiway Tables and Cross Sections of a Multiway Table

In this example, we use the PROBLEM, INPUT, VARIABLE and CATEGORY paragraphs of Example 4F.1 and add the following three TABLE paragraphs to show how to specify tables. These paragraphs are placed before the END paragraph.

```
------------------------------------------
/ TABLE     INDICES ARE AGE, FUNCTION, ANGINA,
                HIGHBP.
/ TABLE     CATVAR IS AGE,      AGE.
            CATVAR IS FUNCTION, ACTIVE.
            CATVAR IS ANGINA,   HIGHBP.
            CATVAR IS HIGHBP,   ANGINA.
/ TABLE     INDICES ARE FUNCTION, ANGINA, HIGHBP.
            CONDITION IS AGE.
------------------------------------------
```

In the first TABLE paragraph a single table is requested by

INDICES ARE AGE, FUNCTION, ANGINA, HIGHBP.

The first variable (AGE) is the column index, the second (FUNCTION) is the fastest changing row index, ..., the last (HIGHBP) is the slowest changing row index. The table is printed in Output 4F.6 (23) .

The second TABLE paragraph describes two tables. Each table has four indices. The first CATVAR statement describes the categorical variables defining the column indices, the second CATVAR statement describes the categorical variables defining the fastest changing row indices, ..., the last CATVAR statement describes the slowest changing row index. The first table has the indices AGE, FUNCTION, ANGINA and HIGHBP and is identical to the table requested by the first TABLE paragraph. The second table has the indices AGE, ACTIVE, HIGHBP and ANGINA (see (24) in Output 4F.6).

The third TABLE paragraph describes a three-way table but also specifies that it be formed from each cross section of a four-way table. That is, a three-way table is produced for each level of the

CONDITIONING variable AGE. These tables are presented in ㉖ in Output 4F.6.

Note: The method used in the first TABLE paragraph (INDICES ARE ...) can describe one table per paragraph; the TABLE paragraph must be repeated for each additional table. The method used in the second paragraph (CATVAR IS ...) can describe many tables at one time provided they all have the same number of dimensions (indices); an additional TABLE paragraph would be required to describe tables with a different number of dimensions. The method used in the third paragraph (CONDITION IS ...) is useful when each cross section is to undergo the same, but separate, analysis; in this example no analysis is requested and therefore the four-way table with AGE as the fourth index provides the same tabulation as does looking at the three-way cross sections requested.

We now describe in more detail the results in Output 4F.6. Circled numbers below correspond to those in the output.

㉙ Interpretation of options specific to P4F. Options that are not specified (such as in the PRINT and FIT paragraphs) are assigned their default values. Only options that cause results to be printed are listed.

⑳ When data are not included in any one of the tables, P4F can list the cases for which the data are omitted and prints an M under the appropriate table number(s). See ②, p. 149, for a more detailed explanation.

Note: A case is included in a table if it has acceptable values for all the indices of the table. Therefore a case can be included in one table but not in another.

㉑ Number of cases read.

㉒ Univariate description for variables that are indices of one or more tables (in this example this includes all variables). See ④, p. 149, for more discussion of the column headings.

㉓ The frequency table requested by the first TABLE paragraph. The totals for each row and each column in a panel of the table are printed. The total frequency and number of cases omitted (none) are printed below the table.

㉔ The two tables requested in the second TABLE paragraph. Tables are sequentially numbered starting from the first TABLE paragraph. Therefore the two tables are labelled TABLE 2 and TABLE 3 respectively.

㉕ The second of the two tables has cases that were not included, therefore a description of the excluded cases is printed. See ⑦, p. 150 for further discussion of this table.

㉖ Cross sections requested in the third TABLE paragraph are printed. Note that in our example each cross section is equivalent to a column in the table requested in the first TABLE paragraph. However, any analysis requested would be separately applied to each cross section.

How to form multiway tables — the TABLE paragraph. Tables can be specified by several methods. In the first TABLE paragraph of Example 4F.6 we specify

INDICES ARE AGE, FUNCTION, ANGINA, HIGHBP.

to describe a four-way table. When INDICES are specified, only one table can be specified in a TABLE paragraph. The dimension of the table is the number of variables specified. The first variable (AGE) is used as the column index, the second as the fastest changing row index, ..., the last (HIGHBP) as the slowest changing row index.

You can also describe an n-way table using COLUMN, ROW and CATVAR statements. The COLUMN variable is the fastest changing (horizontal) index; ROW the next fastest changing (the fastest changing vertical variable). Since there is no standard nomenclature for the third, fourth and higher dimensions, the name CATVAR (categorical variable) is used to describe all higher-way dimensions. The CATVAR statement can be repeated, once for each dimension. Therefore the above four-way table can be described as

```
COLUMN IS AGE.
ROW    IS FUNCTION.
CATVAR IS ANGINA.
CATVAR IS HIGHBP.
```

You may also replace ROW by CATVAR or both ROW and COLUMN by two CATVAR statements; i.e.,

```
CATVAR IS AGE.
CATVAR IS FUNCTION.
CATVAR IS ANGINA.
CATVAR IS HIGHBP.
```

The order of the CATVAR statements determines the order in which the indices of the table are printed. The horizontally printed variable is the COLUMN variable or the first CATVAR variable if COLUMN and ROW are not specified.

As in the example for the two-way table, more than one variable can be specified for each COLUMN, ROW and CATVAR statement. For example

```
/ TABLE    COLUMN = A, B.
           ROW    = C, D.
           CATVAR = E, F.
```

specifies two three-way tables A by C by E and B by D by F. If CROSS is added to this TABLE paragraph, eight tables are produced:

```
A by C by E                 B by C by E
A by C by F                 B by C by F

A by D by E                 B by D by E
A by D by F                 B by D by F
```

That is, every COLUMN index is crossed with every ROW index and these are crossed with every index in each CATVAR statement.

Note: Tables in which the same index appears twice are not formed.

Output 4F.6   Multiway tables formed from data

                    --- BMDP instructions are printed and interpreted ---

***NOTE—REQUESTED OPTIONS ONLY ARE PRINTED BELOW.
       TABLES ARE SEQUENCE NUMBERED ACROSS TABLE PARAGRAPHS.   ⑲

INTERPRETATION OF TABLE PARAGRAPH 1.
----

  1 TABLES ARE REQUESTED —
SYMBOLS ARE INDICATED IN PARENTHESES
TABLE 1 AGE   (A)   BY   FUNCTION   (F)   BY   ANGINA   (A)   BY   HIGHBP   (H)

INTERPRETATION OF PRINT PARAGRAPH — APPLIED TO TABLE PARAGRAPH   1 ABOVE

PRINT TABLE OF   OBSERVED VALUES.
PRINT TABLE OF   EXCLUDED VALUES.
LIST FIRST   5 CASES WITH UNACCEPTABLE VALUES.

INTERPRETATION OF TABLE PARAGRAPH 2.
----

  2 TABLES ARE REQUESTED —
SYMBOLS ARE INDICATED IN PARENTHESES
TABLE 2 AGE   (A)   BY   FUNCTION   (F)   BY   ANGINA   (A)   BY   HIGHBP   (H)
TABLE 3 AGE   (A)   BY   ACTIVE   (A)   BY   HIGHBP   (H)   BY   ANGINA   (A)

INTERPRETATION OF PRINT PARAGRAPH — APPLIED TO TABLE PARAGRAPH   2 ABOVE

PRINT TABLE OF   OBSERVED VALUES.
PRINT TABLE OF   EXCLUDED VALUES.
LIST FIRST   5 CASES WITH UNACCEPTABLE VALUES.

INTERPRETATION OF TABLE PARAGRAPH 3.
----

  1 TABLES ARE REQUESTED —
SYMBOLS ARE INDICATED IN PARENTHESES
TABLE 4 FUNCTION   (F)   BY   ANGINA   (A)   BY   HIGHBP   (H)   GIVEN AGE

INTERPRETATION OF PRINT PARAGRAPH — APPLIED TO TABLE PARAGRAPH   3 ABOVE

PRINT TABLE OF   OBSERVED VALUES.
PRINT TABLE OF   EXCLUDED VALUES.
LIST FIRST   5 CASES WITH UNACCEPTABLE VALUES.

         PRINT LIST OUTPUT— M'S INDICATE TABLES FOR WHICH THE CASE HAS INVALID DATA FOR AT LEAST ONE INDEX.
    CASE NO.   TABLE NUMBER
                 1 2 3 4
        3   M
        6   M
       14   M   ⑳
       22   M
       25   M

NUMBER OF CASES READ.   117   ㉑

                                            N U M B E R   O F   V A L U E S
    VARIABLE ㉒   MEAN   STANDARD   SMALLEST   LARGEST   TOTAL   MISSING   BELOW   ABOVE   NOT EQUAL TO
    NO. NAME   DEVIATION   VALUE   VALUE   FREQUENCY   MINIMUM   MAXIMUM   STATED CODES

    1 AGE   52.32   9.47   34.00   73.00   117   0   0   0   0
    2 FUNCTION   1.68   1.01   0.0   3.00   117   0   0   0   0
    3 ACTIVE   1.59   1.04   0.0   3.00   117   0   0   0   29
    5 ANGINA   0.84   0.37   0.0   1.00   117   0   0   0   0
    6 HIGHBP   0.31   0.46   0.0   1.00   117   0   0   0   0

              --- the CATEGORY paragraph is interpreted ---   (output continued)

Output 4F.6 (continued)

```
*************************
*  TABLE PARAGRAPH  1  *
*************************
```

***** OBSERVED FREQUENCY TABLE 1   ㉓

HIGHBP	ANGINA	FUNCTION	AGE			
			UNDER 51	51-60	OVER 60	TOTAL
NONE	NONE	NONE	1	1	1 I	3
		MINIMAL	3	2	0 I	5
		MODERATE	0	3	1 I	4
		SEVERE	0	1	0 I	1
		TOTAL	4	7	2 I	13
	PRESENT	NONE	5	4	3 I	12
		MINIMAL	4	6	1 I	11
		MODERATE	13	7	9 I	29
		SEVERE	5	8	3 I	16
		TOTAL	27	25	16 I	68
PRESENT	NONE	NONE	0	0	1 I	1
		MINIMAL	2	1	0 I	3
		MODERATE	1	1	0 I	2
		SEVERE	0	0	0 I	0
		TOTAL	3	2	1 I	6
	PRESENT	NONE	2	2	0 I	4
		MINIMAL	4	1	0 I	5
		MODERATE	6	5	0 I	11
		SEVERE	1	6	3 I	10
		TOTAL	13	14	3 I	30

TOTAL OF THE OBSERVED FREQUENCY TABLE IS   117

ALL CASES HAD COMPLETE DATA FOR THIS TABLE.

```
*************************
*  TABLE PARAGRAPH  2  *
*************************
```

***** OBSERVED FREQUENCY TABLE 2   ㉔

--- table 2 is identical to table 1 ---

***** OBSERVED FREQUENCY TABLE 3

ANGINA	HIGHBP	ACTIVE	AGE			
			UNDER 51	51-60	OVER 60	TOTAL
NONE	NONE	VERY	2	1	0 I	3
		NORMAL	1	3	1 I	5
		LIMITED	0	1	0 I	1
		TOTAL	3	5	1 I	9
	PRESENT	VERY	0	0	0 I	0
		NORMAL	1	2	0 I	3
		LIMITED	0	0	0 I	0
		TOTAL	1	2	0 I	3
PRESENT	NONE	VERY	2	1	0 I	3
		NORMAL	14	11	12 I	37
		LIMITED	5	3	1 I	9
		TOTAL	21	15	13 I	49
	PRESENT	VERY	2	1	0 I	3
		NORMAL	8	6	1 I	15
		LIMITED	2	5	2 I	9
		TOTAL	12	12	3 I	27

TOTAL OF THE OBSERVED FREQUENCY TABLE IS   88

29 CASES HAD INCOMPLETE DATA.

***** NUMBER OF EXCLUDED CASES — TABLE 3   ㉕

ACTIVE	AGE					
	IN RANGE	MISSING	TOOSMALL	TOOLARGE	UNCOUNTD	TOTAL
IN RANGE	0	0	0	0	0 I	0
MISSING	0	0	0	0	0 I	0
TOOSMALL	0	0	0	0	0 I	0
TOOLARGE	0	0	0	0	0 I	0
UNCOUNTD	29	0	0	0	0 I	29
TOTAL	29	0	0	0	0 I	29

```
*************************
* TABLE PARAGRAPH   3  *       ⑳
*************************

*****  OBSERVED FREQUENCY TABLE   4

USING LEVEL  ╱UNDER 51   OF VARIABLE    1   AGE
             ********                       *******

HIGHBP   ANGINA                  FUNCTION
------   ------                  --------
                    NONE  MINIMAL MODERATE SEVERE   TOTAL
-----------------------------------------------------------------
NONE     NONE        1       3       0      0 I      4
         PRESENT     5       4      13      5 I     27
                   ---------------------------------I--------
         TOTAL       6       7      13      5 I     31

PRESENT  NONE        0       2       1      0 I      3
         PRESENT     2       4       6      1 I     13
                   ---------------------------------I--------
         TOTAL       2       6       7      1 I     16

         TOTAL OF THE OBSERVED FREQUENCY TABLE IS     47

    ALL CASES HAD COMPLETE DATA FOR THIS TABLE.

USING LEVEL  ╱51-60    OF VARIABLE    1   AGE
             ********                     *******

HIGHBP   ANGINA                  FUNCTION
------   ------                  --------
                    NONE  MINIMAL MODERATE SEVERE   TOTAL
-----------------------------------------------------------------
NONE     NONE        1       2       3      1 I      7
         PRESENT     4       6       7      8 I     25
                   ---------------------------------I--------
         TOTAL       5       8      10      9 I     32

PRESENT  NONE        0       1       1      0 I      2
         PRESENT     2       1       5      6 I     14
                   ---------------------------------I--------
         TOTAL       2       2       6      6 I     16

         TOTAL OF THE OBSERVED FREQUENCY TABLE IS     48

    ALL CASES HAD COMPLETE DATA FOR THIS TABLE.

USING LEVEL  ╱OVER 60   OF VARIABLE    1   AGE
             ********                     *******

HIGHBP   ANGINA                  FUNCTION
------   ------                  --------
                    NONE  MINIMAL MODERATE SEVERE   TOTAL
-----------------------------------------------------------------
NONE     NONE        1       0       1      0 I      2
         PRESENT     3       1       9      3 I     16
                   ---------------------------------I--------
         TOTAL       4       1      10      3 I     18

PRESENT  NONE        1       0       0      0 I      1
         PRESENT     0       0       0      3 I      3
                   ---------------------------------I--------
         TOTAL       1       0       0      3 I      4

         TOTAL OF THE OBSERVED FREQUENCY TABLE IS     22

    ALL CASES HAD COMPLETE DATA FOR THIS TABLE.
```

If a CONDITION statement is included in the TABLE paragraph, then each table is formed at each level of the CONDITION variable (see ⑳ in Output 4F.6). When more than one CONDITION variable is specified, each CONDITION variable is used in turn. The CONDITIONING variable cannot be an index of the table.

For multiway tables, P4F prints the same summaries of values excluded from the tables that were described in Example 4F.1 for two-way tables. These summaries are controlled using the LIST and EXCLUDE instructions.

```
TABLE ─────────────────────────────────────────
  INDices = v list.    either INDICES        none
                       or CATVAR is
                       required
     Names or subscripts of variables used as
     categorical variables to form the multiway
     table. If any variable takes on more than 10
     distinct values, CODES or CUTPOINTS must be
     specified for it in the CATEGORY paragraph. If
     CODES or CUTPOINTS are not specified, P4F
     allocates space for 10 levels; this may cause
     you to exceed the maximum size for a table
     (p. 145) if your table is five-way or higher or
     if you form many four-way tables at one time.
  CATvar = v list.    may be repeated         none
     Names or subscripts used as categorical
     variables to form a multiway table. If any
     variable takes on more than 10 distinct values,
     CODES or CUTPOINTS must be specified for it in
     the CATEGORY paragraph. If CODES or CUTPOINTS
     are not specified, P4F allocates space for 10
     levels; this may cause you to exceed the
     maximum size for a table (p. 145) if your table
     is five-way or higher or if you form many
     four-way tables at one time.
     If CATVAR is repeated, the index in the first
     CATVAR statement varies more rapidly than that
     of the second CATVAR statement, etc. If PAIR is
     specified or preassigned, the number of
     variables specified in every COLUMN, ROW and
     CATVAR statement must be the same.
     Note: The definitions of COLUMN and ROW appear
     on p. 150 and are similar to that of CATVAR,
     except that COLUMN and ROW may appear only once
     in a TABLE paragraph.
  PAIR. or CROSS.                             PAIR
     The tables are formed by PAIRING or CROSSING
     the indices in the ROW, COLUMN and CATVAR
     statements. If PAIR is specified or assumed,
     the number of variables in each ROW, COLUMN and
     CATVAR statement must be the same. If CROSS is
     specified, tables are formed from all
     combinations of the variables in the COLUMN,
     ROW and CATVAR statements in the order
     described above.
  CONDition = v list.                         none
     Names or subscripts of variables used to
     stratify the tables. If more than one is
     specified, each variable is used in turn. A
     table is formed and analyzed at each level
     (code or category) of this variable. If the
     variable takes on more than 10 distinct values,
     CODES or CUTPOINTS must be specified for it in
     the CATEGORY paragraph. See Example 4F.6 for
     its usage.
```

```
PRINT ─────────────────────────────────────────────────
   OBServed.                          OBSERVED/prev.
      The table of observed frequencies is printed
   unless NO OBSERVED is specified.
   LIST = #.                                5/prev.
      The number of cases (#) not included in one or
   more tables that are to be listed against the
   tables from which the cases are excluded.
   EXClude.                           EXCLUDE/prev.
      Following each frequency table from which cases
   are excluded, a two-way frequency table is
   printed that shows the reason for exclusion.
   This additional table can be deleted by
   specifying NO EXCLUDE.

   Note: the PRINT paragraph may be repeated after
   each TABLE paragraph.
```

Example 4F.7 Controlling the Printing of Row and Column Indices — Stacking Variables Together

As indicated in the previous example, the first categorical variable (index) in a table is printed horizontally, the second is the most rapidly changing vertically, etc. It is possible to print more than one categorical variable horizontally (or vertically) by STACKING the indices. Indices that are stacked together are treated as a single composite variable consisting of all possible combinations of the levels of the indices being stacked. For example, if we specify

STACK = ANGINA, HIGHBP.

in the TABLE paragraph and request a table having both ANGINA and HIGHBP as indices, the two indices will be combined into a single index having 4 levels (2 levels for ANGINA x 2 levels for HIGHBP).

Note: In all analyses, indices STACKED together are treated as a single index and the dimension of the table is reduced accordingly.

In our example we replace the TABLE paragraph in Example 4F.1 by

```
-------------------------------------------
/ TABLE    INDICES ARE AGE, INFARCT, ANGINA,
                   HIGHBP.
           STACK IS AGE, INFARCT.
           STACK IS ANGINA, HIGHBP.
-------------------------------------------
```

The first STACK specification forms a new index consisting of all possible combinations of the categories of AGE and INFARCT. Since AGE is the first index in the table (the column variable), the new STACKED variable is treated as the column index. The second STACK statement forms an index consisting

Output 4F.7 Stacking table indices using all combinations of several variables as a single table index

---

--- the features described in ⑲ to ㉒ are printed for this problem ---

```
*************************
* TABLE PARAGRAPH  1  *
*************************
```

***** OBSERVED FREQUENCY TABLE 1

		INFARCT					
		NONE			PRESENT		
HIGHBP	ANGINA	AGE					
		UNDER 51	51-60	OVER 60	UNDER 51	51-60	OVER 60	TOTAL
NONE	NONE	0	1	1	4	6	1 I	13
	PRESENT	12	9	5	15	16	11 I	68
PRESENT	NONE	1	0	0	2	2	1 I	6
	PRESENT	7	5	2	6	9	1 I	30
	TOTAL	20	15	8	27	33	14 I	117

TOTAL OF THE OBSERVED FREQUENCY TABLE IS   117

ALL CASES HAD COMPLETE DATA FOR THIS TABLE.

MINIMUM ESTIMATED EXPECTED VALUE IS   0.41

STATISTIC	VALUE	D.F.	PROB.
PEARSON CHISQUARE	10.809	15	0.7660

of all four possible combinations of ANGINA and HIGHBP.

The resultant table is presented in Output 4F.7. Note that both AGE and INFARCT are listed horizontally and ANGINA and HIGHBP vertically. In contrast to other tables, there are no column totals for each level of HIGHBP (see ㉓ in Output 4F.6); P4F treats both row indices as a <u>single</u> index.

There were initially four indices; but the four indices are stacked into <u>two</u> new indices. Therefore the table is treated as a <u>two-way</u> frequency table. For this reason the Pearson chi-square statistic is printed beneath the table. The degrees of freedom for the chi-square is $15 = (6 - 1)(4 - 1)$ where 6 is the number of levels in the STACKED column index and 4 is the number of levels in the STACKED row index.

```
TABLE
   STACK = v list.    may be repeated          none
      If all the variables in the STACK specification
      appear as indices in the table, a new index is
      created that consists of all possible
      combinations of the levels of the variables in
      the STACK list. An index in one table cannot
      appear in more than one STACK specification. If
      the STACK specification includes the column
      (first) index in the table, the new STACKED
      index is printed horizontally. In all analyses
      the new index is treated as a single index
      whenever any index in the STACK specification
      is referenced.
```

Example 4F.8 Marginal Subtables

A marginal subtable is the original observed frequency table collapsed over one or more indices. In a two-way table it is possible to print the row totals, column totals and the total frequency around the margins of the frequency table. In a three-way or higher table, it is not possible to print all possible marginal subtables compactly about the original table. When requested, P4F can print all (or some) of the marginal subtables.

For the four-way table specified in the following TABLE paragraph we request all two-way tables with a MARGINAL statement in the PRINT paragraph. The TABLE paragraph replaces the TABLE paragraph in the Control Language for Example 4F.1; the PRINT paragraph follows it and is before the END paragraph.

```
-------------------------------------
/ TABLE   INDICES ARE AGE, FUNCTION,
                   ANGINA, HIGHBP.
/ PRINT   MARGINALS ARE 2.
-------------------------------------
```

The results are presented in Output 4F.8.

㉗ The marginal subtable formed by summing over all the indices but AGE in the frequency table. This is followed by the marginal subtable for FUNCTION, etc.

㉘ The marginal subtable indexed by AGE and FUNCTION formed by summing over the remaining indices in the frequency table. The other two-way marginal subtables follow this table.

If MARGINALS ARE 3 were specified, the two-way tables would be followed by all possible three-way tables.

```
PRINT
   MARGinal = #.                               0/prev.
      Print marginal subtables for all dimensions up
      to and including order #.
```

Output 4F.8   Marginal subtables printed by P4F

--- ⑲ to ㉒ and the observed frequency table ㉓ in Output 4F.6 appear here ---

***** MARGINAL SUBTABLE — TABLE 1

	AGE			
	UNDER 51	51–60	OVER 60	TOTAL ㉗
	47	48	22 I	117

***** MARGINAL SUBTABLE — TABLE 1

	FUNCTION			
NONE	MINIMAL	MODERATE	SEVERE	TOTAL
20	24	46	27 I	117

--- similar tables for ANGINA and for HIGHBP ---

***** MARGINAL SUBTABLE — TABLE 1   ㉘

FUNCTION	AGE			
	UNDER 51	51–60	OVER 60	TOTAL
NONE	8	7	5 I	20
MINIMAL	13	10	1 I	24
MODERATE	20	16	10 I	46
SEVERE	6	15	6 I	27
TOTAL	47	48	22 I	117

***** MARGINAL SUBTABLE — TABLE 1

ANGINA	AGE			
	UNDER 51	51–60	OVER 60	TOTAL
NONE	7	9	3 I	19
PRESENT	40	39	19 I	98
TOTAL	47	48	22 I	117

(output continued)

Output 4F.8 (continued)

***** MARGINAL SUBTABLE — TABLE 1

HIGHBP	AGE			
	UNDER 51	51-60	OVER 60	TOTAL
NONE	31	32	18 I	81
PRESENT	16	16	4 I	36
TOTAL	47	48	22 I	117

***** MARGINAL SUBTABLE — TABLE 1

ANGINA	FUNCTION				
	NONE	MINIMAL	MODERATE	SEVERE	TOTAL
NONE	4	8	6	1 I	19
PRESENT	16	16	40	26 I	98
TOTAL	20	24	46	27 I	117

***** MARGINAL SUBTABLE — TABLE 1

HIGHBP	FUNCTION				
	NONE	MINIMAL	MODERATE	SEVERE	TOTAL
NONE	15	16	33	17 I	81
PRESENT	5	8	13	10 I	36
TOTAL	20	24	46	27 I	117

***** MARGINAL SUBTABLE — TABLE 1

HIGHBP	ANGINA		
	NONE	PRESENT	TOTAL
NONE	13	68 I	81
PRESENT	6	30 I	36
TOTAL	19	98 I	117

Example 4F.9 Percentages

P4F can print tables of percentages where the percent can be of the "row" total, the "column" total or of the total frequency. ROW indicates a line in the table and COLUMN a column in a panel.

In order to obtain the percents that are relevant to a specific problem, the order in which the indices are printed can be controlled. (See Examples 4F.6 and 4F.7.)

In this example, percentages of the row totals, of the column totals and of the table total are requested in the PRINT paragraph following the TABLE specification. We insert these paragraphs in the Control Language of Example 4F.1 after the CATEGORY paragraph and before the END paragraph.

```
---------------------------------------
/ TABLE    INDICES ARE AGE, FUNCTION,
                      ANGINA, HIGHBP.
/ PRINT   PERCENTS ARE ROW, COL, TOT.
---------------------------------------
```

The resulting tables are presented in Output 4F.9.

(29) Percentages of row totals. These are percents of the total for each line in the table and not of

Output 4F.9   Percentages in multiway tables

--- (19) to (22) and the observed frequency table (23) in Output 4F.6 appear here ---

***** PERCENTS OF ROW TOTALS — TABLE 1   (29)

HIGHBP	ANGINA	FUNCTION	AGE			
			UNDER 51	51-60	OVER 60	TOTAL
NONE	NONE	NONE	33.3	33.3	33.3 I	100.0
		MINIMAL	60.0	40.0	0.0 I	100.0
		MODERATE	0.0	75.0	25.0 I	100.0
		SEVERE	0.0	100.0	0.0 I	100.0
		TOTAL	30.8	53.8	15.4 I	100.0
	PRESENT	NONE	41.7	33.3	25.0 I	100.0
		MINIMAL	36.4	54.5	9.1 I	100.0
		MODERATE	44.8	24.1	31.0 I	100.0
		SEVERE	31.3	50.0	18.8 I	100.0
		TOTAL	39.7	36.8	23.5 I	100.0
PRESENT	NONE	NONE	0.0	0.0	100.0 I	100.0
		MINIMAL	66.7	33.3	0.0 I	100.0
		MODERATE	50.0	50.0	0.0 I	100.0
		SEVERE	0.0	0.0	0.0 I	100.0
		TOTAL	50.0	33.3	16.7 I	100.0
	PRESENT	NONE	50.0	50.0	0.0 I	100.0
		MINIMAL	80.0	20.0	0.0 I	100.0
		MODERATE	54.5	45.5	0.0 I	100.0
		SEVERE	10.0	60.0	30.0 I	100.0
		TOTAL	43.3	46.7	10.0 I	100.0

the total for a level of the row variable (the latter total is obtained by summing over the columns and over all levels of the third and higher indices).

(30) Percentages of column totals. These are percents of the total for a column in a panel of the table. The definition of column total is similar to that of row total if the two indices are interchanged in the table.

(31) Percentages of the table total. These are percentages of the total frequency in the table (and not of a panel in the table).

```
PRINT
  PERCent = (one or more)                      no/prev.
          NO, ROW, COL, TOT.
    Print tables of percentages.
    NO  - no tables of percentages requested
    ROW - percentages of row totals (in a panel)
    COL - percentages of column totals (in a
          panel)
    TOT - percentages of the total frequency in
          the table
```

USING TABLES AS INPUT AND SAVING TABLES

Example 4F.10 Starting from a Multiway Frequency Table

Tabulated data, such as a table from a government or scientific report, can also be used as input. If the data have already been accumulated into a (multiway) frequency table, it is more efficient to use the table as input than to return to the original data. The tabulated data can be entered in the form of a multiway frequency table (this example) or as a series of cases, each case containing a cell frequency and its indices (Example 4F.11).

Consider a frequency table that has two rows and three columns, such as

```
10  20  30
40  50  60
```

You can record only the frequencies on your data card, e.g.,

```
10  20  30  40  50  60
```

You then need to specify the dimensions of the TABLE in the INPUT paragraph, e.g.,

***** PERCENTS OF COLUMN TOTALS — TABLE 1 (30)

HIGHBP	ANGINA	FUNCTION	AGE UNDER 51	51-60	OVER 60	TOTAL
NONE	NONE	NONE	25.0	14.3	50.0 I	23.1
		MINIMAL	75.0	28.6	0.0 I	38.5
		MODERATE	0.0	42.9	50.0 I	30.8
		SEVERE	0.0	14.3	0.0 I	7.7
		TOTAL	100.0	100.0	100.0 I	100.0
	PRESENT	NONE	18.5	16.0	18.8 I	17.6
		MINIMAL	14.8	24.0	6.3 I	16.2
		MODERATE	48.1	28.0	56.3 I	42.6
		SEVERE	18.5	32.0	18.8 I	23.5
		TOTAL	100.0	100.0	100.0 I	100.0
PRESENT	NONE	NONE	0.0	0.0	100.0 I	16.7
		MINIMAL	66.7	50.0	0.0 I	50.0
		MODERATE	33.3	50.0	0.0 I	33.3
		SEVERE	0.0	0.0	0.0 I	0.0
		TOTAL	100.0	100.0	100.0 I	100.0
	PRESENT	NONE	15.4	14.3	0.0 I	13.3
		MINIMAL	30.8	7.1	0.0 I	16.7
		MODERATE	46.2	35.7	0.0 I	36.7
		SEVERE	7.7	42.9	100.0 I	33.3
		TOTAL	100.0	100.0	100.0 I	100.0

***** PERCENTS OF THE TABLE TOTAL — TABLE 1 (31)

HIGHBP	ANGINA	FUNCTION	AGE UNDER 51	51-60	OVER 60	TOTAL
NONE	NONE	NONE	0.9	0.9	0.9 I	2.6
		MINIMAL	2.6	1.7	0.0 I	4.3
		MODERATE	0.0	2.6	0.9 I	3.4
		SEVERE	0.0	0.9	0.0 I	0.9
		TOTAL	3.4	6.0	1.7 I	11.1
	PRESENT	NONE	4.3	3.4	2.6 I	10.3
		MINIMAL	3.4	5.1	0.9 I	9.4
		MODERATE	11.1	6.0	7.7 I	24.8
		SEVERE	4.3	6.8	2.6 I	13.7
		TOTAL	23.1	21.4	13.7 I	58.1
PRESENT	NONE	NONE	0.0	0.0	0.9 I	0.9
		MINIMAL	1.7	0.9	0.0 I	2.6
		MODERATE	0.9	0.9	0.0 I	1.7
		SEVERE	0.0	0.0	0.0 I	0.0
		TOTAL	2.6	1.7	0.9 I	5.1
	PRESENT	NONE	1.7	1.7	0.0 I	3.4
		MINIMAL	3.4	0.9	0.0 I	4.3
		MODERATE	5.1	4.3	0.0 I	9.4
		SEVERE	0.9	5.1	2.6 I	8.5
		TOTAL	11.1	12.0	2.6 I	25.6

```
        INPUT     TABLE = 3, 2.
```

where 3 is the number of levels of the index that
changes more rapidly (columns in our example) and 2
of the index that changes more slowly (rows).

As a more complex example we use the data in
Table 11.3 on the incidence of peptic ulcer by blood
group in three cities.

Table 11.3 Incidence of Peptic Ulcer by Blood Group
(Woolf, 1955)

City	Illness Bloodgroup	Ulcer		Control	
		O	A	O	A
London		911	579	4578	4219
Manchester		361	246	4532	3775
Newcastle		396	219	6598	5261

We read the Table 11.3 as input and form a frequency
table using the following Control Language.

```
       --------------------------------------
/ PROBLEM      TITLE IS 'WOOLF BLOODGROUPING DATA -
                  EXAMPLE OF TABLE INPUT'.

/ INPUT        VARIABLES ARE 3.
             ↗ TABLE IS 2, 2, 3.
               FORMAT IS '(4F5.0)'.

/ VARIABLE     NAMES ARE BLOODGRP, ILLNESS, CITY.
/ TABLE        INDICES ARE BLOODGRP, ILLNESS, CITY.
/ TABLE        ROW IS ILLNESS.
               COLUMN IS BLOODGRP.
               CONDITION IS CITY.
/ TABLE        ROW IS ILLNESS.
               COLUMN IS BLOODGRP.
/ CATEGORY     CODES(1) ARE 1, 2.
               NAMES(1) ARE 'GROUP O', 'GROUP A'.
               CODES(2) ARE 1, 2.
               NAMES(2) ARE ULCER, CONTROL.
               CODES(3) ARE 1 TO 3.
               NAMES(3) ARE LONDON, MANCHSTR,
                        NEWCASTL.

/ END
    911    579   4578   4219  ⎤  input. is
    361    246   4532   3775  ⎬  multiway
    396    219   6598   5261  ⎦  table
       --------------------------------------
```

The number of VARIABLES in the INPUT paragraph is
the number of categorical variables in the table (3
in our example). The FORMAT describes the entire
table (the entire table is read at one time).

In the above example the 12 cell frequencies are
punched on three cards. (They could be punched on
one card.) P4F determines the number of values to
read from the TABLE statement in the INPUT paragraph
(2x2x3=12). The FORMAT (4F5.0) is equivalent to
(4F5.0/4F5.0/4F5.0) since the format specification
is repeated until all 12 values are read.

The frequency table is read as input and all the
tables requested are formed. The first TABLE
paragraph describes the three-way table that is used
as input. The second TABLE paragraph describes three

two-way cross sections of the original table, a
cross section for each CITY. The third TABLE
paragraph describes the two-way marginal subtable
summed over cities.

The three tables requested by this example are
presented in Output 4F.10. Note that the three-way
frequency table used as input can be analyzed:

③② - as the observed frequency table (Table 1)

③③ - as cross sections of the observed table for
each city (Table 2)

③④ - as a marginal subtable obtained by
collapsing over one or more of the original indices
(city). The index for city is not specified in the
TABLE paragraph.

Note 1: The frequency tables are sequence numbered
across TABLE paragraphs.

Note 2: A two-way cross section of a three-way table
is analyzed as a two-way table.

```
INPut ───────────────────────────────────────────
┌──────────────────────────────────────────────────┐
│ TABLE = # list.     req. if data are       none   │
│                     input as a multi-             │
│                     way table                     │
│  The numbers (#) are the number of levels of      │
│  each of the categorical variables (indices)      │
│  that define the table; their product is the      │
│  number of cells in the table. The first number   │
│  is the number of levels of the fastest varying   │
│  index, the second number of the next fastest,    │
│  etc. The number of VARIABLES should be speci-     │
│  fied as the number of indices; the number of     │
│  CASES is not used; and the FORMAT should de-      │
│  scribe the entire table. Transformations and     │
│  data editing cannot be used with this form of    │
│  input. For example: the multiway table (Table    │
│  11.3) can be written as                           │
│                                                    │
│      911    579   4578   4219    361    246        │
│     4532   3775    396    219   6598   5261        │
│                                                    │
│  where the frequencies are ordered so that Blood   │
│  Group is the fastest varying index, Illness the   │
│  next fastest, and City the slowest. That is, if   │
│  i represents Blood Group, j is Illness, k is      │
│  City and fᵢⱼₖ is the frequency in cell (i,j,k),   │
│  the order of cells is                             │
│                                                    │
└──────────────────────────────────────────────────┘
```

Within the box, the cell order line and TABLE specification read:

$$f_{111}, f_{211}, f_{121}, f_{221}, f_{112}, f_{212}$$

$$f_{221}, f_{222}, f_{113}, f_{213}, f_{123}, f_{223}$$

To read this table as input you must specify

$$\text{TABLE} = 2, 2, 3.$$

in the INPUT paragraph, where the first 2 is
the <u>number of levels</u> of the fastest varying
index, the second 2 is the number of levels of
the next fastest varying index and 3 is the
number of levels of the slowest varying index.

Output 4F.10   Using a frequency table as input to P4F

```
************************
* TABLE PARAGRAPH   1  *
************************
```

***** OBSERVED FREQUENCY TABLE 1 (32)

CITY	ILLNESS	BLOODGRP		
		GROUP O	GROUP A	TOTAL
LONDON	ULCER	911	579 I	1490
	CONTROL	4578	4219 I	8797
	TOTAL	5489	4798 I	10287
MANCHSTR	ULCER	361	246 I	607
	CONTROL	4532	3775 I	8307
	TOTAL	4893	4021 I	8914
NEWCASTL	ULCER	396	219 I	615
	CONTROL	6598	5261 I	11859
	TOTAL	6994	5480 I	12474

TOTAL OF THE OBSERVED FREQUENCY TABLE IS   31675

```
************************
* TABLE PARAGRAPH   2  *
************************
```

***** OBSERVED FREQUENCY TABLE 2 (33)

USING LEVEL   LONDON   OF VARIABLE   3   CITY
             ********   ********

ILLNESS	BLOODGRP		
	GROUP O	GROUP A	TOTAL
ULCER	911	579 I	1490
CONTROL	4578	4219 I	8797
TOTAL	5489	4798 I	10287

MINIMUM ESTIMATED EXPECTED VALUE IS   694.96

STATISTIC	VALUE	D.F.	PROB.
PEARSON CHISQUARE	42.402	1	0.0
YATES CORRECTED CHISQ.	42.037	1	0.0

***** OBSERVED FREQUENCY TABLE 2

USING LEVEL   MANCHSTR   OF VARIABLE   3   CITY
             ********   ********

ILLNESS	BLOODGRP		
	GROUP O	GROUP A	TOTAL
ULCER	361	246 I	607
CONTROL	4532	3775 I	8307
TOTAL	4893	4021 I	8914

MINIMUM ESTIMATED EXPECTED VALUE IS   273.81

STATISTIC	VALUE	D.F.	PROB.
PEARSON CHISQUARE	5.522	1	0.0188
YATES CORRECTED CHISQ.	5.325	1	0.0210

***** OBSERVED FREQUENCY TABLE 2

USING LEVEL   NEWCASTL   OF VARIABLE   3   CITY
             ********   ********

ILLNESS	BLOODGRP		
	GROUP O	GROUP A	TOTAL
ULCER	396	219 I	615
CONTROL	6598	5261 I	11859
TOTAL	6994	5480 I	12474

MINIMUM ESTIMATED EXPECTED VALUE IS   270.18

STATISTIC	VALUE	D.F.	PROB.
PEARSON CHISQUARE	18.187	1	0.0000
YATES CORRECTED CHISQ.	17.833	1	0.0000

```
************************
* TABLE PARAGRAPH   3  *
************************
```

***** OBSERVED FREQUENCY TABLE 3 (34)

ILLNESS	BLOODGRP		
	GROUP O	GROUP A	TOTAL
ULCER	1668	1044 I	2712
CONTROL	15708	13255 I	28963
TOTAL	17376	14299 I	31675

MINIMUM ESTIMATED EXPECTED VALUE IS   1224.27

STATISTIC	VALUE	D.F.	PROB.
PEARSON CHISQUARE	52.921	1	0.0
YATES CORRECTED CHISQ.	52.628	1	0.0

Example 4F.11 Starting from Cell Frequencies and Indices

Input as cell indices and frequencies. The tabulated data can also be organized as sets of cell indices and frequency counts, such as

1	1	1	911		2	2	1	4532
1	1	2	579		2	2	2	3775
1	2	1	4578		3	1	1	396
1	2	2	4219		3	1	2	219
2	1	1	361		3	2	1	6598
2	1	2	246		3	2	2	5261

The data are typed as 12 records, where each record is a set of (3) cell indices and the observed frequency for that cell. The first three numbers represent the categories for CITY, ILLNESS, and BLOODGRP, respectively; the fourth number is the frequency. Note that there can be more than one record for a combination of cell indices.

To read the data, the following Control Language instructions are used.

```
-------------------------------------
/ PROBLEM    TITLE IS 'WOOLF BLOODGROUPING DATA--
            CELL INDICES AND FREQUENCIES ARE INPUT'.

/ INPUT      VARIABLES ARE 4.
            CASES ARE 12.
            FORMAT IS '(3F2.0, F5.0)'.

/ VARIABLE   NAMES ARE CITY, ILLNESS, BLOODGRP, FREQ.
/ TABLE      INDICES ARE BLOODGRP, ILLNESS, CITY.
            COUNT IS FREQ.
/ TABLE      ROW IS ILLNESS.
            COLUMN IS BLOODGRP.
            CONDITION IS CITY.
            COUNT IS FREQ.
/ TABLE      ROW IS ILLNESS.
            COLUMN IS BLOODGRP.
            COUNT IS FREQ.
/ CATEGORY   NAMES(1) ARE LONDON, MANCHSTR, NEWCASTL.
            CODES(1) ARE 1 TO 3.
            NAMES(2) ARE ULCER, CONTROL.
            CODES(2) ARE 1, 2.
            NAMES(3) ARE 'GROUP O', 'GROUP A'.
            CODES(3) ARE 1, 2.

/ END
  1  1  1    911
  1  1  2    579
  1  2  1   4578
  1  2  2   4219         Input is in
  2  1  1    361         form of cell
  2  1  2    246         indices and
  2  2  1   4532         frequencies
  2  2  2   3775
  3  1  1    396
  3  1  2    219
  3  2  1   6598
  3  2  2   5261
-------------------------------------
```

Each categorical variable and the "frequency count" variable are treated as variables (VARIABLE=4). The format describes a case (there are 12 cases, one for each cell in the table) which consists of a set of indices and its frequency count. Therefore, the data are described in the same manner as when each case is an observation. When COUNT=FREQ is specified in the TABLE paragraph in our example, the program accumulates frequencies in the COUNT variable (FREQ) instead of treating each case as one observation.

The tables are printed in Output 4F.11. The frequencies are the same as in Output 4F.10 where the same data were read as a multiway table.

```
TABLE --------------------------------------
   | COUNT = v list.   req. only when data        none
   |                   are input as cell
   |                   indices and frequency
   |                   counts
   | Names or subscripts of variables that contain
   | frequency counts. If more than one variable is
   | specified, tables are formed for each variable
   | separately.
   _____
```

Output 4F.11   Using cell indices and frequencies as input to P4F
```
------------------------------------------------------

      ************************
      * TABLE PARAGRAPH   1  *
      ************************

   *****  OBSERVED FREQUENCY TABLE   1

   VARIABLE    4   FREQ        USED AS COUNT VARIABLE.
                   ********
```

CITY	ILLNESS	BLOODGRP		
		GROUP O	GROUP A	TOTAL
LONDON	ULCER	911	579 I	1490
	CONTROL	4578	4219 I	8797
	TOTAL	5489	4798 I	10287
MANCHSTR	ULCER	361	246 I	607
	CONTROL	4532	3775 I	8307
	TOTAL	4893	4021 I	8914
NEWCASTL	ULCER	396	219 I	615
	CONTROL	6598	5261 I	11859
	TOTAL	6994	5480 I	12474

```
   TOTAL OF THE OBSERVED FREQUENCY TABLE IS     31675

   ALL CASES HAD COMPLETE DATA FOR THIS TABLE.

--- similarly the frequencies of tables 2 and 3 are
   the same as those in tables 2 and 3 in Output
                    4F.10 ---

------------------------------------------------------
```

Example 4F.12 Saving Tables in a BMDP File

You may want to reanalyze data tabulated into a frequency table by requesting additional statistics for a two-way table, fitting different models to a multiway table or looking at cross sections or marginal subtables. If there are many cases, it may be costly to start each analysis from the data; it may be preferable to save the frequency tables tabulated in one analysis in order to reuse them.

In addition to saving the data in a BMDP File for further analysis, P4F can also save the frequency tables. Each frequency table is saved as a separate file. Therefore one analysis can create multiple files. In order to have access to any table in the BMDP File, P4F modifies the CONTENT of the BMDP File for each table to be the word TABLE followed by the sequence number of the table. Note that this use of CONTENT differs slightly from the usual BMDP File usage.

In this example we store tabulated data in ten BMDP Files. We use four TABLE paragraphs to specify the tables and a SAVE paragraph to specify what to store in the file, how to label it and where to write it (see Section 7.1). These paragraphs are inserted after the PROBLEM, INPUT, VARIABLE and CATEGORY paragraphs of Example 4F.1. An END paragraph follows them.

```
-------------------------------------
/ TABLE     COLUMN IS FUNCTION, INFARCT.
           ROW IS ACTIVE, ANGINA.
/ TABLE     COLUMN IS FUNCTION, INFARCT.
           ROW IS ACTIVE, ANGINA.
           CROSS.
/ TABLE     COLUMN IS FUNCTION, INFARCT.
           ROW IS ACTIVE, ANGINA.
           CONDITION IS AGE.
/ TABLE     ROW IS AGE, ACTIVE.
           COLUMN IS ANGINA, HIGHBP.
/ SAVE      CONTENT IS TABLE.
           UNIT IS 9.
           CODE IS KASSERT.
           NEW.
-------------------------------------
```

The ten files are written in the BMDP File named KASSERT. Each table is assigned a BMDP File CONTENT -- TABLE followed by the sequence number of the table where the sequence number is assigned sequentially across TABLE paragraphs. The following tables are stored:

Table		File CONTENT	Paragraph where table is specified
FUNCTION against ACTIVE		TABLE1	1
INFARCT against ANGINA		TABLE2	1
FUNCTION against ACTIVE		TABLE3	2
FUNCTION against ANGINA		TABLE4	2
INFARCT against ACTIVE		TABLE5	2
INFARCT against ANGINA		TABLE6	2
FUNCTION against ACTIVE against AGE		TABLE7	3
INFARCT against ANGINA against AGE		TABLE8	3
AGE against ANGINA		TABLE9	4
ACTIVE against HIGHBP		TABLE10	4

Note: If a CONDITIONING variable is specified, the CONDITIONING variable is saved as an additional dimension to the table; e.g., see Tables 7 and 8 that are defined by the third TABLE paragraph.

In Output 4F.12 a message is written describing each file and that the file has been completed. Output for the requested tables follows. All the BMDP Files are formed before the frequency tables are printed. Therefore if your run terminates before the analysis of the last tables, the tables may still be available in the BMDP Files.

(35) Table 7 is saved as a three-way table FUNCTION by ACTIVE by AGE. This table is requested by the third TABLE paragraph in which AGE is a conditioning variable. In the BMDP File AGE is treated as an additional index to the table (the third index in our example). Multiway tables are saved in a similar manner.

Note: CATEGORY CODES and CUTPOINTS for the table are also saved in the BMDP File.

```
SAVE ─────────────────────────────────
  │ CONTent = (one or both) DATA,TABLE.        DATA
  │   DATA and/or frequency TABLES to be saved in a
  │   BMDP File. When frequency tables are saved, a
  │   CONTENT is generated for each table consisting
  │   of the word TABLE followed by the sequence
  │   number of the table. This CONTENT is printed
  │   when the BMDP file is formed and must be used
  │   to recall a table other than the first.
  ─────────────────────────────────────
```

Output 4F.12   Saving frequency tables in BMDP Files

```
-------------------------------------
     BMDP FILE IS BEING WRITTEN ON UNIT        9
     CODE. . . IS      KASSERT
     CONTENT . IS      TABLE1
     LABEL . . IS
     VARIABLES ARE
          1 FUNCTION      2 ACTIVE


     BMDP FILE ON UNIT  9 HAS BEEN COMPLETED.


     BMDP FILE IS BEING WRITTEN ON UNIT        9
     CODE. . . IS      KASSERT
     CONTENT . IS      TABLE2
     LABEL . . IS
     VARIABLES ARE
          1 INFARCT      2 ANGINA

     BMDP FILE ON UNIT  9 HAS BEEN COMPLETED.


     --- similarly for tables 3 to 6 ---


     BMDP FILE IS BEING WRITTEN ON UNIT        9
     CODE. . . IS      KASSERT
     CONTENT . IS      TABLE7                (35)
     LABEL . . IS
     VARIABLES ARE
          1 FUNCTION      2 ACTIVE      3 AGE

     BMDP FILE ON UNIT  9 HAS BEEN COMPLETED.
```

                                    (output continued)

Output 4F.12 (continued)

```
BMDP FILE IS BEING WRITTEN ON UNIT        9
CODE. . . IS        KASSERT
CONTENT . IS        TABLE8
LABEL . . IS
VARIABLES ARE
      1 INFARCT      2 ANGINA      3 AGE

BMDP FILE ON UNIT  9 HAS BEEN COMPLETED.


BMDP FILE IS BEING WRITTEN ON UNIT        9
CODE. . . IS        KASSERT
CONTENT . IS        TABLE9
LABEL . . IS
VARIABLES ARE
      1 ANGINA      2 AGE

BMDP FILE ON UNIT  9 HAS BEEN COMPLETED.


BMDP FILE IS BEING WRITTEN ON UNIT        9
CODE. . . IS        KASSERT
CONTENT . IS        TABLE10
LABEL . . IS
VARIABLES ARE
      1 HIGHBP      2 ACTIVE

BMDP FILE ON UNIT  9 HAS BEEN COMPLETED.
```

```
************************
* TABLE PARAGRAPH   1  *
************************
```

***** OBSERVED FREQUENCY TABLE   1

ACTIVE		FUNCTION			
	NONE	MINIMAL	MODERATE	SEVERE	TOTAL
VERY	2	4	2	1 I	9
NORMAL	3	13	37	7 I	60
LIMITED	0	1	2	16 I	19
TOTAL	5	18	41	24 I	88

29 CASES HAD INCOMPLETE DATA.

--- a summary of the excluded
        cases appears here ---

***** ANALYSIS OF OBSERVED FREQUENCY TABLE   1

MINIMUM ESTIMATED EXPECTED VALUE IS   0.51

STATISTIC	VALUE	D.F.	PROB.
PEARSON CHISQUARE	48.365	6	0.0000

--- followed by the requested
    analyses for tables 2 to 6 ---

```
************************
* TABLE PARAGRAPH   3  *
************************
```

***** OBSERVED FREQUENCY TABLE   7

USING LEVEL   UNDER 51   OF VARIABLE   1   AGE
            ********   ********

ACTIVE		FUNCTION			
	NONE	MINIMAL	MODERATE	SEVERE	TOTAL
VERY	1	3	2	0 I	6
NORMAL	1	7	14	2 I	24
LIMITED	0	1	2	4 I	7
TOTAL	2	11	18	6 I	37

10 CASES HAD INCOMPLETE DATA.

--- a summary of the excluded
        cases appears here ---

***** ANALYSIS OF OBSERVED FREQUENCY TABLE   7

MINIMUM ESTIMATED EXPECTED VALUE IS   0.32

STATISTIC	VALUE	D.F.	PROB.
PEARSON CHISQUARE	13.703	6	0.0331

--- similar analyses for the other
    two levels of table 7 ---

--- followed by the three tables for
    INFARCT by ANGINA for the UNDER 51,
    51-60 and OVER 60 age groups ---

```
************************
* TABLE PARAGRAPH   4  *
************************

*****  OBSERVED FREQUENCY TABLE   9

AGE              ANGINA
------           ------
              NONE  PRESENT   TOTAL

UNDER 51       7       40 I      47
51-60          9       39 I      48
OVER 60        3       19 I      22
-----------------------I--------
TOTAL         19       98 I     117

      ALL CASES HAD COMPLETE DATA FOR THIS TABLE.

MINIMUM ESTIMATED EXPECTED VALUE IS      3.57

STATISTIC                VALUE   D.F.   PROB.
PEARSON CHISQUARE        0.395      2   0.8209
```

```
*****  OBSERVED FREQUENCY TABLE  10

ACTIVE         HIGHBP
------         ------
              NONE  PRESENT   TOTAL
--------------------------------------
VERY            6       3 I       9
NORMAL         42      18 I      60
LIMITED        10       9 I      19
-----------------------I--------
TOTAL          58      30 I      88

     29  CASES HAD INCOMPLETE DATA.

  --- a summary of the excluded
           cases appears here ---

*****  ANALYSIS OF OBSERVED FREQUENCY TABLE  10

MINIMUM ESTIMATED EXPECTED VALUE IS      3.07

STATISTIC                VALUE   D.F.   PROB.
PEARSON CHISQUARE        1.940      2   0.3791
```

Example 4F.13 Reading a Frequency Table from a BMDP File

Tables that have been saved in a BMDP File can be read and further analyzed by P4F. When there is only one table in the BMDP File or when the first table is wanted, the sequence number of the table may be omitted. Otherwise the CONTENT should be specified as shown in the output when the BMDP File was created (TABLE followed by the sequence number of the table).

In the following Control Language we request as input the second table (TABLE2) saved in Example 4F.12. We omit variable names and category codes and names because they are stored in the files with the tables.

```
--------------------------------------
/ PROBLEM    TITLE IS 'KASSER CORONARY DATA'.
/ INPUT      CODE IS KASSERT.
             CONTENT IS TABLE2.
             UNIT IS 8.
/ TABLE      COLUMN IS 1.
             ROW IS 2.

/ END
--------------------------------------
```

The table specified above is read from the BMDP File and printed in Output 4F.13.

Note: The table in the BMDP File is treated in the same manner as a multiway frequency table read as input. Therefore you can form and analyze a marginal subtable by specifying a subset of the variables (indices), etc. You can use variable names in the TABLE paragraph or you can use subscripts where 1 refers to the column variable (INFARCT) when the table is saved, 2 to the row variable (ANGINA), etc. The subscripts refer to the order of the variables in the table (as in multiway frequency table input) and not to the subscript of the variables in the analysis that created the table.

```
INPUT ---------------------------------
 CONTent = (one only) DATA, TABLE.        DATA
    Read either DATA or a frequency TABLE from a
    BMDP File.
    When a frequency table is to be read from a
    BMDP File, the CONTENT must contain the
    sequence number of the frequency table (see
    SAVE paragraph above).
```

Output 4F.13 Reading a frequency table from a BMDP
File

```
INPUT BMDP FILE
CODE. . . IS     KASSERT
CONTENT . IS     TABLE2
LABEL . . IS
VARIABLES
     1 INFARCT      2 ANGINA
```

```
*************************
 * TABLE PARAGRAPH   1  *
*************************
```

```
*****  OBSERVED FREQUENCY TABLE   1
```

ANGINA	INFARCT		
	NONE	PRESENT	TOTAL
NONE	3	16 I	19
PRESENT	40	58 I	98
TOTAL	43	74 I	117

```
MINIMUM ESTIMATED EXPECTED VALUE IS      6.98
```

STATISTIC	VALUE	D.F.	PROB.
PEARSON CHISQUARE	4.288	1	0.0384
YATES CORRECTED CHISQ.	3.279	1	0.0702

MULTIWAY TABLES — ANALYSIS BY LOG-LINEAR MODELS

Overview with Review of Terms

The purpose of the analysis of a multiway table is to obtain a description of the relationships between the factors of the table, either by forming a model for the data or by testing and ordering the importance of the interactions between the factors. The analysis is based on fitting a (hierarchical) log-linear model to the cell frequencies; that is, the logarithm of the expected cell frequency is written as an additive function of main effects and interactions in a manner similar to the usual analysis of variance model. Detailed discussions of the log-linear model appear in texts by Bishop et al (1975), Fienberg (1977), Plackett (1974) and others.

In the two-way table the test of independence is equivalent to testing the fit of the model,

$$E(f_{ij}) = \alpha_i \beta_j;$$

i.e., the expected cell frequency $E(f_{ij})$ is the product of two terms, one of which depends only on the row (α_i) that the frequency appears in and the other on the column (β_j). In a higher way table the expected cell frequency may be expressed as the product of several terms, each representing a main effect or interaction. Since the logarithm of a product of terms is the sum of the logarithms of the terms, the logarithm of the expected frequency can be expressed as a linear model--the log-linear model.

Before discussing the following examples it may be helpful to review some standard terminology. Consider a four-way $I \times J \times K \times L$ contingency table, where the four indices pertain to categorical variables A,B,C,D, respectively. Let f_{ijkl} be the observed frequency in cell (i,j,k,ℓ) of the table.

P4F performs an analysis of the data based on the assumption that the logarithm of the expected values is a linear function of certain parameters. That is, as in the analysis of variance, the log-linear model may be written as

$$\ln F_{ijk\ell} = \theta + \lambda_i^A + \lambda_j^B + \lambda_k^C + \lambda_\ell^D + \lambda_{ij}^{AB} + \lambda_{ik}^{AC} + \lambda_{i\ell}^{AD}$$

$$+ \lambda_{jk}^{BC} + \lambda_{j\ell}^{BD} + \lambda_{k\ell}^{CD} + \lambda_{ijk}^{ABC} + \lambda_{ij\ell}^{ABD} + \lambda_{ik\ell}^{ACD} + \lambda_{jk\ell}^{BCD} + \lambda_{ijk\ell}^{ABCD}$$

where $F_{ijk\ell} = E(f_{ijk\ell})$ is the expected value of the observed cell frequency and the λ's satisfy the constraints

$$\sum_i \lambda_i^A = 0, \ \ldots, \qquad \sum_i \lambda_{ij}^{AB} = \sum_j \lambda_{ij}^{AB} = 0, \ \ldots,$$

$$\sum_i \lambda_{ijk}^{ABC} = \sum_j \lambda_{ijk}^{ABC} = \sum_k \lambda_{ijk}^{ABC} = 0, \ \ldots,$$

$$\sum_i \lambda_{ijk\ell}^{ABCD} = \sum_j \lambda_{ijk\ell}^{ABCD} = \sum_k \lambda_{ijk\ell}^{ABCD} = \sum_\ell \lambda_{ijk\ell}^{ABCD} = 0.$$

The λ's are called _effects_, with the superscripts indicating the variables to which the effect refers. For example, λ^A means that the effect is due to variable A alone. In identifying an effect, the subscript is omitted. The order of the effect is the number of indices in the superscript. Hence λ^A is a first order effect.

The log-linear model written above is referred to as the <u>saturated</u> model, since it contains all possible effects. By setting certain effects equal to zero, different models are formed. In a <u>hierarchical</u> model a higher order effect cannot be present unless all lower order effects whose indices are subsets of the higher order effect are also included in the model: e.g., if λ^{ABC} is stated (nonzero), it means that λ^{AB}, λ^{BC}, λ^{AC}, λ^A, λ^B, λ^C, θ are all present. Since only hierarchical models are considered, models are described by a minimal set of effects. For example, the full second-order model includes the terms with superscripts $(\theta,A,B,C,D,AB,AC,AD,BC,BD,CD)$ while all the three-way and four-way interactions are set to zero. This model can be described by the minimal set of effects (AB,AC,AD,BC,BD,CD). Including a higher order effect automatically implies including the lower order effects contained by it. That is, (AB) implies (AB,A,B,θ).

Let $F_{ijk\ell}$ be the fitted frequency (expected value) for cell (i,j,k,ℓ) for a particular model under consideration. The goodness-of-fit of the model can be tested using either the usual Pearson goodness-of-fit chi-square statistic

$$\chi^2 = \sum_{i,j,k,\ell} (f_{ijk\ell} - F_{ijk\ell})^2/F_{ijk\ell}$$

or the likelihood ratio statistic

$$G^2 = 2 \sum_{i,j,k,\ell} f_{ijk\ell} \, ln(f_{ijk\ell}/F_{ijk\ell}).$$

Both are asymptotically distributed as chi-square, with n−p degrees of freedom (df), where n is the number of cells, and p is the number of independent parameters estimated.

The likelihood ratio chi-square (G^2) is additive under partitioning for nested models. Two models, M_1 and M_2, are said to be nested if all of the λ effects in M_1 are a subset of the λ's contained in M_2. The difference in G^2 between the two models is a test of the additional effects in M_2 conditional on the effects in M_1. This difference also has an asymptotic chi-square distribution with degrees of freedom equal to the difference in the number of parameters fitted to the two models. This property does not hold for the Pearson chi-square. Therefore, for some of the tests described below, only the likelihood ratio test (G^2) is computed.

The primary purpose of using the log-linear model is to understand the relationships among the factors. We can consider the analysis as divided into three distinct stages:

a) screening for an appropriate model
b) testing, comparing and understanding the models under consideration
c) examining cells or strata with large disparities between observed and expected values under a chosen model.

In Examples 4F.14 to 4F.17 we describe methods of identifying models that should be further tested or compared. In Examples 4F.16 to 4F.19 we describe how to examine user-specified models. One or more log-linear models can be fitted to the observed cell frequencies. For each log-linear model the

test-of-fit of the model is computed. Optional output includes estimates of the log-linear parameters, expected values under the assumed model and several types of residuals based on the differences between the observed and expected values. P4F can add or delete terms from the specified model in a stepwise manner.

In Examples 4F.20 and 4F.21 we describe how to specify cells that contain structural zeros; cells in which observations cannot occur a priori or by design. In the two-way table Goodman (1968) discusses fitting the model of independence to a subset of the cells; he calls the test-of-fit of the model a test of quasi-independence. Such a test is of interest if some cells are known to be zero a priori (observations cannot occur in these cells) or in mobility studies when the diagonal cells (no change) are not part of the model of interest. Structural zeros can also occur in multiway tables, or you may want to fit a model to all but one (or several) cells in the table to see if the model generally fits well. Cells with frequencies to be excluded from being fitted by the model can be specified.

In Examples 4F.22 and 4F.23 we describe how to identify cells (or strata that contain cells) with large differences between the observed and expected values. The model of independence in a two-way table may be appropriate for most but not all of the cell frequencies. For example, the model may fit all cell frequencies except those on the diagonal; or the model may be appropriate for all but one of the cell frequencies when one cell frequency is incorrectly recorded. Similarly, in a multiway table a model may explain the frequencies in most cells of the table. P4F can identify, in a stepwise manner, cells or strata whose frequencies deviate from the expected frequencies under the proposed model. This type of screening can help identify patterns or unusual features in the data.

Example 4F.14 Using Tests of Marginal and Partial Association to Screen Effects

The following examples use data from the Morrison et al (1973) study on the Survival of Breast Cancer Patients (Table 11.4). The data are treated by Bishop et al. (1975, p.103) as a four-way frequency table where one variable (INFL.APP) has four categories:

Minimal Inflammation and Malignant Appearance
Minimal Inflammation and Benign Appearance
Greater Inflammation and Malignant Appearance
Greater Inflammation and Benign Appearance

The table is read as a multiway frequency table in a manner similar to Example 4F.10. In the INPUT paragraph

TABLE = 4, 2, 3, 3.

is specified to indicate that the fastest varying categorical variable (INFL.APP) has four levels, the next fastest (SURVIVED) has two levels, the next fastest (AGE) has three levels and the slowest changing (CENTER) also has three levels.

Table 11.4 Three Year Survival of Breast Cancer Patients According to Two Histologic Criteria, Age and Diagnostic Center. Inflammation is indicated as Minimal or Greater, Appearance is indicated as Malignant or Benign. (Morrison et al., 1973; Bishop et al., 1975, p. 103)

Diagnostic Center	Age	Survived	Minimal Mt	Minimal Bn	Greater Mt	Greater Bn
Tokyo	Under 50	No	9	7	4	3
		Yes	26	68	25	9
	50-69	No	9	9	11	2
		Yes	20	46	18	5
	70 or over	No	2	3	1	0
		Yes	1	6	5	1
Boston	Under 50	No	6	7	6	0
		Yes	11	24	4	0
	50-69	No	8	20	3	2
		Yes	18	58	10	3
	70 or over	No	9	18	3	0
		Yes	15	26	1	1
Glam.	Under 50	No	16	7	3	0
		Yes	16	20	8	1
	50-69	No	14	12	3	0
		Yes	27	39	10	4
	70 or over	No	3	7	3	0
		Yes	12	11	4	1

Key Mt = Malignant
     Bn = Benign

SIMULTANEOUS and ASSOCIATION are options that aid screening for an appropriate model. When the tests of ASSOCIATION are requested, the SIMULTANEOUS tests are automatically printed. We request tests of ASSOCIATION for all interactions, up to and including 4-way, in the FIT paragraph. The instructions are:

```
/ PROBLEM    TITLE IS 'MORRISON BREAST CANCER DATA'.

/ INPUT      VARIABLES ARE 4.
             FORMAT IS '(8F4.0)'.
             TABLE IS 4, 2, 3, 3.

/ VARIABLE   NAMES ARE 'INFL.APP', SURVIVED,
                  AGE, CENTER.
/ CATEGORY   NAMES(1) ARE 'MIN.MAL', 'MIN.BEN',
                  'GRT.MAL', 'GRT.BEN'.
             CODES(1) ARE 1 TO 4.
             NAMES(2) ARE NO, YES.
             CODES(2) ARE 1, 2.
             NAMES(3) ARE UNDER50, '50-69', OVER69.
             CODES(3) ARE 1 TO 3.
             NAMES(4) ARE TOKYO, BOSTON, GLAMORGN.
             CODES(4) ARE 1 TO 3.

/ TABLE      INDICES ARE 'INFL.APP', SURVIVED, AGE,
                  CENTER.
             DELTA IS 0.5.
/ FIT        ASSOCIATION IS 4.

/ END
```

(The cell frequencies from Table 11.4 immediately follow the END paragraph.)

(See end of this P4F section for organization of systems information, BMDP instructions, and data.)

The results are presented in Output 4F.14.

(36) The observed frequency table is printed.

Note: Below the table the message DELTA=0.5 indicates that 0.5 is added to each cell frequency (see p. 161).

(37) Tests of models of full order: A test that all effects greater than order 2 are zero is performed by fitting the model that includes all 0, 1st and 2nd order effects; i.e., (AB,AC,AD,BC,BD,CD) using the notation on p. 176. To test that all effects greater than order 1 are zero, the model fitted includes all 0 and 1st order marginals; i.e., (A,B,C,D).

In the output each line represents a different model. For example, the line beginning with 2 (K-FACTOR = 2) gives the results of fitting all main effects and two-factor interactions; i.e., the test of fit of the model with three-factor and higher interactions set to zero. Since this model is not significant, it may not be necessary to include any three-way interactions in the final model.

(38) The models of full order are nested one within the other. Therefore, we can compute differences between the models in order to test the hypothesis that all interactions of a given order are simultaneously zero. For example, the line beginning with 3 is the difference between the lines beginning with 2 and 3 in (37). Again we see that some (or all) two-factor interactions are necessary, but the three-factor interactions are most likely not necessary. It is possible that the test in (38) for a given order will be significant whereas the parallel test in (37) will not be, since the test in (37) also contains the test that all higher order interactions are also zero.

(39) Tests of partial and marginal association.

Partial association tests that the partial association between a set of factors in an effect λ is zero: this is the difference between fitting a model containing all marginals of the same order as λ and the model containing all marginals of that order except the one being tested. For example, to test that the partial association of A with B is zero, the difference is taken between the fit of the model (AB,AC,AD,BC,BD,CD) and the model (AC,AD,BC,BD,CD) (i.e., λ^{AB} is excluded). The degrees of freedom for this test are given below. Since this test is obtained as the difference between nested models, only the likelihood ratio test G^2 is appropriate.

Marginal association tests that the marginal association between a set of factors in an effect λ is zero. For example, let λ^{AB} be the effect of interest. From the marginal table for variables A and B (i.e., the table is summed over the levels of the remaining categorical variables), the test that $\lambda^{AB}=0$ is performed by fitting the model (A,B) to the resulting two-dimensional table; i.e., the model containing all effects except the effect of interest. If λ^{ABC} is to be tested, the table is

Output 4F.14   Models of full order and tests of association in the multiway table
----

```
*************************
* TABLE PARAGRAPH   1   *
*************************
```

***** OBSERVED FREQUENCY TABLE   1   ⑯36

CENTER	AGE	SURVIVED		INFL.APP			
			MIN.MAL	MIN.BEN	GRT.MAL	GRT.BEN	TOTAL
TOKYO	UNDER50	NO	9	7	4	3 I	23
		YES	26	68	25	9 I	128
		TOTAL	35	75	29	12 I	151
	50-69	NO	9	9	11	2 I	31
		YES	20	46	18	5 I	89
		TOTAL	29	55	29	7 I	120
	OVER69	NO	2	3	1	0 I	6
		YES	1	6	5	1 I	13
		TOTAL	3	9	6	1 I	19
BOSTON	UNDER50	NO	6	7	6	0 I	19
		YES	11	24	4	0 I	39
		TOTAL	17	31	10	0 I	58
	50-69	NO	8	20	3	2 I	33
		YES	18	58	10	3 I	89
		TOTAL	26	78	13	5 I	122
	OVER69	NO	9	18	3	0 I	30
		YES	15	26	1	1 I	43
		TOTAL	24	44	4	1 I	73
GLAMORGN	UNDER50	NO	16	7	3	0 I	26
		YES	16	20	8	1 I	45
		TOTAL	32	27	11	1 I	71
			14	12	3	0 I	29
			27	39	10	4 I	80
		TOTAL	41	51	13	4 I	109
	OVER69	NO	3	7	3	0 I	13
		YES	12	11	4	1 I	28
		TOTAL	15	18	7	1 I	41

TOTAL OF THE OBSERVED FREQUENCY TABLE IS   764

*****DELTA= 0.500   IS ADDED TO EACH CELL FOR ALL ANALYSES

(output continued)

179

Output 4F.14 (continued)

```
***** THE RESULTS OF FITTING ALL K-FACTOR MARGINALS.
      THIS IS A SIMULTANEOUS TEST THAT ALL K+1 AND HIGHER FACTOR INTERACTIONS ARE ZERO.
```

K-FACTOR	D.F.		LR CHISQ	PROB.	PEARSON CHISQ	PROB.	ITERATION
0-MEAN	71		806.49	0.0	1062.63	0.0	
1	63	(37)	174.34	0.00000	181.39	0.00000	2
2	40		39.92	0.47382	40.16	0.46315	4
3	12		9.01	0.70198	8.93	0.70905	5
4	0		0.	1.	0.	1.	

```
***** A SIMULTANEOUS TEST THAT ALL K-FACTOR  INTERACTIONS ARE SIMULTANOUSLY ZERO.
      THE CHI-SQUARES ARE DIFFERENCES IN THE ABOVE TABLE.
```

K-FACTOR	D.F.		LR CHISQ	PROB.	PEARSON CHISQ	PROB.
1	8		632.15	0.0	881.24	0.0
2	23	(38)	134.42	0.0	141.23	0.0
3	28		30.91	0.32115	31.23	0.30686
4	12		9.01	0.70198	8.93	0.70905

```
***** ASSOCIATION OPTION SELECTED FOR ALL TERMS OF ORDER LESS THAN OR EQUAL TO  3
```

EFFECT		D.F.	PARTIAL ASSOCIATION CHISQUARE	PROB	ITER	MARGINAL ASSOCIATION CHISQUARE	PROB	ITER
I.		3	370.15	0.0				
S.		1	152.85	0.0				
A.		2	100.22	0.0				
C.		2	8.94	0.0115				
IS.		3	10.18	0.0171	4	9.48	0.0235	2
IA.	(39)	6	1.47	0.9613	4	3.09	0.7975	2
IC.		6	34.23	0.0000	4	35.41	0.0000	2
SA.		2	4.17	0.1241	4	7.71	0.0211	2
SC.		2	7.79	0.0204	4	10.89	0.0043	2
AC.		4	66.81	0.0000	4	72.21	0.0000	2
ISA.		6	4.83	0.5657	4	7.71	0.2599	3
ISC.		6	4.13	0.6595	4	5.19	0.5200	4
IAC.		12	11.41	0.4944	4	12.35	0.4180	5
SAC.		4	7.48	0.1126	4	8.73	0.0683	4

---

summed over the levels of variable D, and the model (AB,AC,BC) is fitted to the three-dimensional table with elements f_{ijk+}. The tests of marginal association are equal to those of partial association for the main effects and for the highest-order interaction.

The degrees of freedom associated with the chi-square tests of both marginal association and partial association of an effect Z are

$$(I-1)^{\delta^{ZA}} (J-1)^{\delta^{ZB}} (K-1)^{\delta^{ZC}} (L-1)^{\delta^{ZD}}$$

where $\delta^{ZA}=1$ if A is part of Z, and zero otherwise; this is the same formula as for interactions in the analysis of variance. For example, the degrees of freedom for interaction AB are $(I-1)(J-1)$.

The tests of marginal and partial association can be simultaneously used to screen the various interactions to determine whether they are necessary in the model for the data being used (both tests are highly significant), whether they are not necessary (both tests are nonsignificant) or whether they are questionable (one test is significant and the other is not). In a second pass of P4F the models that contain all the necessary terms and relevant combinations of the questionable terms can be fitted, and an appropriate model (or models) for the data can be rapidly chosen. This is further explained in Brown (1976).

Note: The analysis of a log-linear model is similar to that of an unbalanced analysis of variance. The tests of partial and marginal association are equivalent to the increase in the chi-square test-of-fit when the interaction is removed from a model (the model of full order if partial association is tested and the saturated model for a subtable if marginal association is tested). As with unbalanced analysis of variance, the effect of removing two interactions from a model may not be equal to the sum of the two chi-squares printed in the analysis.

From the output we see that the third order interactions are not significant when tested for either partial or marginal association. Therefore they are not needed in the final model. The tests of marginal and partial association are both highly significant for AC and IC; therefore AC and IC belong in the model. Both tests are moderately significant for IS and SC; therefore IS and SC probably belong in the model. One test (marginal association) is significant and the other is not significant for SA; therefore it is doubtful whether SA is needed in the model. Both tests are nonsignificant for IA; therefore IA is not needed in the model. These results give guidelines on the relative importance of the two-factor interactions. We use these guidelines to choose the models to be tested. The models are tested in Example 4F.16.

```
FIT
  SIMULtaneous.                                      no
    Print the simultaneous tests of all effects of
    a given order. These tests are also printed if
    ASSOCIATION is specified.
  ASSOCiation = #.                                    0
    For each interaction that has less than or
    equal to # factors, print the tests that the
    partial and marginal association are each zero.
    Each test requires the fitting of a model by
    iteration, which can be time-consuming in
    high-dimensional tables (5-way or more).
```

Example 4F.15 Testing all Models in a Two or Three-way Table

When the table is two- or three-way, all hierarchical models can be computed by specifying ALL in the FIT paragraph. We illustrate the results using a three-way table from the Morrison Breast Cancer Table. By conditioning on CENTER we analyze a separate three-way table for each city. We replace the TABLE and FIT paragraphs in Example 4F.14 with the following:

Output 4F.15 Fitting all models to the data in a three-way table

```
************************
* TABLE PARAGRAPH   1  *
************************

*****  OBSERVED FREQUENCY TABLE   1

USING LEVEL   TOKYO       OF VARIABLE    4   CENTER
              ********                        ********

AGE      SURVIVED              INFL.APP
-----    -----                 -----
                       MIN.MAL MIN.BEN GRT.MAL GRT.BEN   TOTAL

UNDER50  NO                 9       7       4       3 I     23
         YES               26      68      25       9 I    128
         ---------------------------------------------I---------
         TOTAL             35      75      29      12 I    151

50-69    NO                 9       9      11       2 I     31
         YES               20      46      18       5 I     89
         ---------------------------------------------I---------
         TOTAL             29      55      29       7 I    120

OVER69   NO                 2       3       1       0 I      6
         YES                1       6       5       1 I     13
         ---------------------------------------------I---------
         TOTAL              3       9       6       1 I     19

        TOTAL OF THE OBSERVED FREQUENCY TABLE IS      290

*****DELTA= 0.500    IS ADDED TO EACH CELL FOR ALL ANALYSES
```

(output continued)

Output 4F.15 (continued)

```
***** ALL MODELS ARE REQUESTED—
```

MODEL	DF	LIKELIHOOD-RATIO CHISQ	PROB.	PEARSON CHISQ	PROB.	ITERATIONS
I.	20	241.65	0.0	250.89	0.0	1
S.	22	238.25	0.0	258.48	0.0	1
A.	21	222.19	0.0	269.20	0.0	1
I,S.	19	140.12	0.0	120.09	0.0000	1
S,A.	20	120.66	0.0000	124.65	0.0000	1
A,I.	18	124.06	0.0000	112.67	0.0000	1
I,S,A.	17	22.53	0.1651	22.50	0.1662	1
IS.	16	130.92	0.0000	106.64	0.0000	1
IA.	12	121.53	0.0000	109.63	0.0000	1
SA.	18	113.89	0.0000	115.00	0.0000	1
I,SA.	15	15.76	0.3982	16.12	0.3742	1
S,IA.	11	20.01	0.0452	20.40	0.0401	1
A,IS.	14	13.33	0.5006	13.45	0.4915	1
IS,IA.	8	10.81	0.2129	11.60	0.1698	1
IA,SA.	9	13.24	0.1522	13.40	0.1453	1
SA,IS.	12	6.56	0.8853	6.74	0.8741	1
IS,IA,SA.	6	4.24	0.6445	4.20	0.6495	4

```
        --- similar analysis for the other two levels of center ---
```

```
    -------------------------------------
/ TABLE     INDICES ARE 'INFL.APP', SURVIVED, AGE.
            CONDITION IS CENTER.
            DELTA IS 0.5.
/ FIT       ALL.
    -------------------------------------
```

The models fitted and tested for the first CENTER, TOKYO, are shown in Output 4F.15. Each model is described by its minimal hierarchical form. That is, (IS,IA) represents the log-linear model

$$\theta + \lambda^A + \lambda^I + \lambda^S + \lambda^{IS} + \lambda^{IA}$$

The model (I,S,A) is nonsignificant, therefore we conclude that the model of independence between factors provides an adequate fit to the data.

Note: The first letter of the variable name is used to represent the index. If variable names are not specified, the letters A,B,C are used. You can specify the symbols (see p. 183).

```
FIT ————————————————————————————————
  | ALL.                                            no
  |   Fit all hierarchical models in a two- or three-
  |   way table. If the table is more than three-way,
  \   ALL is not available.
```

Example 4F.16 Specifying Log-linear Models to Test

We now test the fit of five log-linear models to the observed frequencies of the Morrison Breast Cancer Data (Table 11.4). The five models tested are those indicated to be of interest by the tests of partial and marginal association in Example 4F.14. The models are specified in the FIT paragraph. For

this example, we replace the FIT paragraph of the Control Language in Example 4F.14 with the following:

```
    -------------------------------------
/ FIT       MODEL IS AC, IC, S.
            MODEL IS AC, IC, SC.
            MODEL IS AC, IC, SI.
            MODEL IS AC, IC, SC, SI.
            MODEL IS AC, IC, SC, SI, SA.
            MODEL IS AC, IC, SC, SI, SA, AI.
    -------------------------------------
```

Caution: The interaction SI must be used instead of IS since IS is a special word in the Control Language

The statement

```
        MODEL = AC, IC, S.
```

specifies the hierarchical model

$$\theta + \lambda^A + \lambda^I + \lambda^C + \lambda^S + \lambda^{AC} + \lambda^{IC}$$

That is, a model is described by a sequence of superscripts. You need not specify superscripts that are subsets of other superscripts. Therefore the main effects A, I and C are not specified in the above example.

The tests of the models are presented in Output 4F.16. For each model the G^2 and chi-square tests-of-fit are computed, as well as the probability of exceeding the computed test statistic. D.F. are the degrees of freedom for both tests.

The test-of-fit of the model (AC,IC,S) is nonsignificant; therefore this model may be adequate to explain the relationships between the factors.

The difference between the test-of-fit of this model with that of the model (AC,IC,SC) is a test of the two-factor interaction λ^{SC}; G^2 for this test is 66.71-55.83 = 10.88 with 53-51 = 2 degrees of freedom. This is a significant result and therefore we may decide to include λ^{SC} in the model although the test-of-fit of the first model is not significant. Similar comparisons can be made for the other effects.

Note: Each term in a model is described by a series of symbols, one for each index. If VARIABLE NAMES are specified, the symbols are the first letters of the variable names. Otherwise, SYMBOLS must be specified in the TABLE paragraph.

```
TABLE
   SYMBol =     one per INDEX      first character
      c list.   variable, one      of variable
                character each     name
   The SYMBOLS are used as labels for the INDEX
   variables to describe models. The first SYMBOL
   is used for the first INDEX variable, etc. If
   variable names are not specified, the letters
   A,B,C, ... are used. However, either variable
   names must be specified or SYMBOLS must be
   specified in order to state MODELS in the FIT
   paragraph.
   Note: SYMBOLS should be unique if you plan to
   specify MODELS. Otherwise, the faster moving
   index is used when the duplicated SYMBOL is
   specified in the MODEL.
```

```
FIT
   MODEL = c list.    may be repeated          none
      Each c represents the superscripts of the
      effects that define the hierarchical model to
      be fitted to the data. Each superscript must
      contain only SYMBOLS specified in the TABLE
      paragraph or, when SYMBOLS are not specified
      but variable names are, the first letters of
      the variable names. The superscripts are
      separated by commas and terminated by a period.
      For example, the model θ + λ^A + λ^B + λ^C + λ^D +
      λ^AC + λ^BD  can be specified as MODEL = AC, BD.
      More than one model can be specified in one FIT
      paragraph each model must be stated in a
      separate MODEL statement.
```

Example 4F.17 Model Building in a Stepwise Manner

Benedetti and Brown (1978) describe several methods of choosing an appropriate model. One of the methods is stepwise model building starting from a specified model. Stepping can proceed either by ADDING terms to the model or by DELETING terms. The results in Benedetti and Brown indicate that deleting terms from an overspecified model (one that has too many effects in it) is a "safer" procedure than adding terms. However, both ADDING or DELETING terms are possible in P4F.

Output 4F.16   Fitting specified log-linear models by P4F

```
*************************
* TABLE PARAGRAPH   1   *
*************************

*****  OBSERVED FREQUENCY TABLE   1


         --- the observed table is printed in Output 4F.14 ---


*****DELTA= 0.500    IS ADDED TO EACH CELL FOR ALL ANALYSES
```

MODEL	D.F.	LIKELIHOOD-RATIO CHI-SQUARE	PROB	PEARSON CHI-SQUARE	PROB	ITER.
AC,IC,S.	53	66.71	0.0976	67.85	0.0824	2
AC,IC,SC.	51	55.83	0.2982	57.53	0.2464	2
AC,IC,IS.	50	57.23	0.2245	57.52	0.2168	2
AC,IC,SC,IS.	48	45.61	0.5713	45.36	0.5818	4
AC,IC,SC,IS,SA.	46	41.39	0.6654	41.83	0.6476	4
AC,IC,SC,IS,SA,IA.	40	39.92	0.4738	40.16	0.4630	4

P4F can add to or delete from a specified model either simple effects or multiple effects (two or more). By a simple effect is meant a single effect in a log-linear model. For example, the models

$$(A,B,C) \text{ and } (A,BC)$$

differ only by the effect λ^{BC}; therefore they differ by a simple effect. However

$$(A,B,C) \text{ and } (ABC)$$

differ by $\lambda^{AB} + \lambda^{AC} + \lambda^{BC} + \lambda^{ABC}$; therefore they differ by more than a simple effect.

By multiple effects is meant the difference between two models whose expressions differ by a single index. For example, the models

$$(A,B) \text{ and } (AC,B)$$

differ by two effects $\lambda^{C} + \lambda^{AC}$; however, since the expression for the models differs only by the addition of one index (C) to a term already in the model, this change is called the addition of a multiple effect. But the models

$$(A,B,C) \text{ and } (ABC)$$

differ by more than a multiple effect since the terms AB,AC and BC are not in the first model; that is, two indices must be added to a term in the first model to produce the second model.

Adding effects. Starting from each MODEL specified in the FIT paragraph, P4F adds in turn each (simple or multiple) effect. For each "new" model formed by P4F, P4F prints the test-of-fit of the model and the test of significance of the difference between the "new" model and the original model. After fitting all possible "new" models, P4F identifies the "best" model as that for which the test of significance of the difference is most significant (has the smallest tail probability). Since the number of D.F. associated with the difference depends on the additional effect(s) being fitted, the criterion for "best" model is not equivalent to that having the largest chi-square test for the difference. If more than one STEP is specified in the FIT paragraph, P4F replaces the original model by the "best" model and again adds effects. This process is repeated until the maximum number of steps specified is performed, no more effects can be added, or both the test-of-fit of the "best" model and the test of the difference are nonsignificant (their tail probabilities are greater than the criterion PROBABILITY).

We recommend ADD = MULTIPLE rather than SIMPLE since higher order effects may not be reached by the latter option if not all the lower order effects included in the higher order one are significant.

Deleting effects. Starting from each MODEL specified in the FIT paragraph, P4F deletes in turn each (simple or multiple) effect. For each "new" model formed by the program, P4F prints the

test-of-fit of the model and the test of significance of the difference between the "new" model and the original model. After fitting all possible "new" models, P4F identifies the "best" model as that for which the test of significance of the difference is least significant (has the largest tail probability). Since the number of D.F. associated with the difference depends on the effect(s) being deleted, the criterion for "best" model is not equivalent to that having the smallest chi-square test for the difference. If more than one STEP is specified in the FIT paragraph, P4F replaces the original model by the "best" model and again deletes effects. This process is repeated until the maximum number of steps specified is performed, no more effects can be deleted, or both the test-of-fit of the "best" model and the test of the difference are significant (their tail probabilities are less than the criterion PROBABILITY).

We recommend DELETE = SIMPLE rather than MULTIPLE since the effect of MULTIPLE is to delete a second-order interaction and all its higher order relatives; this deletion is very often too extreme.

We illustrate the result of adding and deleting effects (both simple and multiple) by adding the following TABLE and FIT paragraphs after the CATEGORY paragraph of the Control Language of example 4F.14.

```
----------------------------------------
/ TABLE      INDICES ARE 'INFL.APP', SURVIVED, AGE,
                         CENTER.
            DELTA IS 0.5.
/ FIT        MODEL IS AC, IC, SC.
            MODEL IS AISC.
            MODEL IS A, I, S, C.
            ADD = SIMPLE.
            DELETE = SIMPLE.
            STEP IS 5.
/ FIT        MODEL IS AC, IC, SC.
            MODEL IS AISC.
            MODEL IS A, I, S, C.
            ADD = MULTIPLE.
            DELETE IS MULTIPLE.
            STEP IS 5.
----------------------------------------
```

The results are presented in Output 4F.17.

(40) In the first FIT paragraph the model AC, IC, SC is specified and the option ADD = SIMPLE. is designated. P4F adds in turn each of the three remaining two-factor interactions (λ^{IS}, λ^{IA} and λ^{SA} respectively). The smallest p-value for a difference is that due to adding λ^{IS} to the model (p=0.0168). Therefore, the "best" model at the end of STEP 1 is (AC,IS,IC,SC). This "best" model is now used as the base to which effects are added: the two remaining two-factor interactions λ^{IA} and λ^{SA} and the three-factor interaction λ^{ISC}. The smallest p-value for a difference is that of λ^{SA} (p=0.1214) which is not significant; it is greater than the default criterion PROBABILITY (0.05). Also the test-of-fit of the "best" model found (SA,AC,IS,IC,SC) (p=0.6654) is greater than 0.05. Therefore, stepping is terminated.

(41) In the same FIT paragraph DELETE = SIMPLE. is also selected. P4F forms the three models obtained by deleting in turn each of the three two-factor interactions (λ^{IC}, λ^{SC} and λ^{AC} respectively). The least significant difference is that due to deleting

Output 4F.17 Model building by adding and deleting effects (both simple and multiple). Models 1, 2, 4 and 5 are shown for illustration

----
--- the observed frequency table �36 in Output 4F.14 appears here ---

```
****************
*  MODEL  1   *
****************
```

MODEL		D.F.	LIKELIHOOD-RATIO CHI-SQUARE	PROB	PEARSON CHI-SQUARE	PROB	ITER.
AC,IC,SC.		51	55.83	0.2982	57.53	0.2464	2

MODELS FORMED BY ADDING TERMS TO MODEL — AC,IC,SC. ㊵

MODEL	SIMPLE EFFECT	D.F.	LIKELIHOOD-RATIO CHI-SQUARE	PROB	PEARSON CHI-SQUARE	PROB	ITER.
AC,IS,IC,SC.		48	45.61	0.5713	45.36	0.5818	4
DIFF. DUE TO ADDING	IS.	3	10.22	0.0168	12.17	0.0068	
IA,AC,IC,SC.		45	54.33	0.1607	55.77	0.1304	2
DIFF. DUE TO ADDING	IA.	6	1.50	0.9592	1.76	0.9404	
SA,AC,IC,SC.		49	51.61	0.3720	54.72	0.2664	4
DIFF. DUE TO ADDING	SA.	2	4.22	0.1214	2.80	0.2461	

STEP 1.   BEST MODEL FOUND IS — AC,IS,IC,SC.

MODEL	SIMPLE EFFECT	D.F.	LIKELIHOOD-RATIO CHI-SQUARE	PROB	PEARSON CHI-SQUARE	PROB	ITER.
IA,AC,IS,IC,SC.		42	44.09	0.3832	43.79	0.3954	5
DIFF. DUE TO ADDING	IA.	6	1.52	0.9583	1.57	0.9549	
SA,AC,IS,IC,SC.		46	41.39	0.6654	41.83	0.6476	5
DIFF. DUE TO ADDING	SA.	2	4.22	0.1214	3.53	0.1712	
AC,ISC.		42	40.42	0.5403	40.46	0.5386	2
DIFF. DUE TO ADDING	ISC.	6	5.19	0.5200	4.90	0.5572	

STEP 2.   BEST MODEL FOUND IS — SA,AC,IS,IC,SC.

STEPPING STOPS DUE TO CRITERION PROBABILITY (0.050).

MODELS FORMED BY DELETING TERMS FROM MODEL — AC,IC,SC. ㊶

MODEL	SIMPLE EFFECT	D.F.	LIKELIHOOD-RATIO CHI-SQUARE	PROB	PEARSON CHI-SQUARE	PROB	ITER.
AC,I,SC.		57	91.24	0.0027	93.66	0.0016	2
DIFF. DUE TO DELETING	IC.	6	35.41	0.0000	36.13	0.0000	
AC,IC,S.		53	66.71	0.0976	67.85	0.0824	2
DIFF. DUE TO DELETING	SC.	2	10.88	0.0043	10.32	0.0057	
A,IC,SC.		55	128.05	0.0000	127.21	0.0000	2
DIFF. DUE TO DELETING	AC.	4	72.22	0.0000	69.68	0.0000	

STEP 1.   BEST MODEL FOUND IS — AC,IC,S.

MODEL	SIMPLE EFFECT	D.F.	LIKELIHOOD-RATIO CHI-SQUARE	PROB	PEARSON CHI-SQUARE	PROB	ITER.
AC,IC.		54	219.57	0.0	203.87	0.0	2
DIFF. DUE TO DELETING	S.	1	152.86	0.0	136.02	0.0	
AC,I,S.		59	102.12	0.0004	103.15	0.0003	2
DIFF. DUE TO DELETING	IC.	6	35.41	0.0000	35.30	0.0000	
A,IC,S.		57	138.93	0.0000	143.12	0.0000	2
DIFF. DUE TO DELETING	AC.	4	72.22	0.0000	75.27	0.0000	

STEP 2.   BEST MODEL FOUND IS — AC,I,S.

STEPPING STOPS DUE TO CRITERION PROBABILITY (0.050).   (output continued)

Output 4F.17 (continued)

```
****************
*   MODEL  2   *
****************
```

A SATURATED MODEL IS SPECIFIED. THEREFORE EXPECTED FREQUENCIES ARE EQUAL TO OBSERVED FREQUENCIES. TRIVIAL ANALYSES ARE OMITTTED.

MODEL	D.F.	LIKELIHOOD-RATIO CHI-SQUARE	PROB	PEARSON CHI-SQUARE	PROB	ITER.
ISAC.	0	0.0	0.0	0.0	0.0	0

MODELS FORMED BY DELETING TERMS FROM MODEL — ISAC. ㊷

MODEL	SIMPLE EFFECT	D.F.	LIKELIHOOD-RATIO CHI-SQUARE	PROB	PEARSON CHI-SQUARE	PROB	ITER.
SAC,IAC,ISC,ISA.		12	9.01	0.7020	8.93	0.7091	4
DIFF. DUE TO DELETING	ISAC.	12	9.01	0.7020	8.93	0.7091	

STEP 1.   BEST MODEL FOUND IS — SAC,IAC,ISC,ISA.

MODEL	SIMPLE EFFECT	D.F.	LIKELIHOOD-RATIO CHI-SQUARE	PROB	PEARSON CHI-SQUARE	PROB	ITER.
SAC,IAC,ISC.		18	13.84	0.7394	13.53	0.7593	4
DIFF. DUE TO DELETING	ISA.	6	4.83	0.5658	4.60	0.5961	
SAC,IAC,ISA.		18	13.14	0.7833	12.99	0.7923	4
DIFF. DUE TO DELETING	ISC.	6	4.13	0.6595	4.06	0.6685	
SAC,ISC,ISA.		24	20.42	0.6728	20.34	0.6774	4
DIFF. DUE TO DELETING	IAC.	12	11.41	0.4944	11.41	0.4941	
IAC,ISC,ISA.		16	16.49	0.4193	16.51	0.4179	4
DIFF. DUE TO DELETING	SAC.	4	7.48	0.1126	7.58	0.1081	

STEP 2.   BEST MODEL FOUND IS — SAC,IAC,ISA.

MODEL	SIMPLE EFFECT	D.F.	LIKELIHOOD-RATIO CHI-SQUARE	PROB	PEARSON CHI-SQUARE	PROB	ITER.
SAC,IAC,IS.		24	19.81	0.7073	19.51	0.7241	4
DIFF. DUE TO DELETING	ISA.	6	6.67	0.3520	6.52	0.3671	
SAC,IC,ISA.		30	24.55	0.7465	24.31	0.7576	5
DIFF. DUE TO DELETING	IAC.	12	11.41	0.4939	11.33	0.5012	
SC,IAC,ISA.		22	20.10	0.5770	20.36	0.5606	4
DIFF. DUE TO DELETING	SAC.	4	6.96	0.1381	7.37	0.1176	

STEP 3.   BEST MODEL FOUND IS — SAC,IC,ISA.

MODEL	SIMPLE EFFECT	D.F.	LIKELIHOOD-RATIO CHI-SQUARE	PROB	PEARSON CHI-SQUARE	PROB	ITER.
SAC,ISA.		36	57.71	0.0123	58.46	0.0104	2
DIFF. DUE TO DELETING	IC.	6	33.16	0.0000	34.14	0.0000	
SAC,IC,IA,IS.		36	31.24	0.6943	31.72	0.6722	4
DIFF. DUE TO DELETING	ISA.	6	6.69	0.3506	7.41	0.2848	
AC,SC,IC,ISA.		34	32.46	0.5430	32.82	0.5252	4
DIFF. DUE TO DELETING	SAC.	4	7.91	0.0949	8.51	0.0747	

STEP 4.   BEST MODEL FOUND IS — SAC,IC,IA,IS.

--- models chosen in step 5 are printed ---

```
****************
*   MODEL  4   *
****************                                LIKELIHOOD-RATIO        PEARSON
         MODEL                          D.F.  CHI-SQUARE    PROB     CHI-SQUARE    PROB     ITER.
         -----                          ----  ----------    ----     ----------    ----     ----

         AC,IC,SC.                       51      55.83     0.2982      57.53      0.2464      2
```

MODELS FORMED BY ADDING TERMS TO MODEL —   AC,IC,SC.   ㊸

MODEL	MULTIPLE EFFECT	D.F.	LIKELIHOOD-RATIO CHI-SQUARE	PROB	PEARSON CHI-SQUARE	PROB	ITER.
AC,IS,IC,SC.		48	45.61	0.5713	45.36	0.5818	4
DIFF. DUE TO ADDING IS.		3	10.22	0.0168	12.17	0.0068	
IA,AC,IC,SC.		45	54.33	0.1607	55.77	0.1304	2
DIFF. DUE TO ADDING IA.		6	1.50	0.9592	1.76	0.9404	
SA,AC,IC,SC.		49	51.61	0.3720	54.72	0.2664	4
DIFF. DUE TO ADDING SA.		2	4.22	0.1214	2.80	0.2461	
AC,ISC.		42	40.42	0.5403	40.46	0.5386	2
DIFF. DUE TO ADDING ISC.		9	15.41	0.0803	17.07	0.0477	
IAC,SC.		33	41.96	0.1362	42.71	0.1199	2
DIFF. DUE TO ADDING IAC.		18	13.87	0.7377	14.81	0.6746	
SAC,IC.		45	42.89	0.5619	44.34	0.4996	2
DIFF. DUE TO ADDING SAC.		6	12.94	0.0439	13.18	0.0402	

STEP 1.   BEST MODEL FOUND IS — AC,IS,IC,SC.

MODEL	MULTIPLE EFFECT	D.F.	LIKELIHOOD-RATIO CHI-SQUARE	PROB	PEARSON CHI-SQUARE	PROB	ITER.
IA,AC,IS,IC,SC.		42	44.09	0.3832	43.79	0.3954	5
DIFF. DUE TO ADDING IA.		6	1.52	0.9583	1.57	0.9549	
SA,AC,IS,IC,SC.		46	41.39	0.6654	41.83	0.6476	5
DIFF. DUE TO ADDING SA.		2	4.22	0.1214	3.53	0.1712	
AC,ISA,IC,SC.		34	32.46	0.5430	32.82	0.5252	5
DIFF. DUE TO ADDING ISA.		14	13.15	0.5149	12.54	0.5634	
AC,ISC.		42	40.42	0.5403	40.46	0.5386	2
DIFF. DUE TO ADDING ISC.		6	5.19	0.5200	4.90	0.5572	
IAC,IS,SC.		30	31.74	0.3796	32.08	0.3640	4
DIFF. DUE TO ADDING IAC.		18	13.87	0.7377	13.28	0.7746	
SAC,IS,IC.		42	32.67	0.8488	33.25	0.8305	4
DIFF. DUE TO ADDING SAC.		6	12.94	0.0439	12.11	0.0596	

STEP 2.   BEST MODEL FOUND IS — SAC,IS,IC.

MODEL	MULTIPLE EFFECT	D.F.	LIKELIHOOD-RATIO CHI-SQUARE	PROB	PEARSON CHI-SQUARE	PROB	ITER.
IA,SAC,IS,IC.		36	31.24	0.6943	31.72	0.6722	4
DIFF. DUE TO ADDING IA.		6	1.43	0.9643	1.53	0.9576	
ISA,SAC,IC.		30	24.55	0.7465	24.32	0.7576	5
DIFF. DUE TO ADDING ISA.		12	8.11	0.7761	8.94	0.7084	
ISC,SAC.		36	27.48	0.8453	27.34	0.8500	2
DIFF. DUE TO ADDING ISC.		6	5.19	0.5200	5.91	0.4328	
IAC,SAC,IS.		24	19.81	0.7073	19.51	0.7241	4
DIFF. DUE TO ADDING IAC.		18	12.85	0.8003	13.74	0.7460	
ISAC.		0	0.0	1.0000	0.0	1.0000	2
DIFF. DUE TO ADDING ISAC.		42	32.67	0.8488	33.25	0.8305	

STEP 3.   BEST MODEL FOUND IS — ISC,SAC.

STEPPING STOPS DUE TO CRITERION PROBABILITY (0.050).   (output continued)

Output 4F.17 (continued)

MODELS FORMED BY DELETING TERMS FROM MODEL — AC,IC,SC.　㊹

MODEL		MULTIPLE EFFECT	D.F.	LIKELIHOOD-RATIO CHI-SQUARE	PROB	PEARSON CHI-SQUARE	PROB	ITER.
AC,I,SC.			57	91.24	0.0027	93.66	0.0016	2
	DIFF. DUE TO DELETING	IC.	6	35.41	0.0000	36.13	0.0000	
AC,IC,S.			53	66.71	0.0976	67.85	0.0824	2
	DIFF. DUE TO DELETING	SC.	2	10.88	0.0043	10.32	0.0057	
A,IC,SC.			55	128.05	0.0000	127.21	0.0000	2
	DIFF. DUE TO DELETING	AC.	4	72.22	0.0000	69.68	0.0000	

STEP 1.　　　　BEST MODEL FOUND IS — AC,IC,S.

MODEL		MULTIPLE EFFECT	D.F.	LIKELIHOOD-RATIO CHI-SQUARE	PROB	PEARSON CHI-SQUARE	PROB	ITER.
AC,IC.			54	219.57	0.0	203.87	0.0	2
	DIFF. DUE TO DELETING	S.	1	152.86	0.0	136.02	0.0	
AC,I,S.			59	102.12	0.0004	103.15	0.0003	2
	DIFF. DUE TO DELETING	IC.	6	35.41	0.0000	35.30	0.0000	
A,IC,S.			57	138.93	0.0000	143.12	0.0000	2
	DIFF. DUE TO DELETING	AC.	4	72.22	0.0000	75.27	0.0000	

STEP 2.　　　　BEST MODEL FOUND IS — AC,I,S.

STEPPING STOPS DUE TO CRITERION PROBABILITY (　　0.050).

****
*　MODEL 5　*
****

A SATURATED MODEL IS SPECIFIED. THEREFORE EXPECTED FREQUENCIES ARE EQUAL TO OBSERVED FREQUENCIES.
TRIVIAL ANALYSES ARE OMITTTED.

MODEL	D.F.	LIKELIHOOD-RATIO CHI-SQUARE	PROB	PEARSON CHI-SQUARE	PROB	ITER.
ISAC.	0	0.0	0.0	0.0	0.0	0

MODELS FORMED BY DELETING TERMS FROM MODEL — ISAC.　㊺

MODEL		MULTIPLE EFFECT	D.F.	LIKELIHOOD-RATIO CHI-SQUARE	PROB	PEARSON CHI-SQUARE	PROB	ITER.
SAC,I.			51	78.29	0.0083	79.33	0.0067	2
	DIFF. DUE TO DELETING	ISAC.	51	78.29	0.0083	79.33	0.0067	
IAC,S.			35	52.85	0.0270	51.77	0.0337	2
	DIFF. DUE TO DELETING	ISAC.	35	52.85	0.0270	51.77	0.0337	
ISC,A.			46	112.64	0.0000	110.49	0.0000	2
	DIFF. DUE TO DELETING	ISAC.	46	112.64	0.0000	110.49	0.0000	
ISA,C.			46	146.04	0.0000	142.40	0.0000	2
	DIFF. DUE TO DELETING	ISAC.	46	146.04	0.0000	142.40	0.0000	

STEP 1.　　　　BEST MODEL FOUND IS — IAC,S.

STEPPING STOPS DUE TO CRITERION PROBABILITY (　　0.050).

λ^{SC} (p=0.0043). Therefore, the "best" model selected is (AC,IC,S). Using this as the new base model, the least significant difference is obtained by deleting λ^{IC} (p=0.0000). The resulting "best" model is (AC,I,S) whose test of significance is highly significant (p=0.0004). Since both the test of the difference and the test of significance of the "best" model are significant (less than the criterion PROBABILITY), stepping stops.

㊷ The next model specified is saturated (includes all possible effects), therefore no terms can be added to it. On the other hand stepwise deletion is possible. In the first step only one model can be formed - that containing all three-factor interactions. In the second step each three-factor interaction is in turn deleted. The "best" model chosen is obtained by deleting λ^{ISC}. Stepping continues for 5 steps and is terminated when the maximum number of permitted STEPS is performed. Additional steps would be necessary to arrive at a parsimonious model.

㊸ In the second FIT paragraph ADD = MULTIPLE is designated. In addition to the three models obtained in ㊵ above, three additional models are formed that involve multiple effects. For example, (AC,ISC) differs from (AC, IC, SC) by $\lambda^{IS} + \lambda^{ISC}$. Stepping is performed in a manner similar to ㊵ above.

㊹ There is no difference between SIMPLE and MULTIPLE deletion for the first model. This is due to a deliberate modification of the DELETE = MULTIPLE option as described in the following note.

Note: Main effects in a log-linear model test the equality of the marginal cell frequencies. Since this test is usually not of interest we choose to include the main effects in all models. Therefore, when DELETE = MULTIPLE is specified and the elimination of a factor from a two-way or higher-way interaction would lead to a model that does not include the main effect for the factor, the main effect is retained in the model. For example, if I is eliminated from the term IC in the model (AC,IC,SC), then both λ^I and λ^{IC} would be removed from the model. P4F leaves λ^I in the "new" model.

㊺ DELETE = MULTIPLE deletes one index at a time from each term in the model. Therefore, four models are formed starting from the saturated model: (SAC,I), (IAC,S), (ISC,A) and (ISA,C). Note that each model differs from the saturated model by the deletion of one index and the retention of the deleted main effect. Multiple effects are tested each time; these tests correspond to the Wermuth test of zero partial association (Wermuth, 1976). Since the test of each of the "new" models is significant, stepping stops.

In this example the option eliminated too many effects from each model. For this reason we recommend DELETE = SIMPLE rather than DELETE = MULTIPLE.

```
FIT ────────────────────────────────────────
  ADD = (one only)                             no
       SIMPle, MULTiple.
    Builds a MODEL in a stepwise manner starting
    from a specified MODEL by adding single or
    multiple effects at each step (see p. 184).
  DELete = (one only)                          no
       SIMPle, MULTiple.
    Builds model in a stepwise manner starting from
    a specified MODEL by deleting single or
    multiple effects at each step (see p. 184).
    Note: When ADDING or DELETING terms from a
    model, the new model may differ from the
    previous model by a single effect (SIMPLE) or
    by a combination of effects (MULTIPLE) subject
    to the restriction that the more complex model
    differs from the simpler model by a term
    containing only one more index.
  STEP = #.                                     0
    Maximum number of steps for ADDING or DELETING
    effects from a user-specified model or the
    maximum number of cells to be identified as
    extreme in a stepwise manner (p. 201).
  PROBability = #.                        .05/prev.
    Criterion probability to determine a
    significant test-of-fit.
```

Taking interactions into account. The design of an experiment, the planned analysis of the data or results of a preliminary analysis can affect the choice of models to be fitted to the data.

If the number of observations in each of the cells of a subtable is fixed by design, then the interaction containing indices of the subtable should be included in all models; e.g., if in a clinical trial the number of patients to be examined is stratified by sex and age and a prespecified number is to be admitted at each age-sex combination, then the interaction age by sex should be included in all models fitted even if it is not significant.

When there is a dependent variable, such as survival, and several independent variables, such as treatment, age and sex, the models of interest are those that include the interactions between the independent variables; i.e., the interaction treatment by sex by age as well as all lower order relatives. When the dependent variable has only two levels, a model fit that includes all interactions between the independent variables is equivalent to a logistic model.

Note: PLR (p. 330) can be used to fit a logistic regression model.

Interactions can be INCLUDED in all models by specifying

$$INCLUDE = c_1, c_2, \ldots .$$

in the FIT paragraph, where $c_1, c_2, \ldots$ are

specified in the same manner as in the MODEL statement. For example,

INCLUDE = SA.

would include the interaction λ^{SA} and main effects λ^S and λ^A in all models.

INCLUDE = SA, CG.

would include the interactions λ^{SA} and λ^{CG} and main effects λ^S, λ^A, λ^C, λ^G in all models.

Note: INCLUDE affects all models by adding the interactions in the INCLUDE statement to those in all MODEL statements. In addition, INCLUDE also affects the models fitted by SIMULTANEOUS and ASSOCIATION options. Each model of full order (SIMULTANEOUS) is augmented by the terms in the INCLUDE statement as is each pair of models used to compute tests of marginal and partial association. The only models not affected by INCLUDE are when ALL models are printed (2- or 3-way tables).

FIT ─────────────────────────────

> INClude = c_1 , c_2, ...   none
> Terms to be included in all log-linear models fitted to the data. See note above for the effect on all options. c_1, c_2, ... are equivalent to those in a MODEL statement.
>
> The only option not affected is ALL.

The effect of STACKING on log-linear models. STACKING (p. 166) reduces the dimension of the multiway table by "recoding" two or more indices into a single index. All log-linear models are applied to the "recoded" table. If the symbol for any of the STACKED indices is included in a model, then the symbol is replaced by all the symbols representing the STACKED variables. Models generated by P4F (such as by the SIMUL, ASSOC and ALL options), either include all the STACKED variables or none of them.

MULTIWAY TABLES — RESULTS OF FITTING A LOG-LINEAR MODEL

Example 4F.18 Expected Values and Residuals

The chi-square test-of-fit provides an overall indication of how well the model fits the data, that is, how close the expected values under the model are to the observed frequencies. To try to understand the reasons for a significant lack-of-fit, it is often useful to compare the observed and expected values, either directly or in terms of deviates based on the differences between the two.

In this example we request expected values and two types of deviates in the PRINT paragraph. We compute these values for the model found most satisfactory in Example 4F.16; it contains all main effects and three two-way interactions. The following FIT and PRINT paragraphs are inserted in the Control Language of Example 4F.14 after the PROBLEM, INPUT, VARIABLE, CATEGORY and TABLE paragraphs and before the END paragraph.

```
------------------------------------
/ FIT        MODEL IS AC, IC, SC.
/ PRINT      EXPECTED. STANDARDIZED. FREEMAN.
------------------------------------
```

The results are presented in Output 4F.18.

(46) Expected values ($F_{ijk\ell}$) obtained by fitting the log-linear model to the observed frequencies ($f_{ijk\ell}$).

(47) Standardized deviates are the square roots of the components of Pearson's chi-square statistics i.e.,

$$(f_{ijk\ell} - F_{ijk\ell})/F_{ijk\ell}^{\frac{1}{2}} \ .$$

(48) Freeman-Tukey deviates are defined as

$$f_{ijk\ell}^{\frac{1}{2}} + (f_{ijk\ell} + 1)^{\frac{1}{2}} - (4F_{ijk\ell} + 1)^{\frac{1}{2}} \ .$$

They are used as a normalizing transformation when the data have a Poisson distribution.

Other deviates that are available include:

- differences = $f_{ijk\ell} - F_{ijk\ell}$

- components of Pearson's chi-square
  $= (f_{ijk\ell} - F_{ijk\ell})/F_{ijk\ell}^{\frac{1}{2}}$

- components of the likelihood ratio chi-square
  $= 2f_{ijk\ell} \ \ell n(f_{ijk\ell}/F_{ijk\ell}) \ .$

Output 4F.18   Expected (fitted) values and residuals printed by P4F

```
        ************************
        *  TABLE PARAGRAPH   1  *
        ************************

                    --- the observed frequency table is printed as in Output 4F.14 ---

        ****************
        *   MODEL   1   *
        ****************
```

			LIKELIHOOD-RATIO		PEARSON		
MODEL		D.F.	CHI-SQUARE	PROB	CHI-SQUARE	PROB	ITER.
AC,IC,SC.		51	55.83	0.2982	57.53	0.2464	2

***** EXPECTED VALUES USING ABOVE MODEL   ㊶

CENTER	AGE	SURVIVED	INFL.APP				
			MIN.MAL	MIN.BEN	GRT.MAL	GRT.BEN	TOTAL
TOKYO	UNDER50	NO	7.9	15.9	7.5	2.6 I	33.9
		YES	28.1	57.0	26.9	9.2 I	121.1
		TOTAL	35.9	72.9	34.4	11.8 I	155.0
	50-69	NO	6.3	12.7	6.0	2.1 I	27.1
		YES	22.5	45.6	21.5	7.4 I	96.9
		TOTAL	28.7	58.3	27.5	9.4 I	124.0
	OVER69	NO	1.2	2.4	1.1	0.4 I	5.0
		YES	4.2	8.5	4.0	1.4 I	18.0
		TOTAL	5.3	10.8	5.1	1.8 I	23.0
BOSTON	UNDER50	NO	5.4	12.1	2.3	0.7 I	20.6
		YES	10.9	24.4	4.7	1.4 I	41.4
		TOTAL	16.4	36.5	7.0	2.1 I	62.0
	50-69	NO	11.1	24.6	4.7	1.4 I	41.8
		YES	22.2	49.5	9.5	2.9 I	84.2
		TOTAL	33.3	74.2	14.3	4.3 I	126.0
	OVER69	NO	6.8	15.1	2.9	0.9 I	25.6
		YES	13.6	30.3	5.8	1.7 I	51.4
		TOTAL	20.3	45.3	8.7	2.6 I	77.0
GLAMORGN	UNDER50	NO	9.3	10.1	3.5	0.9 I	23.8
		YES	20.0	21.7	7.5	2.0 I	51.2
		TOTAL	29.3	31.9	10.9	2.9 I	75.0
	50-69	NO	14.0	15.2	5.2	1.4 I	35.9
		YES	30.1	32.8	11.3	3.0 I	77.1
		TOTAL	44.1	48.0	16.5	4.4 I	113.0
	OVER69	NO	5.6	6.1	2.1	0.6 I	14.3
		YES	12.0	13.0	4.5	1.2 I	30.7
		TOTAL	17.6	19.1	6.6	1.7 I	45.0

(output continued)

Output 4F.18 (continued)

***** STANDARDIZED DEVIATES =
(OBS - EXP)/SQRT(EXP) FOR ABOVE MODEL ㊼

CENTER	AGE	SURVIVED		MIN.MAL	INFL.APP MIN.BEN	GRT.MAL	GRT.BEN
TOKYO	UNDER50	NO		0.6	-2.1	-1.1	0.6
		YES		-0.3	1.5	-0.3	0.1
	50-69	NO		1.3	-0.9	2.2	0.3
		YES		-0.4	0.1	-0.6	-0.7
	OVER69	NO		1.2	0.7	0.4	0.2
		YES		-1.3	-0.7	0.8	0.1
BOSTON	UNDER50	NO		0.5	-1.3	2.7	-0.2
		YES		0.2	0.0	-0.1	-0.8
	50-69	NO		-0.8	-0.8	-0.6	0.9
		YES		-0.8	1.3	0.3	0.4
	OVER69	NO		1.1	0.9	0.4	-0.4
		YES		0.5	-0.7	-1.8	-0.2
GLAMORGN	UNDER50	NO		2.4	-0.8	0.0	-0.4
		YES		-0.8	-0.3	0.4	-0.3
	50-69	NO		0.1	-0.7	-0.8	-0.8
		YES		-0.5	1.2	-0.2	0.9
	OVER69	NO		-0.9	0.6	1.0	-0.1
		YES		0.1	-0.4	0.0	0.3

***** FREEMAN-TUKEY DEVIATES FROM THE ABOVE MODEL ㊽

CENTER	AGE	SURVIVED		MIN.MAL	INFL.APP MIN.BEN	GRT.MAL	GRT.BEN
TOKYO	UNDER50	NO		0.6	-2.4	-1.1	0.6
		YES		-0.3	1.5	-0.2	0.2
	50-69	NO		1.2	-0.9	1.9	0.4
		YES		-0.4	0.2	-0.6	-0.6
	OVER69	NO		1.1	0.8	0.5	0.3
		YES		-1.4	-0.6	0.8	0.3
BOSTON	UNDER50	NO		0.5	-1.4	2.1	-0.0
		YES		0.2	0.1	0.0	-0.6
	50-69	NO		-0.7	-0.8	-0.5	0.9
		YES		-0.8	1.2	0.4	0.5
	OVER69	NO		1.0	0.9	0.4	-0.2
		YES		0.6	-0.7	-2.1	-0.0
GLAMORGN	UNDER50	NO		2.1	-0.8	0.1	-0.2
		YES		-0.8	-0.2	0.4	-0.2
	50-69	NO		0.2	-0.7	-0.7	-0.6
		YES		-0.4	1.2	-0.2	0.9
	OVER69	NO		-0.8	0.6	0.9	0.1
		YES		0.2	-0.4	0.1	0.4

PRINT

EXPected.   no/prev.
Expected values ($F_{ijk\ell}$) are printed for each MODEL.
STANdardized.   no/prev.
Standardized deviates are printed for each MODEL.
FReeman.   no/prev.
Freeman-Tukey deviates are printed for each MODEL.
DIFFerence.   no/prev.
Differences between the observed and expected values are printed for each MODEL.
CHISQuare.   no/prev.
Components of the Pearson chi-square are printed for each MODEL.
LRCHI.   no/prev.
Components of the likelihood ratio chi-square (G^2) are printed for each MODEL.

Example 4F.19 Estimates of Log-linear Model Parameters and their Standard Errors

Examination of the estimates of the parameters can provide an insight into relationships between the factors. In this example we request the estimates of the log-linear parameters λ and of the multiplicative parameters $\beta = e^{\lambda}$ by specifying LAMBDA and BETA in the PRINT paragraph. These estimates are computed for the model containing all main effects and three two-way interactions. The following paragraphs are inserted after the PROBLEM, INPUT, VARIABLE and CATEGORY paragraphs of the Control Language of Example 4F.14.

```
/ TABLE      INDICES ARE 'INFL.APP.', SURVIVED, AGE,
                CENTER.
             DELTA IS 0.5.
/ FIT        MODEL IS AC, IC, SC.
/ PRINT      LAMBDA. BETA.
```

The results are presented in Output 4F.19.

(49) This message describes the method used to compute the parameter estimates (λ) and their asymptotic standard errors. When there are no structural zeros and the model is direct, i.e., the expected values can be expressed in closed form by a simple expression; the parameter estimates are obtained as described in the following paragraph and the standard errors are computed by the 'delta' method (Lee, 1977). Otherwise, both the parameter estimates and their asymptotic standard errors are obtained by solving a set of linear equations involving $ln(F_{ijk\ell})$ and then inverting the information matrix. More details are found in Appendix A.6.

(50) Estimates of the parameters (lambdas – λ's) in the model. The estimates are computed for all terms in the hierarchical model. Let

$$x_{ijk\ell} = ln\, F_{ijk\ell} .$$

The estimates of the effects are similar to the calculation of main effects and interactions in a factorial analysis of variance, for example,

$$\hat{\lambda}^A_i = \bar{x}_{i\ldots} - \bar{x}_{\ldots}$$

$$\hat{\lambda}^{AB}_{ij} = \bar{x}_{ij\ldots} - \bar{x}_{i\ldots} - \bar{x}_{\cdot j\cdot} - \bar{x}_{\ldots}$$

$$\hat{\lambda}^{ABC}_{ijk} = \bar{x}_{ijk\cdot} - \bar{x}_{ij\ldots} - \bar{x}_{i\cdot k\cdot} - \bar{x}_{\cdot jk} + \bar{x}_{i\ldots}$$

$$+ \bar{x}_{\cdot j\cdot} + \bar{x}_{\cdot\cdot k\cdot} - \bar{x}_{\ldots}$$

where a period (.) indicates the mean of the omitted subscript.

(51) The ratio of the parameter estimates to their asymptotic standard errors. When the model is direct and <u>no</u> expected value is zero, the standard errors are computed by the 'delta' method (Lee, 1977)

Output 4F.19 Parameter estimates in the log linear model

                    --- the observed table is printed as in Output 4F.13 ---

****
*   MODEL 1   *
****

MODEL	D.F.	LIKELIHOOD-RATIO CHI-SQUARE	PROB	PEARSON CHI-SQUARE	PROB	ITER.
AC,IC,SC.	51	55.83	0.2982	57.53	0.2464	2

THE ABOVE MODEL IS DIRECT. (49)

ESTIMATES OF THE LOG-LINEAR PARAMETERS (LAMBDA) IN THE MODEL ABOVE
THETA(MEAN) 1.8260

ESTIMATES OF THE MULTIPLICATIVE PARAMETERS (BETA = EXP(LAMBDA)
EXP(THETA) 6.2088

***** ESTIMATES OF THE LOG-LINEAR PARAMETERS (LAMBDA)
       IN THE MODEL ABOVE

                    INFL.APP
                    -----
                                            (50)
       MIN.MAL MIN.BEN GRT.MAL GRT.BEN

        0.480   1.011   -0.145   -1.346

***** RATIO OF THE LOG-LINEAR PARAMETER ESTIMATES (LAMBDA)
       TO ITS STANDARD ERROR

                    INFL.APP
                    ------
                                            (51)
       MIN.MAL MIN.BEN GRT.MAL GRT.BEN

        6.775   15.730   -1.718 -10.150

(output continued)

Output 4F.19 (continued)

***** ESTIMATES OF THE MULTIPLICATIVE PARAMETERS
(BETA = EXP(LAMBDA)

INFL.APP
------
⑤②

MIN.MAL	MIN.BEN	GRT.MAL	GRT.BEN
1.616	2.748	0.865	0.260

***** ESTIMATES OF THE LOG-LINEAR PARAMETERS
(LAMBDA) IN THE MODEL ABOVE

SURVIVED

NO	YES
-0.456	0.456

***** RATIO OF THE LOG-LINEAR PARAMETER ESTIMATES
(LAMBDA) TO ITS STANDARD ERROR

SURVIVED

NO	YES
-11.548	11.548

***** ESTIMATES OF THE MULTIPLICATIVE PARAMETERS
(BETA = EXP(LAMBDA)

SURVIVED

NO	YES
0.634	1.578

***** ESTIMATES OF THE LOG-LINEAR PARAMETERS
(LAMBDA) IN THE MODEL ABOVE

AGE

UNDER50	50-69	OVER69
0.145	0.444	-0.589

***** RATIO OF THE LOG-LINEAR PARAMETER ESTIMATES
(LAMBDA) TO ITS STANDARD ERROR

AGE

UNDER50	50-69	OVER69
2.627	8.633	-8.649

***** ESTIMATES OF THE MULTIPLICATIVE PARAMETERS
(BETA = EXP(LAMBDA)

AGE

UNDER50	50-69	OVER69
1.156	1.559	0.555

***** ESTIMATES OF THE LOG-LINEAR PARAMETERS
(LAMBDA) IN THE MODEL ABOVE

CENTER

TOKYO	BOSTON	GLAMORGN
0.049	0.001	-0.050

***** RATIO OF THE LOG-LINEAR PARAMETER ESTIMATES
(LAMBDA) TO ITS STANDARD ERROR

CENTER

TOKYO	BOSTON	GLAMORGN
0.596	0.014	-0.586

***** ESTIMATES OF THE MULTIPLICATIVE PARAMETERS
(BETA = EXP(LAMBDA)

CENTER

TOKYO	BOSTON	GLAMORGN
1.050	1.001	0.951

***** ESTIMATES OF THE LOG-LINEAR PARAMETERS
(LAMBDA) IN THE MODEL ABOVE

CENTER	INFL.APP			
	MIN.MAL	MIN.BEN	GRT.MAL	GRT.BEN
TOKYO	-0.368	-0.191	0.214	0.345
BOSTON	0.044	0.315	-0.178	-0.181
GLAMORGN	0.323	-0.123	-0.036	-0.164

***** RATIO OF THE LOG-LINEAR PARAMETER ESTIMATES
(LAMBDA) TO ITS STANDARD ERROR

CENTER	INFL.APP			
	MIN.MAL	MIN.BEN	GRT.MAL	GRT.BEN
TOKYO	-3.862	-2.292	2.012	2.121
BOSTON	0.425	3.385	-1.400	-0.910
GLAMORGN	3.199	-1.287	-0.289	-0.827

***** ESTIMATES OF THE MULTIPLICATIVE PARAMETERS
(BETA = EXP(LAMBDA)

CENTER	INFL.APP			
	MIN.MAL	MIN.BEN	GRT.MAL	GRT.BEN
TOKYO	0.692	0.826	1.238	1.412
BOSTON	1.045	1.370	0.837	0.834
GLAMORGN	1.382	0.884	0.965	0.849

--- similar results for SURVIVED by CENTER ---

***** ESTIMATES OF THE LOG-LINEAR PARAMETERS
(LAMBDA) IN THE MODEL ABOVE

CENTER	AGE		
	UNDER50	50-69	OVER69
TOKYO	0.565	0.043	-0.609
BOSTON	-0.454	-0.043	0.497
GLAMORGN	-0.111	-0.000	0.112

***** RATIO OF THE LOG-LINEAR PARAMETER ESTIMATES
(LAMBDA) TO ITS STANDARD ERROR

CENTER	AGE		
	UNDER50	50-69	OVER69
TOKYO	7.348	0.576	-5.648
BOSTON	-5.755	-0.618	5.757
GLAMORGN	-1.418	-0.003	1.194

***** ESTIMATES OF THE MULTIPLICATIVE PARAMETERS
(BETA = EXP(LAMBDA)

CENTER	AGE		
	UNDER50	50-69	OVER69
TOKYO	1.760	1.044	0.544
BOSTON	0.635	0.958	1.644
GLAMORGN	0.895	1.000	1.118

unless VARIANCE is stated in the PRINT paragraph. In all other cases, the standard error is computed by inverting the information matrix. The latter method gives the correct asymptotic standard errors in all cases; the results of both methods are identical when the log-linear model is direct and there are no zero expected values.

When there is not enough space to form the information matrix, the 'delta' method is used to estimate the standard errors. When the model is not direct and there are no zero expected values, the standard errors produced by the 'delta' method are conservative, i.e., overestimate the asymptotic standard errors. When there are zero expected values, the standard errors produced by the 'delta' method underestimate the asymptotic standard error; the difference may be large when the parameter estimate has the same levels of the indices as those for a cell with a zero expected value.

See Appendix A.7 for a more detailed explanation of the computation of the parameter estimates and their standard errors.

㊼ Estimates of the multiplicative parameters. The log-linear model is obtained by taking the logarithm of a product of factors. The terms in the product are of the form e^λ where λ is a log-linear parameter. P4F prints the values of $\beta = e^\lambda$.

PRINT

LAMBda. no/prev.
Print the estimates of the parameters of the log-linear model, and the estimates divided by their standard error. These estimates are printed only if the tail probability of the test-of-fit of the model exceeds PROBABILITY as specified in the FIT paragraph, i.e., the test-of-fit is nonsignificant.

BETA. no/prev.
Print the estimates of the multiplicative parameters ($\beta = e^\lambda$). These estimates are printed only if the tail probability of the test-of-fit of the model exceeds PROBABILITY as specified in the FIT paragraph.

VARiance. no/prev.
Print the correlation and covariance matrices between the estimates of the parameters. These matrices are printed only if the tail probability of the test-of-fit exceeds PROBABILITY as specified in the FIT paragraph.
Note: When VARIANCE is specified, the standard errors of the parameter estimates are obtained by inverting the information matrix.

Output 4F.20   Using EMPTY to specify structural zeros

```
***********************
* TABLE PARAGRAPH   1  *
***********************
```

***** <u>OBSERVED FREQUENCY TABLE   1</u>   (53)

ASTERISK INDICATES MISSING VALUE

CENTER	AGE	SURVIVED	INFL.APP				
			MIN.MAL	MIN.BEN	GRT.MAL	GRT.BEN	TOTAL
TOKYO	UNDER50	NO	9	7	4	3 I	23
		YES	26	68 *	25 *	9 I	128
		TOTAL	35	75	29	12 I	151
	50-69	NO	9	9	11	2 I	31
		YES	20	46	18	5 I	89
		TOTAL	29	55	29	7 I	120
	OVER69	NO	2	3	1	0 I	6
		YES	1	6	5	1 I	13
		TOTAL	3	9	6	1 I	19
BOSTON	UNDER50	NO	6	7	6	0 I	19
		YES	11	24	4	0 I	39
		TOTAL	17	31	10	0 I	58
	50-69	NO	8	20	3	2 I	33
		YES	18	58	10	3 I	89
		TOTAL	26	78	13	5 I	122
	OVER69	NO	9	18 *	3	0 I	30
		YES	15	26	1	1 I	43
		TOTAL	24	44	4	1 I	73
GLAMORGN	UNDER50	NO	16	7	3	0 I	26
		YES	16	20	8	1 I	45
		TOTAL	32	27	11	1 I	71
	50-69	NO	14	12	3	0 I	29
		YES	27	39	10	4 I	80
		TOTAL	41	51	13	4 I	109
	OVER69	NO	3	7	3	0 I	13
		YES	12	11	4	1 I	28
		TOTAL	15	18	7	1 I	41

TOTAL OF THE OBSERVED FREQUENCY TABLE IS   653
SUMMED OVER   69 CELLS WITHOUT STRUCTURAL ZEROS   (54)

(output continued)

STRUCTURAL ZEROS AND QUASI-INDEPENDENCE

Example 4F.20 Method 1: Defining Empty Cells

The term 'structural zero' is used to refer to a cell whose probability of containing an outcome is known to be zero. Therefore models fit to the data in the table are fitted to all cells except those with structural zeros. If a cell is specified as being a 'structural zero', P4F computes the expected value for each such cell using all cells but those declared as structural zeros. Deviates, such as standardized deviates or Freeman-Tukey deviates, are computed from the observed and expected frequencies.

Cells with positive frequency can also be specified as structural zeros. For cells specified to be structural zeros, P4F computes the equivalent of PRESS residuals for the cells; i.e., the difference between the observed frequency and the expected frequency where the expected frequency is computed from all cells but the cell designated as a structural zero.

The test of quasi-independence in a two-way table is a test of independence limited to a subset of the table. If the cells to be excluded from the subset are specified as structural zeros, the resulting test-of-fit of the model of independence is a test of quasi-independence on the subtable of interest.

There are two ways of describing structural zeros. In the following examples we illustrate the two methods and describe the effect of structural zeros on the analysis. In this example we state the indices of the cells with structural zeros in the TABLE paragraph. To obtain Output 4F.20 we replace the TABLE and FIT paragraphs in the Control Language of Example 4F.14 with the following paragraphs:

```
------------------------------------
/ TABLE      INDICES ARE 'INFL.APP', SURVIVED, AGE,
                CENTER.
             EMPTY ARE 2,2,1,1,  3,2,1,1,  2,1,3,2.
             DELTA IS 0.5.
/ FIT        MODEL IS AC, IC, SC.
             MODEL IS A, I, S, C.
             MODEL IS AI, SI, AC, AS, IC, SC.
/ PRINT      EXPECTED.  STANDARDIZED.  FREEMAN.
------------------------------------
```

Since the table is four-way, the specification

EMPTY ARE 2,2,1,1, 3,2,1,1, 2,1,3,2.

describes three cells with indices (2,2,1,1), (3,2,1,1) and (2,1,3,2) where the first number of the four is the level of the fastest moving index (the COLUMN variable or first INDEX variable—'INFL.APP' in our example), and the last number is the level of the slowest moving index (the last INDEX -- CENTER in our example). If the number of indices in the EMPTY list is not a multiple of the number of indices in the table, P4F prints an error message and stops.

The results are presented in Output 4F.20.

(53) In the observed frequency table, note the asterisks beside three frequencies corresponding to the three cells identified above. The observed frequencies in these cells are excluded from all computations including those involving log-linear models (except for the computation of deviates).

(54) The total frequency in the observed table is computed without the cells declared as structural zeros. Compare this output with that of Output 4F.14. The total is now 653 instead of 764 and the sum is over 69 cells where there are 72 cells in the observed table.

(55) P4F then prints the table of initial fitted values that is used in the iterations to find the expected values under each log-linear model. Note that there are zeros in the cells declared to be EMPTY and ones elsewhere.

(56) The test-of-fit of a model is based on three fewer cell frequencies than the same model in Output 4F.16. Therefore there are fewer degrees of freedom.

(57) Expected values are computed for all cells including those with structural zeros. The expected values are computed for the model fit to the cells without structural zeros and then extrapolated to the remaining cells by a method suggested by Don Oliver and Steve Fienberg (personal communication).

Output 4F.20 (continued)

```
*****  INITIAL FITTED VALUES —
       ZEROS INDICATE STRUCTURAL ZEROS  — TABLE  1
```

ASTERISK INDICATES MISSING VALUE

CENTER	AGE	SURVIVED	MIN.MAL	MIN.BEN	GRT.MAL	GRT.BEN
TOKYO	UNDER50	NO	1	1	1	1
		YES	1	0 *	0 *	1
	50-69	NO	1	1	1	1
		YES	1	1	1	1
	OVER69	NO	1	1	1	1
		YES	1	1	1	1
BOSTON	UNDER50	NO	1	1	1	1
		YES	1	1	1	1
	50-69	NO	1	1	1	1
		YES	1	1	1	1
	OVER69	NO	1	0 *	1	1
		YES	1	1	1	1
GLAMORGN	UNDER50	NO	1	1	1	1
		YES	1	1	1	1
	50-69	NO	1	1	1	1
		YES	1	1	1	1
	OVER69	NO	1	1	1	1
		YES	1	1	1	1

The header also shows INFL.APP spanning the MIN.MAL, MIN.BEN, GRT.MAL, GRT.BEN columns, with circled (55).

```
*****DELTA= 0.500   IS ADDED TO EACH CELL FOR ALL ANALYSES
```

(output continued)

Output 4F.20 (continued)

```
****************
*   MODEL  1   *
****************
```

MODEL		D.F.	LIKELIHOOD-RATIO CHI-SQUARE	PROB	PEARSON CHI-SQUARE	PROB	ITER.
────	⑤⑥	───	────────	────	──────────	───	────
AC,IC,SC.		48	47.95	0.4749	49.58	0.4102	6

***** <u>EXPECTED VALUES USING ABOVE MODEL</u>

ASTERISK INDICATES MISSING VALUE

CENTER	AGE	SURVIVED	INFL.APP ⑤⑦				
─────	─────	─────	─────				
			MIN.MAL	MIN.BEN	GRT.MAL	GRT.BEN	TOTAL
TOKYO	UNDER50	NO	7.8	12.3	7.0	2.6 I	29.6
		YES	23.6	37.4 *	21.1 *	7.8 I	90.0
		TOTAL	31.4	49.8	28.1	10.3 I	119.6
	50-69	NO	8.1	12.8	7.2	2.6 I	30.7
		YES	24.5	38.8	21.9	8.1 I	93.3
		TOTAL	32.6	51.6	29.1	10.7 I	124.0
	OVER69	NO	1.5	2.4	1.3	0.5 I	5.7
		YES	4.5	7.2	4.1	1.5 I	17.3
		TOTAL	6.0	9.6	5.4	2.0 I	23.0
BOSTON	UNDER50	NO	5.3	11.5	2.3	0.7 I	19.8
		YES	11.4	24.5	4.9	1.5 I	42.2
		TOTAL	16.7	36.0	7.2	2.1 I	62.0
	50-69	NO	10.8	23.3	4.6	1.4 I	40.1
		YES	23.1	49.8	9.9	3.0 I	85.9
		TOTAL	34.0	73.1	14.6	4.4 I	126.0
	OVER69	NO	6.2	13.3 *	2.6	0.8 I	22.9
		YES	13.2	28.4	5.6	1.7 I	48.9
		TOTAL	19.3	41.7	8.3	2.5 I	71.8
GLAMORGN	UNDER50	NO	9.3	10.1	3.5	0.9 I	23.8
		YES	20.0	21.7	7.5	2.0 I	51.2
		TOTAL	29.3	31.9	10.9	2.9 I	75.0
	50-69	NO	14.0	15.2	5.2	1.4 I	35.9
		YES	30.1	32.8	11.3	3.0 I	77.1
		TOTAL	44.1	48.0	16.5	4.4 I	113.0
	OVER69	NO	5.6	6.1	2.1	0.6 I	14.3
		YES	12.0	13.0	4.5	1.2 I	30.7
		TOTAL	17.6	19.1	6.6	1.7 I	45.0

Output 4F.20 (continued)

***** <u>STANDARDIZED DEVIATES</u> = (OBS − EXP)/SQRT(EXP) FOR ABOVE MODEL

ASTERISK INDICATES MISSING VALUE

CENTER	AGE	SURVIVED	INFL.APP ⑤⑧			
------	-----	--------	-----			
			MIN.MAL	MIN.BEN	GRT.MAL	GRT.BEN
TOKYO	UNDER50	NO	0.6	−1.4	−0.9	0.6
		YES	0.6	5.1 *	0.9 *	0.6
	50−69	NO	0.5	−0.9	1.6	−0.1
		YES	−0.8	1.2	−0.7	−0.9
	OVER69	NO	0.8	0.7	0.1	0.0
		YES	−1.4	−0.3	0.7	0.0
BOSTON	UNDER50	NO	0.5	−1.2	2.8	−0.2
		YES	0.0	−0.0	−0.2	−0.8
	50−69	NO	−0.7	−0.6	−0.5	0.9
		YES	−1.0	1.2	0.2	0.3
	OVER69	NO	1.3	1.4 *	0.5	−0.3
		YES	0.6	−0.4	−1.7	−0.1
GLAMORGN	UNDER50	NO	2.4	−0.8	0.0	−0.4
		YES	−0.8	−0.3	0.4	−0.3
	50−69	NO	0.1	−0.7	−0.8	−0.8
		YES	−0.5	1.2	−0.2	0.9
	OVER69	NO	−0.9	0.6	1.0	−0.1
		YES	0.1	−0.4	0.0	0.3

--- the analyses for the other models are similar ---

---

⑤⑧ Deviates, in this case standardized deviates, are computed between the original observed frequency and the expected values obtained as described above.

Note 1: If a CONDITION index is specified (i.e., if the tables are cross sections of a higher way table), the number of indices in the table includes the CONDITION variable. That is, you must specify as the last index in each cell (the slowest moving variable) the level of the CONDITION index.

Note 2: Integers must be used to describe the levels of the indices; that is, category names or codes cannot be used.

Note 3: If structural zeros are specified for a two-way table, the two-way table is treated as a multiway table and none of the statistics for two-way tables are printed. Therefore, to obtain the test-of-fit of the model of quasi-independence, you must either specify

```
    / FIT    SIMULTANEOUS.
```

or

```
    / FIT    MODEL = A, B.
```

where A and B are the symbols for the two indices.

TABLE ────────

EMPTY(#) = # list. may be repeated   none
    Indices of cells containing structural zeros in
    the #th table. If the table is n-way then each
    set of n successive numbers defines a cell that
    is a structural zero. If the empty cells are in
    the first table, # is not necessary. If a
    CONDITION variable is specified for the table,
    then the CONDITION index is the slowest moving
    index in the table. (See Note 1 above.)

Output 4F.21   Using the initial fit matrix to specify structural zeros

---

```
*************************
* TABLE PARAGRAPH   1  *
*************************
```

***** <u>OBSERVED FREQUENCY TABLE   1</u>

ASTERISK INDICATES MISSING VALUE

CENTER	AGE	SURVIVED	INFL.APP				
			MIN.MAL	MIN.BEN	GRT.MAL	GRT.BEN	TOTAL
TOKYO	UNDER50	NO	9	7	4	3 I	23
		YES	26	68 *	25 *	9 I	128
		TOTAL	35	75	29	12 I	151
	50-69	NO	9	9	11	2 I	31
		YES	20	46	18	5 I	89
		TOTAL	29	55	29	7 I	120
	OVER69	NO	2	3	1	0 I	6
		YES	1	6	5	1 I	13
		TOTAL	3	9	6	1 I	19
BOSTON	UNDER50	NO	6	7	6	0 I	19
		YES	11	24	4	0 I	39
		TOTAL	17	31	10	0 I	58
	50-69	NO	8	20	3	2 I	33
		YES	18	58	10	3 I	89
		TOTAL	26	78	13	5 I	122
	OVER69	NO	9	18 *	3	0 I	30
		YES	15	26	1	1 I	43
		TOTAL	24	44	4	1 I	73
GLAMORGN	UNDER50	NO	16	7	3	0 I	26
		YES	16	20	8	1 I	45
		TOTAL	32	27	11	1 I	71
	50-69	NO	14	12	3	0 I	29
		YES	27	39	10	4 I	80
		TOTAL	41	51	13	4 I	109
	OVER69	NO	3	7	3	0 I	13
		YES	12	11	4	1 I	28
		TOTAL	15	18	7	1 I	41

TOTAL OF THE OBSERVED FREQUENCY TABLE IS   653
SUMMED OVER   69 CELLS WITHOUT STRUCTURAL ZEROS

--- the remainder of the analysis is identical to that in Output 4F.20 ---

---

Example 4F.21 Method 2: Using the Initial FIT Matrix

In our second example we specify the initial fitted matrix by

        INITIAL ARE   72*1, (6)2*0., (42)0.

This specifies that the sixth and seventh cells are structural zeros followed by 34 cells with observed values followed by another structural zero; the remaining cells are assumed to contain observed values. To use this option we must know how the cells are ordered within the table; they are ordered so that the column index is fastest moving, etc. To obtain Output 4F.21 we replace the TABLE and FIT paragraphs in the Control Language of Example 4F.14 with the following paragraphs:

```
-------------------------------------
/ TABLE    INDICES ARE 'INFL.APP', SURVIVED, AGE,
                CENTER.
          INITIAL ARE 72*1, (6)2*0., (42)0.
          DELTA IS 0.5.

/ FIT      MODEL IS AC, IC, SC.
           MODEL IS A, I, S, C.
           MODEL IS AI, SI, AC, AS, IC, SC.
-------------------------------------
```

Note that only the INITIAL statement differs from Example 4F.20.

The results are presented in Output 4F.21. Note the asterisks beside the three cells assigned structural zeros. Since the same cells are described as structural zeros as Example 4F.20, the results of the two examples are identical.

Note 4: See Note 1 and 3 above in Example 4F.20.

Note 5: INITIAL must be zero or positive numbers. You can specify any initial fit matrix and not only a matrix of zeros and ones.

TABLE ─────────────────────────────────
```
  INITial(#) = # list.    may be repeated    1,1,...
    The table of initial fitted values for the #th
    table. Cells for which a value is not specified
    are assigned the value 1. If the table is for
    the first observed frequency table, # is not
    necessary. If a CONDITION variable is specified
    for the table, then the CONDITION index is the
    slowest moving index in the table.
    Note 6: The effects of EMPTY and INITIAL are
    described in Example 4F.20.
    Note 7: If EMPTY or INITIAL is specified for
    any table in a TABLE paragraph, then the usual
    analysis for two-way tables will not be
    performed for any two-way tables defined in the
    same paragraph whether or not that table
    contains structural zeros. See Note 3 above.
```

IDENTIFYING EXTREME CELLS AND STRATA

Example 4F.22 Extreme Cells

At times a significant chi-square test-of-fit is due to one or a few cells whose expected frequencies are inconsistent with the data in the remaining cells. For example, in mobility tables the test of independence is performed for all frequencies but those on the diagonal.

P4F can identify in a stepwise manner the cells whose frequencies deviate from the expected frequencies under the proposed model - i.e., the cells with the largest Freeman-Tukey deviate or with the largest standardized deviate. After a cell is identified as having the largest deviate, it is treated as a structural zero (Examples 4F.20 and 4F.21) and the model is fit to the remaining cells. P4F can also delete in turn each level of an index to see the effect of the level on the chi-square test-of-fit (Example 4F.23).

In the FIT paragraph we request that standardized deviates be used to identify a maximum of five most extreme cells (STEP = 5.) for two models. We replace the TABLE and FIT paragraphs of the Control Language of Example 4F.14 with these:

```
-------------------------------------
/ TABLE    INDICES ARE 'INFL.APP', SURVIVED, AGE,
                CENTER.

/ FIT      MODEL IS AC, IC, SC.
           MODEL IS A, I, S, C.
           CELL IS STANDARDIZED.
           STEP = 5.
-------------------------------------
```

The results are presented in Output 4F.22.

㊹ The first model has a nonsignificant test-of-fit when compared with the value of PROBABILITY (the α-level for determining an adequate fit - we use the assumed value of .05). Therefore stepping is not performed.

㊺ The second model has a highly significant test-of-fit. Therefore the cell with the maximum standardized deviate is identified. This cell is then considered to have a structural zero and the next cell with the maximum deviate is identified. This process is repeated five times (the maximum number of steps) or until a non-significant test-of-fit is obtained.

Note: The FIT paragraph applies only to multiway tables and to two-way tables with structural zeros (Examples 4F.20 and 4F.21). Therefore, to use this option when the table is two-way, and there are no structural zeros, you must specify

            INITIAL = 1.

in the TABLE paragraph and

            MODEL = A, B.

in the FIT paragraph where A and B are the symbols for the two indices.

Output 4F.22 Identifying extreme cells

```
--- the observed frequency table (36) in Output 4F.14 appears here ---

   *************************
   * TABLE PARAGRAPH   1  *
   *************************

*****  OBSERVED FREQUENCY TABLE  1

****************
*  MODEL  1   *
****************

                                                       LIKELIHOOD-RATIO            PEARSON
   MODEL                                        D.F.  CHI-SQUARE   PROB          CHI-SQUARE   PROB       ITER.
   -----          (59)                          ----  ----------   ----          ----------   ----       -----
   AC,IC,SC.                                     51      55.83    0.2982            57.53    0.2464         2

****** STEPWISE CELL DELETION IS NOT PERFORMED.   P-VALUE OF MODEL FIT ( 0.2982) IS GREATER THAN CRITERION PROB ( 0.0500 )

****************
*  MODEL  2   *
****************

                                                       LIKELIHOOD-RATIO            PEARSON
   MODEL                                        D.F.  CHI-SQUARE   PROB          CHI-SQUARE   PROB       ITER.
   -----          (60)                          ----  ----------   ----          ----------   ----       -----
   A,I,S,C.                                      63     174.34    0.0000           181.39    0.0000         2

***** CRITERION TO SELECT CELLS IS MAXIMUM STANDARDIZED DEVIATE = (OBS. - EXP.) /SQRT(EXP.).

                                 MAXIMUM        FOUND IN CELL
STEP  CHISQUARE  D.F.   PROB    DEVIATION  CENTER    AGE       SURVIVED  INFL.APP
  0      174.34   63  0.00000
                                  4.699    TOKYO     UNDER50   YES       MIN.BEN
  1      147.29   62  0.00000
                                  4.636    TOKYO     UNDER50   YES       GRT.MAL
  2      128.00   61  0.00000
                                  3.907    BOSTON    OVER69    NO        MIN.BEN
  3      115.21   60  0.00002
                                  3.688    TOKYO     UNDER50   YES       GRT.BEN
  4      104.96   59  0.00022
                                  3.607    GLAMORGN  UNDER50   NO        MIN.MAL
  5       94.22   58  0.00186

MAXIMUM NUMBER OF STEPS PERFORMED. STEPPING ENDS.
```

FIT

CELL = (one only) — no
NO, STAN, FR.
Identify extreme cells in a stepwise manner using either the maximum STANDARDIZED deviate or the maximum FREEMAN-TUKEY deviate at each step.

STEP = #. — 0
Maximum number of steps in which extreme cells are to be identified.

PROBability = #. — 0.05/prev.
α - level to determine if the test-of-fit of the model is significant. Stepping stops if the p-value (tail probability) of the test-of-fit is greater than this value.
Note: See note above in (60) if table is two-way.

Example 4F.23 Extreme Strata

In this example we identify strata (levels of an index) containing observed frequencies that differ greatly from the expected frequencies of the two models specified. To do this we use the STRATA instruction in the FIT paragraph. We replace the TABLE and FIT paragraphs of Example 4F.14 with the following:

```
/ TABLE      INDICES ARE 'INFL.APP', SURVIVED, AGE,
                  CENTER.

/ FIT        MODEL  IS AC, IC, SC.
             MODEL  IS A, I, S , C.
             STRATA IS ALL.
```

The results are presented in Output 4F.23.

(61) P4F eliminates each category of each index in turn. In this example P4F first eliminates each level of INFL.APP, then of AGE and lastly of CENTER. The first line in the table shows that if the category MIN.MAL were eliminated and the model (AC,IC,SC) fit to the remaining cells, the test-of-fit of the model (G^2) would be 37.77 (with 36 D.F.) instead of 55.83 (with 51 D.F.) obtained when fitting the same model to the frequencies in the original table. Since the test-of-fit using all cells is nonsignificant, the elimination of strata for this model does not lead to interesting results.

(62) The test-of-fit of the second model (A,I,S,C)

is highly significant. We can then ask if the significance is primarily due to the frequencies of a single category.

(63) If we examine the results of deleting strata for this model (A,I,S,C), we see that the elimination of TOKYO reduces the test-of-fit to 55.59 (with 40 D.F.) from 174.35 (with 63 D.F.). This indicates that the pattern of cell frequencies in TOKYO differs from those in the other two cities.

Note 1: If a variable has only two levels (such as SURVIVAL), its categories are not eliminated.

Note 2: If the observed table is a two-way table, see the note following (60) in the previous example.

Output 4F.23   Identifying extreme strata

--- the observed frequency table (36) in Output 4F.14 appears here ---

```
****************
*   MODEL  1   *
****************
```

MODEL	D.F.	LIKELIHOOD-RATIO CHI-SQUARE	PROB	PEARSON CHI-SQUARE	PROB	ITER.
AC,IC,SC.	51	55.83	0.2982	57.53	0.2464	2

*****DELETION OF STRATA (61)

VARIABLE	CATEGORY	CHISQUARE	D.F.	PROB.
INFL.APP	MIN.MAL	37.77	36	0.38850
INFL.APP	MIN.BEN	29.97	36	0.75001
INFL.APP	GRT.MAL	36.04	36	0.46688
INFL.APP	GRT.BEN	50.96	36	0.05036
AGE	UNDER50	25.23	30	0.71371
AGE	50-69	32.42	30	0.34819
AGE	OVER69	38.54	30	0.13641
CENTER	TOKYO	33.30	34	0.50175
CENTER	BOSTON	35.51	34	0.39699
CENTER	GLAMORGN	42.85	34	0.14190

```
****************
*   MODEL  2   *
****************
```

MODEL	D.F.	LIKELIHOOD-RATIO CHI-SQUARE	PROB	PEARSON CHI-SQUARE	PROB	ITER.
A,I,S,C. (62)	63	174.34	0.0000	181.39	0.0000	2

*****DELETION OF STRATA

VARIABLE	CATEGORY	CHISQUARE	D.F.	PROB.
INFL.APP	MIN.MAL	119.04	46	0.00000
INFL.APP	MIN.BEN	80.11	46	0.00136
INFL.APP	GRT.MAL	142.97	46	0.00000
INFL.APP	GRT.BEN	158.40	46	0.00000
AGE	UNDER50	74.86	40	0.00069
AGE	50-69	141.93	40	0.00000
AGE	OVER69	99.51	40	0.00000
CENTER	TOKYO	55.58	40	0.05164 (63)
CENTER	BOSTON	88.25	40	0.00002
CENTER	GLAMORGN	140.65	40	0.00000

```
┌ FIT ─────────────────────────────────────────────
│ STRATA = ALL.                                none
│   or   = v list.
│   Eliminate in turn each category (stratum) for
│   each index or for the specified indices (list
│   of variable names or numbers). Strata of
│   indices with only two categories are not
│   eliminated.
│   Note: See note above in ⑥⓪ of Example 4F.22
│   if table is two-way.
└────────────────────────────────────────────────
```

SIZE OF PROBLEM

First P4F forms all the frequency tables requested. The maximum number of cells in all tables should not exceed 10,000. Remember that if CODES or CUTPOINTS are not specified for an index, 10 levels are allocated for that index. P4F then copies all the tables but the first to a temporary unit and reallocates space according to the largest table to be analyzed. P4F can analyze two-way tables that are less than 5000 cells and higher-way tables that are less than 3000 cells each.

COMPUTATIONAL METHOD

Appendix A.5 describes the formulas used in the two-way table to compute the test statistics and measures of association, as well as their standard errors.

Appendices A.6 and A.7 give further details of how the log-linear parameters are estimated and their standard errors computed. Two parameters that may be reset in the algorithm to fit the log-linear model are described below.

Convergence of the model-fitting. Each log-linear model is fitted by an algorithm published by Haberman (1972) called iterative proportional fitting. To control the accuracy of the final fit and to limit the maximum number of iterations, the CONVERGENCE criterion and the maximum number of ITERATIONS can be stated. In general, preassigned values can be used.

Note: When there are few observations per cell (the table is sparse), the number of iterations required for convergence tends to increase. At the same time the validity of the chi-square approximation (i.e., the probability) becomes questionable.

```
┌ FIT ─────────────────────────────────────────────
│ CONVergence = #, #.              0.01,0.00001/prev.
│   Maximum permitted absolute difference (the
│   first number) and maximum permitted relative
│   difference (the second number) between every
│   observed and fitted marginal total in the
│   model.
│ ITERation = #.                           20/prev.
│   Maximum number of iterations used to fit any
│   model. An error message is printed if this
│   number is reached.
└────────────────────────────────────────────────
```

ACKNOWLEDGEMENT

The standard errors for the measures of association in the two-way table and the methods of stepwise model-building are the results of fruitful discussions and joint work with Dr. Jacqueline Benedetti. The treatment of marginal and structural zeros, the computation of standard errors for the parameter estimates in the log-linear model and of the degrees of freedom for the log-linear model have been greatly improved with the help of Dr. Camil Fuchs.

SUMMARY

Organization and repetitions of the TABLE, STATISTICS, FIT and PRINT paragraphs. The TABLE paragraph may be repeated as often as desired. The PRINT, STATISTICS and FIT paragraphs apply to the tables described in the preceding TABLE paragraph.

The PRINT and STATISTICS paragraphs can appear only once after any TABLE paragraph. The FIT paragraph can be repeated multiple times after each TABLE paragraph. All tables described in all the TABLE paragraphs in one problem (before the END paragraph) are formed and processed at one time. In these paragraphs, options that continue to apply across problems (/prev.) also apply across TABLE paragraphs until the value of the option is changed in a succeeding paragraph.

Order of Input Cards

```
  // (job card)
  // EXEC BIMED,PROG=BMDP4F        (see Appendix E)
  //SYSIN DD *
  / PROBLEM
  / INPUT
  / VARIABLE
  / TRANSFORM
  / SAVE
  / CATEGORY
* / TABLE
* / FIT
* / PRINT
* / STATISTICS
  / END
      (data)
  // (system card)
```

* These paragraphs may be repeated.

Full sets of BMDP paragraphs (and data, if on cards) can be repeated for additional problems, see Section 5.8.

Paragraph Statement	Preassigned	Comment and Manual Reference
/•TABLE		Tables to be formed; required, may be repeated.
o INDex = v list.	none	Variables defining indices for table ($\leq$ 15), fastest moving (column) index first. 165
or		
o COLumn = v list.	none	Variables defining column categories. 150
o ROW = v list.	none	Variables defining row categories. 150
CATvar = v list.	none	May be repeated. First CATVAR statement contains variable(s) defining third dimension for table(s); second CATVAR, those defining fourth dimension, etc. 151,165
PAIR. or CROSS.	PAIR	PAIR or CROSS row, column and CATVAR variables. 150,165
CONDition = v list.	none	Tables are formed in turn for each level of each condition variable. 165
COUNT = v list.	none	Variables containing frequencies when input is as cell indices and frequencies. Tables are formed for each COUNT variable in turn. 172
EMPTY(#) = # list.	none	Indices of cells that are to be treated as structural zeros in table #. Write sequentially as sets of indices for each cell to be so treated. May be repeated for additional tables. 199
or		
INIT(#) = # list.	all ones	Elements of fit matrix. Zeros indicate cells to be treated as structural zeros in table #. Ones indicate cells that are not structural zeros. May be repeated for additional tables. 201
SYMBols = c list.	first letter of variable names	Symbols to identify indices when specifying models. 183
STACK = v list.	none	Variables to be treated as a single index consisting of all possible combinations of the variables. May be repeated. 167
DELTA = #.	0	Value to be added to each cell before analysis. * 161
/ PRINT		Tables to be printed.
OBServed.	yes	Observed frequency table. * 151,166
EXCluded.	yes	Table of excluded values. * 151,166
LIST = #.	5	List first # cases that were not included in one or more tables. * 151
EXPected.	no	Table of expected (fitted) values. * 158, 192
LAMBda.	no	Table of estimated log-linear parameters and their standard errors. * 195
VARiance.	no	Asymptotic covariances and correlations between estimates of the log-linear parameters. * 195
BETA.	no	Table of estimated multiplicative parameters. * 195
STANdardized.	no	Table of standardized deviates (obs - exp)/exp$^{\frac{1}{2}}$. * 158, 192
FReeman.	no	Table of Freeman-Tukey deviates. * 158, 192
ADJust.	no	Table of adjusted standardized deviates, two-way tables only. * 158
DIFFerence.	no	Table of differences = obs - exp. * 158, 192
CHISQ.	no	Table of components of chi-square. * 158, 192
LRCHI.	no	Table of components of likelihood ratio chi-square. * 158, 192
MARGin = #.	none	Marginal subtables up to order #. * 167
PERCent = (one or more) NO, ROW, COL, TOT.	no	Tables of row, column and total percents. * 151,169
/ STATistics		Statistics to be computed for two-way frequency table. See p. 156 for NO ALL option.
CHISQuare.	yes	Chi-square and related statistics. * 153, 156
CONTingency	no	Contingency coefficient and related statistics. * 155, 156
LRCHI.	no	Likelihood ratio chi-square statistics G^2. * 153, 156
FISHer.	no	Fisher's exact probabilities (when maximum expected value is less than 20). * 155, 156
TETRachoric.	no	Tetrachoric correlation. * 155, 156
CORRelation.	no	Product-moment correlation. * 156
SPEARman.	no	Spearman correlation. * 156
GAMma.	no	Gamma and related measures of association. * 156
LAMBda.	no	Goodman-Kruskal measures of prediction λ and λ^*. * 156
TAUS.	no	Goodman-Kruskal measures of proportional prediction γ. * 156
UNCertainty.	no	Measures of uncertainty. * 156
MCNemar.	no	McNemar's test of symmetry, and kappa, a test of reliability computed for square two-way tables. * 156
MINimum = #.	0	If minimum expected value is less than #, table is collapsed for computation of chi-square and contingency coefficients. * 160
LINEAR.	no	Test of linear trend when table is 2xk or kx2. * 156

(continued)

(continued)

Paragraph Statement	Preassigned	Comment and Manual Reference
/ FIT		Models to be fitted, may be repeated, applies to last previous TABLE paragraph.
ALL.	no	Fit all possible models when table is 2-way or 3-way. 182
SIMULtaneous.	no	Fit models of full order. 181
ASSOCiation = #.	0	Estimate partial and marginal association for all effects of order $\leq$ #. 181
MODEL = c list.	none	Hierarchical models to be fitted, may be repeated. 183
INClude = c list.	none	Effects to be included in all models. 190
ITERation = #.	20	Maximum number of iterations permitted. * 204
CONVergence = #, #.	.01, .00001	Two convergence criterions for the algorithm. * 204
ADD = (one only) SIMPle, MULTiple	no	Add SIMPLE or MULTIPLE terms to the specified model. 189
DELete = (one only) SIMPle, MULTiple	no	Delete SIMPLE or MULTIPLE terms from the specified model. 189
STEP = #.	0	Number of steps to add or delete effects or to eliminate significant cells. 189,202
PROBability = #.	.05	Descriptive level of significance for adequate fit. * 189,202
CELL = (one only) NO, STAN, FR.	no	Identify the extreme cell(s) with the maximum standardized deviate or maximum Freeman-Tukey deviate. 202
STRATA = ALL. or STRATA = v list.	none	Eliminate each stratum in turn for each index, or for specified indices. 204
/ INPUT		
TABLE = # list.	none	When input is a multiway frequency table, number of levels for each index (fastest moving index first) 170
CONTent = (one only) DATA, TABLEn.	DATA	Input from BMDP File may be data or a frequency table previously created. When a table is input, n is the sequence number of the table when created. 175
/ SAVE		
CONTent = (one or both) DATA, TABLE.	DATA	Save data or frequency tables in BMDP File. 173

Key:

/	–indicates paragraph		*	–assigned value remains the same for additional problems
.	–period ends a sentence			
●	–required O –may be required		VT	–number of variables after transformations
v	–variable (name or subscript)		list	–more than one item, often one per var.
g	–group (name or subscript)			
#	–number			Capitalized letters–paragraph or sentence names recognized by BMDP
'c'	–characters (name or parameter) may omit apostrophes if contiguous letters only			Page numbers following refer to this Manual

12
MISSING VALUES
Patterns, Estimation and Correlations

In even the best designed and monitored experiments, observations can be recorded incorrectly or not recorded at all. For example, an animal may die from a cause unrelated to the experiment, a patient may not return for a follow-up visit, a blood sample may be ruined, or the recording equipment may malfunction. When an entire case is missing, the analysis must accommodate the resulting imbalance.

When values for one or more variables are not recorded in some cases, the problem is far more complex. Two possible choices are

- to eliminate all the data for cases that contain any missing values
- to use acceptable values from all cases, including the incomplete cases

The second choice requires a more difficult analysis, but may be necessary when more than a few cases are incomplete.

Cases with known errors (or univariate outliers) can be treated in a similar manner to those with missing values. Univariate outliers may be identified in a preliminary data screening, or they may violate specified limits. Ordinarily they are eliminated from statistical analysis by specifying MINIMUM and MAXIMUM limits for the variables.

In this chapter missing values usually refer to observations that are not recorded, or are improperly recorded. Cases with missing values are those that have one or more observations equal to the missing value code or out of range (as specified in the VARIABLE paragraph or set during data editing, Chapter 6).

Many classical statistical analyses require complete cases (i.e., no missing values). When doing exploratory data analysis, this restriction can be circumvented. For example, regression or factor analysis can start from a correlation matrix rather than from the original data; methods are available to estimate the correlations from all acceptable values. A second approach is to estimate missing observations and then use the "completed" data in an analysis.

In this chapter we describe two programs:

P8D -- Missing Value Correlation   p. 208
PAM -- Description and Estimation of
        Missing Data   p. 217

Either can be used to estimate a correlation matrix when there are missing values in some cases; the resulting matrix can then be input to a subsequent analysis, such as regression or factor analysis. In addition, PAM can replace missing values with estimates based on data present for the case.

P8D computes correlations from data containing missing values in any of four different ways. Computations can be performed using

- only complete cases (COMPLETE); cases with any missing values or values out of range are not used
- all pairs of acceptable values for correlations (CORPAIR); the correlation for each pair of variables is computed using only cases that have acceptable values for both variables
- all pairs of acceptable values for covariances (COVPAIR); the covariance for each pair of variables is computed as in CORPAIR, but variances are computed separately from all acceptable values for each variable (this differs from CORPAIR in the variances used)
- all acceptable values (ALLVALUE); the means and variances are computed from all acceptable values for each variable and the covariances are computed using deviations from these means (this differs from COVPAIR in the means used for the covariances)

The method COMPLETE is the only method of the four that guarantees a correlation matrix that can be inverted (one that is positive semidefinite), and that can be used in factor analysis and for multiple regression. In addition, P8D tabulates the frequencies of existing pairs of variables. The mean and variance of each variable are printed. Case weights can be used in the computations. P8D also provides t tests to help the user determine if the values of a variable depend on the presense or absence of another variable.

PAM can estimate covariances or correlations by one of three methods. It can also replace missing values by estimates based on the acceptable values. To better understand the implication of estimating either the missing values or correlations and using them in an analysis, the extent and the pattern of the missing values can also be examined with PAM. If the pattern of missing data is not random, an analysis of the data can be severely affected.

PAM estimates covariances or correlations using only complete cases (COMPLETE), using all acceptable values (similar to the ALLVALUE option in P8D), or by maximum likelihood. When the ALLVALUE method is used, the eigenvalues are found and, if any eigenvalues are negative, the correlation matrix is reestimated using only positive eigenvalues and their eigenvectors. This guarantees that the correlation matrix is positive semidefinite and can be used in multiple regression and factor analysis. Maximum likelihood is preferred for many analyses but it can be expensive for large problems.

ALLVALUE in PAM will likely be cheaper to run than the pre-1981 P8D unless I/O is much cheaper than CPU in your facility. Costs for the new P8D are comparable to the costs for ALLVALUE in PAM.

PAM can replace missing values by means or by predicted values using regression equations that are computed by any of several methods. In one method (REGR) the squared multiple correlations of each variable with all the other variables are computed; they are a measure of multicollinearity and indicate how well each variable can be estimated from the other variables.

The pattern of missing values is described in a number of ways including a cases-by-variables plot of the location of the missing data. PAM also computes the Mahalanobis distance of each case (including those having missing values) to the mean of all cases (or the group mean when the cases are grouped). PAM prints the frequency and percentage of missing data for each pair of variables. Specified pairs of variables can be plotted against each other. Cases can be grouped and case weights assigned. For each variable in each group PAM computes the sample size, percentage missing, and univariate statistics.

Both P8D and PAM can be used for data description to enhance your understanding of the effect of missing data. Also, they can be used to prepare the data for further analysis

- by computing and saving a covariance or correlation matrix, which is then used as input for further analyses (such as regression or factor analysis)
- by estimating the missing values; the "completed" data are saved and used as input to additional analyses

Subsequent analyses are affected by either of these procedures, as are the usual tests of significance reported. However, the results can be useful in exploratory data analysis.

Control Language

The BMDP instructions to describe the data and variables are common to all BMDP programs and are explained in Chapter 5; the PROBLEM, INPUT and VARIABLE paragraphs are used in the programs discussed in this chapter; the GROUP paragraph can be used in PAM.

If data editing or transformations are necessary, the methods described in Chapter 6 can be used. Data can be read using a FORMAT statement or from a BMDP File (Chapter 7).

A summary of the Control Language instructions common to all BMDP programs is on p. 48; summaries of the Control Language instructions specific to each program described in this chapter follow the general summary. These summaries can be used as indexes to the program descriptions.

P8D

12.1 Correlations with Options for Incomplete Data

Laszlo Engelman

ABSTRACT

P8D computes a matrix of correlations. Several options control which formulas may be used when data are incomplete. A case is incomplete if there are values that are missing or out of range. Throughout this writeup, we consider values out of range as missing values.

There are four formulas that can be used to compute correlations. The COMPLETE method excludes all cases that have any values missing on any of the variables used in the analysis. The other three methods do not delete incomplete cases, but differ in the way they use the values from the incomplete cases.

The CORPAIR method computes the correlation of each pair of variables from the cases for which both variables are present using the formula for correlation given in Chapter 2.

The COVPAIR method computes the covariance (rather than correlation) of each pair of variables from the cases for which both variables are present, using the usual formula for covariance. The correlation matrix for COVPAIR is computed from the COVPAIR covariance matrix in the usual manner of converting covariance matrices to correlation matrices. The COVPAIR and CORPAIR correlations differ in the standard deviations used to convert covariances to correlations. Standard deviations in COVPAIR are computed once for each variable while for CORPAIR a different standard deviation for each variable is required for each correlation of that variable with all other variables.

The ALLVALUE method differs from COVPAIR insofar as the means used in computing the covariance of a pair of variables in the ALLVALUE method are computed using all values of each variable rather than the values on cases for which both variables have been observed.

The choices between the options are not always clear-cut. Some discussion is contained in Frane (BMDP Technical Report No. 45). Briefly, COMPLETE is recommended when the number of complete cases is large; the other methods are needed when the number of complete cases is small. Only COMPLETE guarantees that a correlation matrix is positive semidefinite. For COMPLETE and CORPAIR correlations are within −1 to +1 range. In a sense, ALLVALUE uses more of the information in the data than COVPAIR, which in turn uses more information than CORPAIR. However,

ALLVALUE and COVPAIR tend in practice not to be positive semidefinite more frequently than CORPAIR.

Correlation and covariance matrices can be saved on a BMDP File and used as input to other BMDP programs such as P1M, P4M, P1R, P2R, P6R, P6M and P9R to perform regression, cluster, factor, partial correlation and canonical correlation analysis. These programs (except P1M, Variable Clustering) will terminate with an error message if the input correlation or covariance matrix is not positive semidefinite. An alternative program, PAM, provides correlation and covariance matrices from incomplete data that are smoothed to be sure that they are positive semidefinite.

The user is advised to view results from P8D and any other program with caution unless there is evidence that missing values occur at random.

WHERE TO FIND IT

Example 8D.1 Basic Setup for a Missing Value Correlation Matrix

In our first example P8D computes a correlation matrix for the variables in the Werner blood chemistry data (Table 5.1) using CORPAIR, the preassigned method for estimating the correlations. For this example, no instructions specific to P8D are used: we use instructions that are common to all BMDP programs for describing the data and variables. The explanation of the PROBLEM, INPUT and VARIABLE paragraphs is given in Chapter 5. Our BMDP instructions are:

```
/ PROBLEM   TITLE IS 'WERNER BLOOD CHEMISTRY DATA'.
/ INPUT     VARIABLES ARE 9.
           FORMAT IS '(A4, 5F4.0, 3F4.1)'.
/ VARIABLE  NAMES ARE ID, AGE, HEIGHT, WEIGHT,
                      BRTHPILL, CHOLSTRL, ALBUMIN,
                      CALCIUM, URICACID.
           MAXIMUM IS (6)400.
           MINIMUM IS (6)150.
           LABEL IS ID.
/ END
```

Output 8D.1 The CORPAIR method is used to compute estimates of the correlations for incomplete data. Circled numbers correspond to those in the text

----

--- the BMDP instructions read by P8D are read and interpreted ---

MAXIMUM NUMBER OF MISSING VALUES PER CASE . . .   5

CORRELATION TYPE(S) TO BE COMPUTED
       CORPAIR
                                                                    ①
THE FOLLOWING MATRICES WILL BE PRINTED
       PAIRWISE FREQUENCIES WITH BOTH VARIABLES PRESENT
       CORRELATION MATRIX

NUMBER OF CASES TO PRINT.   10

NUMBER OF CASES READ.   188   ②

VARIABLE				STANDARD	SMALLEST		LARGEST	
NO.	NAME	COUNT	MEAN	DEVIATION	CASE	VALUE	CASE	VALUE
2	AGE	188	33.8191	10.1127	5	19.0000	155	55.0000
3	HEIGHT	186	64.5107	2.4850	25	57.0000	46	71.0000
4	WEIGHT	186	131.6720	20.6604	28	94.0000	142	215.0000
5	BRTHPILL	188	1.5000	0.5013	1	1.0000	2	2.0000
6	CHOLSTRL	186	236.1505	42.5553	33	155.0000	182	390.0000
7	ALBUMIN	186	4.1112	0.3580	37	3.2000	43	5.0000
8	CALCIUM	185	9.9621	0.4795	51	8.6000	89	11.1000
9	URICACID	187	4.7705	1.1572	124	2.2000	138	9.9000

③

PAIRWISE FREQUENCIES WITH BOTH VARIABLES PRESENT

		AGE	HEIGHT	WEIGHT	BRTHPILL	CHOLSTRL	ALBUMIN	CALCIUM	URICACID
		2	3	4	5	6	7	8	9
AGE	2	188							
HEIGHT	3	186	186						
WEIGHT	4	186	184	186					
BRTHPILL	5	188	186	186	188				
CHOLSTRL	6	186	184	184	186	186			
ALBUMIN	7	186	185	184	186	184	186		
CALCIUM	8	185	184	183	185	184	183	185	
URICACID	9	187	185	185	187	185	185	185	187

④

CORPAIR CORRELATION MATRIX

		AGE	HEIGHT	WEIGHT	BRTHPILL	CHOLSTRL	ALBUMIN	CALCIUM	URICACID
		2	3	4	5	6	7	8	9
AGE	2	1.0000							
HEIGHT	3	0.0807	1.0000						
WEIGHT	4	0.2521	0.4759	1.0000					
BRTHPILL	5	0.0	0.1692	0.0738	1.0000				
CHOLSTRL	6	0.3678	0.0199	0.1474	0.0758	1.0000			
ALBUMIN	7	-0.0720	-0.0208	-0.2534	-0.2398	0.0533	1.0000		
CALCIUM	8	-0.0326	0.1485	0.0703	-0.0561	0.2515	0.4535	1.0000	
URICACID	9	0.1776	0.1335	0.3043	0.0247	0.2660	0.0072	0.1949	1.0000

⑤

(See end of this P8D section for organization of systems information, BMDP instructions and data.)

The instructions above specify that values for cholesterol (the sixth variable) below 150 and above 400 should not be used (they are considered missing when the correlations are computed). Blanks in the data file are assumed to be missing values.

The results are presented in Output 8D.1. Circled numbers below correspond to those in the output.

① Interpretation of Control Language instructions specific to P8D. No such instructions are specified in Example 8D.1; therefore, preassigned options are shown.

② Number of cases read. P8D allows you to specify the maximum number of missing values allowed in a case by using the MMV instruction in the VARIABLE paragraph. Cases with more missing values or values out of range are excluded from computations.

③ For each variable the number of acceptable values, mean, standard deviation, and smallest and largest values are computed using all acceptable values for the variable.

④ The frequency n_{ik} of cases for which both variables have acceptable values is reported for each pair of variables.

⑤ Estimates of the correlations by the CORPAIR method (the preassigned method of computing the correlations); any of the methods can be specified.

Specifying the method (TYPE) of computation. The method of computation is specified in the CORRELATION paragraph by a TYPE statement: COMPLETE, CORPAIR, COVPAIR and ALLVALUE can be used. If more than one method is specified, each is used in turn to compute covariances and correlations; if a matrix is to be saved in a BMDP File, only the matrix computed by the first method specified is saved.

```
VARiable ─────────────────────────────
  MMV = #.              [(# of variables +1)/2]
  Maximum number of missing values per case.
  Cases with more missing values are excluded
  from the computations.
```

```
CORRelation ─────────────────────────
  TYPE = (one or more)              CORPAIR/prev.
      COMPLETE, CORPAIR,
      COVPAIR, ALLVALUE.
  The method used to estimate correlations:
  COMPLETE -- only complete cases are used
  CORPAIR  -- only  cases  that  have  acceptable
              values for both variables are used
              to compute correlations
  COVPAIR  -- covariances are computed from cases
              that  have  acceptable  values  for
              both  variables  but  variances  are
              computed from all acceptable values
  ALLVALUE -- all acceptable values are used
  These terms are defined more precisely in the
  Definition section below.
```

Example 8D.2 Printing the Covariance Matrix, a Table of Means and Variances Over Cases Present for Each Pair of Variables and a Table of Two-Sample t Tests where Groups are Defined by the Presence and Absence of Another Variable

The correlation matrix and matrix of pairwise frequencies (n_{ik}) are printed automatically. In addition, you can request a printing of

- the input data
- the covariance matrix (as computed by TYPE above)
- the matrix of means, $\bar{x}_{i(k)}$, for variable i over cases complete for variable i and variable k
- the matrix of variances, $var_{i(k)}$
- the two-sample t tests for equality of means of each variable split into two groups based on the presence and absence of values for another variable
- the matrix of sums of case weights for pairwise complete variables

We print the covariance matrix, the tables of means and variances and the t tests by adding the following PRINT paragraph to the instructions of Example 8D.1 before the END paragraph

```
-------------------------------------
  / PRINT    MEAN.
            VARIANCE.
            COVARIANCE.
            TTEST.
-------------------------------------
```

Output 8D.2   Optional results printed by P8D including a table of two-sample t tests where groups are defined by the presence or absence of another variable

--- univariate statistics ---

MEANS OF COLUMN VARIABLE OVER CASES WHERE ROW VARIABLE IS PRESENT

		AGE 2	HEIGHT 3	WEIGHT 4	BRTHPILL 5	CHOLSTRL 6	ALBUMIN 7	CALCIUM 8	URICACID 9
AGE	2	33.8191	64.5107	131.6720	1.5000	236.1505	4.1112	9.9621	4.7705
HEIGHT	3	33.6989	64.5107	131.3695	1.5054	236.1956	4.1124	9.9592	4.7707
WEIGHT	4	33.7742	64.4837	131.6720	1.5000	236.2065	4.1130	9.9611	4.7470
BRTHPILL	5	33.8191	64.5107	131.6720	1.5000	236.1505	4.1112	9.9621	4.7705
CHOLSTRL	6	33.9301	64.4945	131.4185	1.4946	236.1505	4.1162	9.9640	4.7669
ALBUMIN	7	33.6935	64.5243	131.6848	1.5054	236.1956	4.1112	9.9666	4.7842
CALCIUM	8	33.6702	64.5000	131.1912	1.5027	235.7445	4.1169	9.9621	4.7561
URICACID	9	33.7112	64.4973	131.6000	1.5027	235.6973	4.1124	9.9621	4.7705

⑥

(output continued)

Output 8D.2 (continued)

VARIANCES OF COLUMN VARIABLE OVER CASES WHERE ROW VARIABLE IS PRESENT
---

⑦		AGE 2	HEIGHT 3	WEIGHT 4	BRTHPILL 5	CHOLSTRL 6	ALBUMIN 7	CALCIUM 8	URICACID 9
AGE	2	102.	6.18	427.	0.251	0.181E 04	0.128	0.230	1.34
HEIGHT	3	101.	6.18	419.	0.251	0.183E 04	0.129	0.230	1.35
WEIGHT	4	102.	6.16	427.	0.251	0.183E 04	0.129	0.232	1.30
BRTHPILL	5	102.	6.18	427.	0.251	0.181E 04	0.128	0.230	1.34
CHOLSTRL	6	102.	6.17	425.	0.251	0.181E 04	0.127	0.231	1.30
ALBUMIN	7	101.	6.17	430.	0.251	0.183E 04	0.128	0.221	1.33
CALCIUM	8	98.9	6.21	416.	0.251	0.179E 04	0.128	0.230	1.32
URICACID	9	101.	6.18	428.	0.251	0.178E 04	0.129	0.230	1.34

T-TEST FOR EACH VARIABLE (COLUMN) COMPARING THE VALUES
IN TWO GROUPS. THE GROUPS ARE BASED ON THE ABSENCE OR
PRESENCE OF DATA FOR ANOTHER VARIABLE (ROW). FOUR LINES
(FIVE VALUES) ARE PRINTED FOR EACH PAIR OF VARIABLES
   1)   T   (SEPARATE VARIANCE COMPUTATION),
   2) D.F. (ESTIMATED FOR SEPARATE VARIANCE T),
   3) RATIO OF VARIANCE IN 'ABSENT' GROUP TO
          VARIANCE IN 'PRESENT' GROUP,
   4) SAMPLE SIZES OF 'ABSENT' AND 'PRESENT' GROUPS.
FOR 0 OR 1 MISSING VALUE ONLY THE SAMPLE SIZES ARE GIVEN.   ⑧
VARIANCE RATIOS ARE NOT REPORTED WHEN THE SMALLER DEGREES
OF FREEDOM IS 4 OR LESS.

		AGE 2	HEIGHT 3	WEIGHT 4	BRTHPILL 5	CHOLSTRL 6	ALBUMIN 7	CALCIUM 8	URICACID 9
AGE	2	0.0	0.0	0.0	0.0	0.0	0.0	0.0	0.0
		0.0	0.0	0.0	0.0	0.0	0.0	0.0	0.0
		0.0	0.0	0.0	0.0	0.0	0.0	0.0	0.0
		0 188	0 186	0 186	0 188	0 186	0 186	0 185	0 187
HEIGHT	3	1.41	0.0	1.52	-13.11	-0.71	0.0	0.0	-0.08
		1.0	0.0	1.0	78.5	1.9	0.0	0.0	1.2
		0.0	0.0	0.0	0.0	0.0	0.0	0.0	0.0
		2 186	0 186	2 184	2 186	2 184	1 185	1 184	2 185
WEIGHT	4	0.53	2.49	0.0	0.0	-0.27	-1.07	1.45	6.14
		1.0	1.1	0.0	1.0	1.1	1.1	2.3	1.1
		0.0	0.0	0.0	0.0	0.0	0.0	0.0	0.0
		2 186	2 184	0 186	2 186	2 184	2 184	2 183	2 185
BRTHPILL	5	0.0	0.0	0.0	0.0	0.0	0.0	0.0	0.0
		0.0	0.0	0.0	0.0	0.0	0.0	0.0	0.0
		0.0	0.0	0.0	0.0	0.0	0.0	0.0	0.0
		0 188	0 186	0 186	0 188	0 186	0 186	0 185	0 187
CHOLSTRL	6	-6.18	0.75	4.51	14.35	0.0	-3.05	0.0	0.16
		1.5	1.0	1.2	70.2	0.0	1.1	0.0	1.0
		0.0	0.0	0.0	0.0	0.0	0.0	0.0	0.0
		2 186	2 184	2 184	2 186	0 186	2 184	1 184	2 185
ALBUMIN	7	1.38	0.0	-0.11	-13.11	-0.71	0.0	-0.44	-1.28
		1.0	0.0	1.0	78.5	1.9	0.0	1.0	1.0
		0.0	0.0	0.0	0.0	0.0	0.0	0.0	0.0
		2 186	1 185	2 184	2 186	2 184	0 186	2 183	2 185
CALCIUM	8	0.89	0.66	3.09	-0.50	0.81	-2.57	0.0	1.22
		2.0	1.0	2.1	2.0	1.0	2.2	0.0	1.0
		0.0	0.0	0.0	0.0	0.0	0.0	0.0	0.0
		3 185	2 184	3 183	3 185	2 184	3 183	0 185	2 185
URICACID	9	0.0	0.0	0.0	0.0	0.0	0.0	0.0	0.0
		0.0	0.0	0.0	0.0	0.0	0.0	0.0	0.0
		0.0	0.0	0.0	0.0	0.0	0.0	0.0	0.0
		1 187	1 185	1 185	1 187	1 185	1 185	0 185	0 187

```
CORPAIR  COVARIANCE MATRIX
------------------------
```

		AGE 2	HEIGHT 3	WEIGHT 4	BRTHPILL 5	CHOLSTRL 6	ALBUMIN 7	CALCIUM 8	URICACID 9
AGE	2	102.							
HEIGHT	3	2.03	6.18						
WEIGHT	4	52.7	24.4	427.					
BRTHPILL	5	0.0	0.211	0.765	0.251				
CHOLSTRL	6	158.	2.10	130.	1.62	0.181E 04			
ALBUMIN	7	-0.261	-0.185E-01	-1.87	-0.430E-01	0.813	0.128		
CALCIUM	8	-0.158	0.177	0.696	-0.135E-01	5.13	0.778E-01	0.230	
URICACID	9	2.08	0.384	7.28	0.143E-01	13.1	0.298E-02	0.108	1.34

(⑨ appears in upper right area of the matrix)

Output 8D.2 contains the matrices of means ⑥, variances ⑦, a table containing two-sample t statistics for each variable split into two groups based on the presence or absence of the row variable ⑧, and covariances ⑨ in addition to the results in Output 8D.1.

In the first column of the t test table (⑧ in Output 8D.2) the t value for AGE is -6.18 when the presence and absence of the values of CHOLSTRL is used as a grouping variable. That is, the test compares the average age of the 186 women with acceptable CHOLSTRL values with the average age of the two women whose cholesterol values are missing (these are the extreme values of 50 and 600 that are excluded from the analysis by the MIN and MAX statements specified in the VARIABLE paragraph). From other analyses we know that the average age of all 188 women is around 34 years. The woman with the cholesterol value of 600 is 22 years, the woman with 50 is 25 years. Clearly the average of 22 and 25 is much lower than that for the other 186 women. Thus the women with extreme values are much younger. This discussion illustrates how we use the t test results to identify values that may not be missing randomly. (Here, of course, the situation is contrived because we added the extreme values to the data set.)

PRINT ────────────

FREQuency.   FREQuency/prev.
The matrix of pairwise frequencies, n_{ik}, is printed unless you specify NO FREQUENCY.
CORRelation.   CORRelation/prev.
The correlation matrices computed by the methods specified in TYPE are printed unless you specify NO CORRELATION.
COVAriance.   no/prev.
Print the covariance matrix computed by the same method(s) as described for CORRELATION.
MEAN.   no/prev.
Print the matrix of means, $\bar{x}_{i(k)}$ (i.e., the mean of variable i for cases where variable k has acceptable values). This is computed only if TYPE is COVPAIR or CORPAIR.
Note: Univariate means and standard deviations are always printed.

VARiance.   no/prev.
Print the matrix of variances, $var_{i(k)}$ (i.e., the variance of variable i where variable k has acceptable values). This is only computed if TYPE is CORPAIR.
SUMWeight.   no/prev.
Print the matrix of sums of weights for cases for which the values of variables i and k are both acceptable. This is ignored if a WEIGHT variable is not specified.
TTEST.   no/prev.
Print t test results (for a test of equality of means) for each variable split into two groups based on the presence (group 1) and absence (group 2) of values for another variable.
CASES = #.   10/prev.
The number of input cases to print.

Example 8D.3 Computing a Segment of the Correlation Matrix

You can request that only a portion of the correlation (or covariance matrix) be computed by using the ROW and COLUMN instructions. We add the following CORRELATION paragraph to the instructions in Example 8D.1 before the END paragraph

```
-------------------------------------
/ CORR   TYPE IS ALLVALUE.
        ROWS ARE 2 TO 6.
        COLUMNS ARE 3 TO 9.
-------------------------------------
```

When ROWS and COLUMNS are specified, the matrix is not a complete covariance or correlation matrix, thus

- a rectangular portion of the matrix (not just the lower triangular part) is computed and printed
- the covariance or correlation matrix cannot be saved.

Output 8D.3 A portion of the correlation matrix is computed by P8D using the ALLVALUE method

----

ALLVALUE CORRELATION MATRIX
----

⑩		HEIGHT 3	WEIGHT 4	BRTHPILL 5	CHOLSTRL 6	ALBUMIN 7	CALCIUM 8	URICACID 9
AGE	2	0.0804	0.2524	0.0	0.3676	-0.0716	-0.0321	0.1761
HEIGHT	3	1.0000	0.4713	0.1692	0.0200	-0.0208	0.1488	0.1341
WEIGHT	4	0.4713	1.0000	0.0738	0.1478	-0.2552	0.0698	0.3004
BRTHPILL	5	0.1692	0.0738	1.0000	0.0758	-0.2398	-0.0561	0.0247
CHOLSTRL	6	0.0200	0.1478	0.0758	1.0000	0.0534	0.2504	0.2605

Output 8D.3 contains the results for the ALLVALUE correlation matrix ⑩ .

CORrelation ─────────────────────────

ROW = v list.   all variables
  Names or subscripts of variables used as the rows for the matrices printed.
COLumn = v list.   all variables
  Names or subscripts of variables used as columns for the matrices printed.

<u>Note</u>: The covariance and correlation matrices cannot be saved in a BMDP File when ROW and COLUMN are specified. Also note that if ROW or COLUMN is specified, then the other must also be specified.

<u>Note</u>: In program versions before 1981 ROW and COLUMN were specified in the VARIABLE paragraph.

Example 8D.4 Saving Computed Matrices in a BMDP File

P8D can save the correlation matrix, the covariance matrix, or the data (after transformations are performed) in a BMDP File (Chapter 7). The results saved in a BMDP File can be further analyzed by other programs.

When a covariance or correlation matrix is saved and further analyzed, the effective sample size recorded in the BMDP File is the harmonic mean of the sample sizes of the individual variables (unless TYPE = COMPLETE is specified).

When a BMDP File is read as input and you are creating a second BMDP File to save the data, the two Files must be in different system files and assigned different UNIT numbers.

We add to the Control Language instructions of Example 8D.1 the following paragraphs required to save the correlation matrix. Any BMDP program that accepts a correlation matrix as input also accepts a covariance matrix (and conversely).

```
---------------------------------------
/ SAVE          UNIT IS 9.
               NEW.
               CODE IS WERNER.
               CONTENT IS CORR.
/ CORRELATION  TYPES ARE ALLVALUE, COVPAIR.
---------------------------------------
```

<u>Note</u>: the systems information that precedes the BMDP instructions must contain a card saying where to store the BMDP File. Examples for IBM OS systems are given in Chapter 7. You can also read about allocating space for the system file in Chapter 7.

Output 8D.4 shows that a BMDP File has been created by P8D to contain the correlation matrix. Although the correlation matrix is computed by two methods (TYPE = ALLVALUE, COVPAIR.), only the correlation matrix computed by the first method (ALLVALUE) is saved.

Output 8D.4 Creating a BMDP File to save an ALLVALUE correlation matrix

----

```
---------------------------------------
BMDP FILE IS BEING WRITTEN ON UNIT      9
CODE. . . IS     WERNER
CONTENT . IS     CORR
LABEL . . IS

VARIABLES ARE
    2 AGE       3 HEIGHT    4 WEIGHT    5 BRTHPILL    6 CHOLSTRL
    7 ALBUMIN   8 CALCIUM   9 URICACID


BMDP FILE ON UNIT  9 HAS BEEN COMPLETED.
---------------------------------------
```

SAVE ──────────────────────────────

> CONTent = (one or more)   DATA
>   DATA, COVA, CORR.
> The matrices to be saved in a BMDP File. If
> COVA (covariances) or CORR (correlations) is
> specified, and more than one method of
> computing the correlation matrix is specified,
> only the covariances or correlations computed
> by the first method stated in CORRELATION TYPE
> is saved. COVA and CORR are not saved if
> CORRELATION ROW or COLUMN is specified.

Selecting a Subset of Variables

In common with most BMDP programs, a subset of
the variables can be selected for analysis by P8D;
the variables to be USED are specified in the
VARIABLE paragraph. You can also request the
computation of a portion of the correlation (or
covariance) matrix by specifying ROW and COLUMN
variables in the CORRELATION paragraph, as shown in
Example 8D.3.

Case Weights

Case weights can be used in the computation of
means, variances, covariances and correlations (the
weight for each case is stated by the user and is
stored as a variable in the data matrix). If a case
WEIGHT variable is specified, the formulas used are
given in Appendix A.

VARiable ─────────────────────────

> WEIGHT = v.   no case weights var./prev.
> Name or subscript of the variable that contains
> case weights. The effect case weights have on
> the computations is explained below. If WEIGHT
> is not specified or is set to zero, there are
> no case weights, i.e., each case will have unit
> weight.

Definitions of Correlations from Incomplete Data

For TYPE = COMPLETE, correlations are defined as
in Chapter 2. For correlations computed from
incomplete data,

X_{ij} = value of variable i for case j

n_i = the number of values present for variable i

$\overline{X}_i$ = mean of variable i (using all values that
are present for variable i)

V_i = variance of variable i
$= \Sigma(X_{ij} - \overline{X}_i)^2/(n_i - 1)$
where the sum is taken over all values that
are present for variable i

n_{ik} = the number of cases for which both variable
i and variable k are present

$\overline{X}_{ik} = \Sigma x_{ij}/n_{ij}$
where the sum is taken over all cases for
which both variables i and k are present

$V_{ik} = \Sigma(X_{ij} - \overline{X}_{ik})^2/(n_{ik} - 1)$
where the sum is taken over all cases for
which both variable i and k are present

Note that $\overline{X}_{ik}$ and V_{ik} are the sample mean and
variance of variable i computed from the cases for
which both variables i and k are present.

For COVPAIR, the correlation of variables i and j
is simply the usual correlation computed from the
cases for which both variables have been observed.

The covariances for the different types are

$$COV_{ik}(allvalue) = \Sigma(X_{ij} - \overline{X}_i)(X_{kj} - \overline{X}_k)/(n_{ik} - 1)$$

$$COV_{ik}(covpair) = \Sigma(X_{ij} - \overline{X}_{ik})(X_{kj} - \overline{X}_{ki})/(n_{ik} - 1)$$

$$COV_{ik}(corpair) = COV_{ik}(covpair)\left(\frac{V_{ii}V_{kk}}{V_{ik}V_{ki}}\right)^{\frac{1}{2}}$$

where the sums are taken over all cases for which
both variables i and k are present. Finally, for any
TYPE, the correlation of variables i and j is

$$COR_{ik} = COV_{ik}/(COV_{ii} \cdot COV_{kk})^{\frac{1}{2}} .$$

SIZE OF PROBLEM

The maximum number of variables that can be
analyzed at one time in the available core space by
P8D depends on the methods used to compute the
correlations. For medium sized computer systems, up
to 160 variables can be used when the method is
COMPLETE, 60 variables when it is CORPAIR, and 70
variables otherwise. Appendix B describes how to
increase the capacity of the program.

When the number of variables exceeds the capacity
of the program, P8D rereads the data and calculates
the matrix in manageable blocks. (See the
computational procedure in Appendix A.)

ACKNOWLEDGEMENT

The pre-1981 release of P8D was programmed by
Peter Mundle. The later version of P8D was designed
by Laszlo Engelman with assistance from James Frane
and was programmed by Laszlo Engelman.

SUMMARY

Order of Input Cards

```
// (job card)
// EXEC BIMED,PROG=BMDP8D      (see Appendix E)
//SYSIN DD *
/ PROBLEM
/ INPUT
/ VARIABLE
/ TRANSFORM
/ SAVE
/ CORRELATION
/ PRINT
/ END
    (data, if on cards)
// (system card)
```

Full sets of BMDP paragraphs (and data, if on cards)
can be repeated for additional problems; see Section
5.8.

Paragraph Statement	Preassigned	Comment and Manual Reference
/ VARiable		Additional options to request calculations on particular pairs of the USE variables; results can be printed but not saved. ROW and COL must be used together or both omitted.
WEIGHT = v.	none	Name or subscript of the variable that contains case weights. * 215
MMV = #.	(VT+1)/2	Maximum number of missing values per case. Cases with more than MMV missing values are not used in the computations. 211
/ CORRelation		Optional to control computation.
TYPE = c list.	CORPAIR.	CORPAIR, COVPAIR, ALLVALUE, or COMPLETE, method of computing matrices (see program description above). Only the first matrix specified can be saved on BMDP File (include / SAVE paragraph). * 211
ROW = v list.	all vars.	Names or subscripts of variables used as rows for the printed matrices.
COLumn = v list.	all vars.	Names or subscripts of vairables used as columns for the printed matrices. 214
/ PRINT		Optional to control printing of tables and matrices. 213
FREQuency.	yes	Table of pairwise frequencies. *
CORRelation.	yes	Correlation matrices that have been computed. *
COVAriance.	no	Covariance matrices that have been computed. *
MEAN.	no	Table of pairwise means if / CORR TYPE = COVPAIR or CORPAIR. (Univar. means and standard deviation always printed.) *
VARiance.	no	Table of pairwise variances if / CORR TYPE = CORPAIR. *
SUMWeight	no	Table of sums of weights if / VAR WEIGHT is specified. *
TTEST.	no	Two-sample t-test results for each variable split into groups based on the presence or absence of values of another variable.
CASES = #.	10	Number of cases of the input data to print. *
/ SAVE		Optional to save results for further analyses (regression, discriminant function, clustering, etc.)
CONTent = c list.	DATA	DATA, COVA or CORR. (one or more), the matrices to be saved in a BMDP File. If COVA (covariances) or CORR (correlations) is specified, and more than one method of computing the correlation matrix is specified only the covariances or correlations computed by the first method stated in / CORR TYPE are saved. COVA and CORR are not saved if / CORR ROW and COL are specified. 215
		<u>Note</u>: When a covariance or correlation matrix is saved and further analyzed, the effective sample size recorded in the BMDP File is the harmonic mean of the sample sizes of the individual variables (unless TYPE = COMPLETE is specified).

Key:

/	—indicates paragraph	*	—assigned value remains the same for additional problems
.	—period ends a sentence		
●	—required	VT	—number of variables after transformations
v	—variable (name or subscript)	list	—more than one item, often one per var.
g	—group (name or subscript)		
#	—number		

Capitalized letters—paragraph or sentence names recognized by BMDP

'c' —characters (name or parameter) may omit apostrophes if contiguous letters only

Page numbers following refer to this Manual

PAM

12.2 Description and Estimation of Missing Data

James Frane

ABSTRACT

PAM is designed to fulfill three primary functions:

- to describe the pattern of missing data -- Where are the missing values located? How extensive are they? Do pairs of variables tend to have values missing in the same cases? Are cases with missing values extreme (far from the mean)?
- to estimate the covariance and correlation matrices by either of three computational methods.
- to replace missing values or values out of range by estimated values (using one of several methods). The covariance matrix and the "completed" data matrix can be saved in a BMDP File for further analysis by other programs.

The first function is a preliminary step to the second and third. Usually you will want to use PAM twice; first to look at the pattern and extent of the missing values and then to compute covariances or provide estimates for the missing values. (For further discussion of missing values, see Frane, 1978b.)

PAM replaces invalid values using means, regression on the variable most highly correlated with the missing variable, regression on a highly correlated set of variables, or regression on all available variables. Data can be described and estimated within a group, where group membership is identified by a variable containing a few discrete values. A cases-by-variables graphical display shows the location or pattern of missing values (M) and extreme values (S--too small, B--too big). Output includes summary reports of invalid data by cases, variables and pairs of variables; correlations for dichotomized variables (i.e., 0 if a value is invalid, 1 if it is valid); correlation matrix with its eigenvalues; optional listing for each case that has estimates of missing values and values out of range, the R^2 of the estimated variable with the variables estimating it, and the Mahalanobis D^2 of the case to the mean; and optional plots displaying complete cases and cases with estimates. Critical computations are performed in double precision.

Example AM.1 Basic Setup for Description of Missing Data

PAM is used in this example to describe the pattern of missing values in the Werner blood chemistry data (Table 5.1). There are no instructions in this example specific to PAM; only preassigned options are used.

The explanation of the PROBLEM, INPUT and VARIABLE paragraphs is given in Chapter 5.

```
------------------------------------
/ PROBLEM    TITLE IS 'WERNER BLOOD CHEMISTRY DATA'.
/ INPUT      VARIABLES ARE 9.
            FORMAT IS '(A4, 5F4.0, 3F4.1)'.
/ VARIABLE   NAMES ARE ID, AGE, HEIGHT, WEIGHT,
                       BRTHPILL, CHOLSTRL, ALBUMIN,
                       CALCIUM, URICACID.
            MAXIMUM IS (6)400.
            MINIMUM IS (6)150.
            LABEL IS ID.

/ END
------------------------------------
```

(See end of this PAM section for organization of systems information, BMDP instructions and data.)

When we use only preassigned options, estimates are not computed for the values that are missing. The results of the description of the missing data are presented in Output AM.1. Circled numbers below correspond to those in the output.

(1) Interpretation of BMDP instructions specific to PAM. No such instructions were specified, therefore preassigned options are shown.

(2) For cases that contain missing values or values out of range, a cases-by-variables plot showing the location of missing values (M--missing), values less than the lower limit (S--too small) and values greater than the upper limit (B--too big). In our example, the second case has a value larger than the upper limit for CHOLSTRL and a missing value for CALCIUM.

(3) Number of cases read. You can specify whether computations use only complete cases (cases with no data missing and positive case weight) or all acceptable values.

(4) For variables with missing values or values out of range, the percent of values that are missing or out of range.

(5) Univariate statistics for each variable, including the sample size (number of acceptable observations), mean, standard deviation, coefficient of variation, smallest observed value (not out of range), largest observed value (not out of range), smallest standard score, largest standard score, skewness and kurtosis. (These statistics are defined in Section 2.1.)

(6) Data from the first five cases are printed. The word MISSING replaces missing values, TOOSMALL replaces values less than the lower limit and TOOBIG replaces values greater than the upper limit (see cases 1 and 2). You can request that the data be printed for any number of cases.

(7) For each pair of variables, the sample size (number) of cases containing acceptable values for both variables. Variables having acceptable values for all cases or no acceptable values are omitted from the table. For example, there are 184 cases with acceptable values for both HEIGHT and WEIGHT.

Output AM.1   Description of incomplete data by PAM. Circled numbers correspond to those in the text

----

```
                    WEIGHT VARIABLE . . . . . . . . . . . . . . .
                    GROUPING VARIABLE . . . . . . . . . . . . . .
                    PRECISION . . . . . . . . . . . . . . . . . . DOUBLE
                    TOLERANCE FOR MATRIX INVERSION. . . . . . . . 0.0001000
                    ESTIMATION METHOD . . . . . . . . . . . . . . NONE
                    F TO ENTER LIMIT. . . . . . . . . . . . . .      4.00
   (1)              MISSING VARIABLE LIMIT PER CASE . . . . . . .       7
                    MISSING CASE LIMIT PER VARIABLE . . . . . . .   50.00 PERCENT
                    EIGENVALUE LOWER LIMIT. . . . . . . . . . .   0.00100
                    RIDGE PARAMETER . . . . . . . . . . . . . .   0.0
                    METHOD OF COMPUTING COVARIANCE. . . . . . . . ALLVALUE
                    PRINT CORRELATIONS. . . . . . . . . . . . . . YES
                    PRINT COVARIANCES . . . . . . . . . . . . . . NO
                    PRINT PATTERN OF MISSING DATA . . . . . . . . YES
                    PRINT EIGENVALUES OF CORRELATION MATRIX . . . YES
                    PRINT ESTIMATES OF MISSING VALUES . . . . . . NO
                    PRINT MAHALANOBIS DISTANCES . . . . . . . . . NO
                    PRINT FREQUENCIES AND PERCENTAGES OF MISSING. . YES
                    PRINT INVERSE OF CORRELATION MATRIX . . . . . NO
                    PRINT INVERSE IN FORM OF CORRELATION MATRIX . . NO
                    PRINT SUM OF CASE WEIGHTS . . . . . . . . . . NO
                    PRINT CORRELATIONS OF DICHOTOMIZED VARIABLES. . YES


                    PATTERN OF MISSING DATA AND DATA BEYOND LIMITS
                    COUNT OF MISSING VARIABLES INCLUDES DATA BEYOND LIMITS.
                    THE COLUMN LABELED WT. IS FOR THE CASE WEIGHT, IF ANY. 'M'
                    REPRESENTS A MISSING VALUE. 'B' REPRESENTS A VALUE GREATER
                    THAN THE MAXIMUM LIMIT. 'S' REPRESENTS A VALUE LESS THAN THE
                    MINIMUM LIMIT.
```

```
                                          A H W B C A C U
                                          G E E R H L A R
                                          E I I T O B L I
                                          G G H L U C C
                                          H H P S M I A
                          NO OF     W      T T I T I U C
              CASE   CASE MISS.     T      L R N M I
              LABEL  NO. VARS. GROUP .      L L     D
```

	CASE LABEL	CASE NO.	NO OF MISS. VARS.	GROUP	WT.	AGEHT	HEIGHT	WEIGHT	BRTHWGHT	CHOLSTRL	ALBUMIN	CALCIUM	URICACID
(2)	1946	2	2						B	M			
	1797	4	1						S				
	3	51	1							M			
	2877	86	1					M					
	63	103	2							M M			
	2456	121	2				M		M				
	5	161	1				M						
	1149	185	2				M		M				

```
              NUMBER OF CASES READ. . . . . . . . . . . . . . . .    188
```

(3)
```
              NUMBER OF CASES WITH NO DATA MISSING AND WITH
                   POSITIVE CASE WEIGHT. . . . . . . . . . . . .    180
```

PERCENTAGES OF MISSING DATA FOR EACH VARIABLE IN EACH GROUP

THESE PERCENTAGES ARE BASED ON SAMPLE SIZES AND GROUP SIZES
REPORTED WITH THE UNIVARIATE SUMMARY STATISTICS BELOW.
VARIABLES WITHOUT MISSING DATA ARE NOT INCLUDED.

		1
HEIGHT	3	1.1
WEIGHT	4	1.1
CHOLSTRL	6	1.1
ALBUMIN	7	1.1
CALCIUM	8	1.6
URICACID	9	0.5

④

UNIVARIATE SUMMARY STATISTICS ⑤

VARIABLE	SAMPLE SIZE	MEAN	STANDARD DEVIATION	COEFFICIENT OF VARIATION	SMALLEST VALUE	LARGEST VALUE	SMALLEST STANDARD SCORE	LARGEST STANDARD SCORE	SKEWNESS	KURTOSIS
2 AGE	188	33.81915	10.11269	0.299023	19.00000	55.00000	-1.47	2.09	0.40	-1.01
3 HEIGHT	186	64.51075	2.48507	0.038522	57.00000	71.00000	-3.02	2.61	-0.13	-0.09
4 WEIGHT	186	131.67204	20.66058	0.156909	94.00000	215.00000	-1.82	4.03	1.00	1.69
5 BRTHPILL	188	1.50000	0.50134	0.334223	1.00000	2.00000	-1.00	1.00	0.00	-2.01
6 CHOLSTRL	186	236.15054	42.55551	0.180205	155.00000	390.00000	-1.91	3.62	0.47	0.09
7 ALBUMIN	186	4.11129	0.35797	0.087070	3.20000	5.00000	-2.55	2.48	-0.03	-0.37
8 CALCIUM	185	9.96216	0.47956	0.048138	8.60000	11.10000	-2.84	2.37	-0.11	-0.41
9 URICACID	187	4.77059	1.15723	0.242576	2.20000	9.90000	-2.22	4.43	1.06	2.33

VALUES FOR KURTOSIS GREATER THAN ZERO INDICATE DISTRIBUTIONS
WITH HEAVIER TAILS THAN THE NORMAL DISTRIBUTION.

DATA AFTER TRANSFORMATIONS FOR FIRST   5 CASES

'MISSING' DENOTES A MISSING VALUE, 'TOOBIG' DENOTES A
VALUE THAT EXCEEDS THE MAXIMUM LIMIT, AND 'TOOSMALL'   ⑥
DENOTES A VALUE THAT IS LESS THAN THE MIMINUM LIMIT.

CASE LABEL	NUMBER	WEIGHT	GROUP	2 AGE	3 HEIGHT	4 WEIGHT	5 BRTHPILL	6 CHOLSTRL	7 ALBUMIN
		8 CALCIUM	9 URICACID						
2381	1	1.00000		22.00000	67.00000	144.00000	1.00000	200.00000	4.30000
		9.80000	5.40000						
1946	2	1.00000		22.00000	64.00000	160.00000	2.00000	TOOBIG	3.50000
		MISSING	7.20000						
1610	3	1.00000		25.00000	62.00000	128.00000	1.00000	243.00000	4.10000
		10.40000	3.30000						
1797	4	1.00000		25.00000	68.00000	150.00000	2.00000	TOOSMALL	3.80000
		9.60000	3.00000						
561	5	1.00000		19.00000	64.00000	125.00000	1.00000	158.00000	4.10000
		9.90000	4.70000						

SAMPLE SIZES FOR EACH PAIR OF VARIABLES
(NUMBER OF TIMES BOTH VARIABLES ARE AVAILABLE)   ⑦
IN ORDER TO SAVE SPACE, VARIABLES WITH NO MISSING
DATA OR THAT HAVE NO DATA ARE NOT INCLUDED.

		HEIGHT 3	WEIGHT 4	CHOLSTRL 6	ALBUMIN 7	CALCIUM 8	URICACID 9
HEIGHT	3	186					
WEIGHT	4	184	186				
CHOLSTRL	6	184	184	186			
ALBUMIN	7	185	184	184	186		
CALCIUM	8	184	183	184	183	185	
URICACID	9	185	185	185	185	185	187

(output continued)

Output AM.1 (continued)

PAIRWISE PERCENTAGES OF MISSING DATA

DIAGONAL ELEMENTS ARE THE PERCENTAGES THAT EACH VARIABLE
IS MISSING. OFF-DIAGONAL ELEMENTS ARE THE PERCENTAGES
EITHER VARIABLE IS MISSING.   THESE PERCENTAGES DO NOT INCLUDE
CASES WITH MISSING GROUP OR WEIGHT VARIABLES, CASES WITH
ZERO WEIGHTS, CASES EXCLUDED BY SETTING USE EQUAL TO A
NON-POSITIVE VALUE BY TRANSFORMATIONS, OR CASES WITH GROUPING
VALUES NOT USED. VARIABLES WITH NO MISSING DATA OR THAT
HAVE NO DATA ARE NOT INCLUDED HERE.

⑧

		HEIGHT 3	WEIGHT 4	CHOLSTRL 6	ALBUMIN 7	CALCIUM 8	URICACID 9
HEIGHT	3	1.1					
WEIGHT	4	2.1	1.1				
CHOLSTRL	6	2.1	2.1	1.1			
ALBUMIN	7	1.6	2.1	2.1	1.1		
CALCIUM	8	2.1	2.7	2.1	2.7	1.6	
URICACID	9	1.6	1.6	1.6	1.6	1.6	0.5

CORRELATIONS OF THE DICHOTOMIZED VARIABLES WHERE FOR EACH
VARIABLE ZERO INDICATES THAT THE VALUE WAS MISSING AND ONE
INDICATES THAT THE VALUE WAS PRESENT. VARIABLES WITH NO
MISSING DATA OR WHICH ARE COMPLETELY MISSING ARE NOT
INCLUDED.

⑨

		HEIGHT 3	WEIGHT 4	CHOLSTRL 6	ALBUMIN 7	CALCIUM 8	URICACID 9
HEIGHT	3	1.000					
WEIGHT	4	-0.011	1.000				
CHOLSTRL	6	-0.011	-0.011	1.000			
ALBUMIN	7	0.495	-0.011	-0.011	1.000		
CALCIUM	8	0.401	-0.013	0.401	-0.013	1.000	
URICACID	9	-0.008	-0.008	-0.008	-0.008	0.574	1.000

NOTE THAT THE REMAINING OUTPUT IS FOR THE ORDINARY
CORRELATIONS, NOT THE CORRELATIONS FOR THE
DICHOTOMIZED VARIABLES.

CORRELATIONS

⑩

		AGE 2	HEIGHT 3	WEIGHT 4	BRTHPILL 5	CHOLSTRL 6	ALBUMIN 7	CALCIUM 8	URICACID 9
AGE	2	1.000							
HEIGHT	3	0.080	1.000						
WEIGHT	4	0.252	0.471	1.000					
BRTHPILL	5	0.0	0.169	0.074	1.000				
CHOLSTRL	6	0.368	0.020	0.148	0.076	1.000			
ALBUMIN	7	-0.072	-0.021	-0.255	-0.240	0.053	1.000		
CALCIUM	8	-0.032	0.149	0.070	-0.056	0.250	0.444	1.000	
URICACID	9	0.176	0.134	0.300	0.025	0.260	0.007	0.194	1.000

EIGENVALUES OF CORRELATION MATRIX

```
    2.0016
    1.6239
    1.1823      ⑪
    0.9613
    0.8031
    0.5862
    0.4686
    0.3729
```

⑧ Pairwise percentage of missing data. For each pair of variables in ⑦, PAM prints the percentage of cases in which either variable has a missing value or value out of range. The diagonal elements are the percentages for the individual variables.

⑨ Correlations of dichotomized variables. The correlation of each pair of variables in ⑦ is computed using a dichotomy for each variable; one represents an acceptable value, and zero a value that is missing or out of range. Variables that contain only acceptable values or no acceptable values are not included in this matrix. This correlation matrix (CORRDICH) can be saved in a BMDP File and used in other programs such as factor analysis to further study the pattern of missing values.
Note: all other computations are based on the acceptable observations and not on these dichotomies.

⑩ Correlations. This analysis uses the preassigned method of computing correlations, which is ALLVALUE (see P8D, Definition). When this method is used it is possible that the correlation matrix will not be positive semidefinite. If negative eigenvalues are found, the correlation matrix is recomputed using the positive eigenvalues and their eigenvectors (see below for details).

⑪ Eigenvalues of the correlation matrix.

Options for computing covariances, correlations and statistics. The univariate statistics, covariances and correlations can be computed using

- all acceptable values (ALLVALUE): the mean of each variable is computed from all acceptable values of the variable; deviations from the means are used to compute covariances and correlations (see P8D, Definition)
- maximum likelihood (ML)
- complete cases only (COMPLETE): cases with missing values or values out of range are not used in the computations

When all acceptable values (ALLVALUE) are used, the correlation between two variables can exceed unity since the variances may be computed using more values than the covariances. More generally, the correlation matrix may not be positive semidefinite (i.e., the estimated correlation matrix is not a proper correlation matrix). When the correlation matrix is not positive semidefinite, one or more eigenvalues will be negative, the correlation matrix is then recomputed from the positive eigenvalues and corresponding eigenvectors (Appendix A.9). This guarantees that the "smoothed" correlation matrix is positive semidefinite and can be used in regression and factor analysis. The covariance matrix is also smoothed using the smoothed correlation matrix and the original standard deviations. The maximum likelihood method is described in Orchard and Woodbury (1972) and Beale and Little (1975).
ALLVALUE is the preassigned method. Either ALLVALUE or maximum likelihood is preferred when missing values are not concentrated into a very few cases. However, a check on the effect of the missing data can be made by comparing correlations computed by different methods. The maximum likelihood procedure is more expensive than COMPLETE or

ALLVALUE, but has advantages over COMPLETE when there are many cases with missing values, and advantages over ALLVALUE especially when data are not missing at random.

```
ESTimate ─────────────────────────────────
  TYPE = (one only)                    ALLVALUE/prev.
        ALLVALUE, ML, COMPLETE.
    ALLVALUE uses all acceptable values for each
    variable wherever possible. See P8D (p. 209)
    for a more exact definition. When ALLVALUE is
    used, the correlation matrix may have to be
    smoothed to eliminate negative eigenvalues as
    explained above.
    When ML is specified the program begins with
    the ALLVALUE estimates and iterates to obtain
    the maximum likelihood solution. ML is not
    available in versions dated before 1981.
    When COMPLETE is specified, only cases that
    have valid data for all variables are used in
    the computations of the mean and all other
    univariate statistics, and in the covariances.
  ITeration = #.                              10/prev.
    Maximum number of iterations for ML.
  CONverge = #.                              .01/prev.
    Convergence criterion for ML. Convergence
    criterion is applied to relative charge in
    variances and absolute charge in correlations
    between iterations.
```

Adjustments for correlation matrices with small eigenvalues: smoothing and ridge techniques. Using a correlation matrix with a small eigenvalue, even though it is positive, has undesirable statistical properties (e.g., in regression). You can also smooth the correlation matrix by eliminating the small positive eigenvalues. To do this you specify a limit (EIGEN) on the eigenvalues. Small eigenvalues can also be avoided by means of a "ridge" technique similar to that used in ridge regression: the off-diagonal elements of the correlation matrix are multiplied by the RIDGE value before eigenvalue

```
ESTimate ─────────────────────────────────
  EIGEN = #.                              .001/prev.
    Eigenvalue limit (nonnegative). Correlation
    matrix is smoothed using eigenvalues (and
    corresponding eigenvectors) that are greater
    than EIGEN.
  RIDGE = #.                                  1/prev.
    Value between zero and one. The off-diagonal
    elements of the correlation matrix are
    multiplied by RIDGE before eigenvalue
    smoothing.
```

Example AM.2 Estimation of Missing and Out of Range Values

We specify that the missing values and values out of range are to be replaced by estimates provided by the regression method. Other methods are available and are explained below. We use METHOD = REGR. in this example to more fully illustrate the output available. Other methods may be more appropriate. See discussion below on choosing the METHOD.

Output AM.2 Estimation of missing values by PAM using METHOD = REGR

                          --- results shown in Output AM.1 appear here ---

SQUARED MULTIPLE CORRELATIONS OF EACH VARIABLE WITH ALL OTHER VARIABLES
(MEASURES OF MULTICOLLINEARITY OF VARIABLES)
AND TESTS OF SIGNIFICANCE OF MULTIPLE REGRESSION
DEGREES OF FREEDOM FOR F-STATISTICS ARE   7 AND   180

VARIABLE		R-SQUARED	F-STATISTIC	SIGNIFICANCE
NO.	NAME			(P LESS THAN)
2	AGE	0.198751	6.38	0.00000
3	HEIGHT	0.272510	9.63	0.00000
4	WEIGHT	0.378877	15.69	0.00000
5	BRTHPILL	0.102934	2.95	0.00597
6	CHOLSTRL	0.240848	8.16	0.00000
7	ALBUMIN	0.323993	12.32	0.00000
8	CALCIUM	0.305248	11.30	0.00000
9	URICACID	0.155962	4.75	0.00006

(12)

*** WARNING *** WHEN THE ALLVALUE OPTION IS USED, THE
DEGREES OF FREEDOM USED IN COMPUTING THE ABOVE F STATISTICS
INCLUDE CASES WITH MISSING VALUES. IF THE AMOUNT OF
MISSING DATA IS VERY LARGE, THE SIGNIFICANCE OF THE
F STATISTICS IS EXAGGERATED.

IN THE TABLE BELOW, ESTIMATES THAT ARE LESS THAN THE MINIMUMS
STATED IN THE VARIABLE PARAGRAPH ARE FLAGGED BY THE
LETTER 'S' (SMALL) AFTER THE ESTIMATE. ESTIMATES
GREATER THAN THE MAXIMUMS ARE FLAGGED BY THE LETTER
'B' (BIG).

MAHALANOBIS DISTANCES ARE COMPUTED FROM EACH CASE TO THE
CENTROID OF ITS GROUP. ONLY THOSE VARIABLES WHICH WERE
ORIGINALLY AVAILABLE ARE USED--ESTIMATED VALUES ARE NOT USED.
FOR LARGE MULTIVARIATE NORMAL SAMPLES, THE MAHALANOBIS
DISTANCES HAVE AN APPROXIMATELY CHI-SQUARE DISTRIBUTION WITH
THE NUMBER OF DEGREES OF FREEDOM EQUAL TO THE NUMBER OF
NONMISSING VARIABLES. SIGNIFICANCE LEVELS REPORTED BELOW
THAT ARE LESS THAN .001 ARE FLAGGED WITH AN ASTERISK.

ESTIMATES OF MISSING DATA, MAHALANOBIS D-SQUARED (CHI-SQUARED)   (13)
AND SQUARED MULTIPLE CORRELATIONS WITH AVAILABLE VARIABLES

CASE LABEL	CASE NUMBER	MISSING VARIABLE		ESTIMATE	R-SQUARED	GROUP	CHI-SQ	CHISQ/DF	D.F.	SIGNIFICANCE
2381	1						5.699	0.712	8	0.6810
1946	2	6	CHOLSTRL	237.1477	0.194		11.877	1.979	6	0.0648
1946	2	8	CALCIUM	9.8462	0.262		11.877	1.979	6	0.0648
1610	3						6.299	0.787	8	0.6137
1797	4	6	CHOLSTRL	205.1026	0.241		7.366	1.052	7	0.3918

                     --- similar statistics for cases 5 to 184 ---

1149	185	3	HEIGHT	66.6956	0.265		9.453	1.575	6	0.1497
1149	185	8	CALCIUM	9.8471	0.298		9.453	1.575	6	0.1497
575	186						11.891	1.486	8	0.1561
2271	187						7.625	0.953	8	0.4709
39	188						23.223	2.903	8	0.0031

ESTIMATION OF MISSING DATA COMPLETED

Before estimating missing values it is necessary to thoroughly screen the data and to study the pattern of missing data and correlations; the correlations can be severely affected by extreme values. We suggest that you use P2D (Section 8.2) or P7D (Section 9.2) as well as the screening output from PAM before you choose a method of estimation. It is likely that some transformations such as logarithms may be appropriate. We add an ESTIMATE paragraph to the Control Language of Example AM.1 (before the END paragraph).

```
--------------------------------------
/ ESTIMATE     METHOD IS REGR.
              MINIMUM.
              MAXIMUM.
--------------------------------------
```

The results are presented in Output AM.2. Circled numbers below correspond to those in the output.

⑫ Squared multiple correlations of each variable with all other variables. These indicate approximately the extent that each variable can be estimated from the others by multiple regression. In addition to the squared multiple correlation, the corresponding F statistics and the tail probabilities are printed.

⑬ Estimates of the missing values and values out of range. The squared multiple correlation of the variable estimated with the variables used in the regression equation is printed beside each estimate. For each case, the Mahalanobis D^2 (distance) of the case from the mean is computed; this is labelled CHISQ since for large multivariate normal samples the distribution of D^2 is approximately chi-square. CHISQ/DF is the value of D^2 divided by the number of acceptable values in the case; for large degrees of freedom these values are easier to inspect than the values of CHISQ since their distributions are similar for different degrees of freedom.

As an aid to screening these values, PAM prints the tail area (p-value or probability of exceeding the value of CHISQ) and flags values less than 0.001 with an asterisk. This is not an exact test but can aid in identifying suspicious cases that need to be rechecked. An unusually large number of outliers can indicate that a transformation of the data is necessary; large skewness and kurtosis values can also suggest the need for a transformation.

<u>Methods of estimating missing values.</u> PAM can replace missing values and values out of range by estimates computed by any of the following methods.

MEAN — The mean of the variable is substituted for the missing values. If the cases are classified into groups, the group mean of the variable is substituted.

SINGLE — Each missing value for a variable is estimated by regressing that variable on the variable with which it is most highly correlated, provided the F-to-enter limit is met (see below); otherwise the (group) mean is used.

TWOSTEP — Each missing value for a variable is estimated by regressing that variable on up to two variables selected by stepwise regression (see below). If the F-to-enter limit is <u>not</u> met for either variable, the SINGLE method is used.

STEP — Each missing value for a variable is estimated by regressing that variable on <u>all</u> variables that meet the F-to-enter criterion. Stepwise regression is used to select among the variables that have acceptable values in the case with the missing value.

REGR — Each missing value for a variable is estimated by regressing that variable on all variables that have acceptable values in the case with the missing value. The F-to-enter criterion is not used.

When ML is the covariance TYPE, only the REGR method is available for estimating missing values. Note that REGR estimates of missing values are used in each ML iteration.

The F-to-enter criterion is motivated by an approximate test of the coefficient of any predictor variable. That is, the square of the ratio of the predictor's regression coefficient to its standard error is approximately distributed as an F statistic with one degree of freedom for the numerator. The square of this ratio is compared with the F-to-enter limit (ENTER). This test is affected by the missing values and the procedure of variable selection. We suggest that ENTER not be less than 4.0 to avoid using too many predictor variables (overfitting).

In a stepwise regression of a dependent variable on several others, the variable that has the highest correlation with the dependent variable is chosen first for the regression equation. The variable chosen next is the one with the highest partial correlation with the dependent variable conditional on the variable(s) already in the equation. Additional variables are chosen in the same manner until all variables with acceptable values are used or the F-to-enter criterion is not satisfied.

The choice of method depends on the number of cases, the magnitude of the correlations, the number of missing values, the purpose of estimating the data, the pattern of missing values, etc. When all the correlations are very low it is usually difficult to improve on MEAN. If each variable is highly correlated with another variable and economy is essential, SINGLE may be appropriate. When the number of cases is large and there are many large correlations, REGR is appropriate but may use too many predictor variables (overfitting). STEP or TWOSTEP is appropriate when the correlation matrix contains clusters of moderate or high correlations.

You may prefer STEP to other methods for the same reasons that ordinary stepwise regression is preferred. However, substantially more computation is required than for the other methods. The REGR method is notably cheaper than the STEP, but requires more computation than MEAN, SINGLE and TWOSTEP.

```
ESTimate ─────────────────────────────────
  METHod = (one only)              NONE/prev.
          MEAN, SINGLE, TWOSTEP,
          STEP, REGR,  NONE.
  The method used to estimate and replace missing
  values and values out of range (see below).
  NONE means that there is no estimation of
  missing values. Therefore, to estimate missing
  values a method must be specified. The methods
  are described in detail above. Some of the
  results described in the PRINT paragraph are
  available only for specific methods due to the
  computational techniques used.
```

Estimating and replacing values outside acceptable range limits. Unless you request otherwise, only observations that are equal to the missing value code are estimated. Values out of range are estimated when

MAXIMUM.

and

MINIMUM.

are specified in the ESTIMATE paragraph. MAXIMUM specifies that values greater than the upper limit for the variables are to be estimated; and MINIMUM specifies that values that are less than the lower limit for the variables are to be estimated. (Values greater than the upper limit or less than the lower limit are not used in any computations whether or not they are estimated.)

```
ESTimate ─────────────────────────────────
  MAXimum.                          no/prev.
    Estimate and replace values that are greater
    than the specified upper limits for the
    variables. The values are replaced by the same
    METHOD as missing values.
  MINimum.                          no/prev.
    Estimate and replace values that are less than
    the specified lower limits for the variables.
    The values are replaced by the same METHOD as
    missing values.
```

Limiting the amount of estimation for a case or for a variable. If a case contains too many missing values or values out of range, you may not want to include that case in the computations, or to estimate the missing values for the case. To eliminate such cases, you can specify VLIM as defined below.

If any variable has too many missing values or values out of range, you may not want to compute statistics for it or estimate its missing values. If a pair of variables has too many cases where one or both observations are not acceptable, the estimate of the covariance or correlation for this pair of variables may be poor. Therefore, you can specify the maximum percentage of cases that can have unacceptable observations and yet the computations are performed. If not specified, the preassigned percentage is 50%.

```
ESTimate ─────────────────────────────────
  VLIM = #.                    no. of var./2
    The maximum number of variables with missing
    values or values out of range permitted in a
    case. When the limit is exceeded, the case is
    not used in any computations (means,
    covariances, etc.) and the missing values in
    the case are not estimated.
  CLIM = #.                             50.0
    The maximum percentage of cases that can have
    missing values or values out of range for any
    variable or pair of variables in any group. If
    this limit is exceeded, estimation of missing
    values is not performed. If the COMPLETE method
    of computing covariances is used, this limit is
    applied to the cases with any missing values or
    values out of range.
```

Other options for regression estimation methods. The F-to-enter limit for three METHODS (SINGLE, TWOSTEP and STEP) can be changed. The preassigned value is 4.0 to avoid fitting too many predictor variables. Larger values are sometimes required to avoid overfitting.

The regression equation will include a constant term (intercept) to be estimated unless ZERO is specified.

The regression equation is formed by stepwise inverting (sweeping) the correlation matrix. The TOLERANCE checks that the variable about to be included is not a linear combination of variables already in the regression equation.

```
ESTimate ─────────────────────────────────
  ENTER = #.                       4.0/prev.
    The F-to-enter limit for three METHODS (SINGLE,
    TWOSTEP, and STEP). The F-to-enter value for a
    variable must exceed ENTER for the variable to
    enter the regression equation. F-to-enter is
    the square of the ratio of the coefficient, if
    entered into the regression equation, to its
    standard error.
  ZERO.    Not available          not ZERO /prev.
           when a GROUPING
           variable is specified.
    If ZERO is specified, the regression equation
    used will not have an intercept; i.e., it will
    pass through the origin. The correlation
    matrix, covariance matrix, regression
    statistics, and all but the univariate
    statistics are computed assuming variable means
    are zero.
    Note: this option is rarely used.
  TOLerance = #.    between 0.0      0.0001/prev.
                    and 1.0
    No variable is entered into the regression
    equation whose squared multiple correlation is
    greater than 1.0 minus TOLERANCE. A variable is
    also not entered if, by being entered, it would
    cause one of the variables already in the
    regression equation to violate the TOLERANCE
    check. For IBM 360 and 370 computers, TOLERANCE
    should not be less than $10^{-7}$.
```

Example AM.3 Scatterplots of the Variables and of the Estimated Values

Scatter plots of any pairs of variables can be requested. Two plots are formed for each pair, one showing cases with acceptable values for both variables, the second showing cases with an estimated value for at least one variable. The equations for the two regression lines

$$Y = a + bX$$

$$X = a' + b'Y$$

are printed below each plot. The lengths of both axes of the plot can be adjusted.

We demonstrate these plots by adding the following PLOT paragraph to the Control Language of

Example AM.2 (before the END paragraph).

```
-----------------------------------------
    / PLOT       XVAR IS AGE.
                 YVAR IS CHOLSTRL.
                 SIZE IS 40, 25.
-----------------------------------------
```

The plots are presented in Output AM.3. The plot on the left contains only cases that have acceptable values for both variables; the plot on the right presents only those points for which at least one value is estimated.

```
PLOT ───────────────────────────────────────┐
  XVAR = v list.                        none
    Names or subscripts of variables to be plotted
    along the X-axis (horizontally).
  YVAR = v list.                        none
    Names or subscripts of variables to be plotted
    along the Y-axis (vertically). The first
    variable in XVAR is plotted against the first
    in YVAR, the second against the second, etc.
    Two plots are printed for each pair of
    variables, the first showing cases with
    acceptable values for both variables, and the
    second showing cases with an estimated value
    for at least one of the variables.
  SIZE = #, #.                       50,35/prev.
    The first number is the length of the X-axis,
    and the second is the length of th Y-axis.
```

Output AM.3   Plots printed by PAM

--- results shown in Output AM.2 appear here ---

ON THE FOLLOWING PAGES TWO PLOTS APPEAR FOR EACH PAIR OF VARIABLES FOR WHICH PLOTS HAVE BEEN REQUESTED.   THE FIRST PLOT CONTAINS CASES FOR WHICH NEITHER VARIABLE HAS BEEN ESTIMATED. THE SECOND PLOT CONTAINS CASES FOR WHICH EITHER OR BOTH VARIABLES HAVE BEEN ESTIMATED. IF THE VARIABLE FOR THE X-AXIS HAS BEEN ESTIMATED BUT NOT THE VARIABLE FOR THE Y-AXIS, THE CASE IS PLOTTED WITH AN 'X'. IF THE VARIABLE FOR THE Y-AXIS HAS BEEN ESTIMATED BUT NOT THE VARIABLE FOR THE X-AXIS, THE CASE IS PLOTTED WITH A 'Y'. IF BOTH VARIABLES HAVE BEEN ESTIMATED, A 'B' IS USED. WHEN TWO OR MORE CASES ARE PLOTTED IN THE SAME POSITION AND IF THEY WOULD RECEIVE DIFFERENT PLOT CHARACTERS, THEN AN ASTERISK IS USED.

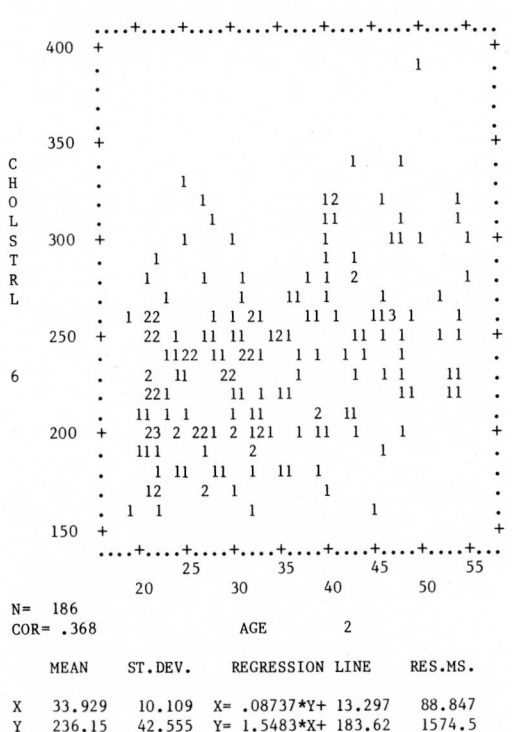

```
N=  186
COR= .368          AGE      2

    MEAN    ST.DEV.   REGRESSION LINE     RES.MS.

X  33.929   10.109   X= .08737*Y+ 13.297    88.847
Y  236.15   42.555   Y= 1.5483*X+ 183.62    1574.5
```

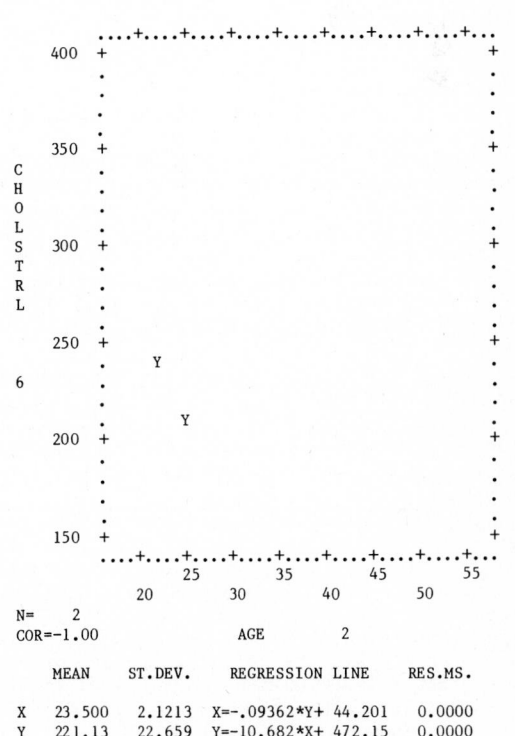

```
N=   2
COR=-1.00          AGE      2

    MEAN    ST.DEV.   REGRESSION LINE     RES.MS.

X  23.500   2.1213   X=-.09362*Y+ 44.201   0.0000
Y  221.13   22.659   Y=-10.682*X+ 472.15   0.0000
```

Example AM.4 Computing Estimates Separately for Each Subpopulation

In Example AM.2 we calculated estimates of the missing values using a regression technique. We do the same in this example except that the estimates are now calculated separately for women using birth control pills and for those who do not. We classify the cases into groups by specifying a GROUPING variable in the VARIABLE paragraph. The group NAMES and CODES are defined in the GROUP paragraph (see Chapter 5). The following instructions are added to those of Example AM.2 before the ESTIMATE paragraph (note that the first instruction, GROUPING IS BRTHPILL, is part of the VARIABLE paragraph.)

```
-------------------------------------
                 ⟋GROUPING IS BRTHPILL.

  / GROUP       CODES(5) ARE      1,   2.
                NAMES(5) ARE NOPILL, PILL.


  / ESTIMATE    METHOD IS REGR.
                MINIMUM.
                MAXIMUM.
-------------------------------------
```

A GROUPING variable modifies the following computations:

- Sample sizes, number of complete cases and percent of "incomplete" cases are printed for each group.
- For each variable the sample size and the percent of missing data are printed for each group.
- For each group a panel of univariate statistics is printed.
- Covariances are computed by using deviations from the group means to produce a pooled within-groups covariance matrix.
- Correlations are computed from the within-groups covariance matrix.
- The pooled (within-groups) covariance matrix and group means are used in the various methods of estimating missing values.
- The group means are used for all the methods of estimating missing values.
- The Mahalanobis distance from each case to the mean of its group is computed.

The results are presented in Output AM.4. They can be compared with those in Output AM.1 and AM.2, for which a GROUPING variable was not specified. The choice of METHOD will depend on the goal of the analysis. See discussion following Example AM.2.

Restrictions and missing codes for the GROUPING variable. The GROUPING variable must be discrete (have a limited number of values). CODES must be specified in the GROUP paragraph for the GROUPING variables. If the groups are NAMED, distinct names must be specified for each group. Note: these requirements are more restrictive than in other programs.

Cases in which the grouping variable is missing (i.e., cases that cannot be assigned to groups) are eliminated from all computations. If the GROUPING variable is missing and GROUP is specified in the ESTIMATE paragraph, the missing value of the GROUPING variable is estimated and the other missing values in that case are estimated as if the GROUPING variable were known to be equal to its estimated value.

Output AM.4

Estimates of missing values are computed separately for each subpopulation. Compare these results with those in Output AM.1 and AM.2

```
-------------------------------------------------------
```

```
WEIGHT VARIABLE . . . . . . . . . . . . . . .
GROUPING VARIABLE . . . . . . . . . . . . . .       5 BRTHPILL
```

PATTERN OF MISSING DATA AND DATA BEYOND LIMITS
COUNT OF MISSING VARIABLES INCLUDES DATA BEYOND LIMITS.
THE COLUMN LABELED WT. IS FOR THE CASE WEIGHT, IF ANY. 'M' REPRESENTS A MISSING VALUE. 'B' REPRESENTS A VALUE GREATER THAN THE MAXIMUM LIMIT. 'S' REPRESENTS A VALUE LESS THAN THE MINIMUM LIMIT.

					A H W C A C U
					G E E H L A R
					E I I O B L I
					G G L U C C
					H H S M I A
		NO OF		W	T T T I U C
CASE	CASE	MISS.		T	R N M I
LABEL	NO.	VARS.	GROUP	.	L D
1946	2	2	PILL		B M
1797	4	1	PILL		S
3	51	1	NOPILL		M
2877	86	1	PILL	M	
63	103	2	NOPILL		M M
2456	121	2	NOPILL	M	M
5	161	1	NOPILL	M	
1149	185	2	NOPILL	M	M

```
NUMBER OF CASES READ. . . . . . . . . . . . . . . .   188

     NUMBER OF CASES WITH NO DATA MISSING AND WITH
        POSITIVE CASE WEIGHT. . . . . . . . . . . . .   180
```

TABLE OF SAMPLE SIZES
(PERCENTAGES OF MISSING INCLUDE CASES WITH ANY VARIABLE MISSING OR BEYOND MAXIMUM OR MINIMUM LIMITS)

GROUP	SIZE	COMPLETE CASES	PERCENT MISSING
NOPILL	94	89	5.3
PILL	94	91	3.2

TABLE OF SAMPLE SIZES, NUMBER MISSING AND PERCENT MISSING FOR ALL GROUPS TAKEN TOGETHER. NUMBER AND PERCENT FOR MISSING INCLUDES VALUES OUTSIDE LIMITS.

VARIABLE NO.	NAME	SAMPLE SIZE	NUMBER MISSING	PERCENT MISSING
2	AGE	188	0	0.0
3	HEIGHT	186	2	1.1
4	WEIGHT	186	2	1.1
6	CHOLSTRL	186	2	1.1
7	ALBUMIN	186	2	1.1
8	CALCIUM	185	3	1.6
9	URICACID	187	1	0.5

SAMPLE SIZES FOR EACH VARIABLE IN EACH GROUP
VARIABLES WITHOUT MISSING DATA ARE NOT INCLUDED.

		NOPILL 1	PILL 2
HEIGHT	3	92	94
WEIGHT	4	93	93
CHOLSTRL	6	94	92
ALBUMIN	7	92	94
CALCIUM	8	92	93
URICACID	9	93	94

PERCENTAGES OF MISSING DATA FOR EACH VARIABLE IN EACH GROUP

THESE PERCENTAGES ARE BASED ON SAMPLE SIZES AND GROUP SIZES
REPORTED WITH THE UNIVARIATE SUMMARY STATISTICS BELOW.
VARIABLES WITHOUT MISSING DATA ARE NOT INCLUDED.

		NOPILL 1	PILL 2
HEIGHT	3	2.1	0.0
WEIGHT	4	1.1	1.1
CHOLSTRL	6	0.0	2.1
ALBUMIN	7	2.1	0.0
CALCIUM	8	2.1	1.1
URICACID	9	1.1	0.0

UNIVARIATE SUMMARY STATISTICS

GROUP IS NOPILL   SIZE IS   94

VARIABLE	SAMPLE SIZE	MEAN	STANDARD DEVIATION	COEFFICIENT OF VARIATION	SMALLEST VALUE	LARGEST VALUE	SMALLEST STANDARD SCORE	LARGEST STANDARD SCORE	SKEWNESS	KURTOSIS
2 AGE	94	33.81915	10.13984	0.299825	19.00000	55.00000	-1.46	2.09	0.40	-1.03
3 HEIGHT	92	64.08696	2.49242	0.038891	57.00000	69.00000	-2.84	1.97	-0.24	-0.34
4 WEIGHT	93	130.15054	18.88693	0.145116	95.00000	195.00000	-1.86	3.43	0.72	0.90
6 CHOLSTRL	94	232.96809	43.49155	0.186685	155.00000	335.00000	-1.79	2.35	0.29	-0.68
7 ALBUMIN	92	4.19783	0.34513	0.082217	3.20000	5.00000	-2.89	2.32	-0.05	-0.03
8 CALCIUM	92	9.98913	0.50349	0.050404	8.60000	11.10000	-2.76	2.21	-0.12	-0.35
9 URICACID	93	4.74194	1.03518	0.218303	2.50000	7.80000	-2.17	2.95	0.50	0.33

VALUES FOR KURTOSIS GREATER THAN ZERO INDICATE DISTRIBUTIONS
WITH HEAVIER TAILS THAN THE NORMAL DISTRIBUTION.

--- univariate statistics for the PILL group ---

--- ⑥ to ⑧ from Output AM.1 appear here ---

CORRELATIONS
(COMPUTED FROM POOLED WITHIN GROUPS COVARIANCE MATRIX)

		AGE 2	HEIGHT 3	WEIGHT 4	CHOLSTRL 6	ALBUMIN 7	CALCIUM 8	URICACID 9
AGE	2	1.000						
HEIGHT	3	0.079	1.000					
WEIGHT	4	0.252	0.464	1.000				
CHOLSTRL	6	0.368	0.008	0.143	1.000			
ALBUMIN	7	-0.071	0.020	-0.245	0.073	1.000		
CALCIUM	8	-0.031	0.160	0.075	0.256	0.441	1.000	
URICACID	9	0.176	0.132	0.299	0.259	0.011	0.195	1.000

EIGENVALUES OF CORRELATION MATRIX

```
1.9758
1.5360
1.1881
0.8093
0.6169
0.4832
0.3907
```

SQUARED MULTIPLE CORRELATIONS OF EACH VARIABLE WITH ALL OTHER VARIABLES
(MEASURES OF MULTICOLLINEARITY OF VARIABLES)
AND TESTS OF SIGNIFICANCE OF MULTIPLE REGRESSION
DEGREES OF FREEDOM FOR F-STATISTICS ARE   6 AND   180

VARIABLE NO. NAME	R-SQUARED	F-STATISTIC	SIGNIFICANCE (P LESS THAN)
2 AGE	0.197489	7.38	0.0
3 HEIGHT	0.248362	9.91	0.0
4 WEIGHT	0.373320	17.87	0.0
6 CHOLSTRL	0.235604	9.25	0.0
7 ALBUMIN	0.280552	11.70	0.0
8 CALCIUM	0.301196	12.93	0.0
9 URICACID	0.154925	5.50	0.00003

*** WARNING *** WHEN THE ALLVALUE OPTION IS USED, THE
DEGREES OF FREEDOM USED IN COMPUTING THE ABOVE F STATISTICS
INCLUDE CASES WITH MISSING VALUES. IF THE AMOUNT OF
MISSING DATA IS VERY LARGE, THE SIGNIFICANCE OF THE
F STATISTICS IS EXAGGERATED.

(output continued)

Output AM.4 (continued)

```
IN THE TABLE BELOW, ESTIMATES THAT ARE LESS THAN THE MINIMUMS
STATED IN THE VARIABLE PARAGRAPH ARE FLAGGED BY THE
LETTER 'S' (SMALL) AFTER THE ESTIMATE.  ESTIMATES
GREATER THAN THE MAXIMUMS ARE FLAGGED BY THE LETTER
'B' (BIG).
```

```
MAHALANOBIS DISTANCES ARE COMPUTED FROM EACH CASE TO THE
CENTROID OF ITS GROUP.  ONLY THOSE VARIABLES WHICH WERE
ORIGINALLY AVAILABLE ARE USED--ESTIMATED VALUES ARE NOT USED.
FOR LARGE MULTIVARIATE NORMAL SAMPLES, THE MAHALANOBIS
DISTANCES HAVE AN APPROXIMATELY CHI-SQUARE DISTRIBUTION WITH
THE NUMBER OF DEGREES OF FREEDOM EQUAL TO THE NUMBER OF
NONMISSING VARIABLES.  SIGNIFICANCE LEVELS REPORTED BELOW
THAT ARE LESS THAN .001 ARE FLAGGED WITH AN ASTERISK.
```

```
ESTIMATES OF MISSING DATA, MAHALANOBIS D-SQUARED (CHI-SQUARED)
AND SQUARED MULTIPLE CORRELATIONS WITH AVAILABLE VARIABLES
```

CASE LABEL	CASE NUMBER	MISSING VARIABLE	ESTIMATE	R-SQUARED	GROUP	CHI-SQ	CHISQ/DF	D.F.	SIGNIFICANCE
2381	1				NOPILL	4.677	0.668	7	0.6993
1946	2	6 CHOLSTRL	237.3527	0.188	PILL	10.793	2.159	5	0.0556
1946	2	8 CALCIUM	9.8481	0.258	PILL	10.793	2.159	5	0.0556
1610	3				NOPILL	5.267	0.752	7	0.6274
1797	4	6 CHOLSTRL	205.2696	0.236	PILL	6.342	1.057	6	0.3860

```
          --- similar statistics for cases 5 to 184 ---
```

CASE LABEL	CASE NUMBER	MISSING VARIABLE	ESTIMATE	R-SQUARED	GROUP	CHI-SQ	CHISQ/DF	D.F.	SIGNIFICANCE
1149	185	3 HEIGHT	66.6665	0.241	NOPILL	8.419	1.684	5	0.1346
1149	185	8 CALCIUM	9.8471	0.294	NOPILL	8.419	1.684	5	0.1346
575	186				PILL	10.813	1.545	7	0.1470
2271	187				NOPILL	6.594	0.942	7	0.4724
39	188				PILL	22.041	3.149	7	0.0025

```
ESTIMATION OF MISSING DATA COMPLETED
```

VARiable ─────────────────────────────────
GROUPing = v.   no grouping/prev.
The name or subscript of the variable used to
classify the cases into groups. A GROUP
paragraph (Section 5.5) must be included to
specify CODES (not CUTPOINTS) for the GROUPING
variable. If the groups are named each name
must be distinct. Grouping the cases modifies
the computations as described above. If
GROUPING is not specified or is set to zero,
there is no grouping variable.

ESTimate ─────────────────────────────────
GROUP.   no
If GROUP is specified, missing values of the
GROUPING variable are estimated. An estimate
for a missing value is first obtained by the
METHOD specified; the CODE of the nearest group
is used as the value of the GROUPING variable.

Example AM.5 How to Save the Covariance Matrix and the Filled-in Data Matrix for Use in Subsequent Multivariate Analyses

PAM can be used to prepare data for another program. The BMDP File (Chapter 7) can be used to save the "completed" data matrix, including the estimates for the missing data, the COVARIANCE matrix and the correlation matrix formed from the dichotomized values (CORRDICH, p. 221). The data or matrices can be further analyzed by other BMDP programs.

PAM is intended primarily to serve as a preprocessor for multivariate analysis. For example, the missing values can be replaced by estimates and then a factor analysis, discriminant analysis, repeated measures analysis of variance or cluster analysis can be requested. The grouping variable, if it is missing, should not ordinarily be estimated. If PAM is used as a preprocessor for regression, estimates of missing data for the independent variables should not be made if the independent variables are fixed. If some independent variables are random, they should be estimated from other random predictors but not from the dependent variable. Missing values of the dependent variable should not ordinarily be estimated prior to regression analysis since the R^2 in the regression analysis would then be inflated. If you estimate missing values of the dependent variable for regression, analysis of variance or analysis of covariance, care should be taken in making inferences on the data with the estimates since the residual mean square will be too small and R^2 too big. Thus, while estimation of missing values may allow exploratory data analysis, rigorous hypothesis testing cannot be performed.

When there are missing data for the dependent variable in a repeated measures analysis of variance (P2V), an entire case is deleted if any dependent variable is missing. PAM may be used to estimate the dependent variable, but bias enters the analysis. However, the bias will be small if the number of missing values is small. In some studies it may be preferable to eliminate cases with missing data; in others, the number of levels of the repeated measures factors may be so large that the number of cases with some missing data may be very large, and so it may be better to estimate missing data. Methods of treating missing data problems are discussed by Frane (1976) and Beale and Little (1975).

In our final example we save the filled-in data and the covariance matrix in a BMDP File (see a) below) and then further analyze COVA by P4M (Factor Analysis, Section 18.1) (see b) below). The estimates of the missing values are made using the regression method STEP. The covariance matrix is computed as described above for ALLVALUE. (If EIGEN or RIDGE is specified, the smoothed or ridged correlation matrices are saved.) It is economical for P4M to start the analysis from the covariance matrix. (The filled-in data matrix is also available in the file for use when P4M computes factor scores for each case.)

a) For our PAM instructions we add a SAVE paragraph to the Control Language of Example AM.2.

```
------------------------------------------
/ ESTIMATE    METHOD IS STEP.
             MINIMUM.
             MAXIMUM.
```

```
/ SAVE       UNIT IS 9.
             NEW.
             CODE IS WERNER.
             CONTENT IS DATA, COVA.
------------------------------------------
```

Note: The systems information that precedes the Control Language must contain a card stating that the BMDP File will be stored on unit 9. In addition, space must be allocated for the system file (Section 7.1).

b) BMDP instructions for using the covariance matrix and filled-in data matrix in a P4M factor analysis with results like those described in Example 4M.1 are:

```
------------------------------------------
/ PROBLEM   TITLE IS 'WERNER BLOOD CHEMISTRY DATA'.
/ INPUT     UNIT IS 9.
            CODE IS WERNER.
            CONTENT IS COVA.

/ END
------------------------------------------
```

Note: The system information to initiate an analysis by P4M must specify a file on unit 9 that has the system file name used when PAM wrote the file.

The results are shown in Output AM.5a and AM.5b.

```
SAVE ─────────────────────────────────────
  CONTent = (one or more)                    DATA
            DATA, COVA, CORRDICH.
  The matrix to be saved:
  DATA      -- the data with missing values
               replaced by estimates, if any.
  COVA      -- the covariance matrix. If a
               GROUPING variable is specified, the
               pooled within-group covariance
               matrix is saved.
  CORRDICH  -- the correlation matrix for the
               dichotomies (see p. 221).
```

Additional Print Options (Covariances, Inverses, Mahalanobis Distance, Eigenvalues, etc.)

Output AM.1 and AM.2 illustrate many of the results that are printed by PAM. Several matrices, such as the covariance matrix and the inverse of the correlation matrix, can also be printed. Some of the matrices, such as those in Output AM.2, depend on whether missing values are estimated, and possibly on the method of estimation. If the preassigned options only are desired (as in Output AM.1 and AM.2), the PRINT paragraph need not be used.

In Output AM.1 the first five cases of the data are printed (⑥). If more (or fewer) cases are wanted,

    CASE = number of cases to print.

can be specified.

You can request any of the MATRICES listed below. However, if you specify any matrices, only those specified are printed.

Output AM.5 a and b   Using PAM to create a BMDP File for the covariance matrix and the filled-in data matrix (a) and using the file in P4M (b)

AM.5 (a)   REQUESTED OUTPUT BMDP FILE. . . . . . UNIT. . .   9
                                                  CODE. . .   WERNER
                                                  LABEL . .
                                                  CONTENT .
                                                             COVA
                                                             DATA

              --- results in Output AM.1 are printed here ---

          BMDP FILE IS BEING WRITTEN ON UNIT   9
          CODE. . . IS   WERNER
          CONTENT . IS   COVA
          LABEL . . IS
          VARIABLES ARE
              2 AGE   3 HEIGHT   4 WEIGHT   5 BRTHPILL   6 CHOLSTRL
              7 ALBUMIN   8 CALCIUM   9 URICACID

  --- the estimates of the missing data appear here. The distance of each case
            from the mean is not printed for METHOD IS STEP ---

          BMDP FILE ON UNIT 9 HAS BEEN COMPLETED.

          BMDP FILE IS BEING WRITTEN ON UNIT   9
          CODE. . . IS   WERNER
          CONTENT . IS   DATA
          LABEL . . IS
          VARIABLES ARE
              1 ID   2 AGE   3 HEIGHT   4 WEIGHT   5 BRTHPILL
              6 CHOLSTRL   7 ALBUMIN   8 CALCIUM   9 URICACID

          BMDP FILE ON UNIT 9 HAS BEEN COMPLETED.

AM.5 (b)   INPUT BMDP FILE
                  CODE. . . IS   WERNER
                  CONTENT . IS   COVA
                  LABEL . . IS

                  VARIABLES
                      2 AGE   3 HEIGHT   4 WEIGHT   5 BRTHPILL   6 CHOLSTRL
                      7 ALBUMIN   8 CALCIUM   9 URICACID

                  VARIABLES TO BE USED
                      2 AGE   3 HEIGHT   4 WEIGHT   5 BRTHPILL   6 CHOLSTRL
                      7 ALBUMIN   8 CALCIUM   9 URICACID

              NUMBER OF VARIABLES TO BE USED.   8

              CORRELATION MATRIX

                            AGE   HEIGHT   WEIGHT   BRTHPILL CHOLSTRL ALBUMIN CALCIUM URICACID
                             2   3   4   5   6   7   8   9

              AGE   2   1.000
              HEIGHT   3   0.080   1.000
              WEIGHT   4   0.252   0.471   1.000
              BRTHPILL   5   0.0   0.169   0.074   1.000
              CHOLSTRL   6   0.368   0.020   0.148   0.076   1.000
              ALBUMIN   7 −0.072   −0.021   −0.255   −0.240   0.053   1.000
              CALCIUM   8 −0.032   0.149   0.070   −0.056   0.250   0.444   1.000
              URICACID   9   0.176   0.134   0.300   0.025   0.260   0.007   0.194   1.000

              --- the results of the factor analysis are printed ---

----

PRINT ─────────────────────────────────
| CASE = #.   5/prev.
| Number of cases for which the data are to be
| printed. In the output missing values are
| replaced by MISSING, values greater than the
| upper limit by TOOBIG and values less than the
| lower limit by TOOSMALL. The data are printed
| after transformations, if any, are performed.
| MATRices = (one or more) PAT, FREQ,
| PAT, FREQ, CORRDICH,   CORRDICH,
| CORR, EIGEN, EST,   CORR,
| DIS, COVA, CREG,   EIGEN,EST,
| SUMW.   DIS/prev.
| The list of matrices to be printed. The
| matrices are
| PAT   -- the pattern of missing data and
| values beyond limits (② in Output
| AM.1). If the number of variables
| exceeds 100, only the first 100
| variables are used.
| FREQ   -- the sample sizes and percentage
| missing or out of range for each
| variable and for each pair of
| variables (⑦ and ⑧). It is
| printed for pairs of variables only
| if TYPE is ALLVALUE.
| CORRDICH -- correlations computed using the
| dichotomies: 1.0 if the value is
| acceptable and 0.0 otherwise (⑨).
| Variables that contain only
| acceptable values or contain no
| acceptable values are not included
| in CORRDICH.
| CORR   -- correlations computed from the
| acceptable values or complete cases
| using the ALLVALUE, or COMPLETE
| methods (⑩). If the method is
| ALLVALUE and the correlation matrix
| is _not_ positive semidefinite, the
| correlation matrix is smoothed
| (recomputed) using only the
| positive eigenvalues and the
| associated eigenvectors (see
| Appendix A.9).
| EIGEN   -- eigenvalues of the correlation
| matrix (⑪). If the method of
| computing correlations is ALLVALUE
| and the correlation matrix is not
| positive semidefinite, both the
| eigenvalues of the original
| correlation matrix and the
| eigenvalues of the smoothed
| (recomputed) correlation matrix are
| printed.
| EST   -- the estimates of the missing data
| (this option is not available if
| the METHOD used is MEAN). If the
| METHOD used is REGR, the
| Mahalanobis distance from the mean
| is also reported for cases that
| contain estimated values.
| DIS   -- the distance of each case from the
| mean is computed (EST reports
| distances for only those cases in
| which values are estimated). Both
| EST and DIS are shown in 13 in
| Output AM.2. DIS is available only
| when the METHOD used in REGR.
| COVA   -- the matrix of covariances. (based
| on the smoothed correlation matrix)
| CREG   -- the inverse of the correlation
| matrix. This is available only if
| the method of estimating missing
| values is REGR.
| RREG   -- the inverse of the correlation
| matrix standardized to have ones on
| the diagonal (in the same way that
| a covariance matrix is converted to
| a correlation matrix). This is
| available only if the method of
| estimating missing values is REGR.
| SUMW   -- matrix of the sum of case weights
| for each pair of variables. It is
| printed only if a case WEIGHT
| variable is specified and if
| ALLVALUE is used to compute
| correlations.
──────────────────────────────────────

The preassigned matrices that are printed if no
specification is given are PAT, FREQ, CORRDICH,
CORR, EIGEN, EST, and DIS. However, if you want only
the univariate statistics and pattern of missing
values, you can specify

        / PRINT   MATRICES ARE PAT, FREQ.

Since the covariance and correlation matrices are
not needed, they are not computed and a lot of
computation is avoided.
Note: If the correlation matrix is not to be
printed and the ESTIMATION METHOD is NONE or MEAN,
then the correlation matrix, covariance matrix,
sample sizes for pairs of variables, etc. will not
be computed and cannot be output to BMDP File. This
results in a considerable reduction in the
computational and computer memory requirements;
e.g., several hundred variables can be screened when
the correlation matrix is not needed.

Case Weights

Cases can be weighted by specifying a WEIGHT
variable in the VARIABLE paragraph. The effect the
weight variable has on computing means, covariances
and correlations is described in P8D (p. 215). The
weighted correlation matrix is used in estimating
missing data; its inverse is used in computing the
Mahalanobis distance.

VARiable ─────────────────────────────
| WEIGHt = v.   no case weights/prev.
| Name or subscript of the variable containing
| weights for each case. The effect case weights
| have on computations is described in P8D
| (p. 215). If WEIGHT is not specified or is set
| to zero, there is no case weight variable.
──────────────────────────────────────

SIZE OF PROBLEM

When correlations are computed or when missing
values are estimated by any METHOD except MEAN,
about 60 variables and 10 groups can be analyzed on

medium sized computer systems. If METHOD is MEAN or NONE and a correlation matrix is not computed, about 130 variables and 10 groups can be analyzed or about 400 variables when there is no grouping variable. Appendix B describes how to increase the capacity of the program.

COMPUTATIONAL METHOD

The data are read and transformations are performed in single precision. Computations are performed in double precision except for the matrix of sum of weights (SUMW), which is computed in single precision.

The data are read in casewise and written on a scratch file unless all cases with missing values can be held in computer memory. Univariate statistics and the covariance matrix are computed using either complete cases only or using all values as in the ALLVALUE option in P8D. (The covariance and correlation matrices are not computed unless the correlation matrix is to be printed).

If the ALLVALUE option is selected, the data are processed twice. During the first pass, the univariate statistics and the covariance matrix for the complete cases are computed using the method of provisional means (Appendix A.2); during the second pass, the ALLVALUE covariance matrix is computed using the covariance matrix for the complete cases and the data for the incomplete cases. If complete cases only are used, the data are read once and the covariance matrix is also computed by the method of provisional means. When a grouping variable is specified, the pooled within-groups covariance matrix is computed.

The maximum likelihood method of estimating the covariance matrix is adapted from Orchard and Woodbury (1972). The methods of estimating missing values are described in Appendix A.10.

If case weights are used, weights are adjusted so that the average nonzero weight is one.

ACKNOWLEDGEMENT

PAM was designed and programmed by James Frane. Subroutines for the maximum likelihood estimation were programmed by Laszlo Engelman.

SUMMARY

Order of Input Cards

```
// (job card)
// EXEC BIMED,PROG=BMDPAM        (see Appendix E)
//SYSIN DD *
/ PROBLEM
/ INPUT
/ VARIABLE
/ GROUP
/ TRANSFORM
/ SAVE
/ ESTIMATE
/ PRINT
/ PLOT
/ END
    (data if on cards)
// (system card)
```

Full sets of BMDP paragraphs (and data, if on cards) can be repeated for additional problems; see Section 5.8.

Paragraph Statement	Preassigned	Comment and Manual Reference
/ VARiable		Additional options to specify case weights and to classify cases into groups.
WEIGht = v.	none	Name or subscript of variable containing weights for each case. * 231
GROUPing = v.	none	Name or subscript of variable to define group membership (must also include /GROUP for CODES, not CUTPOINTS). * 228

- -

/ ESTimate		Optional to estimate invalid values. METHod must be specified. TYPE effects computation of univariate statistics, covariances and correlations.
METHod = c.	NONE.	Specifies how to estimate values that are missing or out of range (one only). (To estimate extreme values see MIN and MAX below). The regression estimates (SINGLE, TWOSTEP and STEP) use the ENTER limit. * 223 MEAN — mean (or group mean) is substituted SINGLE — simple regression estimate using the most highly correlated variable TWOSTEP — regression estimate using up to 2 variables selected by stepwise regression STEP — stepwise regression estimate using all variables that satisfy ENTER limit REGR — regression estimate using all available variables (ENTER limit is ignored) NONE — no estimation of missing values
TYPE = c.	ALLVALUE.	Specifies cases to be included in the computation of means, covariances and correlations (one only). * 221 ALLVALUE — use all cases with acceptable values for variables used. R matrix is smoothed to be positive semidefinite COMPLETE — cases with missing values or values out of range are not used ML — maximum likelihood
ITERation = #.	10.	Maximum number of iterations for ML. * 221
CONverge = #.	.01	Convergence criterion for ML. Convergence criterion is applied to relative charge in variances and absolute charge in correlations between iterations. * 221
RIDGE = #.	none	Multiply each off-diagonal element of the correlation matrix by number specified before eigenvalues are smoothed; the number must be less than one. * 221
EIGEN = #.	0.001	Replace eigenvalues less than # by zero in smoothing the missing value correlation matrix. * 221
MAXimum. MINimum.	no	Treat values greater than those listed as MAX or less than those MIN in / VAR as missing values (i.e., estimated using METH =). If omitted, METH applies only to the estimation of missing values. * 224
GROUP.	no	Compute estimates of the missing values for the GROUPing variable, which must also be specified in / VAR. (The result, using METH = is rounded to the nearest CODE.) * 228
ENTER = #.	4.0.	F-to-enter limit for METH = SINGLE, TWOSTEP or STEP. * 224
ZERO.	no	Compute estimates from regression equation without intercept (zero means are assumed). Option rarely used. * 224
TOLerance = #.	.0001.	Variables are not used in regression estimates whose R^2 (with entered variables) > 1-TOL. * 224
VLIMit = #.	(see note)	Maximum number of variables missing (or out of range) for any case. If exceeded, case is dropped. Note: Preassigned value half the number of variables used.
CLIMit = %.	50.	Maximum percent of cases with missing values permitted for any variable, or any pair of variables (unless METH = MEAN.). If exceeded, no missing values are estimated. * 224

- -

(continued)

(continued)

Paragraph Statement	Preassigned	Comment and Manual Reference
/ PRINT		Optional to request printed output. If omitted, 5 CASES and the matrices underlined below are printed. 231
CASE = #.	5.	Number of cases for which data are printed. *

MATRices = c list.	(see comment)	If MATR is omitted, the matrices underlined below are printed; otherwise only the specified matrices are printed.
		PAT -pattern of missing data and values outside limits
		FREQ -sample size and % missing; printed for pairs of variables only if / EST TYPE = ALLVALUE
		CORRDICH -correlations using dichotomies: 1.0 if value is acceptable, 0.0 otherwise
		CORR -correlations; if / EST TYPE = ALLVALUE, the matrix is computed using only positive eigenvalues
		COVA -covariance matrix
		EIGEN -eigenvalues of correlation matrix; printed for the original matrix and the smoothed matrix if / EST TYPE = ALLVALUE
		EST -estimates of missing data (not available if / EST METH = NONE or MEAN); if METH = REGRESS. Mahalanobis D^2 is reported for cases with estimated values
		SUMW -available only if a case WEIGHT variable is specified and / EST TYPE = ALLVALUE; print matrix of sum of case weights for each pair of variables.
		Options below are available only for / EST METH = REGRESS:
		    DIS -Mahalanobis distance of each case from mean
		    CREG -inverse of the correlation matrix
		    RREG -inverse of the correlation matrix standardized to have 1's on the diagonal

/ PLOT		Optional to specify plots. The first variable in XVAR is plotted against the first variable in YVAR, the second against the second. Two plots are printed for each pair of variables, the first showing cases with acceptable values for both variables, and the second showing cases with an estimated value for at least one variable. 225
XVAR = v list.	none	Names or subscripts of variables to be plotted along the x-axis (horizontally).
YVAR = v list.	none	Names or subscripts of variables to be plotted along the y-axis (vertically).
SIZE = #, #.	50,35.	Width of x-axis (characters); height of y-axis (lines). *
/ SAVE		Additional option required only if a BMDP File is to be created to save special results. 229
CONTent = c list.	DATA.	What to save in BMDP File (one or more): DATA -data; estimates (if any) are inserted for invalid values CORRDICH -correlation matrix for the dichotomies COVA -covariance matrix; pooled within-groups matrix is saved when GROUPING variable is specified

Key:

/	-indicates paragraph		*	-assigned value remains the same for additional problems
.	-period ends a sentence			
●	-required		VT	-number of variables after transformations
v	-variable (name or subscript)		list	-more than one item, often one per var.
g	-group (name or subscript)			
#	-number			Capitalized letters-paragraph or sentence names recognized by BMDP
'c'	-characters (name or parameter) may omit apostrophes if contiguous letters only			Page numbers following refer to this Manual

13
REGRESSION

Regression is used to quantify the relationship between variables when the value of one variable is affected by changes in the values of other variables. The affected variable is the dependent (predicted) variable and the others are the independent (predictor) variables. The correlation between two variables can indicate whether an increase in one variable is associated with an increase in the other variable.

The relationship between a dependent variable y and an independent variable x is linear if the expected value of y can be expressed as $\alpha + \beta x$; i.e.,

$$E(y) = \alpha + \beta x$$

where α and β are the coefficients (parameters) of the regression equation. α is called the intercept and β the slope of the regression.

When there is one independent variable, as in the above equation, the regression is called simple linear regression. The program P6D -- Bivariate (Scatter) Plots -- (Section 10.2) can plot one variable against the other, estimate the regression equation relating the variables, and indicate on the frame of the plot where to draw the regression line. Three programs described in this chapter (P1R, P2R and P9R) can also be used to estimate the parameters of a simple linear regression. P6R (Chapter 18) can be used to obtain regression equations for several dependent variables from the same set of independent variables (multivariate regression).

A model of multiple linear regression is written as

$$E(y) = \alpha + \beta_1 x_1 + \beta_2 x_2 + \ldots$$

where $x_1, x_2, \ldots$ are the independent variables and $\beta_1, \beta_2, \ldots$ their regression coefficients. When the model has this form, the selection of variables to be in the model can be a major problem; data may have been collected on more variables than are necessary in the model, or an important variable that is needed in the model may have been omitted from the study.

In this chapter we describe

These programs differ in four important respects: the criterion for including independent variables in the multiple linear regression, the ability to repeat the analysis on subgroups of the cases and compare the subgroups, the residual analysis available, and the numerical precision used for computations.

We also describe a fifth program

P5R is used when the expected value of the dependent variable can be approximated by a polynomial expression in terms of a single independent variable.

P1R estimates the multiple linear regression equation using all the independent variables. Results are reported only for the equation containing all the variables. The regression can be estimated from all the cases, and also from cases in separate groups if specified. When the cases are in groups, the regression equations are tested for equality across groups. Equality of slopes (with possibly different intercepts) is tested in P1V (Section 15.1).

P2R enters and removes variables from a multiple linear regression equation in a stepwise manner. That is, at each step variables are removed and/or entered into the equation, according to one of four criteria. Forward stepping (beginning with no predictors) and backward stepping (beginning with all predictors) are possible. The order of entry of the variables can be predetermined, partially specified or determined only by the criteria for entry and removal of variables.

P9R identifies "best" subsets of predictor variables or can be used for multiple linear regression without selecting subsets. Best is defined in terms of the sample R-squared, adjusted R-squared, or Mallows' C_p. For example, if adjusted R-squared is chosen, the best subset is the subset that maximizes adjusted R-squared. The number of best subsets (up to ten) can be specified. Thus, not only the best but also the second best, third best, etc. subsets are identified to provide several good alternatives. Computations are performed in double precision.

P4R computes a regression analysis for the dependent variable on a set of principal components computed from the independent variables. The principal components are computed from the original variables (using the covariance matrix). The regression analysis is performed in a stepwise manner and the resulting coefficients are reported in terms of both the principal components and the original or standardized variables. The order of entry of components can be based on the magnitude of eigenvalues or on the absolute value of correlation between the component and the dependent variable.

The methods of variable selection differ in P2R, P9R and P4R. P9R optimizes a criterion by searching the relevant subsets of the variables (not all subsets are computed) by the Furnival and Wilson (1974a,b) algorithm. It can treat at most 27 independent variables and is about as fast as stepwise regression for this number of variables. P2R can treat a much larger problem (about 150 variables) but reports a simple series of solutions (at different steps). P4R is most valuable when subsets of the independent variables are highly correlated or when the number of variables is large relative to the number of cases; the principal components provide linear combinations of the independent variables to be entered stepwise into the regression equation.

The solutions obtained by P2R, P9R and P4R are all based on the data supplied. Other samples from the same population can be expected to lead to other "optimal" solutions that will differ to some degree from each other. This problem is common to all statistical procedures, including these variable selection methods. The alternative subsets provided by P9R may help the analyst evaluate the "uniqueness" of the solution.

P9R uses double precision for many of its computations. The other programs use single precision. The precision can be important when the coefficient of variation is very small or when the correlation matrix for the predictor variables is nearly singular.

Programs P1R, P2R, P4R and P9R estimate the regression coefficients and their standard errors and print the covariance and correlation matrices. They all print and plot predicted values and residuals against the variables. P9R can perform more extensive analyses of residuals than the other programs: it can compute and plot standardized residuals, the residual for each case based upon omitting the case from the regression analysis, and Cook's measure of the influence of each case on the regression equation.

Each program can begin an analysis from the data or from a covariance or correlation matrix. A BMDP File can be created that contains a covariance matrix or that contains residuals and predicted values as well as the data.

Cases with missing values or values out of range are not used by these programs. If too many cases are affected by this restriction, you may first want to read Chapter 12 and use a missing value covariance or correlation matrix as input to these regression programs.

P5R is used when the dependent variable has a nonlinear relationship with one independent variable that can be approximated by a low order polynomial. The degree of the polynomial is determined in a stepwise manner. Orthogonal polynomials are used in the computation. Goodness-of-fit statistics are printed for each polynomial, except the one with the highest degree. The predicted values and residuals can be plotted against the independent variable.

In the regression equations described above we wrote the expected value of y, $E(y)$, rather than y. If we write y, then an error term must be added. That is,

$$E(y) = \alpha + \beta x$$

is equivalent to

$$y = \alpha + \beta x + \varepsilon$$

where ε represents an error term (with mean zero). If the error term has a constant variance across all cases, least squares regression (used by these programs) is the usual method of estimating the coefficients. If the error term's variance is not constant, weighted least squares regression is more appropriate; the data in each case are weighted by the inverse of the variance for that case. All regression programs except P4R allow case weights to be specified.

Some apparently nonlinear relationships between x and y can also be analyzed by linear regression. For example,

$$E(y) = \alpha + \beta/x$$

is nonlinear in x but linear in $z = 1/x$ and

$$E(y) = \alpha + \beta e^x$$

is nonlinear in x but linear in $z = e^x$. The transformation $z = 1/x$ or $z = e^x$ can be done as part of the analysis.

Case weights may be required when a nonlinear function is transformed into a linear function by modifying the dependent variable. For example

$$E(y) = \alpha e^{\beta x} \qquad \text{or} \qquad y = \alpha e^{\beta x} + \varepsilon$$

is often transformed to

$$\ln(y) = \alpha' + \beta x + \varepsilon'$$

where $\alpha' = \ln(\alpha)$ and ε' is the error term for $\ln(y)$. However, if ε in the original equation has constant variance across cases, then ε' <u>cannot</u> have constant variance and case weights are desirable for the latter analysis. If ε' has constant variance across cases, weighting will not be necessary.

Many nonlinear functions cannot be transformed to linear, such as the sum of two exponentials

$$E(y) = \beta_1 e^{\beta_2 x} + \beta_3 e^{\beta_4 x} .$$

Methods of estimating the coefficients of nonlinear regressions are described in Chapter 14.

When there is more than one dependent variable, the interrelations of the variables can be studied by multivariate methods (Chapter 18). Categorical (multinomial) data can be fitted by a log-linear model (Chapter 11, **p. 176**).

P1R

13.1 Multiple Linear Regression

ABSTRACT

P1R estimates a least squares regression equation between a dependent (predicted) variable and one or more independent (predictor) variables. The computations are performed on all the data and, if requested, on subsets or groups of cases. The equality of regression lines across groups is tested. The multiple correlation coefficient, standard error of an estimated value, standardized and unstandardized regression coefficients, significance of coefficient and p values are printed. Data, residuals and predicted values can be plotted in several ways and saved on a BMDP File.

Let y represent the value of the dependent variable and x_1, x_2, ..., x_p the values of the independent variables. P1R estimates by least squares the coefficients β_1, β_2, ..., β_p in the equation

$$y = \alpha + \beta_1 x_1 + \beta_2 x_2 + \cdots + \beta_p x_p + \varepsilon$$

where ε represents the error. That is, it finds a, b_1, b_2, ..., b_p (the estimates of α, β_1, β_2, ..., β_p) that minimize

$$\Sigma(y - a - b_1 x_1 - b_2 x_2 - \cdots - b_p x_p)^2$$

where the summation is over the cases used in the analysis. When case weights are specified,

$$\Sigma w(y - a - b_1 x_1 - b_2 x_2 - \cdots - b_p x_p)^2$$

is minimized, where w is the case weight.

WHERE TO FIND IT

Example 1R.1 Basic Setup for Multiple Linear Regression

In our first example we use P1R to analyze the Werner blood chemistry data (Table 5.1). We specify that CHOLSTRL is the dependent variable and that AGE, WEIGHT and URICACID are independent variables. Only the REGRESS paragraph is specific to P1R, the remaining BMDP instructions are common to all BMDP programs and are described in Chapter 5. Methods for data editing or transformations are given in Chapter 6. We use the following instructions

```
/ PROBLEM    TITLE IS 'WERNER BLOOD CHEMISTRY DATA'.
/ INPUT      VARIABLES ARE 9.
            FORMAT IS '(A4, 5F4.0, 3F4.1)'.
/ VARIABLE   NAMES ARE ID, AGE, HEIGHT, WEIGHT,
                        BRTHPILL, CHOLSTRL, ALBUMIN,
                        CALCIUM, URICACID.
            MAXIMUM IS (6)400.
            MINIMUM IS (6)150.
            LABEL IS ID.

/ REGRESS    DEPENDENT IS CHOLSTRL.
            INDEPENDENT ARE AGE, WEIGHT, URICACID.
/ END
```

(See end of this P1R section for organization of systems information, BMDP instructions and data.)

The results of the above analysis are presented in Output 1R.1. Circled numbers below correspond to those in the output.

The model fitted by P1R is

$$y = a + b_1 x_1 + b_2 x_2 + \cdots + b_p x_p + \varepsilon$$

where

y is the dependent variable
x_1, ..., x_p are the independent variables
b_1, ..., b_p are the regression coefficients
a is the intercept
p is the number of independent variables
ε is the error with mean zero

The predicted value $\hat{y}$ for each case is

$$\hat{y} = a + b_1 x_1 + b_2 x_2 + \cdots + b_p x_p$$

The residual for each case is $(y - \hat{y})$. We have omitted a subscript indicating case number from the formulas.

(1) Only complete cases are used in the computations; i.e., cases that have no missing values or values out of range. Therefore only 180 of the original 188 cases are used. All variables are checked for invalid values unless USE is specified in the VARIABLE paragraph (Section 5.4, p. 42), in

Output 1R.1   Multiple linear regression. Circled numbers correspond to those in the text
----

--- the BMDP instructions read by P1R are printed and interpreted ---


```
REGRESSION INTERCEPT. . . . . . . . . . . . .NON-ZERO
GROUPING VARIABLE . . . . . . . . . . . . . .
WEIGHT VARIABLE . . . . . . . . . . . . . . .
PRINT COVARIANCE MATRIX . . . . . . . . . . .      NO
PRINT CORRELATION MATRIX. . . . . . . . . . .      NO
PRINT CORRELATION OF REGRESSION COEFFICIENTS. .    NO       ①
PRINT RESIDUALS . . . . . . . . . . . . . . .      NO
PRINT NORMAL PROBABILITY PLOT . . . . . . . .      NO
PRINT DETRENDED NORMAL PROBABILITY PLOT . . . .    NO

NUMBER OF CASES READ. . . . . . . . . . . . .     188
       CASES WITH DATA MISSING OR BEYOND LIMITS . .  8
              REMAINING NUMBER OF CASES . . . . . . . .  180
```


VARIABLE ②	MEAN	STANDARD DEVIATION	COEFFICIENT OF VARIATION	MINIMUM	MAXIMUM
2 AGE	33.53819	9.89836	0.29514	19.00000	55.00000
3 HEIGHT	64.46597	2.48213	0.03850	57.00000	71.00000
4 WEIGHT	131.09384	20.49977	0.15637	94.00000	215.00000
5 BRTHPILL	1.50551	0.50136	0.33302	1.00000	2.00000
6 CHOLSTRL	235.83821	42.74364	0.18124	155.00000	390.00000
7 ALBUMIN	4.12052	0.35871	0.08706	3.20000	5.00000
8 CALCIUM	9.96773	0.47279	0.04743	8.80000	11.10000
9 URICACID	4.75551	1.12111	0.23575	2.20000	9.90000


```
REGRESSION TITLE. . . . . . . . . . . . . . .WERNER BLOOD CHEMISTRY DATA
DEPENDENT VARIABLE. . . . . . . . . . . . . .       6 CHOLSTRL
TOLERANCE . . . . . . . . . . . . . . . . . .  0.0100

ALL DATA CONSIDERED AS A SINGLE GROUP

MULTIPLE R          ③   0.4175        STD. ERROR OF EST.          39.1698
MULTIPLE R-SQUARE        0.1743
```

ANALYSIS OF VARIANCE

	SUM OF SQUARES	DF	MEAN SQUARE	F RATIO	P(TAIL)
④ REGRESSION	57004.242	3	19001.414	12.385	0.0
RESIDUAL	270032.000	176	1534.273		

VARIABLE	COEFFICIENT	STD. ERROR	STD. REG COEFF	T	P(2 TAIL)	TOLERANCE
INTERCEPT ⑤	151.42036					
AGE 2	1.38971	0.309	0.322	4.497	0.000	0.915924
WEIGHT 4	0.00289	0.153	0.001	0.019	0.985	0.869294
URICACID 9	7.87099	2.769	0.206	2.843	0.005	0.889443

which case only the variables in the USE statement are checked.

② Univariate statistics are computed for each variable using the complete cases
- mean
- standard deviation
- coefficient of variation
- minimum observed value (not out of range)
- maximum observed value (not out of range)

③ The multiple correlation R is printed (i.e., the correlation of the dependent variable with the predicted value) as well as
- the multiple R^2
- standard error of the estimate: $\{\Sigma(y_j-\hat{y}_j)^2/(N-p)\}^{\frac{1}{2}}$

④ The analysis of variance table for the regression is printed. It contains
- the regression sum of squares: $\Sigma(\hat{y}_j-\bar{y})^2$

- the residual sum of squares: $\Sigma(y_j-\hat{y}_j)^2$

- the F ratio that tests significance of the regression

⑤ A summary table for the regression is printed. It contains
- the coefficient, b_i. The equation is
    CHOLESTRL = 151.42 + 1.390 AGE + .003 WEIGHT
                        + 7.871 URICACID.
- the standard error of the coefficient, $s(b_i)$ (Appendix A.11).
- the standardized regression coefficient, $b_i s_x/s_y$ (the regression coefficient for standardized variables).
- t test for the coefficient, $b_i/s(b_i)$, and the associated two-tailed probability value.
- TOLERANCE $(1 - R_i^2)$ where the multiple R_i^2 is the correlation of independent variable i with the other independent variables (see section on TOLERANCE below).

Specifying the regression -- the REGRESS paragraph. The REGRESS paragraph describes the dependent (predicted) variable and the independent (predictor) variables. This paragraph can be repeated before the END paragraph to specify additional analyses of the same data.

The dependent variable must be specified in the first REGRESS paragraph. If the independent variables are not specified, all other variables are considered as independent except the GROUPING variable, the case WEIGHT variable, the case LABELING variables, or variables not included in a USE statement, if one is specified.

Each regression analysis can be given a separate title.

REGRess ────────────────────────────────────
  DEPENDent = v.   required   none/prev.
    Name or subscript of the dependent (predicted) variable.
  INDEPendent = v list.   (all var./prev.)
    Names or subscripts of the independent (predictor) variables. If not specified, all variables are used as independent variables except those specified as the DEPENDENT, GROUPING, case WEIGHT, or LABELING variables.
  TITLE = 'c'. $\leq$ 160 char.   blank
    Title for the regression analysis.

Example 1R.2 Printing Data, Residuals, Predicted Values, Covariances and Correlations

The data, residuals, and predicted values are printed for each case when DATA is specified in the PRINT paragraph. In addition, the serial correlation of the residuals is printed. P1R can also print the correlation matrix and covariance matrix of the variables and the correlation matrix of the regression coefficients.

To obtain Output 1R.2, we add the following paragraph to the Control Language of Example 1R.1 before the END paragraph (any subset of these instructions may be used):

```
------------------------------------------
/ PRINT    DATA.
          CORRELATION.
          COVARIANCE.
          RREG.
------------------------------------------
```

The additional output requested by these instructions is presented in Output 1R.2.

⑥ The covariance matrix of the variables.

Output 1R.2 Printing covariances, correlations, predicted values and residuals
----

COVARIANCE MATRIX   ⑥

		AGE 2	HEIGHT 3	WEIGHT 4	BRTHPILL 5	CHOLSTRL 6	ALBUMIN 7	CALCIUM 8	URICACID 9
AGE	2	97.9776							
HEIGHT	3	2.1922	6.1610						
WEIGHT	4	51.7972	24.0917	420.2407					
BRTHPILL	5	0.2793	0.2041	0.8236	0.2514				
CHOLSTRL	6	154.5264	1.2157	128.1221	1.9649	1827.0183			
ALBUMIN	7	-0.2802	-0.0052	-1.7253	-0.0423	0.8819	0.1287		
CALCIUM	8	-0.0404	0.1676	0.6272	-0.0149	5.1487	0.0768	0.2235	
URICACID	9	2.3143	0.3489	6.9781	0.0086	13.1294	0.0120	0.0881	1.2569

(output continued)

Output 1R.2 (continued)

CORRELATION MATRIX

⑦		AGE 2	HEIGHT 3	WEIGHT 4	BRTHPILL 5	CHOLSTRL 6	ALBUMIN 7	CALCIUM 8	URICACID 9
AGE	2	1.0000							
HEIGHT	3	0.0892	1.0000						
WEIGHT	4	0.2553	0.4735	1.0000					
BRTHPILL	5	0.0563	0.1640	0.0801	1.0000				
CHOLSTRL	6	0.3652	0.0115	0.1462	0.0917	1.0000			
ALBUMIN	7	-0.0789	-0.0058	-0.2346	-0.2352	0.0575	1.0000		
CALCIUM	8	-0.0086	0.1428	0.0647	-0.0629	0.2548	0.4529	1.0000	
URICACID	9	0.2085	0.1254	0.3036	0.0154	0.2740	0.0299	0.1662	1.0000

--- ③ to ⑤ from Output 1R.1 are printed here ---

CORRELATION MATRIX OF REGRESSION COEFFICIENTS

		AGE 2	WEIGHT 4	URICACID 9	⑧
AGE	2	1.0000			
WEIGHT	4	-0.2060	1.0000		
URICACID	9	-0.1422	-0.2648	1.0000	

LIST OF PREDICTED VALUES, RESIDUALS, AND VARIABLES
    NOTE - NEGATIVE CASE NUMBER DENOTES A CASE WITH MISSING VALUES.
        THE NUMBER OF STANDARD DEVIATIONS FROM THE MEAN IS DENOTED BY UP TO 3 ASTERISKS TO THE RIGHT
           OF EACH RESIDUAL OR VARIABLE.
        MISSING VALUES ARE DENOTED BY MORE THAN THREE ASTERISKS.

⑨

CASE LABEL	NO.	RESIDUAL	PREDICTED VALUE	VARIABLES 2 AGE 8 CALCIUM	3 HEIGHT 9 URICACID	4 WEIGHT	5 BRTHPILL	6 CHOLSTRL	7 ALBUMIN
2381	1	-24.9135	224.9135	22.0000* 9.8000	67.0000* 5.4000	144.0000	1.0000*	200.0000	4.3000
1946	-2	********** ***	239.1275	22.0000* **********	64.0000 7.2000**	160.0000*	2.0000	**********	3.5000*
1610	3	30.4927	212.5073	25.0000 10.4000	62.0000 3.3000*	128.0000	1.0000*	243.0000	4.1000
1797	-4	********** ***	210.2096	25.0000 9.6000	68.0000* 3.0000*	150.0000	2.0000	**********	3.8000
561	5	-57.1798 *	215.1798	19.0000* 9.9000	64.0000 4.7000	125.0000	1.0000*	158.0000*	4.1000

--- similar statistics for cases 6 to 185 ---

575	186	-41.6860 *	261.6860	53.0000* 10.7000*	65.0000 4.6000	140.0000	2.0000	220.0000	4.0000
2271	187	40.2979 *	264.7021	54.0000** 10.3000	66.0000 4.8000	158.0000*	1.0000*	305.0000*	4.2000
39	188	-56.5432 *	276.5432	54.0000** 8.8000**	60.0000* 6.3000*	170.0000*	2.0000	220.0000	3.5000*

SERIAL CORRELATION OF RESIDUALS = -0.0781   ⑩

----

⑦ The correlation matrix of the variables.

⑧ The correlation matrix of the regression coefficients.

⑨ The residual $(y_j - \hat{y}_j)$, predicted value $\hat{y}_j$, and data for each case. A negative case number denotes a case with a missing value; the missing values are replaced by a series of asterisks. Asterisks are also printed when the predicted value or residual cannot be computed due to a missing value in the case. The number of standard deviations that a value

is from the overall mean for the variables is reported by zero, one, two or three asterisks after the value; three asterisks represent three or more standard deviations.

⑩ The serial correlation is defined as

$$\frac{\Sigma (w_j w_{j-1})^{\frac{1}{2}} (y_j - \hat{y}_j)(y_{j-1} - \hat{y}_{j-1})}{\{\Sigma w_j (y_j - \hat{y}_j)^2 \Sigma w_{j-1}(y_{j-1} - \hat{y}_{j-1})^2\}^{\frac{1}{2}}}$$

where the summation is for j=2 to N and w_j is the case weight for the jth case (1.0 if there is no case weight). A large serial correlation indicates a pattern in the residuals. When the data are ordered, for example by time, the pattern can be a result of a change in the method of data collection or an omission of a variable from the regression equation.

```
PRINT ──────────────────────────────────────
   DATA.                                    no/prev.
      The data (after transformation), residuals and
      predicted values are printed. The serial
      correlation of the residuals is also computed.
   CORRelation.                             no/prev.
      The correlation matrix of the variables is
      printed.
   COVAriance.                              no/prev.
      The covariance matrix of the variables is
      printed.
   RREGression.                             no/prev.
      The correlation matrix of the regression
      coefficients is printed. See Appendix A.11 for
      the formula.
```

Example 1R.3 Plots

To produce plots, the following paragraph is added to the Control Language of Example 1R.1 before the END paragraph (we have specified all PLOT options, you may select a subset):

```
--------------------------------------
/ PLOT     RESIDUALS.
           VARIABLE IS URICACID.
           PREP IS AGE.
           NORMAL.
           DNORMAL.
           SIZE IS 40,25.
--------------------------------------
```

The plots are presented in Output 1R.3. The size of all the plots is changed. Those in Output 1R.3 are smaller than the preassigned size (50 characters wide and 35 lines high); they are 40 characters wide and 25 lines high; i.e.,

$$SIZE = 40, 25.$$

is specified in Example 1R.3. Circled numbers below correspond to those in the output.

(11) The residuals $(y_j - \hat{y}_j)$ are plotted against the predicted values (estimates) $\hat{y}_j$. The number of points plotted at each position is printed.

(12) The residuals squared $(y_j - \hat{y}_j)^2$ are plotted against the predicted values (estimates) $\hat{y}_j$. The number of points plotted at each position is printed.

Output 1R.3 Plots available in P1R

PREDICTD

PREDICTD

(output continued)

Output 1R.3 (continued)

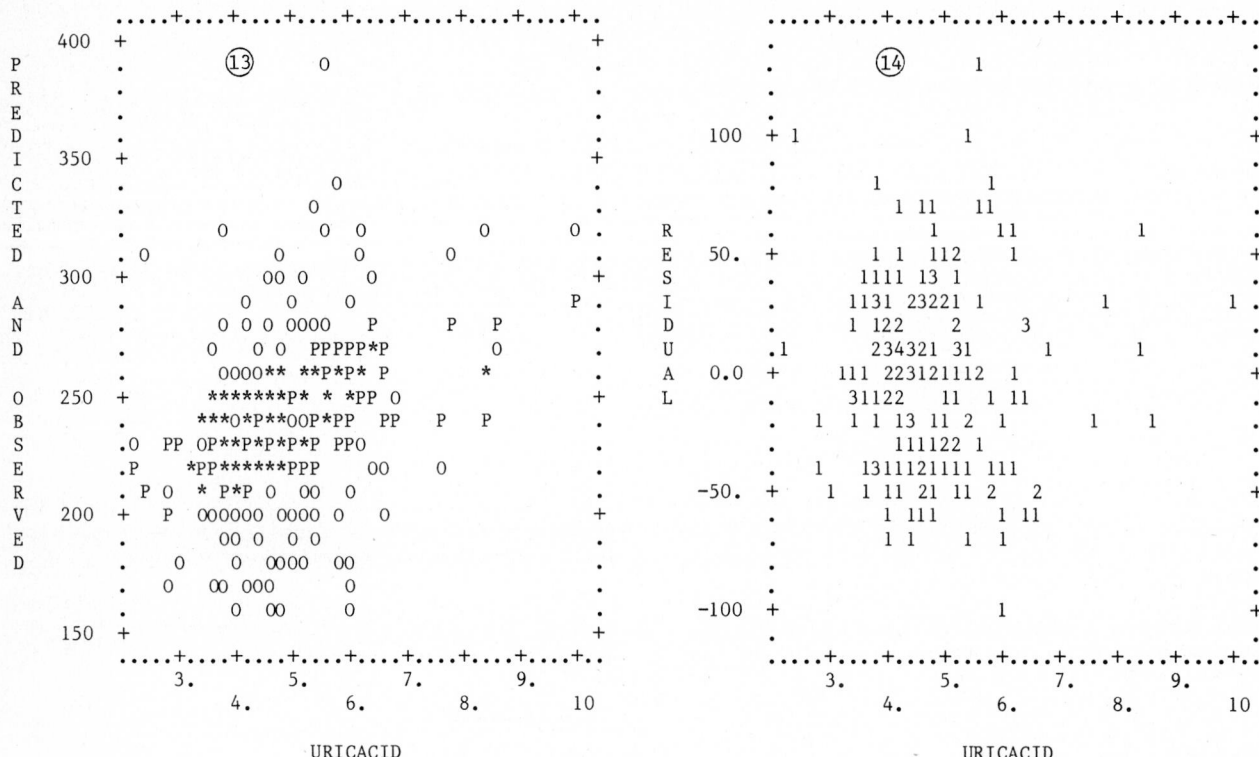

URICACID

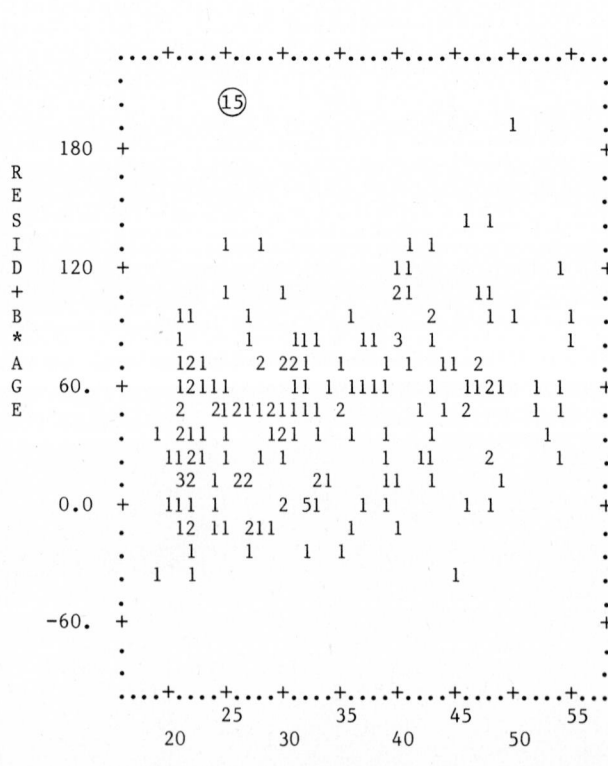

⑬ The observed values of the dependent variable (y_j) and the predicted values $(\hat{y}_j)$ are plotted against the observed values of an independent variable (x_{ij}) (URICACID in our example). O and P, represent observed and predicted values respectively, and * represents an overlap between observed and predicted values.

⑭ The residuals $(y_j - \hat{y}_j)$ are plotted against the observed values of the same independent variable (x_{ij}) as in ⑬. The number of points plotted at each position is printed.

⑮ A partial residual plot (PREP) of an independent variable is printed. This is a plot of the residual plus the contribution of the independent variable to the regression $(y_j - \hat{y}_j + b_i x_{ij})$ against the observed values of that variable (x_{ij}). This type of plot is described by Larsen and McCleary (1972). The number of points plotted at each position is printed.

⑯ A normal probability plot of the residuals is printed. The residual $(\hat{y}_j - y_j)$ is plotted against the expected normal deviate corresponding to its rank. The computation of the expected normal deviate is explained in Section 10.1.

⑰ A detrended normal plot of the residuals (Section 10.1).

NORMAL PROBABILITY PLOT OF RESIDUALS

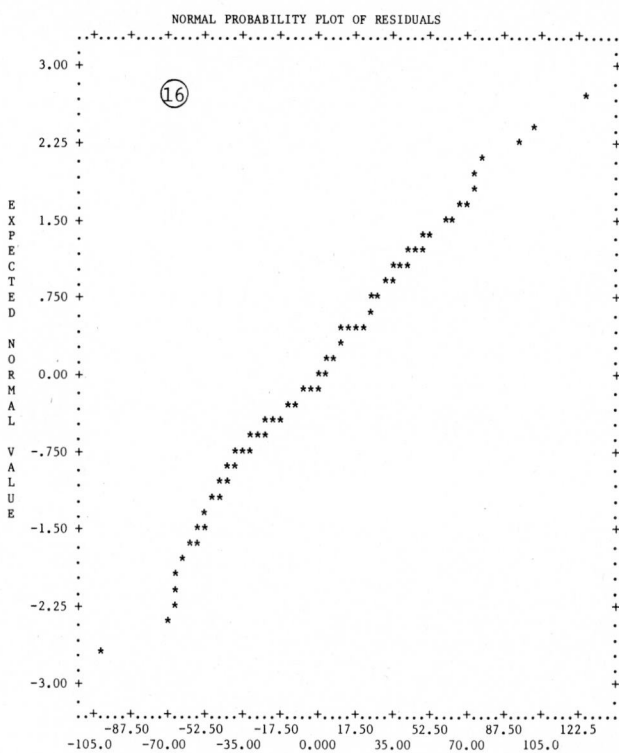

DETRENDED NORMAL PROBABILITY PLOT OF RESIDUALS

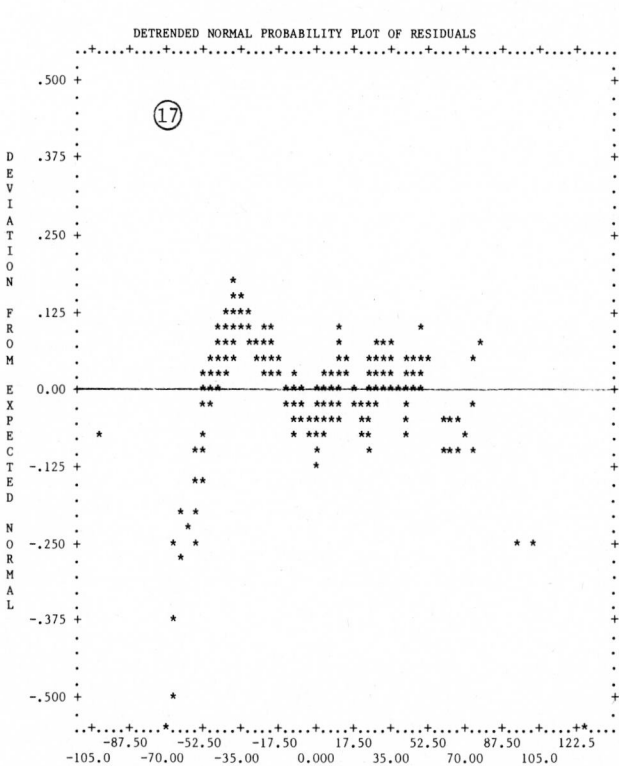

PLOT

RESIDual.   no/prev.
  Plot the residuals $(y-\hat{y})$ and residuals squared $(y-\hat{y})^2$ in separate graphs against the predicted values $\hat{y}$.

VARiable = v list.   none/prev.
  Names or subscripts of variables against which the observed values of the dependent variable y and the predicted values $\hat{y}$ are plotted. Overlaps between observed and predicted values are indicated by asterisks. The residuals $(y-\hat{y})$ are also plotted against the same variables. Each variable is plotted in a separate graph. Note that if a USE sentence is specified in the VARIABLE paragraph, only those variables can be specified in the PLOT paragraph.

SIZE = #,#.   50,35/prev.
  The first number is the number of characters (width) in the horizontal axis and the second number is the number of lines (height) in the vertical axis.

PREP = v list.   none/prev.
  Names or subscripts of variables plotted in partial residual plots. This is a plot of the (residual + coefficient * observed value of independent variable) against the observed value of that independent variable; i.e., $(y - \hat{y} + bx)$ against x.

NORMal.   no/prev.
  Plot a normal probability plot of the residuals.

DNORMal.   no/prev.
  Plot a detrended normal probability plot of the residuals.

Example 1R.4 Separate Analyses of Subpopulations with Test of Equality of Lines Across Groups

In this example we continue using the model

$$CHOLESTRL = a + b_1 AGE + b_2 WEIGHT + b_3 URICACID.$$

but compute separate equations for women who use birth control pills and for those who do not. The equality of the regression lines across groups is tested.

Cases are classified into groups by specifying a GROUPING variable in the VARIABLE paragraph. When a GROUPING variable is stated, the data are first analyzed for all groups combined and then reanalyzed for each group separately. The GROUPING variable is not used as an independent variable. Group NAMES and CODES or CUTPOINTS are defined in the GROUP paragraph (Chapter 5).

The following instructions are added to the Control Language of Example 1R.1 before the REGRESS paragraph (note that the first instruction, GROUPING IS BRTHPILL, is part of the variable paragraph):

```
-------------------------------------
(/ VARIABLE)
            GROUPING IS BRTHPILL.

/ GROUP     CODES(5) ARE        1,  2.
            NAMES(5) ARE NOPILL, PILL.
-------------------------------------
```

Output 1R.4   Separate regression analyses of groups

ALL DATA CONSIDERED AS A SINGLE GROUP   ⑱

MULTIPLE R   0.4175   STD. ERROR OF EST.   39.1698
MULTIPLE R-SQUARE   0.1743

ANALYSIS OF VARIANCE

	SUM OF SQUARES	DF	MEAN SQUARE	F RATIO	P(TAIL)
REGRESSION	57004.242	3	19001.414	12.385	0.0
RESIDUAL	270032.000	176	1534.273		

VARIABLE		COEFFICIENT	STD. ERROR	STD. REG COEFF	T	P(2 TAIL)	TOLERANCE
INTERCEPT		151.42036					
AGE	2	1.38971	0.309	0.322	4.497	0.000	0.915924
WEIGHT	4	0.00289	0.153	0.001	0.019	0.985	0.869294
URICACID	9	7.87099	2.769	0.206	2.843	0.005	0.889443

REGRESSION FOR GROUPS 1 NOPILL ↙   ⑲
   REGRESSION INTERCEPT. . . . . .NON-ZERO
   GROUPING VARIABLE . . . . .BRTHPILL

              --- univariate statistics for group NOPILL ---

   REGRESSION TITLE. . . . . .WERNER BLOOD CHEMISTRY DATA
   DEPENDENT VARIABLE. . . . .   6 CHOLSTRL
   TOLERANCE 0.0100

MULTIPLE R   0.4601   STD. ERROR OF EST.   39.4559
MULTIPLE R-SQUARE   0.2117

ANALYSIS OF VARIANCE

	SUM OF SQUARES	DF	MEAN SQUARE	F RATIO	P(TAIL)
REGRESSION	35528.281	3	11842.758	7.607	0.00014
RESIDUAL	132325.438	85	1556.770		

VARIABLE		COEFFICIENT	STD. ERROR	STD. REG COEFF	T	P(2 TAIL)	TOLERANCE
INTERCEPT		149.80963					
AGE	2	1.72105	0.459	0.379	3.751	0.000	0.906560
WEIGHT	4	-0.14176	0.238	-0.060	-0.595	0.554	0.912072
URICACID	9	9.21686	4.416	0.210	2.087	0.040	0.918725

(output continued)

The results are presented in Output 1R.4. Circled numbers below correspond to those in the output. Three regression analyses are performed:

(18) First P1R analyzes the data in all groups combined.

(19) Then each group is analyzed separately.

(20) Finally a test is made of the equality of the regression lines; when the regression lines (intercepts and slopes) are identical, the total of the sum of squares (SS) of the residuals over the groups will be equal to the SS of the residuals for the analysis of the data prior to grouping.

A test of equality of the regression lines is as follows.

Residual SS within groups = $\sum_{(groups)}$ Residual SS of the group

Total SS = Residual SS of data prior to grouping

Regression SS over groups = Total SS – Residual SS within group

This leads to the F test for equality of regression lines across groups

$$F = \frac{\text{Residual SS over groups}/(\sum p_i + g - p - 1)}{\text{Residual SS within groups}/(N - g - \sum p_i)}$$

where

p = number of independent variables in the regression equation for all groups taken together

p_i = number of independent variables in the regression equation for the i-th group

g = number of groups

N = number of cases in all the groups combined

The p_i's can differ between groups only if one or more variables do not pass the tolerance limit. The F ratio is nonsignificant in our example and therefore we conclude that the two BRTHPILL groups have similar regression equations.

Output 1R.4 (continued)

REGRESSION FOR GROUPS 2 PILL

--- univariate statistics for group PILL ---

```
REGRESSION TITLE. . . . . . . . . . . . . . . .WERNER BLOOD CHEMISTRY DATA
DEPENDENT VARIABLE. . . . . . . . . . . . . .      6 CHOLSTRL
TOLERANCE . . . . . . . . . . . . . . . . . .  0.0100
```

MULTIPLE R	0.3825	STD. ERROR OF EST.	39.1795
MULTIPLE R-SQUARE	0.1463		

ANALYSIS OF VARIANCE

	SUM OF SQUARES	DF	MEAN SQUARE	F RATIO	P(TAIL)
REGRESSION	22885.969	3	7628.656	4.970	0.00313
RESIDUAL	133548.125	87	1535.036		

			STD. REG COEFF	T	P(2 TAIL)	TOLERANCE
INTERCEPT		157.62984				
AGE	2	1.07026	0.423	0.261	2.533	0.013	0.922178
WEIGHT	4	0.10166	0.203	0.054	0.501	0.618	0.834262
URICACID	9	6.72586	3.594	0.200	1.871	0.065	0.860700

ANALYSIS OF VARIANCE OF REGRESSION COEFFICIENTS OVER GROUPS
 (= REDUCTION OF RESIDUALS DUE TO GROUPING)   (20)

	SUM OF SQUARES	DF	MEAN SQUARE	F RATIO	P(TAIL)
REGRESSION OVER GROUPS	4158.438	4	1039.609	0.673	0.61187
RESIDUAL WITHIN GROUPS	265873.563	172	1545.776		

A SIGNIFICANT F RATIO INDICATES THAT THE SLOPES AND/OR INTERCEPTS DIFFER BEYOND CHANCE BETWEEN THE GROUPS

VARiable
  GROUPing = v.   no grouping var./prev.
    Names or subscripts of the variable used to
    classify the cases into groups. If GROUPING is
    not stated or is set to zero, the cases are not
    grouped. If the GROUPING variable takes on more
    than 10 distinct values or codes, CODES or
    CUTPOINTS for the variable must be specified in
    the GROUP paragraph (Section 5.5).

Example 1R.5 Using a Correlation Matrix as Input

Only data can be read by P1R unless a BMDP File
(Chapter 7) is used as input: DATA, a COVARIANCE
matrix, or a CORRELATION matrix can be input from a
BMDP File.

In Chapter 12 we show how to store a correlation
matrix on a BMDP File (Example 8D.3). This
correlation matrix was computed from a data set with
several missing data values. We use this matrix as
input to P1R by substituting the INPUT paragraph
below for the one in Example 1R.1 (and we include
systems information to indicate that the BMDP File
is stored on UNIT 11, Section 7.4).

```
-------------------------------------
/ INPUT    UNIT IS 11.
          CODE IS WERNER.
          CONTENT IS CORR.
-------------------------------------
```

The results are presented in Output 1R.5. Note
that the results differ from those in Output 1R.1
since the correlation matrix in this example also
uses data from the incomplete cases.

When the input is not data, the CONTENT of the
BMDP File must be specified.

When the CONTENT is DATA, COVA or CORR, P1R
recognizes how the input is to be analyzed. Several
BMDP programs create BMDP Files with a different
CONTENT that is not recognized by P1R. You can use
other Files as input to P1R but you must specify in
a TYPE statement how they are to be analyzed (as
DATA, a COVARIANCE or a CORRELATION matrix).

INPut
  CONTent = c.   used only when input   DATA
                  is from a BMDP File
    When the input is not DATA, CONTENT must be
    specified. It must be identical to the CONTENT
    stated in the SAVE paragraph when the BMDP File
    was created.
  TYPE = (one only)   used only if   same as
         DATA,COVA,   input is from   CONTent
         CORR.   BMDP File
    TYPE specifies how the input is analyzed. It
    must be specified when a BMDP File is read as
    input and the CONTENT is not one of the three
    TYPES -- DATA, COVA or CORR. This option is
    rarely used.

Output 1R.5   Using a correlation matrix as input

```
-------------------------------------------------------------------------------------
          INPUT BMDP FILE
          CODE. . . IS     WERNER
          CONTENT . IS     CORR
          LABEL . . IS
          VARIABLES
              2 AGE        3 HEIGHT     4 WEIGHT      5 BRTHPILL     6 CHOLSTRL
              7 ALBUMIN    8 CALCIUM    9 URICACID


          REGRESSION INTERCEPT. . . . . . . . . . . . .NON-ZERO
          GROUPING VARIABLE . . . . . . . . . . . . . . .
          WEIGHT VARIABLE . . . . . . . . . . . . . . . .
          PRINT COVARIANCE MATRIX . . . . . . . . . . .        NO
          PRINT CORRELATION MATRIX. . . . . . . . . . .        NO
          PRINT CORRELATION OF REGRESSION COEFFICIENTS. .      NO
          PRINT RESIDUALS . . . . . . . . . . . . . . .        NO
          PRINT NORMAL PROBABILITY PLOT . . . . . . . .        NO
          PRINT DETRENDED NORMAL PROBABILITY PLOT . . . .      NO

     INPUT CORRELATION OR COVARIANCE MATRIX COMPUTED WITH MISSING DATA.


          VARIABLE
          NO.      NAME    SAMPLE SIZE    SUM OF WEIGHTS

            2 AGE              188.          188.000
            3 HEIGHT           186.          186.000
            4 WEIGHT           186.          186.000
            5 BRTHPILL         188.          188.000
            6 CHOLSTRL         186.          186.000
            7 ALBUMIN          186.          186.000
            8 CALCIUM          185.          185.000
            9 URICACID         187.          187.000


     HARMONIC MEAN OF SAMPLE SIZES     186
```

VARIABLE		MEAN	STANDARD DEVIATION	COEFFICIENT OF VARIATION
AGE	2	33.81914	10.11265	0.29902
HEIGHT	3	64.51074	2.48505	0.03852
WEIGHT	4	131.67204	20.66043	0.15691
BRTHPILL	5	1.50000	0.50133	0.33422
CHOLSTRL	6	236.15053	42.55522	0.18020
ALBUMIN	7	4.11123	0.35796	0.08707
CALCIUM	8	9.96208	0.47955	0.04814
URICACID	9	4.77051	1.15723	0.24258

```
REGRESSION TITLE. . . . . . . . . . . . . .WERNER BLOOD CHEMISTRY DATA
DEPENDENT VARIABLE. . . . . . . . . . . . .        6 CHOLSTRL
TOLERANCE . . . . . . . . . . . . . . . . .   0.0100
```

ALL DATA CONSIDERED AS A SINGLE GROUP

MULTIPLE R	0.4180	STD. ERROR OF EST.	38.9769
MULTIPLE R-SQUARE	0.1747		

ANALYSIS OF VARIANCE

	SUM OF SQUARES	DF	MEAN SQUARE	F RATIO	P(TAIL)
REGRESSION	58531.270	3	19510.422	12.843	0.0
RESIDUAL	276493.875	182	1519.197		

VARIABLE		COEFFICIENT	STD. ERROR	STD. REG COEFF	T	P(2 TAIL)	TOLERANCE
INTERCEPT		152.72365					
AGE	2	1.39409	0.295	0.331	4.732	0.000	0.925233
WEIGHT	4	0.00775	0.149	0.004	0.052	0.958	0.868692
URICACID	9	7.39102	2.612	0.201	2.830	0.005	0.898991

Example 1R.6 Saving Regression Results for Later Analysis (Including Predicted Values, Residuals and the Covariance Matrix)

Both the DATA (including predicted values and residuals) and the COVARIANCE matrix from P1R can be saved in a BMDP File to use as input to a further analysis. Saving the COVARIANCE matrix allows subsequent analyses to start from the computed means and covariances which may result in a substantial reduction of computer costs. Chapter 7 describes BMDP Files and how they are used.

In this example we save the data, the predicted values, the residuals and the covariance matrix by inserting the following SAVE paragraph before the END paragraph of the Control Language in Example 1R.1:

```
-------------------------------------
/ SAVE      UNIT IS 11.
           NEW.
           CODE IS WERNER.
           CONTENT IS DATA,COVA.
-------------------------------------
```

Note that the System Cards that precede the BMDP instructions must contain a card describing where to store the BMDP File (Section 7.3).

Output 1R.6 shows two messages. The first states that the covariance matrix (COVA) is written on UNIT 11 and is completed. The second indicates that a DATA file on UNIT 11 is completed – note that variable 10 is PREDICTD and variable 11 is RESIDUAL.

```
SAVE ─────────────────────────────
  CONTent = (one or both) DATA,COVA.          DATA
    The matrices to be saved in a BMDP File. If
    DATA is specified, the predicted values are
    saved as variable (VT+1) and named PREDICTD and
    the residuals are saved as variable (VT+2) and
    named RESIDUAL where VT is the total number of
    variables (after transformation, if any).

  Note: When a GROUPING variable is specified, the
    predicted values, residuals and covariances are
    saved only from the analysis using all groups
    combined. When the REGRESS paragraph is repeated
    before END, the predicted values and residuals
    from the first regression only are saved.
```

Output 1R.6   Saving the covariance matrix and data in BMDP Files

----

```
        NUMBER OF CASES READ. . . . . . . . . . . . .        188
            CASES WITH DATA MISSING OR BEYOND LIMITS . .        8
                REMAINING NUMBER OF CASES . . . . . . . .      180



    BMDP FILE IS BEING WRITTEN ON UNIT       11
    CODE. . . IS      WERNER
    CONTENT . IS      COVA
    LABEL . . IS
    VARIABLES ARE
            2 AGE        3 HEIGHT     4 WEIGHT     5 BRTHPILL    6 CHOLSTRL
            7 ALBUMIN    8 CALCIUM    9 URICACID


    BMDP FILE ON UNIT 11 HAS BEEN COMPLETED.



        --- univariate statistics and regression analysis appear here ---



    BMDP FILE IS BEING WRITTEN ON UNIT       11
    CODE. . . IS      WERNER
    CONTENT . IS      DATA
    LABEL . . IS
    VARIABLES ARE
            1 ID         2 AGE        3 HEIGHT     4 WEIGHT      5 BRTHPILL
            6 CHOLSTRL   7 ALBUMIN    8 CALCIUM    9 URICACID   10 PREDICTD
           11 RESIDUAL


    BMDP FILE ON UNIT 11 HAS BEEN COMPLETED.
```

Case Weights

When the error variance is not homogeneous but varies from case to case, a weighted least squares estimation is more appropriate; the weight (w) for each case is proportional to the inverse of the variance. In weighted least squares, estimates of the parameters minimize

$$\sum_j w_j (y_j - \hat{y}_j)^2$$

where w_j is the weight for case j.

You can estimate predicted values for cases not used to compute the regression equation by setting their case weights to zero (Appendix C.4).

Case weights affect the computation of the means, variances, covariances and correlations (Section 2.1).

```
VARiable ─────────────────────────────────────
  WEIGHT = v.                    no weight var./prev.
    Name or subscript of the variable containing
    case weights. The weights should be greater
    than or equal to zero. If WEIGHT is not stated
    or is set to zero, there are no case weights.
```

The Intercept in the Regression Equation

The regression equation usually contains an intercept (a constant term), e.g., in

$$y = a + b_1 x_1 + b_2 x_2 + \cdots + b_p x_p$$

a is the intercept. In some problems the intercept must be zero; this can be specified by

$$TYPE = ZERO.$$

in the REGRESS paragraph. When this option is specified, the covariances are the sums of products of observed values instead of the sums of products of deviations from the sample means.

```
REGRess ─────────────────────────────────
  TYPE = (one only)                    NONZERO/prev.
         ZERO, NONZERO.
    If ZERO is specified, the intercept in the
    regression equation is set to zero. TYPE can be
    stated only in the first REGRESS paragraph in
    any problem; it cannot be changed until a new
    problem begins.

    Note: This option is rarely used.
```

TOLERANCE: Inverting the Covariance Matrix

To estimate the parameters of the regression equation P1R must invert the covariance matrix (Appendix A.11). The matrix inversion is performed in a stepwise manner -- at each step an additional independent variable is entered into the regression equation. The variable chosen for entry is the variable with the highest partial correlation with the dependent variable. All independent variables are entered into the regression equation except those that fail the TOLERANCE limit defined below. Use P9R if you need a lower tolerance limit.

REGRess ────────────────────

> TOLerance = #.   between 0.01   0.01/prev.
>   and 1.0
> An independent variable is not entered into the regression equation if it fails to pass the TOLERANCE limit; i.e., if its squared multiple correlation (R^2) with independent variables already in the equation exceeds 1.0 minus TOLERANCE or if its entry will cause the squared multiple correlation of any previously entered variable with the independent variables in the equation to exceed 1.0 minus TOLERANCE. Note that if a zero intercept model is used, then the R^2 is estimated under the assumption that all variables have zero means.

Missing Values

A case with missing values or values outside the maximum or minimum limits for any variable specified in the USE statement of the VARIABLE paragraph is not used in computing the regression equation. Note that if you do not specify a USE statement the program assumes that all variables are used. Thus, unless you specify a USE statement, P1R may exclude cases because of values missing or out of range for variables that are not specified as either the dependent or independent variables. Also if you want to use the maximum number of cases for each regression equation, your USE statement should include only the dependent and independent variables (plus case weight and grouping variables, if any). On the other hand, if you want the same cases to define several different regression equations with different dependent and independent variables, your USE statement should include all of the variables under consideration.

SIZE OF PROBLEM

On medium-sized computer systems P1R can estimate a regression equation containing 145 independent variables. Appendix B describes how the capacity of the program can be increased.

COMPUTATIONAL METHOD

All computations are performed in single precision. Means, standard deviations and covariances are computed by the provisional means method (Appendix A.2). The sum of the cross-products matrix is swept (pivoted) on all independent variables except those that fail the tolerance limit (Appendix A.11). The independent variables are entered into the regression equation one at a time according to the size of their partial correlations; the independent variable with the largest partial correlation is chosen at each step.

ACKNOWLEDGEMENT

P1R was programmed by Douglas Jackson and Jerry Douglas. Later revisions were made by Lanaii Kline.

SUMMARY

Order of Input Cards

```
// (job card)
// EXEC BIMED,PROG=BMDP1R        (see Appendix E)
//SYSIN DD *
/ PROBLEM
/ INPUT
/ VARIABLE
/ TRANSFORM
/ SAVE
/ GROUP
/ REGRESS      (Repeat for subproblems)
/ PRINT
/ PLOT
/ END
    (data if on cards)
// (System Card)
```

Full sets of BMDP paragraphs (and data, if on cards) can be repeated for additional problems; see Section 5.8.

Paragraph Statement	Preassigned	Comment and Manual Reference
/ INPut		Additional input options. 246
TYPE = c.	same as CONT	Type of input, required only if BMDP File content is not DATA, COVA or CORR.
/ VARiable		Additional options to specify case weights and to classify cases into groups.
WEIGHT = v.	none	Name or subscript of variable containing a weight for each case. WEIGHT is used to calculate means, covariances, slopes, etc. Cases with zero weight are not used in computations; their predicted values are calculated. * 248
GROUPing = v.	none	Name or subscript of variable used to define group membership (see also / GROUP). * 246
/●REGRess		Required to specify the equation to be fit (may be repeated).
●DEPENDent = v.	none	Required; name or subscript of dependent variable (the predicted or y variable). * 239
INDEP = v list.	all	Names or subscripts of the independent variables (the predictor of x variables). If not stated, all variables except DEPEND, GROUPING, case WEIGHT, and case LABEL variables are used as INDEP. * 239
TITLE = 'c'.	none	Title to label the output, up to 160 characters. 239
TOLerance = #.	0.01.	Value between 0.001 and 1.0 to prevent loss in accuracy due to inclusion of numerically redundant variables. *249
TYPE = c.	NONZERO.	Either NONZERO (equation with intercept) or ZERO (intercept forced to be 0). * 248
/ PRINT		Optional to request printed output; the listed options are printed only if specified. 241
DATA.	no	Data after transformations, residuals and predicted values, and serial correlation of residuals. *
CORR.	no	Correlation matrix. *
COVA.	no	Covariance matrix. *
RREG.	no	Correlation matrix of the regression coefficients. *
/ PLOT		Optional to produce graphical descriptions. 243
RESIDual.	no	Plot residuals (observed minus predicted value of dependent variable for each case) and residuals squared vs. predicted values. *
VARiables = v list.	none	Two plots are made for each variable in the list (names or subscripts): the observed values and predicted values of the dependent variable and the residuals vs. the listed variable. *
NORMal.	no	Normal probability plot of residuals. *
DNORMal.	no	Detrended version of NORM. *
PREP = v list.	none	Partial residual plot for each variable in list. *
SIZE = #, #.	50,35.	Width of x-axis (characters); height of y-axis (lines). *
/ SAVE		Additional option to save data in a BMDP File. 247
CONTent = c.	DATA.	DATA or COVA (one only). DATA saves predicted values as VT + 1, named PREDICTD; and residuals as VT + 2, named RESIDUAL.

Key:
/	–indicates paragraph	*	–assigned value remains the same for additional problems
.	–period ends a sentence		
●	–required	VT	–number of variables after transformations
v	–variable (name or subscript)	list	–more than one item, often one per var.
g	–group (name or subscript)		
#	–number		Capitalized letters–paragraph or sentence names recognized by BMDP
'c'	–characters (name or parameter) may omit apostrophes if contiguous letters only		Page numbers following refer to this Manual

P2R

13.2 Stepwise Regression

W. J. Dixon
Robert Jennrich

ABSTRACT

P2R computes estimates of the parameters of a multiple linear regression in a stepwise manner by entering or removing variables one at a time from a list of potential predictors. Forward stepping (beginning with no predictors) and backward stepping (beginning with all predictors) are possible. Four criteria are available for stepping. Variables can be forced into the equation. The regression equation can be estimated with or without an intercept. See also P9R for another program that selects variables for multiple regression. Supplementary information is in Hill (1979). The independent variables in stepwise regression analysis can now be grouped so that all variables in a set are entered into or removed from the regression equation in the same step. See Appendix F.4 for further details.

WHERE TO FIND IT

Example 2R.1 Basic Setup for Stepwise Regression

The Werner blood chemistry data (Table 5.1) are used to illustrate the results produced by P2R. We request a stepwise regression with CHOLSTRL as the dependent variable. Only the REGRESS paragraph is specific to P2R. The remaining Control Language instructions are described in Chapter 5. If data editing or transformations are needed, see the methods described in Chapter 6. We use the following instructions:

```
-------------------------------------------
/ PROBLEM   TITLE IS 'WERNER BLOOD CHEMISTRY DATA'.
/ INPUT     VARIABLES ARE 9.
           FORMAT IS '(A4, 5F4.0, 3F4.1)'.
/ VARIABLE  NAMES ARE ID, AGE, HEIGHT, WEIGHT,
                     BRTHPILL, CHOLSTRL, ALBUMIN,
                     CALCIUM, URICACID.
           MAXIMUM IS (6)400.
           MINIMUM IS (6)150.
           LABEL IS ID.

/ REGRESS   DEPENDENT IS CHOLSTRL.

/ END
-------------------------------------------
```

(See end of this P2R section for organization of systems information, BMDP instructions and data.)

The results of this regression analysis are presented in Output 2R.1. The circled numbers below correspond to those in the output.

① Complete cases only are used in the computations; i.e., cases that have no missing values or values out of range. Blanks in the data are assumed to represent missing observations. Therefore only 180 of the original 188 cases are used. All variables are checked for invalid values unless USE is specified in the VARIABLE paragraph (Section 5.3); in which case only the variables specified in the USE statement are checked for acceptable values.

② Univariate statistics for each variable (computed from the complete cases)
- mean
- standard deviation
- coefficient of variation
- skewness
- kurtosis
- smallest observed value (not out of range)
- largest observed value (not out of range)
- smallest standard score
- largest standard score

These statistics are discussed in greater detail in Section 2.1.

③ The interpretation of the REGRESS paragraph. Since only the DEPENDENT variable is specified in Example 2R.1, the remainder of the options take their preassigned values.
- the stepping algorithm is "F"; that is, the entry or removal of the variables from the equation is based on F-to-enter or F-to-remove limits (explained in ⑥ below).

Output 2R.1   Stepwise regression.   Circled numbers correspond to those in the text

----

--- the BMDP instructions read by P2R are printed and interpreted ---

```
REGRESSION INTERCEPT. . . . . . . . . . . . . .NON ZERO
WEIGHT VARIABLE . . . . . . . . . . . . . . .
PRINT COVARIANCE MATRIX . . . . . . . . . . .      NO
PRINT CORRELATION MATRIX. . . . . . . . . . .      NO
PRINT ANOVA AT EACH STEP. . . . . . . . . . .      YES
PRINT STEP OUTPUT . . . . . . . . . . . . . .      YES
PRINT REGRESSION COEFFICIENT SUMMARY TABLE. . .    YES
PRINT PARTIAL CORRELATION SUMMARY TABLE . . . .    NO
PRINT F-RATIO SUMMARY TABLE . . . . . . . . .      NO
PRINT SUMMARY TABLE . . . . . . . . . . . . .      YES
PRINT RESIDUALS AND DATA. . . . . . . . . . .      NO
PRINT CORRELATION OF REGRESSION COEFFICIENTS. .    NO
PRINT NORMAL PROBABILITY PLOT . . . . . . . .      NO
PRINT DETRENDED NORMAL PROBABILITY PLOT . . . .    NO

NUMBER OF CASES READ. . . . . . . . . . . . .      188
    CASES WITH DATA MISSING OR BEYOND LIMITS . .     8        ①
           REMAINING NUMBER OF CASES . . . . . . .  180
```

VARIABLE ②		MEAN	STANDARD DEVIATION	COEFFICIENT OF VARIATION	SKEWNESS	KURTOSIS	SMALLEST VALUE	LARGEST VALUE	SMALLEST STD SCORE	LARGEST STD SCORE
NO.	NAME									
2	AGE	33.5382	9.8984	0.2951	0.4039	-0.9908	19.0000	55.0000	-1.4687	2.1682
3	HEIGHT	64.4660	2.4821	0.0385	-0.1185	-0.0402	57.0000	71.0000	-3.0079	2.6324
4	WEIGHT	131.0938	20.4998	0.1564	1.0572	1.9389	94.0000	215.0000	-1.8095	4.0930
5	BRTHPILL	1.5055	0.5014	0.3330	-0.0220	-2.0106	1.0000	2.0000	-1.0083	0.9863
6	CHOLSTRL	235.8382	42.7436	0.1812	0.4578	0.0640	155.0000	390.0000	-1.8912	3.6067
7	ALBUMIN	4.1205	0.3587	0.0871	-0.0678	-0.3606	3.2000	5.0000	-2.5662	2.4518
8	CALCIUM	9.9677	0.4728	0.0474	-0.0287	-0.5804	8.8000	11.1000	-2.4699	2.3949
9	URICACID	4.7555	1.1211	0.2358	1.1759	2.9185	2.2000	9.9000	-2.2794	4.5887

```
NOTE - KURTOSIS VALUES GREATER THAN ZERO INDICATE A
       DISTRIBUTION WITH HEAVIER TAILS THAN NORMAL
       DISTRIBUTION.


REGRESSION TITLE. . . . . . . . . . . . . . .WERNER BLOOD CHEMISTRY DATA
STEPPING ALGORITHM. . . . . . . . . . . . . .F
MAXIMUM NUMBER OF STEPS . . . . . . . . . . .       18
DEPENDENT VARIABLE. . . . . . . . . . . . . .        6 CHOLSTRL            ③
MINIMUM ACCEPTABLE F TO ENTER . . . . . . . .    4.000,   4.000
MAXIMUM ACCEPTABLE F TO REMOVE. . . . . . . .    3.900,   3.900
MINIMUM ACCEPTABLE TOLERANCE. . . . . . . . . 0.01000
SUBSCRIPTS OF THE INDEPENDENT VARIABLES . . . .  2    3    4    5    7    8    9
```

(output continued)

The regression model fitted to the data is

$$y = a + b_1 x_1 + b_2 x_2 + \cdots + b_p x_p + \varepsilon$$

where

    y is the dependent variable
    $x_1, \ldots, x_p$ are the independent variables
    $b_1, \ldots, b_p$ are the regression coefficients
    a is the intercept
    p is the number of independent variables
    ε is the error with mean zero

The predicted value $\hat{y}$ for each case is

$$\hat{y} = a + b_1 x_1 + b_2 x_2 + \cdots + b_p x_p$$

We have omitted a subscript (j) indicating the case number from the formulas. The residual for each case is $(y_j - \hat{y}_j)$. The number of parameters in the model p' is $p+1$ if the intercept is present and p if the intercept is set to zero. Step 0 includes the correlation listed in column labelled "PARTIAL CORR." of each independent variable with the dependent variable. The F-to-enter value for each independent variable is the F statistic appropriate for testing the significance of the simple linear regression of the dependent variable on each independent variable.

④ Results are printed at each step. We describe the results at Step 1. The multiple correlation R is printed (i.e., the correlation of the dependent variable y with the predicted value $\hat{y}$) as well as
- the multiple R^2
- the adjusted R^2: $R^2 - p(1-R^2)/(N-p')$
                      (Theil, 1971, p. 179)
- the standard error of the estimate:
$$\left\{ \Sigma (y_j - \hat{y}_j)^2 / (N-p') \right\}^{\frac{1}{2}}$$
where N is the number of cases

⑤ The analysis of variance table for the regression is printed containing
- the regression sum of squares: $\Sigma (y_j - \bar{y})^2$

- the residual sum of squares: $\Sigma (y_j - \hat{y}_j)^2$

- the F ratio: this is a test of the significance of the coefficients of the independent variables in the regression equation. Since variables are

Output 2R.1 (continued)

STEP NO.   0
STD. ERROR OF EST.   42.7436

ANALYSIS OF VARIANCE

	SUM OF SQUARES	DF	MEAN SQUARE
RESIDUAL	327036.19	179	1827.018

VARIABLES IN EQUATION						.	VARIABLES NOT IN EQUATION				
VARIABLE	COEFFICIENT	STD. ERROR OF COEFF	STD REG COEFF	TOLERANCE	F TO REMOVE	LEVEL .	VARIABLE	PARTIAL CORR.	TOLERANCE	F TO ENTER	LEVEL
(Y-INTERCEPT	235.838)					. AGE	2	0.36523	1.00000	27.40	1
						. HEIGHT	3	0.01146	1.00000	0.02	1
						. WEIGHT	4	0.14622	1.00000	3.89	1
						. BRTHPILL	5	0.09169	1.00000	1.51	1
						. ALBUMIN	7	0.05751	1.00000	0.59	1
						. CALCIUM	8	0.25477	1.00000	12.36	1
						. URICACID	9	0.27398	1.00000	14.45	1

STEP NO.   1
VARIABLE ENTERED   2 AGE   ④

MULTIPLE R   0.3652
MULTIPLE R-SQUARE   0.1334
ADJUSTED R-SQUARE   0.1285
STD. ERROR OF EST.   39.9024

ANALYSIS OF VARIANCE

		SUM OF SQUARES	DF	MEAN SQUARE	F RATIO
⑤	REGRESSION	43624.605	1	43624.61	27.40
	RESIDUAL	283411.63	178	1592.200	

VARIABLES IN EQUATION							.	VARIABLES NOT IN EQUATION				
VARIABLE		COEFFICIENT	STD. ERROR OF COEFF	STD REG COEFF	TOLERANCE	F TO REMOVE	LEVEL .	VARIABLE	PARTIAL CORR.	TOLERANCE	F TO ENTER	LEVEL
(Y-INTERCEPT		182.943)					.					
AGE	2 ⑥	1.577	0.301	0.365	1.00000	27.40	1 . HEIGHT	3	-0.02279	0.99204	0.09	1
							. WEIGHT	4	0.05887	0.93484	0.62	1
							. BRTHPILL	5	0.07653	0.99683	1.04	1
							. ALBUMIN	7	0.09304	0.99377	1.55	1
							. CALCIUM	8	0.27708	0.99993	14.72	1
							. URICACID	9	0.21727	0.95651	8.77	1

(output continued)

selected for inclusion in the equation in a manner that maximizes the F ratio, the level of significance of the F ratio cannot be obtained from an F distribution. When important variables have <u>not</u> as yet been included in the regression equation, the denominator of the F ratio (the residual mean square error) is inflated.

⑥ Statistics for each independent variable. To the left of the table are the independent variables already entered into the equation (AGE is the only one at Step 1) and to the right are those not yet entered. For the independent variables in the equation, P2R prints
- <u>regression coefficient</u>: b_i

- <u>standard error</u> of the coefficient: $s(b_i)$

- <u>standardized regression coefficient</u>: $b_i s_i / s_y$

  (the regression coefficient for standardized variables)
- <u>tolerance</u> (described on p. 262)
- <u>F-to-remove</u>: this is a test of the regression coefficient. It is equal to $[b_i/s(b_i)]^2$.

It is also the ratio

$$\frac{\text{SS(resi. if var. is removed from equation)} - \text{SS(resi.)}}{\text{SS(residuals)}/(N-p')}$$

where SS is the sum of squares. In two of the criteria for entering and removing variables (p. 258) F-to-remove is compared with the maximum acceptable F-to-remove (in ③) and if it is less than the acceptable limit the variable is removed from the equation. The F-to-remove values are affected by the process of variable selection (variables with large F-to-enter values are selected). Therefore, if an F-to-remove is compared to the critical values of the F distribution, the size of the test is biased (it will usually appear more significant than it really is). The F's-to-remove are helpful in determining the relative importance of the selected variables and as indications of the statistical accuracy with which the coefficients are estimated.
- <u>level</u> (described on p. 257)
For each independent variable not in the equation P2R prints
- <u>partial correlation</u>: the correlation of each

Output 2R.1 (continued)

STEP NO. 2
VARIABLE ENTERED 8 CALCIUM

MULTIPLE R	0.4471
MULTIPLE R-SQUARE	0.1999
ADJUSTED R-SQUARE	0.1909
STD. ERROR OF EST.	38.4482

ANALYSIS OF VARIANCE

	SUM OF SQUARES	DF	MEAN SQUARE	F RATIO
REGRESSION	65382.938	2	32691.47	22.11
RESIDUAL	261653.25	177	1478.267	

VARIABLES IN EQUATION

VARIABLE		COEFFICIENT	STD. ERROR OF COEFF	STD REG COEFF	TOLERANCE	F TO REMOVE	LEVEL
(Y-INTERCEPT		-49.830)					
AGE	2	1.587	0.290	0.367	0.99993	29.87	1
CALCIUM	8	23.320	6.079	0.258	0.99993	14.72	1

VARIABLES NOT IN EQUATION

VARIABLE		PARTIAL CORR.	TOLERANCE	F TO ENTER	LEVEL
HEIGHT	3	-0.06599	0.97141	0.77	1
WEIGHT	4	0.04141	0.93036	0.30	1
BRTHPILL	5	0.09786	0.99294	1.70	1
ALBUMIN	7	-0.03814	0.78926	0.26	1
URICACID	9	0.17924	0.92827	5.84	1

STEP NO. 3
VARIABLE ENTERED 9 URICACID

MULTIPLE R	0.4750
MULTIPLE R-SQUARE	0.2256
ADJUSTED R-SQUARE	0.2124
STD. ERROR OF EST.	37.9329

ANALYSIS OF VARIANCE

	SUM OF SQUARES	DF	MEAN SQUARE	F RATIO
REGRESSION	73789.250	3	24596.41	17.09
RESIDUAL	253246.94	176	1438.903	

VARIABLES IN EQUATION

VARIABLE		COEFFICIENT	STD. ERROR OF COEFF	STD REG COEFF	TOLERANCE	F TO REMOVE	LEVEL
(Y-INTERCEPT		-49.738)					
AGE	2	1.436	0.293	0.333	0.95458	23.99	1
CALCIUM	8	⑦ 20.792	6.088	0.230	0.97040	11.67	1
URICACID	9	6.344	2.625	0.166	0.92827	5.84	1

VARIABLES NOT IN EQUATION

VARIABLE		PARTIAL CORR.	TOLERANCE	F TO ENTER	LEVEL
HEIGHT	3	-0.08324	0.96406	1.22	1
WEIGHT	4	-0.00496	0.86875	0.00	1
BRTHPILL	5	0.09680	0.99272	1.66	1
ALBUMIN	7	-0.03249	0.78831	0.18	1

* * * * * F-LEVELS(4.000, 3.900) OR TOLERANCE INSUFFICIENT FOR FURTHER STEPPING

STEPWISE REGRESSION COEFFICIENTS

VARIABLES / STEP	0 Y-INTCPT	2 AGE	3 HEIGHT	4 WEIGHT	5 BRTHPILL	7 ALBUMIN	8 CALCIUM	9 URICACID
0	235.8382*	1.5772	0.1973	0.3049	7.8169	6.8533	23.0333	10.4459
1 ⑧	182.9431*	1.5772*	-0.3668	0.1182	6.0835	10.3523	23.3203	7.8848
2	-49.8298*	1.5868*	-1.0313	0.0801	7.4891	-4.5760	23.3203*	6.3444
3	-49.7384*	1.4359*	-1.2847	-0.0098	7.2891	-3.8369	20.7920*	6.3444*

NOTE - 1) REGRESSION COEFFICIENTS FOR VARIABLE IN THE EQUATION ARE INDICATED BY AN ASTERISK
2) THE REMAINING COEEFICIENTS ARE THOSE WHICH WOULD BE OBTAINED IF THAT VARIABLE WERE TO ENTER IN THE NEXT STEP

⑨

SUMMARY TABLE

STEP NO.	VARIABLE ENTERED	VARIABLE REMOVED	MULTIPLE R	MULTIPLE RSQ	INCREASE IN RSQ	F-TO-ENTER	F-TO-REMOVE	NUMBER OF INDEPENDENT VARIABLES INCLUDED
1	2 AGE		0.3652	0.1334	0.1334	27.3989		1
2	8 CALCIUM		0.4471	0.1999	0.0665	14.7188		2
3	9 URICACID		0.4750	0.2256	0.0257	5.8421		3

independent variable with the dependent variable removing the effect of variables already in the equation (see Appendix A.11)

- <u>tolerance</u>: a check that the variable is not <u>too</u> highly correlated with one or more variables already in the equation (described on p. 262)

- <u>F-to-enter</u>: F-to-enter tests the coefficient for each variable as if it were entered separately into the equation at the next step. Let SS(residuals) be the sum of squares of residuals at this step and SS(next) be the residual sum of squares after the next independent variable is entered. Then

$$F\text{-to-enter} = \frac{SS(residuals) - SS(next)}{SS(next)/(N-p'-1)} .$$

The F-to-enter for the variable actually entered at the next step is equal to F-to-remove for that variable immediately after being entered. The usual tabled F values (percentiles of the F distribution) should not be used to test the need to include a variable in the model. The distribution of the <u>largest</u> F-to-enter is affected by the number of variables available for selection, their correlation structure and the sample size; and the critical value for the largest F is usually much larger than that for testing one preselected variable. That is, the use of the usual table results in the inclusion of too many variables. A predictive equation with too many variables may perform poorly on new data. See Appendix C.2 and Hill (1979) for further discussion.

- <u>level</u>: used to predetermine the order of entry of variables (described on p. 257).

⑦ At step 3, three variables have entered - the model is

CHOLSTRL = -49.7 + 1.4 AGE + 20.8 CALCIUM + 6.3 URICACID.

The remaining variables have F-to-enter values less than 4.0 (the preassigned value) so the stepping stops. The F-to-remove values of the entered variables are all greater than the remove limit of 3.9, so no variables are removed.

⑧ Stepwise regression coefficients. This table shows the values of the regression coefficients of the variables in the equation (those with asterisks) at each step, and the coefficients of the other variables as if each had been entered separately into the regression equation.

⑨ A summary table reporting the variable entered, the multiple R and the F-to-enter at each step.

<u>Specifying the regression -- the REGRESS paragraph</u>. The REGRESS paragraph describes the dependent and independent variables, the method of entering and removing variables and the method of treating the intercept. This paragraph can be repeated before the END paragraph to specify additional analyses of the same data.

The dependent variable must be specified in the first REGRESS paragraph. If the independent variables are not specified, all other variables are considered as independent except the case WEIGHT variable and variables omitted from a USE statement if specified. The independent variables can be specified and the order of their entry into the

regression equation partially or completely predetermined by an assignment of LEVELS to the variables (p. 257)

Each regression analysis can be given a separate title.

```
REGRess
  DEPENDent = v.   required          none/prev.
    Name or subscript of the dependent (predicted)
    variable.
  INDEPendent = v list        all vars./prev.
    Names or subscripts of the independent
    (predictor) variables. If LEVELS are assigned
    to the variables (p. 257), the LEVELS determine
    both the order of entry of the independent
    variables and which variables are to be
    entered. If neither INDEPENDENT nor LEVEL is
    specified, all variables are used except the
    DEPENDENT variable and the case WEIGHT
    variable, if any.
  TITLE = 'c'.   ≤ 160 char.          blank
    A title for the regression analysis.
```

Example 2R.2 Forward and Backward Stepping

Forward stepping is illustrated in Example 2R.1. At each step the variable with the highest F-to-enter value is included in the equation. The stepping stops when no variable has an F-to-enter value greater than 4.0. (If, at any step, the F-to-remove value for an already entered variable drops below 3.9, it is removed). Starting with all variables in the equation and removing variables one at a time is called backward stepping. Forward and backward stepping do not always produce the same subset, so you may want to examine both solutions.

F-to-enter and F-to-remove limits can each be assigned two values. The first value for each limit controls the forward stepping; the second, the backward stepping. P2R uses the first set of limits to step in the variable - when the forward stepping is completed, the second set is invoked and the backward stepping begins. By assigning very low values to the first pair of values (i.e., the first F-to-enter and the first F-to-remove), all (or almost all) variables are entered into the equation. By assigning high values to the second pair, the variables are removed one by one.

We request both forward and backward stepping by specifying two F-to-enter and two F-to-remove limits in the regression paragraph. The 1 and 0 are used for forward stepping; the 50 and 49 for backward stepping. We also include a title for labeling the output. These instructions are inserted before the END paragraph in the REGRESSION paragraph of Example 2R.1.

```
-------------------------------------
/ REGRESS   DEPENDENT IS CHOLSTRL.
           TITLE IS 'FORWARD STEPPING FOLLOWED BY
           BACKWARD STEPPING'.
           ENTER = 1, 50.
           REMOVE = 0, 49.
-------------------------------------
```

The results are presented in Output 2R.2. First the five variables that pass the F-to-enter limit are entered into the regression. Two variables (WEIGHT and ALBUMIN) do not pass the limit (their

Output 2R.2   Forward and backward stepping

```
REGRESSION TITLE. . . . . . . . . . . . . . .FORWARD STEPPING FOLLOWED BY BACKWARD STEPPING
STEPPING ALGORITHM. . . . . . . . . . . . . .F
MAXIMUM NUMBER OF STEPS . . . . . . . . . . .    18
DEPENDENT VARIABLE. . . . . . . . . . . . . .     6 CHOLSTRL
MINIMUM ACCEPTABLE F TO ENTER . . . . . . . .  1.000,  50.000
MAXIMUM ACCEPTABLE F TO REMOVE. . . . . . . .  0.0  ,  49.000
MINIMUM ACCEPTABLE TOLERANCE. . . . . . . . . 0.01000
SUBSCRIPTS OF THE INDEPENDENT VARIABLES . . . .  2   3   4   5   7   8   9
```

--- results for steps 0 to 4 ---

```
 STEP NO.    5
 VARIABLE ENTERED    3 HEIGHT

 MULTIPLE R           0.4907
 MULTIPLE R-SQUARE    0.2408
 ADJUSTED R-SQUARE    0.2190
 STD. ERROR OF EST.   37.7742

 ANALYSIS OF VARIANCE
                    SUM OF SQUARES     DF   MEAN SQUARE    F RATIO
          REGRESSION  78756.938        5    15751.39       11.04
          RESIDUAL    248279.19       174    1426.892
```

		VARIABLES IN EQUATION					.		VARIABLES NOT IN EQUATION			
			STD. ERROR	STD REG		F TO	.			PARTIAL		F TO	
VARIABLE		COEFFICIENT	OF COEFF	COEFF	TOLERANCE	REMOVE	LEVEL.	VARIABLE		CORR.	TOLERANCE	ENTER	LEVEL
(Y-INTERCEPT		21.526)					.						
AGE	2	1.441	0.293	0.334	0.94823	24.22	1 .	WEIGHT	4	0.03864	0.68591	0.26	1
HEIGHT	3	-1.585	1.176	-0.092	0.93607	1.82	1 .	ALBUMIN	7	-0.01409	0.74640	0.03	1
BRTHPILL	5	8.607	5.736	0.101	0.96390	2.25	1 .						
CALCIUM	8	22.456	6.135	0.248	0.94737	13.40	1 .						
URICACID	9	6.598	2.624	0.173	0.92124	6.32	1 .						

```
 * * * * * F-LEVELS(   1.000,   0.0  ) OR TOLERANCE INSUFFICIENT FOR FURTHER STEPPING
```

--- results for steps 6 to 9 ---

```
 SUMMARY TABLE
```

STEP NO.	VARIABLE ENTERED	REMOVED	MULTIPLE R	RSQ	INCREASE IN RSQ	F-TO-ENTER	F-TO-REMOVE	NUMBER OF INDEPENDENT VARIABLES INCLUDED
1	2 AGE		0.3652	0.1334	0.1334	27.3989		1
2	8 CALCIUM		0.4471	0.1999	0.0665	14.7188		2
3	9 URICACID		0.4750	0.2256	0.0257	5.8421		3
4	5 BRTHPILL		0.4826	0.2329	0.0073	1.6554		4
5	3 HEIGHT		0.4907	0.2408	0.0079	1.8183		5
6		3 HEIGHT	0.4826	0.2329	-0.0079		1.8183	4
7		5 BRTHPILL	0.4750	0.2256	-0.0073		1.6554	3
8		9 URICACID	0.4471	0.1999	-0.0257		5.8421	2
9		8 CALCIUM	0.3652	0.1334	-0.0665		14.7187	1

F-to-enter is less than 1.0). At the sixth step HEIGHT is removed since it had the smallest F-to-remove at the previous step. At subsequent steps the other independent variables are removed.

In this example the variables are removed from the equation by backward stepping in the reverse order from which they were entered. The orders of entry and of removal may not coincide.

REGRess ────────
  ENTER = #,#.   4.0,4.0/prev.
    F-to-enter limits. The first number is used until no more variables can be entered. The second number is then used to remove variables. We describe above how to set them to obtain backward stepping. If only one number is specified, the second number is set equal to it.
  REMOVE = #,#.   3.996,3.996/prev.
    F-to-remove limits. The first number is used until no more variables can be entered. The second number is then used to remove variables. We describe above how to set them to obtain backward stepping. REMOVE must be less than ENTER, or a variable could be entered and removed at alternate steps. If only one number is specified, the second number is set equal to it.

Example 2R.3 Controlling the Order that Variables (or Subsets of Variables) Enter the Model

The order of entering independent variables into an equation can be specified in a LEVEL statement. If LEVEL is not specified, the independent variables are entered as described in the METHOD discussion. It is possible to specify complete ordering or partial ordering for the variables. LEVEL can also be used to eliminate variables from an analysis.

In the LEVEL statement you can assign positive numbers (integers) or zeros to the variables. Variables assigned a level of zero are excluded from the analysis; the level of the DEPENDENT variable is set to zero. Variables assigned a positive value are entered into the equation -- variables with smaller values are entered before variables with larger values. Variables with the same value compete for entry according to the METHOD specified. P2R begins stepping with the lowest positive value of LEVEL and enters all possible variables with that LEVEL before considering variables at the next higher level. Variables not assigned any value for LEVEL are set

to a value greater than the maximum value assigned (one if no LEVEL statement is present).

When variables are eliminated by setting LEVEL=0, the F-to-enter statistic is printed for these variables at each step. When variables are eliminated from the analysis by omitting them from the USE statement in the VARIABLE paragraph, not even their F-to-enter values are computed and printed.

A set of variables (e.g., a set of design variables for a categorial variable) can be assigned the same level and then FORCED to stay in the equation regardless of their F-to-enter values or those of other variables. To illustrate the use of LEVEL and FORCE we modify the REGRESSION paragraph of Example 2R.1:

```
------------------------------------
/ REGRESS   DEPENDENT IS CHOLSTRL.
           TITLE IS 'SPECIFYING ORDER OF ENTRY OF
                   VARIABLES INTO EQUATION'.
           LEVELS ARE 0, 3, 2*2, 2*0, 3*1.
           FORCE IS 1.
------------------------------------
```

Output 2R.3 Using a LEVEL statement to control the order in which variables enter the equation

```
REGRESSION TITLE. . . . . . . . . . . . . .SPECIFYING ORDER OF ENTRY OF VARIABLES INTO EQUATION
STEPPING ALGORITHM. . . . . . . . . . . . .F
MAXIMUM NUMBER OF STEPS . . . . . . . . . . .     18
DEPENDENT VARIABLE. . . . . . . . . . . . .      6 CHOLSTRL
MINIMUM ACCEPTABLE F TO ENTER . . . . . . . .  4.000,   4.000
MAXIMUM ACCEPTABLE F TO REMOVE. . . . . . . .  3.900,   3.900
MINIMUM ACCEPTABLE TOLERANCE. . . . . . . . . 0.01000
FORCED LEVELS . . . . . . . . . . . . . . .      1
SUBSCRIPTS OF THE INDEPENDENT VARIABLES . . . .  2    3    4    5    7    8    9
```

```
STEP NO.   0
STD. ERROR OF EST.   42.7436

ANALYSIS OF VARIANCE
                    SUM OF SQUARES    DF    MEAN SQUARE
          RESIDUAL   327036.19       179    1827.018
```

VARIABLE	COEFFICIENT	STD. ERROR OF COEFF	STD REG COEFF	TOLERANCE	F TO REMOVE	LEVEL	VARIABLE	PARTIAL CORR.	TOLERANCE	F TO ENTER	LEVEL
(Y-INTERCEPT	235.838)										
							AGE 2	0.36523	1.00000	27.40	3
							HEIGHT 3	0.01146	1.00000	0.02	2
							WEIGHT 4	0.14622	1.00000	3.89	2
							BRTHPILL 5	0.09169	1.00000	1.51	0
							ALBUMIN 7	0.05751	1.00000	0.59	1
							CALCIUM 8	0.25477	1.00000	12.36	1
							URICACID 9	0.27398	1.00000	14.45	1

(VARIABLES IN EQUATION / VARIABLES NOT IN EQUATION)

```
STEP NO.    1
VARIABLE ENTERED    9 URICACID
```

--- results for steps 1 to 4 ---

SUMMARY TABLE

STEP NO.	VARIABLE ENTERED	REMOVED	MULTIPLE R	RSQ	INCREASE IN RSQ	F-TO-ENTER	F-TO-REMOVE	NUMBER OF INDEPENDENT VARIABLES INCLUDED
1	9 URICACID		0.2740	0.0751	0.0751	14.4463		1
2	8 CALCIUM		0.3465	0.1201	0.0450	9.0560		2
3	7 ALBUMIN		0.3505	0.1229	0.0028	0.5607		3
4	2 AGE		0.4759	0.2264	0.1036	23.4297		4

The LEVELS instruction separates the variables into four groups:

```
level 1 - ALBUMIN, CALCIUM, URICACID
      2 - HEIGHT, WEIGHT
      3 - AGE
      0 - ID, BRTHPILL, CHOLSTRL (these are not
          used as independent variables)
```

The instruction FORCE IS 1 specifies that LEVEL 1 variables remain in the equation. FORCE IS 2 would include all the variables in LEVEL 1 and LEVEL 2.

Output 2R.3 presents the results from the above analysis. AGE has the highest F-to-enter at Step 0 (and logically would be the first entered), but it is not entered because other variables have a lower LEVEL assigned. First URICACID enters since it has the largest F-to-enter at Step 0 of the three variables at level one (i.e., among ALBUMIN, CALCIUM or URICACID). In the following two steps, CALCIUM and ALBUMIN are entered. ALBUMIN is entered although it violates the F-to-enter limit because FORCE=1 is stated. Variables with a LEVEL less than or equal to FORCE are forced into the equation without regard to the F-to-enter limit and are not removed. Neither HEIGHT nor WEIGHT are entered because they violate the F-to-enter limit and their LEVEL exceeds FORCE. AGE is finally entered.

```
REGRess ─────────────────────────────────────
    LEVEL = # list.   one per var.    highest level
                                       stated + 1
      The first number is the level for the first
      variable, the second is the level for the
      second variable, etc. Note that the levels are
      matched to the variable subscripts (that is,
      the variables read as data) and not to the
      order of variables in the VARIABLE USE
      statement (if given). The effect of LEVEL is
      described above.
    FORCE = #.                            zero/prev.
      If FORCE is not specified or is set to zero,
      there is no forcing. If FORCE is nonzero,
      variables that are assigned a LEVEL less than
      or equal to FORCE are forced into the equation,
      whether or not their F-to-enters are greater
      than the F-to-enter limit. Only the TOLERANCE
      test can be used to stop a forced variable from
      entering the equation.
```

Additional Variable Selection Features (not illustrated)

Methods of entering and removing variables: Any one of four methods can be used for entering or removing variables into or from the equation at each step. The methods are:

F   The variable with the smallest F-to-remove is removed if its F-to-remove is less than the F-to-remove limit. If no variable meets this criterion, the variable with the largest F-to-enter is entered if the F-to-enter exceeds the F-to-enter limit. (F-to-remove and F-to-enter are described on pp. 255 and 256.

FSWAP The variable with the smallest F-to-remove is removed if its F-to-remove is less than the F-to-remove limit. When no variable meets

this criterion, a variable in the equation is exchanged with a variable not yet in the equation if the exchange increases the multiple R. If no variable can be exchanged, a variable is entered as in F.

R   The variable with the smallest F-to-remove is removed if its removal results in a larger multiple R than was previously obtained for the same number of variables. If no variable meets this criterion, a variable is entered as for F.

RSWAP The variable with the smallest F-to-remove is removed by the criterion R. When no variable meets this criterion, a variable in the equation is exchanged with a variable not yet in the equation if the exchange increases the multiple R. If no variable can be exchanged, a variable is entered as in F.

The method F requires the fewest computations (is cheapest), R the next fewest. FSWAP and RSWAP require many more computations; you may want to use P9R (Section 13.3) instead.

Limiting the number of steps. Usually the stepping ends when the F-to-enter, F-to-remove or tolerance limits are violated for all the remaining independent variables. However, it is possible to specify a maximum number of steps; stepping ends when this number is reached.

The model with no intercept. The intercept, a, is usually part of a regression equation; however, in a few problems the intercept must be equal to zero because the regression line must pass through the origin. The intercept can be treated in three ways:
- always in the equation (NONZERO)
- never in the equation (ZERO)
- initially in the equation but may be removed if its F-to-remove is very small (FLOAT)

The adjusted R^2 is printed only when there is an intercept in the regression equation. Note that when ZERO or FLOAT is used, R^2 is computed relative to deviations of the dependent variable from zero rather than from the mean of the dependent variable. Thus in some applications the use of R^2 may not be useful. Evaluation of the regression should then be made only with respect to the residual mean square.

```
REGRess ─────────────────────────────────────
    METHod = (one only)                    F/prev.
        F,FSWAP,R,RSWAP.
      The METHOD used to enter or remove variables.
      The methods are described above.
    STEP = #.           twice the number of var./prev.
      The maximum number of forward and backward
      steps allowed.
    TYPE = (one only)                  NONZERO/prev.
        NONZERO,ZERO,FLOAT.
      The intercept is assumed to be in the equation
      (NONZERO) unless a ZERO intercept or FLOAT is
      specified. If FLOAT is specified, the intercept
      is initially entered into the equation but can
      be removed as any other independent variable.
      Note: The options ZERO and FLOAT are rarely
      used. If the REGRESSION paragraph is repeated
      in one problem, TYPE cannot be changed after
      the first REGRESSION paragraph.
```

Example 2R.4 PRINT Options

Output 2R.1 presents results that are printed automatically. In the following example we illustrate additional tables that can be printed; they are requested in the PRINT paragraph inserted before the END paragraph (the user may select any subset of the options we illustrate).

```
------------------------------------
/ PRINT    DATA.
          COVARIANCE.
          CORRELATION.
          RREG.
          PARTIAL.
          FRATIO.
------------------------------------
```

The additional results are presented in Output 2R.4. Circled numbers below correspond to those in the output.

⑩ COVARIANCE matrix of the variables.

⑪ CORRELATION matrix of the variables.

⑫ Correlation matrix of the regression coefficients of the final regression equation (RREG): defined in Appendix A.11.

⑬ F-to-enter and F-to-remove for each variable at each step (FRATIO): Asterisks indicate variables in the equation (F-to-remove); values without asterisks are F's-to-enter.

⑭ Partial correlations at each step (PARTIAL): Asterisks indicate variables in the equation. The partial correlation of a variable in the equation is its correlation with the dependent variable after removing the effect of the remaining variables in the equation.

Output 2R.4   Optional results printed by P2R

--- covariance matrix ---   ⑩

CORRELATION MATRIX   ⑪

		AGE 2	HEIGHT 3	WEIGHT 4	BRTHPILL 5	CHOLSTRL 6	ALBUMIN 7	CALCIUM 8	URICACID 9
AGE	2	1.0000							
HEIGHT	3	0.0892	1.0000						
WEIGHT	4	0.2553	0.4735	1.0000					
BRTHPILL	5	0.0563	0.1640	0.0801	1.0000				
CHOLSTRL	6	0.3652	0.0115	0.1462	0.0917	1.0000			
ALBUMIN	7	-0.0789	-0.0058	-0.2346	-0.2352	0.0575	1.0000		
CALCIUM	8	-0.0086	0.1428	0.0647	-0.0629	0.2548	0.4529	1.0000	
URICACID	9	0.2085	0.1254	0.3036	0.0154	0.2740	0.0299	0.1662	1.0000

--- results for steps 0 to 3 ---

CORRELATION MATRIX OF REGRESSION COEFFICIENTS

		AGE 2	CALCIUM 8	URICACID 9	
AGE	2	1.0000			⑫
CALCIUM	8	0.0449	1.0000		
URICACID	9	-0.2130	-0.1718	1.0000	

F-TO-ENTER OR F-TO-REMOVE OF EACH VARIABLE AT EACH STEP

VARIABLES STEP	2 AGE	3 HEIGHT	4 WEIGHT	5 BRTHPILL	7 ALBUMIN	8 CALCIUM	9 URICACID	
0	27.3989	0.0234	3.8888	1.5091	0.5908	12.3559	14.4464	⑬
1	27.3989*	0.0920	0.6156	1.0428	1.5454	14.7188	8.7697	
2	29.8695*	0.7697	0.3023	1.7017	0.2564	14.7188*	5.8421	
3	23.9881*	1.2211	0.0043	1.6554	0.1849	11.6655*	5.8421*	

(output continued)

Output 2R.4 (continued)

PARTIAL CORRELATIONS

VARIABLES STEP	2 AGE	3 HEIGHT	4 WEIGHT	5 BRTHPILL	7 ALBUMIN	8 CALCIUM	9 URICACID	
0	0.3652	0.0115	0.1462	0.0917	0.0575	0.2548	0.2740	
1	0.3652*	-0.0228	0.0589	0.0765	0.0930	0.2771	0.2173	⑭
2	0.3800*	-0.0660	0.0414	0.0979	-0.0381	0.2771*	0.1792	
3	0.3463*	-0.0832	-0.0050	0.0968	-0.0325	0.2493*	0.1792*	

SUMMARY TABLE

STEP NO.	VARIABLE ENTERED	REMOVED	MULTIPLE R	RSQ	INCREASE IN RSQ	F-TO- ENTER	F-TO- REMOVE	NUMBER OF INDEPENDENT VARIABLES INCLUDED
1	2 AGE		0.3652	0.1334	0.1334	27.3989		1
2	8 CALCIUM		0.4471	0.1999	0.0665	14.7188		2
3	9 URICACID		0.4750	0.2256	0.0257	5.8421		3

LIST OF PREDICTED VALUES, RESIDUALS, AND VARIABLES

NOTE - NEGATIVE CASE NUMBER DENOTES A CASE WITH MISSING VALUES.
THE NUMBER OF STANDARD DEVIATIONS FROM THE MEAN IS DENOTED BY UP TO 3 ASTERISKS TO THE RIGHT ⑮
OF EACH RESIDUAL OR VARIABLE.
MISSING VALUES ARE DENOTED BY MORE THAN THREE ASTERISKS.

CASE NO. LABEL	PREDICTED	RESIDUAL	WEIGHT	VARIABLES 6 CHOLSTRL	2 AGE	3 HEIGHT	4 WEIGHT	5 BRTHPILL	7 ALBUMIN
1 2381	219.8721	-19.8721	1.000	200.0000	22.0000	67.0000	144.0000	1.0000	4.3000
-2 1946	************	***************	1.000	************	22.0000	64.0000	160.0000	2.0000	3.5000
3 1610	223.3316	19.6684	1.000	243.0000	25.0000	62.0000	128.0000	1.0000	4.1000
-4 1797	204.7949	***************	1.000	************	25.0000	68.0000	150.0000	2.0000	3.8000
5 561	213.2025	-55.2025*	1.000	158.0000	19.0000	64.0000	125.0000	1.0000	4.1000

--- similar statistics for cases 6 to 185 ---

186 575	278.0215	-58.0215*	1.000	220.0000	53.0000	65.0000	140.0000	2.0000	4.0000
187 2271	272.4094	32.5906	1.000	305.0000	54.0000	66.0000	158.0000	1.0000	4.2000
188 39	250.7381	-30.7381	1.000	220.0000	54.0000	60.0000	170.0000	2.0000	3.5000

EACH ASTERISK REPRESENTS ONE STANDARD DEVIATION

LIST OF PREDICTED VALUES, RESIDUALS, AND VARIABLES (CONTINUED)

--- values for variables 8 and 9 are printed in a separate panel ---

----

⑮ The residual ($y_j - \hat{y}_j$), predicted value $\hat{y}_j$, and data for each case. A negative case number denotes a case with a missing value; the missing values are replaced by a series of asterisks. Asterisks are also printed when the predicted value or residual cannot be computed due to a missing value in the case. The number of standard deviations that a value is from the overall mean for the variables is reported by zero, one, two or three asterisks after the value; three asterisks represent three or more standard deviations.

PRINT ─────
  DATA.   no/prev.
    Print the input data, residuals and predicted values.
  COVAriance.   no/prev.
    Print the covariance matrix of the variables.
  CORRelation.   no/prev.
    Print the correlation matrix of the variables.

ANOVA.   ANOVA/prev.
    An analysis of variance table at each step is printed unless you specify NO ANOVA.
STEP.   STEP/prev.
    The results at each step are printed unless you specify NO STEP.
RREGression.   no/prev.
    Print the correlation matrix of the regression coefficients.
COEFficients.   COEFficient/prev.
    The summary table of regression coefficients is printed unless you specify NO COEFFICIENTS.
FRATio.   no/prev.
    Print the summary table of F-to-enter and F-to-remove values.
PARTial.   no/prev.
    Print the summary table of partial correlations.
SUMmary   SUMmary/prev.
    A summary table with the multiple R, R^2, F-to-enter and F-to-remove at each step is printed unless you specify NO SUMMARY.

Plots available in P2R

The plots available in P2R are the same as those in P1R. Examples are presented in Output 1R.3 (p. 241). For a discussion of the plots, please read p. 241. We repeat only the definitions.

```
PLOT ─────────────────────────────────────
  RESIDual.                                no/prev.
     Plot the residuals (y-ŷ) and residuals squared
     (y-ŷ)² in separate graphs against the predicted
     values ŷ.
  VARiable = v list.                       none/prev.
     Names or subscripts of variables against which
     the observed values of the dependent variable y
     and the predicted values ŷ are plotted.
     Overlaps between observed and predicted values
     are indicated by asterisks. The residuals (y-ŷ)
     are also plotted against the same variables.
     Each variable is plotted in a separate graph.
     Note that if a USE sentence is specified in the
     VARIABLE paragraph, only those variables can be
     specified in the PLOT paragraph.
  SIZE = #,#.                              50,35/prev.
     The first number is the number of characters
     (width) in the horizontal axis and the second
     number is the number of lines (height) in the
     vertical axis
  PREP = v list.                           none/prev.
     Names or subscripts of variables plotted in
     partial residual plots. This is a plot of the
     (residual + coefficient * observed value of
     independent variable) against the observed
     value of that independent variable; i.e., (y -
     ŷ + bx) against x.
  NORMal.                                  no/prev.
     Plot a normal probability plot of the
     residuals.
  DNORMal.                                 no/prev.
     Plot a detrended normal probability plot of the
     residuals.
```

Forms of Input

P2R accepts data, a covariance matrix or a correlation matrix as input. The input must be from a BMDP File if it is a covariance or correlation matrix. Example 1R.5 (p. 246) illustrates how to use a CORRELATION matrix as input for P1R; it can also be used for P2R.

When the input is not data, the CONTENT of the BMDP File must be specified. When the CONTENT is DATA, COVA or CORR, P2R recognizes how the input is to be analyzed. Several BMDP programs create BMDP Files with a different CONTENT that is not recognized by P2R. You can use other files as input to P2R but you must specify by a TYPE statement how they are to be analyzed (as DATA, a COVARIANCE or a CORRELATION matrix).

```
INPut ─────────────────────────────────────
  CONTent = c.   used only when input        DATA
                 is from a BMDP File
     When the input is not DATA, CONTENT must be
     specified. It must be identical to the CONTENT
     stated in the SAVE paragraph when the BMDP File
     was created.
  TYPE = (one only)    used only if         same as
         DATA,COVA,    input is from        CONTENT
         CORR.         a BMDP File
     TYPE specifies how the input is analyzed. It
     must be specified when a BMDP File is read as
     input and the CONTENT is not one of the three
     TYPES -- DATA, COVA or CORR. This option is
     rarely used.
```

Saving Regression Results for Later Analyses (including predicted values, residuals and the covariance matrix)

Both the DATA (including predicted values and residuals) and the COVARIANCE matrix from P2R can be saved in a BMDP File to use as input to a further analysis. Saving the COVARIANCE matrix allows subsequent analyses to start from the computed means and covariances, which may result in a substantial reduction of computer costs. Chapter 7 describes BMDP Files and how they are used.

The SAVE paragraph is illustrated for P1R in Example 1R.6, and is the same for P2R. The definition is repeated below.

```
SAVE ─────────────────────────────────────
  CONTent = (one or both) DATA,COVA.         DATA
     The matrices to be saved in a BMDP File. If
     DATA is specified, the predicted values are
     saved as variable (VT+1) and named PREDICTD and
     the residuals are saved as variable (VT+2) and
     named RESIDUAL where VT is the total number of
     variables (after transformation, if any).
```

Weighted Least Squares Regression

When the error variance is not homogeneous but varies from case to case, weighted least squares estimation is more appropriate; the weight (w) for each case is proportional to the inverse of the variance. The user supplies a value to be used as a weight for each case. In weighted least squares, estimates of the coefficients minimize

$$\sum w_j (y_j - \hat{y}_j)^2$$

where w_j is the weight for case j.

You can estimate predicted values for cases not used to compute the regression equation by setting their case weights to zero (See Appendix C.4).

Case weights affect the computation of the means, variances, covariances and correlations (see Section 2.1).

VARiable ─────────────────────────────
> WEIGHT = v.   no weight var./prev.
> Name or subscript of the variable containing
> case weights. The weights should be greater
> than or equal to zero. If WEIGHT is not stated
> or is set to zero, there are no case weights.

TOLERANCE

To estimate the parameters of the regression equation P2R inverts the covariance matrix in a stepwise manner (Appendix A.11). A variable is not entered into the regression equation if it does not pass the TOLERANCE limit defined below. Use P9R if you need a lower tolerance limit.

REGRess ─────────────────────────────
> TOLerance = #.   between 0.01   0.01/prev.
>   and 1.0
> An independent variable is not entered into the
> regression equation if it does not pass the
> TOLERANCE limit; i.e., if its squared multiple
> correlation (R^2) with independent variables
> already in the equation exceeds 1.0 minus
> TOLERANCE, or if its entry will cause the
> squared multiple correlation of any previously
> entered variable with the independent variables
> in the equation to exceed 1.0 minus TOLERANCE.
> Note that if a zero intercept model is used,
> then the R^2 is estimated under the assumption
> that all variables have zero means.

Missing Data

P2R uses complete cases, i.e., when there is a case with missing values or values outside specified MINIMUM or MAXIMUM limits, the case is not used in computing the regression equations. Note that P2R checks the value of all variables that are read unless you specify a subset of the data file using a USE statement in the VARIABLE paragraph. The INDEPENDENT variable list in the REGRESSION paragraph is not used to identify complete cases.

A predicted value is computed for cases where the selected independent variables are complete and the dependent variable is missing. A residual is also obtained for the cases where the dependent variable and all selected independent variables are present. These cases may be deleted from the regression computations because values of the unselected variables are missing.

SIZE OF PROBLEM

P2R can analyze a problem with up to 150 variables included in the analysis. Appendix B describes how to increase the capacity of the program.

COMPUTATIONAL METHOD

All computations are performed in single precision. Means, standard deviations and covariances are computed by the method of provisional means (Appendix A.2). The independent variables are entered into the regression equation or removed from it in a stepwise manner (Appendix A.11) according to the specified (or preassigned) options that you select.

ACKNOWLEDGEMENT

P2R was programmed by Jerry Douglas. Later revisions were made by Lanaii Kline. P2R supersedes BMDO2R; Robert Jennrich guided the development of BMDO2R.

SUMMARY

Order of Input Cards

```
// (job card)
// EXEC BIMED,PROG=BMDP2R        (see Appendix E)
//SYSIN DD *
/ PROBLEM
/ INPUT
/ VARIABLE
/ TRANSFORM
/ SAVE
/ REGRESS          may be repeated
/ PRINT
/ PLOT
/ END
    (data if on cards)
// (system card)
```

Full sets of BMDP paragraphs (and data, if on cards) can be repeated for additional problems; see Section 5.8.

instructions specific to P2R

Paragraph Statement	Preassigned	Comment and Manual Reference
/ INPut		Additional input options. 261
TYPE = c.	same as CONT	Type of input required only if BMDP File content is not DATA, COVA or CORR.
/ VARiable		Additional option to specify case weights. 262
WEIGHT = v.	none	Same as P1R. *
/●REGRess		Required to describe role of variables and to control variable selection (may be repeated).
●DEPendent = v.	none	Required, name or subscript of dependent variable (the predicted or y-variable). * 255
INDEP = v list.	all	Names or subscripts of the independent variables (the predictor or x variables). If not stated, all variables except DEPEND, case WEIGHT, and case LABEL variables are used as INDEP. * 255
TITLE = 'c'.	none	Title to label the output, up to 160 characters. 255

(continued)

Paragraph Statement	Preassigned	Comment and Manual Reference
/ REGRess (continued)		
METHOD = c.	F.	Method for entering or removing variables at each step (one only). * 258
	F	–remove variable with smallest F-to-remove (if no variable qualifies, enter variable with the largest F-to-enter)
	FSWAP	–if no variable meets the removal limit, exchange a variable in the equation with one not yet entered if the exchange increases multiple R; if none does, variables enter as in F
	R	–remove variable with smallest F-to-remove if removal results in larger R than that for the previous smaller set; if it does not, variables enter as in F
	RSWAP	–remove variable as in R; if no variable meets criterion, exchange a variable in the equation with a variable not yet entered if the exchange increases R – if none does, variables enter as in F.
ENTER = #, #.	4.0, 4.0.	F-to-enter and F-to-remove limits. The second number is used for backward stepping. For entering, variables must have F > ENTER limit; and for removing, F < REMOVE limit. * 256
REMOVE = #, #.	3.996, 3.996	
LEVEL = # list.	1, 1, 1,...	Determines order for variables to enter equation. Lower numbers are considered first. Use one number for each variable in the FORMAT list – not the USE list. 258
FORCE = #.	0.	Variables with LEVEL # $\leq$ FORCE # (if FORCE > zero) enter the equation and are not removed (ENTER and REMOVE limits are ignored when FORCE is specified). * 258
TOLerance = #.	.01.	**Value between 0.001 and 1.0 to prevent loss in accuracy due to inclusion of numerically redundant variables. * 262**
STEP = #.	2(VT)	Maximum number of forward and backward steps allowed. * 258
TYPE = c.	NONZERO.	Method (one only) for treating the intercept. ZERO and FLOAT are rarely used. * 258
		NONZERO –always in the equation FLOAT – starts out in the equation
		ZERO –never in the equation but may be removed if its F-to-remove is very small
/ PRINT		Optional to request results to be printed (or omitted). If paragraph is omitted, ANOVA, STEP, COEF and SUM are printed automatically. To appear in the output, the remaining parameters must be specified. 260
ANOVA.	yes	Analysis of variance table for each step *
STEP.	yes	The results at each step are printed in detail for all variables *
COEF.	yes	Summary table of regression coefficients *
SUM.	yes	Summary table with R, R^2, F-to-enter, and F-to-remove for each step *
COVA.	no	Covariance matrix *
CORR.	no	Correlation matrix *
DATA.	no	Input data, residuals and predicted values *
PART.	no	Summary table of partial correlations *
FRATio.	no	Summary table of F-to-enter and F-to-remove *
RREG.	no	Correlations between regression coefficients *
/ PLOT		Optional to produce graphical descriptions. Same as P1R 261
/ SAVE		Additional option to save data in a BMDP File. Same as P1R. 261

Key:

/	–indicates paragraph
.	–period ends a sentence
●	–required
v	–variable (name or subscript)
g	–group (name or subscript)
#	–number
'c'	–characters (name or parameter) may omit apostrophes if contiguous letters only

* –assigned value remains the same for additional problems
VT –number of variables after transformations
list –more than one item, often one per var.

Capitalized letters–paragraph or sentence names recognized by BMDP
Page numbers following refer to this Manual

P9R

13.3 All Possible Subsets Regression

James Frane

ABSTRACT

P9R estimates regression equations for "best" subsets of predictor variables and does extensive residual analysis. The Furnival-Wilson algorithm efficiently identifies the subsets while computing only a small fraction of all possible regressions. Computer costs are comparable to costs for stepwise regression for up to about 25 independent variables. Three criteria are available to define "best": the sample R^2, adjusted R^2, or Mallows' C_p. The user may specify the number of subsets to be identified. Thus, not only the best but also the second best, third best, etc., subsets are identified to provide several good alternatives. The R^2 criterion identifies the M best subsets of each subset size. (Subset size is the number of independent variables included in the equation.) When the adjusted R^2 or Mallows' C_p criterion is chosen, the M best subsets are identified without regard to subset size; for example, if 10 best subsets are requested for 20 independent variables, the best subsets might not include subsets of size 1 or 20. Regression without subset selection is also available. Case weights can be specified.

The average squared residual is printed for cross-validation studies (where some cases have zero weight). Input can be data, a covariance matrix or a correlation matrix. Data are read in single precision; critical computations are done in double precision. Optional output includes, for each case, residuals, standardized residuals, deleted residuals, weighted residuals, predicted values, Mahalanobis distances and Cook's distances, the Durbin-Watson statistic and serial correlation when residuals are computed.

The P9R writeup is supplemented by Frane (1978a) and Hill (1979).

WHERE TO FIND IT

Example 9R.1 Basic Setup for Regression Using Mallows' C_p Criterion for "Best" Subset Selection

The Werner blood chemistry data (Table 5.1) are analyzed to illustrate the results reported by P9R. In Example 9R.1 the REGRESS paragraph is specific to P9R; the other Control Language instructions are described in Chapter 5.

```
        ----------------------------------------
/ PROBLEM    TITLE IS 'WERNER BLOOD CHEMISTRY DATA'.
/ INPUT      VARIABLES ARE 9.
            FORMAT IS '(A4, 5F4.0, 3F4.1)'.
/ VARIABLE   NAMES ARE ID, AGE, HEIGHT, WEIGHT,
                BRTHPILL, CHOLSTRL, ALBUMIN,
                CALCIUM, URICACID.
            MAXIMUM IS (6)400.
            MINIMUM IS (6)150.
            LABEL IS ID.

/ REGRESS    DEPENDENT IS CHOLSTRL.
            INDEPENDENT ARE 2 TO 4, 7 TO 9.
/ END
        ----------------------------------------
```

(See end of this P9R section for organization of systems information, BMDP instructions and data.)

In this example, we use Mallows' C_p as the criterion for subset selection. R^2 is the preassigned criterion. C_p will limit the number of subsets reported. The R^2 criterion would result in reporting the five subsets of each subset size that have the largest values of R^2. The residual analysis subsequent to the selection of variables in the regression equation will be based in this case on the subset that minimizes C_p while a choice of R^2 will use the complete set of independent variables. R^2 is frequently suggested for an initial screening run including a study of residuals. Regardless of which criterion is used for reporting subsets, the final equation you select (after possibly running P9R more than once) should usually include only those independent variables whose coefficients are significantly different from zero. Further discussion of variable selection strategies is given preceding Example 9R.2.

Output 9R.1 presents the results of the analysis by P9R. Circled numbers below correspond to those in the output.

① Interpretation of the REGRESS paragraph and Control Language instructions specific to P9R. Many of the options listed are preassigned.

② Data for the first five cases (after transformation, if any). Only cases used in the computations are printed. If you want other cases printed, you can request them in the PRINT paragraph. The LABEL is the first variable ID read in A4 format.

③ Only complete cases are used in the computations; i.e., cases that have no missing values or values out of range. Therefore only 180 of the original 188 cases are used. The DEPENDENT and INDEPENDENT variables only are checked for acceptable values.

④ Univariate statistics for each variable (computed from the complete cases)
- mean
- standard deviation
- coefficient of variation
- smallest observed value (not out of range)
- largest observed value (not out of range)
- smallest standard score
- largest standard score
- skewness
- kurtosis

These statistics are described in Section 2.1.

Output 9R.1   Results of a regression analysis using Mallows' C_p criterion.   Circled numbers correspond to those in the text
----

--- the BMDP instructions read by P9R are printed and interpreted ---

```
INDEPENDENT VARIABLES ARE
      2 AGE         3 HEIGHT      4 WEIGHT      7 ALBUMIN     8 CALCIUM
      9 URICACID

DEPENDENT VARIABLE. . . . . . . . . . . . . . .      6 CHOLSTRL
NUMBER OF 'BEST' REGRESSIONS. . . . . . . . . .      5
   SELECTION CRITERION . . . . . . . . . . . . . CP
WEIGHT VARIABLE . . . . . . . . . . . . . . .
PRECISION . . . . . . . . . . . . . . . . . . . DOUBLE
TOLERANCE FOR MATRIX INVERSION. . . . . . . . 0.0001000          ①

PRINT CORRELATION MATRIX. . . . . . . . . . . .YES
PRINT COVARIANCE MATRIX . . . . . . . . . . . . NO
PRINT RESIDUALS . . . . . . . . . . . . . . . . NO
PRINT COVARIANCE MATRIX FOR REGRESSION COEFS. . NO
PRINT CORRELATION MATRIX FOR REGRESSION COEFS . NO
MAX. NO. OF VARS. IN ANY REPORTED SUBSET . . .  6
```

DATA AFTER TRANSFORMATIONS   ②

C A S E NO. LABEL	2 AGE	3 HEIGHT	4 WEIGHT	7 ALBUMIN	8 CALCIUM	9 URICACID	6 CHOLSTRL
1 2381	22	67	144	4.300	9.800	5.400	200
3 1610	25	62	128	4.100	10.400	3.300	243
5 561	19	64	125	4.100	9.900	4.700	158
6 2519	19	67	130	4.500	10.500	8.300	255
7 225	20	64	118	3.900	9.500	4	210

```
NUMBER OF CASES READ. . . . . . . . . . . . .     188
   CASES WITH DATA MISSING OR BEYOND LIMITS . .     8          ③
      REMAINING NUMBER OF CASES . . . . . . . .    180
```

SUMMARY STATISTICS FOR EACH VARIABLE
----

	④					SMALLEST	LARGEST		
VARIABLE	MEAN	STANDARD DEVIATION	COEFFICIENT OF VARIATION	SMALLEST VALUE	LARGEST VALUE	STANDARD SCORE	STANDARD SCORE	SKEWNESS	KURTOSIS
2 AGE	33.53889	9.89801	0.295120	19.00000	55.00000	-1.47	2.17	0.40	-0.99
3 HEIGHT	64.46667	2.48211	0.038502	57.00000	71.00000	-3.01	2.63	-0.12	-0.04
4 WEIGHT	131.09444	20.49982	0.156374	94.00000	215.00000	-1.81	4.09	1.06	1.94
7 ALBUMIN	4.12056	0.35872	0.087057	3.20000	5.00000	-2.57	2.45	-0.07	-0.36
8 CALCIUM	9.96778	0.47280	0.047433	8.80000	11.10000	-2.47	2.39	-0.03	-0.58
9 URICACID	4.75556	1.12111	0.235748	2.20000	9.90000	-2.28	4.59	1.18	2.92
6 CHOLSTRL	235.83889	42.74377	0.181241	155.00000	390.00000	-1.89	3.61	0.46	0.06

VALUES FOR KURTOSIS GREATER THAN ZERO INDICATE DISTRIBUTIONS
WITH HEAVIER TAILS THAN THE NORMAL DISTRIBUTION.

(output continued)

Output 9R.1 (continued)

CORRELATIONS
----

(5)		AGE 2	HEIGHT 3	WEIGHT 4	ALBUMIN 7	CALCIUM 8	URICACID 9	CHOLSTRL 6
AGE	2	1.000						
HEIGHT	3	0.089	1.000					
WEIGHT	4	0.255	0.473	1.000				
ALBUMIN	7	-0.079	-0.006	-0.235	1.000			
CALCIUM	8	-0.009	0.143	0.065	0.453	1.000		
URICACID	9	0.209	0.125	0.304	0.030	0.166	1.000	
CHOLSTRL	6	0.365	0.011	0.146	0.057	0.255	0.274	1.000

ABSOLUTE VALUES OF CORRELATIONS IN SHADED FORM

```
    2 AGE        ▉
    3 HEIGHT     .▉
    4 WEIGHT     X▉▉
    7 ALBUMIN    . +▉
    8 CALCIUM    -.▉▉
    9 URICACID   +-▉ -▉
    6 CHOLSTRL   ▉ - XX▉
```

THE ABSOLUTE VALUES OF
THE MATRIX ENTRIES HAVE BEEN PRINTED ABOVE IN SHADED FORM
ACCORDING TO THE FOLLOWING SCHEME

		LESS THAN OR EQUAL TO		0.059
.	0.059	TO AND INCLUDING		0.118
-	0.118	TO AND INCLUDING		0.178
+	0.178	TO AND INCLUDING		0.237
X	0.237	TO AND INCLUDING		0.296
▉	0.296	TO AND INCLUDING		0.355
▉	0.355	TO AND INCLUDING		0.414
▉		GREATER THAN		0.414

FOR EACH SUBSET SELECTED BY YOUR CRITERION, THE R-SQUARED,
ADJUSTED R-SQUARED, MALLOWS' CP, AND THE VARIABLE NAMES ARE
PRINTED. THE REGRESSION COEFFICIENTS AND T-STATISTICS ARE
PRINTED TO THE RIGHT OF THE VARIABLE NAMES.   (6)

MANY OTHER SUBSETS MAY ALSO BE REPORTED THAT ARE NOT
ACCOMPANIED BY REGRESSION COEFFICIENTS AND T-STATISTICS.
SOME OF THESE SUBSETS MAY BE QUITE GOOD ALTHOUGH THEY ARE
NOT NECESSARILY BETTER THAN ANY SUBSET THAT HAS NOT BEEN
PRINTED.

SUBSETS WITH   1 VARIABLES

R-SQUARED	ADJUSTED R-SQUARED	CP	
0.133387	0.128519	19.40	AGE
0.075063	0.069867	32.55	URICACID
0.064901	0.059648	34.84	CALCIUM
0.021378	0.015880	44.65	WEIGHT
0.003305	-0.002294	48.73	ALBUMIN
0.000130	-0.005487	49.44	HEIGHT

(7)

(output continued)

(5) The correlation matrix with the dependent variable listed last. The same matrix is printed in shaded form.

(6) The criterion used is Mallows' C_p (METHOD). The five best subsets of variables according to Mallows' C_p are reported (5 is the preassigned number of subsets to be identified).

(7) Not all subsets of the independent variables are evaluated. At each subset size, P9R reports for up to 10 subsets of independent variables

- squared multiple correlation (R^2): the square of the correlation between the dependent variable y and the predicted value y

- adjusted R^2: $R^2 - p(1-R^2)/(N-p')$
where N is the number of cases and p' is the number of independent variables p (when the intercept is set to zero) or p+1 (when the intercept is not zero)
- Mallows' C_p: $RSS/s^2 - (N-2p')$
where RSS is the residual sum of squares based on the selected independent variables and s^2 is the residual mean square based on the regression using all independent variables

The coefficient of each variable and the coefficient divided by its standard error (the t statistic) are also reported for the best subsets chosen by the criterion.

(8) An analysis of the "best" subset selected by the criterion (the criterion is C_p in our example).

```
                                    SUBSETS WITH    2 VARIABLES
              ADJUSTED                ---------------------------
  R-SQUARED   R-SQUARED      CP

  0.199919    0.190879      6.40   AGE      CALCIUM

  0.174297    0.164968     12.17   AGE      URICACID

  0.140888    0.131181     19.71   AGE      ALBUMIN

  0.136391    0.126632     20.72   AGE      WEIGHT

  0.133837    0.124050     21.30   AGE      HEIGHT
```

--- regressions with 3 and 4 variables appear here. Coefficients and t statistics are reported
for one subset with 3 variables and for three subsets with 4 variables ---

```
                                    SUBSETS WITH    5 VARIABLES
              ADJUSTED                ---------------------------
  R-SQUARED   R-SQUARED      CP

  0.232133    0.210068      5.13   VARIABLE      COEFFICIENT   T-STATISTIC
                                   2 AGE           1.44852         4.91
                                   3 HEIGHT       -1.32644        -1.14
                                   7 ALBUMIN      -4.54807        -0.51
                                   8 CALCIUM      23.2669          3.37
                                   9 URICACID      6.55939         2.48
                                   INTERCEPT      28.3964

  0.232073    0.210006      5.15   AGE    HEIGHT   WEIGHT   CALCIUM   URICACID

  0.226613    0.204389      6.38   AGE    WEIGHT   ALBUMIN  CALCIUM   URICACID

  0.209037    0.186309     10.34   AGE    HEIGHT   WEIGHT   ALBUMIN   CALCIUM

  0.184292    0.160853     15.92   AGE    HEIGHT   WEIGHT   ALBUMIN   URICACID

  0.132863    0.107946     27.51   HEIGHT WEIGHT   ALBUMIN  CALCIUM   URICACID
```

```
                                    SUBSETS WITH    6 VARIABLES
              ADJUSTED                ---------------------------
  R-SQUARED   R-SQUARED      CP

  0.232720    0.206109      7.00   AGE  HEIGHT  WEIGHT  ALBUMIN  CALCIUM  URICACID
```

```
STATISTICS FOR 'BEST' SUBSET
----------------------------
MALLOWS' CP                        2.60        ⑧
SQUARED MULTIPLE CORRELATION     0.22562
MULTIPLE CORRELATION             0.47500
ADJUSTED SQUARED MULT. CORR.     0.21242
RESIDUAL MEAN SQUARE          1438.924527
STANDARD ERROR OF EST.          37.933159
F-STATISTIC                       17.09
NUMERATOR DEGREES OF FREEDOM          3
DENOMINATOR DEGREES OF FREEDOM      176
SIGNIFICANCE (TAIL PROB.)        0.0000
```

NOTE THAT THE ABOVE F-STATISTIC AND
ASSOCIATED SIGNIFICANCE TEND TO BE
LIBERAL WHENEVER A SUBSET OF VARIABLES
IS SELECTED BY THE CP OR ADJUSTED
R-SQUARED CRITERIA.

```
                 -------------------------------------
   VARIABLE      REGRESSION    STANDARD  STAND.   T-   2TAIL    TOL-   CONTRIBUTION
NO.    NAME      COEFFICIENT     ERROR   COEF.   STAT.  SIG.   ERANCE  TO R-SQUARED

   INTERCEPT      -49.7409      60.6922  -1.164  -0.82  0.414
   2 AGE            1.43596      0.293183  0.333   4.90  0.000  0.954582   0.105547
   8 CALCIUM       20.7918       6.08754   0.230   3.42  0.001  0.970402   0.051326
   9 URICACID       6.34439      2.62485   0.166   2.42  0.017  0.928274   0.025705
```

THE CONTRIBUTION TO R-SQUARED FOR EACH VARIABLE IS THE AMOUNT
BY WHICH R-SQUARED WOULD BE REDUCED IF THAT VARIABLE WERE
REMOVED FROM THE REGRESSION EQUATION.

For the best subset P9R prints

- the squared multiple correlation (R^2)
- adjusted R^2
- standard error of estimate ($RMS^{\frac{1}{2}}$)
- F statistic (test of the significance of the regression coefficients; however, its level of significance is sensitive to the method by which the best subset is selected)

For each variable in the best subset P9R prints

- the regression coefficient: b_i
- its standard error: $s(b_i)$ (see Appendix A.11)
- the standardized regression coefficient: $b_i s_i/s_y$ (the regression coefficient for standardized variables)
- t statistic: $b_i/s(b_i)$
- the two-tail level of significance of the t statistic (the level of significance of the test that the coefficient is zero)
- tolerance (described on p. 275)

<u>Specifying the regression.</u> The REGRESS paragraph is required to describe the dependent (predicted) and independent (predictor) variables. This paragraph cannot be repeated in P9R.

REGRess ────────────────────────────

DEPENDent = v.   required   none
   Name or subscript of the dependent (predicted) variable.
INDEPendent = v list.   none
   Names or subscripts of the independent (predictor) variables. If only two variables are specified then METHOD = NONE will be used (described below).

<u>Criterion for selecting the best subset (METHOD).</u> Any of three METHODS can be used as the criterion for the best subset (see Hocking, 1972).

CP: Mallows' C_p (Daniel and Wood, 1971, p. 86) is defined as

$$C_p = \frac{RSS}{s^2} - (N-2p')$$

where

RSS is the residual sum of squares for the best subset being tested
p'   is the number of variables in the subset (including the intercept, if any)
s^2 is the residual mean square based on the regression using all independent variables
     Best is defined as the smallest C_p.

RSQ: multiple correlation squared (R^2)
     Best is defined as the largest R^2.

ADJ: adjusted R^2 is defined as $R^2 - p(1-R^2)/(N-p')$ (Theil, 1971, p. 179). Best is defined as the largest adjusted R^2.

NONE: If you do not want P9R to search for the best subsets, you can specify NONE. An ordinary regression is performed using all independent variables. This option is used when the primary interest is in the residual analysis that is not available in other programs, or when you need computations done in double precision.

When CP is the METHOD used, the criterion

$$C_p = \frac{RSS}{s^2} - (N-2p')$$

can be modified by specifying a value for PENALTY. Without this specification, when an additional variable is entered p increases by one and $-(N-2p')$ increases by two -- two is a penalty for adding a variable. The value specified for PENALTY becomes the coefficient of p in the above formula.

REGRess ────────────────────────────

METHod = (one only)   RSQ/prev.
         CP,RSQ,ADJ,NONE
   Criterion for choosing the best subset. The methods are described above. If NONE is specified, a multiple linear regression analysis is performed using all independent variables (no subsets are identified). If only two independent variables are specified then NONE is assumed.
PENalty = #.   2/prev.
   The penalty for entering an additional variable when the METHOD is CP. Penalty is defined above. Mallows' C_p corresponds to a penalty of 2.
NUMBer = #.   cannot exceed 10   5/prev.
   The number of best subsets to be identified. For CP and ADJ, this number is found for all subset sizes combined. For RSQ this number is found for each subset size.
MAXVar = #.   all
   The maximum number of independent variables to be reported in any selected subset (unless identified as among the best by the CP or ADJ criteria).

<u>Strategies for variable selection.</u> Several strategies can be used to select independent variables. One strategy is to screen a large set of variables and delete those that appear definitely redundant with respect to predicting the dependent variable. Another sample can then be taken and further variables can be deleted. This process might be repeated. The number of variables in the subset and the criterion for selection is highly dependent upon the stage of the research.

It is suggested that in any final selection of variables all the t statistics for the coefficients be highly significant from both the statistical and practical points of view. The preassigned F-to-enter and F-to-remove limits in the stepwise program P2R are 4 and 3.9. This F-to-enter limit suggests that the t statistics for the regression coefficients should be at least two.

The t statistics for the coefficients of the variables for the subset that maximizes adjusted R^2

are all greater than one in absolute value. Maximizing adjusted R^2 is equivalent to minimizing the residual mean square and thereby minimizing the apparent significance level reported for the selected subset (Output 9R.1 ⑧). In the language of stepwise regression, the subset that maximizes adjusted R^2 is such that each variable in the subset has an F-to-remove value greater than one and the remaining variables have F-to-enter values less than one. Subsets larger than the subset that maximizes the adjusted R^2 are not likely to be very good.

The t statistics for the coefficients of the variables for the subset that minimizes C_p tend to be greater than $\sqrt{2}$ in absolute value. In the language of stepwise regression, the subset that minimizes C_p is such that the F-to-remove values for variables in the subset tend to be greater than two and the F-to-enter values for the remaining variables tend to be less than two. Thus neither the adjusted R^2 nor the C_p criteria result in t statistics greater than two. In P9R a restriction can be imposed (approximately) on the coefficients by means of the PENALTY statement in the REGRESS paragraph. The F-to-remove values tend to be greater than the specified value of PENALTY for the best subset.

The problem of variable selection increases as the number of redundant and irrelevant variables increases. Inclusion of such variables permits artifacts in the data to produce spuriously high t statistics, R^2 values and adjusted R^2 values, and spuriously low C_p statistics -- just as spuriously optimistic statistics can result in a stepwise regression. As a general rule of thumb, a smaller number of variables is likely to provide better results in a cross-validation (application of the regression coefficients to new data). A cross-validation can easily be made in this program by means of the case weight variable. The "training"

set should be assigned weights of one and the cross-validation set should be assigned weight zero. If you request that the residuals be printed or plotted, the residual mean square for the training set and the average squared residual for the cross-validation set are printed and can be compared. (See Appendix C.15).

One of the purposes of P9R is to present the user with a wide variety of good subsets. Selection of your final subset will usually be affected by a number of criteria outside the program such as the prevalence of missing values, cost of measuring variables, ease of presentation to others, etc.

Example 9R.2 Printing Covariances, Residuals and Distance Measures

The CORRELATIONS and COVARIANCES between the variables, and the correlations of the estimates of the regression coefficients (RREG) can be printed. In addition, four types of residuals, predicted values and distance measures can be printed. A complete list is given in ⑪ below. These statistics aid in assessing the fit of the data to the regression, the dependence on the independent variables and the sensitivity of the regression equation to the data for each case.

You can specify the number of CASES to print. If not specified, five cases are printed.

In this example we request the covariance matrix, the correlations of the regression coefficient estimates, the four types of residuals and the distance measures by inserting a PRINT paragraph in the Control Language of Example 9R.1 before the END paragraph:

```
----------------------------------------
/ PRINT   MATRICES ARE COVA, RREG, RESI.
----------------------------------------
```

Output 9R.2   Covariance, residuals and distance measures

--- univariate statistics appear here ---

COVARIANCES
----

⑨		AGE 2	HEIGHT 3	WEIGHT 4	ALBUMIN 7	CALCIUM 8	URICACID 9	CHOLSTRL 6
AGE	2	97.9705						
HEIGHT	3	2.1885	6.1609					
WEIGHT	4	51.7924	24.0898	420.2424				
ALBUMIN	7	-0.2804	-0.0052	-1.7254	0.1287			
CALCIUM	8	-0.0406	0.1676	0.6271	0.0768	0.2235		
URICACID	9	2.3140	0.3488	6.9780	0.0120	0.0881	1.2569	
CHOLSTRL	6	154.5175	1.2097	128.1159	0.8815	5.1484	13.1291	1827.0298

--- best subset selected and best subset analyzed ---

CORRELATIONS OF THE ESTIMATES OF THE REGRESSION COEFFICIENTS
----

⑩		AGE 2	CALCIUM 8	URICACID 9
AGE	2	1.000		
CALCIUM	8	0.045	1.000	
URICACID	9	-0.213	-0.172	1.000

(output continued)

Output 9R.2 (continued)

IN THE TABLE BELOW, THE STANDARDIZED RESIDUAL IS THE RESIDUAL
DIVIDED BY ITS STANDARD ERROR. THE COLUMN LABEL DELETED
(PRESS) RESIDUAL CONTAINS THE RESIDUAL FOR EACH CASE FROM
PREDICTING THAT CASE FROM THE OTHER CASES, I.E, THE
RESIDUAL FOR THE CASE AFTER REMOVING THE EFFECT OF
THAT CASE FROM THE REGRESSION COEFFICIENTS. SIMILARLY, THE
ADJUSTED (PRESS) PREDICTED VALUE IS THE PREDICTED VALUE FOR
THE CASE AFTER REMOVING THE EFFECT OF THAT CASE FROM THE
REGRESSION COEFFICIENTS. FOR A DISCUSSION OF COOK'S
DISTANCE, SEE R. D. COOK, TECHNOMETRICS, FEB., 1977.

CASE LABEL	CASE NO.	OBSERVED CHOLSTRL	PREDICTED VALUE	STANDARD ERROR OF PRED.VAL.	RESIDUAL	CASE WEIGHT	WEIGHTED RESIDUAL	STAND- ARDIZED RESIDUAL	DELETED (PRESS) RESIDUAL	ADJUSTED (PRESS) PRED.VAL.	MAHALA- NOBIS DISTANCE	COOK'S DISTANCE
2381	1	200.0000	219.8697	5.1657	-19.8697	1.000	-19.8697	-0.53	-20.2452	220.2452	2.33	0.00
1610	3	243.0000	223.3295	5.8797	19.6705	1.000	19.6705	0.52	20.1547	222.8453	3.31	0.00
1797	4	MISSING	204.7927	5.7056						204.7927	3.06	
561	5	158.0000	213.2000	5.1213	-55.2000	1.000	-55.2000	-1.47	-56.2248	214.2248	2.27	0.01
2519	6	255.0000	248.5149	11.3361	6.4851	1.000	6.4851	0.18	7.1211	247.8789	14.99	0.00
225	7	210.0000	201.8782	5.6138	8.1218	1.000	8.1218	0.22	8.3037	201.6963	2.93	0.00

--- similar statistics and residuals for cases 8 to 182 ---

CASE LABEL	CASE NO.	OBSERVED CHOLSTRL	PREDICTED VALUE	STANDARD ERROR OF PRED.VAL.	RESIDUAL	CASE WEIGHT	WEIGHTED RESIDUAL	STAND- ARDIZED RESIDUAL	DELETED (PRESS) RESIDUAL	ADJUSTED (PRESS) PRED.VAL.	MAHALA- NOBIS DISTANCE	COOK'S DISTANCE
1250	183	250.0000	264.0413	6.5525	-14.0414	1.000	-14.0414	-0.38	-14.4733	264.4733	4.35	0.00
1789	184	265.0000	281.7678	7.0902	-16.7679	1.000	-16.7679	-0.45	-17.3749	282.3749	5.26	0.00
575	186	220.0000	278.0215	8.0304	-58.0215	1.000	-58.0215	-1.57	-60.7439	280.7439	7.03	0.03
2271	187	305.0000	272.4094	6.9854	32.5904	1.000	32.5904	0.87	33.7344	271.2656	5.08	0.01
39	188	220.0000	250.7384	10.3278	-30.7384	1.000	-30.7384	-0.84	-33.1994	253.1994	12.27	0.01

SUMMARY STATISTICS FOR RESIDUALS ⑫

(CASES WITH POSITIVE WEIGHT)
AVERAGE RESIDUAL   -0.0000
RESIDUAL MEAN SQUARE   1438.92452742
AVERAGE DELETED RESIDUAL   0.0324
AVE. SQUARED DELETED RESIDUAL
    (PREDICTION MEAN SQUARE)   1474.14341152
SERIAL CORRELATION   -0.0800
DURBIN-WATSON STATISTIC   2.1543

HISTOGRAM OF STANDARDIZED (STUDENTIZED) RESIDUALS
EACH BIN OF THE HISTOGRAM IS LABELED WITH ITS LOWER LIMIT.
NOTE THAT IF THE COUNT FOR A BIN EXCEEDS 100, ONLY
100 ASTERISKS WILL BE PRINTED.

```
        -2.6    1 *
        -2.4    0
        -2.2    0
        -2.0    1 *
        -1.8    4 ****
        -1.6    8 ********
        -1.4    7 *******
        -1.2    8 ********
        -1.0   14 **************
        -0.8    7 *******
        -0.6   15 ***************
        -0.4   19 *******************
        -0.2    8 ********
         0.0   11 ***********
         0.2   15 ***************
         0.4   16 ****************
         0.6   11 ***********
         0.8    7 *******
         1.0    7 *******
         1.2    6 ******
         1.4    3 ***
         1.6    3 ***
         1.8    6 ******
         2.0    0
         2.2    0
         2.4    0
         2.6    1 *
         2.8    1 *
         3.0    0
         3.2    0
         3.4    1 *              (output continued)
```

The results of the analysis appear in Output 9R.2. Circled numbers below correspond to those in the output.

⑨ The covariance matrix of the variables (the dependent variable is last).

⑩ Correlations of the estimates of the regression coefficients (defined in Appendix A.11) calculated for the best subset.

⑪ The request to print residuals yields the following for each case

- the value of the dependent variable: y
- the predicted value for the dependent variable (predicted from the best subset): $\hat{y}$
- the standard error of the predicted value
- the residual: $y-\hat{y}$
- case weight: w (one if a case WEIGHT is not specified)
- weighted residual: $\sqrt{w}\,(y-\hat{y})$ (if w is zero or one, $y-\hat{y}$ is printed)
- standardized (Studentized) residual (Prescott, 1975): $(y-\hat{y})/(\text{standard error})$
- deleted (PRESS) residual: the residual that would be obtained if the case were omitted from the computation of the regression line (see Appendix A.12 for the formula)
- adjusted (PRESS) predicted value: the predicted value that would be obtained if the cases were omitted from the computation of the regression line (see Appendix A.12).
- Mahalanobis distance: the distance of each case from the mean of all cases used to estimate the regression equation (computed from the values of the independent variables in the best subset, see Appendix A.12 for the formula); a large distance indicates that the case is an outlier in the space defined by the independent variables.

```
-----------------------------------------------------------------
      23.64 IS THE MAXIMUM VALUE OF MAHALANOBIS DISTANCE AMONG CASES WITH
POSITIVE CASE WEIGHT.  THIS OCCURRED FOR CASE NUMBER    138, CASE LABEL = 3312
```

```
-----------------------------------------------------------------
       3.50 IS THE LARGEST STANDARDIZED RESIDUAL (IN ABSOLUTE VALUE) AMONG
CASES WITH POSITIVE CASE WEIGHT.  THIS OCCURRED FOR CASE NUMBER    182, CASE LABEL = 3134
```

```
-----------------------------------------------------------------
       0.08 IS THE MAXIMUM VALUE OF COOK'S DISTANCE AMONG CASES
WITH POSITIVE WEIGHT.  THIS OCCURRED FOR CASE NUMBER    60, CASE LABEL =  152
IF THIS CASE WERE OMITTED, THE REGRESSION COEFFICIENTS WOULD
MOVE FROM THE VALUES REPORTED ABOVE TO THE EDGE OF A    3.08
PERCENT CONFIDENCE ELLIPSOID.
```

```
-----------------------------------------------------------------
COMPARISON OF ESTIMATES OF REGRESSION COEFFICIENTS
(RELATIVE DIFFERENCE IS DIFFERENCE DIVIDED BY ORDINARY COEF.
STANDARD ERROR IS THAT OF ORDINARY COEFFICIENT.)
```

	ORDINARY LEAST SQUARES	OMITTING CASE WITH LARGEST COOK DISTANCE	RELATIVE DIFFERENCE	DIFFERENCE DIVIDED BY STANDARD ERROR
INTERCEPT	-49.740942	-54.433906	-0.0943	0.0773
2 AGE	1.435955	1.498802	-0.0438	-0.2144
8 CALCIUM	20.791836	21.689360	-0.0432	-0.1474
9 URICACID	6.344389	4.916680	0.2250	0.5439

```
-----------------------------------------------------------------
NUMERICAL CONSISTENCY CHECK

RESIDUAL MEAN SQUARES ARE COMPUTED FROM BOTH COVARIANCE MATRIX AND RESIDUALS, AND
RELATIVE DIFFERENCE (DIFFERENCE DIVIDED BY SMALLER OF TWO ESTIMATES) IS COMPUTED.

      RESIDUAL MEAN SQUARES COMPUTED FROM

COVARIANCE MATRIX        RESIDUALS      RELATIVE DIFFERENCE

   0.143892D 04       0.143892D 04        0.118512D-15
```

⑬

- Cook's (1977) distance: a measure of the change in the coefficients of the regression that would occur if the case were omitted from the computation of the coefficients (see Appendix A.12 for the formula).

See Weisberg (1980) for further discussion of the residual analysis.

⑫ Summary statistics for the residuals for cases with positive weights:

- average residual: $\Sigma(y-\hat{y})/N$
- residual mean square: $\Sigma(y-\hat{y})^2/(N-p)$
- average deleted residual: Σ deleted residual/N
- average squared deleted residual: Σ(deleted residual)^2/N
- Durbin-Watson statistic (Theil, 1971, p.199)
- serial correlation
- histogram of standardized residuals

If case weights are specified, the above formulas are modified to include the case weights. Several summary statistics are reported separately for cases with zero case weight (see Appendix C.15). Suspected cases are identified and the regression coefficients are recomputed after removing the effect of the most influential case.

⑬ Numerical consistency check: the residual mean square is computed both from the residuals and from the covariance matrix.

PRINT
  MATRIces = one or more of the   CORR/prev.
                 list below
    Matrices to be printed. If any MATRICES are specified, only those requested are printed.
    CORR: correlation matrix
    COVA: covariance matrix
    RREG: correlations of the estimates of the regression coefficients
    CREG: covariances of the estimates of the regression coefficients
    RESI: residuals, predicted values and related measures as described in ⑪, ⑫ and ⑬ above.
  CASE = #.   5/prev.
    Number of cases of data (after transformations, if any) to be printed.

  SHADE   SHADE./prev.
    To omit shaded correlation matrix state NO SHADE.

Example 9R.3 Plotting Variables, Predicted Values and Residuals

The predicted values, residuals and distance measures are derived variables and are available for plotting. Suppose there are VT variables (after transformations, if any). Then

- the predicted value is kept as variable VT+1 and named PREDICTED
- the residual is kept as variable VT+2 and named RESIDUAL
- the standardized residual is kept as variable VT+3 and named STRESIDL
- the weighted residual is kept as variable VT+4 and named WRESIDUL
- Mahalanobis distance is kept as variable VT+5 and named DISTANCE
- the deleted residual is kept as variable VT+6 and named DELRESID
- Cook's distance is kept as variable VT+7 and named COOKDIST

These new variables can be plotted against each other or against any variable by specifying their name (or subscript) as an XVAR or YVAR variable.

In this example we insert a PLOT paragraph in the Control Language of Example 9R.1 before the END paragraph.

```
/ PLOT    YVAR ARE CHOLSTRL, RESIDUAL, CHOLSTRL,
                RESIDUAL, RESIDUAL.
          XVAR ARE AGE, URICACID, PREDICTD,
                PREDICTD, DELRESID.
          NORMAL.
          SIZE IS 40,25.
```

Each pair of variables in the YVAR and XVAR lists form one plot (e.g., CHOLSTRL versus AGE). The plots are presented in Output 9R.3. Circled numbers below correspond to those in the output. The types of plots shown are:

⑭ One variable against another variable.

⑮ Residuals against a variable.

⑯ A variable against predicted values.

⑰ Residuals against predicted values.

⑱ Residuals against deleted residuals (this plot should be inspected for cases that have a large discrepancy between the residual and deleted residual).

⑲ A normal probability plot of the standardized residuals.

Output 9R.3 Plots of variables, predicted values and residuals

---

IN THE BIVARIATE PLOTS WHICH FOLLOW, A = 10 CASES, B = 11 CASES, ..., AND * = 36 OR MORE CASES.
AN * IN THE BORDER OF ANY PLOT INDICATES A MISSING VALUE OR A VALUE OUT OF RANGE.

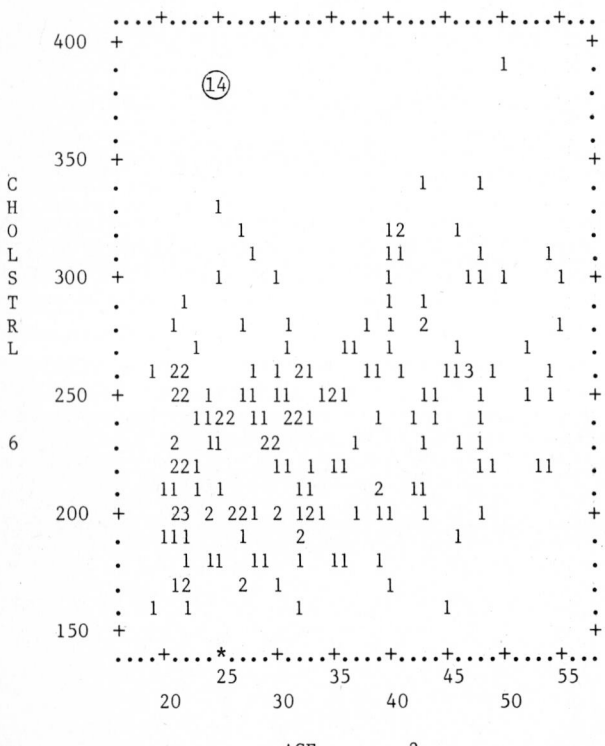

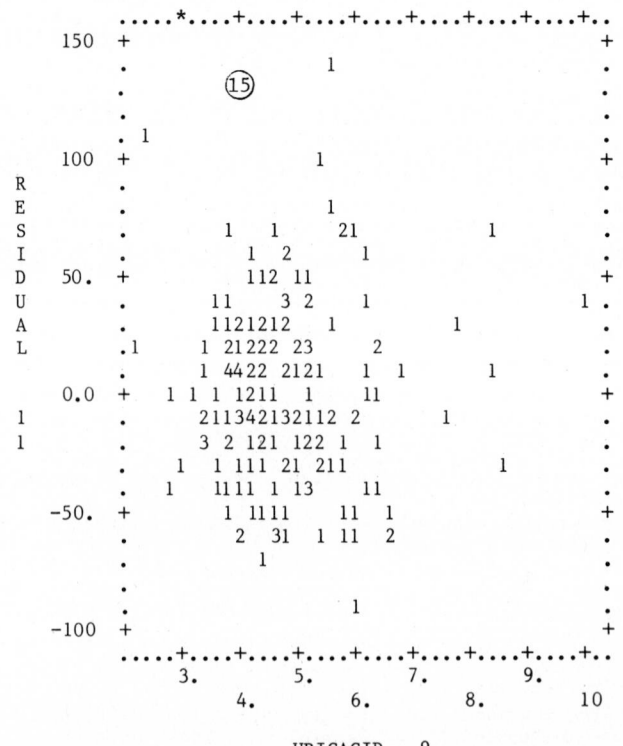

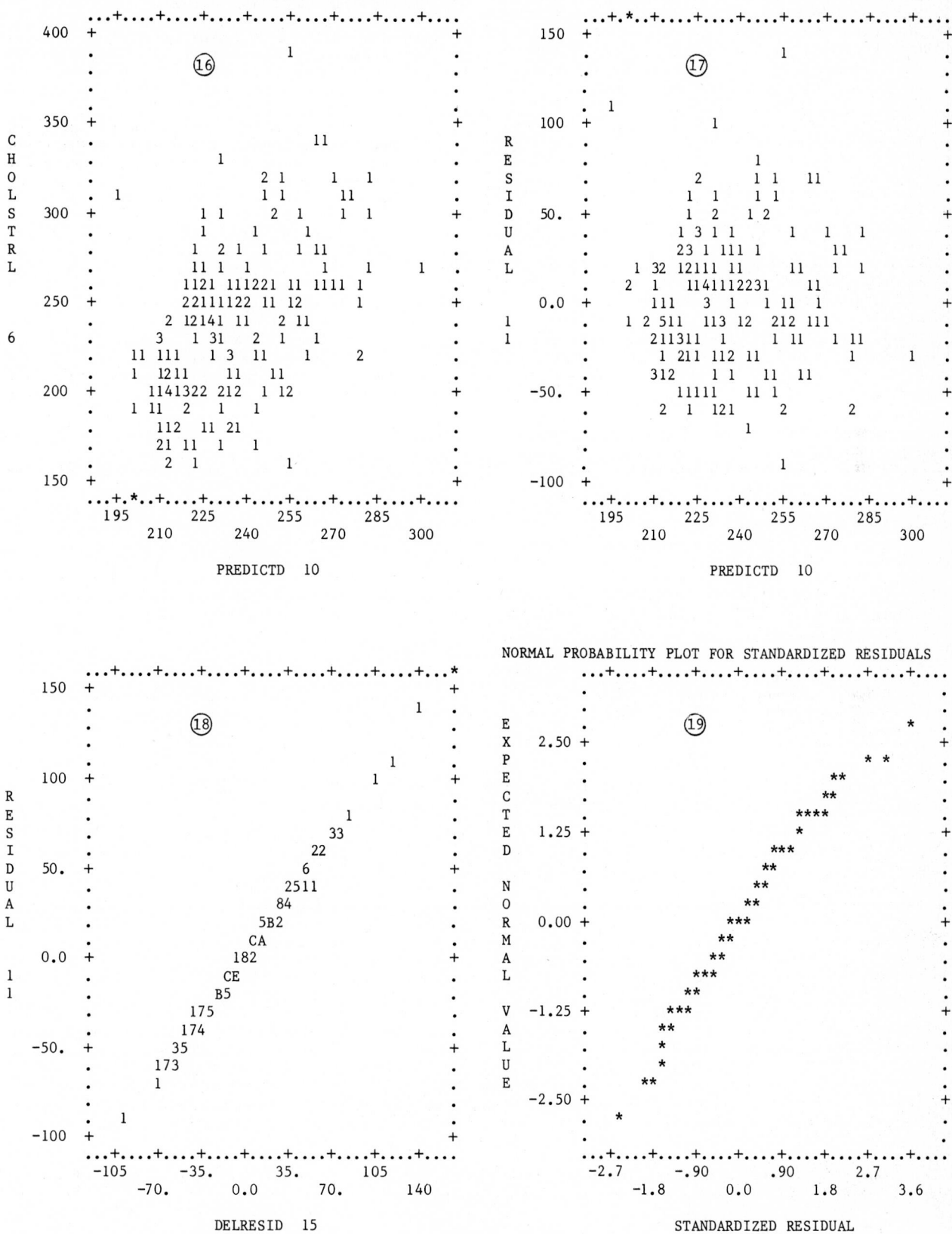

```
PLOT ─────────────────────────────────────────────
   YVAR = v list.                                    none
   Names or subscripts of variables for the Y axes
   of plots.
   XVAR = v list.                                    none
   Names or subscripts of variables for the X axes
   of plots. The first YVAR variable is plotted
   against the first XVAR variable, the second
   against the second, etc. Residuals and
   predicted values can be specified as either
   XVAR or YVAR. See above for how they are named.
   SIZE = #,#.                                   50,35/prev.
   The first number is the number of characters
   (width) in the horizontal axis and the second
   number is the number of lines (height) in the
   vertical axis.
   NORMal.                                        no/prev.
   Print a normal probability plot for the
   standardized (studentized) residuals.
   STATistics.                                    no/prev.
   Print statistics with plots as in program P6D.
   HISTogram.                                     no/prev.
   Print histogram of standardized (studentized)
   residuals.
```

Example 9R.4 Saving the Covariance Matrix, Residuals and Distance Measures for Later Analyses

Both the DATA (including predicted values, residuals and related measures) and the COVARIANCE matrix can be saved in a BMDP File to be used for input to a subsequent analysis. Chapter 7 describes BMDP Files and how they are used.

When DATA are saved, the variables VT+1 to VT+7 as defined in Example 9R.3 are also saved (see Example 9R.2 for a more detailed description of these variables).

In this example we save both the data (including the above variables) and the covariance matrix. A SAVE paragraph is inserted in the Control Language of Example 9R.1 before the END paragraph.

```
------------------------------------------
/ SAVE    UNIT IS 9.
          NEW.
          CODE IS WERNER.
          CONTENT IS DATA, COVA.
------------------------------------------
```

Output 9R.4   Saving the covariance matrix, data, residuals and distance measures in a BMDP File
```
-------------------------------------------------------------------------------------------------

                    REQUESTED OUTPUT BMDP FILE
                        UNIT   =        9
                        CODE   = WERNER
                        LABEL  =
                        CONTENT =
                                  DATA
                                  COVA


                    --------------------------------------------
                    BMDP FILE IS BEING WRITTEN ON UNIT        9
                    CODE. . . IS      WERNER
                    CONTENT . IS      COVA
                    LABEL . . IS

                    VARIABLES ARE
                        2 AGE          3 HEIGHT      4 WEIGHT      7 ALBUMIN     8 CALCIUM
                        9 URICACID     6 CHOLSTRL


                    BMDP FILE ON UNIT  9 HAS BEEN COMPLETED.
                    --------------------------------------------

                        --- the results of the regression analysis appear here ---

                    --------------------------------------------
                    BMDP FILE IS BEING WRITTEN ON UNIT        9
                    CODE. . . IS      WERNER
                    CONTENT . IS      DATA
                    LABEL . . IS

                    VARIABLES ARE
                        1 ID           2 AGE         3 HEIGHT      4 WEIGHT      5 BRTHPILL
                        6 CHOLSTRL     7 ALBUMIN     8 CALCIUM     9 URICACID   10 PREDICTD
                       11 RESIDUAL    12 STRESIDL   13 WRESIDUL   14 DISTANCE   15 DELRESID
                       16 COOKDIST


                    BMDP FILE ON UNIT  9 HAS BEEN COMPLETED.
                    --------------------------------------------

                    NUMBER OF CASES WRITTEN TO FILE      188

-------------------------------------------------------------------------------------------------
```

Note: The System Cards that precede the Control Language must contain a card describing where to store the BMDP File (Section 7.1).

The messages indicating that the BMDP Files are created are shown in Output 9R.4. When the CONTENT is DATA, seven variables are saved in addition to the original variables.

SAVE ─────────────────────────────────
CONTent = (one or both) DATA,COVA.   DATA
    The matrices to be saved in a BMDP File. If
    DATA is specified, the data and the seven
    additional variables described above are saved.
    If COVA is specified, the covariance matrix is
    saved.

Using a Correlation or Covariance Matrix as Input

DATA, a CORRELATION matrix or a COVARIANCE matrix can be used as input to P9R. The input can be from a BMDP File (Chapter 7) but need not be. (In other regression programs the correlation and covariance matrices can only be input from a BMDP File.)

The input of a CORRELATION matrix from a BMDP File is illustrated in Example 1R.5 for P1R; it is similar for P9R.

When P9R reads as input a COVARIANCE or CORRELATION matrix that is not in a BMDP File, it assumes that the matrix is SQUARE unless

SHAPE = LOWER.

is specified in the INPUT paragraph. The matrix is read one row at a time whether it is SQUARE or LOWER. When LOWER is specified, the lower triangular matrix is read. That is, the first value in the first case is read as the first row, the first two values in the second case as the second row, etc. (see Example 4M.6). The TYPE of the input must be specified.

INPut ─────────────────────────────────
CONTent = c. used only when input   DATA
              is from a BMDP File
    If the input is not DATA, CONTENT must be
    specified. It must be identical to the CONTENT
    stated in the SAVE paragraph when the BMDP File
    was created.
TYPE = (one only) DATA,   same as CONTENT;
       COVA, CORR.   otherwise DATA
    The type of input. TYPE must be specified when
    a covariance or correlation matrix is input
    that is not in a BMDP File. TYPE must also be
    specified when a BMDP File is input and the
    CONTENT is not one of the three TYPES: DATA,
    COVA or CORR.
SHAPE = (one only) SQUARE,   SQUARE/prev.
       LOWER.
    SHAPE is required only when a covariance or
    correlation matrix is input that is not a BMDP
    File. LOWER means that a lower triangular
    matrix is input. Each row is read separately
    and must begin in a new record. The FORMAT
    statement must describe the longest (last) row
    in the matrix.

The Model with No Intercept

The regression equation usually contains an intercept (a constant term); e.g., in

$$y = a + b_1 x_1 + b_2 x_2 + \ldots + b_p x_p$$

a is the intercept. In some problems, the intercept must be zero; this can be specified by

ZERO.

in the REGRESS paragraph. This rarely used option affects computations as described in Appendix A.11.

REGRess ─────────────────────────────────
ZERO.   not ZERO/prev.
    If ZERO is specified, the intercept in the re-
    gression equation is set to zero. Note that if
    a zero intercept model is used, then the R^2 is
    estimated under the assumption that all vari-
    ables have zero means.
    Note: this is a rarely used option that affects
    the computations (see Appendix A.11).

A Weight for Each Case

When the error variance is not homogeneous but varies from case to case, weighted least squares estimation is more appropriate; the weight (w) for each case is proportional to the inverse of the variance. In weighted least squares, estimates of the coefficients minimize

$$\sum w_j (y_j - \hat{y}_j)^2$$

where w_j is the weight for case j.

You can estimate predicted values for cases not used to compute the regression equation by setting their case weights to zero. The use of zero case weights to perform a cross-validation is explained in Appendix C.15.

Case weights affect the computation of the means, variances, covariances and correlations (see Section 2.1).

VARiable ─────────────────────────────────
WEIGHT = v.   no weight var./prev.
    Name or subscript of the variable containing
    case weights. The weights should be greater
    than or equal to zero. If WEIGHT is not stated
    or is set to zero, there are no case weights.

TOLERANCE: Inverting the Covariance Matrix

The covariance matrix must be inverted to compute the residual mean square (required for C_p); the equation containing all the independent variables is used. If the squared multiple correlation (R^2) of any independent variable with the other independent variables is too high, the computation of the inverse loses numerical accuracy. Therefore the TOLERANCE limit is used as a check on the largest multiple correlation (TOLERANCE = $1 - R^2$). If the limit is violated, P9R reports a list of the variables in violation and terminates the computations unless the METHOD is NONE. In the latter case, P9R reports a regression equation for a nonredundant subset of predictor variables.

```
REGRess ──────────────────────────────────────
   TOLERANCE = #.                          0.0001/prev.
   If the R² of any independent variable with the
   other    independent    variables    exceeds
   1-TOLERANCE,  the computations  are terminated
   unless the METHOD is NONE. For IBM 360 and 370
   computers,  we suggest  that TOLERANCE be at
   least 10⁻⁴.
```

Missing Values

A case is excluded from the computations if any independent, dependent, or case weight variable is missing or out of range. If only the dependent variable is missing, predicted values are computed for that case; but the case does not affect the regression equation. If you have a large number of missing values, you may want to repeat the analysis with a subset of variables in order to increase the number of cases used.

SIZE OF PROBLEM

When METHOD is NONE, at least 100 independent variables can be included in the analysis for medium-sized computer systems; otherwise, about 27 variables can be used. Computer costs are usually comparable to costs for stepwise regression for up to about 25 independent variables. Appendix B describes how to increase the capacity of the program.

COMPUTATIONAL METHOD

Data are read in single precision. The covariance matrix is computed by the provisional means method (Appendix A.2) in double precision. FORTRAN coding for the best subset algorithm was obtained from Furnival and Wilson (1974a,b). The best subset algorithm uses a mixture of single and double precision and employs both forward and reverse pivots (sweeps, see Appendix A.11). Excessive roundoff error may occur in the best subset algorithm if the R for the dependent variable exceeds .9999 or if the tolerance for any independent variable is less than .0001. To check the results for the best subset, the computations are repeated in double precision with forward pivots only, using a fresh copy of the covariance matrix.

The residuals and related statistics computed for the residual analysis are defined in Appendix A.12.

ACKNOWLEDGEMENT

P9R was designed and programmed by James Frane. FORTRAN coding for the best subset algorithm was obtained from George Furnival and Robert Wilson.

SUMMARY

Order of Input Cards

```
   // (job card)
   // EXEC BIMED,PROG=BMDP9R        (see Appendix E)
   //SYSIN DD *
   / PROBLEM
   / INPUT
   / VARIABLE
   / TRANSFORM
   / SAVE
   / REGRESS
   / PRINT
   / PLOT
   / END
      (data if on cards)
   // (system card)
```

Full sets of BMDP paragraphs (and data, if on cards) can be repeated for additional problems; see Section 5.8.

instructions specific to P9R

Paragraph Statement	Preassigned	Comment and Manual Reference
/ INPut		Additional input options. Same as P6R. 275
/ VARiable		Additional option to specify case weights. 275
WEIGHT = v.	none	Name or subscript of one variable containing a weight for each case. This weight is used in calculating means, covariances, slopes, etc. Cases with zero weight are not used in computations, but their predicted values are calculated. *
/ PRINT		Optional to specify results to be printed. If MATR is specified, only matrices specified are printed. If / PRINT is omitted, CORR is printed, and data for the first 5 cases are listed.
CASE = #.	5.	Number of cases for which data are listed. 271
MATRices = c list.	CORR.	Print one or more of the following matrices: CORR – correlations COVA – covariance RREG – correlations of the regression coefficients CREG – covariances of the regression coefficients RESI – residuals including the 7 values listed under / SAVE CONT = DATA below, and the case weight. 271
MAXVAR = #.		Subsets with more than the number of variables listed are not reported.
SHADE.	yes	Shaded correlation matrix. To omit state NO SHADED. 271

(continued)

(continued)

Paragraph Statement	Preassigned	Comment and Manual Reference
/●REGRess		Required to direct regression.
● DEPENDent = v.	none	Required; name or subscript of the dependent (predicted) variable. 268
● INDEP = v list.	none	Required; names or subscripts of independent (predictor) variables. 268
METHod = c.	CP.	Criteria for choosing the best subset (one only). * 268 CP – Mallows' C_p (see PEN below) RSQ – multiple correlation squared (R^2) ADJ – adjusted R^2 NONE – an ordinary regression using all the independent variables
PENalty = #.	2.	The penalty for entering an additional variable when METH = CP. Mallows' C_p corresponds to a penalty of 2. * 268
NUMber = #.	5.	The number of best subsets to be identified. For CP and ADJ this number is found for all subset sizes combined. For RSQ this number is found for each subset size. * 268
TOLerance = #.	.0001.	**Value less than 1.0 to prevent loss in accuracy due to numerically redundant variables.** * 276
ZERO.	no	Compute covariances and correlations about the origin (zero means assumed). This option is rarely used. * 275
MAXVar = #.	all	Maximum number of independent variables in any selected subset. 268
/ PLOT		Optional to request plots. No plots are printed unless requested. 274
XVAR = v list. YVAR = v list.	none none	Names or subscripts of variables (or predicted values or residuals) to be plotted horizontally (along the x-axis), and variables (or residuals) to be plotted vertically (along the y-axis). The first YVAR is plotted against the first XVAR, the second against the second, etc. Residuals and predicted values are available by name or number as in / SAVE below.
NORMal.	no	Normal probability plot of the standardized residuals. *
SIZE = #, #.	50,35.	Width of x-axis (characters); height of y-axis (lines). *
STATistics.	no	Print mean, standard deviation, correlation and regression equations for each plot, as in P6D. *
HIST.	no	Histogram of standardized residuals. *
/ SAVE		Additional options required only if a BMDP File is created. 275
CONTent = c list.		DATA, COVA (one or both); if COVA is specified the covariance matrix is saved. If DATA is specified, the following are saved after the last variable (VT) for each case. They can be referenced by their name or variable number. PREDICTD – predicted values (VT + 1) RESIDUAL – residuals (VT + 2) STRESIDL – standard residuals (VT + 3) WRESIDUL – weighted residuals (VT + 4) DISTANCE – Mahalanobis' distances (VT + 5) DELRESID – deleted residuals (VT + 6) COOKDIST – Cook's distances (VT + 7)

Key:

/	–indicates paragraph
.	–period ends a sentence
●	–required
v	–variable (name or subscript)
g	–group (name or subscript)
#	–number
'c'	–characters (name or parameter) may omit apostrophes if contiguous letters only

*	–assigned value remains the same for additional problems
VT	–number of variables after transformations
list	–more than one item, often one per var.

Capitalized letters-paragraph or sentence names recognized by BMDP

Page numbers following refer to this Manual

P4R

13.4 Regression on Principal Components

ABSTRACT

P4R computes a regression analysis for a dependent variable on a set of principal components computed from the independent variables. The principal components enter the regression in a stepwise manner and the resulting coefficients are reported in terms of both the principal components and the original or standardized variables. The order of entry of the components is determined by either the magnitude of the eigenvalues or the correlations between the dependent variable and the components. The covariance or correlation matrix can be used to compute the components.

WHERE TO FIND IT

Example 4R.1 Basic Setup for Principal Components Analysis

The Werner blood chemistry data (Table 5.1) are used to illustrate the results produced by P4R. In this example the REGRESS paragraph is specific to P4R; the other Control Language instructions are described in Chapter 5.

```
-------------------------------------
/ PROBLEM    TITLE IS 'WERNER BLOOD CHEMISTRY DATA'.
/ INPUT      VARIABLES ARE 9.
            FORMAT IS '(A4, 5F4.0, 3F4.1)'.
/ VARIABLE   NAMES ARE ID, AGE, HEIGHT, WEIGHT,
                       BRTHPILL, CHOLSTRL, ALBUMIN,
                       CALCIUM, URICACID.
            MAXIMUM IS (6)400.
            MINIMUM IS (6)150.
            LABEL IS ID.

/ REGRESS    DEPENDENT IS CHOLSTRL.
            INDEPENDENT ARE 2 TO 4, 7 TO 9.

/ END
-------------------------------------
```

(See end of this P4R section for organization of system information, BMDP instructions and data.)

The results are presented in Output 4R.1. Circled numbers below correspond to those in the output.

(1) Control Language instructions specific to P4R are interpreted. Preassigned values are reported for some options.

(2) Complete cases only are used in the computations; i.e., cases that have no missing values or values out of range. Therefore only 180 of the original 188 cases are used. All variables are checked for acceptable values unless USE is specified in the VARIABLE paragraph (Section 5.3), in which case only variables specified in the USE statement are checked.

(3) Univariate statistics are computed for each variable using the complete cases
- mean
- standard deviation
- coefficient of variation

(4) The matrix of correlations

(5) Eigenvalues from the correlation matrix of the independent variables. The cumulative proportion of the total variance is the cumulative sum of eigenvalues divided by the total sum of all the eigenvalues.

(6) Eigenvectors corresponding to the eigenvalues.

(7) The total sum of squares $\Sigma(y_j - \bar{y})^2$ and mean square $\Sigma(y_j - \bar{y})/(N - 1)$ for the dependent variable y before the regression analysis.

(8) The correlation between each principal component and the dependent variable.

(9) The regression coefficients of the principal components. Since the principal components are mutually orthogonal, these coefficients do not depend on the order of entry of the components.

(10) Coefficients of the variables
- index of the component entered at each step
- the residual sum of squares at each step:

$$\Sigma(y_j - \hat{y}_j)^2$$

where $\hat{y}$ is the predicted value

Output 4R.1 Regression on principal components. Circled numbers correspond to those in the text

---

--- the BMDP instructions read by P4R are printed and interpreted ---

① REGRESSION TITLE
DEPENDENT VARIABLE(S) 6
INDEPENDENT VARIABLES 2 3 4 7 8 9
COMPUTATION BASED ON CORRELATION MATRIX OF INDEPENDENT VARIABLES
PRINCIPAL COMPONENTS ARE ENTERED IN ORDER OF MAGNITUDE OF CORRELATIONS WITH DEP. VAR
MAXIMUM NUMBER OF COMPONENTS TO ENTER 6
NUMBER OF COMPONENTS TO ENTER LIMITED BY MAGNITUDE OF CORRELATIONS GREATER THAN   0.0100
EIGENVALUE LIMIT. 0.0100

② NUMBER OF CASES READ.   188
   CASES WITH DATA MISSING OR BEYOND LIMITS . .   8
      REMAINING NUMBER OF CASES   180

③
VARIABLE			STANDARD	COEFFICIENT
NO.	NAME	MEAN	DEVIATION	OF VARIATION
2	AGE	33.53819	9.89836	0.29514
3	HEIGHT	64.46597	2.48213	0.03850
4	WEIGHT	131.09384	20.49977	0.15637
5	BRTHPILL	1.50551	0.50136	0.33302
6	CHOLSTRL	235.83821	42.74364	0.18124
7	ALBUMIN	4.12052	0.35871	0.08706
8	CALCIUM	9.96773	0.47279	0.04743
9	URICACID	4.75551	1.12111	0.23575

④ CORRELATION MATRIX

		AGE 2	HEIGHT 3	WEIGHT 4	CHOLSTRL 6	ALBUMIN 7	CALCIUM 8	URICACID 9
AGE	2	1.0000						
HEIGHT	3	0.0892	1.0000					
WEIGHT	4	0.2553	0.4735	1.0000				
CHOLSTRL	6	0.3652	0.0115	0.1462	1.0000			
ALBUMIN	7	-0.0789	-0.0058	-0.2346	0.0575	1.0000		
CALCIUM	8	-0.0086	0.1428	0.0647	0.2548	0.4529	1.0000	
URICACID	9	0.2085	0.1254	0.3036	0.2740	0.0299	0.1662	1.0000

⑤ EIGENVALUES

     1.80863   1.50590   0.97973   0.76741   0.53500   0.40330

CUMULATIVE PROPORTION OF TOTAL VARIANCE OF INDEPENDENT VARIABLES

     0.30144   0.55242   0.71571   0.84361   0.93278   1.00000

⑥ EIGENVECTORS

		1	2	3	4	5	6
2	AGE	0.3723	-0.1154	-0.6265	-0.6646	-0.0298	0.1138
3	HEIGHT	0.5002	0.0704	0.5904	-0.1983	-0.4307	0.4141
4	WEIGHT	0.6195	-0.1382	0.2031	0.0495	0.2965	-0.6822
7	ALBUMIN	-0.1144	0.6952	-0.0595	-0.1902	-0.4789	-0.4843
8	CALCIUM	0.1592	0.6759	0.0368	-0.0408	0.6522	0.2992
9	URICACID	0.4347	0.1502	-0.4613	0.6919	-0.2665	0.1613

⑦ DEPENDENT VARIABLE   6 CHOLSTRL   TOTAL SUM OF SQUARES   327036.25
                                             DEGREES OF FREEDOM   179.
                                             MEAN SQUARE   1827.0181

⑧ CORRELATION BETWEEN PRINCIPAL COMPONENTS AND DEPENDENT VARIABLE
       0.28656   0.15629   -0.31602   -0.07938   0.12736   0.06161

(output continued)

Output 4R.1 (continued)

REGRESSION COEFFICIENTS OF PRINCIPAL COMPONENTS ⑨
CONSTANT   COMPONENTS
(MEAN OF Y)
235.83821   9.10782   5.44370   -13.64672   -3.87329   7.44244   4.14681

COEFFICIENTS OF VARIABLES OBTAINED FROM REGRESSION ON PRINCIPAL COMPONENTS

INDEX OF COMPONENTS ENTERING	RESIDUAL SUM OF SQUARES	F-VALUES REGRESSION MODEL	COMPONENT TO ENTER	R2	CONSTANT	VARIABLES 2 AGE	3 HEIGHT	4 WEIGHT	7 ALBUMIN	8 CALCIUM	9 URICACID
3	0.29438E 06	19.75	19.75	0.0999	408.3958	0.8638	-3.2459	-0.1352	2.2638	-1.0619	5.6149
1	0.26752E 06	19.69	17.77	0.1820	207.1123	1.2064	-1.4106	0.1400	-0.6412	2.0055	9.1462
2	0.25953E 06	15.26	5.42	0.2064	79.5926	1.1429	-1.2562	0.1034	9.9088	9.7873	9.8754
5	0.25423E 06	12.53	3.65	0.2226	96.5079	1.1205	-2.5477	0.2110	-0.0267	20.0535	8.1065
4	0.25217E 06	10.33	1.42	0.2289	68.6327	1.3806	-2.2382	0.2017	2.0270	20.3877	5.7161
6	0.25093E 06	8.75	0.86	0.2327	34.6041	1.4283	-1.5464	0.0637	-3.5720	23.0117	6.3128

⑩ (marker above VARIABLES section)

- F-value for the regression model:

mean square regression/mean square residuals

The degrees of freedom for this F-value are p and N-p-1 where p is the number of components in the regression. This is an overall test of significance for the regression equation.
- F-value component to enter: this is a test of the significance of the coefficient of this component only; the degrees of freedom for this F-value are 1 and N-p-1
- R^2: multiple correlation squared
- the intercept (constant) and coefficients of the original independent variables corresponding to the components already entered

These terms are more precisely explained in Appendix A.13.

Specifying the regression and standardizing the data. The REGRESS paragraph describes the dependent (predicted) variable and the independent variables. This paragraph can be repeated before the END paragraph to specify additional analyses of the same data.

The dependent variable must be specified in the first REGRESS paragraph. If the independent variables are not specified, all variables are treated as independent variables unless a USE statement is specified in the VARIABLE paragraph; only variables listed in the USE statement are included in the analysis.

Each regression analysis can be given a separate title.

The regression can be performed using principal components from either the covariance or correlation matrix: the former corresponds to using the original data, and the latter to standardizing each independent variable by subtracting its mean and then dividing by its standard deviation.

REGRess ─────────────────────
  DEPENDent = v.   none/prev.
    Name or subscript of the dependent (predicted) variable.
  INDEPendent = v list.   all var./prev.
    Names or subscripts of the independent (predictor) variables. If not specified, all variables are used as independent variables except the one specified as the DEPENDENT variable.

TITLE = 'c'.   ≤ 160 char.   blank
  Title for the regression analysis.
STANDardize.   STAND/prev.
  The independent variables are standardized before performing the principal components analysis unless you specify NO STANDARDIZE.

Example 4R.2 Principal Component Scores

Principal component scores for each case are printed if you add the paragraph

---
      / PRINT   SCORE.
---

to the instructions of Example 4R.1 (before the END paragraph).

The scores are printed in Output 4R.2. For each case the coefficients of each principal component are multiplied by the values of variables and the sum is printed. The first six columns in the output correspond to the six principal components. The last column contains the values of the dependent variable.

PRINT ─────────────────────
  SCORE.   no/prev.
    Print the principal component scores and the dependent variable for each case.

Controlling the Entry of the Components

Either of two criteria determine the order of entry of the principal components (eigenvectors):

- Components are entered in the order of the magnitude of the absolute value of their correlations with the dependent variable, the largest is entered first (CORRELATION).
- Components are entered in the order of magnitude of the eigenvalues, the largest is entered first (EIGENVALUE).

The number of components entered into the regression can be restricted by specifying a minimum limit for a component value (correlation or eigenvalue) as an entry requirement. For IBM 360 and 370 computers, the eigenvalue limit should not ordinarily be lowered.

Output 4R.2   Principal component scores

```
         CASE      PRINCIPAL COMPONENT SCORES AND ORIGINAL DEPENDENT VARIABLE(S)
           1  2381      0.4482     0.2557     1.1648     1.0506    -1.1518    -0.6223    200.0000
           3  1610     -0.9843     0.3534     0.5649    -0.1847     1.8846    -0.4958    243.0000
           5   561     -0.6415     0.0434     0.7779     1.1200    -0.0224    -0.1028    158.0000
           6  2519      1.0136     1.8089     0.0325     3.0950    -1.4036     0.9864    255.0000
           7   225     -1.0254    -0.7859     0.9369     0.6914    -0.3268     0.1502    210.0000


         --- similar scores and observed CHOLSTRL values for cases 8 to 185 ---


         186   575      0.9916     0.4243    -0.8846    -1.6245     1.6209     0.9766    220.0000
         187  2271      1.4840     0.2107    -0.6762    -1.6836     0.5511    -0.4643    305.0000
         188    39      1.0775    -2.6829    -2.6220     0.5249     0.1732    -2.3359    220.0000
```

REGRess ────────────────────────────────

CORRelation. or EIGENvalue.   CORR/prev.
   Criterion for entering components into the regression equation. CORR enters the component(s) with the largest correlations(s) first; and EIGEN the component(s) with the largest eigenvalue(s).
LIMIT = $\#_1$, $\#_2$.   0.01,0.01/prev.
   A component is <u>not</u> entered into the regression equation if its correlation (if the criterion is CORR) is less than $\#_1$ or its eigenvalue (for either criterion) is less than $\#_2$. Either limit can be changed. To change the limit for eigenvalue without changing that of correlation, specify LIMIT = (2)$\#_2$.

Saving the Data in a BMDP File

The data (after transformation) can be saved in a BMDP File for further analysis by other programs (Chapter 7). When the data are read from a BMDP File and a new BMDP File is created by P4R, the two Files must be in different system files and on different UNITS.

The predicted values and residuals are <u>not</u> output to BMDP Files. There is no BMDP File covariance matrix input or output.

Plots Available in P4R

The plots available in P4R are

- residuals $(y-\hat{y})$ plotted against the predicted values $\hat{y}$
- residuals squared $(y-\hat{y})^2$ plotted against the predicted values $\hat{y}$
- the observed values of the dependent variable y and the predicted value $\hat{y}$ plotted against the observed values of an independent variable x_i
- the residuals $(y-\hat{y})$ plotted against the observed values of the same independent variable x_i
- a normal probability plot of the residuals
- a detrended normal probability plot of the residuals

All the plots are illustrated in Output 1R.3 for P1R (p. 241). (Only the partial residual plot of P1R is unavailable in P4R.)

PLOT ────────────────────────────────

RESIDual.   no/prev.
   Plot the residuals $(y-\hat{y})$ and residuals squared $(y-\hat{y})^2$ in separate graphs against the predicted values $\hat{y}$.
VARiable = v list.   none/prev.
   Names or subscripts of variables against which the observed values of the dependent variable y and the predicted values $\hat{y}$ are plotted. Overlaps between observed and predicted values are indicated by asterisks. The residuals $(y-\hat{y})$ are also plotted against the same variables. Each variable is plotted in a separate graph.
NORMal.   no/prev.
   Plot a normal probability plot of the residuals.
DNORMal.   no/prev.
   Plot a detrended normal probability plot of the residuals.
SIZE = #,#.   50,35/prev.
   The first number is the number of characters (width) in the horizontal axis and the second number is the number of lines (height) in the vertical axis.

SIZE OF PROBLEM

On medium-sized computers this program can analyze up to 55 variables. Appendix B describes how to increase the capacity of the program.

COMPUTATIONAL METHOD

All computations are performed in single precision. Means, standard deviations and covariances are computed by the method of provisional means (Appendix A.2). The computational procedure for P4R is described in Appendix A.13.

ACKNOWLEDGEMENT

P4R was programmed by Jerry Douglas and Laszlo Engelman.

SUMMARY

Order of Input Cards

```
// (job card)
// EXEC BIMED,PROG=BMDP4R        (see Appendix E)
//SYSIN DD *
/ PROBLEM
/ INPUT
/ VARIABLE
/ TRANSFORM
/ SAVE
/ REGRESS        may be repeated
/ PRINT
/ PLOT
/ END
    (data,if on cards)
// (system card)
```

Full sets of BMDP paragraphs (and data, if on cards)
can be repeated for additional problems; see Section
5.8.

instructions specific to P4R

Paragraph Statement	Preassigned	Comment and Manual Reference
/•REGRess		Required to direct regression (may be repeated).
•DEPENDent = v.	none	Same as P1R. * 280
INDEP = v list.	all	Same as P1R. * 280
TITLE = 'c'.	blank	Same as P1R. 280
STANDardize.	yes	The independent variables are standardized before performing the principal components analysis unless NO STAND is specified. STAND uses the correlation matrix. * 280
CORR or EIGEN.	CORR.	Criterion for entering components (one only): CORR uses largest correlations; EIGEN, largest eigenvalues. * 281
LIMIT = #, #.	.01,.01.	A component is <u>not</u> entered if its correlation is less than the first number (criterion CORR) or its eigenvalue is less than the second number (criterion EIGEN). * 281
- - - - - - - - - -	- - - - -	- -
/ PRINT		Optional to request printed output. 280
SCORE.	no	Print principal component scores and the dependent variable for each case. *
- - - - - - - - - -	- - - - -	- -
/ PLOT		Optional to produce graphical descriptions. Same as P1R, except there is no PREP statement in P4R. * 281

Key:

/	-indicates paragraph		*	-assigned value remains the same for additional problems
.	-period ends a sentence		VT	-number of variables after transformations
•	-required		list	-more than one item, often one per var.
v	-variable (name or subscript)			
g	-group (name or subscript)		Capitalized letters-paragraph or sentence names	
#	-number		recognized by BMDP	
'c'	-characters (name or parameter) may omit apostrophes if contiguous letters only		Page numbers following refer to this Manual	

P5R

13.5 Polynomial Regression

Robert Jennrich
Peter Mundle

ABSTRACT

P5R computes the least squares fit of a polynomial in one independent variable to the dependent variable. The form of the regression equation is

$$y = \beta_0 + \beta_1 x + \beta_2 x^2 + \cdots + \beta_p x^p + e$$

The program reports polynomials of degrees one through a degree specified by the user ($\leq$ 15), with goodness-of-fit statistics for each equation. Computations use orthogonal polynomials (Forsythe 1957). Case weights can be specified. P5R prints, for each polynomial degree, the regression coefficients with standard errors and t values for each orthogonal polynomial, the regression coefficient for each power of the independent variable and residual mean square.

WHERE TO FIND IT

Other Options and Features

Example 5R.1 Basic Setup for Fitting a Polynomial

In our first example we use P5R to fit a polynomial regression in AGE to CHOLSTRL using the Werner blood chemistry data (Table 5.1). The REGRESS paragraph is specific to P5R; the other Control Language instructions are described in Chapter 5.

```
------------------------------------------
/ PROBLEM   TITLE IS 'WERNER BLOOD CHEMISTRY DATA'.
/ INPUT     VARIABLES ARE 9.
           FORMAT IS '(A4, 5F4.0, 3F4.1)'.
/ VARIABLE  NAMES ARE ID, AGE, HEIGHT, WEIGHT,
                      BRTHPILL, CHOLSTRL, ALBUMIN,
                      CALCIUM, URICACID.
           MAXIMUM IS (6)400.
           MINIMUM IS (6)150.
           LABEL IS ID.

/ REGRESS   DEPENDENT IS CHOLSTRL.
           INDEPENDENT IS AGE.

/ END
           ------------------------------------------
```

(See end of this P5R section for organization of systems information, BMDP instructions and data).

The results of this analysis are presented in Output 5R.1. Circled numbers below correspond to those in the output.

① Interpretation of the Control Language instructions specific to P5R. Preassigned values are reported for some options.

② Cases used in the analysis are those that have acceptable values for both the dependent and independent variables; the other variables are not checked for acceptable values. Only 186 of the 188 cases are used in the analysis. Descriptive statistics are printed for the two variables.

Output 5R.1 Polynomial regression. Circled numbers correspond to those in the text

```
------------------------------------------------------------------------------------------------

        --- the BMDP instructions read by P5R are printed and interpreted ---


          REGRESSION TITLE. . . . . . . . . . . . . .WERNER BLOOD CHEMISTRY DATA
          INDEPENDENT VARIABLE. . . . . . . . . . . .  2 AGE
          DEPENDENT VARIABLE. . . . . . . . . . . . .  6 CHOLSTRL
    ①    WEIGHT VARIABLE . . . . . . . . . . . .      0
          DEGREEE OF POLYNOMIAL . . . . . . . . . . .  3
          PRINT CORRELATION MATRIX. . . . . . . . . . NO
          PRINT ORTHOGONAL POLYNOMIAL . . . . . . . . NO


          DATA ARE READ IN SINGLE PRECISION AND COMPUTATIONS ARE
          PERFORMED IN DOUBLE PRECISION USING ORTHOGONAL POLYNOMIALS.


          NUMBER OF CASES READ. . . . . . . . . . . .   188
    ②      CASES WITH DATA MISSING OR BEYOND LIMITS . .     2
              REMAINING NUMBER OF CASES . . . . . . . .   186
```

(output continued)

Output 5R.1 (continued)

RESULTS FOR POLYNOMIAL OF DEGREE 1

POLYNOMIAL COEFFICIENTS	ORTHOGONAL POLYNOMIAL			POLYNOMIAL IN X		
DEGREE	REGRESSION COEFFICIENT	STANDARD ERROR	T VALUE	REGRESSION COEFFICIENT	STANDARD ERROR	T VALUE
0	3220.66394	39.68010	81.17	183.61520	10.21529	17.97
1	212.88457	39.68010	5.37	1.54834	0.28860	5.37

RESIDUAL MEAN SQUARE =   1574.51057 (D.F. = 184)
MULTIPLE R-SQUARE =   0.13527

RESULTS FOR POLYNOMIAL OF DEGREE 2

POLYNOMIAL COEFFICIENTS	ORTHOGONAL POLYNOMIAL			POLYNOMIAL IN X		
DEGREE	REGRESSION COEFFICIENT	STANDARD ERROR	T VALUE	REGRESSION COEFFICIENT	STANDARD ERROR	T VALUE
0	3220.66394	39.75879	81.01	202.80670	38.16605	5.31
1	212.88457	39.75879	5.35	0.38407	2.24922	0.17
2	20.75262	39.75879	0.52	0.01621	0.03106	0.52

RESIDUAL MEAN SQUARE =   1580.76106 (D.F. = 183)
MULTIPLE R-SQUARE =   0.13656

RESULTS FOR POLYNOMIAL OF DEGREE 3   ③

POLYNOMIAL COEFFICIENTS	ORTHOGONAL POLYNOMIAL			POLYNOMIAL IN X		
DEGREE	REGRESSION COEFFICIENT	STANDARD ERROR	T VALUE	REGRESSION COEFFICIENT	STANDARD ERROR	T VALUE
0	3220.66394	39.80178	80.92	311.19559	144.50856	2.15
1	212.88457	39.80178	5.35	-9.47715	12.87791	-0.74
2	20.75262	39.80178	0.52	0.29917	0.36515	0.82
3	-30.95494	39.80178	-0.78	-0.00258	0.00331	-0.78

RESIDUAL MEAN SQUARE =   1584.18168 (D.F. = 182)
MULTIPLE R-SQUARE =   0.13942

GOODNESS OF FIT TEST

FOR THE POLYNOMIAL OF EACH DEGREE, A TEST IS MADE FOR
ADDITIONAL INFORMATION IN THE ORTHOGONAL POLYNOMIALS OF
HIGHER DEGREE. THE NUMERATOR SUM OF SQUARES FOR EACH OF
THESE TESTS IS THE SUM OF SQUARES ATTRIBUTED TO ALL
ORTHOGONAL POLYNOMIALS OF HIGHER DEGREE AND THE DENOMINATOR
SUM OF SQUARES IS THE RESIDUAL SUM OF SQUARES FROM THE FIT
TO THE HIGHEST DEGREE POLYNOMIAL (FIT TO ALL ORTHOGONAL   ④
POLYNOMIALS). A SIGNIFICANT F-STATISTIC THUS INDICATES THAT
A HIGHER DEGREE POLYNOMIAL SHOULD BE CONSIDERED.

DEGREE	SUM OF SQUARES	D.F.	MEAN SQUARE	F	TAIL PROBABILITY
0	46708.71852	3	15569.57284	9.83	0.00
1	1388.87933	2	694.43966	0.44	0.65
2	958.20816	1	958.20816	0.60	0.44
RESID.	288321.06643	182	1584.18168		

③ Results for polynomial of degree 3:
- regression coefficient for each orthogonal polynomial and the standard error of the coefficient (orthogonal polynomials are defined in Appendix A.14)
- the regression coefficient for each power of the independent variable and the standard error of each coefficient; to maximize numerical accuracy in these coefficients, the coefficient of variation for the independent variable should be large (i.e., at least 1).
- for all coefficients, a t value equal to the ratio of the coefficient to its standard error. This can be considered a two-sided test of significance for the coefficient. The regression coefficients of the powers of the independent variable are highly correlated; therefore the estimates of the coefficients may not be stable and the t tests may lack power.
- residual mean square: $\Sigma(y_j-\hat{y}_j)^2/(N-p-1)$
where

  y_j is the value of the dependent variable
  $\hat{y}_j$ is the predicted value estimated by the regression
  p is the degree of the polynomial
  N is the number of cases with a nonzero weight
- the multiple R^2

④ Goodness-of-fit test. This is a test of the lack of fit of the model at each degree, relative to the residual mean square from fitting the polynomial of highest degree. A high value for F is an indication of a poor fit; i.e., more terms are needed.

This run of P5R terminates with a polynomial of degree 3; this is the preassigned maximum degree.

<u>Specifying the regression</u>. The REGRESS paragraph specifies the dependent and independent variables and, if desired, the maximum degree of the

polynomial as well as a title to label the output. It can be repeated <u>after</u> the data cards for additional analyses of the same data (see order of input in the summary, p. 288)

Both the dependent and independent variables must be specified. If the degree is not specified, the maximum degree is cubic (of order three). The use of the DEGREE instruction is illustrated in Example 5R.2.

```
REGRess ─────────────────────────
  DEPENDent = v.      required        none/prev.
    Name or subscript of the dependent (predicted)
    variable.
  INDEPendent = v.    required        none/prev.
    Name or subscript of the independent
    (predictor) variable.
  DEGREE = #.         ≤ 15            3/prev.
    Maximum degree of the polynomial.
  TITLE = 'c'.        ≤ 160 char.     blank
    Title for the analysis.
```

Example 5R.2 Analysis for Degree p, Coefficient for x^p and Correlations

In the following example we request optional results available in P5R. We modify the REGRESS paragraph of Example 5R.1 and add a PRINT paragraph before the END paragraph.

```
/ REGRESS    DEPENDENT IS CHOLSTRL.
             INDEPENDENT IS AGE.
             DEGREE IS 5.

/ PRINT      RREG.
             DEGREE IS 5.
             ORTHPOL.
```

Output 5R.2 Optional results for polynomial regression

RESULTS FOR POLYNOMIAL OF DEGREE 1

CORRELATION MATRIX FOR THE REGRESSION COEFFICIENT(BETA) ESTIMATES

		OTH DEG 1	1ST DEG 2
OTH DEG	1	1.0000	
1ST DEG	2	-0.9586	1.0000

POLYNOMIAL COEFFICIENTS		ORTHOGONAL POLYNOMIAL			POLYNOMIAL IN X		
	DEGREE	REGRESSION COEFFICIENT	STANDARD ERROR	T VALUE	REGRESSION COEFFICIENT	STANDARD ERROR	T VALUE
	0	3220.66394	39.68010	81.17	183.61520	10.21529	17.97
	1	212.88457	39.68010	5.37	1.54834	0.28860	5.37

RESIDUAL MEAN SQUARE =   1574.51057 (D.F. = 184)
MULTIPLE R-SQUARE =   0.13527

--- results for polynomials of degrees 2 to 4 ---

(output continued)

Output 5R.2 (continued)

RESULTS FOR POLYNOMIAL OF DEGREE 5

CORRELATION MATRIX FOR THE REGRESSION COEFFICIENT(BETA) ESTIMATES

		OTH DEG 1	1ST DEG 2	2ND DEG 3	3RD DEG 4	4TH DEG 5	5TH DEG 6
OTH DEG	1	1.0000					
1ST DEG	2	-0.9984	1.0000				
2ND DEG	3	0.9936	-0.9984	1.0000			
3RD DEG	4	-0.9861	0.9939	-0.9985	1.0000		
4TH DEG	5	0.9763	-0.9868	0.9943	-0.9986	1.0000	
5TH DEG	6	-0.9649	0.9779	-0.9879	0.9949	-0.9988	1.0000

POLYNOMIAL COEFFICIENTS   ORTHOGONAL POLYNOMIAL   POLYNOMIAL IN X

DEGREE	REGRESSION COEFFICIENT	STANDARD ERROR	T VALUE	REGRESSION COEFFICIENT	STANDARD ERROR	T VALUE
0	3220.66394	39.78279	80.96	-2887.89075	2292.39126	-1.26
1	212.88457	39.78279	5.35	462.26328	343.87828	1.34
2	20.75262	39.78279	0.52	-26.65226	20.08098	-1.33
3	-30.95494	39.78279	-0.78	0.74445	0.57116	1.30
4	-32.18981	39.78279	-0.81	-0.01007	0.00792	-1.27
5	49.03323	39.78279	1.23	0.00005	0.00004	1.23

RESIDUAL MEAN SQUARE =   0.15827D 04 (D.F. = 180)
MULTIPLE R-SQUARE =   0.14969

⑥
CASE NO.	CASE LABEL	CASE WEIGHT	X VALUE	Y VALUE	PREDICTED VALUE	RESIDUAL	5TH DEG ORTH. POLY. VALUE
1	2381	1.00000	22.00000	200.00000	223.34681	-23.34680	0.05583
2	1946	1.00000	22.00000		223.34681		
3	1610	1.00000	25.00000	243.00000	227.01349	15.98651	0.06458
4	1797	1.00000	25.00000		227.01349		
5	561	1.00000	19.00000	158.00000	198.79582	-40.79581	-0.30192

--- similar statistics for cases 6 to 185 ---

186	575	1.00000	53.00000	220.00000	261.72439	-41.72438	-0.07877
187	2271	1.00000	54.00000	305.00000	264.90981	40.09018	0.03287
188	39	1.00000	54.00000	220.00000	264.90981	-44.90981	0.03287

GOODNESS OF FIT TEST

FOR THE POLYNOMIAL OF EACH DEGREE, A TEST IS MADE FOR
ADDITIONAL INFORMATION IN THE ORTHOGONAL POLYNOMIALS OF
HIGHER DEGREE. THE NUMERATOR SUM OF SQUARES FOR EACH OF
THESE TESTS IS THE SUM OF SQUARES ATTRIBUTED TO ALL
ORTHOGONAL POLYNOMIALS OF HIGHER DEGREE AND THE DENOMINATOR
SUM OF SQUARES IS THE RESIDUAL SUM OF SQUARES FROM THE FIT
TO THE HIGHEST DEGREE POLYNOMIAL (FIT TO ALL ORTHOGONAL
POLYNOMIALS). A SIGNIFICANT F-STATISTIC THUS INDICATES THAT
A HIGHER DEGREE POLYNOMIAL SHOULD BE CONSIDERED.

DEGREE	SUM OF SQUARES	D.F.	MEAN SQUARE	F	TAIL PROBABILITY
0	50149.15995	5	10029.83199	6.34	0.00
1	4829.32076	4	1207.33019	0.76	0.55
2	4398.64959	3	1466.21653	0.93	0.43
3	3440.44143	2	1720.22072	1.09	0.34
4	2404.25769	1	2404.25769	1.52	0.22
RESID.	284880.62500	180	1582.67014		

⑦ ORTHOGONAL POLYNOMIAL EXPANSION

COEFFICIENTS FOR POWERS OF X

POLYNOMIAL / POWERS OF X

	OTH POW	1ST POW	2ND POW	3RD POW	4TH POW	5TH POW
OTH DEG	0.7332E-01					
1ST DEG	-0.2468E 00	0.7273E-02				
2ND DEG	0.9248E 00	-0.5610E-01	0.7812E-03			
3RD DEG	-0.3502E 01	0.3186E 00	-0.9141E-02	0.8322E-04		
4TH DEG	0.1469E 02	-0.1780E 01	0.7766E-01	-0.1450E-02	0.9800E-05	
5TH DEG	-0.5560E 02	0.8453E 01	-0.4987E 00	0.1428E-01	-0.1989E-03	0.1079E-05

286

The results are shown in Output 5R.2. Circled numbers below correspond to those in the output.

⑤ The correlation matrix of the regression coefficients is printed at each step. These are correlations of the coefficients of the powers of the original variable (and not of the orthogonal polynomials). Note the high correlations between the coefficients.

⑥ For each case the following statistics are printed:
- the case weight, if specified
- the value of the independent variable, x_j
- the value of the dependent variable, y_j
- the predicted value, $\hat{y}_j$
- the residual, $y_j - \hat{y}_j$
- the value of the orthogonal polynomial

Blanks in the table are printed when the value is missing or out of range. This table is printed at specified steps (DEGREES of the polynomial specified in the PRINT paragraph).

⑦ Orthogonal polynomial expansion. Each line in the table shows the coefficients of the powers of the independent variable (x) that are used in the orthogonal polynomial. This is obtained by specifying ORTHPOL in the PRINT paragraph.

```
PRINT
  RREG.                              no/prev.
    Print the correlation matrix of the regression
    coefficents of the powers of the independent
    variable.
  DEGREE = # list.                   none/prev.
    Print the table of predicted values and
    residuals at the polynomial DEGREES specified.
  ORThpol.                           no/prev.
    Print the coefficients of the powers of the
    independent variable corresponding to the
    orthogonal polynomials.
```

Plots

The plots available in P5R are
- the observed values of the dependent variable (y_j) and the predicted values ($\hat{y}_j$) plotted against the observed value of the independent variable (x_j)
- the residuals ($y_j - \hat{y}_j$) plotted against the observed value of the independent variable (x_j)
- a normal probability plot of the residuals
- a detrended normal probability plot of the residuals

These plots are illustrated in Output 1R.3(p.241) and are similar for P5R.

```
PLOT
  DEGREE = # list.                   none/prev.
    The degree(s) of the regression at which the
    plots of the dependent variable, predicted
    values, and residuals are plotted against the
    independent variable. If normal plots are
    requested (see NORMAL and DNORMAL below), they
    are also plotted at these DEGREES.
```

```
  NORMal.                            no/prev.
    Print the normal probability plot of the
    residuals (at the DEGREES specified in the PLOT
    paragraph).
  DNORMal.                           no/prev.
    Print the detrended normal probability plot of
    the residuals (at the DEGREES specified in the
    PLOT paragraph).
  SIZE = #,#.                        50,35/prev.
    The first number is the number of characters
    (width) in the horizontal axis and the second
    number is the number of lines (height) in the
    vertical axis.
```

Case Weights

The user can supply a weight for each case. The variable containing this weight is identified in the VARIABLE paragraph. The WEIGHT variable is not used as an independent (predictor) variable. If w is the value of the WEIGHT variable for case j, the weight affects the computation of the mean and covariances as in Section 2.1.

```
VARiable
  WEIGHT = v.                    no weight var./prev.
    Name or subscript of the variable containing
    case weights. The weights should be greater
    than or equal to zero. If WEIGHT is not stated
    or is set to zero, there are no case weights.
```

Input and Saving Results in a BMDP File

P5R can accept only data as input.

When the DATA are saved, the predicted values and residuals are also saved in a BMDP File. The predicted values are saved as variable VT+1 with the name PREDICTD, and the residuals are saved as variable VT+2 with the name RESIDUAL (where VT is the number of variables after transformations).

SIZE OF PROBLEM

The data are kept in memory. On medium sized computer systems, P5R can accommodate approximately 1000 cases. The maximum degree of the polynomial is 15. Appendix B describes how to increase the capacity of the program.

COMPUTATIONAL METHOD

The data are read in single precision and the computations are performed in double precision. The computational procedure is described in Appendix A.14.

ACKNOWLEDGEMENT

P5R was designed by Robert Jennrich and programmed by Peter Mundle. It supersedes BMD05R.

SUMMARY

Order of Input Cards

```
// (job card)
// EXEC BIMED,PROG=BMDP5R      (see Appendix E)
//SYSIN DD *
/ PROBLEM
/ INPUT
/ VARIABLE
/ TRANSFORM
/ SAVE
/ REGRESS
/ PRINT
/ PLOT
/ END
   (data if on cards)

/ REGRESS  ┐
/ PRINT    │ repeat for subproblems
/ PLOT     │
/ END      ┘

// (system card)
```

instructions specific to P5R

Paragraph Statement	Preassigned	Comment and Manual Reference
/ VARiable		Additional option to specify case weights.
WEIGHT = v.	none	Name or subscript of variable containing a weight for each case. Same as P1R. * 287
/●REGRess		Required to direct regression (may be repeated). 285
● DEPendent = v.	none	Name or subscript of the dependent (predicted) variable. *
● INDependent = v.	none	Name or subscript of the independent (predictor) variable. *
TITLE = 'c'.	none	Title, **up to 160** characters, to label output.
DEGREE = #.	3.	Maximum degree of the polynomial (up to 15). *
/ PRINT		Optional to request printed output. The following are printed only when specified (may be repeated). 287
RREG.	no	Correlation matrix of the regression coefficients of the powers of the independent variable. *
DEGREEs = # list.	none	Table of predicted values and residuals at each of the polynomial DEGREES specified. *
ORThpol.	no	Coefficients of the powers of the independent variable corresponding to the orthogonal polynomials. *
/ PLOT		Optional to request plots. No plots are printed unless requested (may be repeated). 287
DEGREEs = # list.	none	The degree(s) which the plots of the dependent variable, predicted values, and residuals are plotted against the independent variable. NORM and DNORM (if specified) are also plotted at these DEGREES. *
NORMal.	no	Normal probability plot of residuals printed at specified DEGREES. *
DNORMal.	no	Detrended normal probability plot printed at specified DEGREES. *
SIZE = #, #.	50,35.	Width of x-axis (characters); height of y-axis (lines). *

Key:

/	–indicates paragraph	*	–assigned value remains the same for additional problems
.	–period ends a sentence		
●	–required	VT	–number of variables after transformations
v	–variable (name or subscript)	list	–more than one item, often one per var.
g	–group (name or subscript)		
#	–number		Capitalized letters–paragraph or sentence names recognized by BMDP
'c'	–characters (name or parameter) may omit apostrophes if contiguous letters only		Page numbers following refer to this Manual

14

NONLINEAR REGRESSION

A regression model is used to quantify a relationship when the value of a variable can be explained by the values of other variables. This chapter discusses methods of estimating the parameters of a nonlinear regression model. Nonlinear models that are linear in the parameters can be fitted as linear regression models; also some nonlinear models can be transformed to linear models. Linear regression models and polynomial models are described in Chapter 13. (For an extensive discussion of nonlinear regression see Jennrich and Ralston, 1978.)

In this chapter we describe three programs used to estimate parameters in nonlinear models by least squares.

P3R -- Nonlinear Regression
PAR -- Derivative-free Nonlinear Regression
PLR -- Stepwise Logistic Regression

P3R and PAR programs can also be used to compute maximum likelihood estimates of the parameters of your model (p. 315). PLR computes maximum likelihood estimates for the logistic model.

P3R estimates the parameters of any of five frequently used nonlinear functions or a multiple linear regression function when you specify a code number for the function and the number of parameters in the model. Other functions can be fitted to the data by specifying both the function and its derivatives by FORTRAN statements. The parameters are estimated by a Gauss-Newton algorithm. Exact linear constraints can be placed on the parameters of the model.

PAR estimates the parameters of any function that can be specified by FORTRAN statements. The derivatives of the function are not used (required). The parameters are estimated by a pseudo-Gauss-Newton algorithm (Ralston and Jennrich, 1977). Upper and lower limits can be specified for linear combinations of the parameters.

Both P3R and PAR can compute weighted least squares estimates. The parameters are estimated by an iterative algorithm. At each iteration the programs print the residual sum of squares and the estimates of the parameters. Once parameter estimates are determined, the programs print estimates of the asymptotic standard deviations of the parameter estimates, and of the correlations between them. The residuals, predicted values, and observed values of all the variables are listed.

Both programs can plot the residuals and predicted values against other variables and print normal probability plots of the residuals. The predicted values and data can be saved in a BMDP File to be further analyzed by other programs.

We recommend P3R if your function is one of six functions available by specifying a code number. A common error in P3R is the incorrect specification of derivatives; so when the derivatives are difficult to specify, we suggest you use PAR. See pps. 302 and 312 for comments on problem size.

PLR investigates the relation between a binary-dependent variable and a set of independent variables. The dependent variable represents events such as success or failure. The independent variables may be categorical in nature or interval-scaled variables. The program provides maximum likelihood estimates of the parameters (β_i) of the linear logistic model

$$E(y) = \theta = \frac{e^{\beta x}}{1+e^{\beta x}}$$

where y denotes the dependent variable and x denotes the independent variables.

The material in this chapter is divided into five sections:

14.1 - Nonlinear Regression -- explains the basic operation of P3R using built-in functions or a FORTRAN function supplied by the user
14.2 - Derivative-free Nonlinear Regression -- explains the basic operation of the derivative-free nonlinear regression program PAR
14.3a - Applications of Nonlinear Regression Algorithms -- includes the maximum likelihood estimation for data from the exponential family of distributions; estimation for data from any distribution.
14.3b - The loss function as an alternate to least squares.
14.3c - Explains models defined by a system of differential equations.
14.4 - System Cards for P3R and PAR
14.5 - Stepwise Logistic Regression

Control Language

The Control Language instructions to describe the data and variables are common to all BMDP programs and are explained in Chapter 5: the PROBLEM, INPUT and VARIABLE paragraphs are used in the nonlinear regression programs.

New in 1981 is a FUN paragraph that allows one to specify within the BMDP instructions using transformation-like statements the function and derivatives for P3R and the function for PAR. The details for P3R are on p. 295 and for PAR are on p. 308.

P3R

14.1 Nonlinear Regression

Robert Jennrich

ABSTRACT

P3R gives least squares estimates of the parameters of a nonlinear function. Six functions (and their derivatives) are built-in. Other functions can be fitted to the data by specifying both the function and its derivatives by BMDP Control Language statements or by FORTRAN statements. Upper and lower limits can be placed on the parameters, and exact linear constraints for the parameters are available. Maximum likelihood estimates can also be computed. When derivatives are difficult or impossible to specify, use PAR. The built-in functions require the same Systems Cards used with other BMDP programs. Functions in FORTRAN require the BIMEDT procedure and a subroutine, P3RFUN, to define the function. This has the same calling sequence as described for PAR except that the vector of parameter derivatives is inserted as the second argument (DF) and the index of the dependent variable (IDEP) is an additional argument in the last position. See Section 14.3 for maximum likelihood estimation.

WHERE TO FIND IT

Other Options and Features

Example 3R.1 Basic Setup for Nonlinear Regression Using a Built-in Function

The data given in Table 14.1 represent radioactivity counts in the blood of a baboon sampled at specified times after an initial bolus injection containing radioactive sulphate.

Table 14.1 Radioactivity in the blood of a baboon named Brunhilda (personal communication from Shires as reported by Jennrich and Bright, 1976).

Counts $\times 10^{-4}$	Case Weights	Time
15.1117	.004379	2
11.3601	.007749	4
9.7652	.010487	6
9.0935	.012093	8
8.4820	.013900	10
7.6891	.016914	15
7.3342	.018591	20
7.0593	.020067	25
6.7041	.022249	30
6.4313	.024177	40
6.1554	.026393	50
5.9940	.027833	60
5.7698	.030039	70
5.6440	.031392	80
5.3915	.034402	90
5.0938	.038540	110
4.8717	.042135	130
4.5996	.047267	150
4.4968	.049453	160
4.3602	.052600	170
4.2668	.054928	180

The counts are recorded in columns 2-8, case weights in columns 10-16 and time in columns 22-24.

We fit the sum of two exponentials

$$y = p_1 e^{p_2 x} + p_3 e^{p_4 x}$$

to the data. This function is one of the six

functions available in P3R by stating BMDP
instructions. To obtain it we specify

        NUMBER IS 1.
        PARAMETERS ARE 4.

in the REGRESS paragraph. The complete set of BMDP
instructions is

```
-------------------------------------
/ PROBLEM    TITLE IS 'RADIOACTIVE SULFATE DATA'.
/ INPUT      VARIABLES ARE 3.
            FORMAT IS '(F8.4, F8.6, F8.0)'.
/ VARIABLE   NAMES ARE COUNT, CASEWT, TIME.

/ REGRESS    DEPENDENT IS COUNT.
            INDEPENDENT IS TIME.
            NUMBER IS 1.
            PARAMETERS ARE 4.
            WEIGHT IS CASEWT.

/ PARAMETER INITIAL ARE 10, -.1, 5, -.01.

/ END
-------------------------------------
```

When the function is not specified by FORTRAN
statements, the Control Language must be preceded by
System Cards to initiate the analysis by P3R. For
IBM OS, the System Cards are

```
//job card
// EXEC  BIMED,PROG=BMDP3R
//SYSIN  DD  *
```

The Control Language is immediately followed by the
data (Table 14.1). The analysis is terminated by
another System Card. For IBM OS, this System Card is

        //

The REGRESS and PARAMETER paragraphs are specific
to P3R. In the REGRESS paragraph we specify the
DEPENDENT variable, the INDEPENDENT variable, the
number of PARAMETERS in the model, the NUMBER identifying the function to be fit, and the variable
that contains case WEIGHTS. INITIAL values for the
parameters are specified in the PARAMETER paragraph.
The remaining BMDP instructions are a general description of the data and variables, as explained in
Chapter 5.

If prior knowledge of the parameters is available, the user may specify prior estimates and ridge
values in the PARAMETER paragraph (see p. 300).

The results of the analysis are presented in
Output 3R.1. Circled numbers below correspond to
those in the output.

① Interpretation of the REGRESS paragraph. Most
of the values reported are preassigned values for
the program.

② Number of cases read. P3R uses only complete
cases in all computations. That is, if the value of
any variable in a case is missing or out of range,
the case is omitted from all computations. If a USE
statement is specified in the VARIABLE paragraph,
only the values of variables in the USE statement
are checked for missing value codes and values out
of range.

③ The means, standard deviations, minimums and
maximums for all variables except the case WEIGHT

Output 3R.1 An analysis of the radioactive sulfate data using P3R. The function is the sum of two exponentials. Circled numbers correspond to those in the text

```
        REGRESSION NUMBER . . . . . . . . . . . . . .        1
        INDEPENDENT VARIABLE(FOR BUILT-IN FUNCTION) . .   TIME
        DEPENDENT VARIABLE. . . . . . . . . . . . .      COUNT
        WEIGHTING VARIABLE. . . . . . . . . . . . .      CASEWT
        NUMBER OF PARAMETERS. . . . . . . . . . . .        4
①      NUMBER OF CONSTRAINTS . . . . . . . . . . .        0
        TOLERANCE FOR PIVOTING. . . . . . . . . . . 0.00000001000
        TOLERANCE FOR CONVERGENCE . . . . . . . . . 0.00001000000
        MAXIMUM NUMBER OF ITERATIONS. . . . . . . .       50
        MAXIMUM NUMBER OF INCREMENT HALVINGS. . . . .       5
        NUMBER OF DATA PASSES PER CASE. . . . . . . .       1
        COMPUTE LOSS FUNCTION . . . . . . . . . . .       NO

        USING THE ABOVE SPECIFICATIONS THIS PROGRAM COULD PROCESS 2009 CASES.

②      NUMBER OF CASES READ. . . . . . . . . . . .       21
```

VARIABLE		MEAN	STANDARD DEVIATION	MINIMUM	MAXIMUM
NO.	NAME				
1	COUNT	5.750695	1.711861	4.266800	15.111699
2	CASEWT	0.035707	0.014208	0.004379	0.054928
3	TIME	97.933350	60.915985	2.000000	180.000000

③ (to left of table)

(output continued)

Output 3R.1 (continued)

④ PARAMETER MAXIMA. . . . . *************** *************** *************** ***************

    PARAMETER MINIMA. . . . . *************** *************** *************** ***************

ITERATION NUMBER	INCREMENT HALVINGS	RESIDUAL SUM OF SQUARES	P(1)	P(2)	P(3)	P(4)
0	0	5.592536	10.000000	-0.100000	5.000000	-0.010000
1	1	0.379743	9.907287	-0.101484	4.947083	0.000353
2	0	0.058245	8.301623	-0.130408	6.940309	-0.003081
3	0	0.018950	9.234010	-0.178251	7.336723	-0.003128
4	0	0.013453	10.542867	-0.211035	7.343436	-0.003137
5	0	0.012897	11.124459	-0.223769	7.364382	-0.003160
6	0	0.012850	11.290754	-0.227774	7.374455	-0.003170
7	0	0.012846	11.336527	-0.228964	7.377789	-0.003174
8	0	0.012845	11.349531	-0.229309	7.378792	-0.003175
9	0	0.012845	11.353256	-0.229409	7.379085	-0.003175
10	0	0.012845	11.354325	-0.229437	7.379169	-0.003176
11	0	0.012845	11.354632	-0.229446	7.379194	-0.003176
12	0	0.012845	11.354720	-0.229448	7.379201	-0.003176
13	0	0.012845	11.354745	-0.229449	7.379203	-0.003176

⑤ (to the left of iteration rows)

⑥ ITERATION 13 HAS THE SMALLEST RESIDUAL SUM OF SQUARES(SUBJECT TO CONSTRAINTS, IF ANY).
   REMAINING CALCULATIONS ARE BASED ON THE RESULTS OF THIS ITERATION.

STANDARD FUNCTION FORM USED WITH IND =   3

F= P(1) EXP(P(2) X(IND)) + P(3) EXP(P(4) X(IND)) + ...

ASYMPTOTIC CORRELATION MATRIX OF THE PARAMETERS

	⑦	P(1) 1	P(2) 2	P(3) 3	P(4) 4
P(1)	1	1.0000			
P(2)	2	-0.8140	1.0000		
P(3)	3	0.1459	-0.5026	1.0000	
P(4)	4	-0.1139	0.4184	-0.8689	1.0000

RESIDUAL MEAN SQUARE   0.0007556065 ⑧

DEGREES OF FREEDOM   17

PARAMETER	ESTIMATE	ASYMPTOTIC STANDARD DEVIATION	TOLERANCE
P(1)	11.354745	0.865841	0.2445360588
P(2)	-0.229449	0.018740	0.1865294094
P(3)	7.379203	0.106597	0.1970591829
P(4)	-0.003176	0.000136	0.2445052536

CASE NO. LABEL	⑨	PREDICTED COUNT	STD DEV OF PRED VALUE	OBSERVED COUNT	RESIDUAL	CASEWT	TIME
1		14.508456	0.362616	15.111699	0.603242	0.004379	2.000000
2		11.821133	0.172042	11.360100	-0.461033	0.007749	4.000000
3		10.106008	0.144709	9.765200	-0.340808	0.010487	6.000000
4		9.005399	0.136218	9.093499	0.088100	0.012093	8.000000
5		8.293257	0.118659	8.481999	0.188742	0.013900	10.000000
6		7.399399	0.078204	7.689099	0.289700	0.016914	15.000000
7		7.040509	0.070454	7.334200	0.293690	0.018591	20.000000
8		6.852661	0.072005	7.059299	0.206638	0.020067	25.000000
9		6.720284	0.071352	6.704100	-0.016184	0.022249	30.000000
10		6.500130	0.065070	6.431299	-0.068831	0.024177	40.000000
11		6.295938	0.057665	6.155399	-0.140538	0.026393	50.000000
12		6.099043	0.051118	5.993999	-0.105043	0.027833	60.000000
13		5.908394	0.045842	5.769799	-0.138595	0.030039	70.000000
14		5.723714	0.042003	5.643999	-0.079716	0.031392	80.000000
15		5.544807	0.039683	5.391500	-0.153309	0.034402	90.000000
16		5.203597	0.039321	5.093800	-0.109798	0.038540	110.000000
17		4.883383	0.043086	4.871699	-0.011684	0.042135	130.000000
18		4.582873	0.048814	4.599600	0.016726	0.047267	150.000000
19		4.439627	0.051932	4.496799	0.057172	0.049453	160.000000
20		4.300858	0.055065	4.360200	0.059342	0.052600	170.000000
21		4.166425	0.058141	4.266800	0.100374	0.054928	180.000000

SERIAL CORRELATION   0.36601   ⑩

----

variable. When a case WEIGHT variable is specified, weighted means and standard deviations are computed.

④ Upper and lower limits for the parameters specified in the PARAMETER paragraph. We did not specify limits so asterisks are printed.

⑤ At each iteration P3R prints

- the number of the iteration
- the number of increment halvings (explained on p. 302)
- the residual sum of squares

$$RSS = \sum w(y-f)^2$$

where y is the observed value of the dependent variable, f is the evaluation of the function, and w is the value of the case weight (the case weight value is 1 if there is no weighting); the summation is over all cases used in the analysis.
- the estimates of the parameters (at step zero they are the initial estimates supplied with the Control Language)

Usually you can suggest better initial estimates for the parameters than those supplied by P3R. The preassigned estimates are zero for all parameters. You must provide initial estimates if the function is undefined at zero or all derivatives are zero when the parameter estimates are zero.

⑥ The iteration at which the smallest residual sum of squares occurs. The smallest may not be at the last iteration since P3R terminates the iteration when the relative change in the sum of squares during five successive iterations is less than a specified (or preassigned) limit. Small differences between the parameter values at the last iteration and at the iteration that produces the smallest residual sum of squares can be attributed

to round-off error; large differences can indicate that a saddle-point or local minimum was found. If the maximum number of iterations is reached, the derivatives may be incorrectly specified.

Note: The remaining computations use the parameter estimates from the iteration printed in the results or, when no iteration is printed, from the last iteration.

⑦ The asymptotic correlation matrix of the parameter estimates. This is obtained by inverting the matrix of the sums of cross products of the derivatives. When the derivatives are too highly correlated, it may not be possible to invert the matrix completely (see Appendix A.15).

⑧ The residual mean square is the residual sum of squares divided by (N-p) where N is the number of cases with nonzero weight and p is the number of independent parameters estimated.
   This is followed by the asymptotic standard deviations of the parameter estimates. A zero indicates a problem with the estimate: the estimate may lie on a boundary of the permissible parameter space (equal to its specified upper or lower limit), there may be extremely high correlations among the estimated parameters, or the estimate is so poor that if it is changed the value of the function is not affected.

⑨ For each case, P3R prints

- the predicted value (value of the function) $f = f(x_1, x_2, \ldots, p_1, p_2, \ldots)$
- the standard deviation of the predicted value (Appendix A.15)
- the observed value of the dependent variable y
- the residual (y-f)
- the case weight, w
- the values of the independent variables $x_1, x_2, \ldots$

⑩ The serial correlation of the residuals

$$\frac{\sum\limits_{j=2}^{N} (w_j w_{j-1})^{\frac{1}{2}} (y_j - f_j)(y_{j-1} - f_{j-1})}{\left\{ \sum\limits_{2}^{N} w_j (y_j - f_j)^2 \; \sum\limits_{1}^{N-1} w_j (y_j - f_j)^2 \right\}^{\frac{1}{2}}}$$

The REGRESS paragraph -- describing the nonlinear function. The REGRESS paragraph describes the function, the dependent variable and number of parameters. It is required and can be repeated after the data to describe additional analyses of the same data (see order of input in the summary at the end of this section).

Built-in functions. Six functions (and their derivatives) are available in P3R by specifying their code NUMBER in the REGRESS paragraph. The six are:

Code Number	Function
1	$f_1 = \begin{cases} p_1 e^{p_2 x} + p_3 e^{p_4 x} + \ldots + p_{m-1} e^{p_m x} \\ \qquad \text{if m is even} \\[1em] p_1 e^{p_2 x} + p_3 e^{p_4 x} + \ldots + p_m \\ \qquad \text{if m is odd} \end{cases}$
2	$f_2 = 1/f_1$
3	$f_3 = p_1 + p_2 e^{p_3 x} + (p_4 + p_5 e^{p_6 x}) \sin(p_7 + p_8 x)$

$m = 8$
(good initial estimates are needed for this function)

$$4 \qquad f_4 = \begin{cases} \dfrac{p_1 + p_3 x + p_5 x^2 + \ldots + p_m x^{(m-1)/2}}{1 + p_2 x + p_4 x^2 + \ldots + p_{m-1} x^{(m-1)/2}} \\ \qquad \text{if m is odd} \\[1.5em] \dfrac{p_1 + p_3 x + p_5 x^2 + \ldots + p_{m-1} x^{(m/2)-1}}{1 + p_2 x + p_4 x^2 + \ldots + p_m x^{(m/2)}} \\ \qquad \text{if m is even} \end{cases}$$

$$5 \qquad f_5 = p_1 x^{p_2} e^{p_3 x} + p_5 x^{p_6} e^{p_7 x} + \cdots$$

if m is not a multiple of 4, the additional parameters are treated as zero

$$6 \qquad f_6 = p_1 x_1 + p_2 x_2 + p_3 x_3 + \cdots$$

for constrained linear regression; for an intercept, one of the variables should be a vector of ones; total number of independent variables = m. In the input data, the dependent variable must be listed after the independent variables

where

m = number of parameters
x = the value of the independent variable.

You must specify the DEPENDENT variable, the INDEPENDENT variable and the number of PARAMETERS in addition to the code NUMBER for each function. You can fix or restrict values of the parameters by specifying upper and lower limits for them. A TITLE can also be given.

In Example 3R.1 we specify

```
/ REGRESS   DEPENDENT IS COUNT.
            INDEPENDENT IS TIME.
            NUMBER IS 1.
            PARAMETERS ARE 4.
```

as well as a WEIGHT variable

```
            WEIGHT IS CASEWT.
```

Note: The IBM OS System Cards for any of the six functions are the same as in Example 3R.1. If the function is specified by FORTRAN statements, the IBM OS System Cards are described in Section 14.4.

REGRess ─────────

NUMBer = #.   none/prev.
   The code NUMBER of one of the six functions available in P3R. The number must be specified in the first REGRESS paragraph when one of the six nonlinear functions is desired. When you specify a nonlinear function by FORTRAN statements, NUMBER is passed to the subroutine that evaluates the function, and can then be used as an index in your subroutine. NUMBER need not be specified when your function is stated in FORTRAN.

DEPENDent = v.   required   none/prev.
   Name or subscript of the dependent (predicted) variable.

INDEPendent = v.   1/prev.
   Name or subscript of the independent (predictor) variable; needed only if you request any of the six nonlinear functions available in P3R. It is ignored (not used even if stated) if you specify the function by FORTRAN statements.

PARAMeter = #.   required   none/prev.
   The number of parameters in the regression function.

TITLE = 'c'. $\leq$ 160 char.   blank
   Title for the analysis.

Functions specified in BMDP Control Language. If your function is not one of the built-in functions, you can specify your function and derivatives in the FUN paragraph provided your version of BMDP is dated March 1981 or later. In Example 3R.1, the alternate specification is

```
/ FUN    DF1 = EXP(P2*TIME).
         DF2 = P1*TIME*DF1.
         DF3 = EXP(P4*TIME).
         DF4 = P2*TIME*DF3.
         F = P1*DF1 + P3*DF3.
```

where P1, P2, P3, P4 are assumed names for the parameters; DF1, DF2, DF3, and DF4 are names assigned by P3R to the derivatives; and F denotes the function.

Functions of the parameters may be specified in the FPARM paragraph. An example is

```
/ FPARM  G1 = P1 + P3.    G2 = P2 - P4*P4.
         D11 = 1. D12 = 0. D13 = 1. D14 = 0.
         D21 = 0. D22 = 1. D23 = 0. D24 = -2*P4.
/ REGRESS   FPARM = 2.
```

where G1, G2 are the assumed names of the functions and the D's are derivatives with respect to the parameters. The number of functions of parameters must be specified in the FPARM sentence of the REGRESSION paragraph. The program evaluates the functions at each iteration, estimates their standard deviations, and includes them in the correlation matrix of the parameters (Landaw et al., 1982).

If parameter NAMES are specified in the PARAMETER paragraph, these names must be used in the FUN and FPARM paragraphs also.

Rules for the FUN paragraph are similar to those for the TRANSFORMATION paragraph except that the case USE variable is not available and only those variables specified in the USE list of the variable paragraph can be used. When the FUN paragraph is used, the NUMBER statement in the REGRESSION paragraph is not used.

Example 3R.2 Basic Setup for Specifying a Nonlinear Function in FORTRAN

We fitted the sum of two exponentials to the data in Table 14.1 by using one of the nonlinear functions available in P3R. Now we repeat the analysis by specifying the function and its derivatives in FORTRAN. The sum of two exponentials is

$$f = p_1 e^{p_2 t} + p_3 e^{p_4 t}$$

The derivatives are

$$\frac{\partial f}{\partial p_1} = e^{p_2 t} \qquad \frac{\partial f}{\partial p_2} = p_1 t e^{p_2 t} = p_1 t \frac{\partial f}{\partial p_1}$$

$$\frac{\partial f}{\partial p_3} = e^{p_4 t} \qquad \frac{\partial f}{\partial p_4} = p_3 t e^{p_4 t} = p_3 t \frac{\partial f}{\partial p_3}$$

Note that $f = p_1 \frac{\partial f}{\partial p_1} + p_3 \frac{\partial f}{\partial p_3}$.

In our data the independent variable TIME is the third variable $X(3)$. Therefore we write the function and derivatives as follows:

FORTRAN statements to define function and derivatives (beginning in column 7)

```
     DF(1) = DEXP(P(2)*X(3))
     DF(2) = P(1)*X(3)*DF(1)
     DF(3) = DEXP(P(4)*X(3))
     DF(4) = P(3)*X(3)*DF(3)
     F = P(1)*DF(1) + P(3)*DF(3)
```

BMDP instructions

```
/ PROBLEM    TITLE IS 'RADIOACTIVE
                       SULFATE DATA'.
/ INPUT      VARIABLES ARE 3.
             FORMAT IS '(F8.4, F8.6, F8.0)'
/ VARIABLE   NAMES ARE COUNT, CASEWT, TIME.

/ REGRESS    DEPENDENT IS COUNT.
             PARAMETERS ARE 4.
             WEIGHT IS CASEWT.

/ PARAMETER  INITIAL ARE 10, -.1, 5, -.01.

/ END
```

When the function and its derivatives are specified by FORTRAN statements, the FORTRAN statements must be preceded by System Cards to initiate the analysis by P3R. Different System Cards may be used for various systems (IBM, CDC, VAX, etc.). The usual IBM System Cards are

```
     //job card
     //   EXEC  BIMEDT,PROG=BMDP3R
     //FUN DD  *
```

The FORTRAN statements are immediately followed by another System Card. For IBM OS systems this card is

```
     //GO.SYSIN  DD  *
```

This System Card is followed by the Control Language instructions. The Control Language instructions are in turn followed by the data (Table 14.1). The analysis is terminated by a final System Card. For IBM OS systems, this System Card is

```
     //
```

Section 14.5 discusses System Cards in greater detail.

In the above Control Language instructions NUMBER and INDEPENDENT are not included as in Example 3R.1.

The results are presented in Output 3R.2. Small differences between Output 3R.1 and 3R.2 are due to the limited accuracy of computations performed on the computer (slightly different round-off error).

Specifying a function by FORTRAN statements. You are not limited to the six functions described above. Any function can be fitted to the data if you can specify, in FORTRAN, both the function and its derivatives with respect to the parameters. The FORTRAN subroutine containing the function and its derivatives temporarily becomes part of P3R and replaces the subroutine containing the six functions described above. (You cannot use both -- one of the six functions and a FORTRAN-specified function -- in the same job.)

The FORTRAN subroutine is called once for each case during each iteration (or halving). The first

Output 3R.2   FORTRAN statements are used to define a nonlinear function and its derivatives. The problem is the same as that in Example 3R.1

ITERATION NUMBER	INCREMENT HALVINGS	RESIDUAL SUM OF SQUARES	P(1)	P(2)	P(3)	P(4)
0	0	5.592536	10.000000	−0.100000	5.000000	−0.010000
1	1	0.379743	9.907287	−0.101484	4.947083	0.000353
2	0	0.058245	8.301623	−0.130408	6.940309	−0.003081
3	0	0.018950	9.234010	−0.178251	7.336723	−0.003128
4	0	0.013453	10.542867	−0.211035	7.343436	−0.003137
5	0	0.012897	11.124459	−0.223769	7.364382	−0.003160
6	0	0.012850	11.290754	−0.227774	7.374455	−0.003170
7	0	0.012846	11.336527	−0.228964	7.377789	−0.003174
8	0	0.012845	11.349531	−0.229309	7.378792	−0.003175
9	0	0.012845	11.353256	−0.229409	7.379085	−0.003175
10	0	0.012845	11.354325	−0.229437	7.379169	−0.003176
11	0	0.012845	11.354632	−0.229446	7.379194	−0.003176
12	0	0.012845	11.354720	−0.229448	7.379201	−0.003176
13	0	0.012845	11.354745	−0.229449	7.379203	−0.003176

ITERATION   13 HAS THE SMALLEST RESIDUAL SUM OF SQUARES(SUBJECT TO CONSTRAINTS, IF ANY). REMAINING CALCULATIONS ARE BASED ON THE RESULTS OF THIS ITERATION.

ASYMPTOTIC CORRELATION MATRIX OF THE PARAMETERS

		P(1) 1	P(2) 2	P(3) 3	P(4) 4
P(1)	1	1.0000			
P(2)	2	−0.8140	1.0000		
P(3)	3	0.1459	−0.5026	1.0000	
P(4)	4	−0.1139	0.4184	−0.8689	1.0000

RESIDUAL MEAN SQUARE   0.0007556065

DEGREES OF FREEDOM   17

PARAMETER	ESTIMATE	ASYMPTOTIC STANDARD DEVIATION	TOLERANCE
P(1)	11.354745	0.865841	0.2445360588
P(2)	−0.229449	0.018740	0.1865294094
P(3)	7.379203	0.106597	0.1970591829
P(4)	−0.003176	0.000136	0.2445052536

----

three statements of the subroutine are

```
      SUBROUTINE P3RFUN(F,DF,P,X,N,KASE,NVAR,NPAR,
     *                  IPASS,XLOSS,IDEP)
      IMPLICIT REAL*8 (A-H,O-Z)
      DIMENSION DF(NPAR),P(NPAR),X(NVAR)
```

where the following values should not be changed

NPAR - the number of parameters in the function
NVAR - the total number of variables (not the number of independent variables); the sum of the variables read as data and those added by transformations, if any
KASE - the sequence number of the case for which the function is being evaluated
IPASS - pass number; this is used when the function evaluation requires more than one pass at the data (IPASS is primarily useful with maximum likelihood estimation and is explained in Section 14.3; otherwise it can be ignored). In addition, after convergence is reached in any analysis, the function subroutine is called as part of the final report of results. When this final report is made, IPASS is set equal to 1000. IPASS thus serves as a flag to you so that you can produce additional reports, e.g., calculate functions of the parameters
P(1),P(2),...,P(NPAR) - the current values of the parameters

The following values are usually not changed

X(1),X(2),...,X(NVAR) - the observed values of <u>all</u> the variables in the order that they appear in the data matrix
N   - the NUMBER specified in the REGRESS paragraph. It can be used to select functions in your FORTRAN subroutine
XLOSS - a utility or loss function to replace the residual sum of squares as a criterion for convergence (XLOSS is primarily useful for maximum likelihood estimation and is explained in Section 14.3; otherwise it can be ignored)
IDEP - index of the dependent variable

The following <u>must</u> be evaluated in the subroutine

F   - the value of the function for this case (f)
DF(1),DF(2),...,DF(NPAR) - the values of the derivatives of the function with respect to the parameters ($\partial f/\partial p_i$)

The rules of FORTRAN apply in the subroutine (and <u>not</u> the rules of BMDP Control Language). Any FORTRAN statements and functions can be used. The second statement, IMPLICIT REAL*8, specifies that all real values are in double precision. If you are not using an IBM 360/370 computer, you must include all real variables in a DOUBLE PRECISION statement. All FORTRAN functions can be called; double precision versions of the functions should be used. (In some CDC and Burroughs versions, double precision is not used.)

Example 3R.3 A Radioimmunoassay Problem

We use data from an insulin radioimmunoassay that are presented in Table 14.2 (Brown et al., 1974).

Table 14.2   Activity corresponding to levels of insulin standard (Brown et al., 1974).

Insulin Standard	Counts x 10^{-3}
0	9.274
0	9.522
5	8.082
5	8.354
10	7.296
10	7.518
25	5.864
25	5.974
50	4.396
50	4.110
100	2.830
100	2.674
200	1.798
200	1.566

The insulin standard is recorded in columns 4-6 and counts in columns 8-12.

The empirical function appropriate to the data is

$$f = \frac{1}{p_1 x + p_2} + p_3$$

(Taljedal and Wold, 1970). The derivatives are

$$\frac{\partial f}{\partial p_1} = -\frac{x}{(p_1 x + p_2)^2} \quad ; \quad \frac{\partial f}{\partial p_2} = -\frac{1}{(p_1 x + p_2)^2} \quad ; \quad \frac{\partial f}{\partial p_3} = 1.$$

The independent variable x is the first variable.

Note that if p_1 and p_2 are zero the function is not defined; therefore initial estimates of the parameters must be specified.

The function and its derivatives are specified with the following BMDP instructions.

<u>FORTRAN definition of function and derivatives</u>
<u>(beginning in column 7):</u>

```
      DF(3) = 1.0
      A = P(1)*X(1) + P(2)
      IF(A.LE.0.0) A = 0.000001
      F = 1.0/A + P(3)
      DF(2) = -1.0/A**2
      DF(1) = X(1)*DF(2)
```

BMDP instructions:

```
/ PROBLEM   TITLE IS 'INSULIN DATA'.
/ INPUT     VARIABLES ARE 2.
            FORMAT IS '(F6.0, F6.3)'.
/ VARIABLE  NAMES ARE STANDARD, COUNT.

/ REGRESS   DEPENDENT IS COUNT.
            PARAMETERS ARE 3.

/ PARAMETER INITIAL ARE 0.01, 0.1, 5.
/ END
```

Output 3R.3 An analysis of the insulin radioimmunoassay data by P3R

NUMBER OF CASES READ.   14

VARIABLE			STANDARD		
NO.	NAME	MEAN	DEVIATION	MINIMUM	MAXIMUM
1	STANDARD	55.714249	69.637985	0.0	200.000000
2	COUNT	5.661283	2.773079	1.566000	9.521999

PARAMETER MAXIMA. . . . . ************** ************** **************

PARAMETER MINIMA. . . . . ************** ************** **************

ITERATION NUMBER	INCREMENT HALVINGS	RESIDUAL SUM OF SQUARES	P(1)	P(2)	P(3)
0	0	168.067877	0.010000	0.100000	5.000000
1	0	7.070914	0.002958	0.120812	1.312471
2	0	0.319400	0.002667	0.107692	0.137567
3	0	0.249154	0.002694	0.108966	0.138173
4	0	0.249144	0.002694	0.108981	0.138054
5	0	0.249144	0.002694	0.108981	0.138048
6	0	0.249144	0.002694	0.108981	0.138048
7	0	0.249144	0.002694	0.108981	0.138048
8	5	0.249144	0.002694	0.108981	0.138048
7	0	0.249144	0.002694	0.108981	0.138048

ITERATION   7 HAS THE SMALLEST RESIDUAL SUM OF SQUARES(SUBJECT TO CONSTRAINTS, IF ANY).
REMAINING CALCULATIONS ARE BASED ON THE RESULTS OF THIS ITERATION.

ASYMPTOTIC CORRELATION MATRIX OF THE PARAMETERS

			P(1)	P(2)	P(3)
			1	2	3
P(1)	1		1.0000		
P(2)	2		0.7446	1.0000	
P(3)	3		0.9357	0.8830	1.0000

RESIDUAL MEAN SQUARE   0.0226494893

DEGREES OF FREEDOM   11

PARAMETER	ESTIMATE	ASYMPTOTIC STANDARD DEVIATION	TOLERANCE
P(1)	0.002694	0.000220	0.0942260705
P(2)	0.108981	0.002070	0.1667713025
P(3)	0.138048	0.186350	0.0465876330

CASE NO. LABEL	PREDICTED COUNT	STD DEV OF PRED VALUE	OBSERVED COUNT	RESIDUAL	STANDARD
1	9.313979	0.088011	9.273999	-0.039981	0.0
2	9.313979	0.088011	9.521999	0.208019	0.0
3	8.304730	0.056879	8.082000	-0.222731	5.000000

--- similar statistics for cases 4 to 11 ---

12	2.781170	0.059201	2.674000	-0.107170	100.000000
13	1.681972	0.091104	1.797999	0.116027	200.000000
14	1.681972	0.091104	1.566000	-0.115972	200.000000

SERIAL CORRELATION   -0.42374

The IBM OS System Cards required for this analysis are the same as described for Example 3R.2 and are discussed in greater detail in Section 14.4. The data for this example are in Table 14.2.

The results of the analysis are presented in Output 3R.3.

Example 3R.4 Plots of the Residuals and Predicted Values

In the PLOT paragraph you can specify the following plots:

- predicted and observed values of the dependent variable and residuals against specified variables
- residuals and residuals squared against the predicted values
- a normal probability plot of the residuals
- a detrended normal probability plot of the residuals

The plots and normal probability plots available in P3R are described in Section 10.1. The residuals and predicted values plotted are those printed in the results and we request them by inserting the following PLOT paragraph in the Example 3R.1 instructions before the END paragraph

```
----------------------------------------
    / PLOT    VARIABLE IS TIME.
             RESIDUAL.
             SIZE = 40, 25.
----------------------------------------
```

The plots are shown in Output 3R.4.

```
PLOT ─────────────────────────────
  RESIDual.                          no/prev.
     The residuals (y-f) and residuals squared
     (y-f)² are plotted against the predicted values
     (the value of the function f) in separate
     plots.
  VARiable = v list.                 none/prev.
     Names or subscripts of variables against which
     the observed values of the dependent variable y
     and the predicted values f are plotted in one
     graph. In a second graph the residuals (y-f)
     are plotted against these variables.
  NORMal.                            no/prev.
     Normal probability plot of the residuals is
     printed. If case weights are specified,
     weighted residuals are used in this plot.
  DNORMal.                           no/prev.
     Detrended normal probability plot of the
     residuals is printed. If case weights are
     specified, weighted residuals are used in this
     plot.
  SIZE = #, #.                       50,35/prev.
     The first number is the number of characters
     (width) in the horizontal axis and the second
     number is the number of lines (height) in the
     vertical axis.
```

Output 3R.4 Plots of residuals, predicted and observed values from the sum of exponentials model using the radioactive sulfate data of Brunhilda the baboon

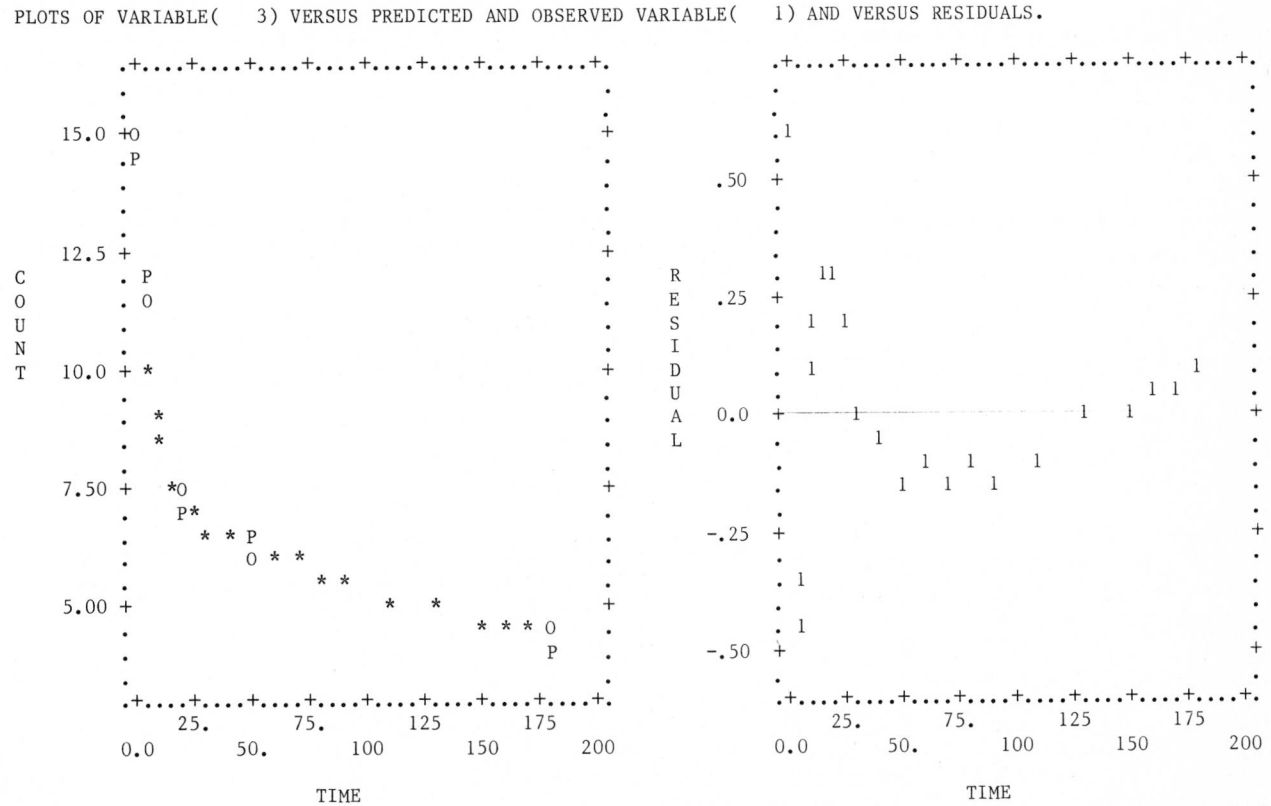

(output continued)

Output 3R.4 (continued)

PLOTS OF PREDICTED VARIABLE COUNT   VERSUS RESIDUALS AND VERSUS RESIDUALS SQUARED

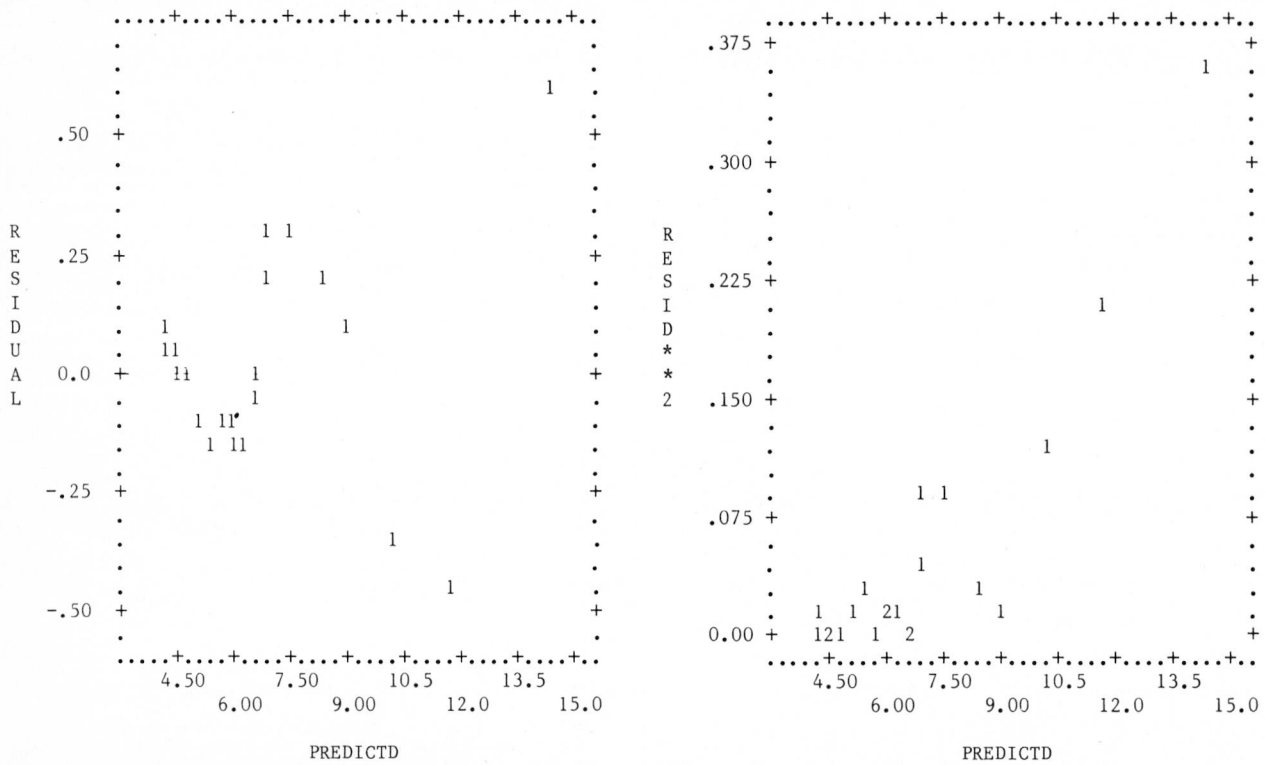

PREDICTD   PREDICTD

Describing the Parameters: Initial Estimates, Upper and Lower Limits

The PARAMETER paragraph is used to specify initial estimates for the parameters. An upper and lower limit and a name can be specified for each parameter, and exact linear constraints can be imposed.

P3R provides initial values (zeros) for the parameters. These may be a very poor starting point; e.g., in the insulin radioimmunoassay, Example 3R.3, the function is undefined when the parameters are all zero. Initial values must be specified when the function is undefined, or all derivatives are zero when all parameters are zero. Nonzero initial values are required for function number 3, p. 294.

Usually you can specify improved initial values by a little forethought. Improved values reduce the computation required, and increase the likelihood of finding a global solution when there are local minimums to the residual sum of squares. To provide reasonable initial values:
- use the solution from a similar analysis or from an analysis by a different method
- if you cannot choose an exact value, choose a reasonable range for the parameter and pick a value close to the limit nearer zero (but preferably not zero and not a specified boundary); this limit is usually more precisely estimated.
- be sure to use initial values that have the correct sign; e.g., for built-in function #1, p_1 and p_3 are usually positive, p_2 and p_4 are usually negative
- if you still cannot decide, use arbitrary nonzero numbers such as ±1, ±2, ±3,... depending on whether you think the parameters are positive or negative

You can specify upper and lower limits for the parameters. Limits can be used to restrict a parameter to a given range in order to avoid a local minimum, a value of the parameter for which the function is undefined, or an interval where a change in the parameter does not affect the function (i.e., its estimated derivative is zero). You can fit the value of a parameter by setting its upper and lower limits to the fixed value.

You can specify names for the parameters to be used in the printed results. You can specify upper and lower limits and names for any subset of the parameters by using the tab feature (p. 29).

To incorporate prior knowledge of some parameters and their standard errors in the analysis, use the PRIOR and RIDGE statements (Landaw et al., 1982). PRIOR values are the estimates and RIDGE values should be σ^2/σ_i^2, where σ^2 is an estimate of the (weighted) residual mean square and σi is the standard error of the i'th parameter's prior estimate (see A.15). For example, if previous information gives 0.2 ± 0.04 and 0.05 ± 0.01 as the estimate ± S.E. for the 2nd and 4th parameter, respectively, and $\sigma^2 = 4$, specify

        PRIOR = (2) 0.2, (4) 0.05.
        RIDGE = (2) 2500, (4) 40000.

You may have to make a preliminary run to estimate σ^2. If case weights (p. 302) are precisely equal to the inverse of the error variance, then $\sigma^2 = 1$.

PARAMeter ─────────────────────────────
> INITial = # list.   one per   0.0,0.0,.../prev.
>   parameter
>   Initial values for the parameter estimates. The
>   values must satisfy lower and upper limits (if
>   specified) for the parameters. Good initial
>   estimates are important to avoid saddlepoints
>   or local minimums of the residual sum of
>   squares.
>   <u>Note</u>: If the final sum of squares seems too
>   large, if there appear to be unusual features
>   in the estimates of the parameters or
>   residuals, or if system error messages, such as
>   underflow, overflow or divide check are
>   printed, you should check
>
>   - the formulas of your derivatives
>   - the FORTRAN statements that specify the
>   function and derivatives
>   - whether the function (or derivatives)
>   evaluated using the initial values of the
>   parameters and at the largest or smallest
>   data values is extremely large or small
>
>   If no error is found, you should try different
>   initial values.
> MAXimum = # list.   one per   none/prev.
>   parameter
>   Upper limits for the parameters.
> MINimum = # list.   one per   none/prev.
>   parameter
>   Lower limits for the parameters.
> NAME = c list.   one per   p(1),P(2),.../prev.
>   parameter
>   Names for the parameters.

Constraints on the Parameters

Exact linear equality constraints can be specified on the parameters. Let $p_1, p_2, \ldots$ represent the values of the parameters. Then an exact linear equality constraint has the form

$$b_1 p_1 + b_2 p_2 + \ldots = c$$

where b_1, b_2, ... are specified coefficients and c is a specified constant. For example

$$p_1 + p_2 + p_3 = 1$$

and

$$2p_3 - p_5 = 3$$

are both constraints. A linear inequality constraint can also be obtained by using a linear equality constraint with limits on parameters. For example, suppose you want $0 \le p_1 + p_2 + p_3 \le 1$, you specify CONSTRAINT = $p_1 + p_2 + p_3 - p_4 = 0$ and MINIMUM = 0, and MAXIMUM = 1 for p_4.

When constraints are used, the number of constraints must be specified in the REGRESS paragraph; the constraints are specified in the PARAMETER paragraph.

The two constraints, $p_1 + p_2 + p_3 = 1$ and $2p_3 - p_5 = 3$, are specified as

```
/ REGRESS    CONSTRAINT = 2.
/ PARAMETER  CONSTRAINT = 1, 1, 1.     k = 1.
             CONSTRAINT = (3)2, (5)-1.  k = 3.
```

REGRess ─────────────────────────────
> CONSTraint = #.   none/prev.
>   Number of exact linear equality constraints on
>   the parameters that are specified in the
>   PARAMETER paragraph.

PARAMeter ─────────────────────────────
> CONSTraint =   may be   0.0,0.0,.../prev.
>   # list.   repeated
>   Coefficients of the parameters in one
>   constraint. The first number is the coefficient
>   of the first parameter, etc. This statement can
>   be repeated in the same PARAMETER paragraph to
>   specify additional constraints. If any
>   CONSTRAINT is specified, all CONSTRAINTS
>   specified in previous PARAMETER paragraphs are
>   cancelled.
> K = #.   may be repeated   0.0/prev.
>   # is the value on the right hand side of the
>   equal sign for the <u>preceding</u> CONSTRAINT.
>
>   <u>Note</u>: The value of K is applied to the CONSTRAINT
>   statement preceding it, i.e., you should write
>   your CONSTRAINT and K statements in pairs. When
>   constraints are specified, the upper and lower
>   limits for some of the parameters may be
>   violated. Any such violation is easily detected
>   by inspecting the parameter estimates.

Printing Observed Values, Predicted Values and Residuals

For each case P3R prints the predicted value (value of the function), its standard error, the value of the dependent variable, the residuals, and the observed values of the specified variables (see ⑨ in Output 3R.1). You can specify whether or not to print this list and, if so, which variables to include in the list. All computed values use the chosen estimates of the parameters (see ⑥) in Output 3R.1).

If you specify

PRINT = 0.

in the REGRESS paragraph, the residuals, predicted values and data are not printed.

You can also specify

PRINT = v list.

using the names or subscripts of variables whose observed values are to be printed for each case; the predicted value, its standard error, the value of the dependent variable, and the residual are also printed. The values of variables not specified in the v list are <u>not</u> printed.

REGRess ─────────────────────────────
> PRINT = v list.   all variables/prev.
>   The names or subscripts of variables whose
>   observed values are printed for each case. In
>   addition to the observed values, the predicted
>   values, its standard error, the value of the
>   dependent variable and the residual are also
>   printed. If PRINT = 0 is specified, residuals,
>   predicted values and data are <u>not</u> printed.

Saving the Data, Residuals and Predicted Values

When DATA are saved, the predicted values and residuals from the first analysis in a problem are also saved in a BMDP File. The predicted values are saved as variable VT+1 with the name PREDICTD and the residuals are saved as variable VT+2 with the name RESIDUAL (where VT is the number of variables after transformation).

The predicted values and residuals are computed using the chosen estimates of the parameters (see ⑥ in Output 3R.1). If you alter the value of any variable (such as the case WEIGHT variable) in the FORTRAN subroutine, the values of these variables are also computed and saved using the chosen estimates of the parameters.

Case Weights

When the error variance is not homogeneous but varies from case to case, weighted least squares estimation is more appropriate; the weight (w) for each case is proportional to the inverse of the variance. In weighted least squares, the quantity minimized is

$$\Sigma w(y - f)^2$$

where the sum is over all cases read.

The variance may be expressed in terms of the function f; the case weight will vary from iteration to iteration as the estimates of the parameter change. The variable $X(i)$, where i is the subscript of the case WEIGHT variable, can be modified in the FORTRAN subroutine describing the function. This is known as iteratively reweighted least squares and is used in maximum likelihood estimation (Section 14.3).

In P3R, the case WEIGHTS are specified in the REGRESS paragraph.

```
REGRess ─────────────────────────────────────────
│  WEIGHT = v.                     no weight var./prev.
│  Name or subscript of the variable containing
│  case weights. If WEIGHT is not stated or is set
│  to zero, there are no case weights.
 ──────────────────────────────────────────────────
```

Values Used in the Gauss-Newton Algorithm

The function is fitted by an iterative algorithm. The algorithm declares that a solution has been reached when

$$\left| (RSS^{(k+1)} - RSS^{(k)})/RSS^{(k+1)} \right| < C$$

for five successive values of k, where $RSS^{(k)}$ is the residual sum of squares at iteration k, and C is the value of the CONVERGENCE criterion.

When the CONVERGENCE criterion is set to a value less than zero, the maximum number of ITERATIONS is used and the parameter estimates used in the computation of the standard errors, asymptotic correlations, residuals and predicted values are from the last iteration; if a BMDP File is created, these residuals and predicted values are saved.

If the residual sum of squares increases between two iterations, the increment size is halved and the residual sum of squares is recomputed and tested against the residual sum of squares at the previous iteration. This halving is repeated until the residual sum of squares is less than that at the previous iteration or the maximum number of HALVINGS is reached. At each iteration the number of increment halvings performed is printed.

TOLERANCE is used to guard against the problem of near singularity when inverting the matrix of sums of cross products of the derivatives. A parameter estimate is not changed at an iteration if more than (1 - TOLERANCE) proportion of the sum of squares of partial derivatives with respect to that parameter can be expressed with partial derivatives of other parameters.

```
REGRess ─────────────────────────────────────────
│  CONVerge = #.                          0.00001/prev.
│  Value of the convergence criterion C as
│  described above.
│  ITERation = #.                             50/prev.
│  Maximum number of iterations. If convergence
│  has not occurred by this number of iterations,
│  the algorithm is terminated.
│  Note: If linear CONSTRAINTS are specified, they
│  are solved on the first iteration for some of
│  the parameters in terms of the other
│  parameters; at least two iterations are
│  required even for a linear function.
│  HALVing = #.          > 0                    5/prev.
│  The maximum number of increment halvings as
│  described above.
│  TOLerance = #.   .00001 < # < 1.0      0.001/prev.
│  A check for near singularity as described
│  above. A more complete discussion of tolerance
│  is given in Appendix A.11.
 ──────────────────────────────────────────────────
```

SIZE OF PROBLEM

The maximum problem size that P3R can analyze is a function of the number of cases (C), the total number of variables (V), and the number of parameters (P). The following table indicates the maximum number of cases for various combinations of P and V. Appendix B describes how to increase the capacity of the program.

total variables V	2	3	4	5	10	20
parameters P	10	20	20	20	20	20
cases C	1700	1500	1350	1200	800	480

COMPUTATIONAL METHOD

All computations are in double precision. Means and standard deviations are computed by the method of provisional means (Appendix A.2). The parameters are estimated by a modified Gauss-Newton algorithm (Appendix A.15).

ACKNOWLEDGEMENT

P3R was programmed by Steve Chasen and later substantially enhanced by Paul Sampson. Improvements were also made by Jerry Toporek.

SUMMARY

Order of Input Cards

A. Built-in function or a function specified in the
   FUN paragraph

```
//job card                          ] IBM OS
//  EXEC  BIMED,PROG=BMDP3R         ] System Cards
//SYSIN  DD  *
/ PROBLEM                           ]
/ INPUT
/ VARIABLE
/ TRANSFORM                          BMDP
/ SAVE                               instructions
/ REGRESS
/ PARAMETER
/ FUN
/ PLOT
/ END                               ]
   (data, if on cards)
/ REGRESS      ] repeat for
/ PARAMETER    | additional
/ FUN          | analyses of
/ END          ] the same data

//                                  ] IBM OS
                                    ] System Cards
```

JCL for additional FORTRAN units should be placed in
front of the //SYSIN card; for unit 8, type:

```
//FT08F001  DD...
```

B. Function specified by FORTRAN statements

```
//job card                          ] IBM OS
//  EXEC  BIMEDT,PROG=BMDP3R        ] System Cards
//FUN DD  *                         ]

FORTRAN statements, for IBM OS     ] Function
do not include SUBROUTINE and      | specified
DIMENSION statements at            | in FORTRAN
beginning and RETURN and END       |
at end                             ]

//GO.SYSIN  DD  *                   ] IBM OS
                                    ] System Cards
/ PROBLEM                           ]
/ INPUT
/ VARIABLE
/ TRANSFORM
/ SAVE                               BMDP
/ REGRESS                            instructions
/ PARAMETER
/ PLOT
/ END                               ]
   (data, if on cards)
/ REGRESS      ] repeat for
/ PARAMETER    | additional analyses
/ END          ] of the same data

//                                  ] IBM OS
                                    ] System Cards
```

JCL for additional FORTRAN units should be placed in
front of the //GO.SYSIN card; for unit 8, type:

```
//GO.FT08F001 DD...
```

Paragraph Statement	Preassigned	Comment and Manual Reference
/●REGRess		Required to direct regression (may be repeated after data). Options describe the role of the variables in the equation, identify the built-in function to be used (if any) and specify the number of parameters.
● NUMBer = #.	none	Must be specified when a built-in function is used. Code number selects built-in function: 294 1. sum of exponentials 4. rational polynomials 2. one/(sum of exponentials) 5. growth function 3. exponentially damped 6. constrained linear regression sine wave
● PARAMeters = #.	none	The number of parameters in the regression function. * 294
● DEPENDent = v.	none	Required; name or subscript of the dependent (predicted) variable. * 294
o INDEPendent = v.	1.	Name or subscript of the independent (predictor) variable. Use only with built-in functions. * 294
TITLE = 'c'.	none	Title, up to 160 characters, to label the output. 294
PRINT = v list.	all	Names or subscripts of variables whose observed values are printed for each case. The predicted value, its standard error and residual are also printed. PRINT = 0. specifies that no casewise information be printed. * 301
WEIGHT = v.	none	Name or subscript of variable containing case weights. A case weight variable can be used for iteratively reweighted least squares (e.g., maximum likelihood estimation – see page 315). * 302
CONSTraint = #.	none	Number of exact linear equality constraints on the parameters specified in /PARAM. * 301
CONVerge = #.	.0001.	Value of convergence criterion used to decide if a solution has been reached. If set to a negative value, the number of ITER is used. *
ITERations = #.	50.	Maximum number of iterations. * 302
HALVIngs = #.	5.	Maximum number of increment halvings. * 302
TOLerance = #.	10^{-8}.	Singularity check at each iteration; controls the degree of singularity tolerated before a parameter is ignored. 302
Options for special situations		(See pp. 315–323 for description and example.)
PASS = #.	1.	The number of times the data are passed to subroutine FUN. 321
MEANSQuare = #.	none	Use MEANSQ value in place of residual mean square to compute information theory standard errors. * 315
LOSS.	no	Replace the last square criterion with loss function (specified as XLOSS in subroutine FUN; the convergence criterion is applied to the sum of XLOSS). * 323
FPARM = #.	none	Number of functions of parameters specified in FPARM paragraph. 295
/oFUN		Use rules of the TRANSFORM paragraph to specify the function and its derivatives. 295
/ FPARM		Use rules of the TRANSFORM paragraph to define functions of parameters and their derivatives. 295
/ PARAMeter		Optional to control estimates for the parameters (may be repeated). 301
INITial = # list.	all zero	One number per parameter. Initial values for parameter estimates. Must satisfy MAX and MIN below.
MAXimums = # list.	none	Upper limits for the parameters; one number per parameter. *
MINimums = # list.	none	Lower limits for the parameters; one number per parameter. *
NAMEs = list.	P(1),P(2),...	Names, up to 8 characters each, for the parameters. *
CONSTraint = # list.	none	List contains the coefficients of the parameters in one constraint. The first number is the coefficient of the first parameter, etc.
K = #.	no	The number for K is the value for the right side of the equal sign for the preceding CONST statement. *
PRIOR = # list.	none	One number per parameter. Prior estimate of parameter value.
RIDGE = # list.	none	One number per parameter. Ridge values corresponding to the parameters with prior estimates. 300
/ PLOT		Optional to produce graphical descriptions. Same as P1R except there is no PREP statement in P3R. 299

Key:

/	–indicates paragraph	*	–assigned value remains the same for additional problems
.	–period ends a sentence		
●	–required o –may be required	VT	–number of variables after transformations
v	–variable (name or subscript)	list	–more than one item, often one per var.
g	–group (name or subscript)		
#	–number	Capitalized letters –paragraph or sentence names recognized by BMDP
'c'	–characters (name or parameter) may omit apostrophes if contiguous letters only		Page numbers following refer to this Manual

PAR

14.2 Derivative-Free Nonlinear Regression

Mary Ralston

ABSTRACT

PAR estimates the parameters of a nonlinear function by least squares and can be used to compute maximum likelihood estimates. The program is appropriate for a wide variety of functions that are not linear in the parameters, and for which derivatives are difficult to specify or costly to compute. The regression function must be specified by FORTRAN statements; the derivatives are not specified (see also P3R). Upper and lower limits may be specified on the individual parameters or for arbitrary linear combinations of the parameters. Examples 3R.2 and 3R.3 are reanalyzed using PAR.

In the 1981 release of BMDP, the user may specify the function using transformation statements within the FUN paragraph.

WHERE TO FIND IT

Example AR.1 Reanalysis of Example 3R.2

The data for the first example are in Table 14.1. As in Example 3R.2, the sum of the two exponentials

$$f = p_1 e^{p_2 t} + p_3 e^{p_4 t}$$

is fitted to the data. The function can be specified by a FORTRAN statement and followed by Control Language. (In versions dated March 1981 or later, you can specify the function in the FUN paragraph. See below.) PAR uses double precision for all computations. Therefore, the double precision versions of functions should be used (e.g., DEXP, not EXP).

```
------------------------------------
FORTRAN statement of function:

    F = P(1)*DEXP(P(2)*X(3))
  *   + P(3)*DEXP(P(4)*X(3))

BMDP instructions:

/ PROBLEM     TITLE IS 'RADIOACTIVE SULFATE DATA'.
/ INPUT       VARIABLES ARE 3.
              FORMAT IS '(F8.4, F8.6, F8.0)'.
/ VARIABLE    NAMES ARE COUNT, CASEWT, TIME.

/ REGRESS     DEPENDENT IS COUNT.
              WEIGHT IS CASEWT.
              PARAMETERS ARE 4.

/ PARAMETER INITIAL ARE 10, -.1, 5, -.01.

/ END
------------------------------------
```

When the function is specified in BMDP Control Language, you would include the following:

```
/ FUN   F = P1*EXP(P2*TIME) + P3*EXP(P4*TIME).
```

When the function is specified by FORTRAN statements, they must be preceded by System Cards to initiate the analysis. The IBM OS System Cards are

```
//job
// EXEC  BIMEDT,PROG=BMDPAR
//FUN DD *
```

Functions of the parameters may be specified in the FPARM paragraph. An example is

```
/ FPARM  G1 = P1/P2 + P3/P4.  G2 = P1 + P3.
```

where G1 and G2 are assumed names of the functions. PAR evaluates the functions at each iteration, estimates their standard deviation, and includes them in the correlation matrix of the parameters (Landaw et al., 1982).

The FORTRAN statements are immediately followed by another System Card. FOR IBM OS, this card is

    //GO.SYSIN DD *

This System Card is followed by the Control Language instructions, which are in turn followed by the data (Table 14.1). The analysis is terminated by a final System Card. For IBM OS, this System Card is

    //

System Cards are discussed in more detail in 14.4.

The REGRESS and PARAMETER paragraphs are specific to PAR. In the REGRESS paragraph, we specify the DEPENDENT variable, the number of PARAMETERS and the case WEIGHT variable. In the PARAMETER paragraph, INITIAL values for the parameters must be stated.

If prior knowledge of the parameters is available, the user may specify prior estimates and ridge values in the PARAMETER paragraph.

The results are presented in Output AR.1. Circled numbers below correspond to those in the output.

① Interpretation of the REGRESS paragraph. Most values reported are preassigned for the programs.

② Lower (MINIMUM) and upper (MAXIMUM) limits and the initial values specified for the parameters. As no limits were specified, asterisks are printed.

③ Number of cases read. PAR uses only complete cases in all computations. That is, if the value for any variable in a case is missing or out of range, the case is omitted from the computations. If a USE statement is specified in the VARIABLE paragraph, only the values of variables in the USE statement are checked for missing values and values out of range.

④ The mean, standard deviation, minimum and maximum for each variable. When a case WEIGHT variable is specified, as in our example, weighted means and weighted standard deviations are computed.

⑤ At each iteration PAR prints

- the number of the iteration
- the number of increment halvings (explained on p. 312)
- the residual sum of squares RSS = $\Sigma w(y-f)^2$

where y is the observed value of the dependent variable in case j, f is the evaluation of the function, and w is the value of the case weight (the case weight value is 1 if there is no weighting); the summation is over all cases used in the analysis.

⑥ The minimum residual sum of squares and estimates of the parameters. Small differences between the parameter values at the last iteration and at the iteration that produces the smallest

---

Output AR.1   An analysis of the radioactive sulfate data using PAR. The function is the sum of 2 exponentials. Circled numbers correspond to those in the text

---

```
            REGRESSION TITLE


            REGRESSION NUMBER . . . . . . . . . . . . . . .        0
            DEPENDENT VARIABLE. . . . . . . . . . . . . .       COUNT
            WEIGHTING VARIABLE. . . . . . . . . . . . . .       CASEWT
            NUMBER OF PARAMETERS. . . . . . . . . . . . .        4
  ①        NUMBER OF CONSTRAINTS . . . . . . . . . . . .        0
            TOLERANCE FOR PIVOTING. . . . . . . . . . . . 1.0E-08
            TOLERANCE FOR CONVERGENCE . . . . . . . . . . 1.0E-05
            MAXIMUM NUMBER OF ITERATIONS. . . . . . . . .       50
            MAXIMUM NUMBER OF INCREMENT HALVINGS. . . . .        5


            PARAMETERS TO BE ESTIMATED

                         1 P(1)          2 P(2)           3 P(3)          4 P(4)
            MINIMUM  ****************  ****************  ****************  ****************
  ②        MAXIMUM  ****************  ****************  ****************  ****************
            INITIAL      10.000000        -0.100000         5.000000        -0.010000


            USING THE ABOVE SPECIFICATIONS THIS PROGRAM COULD USE UP TO 3373 CASES.


  ③        NUMBER OF CASES READ. . . . . . . . . . . . .       21


            VARIABLE                 STANDARD
            NO. NAME        MEAN      DEVIATION      MINIMUM        MAXIMUM

            1   COUNT      5.750695    1.711861      4.266800      15.111699
  ④        3   TIME      97.933350   60.915985      2.000000     180.000000
            2   CASEWT          NOT COMPUTED         0.004379       0.054928
```

⑤

ITER. NO.	INCR. HALV.	RESIDUAL SUM OF SQUARES	PARAMETERS 1 P(1)	2 P(2)	3 P(3)	4 P(4)
0	0	6.116142	10.000000	-0.100000	5.000000	-0.011000
0	0	5.680311	10.000000	-0.110000	5.000000	-0.010000
0	0	5.592536	10.000000	-0.100000	5.000000	-0.010000
0	0	5.561262	11.000000	-0.100000	5.000000	-0.010000
0	0	4.992193	10.000000	-0.100000	5.500000	-0.010000
1	1	0.913285	10.102698	-0.100470	5.023928	0.001340
2	0	0.259233	7.585941	-0.166839	8.652808	-0.004084
3	0	0.110177	8.947056	-0.169415	6.950855	-0.003428
4	0	0.028216	9.058777	-0.173112	7.156355	-0.002707
5	3	0.019025	9.163389	-0.174800	7.168309	-0.002908
6	0	0.015920	10.137881	-0.189985	7.216169	-0.002973
7	5	0.015658	10.186379	-0.191123	7.233585	-0.003014
8	1	0.015283	10.686998	-0.209210	7.339658	-0.003235
9	0	0.013070	10.844036	-0.219042	7.367585	-0.003166
10	0	0.013050	10.859483	-0.219715	7.363721	-0.003158
11	0	0.013002	11.324760	-0.226622	7.331683	-0.003118
12	0	0.012934	11.195494	-0.223120	7.347094	-0.003136
13	0	0.012853	11.289281	-0.227599	7.374182	-0.003174
14	2	0.012853	11.291146	-0.227602	7.374532	-0.003175
15	0	0.012849	11.297230	-0.228215	7.377354	-0.003171
16	0	0.012848	11.305405	-0.228237	7.376182	-0.003172
17	0	0.012847	11.334945	-0.228658	7.374821	-0.003170
18	0	0.012846	11.336476	-0.228826	7.376317	-0.003172
19	0	0.012846	11.348867	-0.229183	7.379221	-0.003176
20	0	0.012845	11.346282	-0.229193	7.378816	-0.003175
21	3	0.012845	11.346608	-0.229221	7.378938	-0.003175
22	0	0.012845	11.356826	-0.229422	7.378522	-0.003175
23	0	0.012845	11.352948	-0.229367	7.378706	-0.003175
24	0	0.012845	11.353100	-0.229383	7.378853	-0.003175
25	0	0.012845	11.354609	-0.229426	7.379203	-0.003176

THE RESIDUAL SUM OF SQUARES (= 1.284532E-02) WAS SMALLEST WITH THE FOLLOWING PARAMETER VALUES ⑥

1 P(1)	2 P(2)	3 P(3)	4 P(4)
11.3546	-0.229426	7.37920	-3.175618D-03

ESTIMATE OF ASYMPTOTIC CORRELATION MATRIX

		P(1) 1	P(2) 2	P(3) 3	P(4) 4	⑦
P(1)	1	1.0000				
P(2)	2	-0.8139	1.0000			
P(3)	3	0.1460	-0.5028	1.0000		
P(4)	4	-0.1140	0.4187	-0.8689	1.0000	

THE ESTIMATED MEAN SQUARE ERROR IS 7.5561E-04 ⑧

ESTIMATES OF ASYMPTOTIC STANDARD DEVIATIONS OF PARAMETER ESTIMATES WITH   17 DEGREES OF FREEDOM ARE

⑨

1 P(1)	2 P(2)	3 P(3)	4 P(4)
0.865788	1.873086D-02	0.106594	1.362988D-04

CASE NO. NAME ⑩	RESIDUAL	OBSERVED 1 COUNT	PREDICTED 1 COUNT	STD. DEV. PREDICTED	2 CASEWT	3 TIME
1	0.603008	15.111699	14.508691	0.362641	0.004379	2.000000
2	-0.461383	11.360100	11.821483	0.171988	0.007749	4.000000
3	-0.341157	9.765200	10.106357	0.144654	0.010487	6.000000

--- similar statistics for cases 4 to 18 ---

19	0.057188	4.496799	4.439611	0.051932	0.049453	160.000000
20	0.059359	4.360200	4.300841	0.055064	0.052600	170.000000
21	0.100391	4.266800	4.166409	0.058141	0.054928	180.000000

residual sum of squares can be attributed to round-off error; large differences can indicate that a saddle-point or local minimum was found. If the minimum residual sum of squares does not occur within the last (P+1) iterations (where P is the number of parameters), the last iteration is used in the remaining computations even though it is <u>not</u> the minimum.

<u>Note</u>: The remaining computations use the parameter estimates printed in ⑥.

⑦ The asymptotic correlation matrix of the parameter estimates. The matrix computation is described in Appendix A.16.

⑧ The mean square error is equal to the residual sum of squares divided by (N-p) where N is the number of cases with nonzero weights, and p is the number of independent parameters in the function.

⑨ The asymptotic standard deviations (standard errors) of the parameter estimates. A zero indicates a problem with the estimate: the estimate may lie on a boundary of the permissible parameter space (equal to its specified upper or lower limit), there may be extremely high correlations among the estimated parameters, or the estimate is so poor that if it is changed the value of the function is not affected. If an estimate lies on a boundary, PAR prints a message describing the boundary. It must be stressed that these asymptotic standard deviations are estimates and their accuracy is highly dependent on sample size. They must be viewed with reservation when there are step halvings among the last m steps where m is the number of parameters.

⑩ For each case, PAR prints

- the residual, y-f
- the observed value of the dependent variable, y
- the predicted value, f, which is the value of the function
- the standard error of the predicted value (see Appendix A.16)
- the values of the independent variables and the case WEIGHT variable

<u>Specifying the regression function in BMDP Control Language</u>. In versions of BMDP dated March 1981 or later, the function to be fit can be defined in the FUN paragraph. The FUN paragraph follows the same general rules as the TRANSFORMATION paragraph except that the case USE variable is not available and only those variables that are included in the USE statement of the VARIABLE paragraph can be referenced.

The use of the FUN paragraph is illustrated using the problem described in Example AR.1. We would include the following:

```
/ FUN    F = P1*EXP(P2*TIME) + P3*EXP(P4*TIME).
```

where P1, P2, P3 and P4 are the predefined names for the parameters. If you give names to the parameters, you should use them in the FUN paragraph. For IBM systems we use the BIMED procedure instead of the BIMEDT procedure.

<u>Specifying the regression function in FORTRAN</u>. Any function can be fitted to the data if you specify it by FORTRAN statements. The FORTRAN subroutine that contains the function temporarily becomes part of program PAR. The FORTRAN subroutine is called once for each case during each iteration (or halving). The calling sequence of the subroutine is

```
SUBROUTINE FUN(F,P,X,N,KASE,NVAR,NPAR,IPASS,XLOSS)
IMPLICIT REAL*8 (A-H,O-Z)
DIMENSION P(NPAR),X(NVAR)
```

where the following values should not be changed

NPAR - the number of parameters in the function
NVAR - the total number of variables (not the number of independent variables), the sum of the variables read and those added by transformations, if any; if USE is specified in the VARIABLE paragraph, NVAR is the largest subscript of any variable in the USE statement
KASE - the sequence number of the case for which the function is being computed
IPASS - this is used only when the function evaluation requires two passes at the data (IPASS is primarily useful with maximum likelihood estimation and is explained in Section 14.3; otherwise it can be ignored)
P(1),P(2),...,P(NPAR) - the current values of the parameters

The following values are usually not changed

X(1),X(2),...,X(NVAR) - the observed values of all the variables in the order that they appear in the data matrix.
N - the NUMBER specified in the REGRESS paragraph. It can be used to select functions in your FORTRAN subroutine
XLOSS - a utility or loss function to replace that of least squares as a criterion for convergence (XLOSS is primarily useful for maximum likelihood estimation and is explained in Section 14.3; otherwise it can be ignored)

The following must be evaluated in the subroutine

F - the value of the function for this case

The rules of FORTRAN apply in the subroutine (not the rules of Control Language). The second statement, IMPLICIT REAL*8, specifies that all real values are in double precision. If you are not using an IBM 360/370 computer, you must include all real variables in a DOUBLE PRECISION statement. All FORTRAN functions can be called; double precision versions of the functions should be used.

Example AR.2 Reanalysis of Example 3R.3

The radioimmunoassay data in Table 14.2. The empirical function appropriate to the data is

$$f = \frac{1}{P_1 x + P_2} + P_3$$

The independent variable x is the first variable. In FORTRAN we code the function as shown below and add the Control Language.

Output AR.2   Reanalysis of the insulin data by PAR

VARIABLE NO.	NAME	MEAN	STANDARD DEVIATION	MINIMUM	MAXIMUM
1	STANDARD	55.714249	69.637985	0.0	200.000000
2	COUNT	5.661283	2.773079	1.566000	9.521999

ITER. NO.	INCR. HALV.	RESIDUAL SUM OF SQUARES	PARAMETERS 1 P(1)	2 P(2)	3 P(3)
0	0	217.461414	0.010000	0.100000	5.500000
0	0	168.067877	0.010000	0.100000	5.000000
0	0	158.658378	0.011000	0.100000	5.000000
0	0	140.590615	0.010000	0.110000	5.000000
1	0	9.919630	0.002656	0.123317	1.349150
2	3	9.483507	0.002401	0.121014	1.124498
3	0	3.449059	0.001704	0.107005	-0.222941
4	0	3.157619	0.003174	0.110235	-0.029835
5	0	2.250136	0.003094	0.109053	-0.027015
6	0	0.259108	0.002668	0.108362	0.078093
7	0	0.250936	0.002635	0.108500	0.085251
8	2	0.250609	0.002642	0.108577	0.091252
9	0	0.249209	0.002687	0.108991	0.136127
10	0	0.249145	0.002693	0.108974	0.137429
11	2	0.249145	0.002693	0.108974	0.137429
12	0	0.249145	0.002693	0.108976	0.137550
13	0	0.249144	0.002694	0.108984	0.138409
14	0	0.249144	0.002694	0.108981	0.138045
15	4	0.249144	0.002694	0.108981	0.138046

THE RESIDUAL SUM OF SQUARES (=   0.249144   ) WAS SMALLEST WITH THE FOLLOWING PARAMETER VALUES

1 P(1)	2 P(2)	3 P(3)
2.693592D-03	0.108981	0.138046

ESTIMATE OF ASYMPTOTIC CORRELATION MATRIX

		P(1) 1	P(2) 2	P(3) 3
P(1)	1	1.0000		
P(2)	2	0.7459	1.0000	
P(3)	3	0.9365	0.8828	1.0000

THE ESTIMATED MEAN SQUARE ERROR IS   2.2649E-02

ESTIMATES OF ASYMPTOTIC STANDARD DEVIATIONS OF PARAMETER ESTIMATES WITH   11 DEGREES OF FREEDOM ARE

1 P(1)	2 P(2)	3 P(3)
2.202094D-04	2.070125D-03	0.186364

CASE	OBSERVED	PREDICTED 2 COUNT	STD. DEV. PREDICTED	1 STANDARD
1	-0.039980	9.273999	9.313979	0.087987	0.0
2	0.208020	9.521999	9.313979	0.087987	0.0
3	-0.222732	8.082000	8.304731	0.056890	5.000000
4	0.049268	8.353999	8.304731	0.056890	5.000000
5	-0.199496	7.296000	7.495496	0.054249	10.000000
6	0.022504	7.518000	7.495496	0.054249	10.000000
7	0.054465	5.863999	5.809535	0.066492	25.000000
8	0.164465	5.974000	5.809535	0.066492	25.000000
9	0.153880	4.396000	4.242119	0.061860	50.000000
10	-0.132120	4.110000	4.242119	0.061860	50.000000
11	0.048829	2.830000	2.781171	0.059216	100.000000
12	-0.107172	2.674000	2.781171	0.059216	100.000000
13	0.116027	1.797999	1.681972	0.091098	200.000000
14	-0.115972	1.566000	1.681972	0.091098	200.000000

```
------------------------------------
FORTRAN to define function:

    A = P(1)*X(1) + P(2)
    IF(A.LE.0.0) A = 0.000001
    F = 1.0/A + P(3)

BMDP instructions:

/ PROBLEM     TITLE IS 'INSULIN DATA'.
/ INPUT       VARIABLES ARE 2.
              FORMAT IS '(F6.0, F6.3)'.
/ VARIABLE    NAMES ARE STANDARD, COUNT.

/ REGRESS     DEPENDENT IS COUNT.
              PARAMETERS ARE 3.

/ PARAMETER   INITIAL ARE 0.01, 0.1, 5.

/ END
              ------------------------------------
```

The System Cards required for this analysis are the same as described for Example AR.1 and are discussed in greater detail in Section 14.4. The data for this example are in Table 14.2.

The results of the analysis are presented in Output AR.2.

Describing the nonlinear function -- the REGRESS paragraph. The REGRESS paragraph describes the dependent variable and the number of parameters. It is required and can be repeated after the data to describe additional analyses of the same data (see the order of input in the summary at the end of this section).

```
REGRess ------------------------------------
  DEPENDent = v.   required          none/prev.
    Name or subscript of the dependent (predicted)
    variable.
  PARAMeter = #.   required          none/prev.
    The number of parameters in the regression
    function.
  TITLE = 'c'.      < 160 char.          blank
    Title for this analysis.
  NUMBer = #.                        none/prev.
    The value of NUMBER is passed to the FORTRAN
    subroutine that defines the function. It can be
    used to select among functions coded in that
    subroutine.
```

PLOTS of the Residuals and Predicted Values

In the PLOT paragraph you can specify the following plots:

- predicted and observed values of the dependent variable and residuals against specified variables
- residuals and residuals squared against the predicted values
- a normal probability plot of the residuals
- a detrended normal probability plot of the residuals

The residuals and predicted values plotted are those printed in the results.

These plots are illustrated in Output 1R.3 of Section 13.1. They are specified as follows:

```
PLOT ------------------------------------
  RESIDual.                              no/prev.
    The residuals (y-f) and residuals squared
    (y-f)$^2$ are plotted against the predicted values
    f in separate plots.
  VARiable = v list.                   none/prev.
    Names or subscripts of variables against which
    the observed values of the dependent variable y
    and the predicted values f are plotted in one
    graph. In a second graph the residuals (y-f)
    are plotted against these variables.
  NORMal.                                no/prev.
    Normal probability plot of the residuals is
    printed.
  DNORMal.                               no/prev.
    Detrended normal probability plot of the
    residuals is printed.
  SIZE = #, #.                      50,35/prev.
    The first number is the number of characters
    (width) in the horizontal axis and the second
    number is the number of lines (height) in the
    vertical axis.
```

Describing the Parameters— Initial Values, Upper and Lower Limits, etc.

The PARAMETER paragraph is required to specify initial values for the parameters. An upper and lower limit and a name can be specified for each parameter. Upper and lower limits can also be specified for linear combinations of the parameters.

Initial values for the parameters must be specified. Here are some suggestions to help you provide reasonable initial values:

- use the solution from a similar analysis or from an analysis by a different method
- if you cannot choose an exact value, choose a reasonable range for the parameter and pick a value close to the limit nearer zero (but preferably not zero and not a specified boundary); this is the limit that is usually more precisely estimated.
- if you still cannot decide, use arbitrary nonzero numbers such as ± 1, ± 2, ± 3,... depending on whether you think the parameters are positive or negative

You can specify upper and lower limits for the parameters. Limits can be used to restrict a parameter to a given range in order to avoid a local minimum, a value of the parameter for which the function is undefined, or an interval where a change in the parameter does not affect the function (i.e., its estimated derivative is zero).

You can specify names for the parameters to be used in the printed results.

In PAR you can specify that some parameters are fixed at their initial values. Then the initial value is used as the value of the parameter throughout the analysis.

PAR computes the function using the initial values of the parameters and then computes additional initial values of the parameters to obtain several values of the function (Appendix A.16). DELTA is used to compute the additional initial values of the parameters.

PARAMeter ───────────────────────────
> INITial = # list.   required,   none/prev.
>   one per parameter
> Initial values for the parameter estimates. The
> values must be within (but not equal to)
> specified lower and upper limits for the
> parameters. Good initial estimates are
> important to avoid saddle-points or local
> minimums of the residual sum of squares.
> Note: If the final sum of squares seems too
> large, if there appear to be unusual features
> in the estimates of the parameters or
> residuals, or if system error messages, such as
> underflow, overflow or divide check, are
> printed, you should check
>
> - the FORTRAN statements that specify the
> function
> - whether the function evaluated using the
> initial values of the parameters and at the
> largest or smallest data values is extremely
> large or small.
>
> If no error is found, you should try different
> initial values.
> MAXimum = # list.   one per   none/prev.
>   parameter
> Upper limits for the parameters.
> MINimum = # list.   one per   none/prev.
>   parameter
> Lower limits for the parameters.
> NAME = c list.   one per   P(1),P(2),.../prev.
>   parameter
> Names for the parameters. The preassigned names
> cannot be used in Control Language
> instructions.
> FIXED = parameter names or subscripts.   none
> Parameters to be held fixed at their initial
> values.
> DELTA = # list.   .1*INIT(I)
>   when INIT(I) ≠ 0 / prev.
>   .01 otherwise
> Step size used to compute additional starting
> values of the function. You will rarely need to
> specify DELTA.

CONSTRAINTS on the Parameters

Upper and lower limits for each parameter can be
specified as described above.

Upper and lower limits can also be specified for
linear combinations of the parameters. Let p_1, p_2,
... represent the values of the parameters. The
constraints have the form

$$c_1 \leq b_1 p_1 + b_2 p_2 + \ldots \leq c_2$$

where b_1, b_2, ... are known coefficients and c_1 and
c_2 are constants. For example, $p_2 \leq p_4$ can be
written as

$$p_2 - p_4 \leq 0$$

When constraints are used, the number of
constraints must be specified in the REGRESS
paragraph. The constraints are specified in the
PARAMETER paragraph.

REGRess ───────────────────────────
> CONSTraint = #.   none/prev.
> Number of linear constraints on the parameters
> that are specified in the PARAMETER paragraph.

PARAMeter ───────────────────────────
> CONSTraint =   may be   0.0,0.0,.../prev.
>   # list.   repeated
> Coefficients of the parameters in one
> constraint. The first number is the coefficient
> of the first parameter, etc. This statement can
> be repeated in the same PARAMETER paragraph to
> specify additional constraints. If any
> CONSTRAINT is specified, all CONSTRAINTS
> specified in previous PARAMETER paragraphs are
> cancelled.
> LIMIT = #, #.   may be repeated   -∞,∞/prev.
> The first number is the lower limit and the
> second number is the upper limit for the linear
> combination of parameters specified in the
> preceding CONSTRAINT statement. If only one
> number is specified, it is used as a lower
> limit. An upper limit without a lower limit is
> specified as LIMIT = (2)#.
>
> Note: The LIMITS are applied to the CONSTRAINT
> statement preceding it, i.e., you should write
> your CONSTRAINT and LIMIT statements in pairs.
> The INITIAL values of the parameters must satisfy
> the specified upper and lower limits for the
> parameters and for specified linear combinations
> of the parameters.

Printing Observed Values, Predicted Values and Residuals

For each case, PAR prints the predicted value
(value of the function), its standard error, the
value of the dependent variable, the residuals and
the observed values of the specified variables (see
⑩ in Output AR.1). You can specify whether or not
to print this list and, if so, which variables to
include in the list. All computed values use the
chosen estimates of the parameters (see note
p. 308).

If you specify

PRINT = 0.

in the REGRESS paragraph, no results are printed for
each case. You can specify

PRINT = v list.

using the names or subscripts of variables whose
observed values are to be printed for each case; the
predicted value, its standard error, the value of
the dependent variable and the residual are also
printed. The values of variables not specified in
the v list are not printed.

REGRess ───────────────────────────
> PRINT = v list.   all variables/prev.
> The names or subscripts of variables whose
> observed values are printed for each case. In
> addition to the observed values, the predicted
> value, its standard error, the value of the
> dependent variable and the residual are also
> printed. If PRINT = 0 is specified, residuals,
> predicted values and data are not printed.

Saving the Data and Predicted Values

When DATA are saved, the predicted values and their standard errors (but <u>not</u> the residuals) are also stored in the BMDP File. PAR allows you to save predicted values from more than one analysis of the same data. To do so you must specify in the SAVE paragraph the NUMBER of the analyses for which the predicted values are to be saved; otherwise only the predicted value from the first analysis is saved. The predicted values from the first analysis are saved as variable VT+1 with the name PREDICT1; standard errors of the predicted values as variable VT+2 with the name STDPRED1, the predicted values from the second analysis as variable VT+3 with the name PREDICT2, etc.

The predicted values and the standard errors are computed using the chosen estimates of the parameters (see note, p. 308). If you alter the value of any variable (such as the case WEIGHT variable) in the FORTRAN subroutine, the values of these variables are also computed and saved using the chosen estimates of the parameters.

```
SAVE
  NUMBer = #.                                          1
    Number of analyses (subproblems) from which the
    predicted values and their standard errors are
    to be saved in a BMDP File (along with the
    data). If not specified or if set to one, only
    the results from the first analysis are saved.
```

Case Weights

When the error variance is not homogeneous but varies from case to case, weighted least squares estimation is more appropriate; the weight (w) for each case is proportional to the inverse of the variance. In weighted least squares, the quantity minimized is

$$\Sigma\, w(y - f)^2$$

where the sum is over all cases read.

The variance may be expressed in terms of the function f; the case weight will vary from iteration to iteration as the estimates of the parameters change. The variable X(i), where i is the subscript of the case WEIGHT variable, can be modified in the FORTRAN subroutine describing the function. This is known as iteratively reweighted least squares and is used in maximum likelihood estimation (Section 14.3).

In PAR, the case WEIGHTS are specified in the REGRESS paragraph.

```
REGRess
  WEIGHT = v.                          no weight var./prev.
    Name or subscript of the variable containing
    case weights. If WEIGHT is not stated or is set
    to zero, there are no case weights.
```

Values Used in the Pseudo-Gauss-Newton Iteration

The function is fitted by an iterative algorithm. The algorithm decides that a solution has been reached when

$$\left| (\text{RSS}^{(k+1)} - \text{RSS}^{(k)})/\text{RSS}^{(k+1)} \right| < C$$

for five successive values of k, where $\text{RSS}^{(k)}$ is the residual sum of squares at step k, and C is the value of the CONVERGENCE criterion.

The algorithm can also be stopped if it exceeds a specified number of ITERATIONS.

If the residual sum of squares increases between two iterations, the increment size is halved and the residual sum of squares is recomputed and tested against the residual sum of squares at the previous iteration. This HALVING is repeated until the residual sum of squares is less than that of the previous halving or the maximum number of halvings is reached. At each iteration the number of increment halvings performed is printed.

TOLERANCE is used to guard against round-off errors in critical portions of the computations.

```
REGRess
  CONVergence = #.                          0.00001/prev.
    Value of the convergence criterion C, as
    described above.
  ITERation = #.                                  50/prev.
    Maximum number of iterations. If convergence
    has not occurred by this number of iterations,
    the algorithm is terminated.
  HALVing = #.        > 0                           5/prev.
    The maximum number of increment halvings as
    described above.
  TOLerance = #.                              10^{-8}/prev.
    A check for round-off errors. See Appendix
    A.16.
```

SIZE OF PROBLEM

The amount of data that PAR can analyze on medium-sized computer systems is a function of the number of cases used in the analysis (C), the largest subscript of the variables in the USE list (V), and the number of parameters estimated (total parameters – number of fixed parameters)(P). The following table indicates approximately how many cases can be used for various values of P and V.

V+P	5	10	15	20
C	930	560	400	300

Appendix B describes how to increase the capacity of the program.

COMPUTATIONAL METHOD

The computations are performed in double precision. The pseudo-Gauss-Newton algorithm is described in Appendix A.16.

ACKNOWLEDGEMENT

PAR was designed and programmed by Mary Ralston. Later improvements were made by Paul Sampson and Jerry Toporek.

SUMMARY

Order of Input Cards

A. Function specified as a transformation in the
    FUN paragraph

```
// (job card)                          ⎤ IBM OS
// EXEC   BIMED,PROG=BMDPAR             ⎦ System Cards
//SYSIN DD *
/ PROBLEM                              ⎤
/ INPUT
/ VARIABLE
/ TRANSFORM
/ SAVE                                   BMDP
/ REGRESS                                instructions
/ PARAMETER
/ FUN
/ PLOT
/ END                                  ⎦
   (data, if on cards)
/ REGRESS     ⎤ repeat for
/ PARAMETER     additional
/ FUN           analyses of
/ END         ⎦ the same data

//                                     ⎤ IBM OS
                                       ⎦ System Cards
```

B. Function specified by FORTRAN statements

```
// (job card)                          ⎤ IBM OS
// EXEC   BIMEDT,PROG=BMDPAR            ⎦ System Cards
//FUN DD  *

FORTRAN statements, for IBM OS        ⎤ Function
do not include SUBROUTINE and           specified
DIMENSION statements at                 in FORTRAN
beginning and RETURN and END
at end                                ⎦

//GO.SYSIN  DD  *                       ⎤ IBM OS
                                        ⎦ System Cards
/ PROBLEM                              ⎤
/ INPUT
/ VARIABLE
/ TRANSFORM
/ SAVE                                   BMDP
/ REGRESS                                instructions
/ PARAMETER
/ PLOT
/ END                                  ⎦
   (data, if on cards)
/ REGRESS     ⎤ repeat for
/ PARAMETER     additional analyses
/ END         ⎦ of the same data

//                                     ⎤ IBM OS
                                       ⎦ System  Cards
```

instructions specific to PAR

Paragraph Statement	Preassigned	Comment and Manual Reference
/●REGRess		Required to direct regression (may be repeated).
●DEPENDent = v.	none	Required; name or subscript of the dependent (predicted) variable. * 310
●PARAMeters = #.	none	Required; the number of parameters in the regression function. * 310
TITLE = 'c'.	none	Title, up to 160 characters, to label the output. 310
NUMBer = #.	none	The value of NUMB is passed to the FORTRAN subroutine that defines the function. Use it to select among functions coded in the subroutine. *
PRINT = v list.	all	Names or subscripts of variables whose observed values are printed for each case. The predicted value, its standard error and residual are also printed. PRINT = 0 specifies that no casewise information be printed. * 311
WEIGHT = v.	none	Name or subscript of variable containing case weights (see P3R). * 312
CONSTraint = #.	0.	Number of linear inequality constraints on the parameters that are specified in / PARAM. * 311
CONVergence = #.	.00001.	Value of convergence criterion used to decide if a solution has been reached. * 312
ITERations = #.	50.	Maximum number of iterations. * 312
HALVings = #.	5.	Maximum number of increment halvings. * 312
TOLerance = #.	10^{-8}.	A check for round-off errors (see P3R). * 312
FPARM = #.	none	Number of functions of parameters specified in the FPARM paragraph. 295

Options for special situations like maximum likelihood estimation:

PASS = #.	1.	The number of times the data are passed to subroutine FUN. *321
MEANSQuare = #.	none	Needed to obtain information theory standard errors. * 315
LOSS.	no	Replace the latest squares criterion with user-specified loss function (specified as XLOSS in subroutine FUN; the convergence criterion is applied to the sum of XLOSS). * 323

(continued)

(continued)

Paragraph Statement	Preassigned	Comment and Manual Reference
/●PARAMeter		Required to specify initial values for the parameters (may be repeated.) 311
●INITial = # list.	none	One number per parameter used as initial value for parameter estimate. Good initial estimates are important. *
MAXimums = # list.	none	Upper limits for the parameters; one number per parameter. *
MINimums = # list.	none	Lower limits for the parameters; one number per parameter. *
NAMEs = c list.	P(1),P(2), etc.	Name, up to 8 characters, for the parameters, one name per parameter. *
DELTA = # list.	none	Step size used to compute additional starting values of the function. DELTA is rarely needed. If omitted, the program decides.
FIXED = c list.	none	Parameter names or subscripts (not $P(1)$, $P(2)$, ...) of parameters to be held fixed at their initial values. *
CONSTraint = # list.	zeros	Coefficients and limits of inequality constraints on the parameters.
LIMITs = #, #.	none	The number of constraints must be specified in / REGR. The CONST statement contains the coefficients of the parameters in one constraint. The first number is the coefficient of first parameter, etc. In LIMIT, the first number is the lower limit, the second the upper limit for the combination of parameters specified in preceding CONST. The CONST and LIMIT statements must be in pairs. INITIAL values for the parameters must satisfy these constraints. *
PRIOR = # list.	none	One number per parameter. Prior estimate of parameter value.
RIDGE = # list.	none	One number per parameter. Ridge values corresponding to the parameters with prior estimates. 300
/oFUN		Use rules of the TRANSFORM paragraph to specify the function.
/ FPARM		Use rules of the TRANSFORM paragraph to define functions of parameters. 305
/ PLOT		Optional to produce graphical descriptions. 310
RESIDual.	no	Residuals (observed minus predicted value of dependent variable for each case) and residuals squared vs. predicted values. *
VARiables = v list.	none	Two plots are made for each variable in the list: observed values and predicted values of the dependent variable vs. each listed variable; residuals vs. each listed variable. Use variable name or subscript.*
NORMal.	no	Normal probability plot of residuals. *
DNORMal.	no	Detrended version of NORM. *
SIZE = #, #.	50,35.	Width of x-axis (characters); height of y-axis (lines). *
/ SAVE		Additional option to save predicted values and their standard errors (but not residuals) with the DATA when a BMDP File is created. 312
NUMBer = #.	1.	Number of analyses (/ REGR, / PARAM, / END) from which the predicted values and standard errors are to be saved in a BMDP File. The predicted values from the first analysis are saved after the data as variable VT+1 with name PREDICT1, the standard errors as VT+2 with name STDPRED1. Values from the second analysis are stored as VT+3 and VT+4 and are named PREDICT2 and STDPRED2, respectively.

Key:

/	–indicates paragraph	*	–assigned value remains the same for additional problems
.	–period ends a sentence		
o	–required ● –may be required	VT	–number of variables after transformations
v	–variable (name or subscript)	list	–more than one item, often one per var.
g	–group (name or subscript)		
#	–number		Capitalized letters –paragraph or sentence names recognized by BMDP
'c'	–characters (name or parameter) may omit apostrophes if contiguous letters only		Page numbers following refer to this Manual

14.3 *Applications of Nonlinear Regression Algorithms*

14.3a Maximum Likelihood Estimation

Estimation for Data from the Exponential Family of Distributions

Jennrich and Moore (1975) show how maximum likelihood estimates of parameters from a distribution in the exponential family can be obtained from the minimization of

$$(Y-F) \; \Sigma^{-1} (Y-F)'$$

where

Y   is a row vector containing the observed values of the dependent variable

F   is a row vector containing the values of the function evaluated at the true parameter values (the expected values of the dependent variable),

and

Σ^{-1} is the inverse of the covariance matrix of Y

Usually Σ^{-1} is a diagonal matrix; each diagonal element can be replaced by a case weight equal to the inverse of the variance of the dependent variable for that case.

Let y_1, y_2, ..., y_N be N mutually independent observed values of the dependent variable. Let the predicted value of y_j be $f(X_j, \theta)$, where X_j represents the data vector of the independent variables for case j and θ represents the vector of parameters p_1, p_2, ... in the model. Let the weight w_j for the data in case j be

$$w_j = 1/[\text{variance}(y_j)] \; .$$

The weight may be a function of the values of the variables and estimates of the parameters. Then in subroutine P3RFUN or FUN we define

$$F \equiv f(X_j, \theta)$$

$$X(\text{subscript of case weight variable}) \equiv w_j$$

$$= w_j(X_j, \theta)$$

and in P3R we require the partial derivatives

$$DF(I) \equiv \partial f(X_j, \theta)/\partial p_i \; .$$

Jennrich and Moore show that if the standard deviations are rescaled by setting the residual mean square equal to one, the standard deviations of the estimates are the usual information theory standard errors.

ABSTRACT

Parameters of a model can be estimated by the maximum likelihood method with both P3R and PAR. We describe two methods of modifying the least squares algorithm so it can be used for maximum likelihood. The first method is appropriate for data that are sampled from a distribution belonging to the exponential family -- such as normal, binomial, multinomial, Poisson and gamma distributions. The method provides a meaningful residual analysis and standard errors for the parameter estimates. The second method provides estimates of the parameters only. It is appropriate for data sampled from any distribution. However, it has no residual analysis. In our discussion we assume you are familiar with either P3R (Section 14.1) or PAR (Section 14.2).

Other applications include user-supplied loss function for use in likelihood ratio computations and the solution of models defined by a system of differential equations (e.g., pharmacokinetic models).

REGRess ─────
MEANSQuare = #.   none/prev.
    If specified, the value of MEANSQUARE is used in place of the residual mean square to compute estimates of the asymptotic standard deviations.

The data must be sampled from a distribution in the exponential family (see Lehman, 1959, p. 50 for a definition). This family includes the normal, binomial, multinomial, gamma and Poisson as well as other distributions.

Jennrich and Moore assume that the parameter estimates correspond to a solution where the derivatives are zero. However, P3R and PAR use criteria for convergence based on sums of squares and not on the values of the derivatives. It is possible to disconnect the convergence criterion by specifying

$$\text{HALVING} = 0.$$

in the REGRESS paragraph of PAR, or

$$\text{CONVERGENCE} = -1.0.$$
$$\text{HALVING} = 0.$$

in the REGRESS paragraph of P3R, and to terminate the algorithm in P3R by specifying the maximum number of iterations. (Ten iterations are usually sufficient.)

Example 3R.5 Using P3R to Fit a Logistic Model

Logistic models can be analyzed directly using PLR, Section 14.5. P3R can also be used as discussed by Jennrich and Moore (1975). We briefly present an example using the notation described above. The data are from Cox (1970, p. 86); at a specified time (t), a number of objects (n) are tested and the failures (s) recorded.

t	s	n
7	0	55
14	2	157
27	7	159
51	3	16

Cox fitted the data (s_i) by the logistic model

$$f_i = n_i e^{p_1 + p_2 t_i} / (1 + e^{p_1 + p_2 t_i})$$

If the s_i are assumed to be from independent binomial distributions, then

$$\text{var}(s_i) = f_i (n_i - f_i)/n_i .$$

Therefore

$$w_i = 1/\text{var}(s_i) = n_i/[f_i(n_i - f_i)]$$

The derivatives are

$$\frac{\partial f_i}{\partial p_1} = f_i/(1 + e^{p_1 + p_2 t_i}) \quad \text{and} \quad \frac{\partial f_i}{\partial p_2} = t_i f_i/(1 + e^{p_1 + p_2 t_i}).$$

Therefore we specify the following FORTRAN subroutine and BMDP instructions for P3R (in versions dated March 1981 and later, you can use the FUN paragraph instead of the FORTRAN):

FORTRAN statements to define function, derivatives, case weights:

```
        XNUMER = DEXP(P(1) + P(2)*X(1))
        DENOM = 1.0 + XNUMER
        F = X(3)*XNUMER/DENOM
        DF(1) = F/DENOM
        DF(2) = X(1)*F/DENOM
        X(4) = DENOM/F
```

BMDP instructions:

```
/ PROBLEM    TITLE IS 'COX DATA'.
/ INPUT      VARIABLES ARE 4.
             FORMAT IS '(4F5.0)'.
/ VARIABLES  NAMES ARE TIME, UNREADY, TESTED, CASEWT.

/ REGRESS    DEPENDENT IS UNREADY.
             PARAMETERS ARE 2.
             WEIGHT IS CASEWT.
             ITERATIONS ARE 10.
             HALVING IS 0.
             CONVERGENCE IS -1.0.
             MEANSQUARE IS 1.0.

/ PARAMETER INITIAL ARE 0.0, 0.0.

/ END
```

Data:

```
     7    0    55    1
    14    2   157    1
    27    7   159    1
    51    3    16    1
```

The System Cards required for this analysis are the same as described for Example 3R.2 and are discussed in greater detail in Section 14.4.

In this example we add to the data a fourth variable that contains iteratively computed case weights. P3R checks that the sum of the case weights is positive. Therefore the case weights must not be initialized to zero. In the REGRESS paragraph we turn off the convergence criterion (CONVERGENCE is -1.0 and HALVING is 0), terminate the algorithm after 10 iterations and rescale the mean square error to 1.0.

The results of the analysis are given in Output 3R.5. The parameter estimates used in the computation of residuals and standard errors are from the last iteration when CONVERGENCE is set to a value less than zero; the maximum likelihood estimates for the parameters are obtained from the last iteration (①) in Output 3R.5).

Output 3R.5 Maximum likelihood. Analysis of the Cox data by P3R using iteratively reweighted least squares

----

NUMBER OF CASES READ.   4

VARIABLE NO. NAME	MEAN	STANDARD DEVIATION	MINIMUM	MAXIMUM
1 TIME	24.750000	19.362762	7.000000	51.000000
2 UNREADY	3.000000	2.943920	0.0	7.000000
3 TESTED	96.750000	72.499969	16.000000	159.000000
4 CASEWT	1.000000	0.0	1.000000	1.000000

PARAMETER MAXIMA. . . . . *************** **************

PARAMETER MINIMA. . . . . *************** **************

ITERATION NUMBER	INCREMENT HALVINGS	RESIDUAL SUM OF SQUARES	P(1)	P(2)
0	0	342.584615	0.0	0.0
1	0	37.906692	-2.150288	0.013802
2	0	8.470283	-3.504031	0.036062
3	0	1.528108	-4.674594	0.063338
4	0	0.657320	-5.288439	0.077877
5	0	0.673094	-5.410884	0.080603
6	0	0.674874	-5.415172	0.080696
7	0	0.674876	-5.415177	0.080696
8	0	0.674876	-5.415177	0.080696
9	0	0.674876	-5.415177	0.080696
10	0	0.674876	-5.415177	0.080696 ①

ASYMPTOTIC CORRELATION MATRIX OF THE PARAMETERS

		P(1) 1	P(2) 2
P(1)	1	1.0000	
P(2)	2	-0.9101	1.0000

RESIDUAL MEAN SQUARE   0.3374379873

DEGREES OF FREEDOM   2

THE SPECIFIED VALUE OF THE RESIDUAL MEAN SQUARE(1.000), NOT THE COMPUTED VALUE, IS USED IN COMPUTING STANDARD
DEVIATIONS FOR PARAMETERS AND PREDICTED VALUES.

PARAMETER	ESTIMATE	ASYMPTOTIC STANDARD DEVIATION	TOLERANCE
P(1)	-5.415177	0.727541	0.1716535029
P(2)	0.080696	0.022356	0.1716535029

CASE NO. LABEL	PREDICTED UNREADY	STD DEV OF PRED VALUE	OBSERVED UNREADY	RESIDUAL	CASEWT	TIME	TESTED
1	0.427087	0.249470	0.0	-0.427087	2.359767	7.000000	55.000000
2	2.132166	0.970174	2.000000	-0.132166	0.475464	14.000000	157.000000
3	6.013250	1.776600	7.000000	0.986749	0.172836	27.000000	159.000000
4	3.427495	1.521988	3.000000	-0.427496	0.371297	51.000000	16.000000

SERIAL CORRELATION   -0.36924

Example AR.3 Using PAR to Fit a Logistic Model

A similar analysis to that performed above using P3R can be done with PAR by omitting the two statements beginning DF(1) and DF(2) in the FORTRAN subroutine. The FORTRAN statements and BMDP instructions for PAR are

----

FORTRAN statements to define function, case weights:

```
    XNUMER = DEXP(P(1) + P(2)*X(1))
    DENOM = 1.0 + XNUMER
    F = X(3)*XNUMER/DENOM
    X(4) = DENOM/F
```

BMDP instructions:

```
/ PROBLEM    TITLE IS 'COX DATA'.
/ INPUT      VARIABLES ARE 4.
             FORMAT IS '(4F5.0)'.
/ VARIABLE   NAMES ARE TIME, UNREADY, TESTED, CASEWT.

/ REGRESS    DEPENDENT IS UNREADY.
             PARAMETERS ARE 2.
             WEIGHT IS CASEWT.
             HALVING IS 0.
             MEANSQUARE IS 1.0.

/ PARAMETER  INITIAL ARE 0.0, 0.0.

/ END
```

The System Cards required for this analysis are the same as described for Example AR.1 and are discussed in greater detail in Section 14.4. We do not show the output.

Example 3R.6 Using P3R to Fit a Model of Quasi-independence

The Multiway Frequency Tables program P4F (Chapter 11) can be used to fit a multinomial model to data in a multiway table. However, when a cell in the table has zero frequency a priori (i.e., it is known that no observation can be recorded in the cell), the method used with P4F provides only approximate standard deviations for the estimates of the parameters in the log-linear model. P3R or PAR can be used to obtain improved estimates of the standard deviations.

We now show how P3R can be used to fit a multinomial model to data in a multiway frequency table when a cell in the table has zero frequency a priori. The data in Table 14.3 are from a sensitivity test of fibers (Frank and Pfaffman, 1969). One outcome that corresponds to no sensitivity to any of the four stimuli can occur when the fiber is dead. The data for this outcome are not included in the computations. The cell corresponding to this outcome is analyzed as if the outcome were a structural zero.

Table 14.3 Data on sensitivity of Chorda tympani fibers in rat's tongue to four taste stimulus sources (Frank and Pfaffman, 1969) as reported in Fienberg, 1972, and Bishop et al., 1975, p.221)

S	Q	H N	Yes Yes	Yes No	No Yes	No No
Yes	Yes	2	0	1	0
Yes	No	1	3	3	2
No	Yes	3	3	0	1
No	No	3	1	4	-

Key: Shows sensitivity to
    H: hydrogen chloride   Q: quinine
    N: sodium chloride   S: sucrose

No sensitivity to any stimulus can result from a dead fiber. Therefore the cell corresponding to No for all four tests has no observations.

The model to be fitted to the data is the log-linear model corresponding to independence between the stimuli, i.e.,

$$f = k \ \exp(p_1 x_1 + p_2 x_2 + p_3 x_3 + p_4 x_4)$$

where k is a normalizing constant and the X_i's are design variables. We know that the sum of the f's over all the cells must correspond to the total frequency (N = 27). This constraint can be imposed on the function by rewriting it as

$$f = \frac{N \ \exp(p_1 x_1 + p_2 x_2 + p_3 x_3 + p_4 x_4)}{\Sigma \ \exp(p_1 x_1 + p_2 x_2 + p_3 x_3 + p_4 x_4)}$$

and the derivatives of f with respect to the parameters as

$$\frac{\partial f}{\partial p_i} = f \left[x_i - \frac{\Sigma \ x_i \exp(p_1 x_1 + p_2 x_2 + p_3 x_3 + p_4 x_4)}{\Sigma \ \exp(p_1 x_1 + p_2 x_2 + p_3 x_3 + p_4 x_4)} \right]$$

where the summations are over all cells except the one containing the structural zero.

For a multinomial distribution the case weight is the inverse of the expected value of the dependent variable; i.e.,

$$w = 1/f.$$

Since the covariance matrix of the dependent variable is singular, the case weights are obtained from the generalized inverse.

We therefore specify the FORTRAN statements as

FORTRAN statements of function, derivatives, case weights:

```
      DIMENSION PART(4)
      IF(IPASS.EQ.2) GO TO 10
C
      IF(KASE.GT.1) GO TO 2
      DO 1 I = 1,4
    1 PART(I) = 0.0
      SUM = 0.0
C
    2 TEMP = DEXP(X(1)*P(1) + X(2)*P(2) + X(3)*P(3)
     *       + X(4)*P(4))
      SUM = SUM + TEMP
      DO 3 I = 1,4
    3 PART(I) = PART(I) + X(I)*TEMP
      RETURN
C
   10 F = 27.0*DEXP(X(1)*P(1) + X(2)*P(2)
     *    + X(3)*P(3) + X(4)*P(4))/SUM
      X(6) = 1.0/F
      DO 12 I = 1,4
   12 DF(I) = F*(X(I) - PART (I)/SUM)
```

BMDP instructions:

```
/ PROBLEM      TITLE IS 'RAT TASTE-BUDS'.
/ INPUT        VARIABLES ARE 6.
              FORMAT IS '(6F4.0)'.
/ VARIABLE     NAMES ARE H, N, S, Q, FREQ, WT.

/ REGRESS      DEPENDENT IS FREQ.
              PARAMETERS ARE 4.
              WEIGHT IS WT.
              ITERATIONS ARE 10.
              HALVING IS 0.
              CONVERGENCE IS -1.
              MEANSQUARE IS 1.
              PASS IS 2.

/ END
```

Data:

```
  1   1   1   1   2   1
  1   1   1  -1   1   1
  1   1  -1   1   3   1
  1   1  -1  -1   3   1
  1  -1   1   1   0   1
  1  -1   1  -1   3   1
  1  -1  -1   1   3   1
  1  -1  -1  -1   1   1
 -1   1   1   1   1   1
 -1   1   1  -1   3   1
 -1   1  -1   1   0   1
 -1   1  -1  -1   4   1
 -1  -1   1   1   0   1
 -1  -1   1  -1   2   1
 -1  -1  -1   1   1   1
```

The System Cards required for this analysis are the same as described for Example 3R.2 and are discussed in greater detail in Section 14.4.

The first four variables of the data are design variables for H, N, S and Q, respectively, the fifth is the observed frequency, and the sixth is the iteratively computed case weight variable.

When the statement

$$PASS = 2.$$

is specified in the REGRESS paragraph, the subroutine P3RFUN is called twice for each case on each iteration. First P3R calls subroutine P3RFUN once for each case, with IPASS set to 1. On this pass

$$\sum_{(\text{all cases})} \exp(p_1 x_1 + p_2 x_2 + p_3 x_3 + x_4 p_4)$$

$$\sum_{(\text{all cases})} x_i \exp(p_1 x_1 + p_2 x_2 + p_3 x_3 + p_4 x_4)$$

$$i = 1, 2, 3, 4$$

are computed. Then P3R calls subroutine P3RFUN once

Output 3R.6   Fitting a quasi-independent model by P3R

```
            NUMBER OF CASES READ. . . . . . . . . . . . .    15

            VARIABLE                STANDARD
            NO. NAME      MEAN       DEVIATION    MINIMUM      MAXIMUM

               1  H       0.066667   1.032795    -1.000000    1.000000
               2  N       0.066667   1.032795    -1.000000    1.000000
               3  S       0.066667   1.032795    -1.000000    1.000000
               4  Q       0.066667   1.032795    -1.000000    1.000000
               5  FREQ    1.799996   1.320171     0.0         4.000000
               6  WT      1.000000   0.0          1.000000     1.000000


            PARAMETER MAXIMA. . . . . . . . . .  ************** ************** ************** **************

            PARAMETER MINIMA. . . . . . . . . .  ************** ************** ************** **************
```

(output continued)

Output 3R.6 (continued)

ITERATION NUMBER	INCREMENT HALVINGS	RESIDUAL SUM OF SQUARES	P(1)	P(2)	P(3)	P(4)
0	0	13.555556	0.0	0.0	0.0	0.0
1	0	10.054183	0.094697	0.164141	-0.183081	-0.321970
2	0	10.075411	0.099936	0.169944	-0.177120	-0.323578
3	0	10.075471	0.099935	0.169946	-0.177127	-0.323588
4	0	10.075471	0.099935	0.169946	-0.177127	-0.323588
5	0	10.075471	0.099935	0.169946	-0.177127	-0.323588
6	0	10.075471	0.099935	0.169946	-0.177127	-0.323588
7	0	10.075471	0.099935	0.169946	-0.177127	-0.323588
8	0	10.075471	0.099935	0.169946	-0.177127	-0.323588
9	0	10.075471	0.099935	0.169946	-0.177127	-0.323588
10	0	10.075471	0.099935	0.169946	-0.177127	-0.323588

ASYMPTOTIC CORRELATION MATRIX OF THE PARAMETERS

		P(1) 1	P(2) 2	P(3) 3	P(4) 4
P(1)	1	1.0000			
P(2)	2	0.1270	1.0000		
P(3)	3	0.0930	0.0988	1.0000	
P(4)	4	0.0811	0.0862	0.0631	1.0000

RESIDUAL MEAN SQUARE   0.9159518480

DEGREES OF FREEDOM   11

THE SPECIFIED VALUE OF THE RESIDUAL MEAN SQUARE(1.000), NOT THE COMPUTED VALUE, IS USED IN COMPUTING STANDARD DEVIATIONS FOR PARAMETERS AND PREDICTED VALUES.

PARAMETER	ESTIMATE	ASYMPTOTIC STANDARD DEVIATION	TOLERANCE
P(1)	0.099935	0.198539	0.9729672581
P(2)	0.169946	0.202204	0.9711291130
P(3)	-0.177127	0.195491	0.9812411297
P(4)	-0.323588	0.200759	0.9851536718

CASE NO. LABEL	PREDICTED FREQ	STD DEV OF PRED VALUE	OBSERVED FREQ	RESIDUAL	WT	H	N	S
1	1.324368	0.089693	2.000000	0.675632	0.755077	1.000000	1.000000	1.000000
2	2.529727	0.089693	1.000000	-1.529727	0.395299	1.000000	1.000000	1.000000
3	1.887378	0.089693	3.000000	1.112621	0.529835	1.000000	1.000000	-1.000000

--- similar statistics for cases 4 to 12 ---

13	0.771957	0.089693	0.0	-0.771957	1.295409	-1.000000	-1.000000	1.000000
14	1.474545	0.089693	2.000000	0.525455	0.678175	-1.000000	-1.000000	1.000000
15	1.100127	0.089693	1.000000	-0.100128	0.908985	-1.000000	-1.000000	-1.000000

CASE	Q
1	1.000000
2	-1.000000
3	1.000000

--- cases 4 to 12 are omitted ---

13	1.000000
14	-1.000000
15	1.000000

SERIAL CORRELATION   -0.50722

for each case to compute the function value F and the derivatives DF(I) in the second pass.

When PASS is not specified in the REGRESS paragraph, subroutine P3RFUN is called only once for each case and the function value F and derivatives DF(I) must be computed in this one pass.

The following definition of PASS is appropriate for both P3R and PAR.

```
REGRess ─────────
  │ PASS = #.                                    1/prev.
  │   The number of times the data are passed to
  │   subroutine P3RFUN. When # is greater than one,
  │   - on each cycle through the case, IPASS is set
  │     to the number of the cycle
  │   - the function (and derivatives) must be
  │     computed on the last cycle (IPASS set to #)
  │     through the cases
  ╰─
```

The results of the analysis of this example are presented in Output 3R.6. When CONVERGE is assigned a negative value, as in our example, the estimates of the parameters from the last iteration are used in the computation of asymptotic standard deviations, correlations, and predicted values.

Example AR.4 Using PAR to Fit a Model of Quasi-independence

A similar analysis to the above can be obtained with PAR by increasing the number of ITERATIONS to 25 and using the following FORTRAN statements and Control Language instructions:

FORTRAN statements of function, case weight:

```
      IF(IPASS.EQ.2) GO TO 10.
C
      IF(KASE.EQ.1) SUM = 0.0
C
      TEMP = DEXP(X(1)*P(1) + X(2)*P(2) + X(3)*P(3)
     *       + X(4)*P(4))
      SUM = SUM + TEMP
      RETURN
C
   10 F = 27.0*DEXP(X(1)*P(1) + X(2)*P(2)
     *     + X(3)*P(3) + X(4)*P(4))/SUM
      X(6) = 1.0/F
```

BMDP instructions:

```
/ PROBLEM     TITLE IS 'RAT TASTE-BUDS'.
/ INPUT       VARIABLES ARE 6.
             FORMAT IS '(6F4.0)'.
/ VARIABLE    NAMES ARE H, N, S, Q, FREQ, WT.

/ REGRESS     DEPENDENT IS 5.
             PARAMETERS ARE 4.
             WEIGHT IS 6.
             HALVING IS 0.
             MEANSQUARE IS 1.
             PASS IS 2.

/ PARAMETER   INITIAL = 4*0.0.

/ END
```

The System Cards required for this analysis are the same as described for Example AR.1 and are discussed in greater detail in Section 14.4.

The output for this problem is essentially the same as Output 3R.6.

Estimation for Data from Any Distribution

This method is appropriate for maximum likelihood estimation based on a random sample from any distribution. The normal equations solved to maximize the likelihood are

$$\sum \frac{\partial \ln\, g(X_j, \theta)}{\partial p_i} = 0 \qquad i=1,2,\ldots$$

where $g(X_j, \theta)$ is the probability density of the data vector in case j and θ is the vector of parameters. Let

$$f = \ln\, g(X_j, \theta)\ .$$

The normal equations can be written

$$\sum \frac{\partial f}{\partial p_i} = 0 \qquad i=1,2,\ldots$$

or

$$\sum \frac{\partial f}{\partial p_i}(y-f) = 0 \qquad i=1,2,\ldots$$

when y−f is identically one and the summation is over all cases. If we define a new variable (and call it the dependent variable),

$$X(\text{subscript of dependent variable}) = y = f + 1,$$

then y−f is identically one. Therefore, the nonlinear regression programs solve the maximum likelihood normal equations if in the P3RFUN subroutine we set

$$F = f = \ln\, g(X, \theta)$$

$$X(\text{subscript of dependent variable}) = F + 1$$

and (in P3R)

$$DF(i) = \frac{\partial f}{\partial p_i} = \frac{\partial \ln\, g(X, \theta)}{\partial p_i}\ .$$

Their solution yields maximum likelihood estimates for $p_1, p_2, \ldots$ and standard errors for the estimates. However, the residual analysis is meaningless because each residual (y−f) is one.

Output 3R.7   Reanalysis of the Cox data by P3R using the second method of maximum likelihood estimation. Compare these results with those in Output 3R.5.

```
NUMBER OF CASES READ. . . . . . . . . . . . .      7
```

VARIABLE			STANDARD		
NO.	NAME	MEAN	DEVIATION	MINIMUM	MAXIMUM
1	TIME	19.875931	10.718314	7.000000	51.000000
2	UNREADY	0.031008	0.187227	0.0	1.000000
3	TESTED	130.193771	50.466080	2.000000	155.000000
4	DUMMY	0.0	0.0	0.0	0.0

```
PARAMETER MAXIMA. . . . . . . . . . .  ************** **************

PARAMETER MINIMA. . . . . . . . . . .  ************** **************
```

ITERATION NUMBER	INCREMENT HALVINGS	RESIDUAL SUM OF SQUARES	P(1)	P(2)
0	0	387.000000	0.0	0.0
1	0	387.000000	-2.150290	0.013802
2	0	387.000000	-8.514570	0.155964
3	0	387.000000	-6.481939	0.100283
4	0	387.000000	-5.614957	0.083388
5	0	387.000000	-5.408093	0.080216
6	0	387.000000	-5.417967	0.080780
7	0	387.000000	-5.414591	0.080677
8	0	387.000000	-5.415306	0.080700
9	0	387.000000	-5.415149	0.080695
10	0	387.000000	-5.415183	0.080696

```
ASYMPTOTIC CORRELATION MATRIX OF THE PARAMETERS

                  P(   1)     P(   2)
                    1          2

P(   1)    1      1.0000
P(   2)    2     -0.9265      1.0000


RESIDUAL MEAN SQUARE          77.3999938965

DEGREES OF FREEDOM            5

THE SPECIFIED VALUE OF THE RESIDUAL MEAN SQUARE(   1.000), NOT THE COMPUTED VALUE, IS USED IN COMPUTING STANDARD
DEVIATIONS FOR PARAMETERS AND PREDICTED VALUES.
```

PARAMETER	ESTIMATE	ASYMPTOTIC STANDARD DEVIATION	TOLERANCE
P(1)	-5.415183	0.796911	0.1415426823
P(2)	0.080696	0.024637	0.1415426823

CASE NO. LABEL	PREDICTED DUMMY	STD DEV OF PRED VALUE	OBSERVED DUMMY	RESIDUAL	TESTED	TIME	UNREADY
1	-0.007795	0.004973	0.992204	1.000000	55.000000	7.000000	0.0
2	-0.013674	0.006718	0.986326	1.000000	155.000000	14.000000	0.0
3	-4.299110	0.487942	-3.299110	1.000000	2.000000	14.000000	1.000000
4	-0.038553	0.011672	0.961447	1.000000	152.000000	27.000000	0.0
5	-3.274939	0.296942	-2.274939	1.000000	7.000000	27.000000	1.000000
6	-0.241077	0.128235	0.758923	1.000000	13.000000	51.000000	0.0
7	-1.540755	0.470380	-0.540756	1.000000	3.000000	51.000000	1.000000

```
SERIAL CORRELATION        0.79329
```

Example 3R.7 Using P3R to Fit a Binomial Model

We now reanalyze the Cox data given in Example 3R.5 (p. 316) by maximum likelihood. We must consider each binary outcome as a separate case. Therefore, each case contains a zero or one to indicate success or failure. However, it is not necessary to replicate identical cases; we can use the weight variable to indicate frequency of outcome. The data are shown below.

Now let x be a binary outcome (zero or one) for each case. Then x has the binomial distribution

$$f = \ell n g(x_i, \theta) = x_i \, \ell n \theta + (1-x_i) \, \ell n (1-\theta)$$

except for a constant, where

$$\theta = e^{p_1 + p_2 t} / (1 + e^{p_1 + p_2 t})$$

is the parameter of the binomial distribution. Then

$$\frac{\partial f}{\partial p_1} = \frac{x_i}{\theta} \frac{\partial \theta}{\partial p_1} - \frac{1-x_i}{1-\theta} \frac{\partial \theta}{\partial p_1} = x_i - \theta$$

$$\frac{\partial f}{\partial p_2} = t(x_i - \theta) \ .$$

We specify the FORTRAN statements and BMDP instructions as:

FORTRAN statements for function, derivatives:

```
    XNUMER = DEXP(P(1) + P(2)*X(1))
    DENOM = 1.0 + XNUMER
    THETA = XNUMER/DENOM
    F = X(2)*DLOG(THETA)
   *    + (1.0-X(2))*DLOG(1.0-THETA)
    DF(1) = X(2) - THETA
    DF(2) = X(1)*(X(2) - THETA)
    X(4) = F + 1.0
```

BMDP instructions:

```
/ PROBLEM    TITLE IS 'COX DATA'.
/ INPUT      VARIABLES ARE 4.
             FORMAT IS '(4F5.0)'.
/ VARIABLES  NAMES ARE TIME, UNREADY, TESTED, DUMMY.

/ REGRESS    DEPENDENT IS DUMMY.
             PARAMETERS ARE 2.
             WEIGHT IS TESTED.
             ITERATIONS ARE 10.
             HALVING IS 0.
             CONVERGENCE IS -1.0.
             MEANSQUARE IS 1.0.

/ PARAMETER  INITIAL ARE 0.0, 0.0.

/ END
```

Data:

```
  7   0   55    0
 14   0  155    0
 14   1    2    0
 27   0  152    0
 27   1    7    0
 51   0   13    0
 51   1    3    0
```

The System Cards required for this analysis are the same as described for Example 3R.2 and are discussed in greater detail in Section 14.4.

The first variable in the data is TIME, the second is binary outcome, the third is the frequency of the outcome, and the last is a dummy variable. The case weight variable records the frequency. The dependent variable is recalculated at each iteration. The results of the analysis are presented in Output 3R.7.

14.3b The Loss Function as an Alternate to Least Squares

You can specify your own loss function, such as minus the logarithm of the likelihood, to replace the least squares criterion by both P3R and PAR. You must specify LOSS in the REGRESS paragraph, and then for each case compute XLOSS in subroutine P3RFUN (or FUN in PAR). XLOSS is then summed over all the cases and used in place of the sum of squares in the criterion for CONVERGENCE.

```
REGRess ─────────────────────────────────
  LOSS.                          no/prev.
     A loss function is computed for each case in
  subroutine P3RFUN. In subroutine P3RFUN (or FUN
  in PAR) the loss function is called XLOSS.
  XLOSS is summed over all cases. If the minimum
  sum of XLOSS corresponds to the estimates that
  you want, the CONVERGENCE criterion can remain
  positive as well as the value of HALVING. Then
  P3R and PAR apply the criterion of convergence
  to the sum of XLOSS.
─────────────────────────────────────────
```

We recommend the use of LOSS, especially with the second method of maximum likelihood estimation.

Example AR.5 Using PAR with a Loss Function

We reanalyze the Cox data using a loss function in PAR.

FORTRAN statements for function, derivatives:

```
    XNUMER = DEXP(P(1) + P(2)*X(1))
    DENOM = 1.0 + XNUMER
    THETA = XNUMER/DENOM
    F = X(2)*DLOG(THETA)
   *    + (1.0-X(2))*DLOG(1.0 - THETA)
    X(4) = F + 1.0
    XLOSS = -F*X(3)
```

Output AR.5   Reanalysis of the Cox data using a loss function

---

NUMBER OF CASES READ.   7

VARIABLE NO.	NAME	MEAN	STANDARD DEVIATION	MINIMUM	MAXIMUM
1	TIME	19.875931	10.718314	7.000000	51.000000
2	UNREADY	0.031008	0.187227	0.0	1.000000
4	DUMMY	0.0	0.0	0.0	0.0
3	TESTED	NOT COMPUTED		2.000000	155.000000

ITER. NO.	INCR. HALV.	LOSS FUNCTION	PARAMETERS 1 P(1)	2 P(2)
0	0	305.385142	0.0	0.010000
0	0	270.067796	0.010000	0.0
0	0	268.247959	0.0	0.0
1	0	76.653071	-2.031117	0.007611
2	2	74.663518	-2.175420	0.012859
3	0	52.532254	-6.706947	0.087562
4	5	52.525842	-6.856091	0.092677
5	2	51.069111	-6.604997	0.091062
6	0	48.049263	-5.878115	0.087847
7	5	48.002807	-5.730406	0.083012
8	0	47.877357	-5.183812	0.078932
9	2	47.862700	-5.231653	0.080376
10	2	47.850837	-5.189227	0.078658
11	0	47.688867	-5.440190	0.080980
12	2	47.687708	-5.428618	0.081282
13	5	47.688858	-5.449539	0.081938
14	0	47.687897	-5.413300	0.080968
15	1	47.687478	-5.401210	0.080355
16	2	47.687388	-5.405521	0.080486
17	1	47.687297	-5.413609	0.080600
18	3	47.687291	-5.415186	0.080652
19	2	47.687288	-5.414283	0.080634

THE LOSS FUNCTION (=   47.6873   ) WAS SMALLEST WITH THE FOLLOWING PARAMETER VALUES

1 P(1)	2 P(2)
-5.41428	8.063412D-02

ESTIMATE OF ASYMPTOTIC CORRELATION MATRIX

		P(1) 1	P(2) 2
P(1)	1	1.0000	
P(2)	2	-0.9265	1.0000

THE ESTIMATED MEAN SQUARE ERROR IS   9.537
THE SPECIFIED VALUE OF THE MEAN SQUARE ERROR (1.000)NOT THE COMPUTED VALUE IS USED IN COMPUTING STANDARD DEVIATIONS

ESTIMATES OF ASYMPTOTIC STANDARD DEVIATIONS OF PARAMETER ESTIMATES WITH   5 DEGREES OF FREEDOM ARE

1 P(1)	2 P(2)
0.796932	2.463822D-02

BMDP instructions:

```
/ PROBLEM    TITLE IS 'COX DATA'.
/ INPUT      VARIABLES ARE 4.
             FORMAT IS '(4F5.0)'.
/ VARIABLES  NAMES ARE TIME, UNREADY, TESTED, DUMMY.

/ REGRESS    DEPENDENT IS DUMMY.
             PARAMETERS ARE 2.
             WEIGHT IS TESTED.
             MEANSQUARE IS 1.0.
             LOSS.

/ PARAMETER  INITIAL ARE 0.0, 0.0.

/ END
```

Data:

```
 7    0    55    0
14    0   155    0
14    1     2    0
27    0   152    0
27    1     7    0
51    0    13    0
51    1     3    0
------------------------------------
```

The System Cards required for this analysis are the same as described for Example AR.1 and are discussed in greater detail in Section 14.4.

The results are presented in Output AR.5. In our example we define XLOSS as $-F*X(3)$; i.e., as minus the logarithm of the likelihood multiplied by the frequency of the likelihood (the case weight is the frequency). Since the data are multinomial, twice the final value of the loss function is the likelihood ratio statistic; i.e., $-2\ln$ (maximum likelihood).

Likelihood ratio test. More generally, two models, one containing the other, can be compared by computing loss functions, $-2\ln$(maximum likelihood), for each model. The difference between the loss functions provides a likelihood ratio test of the hypothesis that the additional parameters are zero. Under the appropriate large sample assumptions, this difference has a chi-square distribution with degrees of freedom equal to the difference in the number of parameters in the two models.

14.3c Models Defined by a System of Differential Equations

In many nonlinear regression applications the regression function f is implicitly defined by a system of differential equations. The BMDP library contains a number of subroutines, primarily a numerical integrator, that make it possible to use PAR to fit functions so defined. In our discussion it is assumed the user is familiar with PAR (Section 14.2).

Example AR.6 Using PAR to Fit a Pharmacokinetic Model

Kaplan et al. (1972) used a two compartment open model:

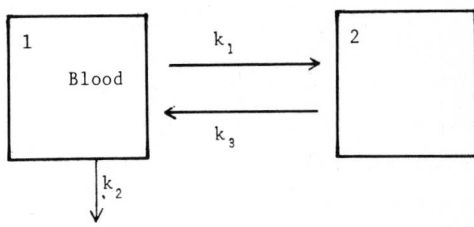

to study the pharmacokinetic profile of sulfisoxazole. Subjects were given an intravenous injection of the drug at time t = 0 and concentrations y of the drug in the blood were measured at various times following injection:

t	y	t	y
.25	215.6	3.00	101.2
.50	189.2	4.00	88.0
.75	176.0	6.00	61.6
1.00	162.8	12.00	22.0
1.50	138.6	24.00	4.4
2.00	121.0	48.00	0.0

The differential equations that describe the compartment model are:

$$\frac{dz_1}{dt} = -(k_1 + k_2)z_1 + k_3 z_2$$

$$\frac{dz_2}{dt} = k_1 z_1 - k_3 z_2 \ .$$

The initial conditions are:

$$z_1(0) = C_0$$

$$z_2(0) = 0$$

where C_0 is the concentration at time t = 0. The function f to be fitted to the data is given by:

$$f = z_1(t)$$

where $z_1(t)$ is the value of z_1 at time t. This depends on the differential equations which in turn depend on the unknown parameters

$$p_1 = k_1, \quad p_2 = k_2, \quad p_3 = k_3, \quad \text{and} \quad p_4 = C_0 \ .$$

The collection of subroutines in the BMDP library named DEFUN is designed to carry out numerical integrations and aid in the evaluation of regression functions when the latter are defined by differential equations. To use these subroutines for our example we specify the following FORTRAN subroutine and Control Language instructions:

FUN subroutine:

```
    CALL  DEFUN(F,P,X,N,KASE,NVAR,NPAR,IPASS,XLOSS)
    RETURN
    END
```

DIFEQ subroutine lead in:

```
    SUBROUTINE DIFEQ(F,P,X,N,KASE,NVAR,NPAR,
   *                 IPASS,XLOSS)
    IMPLICIT REAL*8 (A-H, O-Z)
    COMMON/DECON/ Z(10),DZ(10),T,NEQN,IGO,IT,NEW
    DIMENSION X(NVAR),P(NPAR)
    GO TO (100,200,300),IGO
```

Set initial values:

```
C
  100 CONTINUE
    IT = 1
    NEQN = 2
    Z(1) = P(4)
    Z(2) = 0.0
    RETURN
```

Define differential equations:

```
C
  200 CONTINUE
    DZ(1) = -(P(1) + P(2))*Z(1) + P(3)*Z(2)
    DZ(2) = P(1)*Z(1) - P(3)*Z(2)
    RETURN
```

Define regression function:

```
C
  300 CONTINUE
    F = Z(1)
```

BMDP instructions:

```
/ PROBLEM      TITLE IS 'KAPLAN ET AL'.
/ INPUT        VARIABLES ARE 2.
              FORMAT IS '(F5.0, 5X, F5.0)'.
/ VARIABLES    NAMES ARE TIME, SULFISOX.

/ REGRESS      DEPENDENT IS SULFISOX.
              PARAMETERS ARE 4.
/ PARAMETER    NAMES ARE K1, K2, K3, CO.
              INTITIAL ARE .5, .5, .5, 240.
/ END
```

Data:

```
    0.25      215.6
    0.50      189.2
    0.75      176.0
    1.00      162.8
    1.50      138.6
    2.00      121.0
    3.00      101.2
    4.00       88.0
    6.00       61.6
   12.00       22.0
   24.00        4.4
   48.00        0.0
```

The System Cards required for this example are the same as described for Example AR.1 and are discussed in greater detail in Section 14.4.

The FUN subroutine simply contains a call to DEFUN, which has the same argument list as FUN. (See Section 14.2, Specifying a Regression Function in FORTRAN.) The RETURN and END statements for the FUN subroutine must be supplied. This differs from its standard use. The DIFEQ subroutine is given in full except that its RETURN and END statements are omitted. The DIFEQ subroutine lead-in should be reproduced exactly as displayed in the example, except that on non-IBM machines, the "IMPLICIT REAL*8" statement may have to be replaced by explicit double precision declarations. The problem-specific statements that follow the 100 CONTINUE statement

```
    IT = 1
    NEQN = 2
    Z(1) = P(4)
    Z(2) = 0.0
```

indicate that the time variable is the first variable in each case, that there are two differential equations in the defining system, and that the initial values of z_1 and z_2 are $p_4 = C_0$ and zero, respectively.

The statements that follow the 200 CONTINUE statement

```
    DZ(1) = -(P(1) + P(2))*Z(1) + P(1)*Z(2)
    DZ(2) = P(2)*Z(1) - P(3)*Z(2)
```

define the system of differential equations. Finally, the statement that follows the 300 CONTINUE statement

```
    F = Z(1)
```

defines the regression function.

The results of the above analysis are given in Output AR.6. Circled numbers below correspond to those in the output.

① The program converged in 17 iterations from rather arbitrary starting values. The initial value of $C_0 = 240$ was obtained from a rough sketch of y versus t and initial values for the transfer rates $k_1 = k_2 = k_3 = 0.5$ were chosen to guarantee a fair amount of activity in the compartments in a span of two or three time units, something also suggested by the rough sketch.

② Parameter estimates, standard errors of estimate, and correlations are given.

③ The usual listing of residuals, observed values, predicted values, etc.

Although not requested here, it would also be useful to request a printer plot of the data and the fit against time.

Further examples and details about the DEFUN subroutines are given in BMDP Technical Report No. 58 (Ralston et al., 1979). These include restrictions on the number of components z_i in the system of differential equations (10), methods of handling discontinuities in the $z_i(t)$ and their derivatives, and a variety of default settings for the integrator and how to override them.

Output AR.6   Using PAR to fit a Pharmacokinetic Model

NUMBER OF CASES READ.   12

VARIABLE NO.	NAME	MEAN	STANDARD DEVIATION	MINIMUM	MAXIMUM
1	TIME	8.583330	14.171165	0.250000	48.000000
2	SULFISOX	106.699951	73.407578	0.0	215.599991

①

ITER. NO.	INCR. HALV.	RESIDUAL SUM OF SQUARES	PARAMETERS 1 K1	2 K2	3 K3	4 CO
0	0	29586.387050	0.500000	0.550000	0.500000	240.000000
0	0	27500.411545	0.550000	0.500000	0.500000	240.000000
0	0	25631.141118	0.500000	0.500000	0.500000	240.000000
0	0	24665.452310	0.500000	0.500000	0.550000	240.000000
0	0	19117.332662	0.500000	0.500000	0.500000	264.000000
1	1	1852.320205	0.592334	0.170752	0.671566	253.617798
2	0	153.391744	0.374841	0.262976	1.309015	249.705890
3	1	69.019170	0.368671	0.233096	1.220007	246.878250
4	0	47.951072	0.387475	0.236729	1.180137	249.335999
5	2	46.798509	0.384958	0.237859	1.174799	249.424986
6	3	46.641518	0.378697	0.236651	1.159550	248.924654
7	0	36.065926	0.298457	0.228696	0.905698	243.009126
8	0	34.857020	0.314190	0.228036	0.902472	243.951261
9	0	34.545372	0.311658	0.227889	0.909565	243.856984
10	1	34.507441	0.310026	0.227737	0.912106	243.567083
11	0	34.403277	0.311978	0.227948	0.915067	243.619555
12	0	34.380636	0.314986	0.228541	0.926133	243.872956
13	4	34.380634	0.314975	0.228545	0.926139	243.872622
14	0	34.380306	0.314699	0.228507	0.925325	243.849365
15	5	34.380310	0.314689	0.228506	0.925336	243.847691
16	5	34.380304	0.314663	0.228506	0.925315	243.847654
17	0	34.380251	0.314517	0.228482	0.924715	243.836798

THE RESIDUAL SUM OF SQUARES (=   34.3802   ) WAS SMALLEST WITH THE FOLLOWING PARAMETER VALUES

②

1 K1	2 K2	3 K3	4 CO
0.314517	0.228482	0.924715	243.837

ESTIMATE OF ASYMPTOTIC CORRELATION MATRIX

		K1 1	K2 2	K3 3	CO 4
K1	1	1.0000			
K2	2	0.6591	1.0000		
K3	3	0.8451	0.8041	1.0000	
CO	4	0.9199	0.6936	0.6983	1.0000

THE ESTIMATED MEAN SQUARE ERROR IS   4.298

ESTIMATES OF ASYMPTOTIC STANDARD DEVIATIONS OF PARAMETER ESTIMATES WITH   8 DEGREES OF FREEDOM ARE

1 K1	2 K2	3 K3	4 CO
5.061517D-02	7.933159D-03	0.153338	4.54750

③

CASE NO.	NAME	RESIDUAL	OBSERVED 2 SULFISOX	PREDICTED 2 SULFISOX	STD. DEV. PREDICTED	1 TIME
1		0.838004	215.599991	214.761987	1.895536	0.250000
2		-3.045995	189.199997	192.245992	1.119609	0.500000
3		1.477066	176.000000	174.522934	1.167996	0.750000
4		2.483595	162.799988	160.316393	1.180304	1.000000
5		-0.414961	138.599991	139.014952	1.051753	1.500000
6		-2.609316	121.000000	123.609316	1.085922	2.000000
7		-0.488130	101.199997	101.688127	1.234437	3.000000
8		2.438239	88.000000	85.561761	1.168549	4.000000
9		-0.024508	61.599991	61.624499	1.263988	6.000000
10		-1.331930	22.000000	23.331930	1.575764	12.000000
11		1.051933	4.400000	3.348067	0.574504	24.000000
12		-0.068927	0.0	0.068927	0.026283	48.000000

14.4 System Cards for P3R and PAR

ABSTRACT

When the function to be fitted to the data by P3R can be specified by function NUMBER in Control Language, the necessary IBM OS System Cards are shown in Example 3R.1.

When the function to be fitted to the data by P3R or PAR is specified in the FORTRAN subroutine P3RFUN or FUN respectively, the subroutine must be temporarily appended to the BMDP program. We first describe how this is done in general terms, and then specify the System Cards for IBM OS systems.

The BMDP programs are written in FORTRAN. The FORTRAN code is compiled (translated) on the computer into executable code prior to doing an analysis. Almost all computer facilities maintain the BMDP programs in executable code, greatly reducing the time used by the program (and hence its cost). When you specify the function in FORTRAN in subroutine P3RFUN or FUN, the subroutine must also be compiled into executable code; the code must then be combined with that of the BMDP program prior to the analysis.

System Cards can vary so you should check with your computing facility consultant for the proper System Cards to use. Space is provided on the page opposite the inside back cover for you to write the cards required at your facility.

System Cards Used for IBM OS

The first cards in the deck for P3R are the System Cards

```
//job card
// EXEC  BIMEDT,PROG=BMDP3R
   (Note:  Remember the T on BIMEDT)
//FUN DD  *
```

followed by FORTRAN statements that define the function and its derivatives.

Note: At HCF the first three FORTRAN statements beginning

```
SUBROUTINE P3RFUN...
IMPLICIT REAL*8...
DIMENSION...
```

and the last two statements

```
RETURN
END
```

must be omitted; they are provided by the computer. Check whether these statements are needed at your facility.

The FORTRAN statements of the function and its derivatives are followed by a System Card

```
//GO.SYSIN DD *
```

Next are the Control Language instructions and data, if on cards, and then a System Card to terminate the program. This is followed by

```
//
```

For PAR the order of cards is similar except the second System Card is

```
// EXEC BIMEDT,PROG=BMDPAR
```

and the first three FORTRAN statements that begin

```
SUBROUTINE FUN...
IMPLICIT REAL*8...
DIMENSION...
```

as well as the last two statements

```
RETURN
END
```

must be omitted; they are ordinarily provided by the computer. Check whether these statements are needed at your facility.

If you are reading from a BMDP File, creating a BMDP File, or reading data from a disk or magnetic tape, the System Card to describe the UNIT

```
//GO.FTyyF001  DD ...
```

must be placed immediately before the

```
//GO.SYSIN  DD  *
```

The order of cards is as follows if you specify transformations in a FORTRAN subroutine:

```
//job card
// EXEC BIMEDT,PROG=BMDP3R   (or PAR)
//TRANSF  DD  *
```

This is followed by FORTRAN statements describing the transformations (Section 6.4). Next is a System Card

```
//FUN DD    *
```

The sequence of cards that follow //FUN DD * is as described above.
    The entire input deck for Example 3R.2 is:

IBM OS System Cards:

```
//job card
// EXEC BIMEDT,PROG=BMDP3R
//FUN DD *
```

FORTRAN statements:

```
C
      DF(1) = DEXP(P(2)*X(3))
      DF(2) = P(1)*X(3)*DF(1)
      DF(3) = DEXP(P(4)*X(3))
      DF(4) = P(3)*X(3)*DF(3)
      F = P(1)*DF(1) + P(3)*DF(3)
C
```

HCF System Card:

```
//GO.SYSIN  DD  *
```

BMDP instructions:

```
/ PROBLEM    TITLE IS 'RADIOACTIVE SULFATE DATA'.
/ INPUT      VARIABLES ARE 3.
             FORMAT IS '(F8.4, F8.6, F8.0)'
/ VARIABLE   NAMES ARE COUNT, CASEWT, TIME.

/ REGRESS    DEPENDENT IS COUNT.
             PARAMETERS ARE 4.
             WEIGHT IS CASEWT.

/ PARAMETER   INITIAL ARE 10, -.1, 5, -.01.

/ END
```

Data from Table 14.1:

```
15.1117 .004379      2
11.3601 .007749      4
 9.7652 .010487      6
 9.0935 .012093      8
 8.4820 .013900     10
 7.6891 .016914     15
 7.3342 .018591     20
 7.0593 .020067     25
 6.7041 .022249     30
 6.4313 .024177     40
 6.1554 .026393     50
 5.9940 .027833     60
 5.7698 .030039     70
 5.6440 .031392     80
 5.3915 .034402     90
 5.0938 .038540    110
 4.8717 .042135    130
 4.5996 .047267    150
 4.4968 .049453    160
 4.3602 .052600    170
 4.2668 .054928    180
```

IBM OS System Card:

```
//
```

PLR

14.5 Stepwise Logistic Regression

Laszlo Engelman

ABSTRACT

PLR selects predictor (independent) variables in a stepwise manner, and estimates the coefficients for a logistic regression. The dependent (outcome or response) variable is a binary variable coded as 0 or 1. The predicted proportion of successes (s/n) follows the logistic model $\exp(U)/(1 + \exp(U))$, where s is the sum of the binary (0,1) dependent variable, n is the total sample size and U is a linear function of one or more independent variables. The dependent variable records events such as success or failure, response or no response, etc. The independent variables can be categorical or continuous. The program generates design variables for the categorical variables and their interactions. For example, two design variables are generated for a categorical variable with three categories. The design variables for each categorical variable (or interaction term) are considered as a set. At each step in the stepping process, a continuous variable or one set of design variables is added to or removed from the model. A hierarchical rule allows an interaction into the model only if all its lower-order interactions and main effects are in the model (the rule can be negated). The step selections are based on either the maximum likelihood ratio (MLR) or an approximate asymptotic covariance estimate (ACE). The latter is considerably faster (more economical) and is recommended for the initial run of large problems. Output includes, at each step, the log-likelihood, the change in log-likelihood from the previous step, and three goodness-of-fit χ^2 statistics; a summary report includes histograms of predicted probabilities of each group and a table of correct and incorrect classifications using different cutpoints on the computed probabilities. Also for each distinct pattern of all variables considered, or for those actually selected, output includes frequency of successes and failures, predicted probability, observed proportion, log odds, and standardized residuals; scatter plots of the proportions of the first group vs. the predicted probability of the first group, and the proportion of the first group vs. the predicted log odds.

Example LR.1 Basic Setup for Logistic Regression Using Tabulated Data

The data are from Cox (1970, p. 86): at a specified time (t) a number of objects (n) are tested and the number of failures (f) recorded.

t	f	n
7	0	55
14	2	157
27	7	159
51	3	16

We want to estimate the parameters (p_i) of a model that will predict the proportion of failures (f_i/n_i) at each time:

$$E\left(\frac{f}{n}\right) = \frac{e^{p_1 + p_2 t}}{1 + e^{p_1 + p_2 t}}$$

where $E\left(\frac{f}{n}\right)$ is the predicted proportion. The Control Language instructions are as follows:

```
/ PROBLEM    TITLE IS 'DATA FROM D.R.COX (1970
                      P. 86).'.
/ INPUT      VARIABLES ARE 3.
             FORMAT IS '(3F4.0)'.
/ VARIABLE   NAMES ARE TIME, FAIL, NUMBER.
/ REGRESS    COUNT  IS NUMBER.
             FCOUNT IS FAIL.
             INTERVAL IS TIME.
/ PRINT      CELL = ALL.
/ END
```

(See end of this PLR section for organization of systems information, BMDP instructions and data.)

The REGRESS paragraph is specific to PLR; the REGRESS paragraph specifies the DEPENDENT and INDEPENDENT variables, the MODEL, the METHOD of variable selection and associated limits. The PRINT paragraph controls the results to be printed. The results of the analysis are presented in Output LR.1. Circled numbers below correspond to those in the output.

① Interpretation of the REGRESS paragraph. Most of the values reported are preassigned values. The values for the first ten cases are printed. The user

may control the number of cases printed using CASE option in the PRINT paragraph.

② The number of cases read and number of responses they represent.

③ The minimum, maximum, mean, standard deviation, skewness and kurtosis are reported for all interval-scaled variables. For categorical variables the data values and their frequencies are reported along with the design variables that are generated for each categorical variable (see Example LR.2).

Output LR.1   A logistic regression analysis of D.R. Cox data by PLR. Circled numbers correspond to those in the text

--- the BMDP instructions read by PLR are printed and interpreted ---

```
DEPENDENT VARIABLE. . . . . . . . . . . . . . .   0
       COUNT VARIABLE. . . . . . . . . . . . . .   3 NUMBER
      SCOUNT VARIABLE. . . . . . . . . . . . . .   0
      FCOUNT VARIABLE. . . . . . . . . . . . . .   2 FAIL                    ①
METHOD TO SELECT NEXT TERM TO REMOVE OR ENTER .   ACE
HIERARCHICAL TERM INCLUSION RULE USED . . . . .   SING
REMOVE LIMIT (P-VALUE MUST BE GREATER). . . . .   0.1500  0.1500
ENTER LIMIT (P-VALUE MUST BE LESS). . . . . . .   0.1000  0.1000
TOLERANCE . . . . . . . . . . . . . . . . . . .   0.0001000
CONVERGENCE CRITERION . . . . . . . . . . . . .   0.0001000
MAXIMUM NUMBER OF ITERATIONS. . . . . . . . . .   10
              STEP HALVINGS . . . . . . . .      5
```

```
C A S E        1       2       3
NO. LABEL     TIME    FAIL   NUMBER
_____ _____  _____  _____  _____

  1            7       0       55
  2           14       2      157
  3           27       7      159
  4           51       3       16

NUMBER OF CASES READ. . . . . . . . . . . . .    4
```

```
TOTAL NUMBER OF RESPONSES USED IN THE ANALYSIS   387
                    SUCCESS . . . . . .         375
                    FAIL    . . . . . .          12    ②

NUMBER OF DISTINCT COVARIATE PATTERNS . . . . .   4
```

DESCRIPTIVE STATISTICS OF INDEPENDENT VARIABLES
-- ③

VARIABLE NO. N A M E	MINIMUM	MAXIMUM	MEAN	STANDARD DEVIATION	SKEWNESS	KURTOSIS
1 TIME	7.0000	51.0000	19.8760	9.9361	1.0290	1.5394

(output continued)

Output LR.1 (continued)

```
STEP NUMBER    0
---------------

                        LOG LIKELIHOOD =     -53.494
GOODNESS OF FIT CHI-SQ  (2*O*LN(O/E)) =     12.710   D.F.=    3  P-VALUE= 0.005
GOODNESS OF FIT CHI-SQ  ( C.C.BROWN ) =      0.0     D.F.=    0  P-VALUE= 1.000


                                      STANDARD
          TERM          COEFFICIENT    ERROR     COEFF/S.E.

CONSTANT                    3.4420    0.2933      11.74


STATISTICS TO ENTER OR REMOVE TERMS
-----------------------------------
                    APPROX.                   APPROX.
          TERM      F TO    D.F. D.F.         F TO    D.F. D.F.
                    ENTER                     REMOVE                P-VALUE

TIME                15.63    1    385                              0.0001
CONSTANT                                      137.41   1    385    0.0000
CONSTANT                                      IS IN                        MAY NOT BE REMOVED.


STEP NUMBER    1                  TIME                 IS ENTERED
---------------
```
④
```
                        LOG LIKELIHOOD =     -47.687
IMPROVEMENT CHI-SQUARE  (2*(LN(MLR) ) =     11.614   D.F.=    1  P-VALUE= 0.001
GOODNESS OF FIT CHI-SQ  (2*O*LN(O/E)) =      1.096   D.F.=    2  P-VALUE= 0.578
GOODNESS OF FIT CHI-SQ  ( D. HOSMER ) =      0.474   D.F.=    1  P-VALUE= 0.491
GOODNESS OF FIT CHI-SQ  ( C.C.BROWN ) =      1.004   D.F.=    2  P-VALUE= 0.605


                                      STANDARD
          TERM          COEFFICIENT    ERROR     COEFF/S.E.

TIME            ⑤     -0.80696E-01  0.2236E-01   -3.610
CONSTANT               5.4152       0.7275        7.443


CORRELATION MATRIX OF COEFFICIENTS
----------------------------------


              TIME      CONSTANT

TIME          1.000                   ⑥
CONSTANT     -0.910      1.000




STATISTICS TO ENTER OR REMOVE TERMS
-----------------------------------           ⑦
                    APPROX.                   APPROX.
          TERM      F TO    D.F. D.F.         F TO    D.F. D.F.
                    ENTER                     REMOVE                P-VALUE

TIME                                          14.48    1    384    0.0002
CONSTANT                                      IS IN                        MAY NOT BE REMOVED.


NO TERM PASSES THE REMOVE AND ENTER LIMITS (  0.1500   0.1000  ) .
```

SUMMARY OF STEPWISE RESULTS

STEP NO	TERM ENTERED ⑧	DF	TERM REMOVED	LOG LIKELIHOOD	IMPROVEMENT CHI-SQUARE	P-VALUE	GOODNESS OF FIT CHI-SQUARE	P-VALUE
0				-53.494			12.710	0.005
1	TIME	1		-47.687	11.614	0.001	1.096	0.578

SUMMARY DESCRIPTION OF CELLS. CELLS ARE FORMED BY ALL POSSIBLE COMBINATIONS OF VALUES OF ALL VARIABLES.

NUMBER SUCCESS	NUMBER FAIL	OBSERVED PROPORTION SUCCESS	PREDICTED PROB. OF SUCCESS	S.D. OF PREDICTED PROB.	OBS-PRED ------- S.D.RES.	PRED. LOG ODDS	TIME
13	3	0.8125	0.7858	0.0951	0.6964	1.300	51.00
152	7	0.9560	0.9622	0.0112	-0.6085	3.236	27.00 ⑨
155	2	0.9873	0.9864	0.0062	0.1226	4.285	14.00
55	0	1.0000	0.9922	0.0045	0.7103	4.850	7.00

MINIMUM EXPECTED CELL FREQUENCY   =   0.43
NUMBER OF EXPECTED VALUES LESS THAN 5.0 =   3

---

④ At each step in the output the program reports the log-likelihood and the results for four tests.

- The improvement chi-square tests the hypothesis that the term entered (removed) at that step significantly improves prediction; computed from the log of the ratio of the current versus previous likelihood function values. However, significance is not based on stepwise selection of terms. A small p-value indicates a significant improvement at the step.
- The goodness-of-fit chi-square can be used to test the hypothesis that the model at that step fits the data adequately. This is computed from the observed versus predicted frequencies at each cell in the data. This test can give misleading results when cell frequencies are small (e.g., less than 5).
- The 'Hosmer' goodness-of-fit test compares the observed and predicted frequencies of ten cells. Cells are defined by the predicted values (see Hosmer, D.W. and Lemeshow, S., 'Goodness-of-fit tests for the multiple logistic regression model'). A small p-value means that the predicted values do not fit the data.
- The 'C.C. Brown' goodness-of-fit test compares the fit of data to the logistic or to some alternate member of the family of models as defined by R.L. Prentice (see 'A Generalization of the Probit and Logit Methods for Dose Response Curves,' *Biometrics* 32, pp. 761-768). A small p-value indicates that the logistic model is not appropriate for the data.

⑤ The regression coefficients, standard errors of coefficients and their ratio are reported at each step.

⑥ The asymptotic correlation matrix is printed at each step.

⑦ All terms for entry or removal into the model at the completion of each step. If the term selected is based on the asymptotic covariance matrix, then the F statistics are printed; if selection is based on maximum likelihood ratios, then the chi-square statistics are printed.

⑧ A summary table of the previously reported statistics and p-values is printed at completion of the stepping process.

⑨ The frequencies of successes, failures, predicted probability, observed proportion, standardized residuals and log odds are printed for each distinct pattern of the independent variables. In this example we only have one independent variable, time. When there are several independent variables and only a subset is included in the model, this display is also printed for the distinct patterns formed from the variables included in the model.

We omit the remaining output produced with this basic setup: scatter plots of the observed proportions versus the predicted probabilities and the observed proportions versus the log odds, histograms of the predicted probabilities for each group and a table of correct and incorrect classifications resulting from placing different cutpoints on the computed probabilities. The scatter plots are of interest when there are many distinct combinations of the independent variables (cells) and the frequency of each cell is greater than one (the observed proportion is between 0 and 1). A point is plotted for each cell. In the plot of observed proportions versus predicted probabilities it would be preferable for points to fall along a straight line extending from the lower left to the upper right. Ideally, the points for each cell value in the log odds plot should fall along a logistic shaped curve (a tipped S shape extending from the lower left to the upper right). The histograms of predicted probabilities are useful when the independent variables contain many distinct values. From them one can assess the overlap between the predicted probabilities for the failure group and the success group.

Input forms for the dependent variable. The dependent variable or outcome can be recorded in any of three ways:

1) a response (1 or 0 - success or failure) is given for each case (see Example LR.2). Use the parameter DEPENDENT.

2) each record has a tally for a pattern of covariates (independent variables). The variable identified by the parameter DEPENDENT contains the response and the variable identified by COUNT contains the tally.

3) each record has a tally for a pattern of covariates, and any two of the following three parameters designate variables containing counts: COUNT (the total observations in the cell), SCOUNT (the tally of successes), FCOUNT (the tally of failures). (See Example LR.1.)

If DEPENDENT is specified, its values are assumed to be 1 (success) and 0 (failure), unless grouping information for the dependent variable is given in the GROUP paragraph. The first group (code or interval) is assumed to be the success group (y = 1) and the second, the failure (y = 0). The dependent variable's groups may be named using the NAME sentence of the GROUP paragraph.

Identifying the categorical and interval-scaled independent variables. Independent variables can be either INTERVAL-scaled or CATEGORICAL. For example, if you want to estimate the probability of reoccurrence of a malignancy from sex, hospital and age:

Reoccurrence	Sex	Hospital	Age
0	1	1	67
0	2	3	72
0	2	2	59
1	2	1	68
1	1	1	69
0	1	3	63
.	.	.	.
.	.	.	.
.	.	.	.

You would state

```
/ REGRESSION    DEPENDENT   = REOCCUR.
                INTERVAL    = AGE.
                CATEGORICAL = SEX, HOSPITAL.
```

Variables that are interval-scaled must be declared as such in the INTERVAL statement. All variables read in as input (other than DEPENDENT, COUNT, SCOUNT, FCOUNT or INTERVAL) are assumed to be categorical independent variables.

The number of variables used in a particular analysis can be restricted by the USE statement in the VARIABLE paragraph or in the MODEL statement in the REGRESSION paragraph.

REGRess ——————
DEPENDent = v.   none
Name or subscript of the dependent variable. The grouping information (CODES or CUTPOINTS in the GROUP paragraph) for this variable should define two groups. When CODES or CUTPOINTS are specified in the GROUP paragraph the first group stated is assumed to be the success group. If grouping information is not given the preassigned code values are 1 (success) and 0 (failure). If DEPEND or DEPEND and COUNT are not specified, two of the following three parameters must be specified to define the outcomes.

COUNT = v.   none
Name or subscript of the input variable containing the n_v counts. If COUNT is not specified, each input case is assumed to have n =1.

SCOUNT = v.   none
Name or subscript of the input variable containing the s_j counts if one of the input variables is the number of successes with the recorded variable values.

FCOUNT = v.   none
Name or subscript of the input variable containing the f_j counts if one of the input variables is the number of failures with the recorded variable values.

Acceptable combinations of the above four parameters are:

```
DEPEND
DEPEND and COUNT
COUNT and SCOUNT
COUNT and FCOUNT
SCOUNT and FCOUNT
```

INTERval = v list.   none
Names or subscripts of interval-scaled variables. Variables not listed are assumed to be categorical variables.

CATEGorical = v list.   all, but INTER, DEPEND, COUNT, SCOUNT, FCOUNT
Names or subscripts of categorical variables; the program generates sets of design variables for these variables.

Example LR.2 Basic Setup for Logistic Regression Using One Subject per Case

We use the Kasser coronary data (Table 11.1) to see if age, history of angina pectoris (ANGINA: yes, no), history of high blood pressure (HIGH BP: yes, no) and functional status (FUNCTION: none, minimal, moderate, and more than moderate) can be used to predict the probability of past myocardial infarction (INFARCT: yes, no). If all these predictors are found useful, U(X) has the form (see Abstract):

$b_0 + b_1$ AGE + b_3 ANGINA + b_3 HIGH BP + b_4 FUNCTION

where categorical variables are replaced by their corresponding design variable sets.

The preassigned procedure for PLR is to compute the estimates of the parameters in a stepwise manner. That is, variables are entered (or removed) into the equation one at a time, selecting the most useful variable first. (The user may initiate the analysis with particular variables and interactions -- see MODEL below). It is often of interest to select a useful subset of the independent variables: PLR, like P2R, has preassigned values for controlling the stepping (REMOVE and ENTER).

The INPUT, VARIABLE and GROUP paragraphs in the following BMDP instructions are explained in Chapter 5. For this analysis we do not want to use an input variable named ACTIVE that has a number of unknown responses. We use the USE statement in the VARIABLE paragraph to restrict the analysis to the five variables of interest. In the REGRESSION paragraph we state that INFARCT is the dependent variable and that AGE is an interval-scaled variable. All other variables in the USE list are assumed to be categorical and the program will automatically generate a set of design variables for each one.

```
/ PROBLEM    TITLE IS 'KASSER CORONARY DATA'.
/ INPUT      VARIABLES ARE 6.
            FORMAT IS '(6F4.0)'.
```

```
/ VARIABLE   NAMES ARE AGE, FUNCTION, ACTIVE,
            INFARCT, ANGINA, 'HIGH BP'.
            USE = 1, 2, 4 TO 6.

/ GROUP      CODES(4) = 0, 1.
            NAMES(4) = NO, YES.

/ REGRESS    DEPEND IS INFARCT.
            INTERVAL IS AGE.

/ PRINT      CELL = MODEL.  PLOT.

/ PLOT       SIZE = 50, 35.

/ END        ------------------------------------
```

(See page 342 for organization of systems information, BMDP instructions and data.)

The results of the logistic regression analysis are presented in Output LR.2. The circled numbers below correspond to those in the output.

(10) The categorical variables are interpreted.

(11) The program reads responses for 117 subjects. There are 101 distinct combinations (cells) of the independent variables: several people have the same

Output LR.2   A logistic regression analysis of the Kasser Coronary data

----

VARIABLE NO. NAME	MINIMUM LIMIT	MAXIMUM LIMIT	MISSING CODE	CATEGORY CODE	CATEGORY NAME	INTERVAL RANGE GREATER THAN	LESS THAN OR = TO
4 INFARCT		(10)		0.00000	NO		
				1.00000	YES		

```
TOTAL NUMBER OF RESPONSES USED IN THE ANALYSIS     117
                          NO     . . . . . .     43
                          YES    . . . . . .     74

NUMBER OF DISTINCT COVARIATE PATTERNS . . . . .    101
```

(11)

DESCRIPTIVE STATISTICS OF INDEPENDENT VARIABLES

VARIABLE NO. N A M E	MINIMUM	MAXIMUM	MEAN	STANDARD DEVIATION	SKEWNESS	KURTOSIS
1 AGE	34.0000	73.0000	52.3162	9.4746	0.0568	−0.5646

VARIABLE NO. N A M E	VALUE OR INTERVAL	FREQ	DESIGN VARIABLES (1)	(2)	(3)
2 FUNCTION	0	20	−1	−1	−1
	1	24	1	0	0
	2	46	0	1	0
	3	27	0	0	1
5 ANGINA	0	19	−1		
	1	98	1		
6 HIGHBP	0	81	−1		
	1	36	1		

(output continued)

Output LR.2 (continued)

```
STEP NUMBER   0
---------------

                      LOG LIKELIHOOD =    -76.941
GOODNESS OF FIT CHI-SQ  (2*O*LN(O/E)) =   140.020  D.F.= 100  P-VALUE= 0.005
GOODNESS OF FIT CHI-SQ  ( C.C.BROWN ) =     0.0    D.F.=   0  P-VALUE= 1.000

                                  STANDARD
         TERM          COEFFICIENT  ERROR   COEFF/S.E.

CONSTANT               -0.54287    0.1918     -2.831


STATISTICS TO ENTER OR REMOVE TERMS
-----------------------------------
                APPROX.             APPROX.
     TERM       F TO   D.F. D.F.    F TO   D.F. D.F.
                ENTER               REMOVE              P-VALUE

AGE             0.31    1   115                         0.5814
FUNCTION        0.26    3   113                         0.8537
ANGINA          4.38    1   115                         0.0387
HIGH BP         0.53    1   115                         0.4666
CONSTANT                            7.95    1   115     0.0057
CONSTANT                            IS IN                        MAY NOT BE REMOVED.

STEP NUMBER   1             ANGINA            IS ENTERED
---------------    (12)

                      LOG LIKELIHOOD =    -74.553
IMPROVEMENT CHI-SQUARE  (2*(LN(MLR) ) =     4.776  D.F.=   1  P-VALUE= 0.029
GOODNESS OF FIT CHI-SQ  (2*O*LN(O/E)) =   135.243  D.F.=  99  P-VALUE= 0.009
GOODNESS OF FIT CHI-SQ  ( C.C.BROWN ) =     0.0    D.F.=   0  P-VALUE= 1.000

                                  STANDARD
         TERM          COEFFICIENT  ERROR   COEFF/S.E.

ANGINA                  0.64461    0.3296      1.956
CONSTANT               -1.0162     0.3296     -3.083


CORRELATION MATRIX OF COEFFICIENTS
----------------------------------


          ANGINA    CONSTANT

ANGINA     1.000
CONSTANT  -0.806     1.000


STATISTICS TO ENTER OR REMOVE TERMS
-----------------------------------
                APPROX.             APPROX.
     TERM       F TO   D.F. D.F.    F TO   D.F. D.F.
                ENTER               REMOVE              P-VALUE

AGE             0.25    1   114                         0.6208
FUNCTION        0.57    3   112                         0.6348
ANGINA                              3.77    1   114     0.0548
HIGH BP         0.57    1   114                         0.4501
CONSTANT                            IS IN                        MAY NOT BE REMOVED.


NO TERM PASSES THE REMOVE AND ENTER LIMITS (  0.1500  0.1000 ) .
```

SUMMARY OF STEPWISE RESULTS

STEP NO	TERM ENTERED	DF	TERM REMOVED	LOG LIKELIHOOD	IMPROVEMENT CHI-SQUARE	P-VALUE	GOODNESS OF FIT CHI-SQUARE	P-VALUE
0				-76.941			140.020	0.005
1	ANGINA	1		-74.553	4.776	0.029	135.243	0.009

SUMMARY DESCRIPTION OF CELLS. CELLS ARE FORMED BY ALL POSSIBLE COMBINATIONS OF VALUES OF VARIABLES IN THE MODEL.

NUMBER NO	NUMBER YES	OBSERVED PROPORTION NO	PREDICTED PROB. OF NO	S.D. OF PREDICTED PROB.	OBS-PRED ------- S.D.RES.	PRED. LOG ODDS	ANGINA
3	16	0.1579	0.1597	0.0840	-28.8740	-1.661	0.0
40	58	0.4082	0.4082	0.0496	-0.0030	-0.372	1.00

MINIMUM EXPECTED CELL FREQUENCY   =   3.03
NUMBER OF EXPECTED VALUES LESS THAN 5.0 =   1

(output continued)

age, function status and histories of angina and high blood pressure. Descriptive statistics are printed for the interval variables (AGE) and a frequency is listed for each code of the categorical variables. When CODES or CUTPOINTS are specified, the category index is the order of the category, not the actual value of the code, e.g., for angina, the codes are 0 and 1; if these codes had been specified in the GROUP paragraph, the respective indices would be 1 and 2.

For k categories, k-1 design variables are generated. Three types of design variables are available (see design variables, page 000). Unless otherwise stated, the program generates the "MARGINAL" type of design variable. If a subject is in the first of four possible categories, then the design variables are -1, -1, -1; if he is in the second category, 1, 0, 0; if in the third, 0,1,0; etc. Note that the first design variable used "marginally" yields the contrast between the first and second categories.

(12) ANGINA is entered in the model at step 1: it has the lowest p-value (largest approximate F-to-enter) at step 0. Its presence provides a significant improvement over the constant above at step 0 (IMPROVEMENT CHI-SQUARE of 4.777, p-value .029). If a categorical variable were most important, its design variables would be entered as a set at this step. The first goodness-of-fit chi-square test is meaningless for this problem because we have so many distinct cells (covariate patterns -- 101 for 117 subjects) - chi-square tests are unreliable when more than a few cells have expected frequencies less than 5.0. The Hosmer test indicates that the predicted values fit the observed values well. From the Brown test we see that the logistic model is adequate for these data. The model is now

$$\text{Probability of no infarct} = \frac{e^{-1.016+.645 \text{ angina}}}{1 + e^{-1.016+.645 \text{ angina}}}.$$

The value of the coefficient divided by its standard error (COEFF/s.e.) is printed for each variable. These can be read roughly as t statistics. For a useful variable, we do not like to see these values drop below 2.0. No candidate variables have p-values for entry below .15 and angina does not have a p-value for removal greater than .10, so the stepping stops. Information in this sample for age, high blood pressure, etc. will not improve the prediction.

(13) The results for the cells formed using all combinations of only those variables entered in the model. Only ANGINA entered, so there are only two cells with values 0 (no angina) and 1 (yes angina). If the interval variable AGE entered the model, the actual value of age would be printed. The user can control how the independent variables and/or the proportion of success are sorted by using the SORT instruction in the PRINT paragraph.

Output LR.2 (continued)

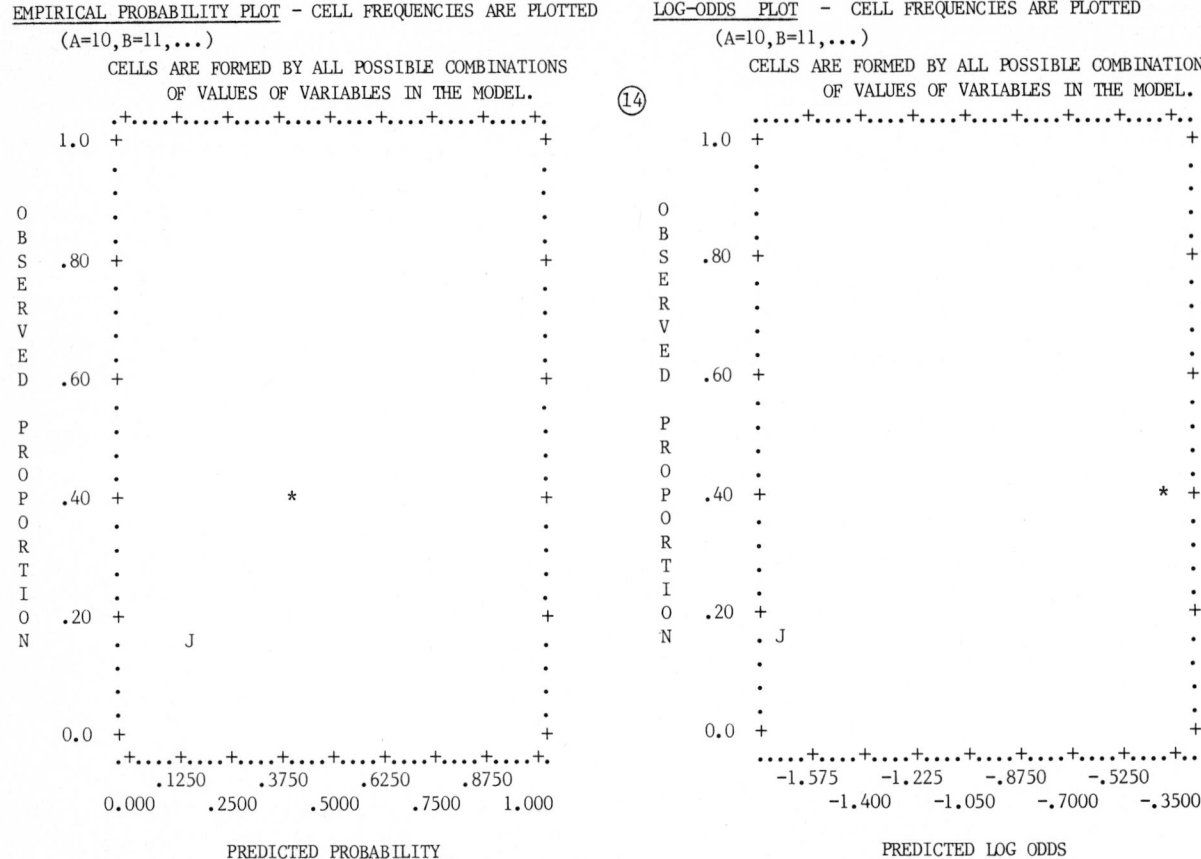

EMPIRICAL PROBABILITY PLOT - CELL FREQUENCIES ARE PLOTTED
    (A=10,B=11,...)
        CELLS ARE FORMED BY ALL POSSIBLE COMBINATIONS
            OF VALUES OF VARIABLES IN THE MODEL.

                        PREDICTED PROBABILITY

LOG-ODDS PLOT - CELL FREQUENCIES ARE PLOTTED
    (A=10,B=11,...)
        CELLS ARE FORMED BY ALL POSSIBLE COMBINATIONS
            OF VALUES OF VARIABLES IN THE MODEL.

                        PREDICTED LOG ODDS

⑭ For the data with only two cells, the scatter plots of the observed probabilities versus the predicted probabilities and the observed probabilities versus the log odds are not interesting. In the plot on the left the lower point (J) plots the probabilities of an infarct for those with no angina; the asterisk represents the proportions for those with angina. We omit the remainder of the output.

Specifying the Model

The model consists of all the terms you want to consider in the analysis. A "term" is an independent variable or an interaction of independent variables. The terms to be considered are specified in the MODEL statement.

                MODEL = AGE, SEX*RACE

Interactions are stated with asterisks connecting the names of the variables. When an interaction is in the model, its components are assumed to be in the model as well. Thus the above example will consider the terms: AGE, SEX, RACE and the interaction of SEX and RACE. A constant term is also included in the model.

For each term listed in the MODEL statement (and for the constant term) you can state whether the term should be included or excluded at the start of the stepping process. For example, the statement

        START = OUT, IN.   CONSTANT = OUT.

added to the above MODEL statement causes AGE to be OUT, the interaction of SEX and RACE to be IN, and the CONSTANT term to be OUT at the start of the computations. The interaction being IN implies that both main effects (SEX and RACE) are also IN.
    You can also specify how many times each term is allowed to move in or out of the model. The two statements

        MOVE = 2, 0.   and   CMOVE = 2.

used with the MODEL statement above allow AGE and CONSTANT to move twice, but SEX, RACE and the interaction of SEX and RACE are not allowed to move. The above statements, all taken together, allow AGE and CONSTANT to be in or out of the final model, but SEX, RACE and the interaction of SEX and RACE will be in the final model. This occurs because AGE and CONSTANT are allowed to be IN or OUT, but the other terms are included at the start and are not allowed to move out.

Since the significance of a term is approximated, the computed significance for entry may not equal the significance computed after entry. The MOVE limit prevents cycling a term in and out of the model.

Design Variables

PLR generates design variables for each categorical variable. These are used in the model instead of the value or category numbers recorded for the covariate. Generated design variables either contrast the first category with later categories, or are orthogonal polynomial components. Assuming three categories, PLR generates two design variables, D_1 and D_2, of one of the following types:

	D_1	D_2	
category 1	-1	-1	Each design variable used without the
category 2	1	0	other(s) contrasts a category with
category 3	0	1	the first category (marginally).
category 1	0	0	Each design variable used with the
category 2	1	0	other(s) contrasts a category with
category 3	0	1	the first category (partially).
category 1	-.7071	.4082	The first is the linear, the second
category 2	0.0	-.8165	is the quadratic component of equally
category 3	.7071	.4082	spaced categories of equal size.

PLR accepts DVAR = MARG., DVAR = PART., or DVAR = ORTH. If not stated, DVAR = MARG. is assumed.

The option DVAR = ORTH. generates orthogonal components appropriate for the values of the design variables. For example, if the covariate's values are unequally spaced, e.g., 1, 4, 9, then the design variables generated are

$$
\begin{array}{rr}
-.6415 & .5051 \\
-.1166 & -.8081 \\
.7582 & .3030
\end{array}
$$

However, inequality of category sizes will not affect design variable generation.

The DVAR = ORTH. option is only used for covariates with fewer than 12 categories. For covariates with more than 11 categories, PLR uses DVAR = MARG.

REGRess ─────────

> MODEL = v list.   all main effects
> Independent variables and their interactions to be considered for the model. Asterisks between the variable names indicate interactions, e.g.,
>
> RACE*SEX*TREAT
>
> refers to a three-way interaction of RACE, SEX and TREAT variables. Only the highest order interactions need be stated; lower order terms (RACE*SEX, RACE*TREAT, SEX*TREAT, RACE, SEX, TREAT) are generated by the program. If MODEL is not specified, each variable in the VARIABLE USE list except those used as DEPENDENT, COUNT, FCOUNT and SCOUNT variables, is considered for the model. No interaction term is assumed. An additional term, CONSTANT, is added to the MODEL by the program. For interval-scaled variables, the word "interaction" means "product."*
> START = list of IN or OUT   IN,...,IN
>   (or 2 for IN, 1 for OUT).
> Indicates whether a term in the MODEL statement is included at the beginning of the stepwise process. Use one word for each term specified in the MODEL statement.*
> CONSTANT = IN or OUT   IN
>   (or 2 for IN, 1 for OUT).
> Indicates whether the CONSTANT term is included

at the beginning of the stepwise process.
> MOVE = # list.   0,...,0
> Use one number for each term in the MODEL to indicate the maximum number of times the corresponding term in the MODEL statement can be moved into or out of the model. No term is allowed to move unless stated otherwise.*
> CMOVE = #.   0
> The maximum number of times the CONSTANT may be moved into or out of the model. If not specified, the CONSTANT is not allowed to move.
> DVAR = (one only) MARG,   MARG/ prev.
>   PART, or ORTH.
> Controls the type of design variables generated for categorical covariates. See Design Variables, above.
> * Note that if a MODEL statement is not given, then each covariate is assumed to be out of the model at the start of computations, and it is assumed that each is allowed to move twice.

Methods for Entering and Removing Variables and Forward and Backward Stepping

At each step the set of coefficients β for the included terms are estimated as the value that maximizes the likelihood function. After estimating β, a decision is made whether to enter or remove any term in the next step, based on either

MLR--the log of the ratios of the maximized likelihood functions

$$\chi^2 \cong 2\left|\log(L(\beta \text{ current})/L(\beta \text{ candidate}))\right|$$

or

ACE--an estimate of the asymptotic covariance matrix of β, from which an approximate F value is computed

MLR is more reliable; however, ACE can be considerably less expensive in computational time, especially when the number of terms is large (10 or more).

After the approximate χ^2 or F values are obtained the tail area probabilities are computed and the term with the largest p-value is removed if it is larger than the specified REMOVE limit. If no term has a p-value larger than this limit, the term with the smallest p-value is entered if its p-value is less than the ENTER limit and its tolerance is greater than the TOLERANCE limit.

You can state 2 values for ENTER and REMOVE limits. After all terms are entered that can be entered according to the first ENTER and REMOVE limits, they can be removed from the model according to the second ENTER and REMOVE limits. (Example 2R.2 demonstrates this type of forward and backward stepping.)

REGRess ─────────

> METHOD = (one only) ACE, MLR.   ACE/prev.
> The method used for assessing the significance of each term in selecting the one to be removed or entered in the next step.
>   ACE (asymptotic covariance estimate)
>   MLR (maximum likelihood method)
> TOLerance = #.   0.0001/prev.
> A value used as the tolerance limit in the inversion of the cross product of partial derivatives matrix. The cross product matrix and its inversion are computed in double precision.
> REMOVE = #₁, #₂.   0.15,0.15/prev.
> Two values used as limits of p-values to remove terms.

ENTER = #₁, #₂.   0.10,0.10/prev.

Two values used as limits of p-values to enter terms.

Note: Stepping of terms is controlled by the 1st REMOVE and ENTER limits. When no further terms can be moved with these, PLR switches to the 2nd REMOVE and ENTER limits and resumes the stepping.

Values Used to Control the Maximum Likelihood Computations

Maximum likelihood estimates are computed by an iterative process (Jennrich and Moore, 1975). When the relative improvement of the likelihood function is less than the value of the CONVERGENCE criterion, the algorithm deems the solution attained. The algorithm can be stopped if an excessive number of ITERATIONS is needed to meet the CONVERGENCE criterion.

When there is no improvement in the likelihood function between successive iterations, the computed correction to the parameters is halved and the likelihood function is recomputed. This halving is repeated until the likelihood function is greater than that in the previous iteration, or until the maximum number of HALVINGS is reached.

REGRess ───

CONVergence = #.   .0001/prev.

A no. used as the convergence criterion of the likelihood function. The function is said to have "no improvement" if the relative improvement is less than the CONVERGENCE criterion.

ITERation = #.   10/prev.

Maximum no. of iterations to maximize the likelihood function.

HALving = #.   5/prev.

The maximum number of step halvings allowed.

The Hierarchical Rule for Moving Variables and Interactions

The hierarchical rule is as follows: an interaction is considered for entry into the model only if all its lower-order interactions and main effects are in the model. Conversely, an interaction term is a candidate for removal only if the model does not have a higher-order interaction that contains the term. For example, if I, J and K are explanatory variables, I*J*K enters only if I, J, K, I*J, I*K and J*K are all in the model; I may be removed only if I*J, I*K and I*J*K are not in the model.

This rule is optional. Negating it (RULE=NONE) allows any term to be entered or removed at any time. If you use SINGLE, only 1 term can be moved into or out of the model at 1 step. If you allow more than 1 term to be moved at 1 step, each term can move other terms with it to meet the requirements of the rule. For example, if I and I*J are in the model, I can be removed if it takes I*J with it.

REGRess ───

RULE = (one only) NONE, SINGLE,   SING/prev.
                  MULTIPLE.

Type of hierarchical rule to be used in entering and removing variables and their interactions from the model.

NONE   -the hierarchical rule is not enforced, i.e., any term can be entered or

removed from the model at any time.

SINGle   -only 1 term can be moved at 1 step; a term can be entered if all its lower-order interactions are already in the model, or a term can be removed if none of its higher-order interactions are already in the model.

MULTiple -any term can be moved at any step, but with each term, all other terms needed to keep the hierarchy will also be moved.

Controlling the Printed Output

At the end of the analysis, a summary description and scatterplots are printed for each "distinct pattern of independent variables." A distinct pattern of independent variables (or a cell) can be either

- all responses for which all the variables considered for moving in or out of the model have the same value,

or

- all responses for which all the variables included in the final model have the same value.

The predicted values are probabilities and so range between 0 and 1. Two HISTOGRAMS can be requested, one for each outcome group. The histograms indicate if the probabilities computed for one outcome are (in general) greater than those for the other.

A table of correct and incorrect classifications, at various cutpoints on the computed probabilities, is also reported.

PRINT ──

CELLS = (one or more) ALL, MODEL,   BOTH/prev.
                      BOTH, NONE.

Cells included in summary report are defined by

ALL   (all variables considered for the model)
MODEL (all variables included in the model)
BOTH   (all variables considered, and included;
        2 sets of reports)
NONE   (summary report on cells is not printed)

SORT = (one only) NONE, PROP,   BOTH/prev.
                  VAR or BOTH.

How cells are sorted in the summary report.

NONE   (unsorted)
PROP   (sorted by proportion of success)
VAR   (sorted by values of variables)
BOTH   (sorted by both proportion of success
        and values of variables)

PLOT.   yes/prev.

Print empirical probability plot and log-odds plots of cells. To negate state NO PLOT.

HISTogram.   yes/prev.

For both groups print histograms of the predicted probabilities of each subject in the first group (useful when the independent variables are interval-scaled). Use NO HIST to omit.

CASE = #.   10/prev.

The number of input cases to be printed.

CORR.   CORR/prev.

Controls printing of the correlation matrix of the parameters. To negate state NO CORR.

Note: In versions before 1981, CELL, SORT, PLOT and HIST were specified in the REGRESS paragraph.

<u>Cross validation.</u> The result of computations can be evaluated on cases not entering the estimation process when specifying the outcome with the COUNT, SCOUNT, or FCOUNT parameter. Cases with zero COUNT, SCOUNT, or FCOUNT do not affect parameter estimation and can be considered for the cross validation. To print output for these cases, specify CELL = ALL or BOTH in the PRINT paragraph.

The COST Matrix for Selecting Appropriate Cutpoints on the Probabilities.

If the misclassification of an outcome into the other group COSTS more than the misclassification of the other outcome into the first group, the selection of appropriate cutpoints on the probabilities should be based on a weighted consideration of the different types of misclassifications. To help with computing the loss at each cutpoint, a 2x2 COST matrix can be requested.

REGRess ──────

COST = A, B, C, D.   0,-1,-1,0/prev.
Numbers indicating the relative gain (or loss) for correctly (or incorrectly) classifying a case. The four values from a 2x2 matrix are:

	Predicted group	
	J	K
observed group J	A	C
K	B	D

A (usually $\geq$ 0) is the gain for classifying a case in group J correctly
B (usually $\leq$ 0) is the loss for misclassifying a case in group K
C (usually $\leq$ 0) is the loss for misclassifying a case in group J
D (usually $\geq$ 0) is the gain for classifying a case in group K correctly.

Controlling Plot Size (new in 1981)

The preassigned plot size (60 characters wide, 40 lines high) can be changed by stating, for example,

SIZE = 40, 25.

PLOT ──────

SIZE = #, #.   60,40/prev.
The first number is the number of characters (width) in the horizontal axis, the second is the no. of lines (height) in the vertical axis.

Controlling Computation Time

The user may specify a limit on the computation time. When the limit is reached, the program will print results available at that time.

PROBLEM ──────

TIME = #.   No limit/prev.
# is the limit on seconds for the program to terminate. The final report is then printed.

Saving Data on BMDP Files

PLR can save the data with the predicted probabilities attached as an additional variable or the cellwise tabulated data with seven additional variables.

SAVE ──────

CONTENT = (one or both) DATA, CELL.   DATA
DATA - (all input variables plus predicted values are saved.)
CELL - If CELL is requested, the summary description for each cell (distinct pattern of the independent variables) is saved (in the order listed) after the values of the p independent variables.

SUCCESS - total number of successes for the pattern (p+1) (the name SUCCESS is replaced by the first name given to the dependent variable in the GROUP paragraph or the NAME given to SCOUNT in the variable paragraph)
FAIL   - total number of failures for the pattern (p+2) (the dependent variable NAME, if given, in the GROUP paragraph overrides the name FAIL - as also does the NAME given FCOUNT in the variable paragraph)
OBSPROP - observed proportion of successes (p+3)
PREDPROP - predicted probability of success (p+4)
SEPRED   - standard deviation of the predicted probability (p+5)
STDRESID - the observed minus the predicted probability divided by the standard error (p+6)
LOGODDS - predicted log odds (p+7)

SIZE OF PROBLEM

PLR analyzes up to tenth-order interactions. The program stores each distinct covariate pattern in computer memory. When the total storage space is 15,000 (M=15,000) the program can handle approximately 160 distinct patterns with 50 variables without interactions, or 1,300 patterns with 10 variables without interactions.

COMPUTATIONAL METHOD

The data are read in single precision. Computations are performed in double precision.
The computational procedure is described in Appendix A.28.

ACKNOWLEDGEMENT

PLR was designed and programmed by Laszlo Engelman. Contributions to the design were made by Alan Forsythe, Ray Mickey, Frank Massey and Virginia Clark.

SUMMARY

Order of Input Cards

```
// (job card)
// EXEC BIMED,PROG=BMDPLR        (see Appendix E)
//SYSIN DD *
/ PROBLEM
/ INPUT
/ VARIABLE
/ GROUP
/ TRANSFORM
/ SAVE
/ REGRESSION
/ PRINT
/ END
    (data, if on cards)
// (system card)
```

Full sets of BMDP paragraphs (and data, if on cards)
can be repeated for additional problems; see Section
5.8.

instructions specific to PLR

Paragraph Statement	Preassigned	Comment and Manual Reference
/ GROUP		Additional option to define groups. Use CODE or CUTP to define two groups for the dependent variable if it does not have the values 1.0 and 0.0. NAMES are given to the two groups to label the output. 43
/•REGRess		Required; each record of the input data can represent the dependent and independent variables for a single case. For data that has already been grouped into cells by patterns of independent variables, each record can represent a group of cases in one of two ways: DEPEND and COUNT, or any two of SCOUNT, FCOUNT, or COUNT.
o DEPENDent = v.	none	Name or subscript of dependent variable. If not 0 (failure) or 1 (success), use GROUP paragraph to define two groups. 334
o COUNT = v.	none	Name or subscript of variable that states the number of cases summarized by this record. 334
o SCOUNT = v.	none	Name or subscript of the variable containing the number of failures for the subjects with the pattern of independent variables recorded for that case. Use with FCOUNT or COUNT. 334
o FCOUNT = v.	none	Name or subscript of the variable containing the number of successes for the subjects with the pattern of independent variables recorded for that case. Use with SCOUNT or COUNT. 334
INTERval = v list.	none	Names or subscripts of the interval-scaled variables. 334
CATEGorical = v list.	(see comment)	Names or subscripts of categorical variables; the program generates a set of design variables for each variable listed. If omitted, all variables are assumed categorical except DEPEND, COUNT, SCOUNT, FCOUNT and those listed in INTERVAL. 334
DVAR = c.	MARG.	MARG, PART, or ORTH, specifying the type of design variables to be generated for categorical covariates. 339
MODEL = v list.	all main effects	Specifies the terms available for consideration in the model. Use names or subscripts. Interactions are stated by connecting the names of the variables with asterisks. Only the highest order interactions need to be stated. A constant term is added to the model by the program. For interval-scaled variables the word "interaction" means "product." 339
START = c list.	IN, IN,...*	IN or OUT (or 2 or 1), one for each term specified in the MODEL statement, indicating whether the term is to be included at the beginning of the stepwise process. 339
CONSTant = c.	IN.	IN or OUT (or 2 or 1), indicating if the CONST is included at the beginning of the stepping. 339
MOVE = # list.	0, 0,...*	One number for each term in MODEL to indicate how many times the term can move into or out of the model. 339
CMOVE = #.	0.	The number of times the CONST can move into or out of the model. 339
METHOD = c.	ACE.	ACE (asymptotic covariance estimate) or MLR (maximum likelihood ratio) (one only) for entering or removing terms at each step. * 339

* If MODEL is not stated, then the default for START is OUT,OUT,... and MOVE is 2,2....

(continued)

(continued)

Paragraph Statement	Preassigned	Comment and Manual Reference
/ REGRess (continued)		
RULE = c.	SING.	Rule for entering and removing variables and their interactions (one only). * 340
		SING - hierarchical rule (only a single term can move at a step); a term is entered only if all its lower order interactions are in, or removed if its higher order interactions are out
		NONE - any term can be entered or removed
		MULT - hierarchical rule (moves all terms needed to maintain the hierarchy)
ENTER = #, #.	.10, .10.	Limits for the tail area probabilities (p-value) for the approximate χ^2 or F values used to control entry or removal of terms. The first number is used for forward stepping, the second for backward stepping
REMOVE = #, #.	.15, .15.	No backward stepping when #1 = #2. The term with the largest p-value > REMOVE is removed first. If no term in the model has p-value larger than the REMOVE limit, the term with the smallest p-value < ENTER is entered. * 339
TOLerance = #.	.0001	Singularity check at each iteration; controls the amount of numerical accuracy. * 339
CONVergence = #.	.0001.	Value of the convergence criterion of the likelihood function. * 340
ITERations = #.	10.	Maximum number of iterations to maximize the likelihood function. * 340
HALVings = #.	5.	Maximum number of stephalvings allowed. * 340
COST = A,B,C,D.	0.,-1.,-1.,0.	"Cost" information can be included in computing the "loss" due to misclassification. * 341
/ SAVE		Additional option required only if a BMDP File of cells is to be created.
CONTent = c list.	DATA.	DATA, CELL (one or both). If CELL is requested, the summary description for each cell (distinct pattern of the independent variables) is saved after the values of the VT independent variables 341
		SUCCESS - total number of successes (VT+1); SUCCESS is replaced by first name specified for DEPEND variable in / GROUP, or name of SCOUNT variable
		FAIL - total number of failures (VT+2) FALL is replace by second name specified for DEPEND variable in / GROUP, or name of FCOUNT variable
		OBSPROP - observed proportion of successes (VT+3)
		PREDPROP - predicted probability of successes (VT+4)
		SEPRED - standard deviation of predicted probability (VT+5)
		STDRESID - observed minus predicted probability divided by standard error (VT+6)
		LOGODDS - predicted log odds (VT+7)
/ PROBLEM		
TIME = #.	no limit	# is the limit on seconds for the program to terminate. The final report is then printed. * 341
/ PLOT		
SIZE = #, #.	60,40	The first number is the number of characters (width) in the horizontal axis and the second number is the number of lines (height) in the vertical axis. * 341

(continued)

(continued)

Paragraph Statement	Preassigned	Comment and Manual Reference
/ PRINT		Optional, see p. 340.
CORR.	CORR.	Controls printing of the correlation matrix of the parameters. To negate state NO CORR. *
COVA.	NO COVA.	Controls printing of the covariance matrix of the paameters. To print, state COVA.*
CELL = c.	NONE.	Controls formation of cells (distinct pattern of independent variables) in summary report (one only): * BOTH – use both ALL and MODEL, yields 2 reports ALL – use patterns of all variables considered MODEL – use only varibles included in the model NONE – no report
SORT = c.	BOTH.	How cells are sorted in the summary reports (one only): * BOTH – sorted by both PROP and VAR PROP – sorted by proportion of success VAR – sorted by the values of the independent variables NONE – unsorted
HISTogram.	NO HIST.	For both groups print histograms of the predicted probabilities of each subject in the first group (useful when independent variables are interval-scaled). *
PLOT.	NO HIST.	Print scatter plots of observed proportion vs. the predicted proportion, and the observed proportion vs. the predicted log odds. Points are plotted for patterns as specified in CELL above. *
COST.	NO COST.	Controls printing of table of cost matrices. To print, state COST. *
CASE = #.	10	The number of input cases to be printed. *

Key:

/	–indicates paragraph	*	–assigned value remains the same for additional problems
.	–period ends a sentence		
●	–required o –may be required	VT	–number of variables after transformations
v	–variable (name or subscript)	list	–more than one item, often one per var.
g	–group (name or subscript)		
#	–number		Capitalized letters–paragraph or sentence names recognized by BMDP
'c'	–characters (name or parameter) may omit apostrophes if contiguous letters only		Page numbers following refer to this Manual

15

ANALYSIS OF VARIANCE AND COVARIANCE

In this chapter we describe five programs that estimate means, variances and regression coefficients and test hypotheses by an analysis of variance (ANOVA) or covariance. They are

P1V performs a one-way ANOVA for each dependent variable to test the equality of group means. If covariates (independent variables) are specified, an analysis of covariance is performed for each dependent variable; the coefficients of the covariates are tested for equality between groups. The equality of means (or adjusted means) between each pair of groups is tested by t statistics. If linear contrasts are specified for the group means, the significance of each contrast is tested by a t test. Scatter plots of each dependent variable, predicted value and residual against the independent variables (covariates) and of residuals against predicted values can be requested.

A one-way ANOVA can also be computed with P7D (Section 9.2) or P9D (Section 9.3). P7D also computes an ANOVA test that does not assume the group variances are equal and plots side-by-side histograms for the groups. Two-way analysis of variance is also available in P7D. Bonferroni probabilities are available for all pairwise comparisons and the program has a diagnostic plot option to aid in the selection of a variance stabilizing transformation. When only two groups are being computed, P3D (Section 9.1) computes two-sample t tests assuming equal or unequal group variances. New in the 1979 BMDP release of P3D is a robust trimmed t test.

P2V performs an analysis of variance or covariance for a wide variety of fixed effects models and for repeated-measures models with equal or unequal cell sizes. Fixed effects models that can be analyzed include factorial designs, Latin squares, fractional factorials, etc.; you can specify the analysis of variance components in the design.

Repeated-measures models are designs in which repeated measurements are made of the same variable for each subject (or case). Split-plot models can be analyzed similarly; a plot is analogous to a subject. If there are two measurements for each subject, the analysis of the within-subjects factors is similar to a paired comparison t test. In a repeated-measures model a distinction is made between variables that classify the cases into groups (grouping factors) and repeated measures of the same variable: grouping factors may be sex, race, disease or control-treatment. A within-subjects factor might be the time of the measurement if a measurement is repeated on each subject at fixed intervals or a treatment factor if each subject receives each treatment. Grouping factors refer to "between subject" effects and repeated-measures factors refer to "within subject" effects. A basic reference for repeated-measures models is Winer (1971). In split-plot designs, factors for main plot treatments are grouping factors and subplot factors correspond to within factors.

Repeated-measures models are a special class of mixed models. The grouping and within factors are all fixed effect factors. A factor for subjects (cases), although not explicitly defined, is the only random effects factor. Each subject is observed at all combinations of the within factors (i.e., is crossed with the within factors), but at only one level of each grouping factor (i.e., is nested within the grouping factors).

P4V extends P2V to multivariate analysis of variance and covariance, including both univariate and multivariate approaches to repeated measures. P4V also tests a wider variety of hypotheses than P2V through the use of cell weights. Multivariate analysis of variance is also included as part of the discriminant analysis program, P7M.

P8V and P3V analyze mixed models. P8V treats equal cell-size problems and uses the Cornfield-Tukey formulas to general expected mean squares, variance components and F statistics. P3V handles unbalanced designs using maximum likelihood estimation.

Control Language

The BMDP instructions to describe the data and variables are common to all BMDP programs and are explained in Chapter 5; the PROBLEM, INPUT, VARIABLE and GROUP paragraphs are used in the programs discussed in this chapter. If data editing or transformations are necessary, the methods described in Chapter 6 can be used. Data can be read using a FORMAT statement or from a BMDP File (Chapter 7).

A summary of the Control Language instructions common to all BMDP programs is on p. 48; summaries of the Control Language instructions specific to each program described in this chapter follow each program. These summaries can be used as indexes to the program descriptions.

P1V

15.1 One-Way Analysis of Variance and Covariance

Laszlo Engelman

ABSTRACT

P1V performs a one-way analysis of variance (ANOVA) for each dependent variable; i.e., it tests the equality of group means or adjusted group means when covariates are specified. The slopes of the covariates are tested for equality (parallelism) among groups. The equality of means (or adjusted means) between each pair of groups is tested by t statistics. User-specified linear contrasts of group means can be tested by a t test. Output includes optional within-group statistics - minimum and maximum values and covariance and correlation matrices. When covariates are specified, output options also include regression coefficients, standard errors and t-values; group means, adjusted group means and standard errors; within-group slope for each covariate; optional correlations between regression coefficients or between adjusted group means.

Each dependent variable, predicted value and residual can be plotted against the independent variables (covariates). Residuals can be plotted against predicted values.

A one-way ANOVA can also be obtained with P7D (Section 9.2). P7D also computes an ANOVA test that does not assume equal group variances and provides side-by-side histograms of the data in the groups, plots cell standard deviations vs. cell means, computes t-tests for each pair of means and reports Bonferroni probabilities.

WHERE TO FIND IT

Example 1V.1 Basic Setup for One-way ANOVA

In our first example we specify that the variable used to classify cases into groups (the GROUPING variable) is BRTHPILL and that the DEPENDENT variables are LOGCHOL and CALCIUM. That is, a one-way ANOVA is to be computed for LOGCHOL and for CALCIUM using the groups specified by BRTHPILL.

The Werner blood chemistry data (Table 5.1) are used to illustrate results computed by P1V. Cholesterol is usually analyzed on a logarithmic scale. In the examples in this section we transform cholesterol (CHOLSTRL) to $\log_{10}$ (cholesterol) by stating in the TRANSFORM paragraph

```
/ TRANSFORM    LOGCHOL IS LOG(CHOLSTRL).
```

and ADDING one variable in the VARIABLE paragraph. We could replace the value of CHOLSTRL by its logarithm, but we choose to add a new variable with a new name (LOGCHOL) to avoid confusion in labeling the results. Control Language transformations are described in Section 6.1.

The other BMDP instructions are described in Chapter 5.

```
------------------------------------
/ PROBLEM    TITLE IS 'WERNER BLOOD CHEMISTRY DATA'.
/ INPUT      VARIABLES ARE 9.
            FORMAT IS '(A4, 5F4.0, 3F4.1)'.
/ VARIABLE   NAMES ARE ID, AGE, HEIGHT, WEIGHT,
                  BRTHPILL, CHOLSTRL, ALBUMIN,
                  CALCIUM, URICACID, LOGCHOL.
            MAXIMUM IS (6)400.
            MINIMUM IS (6)150.
            LABEL IS ID.
            ADD IS 1.
            GROUPING IS BRTHPILL.

/ GROUP      CODES(5) ARE      1,    2.
            NAMES(5) ARE NOPILL, PILL.

/ TRANSFORM LOGCHOL = LOG(CHOLSTRL).

/ DESIGN     DEPENDENT ARE LOGCHOL, CALCIUM.

/ END
------------------------------------
```

(See end of this P1V section for organization of systems information, BMDP instructions and data.)

The results are presented in Output 1V.1. Circled numbers below correspond to those in the output.

① Number of cases read. Only complete cases are used in the analysis; i.e., cases that have no missing values or values out of range. All variables are checked unless a USE statement is specified in the VARIABLE paragraph, in which case only the variables in the USE statement are checked. In addition, if CODES are specified for the GROUPING variable, a case is included only if the value of the GROUPING variable is equal to one of the specified CODES. 180 of the 188 cases are used in the analysis because eight cases have one or more values missing or out of range.

② The number of cases in each group is listed.

Output 1V.1   One-way analysis of variance. Circled numbers correspond to those in the text

----

                    --- the BMDP instructions read by P1V are read and interpreted ---

*** CONTROL LANGUAGE TRANSFORMATIONS ARE PERFORMED ***

    GROUPING VARIABLE IS. . . . . .BRTHPILL

    NUMBER OF CASES READ.   188
        CASES WITH DATA MISSING OR BEYOND LIMITS . .   8   ①
            REMAINING NUMBER OF CASES   180
    NUMBER OF GROUPS FOUND.   2

                        BEFORE TRANSFORMATION   INTERVAL RANGE
    VARIABLE   MINIMUM   MAXIMUM   MISSING   CATEGORY CATEGORY   GREATER   LESS THAN
    NO. NAME   LIMIT   LIMIT   CODE   CODE   NAME   THAN   OR EQUAL TO
     5   BRTHPILL   1.00000   NOPILL
                                                       2.00000   PILL

NUMBER OF CASES PER GROUP

NOPILL   89.   ②
PILL   91.
TOTAL   180.

****
****

ESTIMATES OF MEANS
------------------   ③

                  NOPILL   PILL   TOTAL
                     1   2   3

    CALCIUM   8   9.9977   9.9384   9.9678
    LOGCHOL 10   2.3576   2.3734   2.3656

ONE WAY ANALYSIS OF VARIANCE FOR VARIABLE LOGCHOL
****
ANALYSIS OF VARIANCE
                      ④

    SOURCE OF VARIANCE   D.F.   SUM OF SQ.   MEAN SQ.   F-VALUE   TAIL AREA PROBABILITY
    EQUALITY OF CELL MEANS   1   0.0111   0.0111   1.8265   0.1783
        ERROR   178   1.0857   0.0061

T-TEST MATRIX FOR GROUP MEANS ON   178 DEGREES OF FREEDOM

              NOPILL   PILL
                 1   2   ⑤

    NOPILL   1   0.0
    PILL   2   1.3515   0.0

PROBABILITIES FOR THE T-VALUES ABOVE

              NOPILL   PILL
                 1   2

    NOPILL   1   1.0000
    PILL   2   0.1783   1.0000

----

③ For each group the mean is printed, as well as the mean for all the cases (TOTAL). Let x_{ij} represent the jth observation in the ith group. Then the mean of the ith group is $\bar{x}_i = \Sigma_j x_{ij}/n_i$ where n_i is the number of cases in the group. The overall mean (TOTAL) is $\bar{x} = \Sigma\Sigma x_{ij}/N$ where $N = \Sigma n_i$ is the total frequency.

④ One-way analysis of variance (for LOGCHOL). The equality of the group means is tested by the classical one-way analysis of variance (F statistic). The degrees of freedom of the F statistic are g-1 and N-g, where g is the number of groups. The between sum of squares (between cell means) is

$$BSS = \Sigma n_i(\bar{x}_i - \bar{x})^2 \quad .$$

and the error sum of squares is

$$ESS = \Sigma\Sigma(x_{ij} - \bar{x}_i)^2 \quad .$$

The F statistic (F-value) is

$$F = \frac{BSS/(g-1)}{ESS/(N-g)} \quad .$$

The tail area probability is the probability of exceeding the value of the F statistic when the data are sampled from normal distributions with equal population variances. The probability (size of the test) can be severely affected when the groups have different population variances (Brown and Forsythe, 1974a). P7D, Section 9.2, computes a one-way ANOVA statistic that does not assume homogeneity of variances.

⑤ A t test is computed between each pair of groups to test the equality of group means. When there are no covariates this t statistic is

$$\frac{(\bar{x}_i - \bar{x}_k)\Big/\left(\frac{1}{n_i} + \frac{1}{n_k}\right)^{\frac{1}{2}}}{\{ESS/(N-g)\}^{\frac{1}{2}}} \quad .$$

The numerator is that of the two-sample t test, but the denominator uses the error mean square from the ANOVA. The probabilities computed for the t values are the probabilities of exceeding the absolute values of the t test based on a t variable with N-g degrees of freedom. The probabilities correspond to two-sided tests of the hypothesis that the means of each pair of groups are equal. These probabilities are presented for descriptive purposes. When multiple tests are performed, the procedures in Miller (1966) should be considered.

Specifying an analysis of variance or covariance. Cases are classified into groups by the values of a GROUPING variable. You must specify the GROUPING variable in the VARIABLE paragraph. When CODES or CUTPOINTS are necessary to describe the groups or

when you want to name the groups (to make the results easier to read), you must also include a GROUP paragraph.

VARiable ─────────────────────
　GROUPing = v.　　required　　　　　　no grouping
　　　　　　　　　　　　　　　　　　　　var./prev.
　　Name or subscript of variable used to classify cases into groups. If the GROUPING variable has more than ten distinct values, CODES or CUTPOINTS must be specified in a GROUP paragraph (Section 5.5).

The variables to be analyzed are described in a DESIGN paragraph, which can be repeated before the END paragraph to specify additional analyses of the same data. When

/ DESIGN

only is specified, a one-way analysis of variance is computed for all variables except the GROUPING variable.

You can specify the DEPENDENT variables for which the analysis of variance (no covariates) or analysis of covariance are computed. You can also specify the INDEPENDENT variables (covariates) (see Example 1V.2).

DESIGN ─────────────────────
　DEPENDent = v list.　　　all except GROUPing and
　　　　　　　　　　　　　　　INDEPendent variables
　　Names or subscripts of variables to be analyzed by a one-way analysis of variance or covariance. Each dependent variable is analyzed separately.
　INDEPendent = v list.　　　　　　　　　none
　　Names or subscripts of variables to be used as covariates. If none are specified, a one-way analysis of variance is computed.
　TITLE='c'.　　$\leq$ 160 char.　　　blank
　　A title for the analysis.

Selecting GROUPS

You can select groups to be included in the analysis by specifying the GROUPS to be compared in the DESIGN paragraph. If GROUPS are not specified, all the groups are compared in the analysis.

DESIGN ─────────────────────
　GROUP = g list.　　　　　all groups/prev.
　　Group NAMES (from the GROUP paragraph) or group subscripts. A group subscript is the sequence number of the code or interval that defines the group (not the value of its CODE or CUTPOINT). The groups specified are compared by the analysis of variance or covariance.

Output 1V.2   One-way analysis of covariance

ESTIMATES OF MEANS

		NOPILL 1	PILL 2	TOTAL 3
AGE	2	32.9772	34.0876	33.5385
HEIGHT	3	64.0559	64.8678	64.4663
WEIGHT	4	129.4379	132.7140	131.0941
CALCIUM	8	9.9977	9.9384	9.9678
LOGCHOL	10	2.3576	2.3734	2.3656

DEPENDENT VARIABLE IS LOGCHOL
****

COVARIATE	REG.COEFF.	STD.ERR.	T-VALUE
AGE	0.00269	0.00057	4.68296 ⑥
HEIGHT	-0.00251	0.00253	-0.98909
WEIGHT	0.00033	0.00031	1.04947

GROUP	N	GRP.MEAN	ADJ.GRP.MEAN	STD.ERR.
NOPILL	89.	2.35763	2.35865	0.00783 ⑦
PILL	91.	2.37336	2.37236	0.00774

ANALYSIS OF VARIANCE

SOURCE OF VARIANCE ⑧	D.F.	SUM OF SQ.	MEAN SQ.	F-VALUE	TAIL AREA PROBABILITY
EQUALITY OF ADJ. CELL MEANS	1	0.0082	0.0082	1.5294	0.2179
ZERO SLOPE	3	0.1453	0.0484	9.0126	0.0000
ERROR	175	0.9404	0.0054		
EQUALITY OF SLOPES	3	0.0163	0.0054	1.0113	0.3891
ERROR	172	0.9241	0.0054		

SLOPE WITHIN EACH GROUP
----
⑨

		NOPILL 1	PILL 2
AGE	2	0.0035	0.0019
HEIGHT	3	-0.0003	-0.0053
WEIGHT	4	-0.0001	0.0007

T-TEST MATRIX FOR ADJUSTED GROUP MEANS ON   175 DEGREES OF FREEDOM

		NOPILL 1	PILL 2	⑩
NOPILL	1	0.0		
PILL	2	1.2366	0.0	

PROBABILITIES FOR THE T-VALUES ABOVE

		NOPILL 1	PILL 2
NOPILL	1	1.0000	
PILL	2	0.2179	1.0000

Example 1V.2 Analysis of Covariance

In an analysis of covariance, you must also specify the covariates. The covariates are specified as INDEPENDENT variables. This instruction is added to the DESIGN paragraph of the Control Language in Example 1V.1.

```
------------------------------------
/ DESIGN  DEPENDENT ARE LOGCHOL, CALCIUM.
          INDEPENDENT ARE AGE, HEIGHT, WEIGHT.
------------------------------------
```

The results are presented in Output 1V.2. Circled numbers below correspond to those in the output.

⑥ The first DEPENDENT variable is LOGCHOL. The model fitted to the data is

$$y_{ij} = \mu_i + \beta_1(x_{1ij} - \bar{x}_1) + \beta_2(x_{2ij} - \bar{x}_2) + \cdots$$

where x_{nij} is the jth value in the ith group for the nth covariate. The estimates of $\beta_m (\hat{\beta}_m)$ are printed as the regression coefficients. The standard error of the estimate is printed in the second column. The t value is the ratio of $\hat{\beta}$ to its standard error; it can be used as a test of the significance of the regression coefficient.

⑦ For each group the group mean $\bar{y}_i$ is printed. The adjusted group mean is

$$\hat{\mu}_i = \bar{y}_i + \sum_m \hat{\beta}_m(\bar{x}_m - \bar{x}_{mi}) .$$

The standard error of the adjusted group mean is also printed.

⑧ The analysis of variance is now an analysis of covariance. The computational formulas are in Appendix A.17.
The analysis of covariance is patterned after the analysis described in Dixon and Massey (1969, Chapter 12).
The first test in the analysis of variance table is for the equality of the adjusted cell means, i.e., the test that μ_i are equal in the model in ⑥. The second test is for zero slope for the covariates, i.e., the test that the coefficients β_m are zero (the μ_i can be different).
The third test in the analysis of variance table uses the model

$$y_{ij} = \mu_i + \beta_{1i}(x_{1ij} - \bar{x}_1) + \beta_{2i}(x_{2ij} - \bar{x}_2) + \cdots$$

and tests whether

$$\beta_{11} = \beta_{12} = \cdots = \beta_{1g}$$
$$\beta_{21} = \beta_{22} = \cdots = \beta_{2g}$$

etc.

i.e., tests the equality of the coefficients for each covariate between groups. When this test is significant, the data do not fit the model in ⑥ and hence the first two tests are inappropriate. When the third test is significant, the residual plots described on p.352 may identify whether there are extreme values in your data or whether a transformation of the data is needed before doing a reanalysis.

⑨ The slope within each group is the regression coefficient for each covariate in the model

$$y_{ij} = \mu_i + \beta_{1i}(x_{1ij} - \bar{x}_1) + \beta_{2i}(x_{2ij} - \bar{x}_2) + \cdots$$

⑩ The tests for adjusted group means are t tests between the adjusted means for each pair of group means. In the second panel the two-tailed probabilities are printed. The usual caution is needed in concluding significance when multiple tests are made.

Example 1V.3 Plots

To illustrate the PLOTS produced by P1V we add the instruction PLOT to the DESIGN paragraph as follows:

```
------------------------------------
/ DESIGN   DEPENDENT IS LOGCHOL.
           INDEPENDENT ARE AGE, HEIGHT, WEIGHT.
           PLOT.
------------------------------------
```

In Output 1V.3 the following scatter plots are printed:

⑪ the observed value (0) and the predicted value (P) of the dependent variable (LOGCHOL) against each independent variable (AGE is shown) for each group separately; asterisks indicate overlap between observed and predicted values

⑫ the residual (R=0-P) against the same independent variable for each group separately

⑬ the residual (R) against the predicted value for each group

⑭ the squared residual $(S=R^2)$ against the predicted value for each group

```
DESIGN ─────────────────────────────
  PLOT.                                  no
    When PLOT is specified, the following scatter
    plots are printed:
    - observed values of the dependent variable,
    predicted values, and residuals against each
    covariate for each group separately
    - residuals and residuals squared against the
    predicted values for each group separately
```

Output 1V.3   Plots of the covariates

OBSERVED, PREDICTED VALUES AND RESIDUALS OF THE DEPENDENT VARIABLE
VERSUS EACH COVARIATE FOR EACH GROUP

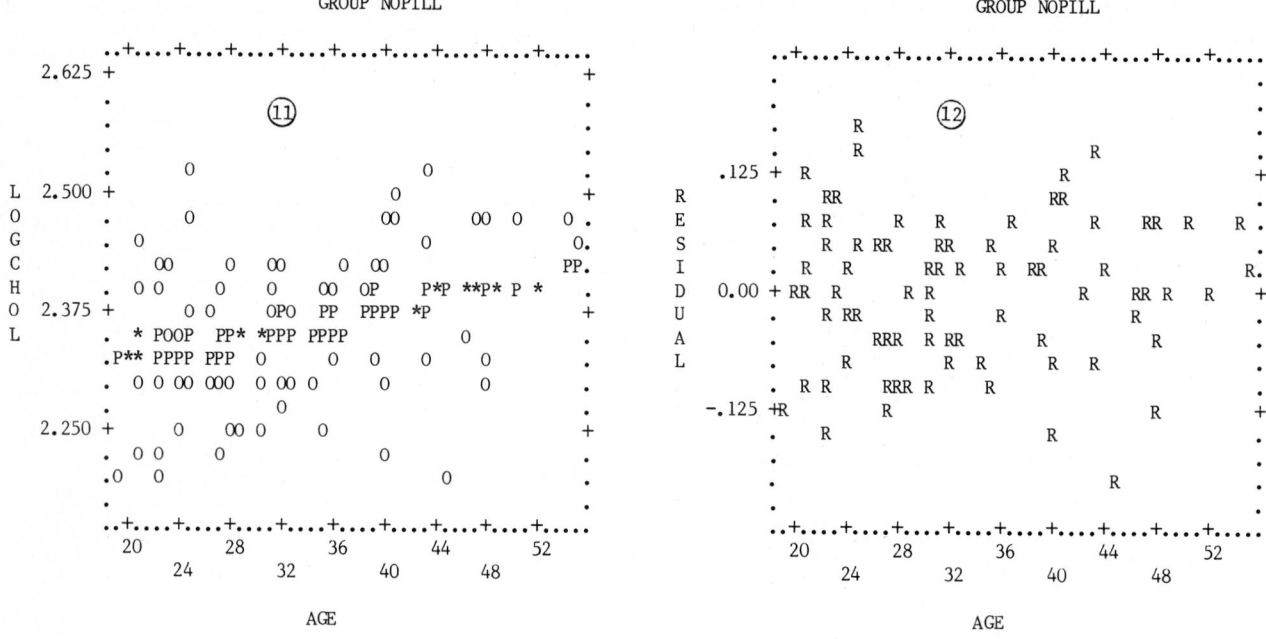

--- similar plots are printed for group PILL ---

--- four plots for HEIGHT and WEIGHT appear here ---

PREDICTED DEPENDENT VAR. VS RESIDUALS FOR EACH GROUP.

--- similar plots are printed for group PILL ---

Example 1V.4 Contrasts

You can specify contrasts (linear combinations of the means μ_i); P1V tests whether each contrast is zero (but not whether all contrasts simultaneously are zero).

In our example we classify the cases according to four AGE groupings. The one-way analysis of covariance yields a highly significant F value for the test of equality of adjusted cell means (see Output 1V.4). We are interested in knowing if the AGE effect is primarily linear or if it has a significant nonlinear component. Therefore we specify three CONTRASTS on the adjusted group means:

-3,	-1,	1,	3	linear effect
-1,	1,	1,	-1	quadratic effect
-1,	3,	-3,	1	cubic effect

These contrasts test hypotheses about the group means. (Although these contrasts are orthogonal in terms of their coefficients, their sums of squares may not be orthogonal if the number of observations differs between groups or if there are covariates.) We replace the GROUP paragraph of Example 1V.1 by

```
-------------------------------------
/ GROUP    CUTPOINTS(2) ARE 25, 35, 45.
          NAMES(2) ARE '25ORLESS', '26 to 35',
                       '36 to 45', 'OVER 45'.
-------------------------------------
```

and add the contrast specifications to the DESIGN paragraph. The DESIGN paragraph as modified is as follows:

```
-------------------------------------
/ DESIGN   DEPENDENT IS LOGCHOL.
          INDEPENDENT ARE HEIGHT, WEIGHT.
          CONTRAST IS -3, -1,  1,  3.
          CONTRAST IS -1,  1,  1, -1.
          CONTRAST IS -1,  3, -3,  1.
-------------------------------------
```

(15) The results are presented in Output 1V.4. The last panel in the results presents the contrast, its t value and the probability of exceeding t (P(T) is a two-tailed probability). The t value is computed as the ratio of $\Sigma c_m \hat{\mu}_m$ to its standard error where c_1, c_2,... are the coefficients in the contrast and $\hat{\mu}_1$, $\hat{\mu}_2$,... are the adjusted group means. The formula for the standard error is given in Appendix A.17.

```
DESIGN
  CONTRast = # list.   may be repeated        none
    Coefficients used to define a contrast on the
    adjusted group means (or the group means if
    there are no covariates). CONTRAST = may be
    repeated in the DESIGN paragraph to specify
    additional contrasts on the adjusted group
    means. Each contrast is tested by a two-sided t
    test.
```

Output 1V.4 Testing user specified contrasts across group means (the test results appear in (15) below)

```
          GROUPING VARIABLE IS. . . . . . . . . . . . .AGE

          NUMBER OF CASES READ. . . . . . . . . . . .      188
              CASES WITH DATA MISSING OR BEYOND LIMITS . .    8
                 REMAINING NUMBER OF CASES . . . . . . . .  180
          NUMBER OF GROUPS FOUND. . . . . . . . . . . .      4
```

		BEFORE	TRANSFORMATION				INTERVAL	RANGE
VARIABLE		MINIMUM	MAXIMUM	MISSING	CATEGORY	CATEGORY	GREATER	LESS THAN
NO.	NAME	LIMIT	LIMIT	CODE	CODE	NAME	THAN	OR EQUAL TO
2	AGE					25ORLESS		25.00000
						26 TO 35	25.00000	35.00000
						36 TO 45	35.00000	45.00000
						OVER 45	45.00000	

```
          NUMBER OF CASES PER GROUP
          -------------------------
          25ORLESS   50.
          26 TO 35   59.
          36 TO 45   41.
          OVER 45    30.
          TOTAL     180.
```

(output continued)

Output 1V.4 (continued)

DEPENDENT VARIABLE IS LOGCHOL
****

COVARIATE	REG.COEFF.	STD.ERR.	T-VALUE
HEIGHT	-0.00183	0.00252	-0.72638
WEIGHT	0.00037	0.00031	1.17551

GROUP	N	GRP.MEAN	ADJ.GRP.MEAN	STD.ERR.
25ORLESS	50.	2.34059	2.34245	0.01059
26 TO 35	59.	2.34643	2.34680	0.00960
36 TO 45	41.	2.38815	2.38685	0.01157
OVER 45	30.	2.41412	2.41206	0.01358

ANALYSIS OF VARIANCE

SOURCE OF VARIANCE	D.F.	SUM OF SQ.	MEAN SQ.	F-VALUE	TAIL AREA PROBABILITY
EQUALITY OF ADJ. CELL MEANS	3	0.1247	0.0416	7.6562	0.0001
ZERO SLOPE	2	0.0077	0.0039	0.7103	0.4929
ERROR	174	0.9446	0.0054		
EQUALITY OF SLOPES	6	0.0144	0.0024	0.4341	0.8553
ERROR	168	0.9302	0.0055		

SLOPE WITHIN EACH GROUP

		25ORLESS	26 TO 35	36 TO 45	OVER 45
		1	2	3	4
HEIGHT	3	-0.0016	-0.0044	-0.0059	0.0052
WEIGHT	4	0.0003	0.0003	0.0006	0.0003

T-TEST MATRIX FOR ADJUSTED GROUP MEANS ON 174 DEGREES OF FREEDOM

		25ORLESS	26 TO 35	36 TO 45	OVER 45
		1	2	3	4
25ORLESS	1	0.0			
26 TO 35	2	0.3045	0.0		
36 TO 45	3	2.8054	2.6611	0.0	
OVER 45	4	3.9975	3.9191	1.4236	0.0

PROBABILITIES FOR THE T-VALUES ABOVE

		25ORLESS	26 TO 35	36 TO 45	OVER 45
		1	2	3	4
25ORLESS	1	1.0000			
26 TO 35	2	0.7611	1.0000		
36 TO 45	3	0.0056	0.0085	1.0000	
OVER 45	4	0.0001	0.0001	0.1564	1.0000

T-VALUES FOR CONTRASTS IN ADJUSTED GROUP MEANS

CONTRAST NUMBER	T	P(T) (15)	GROUP 25ORLESS	GROUP 26 TO 35	GROUP 36 TO 45	GROUP OVER 45
1	4.5542	0.0000	-3.0000	-1.0000	1.0000	3.0000
2	-0.9193	0.3592	-1.0000	1.0000	1.0000	-1.0000
3	-1.0512	0.2946	-1.0000	3.0000	-3.0000	1.0000

Example 1V.5 Additional Descriptive Statistics Printed for Each Cell

A PRINT paragraph is added before the END paragraph to the Control Language presented in Example 1V.2.

```
------------------------------------
/ PRINT    MAXIMUM.
           MINIMUM.
           MEAN.
           CORRELATION.
           TOTAL.
           BETWEEN.
           WITHIN.
           RREG.
           MCORRELATION.
------------------------------------
```

The additional results are presented in Output 1V.5. Circled numbers below correspond to those in the output.

(16) MINIMUM: The observed minimums for all variables in each group are printed.

(17) MAXIMUM: The observed maximums for all variables in each group are printed.

(18) MEAN: The means for all variables in each group are printed.

Output 1V.5 Within cell descriptive statistics printed by P1V

```
NUMBER OF CASES PER GROUP
-------------------------
NOPILL    89.
PILL      91.
TOTAL    180.
```

OBSERVED MINIMA

(16)		NOPILL 1	PILL 2
AGE	2	19.0000	19.0000
HEIGHT	3	57.0000	59.0000
WEIGHT	4	95.0000	94.0000
BRTHPILL	5	1.0000	2.0000
CHOLSTRL	6	155.0000	160.0000
ALBUMIN	7	3.2000	3.2000
CALCIUM	8	9.0000	8.8000
URICACID	9	2.7000	2.2000
LOGCHOL	10	2.1903	2.2041

OBSERVED MAXIMA

(17)		NOPILL 1	PILL 2
AGE	2	55.0000	55.0000
HEIGHT	3	69.0000	71.0000
WEIGHT	4	195.0000	215.0000
BRTHPILL	5	1.0000	2.0000
CHOLSTRL	6	335.0000	390.0000
ALBUMIN	7	5.0000	4.7000
CALCIUM	8	11.1000	10.8000
URICACID	9	7.8000	9.9000
LOGCHOL	10	2.5250	2.5911

ESTIMATES OF MEANS

(18)		NOPILL 1	PILL 2
AGE	2	32.9772	34.0876
HEIGHT	3	64.0559	64.8678
WEIGHT	4	129.4379	132.7140
BRTHPILL	5	1.0000	2.0000
CHOLSTRL	6	231.8873	239.7030
ALBUMIN	7	4.2056	4.0373
CALCIUM	8	9.9977	9.9384
URICACID	9	4.7382	4.7725
LOGCHOL	10	2.3576	2.3734

(output continued)

Output 1V.5 (continued)

CORRELATION MATRIX   GROUP NOPILL
----

⑲		AGE 2	HEIGHT 3	WEIGHT 4	CHOLSTRL 6	ALBUMIN 7	CALCIUM 8	URICACID 9	LOGCHOL 10
AGE	2	1.0000							
HEIGHT	3	0.1088	1.0000						
WEIGHT	4	0.2456	0.4278	1.0000					
CHOLSTRL	6	0.4132	0.0303	0.0790	1.0000				
ALBUMIN	7	-0.1350	0.1815	-0.2332	0.0505	1.0000			
CALCIUM	8	-0.0904	0.2805	0.0374	0.3033	0.4731	1.0000		
URICACID	9	0.2312	0.1205	0.2184	0.2843	0.1033	0.1482	1.0000	
LOGCHOL	10	0.4048	0.0273	0.0787	0.9948	0.0333	0.2958	0.2634	1.0000

CORRELATION MATRIX   GROUP PILL

		AGE 2	HEIGHT 3	WEIGHT 4	CHOLSTRL 6	ALBUMIN 7	CALCIUM 8	URICACID 9	LOGCHOL 10
AGE	2	1.0000							
HEIGHT	3	0.0548	1.0000						
WEIGHT	4	0.2578	0.5072	1.0000					
CHOLSTRL	6	0.3137	-0.0397	0.1934	1.0000				
ALBUMIN	7	-0.0062	-0.1133	-0.2158	0.1134	1.0000			
CALCIUM	8	0.0784	0.0217	0.0992	0.2175	0.4301	1.0000		
URICACID	9	0.1920	0.1296	0.3587	0.2695	-0.0185	0.1866	1.0000	
LOGCHOL	10	0.3084	-0.0537	0.1885	0.9927	0.1154	0.2532	0.2573	1.0000

```
**********************************************************************************************
**********************************************************************************************
```

ESTIMATES OF MEANS

		NOPILL 1	PILL 2	TOTAL 3
AGE	2	32.9772	34.0876	33.5385
HEIGHT	3	64.0559	64.8678	64.4663
WEIGHT	4	129.4379	132.7140	131.0941
LOGCHOL	10	2.3576	2.3734	2.3656

VARIANCE-COVARIANCE MATRIX   TOTAL

D.F.= 179.

⑳		AGE 2	HEIGHT 3	WEIGHT 4	LOGCHOL 10
AGE	2	97.9736			
HEIGHT	3	2.1902	6.1609		
WEIGHT	4	51.7948	24.0906	420.2422	
LOGCHOL	10	0.2784	0.0011	0.2280	0.0061

VARIANCE-COVARIANCE MATRIX   BETWEEN

D.F.= 1.

㉑		AGE 2	HEIGHT 3	WEIGHT 4	LOGCHOL 10
AGE	2	55.4789			
HEIGHT	3	40.5670	29.6632		
WEIGHT	4	163.6814	119.6863	482.9153	
LOGCHOL	10	0.7862	0.5749	2.3195	0.0111

VARIANCE-COVARIANCE MATRIX   WITHIN

D.F.= 178.

㉒		AGE 2	HEIGHT 3	WEIGHT 4	LOGCHOL 10
AGE	2	98.2124			
HEIGHT	3	1.9746	6.0289		
WEIGHT	4	51.1662	23.5536	419.8899	
LOGCHOL	10	0.2756	-0.0021	0.2162	0.0061

CORRELATION MATRIX FOR THE REGRESSION COEFFICIENTS

㉓		AGE 2	HEIGHT 3	WEIGHT 4
AGE	2	1.0000		
HEIGHT	3	0.0430	1.0000	
WEIGHT	4	-0.2429	-0.4641	1.0000

CORRELATION MATRIX FOR THE ADJUSTED GROUP MEANS

㉔		NOPILL 1	PILL 2
NOPILL	1	1.0000	
PILL	2	-0.0146	1.0000

--- analysis for CHOLSTRL appears here ---

----

⑲ CORRELATION: The correlations between all variables except the GROUPING variable in each group are printed. The covariances are printed if COVARIANCE is specified.

⑳ TOTAL
㉑ BETWEEN   } are three variance-covariance matrices computed using all variables (DEPENDent and INDEPendent) in the analysis
㉒ WITHIN

When TOTAL is specified, the variances and covariances are computed without regard to the grouping; that is, the sum of squares between two variables x and y is computed as

$$SS_{TOTAL} = \Sigma\Sigma\ (x_{ij} - \bar{x})(y_{ij} - \bar{y})\ .$$

The number of degrees of freedom is N-1, where N is the number of cases.
When WITHIN is specified, the variances and covariances are computed from the pooled within-group sum of squares; that is

$$SS_{WITHIN} = \Sigma\Sigma\ (x_{ij} - \bar{x}_i)(y_{ij} - \bar{y}_i)\ .$$

The number of degrees of freedom is N-g.
The BETWEEN sum of squares is computed as the difference between the TOTAL and WITHIN sums of squares; that is,

$$SS_{BETWEEN} = SS_{TOTAL} - SS_{WITHIN}\ .$$

The number of degrees of freedom is g-1.

㉓ RREGRESSION: Correlations between the estimates of the regression coefficients (coefficients of the covariates) are printed.

㉔ MCORRELATION: Correlations between the adjusted group means are printed.

PRINT
MINimum.   no/prev.
  Print minimums for all variables in each group.
MAXimum.   no/prev.
  Print maximums for all variables in each group.
MEAN.   no/prev.
  Print means for all variables in each group.
COVAriance.   no/prev.
  Print covariances between all variables in each group except the GROUPING variable.
CORRelation.   no/prev.
  Print correlations between all variables in each group except the GROUPING variable.
TOTal.   no/prev.
  Print variance-covariance matrix for the DEPENDENT and INDEPENDENT variables. It is computed with no grouping (see explanation above).
BETween.   no/prev.
  Print variance-covariance matrix for the DEPENDENT and INDEPENDENT variables. It is computed from the difference between the total and pooled variance-covariance matrices (see explanation above).

WIThin.   no/prev.
  Print variance-covariance matrix for the DEPENDENT and INDEPENDENT variables. It is computed from the pooled within-group sum of squares (see explanation above).
RREGression.   no/prev.
  Print correlations between the estimates of the coefficients of the covariates.
MCORrelation.   no/prev.
  Print the correlations between the adjusted group means.

SIZE OF PROBLEM

The maximum problem that can be analyzed at most facilities depends on the number of groups (G) and the total number (V) of INDEPENDENT and DEPENDENT variables.

If V is less than or equal to	10	15	20	15	30
Then G can be as high as	58	27	13	27	3

Appendix B describes how to increase the capacity of the program.

COMPUTATIONAL METHOD

All computations are performed in single precision. Means, standard deviations and covariances are computed by the method of provisional means (Appendix A.2). The computations performed by P1V are described in Appendix A.17.

ACKNOWLEDGEMENT

P1V was designed by Laszlo Engelman and programmed by Laszlo Engelman and Koji Yamasaki.

SUMMARY

Order or Input Cards

```
// (job card)
// EXEC BIMED,PROG=BMDP1V        (see Appendix E)
//SYSIN DD *
/ PROBLEM
/ INPUT
/ VARIABLE
/ GROUP
/ TRANSFORM
/ SAVE
/ DESIGN      ] Repeat for subproblems
/ PRINT
/ END
    (data if on cards)
// (system card)
```

Full sets of BMDP paragraphs (and data, if on cards) can be repeated for additional problems; see Section 5.8.

357

Paragraph Statement	Preassigned	Comment and Manual Reference
/●VARiable		Required to classify cases into groups.
●GROUPing = v.		Name or subscript of variable used to define group membership. (See also / GROUP.) * 349
- - - - - - - - - -	- - - - - -	- -
/●DESIGN		Required to describe variables to be analyzed (may be repeated). When / DESIGN is specified with no parameters a one-way ANOVA is **computed** for all variables except the GROUPING variable.
●DEPENDent = v list.	all except **GROUPing**, INDEP	Names or subscripts of variables to be analyzed by a one-way analysis of variance or covariance. Each variable in the list is analyzed separately. 349
INDEP = v list.	none	Names or subscripts of variables to be used as covariates. If no variables are specified, a one-way analysis of variance is computed.
GROUPs = g list.	all groups	Group NAMES (from / GROUP) or subscripts (by order - not by CODE or CUTP value) to be compared in the analysis of variance or covariance. *
TITLE = 'c'.	**blank**	Title, up to 160 characters, to label the output. 349
PLOT.	no	Print 4 plots for each group for each covariate: observed and predicted values vs. covariates, residual vs. covariate, residual vs. predicted value and residual squared vs. predicted value. 351
CONTRast = # list.	none	Coefficients used to define a contrast on the (adjusted) group means for test (may be repeated). 353
- - - - - - - - - -	- - - - - -	- -
/ PRINT		Optional to specify printed output. The following options are not printed unless specified. 357
MINimum.	no	Minimum for each variable in each group. *
MAXimum.	no	Maximum for each variable in each group. *
MEAN.	no	Means for each variable in each group. *
COVAriance.	no	Covariances between all variables in each group, except the GROUPING variable. *
CORRelation.	no	Correlations between all variables in each group, except the GROUPING variable. *
TOTal.	no	Covariance matrix for DEPEND and INDEP variables; computed with no grouping.
BETween.	no	Covariance matrix for DEPEND and INDEP variables; the difference between TOT and WITH. *
WITHin.	no	Pooled within-group covariance matrix for the DEPEND and INDEP variables. *
RREGression.	no	Correlations between the estimates of the coefficients of the covariates. *
MCORrelation.	no	Correlations between the adjusted group means. *

Key:

/	-indicates paragraph	*	-assigned value remains the same for additional problems
.	-period ends a sentence		
●	-required	VT	-number of variables after transformations
v	-variable (name or subscript)	list	-more than one item, often one per var.
g	-group (name or subscript)		
#	-number		Capitalized letters-paragraph or sentence names recognized by BMDP
'c'	-characters (name or parameter) may omit apostrophes if contiguous letters only		Page numbers following refer to this Manual

P2V

15.2 Analysis of Variance and Covariance Including Repeated Measures

Robert Jennrich
Paul Sampson
James Frane

ABSTRACT

P2V performs an analysis of variance or covariance for a wide variety of fixed effects models and for repeated-measures (split-plot, changeover) models with equal or unequal cell sizes. Fixed effects models that can be analyzed include factorial designs, Latin squares, fractional factorials, etc; you can specify the analysis of variance components in the model. Multivariate analysis of variance and covariance is available in P4V.

In repeated-measures models, repeated measurements are made of the same variable for each subject (or case) at different times under possibly different conditions. Split-plot models can be analyzed similarly; a plot is analogous to a subject. If there are two measurements for each subject, the analysis is similar to a paired-comparison t test. In a repeated-measures model a distinction is made between a factor that classifies the subjects into groups (grouping factor) and a factor for which each subject is measured at all levels (within-subjects factor). Sex, race, disease or treatment could be a grouping factor. A within-subjects factor might be the time of the measurement if a measurement is made on each subject at fixed intervals or a course of treatment if each subject receives each treatment. Grouping factors refer to "between group" effects and within-subjects factors refer to effects measured by differences "within subject". A basic reference for repeated-measures models is Winer (1971). In split-plot designs, factors for main plot treatments are grouping factors and subplot factors are within-subject factors. The P2V writeup is supplemented by Frane (1980a).

Repeated-measures models are a special class of mixed models. The grouping and within-subjects factors are all fixed-effects factors. A factor for

subjects (cases), implicitly defined, is the only random effects factor. Each subject is observed at all combinations of the within-subject factor levels, but at only one level of each grouping factor. (In the language of mixed models, the implicit subject factor is nested in the grouping factors and crossed with the within-subjects factors.) Grouping factors are also called between-groups or whole-plot factors. Within-subjects factors are also called trial factors, split-plot factors, repeated-measures factors, or simply within factors.

P2V can analyze models that have grouping factors or within factors or both. Other mixed models can be analyzed if the design is balanced (equal number of observations in each cell) and if you select the appropriate error term to test each analysis of variance component. For mixed models with equal cell sizes, see program P8V. For unbalanced mixed models, see P3V. Both the grouping factors and the within factors must be crossed (not nested) in P2V. P2V uses the univariate approach to repeated measures. Many statisticians prefer a multivariate analysis of variance approach as is available in P4V.

There are many aspects to the analysis of variance and covariance. We have chosen to present a number of the most frequently used designs. (See the list below in WHERE TO FIND IT.)

One of the examples may be similar to the design that you need. If so, you can skip the discussion of many of the other examples. We describe several examples in greater detail to explain the sums of squares and test statistics computed by P2V. If your example has any grouping factors, we recommend that you read Example 2V.1, and if it has any within factors we recommend that you read Example 2V.6 (one grouping factor and one within factor).

When there are two or more within factors, the factors must be crossed and each subject must be observed at <u>all</u> possible combinations of the within factors. (If not, see Frane, 1980a.) When there are two or more grouping factors, the grouping factors must also be crossed; i.e., the levels of a grouping factor must be repeated at all levels of the other grouping factor.

A covariate can be constant or it can vary across the levels of a within factor for a given subject. Covariates are assumed to be linearly related to the dependent variable.

A case consists of all the data for one subject or experimental unit. There are two ways to specify a design for the analysis of variance (ANOVA) table. In the examples we illustrate both methods.

- One way is to specify the grouping factors (GROUPING), the covariates (COVARIATES), the dependent variables (DEPENDENT) (when there are repeated measures, i.e., within factors, each repeated measure is a dependent variable), and the number of levels (observations) of each within factor (LEVEL).

- A second way to state the design is to specify a FORM statement. In the FORM statement G represents a grouping variable, Y the dependent variable, X a covariate and D a deleted variable (deleted variables are not used in the analysis).

FIXED EFFECTS FACTORIAL DESIGNS (GROUPING VARIABLES ONLY)

Example 2V.1 Basic Setup for a Two-way ANOVA

In this example we analyze the systolic blood pressure data in Table 15.1 (Afifi and Azen, 1972, p.166, and Kutner, 1974). There are two GROUPING factors, TREATMNT (called Drug by Kutner) and DISEASE -- with four TREATMNT groups and three DISEASE groups. Afifi and Azen and Kutner analyze the difference in systolic blood pressures (SYSINCR). For the analysis we think of the SYSINCR values being arranged in these cells

```
                    TREATMNT
                 1  2  3  4
              ┌──┬──┬──┬──┐
           1  │  │  │  │  │
              ├──┼──┼──┼──┤
  DISEASE  2  │  │  │  │  │
              ├──┼──┼──┼──┤
           3  │  │  │  │  │
              └──┴──┴──┴──┘
```

Table 15.1   Data from Afifi and Azen (1972, p.166) omitting the same cases omitted by Kutner (1974)

TREATMNT	DISEASE	SYSINCR	TREATMNT	DISEASE	SYSINCR	TREATMNT	DISEASE	SYSINCR	TREATMNT	DISEASE	SYSINCR
1	1	42	1	3	24	2	3	4	4	1	24
1	1	44	2	1	28	2	3	16	4	1	9
1	1	36	2	1	23	3	1	1	4	1	22
1	1	13	2	1	34	3	1	29	4	1	-2
1	1	19	2	1	42	3	1	19	4	1	15
1	1	22	2	1	13	3	2	11	4	2	27
1	2	33	2	2	34	3	2	9	4	2	12
1	2	26	2	2	33	3	2	7	4	2	12
1	2	33	2	2	31	3	2	1	4	2	-5
1	2	21	2	2	36	3	2	-6	4	2	16
1	3	31	2	3	3	3	3	21	4	2	15
1	3	-3	2	3	26	3	3	1	4	3	22
1	3	25	2	3	28	3	3	9	4	3	7
1	3	25	2	3	32	3	3	3	4	3	25
									4	3	5
(cont'd)			(cont'd)			(cont'd)			4	3	12

Note: TREATMNT corresponds to drugs and is coded 1 to 4. DISEASE is coded 1 to 3. SYSINCR is the increase in systolic pressure (mmHg) due to treatment. TREATMNT is recorded in column 3, DISEASE in column 6 and SYSINCR in columns 8-9.

In our example we use SYSINCR as the DEPENDENT variable in order to obtain the same results as Kutner; however, given the original data, we could alternatively analyze the percentage change in systolic blood pressure with the original blood pressure as a covariate or perform the latter analysis using the logarithm of blood pressure. Note that when there are only two grouping factors, a more detailed analysis can be obtained with P7D.

In the ANOVA table the main effect of each grouping factor is identified by the name of the grouping variable as specified in the VARIABLE paragraph. The first character of the grouping variable names are used to label interactions; therefore the two grouping variables are given names that begin with different letters. In BMDP instructions only the DESIGN paragraph is specific to P2V. The other BMDP instructions are explained in Chapter 5.

```
/ PROBLEM   TITLE IS 'KUTNER SYSTOLIC BLOOD PRESSURE
                      DATA'.
/ INPUT     VARIABLES ARE 3.
            FORMAT IS '(3F3.0)'.
/ VARIABLE  NAMES ARE TREATMNT, DISEASE, SYSINCR.
/ DESIGN    DEPENDENT IS SYSINCR.
            GROUPING ARE TREATMNT, DISEASE.

/ GROUP     CODES(1) ARE     1,     2,     3,     4.
            NAMES(1) ARE DRUG1, DRUG2, DRUG3, DRUG4.
            CODES(2) ARE     1,     2,     3.
            NAMES(2) ARE DISEASE1, DISEASE2, DISEASE3.

/ END
```

(See end of this P2V Section for organization of systems information, BMDP instructions and data)

If the FORM statement is used, the DESIGN paragraph is written

/ DESIGN   FORM IS '2G,Y'.

2G specifies that the first two variables are grouping factors, and Y specifies that the third variable is the dependent variable.

The results are presented in Output 2V.1. Circled numbers below correspond to those in the output.

① The DESIGN paragraph is interpreted by P2V.

② Number of cases read. Only cases containing acceptable values for all variables specified in the DESIGN paragraph are used in the analysis. An acceptable value is a value that is not missing or out of range. In addition, if CODES are specified for any GROUPING factors (variables), a case is included only if the value of the GROUPING factor is equal to a specified CODE.

③ The frequency (COUNT) of observations in each cell is printed.

Output 2V.1   A two-way analysis of variance by P2V. Circled numbers correspond to those in the text

----

--- the BMDP instructions read by P2V are printed and interpreted ---

DESIGN SPECIFICATIONS

```
        GROUP =   1   2    ①
        DEPEND =   3
```

VARIABLE NO. NAME	MINIMUM LIMIT	MAXIMUM LIMIT	MISSING CODE	CATEGORY CODE	CATEGORY NAME	GREATER THAN	LESS THAN OR = TO
1 TREATMNT							
				1.00000	DRUG1		
				2.00000	DRUG2		
				3.00000	DRUG3		
				4.00000	DRUG4		
2 DISEASE							
				1.00000	DISEASE1		
				2.00000	DISEASE2		
				3.00000	DISEASE3		

GROUP STRUCTURE   ③

TREATMNT	DISEASE	COUNT
DRUG1	DISEASE1	6.
DRUG1	DISEASE2	4.
DRUG1	DISEASE3	5.
DRUG2	DISEASE1	5.
DRUG2	DISEASE2	4.
DRUG2	DISEASE3	6.
DRUG3	DISEASE1	3.
DRUG3	DISEASE2	5.
DRUG3	DISEASE3	4.
DRUG4	DISEASE1	5.
DRUG4	DISEASE2	6.
DRUG4	DISEASE3	5.

NUMBER OF CASES READ.   58   ②

(output continued)

Output 2V.1 (continued)

CELL MEANS FOR 1-ST DEPENDENT VARIABLE ④

TREATMNT= DISEASE =	DRUG1 DISEASE1	DRUG1 DISEASE2	DRUG1 DISEASE3	DRUG2 DISEASE1	DRUG2 DISEASE2	DRUG2 DISEASE3	DRUG3 DISEASE1	DRUG3 DISEASE2	DRUG3 DISEASE3	DRUG4 DISEASE1
SYSINCR	29.33333	28.25000	20.40000	28.00000	33.50000	18.16667	16.33333	4.40000	8.50000	13.60000
COUNT	6	4	5	5	4	6	3	5	4	5

TREATMNT= DISEASE =	DRUG4 DISEASE2	DRUG4 DISEASE3	MARGINAL
SYSINCR	12.83333	14.20000	18.87931
COUNT	6	5	58

STANDARD DEVIATIONS FOR 1-ST DEPENDENT VARIABLE

TREATMNT= DISEASE =	DRUG1 DISEASE1	DRUG1 DISEASE2	DRUG1 DISEASE3	DRUG2 DISEASE1	DRUG2 DISEASE2	DRUG2 DISEASE3	DRUG3 DISEASE1	DRUG3 DISEASE2	DRUG3 DISEASE3	DRUG4 DISEASE1
SYSINCR	13.01794	5.85235	13.37161	10.97725	2.08167	12.52863	14.18920	6.91375	9.00000	10.54988

TREATMNT= DISEASE =	DRUG4 DISEASE2	DRUG4 DISEASE3
SYSINCR	10.34247	8.92749

ANALYSIS OF VARIANCE FOR 1-ST ⑤
DEPENDENT VARIABLE - SYSINCR

	SOURCE	SUM OF SQUARES	DEGREES OF FREEDOM	MEAN SQUARE	F	TAIL PROB.
	MEAN	20037.61301	1	20037.61301	181.41	0.0000
	TREATMNT	2997.47186	3	999.15729	9.05	0.0001
	DISEASE	415.87305	2	207.93652	1.88	0.1637
	TD	707.26626	6	117.87771	1.07	0.3958
1	ERROR	5080.81667	46	110.45254		

----

④ The mean, frequency and standard deviation of each cell for each dependent variable are printed.

⑤ An ANOVA table is printed.

The sums of squares in the one-way ANOVA are well known. The sums of squares in the two-way, or higher, ANOVA depend upon the hypothesis of interest unless each cell contains the same number of observations. The hypotheses tested by P2V are the same for equal or unequal cell size problems, and are not affected by losing some of the cases. Although the hypotheses tested are independent, the sums of squares for unequal cell size problems are not in general orthogonal. Orthogonal sums of squares methods (or "sequential" methods) test hypotheses that are functions of cell sizes; P2V does not use a sequential method. For more detailed discussions, see Kutner (1974) and Speed and Hocking (1976). (The hypotheses tested by P2V for the main effects are labelled A and B by Kutner and H1 and H2 by Speed and Hocking.) They, as well as others,

recommend these hypotheses for experimental data. Searle (1971, pp. 316-317) points out that sequential methods test hypotheses that depend on the cell sizes and cautions against their use. More general hypotheses can be tested in BMDP4V.

Hypotheses tested. In our example of a two-way ANOVA, let $E(Y_{ij}) = \mu_{ij}$ where Y_{ij} is an observation of the group (i,j). The test of equality of row means is the test that

$$\Sigma_j \mu_{ij} = \Sigma_j \mu_{kj} \qquad \text{for all } i, k.$$

The test of equality of column means is the test that

$$\Sigma_i \mu_{ij} = \Sigma_i \mu_{i\ell} \qquad \text{for all } j, \ell.$$

The test of no interaction is the test that

$$\mu_{ij} + \mu_{kl} = \mu_{il} + \mu_{kj} \qquad \text{for all } i \neq k \text{ and } j \neq l.$$

The test labelled MEAN is the test that

$$\Sigma_i \Sigma_j \mu_{ij} = 0 .$$

The test for MEAN is usually not of interest unless the dependent variable is the difference between two measurements. Note that this is a test of the average population cell mean; it is not a test of whether the average of all observations has zero expected value. The latter test would be a test of whether $\Sigma n_{ij}\mu_{ij} = 0$, where n_{ij} is the number of cases in cell i,j. (Such a test can be obtained in P4V.)

If the model is written

$$E(Y_{ij}) = \mu + \alpha_i + \beta_j + \gamma_{ij}$$

with the usual constraints

$$\Sigma_i \alpha_i = 0, \qquad \Sigma_j \beta_j = 0, \qquad \Sigma_i \gamma_{ij} = \Sigma_j \gamma_{ij} = 0,$$

the hypotheses described above can also be stated as

$$\alpha_i = 0 \qquad \text{for all } i$$
$$\beta_j = 0 \qquad \text{for all } j$$
$$\gamma_{ij} = 0 \qquad \text{for all } i, j$$

and

$$\mu = 0$$

respectively.

Computationally, P2V obtains each sum of squares as the difference in the residual sums of squares of two regression models. For each grouping variable with l levels, P2V generates $(l-1)$ dummy variables. Interactions between grouping variables are represented by the products of their dummy variables. P2V first fits the regression model containing all the dummy variables for the grouping variables and their interactions and then the model containing all dummy variables but those of the main effect or interaction being tested; the difference between residual sums of squares of the two models is the sum of squares reported. A more detailed computational procedure is provided in Appendix A.18.

P2V assumes that all interactions are to be included in the ANOVA model. You can also specify the effects or interactions of the grouping variables to be included in the model, e.g., you may wish to specify a model with main effects but no interactions.

Example 2V.2 Two Grouping Factors and Two Covariates

We analyze the logarithm of CHOLSTRL (LOGCHOL) from the Werner blood chemistry data (Table 5.1). We specify that the COVARIATES are the logarithms of height (LOGHGHT) and of weight (LOGWGHT). The logarithms are obtained by Control Language

transformations in the TRANSFORM paragraph and the three logarithms are ADDED as new variables in the VARIABLE paragraph. The two GROUPING factors are AGE (four age groupings) and BRTHPILL (two levels).

```
/ PROBLEM    TITLE IS 'WERNER BLOOD CHEMISTRY DATA'.
/ INPUT      VARIABLES ARE 9.
            FORMAT IS '(A4,5F4.0,3F4.1)'.
/ VARIABLE   NAMES ARE ID, AGE, HEIGHT, WEIGHT,
               BRTHPILL, CHOLSTRL, ALBUMIN,
               CALCIUM, URICACID, LOGHGHT,
               LOGWGHT, LOGCHOL.
            MAXIMUM IS (6)400.
            MINIMUM IS (6)150.
            LABEL IS ID.
            ADD IS 3.

/ TRANSFORM  LOGHGHT = LOG(HEIGHT).
            LOGWGHT = LOG(WEIGHT).
            LOGCHOL = LOG(CHOLSTRL).
/ DESIGN     DEPENDENT IS LOGCHOL.
            GROUPING ARE AGE, BRTHPILL.
            COVARIATES ARE LOGHGHT, LOGWGHT.

/ GROUP      CODES(5) ARE        1,    2.
            NAMES(5) ARE  NOPILL, PILL.
            CUTPOINTS(2) ARE  25, 35, 45.
            NAMES(2) ARE '25ORLESS', '26 TO 35',
                        '36 TO 45', 'OVER 45'.

/ END
```

Using the FORM statement, the DESIGN paragraph is written

```
/ DESIGN    FORM IS 'D,G,2D,G,4D,2X,Y'.
```

The first D deletes the first variable. The second variable (AGE) is used as a grouping factor. The third and fourth variables are also deleted. The fifth variable (BRTHPILL) is another grouping factor. The four blood chemistry measurements (variables 6 to 9) are deleted. Two new variables (10 and 11), LOGHGHT and LOGWGHT, are used as covariates. The twelfth variable (LOGCHOL) is the dependent variable.

The results are presented in Output 2V.2. Circled numbers below correspond to those in the output.

⑥ Analysis of covariance for each dependent variable. The model for this analysis of covariance can be written as

$$E(Y_{ij}) = \mu_{ij} + \beta_1 x_{1ij} + \beta_2 x_{2ij}$$

or

$$E(Y_{ij}) = \mu + \alpha_i + \gamma_j + (\alpha\gamma)_{ij} + \beta_1 x_{1ij} + \beta_2 x_{2ij}$$

where α_i and γ_j represent the main effects and $(\alpha\gamma)_{ij}$ the interaction of the grouping variables and β_1 and β_2 are the coefficients of the covariates. The usual constraints apply to α_i, γ_j and $(\alpha\gamma)_{ij}$.

The hypotheses tested are independent, but the sums of squares may not be orthogonal. For example, the sums of squares for each covariate do not add up to the sum of squares for all covariates. The sum of squares used in the test of each hypothesis (each covariate, all covariates, each analysis of variance component) can be obtained as the difference in the residual sums of squares of two models; one in which all covariates and effects are fitted and the other in which the covariate(s) or effect of interest is set to zero.

See the previous problem for a more detailed discussion of the hypotheses tested for main effects.

The regression coefficients are estimates of the coefficients for the covariates when all effects and covariates in the model are fitted.

⑦ Adjusted cell means. The adjusted mean for cell (i,j) is

$$\hat{\mu}_{ij} = \overline{Y}_{ij} + \hat{\beta}_1(\overline{x}_1 - \overline{x}_{1ij}) + \hat{\beta}_2(\overline{x}_2 - \overline{x}_{2ij}) + \cdots$$

where $\overline{Y}_{ij}$, $\overline{x}_{1ij}$, $\overline{x}_{2ij}$ are means computed for cell (i, j), $\overline{x}_1$ and $\overline{x}_2$ are means computed for all cases, and $\hat{\beta}_1$ and $\hat{\beta}_2$ are the least squares estimates of β_1 and β_2. That is, an adjusted cell mean is the mean of the dependent variable adjusted for covariates, evaluated using grand means of the covariates. The regression coefficients are assumed to be constant across groups (and within factors if present) when the adjusted cell means are computed.

Example 2V.3 Latin Square

Cochran and Cox (1957, p.121) give an example of a 6x6 Latin square. Data can be read into P2V as four variables. The first three specify the levels of the factors (or grouping variables) and the fourth is the dependent variable. The data for this example are:

1	1	6	3.5		4	1	4	6.6
1	2	2	8.9		4	2	1	4.5
1	3	3	9.6		4	3	2	3.7
1	4	4	10.5		4	4	5	3.7
1	5	5	3.1		4	5	6	-3.3
1	6	1	5.9		4	6	3	3.0
2	1	2	4.2		5	1	3	4.1
2	2	6	1.9		5	2	5	2.4
2	3	5	3.7		5	3	4	6.0
2	4	3	10.2		5	4	1	5.1
2	5	1	7.2		5	5	2	3.5
2	6	4	7.6		5	6	6	4.0
3	1	1	6.7		6	1	5	3.8
3	2	4	5.8		6	2	3	5.8
3	3	6	-2.7		6	3	1	7.0
3	4	2	4.6		6	4	6	3.8
3	5	3	4.0		6	5	4	5.0
3	6	5	-0.7		6	6	2	8.6

For the analysis the values of the dependent variable could be arranged in this structure

factor 2

		1	2	3	4	5	6
	1	6	2	3	4	5	1
	2	2	6	5	3	1	4
factor 1	3	1	4	6	2	3	5
	4	4	1	2	5	6	3
	5	3	5	4	1	2	6
	6	5	3	1	6	4	2

where the level of the third grouping factor is displayed in each cell. For example, 5.9, the value of the dependent variable for the fifth case in the file belongs in the cell in the upper right corner: for factor 1 it has level 1, for factor 2 it has level 6 and for factor 3 it has level 1 (the value

Output 2V.2 Two-way analysis of variance with two covariates by P2V

ANALYSIS OF VARIANCE FOR 1-ST ⑥
DEPENDENT VARIABLE - LOGCHOL

SOURCE	SUM OF SQUARES	DEGREES OF FREEDOM	MEAN SQUARE	F	TAIL PROB.	REGRESSION COEFFICIENTS
AGE	0.12971	3	0.04324	7.99	0.0001	
BRTHPILL	0.00321	1	0.00321	0.59	0.4425	
AB	0.01734	3	0.00578	1.07	0.3644	
1-ST COVAR	0.00354	1	0.00354	0.65	0.4200	-0.31073
2-ND COVAR	0.00927	1	0.00927	1.71	0.1924	0.13244
ALL COVARIATES	0.00943	2	0.00472	0.87	0.4203	
ERROR	0.93120	172	0.00541			

ADJUSTED CELL MEANS FOR 1-ST DEPENDENT VARIABLE ⑦

AGE =	25ORLESS	25ORLESS	26 TO 35	26 TO 35	36 TO 45	36 TO 45	OVER 45	OVER 45
BRTHPILL=	NOPILL	PILL	NOPILL	PILL	NOPILL	PILL	NOPILL	PILL
LOGCHOL	2.33968	2.34620	2.32726	2.36695	2.38733	2.38634	2.41828	2.40799

----

written in the cell above). The design can be specified as

```
/ DESIGN    GROUPING ARE 1, 2, 3.
            DEPENDENT IS 4.
```

or as

```
/ DESIGN    FORM IS '3G, Y'.
```

P2V fits the data by a full factorial model (all main effects and interactions) in the grouping factors unless you specify otherwise. For a Latin square design the model will usually contain only main effects. You can state in the DESIGN paragraph either the effects <u>included</u> in the model

```
INCLUDED ARE 1, 2, 3.
```

or the effects <u>excluded</u> from the model

```
EXCLUDED ARE 12, 13, 23, 123.
```

The choice between the two statements is a matter of convenience. Indices in the INCLUDE and EXCLUDE statements refer to the sequential order of the grouping variables (<u>not</u> to the subscripts of the grouping variables). For example, if the subscripts of the grouping variables were 2, 3 and 4, we would still write

```
INCLUDED ARE 1, 2, 3.
```

(Output is not shown.)

Example 2V.4 Incomplete Blocks

John (1971, p.135) discusses an example of a partially confounded incomplete block design. There are eight blocks. Each block contains observations at four combinations of the levels of three treatment (grouping) factors. Suppose the data are recorded as five variables such that the first variable is the block number, the next three are the levels (0 or 1) of the three treatment factors, and the last variable is the response (observation). The data for this example are:

1	0	0	0	101		5	0	0	0	87
1	1	0	1	373		5	1	0	1	324
1	0	1	1	398		5	0	1	0	279
1	1	1	0	291		5	1	1	1	471
2	0	0	1	312		6	0	0	1	323
2	1	0	0	106		6	1	0	0	128
2	0	1	0	265		6	0	1	1	423
2	1	1	1	450		6	1	1	0	334
3	0	0	0	106		7	0	0	0	131
3	1	1	0	306		7	1	0	0	103
3	0	0	1	324		7	0	1	1	445
3	1	1	1	449		7	1	1	1	437
4	0	1	0	272		8	0	0	1	324
4	1	0	0	89		8	1	0	1	361
4	0	1	1	407		8	0	1	0	302
4	1	0	1	338		8	1	1	0	272

A diagram of this design is

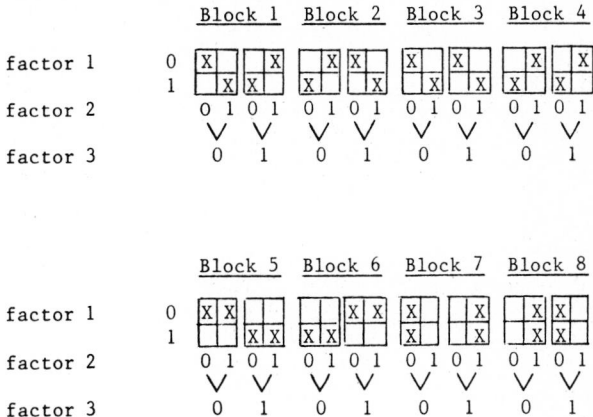

The design can be specified either as

```
/ DESIGN    GROUPING ARE 1 TO 4.
            DEPENDENT IS 5.
```

or

```
/ DESIGN    FORM IS '4G,Y'.
```

As in the Latin square design above, the effects in the model must be specified; otherwise the model has more parameters than can be estimated. For John's example we specify

```
INCLUDED ARE 1, 2, 3, 4, 23, 24, 34, 234.
```

The model contains the main effect for block, and all main effects and interactions of the three treatment factors; the model does not contain any interactions of the block effect with treatment effects.

(Output is not shown.)

Example 2V.5 Fractional Factorial 2^{n-k}

A fractional factorial design is specified in a manner similar to the incomplete block design. John (1971, p. 154) gives a numerical example of a 2^{4-1} design where the mean effect is confounded with the fourth order interaction. Suppose the data are recorded as five variables, four design variables (grouping factors) and the dependent variable. The data for this example are

0	0	0	0	7		1	0	0	1	8
1	1	0	0	1		0	1	0	1	12
1	0	1	0	12		0	0	1	1	6
0	1	1	0	14		1	1	1	1	6

A diagram of this design with data values is

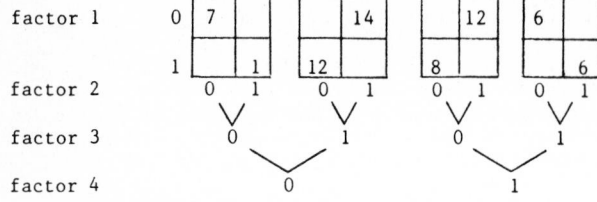

The design is specified either as

    / DESIGN   GROUPING ARE 1 TO 4.
                DEPENDENT IS 5.
 or
    / DESIGN   FORM IS '4G,Y'.

In addition, the effects in the model must be specified; otherwise the model would have more parameters than could be estimated. The model for the above design contains all main effects (they are confounded with third order interactions) and three two-factor interactions (each is confounded with a second two-factor interaction). Therefore we describe the model to P2V as

    INCLUDED ARE 1, 2, 3, 4, 12, 13, 23.

(Output is not shown.)

REPEATED-MEASURES DESIGNS

Example 2V.6 One Grouping Factor and One Within Factor

Table 15.2 Numerical example from Winer (1971, p. 525)

a	b_1	b_2	b_3	b_4
1	0	0	5	3
1	3	1	5	4
1	4	3	6	2
2	4	2	7	8
2	5	4	6	6
2	7	5	8	9

Note: There are two groups (a=1 and a=2). b_1, b_2, b_3, b_4 are the repeated measures for each subject (case).

The data (Table 15.2) are from Winer (1971, p. 525). Six subjects are divided into two groups according to the <u>method</u> (the grouping factor) used to calibrate dials. Each subject has four accuracy scores, one for each shape (the within factor) of the dials. The data for each subject comprise a

case. The analysis of the data is requested with the following:

```
-------------------------------------
/ PROBLEM     TITLE IS 'WINER, PAGE 525, CALIBRATION
                 OF DIALS'.
/ INPUT       VARIABLES ARE 5.
              FORMAT IS '(5F2.0)'.

/ VARIABLE    NAMES ARE METHOD, ACCURCY1, ACCURCY2,
                 ACCURCY3, ACCURCY4.

/ DESIGN      DEPENDENT ARE 2 TO 5.
              LEVEL IS 4.
              GROUPING IS METHOD.
              NAME IS SHAPE.

/ END
 1 0 0 5 3
 1 3 1 5 4
 1 4 3 6 2
 2 4 2 7 8
 2 5 4 6 6
 2 7 5 8 9
-------------------------------------
```

In the DESIGN paragraph, LEVEL = 4 specifies that there are four levels in the within factor. Each case contains the value of the GROUPING variable and values of the dependent variable for all the levels of the within factor on a subject.

Using the FORM statement, the DESIGN paragraph is written

    / DESIGN   FORM IS 'G,4(Y)'.
               NAME IS SHAPE.

G specifies that the first variable is a GROUPING factor, and 4(Y) that the next four variables contain the values of the dependent variables for the four levels of the within factor SHAPE. (If 4Y is written, instead of 4(Y), the four variables are considered to be different dependent variables, each of which is analyzed by a separate ANOVA. Note that it is sometimes desirable to perform both analyses.)

The analysis of variance table is presented in Output 2V.6. The model for this repeated measures design is

$$y_{ijk} = \mu + \alpha_i + \pi_{k(i)} + \beta_j + (\alpha\beta)_{ij} + (\beta\pi)_{jk(i)}$$

where

α_i represents the grouping factor

$\pi_{k(i)}$ represents subjects with the grouping factor (used to obtain the error term for the grouping factor)

β_j represents the within factor

$(\alpha\beta)_{ij}$ represents the interaction between the grouping factor and the within factor

and $(\beta\pi)_{jk(i)}$ represents the interaction of the within factor and the subjects within the grouping factor (used to obtain the error term for the within factor and for the interaction of the grouping factor and within factor)

We have the usual constraints that α_i, $\pi_{k(i)}$, β_j, $(\alpha\beta)_{ij}$, and $(\beta\pi)_{jk(i)}$ each sums to zero on every index. An error term $\varepsilon_{m(ijk)}$ can be added to the above model to represent experimental error within the individual observation; however, it cannot be estimated independently of $(\beta\pi)_{jk(i)}$. Winer (1971, p.518) describes this model in more detail.

Explanation of a repeated-measures analysis. Suppose there are only two measures Y_1 and Y_2 in each case (subject); i.e., the design has one trial factor with two levels. P2V computes two analyses of variance. The first is to test whether the expectation of the sum $P_0 = (Y_1 + Y_2)/\sqrt{2}$ is zero. The second is to test whether the expectation of the difference $P_1 = (Y_1 - Y_2)/\sqrt{2}$ is zero. This latter test is equivalent to a paired comparison t test (as computed by P3D, Section 9.1). (The denominator, $\sqrt{2}$, is chosen to make the sum of squares of the coefficients equal to one.)

Now suppose we have two groups of subjects and one within factor with two levels. P2V again computes the sums $P_0 = (Y_1 + Y_2)/\sqrt{2}$ and the differences $P_1 = (Y_1 - Y_2)/\sqrt{2}$ of the two repeated measures. Two analysis of variance tables are printed by P2V. The first table is an analysis of P_0; it contains a test for the grand mean of P_0 (labelled MEAN in the results) and a test of equality of means between the two groups (a test of the group effect). The latter test is equivalent to a two-sample t test to compare the two group means for P_0. The second analysis of variance table is an analysis of P_1; it contains a test of the mean of P_1 (a test of the within factor) and the second tests the equality of means for P_1 between the two groups (a test of the interaction between the grouping factor and the within factor).

Now suppose there is one grouping factor and one within factor with three levels. The data will contain four variables for each subject or case -- the value of the grouping factor and three values for the dependent variable (Y_1, Y_2, and Y_3). Again P2V computes two analyses of variance. The first is for $P_0 = (Y_1 + Y_2 + Y_3)/\sqrt{3}$. The second can be decomposed into two parts: $P_1 = (Y_1 - Y_3)/\sqrt{2}$ and $P_2 = (Y_1 - 2Y_2 + Y_3)/\sqrt{6}$. P_1 and P_2 are the orthogonal

polynomial decomposition of Y_1, Y_2, Y_3 into linear and quadratic components. (P_0 is the mean.) An analysis of variance is performed for both P_1 and P_2, but the individual analyses are not printed unless ORTHOGONAL is stated in the DESIGN paragraph. P2V pools the results for P_1 and P_2 by adding the sums of squares for each effect from the individual analyses. Similarly, the error sum of squares is the sum of the error sums of squares for P_1 and P_2. (We show the individual analyses in Output 2V.8.)

The ANOVA table in Output 2V.6 has two parts. The top part is the analysis of $P_0 = (Y_1 + Y_2 + Y_3 + Y_4)/\sqrt{4}$; it contains the test for between-groups (whole-plot) effects. MEAN provides a test that the mean of P_0 is zero, which is usually not of interest. METHOD is the grouping factor. The first line labelled ERROR reports the within-group sum of squares for P_0.

The second part of the ANOVA table presents the analysis of the within factor SHAPE and the interaction of the trial and grouping factors (SM). As explained above, the analysis is by an orthogonal decomposition into

$$P_1 = (3Y_1 + Y_2 - Y_3 - 3Y_4)/\sqrt{20}$$

$$P_2 = (Y_1 - Y_2 - Y_3 + Y_4)/\sqrt{4}$$

$$P_3 = (Y_1 - 3Y_2 + 3Y_3 - Y_4)/\sqrt{20}$$

each of which is analyzed separately and then the sums of squares are pooled.

The pooling of the sums of squares for the orthogonal polynomial components assumes that these components are statistically independent and have the same variance. Unless requested otherwise, a test of this assumption (symmetry test, Anderson, 1958, p. 259) is made. In addition, two adjustments are made to the degrees of freedom for the tests of the repeated-measures factor and its interaction with the grouping factor. These adjustments are due to Greenhouse and Geisser (1959) and Huynh and Feldt (1976). For more discussion, see Frane (1980a).

Output 2V.6 One grouping factor and one trial factor analyzed by P2V. Only the ANOVA table is shown
----

ANALYSIS OF VARIANCE FOR 1-ST
DEPENDENT VARIABLE - ACCURCY1 ACCURCY2 ACCURCY3 ACCURCY4

	SOURCE	SUM OF SQUARES	DEGREES OF FREEDOM	MEAN SQUARE	F	TAIL PROB.	GREENHOUSE GEISSER PROB.	HUYNH FELDT PROB.
	MEAN	477.04167	1	477.04167	111.16	0.0005		
	METHOD	51.04167	1	51.04167	11.89	0.0261		
1	ERROR	17.16667	4	4.29167				
	SHAP	47.45833	3	15.81944	12.80	0.0005	0.0099	0.0011
	SM	7.45833	3	2.48611	2.01	0.1662	0.2152	0.1791
2	ERROR	14.83333	12	1.23611				

ERROR TERM	EPSILON FACTORS FOR DEGREES OF FREEDOM ADJUSTMENT	
	GREENHOUSE-GEISSER	HUYNH-FELDT
2	0.4751	0.8483

Repeated measures for multiple dependent variables. In many experiments, each of several dependent variables is measured at each of several times. A repeated-measures analysis of each of these dependent variables can easily be requested. For example, if we had three dependent variables in the above example, then there would be 13 variables in all. In a typical experiment, data would be recorded in the following form:

$$G, U_1, V_1, W_1, U_2, V_2, W_2, U_3, V_3, W_3, U_4, V_4, W_4$$

U, V, and W denote the three variables, and their subscripts denote the level of the within factor. The design could be specified as

```
/ DESIGN   FORM = 'G,4(3Y)'.
```

The expression 4(3Y) means that each of three variables has been measured four times and that the first measurements of all three variables are recorded in the data matrix before any of the second measurements. The design could also be specified by

```
/ DESIGN   DEPEND = 2 TO 13.
           LEVEL = 4.
           GROUPING = 1.
```

Example 2V.7 Two Grouping Factors and One Within Factor

Table 15.3 Numerical example from Winer (1971, p. 564)

a	b	c 1	2	3	4
1	1	18	14	12	6
1	1	19	12	8	4
1	1	14	10	6	2
1	2	16	12	10	4
1	2	12	8	6	2
1	2	18	10	5	1
2	1	16	10	8	4
2	1	18	8	4	1
2	1	16	12	6	2
2	2	19	16	10	8
2	2	16	14	10	9
2	2	16	12	8	8

Note: There are two grouping factors (a and b) each having two levels. 1, 2, 3, 4 under c are the repeated measures for each subject (case). The data below are recorded in fields of three characters each.

The data (Table 15.3) are from Winer (1971, p. 564). There are two GROUPING factors, ANXIETY and TENSION -- each has two levels. The experiment is repeated four times for each subject (called blocks of trials by Winer and NAMED B in this example); the number of ERRORS is recorded as the DEPENDENT variable. The data for each subject comprise a case. The Control Language and data follow:

```
--------------------------------------
/ PROBLEM    TITLE IS 'WINER, PAGE 564, LEARNING
                      DATA'.
/ INPUT      VARIABLES ARE 6.
             FORMAT IS '(6F3.0)'.
/ VARIABLE   NAMES ARE ANXIETY, TENSION, ERRORS1,
                       ERRORS2, ERRORS3, ERRORS4.
/ DESIGN     GROUPING ARE ANXIETY, TENSION.
             DEPENDENT ARE 3 TO 6.
             LEVEL IS 4.
             NAME IS B.
/ GROUP      CODES(1) ARE    1,    2.
             NAMES(1) ARE  LOW, HIGH.
             CODES(2) ARE    1,    2.
             NAMES(2) ARE NONE, HIGH.
/ END
  1  1 18 14 12  6
  1  1 19 12  8  4
  1  1 14 10  6  2
  1  2 16 12 10  4
  1  2 12  8  6  2
  1  2 18 10  5  1
  2  1 16 10  8  4
  2  1 18  8  4  1
  2  1 16 12  6  2
  2  2 19 16 10  8
  2  2 16 14 10  9
  2  2 16 12  8  8
--------------------------------------
```

Using the FORM statement, the DESIGN paragraph is written

```
/ DESIGN   FORM IS '2G,4(Y)'.
           NAME IS B.
```

The first two variables are GROUPING factors and the next four contain the values of the dependent variable at the four levels of the trial factor.

The ANOVA table is presented in Output 2V.7. There are two panels. In the upper panel the grouping main effects and their interaction are tested; this analysis is similar to that explained for Example 2V.1 above, where

$$P_0 = (Y_1 + Y_2 + Y_3 + Y_4)/\sqrt{4}$$

is analyzed as the dependent variable. The analysis in the lower panel is similar to that described for Example 2V.6 above.

Output 2V.7   Two grouping factors and one repeated measure analyzed by P2V. Only the ANOVA table is shown

----

ANALYSIS OF VARIANCE FOR 1-ST
DEPENDENT VARIABLE - ERRORS1 ERRORS2 ERRORS3 ERRORS4

	SOURCE	SUM OF SQUARES	DEGREES OF FREEDOM	MEAN SQUARE	F	TAIL PROB.	GREENHOUSE GEISSER PROB.	HUYNH FELDT PROB.
	MEAN	4800.00000	1	4800.00000	465.45	0.0000		
	ANXIETY	10.08333	1	10.08333	0.98	0.3517		
	TENSION	8.33333	1	8.33333	0.81	0.3949		
	AT	80.08333	1	80.08333	7.77	0.0237		
1	ERROR	82.50000	8	10.31250				
	B	991.50000	3	330.50000	152.05	0.0000	0.0	0.0
	BA	8.41667	3	2.80556	1.29	0.3003	0.3002	0.3015
	BT	12.16667	3	4.05556	1.87	0.1624	0.1967	0.1693
	BAT	12.75000	3	4.25000	1.96	0.1477	0.1847	0.1550
2	ERROR	52.16667	24	2.17361				

ERROR TERM	EPSILON FACTORS FOR DEGREES OF FREEDOM ADJUSTMENT	
	GREENHOUSE-GEISSER	HUYNH-FELDT
2	0.5361	0.9023

Output 2V.8   Decomposition of the ANOVA table in Output 2V.7

ANALYSIS OF VARIANCE FOR 1-ST
DEPENDENT VARIABLE - ERRORS1 ERRORS2 ERRORS3 ERRORS4

	SOURCE	SUM OF SQUARES	DEGREES OF FREEDOM	MEAN SQUARE	F	TAIL PROB.	GREENHOUSE GEISSER PROB.	HUYNH FELDT PROB.
	MEAN	4800.00000	1	4800.00000	465.45	0.0000		
	ANXIETY	10.08333	1	10.08333	0.98	0.3517		
	TENSION	8.33333	1	8.33333	0.81	0.3949		
	AT	80.08333	1	80.08333	7.77	0.0237		
1	ERROR	82.50000	8	10.31250				
	B(1)	984.15000	1	984.15000	247.84	0.0000		
	B(1)A	1.66667	1	1.66667	0.42	0.5352		
	B(1)T	10.41667	1	10.41667	2.62	0.1440		
	B(1)AT	9.60000	1	9.60000	2.42	0.1586		
	ERROR	31.76667	8	3.97083				
	B(2)	6.75000	1	6.75000	3.41	0.1020		
	B(2)A	3.00000	1	3.00000	1.52	0.2532		
	B(2)T	0.08333	1	0.08333	0.04	0.8425		
	B(2)AT	0.33333	1	0.33333	0.17	0.6923		
	ERROR	15.83333	8	1.97917				
	B(3)	0.60000	1	0.60000	1.05	0.3353		
	B(3)A	3.75000	1	3.75000	6.57	0.0335		
	B(3)T	1.66667	1	1.66667	2.92	0.1259		
	B(3)AT	2.81667	1	2.81667	4.93	0.0571		
	ERROR	4.56667	8	0.57083				
	B	991.50000	3	330.50000	152.05	0.0000	0.0	0.0
	BA	8.41667	3	2.80556	1.29	0.3003	0.3002	0.3015
	BT	12.16667	3	4.05556	1.87	0.1624	0.1967	0.1693
	BAT	12.75000	3	4.25000	1.96	0.1477	0.1847	0.1550
2	ERROR	52.16667	24	2.17361				

ERROR TERM	EPSILON FACTORS FOR DEGREES OF FREEDOM ADJUSTMENT	
	GREENHOUSE-GEISSER	HUYNH-FELDT
2	0.5361	0.9023

Example 2V.8 An Ordered Within Factor Broken into Orthogonal Components

When the levels of a within factor are ordered, the analysis in the lower panel of Example 2V.7 can be better understood if we add ORTHOGONAL to the BMDP instructions so that the DESIGN paragraph reads as follows:

```
-----------------------------------
/ DESIGN    GROUPING ARE ANXIETY, TENSION
           DEPENDENT ARE 3 TO 6.
           LEVEL IS 4.
           NAME IS B.
           ORTHOGONAL.
-----------------------------------
```

The ANOVA table in Output 2V.8 contains the analysis of the orthogonal components. The first and last panels are identical to those in Output 2V.7. The second panel contains the sums of squares for the analysis of the linear component, $B(1)$, the third panel that of the quadratic component, $B(2)$, and the fourth panel that of the cubic component, $B(3)$. Each sum of squares in the last panel is the sum of the sums of squares in the corresponding lines of the middle three panels. Note that there is never a Greenhouse-Geisser or Huynh-Feldt adjustment to degrees of freedom for the tests involving individual orthogonal polynomial components since the symmetry assumption is not required for the individual components.

Example 2V.9 Split-plot Designs

The above repeated-measures analysis (Example 2V.7) can also be used to obtain a split-plot analysis when the two grouping factors are the main plot or whole plot treatments and the within factor is the subplot treatment. Often one of the main plot effects is a blocking factor. The repeated measures model described above contains an interaction of the blocking effect with the subplot treatment. If this interaction is assumed to be zero and the design is balanced (the same number of observations in each cell), you can pool the sum of squares of this interaction with the error sum of squares. For example, Snedecor and Cochran (1967, p. 370) consider a split-plot design with randomized blocks. The model is

$$Y_{ijk} = \mu + M_i + B_j + e_{ij} + T_k + (MT)_{ik} + d_{ijk}$$

where M is a main plot treatment, B is a block effect, T is a subplot treatment, e is the main plot error and d is the subplot error. If the main plot treatment (M) is recorded as the first variable, the block effect (B) as the second and subplots as the levels (say four) of the within factor (as described for the above repeated measures model), then the DESIGN paragraph may be written as

```
/ DESIGN    GROUPING ARE 1, 2.
           DEPENDENT ARE 3 TO 6.
           LEVEL IS 4.
           NAME IS S.
           EXCLUDE IS 12.
```

The analysis of variance table would then be similar to that in Output 2V.7 (except that M replaces A, B replaces T and T replaces B). Since the above model does not contain the interactions $(MB)_{ij}$ and $(BT)_{jk}$, we can pool the sum of squares reported for BT with that for d (the ERROR in the last panel) when the design is balanced. The interactions MB and MBT are not estimated because MB is EXCLUDED. No separate output is shown.

An alternate way of analyzing this model when the design is balanced is to specify grouping factors only and choose the proper error term. For the Snedecor and Cochran model you could specify the DESIGN paragraph

```
/ DESIGN    GROUPING ARE 1, 2, 3.
           DEPENDENT IS 4.
           INCLUDE IS 1, 2, 3, 12, 23.
```

where variable 1 is the blocking factor, 2 the main plot treatment, 3 the subplot treatment and 4 the yield. The INCLUDE statement indicates that the model includes three main effects and two interactions. The interactions are between main plot treatments and blocks used as the error test for testing main plot treatment effects and between main plot treatments and subplot treatments. Note that this form of input requires that you select the proper error term for testing main plot treatment and blocking effects. The tests provided by P2V are for a fixed effects model and are the proper tests for subplot treatment effects and for the interaction of main and subplot treatment effects but not the proper test for main plot or block effects. See Frane (1980a) for further discussion of blocking and split-plots.

Example 2V.10 One Grouping Factor and Two Within Factors

Table 15.4   Numerical example from Winer (1971, p. 546)

a	b₁ c_1	c_2	c_3	b₂ c_1	c_2	c_3	b₃ c_1	c_3	c_3
									(Periods) / (Dials)
1	45	53	60	40	52	57	28	37	46
1	35	41	50	30	37	47	25	32	41
1	60	65	75	58	54	70	40	47	50
2	50	48	61	25	34	51	16	23	35
2	42	45	55	30	37	43	22	27	37
2	56	60	77	40	39	57	31	29	46

Note: a is a grouping variable with two levels. Periods and dials are two within factors. The grouping variable (a) is recorded below in the first field; the repeated measures are recorded in two character entries for each of nine entries.

The data (Table 15.4) are from Winer (1971, p. 546). Subjects are grouped according to two noise levels under which they monitor three dials. Accuracy scores are obtained for calibrating each dial during three time periods. There is one GROUPING variable (NOISE) and two within factors, each with three levels. The BMDP instructions and data follow:

```
-------------------------------------
/ PROBLEM    TITLE IS 'WINER, PAGE 546, NOISE DATA'.

/ INPUT      VARIABLES ARE 10.
             FORMAT IS '(10F3.0)'.
/ VARIABLE   NAMES ARE NOISE, B1C1, B1C2, B1C3,
                       B2C1, B2C2, B2C3,
                       B3C1, B3C2, B3C3.

/ DESIGN     GROUPING IS NOISE.
             DEPENDENT ARE 2 TO 10.
             LEVELS ARE 3, 3.
             NAMES ARE PERIOD, DIAL.
/ GROUP      CODES(1) ARE 1, 2.
             NAMES(1) ARE A1, A2.

/ END
  1 45 53 60 40 52 57 28 37 46
  1 35 41 50 30 37 47 25 32 41
  1 60 65 75 58 54 70 40 47 50
  2 50 48 61 25 34 51 16 23 35
  2 42 45 55 30 37 43 22 27 37
  2 56 60 77 40 39 57 31 29 46
-------------------------------------
```

In this example the LEVELS statement in the DESIGN paragraph states that there are two within factors, each with three levels. The first 3 refers to the number of levels of PERIOD and the second to the number of levels of DIAL. The number of levels of the more slowly varying index (PERIOD) is stated first.

Using the FORM statement, the DESIGN paragraph is written

```
/ DESIGN    FORM = 'G,3(3(Y))'.
            NAME = PERIOD, DIAL.
```

The first variable is the grouping factor. The next nine variables contain the repeated measures for a subject. (3(Y)) specifies that the inner trial factor (dial calibration) has three levels and is recorded as three successive variables. 3(3(Y)) specifies that the outer within factor (time period) has three levels and is recorded in three sets of three variables; each set varies over the three levels of the inner within factor. The first NAME for the within factors applies to the outer factor and the second NAME to the inner.

The ANOVA table is presented in Output 2V.10. In the top panel the grouping variable (NOISE) is tested as described previously. The main effect of each within factor appears in a separate panel since the appropriate error term for each effect differs (see Winer, 1971, p. 540).

Output 2V.10   One grouping factor and two repeated measures analyzed by P2V.   Only the ANOVA table is shown

```
ANALYSIS OF VARIANCE FOR  1-ST
DEPENDENT VARIABLE - B1C1   B1C2   B1C3   B2C1   B2C2   B2C3   B3C1   B3C2   B3C3
```

	SOURCE	SUM OF SQUARES	DEGREES OF FREEDOM	MEAN SQUARE	F	TAIL PROB.	GREENHOUSE GEISSER PROB.	HUYNH FELDT PROB.
	MEAN	105868.16667	1	105868.16667	169.99	0.0002		
	NOISE	468.16667	1	468.16667	0.75	0.4348		
1	ERROR	2491.11111	4	622.77778				
	PERI	3722.33333	2	1861.16667	63.39	0.0000	0.0003	0.0000
	PN	333.00000	2	166.50000	5.67	0.0293	0.0569	0.0293
2	ERROR	234.88889	8	29.36111				
			2	1185.16667	89.82	0.0000	0.0000	0.0000
	DN	50.33333	2	25.16667	1.91	0.2102	0.2152	0.2102
3	ERROR	105.55556	8	13.19444				
	PD	10.66667	4	2.66667	0.34	0.8499	0.7295	0.8499
	PDN	11.33333	4	2.83333	0.36	0.8357	0.7156	0.8357
4	ERROR	127.11111	16	7.94444				

```
ERROR         EPSILON FACTORS FOR DEGREES OF FREEDOM ADJUSTMENT
TERM
              GREENHOUSE-GEISSER    HUYNH-FELDT
  2                0.6476             1.0000
  3                0.9171             1.0000
  4                0.5134             1.0000
```

The analysis of the two within factors is again by orthogonal polynomial decomposition. Let us represent the data in the table as

	Dial		
	Y_{11}	Y_{12}	Y_{13}
Period	Y_{21}	Y_{22}	Y_{23}
	Y_{31}	Y_{32}	Y_{33}

Then let

$$P_{10} = (Y_{31}+Y_{32}+Y_{33}-Y_{11}-Y_{12}-Y_{13})/\sqrt{6}$$

linear component in Period

$$P_{20} = (Y_{31}+Y_{32}+Y_{33}-2Y_{21}-2Y_{22}-2Y_{23}+Y_{11}+Y_{12}+Y_{13})/\sqrt{18}$$

quadratic component in Period

P_{01} and P_{02} the corresponding linear and quadratic components is Dial

and let P_{11}, P_{12}, P_{21}, P_{22} be the orthogonal decomposition of the interaction between Period and Dial; the coefficients of P_{ij} are obtained from the vector cross product of P_{io} and P_{oj}; i.e., the product of the corresponding coefficients in P_{io} and P_{oj}.

Then the second panel in the ANOVA table in Output 2V.10 is obtained by summing the sums of squares in the analyses of P_{10} and P_{20} (the orthogonal decomposition of Period). The third panel is obtained from the analysis of P_{01} and P_{02} and the last panel from the analyses of P_{11}, P_{12}, P_{21}, and P_{22}. Since there are three repeated-measures analysis of variance tables, there are three different tests of symmetry and three different Greenhouse-Geisser and Huynh-Feldt adjustments to degrees of freedom.

Example 2V.11 Two Within Factors (no grouping factor)

We now reanalyze the data in Table 15.4 without a grouping factor.

```
-------------------------------------
/ PROBLEM    TITLE IS 'WINER, PAGE 546, NOISE DATA'.
/ INPUT      VARIABLES ARE 10.
            FORMAT IS '(10F3.0)'.
/ VARIABLE   NAMES ARE NOISE, B1C1, B1C2, B1C3,
                       B2C1, B2C2, B2C3,
                       B3C1, B3C2, B3C3.

/ DESIGN     DEPENDENT ARE 2 TO 10.
            LEVELS ARE 3, 3.
            NAMES ARE PERIOD, DIAL.

/ END
1  45 53 60 40 52 57 28 37 46
1  35 41 50 30 37 47 25 32 41
1  60 65 75 58 54 70 40 47 50
2  50 48 61 25 34 51 16 23 35
2  42 45 55 30 37 43 22 27 37
2  56 60 77 40 39 57 31 29 46
-------------------------------------
```

Output 2V.11   Analysis of two trial factors by P2V. Only the ANOVA table is presented

---

ANALYSIS OF VARIANCE FOR 1-ST
DEPENDENT VARIABLE — B1C1   B1C2   B1C3   B2C1   B2C2   B2C3   B3C1   B3C2   B3C3

	SOURCE	SUM OF SQUARES	DEGREES OF FREEDOM	MEAN SQUARE	F	TAIL PROB.	GREENHOUSE GEISSER PROB.	HUYNH FELDT PROB.
	MEAN	105868.16667	1	105868.16667	178.88	0.0000		
1	ERROR	2959.27778	5	591.85556				
	PERI	3722.33333	2	1861.16667	32.77	0.0000	0.0006	0.0002
2	ERROR	567.88889	10	56.78889				
	DIAL	2370.33333	2	1185.16667	76.03	0.0000	0.0000	0.0
3	ERROR	155.88889	10	15.58889				
	PD	10.66667	4	2.66667	0.39	0.8166	0.6931	0.7899
4	ERROR	138.44444	20	6.92222				

ERROR TERM	EPSILON FACTORS FOR DEGREES OF FREEDOM ADJUSTMENT	
	GREENHOUSE–GEISSER	HUYNH–FELDT
2	0.6665	0.8179
3	0.7925	1.0000
4	0.5083	0.8596

Using the FORM statement, the DESIGN paragraph is written

```
/ DESIGN    FORM IS 'D,3(3(Y))'.
            NAME  = PERIOD, DIAL.
```

That is, the letter D is used to indicate that the first variable is deleted.

The resulting ANOVA table is presented in Output 2V.11 without a grouping factor. The sums of squares for P, D, and PD are the same as in Output 2V.10. The error sums of squares in Output 2V.11 are equal to the error sums of squares plus the sums of squares of the grouping factor in Example 2V.10.

Example 2V.12 One Grouping Variable, One Within Factor and One Covariate Changing Over Trials

This design can be used, for example, when body temperature is measured with blood pressure as a covariate on each of two days. The subjects are classified into three disease groups. Disease is the grouping factor, temperature the dependent variable, blood pressure the covariate, and days the within factor.

Winer (1971, p. 806) presents an artificial example that has this type of design. His data (Table 15.5) are used for this example.

Table 15.5 A numerical example from Winer (1971, p. 806)

a	b_1		b_2	
	X	Y	X	Y
1	3	8	4	14
1	5	11	9	18
1	11	16	14	22
2	2	6	1	8
2	8	12	9	14
2	10	9	9	10
3	7	10	4	10
3	8	14	10	18
3	9	15	12	22

Note: a is a grouping variable with three levels and is recorded in the first field. The repeated measures are recorded in four fields of three characters each.

Output 2V.12 One grouping variable, one repeated measure and one covariate analyzed by P2V. Only the ANOVA table is presented

----

ANALYSIS OF VARIANCE FOR 1-ST
DEPENDENT VARIABLE - B1Y   B2Y

	SOURCE	SUM OF SQUARES	DEGREES OF FREEDOM	MEAN SQUARE	F	TAIL PROB.	REGRESSION COEFFICIENTS
	GROUP	54.25900	2	27.12950	3.06	0.1357	
	1-ST COVAR	132.62951	1	132.62951	14.95	0.0118	0.84747
1	ERROR	44.37049	5	8.87410			
	B	31.54703	1	31.54703	52.61	0.0008	
	BG	2.33929	2	1.16964	1.95	0.2365	
	1-ST COVAR	10.00198	1	10.00198	16.68	0.0095	0.84524
2	ERROR	2.99802	5	0.59960			

POOLED REGRESSION COEFFICIENTS

   1-ST COVARIATE   0.84629

ADJUSTED CELL MEANS FOR 1-ST DEPENDENT VARIABLE

	GROUP =	A1	A2	A3
	B			
B1Y	1	12.65401	9.70524	12.57685
B2Y	2	16.73056	11.65401	15.67933

The Control Language and data appear as follows:

```
--------------------------------------
/ PROBLEM     TITLE IS 'WINER, PAGE 806, NUMERICAL
                       EXAMPLE'.
/ INPUT       VARIABLES ARE 5.
              FORMAT IS '(5F3.0)'.
/ VARIABLE    NAMES ARE GROUP, B1X, B1Y, B2X, B2Y.

/ DESIGN      GROUPING IS GROUP.
              DEPENDENT ARE B1Y, B2Y.
              COVARIATES ARE B1X, B2X.
              LEVEL IS 2.
              NAME IS B.

/ GROUP       CODES(1) ARE  1,  2,  3.
              NAMES(1) ARE A1, A2, A3.

/ END
   1  3  8  4 14
   1  5 11  9 18
   1 11 16 14 22
   2  2  6  1  8
   2  8 12  9 14
   2 10  9  9 10
   3  7 10  4 10
   3  8 14 10 18
   3  9 15 12 22
--------------------------------------
```

When COVARIATES are stated and there is a within factor, the COVARIATES are paired with the DEPENDENT variables. That is, the first COVARIATE is treated as the covariate for the first level of the within factor and the second COVARIATE for the second level.

Using the FORM statement, the DESIGN paragraph is written

```
      / DESIGN   FORM = 'G,2(X,Y)'.
                 NAME IS B.
```

The first variable is a grouping factor. Then there are two pairs of variables -- a covariate followed by a dependent variable. 2( ) indicates that there are two levels to the within factor.

The ANOVA table is presented in Output 2V.12. There are two panels in the ANOVA table. The top panel contains the analysis of the grouping factor and the bottom panel contains the analysis of the within factor and of the interaction of the within factor with the grouping factor.

The analysis of covariance uses the same orthogonal decomposition as the ANOVA. First the covariate is averaged for each case; we denote the average of the covariate by Q_0 and that of the dependent variable by P_0. Then an analysis of covariance is performed on P_0 using Q_0 as the covariate. This is reported in the first panel.

Then the covariate is decomposed into orthogonal polynomials $Q_1, Q_2, \ldots$ in parallel with the decomposition of the dependent variable into $P_1, P_2, \ldots$. If the orthogonal polynomial decomposition is requested, a separate analysis of covariance is computed for each P_i using Q_i as a covariate. To obtain the lower panel of Output 2V.12, P2V pools the covariance matrices for the polynomials of degree one and higher that contain covariances between the dependent variable, dummy variables generated for grouping variables, and the covariate(s).

This pooled estimate of the covariance matrix is used to compute an analysis of covariance for the trial factor (Appendix A.18).

The beta estimates in the ANOVA table are the coefficients of the covariate; the coefficient in the lower panel is a weighted average of the regression of P_1 on Q_1, P_2 on Q_2, etc.

The "pooled regression coefficient" (below the ANOVA table) is obtained from the weighted pooled cross-product matrix (the weights are the inverses of the error mean squares). The pooled regression coefficients are used to compute adjusted cell means. See Appendix A.18, steps 6 and 7.

Output 2V.13   One grouping variable, one repeated measure and one covariate analyzed by P2V.   Only the ANOVA table is presented

```
--------------------------------------------------------------------------------------------------
```

ANALYSIS OF VARIANCE FOR 1-ST
DEPENDENT VARIABLE - B1Y   B2Y

	SOURCE	SUM OF SQUARES	DEGREES OF FREEDOM	MEAN SQUARE	F	TAIL PROB.	REGRESSION COEFFICIENTS
	GROUP	44.49160	1	44.49160	3.63	0.1151	
	1-ST COVAR	166.57680	1	166.57680	13.59	0.0142	1.02194
1	ERROR	61.29820	5	12.25964			
	B	85.56250	1	85.56250	80.53	0.0001	
	BG	0.56250	1	0.56250	0.53	0.4943	
2	ERROR	6.37500	6	1.06250			

ADJUSTED CELL MEANS FOR 1-ST DEPENDENT VARIABLE

	GROUP =	A1	A2
	B		
B1Y	1	14.63323	18.36677
B2Y	2	10.38323	13.36677

```
-------------------------------------------------------------------------------------------------------
```

Example 2V.13 One Grouping Variable, One Within Factor and One Covariate Constant Over the Levels of the Within Factor

This design can be used, for example, when body temperature is measured for each subject on two different days and age is used as a covariate. The subjects are classified by sex. Sex is the grouping factor, temperature the dependent variable, age the covariate and day the within factor.

Winer (1971, p. 803) presents an artificial example with a similar design. His data (Table 15.6) are used in the following example.

Table 15.6 A numerical example from Winer (1971, p. 803)

a	X	Y_1	Y_2
1	3	10	8
1	5	15	12
1	8	20	14
1	2	12	6
2	1	15	10
2	8	25	20
2	10	20	15
2	2	15	10

Note: a is a grouping factor, X is a covariate that is constant over trials, and Y_1 and Y_2 are two repeated measures. The grouping factor is recorded in the first field, the covariate in the second field and the repeated measures in the third and fourth fields.

The Control Language and data follow:

```
------------------------------------
/ PROBLEM    TITLE IS 'WINER, PAGE 803, NUMERICAL
                EXAMPLE'.
/ INPUT      VARIABLES ARE 4.
             FORMAT IS '(4F3.0)'.
/ VARIABLE   NAMES ARE GROUP, X, B1Y, B2Y.

/ DESIGN     GROUPING IS GROUP.
             DEPENDENT ARE B1Y, B2Y.
             COVARIATE IS X, X.
             LEVEL IS 2.
             NAME IS B.

/ GROUP      CODES(1) ARE  1,  2.
             NAMES(1) ARE A1, A2.

/ END
   1  3 10  8
   1  5 15 12
   1  8 20 14
   1  2 12  6
   2  1 15 10
   2  8 25 20
   2 10 20 15
   2  2 15 10
------------------------------------
```

In the DESIGN paragraph two COVARIATES must be stated to match the number of levels in the within factor. Since the covariate is constant over trials, we repeat the subscript of the covariate.

Using the FORM statement, the DESIGN paragraph is written

```
/ DESIGN    FORM = 'G,X,2(Y)'.
            NAME IS B.
```

Since the covariate, X, is specified outside the parentheses, it is constant over repeated measures and is used only to test between group effects.

The ANOVA table is presented in Output 2V.13. The covariate does not vary across trials, therefore it is not included in the lower panel that analyzes the differences among the levels of the within factors. Otherwise, the ANOVA table is similar to that in Output 2V.12.

Specifying the Design

The design can either be given in terms of a FORM statement or in terms of GROUP, LEVEL, DEPEND and COVA statements. The FORM statement is frequently more convenient for repeated-measures designs and the latter method is usually more convenient otherwise.

Rules for the GROUP, LEVEL, DEPEND and COVA statements. The GROUP statement lists the variables that specify the levels of the grouping factors to which a subject belongs.

The LEVEL statement is used only for repeated measures models. The number of values in the LEVEL statement is the number of within factors; the values of the LEVEL statement specify the number of levels in each within factor. For example,

```
LEVEL = 4, 3.
```

specifies two within factors with four levels in the first and three levels in the second.

P2V can analyze _several_ dependent variables in parallel; the same analysis is performed on each dependent variable. The DEPENDENT statement serves two functions in P2V.

- It implicitly indicates the number of dependent variables.
- It specifies the variables to be used as repeated measures or as dependent variables.

Suppose T is the product of the numbers of levels of the within factors; e.g., if we have two within factors with four and three levels respectively, then T = 12; if there are no within factors, T is one. The DEPENDENT statement must list either exactly T variables or kT variables, where k is an integer. If k is greater than one, k is the number of dependent variables. When both k and T are greater than one, the variables in the DEPENDENT statement must be ordered as in the following example. Suppose k is 2 and T is 4; then the repeated measures for the first analysis are recorded in the first, third, fifth and seventh variables listed as DEPENDENT variables and the repeated measures for the second analysis are the even-numbered variables.

For repeated-measures models the order of variables specified in the DEPENDENT statement must correspond to the order implied in the LEVEL statement. If LEVEL = 2, 3. and DEPEND = 1 TO 6., the data are read by P2V as

$$Y_{11}, Y_{12}, Y_{13}, Y_{21}, Y_{22}, Y_{23}$$

where Y_{ij} denotes the value of the dependent variable for the ith level of the first within factor and the jth level of the second. The index corresponding to the first within factor varies more slowly than that of the second within factor; all levels of the second within factor appear as blocks at each level of the first factor. DEPEND = 3, 1, 2, 4, 5, 6. indicates that the data are recorded in an "unnatural" order as $Y_{12}, Y_{13}, Y_{11}, Y_{21}, Y_{22}, Y_{23}$.

In a repeated-measures model the number of values in the DEPENDENT statement is a whole number multiple of the product of the numbers in the LEVEL statement; e.g., if LEVEL = 2, 3., the number of values in the DEPENDENT statement must be a multiple of 2 x 3 = 6. If there are 12 values in the DEPENDENT statement, there are two distinct dependent variables, and an analysis of variance is made for each. If DEPEND = 1 TO 12., the first dependent variable is assumed to be variables 1, 3, 5, 7, 9, 11; the second to be variables 2, 4, 6, 8, 10, 12.

The number of values in the COVARIATE statement is a whole number multiple of the product of the numbers in the LEVEL statement, if any.

```
GROUP = 1.        DEPEND = 2 TO 7.
LEVEL = 2, 3.     COVA = 8 TO 19.
```

indicates 12 values for covariates. Since the product of the number of levels is six, there are two distinct covariates. The first covariate is assumed to be variables 8, 10, 12, 14, 16, 18; the second to be variables 9, 11, 13, 15, 17, 19. In this example, the covariates are measured each time the dependent variable is measured. If there are two distinct dependent variables, the covariates are applied to both of them.

When a covariate is not measured for every level of a within factor, the index of that covariate must be repeated in the COVARIATE statement (see Example 2V.10).

```
GROUP = 1.        DEPEND = 2 TO 7.
LEVEL = 2, 3.     COVA = 8,9,10,8,9,10.
```

indicates that the covariate is measured separately for each level of the second factor (three levels) but remains unchanged for the first factor (two levels).

DESIGN ─────────────────────────────────

GROUPing = v list.   none/prev.
    Names or subscripts of the GROUPING factors (variables). If the GROUPING variable takes on more than 10 distinct values, CODES or CUTPOINTS must be specified in a GROUP paragraph (Section 5.5). When CODES or CUTPOINTS are not specified, the cell means and standard deviations are not sorted before being printed.
DEPENDent = v list.   none/prev.
    Names or subscripts of the dependent variables, or of the variables that record an observation at any level, or combination of levels, of the within-subject factors. (See above for a more detailed explanation.)
LEVEL = # list.   none/prev.
    Number of levels in the within-subject factors. LEVELS is specified only for repeated-measures models. The first number is that for the slowest changing factor, the second for the next slowest changing, etc. That is, the data are organized so that all the levels of the second factor appear at each level of the first factor.
COVAriates = v list.   none/prev.
    Names or subscripts of the covariates. The covariates are paired with the repeated measures (see above for a more detailed explanation).

Note: If any of GROUPING, DEPENDENT, LEVELS or COVARIATES is stated, those not stated are set to none. All four are ignored if FORM is stated.

Rules for the FORM statement

    G = a grouping variable
    Y = a dependent variable
    X = a covariate
    D = a deleted variable (a variable not used in the analysis)

The number of within factors is indicated by the number of pairs of parentheses. Parentheses must be nested and the symbol Y must appear in the innermost nest: 4(2(Y)) is allowed but 4(Y),2(Y) is meaningless. The number of levels of a within factor is the number preceding the parentheses corresponding to that factor. 4(2(Y)) specifies two within factors with four levels in the first factor and two levels in the second.

The variables in the FORM statement are in the same order as the input variables. FORM = '3(2(Y)),G'. specifies that the grouping variable is the seventh variable and that the dependent variable is measured six times, corresponding to the levels of two within factors. The data are arranged so the levels of the second factor "move fastest". For each case the variables are

$$Y_{11}, Y_{12}, Y_{21}, Y_{22}, Y_{31}, Y_{32}, G$$

where Y_{ij} is the value of the dependent variable for

the ith level of the first factor and the jth level of the second.

The symbol D is used to indicate that a variable is not used. The statement

FORM = 'D,G,2D,2(D,Y)'.

indicates that the second variable is a grouping variable and the dependent variable is recorded as variables six and eight. The remaining variables (1, 3, 4, 5, 7) are not used.

If several dependent variables (temperature, blood pressure, weight, etc.) are to be analyzed separately, the number of distinct dependent variables should immediately precede the symbol Y: 3(2(4Y)) designates four dependent variables; each is measured at all levels of two within factors. Four analyses of variance are performed. The data are arranged as

$$Y_{111}, Y_{112}, Y_{113}, Y_{114}, Y_{121}, \ldots, Y_{124}, Y_{211}, \ldots$$

where Y_{ijk} is the value of the kth dependent variable for the ith level of the first within factor and the jth level of the second. We say that the index corresponding to the dependent variable "moves fastest". If covariates are included, e.g., 3(2X, 4Y), an analysis of covariance is performed for each of the four dependent variables using both covariates.

DESIGN ─────────

FORM = 'c'.   none/prev.
  The FORM for the design. See above for an explanation. The statement can be up to 100 characters. If FORM is specified, GROUPING, LEVELS, DEPENDENT and COVARIATES are ignored. When a GROUPING variable takes on more than 10 distinct values, CODES or CUTPOINTS must be specified in a GROUP paragraph. When CODES or CUTPOINTS are not specified, the cell means and standard deviations are not sorted before printing.

The following statements illustrate the two ways of specifying the role of the variables; each pair specifies the same design.

	Method 1			-- or -- Method 2
GROUP = 1.	DEPEND = 2,3,4.	–	LEVEL = 3.	FORM = 'G,3(Y)'.
GROUP = 1,2.	DEPEND = 3 TO 8.	–	LEVEL = 2, 3.	FORM = '2G,2(3(Y))'.
GROUP = 1.	DEPEND = 2 TO 9.	–	LEVEL = 2.	FORM = 'G,2(4Y)'.
GROUP = 1.	DEPEND = 3,5,7.	COVA = 2,4,6.	LEVEL = 3.	FORM = 'G,3(X,Y)'.
GROUP = 1,10.	DEPEND = 5,7,9.	COVA = 3,4,3,6,3,8.	LEVEL = 3.	FORM = 'G,D,X,3(X,Y),G'.
GROUP = 1.	DEPEND = 3,4,6,7,9,10.	COVA = 2,2,5,5,8,8.	LEVEL = 3, 2.	FORM = 'G,3(X,2(Y))'.
GROUP = 1, 2.	DEPEND = 3.	–	–	FORM = '2G,Y'.
–	DEPEND = 1 TO 3.	–	LEVEL = 3.	FORM = '3(Y)'.
–	DEPEND = 4,5,9,10.	COVA = 1,2,3,6,7,8.	LEVEL = 2.	FORM = '2(3X,2Y)'.

Not all design specifications can be given by a FORM statement. For example, there is no FORM statement equivalent to

DEPEND = 1 TO 4.   COVA = 5 TO 8.   LEVEL = 4.

(The COVARIATES in variables 5 to 8 are paired with the levels of the within factor.)

Complex designs. Very complex designs can also be specified. Suppose there are two grouping factors: sex and hospital. There are two within factors: day with three levels and time with levels a.m. and p.m. There are two dependent variables: systolic and diastolic blood pressure. A separate analysis of variance will be made for each. There are three covariates: age (measured only once for each subject), weight (measured once a day), and temperature (measured each time blood pressure is taken). Altogether there are 24 variables. Data for such a design could be arranged as shown below.

| GROUPS | | | Day 1 | | | | | | | Day 2 | | | | | | | Day 3 | | | | | | |
| | | | AM | | | | PM | | | AM | | | | PM | | | AM | | | | PM | | |
H	S	A	Wt	T	BPS	BPD	T	BPS	BPD	Wt	T	BPS	BPD	T	BPS	BPD	Wt	T	BPS	BPD	T	BPS	BPD
1	1																						
1	1																						
1	1																						
1	1																						
1	1																						
1	1																						
1	2																						
1	2																						
1	2																						
1	2																						
1	2																						
1	2																						
2	1																						
2	1																						
2	1																						
2	1																						
2	2																						
2	2																						
2	2																						
2	2																						
2	2																						

```
1  2   3   4  5  6   7    8  9  10   11 12 13  14   15 16  17   18 19 20  21   22 23  24
```

The row of numbers immediately above refers to the indices of the variables.

```
Key:  H    = hospital
      S    = sex
      A    = age
      Wt   = weight
      T    = temperature
      BPS  = blood pressure, systolic
      BPD  = blood pressure, diastolic
```

We could state the design as

```
GROUP = 1,2.
LEVEL = 3,2.
DEPEND = 6,7,9,10,13,14,16,17,20,21,23,24.
COVA = 3,4,5,3,4,8,3,11,12,3,11,15,3,18,19,3,18,22.
```

or more simply as

```
FORM = '2G,X,3(X,2(X,2Y))'.
```

Names for the Grouping and Within-Subject Factors

The first letters of the names of the grouping and within factors are used to label interactions in the ANOVA tables. Therefore, the results can be more easily interpreted if each name begins with a distinct letter. Names for the grouping factors are specified as variable names in the VARIABLE paragraph. Names for the within factors are specified in the DESIGN paragraph (see Examples 2V.6 to 2V.13).

```
DESIGN ─────────────────────────────────────
  NAME = c list.                    R,S,T,.../prev.
    Names of within factors (up to four characters
    each). Names are used to label the output and
    should be specified when there is more than one
    factor. The first NAME is for the first factor
    specified in the LEVEL statement or the first
    (leftmost) factor in the FORM statement, the
    second for the second factor, etc. Only the
    first character of the name is used in the
    ANOVA table; therefore each NAME should begin
    with a different letter and also differ from
    the first letters of the names of the GROUPING
    variables.
```

Orthogonal Decomposition of Within-Subject Factors

The analysis of the within factors in a
repeated-measures design involves an orthogonal
polynomial decomposition for the within factors.
This is described in detail on pp. 367, 372 and in
Appendix A.18. The ANOVA tables corresponding to the
ANOVA of each orthogonal polynomial are printed.

ORTHOGONAL.

is specified in the DESIGN paragraph. This option is
illustrated in Output 2V.8.

The orthogonal decomposition is of interest only
when the levels of the within factor are ordered
(such as by time or dosage).

Unless you specify otherwise, the levels of each
within factor are spaced equally; i.e., 1, 2, 3,
... . You can specify unequal spacing by a POINT
statement.

```
DESIGN ─────────────────────────────────────
  ORTHogonal.                          no/prev.
    Print the ANOVA or analysis of covariance
    tables corresponding to the analysis of each
    orthogonal polynomial.
  POINT(#) = # list.                   1,2,3....
    Spacing for the levels of the within factor. #
    is the subscript of the within factor; 1
    specifies the first within factor in the LEVEL
    or FORM statement, 2 is the second, etc. The
    numbers are the values assigned to the levels
    of the within factor to obtain unequal spacing
    in the orthogonal decomposition.
```

Test of Symmetry of Orthogonal Components and Adjustments to Degrees of Freedom

Assumptions required for the validity of F-tests
in the fixed effects analysis of variance model are
that the observations are mutually independent,
normally distributed, and have equal variance. In
the repeated-measures model, measures made on the
same subject are usually correlated. As a
consequence, F tests are made in a way that allows
some relaxation of the assumption of complete
independence. The independence assumption is
replaced by symmetry assumptions, one for each error
sum of squares for which there is more than one
degree of freedom for a within factor. (F tests in

an orthogonal polynomial breakdown or those that
include only two levels of a repeated measure do not
require the symmetry assumption.) In all other cases
the assumption can be tested by specifying

SYMMETRY.

in the DESIGN paragraph. These tests are based on a
sphericity test found in Anderson (1958, p. 259).
Specifically, they test the hypothesis that the
orthogonal polynomials for any within factor are
independent and have equal variances. A related
concept is that of compound symmetry (Winer, 1971,
pp. 594-599). Compound symmetry is a sufficient but
not necessary condition. The symmetry test of P2V is
a sufficient and necessary condition; it is less
restrictive than compound symmetry.

This test should be viewed with the following
reservations: it has low power for small sample
sizes. For large sample sizes, the test is likely to
show significance although the effect on the
analysis of variance may be negligible. The
sphericity test can be very sensitive to outliers.

When there is reason to doubt the symmetry
assumption, either because of the sphericity test or
because of compelling theoretical considerations,
such as the fact that the within factor is time, for
which there is a suspected carryover effect from one
level of the within factor to the next, tests can be
made by reducing the degrees of freedom contributed
by the within factors. These adjustments are due to
Greenhouse and Geisser (1959) and Huynh-Feldt. See
Frane (1980a) for more discussion.

```
DESIGN ─────────────────────────────────────
  SYMmetry.                            yes/prev.
    A test for the symmetry assumption for within
    factors. In versions dated before 1980, the
    assumed value is NO rather than YES.
```

Alternate Models with More than One Grouping Factor (pooling interactions)

When there are several grouping factors, P2V fits
all possible interactions of the grouping factors
unless you specify otherwise. Some designs use only
a subset of the interactions; e.g., Latin squares,
incomplete blocks and fractional factorials.

You can specify either the main effects and
interactions to be included in the model or the
interactions to be excluded from the model. For
example, if there are two grouping factors (Example
2V.1) you can specify a model that includes only
main effects by specifying

INCLUDE = 1,2.

or

EXCLUDE = 12.

in the DESIGN paragraph. For example, if we add the
sentence INCLUDE = 1,2. to the DESIGN paragraph of
Example 2V.1, we would obtain a test of the main
effect for each grouping factor assuming that the
interaction is zero.

```
DESIGN ─────────────────────────────────
   │         ┌─ INCLude=# list.    include all main
   │(one only)│                    effects and
   │         └─ EXCLude=# list.    interactions for
   │                               grouping factors
        The numbers are terms to be included or
        excluded from the model for the grouping
        factors. The grouping factors are represented
        by the numbers 1, 2, 3, ... (and not by the
        subscripts of the grouping variables).
        Interactions are specified as 12, 13, 123, ...
        etc. For example, when there are three grouping
        factors, both

                    INCLUDE = 1, 2, 3, 12, 13.
        and
                    EXCLUDE = 23, 123.

        specify models that contain all main effects
        and two of the two-factor interactions. The
        within factors part of the model, if any, will
        include interactions of each term of the
        grouping part of the model with the within
        factors.
```

Printing and Plotting Cell Means and Standard Deviations

Cell means and standard deviations are printed unless you request NO MEAN. Plots of cell standard deviations versus cell means on standard and logarithmic scales are used to determine the appropriate transformation for stabilizing the cell variances. (See discussion in P7D.)

```
DESIGN ─────────────────────────────────
   │ MEAN.                            yes/prev.
   │   Print cell means and standard deviations.
```

```
PLOT ───────────────────────────────────
   │ MEAN.                             no/prev.
   │   Diagnostic plots are printed of the cell
   │   standard deviation versus the cell mean on both
   │   a standard and a logarithmic scale.
```

RESIDUALS AND PREDICTED VALUES

Example 2V.14 Printing and Saving Predicted Values and Residuals

Predicted values and residuals can be printed or saved in a BMDP File to be further analyzed or plotted by other BMDP programs (e.g., P5D and P6D in Chapter 10). When there are no within factors, there is only one predicted value for each case (the estimate of its expected value). The residual is the difference between the observed and predicted values. When there are within factors, two sets of predicted values can be estimated in terms of

- the coefficients of the orthogonal polynomials used in the computation of the sums of squares (see Appendix A.18); a predicted value and residual is computed for each orthogonal polynomial and for products of orthogonal polynomials corresponding to interactions
- the means and deviations from the means

You can choose between the two sets of parameters by stating

RESIDUALS ARE ORTH.

or

RESIDUALS ARE MEAN.

in the DESIGN paragraph.

The predicted values and residuals are printed when PRINT. is specified in the DESIGN paragraph. (The preassigned option is MEAN.) Residuals are saved with the data in a BMDP File when you specify a SAVE paragraph (Section 7.3). You can save the data without the residuals if you specify

NO RESIDUAL.

in the SAVE paragraph.

When the option MEAN is used, the residuals and predicted values are computed both for individual cells and for all marginals of the within factors. Therefore, the number of pairs of predicted values and residuals is the product $(1 + \ell_1)(1 + \ell_2)...$ where ℓ_1 is the number of levels of the first within factor, etc. When the orthogonal polynomial option is selected, the number of pairs of predicted values and residuals is the product $\ell_1 \ell_2...$

Details of the methods of computing residuals are given in Appendix A.18. As an example, consider a design with one grouping factor, one within factor and one covariate (measured at each level of the within factor). The model for computing predicted values and residuals when

RESIDUALS ARE MEAN.

is

$$y_{ijk} = \mu + \alpha_i + \beta_0 x_{i \cdot k} + \pi_{k(i)} + \gamma_j + (\alpha\gamma)_{ij}$$
$$+ \beta_1 (x_{ijk} - x_{i \cdot k}) + (\gamma\pi)_{jk(i)}$$

where i denotes group, j denotes level of the within factor, k denotes subjects (nested in groups), $x_{i \cdot k}$ indicates that the covariate has been averaged over the levels of the within factor, $\pi_{k(i)}$ is a between groups error component and $(\beta\pi)_{jk(i)}$ is a within subjects error component. This is the model for Example 2V.12. First, there is a predicted value and residual for the <u>between groups part of the model</u>:

$$y_{i \cdot k} = \mu + \alpha_i + \beta_0 x_{i \cdot k} + \pi_{k(i)} \cdot$$

This part of the model is a simple fixed effects model for which we compute the usual predicted value and residual. The predicted value for this part of the model is named PO and the residual is named RO. They are computed as

$$PO = \hat{\mu} + \hat{\alpha}_i + \hat{\beta}_0 x_{i \cdot k}$$

$$RO = y_{i \cdot k} - PO \cdot$$

The <u>within subjects part of the model</u> can be written

$$y_{ijk} - y_{i \cdot k} = \gamma_j + (\alpha\gamma)_{ij} + \beta_1(x_{ijk} - x_{i \cdot k}) + (\gamma\pi)_{jk(i)} \ .$$

For each level of the within factor, we have a predicted value and residual:

$$P_j = \hat{\gamma}_i + (\hat{\alpha\gamma})_{ij} + \hat{\beta}_1(x_{ijk} - x_{i \cdot k})$$

$$R_j = y_{ijk} - y_{i \cdot k} \ .$$

Thus,

$$y_{ijk} = PO + RO + P_j + R_j \ .$$

In the following examples, a and b, we print and save the residuals and predicted values, first using the preassigned option

RESIDUAL = MEAN.

and then specifying in the DESIGN paragraph

RESIDUAL = ORTH.

For example a, the instructions of Example 2V.4 are modified as follows

```
/ PROBLEM    TITLE IS 'WINER, PAGE 546, NOISE DATA'.
/ INPUT      VARIABLES ARE 10.
             FORMAT IS '(10F3.0)'.
/ VARIABLE   NAMES ARE NOISE, B1C1, B1C2, B1C3,
                       B2C1, B2C2, B2C3,
                       B3C1, B3C2, B3C3.

/ DESIGN     GROUPING IS NOISE.
             DEPENDENT ARE 2 TO 10.
             LEVELS ARE 3, 3.
             NAMES ARE PERIOD, DIAL.
             PRINT.

/ GROUP      CODES(1) ARE  1,  2.
             NAMES(1) ARE A1, A2.

/ SAVE       UNIT IS 10.
             NEW.
             CODE IS WINER.
             RESIDUAL.

/ END
```

Note: The System Cards that precede the Control Language must contain a card describing where to store the BMDP File (Section 7.3). In addition space must be allocated for the system file (Section 7.3). (See end of this P2V section for organization of systems information, BMDP instructions and data.)

For example b, we add a RESIDUAL statement to the DESIGN paragraph above.

```
/ DESIGN     GROUPING IS NOISE.
             DEPENDENT ARE 2 TO 10.
             LEVELS ARE 3, 3.
             NAMES ARE PERIOD, DIAL.
             RESIDUAL = ORTH.
             PRINT.
```

The results are presented in Outputs 2V.14a and b.

Note that the predicted values are labelled P followed by two numbers since there are two repeated measures and that the residuals are labelled R followed by two numbers. For example, RESID = MEAN is used, P00 denotes the predicted values for the average over all levels of the repeated measure and P13 denotes the predicted value for the first level of the first within factor and the third level of the second within factor. When RESID = ORTH is used, P00 denotes the predicted value for the product of the zero degree orthogonal polynomials for each of the within factors and P13 denotes the predicted value for the product of the linear component of the first within factor and the cubic component of the second within factor.

Note that in either case, a numerical consistency check is computed to compare the estimates of residual sums of squares computed from covariance matrices and from the residuals themselves. A relative error of zero for the difference indicates high numerical accuracy.

```
DESIGN
  RESIdual = (one only)              MEAN/prev.
             MEAN, ORTH.
  Method of computing residuals and predicted
  values.
  PRINT.                             no/prev.
  Print the residuals and predicted values.
```

```
SAVE
  RESIdual.                          RESI/prev.
  The residuals and predicted values are saved in
  a BMDP File if one is created unless you
  specify NO RESIDUAL. If saved, each case in the
  File contains the data, followed by the
  predicted values, followed by the residuals.
  See the following examples for how the
  predicted values and residuals are labelled.
```

Output 2V.14a   A BMDP File is created and the residuals are printed by P2V   (RESIDUALS = MEAN)

```
----------------------------------------------
BMDP FILE IS BEING WRITTEN ON UNIT      10
CODE. . . IS     WINER
CONTENT . IS     DATA
LABEL . . IS

VARIABLES ARE
    1 NOISE      2 B1C1      3 B1C2      4 B1C3      5 B2C1
    6 B2C2       7 B2C3      8 B3C1      9 B3C2     10 B3C3
   11 P00       12 P10      13 P20      14 P30      15 P01
   16 P02       17 P03      18 P11      19 P12      20 P13
   21 P21       22 P22      23 P23      24 P31      25 P32
   26 P33       27 R00      28 R10      29 R20      30 R30
   31 R01       32 R02      33 R03      34 R11      35 R12
   36 R13       37 R21      38 R22      39 R23      40 R31
   41 R32       42 R33
```

CASE	NOISE	P00	P10	P20	P30	P01	P02	P03	P11	P12
		P13	P21	P22	P23	P31	P32	P33	R00	R10
		R20	R30	R01	R02	R03	R11	R12	R13	R21
		R22	R23	R31	R32	R33				
1	A1	47.22221	6.55556	2.22222	-8.77778	-7.11111	-0.77778	7.88889	0.0	0.0
		0.0	0.33333	-1.00000	0.66667	-0.33333	1.00000	-0.66667	-0.77778	-0.33333
		1.00000	-0.66667	-1.66667	1.66667	0.0	1.11111	-0.55556	-0.55556	-1.22222
		2.44444	-1.22222	0.11111	-1.88889	1.77778				
2	A1	47.22221	6.55556	2.22222	-8.77778	-7.11111	-0.77778	7.88889	0.0	0.0
		0.0	0.33333	-1.00000	0.66667	-0.33333	1.00000	-0.66667	-9.66667	-2.11111
		-1.77778	3.88889	-0.44444	-0.11111	0.55556	0.55556	-0.11111	-0.44444	-0.77778
		0.88889	-0.11111	0.22222	-0.77778	0.55556				
3	A1	47.22221	6.55556	2.22222	-8.77778	-7.11111	-0.77778	7.88889	0.0	0.0
		0.0	0.33333	-1.00000	0.66667	-0.33333	1.00000	-0.66667	10.44444	2.44444
		0.77778	-3.22222	2.11111	-1.55556	-0.55556	-1.66667	0.66667	1.00000	2.00000
		-3.33333	1.33333	-0.33333	2.66667	-2.33333				
4	A2	41.33333	13.55556	-1.77778	-11.77778	-6.66667	-3.33333	10.00000	1.11111	-0.55556
		-0.55556	-1.22222	0.44444	0.77778	0.11111	0.11111	-0.22222	-3.22222	1.33333
		0.33333	-1.66667	-1.11111	0.22222	0.88889	3.66667	-1.33333	-2.33333	-2.66667
		0.0	2.66667	-1.00000	1.33333	-0.33333				
5	A2	41.33333	13.55556	-1.77778	-11.77778	-6.66667	-3.33333	10.00000	1.11111	-0.55556
		-0.55556	-1.22222	0.44444	0.77778	0.11111	0.11111	-0.22222	-3.77778	-3.77778
		0.88889	2.88889	0.44444	2.11111	-2.55556	-0.22222	-0.55556	0.77778	0.77778
		1.11111	-1.88889	-0.55556	-0.55556	1.11111				
6	A2	41.33333	13.55556	-1.77778	-11.77778	-6.66667	-3.33333	10.00000	1.11111	-0.55556
		-0.55556	-1.22222	0.44444	0.77778	0.11111	0.11111	-0.22222	7.00000	2.44444
		-1.22222	-1.22222	0.66667	-2.33333	1.66667	-3.44444	1.88889	1.55556	1.88889
		-1.11111	-0.77778	1.55556	-0.77778	-0.77778				

```
BMDP   FILE ON UNIT 10 HAS BEEN COMPLETED.
----------------------------------------------
NUMBER OF CASES WRITTEN TO FILE        6
```

ERROR TERM	SUM OF SQUARES	RECOMPUTED FROM RESIDUALS	RELATIVE ERROR
1	2491.11111	2491.11111	-0.00000
2	234.88889	234.88889	0.00000
3	105.55556	105.55556	-0.00000
4	127.11111	127.11111	-0.00000

Output 2V.14b   A BMDP File is created and the residuals are printed by P2V (RESIDUALS = ORTH)

ANALYSIS OF VARIANCE FOR 1-ST
DEPENDENT VARIABLE - B1C1   B1C2   B1C3   B2C1   B2C2   B2C3   B3C1   B3C2   B3C3

	SOURCE	SUM OF SQUARES	DEGREES OF FREEDOM	MEAN SQUARE	F	TAIL PROB.	GREENHOUSE GEISSER PROB.	HUYNH FELDT PROB.
	MEAN	105868.16667	1	105868.16667	169.99	0.0002		
	NOISE	468.16667	1	468.16667	0.75	0.4348		
1	ERROR	2491.11111	4	622.77778				
	PERI	3722.33333	2	1861.16667	63.39	0.0000	0.0003	0.0000
	PN	333.00000	2	166.50000	5.67	0.0293	0.0569	0.0293
2	ERROR	234.88889	8	29.36111				
	DIAL	2370.33333	2	1185.16667	89.82	0.0000	0.0000	0.0000
	DN	50.33333	2	25.16667	1.91	0.2102	0.2152	0.2102
3	ERROR	105.55556	8	13.19444				
	PD	10.66667	4	2.66667	0.34	0.8499	0.7295	0.8499
	PDN	11.33333	4	2.83333	0.36	0.8357	0.7156	0.8357
4	ERROR	127.11111	16	7.94444				

ERROR TERM	EPSILON FACTORS FOR DEGREES OF FREEDOM ADJUSTMENT			ERROR SUM OF SQUARES	CORRESPONDING RESIDUALS
	GREENHOUSE-GEISSER	HUYNH-FELDT			
2	0.6476	1.0000		1	R00
3	0.9171	1.0000		2	R10, R20
4	0.5134	1.0000		3	R01, R02
				4	R11, R12, R21, R22

BMDP FILE IS BEING WRITTEN ON UNIT   10
CODE. . . IS   WINER
CONTENT . IS   DATA
LABEL . . IS

VARIABLES ARE
     1 NOISE   2 B1C1   3 B1C2   4 B1C3   5 B2C1
     6 B2C2   7 B2C3   8 B3C1   9 B3C2   10 B3C3
    11 P00   12 P10   13 P20   14 P01   15 P02
    16 P11   17 P12   18 P21   19 P22   20 R00
    21 R10   22 R20   23 R01   24 R02   25 R11
    26 R12   27 R21   28 R22

CASE	NOISE	P00 / R00	P10 / R10	P20 / R20	P01 / R01	P02 / R02	P11 / R11	P12 / R12	P21 / R21	P22 / R22
1	A1	141.66666	18.77942	-4.71404	-18.37117	1.64992	-0.16667	0.86603	0.28868	-1.50000
		-2.33333	0.40825	-2.12132	-2.04124	-3.53553	1.66667	-1.15470	-0.00000	3.66667
2	A1	141.66666	18.77942	-4.71404	-18.37117	1.64992	-0.16667	0.86603	0.28868	-1.50000
		-28.99998	-7.34847	3.77124	-1.22474	0.23570	0.66667	-0.57735	0.57735	1.33333
3	A1	141.66666	18.77942	-4.71404	-18.37117	1.64992	-0.16667	0.86603	0.28868	-1.50000
		31.33333	6.94022	-1.64992	3.26599	3.29983	-2.33333	1.73205	-0.57735	-5.00000
4	A2	123.99998	31.02686	3.77124	-20.41240	7.07107	0.66667	0.57735	1.73205	0.66667
		-9.66667	3.67423	-0.70711	-2.44949	-0.47140	3.33333	2.30940	4.61880	-0.00000
5	A2	123.99998	31.02686	3.77124	-20.41240	7.07107	0.66667	0.57735	1.73205	0.66667
		-11.33333	-8.16497	-1.88562	3.67423	-4.47834	0.33333	0.00000	-2.30940	1.66667
6	A2	123.99998	31.02686	3.77124	-20.41240	7.07107	0.66667	0.57735	1.73205	0.66667
		21.00000	4.49073	2.59272	-1.22474	4.94975	-3.66667	-2.30940	-2.30940	-1.66667

BMDP   FILE ON UNIT 10 HAS BEEN COMPLETED.

NUMBER OF CASES WRITTEN TO FILE   6

ERROR TERM	SUM OF SQUARES	RECOMPUTED FROM RESIDUALS	RELATIVE ERROR
1	2491.11111	2491.11111	-0.00000
2	234.88889	234.88889	0.00000
3	105.55556	105.55556	-0.00000
4	127.11111	127.11111	0.00000

Output 2V.15   In one computer run, residuals and predicted values are passed to P6D for plotting

----

--- ① to ④ in Output 2V.1 appear here ---

ANALYSIS OF VARIANCE FOR 1-ST
DEPENDENT VARIABLE - SYSINCR

	SOURCE	SUM OF SQUARES	DEGREES OF FREEDOM	MEAN SQUARE	F	TAIL PROB.
	MEAN	20037.61301	1	20037.61301	181.41	0.0000
	TREATMNT	2997.47186	3	999.15729	9.05	0.0001
	DISEASE	415.87305	2	207.93652	1.88	0.1637
	TD	707.26626	6	117.87771	1.07	0.3958
1	ERROR	5080.81667	46	110.45254		

BMDP FILE IS BEING WRITTEN ON UNIT   3
CODE. . . IS   KUTNER
CONTENT . IS   DATA
LABEL . . IS

VARIABLES ARE
     1 TREATMNT   2 DISEASE   3 SYSINCR   4 PREDICTD   5 RESIDUAL

BMDP   FILE ON UNIT 3 HAS BEEN COMPLETED.

NUMBER OF CASES WRITTEN TO FILE   58

ERROR TERM	SUM OF SQUARES	RECOMPUTED FROM RESIDUALS	RELATIVE ERROR
1	5080.81667	5080.81667	-0.00000

BMDP6D - BIVARIATE (SCATTER) PLOTS
DEPT. OF BIOMATHEMATICS
UNIVERSITY OF CALIFORNIA, LOS ANGELES, CA 90024
(213)-825-5940   TWX UCLA LSA
PROGRAM REVISED MAY   1980
MANUAL REVISED — 1979
COPYRIGHT (C) 1980 REGENTS OF UNIVERSITY OF CALIFORNIA

--- the P6D instructions are printed and interpreted ---

INPUT BMDP FILE
CODE. . . IS   KUTNER
CONTENT . IS   DATA
LABEL . . IS
VARIABLES
     1 TREATMNT   2 DISEASE   3 SYSINCR   4 PREDICTD   5 RESIDUAL

     VARIABLES TO BE USED
     1 TREATMNT   2 DISEASE   3 SYSINCR   4 PREDICTD   5 RESIDUAL

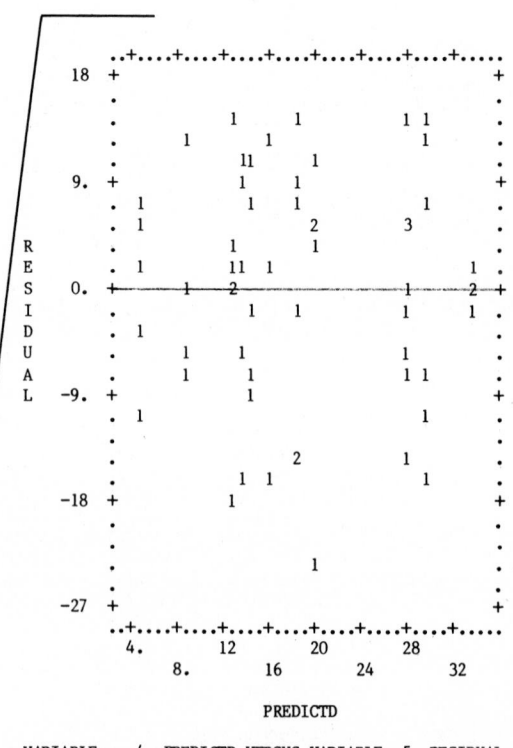

VARIABLE   4 PREDICTD VERSUS VARIABLE 5 RESIDUAL

Example 2V.15 Using Program P6D to Plot the Residuals and Predicted Values

Two types of plots are frequently desirable. First, plots of cell standard deviations versus cell means on standard and logarithmic scale as produced in P7D. See the discussion for this plot in the P7D writeup, p. 112. In P2V, these plots are requested by stating / PLOT MEAN.

Secondly, it is desirable to produce plots of predicted values and residuals. Such plots are not available in P2V as of 1981, but can be easily obtained as shown in this example by saving the predicted values and residuals and requesting plots in P6D. P5D and P7D can also be used to produce histograms and normal probability plots. This example uses the scratch unit number three that is available in the BIMED procedure for IBM and similar systems. The Kutner data of Example 2V.1 are used.

```
// EXEC    BIMED,PROG=BMDP2V
//SYSIN   DD  *
/ PROB
/ INPUT    VAR = 3.
            FORMAT = '(3F3.0)'.
/ VAR      NAMES = TREATMNT, DISEASE, SYSINCR.
/ DESIGN   DEPEND = SYSINCR.
            GROUPING = TREATMNT, DISEASE.
/ SAVE     NEW.
            UNIT = 3.
            CODE = KUTNER.
            RESIDUAL.
/ END
    (data records)
// EXEC    BIMED,PROG=BMDP6D
//SYSIN   DD  *
/ PROB
/ INPUT    UNIT = 3.
            CODE = KUTNER.
/ PLOT     XVAR = PREDICTD.
            YVAR = RESIDUAL.
            SIZE = 40, 25.
/ END
```

The results are shown in Output 2V.15.

Predicted values and residuals can also be plotted for repeated-measures analysis. Note that there are several different predicted values and corresponding residuals for repeated-measures analysis. For example, in Example 2V.6, there are predicted values and residuals for each level of each factor and for each cell determined by the set of within factors. In particular, P10, P20, P30, and R10, R20, and R30 are the predicted values and residuals for the three levels of the first within factor. Each predicted value can be plotted versus the corresponding residual as above. We can also plot all predicted values and residuals in the same plot with the COMMON. option in P6D:

```
/ PLOT    XVAR = P10, P20, P30.
           YVAR = R10, R20, R30.
           COMMON.
```

TOLERANCE

The matrix of sums of cross products must be pivoted (swept) on the covariates and dummy variables for the grouping factors, if any. The tolerance limit is used to avoid pivoting when pivoting will cause a loss in accuracy in the results (Appendix A.11). The tolerance limit rarely needs to be changed. For IBM 360 and 370 computers, the tolerance limit should not ordinarily be lowered.

DESIGN
> TOLerance = #.   0.0001/prev.
>   Tolerance limit for pivoting. This rarely needs to be changed.

Case Weights

A case weight variable can be used as in the regression programs, e.g., P9R. Case weights are used when the variances of the residuals are known to be different. This occurs, for example, when the cases that are input are actually averages of groups of cases. In this circumstance, the case weights are usually the numbers of observations used in defining the averages.

If the weight for a case is equal to zero, the case is not used in the computations of any statistics except predicted values and residuals. Note that the total number of degrees of freedom is equal to the number of cases with positive case weight.

VARiable
> WEIGht = v.   none/prev.
>   The case weight variable, if any. (The case weight option is not available in versions dated before 1980.)

SIZE OF PROBLEM

P2V can analyze up to nine within factors and nine grouping factors. The number of dependent variables plus covariates that can be analyzed is a function of the number of cells ($C = \ell_1 \ell_2 ...$) formed by the grouping factors (where ℓ is the number of levels of the ith grouping factor), and the number of within factors ($T = t_1 t_2 ...$). The following table gives a rough guideline to the maximum number of dependent variables and covariates (V) for medium-sized computer systems.

C	0	0	50	100	50
T	50	100	0	0	50
V	11	4	40	16	1

Appendix B describes how to increase the capacity of the program.

COMPUTATIONAL METHOD

All computations are performed in double precision. Means, standard deviations and covariances are computed by the method of provisional means (Appendix A.2). The computations performed by P2V are described in Appendix A.18.

ACKNOWLEDGEMENT

P2V was designed by Robert Jennrich and Paul Sampson with major contributions from Alan Forsythe and James Frane. It was programmed by Paul Sampson.

SUMMARY

Order of Input Cards

```
// (job card)
// EXEC BIMED,PROG=BMDP2V        (see Appendix E)
//SYSIN DD *
/ PROBLEM
/ INPUT
/ VARIABLE
/ TRANSFORM
/ SAVE
/ DESIGN
/ GROUP
/ END
   (data, if on cards)
// (system card)
```

Full sets of BMDP paragraphs (and data, if on cards)
can be repeated for additional problems; see Section
5.8.

instructions specific to P2V

Paragraph Statement	Preassigned	Comment and Manual Reference
/ VARIABLE		
WEIGht = v.	none	Case weight. * 385
/●DESIGN		Required to specify design by either (FORM) or (GROUP, DEPEND, LEVEL and COVA). If FORM is used, parameters for GROUP, etc. are ignored. INCLUDE and EXCLUDE indicate which effects are to be in the ANOVA model, thereby affecting the error term.
○FORM = 'symbol list'.	none	The FORM of the design, up to 100 characters. Use symbols G (grouping variable), Y (dependent variable), X (covariate) and D (variable not used). The number of nested pairs of parentheses indicates the number of within factors, the symbol Y must appear in the innermost nest. * 377
○GROUPing = v list.	none	Names or subscripts of the GROUPing variables (factors). (See / GROUP) *
○DEPENDent = v list.	none	Names or subscripts of the dependent variables, i.e., the variables that are the measurements or within-subject factors values being tested. *
LEVELs = # list.	none	Number of levels of the within factors. Specify only for repeated-measures variables. The first number is for the slowest changing factor, the second for the next slowest changing, etc. * 376
COVAriates = v list.	none	Names or subscripts of the covariates. The covariates are paired with the within factors, i.e., the first covariate listed is index of that covariate must be repeated. * 376
INCLude = # list. ⎫ EXCLude = # list. ⎭	see comment	Terms to be included or excluded from the model for the grouping factors Use with designs that do not fit all possible interactions of the grouping factors; e.g., Latin squares, incomplete blocks and fractional factorials. Specify the main effects and interactions to be included in the model OR the interactions to be excluded. The grouping factors are identified by the numbers 1, 2, 3 (the order as defined in / DESIGN GROUP or FORM - not the subscript of the grouping variable). Interactions are specified as 12, 13, 23, 123, etc. 380
NAMEs = c list.	R, S, T,...	Names of within factors, up to 3 characters each, to label the output when more than one within factor is specified. (Only the first character is used in the ANOVA table.) The first NAME is for the first within factor in the LEVEL statement, or the leftmost within factor in the FORM statement, etc. * 379
ORTHogonal.	no	Print the ANOVA or analysis of covariance tables for each orthogonal polynomial of the within factors. The orthogonal decomposition into linear quadratic, etc., components is of interest only when the levels of the within factors are ordered (e.g., time or dosage). * 379

(continued)

(continued)

Paragraph Statement	Preassigned	Comment and Manual Reference
/ DESIGN (continued)		
POINT(j) = # list.	equal spacing	Spacing for the levels of the within factor j, where j = 1 is the first factor in the LEVEL or FORM statement, j = 2 the second, etc. The numbers are the values assigned to the levels of the within factor to obtain unequal spacing in the orthogonal decomposition. 379
SYMmetry.	yes	A test for compound symmetry of orthogonal components of within factors. See p. 379 regarding reservations about the test. *
MEAN.	yes	Print cell means and standard deviations. 380
RESIduals = c.	MEAN.	Method for estimating predicted values and residuals for printing or saving (one only): * 381 MEAN - use means and deviations from means ORTH - use each orthogonal polynomial and their products that correspond to interactions
PRINT.	no	Print the residuals and predicted values. * 381
TOLerance = #.	.0001.	Tolerance limit, used to avoid pivoting that results in a loss of accuracy. This rarely needs to be changed. * 385
/ PLOT		
MEAN.	no	Plot of cell means vs. cell standard deviations. * 380
/ SAVE		Additional option required only if BMDP File is created.
RESIdual.	yes	When a BMDP File is created, the residuals and predicted values are saved after the data for each case. When RESIDUAL = MEAN. is specified, the number of pairs of predicted values and residuals is the product of the number of levels of the within factors. * 381

Key:

/	-indicates paragraph		*	-assigned value remains the same for additional problems
.	-period ends a sentence			
●	-required O -may be required		VT	-number of variables after transformations
v	-variable (name or subscript)		list	-more than one item, often one per var.
g	-group (name or subscript)			
#	-number			Capitalized letters-paragraph or sentence names recognized by BMDP
'c'	-characters (name or parameter) may omit apostrophes if contiguous letters only			Page numbers following refer to this Manual

P4V

15.3 General Univariate and Multivariate Analysis of Variance and Covariance, Including Repeated Measures (URWAS)

Michael Davidson
Jerome Toporek

ABSTRACT

P4V is a general purpose analysis of variance and covariance program. It handles both univariate and multivariate analyses. Repeated measures, split-plot, and changeover designs are included. Both univariate and multivariate tests are given for repeated-measures designs, including multivariate tests for repeated measurement of several different dependent variables. The Greenhouse-Geisser and Huynh-Feldt adjustments to the univariate approach to repeated measures are reported.

Effective use of the advanced features of this program requires more than a casual background in analysis of variance, e.g., its multivariate analysis of variance features are intended for those who already have a background in multivariate analysis of variance.

Factor level weights or cell weights are specified to indicate the importance to be given to each level of each factor or to each cell in determining the sums of squares to be computed and the hypotheses to be tested. Weights thus give a flexibility to P4V that enables it to carry out analyses performed by other popular analysis of variance programs as well as analyses not easily obtained by other programs.

This writeup for P4V is supplemented by BMDP Technical Reports 56, 59, 67, 69 and 75. We strongly urge reading these technical reports if your analysis is more complex than the examples given here. Several options are described in complete detail only in Technical Report 67.

WHERE TO FIND IT

Many features found in P4V are described in detail only in BMDP Technical Reports 56, 59, 67, 69 and 75. TR 67 is the complete user's manual for P4V. TR 56 is an annotated computer output. TR 59 discusses the design philosophy of P4V. TR 69 discusses repeated measures designs, and TR 75 discusses the multivariate approach to repeated measures. Some of the topics discussed in detail in TR 67, but not discussed or covered only briefly here include:

- nested grouping factors
- nested repeated-measures factors
- monitoring of numerical accuracy
- multivariate ANOVA with repeated measures for each variate (distinct dependent variable)
- empty cells
- user definition of effects to be tested
- user defined orthogonalization of effects
- applications with unequal cell weights
- specifying models with the structure formula procedure (symbolic description of design)
- use of simple effects
- automatic averaging of available variables, especially for incomplete data

Abbreviations Used in P4V Output

WCP	- within contrast pooled (for univariate approach to repeated measures)
SS	- sum of squares
MS	- mean square
LRATIO	- likelihood ratio for multivariate test
TSQ	- Hotelling's T-squared
TZSQ	- Hotelling's generalized T-squared
MXROOT	- maximum root
ALL	- all variates combined in multivariate test
DFH	- degrees of freedom for hypothesis in multivariate test
DFE	- degrees of freedom for error in multivariate test
HE EVALS	- eigenvalues for canonical analysis using hypothesis and residual covariance matrices
HT EVALS	- eigenvalues for canonical analysis using hypothesis and total covariance matrices
S	- the minimum of DFH and the rank of the total covariance matrix
T	- the maximum of DFH and the rank of the total covariance matrix

Example 4V.1 Two-way Analysis of Variance

The Kutner data used to illustrate P2V is also used to illustrate P4V. As discussed in their writeups, P2V and P7D always give each population cell mean equal importance or weight (see p. 362 and p. 109). In this example, we first perform an analysis with equal weights and then show analyses with unequal cell weights.

The BMDP instructions for P4V are in two parts: the first part (Data Definition instructions) defines the input data; the second part (Analysis instructions) defines the analysis to be performed. Note that the slash must come at the end of each paragraph of Analysis instructions, rather than at the beginning.

The setup for the Kutner data is

```
----------------------------------------
/ PROBLEM   TITLE IS 'KUTNER, TWO-WAY ANOVA, UNEQUAL
                     CELL SIZES'.
/ INPUT     VARIABLES ARE 3.
            FORMAT IS FREE.

/ VARIABLE  NAMES ARE TREATMNT, DISEASE, SYSINCR.

/ BETWEEN   FACTORS ARE TREATMNT, DISEASE.
            CODES(1) ARE 1 TO 4.
            NAMES(1) ARE DRUG1, DRUG2, DRUG3, DRUG4.
            CODES(2) ARE 1 TO 3.
            NAMES(2) ARE DISEASE1, DISEASE2,
                        DISEASE3.

/ WEIGHTS   BETWEEN ARE EQUAL.

/ PRINT     MARGINALS ARE ALL.

/ END
   (data records go here)
/END

ANALYSIS   PROCEDURE IS FACTORIAL. /
END /
/ WEIGHTS   BETWEEN ARE SIZES.
/ PRINT     MARGINALS ARE NONE. NO CELLS.
/ END
ANALYSIS PROCEDURE IS FACTORIAL. /
----------------------------------------
```

(See end of this P4V section for organization of systems information, BMDP instructions and data.)

Our discussion of these instructions is organized to follow the operation of the program. We first discuss the data definition instructions and the output produced from this interpretation; we then discuss the analysis instructions and present output of the results.

The Data Definition instructions include BETWEEN and WEIGHT paragraphs in addition to such standard paragraphs as PROBLEM, INPUT and VARIABLE. The BETWEEN paragraph is used to describe the grouping factors. The CODE and NAME statements can alternatively be placed in a GROUP paragraph. The subscripts of the CODE and NAME statements in the BETWEEN paragraph refer to the index of the factors mentioned in the BETWEEN paragraph, not the index of the variables as defined in the INPUT and VARIABLE paragraphs (although in this example they are the same).

Specifying cell weights. One of the unique features of P4V is the flexibility the user has to give weight or importance to each cell when defining sums of squares and hypotheses to be tested. In P2V and P7D, we automatically give each cell the same importance, thereby providing classical Yates' hypotheses for balanced or unbalanced data. In P4V you must state the importance of each cell. If each cell is to have the same weight, you can simply specify

BETWEEN ARE EQUAL.

in the WEIGHT paragraph as we have done above. Weights are specified separately for between (grouping) factors and for within (repeated-measures) factors. An example of the latter is given in Example 4V.3.

We include the optional PRINT paragraph to obtain statistics for each cell and for all marginals of combinations of factors.

The cards or records containing data follow the P4V Data Definition instructions unless they are on a separate tape or disk file. Before any analysis is performed, P4V reads the Data Definition instructions and the data and computes descriptive statistics for each cell. The results are presented in Output 4V.1. Circled numbers below correspond to those in the output.

① The cells of the analysis of variance design are described. The cell weight for each cell is 1.0 since we specify cell weights to be equal. The

Output 4V.1 Two-way analysis of variance – Kutner data

```
------------------------------------------------------
```

	BETWEEN DESIGN:				
①	CELL NO.	WEIGHT	SIZE	TREATMNT	DISEASE
	1	1.00000	6	1 DRUG1	1 DISEASE1
	2	1.00000	4	1 DRUG1	2 DISEASE2
	3	1.00000	5	1 DRUG1	3 DISEASE3
	4	1.00000	5	2 DRUG2	1 DISEASE1
	5	1.00000	4	2 DRUG2	2 DISEASE2
	6	1.00000	6	2 DRUG2	3 DISEASE3
	7	1.00000	3	3 DRUG3	1 DISEASE1
	8	1.00000	4	3 DRUG3	2 DISEASE2
	9	1.00000	4	3 DRUG3	3 DISEASE3
	10	1.00000	5	4 DRUG4	1 DISEASE1
	11	1.00000	6	4 DRUG4	2 DISEASE2
	12	1.00000	4	4 DRUG4	3 DISEASE3

(output continued)

Output 4V.1 (continued)

(2) SUMMARY STATISTICS FOR VARIATE(S):

VARIATE	COUNT	MEAN	VARIANCE	STD.DEV.	WTD.MEAN	MAXIMUM	MINIMUM
SYSINCR	56	19.21	166.3	12.89	18.95	44.00	-6.000

LEVEL 1 MARGINALS

(3)

FACTOR	LEVEL	COUNT	MEAN	VARIANCE	STD.DEV.	WTD.MEAN	MAXIMUM	MINIMUM
TREATMNT	DRUG1	15	26.07	136.4	11.68	25.99	44.00	-3.000
	DRUG2	15	25.53	135.0	11.62	26.56	42.00	3.000
	DRUG3	11	8.909	110.1	10.49	9.528	29.00	-6.000
	DRUG4	15	13.60	92.97	9.642	13.73	27.00	-5.000
DISEASE	DISEASE1	19	22.79	173.2	13.16	21.82	44.00	-2.000
	DISEASE2	18	18.83	186.7	13.67	19.58	36.00	-6.000
	DISEASE3	19	16.00	134.0	11.58	15.45	32.00	-3.000

(4) CELL STATISTICS

==

FACTOR	LEVEL
TREATMNT	DRUG1

==>

FACTOR	LEVEL	COUNT	MEAN	VARIANCE	STD.DEV.	WTD.MEAN	MAXIMUM	MINIMUM
DISEASE	DISEASE1	6	29.33	169.5	13.02	29.33	44.00	13.00
	DISEASE2	4	28.25	34.25	5.852	28.25	33.00	21.00
	DISEASE3	5	20.40	178.8	13.37	20.40	31.00	-3.000

==

FACTOR	LEVEL
TREATMNT	DRUG2

==>

FACTOR	LEVEL	COUNT	MEAN	VARIANCE	STD.DEV.	WTD.MEAN	MAXIMUM	MINIMUM
DISEASE	DISEASE1	5	28.00	120.5	10.98	28.00	42.00	13.00
	DISEASE2	4	33.50	4.333	2.082	33.50	36.00	31.00
	DISEASE3	6	18.17	157.0	12.53	18.17	32.00	3.000

==

FACTOR	LEVEL
TREATMNT	DRUG3

==>

FACTOR	LEVEL	COUNT	MEAN	VARIANCE	STD.DEV.	WTD.MEAN	MAXIMUM	MINIMUM
DISEASE	DISEASE1	3	16.33	201.3	14.19	16.33	29.00	1.000
	DISEASE2	4	3.750	60.92	7.805	3.750	11.00	-6.000
	DISEASE3	4	8.500	81.00	9.000	8.500	21.00	1.000

==

FACTOR	LEVEL
TREATMNT	DRUG4

==>

FACTOR	LEVEL	COUNT	MEAN	VARIANCE	STD.DEV.	WTD.MEAN	MAXIMUM	MINIMUM
DISEASE	DISEASE1	5	13.60	111.3	10.55	13.60	24.00	-2.000
	DISEASE2	6	12.83	107.0	10.34	12.83	27.00	-5.000
	DISEASE3	4	14.75	104.3	10.21	14.75	25.00	5.000

(output continued)

column labeled SIZE is the number of cases in each cell. The TREATMNT and DISEASE columns indicate the group number and group name for the level of each factor.

② Summary statistics are reported. The column labeled MEAN contains the mean of all the cases. The VARIANCE column contains the usual unbiased estimate of variance obtained by dividing the sum of squared deviations from the mean by the number of cases minus one. Note that the variance and standard deviation are computed using all cases as a single sample. The WTD.MEAN is the weighted average of the cell means. In our example, it is the simple average of the cell means because we specify that cell weights are equal. It is the mean of all the cases if cell sizes are equal or if we state that cell sizes are to be used as weights.

After reporting the statistics for all the cases as a single sample, statistics are reported for each level of each factor ③, and for each cell ④. More generally, we obtain statistics for all marginals of all combinations of factors since we request MARGINALS ARE ALL. in the PRINT paragraph.

The Analysis instructions. After the cell statistics are reported, P4V reads and processes the Analysis paragraphs one at a time. Note that the slash (/) for the Analysis paragraphs is placed at the end rather than at the beginning of the paragraphs. This modification facilitates interactive use. The slash is used both to signal the end of the paragraph and to begin processing. When running the program interactively, you specify new Analysis instructions after seeing the results of previous Data Definition and Analysis instructions.

In this example, we simply request the FACTORIAL procedure in the ANALYSIS paragraph to generate instructions defining the analysis of variance effects. Alternatively effects to be included in the ANOVA model can be specified by the user. By default, P4V generates statements that define typical effects. Each effect corresponds to a DESIGN or INTERACT paragraph generated by P4V ⑤. In our example, P4V generates three DESIGN paragraphs and an INTERACT paragraph.

⑥ The first DESIGN paragraph generated defines the overall or grand mean effect as indicated in the NAME statement of that paragraph. The TYPE statement indicates that the "grand mean" refers to a between-subject effect (not within or repeated-measures effect). This effect is defined as a "contrast" (as opposed to "regression" as discussed later and in TR 67). MODEL. and CODE =

Output 4V.1 (continued)

```
ANALYSIS  PROCEDURE IS FACTORIAL. /      ⑤


FACTORIAL PROCEDURE .....

THE FOLLOWING STATEMENTS HAVE BEEN GENERATED:



DESIGN  TYPE IS BETWEEN, CONTRAST.  MODEL.      ⑥
   CODE IS CONST.  NAME IS 'OVALL: GRAND MEAN'./


DESIGN  FACTOR IS TREATMNT.       ⑦
   CODE IS EFFECT.  NAME IS 'T: TREATMNT'./


DESIGN  FACTOR IS DISEASE.         ⑧
   CODE IS EFFECT.  NAME IS 'D: DISEASE'./


INTERACT EFFECTS ARE T,D.      ⑨
   NAME IS TD./


ANALYSIS  /    ⑩


END OF PROCEDURE-GENERATED STATEMENTS.
USER-SUPPLIED ANALYSIS CONTROL STATEMENTS RESUME
FOLLOWING ANALYSIS OUTPUT.
```

```
=================================================================

 --- ANALYSIS SUMMARY ---

THE FOLLOWING EFFECTS ARE COMPONENTS OF THE SPECIFIED
LINEAR MODEL FOR THE BETWEEN DESIGN.  ESTIMATES AND TESTS
OF HYPOTHESES FOR THESE EFFECTS CONCERN PARAMETERS OF THAT MODEL.

    OVALL: GRAND MEAN
    T: TREATMNT
    D: DISEASE
    TD                            ⑪
=================================================================

EFFECT    VARIATE      STATISTIC        F      DF        P
-----------------------------------------------------------------

OVALL: GRAND MEAN

     SYSINCR
               SS=    19273.9
               MS=    19273.9      167.39   1,   44  0.0000

T: TREATMNT

     SYSINCR
               SS=    2901.76
               MS=    967.253       8.40   3,   44  0.0002

D: DISEASE

     SYSINCR
               SS=    378.592
               MS=    189.296       1.64   2,   44  0.2049

TD

     SYSINCR
               SS=    708.623
               MS=    118.104       1.03   6,   44  0.4215


ERROR
     SYSINCR
               SS=    5066.3167
               MS=    115.14356

=================================================================
```

(output continued)

CONST. are also discussed later and in TR 67. They can be ignored in basic applications.

⑦ The second DESIGN paragraph is used to describe the main effect for the first between factor (grouping variable), TREATMNT.

⑧ The third DESIGN paragraph describes the second between factor.

⑨ The INTERACT paragraph describes the interaction of two factors.

⑩ The ANALYSIS paragraph with no statements is a signal that the description of the analysis to be performed has been completed and that the analysis of variance computations will now begin.

Remember that the Control Language paragraphs in ⑥ through ⑩ are supplied by the program in

Output 4V.1 (continued)

```
=========================================================================

⑫       --- ANALYSIS SUMMARY ---


THE FOLLOWING EFFECTS ARE COMPONENTS OF THE SPECIFIED
LINEAR MODEL FOR THE BETWEEN DESIGN.  ESTIMATES AND TESTS
OF HYPOTHESES FOR THESE EFFECTS CONCERN PARAMETERS OF THAT MODEL.

            OVALL: GRAND MEAN
            TD
            T|D
            D|T

THE FOLLOWING EFFECTS INVOLVE WEIGHTED COMBINATIONS OF CELL MEANS.
THEY ARE NOT COMPONENTS OF THE LINEAR MODEL FOR THE BETWEEN DESIGN.

            T: TREATMNT
            D: DISEASE


=========================================================================

EFFECT    VARIATE      STATISTIC        F       DF        P
-------------------------------------------------------------------------

OVALL: GRAND MEAN

        SYSINCR
                    SS=      20674.6
                    MS=      20674.6       179.55   1,   44   0.0000

T: TREATMNT

        SYSINCR
                    SS=      2944.25
                    MS=      981.418       8.52     3,   44   0.0001

D: DISEASE

        SYSINCR
                    SS=      441.771
                    MS=      220.885       1.92     2,   44   0.1589

TD

        SYSINCR
                    SS=      708.623
                    MS=      118.104       1.03     6,   44   0.4215

T|D

        SYSINCR
                    SS=      2928.72
                    MS=      976.240       8.48     3,   44   0.0001

D|T

        SYSINCR
                    SS=      426.237
                    MS=      213.118       1.85     2,   44   0.1691


ERROR
        SYSINCR
                    SS=      5066.3167
                    MS=      115.14356


=========================================================================
```

response to a request by the user for the FACTORIAL procedure. User-supplied paragraphs for specification of special contrasts and other hypotheses are illustrated later.

⑪ A conventional analysis of variance table is reported. The analysis of variance is preceded by a summary listing the effects to be tested. We suggest that you examine this summary to see which effects are present and to verify their roles, especially for complex models. Since we have stated that the between weights are equal, the hypotheses tested here are exactly the same as those tested in P2V. In particular, the hypothesis for column effects (DISEASE) is

$$\mu_{11} + \mu_{21} + \mu_{31} + \mu_{41}$$
$$= \mu_{12} + \mu_{22} + \mu_{32} + \mu_{42}$$
$$= \mu_{13} + \mu_{23} + \mu_{33} + \mu_{43}$$

where μ_{ij} denotes the population cell mean for cell ij.

Equal weights are frequently (though not always) appropriate for experimental data in which all levels of all factors have been determined by the experimenter (e.g., are treatment factors) rather than determined as some prior grouping of subjects or experimental units (e.g., blocking factors). Such prior groupings may be age, sex, socioeconomic status, or, as in our example, disease group. When defining the main effects of a treatment factor, it may be appropriate to give different weight to the different levels of the factors defining groups, e.g., the levels of the disease factor could be weighted according to the prevalence of the disease. (Note that the prevalence may or may not be reflected in the cell size.) To request an analysis with equal weight for each level of TREATMNT and unequal weights for the levels of DISEASE, we replace the WEIGHT paragraph above by a statement such as

/ WEIGHT   DISEASE = 1, 3, 4.

This statement specifies that the main effects for TREATMNT are defined by contrasts among the weighted sums

$$s_1 = 1\mu_{11} + 3\mu_{12} + 4\mu_{13}$$
$$s_2 = 1\mu_{21} + 3\mu_{22} + 4\mu_{23}$$
$$s_3 = 1\mu_{31} + 3\mu_{32} + 4\mu_{33}$$
$$s_4 = 1\mu_{41} + 3\mu_{42} + 4\mu_{43}$$

where μ_{ij} denotes the population cell mean for cell ij. The TREATMNT null hypothesis is therefore that all contrasts among the s_i's are zero, i.e., that $s_1 = s_2 = s_3 = s_4$. The contrasts defining the main effect for DISEASE and the interaction stay the same as for the equal cell weights analysis given previously.

A different cell weight can be given to each cell. Cell sizes (cell frequencies) are often used as the cell weights when each analysis of variance factor is observed rather than determined by the experimenter, i.e., when every factor refers to a prior grouping of subjects or cases. For example, if

patients are grouped according to age and diagnosis, and the cell sizes are proportional to the population sizes for the cells defined by age and diagnosis, then we may want to perform an analysis with cell sizes as cell weights. In this case, the contrast defining the main effect for diagnosis (column effect with two levels), would be

$$\frac{n_{11}\mu_{11} + n_{21}\mu_{21} + n_{31}\mu_{31}}{n_{11} + n_{21} + n_{31}} - \frac{n_{12}\mu_{12} + n_{22}\mu_{22} + n_{32}\mu_{32}}{n_{12} + n_{22} + n_{32}} = 0$$

The above hypothesis states that the average of all subjects for the first diagnosis category is the same as that for the second. To request that cell sizes be used as cell weights, specify BETWEEN ARE SIZES. in the WEIGHT paragraph.

Each of the above analyses includes tests of main effects in the presence of possible interactions. Some statisticians prefer tests of main effects only when interactions are assumed to be zero, when the test of interaction is not significant, or when the magnitude of the interaction is small even if statistically significant. Often in such cases, the test of main effects is desired with the interaction sum of squares included in the error sum of squares so that a test of main effects becomes a test of whether the main effect is large relative to the total interaction and within-cell variation. To request an analysis without interaction in the model specify DEPTH = 1. in the ANALYSIS paragraph. This DEPTH statement requests analysis of main effects only. If you have three factors and want all effects up to and including two-way interactions in the model, state DEPTH = 2.

Specifying the interactions to be included in the model can be done by using the STRUCTURE procedure rather than the FACTORIAL procedure. For example, a three-way ANOVA for main effects for factors A, B, and C and the BC interaction can be requested by stating

        ANALYSIS   PROCEDURE IS STRUCTURE.
        BFORM IS 'A + B*C'.   /

Because some statisticians do not test for main effects when interactions are significant, they prefer that the sums of squares reported for main effects be the sums of squares obtained from a model not including interaction. For two-way ANOVA, this can be done in P4V in any of three ways:

- Perform an analysis without interaction (e.g. PROC = FACT. DEPTH = 1.) with any set of cell weights.
- Perform an analysis without interaction with no weights specified (since the sums of squares reported are invariant to the choice of weights).
- Perform .an analysis with interaction and with unequal cell weights.

In the first and third cases, two sums of squares are reported for each main effect.

⑫ The input to our current example includes a subproblem defined by the final four lines of our instructions. The factors are called T and D (TREATMNT and DISEASE). Sample size cell weights are requested. There are two sums of squares for TREATMNT, labeled T and T|D. The T sum of squares is used for testing the hypothesis or population cell means defined by the contrast given above which uses cell sizes as weights. The sum of squares $T|D$ is the sum of squares obtained for T with no interaction in the model and cell weights equal. This sum of squares is sometimes called the "T adjusted for D" sum of squares because it is equal to the decrease in the residual sum of squares that results from adding the main effect for factor T to an ANOVA model containing only the grand mean and the main effect for factor D.

In summary, whenever interaction is included in the model and unequal cell weights are used, the sums of squares labeled simply T or D are the sums of squares appropriate for testing the contrasts defined by the cell weights while the $T|D$ and $D|T$ sums of squares are for testing T and D when the interaction effects are small or insignificant. From this point of view, unequal weights provide a convenient method for testing a progression of increasingly simpler models in a single run. The $T|D$ sum of squares is omitted whenever it is equal to the T sum of squares.

<u>Choosing cell weights.</u> Many experiments in the biological, behavioral, and health sciences involve a mixture of experimental and observational factors. In some instances the observational factors are called blocking factors. In these experiments, treatments are randomly assigned to experimental units within a block of units. It is usually assumed that there are no interactions between treatment factors and blocking factors. In these circumstances, it may be appropriate to simply specify equal cell weights if cell weights are equal for the treatment part of the model and proportional for the blocking factor part of the model and it can be assumed that there is no interaction between blocking and treatment factors. In this case, the sums of squares are independent of the particular weights chosen for the blocking factor.

In many experiments however, interactions do exist between the observational factors and the treatments and the main purpose of an experiment may be to study the interactions between treatments and factors such as sex, age, cultural background, etc.

Whenever there is an observational factor, it is likely that the levels of the factor do not occur with equal frequency or importance. It is also likely that the importance of population size may not be proportional to the sample size. For example, sex may be one of your factors, but the study may include more females than males. Also, you may wish to stress results for males more than for females because the object of the study, e.g., heart disease, may affect more males than females.

The following general rule may help in assigning cell weights: give equal weight to each level of any factor whose level is assigned by the experiment (e.g. a treatment) and give unequal weights to levels of observed factors such as disease, sex, and age. (Note that while the number of male and female humans may be roughly equal, the same is not true for other animals or for subpopulations with particular diseases or occupations.)

Under special circumstances, some tests are independent of cell weights. For example, if cell weights are given in terms of the levels of the factors (proportional cell weights) for a two-way ANOVA without interaction, then the tests for main effects are independent of the cell weights.

Example 4V.2 Multivariate Analysis of Variance

The Werner blood chemistry data are used to illustrate a two-way multivariate analysis of variance with two dependent variables. The grouping variables are AGE and BRTHPILL. The dependent variables are CHOLSTRL and ALBUMIN. The setup for P4V is

```
-------------------------------------
/ PROBLEM    TITLE IS 'WERNER, TWO-WAY MANOVA'.
/ INPUT      VARIABLE ARE 9.
            FORMAT IS '(A4, 5F4.0, 3F4.1)'.

/ VARIABLE   NAMES ARE ID, AGE, HEIGHT, WEIGHT,
                BRTHPILL, CHOLSTRL, ALBUMIN,
                CALCIUM, URICACID.
            MAX IS (6)400.
            MIN IS (6)150.
            LABEL IS ID.
            USED ARE AGE, BRTHPILL, CHOLSTRL,
                ALBUMIN.

/ BETWEEN    FACTORS ARE AGE, BRTHPILL.
            CUTPOINTS(AGE) ARE 25, 35, 45.
            NAMES(AGE) ARE '25ORLESS', '26 TO 35',
                '36 TO 45', OVER45.
            CODES(BRTHPILL) ARE 1, 2.
            NAMES(BRTHPILL) ARE NOPILL, PILL.

/ WEIGHTS    BETWEEN ARE EQUAL.

/ END
    (data records go here)
/END
ANALYSIS PROCEDURE IS FACTORIAL. /
-------------------------------------
```

The USE statement is included in the VARIABLE paragraph to indicate the subset of variables that will be needed. The analysis can be performed without the USE satement, but some unnecessary computation will be avoided if it is included. Moreover, if we did not include the USE statement, we would need to mention the dependent variable in the ANALYSIS paragraph. (The USE statement is also important if there are missing values. A case will not be used if any of its variables are missing or out of range.)

The FACTOR statement in the BETWEEN paragraph indicates the grouping factors. P4V assumes that all variables included in the USE statement are dependent variables except those included in the FACTOR statement. The remainder of the Control Language for this example is the same as for Example 4V.1.

The results for the main effect for age are given in Output 4V.2. The remainder of the output (not shown) is similar to that for Example 4V.1. For example, summary statistics for the entire sample, marginal statistics, and cell statistics can be requested for each dependent variable.

The analysis of variance table contains several parts for each effect. We have presented only the results for the main effect for age. There are two subsections: all dependent variables taken in a single multivariate analysis and then each dependent variable in a univariate analysis.

⑬ The subsection labeled ALL contains the multivariate analysis. There are several

multivariate statistics. LRATIO denotes Wilks'
lambda likelihood ratio statistic. The F statistic
associated with LRATIO is Rao's approximation as in
P7M (Rao, 1973, Section 8c.5). TRACE is the
Hotelling-Lawley trace. TZSQ is Hotellings
generalized T-zero squared statistic. CHISQ is
Tiku's (1971) approximate chisquare for testing the
significance of TRACE and TZSQ. MXROOT is Roy's
largest root statistic, whose p-value is computed as
in Harris (1975).

(14) Univariate tests are presented for each
dependent variable.

We have analyzed the data considering age as a
categorical variable. The analysis does not
investigate the possible trend across the age
categories.

Example 4V.3 Repeated Measures

P4V provides both a univariate and multivariate
approach to repeated measures (split-plot,
changeover). The univariate approach (when equal
cell weights are chosen) is the same as that used in
P2V. The multivariate approach to repeated measures
is introduced as an example. In the description of
P2V, we considered an example from Winer (1971, p.
525) in which there was one grouping factor with two
levels and one within-subjects factor with four
levels. The model can be written as

$$Y_{ijk} = \mu_{ij} + e_{ijk}$$

or equivalently as

$$Y_{ijk} = \mu + \alpha_i + \beta_j + \gamma_{ij} + e_{ijk}$$

where the subscript i denotes group (method in
Winer's example), j denotes trial or level of the
within factor (shape), and k denotes subject (nested

in method). The test of the main effect for the
within factor (for equal cell weights) is a test
that $\beta_j = 0$, i.e., that

$$\mu_{11} + \mu_{21} = \mu_{12} + \mu_{22} = \mu_{13} + \mu_{23} = \mu_{14} + \mu_{24} \quad .$$

The same hypothesis is tested in the univariate
and multivariate approaches, but the approaches
differ in their assumptions about the residuals
e_{ijk}. The univariate approach to repeated measures
is discussed in Winer (1971) and in Frane (1980).
The multivariate approach to repeated measures is
discussed in Morrison (1967), Bock (1975), and
Davidson (1972, 1980). Note that the univariate and
multivariate approaches each have their own
advantages and disadvantages so that one approach
cannot be universally recommended over the other.

Briefly, the univariate approach has a more
restrictive assumption regarding the variances and
covariances of the repeated measurements. Violation
of this assumption may result in a less powerful
test when there is an effect, or result in a test
that is liberal (i.e., one that rejects the null
hypothesis of no difference too frequently). On the
other hand, if the assumption is met (as it
frequently is), the univariate approach is more
powerful, especially in small samples. Moreover, the
univariate approach easily accommodates covariates
as well as tests for carryover (residual) effects,
period effects, and order effects, which do not have
a clear definition in the multivariate approach. The
multivariate approach is more flexible in the
assumption regarding the covariance matrix for the
repeated measurements, but it does require that the
repeated measurements have a multivariate normal
distribution. Violation of this assumption can be
very serious (e.g., the presence of multivariate
outliers). In P4V, we prefer to present both
solutions. The univariate approach also requires
multivariate normality, but the approaches differ in
the way that they are sensitive to the assumption.

Output 4V.2   Multivariate analysis of variance - Werner data tests for age effect

EFFECT	VARIATE	STATISTIC		F	DF	P
A: AGE						
(13) -ALL----		LRATIO=	0.828204	5.77	6, 350.00	0.0000
		TRACE=	0.203573			
		TZSQ=	35.8288			
		CHISQ =	32.69		5.412	0.0000
		MXROOT=	0.154275			0.0000
(14)	CHOLSTRL					
		SS=	48209.8			
		MS=	16069.9	10.07	3, 176	0.0000
	ALBUMIN					
		SS=	0.525631			
		MS=	0.175210	1.45	3, 176	0.2290

The P4V setup for the Winer (1971, p. 525) example is

```
-------------------------------------
/ PROBLEM     TITLE IS 'WINER, P. 525'.
/ INPUT       VARIABLES ARE 5.
             FORMAT IS FREE.

/ VARIABLE    NAMES ARE METHOD, ACCURACY, ACCURCY2,
             ACCURCY3, ACCURCY4.

/ BETWEEN     FACTOR IS METHOD.
             CODES ARE 1, 2.
             NAMES ARE FIRST, SECOND.

/ WITHIN      FACTOR IS SHAPE.
             CODES ARE 1 TO 4.
             NAMES ARE SHAPE1, SHAPE2, SHAPE3,
             SHAPE4.

/ WEIGHTS     BETWEEN ARE EQUAL.
             WITHIN ARE EQUAL.
/ END
 1 0 0 5 3
 1 3 1 5 4
 1 4 3 6 2
 2 4 2 7 8
 2 5 4 6 6
 2 7 5 8 9
/END
ANALYSIS PROCEDURE IS FACTORIAL./
-------------------------------------
```

The subjects are divided into two groups according to METHOD. An accuracy score for each subject is recorded for each of four experimental conditions. These four scores are the four variables ACCURACY, ACCURCY2, ACCURCY3, ACCURCY4. The four conditions are named SHAPE1, SHAPE2, SHAPE3, and SHAPE4. They are the four levels of the within factor that we call SHAPE. The first variable is named ACCURACY rather than ACCURCY1, since the name of the first variable is used to label the common dependent variable (called the VARIATE in P4V) represented in all four variables. The WITHIN paragraph describes the within factor. In basic applications, the CODE statement in the WITHIN paragraph merely serves to indicate the fact that there are four levels in the within factor. (These codes do not appear in the data file.) Weights for the within factor are required and are stated in the WEIGHT paragraph. If the within factor is a treatment (as opposed to an ordered or continuous variable like time), then equal weights will likely be appropriate. If the within factor is time (and often dose), unequal weights may be appropriate. We may wish to stress the results for the first time period or for the initial dose.

In our example with a single between factor and a single within factor, the within weights affect only the test of the between factor (and grand mean) and the between weights affect only the test of the within factor since each set of weights specifies how the levels of one factor are to be averaged when performing tests of the other factor.

Results for Example 4V.3 are given in part in Output 4V.3.

(15) P4V performs between groups tests using univariate analysis of variance with the (weighted) sum (over repeated measures) of the dependent variable, i.e., the test for METHOD is obtained by taking the sum of the four dependent variables ACCURACY, ACCURCY2, ACCURCY3, and ACCURCY4 (and normalizing by dividing by two).

(16) The repeated-measures or within-subjects tests are given under the section labeled WITHIN EFFECT: S: SHAPE. Tests are given for the main effect for SHAPE (labeled S) and the interaction of SHAPE with METHOD (labeled (S) X (M: METHOD)). For each of these effects, there are several statistics. TSQ is Hotelling's T-squared statistic as in multivariate analysis of variance. TSQ is a test of the equality of the four means for SHAPE considering the four scores for SHAPE to have a four-variable multivariate normal distribution. In this simple example, the Wilks' lambda, Roy's largest root, and Hotelling-Lawley trace test statistics are equivalent to Hotelling's T-squared and are not reported separately. If the grouping variable has more than two groups, then the test for the group by within factor interaction has all the separate multivariate tests.

WCP SS (Within Contrast Pooled, i.e., the pooling of the sums of squares corresponding to a set of orthogonal contrasts for the level of a repeated-measures factor) and WCP MS refer to the sum of squares and mean squares for the univariate analysis of repeated measures. They are equal to those reported in BMDP2V since our example uses equal cell weights. Below WCP MS appear the results for the Greenhouse-Geisser (Imhof) adjustment to degrees of freedom, which yields a conservative test (see Frane, 1980, for general discussion of this test). Briefly, the GGI adjustment reduces the numerator and denominator degrees of freedom to adjust for the fact that the classical univariate approach to repeated measures tends to be liberal (appears too significant) in some analyses. Conditions under which it is appropriate to use the conservative approach are discussed in Frane (1980). The Huynh-Feldt approach to this same problem is also reported, as in P2V.

In Example 4V.3, we use equal cell weights for both the between (grouping) and the within (repeated-measures) factor. As in Example 4V.1, we could specify that the between weights are cell sizes or we could give specific weights.

As in P2V, multiple grouping factors and multiple within-subjects factors are possible. One of our examples for P2V has <u>two grouping factors and one</u>

Output 4V.3 Repeated measures analysis of variance - Winer, p.525

```
========================================================================

    --- ANALYSIS SUMMARY ---

THE FOLLOWING EFFECTS ARE COMPONENTS OF THE SPECIFIED
LINEAR MODEL FOR THE BETWEEN DESIGN.  ESTIMATES AND TESTS
OF HYPOTHESES FOR THESE EFFECTS CONCERN PARAMETERS OF THAT MODEL.

        OVALL: GRAND MEAN
        M: METHOD

THE FOLLOWING EFFECTS ARE COMPONENTS OF THE SPECIFIED
LINEAR MODEL FOR THE WITHIN  DESIGN.  ESTIMATES AND TESTS
OF HYPOTHESES FOR THESE EFFECTS CONCERN PARAMETERS OF THAT MODEL.

        OBS: WITHIN CASE MEAN
        S: SHAPE

EFFECTS CONCERNING PARAMETERS OF THE COMBINED BETWEEN AND
WITHIN MODELS ARE THE COMBINATIONS (INTERACTIONS) OF EFFECTS
IN BOTH MODELS.

========================================================================

WITHIN EFFECT: OBS: WITHIN CASE MEAN

EFFECT   VARIATE      STATISTIC         F       DF      P
--------------------------------------------------------------

 OVALL: GRAND MEAN

        ACCURACY
                SS=        477.042
                MS=        477.042     111.16   1,    4  0.0005

 M: METHOD

        ACCURACY
                SS=        51.0417
                MS=        51.0417      11.89   1,    4  0.0261


 ERROR
        ACCURACY
                SS=        17.166667
                MS=        4.2916667

========================================================================

WITHIN EFFECT: S: SHAPE

EFFECT   VARIATE      STATISTIC         F       DF      P
--------------------------------------------------------------

  S

        ACCURACY
                TSQ=       154.129      25.69   3,    2  0.0377
                WCP SS=    47.4583
                WCP MS=    15.8194      12.80   3,   12  0.0005
                GREENHOUSE-GEISSER ADJ. DF  12.80 1.43,  5.70 0.0099
                HUYNH-FELDT ADJUSTED DF     12.80 2.55, 10.18 0.0011

 (S) X (M: METHOD)

        ACCURACY
                TSQ=       19.8795       3.31   3,    2  0.2404
                WCP SS=    7.45833
                WCP MS=    2.48611       2.01   3,   12  0.1662
                GREENHOUSE-GEISSER ADJ. DF   2.01 1.43,  5.70 0.2152
                HUYNH-FELDT ADJUSTED DF      2.01 2.55, 10.18 0.1791


 ERROR
        ACCURACY
                WCP SS=    14.833333
                WCP MS=    1.2361111

                GGI EPSILON=   0.47514
                H-F EPSILON=   0.84835


========================================================================
```

within factor (Winer, 1971, p. 564). The corresponding P4V setup is

```
/ PROBLEM     TITLE = 'WINER, P. 564'.
/ INPUT       VARIABLES = 6.
             FORMAT = FREE.

/ VARIABLE    NAMES = ANXIETY, TENSION, ERRORS,
                     ERRORS2, ERRORS3, ERRORS4.

/ BETWEEN     FACTORS = ANXIETY, TENSION.
             CODES(1) = 1, 2.
             NAMES(1) = LOW, HIGH.
             CODES(2) = 1, 2.
             NAMES(2) = NONE, HIGH.

/ WITHIN      FACTOR = B.
             CODES = 1 TO 4.
             NAMES = B1, B2, B3, B4.

/ WEIGHTS     BETWEEN = EQUAL.
             WITHIN = EQUAL.

/ END
   (data records)
/END
ANALYSIS  PROC = FACTORIAL./
```

Another P2V example has one grouping and two within factors (Winer, 1971, p. 546). The P4V setup is

```
/ PROBLEM     TITLE = 'WINER, P. 546'.
/ INPUT       VARIABLES = 10.
             FORMAT = FREE.

/ VARIABLE    NAMES = NOISE, ACCURACY, ACCRCY12,
                     ACCRCY13, ACCRCY21,
                     ACCRCY22, ACCRCY23,
                     ACCRCY31, ACCRCY32,
                     ACCRCY33.

/ BETWEEN     FACTOR = NOISE.
             CODES  = 1, 2.
             NAMES  = NOISE1, NOISE2.

/ WITHIN      FACTORS = PERIOD, DIAL.
             CODES(1) = 1 TO 3.
             NAMES(1) = PERIOD1, PERIOD2, PERIOD3.
             CODES(2) = 1 TO 3.
             NAMES(2) = DIAL1, DIAL2, DIAL3.

/ WEIGHTS     BETWEEN = EQUAL.
             WITHIN = EQUAL.

/ END
   (data records)
/END
ANALYSIS   PROC = FACTORIAL./
```

Multivariate analysis of variance for multiple dependent variables each with repeated measures can also be obtained. The P4V setup for multiple dependent variables and one within factor is similar to the setup for a single dependent variable and two within factors. In other words, the multiple dependent variables can be considered to constitute a special kind of within-subjects factor. In terms of the structure of the data matrix within factors are factors that describe the organization of variables either into repeated-measures factors or into distinct dependent variables and covariates. If we take the DIAL factor above to represent three distinct dependent variables, we call each dependent variable a VARIATE. The P4V Control Language for DIAL replaced by three dependent variables would be the same as that given above except for the WITHIN paragraph, which would become

```
/ WITHIN    FACTORS = PERIOD, VARIATES.
           CODES(1) = 1 TO 3.
           NAMES(1) = PERIOD1, PERIOD2, PERIOD3.
           CODES(2) = 1 TO 3.
           NAMES(2) = DIAL1, DIAL2, DIAL3.
```

Univariate and multivariate approaches to repeated measures are reported for each dependent variable (variate). In addition, a multivariate analysis of variance using the three dependent variables would also be reported for each effect of the ANOVA model.

Example 4V.4 Analysis of Covariance

The Werner data used in the analysis of covariance example of P2V and in Example 4V.2 are used to illustrate the P4V analysis of covariance. The P4V setup for a two-way analysis of covariance with two covariates and two dependent variables is

```
------------------------------------
/ PROBLEM    TITLE IS 'WERNER, MULTIVARIATE ANALYSIS
                  OF COVARIANCE'.
/ INPUT      VARIABLES ARE 9.
            FORMAT IS '(A4, 5F4.0, 3F4.1)'.

/ VARIABLE   NAMES ARE ID, AGE, HEIGHT, WEIGHT,
                  BRTHPILL, CHOLSTRL, ALBUMIN,
                  CALCIUM, URICACID.
            MAX IS (6)400.
            MIN IS (6)150.
            LABEL IS ID.
            USED ARE AGE, HEIGHT, WEIGHT, BRTHPILL,
                  CHOLSTRL, ALBUMIN, CALCIUM,
                  URICACID.

/ BETWEEN    FACTORS ARE AGE, BRTHPILL.
            CUTPOINTS(AGE) ARE 25, 35, 45.
            NAMES(AGE) ARE '25ORLESS', '26 TO 35',
                  '36 TO 45', OVER45.
            CODES(BRTHPILL) ARE 1, 2.
            NAMES(BRTHPILL) ARE NOPILL, PILL.

/ WEIGHTS    BETWEEN ARE EQUAL.
/ END

(data records go here)

/END
ANALYSIS PROCEDURE IS FACTORIAL.
         DEPENDENT ARE CHOLSTRL, ALBUMIN.
         COVARIATES ARE HEIGHT, WEIGHT.  /
------------------------------------
```

Results for Example 4V.4 are given in Output 4V.4.

(17) The section of the table labeled COVARIATES contains the multivariate analysis of covariance test of the significance of the regression of the dependent variable on the covariates, forcing the effects of AGE, BRTHPILL, and their interaction into the regression model, i.e., the test of the covariates is the multivariate analysis of covariance test of whether the covariates contain any significant information (over and above the information already contained in AGE and BRTHPILL) for estimating the dependent variables. This covariate section contains three subsections. The first is for both dependent variables, and the other two are for each of the dependent variables separately. Since we have used equal weights, the latter two subsections report the same tests as those given in BMDP2V.

Beneath the section for covariates, reports are given for the grand mean, main effect of AGE and BRTHPILL, and the interaction as in the multivariate analysis of variance of Example 4V.2. In this analysis age is considered as a categorical variable. No analysis is made for possible trends across the age categorical variable.

Output 4V.4   Analysis of covariance - Werner data

```
========================================================

  --- ANALYSIS SUMMARY ---

THE FOLLOWING EFFECTS ARE COMPONENTS OF THE SPECIFIED
LINEAR MODEL FOR THE BETWEEN DESIGN.  ESTIMATES AND TESTS
OF HYPOTHESES FOR THESE EFFECTS CONCERN PARAMETERS OF THAT MODEL.

        COVARIATES
        OVALL: GRAND MEAN
        A: AGE
        B: BRTHPILL
        AB

========================================================
```

EFFECT	VARIATE	STATISTIC		F	DF	P
COVARIATES						
	-ALL----					
		LRATIO=	0.912436	3.99	4, 340.00	0.0036
		TRACE=	0.959668D-01			
(17)		TZSQ=	16.4103			
		CHISQ =	15.08		3.660	0.0033
		MXROOT=	0.875636D-01			0.0020
	CHOLSTRL					
		SS=	2393.26			
		MS=	1196.63	0.74	2, 171	0.4780
	ALBUMIN					
		SS=	1.53704			
		MS=	0.768518	6.70	2, 171	0.0016
OVALL: GRAND MEAN						
	-ALL----					
		TSQ=	29.1478	14.49	2, 170	0.0
	CHOLSTRL					
		SS=	18569.1			
		MS=	18569.1	11.50	1, 171	0.0009
	ALBUMIN					
		SS=	2.45289			
		MS=	2.45289	21.39	1, 171	0.0
A: AGE						
	-ALL----					
		LRATIO=	0.847805	4.88	6, 340.00	0.0001
		TRACE=	0.176452			
		TZSQ=	30.1734			
		CHISQ =	27.42		5.395	0.0001
		MXROOT=	0.135637			0.0001
	CHOLSTRL					
		SS=	42690.1			
		MS=	14230.0	8.81	3, 171	0.0000
	ALBUMIN					
		SS=	0.383185			
		MS=	0.127728	1.11	3, 171	0.3450
B: BRTHPILL						
	-ALL----					
		TSQ=	9.51355	4.73	2, 170	0.0100
	CHOLSTRL					
		SS=	448.287			
		MS=	448.287	0.28	1, 171	0.5989
	ALBUMIN					
		SS=	0.990253			
		MS=	0.990253	8.63	1, 171	0.0038
AB						
	-ALL----					
		LRATIO=	0.965800	0.99	6, 340.00	0.4288
		TRACE=	0.352615D-01			
		TZSQ=	6.02972			
		CHISQ =	5.32		5.395	0.4274
		MXROOT=	0.294438D-01			0.4006
	CHOLSTRL					
		SS=	5435.91			
		MS=	1811.97	1.12	3, 171	0.3415
	ALBUMIN					
		SS=	0.240255			
		MS=	0.800849D-01	0.70	3, 171	0.5543
ERROR						
	CHOLSTRL					
		SS=	276050.07			
		MS=	1614.3279			
	ALBUMIN					
		SS=	19.610642			
		MS=	0.11468212			

```
========================================================
```

Example 4V.5 Repeated Measures with Covariates

Repeated-measures analysis of covariance can be performed as in P2V. P4V also allows cell weights. The use of cell weights is described in previous examples. Sometimes a covariate is measured only once per experimental unit and sometimes a covariate is measured each time that the dependent variable is measured, i.e, the covariate has different values for the different levels of the repeated-measures factor. If the covariate is measured only once, both univariate and multivariate approaches to repeated-measures analysis of covariance are clear. Unfortunately the multivariate approach to repeated measures analysis of covariance has not been clearly defined when covariates are measured at each level of a repeated measures factor with more than two levels (Davidson, 1980) and so P4V is limited to the univariate approach for such designs. (The univariate and multivariate analysis of variance and covariance tests are identical whenever there are only two levels in the repeated-measures factor.)

We first consider the repeated-measures analysis of covariance example discussed in P2V (Winer, 1971, p. 806). The P4V setup is

```
-----------------------------------------
/ PROBLEM     TITLE IS 'WINER, P. 806, REPEATED-
                       MEASURES ANCOVA'.
/ INPUT       VARIABLES ARE 5.
             FORMAT IS FREE.

/ VARIABLE    NAMES ARE GROUP, COVARIAT, YIELD,
                       COVA2, YIELD2.

/ BETWEEN     FACTOR IS GROUP.
             CODES ARE 1 TO 3.
             NAMES ARE A1, A2, A3.

/ WITHIN      FACTORS ARE B, VARIATES.
             CODES(1) ARE 1, 2.
             NAMES(1) ARE B1, B2.
             CODES(2) ARE 1, 2.
             NAMES(2) ARE COVARIAT, YIELD.

/ WEIGHTS     BETWEEN ARE EQUAL.
             WITHIN  ARE EQUAL.

/ END
  1  3  8  4 14
  1  5 11  9 18
  1 11 16 14 22
  2  2  6  1  8
  2  8 12  9 14
  2 10  9  9 10
  3  7 10  4 10
  3  8 14 10 18
  3  9 15 12 22
/END
ANALYSIS     PROCEDURE IS FACTORIAL.
             COVARIATE IS COVARIAT.  /
-----------------------------------------
```

The BETWEEN paragraph specifies the grouping factor and the WITHIN paragraph describes the role of the remaining four variables. These four variables define two levels of a repeated-measures factor called B and for each level of factor B there are two variables, the covariate and the dependent variable. These two variables are called VARIATES. In P4V, a VARIATE is a variable that is represented several times for each case. Each of the VARIATES in our example has two variables since each VARIATE has been measured twice. In our example, the names of the VARIATES are specified in the NAMES(2) statement in the WITHIN paragraph. The CODES(1) statement specifies two codes so there are two levels of the repeated-measures factor. Since B is mentioned first in the FACTOR statement, the variables are arranged so that all the variables pertaining to the first level of B are listed before any of the variables of the second level of B.

Results are presented in Output 4V.5. Most of the output is similar to previous output.

(18) The section of the output labeled WITHIN EFFECT: OBS: WITHIN CASE MEAN refers to the between-groups effects that are tested by computing the mean of all observations for each case. This portion of the output reports the analysis of covariance using averages over levels of the repeated-measures factor of the dependent variable and of the covariate. This analysis of covariance is the same as the ordinary fixed effects analysis of covariance computed on the averages.

(19) This portion of the table reports the results for the within factor, B.

When the covariate is <u>not measured for each level of the within factor</u>, e.g., as in the P2V example from Winer (p. 803), the P4V setup is

```
/ PROBLEM     TITLE IS 'WINER, P. 803, REPEATED-
                       MEASURES ANCOVA'.
/ INPUT       VARIABLES ARE 4.
             FORMAT IS FREE.

/ VARIABLE    NAMES ARE GROUP, COVARIAT, YIELD,
                       YIELD2.

/ BETWEEN     FACTOR IS GROUP.
             CODES ARE 1, 2.
             NAMES ARE A1, A2.

/ WITHIN      FACTORS ARE B, VARIATES.
             USE = COVARIAT, YIELD, COVARIAT,
                   YIELD2.
             CODES(1) ARE 1, 2.
             NAMES(1) ARE B1, B2.
             CODES(2) ARE 1, 2.
             NAMES(2) ARE COVARIAT, YIELD.
/ WEIGHTS     BETWEEN ARE EQUAL.
/ END
  1  3 10  8
  1  5 15 12
  1  8 20 14
  1  2 12  6
  2  1 15 10
  2  8 25 20
  2 10 20 15
  2  2 15 10
/END
ANALYSIS     PROCEDURE IS FACTORIAL.
             COVARIATE IS COVARIAT.     /
```

Output is similar to that of Example 4V.5 except that there is no covariate effect in the within-subjects section of the analysis of covariance table because the covariate is constant across the levels of the within factor.

Output 4V.5   Repeated measures with covariates – Winer p. 806

```
=================================================================
   --- ANALYSIS SUMMARY ---

THE FOLLOWING EFFECTS ARE COMPONENTS OF THE SPECIFIED
LINEAR MODEL FOR THE BETWEEN DESIGN.  ESTIMATES AND TESTS
OF HYPOTHESES FOR THESE EFFECTS CONCERN PARAMETERS OF THAT MODEL.

        COVARIATE
        OVALL: GRAND MEAN
        G: GROUP

THE FOLLOWING EFFECTS ARE COMPONENTS OF THE SPECIFIED
LINEAR MODEL FOR THE WITHIN  DESIGN.  ESTIMATES AND TESTS
OF HYPOTHESES FOR THESE EFFECTS CONCERN PARAMETERS OF THAT MODEL.

        OBS: WITHIN CASE MEAN
        B

EFFECTS CONCERNING PARAMETERS OF THE COMBINED BETWEEN AND
WITHIN MODELS ARE THE COMBINATIONS (INTERACTIONS) OF EFFECTS
IN BOTH MODELS.

=================================================================
WITHIN EFFECT:
        OBS: WITHIN CASE MEAN
```

(18)

EFFECT	VARIATE	STATISTIC		F	DF		P
COVARIATE							
	YIELD						
		SS=	132.630				
		MS=	132.630	14.95	1,	5	0.0118
OVALL: GRAND MEAN							
	YIELD						
		SS=	128.789				
		MS=	128.789	14.51	1,	5	0.0125
G: GROUP							
	YIELD						
		SS=	54.2590				
		MS=	27.1295	3.06	2,	5	0.1357
ERROR	YIELD						
		SS=	44.370487				
		MS=	8.8740975				

```
=================================================================
WITHIN EFFECT:
        B
```

(19)

EFFECT	VARIATE	STATISTIC		F	DF		P
COVARIATE							
	YIELD						
		SS=	10.0020				
		MS=	10.0020	16.68	1,	5	0.0095
B							
	YIELD						
		SS=	31.5470				
		MS=	31.5470	52.61	1,	5	0.0008
(B) X (G: GROUP)							
	YIELD						
		SS=	2.33929				
		MS=	1.16964	1.95	2,	5	0.2365
ERROR	YIELD						
		SS=	2.9980159				
		MS=	0.59960317				

```
=================================================================
```

DESCRIBING THE DATA

Selecting Variables to be Used

P4V can perform many analyses of the same input data within a single problem. You can also request subproblems within a problem after seeing some of the results. For this reason, it is desirable to state which of the input variables will be needed, especially when the number of variables in your input file is large and/or there are incomplete cases. Statistics are computed for each cell for each variable that is specified in the analysis and the pooled within-groups covariance matrix is computed for all these variables. P4V assumes that all of the input variables (after transformations) are to be used unless you state the variables to be used in the VARIABLE paragraph.

```
VARiable ─────────────────────────────────────
│  USE = v list.                         all/all
│  Names and/or subscripts of varibles to be used.
```

Describing Between-groups Factors

Ordinary fixed-effects analysis of variance contains only between-groups factors, i.e., the factors for ordinary analysis of variance are between-groups factors. The levels of these factors are recorded as variables in the data. The variables indicating how cases are grouped are specified and described in the BETWEEN paragraph. See Example P4V.1 for more discussion.

```
BETween ───────────────────────────────────────
│  FACTor = v list.                        none/none
│    Names and/or indices of variables specifying
│    the between-groups factors.
│  CODE(#) = # list.                            none
│    Category codes for factor # in the above list
│    of factors.
│  CUTPoints(#) = # list.                       none
│    Category cutpoints for factor # in the above
│    list of factors.
│
│  Note: See Example 4V.1 for the distinction
│  between these CODES and CUTPOINTS and those
│  specified in the GROUP or CATEGORY paragraph.
│
│  NAME(#) = c list.
│    Factor level names for factor # in the above
│    list of factors.
│  ORDer(#) = # or c list.         order of appearance
│                                    of cells in input
│                                    data file
│    Order of cells according to factor-level codes
│    or names. One ORDER sentence for each factor;
│    one entry in each ORDER list for each cell. If
│    ORDER is specified for one factor, it must be
│    specified for all factors. ORDER statements are
│    handy when your data are not sorted by factor
│    levels to be sure that cells are in a known
│    order when supplying explicit cell weights in
│    the WEIGHT paragraph, or coefficient VALUES in
│    the DESIGN paragraph.
```

The usual GROUP paragraph can also be used instead of specifying CODES, CUTPOINTS, and NAMES in the BETWEEN paragraph.

Describing the Within-subjects (Repeated-measures) Factors

Within-subjects factors are used for repeated measures, split-plot, and crossover designs in which each case (experimental unit) is measured under more than one condition or at more than one time. In P4V (as in P2V), the multiple measurements for each case are recorded as separate variables within that case rather than as separate cases. The WITHIN paragraph describes how a set of variables defines a within-cases (repeated-measures) factor. See Example 4V.3 for an example with discussion. Most of the parameters of the WITHIN paragraph are similar to the corresponding parameters of the BETWEEN paragraph discussed above.

```
WITHin ─────────────────────────────────────────
│  FACTor = c list.                        none/none
│    List of names for labeling the within-subjects
│    factors. The order of factors in this statement
│    establishes the factor numbers for other
│    statements below.
│  CODE(#) = # list.
│    Category codes for factor # in the above list
│    of factors.
│  CUTPoints(#) = # list.
│    Category cutpoints for factor # in the above
│    list of factors.
│
│  Note: See Example 4V.1 for the distinction
│  between these CODES and CUTPOINTS and those
│  specified in the GROUP or CATEGORY paragraph.
│
│  Note: CODES or CUTPOINTS are required, but the
│  values stated can be arbitrary unless factor name
│  statements are used as described below.
│
│  NAME(#) = c list.
│    Factor level names for factor # in the above
│    list of factors. NAMES are important for
│    labeling cell and marginal statistics.
│  USE = v list.          all variables specified in
│                         USE statement of VARIABLE
│                         paragraph except between
│                         factor variables
```

P4V assumes that the variables indicated above have been listed according to the levels of the within-cases factors specified above. In Example 4V.5 the WITHIN factors are B and VARIATES. Note that VARIATES is a reserved factor name for indicating that two or more variables represent a single conceptual variable that we call a VARIATE in P4V. The variables used are COVARIAT, YIELD, COVA2, and YIELD2. COVARIAT and COVA2 constitute one VARIATE and YIELD and YIELD2 constitute a second VARIATE. Note that the actual role of each VARIATE is not defined until the ANALYSIS paragraph is given and that the role of a VARIATE can change with successive ANALYSIS paragraphs. P4V assumes that the first within-factor index moves slowest in the sense that the first two variables refer to the first level of the first factor (B) and the second two variables refer to the second level of factor B. Similarly, since VARIATES is indicated as the second (and last) within factor, each consecutive pair of variables corresponds to the two levels of the VARIATES factor. We say that the levels of the first mentioned factor in the FACTOR statement move slowest and the levels of the last mentioned factor move fastest. Sometimes the order of the variables is different from that needed by the program. In that case there are three ways to properly assign input variables to the levels of within factors. For example, suppose the variables are recorded in the order YIELD, COVARIAT, COVA2, YIELD2. We could state

USE = COVARIAT, YIELD, COVA2, YIELD2.

in the WITHIN paragraph, temporarily reordering the variables for this subproblem. Alternatively, we can state

USE = GROUP, COVARIAT, YIELD, COVA2, YIELD2.

in the VARIABLE paragraph, which would reorder the variables for the entire problem. The third alternative is to explicitly assign input variables to levels of the within factors. We use the factor name statements in the WITHIN paragraph whereby we state the level (code or name) each variable has for each factor. Thus for the recorded order given above, we can state

B = 1, 1, 2, 2.

indicating that YIELD and COVARIAT refer to the code value 1 of the first factor and that COVA2 and YIELD2 refer to the code value 2, and

VARIATES = 2, 1, 1, 2.

indicating that YIELD and YIELD2 refer to the code value 2 of the second factor and that COVARIAT and COVA2 refer to the code value 1 of the second factor. Note that it is usually easier to employ the USE statement in either the VARIABLE or WITHIN paragraphs than to employ these factor name statements. The factor name statements are, however, quite useful for applications where WITHIN CUTPOINTS are desired.

```
WITHin
  (factorname) = # list or c list.
    List of factor level codes or names, one for
    each variable used, except for grouping
    variables, specifying the level of the
    specified factor that is associated with each
    variable. Note that the codes specified here
    correspond to the CODES specified in the WITHIN
    paragraph and that "factorname" refers to your
    name for the factor as specified in the FACTOR
    statement.
```

In the example above, we use factor level codes of 1 and 2. This is frequently appropriate, but in other instances it is advantageous to give other codes so that the output is labeled more completely. For example, if data are gathered in consecutive years, then we could have codes for the within factor that are equal to the year, e.g., 1977, 1978, 1979, etc.

Sometimes cutpoints are useful for the within factors. If a dependent variable has been measured at times 1, 3, 5, 9, and 15, we can define a within factor from these five variables by specifying one or more cutpoints, e.g., a cutpoint of 7 would define a within factor with two levels. The first level would be defined by the average at times 1, 3 and 5, and the second level is defined by the average at times 9 and 15. Note that these cutpoints refer to the assignment of variables to levels of a within factor based on the values in a factor name sentence.

Cell weights, discussed below, can be used to specify the importance to be given to each level of a within factor.

Requesting Cell and Marginal Statistics

Statistics can be requested for each cell defined by the BETWEEN and WITHIN paragraphs and/or for selected marginals. Statistics include mean, standard deviation, weighted mean, and maximum and minimum values. See Example 4V.1.

```
PRINt
  CELLS.                              CELLS/CELLS
    Request to print statistics for all cells.
  MARGinals = NONE. or                NONE/prev.
             ALL. or                  subproblem
             #1, #2, ....
    Request to print no statistics, statistics for
    all marginals of all factors, or to print
    statistics for all combinations of #1 factor
    levels, #2 factor levels, etc.
```

Cell Weights

Cell weights are used in P4V to specify the importance to be given to each cell or level of each factor in defining the sums of squares and hypotheses to be tested. Cell weights should not be confused with the case weights available in P2V. Case weights reflect the accuracy with which the dependent variable has been measured for a particular case (e.g., the sample size when each case is the average of several measurements). In P4V, cell weights must be given for most analyses; they are frequently unequal when one or more factors have levels that are not of equal interest (e.g., sex when a disease is much more prevalent for one sex). Cell weights are sometimes used for unbalanced data when the imbalance is a reflection of the fact that the categories are not equally important. Cell weights are discussed in Example 4V.1.

```
WEIGHTS ─────────────────────────────────────────────────
  │ BETWeen = EQUAL. or         NONE/prev.,
  │           NONE. or          if BETWEEN design
  │           SIZES. or         is unchanged from
  │           # list,           prev. subpopula-
  │           one for each      tion
  │           cell of the
  │           between design
  │   Cell weights for the between-groups part of the
  │   design, one for each cell. EQUAL specifies that
  │   all weights are equal to one and SIZES says
  │   that the cell size is the cell weight. If no
  │   weights are given, P4V will do only those
  │   portions of the analysis that do not depend on
  │   cell weights.
  │ WITHin = EQUAL. or           same as for
  │          NONE. or            BETWEEN
  │          SIZES. or
  │          # list, one for each cell
  │          of the within design
  └─────────────────────────────────────────────────
```

In many applications, the importance of each cell
can be defined in terms of the levels of each of the
factors. In such circumstances, the factor name
statement is usually easier to state than the
individual cell weights. If a factor name statement
is used for one of the between or within factors,
then the BETWEEN or WITHIN weight statement is not
used. If a factor name statement is used for any
between or within factor, then it is not necessary
to give factor name statements for other factors in
that part of the design (between or within) provided
the weights for the unmentioned factors are equal.

```
WEIGHTS ─────────────────────────────────────────────────
  │ (factor name) = EQUAL.,      same as for
  │                 SIZES. or    BETWEEN
  │                 # list,
  │                 one for each
  │                 each of the
  │                 specified factor
  │   Weights for each level of the factor. Cell
  │   weights are then computed as the product of the
  │   factor level weights. Note that factor name
  │   sentences are supplied as alternatives to
  │   either (or both) of the BETWEEN and WITHIN
  │   sentences.
  └─────────────────────────────────────────────────
```

SPECIFYING THE ANALYSIS

Requesting an Analysis of Variance

In the BETWEEN and WITHIN paragraphs, we define a
number of between groups and/or within-cases
factors. After data are read and cell and marginal
statistics are computed, P4V performs any number of
analyses of variance and covariance. Usually,
analyses are requested through use of the ANALYSIS
paragraph. For most common analyses, you would
simply include the following:

ANALYSIS PROCEDURE IS FACTORIAL./

See Example 4V.1 for a discussion. Remember that the
slash should be placed at the end of the paragraph
rather than at the beginning.

The factorial procedure performs a standard
analysis with all interactions of all factors unless
you request otherwise in the DEPTH statement.

If you have a repeated-measures (within-subjects)
design, P4V assumes that you want to see both the
univariate and multivariate tests. If you wish, the
multivariate test or the univariate test can be
suppressed. Similarly, if you have multiple
dependent variables for an ordinary analysis of
variance, P4V will perform both univariate and
multivariate analysis of variance tests unless you
request that the multivariate test be omitted.
Control is provided to allow results for the
univariate approach to repeated measures to be
reported as well as estimates of parameters.

```
ANALYsis ─────────────────────────────────────────────────
  │ PROCedure = FACTorial,            none/none
  │             STRUCture, or
  │             SIMPLE.
  │   Method of requesting the analysis of variance.
  │   For most common applications, use FACTORIAL.
  │   The use of STRUCTURE and SIMPLE are described
  │   later. Note that this statement is usually
  │   required unless you have specified your own
  │   DESIGN paragraphs.
  │ DEPTh = #.                        100/100
  │   Maximum order of interaction to be generated by
  │   the procedure. The assumption is that
  │   interactions of all orders are computed. DEPTH
  │   = 1 specifies main effects only.
  │ MTYPE.                        MTYPE/prev. ANALYSIS
  │                                   paragraph
  │   Request to obtain multivariate tests for
  │   repeated-measures designs. To obtain the
  │   univariate tests only, state NO MTYPE.
  │ MULTivariate.                 MULT/prev. ANALYSIS
  │                                   paragraph
  │   Request for multivariate analysis of variance
  │   when there are multiple dependent variables. To
  │   obtain univariate tests for each variable only,
  │   state NO MULT.
  │ WCP = OPTional.              OPTIONAL/prev. ANAL
  │       SUPpressed.                 paragraph
  │       ASSumed.
  │   Requests control over statistics for the
  │   univariate (within contrast pooled sum of
  │   squares) approach to repeated measures.
  │   OPTIONAL requests all of the statistics.
```

SUPPRESSED requests that the statistics not be printed. ASSUMED indicates that the univariate approach to repeated measures is assumed to be appropriate for the data at hand and so the multivariate statistic, Greenhouse-Geisser, and and Huynh-Feldt statistics are not reported.

ESTimation. NO EST/prev. ANAL paragraph

Request to print parameter estimates and estimated cell means. (In two-way ANOVA, the parameter estimates refer to the $\mu + \alpha + \beta + \alpha*\beta$ interaction parameterization of the ANOVA model.)

Dependent Variables and Covariates

Covariates are discussed in Examples 4V.4 and 4V.5.

P4V assumes that all variables specified as being used in the VARIABLE or WITHIN paragraph are to be treated as dependent variables except between-groups factors (grouping factors) and covariates. Sometimes you may wish to perform a series of analyses using different subsets of variables. If so, you need to specify which variables are to be used as dependent variables in each ANALYSIS paragraph.

ANALysis ————
COVAriates = v list. none/prev. ANALYSIS paragraph
List of variables that are covariates.
DEPENdent = v list. all except grouping vars. and cova./ prev. ANALYSIS paragraph
List of variables to be used as dependent variables.

Controlling What is Printed

In Output 4V.1 we show program-generated statements specifying the model to be analyzed. If you specify NO GEN. in the ANALYSIS paragraph, these statements are not printed.

ANALysis ————
GEN. GEN./prev.
Request to print program-generated statements specifying the model to be analyzed. If LEVEL = BRIEF or MINIMAL in the PRINT paragraph, P4V assumes NO GEN.

In Output 4V.1 we show a table of cells. This table can be suppressed. For repeated-measures analyses an input variable assignment chart is printed. However, if you state LEVEL = MINIMAL. in the PRINT paragraph, then neither is printed.

Incomplete Designs

Many experiments are designed so that not all possible cells have data. For example, in a design with three grouping factors with six levels in each, there are 6 x 6 x 6 = 216 possible cells; but a Latin square of order six has only 36 cells with data. The FACTORIAL procedure assumes that all interactions of all factors are to be included in the ANOVA model. The DEPTH statement or the STRUCTURE formula procedure can be used to request analyses that do not have all possible interactions. In the description of P2V, we described analysis for a Latin square of order six. The P4V setup for the same analysis is

```
/ PROBLEM    TITLE = 'LATIN SQUARE FROM COCHRAN AND
                      COX'.

/ INPUT      VARIABLES ARE 4.
             FORMAT = FREE.

/ VARIABLE   NAMES = ORDER, AREA, SAMPLER, Y.

/ BETWEEN    FACTORS ARE ORDER, AREA, SAMPLER.
             CODES(1) = 1 TO 6.
             CODES(2) = 1 TO 6.
             CODES(3) = 1 TO 6.

/ WEIGHTS    BETWEEN ARE EQUAL.

/ END
     1 1 6 3.5
     1 2 2 4.2
     .
     .
     .
/END
ANALYSIS     PROC = FACTORIAL.
             DEPTH = 1./
```

The DEPTH statement is discussed above. Alternatively, you can replace the last two lines of the Control Language above by

```
ANALYSIS     PROC = STRUCTURE.
             BFORM = 'ORDER + AREA + SAMPLER'./
```

The Data Definition instructions (before the data) are similar to those given previously. The first three variables are the grouping variables and the fourth variable is the dependent variable. The BFORM statement is used in the STRUCTURE procedure to indicate those main effects and interactions to be included in the model. Another example is given in the next section.

Selecting Main Effects and Interactions in Your Model

We discuss the DEPTH parameter above as a way of limiting interactions to a certain degree. More general models can be specified by means of the STRUCTURE procedure. The STRUCTURE procedure is discussed in detail in BMDP TR 67. We give only a basic introduction here to allow you to specify commonly-used factorial (as opposed to nested) designs that do not have all possible interactions. For our present purposes, the STRUCTURE procedure is best described by way of example. If we have a four-way analysis of variance with factors A, B, C, D and if we want all main effects plus all two-way interactions between factors B, C, and D, then we specify

```
ANALYSIS    PROCEDURE IS STRUCTURE.
            BFORM IS 'A + B + C + D + B.C + B.D
                + C.D'./
```

Thus the appearance of a single factor name indicates the main effect for the factor. A list of factor names separated by periods indicates the interactions of the factors, e.g., B.C.D would indicate a three-way interaction. Some simplification is permitted. If we want all interactions among B, C, and D but no interactions with A, we could state 'A + B*C*D'. Use of the structure procedure is particularly appropriate when we know beforehand that certain interactions are not of interest.

We may want to eliminate one or more interactions or main effects as a result of examining the results from a previous analysis paragraph. Suppose we make a first analysis with main effects and interactions for all four of the above factors and then want to look at the analysis for a model with main effects for all four of these factors plus the two-way interactions for the last three factors. We can state

```
ANALYSIS    PROC IS STRUC.
            BFORM IS 'A + B + C + D + B.C + B.D
                + C.D'./
```

after the current ANALYSIS paragraph.

In a typical interactive run of P4V, we may use a sequence of ANALYSIS paragraphs (especially if the data are unbalanced with respect to cell sizes or cell weights) to select a simple model in a stepwise manner (using backward stepping) where the deletion of a variable or effect is done interactively.

More general discussion of models with some possible interactions omitted (unsaturated models) is given in TR 67 in terms of the BMT option of the ANALYSIS paragraph.

You may also wish to select covariates; for example, the BC interaction could be eliminated and a different subset of covariates used. The BMDP instructions to do this are

```
ANALYSIS    PROC IS STRUC.
            FORM IS 'A + B + C + D + B.D + C.D'.
            DEPENDENT IS ....
            COVARIATES ARE ..../
```

In any one step, one or more terms can be deleted and/or the selection of covariates and dependent variables can be changed. In Example 4V.4, we describe a multivariate analysis of covariance with two dependent variables, two covariates, and two

grouping factors. Interaction of the grouping factors is also included. This analysis could be accomplished with the following instructions

```
ANALYSIS PROC IS FACTORIAL. COVA IS WEIGHT. /
```

to repeat the analysis with WEIGHT as the only covariate, then

```
ANALYSIS PROC IS STRUC. BFORM IS 'AGE + BRTHPILL'. /
```

for an analysis with main effects only, then

```
ANALYSIS PROC IS STRUC. BFORM IS AGE./
```

for an analysis without BRTHPILL, then

```
ANALYSIS PROC IS STRUC. BFORM IS AGE. COVA IS NONE./
```

to delete the last covariate, and then

```
ANALYSIS PROC IS STRUC. BFORM IS AGE.
            DEPEND IS CHOLSTRL./
```

to produce a report for CHOLSTRL only. At this point, CHOLSTRL is the only dependent variable, there are no covariates, and we have only the main effect for AGE. Note that the instructions are the same for both interactive and batch use. The advantage of interactive use is that the results of each analysis can be seen before specifying the next analysis.

Contrasts using 1, −1 and 0 coefficients. Contrasts can be used to define the ANOVA hypotheses to be tested and/or to request tests in addition to those in the ANOVA table. This discussion is restricted to analyses with equal cell weights. For a more general discussion, see Davidson and Toporek TR 67.

Suppose we have a one-way ANOVA and want to contrast the first cell with each of the others. In Example 4V.2, we have a two-way ANOVA; if we ignore BRTHPILL usage, we have a one-way ANOVA with AGE as the grouping factor. There are four levels for AGE so there are three contrasts. The following instructions can be used:

```
DESIGN      TYPE = BETWEEN, CONTRAST.
            CODE = READ.
            VALUES = 1, −1, 0, 0.
            NAME = AGE12./
DESIGN      VALUES = 1, 0, −1, 0.
            NAME = AGE13./
DESIGN      VALUES = 1, 0, 0, −1.
            NAME = AGE14./
ANALYSIS    PROC = FACTORIAL./
```

There are two items specified in the TYPE statement above. BETWEEN indicates that we are specifying a contrast for the between-groups part of the model. CONTRAST indicates that the contrast is specified simply in terms of ones, zeros, and minus ones, indicating whether the cell is to be given a positive, zero, or negative coefficient. The VALUES statement lists the values that define the contrast. (In this VALUES statement, the coefficients sum to zero. If they did not, they would be adjusted so that they would; e.g., VALUES = 1, 1, -1, 0. would be converted to the actual contrast 1/2, 1/2, -1, 0.) (The PRINT statement in the DESIGN paragraph causes the actual contrast to be printed.) The NAME statement gives a name to the effect defined by the VALUES. This name is used in labeling the results and in referencing the effect in other instructions.

The ANALYSIS paragraph above requests the FACTORIAL procedure. This results in tests of the above contrasts plus the usual ANOVA table. To obtain only the tests of the contrasts, omit the request for the FACTORIAL procedure.

The following instructions are equivalent to the instructions above

```
DESIGN     TYPE = BETWEEN, CONTRAST.
           LEVELS = 25, 35.
           CODE = EFFECT.
           NAME = AGE12./
DESIGN     LEVELS = 25, 45.
           NAME = AGE13./
DESIGN     LEVELS = 25, OVER45.
           NAME = AGE14./
```

In this set of instructions, we define the contrasts with the first cell by merely mentioning the levels of the factor that are used in each contrast, e.g., LEVELS = 25, 35. refers to the fact that the first two CUTPOINTS for AGE are 25 and 35 so the first contrast generated has 1 for the first level, -1 for the second, and zeros for the other levels. The levels can be referenced by either the upper cutpoint of the level or the NAME of the level. OVER45 is the name of the last level of AGE, which has no upper endpoint.

Regression contrasts. To specify contrasts for the linear and quadratic trend for AGE, the instructions are

```
DESIGN     TYPE = BETWEEN, REGRESSION.
           CODE = READ.
           VALUES = -3, -1, 1, 3.
           NAME = AGELINR./
DESIGN     VALUES = 1, -1, -1, 1.
           NAME = AGEQUAD./
ANALYSIS   PROC = FACTORIAL./
```

REGRESSION in the TYPE statement indicates that we are specifying the coefficients directly (rather than indirectly using signs of the coefficients as in the previous CONTRAST in the TYPE statement). The first DESIGN paragraph specifies linear trend and the second specifies quadratic trend.

In the trend example above, we specify orthogonal polynomial coefficients. It is easy to specify these coefficients for low order polynomials, but it is not so simple when the number of levels in the factor is large or when intervals or cell weights are unequal. To facilitate the specification for a large number of levels, use the ORTHO paragraph. (Other applications of the ORTHO paragraph are discussed in TR 67). Our instructions could be

```
DESIGN     TYPE = BETWEEN, REGRESSION.
           CODE = CONST.
           NAME = AGECONST./
DESIGN     CODE = READ.
           VALUES = 1,2,3,4.
           NAME = AGELINR./
ORTHO      EFFECT = AGELINR.
           BASE = AGECONST./
DESIGN     VALUES = 1,4,9,16.
           NAME = AGEQUAD./
ORTHO      EFFECT = AGEQUAD.
           BASE = AGECONST,AGELINR./
ANALYSIS   PROC = FACTORIAL./
```

The first DESIGN paragraph above requests the generation of an effect called AGECONST, which is defined simply as a vector of ones (CODE = CONST.). The second DESIGN paragraph generates linear trend merely as the numbers one to four. This is then transformed by the first ORTHO paragraph to be equivalent to the contrast -3, -1, 1, 3 by orthogonalizing it to the AGECONST effect. The third DESIGN paragraph initially defines the quadratic effect as the squares of the coefficients in the second DESIGN paragraph. The second ORTHO paragraph then orthogonalizes them to the first two effects so that they define the second order orthogonal polynomial. It is important to note in this example that cell weights are equal. If cell weights are not equal, refer to the extended discussion in TR 67 since orthogonalization is done with respect to weights, i.e., the results of orthogonalization will differ from those we stated above when weights are not equal.

Another method for obtaining orthogonal polynomial effects employs the STRUCTURE procedure. We could use the three DESIGN paragraphs above for AGELINR and AGEQUAD, followed by

```
ANALYSIS   PROC = STRUCTURE.
           BFORM = 'AGELINR/AGEQUAD'.
```

The BFORM statement requests that the AGELINR effect be defined after orthogonalization with respect to AGECONST, and that the AGEQUAD effect be defined after orthogonalization with respect to AGECONST and AGELINR.

With more than one factor, you may wish to define a contrast in one factor but not the other (see Example 4V.2). If we wish to retain BRTHPILL in the ANOVA model and test for linear and quadratic trend for AGE, we can state

```
DESIGN   FACTOR = AGE.
         TYPE = BETWEEN, REGRESSION.
         CODE = READ.
         VALUES = -3, -1, 1, 3.
         NAME = AGELINR./
DESIGN   FACTOR = AGE.
         VALUES = 1, -1, -1, 1.
         NAME = AGEQUAD./
ANALYSIS PROC = STRUC.
         BFORM = '(AGELINR + AGEQUAD)*BRTHPILL'./
```

We include the FACTOR statement above because it is necessary when there is more than one factor in the model to indicate the factor or factors for which the VALUES apply. The STRUCTURE procedure crosses the specified contrasts on AGE with the standard contrast for BRTHPILL, generating five lines in the ANOVA table: AGELINR, AGEQUAD, BRTHPILL, AGELINR x BRTHPILL, and AGEQUAD x BRTHPILL. If we state PROC = FACTORIAL, then the ANOVA table would have entries for AGELINR, AGEQUAD, AGE, BRTHPILL, and AGE x BRTHPILL.

We can also obtain tests of AGE trend for each BRTHPILL group separately. For example, to obtain the linear trend for the BRTHPILL group, state

```
DESIGN    FACTOR = BRTHPILL,AGE.
          LEVEL(1) = 1.
          TYPE = BETWEEN, REGRESSION.
          CODE = READ.
          VALUES = -3, -1, 1, 3.
          NAME = AGELINR./
```

Simple Effects

After discovering that there is a significant interaction, we may want to examine simple effects, i.e., effects of one or more factors holding other factors fixed. In Example 4V.1, we perform a two-way ANOVA. If the interaction is significant, we can follow the initial analysis by a request for simple effects of BRTHPILL as follows:

```
ANALYSIS    PROC = SIMPLE.
            HOLD = AGE./
```

The effect of BRTHPILL is tested at each level of AGE.

When there are more than two factors, they can be held fixed in more than one way. The simple effects are obtained for all factors holding each factor fixed, that is included in the HOLD statement. For example, if we have factors A, B, and C, and state HOLD = A, B., then for each level of A we obtain tests for B, C, and BC; and at each level of B, we get tests for A, C, and AC. For simple effects of C for each combination of A and B, state

```
ANALYSIS    PROC = SIMPLE.
            HOLD = A, B.
            COMBINE = 2./
```

```
ANALysis ─────────────────────────────────────
│ PROCedure = SIMPLE.              no procedure
│   Request for simple procedure.
│ HOLD = name list.               all factors
│   List of factors to be held fixed. If PROC =
│   SIMPLE. and HOLD is not stated, then simple
│   effects are obtained for holding all factors
│   fixed, the number of COMBINE factors at a time.
│ COMBINE = #.                             1
│   Maximum number of factors to be held fixed
│   simultaneously when PROC = SIMPLE.
```

ACKNOWLEDGEMENT

P4V was designed and written by Michael Davidson and Jerome Toporek. Initial development was done as URWAS, the University of Rochester Weighted Analysis of Variance System, while Michael Davidson was a member of the departments of Psychology and Statistics at the University of Rochester and Jerome Toporek was a member of the University of Rochester Computing Center. James Frane and Jerome Toporek are responsible for this writeup.

SUMMARY

Order of Input Cards

```
// (job card)
// EXEC BIMED,PROG=BMDP4V        (see Appendix E)
//SYSIN DD *
/ PROBLEM
/ INPUT
/ VARIABLE
/ TRANSFORM
/ SAVE
/ BETWEEN
/ WITHIN
/ WEIGHTS
/ PRINT
/ END
   (data, if on cards)
DESIGN.../
INTERACT.../
ORTH.../
DELETE.../        may be repeated
CONVERT.../
PRINT.../
ANALYSIS.../
END /
```

may be repeated (without new data)

The DESIGN, INTERACT, ORTH, DELETE, CONVERT, PRINT, and ANALYSIS paragraphs can be repeated in any order before the END paragraph. Note that these paragraphs are executed one at a time and that the slash must come at the end of each of these paragraphs. The END paragraph signals the end of the current analysis.

The BETWEEN, WITHIN, WEIGHTS, and PRINT paragraphs can then be respecified for a subproblem using the same data.

Full sets of BMDP paragraphs (and data, if on cards) can be repeated for additional problems; see Section 5.8.

Part I: Instructions in the Data Definition Paragraphs

The Data Definition instructions appear before data (when the data are in the same file as the Control Language) and the Analysis and Model instructions (described later) come after the data. Only the Data Definition instructions specific to P4V are given below. Note the importance of the USE statement in the VARIABLE paragraph when only a subset of the variables is requested. None of the program-specific parameters default from problem to problem. Defaulting to previous (*) means defaulting to the previous subproblem.

Since P4V has a large number of options, we have placed a (um) to the left of any parameter that you are likely to find useful for ordinary univariate and multivariate analysis of variance and covariance. We have placed an (rm) to the left of options that you are likely to choose for repeated-measures designs.

Options labeled TR 67 are discussed only in Davidson and Toporek (BMDP Technical Report 67, 1981).

Paragraph Statement	Preassigned	Comment and Manual Reference
/ PROBlem		Parameters related to computational accuracy.
DIGITS = #.	6	Minimum acceptable number of numerically accurate digits in computations (TR 67).
POWer = # or INF.	2	Parameter for numerical accuracy monitoring (TR 67).
/ VARiable		Selecting variables. 402
(um) USE = v list.	all	Variables to be used. Note that substantial savings in computation can be made by employing the USE statement when only a small subset of the input variables are needed. Also important when there are missing values.
/ PRINt		Print statistics. 403
(um) CELLS.	CELLS.	Print statistics for each cell. *
(um) MARGINALS = NONE. or ALL. or # list.	NONE.	Print statistics for no marginals of factors, all marginals of factors, or for combinations of factors. *
/ BETWeen		Between groups specification. 402
(um) FACTor = v list.	none	Grouping variables. *
(um) CODE(n) = # list.	none	Factor level codes for the nth factor listed in the FACTOR statement. *
(um) CUTPoint(n) = # list.	none	Factor level cutpoints for the nth factor listed in the FACTOR statement. *
(um) NAME(n) = c list.	code or cutp.values	Factor level names for the nth factor listed in the FACTOR statement. *
ORDER(n) = # list or name list.	order of appearance of cells in data	Order of cells according to factor level names or codes. If given, must be stated for all factors.
/ WITHin		Within-cases specification. 402
(rm) FACTor = c list.	none	Names of within-cases (repeated-measures) factors. *
(rm) CODE (v list) = # list.	As for the BETWEEN paragraph	
(rm) CUTPoint (v list) = # list.	As for the BETWEEN paragraph	
(rm) NAME (v list) = c list.	As for the BETWEEN paragraph	
(factorname) = # list or c list.		Assignment of levels of within-subjects factors to each variable. See p. 403
(um) USE = v list.	USE from VAR para.	Variables to be used in this subproblem. *

(continued)

(continued)

Paragraph Statement	Preassigned	Comment and Manual Reference
/ WEIGhts		Cell weight specification. 404
(um) BETWeen =	NONE	Weights for cells defined by between groups factors. See pp. 389, 394
EQUAL. or		
SIZES. or		
NONE. or		
# list.		
(rm) WITHin = ...		As for the BETWeen statement above
(um) (factorname)	EQUAL for	Weights defined for levels of each factor. See p. 404
= EQUAL. or	factors	
SIZES. or	not mentioned.	
# list.		

- -

Following the analysis paragraphs described in Parts II and III below, the PRINT, BETWEEN, WITHIN, and WEIGHTS paragraphs can be repeated followed by new analysis paragraphs as a subproblem. Any number of subproblems is permitted.

- -

Part II: Instructions in the ANALYSIS Paragraph

The analysis instructions appear after the data. The analysis instructions are executed one paragraph at a time. ANALYSIS paragraphs can be repeated any number of times within a subproblem. This feature is especially advantageous for comparing various models. In particular, models can be built in a stepwise manner by running P4V interactively. It is essential to remember that the slash comes at the end of each ANALYSIS paragraph since each of these paragraphs is executed one at a time. The slash at the end of the paragraph is the signal to the program to begin execution of the instructions in the paragraph. The next paragraph must then begin on a new line.

In the chart below, the * indicates the previous occurrence of the option in the current problem. Analysis options do not default to those of a previous problem.

The paragraphs described here and in Part III below can be repeated any number of times and in any order (although the analysis performed depends, of course, on the order given). To terminate the Analysis instrucitons and begin either a new problem or subproblem, supply an END paragraph. If you have no new problem or subproblem do not supply the END paragraph. If you are running P4V interactively, supply a FINISH paragraph to terminate.

The Analysis instructions are discussed in greater detail in TR 67.

The ANALYSIS paragraph with a PROCEDURE statement provides a "ready-made" analysis that can be "tailored" further by the use of the paragraphs described in Part III below.

Paragraph Statement	Preassigned	Comment and Manual Reference
ANALysis		Analysis specification (slash at end of paragraph).
(um) PROCedure =	none	Request for one of the standard procedures. 404,408
FACTorial.,		
SIMPle. or		
STRUcture.		
(um) DEPENdent =	See p. 405	List of dependent variables. *
v list.		
(um) COVAriates =	none	List of covariates. * 405
v list.		
UNISUM.	NO UNISUM.	Print univariate summary table. Appendix F
(um) DEPTh = #.	100	Maximum order of interaction. 405
(um) MULTivariate.	MULT.	Request for multivariate statistics. * 404
(rm) MTYPE.	MTYPE.	Request for multivariate approach to repeated measures. * 404
ESTimates.	NO EST.	Print parameter and cell mean estimates. 405
WCP =	OPT.	Control over univariate approach to repeated measures. (WCP: within contrast pooled sum of squares.) 404
OPTional.,		
SUPPressed.		
or ASSUmed.		
PRANge =	FULL.	Limits the selected PROCEDURE to generate just the between or within part of the design. See TR 67.
FULL.,		
BETWeen. or		
WITHin.		

(continued)

(continued)

Paragraph Statement	Preassigned	Comment and Manual Reference
ANALysis (continued)		
BMT = ASSUmed., TEST. or SATurated.	ASSUmed.	Technique for dealing with unsaturated models (more cells with data than ANOVA parameters). (BMT: between model technique)
EVALues.	NO EVAL.	Request to print eigenvalues associated with multivariate tests. *
VECTors.	NO VECT.	Request to print eigenvectors associated with multivariate tests. *
DISPersion.	NO DISP.	Request to print multivariate dispersion matrices. *
BFORM = 'c'.	all	Formula to request which main effects and interactions are used for the between groups part of the design when PROC = STRUCTURE.
WFORM = 'c'.	all interactions	Formula to request which main effects and interactions are used for the within-cases part of the design when PROC = STRUCTURE.
HOLD = name list.	all factors	List of factors to be held fixed when PROC = SIMPLE. 408
COMBine = #.	1	Maximum number of factors to be held fixed simultaneously when PROC = SIMPLE. 408
SIDE.	SIDE.	Method of orthogonalization when PROC = STRUC. *
KEEP.	NO KEEP.	Request to keep design matrices for use after this analysis. *
GEN.	GEN. (NO GEN. if PRINT LEVEL is less than NORMAL.)	Request to print program generated instructions. 405

<u>Note</u>: The remaining options in the ANALYSIS paragraph will generally require a more extensive background in the foundations of general linear models.

Paragraph Statement	Preassigned	Comment and Manual Reference
PRINt.	NO PRIN.	Print design matrices. *
MODEL.	MODEL.	See BMDP TR 67. *
BMODEL = name list.	matrices with model parameter set	List of names of matrices that define the between-groups part of the model. (TR 67)
WMODEL = name list.	matrices with model parameter set	List of names of matrices that define the within-cases part of the model. (TR 67)

Part III: Customizing the Model

The use of the remaining paragraphs requires considerable familiarity with the basic foundations of general linear models. The use of these paragraphs will enable the user to "customize" and "fine-tune" an analysis to represent more closely his experimental design, e.g., the MODEL to be analyzed. Detailed discussion of each of the following paragraphs is given in TR 67, but not in this manual. When you use any of these paragraphs, they will come before an ANALYSIS paragraph. The presence of the ANALYSIS paragraph will cause an analysis to be performed based on the analysis of variance design information requested and defined by the following paragraphs. These paragraphs, as well as the ANALYSIS paragraph, require the slash to be placed at the end of the paragraph rather than at the beginning.

Paragraph Statement	Preassigned	Comment and Manual Reference
DESIgn		Design matrix specification for main effects (slash at end of paragraph).
FACTor = name list.	none; single factor if only one exists	Factor names whose level combinations are assigned design matrix values.
LEVEL(n) = name list or codes.	all levels	Levels of factor n to be included in assigning design matrix values where n refers to the position of the factor in the FACTOR statement above.
TYPE = BETWeen. or WIThin. and either CONTrast. or REGRession.	none	Whether the design matrix is for the between or within part of the model and whether the design matrix is of contrast or regression type. *

(continued)

(continued)

Paragraph Statement	Preassigned	Comment and Manual Reference
DESIgn (continued)		
CODE = CONST., INDicate., EFFect., HELMert. or READ.	HELM.	See TR 67. * CONST - a single column of ones IND - one column for each specified level combination; each has ones for those cells with that combination EFFECT - one fewer column than the number of level combinations; each combination contrasted with the last HELMERT - Helmert contrasts among specified level combinations READ - read with VALUES statement
VALues = # list.	none	Design matrix, read rowwise, when CODE = READ.
NAME = 'c'.	none; name of factor if only one	Name assigned to design matrix, either short or long form.
CONVert.	NO CONV.	Request to convert design matrix to regression type. *
MODel.	NO MOD.	Design matrix is part of analysis of variance model. NO MOD implies that the design matrix defines one or more contrasts to be tested in addition to the regular model, if any. *
PRINt.	NO PRIN.	Request to print design matrix. *

- -

INTeract		Design matrix specification for interactions. (Slash at end of paragraph)
EFFects = c_1, c_2.	none	Generate design matrix as the interaction of effects defined by design matrices c_1 and c_2.
NAME = c.	none	Name for generated design matrix.
CONVert.	As in DESign paragraph.	
MODel.	As in DESign paragraph.	
PRINt.	As in DESign paragraph.	

- -

ORTHogonalize		Orthogonalization of ANOVA effects. (Slash at end of paragraph)
EFFect = c.	none	Name of design matrix to be orthogonalized.
BASE = c list.	none	Names of design matrices to which the matrix above is to made orthogonal.
NAME = c.	same name as EFFECT	Name of result. If not given, the original design matrix is replaced.
MODel.	same as for EFFECT matrix	If MODEL is requested or design matrix of EFFECT statement was in model, then new matrix is in model and the old EFFECT matrix is removed.
PRINt.	NO PRIN.	Print resulting design matrix. *
SIDE.	NO SIDE.	Requests orthogonalization by discovery and imbedding of side conditions. See TR 67. *

- -

DELete		Deletion of effects from ANOVA model. (Slash at end of paragraph)
ALL. or BETWeen. or WITHin. or NAMES = c list.	All matrices are deleted if DELETE paragraph present but no option is selected.	Request to delete some or all design matrices.

- -

CONVert		Parameters of the CONVERT paragraph are the same as those of the DELETE paragraph. The CONVERT paragraph requests conversion of specified design matrices to regression type. (Slash at end of paragraph)

- -

PRINt		Parameters of the PRINT paragraph are the same as those of the DELETE paragraph. The PRINT paragraph requests printing of specified design matrices. (Slash at end of paragraph)

Key:

/	–indicates paragraph	*	–assigned value remains the same for additional <u>subproblems</u>
.	–period ends a sentence		
●	–required	VT	–number of variables after transformations
v	–variable (name or subscript)	list	–more than one item, often one per variable
g	–group (name or subscript)		
#	–number	Capitalized letters - paragraph or sentence names recognized by BMDP
'c'	–characters (name or parameter) may omit apostrophes if contiguous letters only	Page numbers following refer to this Manual

P3V

15.4 General Mixed Model Analysis of Variance

Robert Jennrich
Paul Sampson

ABSTRACT

P3V uses the maximum likelihood (ML) and restricted maximum likelihood (REML) approaches to the fixed and random coefficients model. The program handles mixed models of quite arbitrary form without requiring the balance demanded by P2V and P8V. For balanced data, REML estimates of mean and variance components agree with those obtained from classical analysis of variance whenever the latter produces nonnegative variance component estimates. For other situations this program is somewhat experimental in nature, since maximum likelihood experience with the general mixed model is limited. The fixed effects sum to zero and the random effects are assumed to be sampled from normal populations with zero means. You specify the hypotheses to be tested.

Output includes estimates of the parameters of the model, their asymptotic standard errors, t statistics and probabilities; the value of minus two times the logarithm of the likelihood function; an estimate of the parameter covariance matrix; a printout of program-generated dummy variables; an observed and predicted mean for each cell defined by the fixed effects with the standard error of the predicted cell mean; a predicted cell mean covariance matrix; pairwise tests for predicted cell means, residuals; and parameter estimates for specified hypotheses (submodels), log likelihoods and likelihood ratio tests with degrees of freedom and tail probability.

Our description of P3V assumes that you are familiar with the fixed and random coefficients formulation of the general mixed model (e.g., Jennrich and Sampson, 1976; Harville, 1977). An example of a mixed model is

$$y_{ijk} = \mu + \alpha_i + b_j + c_{ij} + \beta x_{ijk} + e_{ijk}$$

where

y_{ijk} is the value of the dependent variable

μ is a fixed effect

α_i is a fixed effect

b_j is a random effect (it is assumed to be sampled from a normal distribution with mean zero and variance σ_b^2)

c_{ij} is a random effect corresponding to an interaction (it is assumed to be sampled from a normal distribution with mean zero and variance σ_c^2)

β is the coefficient of the covariate x

e_{ijk} is a random effect corresponding to the error (it is assumed to be sampled from a normal distribution with mean zero and variance σ_e^2)

A more general model can have several fixed effects, random effects and covariates.

If there are no random effects (other than e), the classical analysis should be obtained by P7D, P1V, P2V, or P4V.

We demonstrate the results obtained with P3V by the three examples below. Our discussion raises a number of questions about the relation between conventional analysis of variance and maximum likelihood analysis as well as questions about model definition and testing strategies. We purposely try to make these questions conspicuous. We feel this is appropriate since experience with maximum likelihood analysis of the general mixed model is limited.

The user is cautioned that P3V can be expensive if the number of parameters in the model is large. We therefore suggest trying a simpler model first if you have a large model.

WHERE TO FIND IT

- specifying the model: the design paragraph
- specifying hypotheses to be tested
- restricted maximum likelihood
- initial estimates for the parameters
- case weights

Example 3V.1 Repeated Measures with One Covariate

As our first example we reanalyze the data in Table 15.5 (p. 373). The data are from a numerical example (Winer, 1971, p. 806) of a repeated measures model with one covariate. The model can be written

$$y_{ijk} = \mu + \alpha_i + \beta_j + \gamma_{ij} + \beta x_{ijk} + d_{ik} + e_{ijk}$$

where α_i, β_j, γ_{ij} are fixed effects that sum to zero on all i and j and the d_{ik} and e_{ijk} represent independent normal samples from populations with variances σ_d^2 and σ_e^2.

The BMDP instructions and data follow. The model is described by a DESIGN paragraph in which you specify the DEPENDENT variable, variables that are COVARIATES, effects and interactions that are FIXED and how to name them (FNAME), and RANDOM effects and how to name them (RNAME). The submodels are specified in a HYPOTHESIS paragraph in which you specify the terms in the model that are zero. The instructions in the INPUT, VARIABLE and GROUP paragraphs are common to all programs and are described in Chapter 5. Note that the fixed effect μ and random component e_{ijk} are provided automatically and should not be specified.

```
--------------------------------------
/ PROBLEM      TITLE IS 'REPEATED MEASURES WITH
                   COVARIATE - WINER,
                       PAGE 806'.
/ INPUT        VARIABLES ARE 5.
               FORMAT IS '(5F3.0)'.
/ VARIABLE     NAMES ARE GROUP, SUBJECT, TREATMNT,
                   BLOODPRS, TEMPRTUR.
/ GROUP        CODES(1) ARE 1 TO 3.
               CODES(3) ARE 1 TO 2.

/ DESIGN       DEPENDENT IS TEMPRTUR.
               FIXED     IS GROUP.
               FIXED     IS TREATMNT.
               FIXED     IS GROUP, TREATMNT.
               FNAMES    ARE GROUP, TREATMNT,'GRP*TRT'.
               COVARIATE IS BLOODPRS.
               RANDOM    IS GROUP, SUBJECT
               RNAME     IS 'SBJ*GRP'.

/ HYPOTHESIS   FIXED IS 3.
/ HYPOTHESIS   FIXED IS 1.
/ HYPOTHESIS   FIXED IS 2.
/ HYPOTHESIS   RANDOM IS 1.
/ HYPOTHESIS   FIXED IS 1, 3.
/ HYPOTHESIS   FIXED IS 2, 3.

/ END
   1  1  1   3   8        2  2  2   9  14
   1  1  2   4  14        2  3  1  10   9
   1  2  1   5  11        2  3  2   9  10
   1  2  2   9  18        3  1  1   7  10
   1  3  1  11  16        3  1  2   4  10
   1  3  2  14  22        3  2  1   8  14
   2  1  1   2   6        3  2  2  10  18
   2  1  2   1   8        3  3  1   9  15
   2  2  1   8  12        3  3  2  12  22
--------------------------------------
```

(See end of this P3V section for organization of systems information, BMDP instructions and data.)

The results are presented in Output 3V.1. Circled numbers below correspond to those in the output.

① Number of cases read. Only cases containing acceptable values for all variables specified in the DESIGN paragraph are used in the analysis. An acceptable value is a value that is not missing or out of range. In addition, if CODES are specified for any fixed effects factors, a case is included only if the value of the fixed effects factor is equal to a specified code.

② Univariate statistics for each cell. Cells are formed for all combinations of levels of the fixed effects (GROUP and TREATMENT in our example -- the level of the first fixed effect specified, GROUP, appears first in the cell index). For each cell the mean, standard deviation, coefficient of variation, and the cell count (sample size) are printed for the dependent variable and for the covariate(s) (BLOODPRS in our example).

③ Estimates of the parameters of the model, their asymptotic standard errors, the ratios of the estimates to their standard errors (t-like statistics) and two-tailed probabilities obtained from the normal distribution. GROUP appears twice in the list of parameters -- P3V generates $k-1$ dummy variables for a fixed effect when the fixed effect has k levels (the two dummy variables for GROUP take on the values 1, 0, -1 and 0, 1, -1 at the three levels of GROUP); the estimate of the coefficient of each dummy variable is printed as a separate line in the table. Similarly, two lines that appear for GRP*TRT, the interaction of GROUP and TREATMNT, correspond to the two degrees of freedom for the interaction (see Appendix A).

④ $-2 \ln$ (maximum likelihood) is minus 2 times the logarithm of the likelihood evaluated at the maximum likelihood estimates of the parameters.

⑤ Variance-covariance matrix of the estimates of the parameters. Again two rows (and two columns) appear for both GROUP and GRP*TRT; they correspond to the two dummy variables generated for these effects.

⑥ Dummy variables generated by P3V. The first dummy variable (the first column) contains only ones and represents the mean effect. The second and third dummy variables represent the group effects. The fourth dummy variable represents the treatment effect and the last two represent the group by treatment interactions.

⑦ For each cell defined by the fixed effects P3V prints the cell mean, the predicted cell mean (using the estimated parameters and evaluated at the grand mean of the covariate), and the standard error of the predicted cell mean.

⑧ Variance-covariance matrix for the predicted cell means.

⑨ Pairwise tests for the predicted cell means. These are t-like ratios of the difference between each pair of means divided by the estimate of the standard deviation of their difference.

⑩ Residual analysis. For each case P3V prints the

- cell to which it belongs
- observed value y of the dependent variable
- predicted value $\hat{y}$
- standard deviation of the predicted value
- residual $(y-\hat{y})$
- standard deviation of the residual
- the ratio of the residual to its standard deviation (the standardized residual)

⑪ Each HYPOTHESIS paragraph defines a submodel to be tested. The effect or effects specified in the HYPOTHESIS paragraph are set to zero and the parameters in the model are reestimated. In the first HYPOTHESIS paragraph, the third FIXED effect is set to zero -- the third FIXED effect in the example is GRP*TRT. Therefore the parameter estimates corresponding to GRP*TRT are zero. The remaining estimates can be compared to those of the complete model ③ to examine the effect of setting GRP*TRT to zero.

Output 3V.1 General mixed model analysis of variance. Circled numbers correspond to those in the text

----

--- the BMDP instructions read by P3V are printed and interpreted ---

NUMBER OF CASES READ.   18   ①

CELL INFORMATION FOR VARIABLE TEMPRTUR

CELL	MEAN	ST.DEV.	COEF. OF VARIATION	COUNT	GROUPING VARIABLES GROUP	TREATMNT
1,1	11.66667	4.04145	0.34641	3.00000	* 1.0000	* 1.0000
1,2	18.00000	4.00000	0.22222	3.00000	* 1.0000	* 2.0000
2,1	9.00000	3.00000	0.33333	3.00000	* 2.0000	* 1.0000
2,2	10.66667	3.05505	0.28641	3.00000	* 2.0000	* 2.0000
3,1	13.00000	2.64575	0.20352	3.00000	* 3.0000	* 1.0000
3,2	16.66667	6.11010	0.36661	3.00000	* 3.0000	* 2.0000

②

--- univariate statistics for BLOODPRS ---

DEPENDENT VARIABLE TEMPRTUR

PARAMETER	ESTIMATE	STANDARD DEVIATION	EST/ST.DEV.	TWO-TAIL PROBABILITY (ASYMPTOTIC THEORY)
ERR.VAR.	0.3331146001	0.1570317284		
BLOODPRS	0.8462912570	0.1121652309	7.5450401306	0.0
CONSTANT	6.8194822389	0.9907456454	6.8831815720	0.0
GROUP	1.5256181238	0.7403623784	2.0606365204	0.039
GROUP	-2.4870420763	0.7485773287	-3.3223581314	0.001
TREATMNT	-1.5212988159	0.1471449164	-10.3387784958	0.0
GRP*TRT	-0.5169795080	0.2138914818	-2.4170169830	0.016
GRP*TRT	0.5469169398	0.2064081061	2.6496868134	0.008
SBJ*GRP	2.2984841011	1.1646812100		

③

-2*LOG(MAXIMUM LIKELIHOOD)   55.54656982   ④

VARIANCE-COVARIANCE MATRIX OF THE PARAMETERS   ⑤

	ERR.VAR.	BLOODPRS	CONSTANT	GROUP	GROUP	TREATMNT	GRP*TRT	GRP*TRT
ERR.VAR.	0.0247							
BLOODPRS	-0.0	0.0126						
CONSTANT	-0.0	-0.0944	0.9816					
GROUP	-0.0	-0.0021	0.0157	0.5481				
GROUP	-0.0	0.0126	-0.0944	-0.2760	0.5604			
TREATMNT	-0.0	0.0063	-0.0472	-0.0010	0.0063	0.0217		
GRP*TRT	-0.0	0.0105	-0.0786	-0.0017	0.0105	0.0052	0.0457	
GRP*TRT	-0.0	-0.0084	0.0629	0.0014	-0.0084	-0.0042	-0.0255	0.0426
SBJ*GRP	-0.0123	-0.0	-0.0	-0.0	-0.0	-0.0	-0.0	-0.0

	SBJ*GRP
SBJ*GRP	1.3565

CELL	GROUPING VARIABLES GROUP	TREATMNT	DUMMY VARIABLES					
1,1	* 1.0000	* 1.0000	1.	1.	0.	1.	1.	0.
1,2	* 1.0000	* 2.0000	1.	1.	0.	-1.	-1.	0.
2,1	* 2.0000	* 1.0000	1.	0.	1.	1.	0.	1.
2,2	* 2.0000	* 2.0000	1.	0.	1.	-1.	0.	-1.
3,1	* 3.0000	* 1.0000	1.	-1.	-1.	1.	-1.	-1.
3,2	* 3.0000	* 2.0000	1.	-1.	-1.	-1.	1.	1.

⑥

CELL	OBSERVED MEAN	PREDICTED MEAN	SD.DEV. PRED.
1,1	11.6667	12.6540	0.9457
1,2	18.0000	16.7305	0.9516
2,1	9.0000	9.7052	0.9412
2,2	10.6667	11.6540	0.9457
3,1	13.0000	12.5769	0.9383
3,2	16.6667	15.6793	0.9457

⑦

(output continued)

(12) P3V prints $-2 \ell n$ (maximum likelihood) for this model. The difference between this statistic and that in (4) is a test of the significance of the GRP*TRT interaction.

(13) The difference between the two values for $-2 \ell n$ (maximum likelihood) is printed. This is a likelihood ratio test of the parameters that are set to zero (GRP*TRT in our example). Its degrees of freedom (number of mathematically independent parameters set to zero) and tail probability are printed. The probability is obtained from a chi-square distribution (the asymptotic distribution of the difference) with degrees of freedom printed.

(14) Similar results are obtained for the other HYPOTHESIS paragraphs, but are not reproduced here.

(15) The last two HYPOTHESIS paragraphs test whether each main effect and the interaction are simultaneously zero. Such tests are of interest when hierarchical models are desired. (Hierarchical models include interactions only when corresponding lower order interactions and main effects are included.) Suppose, for example, that we wish to perform tests at the .01 level. Since the likelihood ratio chi-square for the group-treatment interaction is barely significant at the .05 level, we may wish to test whether the group main effect and the group-treatment interaction are both zero. This is done by specifying the fifth hypothesis.

Some statisticians may want to test group effects assuming interaction effects are zero. This can be done by comparing the model for the first hypothesis (all effects except group-treatment interaction) with the model for the fifth hypothesis (no group effect and no interaction). This test is performed by subtracting the corresponding values of -2 (maximum likelihood) or, equivalently, by subtracting the chi-square values and the corresponding degrees of freedom. For this example $12.536 - 6.081 = 6.455$ with two degrees of freedom.

Output 3V.1 (continued)

VARIANCE-COVARIANCE MATRIX OF PREDICTED CELL MEANS

	1,1	1,2	2,1	2,2	3,1	3,2
1,1	0.8943					
1,2	0.7441	0.9055				
2,1	0.0122	-0.0157	0.8859			
2,2	0.0171	-0.0220	0.7784	0.8943		
3,1	-0.0073	0.0094	-0.0052	-0.0073	0.8803	
3,2	-0.0171	0.0220	-0.0122	-0.0171	0.7735	0.8943

(8)

PAIRWISE TESTS FOR PREDICTED CELL MEANS

	1,1	1,2	2,1	2,2	3,1	3,2
1,1	0.0					
1,2	7.3035	0.0				
2,1	-2.2254	-5.2034	0.0			
2,2	-0.7550	-3.7386	4.1224	0.0		
3,1	-0.0577	-3.1248	2.1543	0.6899	0.0	
3,2	2.2407	-0.7933	4.4470	2.9814	6.5021	0.0

(9)

RESIDUAL ANALYSIS

CELL	OBSERVED TEMPRTUR	PREDICTED TEMPRTUR	ST.DEV. PRED.	OBSERVED- PREDICTED	ST.DEV. O-P	(O-P)/ ST.DEV.
1,1	8.0000	8.8457	1.0085	-0.8457	1.2707	-0.666
1,2	14.0000	13.7685	1.0917	0.2315	1.1999	0.193
1,1	11.0000	10.5383	0.9485	0.4617	1.3161	0.351
1,2	18.0000	18.0000	0.9366	0.0000	1.3245	0.000
1,1	16.0000	15.6160	1.0729	0.3840	1.2167	0.316
1,2	22.0000	22.2314	1.0917	-0.2314	1.1999	-0.193
2,1	6.0000	5.0506	1.0729	0.9494	1.2167	0.780
2,2	8.0000	6.1531	1.1113	1.8469	1.1818	1.563
2,1	12.0000	10.1284	0.9485	1.8716	1.3161	1.422
2,2	14.0000	12.9234	0.9832	1.0766	1.2903	0.834
2,1	9.0000	11.8210	1.0085	-2.8210	1.2707	-2.220
2,2	10.0000	12.9234	0.9832	-2.9234	1.2903	-2.266
3,1	10.0000	12.1537	0.9433	-2.1537	1.3198	-1.632
3,2	10.0000	12.7173	1.0729	-2.7173	1.2167	-2.233
3,1	14.0000	13.0000	0.9366	1.0000	1.3245	0.755
3,2	18.0000	17.7950	0.9485	0.2050	1.3161	0.156
3,1	15.0000	13.8463	0.9433	1.1537	1.3198	0.874
3,2	22.0000	19.4876	1.0085	2.5124	1.2707	1.977

(10)

```
CONSTRAINED MODEL - HYPOTHESIS NUMBER  1
```

PARAMETER	ESTIMATE	STANDARD DEVIATION	EST/ST.DEV.	TWO-TAIL PROBABILITY (ASYMPTOTIC THEORY)	
ERR.VAR.	0.6240477058	0.2941789097			
BLOODPRS	0.9561385097	0.1200782227	7.9626302719	0.0	
CONSTANT	5.9956278439	1.0480499202	5.7207460403	0.0	⑪
GROUP	1.5073102484	0.7583568356	1.9875993729	0.047	
GROUP	-2.3771948236	0.7675437108	-3.0971450806	0.002	
TREATMNT	-1.4663751896	0.1956374501	-7.4953699112	0.0	
GRP*TRT	0.0	0.0			
GRP*TRT	0.0	0.0			
SBJ*GRP	2.2741467053	1.2279736733			

```
-2*LOG(MAXIMUM LIKELIHOOD)     61.62792969   ⑫
```

VARIANCE-COVARIANCE MATRIX OF THE PARAMETERS

	ERR.VAR.	BLOODPRS	CONSTANT	GROUP	GROUP	TREATMNT	GRP*TRT	GRP*TRT
ERR.VAR.	0.0865							
BLOODPRS	-0.0	0.0144						
CONSTANT	-0.0	-0.1081	1.0984					
GROUP	-0.0	-0.0024	0.0180	0.5751				
GROUP	-0.0	0.0144	-0.1081	-0.2898	0.5891			
TREATMNT	-0.0	0.0072	-0.0541	-0.0012	0.0072	0.0383		
GRP*TRT	-0.0	-0.0	-0.0	-0.0	-0.0	-0.0	-0.0	
GRP*TRT	-0.0	-0.0	-0.0	-0.0	-0.0	-0.0	-0.0	-0.0
SBJ*GRP	-0.0433	-0.0	-0.0	-0.0	-0.0	-0.0	-0.0	-0.0

	SBJ*GRP
SBJ*GRP	1.5079

```
LIKELIHOOD RATIO TEST

CHI-SQUARE =      6.081
                           ⑬
DEGREES OF FREEDOM    2

PROBABILITY    0.048


CONSTRAINED MODEL - HYPOTHESIS NUMBER  2

  --- results for hypothesis 2 ---

LIKELIHOOD RATIO TEST

CHI-SQUARE =      7.343
                           ⑭
DEGREES OF FREEDOM    2

PROBABILITY    0.025


CONSTRAINED MODEL - HYPOTHESIS NUMBER  3

  --- results for hypothesis 3 ---

LIKELIHOOD RATIO TEST

CHI-SQUARE =     24.109

DEGREES OF FREEDOM    1

PROBABILITY    0.000
```

```
CONSTRAINED MODEL - HYPOTHESIS NUMBER  4

  --- results for hypothesis 4 ---

LIKELIHOOD RATIO TEST

CHI-SQUARE =     12.952

DEGREES OF FREEDOM    1

PROBABILITY    0.000


CONSTRAINED MODEL - HYPOTHESIS NUMBER  5

  --- results for hypothesis 5 ---

LIKELIHOOD RATIO TEST

CHI-SQUARE =     12.536
                           ⑮
DEGREES OF FREEDOM    4

PROBABILITY    0.014


CONSTRAINED MODEL - HYPOTHESIS NUMBER  6

  --- results for hypothesis 6 ---

LIKELIHOOD RATIO TEST

CHI-SQUARE =     24.659

DEGREES OF FREEDOM    3

PROBABILITY    0.000
```

The results for the maximum likelihood analysis by P3V can be compared to the results for the repeated measures analysis by P2V (Output 2V.12). For both analyses, the main effect for group and the group x treatment interaction were nonsignificant and the treatment effect was significant at the .001 level. In P3V, the significance of the covariate is judged in terms of its asymptotic standard error. In P2V, the significance of the covariate is assessed via F tests separately for between-group effects and for the within-subjects effects.

Example 3V.2 A Random Effects Model

As a second example we analyze the data in Table 15.7 from Bowker and Lieberman (1963, p. 362). The values of the dependent variable are the lifetimes of electronic components tested in three randomly selected ovens at two randomly selected temperatures.

Table 15.7   Life times of electronic components (Bowker and Lieberman, 1963, p. 362)

Oven

Temperature	1	2	3
1	237	208	192
	254	178	186
	246	187	183
2	178	146	142
	179	145	125
	183	141	136

The model for this analysis is

$$y_{ijk} = \mu + a_i + b_j + c_{ij} + e_{ijk}$$

where $i = 1, 2$; $j = 1, 2, 3$; and $k = 1, 2, 3$. Here the a_i, b_j, c_{ij} and e_{ijk} are independent samples from Gaussian populations with zero means and variances σ_a^2, σ_b^2, σ_c^2, and σ_e^2 respectively. The conventional analysis of these data (as could be obtained using P8V) is shown in Table 15.8.

To obtain maximum likelihood estimates for the parameters in the above model we specify the following BMDP instructions.

```
----------------------------------------
/ PROBLEM      TITLE IS 'BOWKER AND LIEBERMAN -
                  RANDOM EFFECTS'.
/ INPUT        VARIABLES ARE 3.
               FORMAT IS '(3F4.0)'.
/ VARIABLE     NAMES ARE OVEN, TEMPRTUR, LIFETIME.

/ DESIGN       DEPENDENT IS LIFETIME.
               RANDOM    IS OVEN.
               RANDOM    IS TEMPRTUR.
               RANDOM    IS OVEN, TEMPRTUR.
               RNAMES    ARE OVEN, TEMPRTUR,
                           'OVEN*TMP'.

/ HYPOTHESIS   RANDOM IS 1.
/ HYPOTHESIS   RANDOM IS 2.
/ HYPOSHESIS   RANDOM IS 3.

/ END
    1     1     237    3   1   192     2   2   146
    1     1     254    3   1   186     2   2   145
    1     1     246    3   1   183     2   2   141
    2     1     208    1   2   178     3   2   142
    2     1     178    1   2   179     3   2   125
    2     1     187    1   2   183     3   2   136
----------------------------------------
```

The results are presented in Output 3V.2. We summarize the tests of the variance components in Table 15.9.

The number of degrees of freedom for σ_a^2 is two (rather than one) because when σ_a^2 is set equal to zero, the estimate of σ_b^2 was also zero.

The variance components for the main effects differ somewhat from the analysis of variance results but agree exactly with the maximum likelihood results given by Hartley and Vaughn (1972). In both cases, the large components are associated with the temperature and oven main effects. The chi-square values are likelihood ratio statistics for the hypothesis that the corresponding variance component is zero. Clearly, these tests lead to less significance than the conventional analysis of variance tests, so this may not be the best way to test the significance of a variance component.

Table 15.8   Random Effects Model Analysis of Variance

Source	d.f.	Mean Sq.	Expected Mean Sq.	F-value	Variance Component
temp	1	13667.56	$\sigma_e^2 + 3\sigma_c^2 + 9\sigma_a^2$	99.5**	1503.
oven	2	4823.17	$\sigma_e^2 + 3\sigma_c^2 + 6\sigma_b^2$	35.1*	781.
temp x oven	2	137.39	$\sigma_e^2 + 3\sigma_c^2$	2.0	23.
error	12	69.78	σ_e^2		70.

* means significant at the 5% level
** at 1%, and
*** at 0.1%

418

Table 15.9 Maximum Likelihood Analysis for the Random Effects Model

Variance Component	Estimate	Standard Error	d.f.	Likelihood Ratio χ^2
σ_a^2	893	1075	2	4.74
σ_b^2	664	674	1	4.00*
σ_c^2	23	47.0	1	.46
σ_e^2	70	28.3		

Output 3V.2 Analysis of a random effects model

NUMBER OF CASES READ.   18

DEPENDENT VARIABLE LIFETIME

PARAMETER	ESTIMATE	STANDARD DEVIATION	EST/ST.DEV.	TWO-TAIL PROBABILITY (ASYMPTOTIC THEORY)
ERR.VAR.	69.7777777778	28.4866584901		
CONSTANT	180.3333333333	25.9904318931	6.9384508133	0.0
OVEN	664.2788652980	674.4496845039		
TEMPRTUR	892.7998580675	1075.0786174784		
OVEN*TMP	22.7987358909	47.0256706144		

-2*LOG(MAXIMUM LIKELIHOOD)   146.94613647

VARIANCE-COVARIANCE MATRIX OF THE PARAMETERS

	ERR.VAR.	CONSTANT	OVEN	TEMPRTUR	OVEN*TMP
ERR.VAR.	811.4895				
CONSTANT	-0.0	675.5024			
OVEN	0.0000	-0.0	454882.3750		
TEMPRTUR	-0.0000	-0.0	-94041.3750	1155794.0000	
OVEN*TMP	-270.4963	-0.0	-1020.2092	-495.4041	2211.4136

RESIDUAL ANALYSIS

CELL	OBSERVED LIFETIME	PREDICTED LIFETIME	ST.DEV. PRED.	OBSERVED-PREDICTED	ST.DEV. O-P	(O-P)/ ST.DEV.
	237.0000	180.3333	25.9904	56.6667	31.2114	1.816
	254.0000	180.3333	25.9904	73.6667	31.2114	2.360
	246.0000	180.3333	25.9904	65.6667	31.2114	2.104
	208.0000	180.3333	25.9904	27.6667	31.2114	0.886
	178.0000	180.3333	25.9904	-2.3333	31.2114	-0.075
	187.0000	180.3333	25.9904	6.6667	31.2114	0.214
	192.0000	180.3333	25.9904	11.6667	31.2114	0.374
	186.0000	180.3333	25.9904	5.6667	31.2114	0.182
	183.0000	180.3333	25.9904	2.6667	31.2114	0.085
	178.0000	180.3333	25.9904	-2.3333	31.2114	-0.075
	179.0000	180.3333	25.9904	-1.3333	31.2114	-0.043
	183.0000	180.3333	25.9904	2.6667	31.2114	0.085
	146.0000	180.3333	25.9904	-34.3333	31.2114	-1.100
	145.0000	180.3333	25.9904	-35.3333	31.2114	-1.132
	141.0000	180.3333	25.9904	-39.3333	31.2114	-1.260
	142.0000	180.3333	25.9904	-38.3333	31.2114	-1.228
	125.0000	180.3333	25.9904	-55.3333	31.2114	-1.773
	136.0000	180.3333	25.9904	-44.3333	31.2114	-1.420

(output continued)

Output 3V.2 (continued)

CONSTRAINED MODEL — HYPOTHESIS NUMBER 1

PARAMETER	ESTIMATE	STANDARD DEVIATION	EST/ST.DEV.	TWO-TAIL PROBABILITY (ASYMPTOTIC THEORY)
ERR.VAR.	69.7777777778	28.4866584901		
CONSTANT	180.3333333333	19.4847201927	9.2551145554	0.0
OVEN	0.0	0.0		
TEMPRTUR	483.7222222224	783.9155255221		
OVEN*TMP	803.5000000000	584.6841898914		

-2*LOG(MAXIMUM LIKELIHOOD)   150.94934082

VARIANCE-COVARIANCE MATRIX OF THE PARAMETERS

	ERR.VAR.	CONSTANT	OVEN	TEMPRTUR	OVEN*TMP
ERR.VAR.	811.4895				
CONSTANT	-0.0	379.6543			
OVEN	-0.0	-0.0	-0.0		
TEMPRTUR	-0.0000	-0.0	-0.0	614523.5000	
OVEN*TMP	-270.4963	-0.0	-0.0	-113921.7500	341855.5625

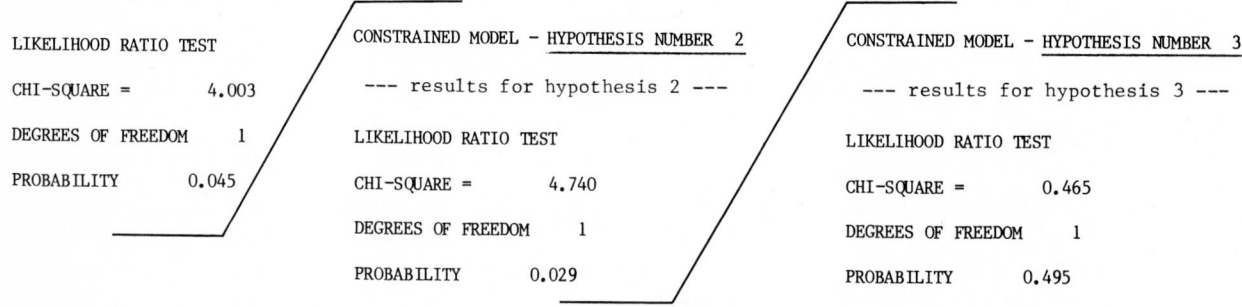

LIKELIHOOD RATIO TEST

CHI-SQUARE =   4.003

DEGREES OF FREEDOM   1

PROBABILITY   0.045

CONSTRAINED MODEL — HYPOTHESIS NUMBER 2

--- results for hypothesis 2 ---

LIKELIHOOD RATIO TEST

CHI-SQUARE =   4.740

DEGREES OF FREEDOM   1

PROBABILITY   0.029

CONSTRAINED MODEL — HYPOTHESIS NUMBER 3

--- results for hypothesis 3 ---

LIKELIHOOD RATIO TEST

CHI-SQUARE =   0.465

DEGREES OF FREEDOM   1

PROBABILITY   0.495

Example 3V.3 Mixed Model Analysis of Variance

It seems natural to consider a model in which the temperature component in the above example is fixed, i.e., a mixed model of the form

$$y_{ijk} = \mu + \alpha_i + b_j + c_{ij} + e_{ijk}$$

where now both μ and α_i are fixed, the α_i sum to zero and the components b_j, c_{ij}, e_{ijk} are as before. There are at least two schools of thought regarding c_{ij}. One school assumes, as we have, that the c_{ij} are independent. The other assumes that the c_{ij} sum to zero on i. Our choice is based on a desire to make our results comparable with previously published results rather than a strong preference for one school over the other. Under the assumption that the c_{ij} are independent, the analysis of variance table using the mixed model is identical to that given for the random effects model except that the definition of σ_a^2 is changed to $\sigma_a^2 = \alpha_1^2 + \alpha_2^2$.

To obtain a maximum likelihood analysis we add a GROUP paragraph to the instructions in Example 3V.1 and replace the DESIGN and HYPOTHESIS paragraphs as

follows:

```
/ PROBLEM      TITLE IS 'BOWKER AND LIEBERMAN -
                         MIXED MODEL'.
/ INPUT        VARIABLES ARE 3.
               FORMAT IS '(3F4.0)'.
/ VARIABLE     NAMES ARE OVEN, TEMPRTUR, LIFETIME.
/ GROUP        CODES(2) ARE 1, 2.
/ DESIGN       DEPENDENT IS LIFETIME.
               FIXED      IS TEMPRTUR.
               FNAME      IS TEMPRTUR.
               RANDOM     IS OVEN.
               RANDOM     IS OVEN, TEMPRTUR.
               RNAMES     ARE OVEN, 'OVEN*TMP'.
/ HYPOTHESIS   FIXED IS 1.
/ HYPOTHESIS   RANDOM IS 1.
/ HYPOTHESIS   RANDOM IS 2.
/ END
```

The results are presented in Output 3V.3. We summarize the results as follows in Table 15.10.

Treating the temperature effect as fixed clearly establishes its significance and more clearly establishes that of the random oven effect. Indeed both are now more clearly established than by either the conventional random or mixed model analysis of variance.

Another strategy for testing the fixed temperature effect can be based on treating

$$\hat{\alpha}_1/\text{st}\hat{d}\,\hat{\alpha}_1 = 12.2$$

as a t statistic with 16 degrees of freedom. This test seems to give even greater significance than the χ^2 likelihood ratio test.

One way to resolve the c_{ij} controversy in a mixed model is to assume $\sigma_c^2=0$ motivated by the fact that

its estimate is very small. This leads to the conventional analysis of variance shown in Table 15.11.

Results in this table are the same as those given previously except that the interaction sum of squares are pooled with the error sum of squares.

Clearly for testing significance with a conventional analysis of variance, the pooling that results from the assumption that $\sigma_c^2=0$ has a good effect without greatly affecting the variance component estimates. The maximum likelihood analysis with $\sigma_c^2=0$ is summarized as in Table 15.12.

As in the conventional analysis of variance, the tests become more significant when σ_c^2 is assumed to be zero. The component estimates are about the same as those in the previous maximum likelihood analysis.

Table 15.10 Maximum Likelihood Analysis for the Mixed Model

Mean or Variance Component	Estimate	Standard Error	d.f.	Likelihood Ratio χ^2
α_1	27.6	2.26	1	11.88
σ_b^2	520.6	437.75	1	6.68
σ_c^2	7.3	26.68	1	.09
σ_e^2	70.0			

Table 15.11 Mixed Model Analysis of Variance with no Interaction

Source	d.f.	Mean Sq.	Expected Mean Sq.	F-value	Variance Component
temp	1	13667.56	$\sigma_e^2+9\sigma_a^2$	172.0	1509
oven	2	4823.17	$\sigma_e^2+6\sigma_b^2$	60.7	791
error	14	79.44	σ_e^2		79

Table 15.12 Maximum Likelihood Analysis for the Mixed Model with no Interaction

Mean or Variance Component	Estimate	Standard Error	d.f.	Likelihood Ratio χ^2
α_1	27.6	2.03	1	38.8
σ_b^2	523.6	437.59	1	26.3
σ_e^2	74.1	27.07		

Output 3V.3   Analysis of a mixed model

NUMBER OF CASES READ.   18

DEPENDENT VARIABLE LIFETIME

PARAMETER	ESTIMATE	STANDARD DEVIATION	EST/ST.DEV.	TWO-TAIL PROBABILITY (ASYMPTOTIC THEORY)
ERR.VAR.	69.7777777778	28.4866584901		
CONSTANT	180.3333333333	13.3654705293	13.4924783707	0.0
TEMPRTUR	27.5555555556	2.2557653615	12.2156124115	0.0
OVEN	520.6419753086	437.7440521060		
TEMPRTUR	7.2716049383	26.6756062595		

-2*LOG(MAXIMUM LIKELIHOOD)   139.80477905

CONSTRAINED MODEL - HYPOTHESIS NUMBER   1

LIKELIHOOD RATIO TEST

CHI-SQUARE =   11.881

DEGREES OF FREEDOM   1

PROBABILITY   0.001

CONSTRAINED MODEL - HYPOTHESIS NUMBER   2

LIKELIHOOD RATIO TEST

CHI-SQUARE =   6.685

DEGREES OF FREEDOM   1

PROBABILITY   0.010

CONSTRAINED MODEL - HYPOTHESIS NUMBER   3

LIKELIHOOD RATIO TEST

CHI-SQUARE =   0.094

DEGREES OF FREEDOM   1

PROBABILITY   0.760

Example 3V.4 Nesting

Nested models can also be analyzed. Suppose we have a two-factor experiment with factor B nested in factor A. Suppose further that A has three levels. Data for this example could appear as

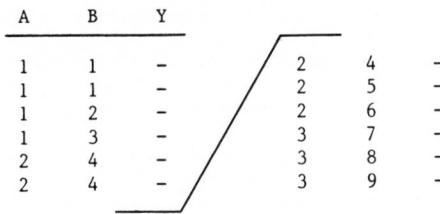

A	B	Y		A	B	Y
1	1	-		2	4	-
1	1	-		2	5	-
1	2	-		2	6	-
1	3	-		3	7	-
2	4	-		3	8	-
2	4	-		3	9	-

Note that any given level of B appears at only one level of A. This fact implies that B is nested in A. If B were crossed with A, then levels 4, 5, 6, and levels 7, 8, and 9 of B would have to actually be levels 1, 2, and 3. The levels of B are similar then to subject identification numbers in an experiment where subjects are nested in the levels of a treatment factor. Each subject is given a distinct subject number; two different subjects cannot have the same subject number whatever their assignment to levels of the treatment factor.

In this example, there is an implicit third factor or index that is nested in B. This is seen from the fact that there is more than one case for some levels of B. This third index is used in defining the residual variance.

P3V will provide estimates of

the constant (mean or intercept),
the variance component for A,
the variance component for B, and
the residual variance.

Appropriate Control Language for analyzing the above data follows:

```
-----------------------------------
/ INPUT    VAR = 3.
          FORMAT = FREE.
/ VAR     NAMES = A, B, Y.
/ DESIGN  FIXED = A.
          RANDOM = A,B.
          DEPEND = Y.
          RNAME = 'A*B'.
/ END
-----------------------------------
```

We do not show output for this example.

Specifying the Model: The DESIGN Paragraph

The DESIGN paragraph is used to specify the DEPENDENT variable, COVARIATES, FIXED effects components, RANDOM effects components, and names for the components (FNAME and RNAME respectively).

Each value of the DEPENDENT variable appears in a distinct case; there can only be one dependent variable. In P3V each repeated measure for a subject is recorded as a separate case. (This differs from P2V where multiple dependent variables can be present to represent repeated measures for a subject.)

The model is described by a sequence of FIXED and RANDOM component statements. Each component in the model (except the grand mean and the error) must be specified as either FIXED or RANDOM in separate statements; each statement corresponds to a line in an ANOVA table. You can name the FIXED and RANDOM components by FNAME and RNAME statements, respectively. Ordinarily you will probably want to give main effects the same name as the variable that defines the component. The main purpose of the FNAME and RNAME statements is to allow you to name the interactions. The names of the components are specified in the <u>same</u> sequence as that in which the components are defined. In our first example (Example 3V.1) the DESIGN paragraph is

```
/ DESIGN   DEPENDENT IS TEMPRTUR.
           FIXED      IS GROUP.
           FIXED      IS TREATMNT.
           FIXED      IS GROUP, TREATMNT.
           FNAMES     ARE GROUP, TREATMNT, 'GRP*TRT'.
           COVARIATE IS BLOODPRS.
           RANDOM     IS GROUP, SUBJECT.
           RNAME      IS 'SBJ*GRP'.
```

Therefore the FNAMES GROUP, TREATMNT and GRP*TRT are for the GROUP, TREATMNT and GROUP x TREATMNT interactions, respectively, and the RNAME SBJ*GRP is for SUBJECTS in the GROUPS component.

DESIGN ───

DEPENDent = v.   required   none/prev.
    Name or subscript of the dependent variable.
COVARiate = v list.   none/prev.
    Names or subscripts of the covariates.
FIXED = v list.   may be repeated   none/prev.
    Names or subscripts of variables that define a fixed effects component (main effect or interaction). Each FIXED statement corresponds to a line in an ANOVA table.
    <u>Note</u>: You <u>must</u> specify CODES or CUTPOINTS in the GROUP paragraph (Section 5.5) for each variable in a FIXED statement.
FNAME = c list.   FIX(subscript)/prev.
    Names for the FIXED components. The first name is for the fixed component defined by the first FIXED statement, the second name for the second fixed component, etc. Note that all names are specified in one FNAMES statement. If FNAMES is not specified, FIX(subscript) is used to label the results, where subscript is the sequence number of the FIX statement defining the component.
RANDom = v list. may be repeated   none/prev.
    Names or subscripts of variables that define a random effects component (main effect or interaction). Each RANDOM statement corresponds to a line in an ANOVA table. You should specify at least one random component; otherwise you should use BMDP2V.
RNAME = c list.   RAND(subscript)/prev.
    Names for the RANDOM component. The first name is for the random component defined by the first RANDOM statement, the second name for the second random component, etc. Note that all names are specified in one RNAMES statement. If RNAMES is not specified, RAND(subscript) is used to label the results where subscript is the sequence number of the RAND statement defining the component.

Specifying Hypotheses to be Tested

Each hypothesis to be tested (or each submodel to be evaluated) must be specified in a separate HYPOTHESIS paragraph; no hypotheses are tested automatically. The HYPOTHESIS paragraph can be repeated to specify additional submodels. The HYPOTHESES paragraph is not used if METHOD = REML is specified in the DESIGN paragraph.

Each hypothesis is specified by one FIXED and/or one RANDOM statement that specify the components to be set to zero. Components are identified by the sequence number in which they are specified in the DESIGN paragraph. For example, the statements

FIX = 1, 3.   RANDOM = 1.

in the HYPOTHESIS paragraph specifies that two fixed effects components defined in the first and third FIXED statements and the random component defined by the first RANDOM statement in the DESIGN paragraph are all to be set to zero.

```
HYPOTHesis ─────────────────────────────────
   FIXed = # list.                         none
      The fixed components to be set to zero in the
      hypothesis  to  be  tested  (or  submodel
      evaluated). Each fixed component is identified
      by the sequence number of the FIXED statement
      in which it is defined.
   RANDom = # list.                        none
      The random components to be set to zero in the
      hypothesis  to  be  tested  (or  submodel
      evaluated). Each random component is identified
      by the sequence number of the RANDOM statement
      in which it is defined.
```

Restricted Maximum Likelihood

The three examples shown for P3V have used (unrestricted) maximum likelihood estimates. P3V can also be used for restricted maximum likelihood or REML estimates (see, for example, Corbeil and Searle, 1976). If data are balanced and if the conventional analysis of variance estimates of the variance components are all nonnegative, then the conventional ANOVA estimates are identical to the REML estimates (Jennrich, unpublished).

```
DESIGN ──────────────────────────────────────
   METHod = (one only) ML, REML            ML/prev.
      Parameter  estimates  are  obtained  by
      (unrestricted) maximum likelihood estimation
      (ML)  or  by  restricted  maximum  likelihood
      (REML). ML estimates are obtained unless REML
      is specified.
```

Initial Estimates for the Parameters

The maximum likelihood estimates are found by iteration. You can specify initial estimates for the parameters.

```
DESIGN ──────────────────────────────────────
   PARAMeters = # list.         all 0.0 except $\sigma_e^2$ =
                                variance of dependent
                                variable/prev.
      Initial estimates for the parameters. The first
      parameter is the variance of the error, $\sigma_e^2$.
      Next are coefficients of the covariates in the
      order stated in the COVARIATE statement (if
      any). These are followed by the fixed and
      random components in the sequence stated in the
      DESIGN paragraph. Remember that the parameters
      for any fixed effects component are the
      coefficients of the dummy variables; therefore
      if the component has more than one degree of
      freedom, it also has more than one coefficient.
```

Maximum Number of Iterations

The maximum number of iterations for the algorithm to obtain maximum likelihood estimates is preassigned to 30. You can raise or lower this limit.

```
DESIGN ──────────────────────────────────────
   MAXIT = #.                               30/prev.
      Maximum number of iterations.
```

Number of Levels for Components

The main effect for a fixed effects component is defined by codes, categories or levels of a grouping variable. The codes or categories can be defined by CODES or CUTPOINTS in a GROUP paragraph (Section 5.5). If each value of the grouping variable corresponds to a distinct category for the fixed effect, you can specify the number of LEVELS in the GROUP paragraph and not CODES or CUTPOINTS. Either the number of LEVELS or CODES or CUTPOINTS must be specified for each grouping variable that defines a fixed component main effect. If the number of levels in a random effects component main effect is greater than 100, LEVELS or CODES or CUTPOINTS must be specified.

```
GROUP ───────────────────────────────────────
   LEVEL (#_1) = #_2.   may be repeated        none
      #_2 is the number of levels of the variable with
      subscript #_1. LEVEL is required for any
      variable that defines a fixed component main
      effect (or random component main effect with
      more than 100 levels) and for which neither
      CODES nor CUTPOINTS are stated in the GROUP
      paragraph (Section 5.5).
```

Case Weights

The analysis can be weighted by the values of a case WEIGHT variable.

```
VARiable ─────────────────────────────────────
   WEIGHT = v.                             none/prev.
      Name or subscript of variable that contains
      case weights. If not specified or set to zero,
      there are no case weights.
```

SIZE OF PROBLEM

The maximum problem that P3V can analyze at most facilities is a complex function of the number of variables, covariates, groups and total number of dummy variables generated for the fixed and random effects. The following provides a rough guide to the capacity of P3V. Let vv be the total number of variables used in the analysis (the number of variables read as input and the number of dummy variables generated by P3V) and let g be the total number of groups (cells) in the ANOVA model. Then P3V can analyze the following combinations of vv and g

vv	10	20	50	75
g	100	90	65	30

Appendix B describes how to increase the capacity of the program.

COMPUTATIONAL METHOD

The data are read in single precision. Computations are performed in double precision. The means, variances and cross products are computed by the method of provisional means (Appendix A.2). The computations performed by P3V are described in Appendix A.19. They are based on a combination Fisher-scoring and Newton-Raphson algorithm (Jennrich and Sampson, 1976).

ACKNOWLEDGEMENT

P3V was designed by Robert Jennrich and Paul Sampson with major contributions from R.L. Anderson. It was programmed by Paul Sampson.

SUMMARY

Order of Input Cards

```
// (job card)
// EXEC BIMED,PROG=BMDP3V        (see Appendix E)
//SYSIN DD *
/ PROBLEM
/ INPUT
/ VARIABLE
/ TRANSFORM
/ SAVE
/ DESIGN
/ HYPOTHESIS        repeat for subproblems
/ GROUP
/ END
    (data, in on cards)
// (system card)
```

Full sets of BMDP paragraphs (and data, if on cards) can be repeated for additional problems; see Section 5.8.

Paragraph Statement	Preassigned	Comment and Manual Reference
/ VARiable		Additional option to specify case weights.
WEIGHT = v.	none	Name or subscript of variable containing case weights. * 424
/●DESIGN		Required to specify which components (main effects and interactions) are fixed or random, the dependent variable and name for each component. Use separate statements to specify each component in the model as either FIXED or RANDOM (omit the grand mean and the error term). A two-factor interaction is denoted by two variables separated by a comma.
● DEPENDent = v.	none	Name or subscript of the dependent variable. * 423
o FIXed = v list.	none	Names or subscripts of variables that define a fixed effects component (main effect or interaction). Repeat for each fixed effect component in the model. / GROUP CODE or CUTP must be specified for each variable in the FIX list. * 423
o RANDom = v list.	none	Names or subscripts of variables that define a random effects component. Repeat for each component (main effect or interaction). *
COVAriate = v list.	none	Names or subscripts of the covariates. * 426
FNAMEs = c list.	F(1),F(2), etc.	Names for the FIX components. The first name is for the component in the first FIX statement, the second for the second component, etc. (All names are specified in one statement.) * 426
RNAMEs = c list.	R(1),R(2), etc.	Names for the RAND components. The first name is for the component in the first RAND statement, the second for the second component, etc. (All names are specified in one statement.) * 426
METHod = c.	ML.	Method of estimating parameters (one only). ML or REML (see program definition above). * 424
PARAMeters = # list.	1,0,0,0,etc.	Initial estimates for the parameters. The first number is the variance of the error term. Next are the coefficients of the covariates (same order as in COVA statement). The fixed and random components follow (the sequence stated in / DESIGN). Parameters for fixed effect components are the coefficients of the dummy variables (one per degree of freedom). * 424
MAXIT = #.	30.	Maximum number of iterations. * 424
/ HYPOTHesis		Optional to specify each hypothesis to be tested (each submodel to be evaluated) in a separate HYPOTH paragraph, using one FIX and/or one RAND statement to indicate which components are set to zero (can be repeated).
FIXed = # list.	none	Set specified fixed components to zero. Use order of components in / DESIGN FIX. 424
RANDom = # list.	none	Set specified random components to zero. Use order of components in / DESIGN RAND. 424
/ GROUP		Additional option for fixed effects. 424
LEVEL(j) = #.	none	The number of levels for variable j. LEVEL is required for any variable that defines a fixed main effect for which neither CODE nor CUTP is stated. *

Key:

/	—indicates paragraph
.	—period ends a sentence
●	—required o —may be required
v	—variable (name or subscript)
g	—group (name or subscript)
#	—number
'c'	—characters (name or parameter) may omit apostrophes if contiguous letters only

* —assigned value remains the same for additional problems
VT —number of variables after transformations
list —more than one item, often one per var.

Capitalized letters—paragraph or sentence names recognized by BMDP
Page numbers following refer to this Manual

- preassigned (default) options
- cell and marginal means and residuals
- multiple dependent variables
- finite population size
- selecting a subset of variables
- missing values and subsets of cases
- transformations

Example 8V.1 Two Crossed Random Factors

Winer (1971, p. 288) discusses an example with two analysis of variance indices, or factors: subjects and judges. Each judge rates each subject. If the subjects and evaluators are both random samples, the analysis of variance model can be written as

$$Y_{ij} = \mu + a_i + b_j + e_{ij}, \qquad \begin{array}{l} i=1,\ldots,n, \\ j=1,\ldots,k \end{array}$$

where

Y_{ij} = observed measurement

μ = grand mean

a_i = subject effect

b_j = judge effect

e_{ij} = error of measurement

There are six subjects and four judges. The rows of the data matrix correspond to the subjects (cases) and the columns to the judges. The data are input so that each variable corresponds to the scores given by a single judge. The LEVEL statement in the DESIGN paragraph specifies that there are six levels (subjects) in the first factor and four levels (judges) in the second. The RANDOM statement indicates that both factors are random. The Control Language and data follow:

```
----------------------------------------
/ PROBLEM     TITLE IS 'WINER, P. 288'.
/ INPUT       VARIABLES ARE 4.
             FORMAT IS '(4F2.0)'.

/ VARIABLE    NAMES ARE JUDGE1, JUDGE2,
             JUDGE3, JUDGE4.

/ DESIGN      LEVELS ARE 6, 4.
             NAMES ARE SUBJECTS, JUDGES.
             RANDOM ARE SUBJECTS, JUDGES.
             MODEL IS 'S,J'.

/ END
 2 4 3 3
 5 7 5 6
 1 3 1 2
 7 9 9 8
 2 4 6 1
 6 8 8 4
----------------------------------------
```

(See end of this P8V section for organization of systems information, BMDP instructions and data.)

NAMES are used both for labeling the results and for specifying the nesting and crossing relationships among the factors in the MODEL statement. Note that the MODEL is enclosed in

P8V

15.5 General Mixed Model Analysis of Variance — Equal Cell Sizes

Robert Jennrich
Paul Sampson

ABSTRACT

P8V performs an analysis of variance for any complete design with equal cell sizes. This includes nested, crossed, and partially crossed designs for fixed-effects models, mixed models (including repeated measures), and random-effects models. Separate analyses can be performed for several dependent variables. Factors are nested or crossed, and effects are random or fixed. P8V prints expected mean squares defined in terms of variance components. A careful organization of the input data is important (see the sections below on Data Entry and Rules for Specifying the Analysis). Output also includes estimates of variance components and optional cell means, marginal means, residuals and other cell deviations from marginal means. The expected mean squares are derived from the Cornfield and Tukey (1956) formulas; P8V derives F statistics from these formulas. Many different models can be analyzed in P8V; the operation is best described by examples of the models. Following the examples we provide general rules for specifying models and for requesting optional results.

Output 8V.1   Analysis of two crossed random factors. Circled numbers correspond to those in the text

----

--- the BMDP instructions read by 8V are printed and interpreted ---

ANALYSIS OF VARIANCE DESIGN   (1)

INDEX	SUBJECTS	JUDGES
NUMBER OF LEVELS	6	4
POPULATION SIZE	INF	INF

MODEL   S,J

ESTIMATES OF VARIANCE COMPONENTS   (3)

(1)	21.35000
(2)	5.81667
(3)	0.76667
(4)	1.23333

ANALYSIS OF VARIANCE FOR DEPENDENT VARIABLE 1   (2)

	SOURCE	ERROR TERM	SUM OF SQUARES	D.F.	MEAN SQUARE	F	PROB.	EXPECTED MEAN SQUARE
1	MEAN		541.500	1	541.5000			24(1) + 4(2) + 6(3) + (4)
2	SUBJECTS	SJ	122.500	5	24.5000	19.86	0.0000	4(2) + (4)
3	JUDGES	SJ	17.500	3	5.8333	4.73	0.0162	6(3) + (4)
4	SJ		18.500	15	1.2333			(4)

- -

GRAND MEAN   4.75000

CELL AND MARGINAL MEANS

S =	1	2	3	4	5	6
	3.00000	5.75000	1.75000	8.25000	3.25000	6.50000

J =	1	2	3	4
	3.83333	5.83333	5.33333	4.00000

	J =	1	2	3	4
S =	1	2.00000	4.00000	3.00000	3.00000
	2	5.00000	7.00000	5.00000	6.00000
	3	1.00000	3.00000	1.00000	2.00000
	4	7.00000	9.00000	9.00000	8.00000
	5	2.00000	4.00000	6.00000	1.00000
	6	6.00000	8.00000	8.00000	4.00000

- -

CELL DEVIATIONS

X(S.)   - X(..)

S =	1	2	3	4	5	6
	-1.75000	1.00000	-3.00000	3.50000	-1.50000	1.75000

X(.J)   - X(..)

J =	1	2	3	4
	-0.91667	1.08333	0.58333	-0.75000

X(SJ)   - X(.J)   - X(S.)   + X(..)

	J =	1	2	3	4
S =	1	-0.08333	-0.08333	-0.58333	0.75000
	2	0.16667	0.16667	-1.33333	1.00000
	3	0.16667	0.16667	-1.33333	1.00000
	4	-0.33333	-0.33333	0.16667	0.50000
	5	-0.33333	-0.33333	2.16667	-1.50000
	6	0.41667	0.41667	0.91667	-1.75000

----

apostrophes ('S,J') and that the first letter of each name is used. In our example, the two factors are crossed because each judge rates each subject.

Data entry. Other BMDP programs (7D, 1V, 2V, 3V, and 4V) do not require that input (cases) be arranged in a specific order: they use GROUP CODES or CUTPOINTS to sort data into the appropriate design structure (cells). P8V does not use GROUPING information; it uses the LEVEL statement to recognize the design structure in the input data. The order of the two numbers in the LEVEL statement is essential. For our example (LEVELS ARE 6, 4.), as you read the numbers in the rows of the data matrix, you read the data for all four levels of the second factor (JUDGES) at the first level of the first factor (SUBJECTS) before reading any data for the second level of the first factor. If we denote the data for the present example by Y_{ij} where i indicates the level of the first factor and j the level of the second, then the data are arranged as follows:

$$
\begin{matrix}
Y_{11} & Y_{12} & \cdots & Y_{1k} \\
Y_{21} & Y_{22} & \cdots & Y_{2k} \\
\cdot & & & \\
\cdot & & & \\
\cdot & & & \\
Y_{n1} & Y_{n2} & \cdots & Y_{nk} & .
\end{matrix}
$$

For these data we specify LEVELS ARE N,K.

The results are presented in Output 8V.1. Circled numbers below correspond to those in the output.

① The DESIGN paragraph is interpreted by P8V.

② The ANOVA table is printed, together with the expected mean squares. The line for the mean is not usually of interest. The line for the subjects effect, SUBJECTS, indicates that the mean square for

SJ would be used for any test of the magnitude of the SUBJECTS effect. The expected mean square for SUBJECTS includes two variance components: $4\sigma_a^2$, four times the variance component for subjects; and σ_e^2, the variance component for error of measurement. The line for JUDGES is similar to that for SUBJECTS. The line for SJ is used as the error term for tests of SUBJECTS or JUDGES effects. For example, the test for the SUBJECTS effect is obtained by dividing the mean square for SUBJECTS by the mean square for SJ.

③ Estimates of variance components are reported. The first variance component corresponds to the grand mean and is usually not of interest. The second is the estimate of σ_a^2, the subject variance; the third is the estimate of σ_b^2, the judge variance; and the last is the estimate of σ_e^2, the error of measurement.

Reliability (internal consistency). Analysis of variance can also be used to compute reliability estimates (see Winer, 283–296). Using Winer's method (p. 290) we can compute the estimate of reliability of the mean of the four judges as

$$
r_4 = \frac{4\hat{\theta}}{1 + 4\hat{\theta}} \qquad \text{where} \quad \hat{\theta} = \hat{\sigma}_a^2 / \hat{\sigma}_e^2 .
$$

We can also compute r as (F−1)/F where F is the analysis of variance F statistic for testing equality of subject means.

Example 8V.2 Two Nested Random Factors

Using the Winer data (p. 288) we can define a nested design by changing the MODEL statement in the DESIGN paragraph to specify that the subjects are nested in judges; i.e., there are separate subjects for each judge. The replacement specification is:

```
----------------------------------------
            MODEL IS 'J,S(J)'.
----------------------------------------
```

Output 8V.2 Analysis of two nested random factors

```
          ANALYSIS OF VARIANCE DESIGN


     INDEX            SUBJECTS  JUDGES
     NUMBER OF LEVELS    6        4
     POPULATION SIZE    INF      INF


     MODEL     J, S(J)                              ESTIMATES OF VARIANCE COMPONENTS

                                                    (1)          22.31944
                                                    (2)          -0.20278
                                                    (3)           7.05000


     ANALYSIS OF VARIANCE FOR DEPENDENT VARIABLE   1
```

	SOURCE	ERROR TERM	SUM OF SQUARES	D.F.	MEAN SQUARE	F	PROB.	EXPECTED MEAN SQUARE
1	MEAN	JUDGES	541.500	1	541.5000	92.83	0.0024	24(1) + 6(2) + (3)
2	JUDGES	S(J)	17.500	3	5.8333	0.83	0.4943	6(2) + (3)
3	S(J)		141.000	20	7.0500			(3)

Example 8V.3 Fixed Effect (A One-Way ANOVA)

If J denotes a fixed-effect rather than a random factor, we have a one-way analysis of variance. The input for this analysis using the same data as in Examples 8V.1 and 8V.2 is shown below with the results in Output 8V.3.

```
------------------------------------
/ PROBLEM      TITLE IS 'WINER, P. 288'.
/ INPUT        VARIABLES ARE 4.
              FORMAT IS '(4F2.0)'.

/ VARIABLE     NAMES ARE JUDGE1, JUDGE2,
              JUDGE3, JUDGE4.

/ DESIGN       LEVELS ARE 6, 4.
              NAMES ARE SUBJECTS, J.
              RANDOM IS SUBJECTS.
              FIXED IS J.
              MODEL IS 'J, S(J)'.

/ END
------------------------------------
```

Example 8V.4 Repeated Measures: One Grouping Factor and One Within Factor

P8V can also be used to analyze repeated-measures designs. The input in Example 8V.4 is used to analyze Winer's repeated-measures data (p. 525). The input contains three factors, A, B, and S, where A and B denote fixed effects and S is random and denotes subjects or experimental units. Factor B has repeated measures, so S is nested in A but crossed with B. S is nested in A because each level of A has different subjects. S is crossed with B because every subject is measured for every level of B. A is a grouping factor because it indicates how subjects

or experimental units are grouped. B is a within-subjects, or repeated-measures factor. A is crossed with B. As in Example 8V.1, the order of the numbers in the LEVEL statement is essential. As you read the data, the slowest moving index must correspond to the first number in the LEVEL statement. The slowest moving index is the one for factor A since all data for level one of A appear before any data for level two. S has the second slowest moving index. B has the fastest moving index since each card contains all levels of B for one subject in one group. Hence the LEVEL statement indicates that there are two groups with three subjects in each group, and that each subject is measured four times. Results are shown in Output 8V.4. (These data are also analyzed in Example 2V.6). Note that P8V does not use a GROUPING variable like P2V to divide the subjects into two groups for factor A.

```
------------------------------------
/ PROBLEM      TITLE IS 'WINER, P. 525'.
/ INPUT        VARIABLES ARE 4.
              FORMAT IS '(4F2.0)'.

/ VARIABLE     NAMES ARE B1, B2, B3, B4.

/ DESIGN       LEVELS ARE 2, 3, 4.
              NAMES ARE A, S, B.
              FIXED ARE A, B.
              RANDOM IS S.
              MODEL IS 'A, B, S(A)'.

/ END
0 0 5 3
3 1 5 4
4 3 6 2
4 2 7 8
5 4 6 6
7 5 8 9
------------------------------------
```

Output 8V.3 One-way analysis of variance

ANALYSIS OF VARIANCE DESIGN

INDEX	SUBJECTS	J
NUMBER OF LEVELS	6	4
POPULATION SIZE	INF	4

MODEL   J, S(J)

ESTIMATES OF VARIANCE COMPONENTS

(1)	22.26875
(2)	−0.20278
(3)	7.05000

ANALYSIS OF VARIANCE FOR DEPENDENT VARIABLE 1

	SOURCE	ERROR TERM	SUM OF SQUARES	D.F.	MEAN SQUARE	F	PROB.	EXPECTED MEAN SQUARE
1	MEAN	S(J)	541.500	1	541.5000	76.81	0.0000	24(1) + (3)
2	J	S(J)	17.500	3	5.8333	0.83	0.4943	6(2) + (3)
3	S(J)		141.000	20	7.0500			(3)

Example 8V.5 Repeated Measures: Two Repeated Measures

If both A and B had repeated measures, S would be crossed with A and B. Our model is specified by replacing the MODEL designated in Example 8V.4 by

```
-------------------------------------
            MODEL IS 'A, B, S'.
-------------------------------------
```

Example 8V.6 Repeated Measures: One Grouping Factor and Two Within Factors

Winer (p. 546) also describes a repeated-measures example with three fixed-effects factors (A,B,C) and one random factor (S), for subjects. There are repeated measures for factors B and C; i.e., subjects are nested in groups (A) and crossed with B and C. A has two levels and B, C and S each have three levels. The data are arranged so that A moves

Output 8V.4   An analysis with one grouping factor and one repeated measure

----

```
            ANALYSIS OF VARIANCE DESIGN


    INDEX              A        S        B
    NUMBER OF LEVELS   2        3        4                    ESTIMATES OF VARIANCE COMPONENTS
    POPULATION SIZE    2       INF       4
                                                              (1)          19.69792
    MODEL      A, B, S(A)                                     (2)           3.89583
                                                              (3)           2.43056
                                                              (4)           1.07292
                                                              (5)           0.41667
                                                              (6)           1.23611
```

```
    ANALYSIS OF VARIANCE FOR DEPENDENT VARIABLE  1
```

	SOURCE	ERROR TERM	SUM OF SQUARES	D.F.	MEAN SQUARE	F	PROB.	EXPECTED MEAN SQUARE
1	MEAN	S(A)	477.0417	1	477.0417	111.16	0.0005	24(1) + 4(4)
2	A	S(A)	51.0417	1	51.0417	11.89	0.0261	12(2) + 4(4)
3	B	SB(A)	47.4583	3	15.8194	12.80	0.0005	6(3) + (6)
4	S(A)		17.1667	4	4.2917			4(4)
5	AB	SB(A)	7.4583	3	2.4861	2.01	0.1662	3(5) + (6)
6	SB(A)		14.8333	12	1.2361			(6)

Output 8V.5   Analysis of two repeated measures

```
            ANALYSIS OF VARIANCE DESIGN


    INDEX              A        S        B
    NUMBER OF LEVELS   2        3        4                    ESTIMATES OF VARIANCE COMPONENTS
    POPULATION SIZE    2       INF       4
                                                              (1)          19.57292
    MODEL      A, B, S                                        (2)           4.14583
                                                              (3)           0.91146
                                                              (4)           2.37500
                                                              (5)           0.32292
                                                              (6)           0.52778
                                                              (7)           0.78472
                                                              (8)           0.90278
```

```
    ANALYSIS OF VARIANCE FOR DEPENDENT VARIABLE  1
```

	SOURCE	ERROR TERM	SUM OF SQUARES	D.F.	MEAN SQUARE	F	PROB.	EXPECTED MEAN SQUARE
1	MEAN	S	477.0417	1	477.04167	65.42	0.0149	24(1) + 8(3)
2	A	AS	51.0417	1	51.04167	39.52	0.0244	12(2) + 4(5)
3	S		14.5833	2	7.29167			8(3)
4	B	SB	47.4583	3	15.81944	10.08	0.0093	6(4) + 2(7)
5	AS		2.5833	2	1.29167			4(5)
6	AB	ASB	7.4583	3	2.48611	2.75	0.1345	3(6) + (8)
7	SB		9.4167	6	1.56944			2(7)
8	ASB		5.4167	6	0.90278			(8)

```
        --- the estimates of the variance components appear here ---
```

----

slowest, then S, then B and then C (C moves fastest). The complete input is shown below and the results are in Output 8V.6. (These data are also analyzed in Example 2V.10, p. 370.)

The Winer data are arranged in a tyical manner for repeated measures. The indices for the within factors move fastest, for subjects the next fastest and for the between-groups effects they move slowest. Hence, when this is the case, one way to check your setup for repeated measures is to be sure that in your NAME statement in the DESIGN paragraph the grouping factors are given first, then subjects, and then the within-subjects factors.

```
--------------------------------------------
/ PROBLEM      TITLE IS 'WINER, P. 546'.
/ INPUT        VARIABLES ARE 9.
               FORMAT IS "(9F3.0)'.

/ VARIABLE     NAMES ARE B1C1, B1C2, B1C3,
                         B2C1, B2C2, B2C3,
                         B3C1, B3C2, B3C3.
/ DESIGN       LEVELS ARE 2, 3, 3, 3.
               NAMES ARE A, S, B, C.
               FIXED ARE A, B, C.
               RANDOM IS S.
               MODEL IS 'A, S(A), B, C'.

/ END
 45 53 60 40 52 57 28 37 46
 35 41 50 30 37 47 25 32 41
 60 65 75 58 54 70 40 47 50
 50 48 61 25 34 51 16 23 35
 42 45 55 30 37 43 22 27 37
 56 60 77 40 39 57 31 29 46
--------------------------------------------
```

Example 8V.7 Repeated Measures: Two Grouping Factors and One Repeated Measure

A repeated-measures design with four factors is also given in Winer (p. 564): A, B, C and S, where S denotes subjects. Factor C has repeated measures, so the MODEL statement is

$$\text{MODEL IS 'A, B, C, S(AB)'.}$$

We do not show the output for this example.

Example 8V.8 Complex Design

Bennett and Franklin (1954, p. 422) give a complex design with six factors:

A	random with	3	levels
I	" "	4	"
K	" "	2	"
L	fixed	2	"
J	random "	4	"
M	fixed "	2	"

The P8V MODEL statement for this design is

$$\text{MODEL IS 'I, L, M, J(I), K(IJ), A(IJKLM)'.}$$

Output 8V.6 Analysis of one grouping factor and two repeated measures

----

ANALYSIS OF VARIANCE DESIGN

INDEX	A	S	B	C
NUMBER OF LEVELS	2	3	3	3
POPULATION SIZE	2	INF	3	3

MODEL   A, S(A), B, C

ESTIMATES OF VARIANCE COMPONENTS

(1)	1948.98868
(2)	-5.72634
(3)	101.76698
(4)	65.10957
(5)	69.19753
(6)	15.23765
(7)	1.33025
(8)	-0.87963
(9)	9.78704
(10)	4.39815
(11)	-1.70370
(12)	7.94444

ANALYSIS OF VARIANCE FOR DEPENDENT VARIABLE 1

	SOURCE	ERROR TERM	SUM OF SQUARES	D.F.	MEAN SQUARE	F	PROB.	EXPECTED MEAN SQUARE
1	MEAN	S(A)	105868.167	1	105868.1667	169.99	0.0002	54(1) + 9(5)
2	A	S(A)	468.167	1	468.1667	0.75	0.4348	27(2) + 9(5)
3	B	SB(A)	3722.333	2	1861.1667	63.39	0.0000	18(3) + 3(9)
4	C	SC(A)	2370.333	2	1185.1667	89.82	0.0000	18(4) + 3(10)
5	S(A)		2491.111	4	622.7778			9(5)
6	AB	SB(A)	333.000	2	166.5000	5.67	0.0293	9(6) + 3(9)
7	AC	SC(A)	50.333	2	25.1667	1.91	0.2102	9(7) + 3(10)
8	BC	SBC(A)	10.667	4	2.6667	0.34	0.8499	6(8) + (12)
9	SB(A)		234.889	8	29.3611			3(9)
10	SC(A)		105.556	8	13.1944			3(10)
11	ABC	SBC(A)	11.333	4	2.8333	0.36	0.8357	3(11) + (12)
12	SBC(A)		127.111	16	7.9444			(12)

--- the estimates of the variance components appear here ---

This model specifies that

I, L, and M are crossed

J is nested in I and is crossed with all other factors

K is nested in I and J and is crossed with all other factors

A is nested in all other factors

We do not show the output for this example.

General Rules for Specifying the Analysis

The general rules will be understood more easily if you first read the examples above.

The INPUT and DESIGN paragraphs require special attention in P8V. The INPUT paragraph is essentially the same in P8V as in other BMDP programs except that the number of input variables must be stated so they correspond <u>exactly</u> to the number of items in the variable format.

P8V differs from P2V and other BMDP programs insofar as subjects, or experimental units, are an explicit factor in P8V. Thus a design with three factors for P2V will have four factors in P8V. (Compare example 8V.4 and 2V.6.) You must specify the number of levels in each factor. The order of the factors in the LEVEL statement must correspond to the order of the data. (Read the Data entry section above for a detailed explanation.) Data are ordered so that the first factor in the LEVEL statement has the slowest moving index in the data matrix.

Each factor is given a one-character symbol to label the output. The order of the symbols must correspond to the order of the factors in the LEVEL statement.

The MODEL statement specifies the nesting and crossing relationships: factor A is crossed with factor B if the levels of A mean the same thing at each level of B; two experimentally determined factors are usually crossed; A is nested in B if the levels of A mean different things at each level of B (e.g., when A denotes experimental units and different experimental units are used for each level of B). Crossed factors are separated by commas in the MODEL statement and nesting is denoted by parentheses. A(B) means that A is nested in B and crossed with all other factors.

You must specify which factors are fixed and which are random. The indices in the FIXED and RANDOM statements correspond to the order given in the LEVEL and NAME statements; e.g., if the second factor in the LEVEL statement is fixed and the first and third are random, state

FIXED = 2.
RANDOM = 1, 3.

<u>Preassigned (default) options</u>. Basically, there are no options for the DESIGN paragraph. Everything must be stated in the first problem. In subsequent problems if you omit the DESIGN paragraph all options remain the same as stated in the first problem; if you include a DESIGN paragraph everything must be restated (i.e., individual parameters are not carried over).

DESign ────
| LEVels = # list. | must be stated none |

The number of levels in each factor; the factor with the slowest moving index is stated first.
| NAMEs = c list. | must be stated none |

Names for the factors. The first character of each name must be unique.
| FIXed = c list. | must be stated if any |

Names or indices for fixed factors (must correspond to those in the LEVEL statement).
| RANdom = c list. | must be stated none |

Names or indices for random factors.
| MODel = c list. | must be stated none |

Analysis of variance model to specify the nesting and crossing relaionships; only the first character of each NAME is used.

Cell and Marginal Means and Residuals

Cell means and cell deviations are printed for all main effects and second order interactions. Additional cell means, marginal means, residuals and other cell deviations from marginal means are requested by including a PRINT statement in the DESIGN paragraph. To analyze a repeated-measures design with factors A, B, C and S, a PRINT statement is added to the DESIGN paragraph of Example 8V.6:

PRINT IS ABC.

Since S is not included, the marginal means and deviations are computed using the averages over the levels of S (subjects); i.e., the means, marginal means, residuals, and marginal deviations are produced for an analysis where the dependent variable is the average over the levels of S. To request only the marginal means and deviations for each factor, state

PRINT = 'A, B, C'.

For all marginal means and deviations, state

PRINT = 'ASBC'.

DESign ────
| PRINT = 'c list'. | none |

Each c denotes the highest order set of marginal means and deviations to be printed; use only the first character of each NAME.

Multiple Dependent Variables

For analysis of variance for each of several dependent variables you can read all your data into P8V at once. The values of all the dependent variables for one analysis of variance cell must be contiguous in your data matrix. For example, if you have three dependent variables, every third value in your data matrix must be for the same dependent variable. The number of dependent variables is specified in the NDEP statement of the DESIGN paragraph.

```
DESign ─────────────────────────────────────────────┐
  NDEP = #.                                       1
    The number of dependent variables.
└──────────────────────────────────────────────────┘
```

```
DESign ─────────────────────────────────────────────┐
  DEPend = v list.                        all vars.
    Names or subscripts of variables to be used.
└──────────────────────────────────────────────────┘
```

Finite Population Sizes

Usually, random factors are assumed to be samples from theoretically infinite population sizes. The population size is also assumed to be infinite when it is very much larger than the sample size; e.g., when experimental units are human subjects. In some instances, it is important to specify that the population size for each random factor is in fact finite. This is done in the POPSIZE statement. If the POPSIZE statement is used, the FIXED and RANDOM statements should not be used. For example, in the statements

LEVEL = 5, 6, 7.
POPSIZE = 0, 20, 7.

the first and second factors are random and the third is fixed. The first factor is a sample from an infinite population, the second from finite population of size 20, and the third is a fixed factor.

```
DESign ─────────────────────────────────────────────┐
  POPsize = # list.                           none
    Population size for each factor. The order of
    factors corresponds to that in the LEVEL
    statement. For fixed factors, the population
    size equals the number of levels. For random
    factors, the population size is larger. A zero
    is used to denote an infinite population size.
└──────────────────────────────────────────────────┘
```

Selecting a Subset of Variables

If you wish to process a subset of variables, you can specify which variables to use in the DEPEND statement in the DESIGN paragraph. For example, if you read 11 variables and want to use only variables 2, 4, 6, 8 and 10, you state DEPEND = 2, 4, 6, 8, 10. or DEPEND = 2 TO 10 BY 2. The five variables chosen, could, for example, correspond to five levels of a repeated-measures factor or to the levels of a within-plot treatment.

Missing Values and Subsets of Cases

The number of cases to read in P8V is determined by the number of variables used and the product of the number of levels in the factors. In Example 8V.4 the product of the number of levels is 2 x 3 x 4 = 24 and the number of variables is 4 so P8V knows that it needs 24/4 = 6 cases. An error message is printed if the data are insufficient. Since P8V requires equal cell sizes, missing values are a frequent cause of data being insufficient.

If values are missing in a case for any of the variables to be used, the case is automatically eliminated from the analysis. For example, if one of the judges in Example 8V.1 did not rate one of the subjects, the data for that subject (case) would be eliminated automatically. To perform an analysis in this situation we could either

a. reduce the number of levels for subjects from 6 to 5
b. eliminate the judge with the missing score by specifying only 3 levels for judges, and include a DEPEND statement in the DESIGN paragraph
c. reformat the data so that there is one observation (data value) per case and use P3V; in some instances it may be possible to use P2V.

Subsets of cases can also be selected by means of the case USE, OMIT and DELETE statements in the TRANSFORM paragraph.

The important thing to remember is that the product of the number of levels must equal the number of variables used times the number of cases used.

Transformations

Special attention must be given to transformations in P8V. If, for example, you want to use a logarithmic transformation, you must be sure to apply it to all the variables in an analysis. For example, if the levels of one factor correspond to three variables in a single case, all three variables should have the same transformations.

SIZE OF PROBLEM

On medium-sized computer systems P8V can perform analyses with up to 10 factors. Storage requirements are a complex function of the number of dependent variables, the number of analysis of variance components, etc. Appendix B contains an explanation of how to increase the program capacity.

COMPUTATIONAL METHOD

All computations are performed in double precision. Details are given in Appendix

ACKNOWLEDGEMENT

P8V was designed by Robert Jennrich and Paul Sampson and was programmed by Paul Sampson.

SUMMARY

Order of Input Cards

```
// (job card)
// EXEC BIMED,PROG=BMDP8V          (see Appendix E)
//SYSIN DD *
/ PROBLEM
/ INPUT
/ VARIABLE
/ TRANSFORM
/ DESIGN
/ END
    (data, in on cards)
// (system card)
```

Full sets of BMDP paragraphs (and data, if on cards) can be repeated for additional problems; see Section 5.8.

Paragraph Statement	Preassigned	Comment and Manual Reference
/INPut		In this program grouping variables are not used to identify cell membership; the structure of the analysis determines the layout of the data. The LEVEL parameter in / DESIGN is used to specify the organization of the data. The number of cases (records) times the number of variables used must equal the product of the numbers in / DESIGN LEVEL times NDEP.
/ GROUP		This paragraph is not used. The levels of each ANOVA factor are definedby the arangement of the input data and by using / DESIGN LEVEL.
/●DESIGN		Required to specify the design. P8V differs from programs like P2V in that the subjects for the experimental units are also specified as factors; e.g., a design with 3 factors in P2V has four factors in P8V. The first symbol of each factor NAME is used to designate the model. The MOD parameter is used to indicate the relationships between factors (nested and crossed). The LEVEL statement determines the organization of the data with respect to the factors. The parameters FIX and RAND denote which factors are fixed and which are random. In the MOD specification crossed factors are separated by commas and nested factors are denoted with parentheses. 'B,A(B)' means that A is nested in B (like houses in a census tract); 'A,B' means that A is crossed with B. Note that the order of the numbers in the LEVEL statement tells how to read the data: data are ordered so the first factor in the LEVEL statement has the slowest moving index in the data matrix; the second the next slowest, etc. 433
● LEVELs = # list.	none	The number of levels in each factor; determines the structure of the input data.
● NAMEs = c list.	none	Names for the factors. The first character must be unique. Order same as that in the LEVEL list.
● RANdom = c list.	none	Names or order of random factors (must correspond to the order in LEVEL). Omit if POP is used.
● FIXed = c list.	none	Names or order of fixed factors (must correspond to the order in LEVEL). Omit if POP is used.
● MODel = c list.	none	Specifies nesting and crossing relationships in the model. Use first character of each name.
PRINT = c list.	none	Each term in the list denotes a set of marginal means and cell deviations to be printed. The list must be a string of first characters of the factor NAMES. Results are averaged over factors not listed.
NDEPendent = #.	1.	The number of dependent variables. Data must be arranged by cells, with all the dependent variables for that cell given before the next cell is input.
POPsize = # list.	none	May be used instead of FIX or RAND to indicate the population size for each factor. The order must correspond to that in the LEVEL statement. For fixed factors, POP equals the number of levels. For random factors, POP is larger. Use zero to denote an infinite population size.
DEPendent = v list.	all vars.	Names or subscripts of variables to be used. Order must be that used in FORMAT. Use to process a subset of variables or to omit a variable with missing values.

Key:

/	–indicates paragraph	*	–assigned value remains the same for additional problems
.	–period ends a sentence		
●	–required	VT	–number of variables after transformations
v	–variable (name or subscript)	list	–more than one item, often one per var.
g	–group (name or subscript)		
#	–number		Capitalized letters–paragraph or sentence names recognized by BMDP
'c'	–characters (name or parameter) may omit apostrophes if contiguous letters only		Page numbers following refer to this Manual

16

NONPARAMETRIC ANALYSIS

P3S
Nonparametric Statistics

ABSTRACT

The statistics computed by P3S are appropriate for four different problems.

- The sign test and Wilcoxon signed-rank test compare the difference in location of two populations based on paired observations.
- The Mann-Whitney rank sum test and the Kruskal-Wallis one-way analysis of variance compare the differences in location of two or more populations based on independent samples from each population.
- The Friedman two-way analysis of variance compares the average ranks assigned to different objects by tests or by several judges. Kendall's coefficient of concordance is a normalization of the Friedman statistic.
- The Kendall and Spearman rank correlations estimate the correlations between two variables based on the ranks of the observations and not on the data values.

These statistics are discussed in many texts such as Hollander and Wolfe (1973), Conover (1971), Hajek (1969), and Lehmann (1975).

Each of the above statistics has a parallel parametric test that is based on the assumption that the data are normally distributed. The sign and Wilcoxon tests correspond to the paired t test, and the Mann-Whitney test corresponds to the two-sample t test that assumes equal variances for both populations. The t tests are discussed in P3D -- Comparison of Two Groups with t Tests (Section 9.1). The Kruskal-Wallis test corresponds to the one-way analysis of variance (see P7D, Section 9.2 or P1V, Section 15.1). The Friedman test corresponds to the test for a specific main effect in a two-way analysis of variance. The two rank correlations have a parallel in the usual product-moment correlation coefficient.

Except for dropping the assumption that the data are normally distributed, the nonparametric test statistics have assumptions similar to their parametric counterparts. For example, the Mann-Whitney test assumes that the samples are obtained from distributions that are identical under the null hypothesis; the two-sample t (with pooled variance) makes the same assumption and also assumes that the data are normally distributed. The actual sizes of the Mann-Whitney test and the two-sample t test just mentioned are a function of the ratio of the scale parameters (variances) of both groups (Pratt, 1964).

Several nonparametric tests and measures are also available in P4F.

Example 3S.1 The Sign Test and the Wilcoxon Signed-rank Test

To illustrate an analysis produced by P3S we use the data in Table 16.1 (corrected version of data from Siegel, 1956, p. 233). The data are the relative ranks of 20 mothers (from 1 to 20) assigned by staff members. We first ask if one mother differs from another in her average ranking. It is appropriate to simultaneously test the total rankings of the mothers for equality. This is done in Example 3S.2.

Table 16.1 Data from Siegel (1956, p. 253)

		1	2	3	4	5	6	7	8	9	10	11	12	13	14	15	16	17	18	19	20
	1	1	2	3	4	5	6	7	8	9	10	11	12	13	14	15	16	17	18	19	20
J	2	5	1	16	8	9	2	6	10	4	3	11	13	7	12	17	18	19	15	14	20
	3	3	2	7	5	14	9	15	16	6	11	8	10	1	4	19	12	20	13	17	18
u	4	8	3	10	11	4	2	5	13	9	1	14	7	6	15	16	12	19	17	18	20
	5	2	1	16	8	15	4	6	9	7	10	11.5	5	3	17	11.5	14	19	18	13	20
d	6	16	17	5	13	15	11	7	4	9	2	18	3	6	1	19	12	10	8	14	20
	7	12	9	14	6	7	2	3	10	5	4	17	8	1	15	13	16	18	11	20	19
g	8	11	2	13	10	7	3	4	14	6	5	17	9	1	12	8	16	20	15	18	19
	9	9.5	2	15	6	5	7	8	11	9.5	3	13	4	1	14	12	15	20	19	17	18
e	10	2	4	16	3	10	6	14	17	15	7	19	9	1	8	5	13	11	18	12	20
	11	11	14	12	8	7	2	5	10	3	4	13	9	1	18	6	15	19	16	17	20
s	12	8	1	13	3	5	2	14	9	6	10	15	11	19	4	7	12	18	17	16	20
	13	5	3	13	2	8	1	9	12	4	6	14	10	11	7	15	18	16	17	19	20

Note: Each case contains the rankings of one judge for all 20 mothers. The first ranking is recorded in columns 2-3, the second in 5-6, etc; the number of the judge is not recorded on the data card.

In the first example we request a comparison of all possible pairs of the first four mothers; this is the nonparametric analog of a matched pairs t test for each pair of mothers. We restrict the analysis to four mothers to reduce the printed results. In the example the observed values are ranks. The data need <u>not</u> be ranks; P3S will rank the data in order to perform the test.

Only the TEST paragraph is specific to P3S, the remaining instructions to describe the data and variables are common to all BMDP programs and are explained in Chapter 5: the PROBLEM, INPUT, VARIABLE and GROUP paragraphs are used in P3S. If data editing or transformations are necessary, the methods described in Chapter 6 can be used. If a BMDP File is read as input (Chapter 7) and a new BMDP File is created in the same problem, the two Files must be in different system files and must have different UNIT numbers. The Control Language instructions for this example are

```
/ PROBLEM    TITLE IS 'SIEGEL RANK DATA'.
/ INPUT      VARIABLES ARE 20.
             FORMAT IS '(20F3.0)'.

/ TEST       TITLE IS 'SIGN TEST AND WILCOXON TEST'.
             VARIABLES ARE 1 TO 4.
             SIGN.
             WILCOXON.

/ END
```

(See end of this P3S section for organization of systems information, BMDP instructions and data.)

The results are reproduced in Output 3S.1. Circled numbers below correspond to those in the output. The variables (mothers) are not named in the BMDP instructions. Therefore they are named X(subscript).

① The number of cases read is 13. Only complete cases are used in the computations; i.e., cases that have no missing values or values out of range. All variables are checked for acceptable values unless USE is specified in the VARIABLE paragraph (Section 5.4), in which case only the variables specified in the USE statement are checked.

② Univariate statistics for each variable
   - mean
   - standard deviation
   - minimum observed value (not out of range)
   - maximum observed value (not out of range)

③ The sign test is computed for each pair of variables. The difference between the values of the variables in each pair is calculated for each case and the number of differences that are positive (N_+) and negative (N_-) are recorded. Let the total number of nonzero differences be $N_T = N_+ + N_-$. Then N_T is printed in the top panel of the results for the sign test. The lesser of N_+ and N_- (say N_{min}) is printed in the second panel. In the third panel P3S reports the level of significance of the sign test corresponding to a two-sided test of the hypothesis that the + and - signs of the differences are equally probable (each sign has probability $\frac{1}{2}$).

When N_T is less than or equal to 25, the probability p is computed from the binomial distribution

$$P = (\tfrac{1}{2})^{N_T - 1} \sum_{j=0}^{N_{min}} \frac{N_T!}{j!(N_T - j)!} \cdot$$

When N_T exceeds 25, the two-sided probability is calculated from the normal approximation

$$z = \left(N_{min} - N_T/2 + \tfrac{1}{2}\right) \Big/ \left(N_T/4\right)^{\frac{1}{2}} \cdot$$

Output 3S.1 Sign and Wilcoxon tests by P3S. Circled numbers correspond to those in the text. We omit the printing and interpretation of the instructions
----

(1) PERFORM SIGN TEST
PERFORM WILCOXON SIGNED RANKS TEST

NUMBER OF CASES READ.   13

(2)

VARIABLE		MEAN	STANDARD	MINIMUM	MAXIMUM
NO.	NAME		DEVIATION		
1	X(1)	7.192305	4.616720	1.000000	16.000000
2	X(2)	4.692305	5.265999	1.000000	17.000000

--- statistics for variables 3 to 18 ---

| 19 | X(19) | 16.461487 | 2.503842 | 12.000000 | 20.000000 |
| 20 | X(20) | 19.538406 | 0.776253 | 18.000000 | 20.000000 |

SIGN TEST RESULTS
(3)

NUMBER OF NON-ZERO DIFFERENCES

		X(1)	X(2)	X(3)	X(4)
		1	2	3	4
X(1)	1	0			
X(2)	2	13	0		
X(3)	3	13	13	0	
X(4)	4	13	13	13	0

SMALLER NUMBER OF LIKE-SIGNED DIFFERENCES

		X(1)	X(2)	X(3)	X(4)
		1	2	3	4
X(1)	1	0			
X(2)	2	4	0		
X(3)	3	1	2	0	
X(4)	4	6	5	3	0

LEVEL OF SIGNIFICANCE OF SIGN TEST USING NORMAL APPROXIMATION (TWO-TAIL)

		X(1)	X(2)	X(3)	X(4)
		1	2	3	4
X(1)	1	1.0000			
X(2)	2	0.2668	1.0000		
X(3)	3	0.0034	0.0225	1.0000	
X(4)	4	1.0000	0.5811	0.0923	1.0000

(output continued)

Output 3S.1 (continued)

WILCOXON SIGNED RANKS TEST RESULTS

④

NUMBER OF NON-ZERO DIFFERENCES

		X(1)	X(2)	X(3)	X(4)
		1	2	3	4
X(1)	1	0			
X(2)	2	13	0		
X(3)	3	13	13	0	
X(4)	4	13	13	13	0

SMALLER SUM OF LIKE-SIGNED RANKS

		X(1)	X(2)	X(3)	X(4)
		1	2	3	4
X(1)	1	0.0			
X(2)	2	18.00	0.0		
X(3)	3	10.50	11.00	0.0	
X(4)	4	36.50	25.00	10.50	0.0

LEVEL OF SIGNIFICANCE OF WILCOXON SIGNED RANKS TEST USING NORMAL APPROXIMATION (TWO-TAIL)

		X(1)	X(2)	X(3)	X(4)
		1	2	3	4
X(1)	1	1.0000			
X(2)	2	0.0546	1.0000		
X(3)	3	0.0144	0.0159	1.0000	
X(4)	4	0.5294	0.1520	0.0144	1.0000

----

④ The Wilcoxon signed rank test is computed for each pair of variables. The Wilcoxon statistic is used to test the hypothesis that two populations have the same location parameter (mean) under the assumption that both variables have the same distribution.

Let d_j be the difference between the two variables for case j. The absolute values of all nonzero d_j's are ranked; the average rank is assigned when two or more $|d_j|$'s are tied. The sum of the ranks associated with positive differences R_+ and the sum of the ranks associated with negative differences R_- are calculated. The test statistic R_{min} is the lesser of R_+ and R_-.

In the first panel of the results the number of nonzero differences is printed (N_T in ③ above). The second panel gives the value of R_{min}. In the third panel P3S reports the level of significance of the Wilcoxon signed rank test corresponding to a two-sided test of the hypothesis that the populations have the same location parameter. The probability is computed by a normal approximation for the distribution of R_{min}:

$$ z = \left[R_{min} - \frac{N_T(N_T+1)}{4} \right] \Bigg/ \left[\frac{N_T(N_T+1)(2N_T+1)}{24} \right]^{\frac{1}{2}} $$

For small sample sizes ($N \le 20$) exact levels of significance are tabulated in Dixon and Massey (1969, Table A-19).

Specifying the test — the TEST paragraph. The TEST paragraph is required in P3S to specify the statistics to be computed. The TEST paragraph may be repeated for additional analyses of the same data. The TEST paragraph can be used to specify a TITLE for each analysis and to select the VARIABLES to be included in the computations.

TEST

TITLE = 'c'. $\le$ 160 char.   blank
    A title for the analysis.
VARiable = v list.   all var. except
                          the GROUPing var.
    Names or subscripts of variables to be included
    in the analysis.
SIGN.   no/prev.
    Compute the sign test between all possible
    pairings of the variables.
WILCoxon.   no/prev.
    Compute the Wilcoxon signed rank test between
    all possible pairings of the variables.
FRIEDman   no/prev.
    Compute the Friedman two-way analysis of
    variance and the Kendall coefficient of
    concordance.
KRUskal.   no/prev.
    The Kruskal-Wallis one-way analysis of variance
    is computed and, if there are only two groups,
    the Mann-Whitney (Wilcoxon) rank sum statistic
    is also computed.
    Note: When KRUSKAL is specified, the other
    statistics available in P3S (sign test,
    Wilcoxon test, Friedman two-way analysis of
    variance and the correlations) are not computed
    even if requested.
KENDall.   no/prev.
    Compute the Kendall rank correlation
    coefficient.
SPEARman.   no/prev.
    Compute the Spearman rank correlation
    coefficient.

440

Example 3S.2 Friedman's Two-way Analysis of Variance and Kendall's Coefficient of Concordance

We use the data in Table 16.1 (Siegel, 1956, p. 233) to illustrate the FRIEDMAN two-way analysis of variance for k matched samples. Each judge ranked twenty mothers from 1 to 20. The hypothesis to be tested is that the average rank for each mother is equal to the average rank of the other mothers.

Let R_i be the sum of the ranks for the ith variable (i=1,...,20 in our example). The Friedman statistic is

$$X = \frac{12}{Nk(k+1)} \sum_{i=1}^{k} R_i^2 - 3N(k+1)$$

where k is the number of variables and N is the number of cases. The level of significance of X is obtained from the chi-square distribution with k-1 degrees of freedom. This level of significance is appropriate except for very small sample sizes.

The data read by P3S do not need to be ranks; they can be test scores or other measures. For each case P3S ranks the results across variables. That is, a case corresponds to a judge or test. The values each judge or test gives to the variables are ranked by P3S.

The Kendall coefficient of concordance W is

$$W = X/\{N(k-1)\}.$$

The level of significance of W is the same as that of the Friedman X.

To obtain the Friedman and Kendall statistics we use the instructions of Example 3S.1 and specify FRIEDMAN. in the TEST paragraph. The TEST paragraph now reads as follows:

```
------------------------------------
/ TEST      TITLE IS 'FRIEDMAN TEST AND KENDALL
                     COEFFICIENT OF CONCORDANCE'.
           FRIEDMAN.
------------------------------------
```

The results are shown in Output 3S.2. For each variable the sum of the ranks is printed. This is followed by the value of X and its level of significance. Finally, the value of W is printed. Ranks need not be used as input data. P3S ranks the values given to the variables in each case before computing the Friedman test.

Output 3S.2 Friedman test performed by P3S

PERFORM FRIEDMAN TWO WAY ANALYSIS OF VARIANCE TEST

NUMBER OF CASES READ.   13

FRIEDMAN TWO WAY ANALYSIS OF VARIANCE TEST RESULTS

VARIABLE		RANK
NO.	NAME	SUM
1	X(1)	93.5
2	X(2)	61.0
3	X(3)	154.0
4	X(4)	87.0
5	X(5)	111.0
6	X(6)	57.0
7	X(7)	103.0
8	X(8)	143.0
9	X(9)	92.5
10	X(10)	76.0
11	X(11)	181.5
12	X(12)	110.0
13	X(13)	71.0
14	X(14)	141.0
15	X(15)	163.5
16	X(16)	189.0
17	X(17)	226.0
18	X(18)	202.0
19	X(19)	214.0
20	X(20)	254.0

FRIEDMAN TEST STATISTIC = 146.53394
LEVEL OF SIGNIFICANCE = 0.0   ASSUMING CHI-SQUARE DISTRIBUTION WITH   19 DEGREES OF FREEDOM

KENDALL COEFFICIENT OF CONCORDANCE = 0.59325

Example 3S.3 The Mann-Whitney Rank-sum Test and Kruskal-Wallis One-way Analysis of Variance

The Mann-Whitney rank-sum test is the nonparametric version of the two-sample t test for independent samples. The Kruskal-Wallis (1952) statistic tests the equality of the location parameters (means) for two or more independent samples.

Let N observations be classified by a GROUPING variable into g groups; the jth group contains n observations. All the values for each variable are ranked from 1 to N; tied values are assigned average rank for the tied values. Let R be the sum of the ranks for each group. The Kruskal-Wallis statistic is

$$H = \frac{12}{N(N+1)} \sum_{j=1}^{g} \frac{R_j^2}{n_j} - 3(N+1) \quad .$$

If values are tied, H is modified to

$$H' = H \left/ \left[1 - \frac{\Sigma^*(t_i^3 - t_i)}{N^3 - N} \right] \right.$$

where t_i is the number of observations tied with a single value, and Σ^* is the sum over all distinct values for which a tie exists. The level of significance of H is obtained from the chi-square distribution with (k-1) degrees of freedom. This level of significance is appropriate except for very small sample sizes.

When there are only two groups, the Mann-Whitney (Wilcoxon) statistic U is also reported.

$$U = R_1 - \frac{n_1(n_1+1)}{2} \quad .$$

The level of significance of U is the same as that of H and corresponds to a two-tail probability.

The Werner blood chemistry data (Table 5.1) are used to illustrate the Kruskal-Wallis and Mann-Whitney statistics. The data are classified into two groups by BRTHPILL (see for comparison, Example 3D.1). The Control Language follows:

```
----------------------------------------
/ PROBLEM    TITLE IS 'WERNER BLOOD CHEMISTRY DATA'.
/ INPUT      VARIABLES ARE 9.
            FORMAT IS '(A4, 5F4.0, 3F4.1)'..
/ VARIABLE   NAMES ARE ID, AGE, HEIGHT, WEIGHT,
                      BRTHPILL, CHOLSTRL, ALBUMIN,
                      CALCIUM, URICACID.
            MAXIMUM IS (6)400.
            MINIMUM IS (6)150.
            BLANKS ARE MISSING.
            LABEL IS ID.
            GROUPING IS BRTHPILL.

/ GROUP      CODES(5) ARE      1,    2.
            NAMES(5) ARE NOPILL, PILL.

/ TEST       TITLE IS 'KRUSKAL-WALLIS TEST'.
            KRUSKAL.

/ END
----------------------------------------
```

(See end of this P3S section for organization of systems information, BMDP instructions and data.)

The results appear in Output 3S.3. For each variable analyzed a panel of results is printed. First the frequency n_j and rank sum R_j are printed for each group. Then the Kruskal-Wallis statistic and its level of significance are printed. When there are two groups, as in our example, the Mann-Whitney statistic and its level of significance are printed.

> VARiable ─────
> GROUPing.   no grouping var./prev.
>   Name or subscript of the GROUPING variable used
>   to classify the cases into groups. If GROUPING
>   is not specified or is set to zero, the cases
>   are not grouped. If the GROUPING variable takes
>   on more than 10 distinct values or codes, CODES
>   or CUTPOINTS must be specified in the GROUP
>   paragraph (Section 5.5).

Output 3S.3 Mann-Whitney and Kruskal-Wallis tests by P3S

```
        GROUPING VARIABLE . . . . . . . . . . . . . .BRTHPILL
        PERFORM KRUSKAL-WALLIS H TEST


        NUMBER OF CASES READ. . . . . . . . . . . . .    188
            CASES WITH DATA MISSING OR BEYOND LIMITS . .      8
            REMAINING NUMBER OF CASES . . . . . . . .    180
```

VARIABLE		MEAN	STANDARD DEVIATION	MINIMUM	MAXIMUM
NO.	NAME				
2	AGE	33.538193	9.898361	19.000000	55.000000
3	HEIGHT	64.465973	2.482127	57.000000	71.000000
4	WEIGHT	131.093842	20.499771	94.000000	215.000000
5	BRTHPILL	1.505514	0.501360	1.000000	2.000000
6	CHOLSTRL	235.838211	42.743637	155.000000	390.000000
7	ALBUMIN	4.120516	0.358715	3.200000	5.000000
8	CALCIUM	9.967734	0.472791	8.799999	11.099999
9	URICACID	4.755512	1.121115	2.200000	9.900000

VARIABLE				INTERVAL RANGE		
	BEFORE TRANSFORMATION					
VARIABLE	MINIMUM	MAXIMUM	MISSING	CATEGORY	CATEGORY	GREATER	LESS THAN
NO. NAME	LIMIT	LIMIT	CODE	CODE	NAME	THAN	OR EQUAL TO

```
  5   BRTHPILL                                1.00000    NOPILL
                                              2.00000    PILL


  6   CHOLSTRL  150.00000   400.00000
```

KRUSKAL-WALLIS ONE WAY ANALYSIS OF VARIANCE TEST RESULTS

```
VARIABLE    2 AGE
  GROUP         FREQUENCY      RANK
NO. NAME                      SUM
  1   NOPILL      89         7822.5
  2   PILL        91         8467.5

KRUSKAL-WALLIS TEST STATISTIC =   0.44084
LEVEL OF SIGNIFICANCE = 0.5067 USING CHI-SQUARE DISTRIBUTION WITH    1 DEGREES OF FREEDOM

MANN-WHITNEY TEST STATISTIC = 3817
LEVEL OF SIGNIFICANCE = 0.5067 USING NORMAL TWO-TAIL APPROXIMATION
```

--- results for variables 3 and 4 ---

```
VARIABLE    6 CHOLSTRL
  GROUP         FREQUENCY      RANK
NO. NAME                      SUM
  1   NOPILL      89         7678.0
  2   PILL        91         8612.0

KRUSKAL-WALLIS TEST STATISTIC =   1.16060
LEVEL OF SIGNIFICANCE = 0.2813 USING CHI-SQUARE DISTRIBUTION WITH    1 DEGREES OF FREEDOM

MANN-WHITNEY TEST STATISTIC = 3673
LEVEL OF SIGNIFICANCE = 0.2813 USING NORMAL TWO-TAIL APPROXIMATION
```

```
VARIABLE    7 ALBUMIN
  GROUP         FREQUENCY      RANK
NO. NAME                      SUM
  1   NOPILL      89         9129.5
  2   PILL        91         7160.5

KRUSKAL-WALLIS TEST STATISTIC =   9.52726
LEVEL OF SIGNIFICANCE = 0.0020 USING CHI-SQUARE DISTRIBUTION WITH    1 DEGREES OF FREEDOM

MANN-WHITNEY TEST STATISTIC = 5124
LEVEL OF SIGNIFICANCE = 0.0020 USING NORMAL TWO-TAIL APPROXIMATION
```

--- results for variables 8 and 9 ---

Example 3S.4 The Kendall and Spearman Rank Correlations

The Kendall and Spearman rank correlations are correlations based on the ranks of the observations and not on their observed values. When the variables are categorical (take on very few values) you may prefer to use P4F (Chapter 11); P4F also computes standard errors for the correlations.

Let $r_1, r_2, \ldots, r_N$ represent the ranks of the values of one variable and $s_1, s_2, \ldots, s_N$ the ranks of the second variable. The Kendall rank correlation t_b is defined as

$$t_b = \frac{P-Q}{N(N-1)}$$

where

P = twice the number of pairs of rankings such that both $r_j > r_k$ <u>and</u> $s_j > s_k$ (agreements in rank order)

Q = twice the number of pairs of rankings such that both $r_j > r_k$ <u>and</u> $s_j < s_k$ (disagreement in rank order).

When rankings are tied, the formula for t_b is

$$t_b = \frac{P-Q}{\{[N(N-1)-T_1]\,[N(N-1)-T_2]\}^{\frac{1}{2}}}$$

Output 3S.4 The Kendall and Spearman rank correlation coefficients computed by P3S

```
COMPUTE KENDALL RANK CORRELATION COEFFICIENT(S)
COMPUTE SPEARMAN RANK CORRELATION COEFFICIENT(S)



NUMBER OF CASES READ. . . . . . . . . . . . .     188
      CASES WITH DATA MISSING OR BEYOND LIMITS . .       8
            REMAINING NUMBER OF CASES . . . . . . . .     180
```

KENDALL RANK CORRELATION COEFFICIENTS

		AGE 2	HEIGHT 3	WEIGHT 4	BRTHPILL 5	CHOLSTRL 6	ALBUMIN 7	CALCIUM 8	URICACID 9
AGE	2	1.0000							
HEIGHT	3	0.0654	1.0000						
WEIGHT	4	0.1847	0.3822	1.0000					
BRTHPILL	5	0.0413	0.1313	0.0413	1.0000				
CHOLSTRL	6	0.2355	-0.0175	0.0930	0.0664	1.0000			
ALBUMIN	7	-0.0475	0.0088	-0.1782	-0.1956	0.0487	1.0000		
CALCIUM	8	-0.0079	0.1324	0.0579	-0.0447	0.2061	0.3412	1.0000	
URICACID	9	0.1412	0.1094	0.1983	-0.0235	0.1579	0.0368	0.1186	1.0000

SPEARMAN RANK CORRELATION COEFFICIENTS

		AGE 2	HEIGHT 3	WEIGHT 4	BRTHPILL 5	CHOLSTRL 6	ALBUMIN 7	CALCIUM 8	URICACID 9
AGE	2	1.0000							
HEIGHT	3	0.0918	1.0000						
WEIGHT	4	0.2645	0.5050	1.0000					
BRTHPILL	5	0.0497	0.1521	0.0497	1.0000				
CHOLSTRL	6	0.3418	-0.0279	0.1387	0.0805	1.0000			
ALBUMIN	7	-0.0706	0.0116	-0.2534	-0.2307	0.0723	1.0000		
CALCIUM	8	-0.0079	0.1841	0.0875	-0.0532	0.3033	0.4674	1.0000	
URICACID	9	0.2058	0.1473	0.2857	-0.0284	0.2275	0.0532	0.1657	1.0000

----

where

$$T = \Sigma^* t_i (t_i - 1)$$

and t_i is the number of observations tied with a single value and the sum Σ^* is over all distinct values for which a tie exists. T_1 is the total for the first variable and T_2 for the second variable.

The Spearman rank correlation r_s is defined as

$$r_s = 1 - \frac{6D}{N^3 - N}$$

where

$$D = \Sigma (r_j - s_j)^2 \quad .$$

When rankings are tied, r_s is modified to

$$r_s = \frac{A + B - D}{2\sqrt{AB}}$$

where

$$A = (N^3 - N - T_1)/12 \quad \text{and} \quad B = (N^3 - N - T_2)/12$$

and $T = \Sigma^* (t_i^3 - t_i)$. t_i is the number of observations tied with a single value and the sum Σ^* is over all distinct values for which a tie exists. T_1 is the total for the first variable and T_2 for the second variable.

The Werner blood chemistry data (Table 5.1) are used in the following example to illustrate the Kendall and Spearman rank correlations.

```
/ PROBLEM    TITLE IS 'WERNER BLOOD CHEMISTRY DATA'.
/ INPUT      VARIABLES ARE 9.
            FORMAT IS '(A4, 5F4.0, 3F4.1).
/ VARIABLE   NAMES ARE ID, AGE, HEIGHT, WEIGHT,
                       BRTHPILL, CHOLSTRL, ALBUMIN,
                       CALCIUM, URICACID.
            MAXIMUM IS (6)400.
            MINIMUM IS (6)150.
            BLANKS ARE MISSING.
            LABEL IS ID.

/ TEST       TITLE IS 'KENDALL AND SPEARMAN
                    CORRELATIONS'.
            KENDALL.
            SPEARMAN.

/ END
```

The correlations are presented in Output 3S.4.

SIZE OF PROBLEM

P3S keeps the data in memory (all the data, not just for the variables used). Therefore the maximum problem that can be analyzed is a function of the number of cases and the number of variables. The size of the maximum problem also depends on the statistics to be computed. The following is a rough guide for medium-sized computer systems.

number of variables	10	20	50	100
maximum number of cases when				
KRUSKAL is specified	950	530	200	105
FRIEDMAN is specified	550	300	115	55
KENDALL and SPEARMAN, or SIGN and WILCOXON are specified	750	420	70	–

Appendix B describes how to increase the capacity of the program.

COMPUTATIONAL METHOD

All computations are performed in single precision. Means and standard deviations are computed by the method of provisional means (Appendix A.2).

ACKNOWLEDGEMENT

P3S was programmed by Steve Chasen.

SUMMARY

Order of Input Cards

```
// (job card)
// EXEC BIMED,PROG=BMDP3S      (see Appendix E)
//SYSIN DD *
/ PROBLEM
/ INPUT
/ VARIABLE
/ GROUP
/ TRANSFORM
/ SAVE
/ TEST
/ END
    (data if on cards)
/ TEST ┐ Repeat for
/ END  ┘ subproblems.
```

Full sets of BMDP paragraphs (and data, if on cards)
can be repeated for additional problems; see Section
5.8.

instructions specific to P3S

Paragraph Statement	Preassigned	Comment and Manual Reference
/ VARiable		Additional option to classify cases into groups.
GROUPing = v.		Name or subscript of variable used to classify cases into groups for the Mann-Whitney and Kruskal-Wallis tests. (See also / GROUP.) * 442
/●TEST		Required to specify one or more tests using the parameters listed below. 440 When KRU. is specified the other statistics are not computed, even if requested (can be repeated).
SIGN.	no	Sign test between all pairs of variables. *
WILCOXon.	no	Wilcoxon signed-rank test between all pairs of variables. *
FRIEDman.	no	Friedman two-way analysis of variance and the Kendall coefficient of concordance. *
KRUskal.	no	Kruskal-Wallis one-way ANOVA and, if there are only two groups, the Mann-Whitney (Wilcoxon rank-sum) statistic. *
KENDall.	no	Kendall rank-correlation coefficient. *
SPEARman.	no	Spearman rank-correlation coefficient. *
VARiables = v list.	all	Names or subscripts of variables to be included in the analysis. *
TITLE = 'c'.		Title, up to 160 characters, to label the output.

Key:

/	-indicates paragraph
.	-period ends a sentence
●	-required
v	-variable (name or subscript)
g	-group (name or subscript)
#	-number
'c'	-characters (name or parameter) may omit apostrophes if contiguous letters only

* -assigned value remains the same for additional problems
VT -number of variables after transformations
list -more than one item, often one per var.

Capitalized letters-paragraph or sentence names recognized by BMDP
Page numbers following refer to this Manual

17

CLUSTER ANALYSIS

In this chapter we describe four BMDP programs that form clusters of variables (characteristics) or cases (observations) or both.

Most of the methods used in these programs are discussed in Hartigan (1975).

P1M forms clusters of variables based on a measure of association or similarity between the variables (such as correlation), or on a measure of distance separating the variables. The clusters are formed by P1M according to a linkage (amalgamation) rule that determines the similarity of any two clusters of variables. Initially each cluster contains one variable only. At each step the two most similar clusters are joined to form a new cluster, until all variables are in one cluster. P1M prints a tree diagram to illustrate the sequence of clusters formed and a summary table for the clustering process. The correlation matrix is also represented by overprinting (shade) after sorting the variables according to the clustering process. Factor analysis (P4M, p. 480) is a related technique.

P2M forms clusters of cases by one of four distance criteria. The stepwise procedure to form the clusters is similar to that described above for P1M except that cases (not variables) are grouped into clusters. Algorithms for joining cases include single linkage, centroid linkage or the kth nearest neighbor density estimator. P2M prints either a vertical or horizontal tree diagram to describe the sequence of clusters formed. The means of the variables for the cluster formed at each step are printed. The distance matrix is also represented by overprinting after sorting the cases according to the clustering process.

PKM, K–means clustering, provides an alternative to P2M for clustering cases. P2M uses a hierarchical or tree technique while PKM establishes a fixed number of homogeneous groups of cases using Euclidean distances. Four methods of standardization are available. A variety of statistics and graphical displays describes the differences between the clusters. Cluster membership is indicated in the output BMDP File.

P3M forms clusters of both the cases and variables in a data matrix simultaneously. The method of clustering variables and cases used in P3M is primarily appropriate when each variable has very few distinct values. An iterative technique is used to identify blocks (cases by variables) that have a similar pattern over a set of variables for each case. The cases in each block can be viewed as clusters of variables. P3M prints a block diagram to describe the blocks identified. It also prints two tree diagrams (one for the cases and one for the variables) to illustrate the sequence in which the cases and variables are grouped into clusters.

Control Language

The Control Language instructions to describe the data and variables are common to all BMDP programs and are explained in Chapter 5: the PROBLEM, INPUT, and VARIABLE paragraphs are used in the programs discussed in this chapter.

If data editing or transformations are necessary, the methods described in Chapter 6 can be used. Data can be read using a FORMAT statement or from a BMDP File (Chapter 7). If a BMDP File is read as input and a new BMDP File is created in the same problem, the two Files must be in different system files and must have different UNIT numbers.

P1M

17.1 Cluster Analysis of Variables

John Hartigan

ABSTRACT

P1M provides four measures of similarity (association) for clustering variables, and three criteria for linking or combining clusters. Input can be data or a matrix with measures of association or distance. Initially each variable is considered as a separate cluster; then the two most similar variables are joined to form a cluster. The amalgamating process continues in a stepwise fashion (joining variables or clusters of variables) until a single cluster is formed that contains all the variables. Output includes a summary table of the clusters formed; a tree showing the clusters formed at each step, with an explanation of the clustering process; shaded correlation matrix display and correlation matrix (optional).

WHERE TO FIND IT

Example 1M.1 Basic Setup for Clustering Variables

In our first example we use the preassigned options: the measure of similarity is the absolute value of the correlation and the clusters are joined using the minimum distance rule (single linkage). No instructions specific to P1M are used: the PROBLEM, INPUT and VARIABLE paragraphs are common to all programs and are explained in Chapter 5.

Table 17.1 Data from Jarvik's smoking questionnaire, administered to 110 subjects (Dr. M. E. Jarvik, unpublished)

```
3 2 1 3 2 2 1 3 2 2 3 2    2 1 2 2 3 2 2 3 2 2 2 2
4 2 5 3 5 4 5 4 3 4 4 5    3 2 2 3 3 3 2 3 3 4 2 2
5 3 4 4 5 5 4 5 3 4 3 4    3 2 4 2 5 3 5 3 3 3 2 5
4 2 4 3 5 4 4 4 3 4 3 5    3 2 5 3 5 3 5 3 3 4 2 5
4 2 4 3 4 2 4 4 2 4 3 4    3 3 5 5 5 3 5 4 3 5 3 5
3 2 3 1 3 2 3 3 2 3 3 4    2 2 2 1 3 2 3 2 2 1 2 1
4 2 4 2 4 3 3 3 2 3 3 4    3 2 4 4 4 3 3 3 2 3 3 4
3 2 3 2 4 2 3 3 2 3 3 4    3 3 4 3 4 4 4 3 3 3 3 4
3 2 3 2 4 4 3 3 2 3 3 4    3 3 3 5 3 3 3 4 3 5 3 3
3 2 4 1 4 3 4 3 2 3 3 4    3 2 3 3 2 3 2 3 2 3 2 3
5 5 1 4 1 4 1 5 4 5 5 1    2 2 3 3 2 2 2 2 2 2 2 3
1 1 2 3 3 3 3 2 1 3 1 2    2 4 5 4 4 2 5 3 2 4 3 5
2 1 3 4 4 3 4 2 1 4 1 4    2 1 3 1 3 2 4 2 1 1 2 3
2 1 3 4 4 2 3 3 1 4 1 4    1 2 5 2 4 2 5 2 3 3 3 3
2 1 4 3 4 2 4 2 1 3 1 4    2 2 5 4 4 2 4 4 2 5 3 3
3 1 3 4 4 2 4 1 3 1 4 1    3 2 4 4 4 1 4 3 2 4 2 5
3 2 4 4 4 2 4 3 3 4 2 4    1 1 3 1 3 2 3 1 2 2 2 3
2 2 4 3 4 2 4 3 3 4 2 5    2 2 3 1 4 2 3 1 3 2 3 2
3 2 4 4 5 2 5 3 3 4 2 5    1 1 2 3 2 1 2 3 1 4 2 1
3 2 4 4 5 3 5 3 3 3 2 5    2 1 3 3 4 2 3 3 1 3 2 4
3 3 5 4 5 2 4 2 4 2 4 5    2 2 2 2 2 1 2 2 2 2 2 1
3 1 3 3 4 2 2 3 2 4 2 4    2 1 3 2 3 1 3 1 1 2 1 3
3 1 3 1 3 2 3 2 2 1 1 3    1 1 3 1 3 1 3 1 1 2 2 3
3 2 4 2 4 2 4 3 2 2 3 4    1 1 4 1 3 1 4 1 1 1 1 4
3 2 5 2 4 2 5 2 2 3 2 5    1 1 3 1 3 1 3 1 1 1 1 3
3 2 5 2 5 3 5 2 2 3 2 5    1 1 4 1 4 1 5 1 1 1 2 4
4 3 5 3 5 4 5 4 3 3 3 5    1 1 1 2 4 1 5 1 1 2 2 5
3 2 5 2 5 2 5 3 2 3 3 5    1 1 4 3 3 1 4 2 1 4 2 4
4 3 5 3 5 3 5 4 3 3 3 5    1 1 3 3 3 1 3 1 1 3 2 2
3 2 5 1 5 3 5 3 2 3 3 5    1 1 3 2 3 1 2 1 1 2 2 1
3 2 5 2 5 3 5 3 2 3 3 5    2 2 2 2 3 2 3 2 2 2 2 2
4 2 5 3 5 3 5 4 2 3 3 5    2 2 4 3 4 3 4 3 3 4 3 4
2 1 5 2 5 1 5 3 1 3 2 5    4 4 4 4 5 4 4 4 3 4 4 5
1 2 2 2 2 1 3 2 3 3 2 2    4 5 4 3 5 4 4 4 4 4 4 5
3 2 4 3 4 2 4 2 3 3 2 4    4 4 4 5 5 4 4 4 3 4 4 5
2 2 3 2 4 2 4 3 3 4 2 5    2 3 3 2 4 3 3 3 3 3 3 3
2 2 3 2 4 2 4 2 3 3 2 4    4 3 3 4 3 4 4 3 3 4 3 4
3 2 2 3 4 2 4 3 2 4 2 4    4 4 4 3 5 4 5 5 4 4 4 5
4 4 5 4 5 4 5 4 4 4 4 5    4 3 4 4 5 3 4 5 3 5 3 4
2 2 3 2 2 2 3 2 2 2 2 3    4 3 4 3 4 4 4 4 3 4 4 5
2 2 3 2 3 2 4 2 2 2 2 3    5 1 2 4 3 1 2 5 2 4 2 3
2 2 3 2 4 3 3 3 2 3 3 3    2 2 1 1 2 2 1 2 2 3 2 1
4 2 1 2 2 3 1 4 2 3 2 1    5 2 1 3 1 1 2 4 2 4 1 1
2 1 2 3 2 2 1 3 2 3 3 1    2 2 2 1 2 1 3 2 2 2 1 2
4 3 1 3 1 3 1 3 3 3 3 1    2 2 4 3 3 1 4 2 2 3 1 5
2 2 4 3 4 3 4 3 3 3 3 4    3 2 5 4 4 2 4 2 2 4 2 5
4 2 4 3 4 3 4 3 2 3 3 4    1 1 4 1 3 2 3 2 2 2 2 4
2 3 4 3 4 4 2 2 4 2 5      2 1 4 1 4 2 4 2 2 2 2 4
4 4 3 3 3 3 4 3 3 3 3      2 2 3 2 3 2 4 2 2 2 2 4
4 4 2 3 4 2 3 3 3 3 3      4 1 1 4 2 1 2 4 2 4 2 2
2 4 3 3 2 4 3 4 3 3 4 3    4 2 3 3 3 2 3 3 2 3 2 4
3 4 2 3 2 3 2 3 3 3 3 2    2 2 3 1 4 2 2 2 2 3 2 1
3 3 3 2 2 4 3 2 3 3 3 2
3 4 2 3 3 4 2 3 3 3 3 2
```

The data consist of the answers to 12 questions – each coded 1 to 5 such that a high score represents a desire to smoke. The 12 questions (and their NAMES) are concentration (CONCENTR), annoyance (ANNOY), desire to smoke – first wording (SMOKING1), sleepiness (SLEEPY), desire to smoke – second wording (SMOKING2), tenseness (TENSE), desire to smoke – third wording (SMOKING3), alertness (ALERT), irritability (IRRITABL), tiredness (TIRED), contentedness (CONTENT), desire to smoke – fourth wording (SMOKING4). The data are recorded in columns 2, 4, 6, etc. and are read using the format (12F2.0).

The data (Table 17.1) used are from Jarvik's questionnaire on smoking. The four items labeled "smoking" are direct questions concerning the subject's desire to have a cigarette. The remainder of the questions relate to the psychological and physical state of the subject. Each question is scored on a scale from one to five where a low score is "good" and a high score is "bad." Here we analyze only 12 questions from the original study to simplify the presentation. In the early stages of questionnaire development, the investigators want to verify that questions designed to measure a specific dimension (e.g., desire to smoke) do so. They use cluster analysis or a factor analysis as an aid in the process. A realistic study should have a large number of questions. We use only 12 as an illustration.

The instructions for clustering the 12 questions are:

```
------------------------------------
/ PROBLEM     TITLE IS 'JARVIK SMOKING DATA'.
/ INPUT       VARIABLES ARE 12.
             FORMAT IS '(12F2.0)'.
/ VARIABLE    NAMES ARE CONCENTR, ANNOY, SMOKING1,
             SLEEPY, SMOKING2, TENSE,
             SMOKING3, ALERT, IRRITABL,
             TIRED, CONTENT, SMOKING4.

/ END
------------------------------------
```

(See end of this P1M section for organization of systems information, BMDP instructions and data.)

The results of the analysis are presented in Output 1M.1. Circled numbers below correspond to those in the output.

① The measure of similarity used in this analysis is the absolute value of the correlation (the preassigned measure). The linkage rule is single (the preassigned rule); i.e., at each step the two clusters that are combined have the minimum single linkage (the minimum distance or maximum similarity) between any two variables that are not in the same cluster. These terms are described in more detail below and on p. 452.

② The number of cases read. P1M uses complete cases only in all computations; if a case has a missing value or a value out of range, the entire case is omitted. If there is a USE statement (Section 5.4), only variables in the USE statement are checked for acceptable values.

③ The mean and standard deviation for each variable are printed.

④ A summary table of the clusters formed.

⑤ A tree showing the clusters formed at each step.

⑥ An interpretation of the values in the tree.

⑦ An explanation of the clustering process shown in the tree (printed only for the first problem).

⑧ The shaded correlation matrix. This display is explained in Example 1M.3.

The absolute value of the correlation is used in this example as the measure of similarity for the results in ④, ⑤, and ⑥. The correlations are recoded to a similarity measure between 0 and 100, where a correlation of 0.0 is recoded to zero (minimum similarity). Table ⑥ lists the recoded values 0, 5, 10, ..., 100 and the value of the correlation for which the recoded value is obtained. We call the recoded values the measure of similarity between each pair of variables.

Conceptually, the explanation is easier if we view each variable that is not yet in a cluster as a cluster by itself. The similarity between each pair of clusters is then computed. When more than one variable is in a cluster, the similarity between clusters is computed as the maximum over all possible pairings of variables between the two clusters. (Single linkage is the method used in our example.) At each step the two clusters with the maximum similarity, using the amalgamation rule (single linkage), are combined. The stepping terminates when only one cluster remains.

The tree diagram ⑤ shows the clusters that were formed during the stepping. The horizontal and diagonal lines determine the clusters. For example, CONCENTR and ALERT form one cluster; all the variables listed from CONCENTR to TIRED form a second cluster; ANNOY and IRRITABL are a third. Also, we can see that CONCENTR and ALERT form one cluster, SLEEPY and TIRED form a second cluster, and then the two clusters are combined.

The numbers superimposed on the tree diagram ⑤ are the recoded measures of similarity (the correlations recoded as shown in ⑥) between each pair of variables. The first number in each line is the measure of similarity of the variable to the left of the line with the one immediately below it, the second is with the second variable below it, etc.

The similarity between two clusters at the time they are joined is read from the table in ④. Each horizontal or diagonal line in the tree diagram ⑤ starts at one variable and ends at the intersection with a line from another variable. The cluster determined by the pair of lines is then listed beside the first variable in ④. The other boundary of the cluster is the second variable. The number of items is the number of variables in the cluster. The final column in ④ is the value of the similarity at the step when the cluster is formed.

Output 1M.1 Cluster analysis of the Jarvik smoking questionnaire data. Circled numbers correspond to those in the text

----

--- the BMDP instructions read by P1M are printed and interpreted ---

(1) PROCEDURE MEASURE . . . . .ABSCORR
     PROCEDURE AMALGAMATION RULE IS MINIMUM DISTANCE (SINGLE LINKAGE)

(2) NUMBER OF CASES READ.   110

(3)
VARIABLE NAME	NO.	MEAN	STANDARD DEVIATION
CONCENTR	1	2.691	1.073
ANNOY	2	2.118	0.974
SMOKING1	3	3.364	1.131
SLEEPY	4	2.609	1.024
SMOKING2	5	3.582	1.061
TENSE	6	2.445	0.992
SMOKING3	7	3.427	1.161
ALERT	8	2.809	1.018
IRRITABL	9	2.218	0.783
TIRED	10	3.091	0.953
CONTENT	11	2.455	0.842
SMOKING4	12	3.500	1.276

(4)
VARIABLE NAME	NO.	OTHER BOUNDARY OF CLUSTER	NUMBER OF ITEMS IN CLUSTER	DISTANCE OR SIMILARITY WHEN CLUSTER FORMED
CONCENTR	1	12	12	30.07
ALERT	8	1	2	80.21
SLEEPY	4	10	2	79.82
TIRED	10	1	4	69.85
ANNOY	2	6	4	72.48
IRRITABL	9	2	2	79.61
CONTENT	11	2	3	73.92
TENSE	6	1	8	60.54
SMOKING1	3	12	4	80.98
SMOKING2	5	12	3	81.65
SMOKING3	7	12	2	84.53
SMOKING4	12	1	12	30.07

(5) TREE PRINTED OVER ABSOLUTE CORRELATION MATRIX.
     CLUSTERING BY MINIMUM DISTANCE METHOD.

```
     VARIABLE
NAME       NO.
                  --------------------------------/
CONCENTR(  1) 80/45  51/56  59  49  57/ 8  19   4  22/
               /      /         /         /         /
              /      /         /         /         /
ALERT    (  8)/60  69/57  60  60  59/10  22   3  20/
              /      /         /         /         /
           ----/                  /         /      /
SLEEPY   (  4) 79/35  33  24  27/13  21  12  27/
               /         /         /         /
              /         /         /         /
TIRED    ( 10)/41  42  39  36/19  27  13  27/
              /                  /         /
           ----------/              /      /
ANNOY    (  2) 79/73/70/14  11   6  12/
             / / /                  /
            / / /                  /
IRRITABL (  9)/69/72/18  22  10  15/
             / / /                  /
            / / /                  /
CONTENT  ( 11)/71/23  23   9  17/
             /                  /
            /                  /
TENSE    (  6)/22  30  12  21/
             /                  /
          ----------/
SMOKING1(  3) 78  80  77/
           -------/
SMOKING2(  5) 81  81/
         ---/
SMOKING3(  7) 84/
SMOKING4( 12)/
```

(6) THE VALUES IN THIS TREE HAVE BEEN SCALED 0 TO 100 ACCORDING TO THE FOLLOWING TABLE

VALUE ABOVE	CORRELATION	VALUE ABOVE	CORRELATION
0	0.000	50	0.500
5	0.050	55	0.550
10	0.100	60	0.600
15	0.150	65	0.650
20	0.200	70	0.700
25	0.250	75	0.750
30	0.300	80	0.800
35	0.350	85	0.850
40	0.400	90	0.900
45	0.450	95	0.950

--- (7) an explanation of the clustering process ---

--- (8) the shaded correlation matrix appears here (see Output 1M.3) ---

----

Output 1M.2   Using the average linkage rule to join clusters

----

```
         PROCEDURE MEASURE . . . . . . . . . . . . . .ANG
         PROCEDURE AMALGAMATION RULE IS AVERAGE DISTANCE (AVERAGE LINKAGE)



         NUMBER OF CASES READ. . . . . . . . . . . .    110



--- means and standard deviations for each variable ---



          VARIABLE      OTHER BOUNDARY     NUMBER OF ITEMS    DISTANCE OR SIMILARITY
NAME        NO.         OF CLUSTER          IN CLUSTER        WHEN CLUSTER FORMED
CONCENTR     1              12                  12                 61.80
ALERT        8               1                   2                 90.10
ANNOY        2               6                   4                 89.18
IRRITABL     9               2                   2                 89.80
CONTENT     11               2                   3                 87.90
TENSE        6               1                   6                 84.00
SLEEPY       4              10                   2                 89.91
TIRED       10               1                   8                 76.49
SMOKING1     3              12                   4                 92.03
SMOKING2     5              12                   3                 92.41
SMOKING3     7              12                   2                 92.26
SMOKING4    12               1                  12                 61.80



TREE PRINTED OVER CORRELATION MATRIX (SCALED 0-100).
CLUSTERING BY AVERAGE DISTANCE METHOD.
   VARIABLE
NAME     NO.   -------------------------------/
CONCENTR(  1) 90/78 79 74 78/72 75/54 59 52 61/
              /      /     /    /           /
              /      /   / /   /           /
ALERT   (  8)/78 80 80 79/80 84/55 61 51 60/
              /        /     /  /          /
           ----------/     /  /          /
ANNOY   (  2) 89/86/85/67 70/57 55 53 56/
              / /  /  /    /           /
             / /  /  /    /           /
IRRITABL(  9)/84/86/66 71/59 61 55 57/
             / /  /    /           /
            / /  /    /           /
CONTENT (  11)/85/62 69/61 61 54 58/
             /    /   /           /
            /    /   /           /
TENSE   (  6)/63 68/61 65 56 60/
             /        /       /
           ----/     /       /
SLEEPY  (  4) 89/56 60 56 63/
             /             /
            /             /
TIRED   ( 10)/59 63 56 63/
             /          /
          ----------/
SMOKING1(  3) 89 90 88/
             /        /
          -------/
SMOKING2(  5) 90 90/
             /     /
          ----/
SMOKING3(  7) 92/
             /
            /
SMOKING4( 12)/
```

THE VALUES IN THIS TREE HAVE BEEN SCALED 0 TO 100
ACCORDING TO THE FOLLOWING TABLE

VALUE ABOVE	CORRELATION	VALUE ABOVE	CORRELATION
0	-1.000	50	0.000
5	-0.900	55	0.100
10	-0.800	60	0.200
15	-0.700	65	0.300
20	-0.600	70	0.400
25	-0.500	75	0.500
30	-0.400	80	0.600
35	-0.300	85	0.700
40	-0.200	90	0.800
45	-0.100	95	0.900

--- explanation of the clustering ---

Example 1M.2 Measures of Similarity and Linkage Rules

The PROCEDURE paragraph is used to select variables for the analysis, the measure of similarity, and the linkage rule to combine (amalgamate) clusters. This paragraph can be repeated (after the data, when the data are on cards) to specify additional analyses of the same data (see the order of input in the summary, p. 454).

The MEASURE of similarity can be the value of the CORRELATION or the absolute value of the correlation ABSCORR, or it can be obtained from a measure of distance such as the ANGLE between two variables (arccosine of the correlation) or the acute angle corresponding to the arccosine of the absolute value of the correlation ABSANG.

The LINKAGE rule (the criterion for combining two clusters) can be the minimum distance or maximum similarity over all pairings of the variables between the two clusters (SINGLE linkage), the maximum distance or minimum similarity (COMPLETE linkage), or the average distance or similarity (AVERAGE linkage). The average similarity is the arithmetic average of the similarity s_{ij} using all possible pairings of the variables between the two clusters.

$$\Sigma\Sigma s_{ij}/IJ$$

where variable i is contained by the first cluster and variable j by the second cluster, and I and J are the number of variables in the two clusters. (However, when the measure of similarity is derived from an angle, i.e., ANG or ABSANG, average similarity is computed as

$$\frac{\Sigma_i \Sigma_j \ s_{ij}}{\Sigma_i \Sigma_k \ s_{ik} \ \Sigma_j \Sigma_m \ s_{jm}}$$

where s_{ij} = cos(angle between variables i and j), and i, k are in the first cluster and j, m in the second cluster.) Thus, CORR and ANG can differ when the LINKAGE IS AVERAGE.

Variables to be analyzed can be selected either by a USE statement in the VARIABLE paragraph or by a VARIABLE statement in the PROCEDURE paragraph.

In this example we use the angle between two variables as the measure of similarity and choose the AVERAGE criterion for combining clusters. We insert a PROCEDURE paragraph in the Control Language of Example 1M.1 before the END paragraph:

```
----------------------------------------
/ PROCEDURE      MEASURE IS ANG.
                LINKAGE IS AVE.
----------------------------------------
```

The results are presented in Output 1M.2. The tree diagram is printed over the recoded correlation matrix rather than the arccosine of the correlation. That is, if ANG or ABSANG is specified and the angle is obtained as a function of the correlation, the correlations are printed in the results.

```
PROCedure ─────────────────────────────
  MEASure = (one only)              ABSCORR/prev.
    ABSCORR, CORR,
    ANG, ABSANG,
    The measure of similarity used to combine
    variables into clusters. The definitions of
    these terms are given above.

  Note:  If TYPE = SIMI or TYPE = DIST is specified
  in the INPUT paragraph (p. 454), MEASURE is not
  used. If / INPUT  TYPE = ANG, the assumed
  MEASURE is ABSANG.

  LINKage = (one only)                SINGLE/prev.
            SINGLE, AVE, COMP.
    The criterion used to combine (amalgamate)
    clusters. The possible criteria are maximum
    similarity (minimum distance, SINGLE linkage),
    minimum similarity (maximum distance, COMPLETE
    linkage), or average similarity (average
    distance, AVERAGE linkage). AVERAGE linkage is
    defined above.
  VARiable = v list.            all variables/prev.
    Names or subscripts of variables to be used in
    the analysis. Note that the variables to be
    clustered default to those specified in a
    previous PROCEDURE paragraph in the same
    problem; otherwise to the variables in
    / VAR   USE.
```

Example 1M.3 A Shaded Matrix Display of Correlations

The correlation matrix is printed when CORRELATION is specified in the PRINT paragraph. The correlation matrix can also be printed in SHADED form: the variables are sorted into the order specified in the tree diagram and the correlation matrix is then printed with codes replacing the correlations. These options are requested by adding the following PRINT paragraph to the Control Language of Example 1M.1 before the END paragraph.

```
----------------------------------------
/ PRINT      CORRELATION.
             SHADE.
----------------------------------------
```

The results are presented in Output 1M.3. The codes used in the shaded correlation matrix are explained below the matrix.

If you are using a terminal or your printer does not allow overprinting, the shaded matrix can be printed using five symbols of varying density by specifying NCUT in the PRINT paragraph.

Some users prefer to see the shaded correlation matrix without the cluster tree (NO TREE), or to suppress the detailed explanation of the cluster tree (NO EXPL).

```
PRINT ─────────────────────────────────
  │ CORRelation.                              no/prev.
  │   Print the correlation matrix.
  │ SHADE.                                  SHADE/prev.
  │   Print the correlation matrix in shaded form
  │   after reordering the variables to correspond
  │   with the tree diagram. The printed codes are
  │   formed by overprinting (printing the same line
  │   more than once); this may not be possible at
  │   some facilities. (In versions dated before
  │   1980, the assumption is not to print the shaded
  │   correlation matrix.)
  │ NCUT = #.                                   8/prev.
  │   The number is either 8, 11 or 5. Eight is used
  │   with overprinting, 5 is used to obtain shaded
  │   correlation if your printer does not permit
  │   overprinting. Eleven indicates that the first
  │   digit of each correlation is to be used as the
  │   shading symbol.
  │ TREE.                                     TREE/prev.
  │   Print cluster tree. The tree is printed unless
  │   you state NO TREE.
  │ EXPLain.                                  EXPL./prev.
  │   Print detailed explanation of cluster tree. The
  │   explanation is printed unless you state NO
  │   EXPL.
  └─────────────────────────────────────────
```

Types of Input

Input can be either from a BMDP File or from other files including cards. Input from a BMDP File can be data, a correlation matrix or a covariance matrix. Note that if a covariance matrix is input, then it is converted to a correlation matrix before clustering.

If the input is not from a BMDP File, the input can be data or a matrix that contains either measures of similarity or measures of distance between the variables. A matrix of this form can be a covariance matrix, a correlation matrix, a matrix of angles with distance in radians, or a general similarity or distance matrix. When a matrix, other than data, is read as input, it must be input one row at a time; the FORMAT statement describes one row of the matrix. Unlike several other BMDP programs, the matrix must be input as a square array; it is not sufficient to input the lower half. The TYPE of input must be specified when the input is not from a BMDP File unless the input is data.

Output 1M.3 Using a shaded matrix to display correlations

CORRELATIONS

		CONCENTR 1	ANNOY 2	SMOKING1 3	SLEEPY 4	SMOKING2 5	TENSE 6	SMOKING3 7	ALERT 8	IRRITABL 9	TIRED 10
CONCENTR	1	1.0000									
ANNOY	2	0.5618	1.0000								
SMOKING1	3	0.0859	0.1438	1.0000							
SLEEPY	4	0.4570	0.3596	0.1398	1.0000						
SMOKING2	5	0.1997	0.1192	0.7851	0.2113	1.0000					
TENSE	6	0.5790	0.7047	0.2223	0.2726	0.3007	1.0000				
SMOKING3	7	0.0407	0.0604	0.8098	0.1264	0.8165	0.1200	1.0000			
ALERT	8	0.8021	0.5779	0.1007	0.6056	0.2226	0.5939	0.0386	1.0000		
IRRITABL	9	0.5945	0.7961	0.1894	0.3365	0.2213	0.7248	0.1085	0.6054	1.0000	
TIRED	10	0.5120	0.4130	0.1987	0.7982	0.2736	0.3643	0.1386	0.6985	0.4281	1.0000
CONTENT	11	0.4921	0.7392	0.2391	0.2400	0.2352	0.7113	0.0998	0.6051	0.6974	0.3937
SMOKING4	12	0.2278	0.1218	0.7754	0.2774	0.8129	0.2139	0.8453	0.2012	0.1562	0.2714

		CONTENT 11	SMOKING4 12
CONTENT	11	1.0000	
SMOKING4	12	0.1708	1.0000

ABSOLUTE VALUES OF CORRELATIONS IN SORTED AND SHADED FORM

```
 1 CONCENTR  █
 8 ALERT     ██
 4 SLEEPY    XX█               THE ABSOLUTE VALUES OF
10 TIRED     X█████           THE MATRIX ENTRIES HAVE BEEN PRINTED ABOVE IN SHADED FORM
 2 ANNOY     XX++█            ACCORDING TO THE FOLLOWING SCHEME
 9 IRRITABL  XX+X██                          LESS THAN OR EQUAL TO      0.106
11 CONTENT   XX-+████          .       0.106  TO AND INCLUDING          0.211
 6 TENSE     XX-+████          -       0.211  TO AND INCLUDING          0.317
 3 SMOKING1  ....--█           +       0.317  TO AND INCLUDING          0.423
 5 SMOKING2  .-.-.---██        X       0.423  TO AND INCLUDING          0.528
 7 SMOKING3  .. .███           N       0.528  TO AND INCLUDING          0.634
12 SMOKING4  -.--...-████      █       0.634  TO AND INCLUDING          0.740
                               █              GREATER THAN              0.740
```

```
INPut ─────────────────────────────────────────────────┐
   TYPE = (one only)                              DATA
      DATA, COVA, CORR, ANG, SIMI, DIST.
      The type of input.
      DATA -- data
      COVA -- a covariance matrix
      CORR -- a correlation matrix
      ANG  -- an angular distance matrix measured in
              radians
      SIMI -- a matrix of similarities
      DIST -- a matrix of distances
      TYPE need not be specified if data are input.

   Note: If SIMI or DIST is specified, MEASURE in
   the PROCEDURE paragraph is not used.
```

Saving the Data or Correlation Matrix in a BMDP File

The correlation matrix or covariance matrix may be saved for analysis in other programs or reanalysis in P1M - e.g., with a different linkage rule.

The SAVE paragraph is illustrated in Example 4M.5. Also see Chapter 7.

```
SAVE ──────────────────────────────────────────────────┐
   CONTent = (one or both)                        DATA
             DATA, CORR.
      The matrices to be saved in a BMDP File.
      DATA -- data
      CORR -- the correlation matrix
```

SIZE OF PROBLEM

For medium-sized computer systems P1M can easily analyze up to 140 variables. Appendix B describes how to increase the capacity of the program.

COMPUTATIONAL METHOD

Means, standard deviations and correlations are computed in single precision by the method of provisional means (Appendix A.2). The method of shading the correlation matrix is similar to that of Ling (1973). The method of forming clusters is described on pp. 449 and 452.

ACKNOWLEDGEMENT

P1M was designed by John Hartigan and programmed by Howard Gilbert and Steve Chasen. Later revisions were made by James Frane.

SUMMARY

Order of Input Cards

```
   // (job card)
   // EXEC BIMED,PROG=BMDP1M       (see Appendix E)
   //SYSIN DD *
   / PROBLEM
   / INPUT
   / VARIABLE
   / TRANSFORM
   / SAVE
   / PROCEDURE
   / PRINT
   / END
       (data if on cards)
   / PROCEDURE
   / END
   // (system card)
```

Full sets of BMDP paragraphs (and data, if on cards) can be repeated for additional problems; see Section 5.8.

Paragraph Statement	Preassigned	Comment and Manual Reference
/●INPut		Additional option to specify type of input. 454
TYPE = c.	DATA.	Specifies input. When a matrix other than data is read it must be input one row at a time; the FORMAT describes one row of the matrix. Only DATA can be input from a BMDP File (one only). * DATA - data ANG - angular distance matrix in radians COVA - covariance matrix SIMI - matrix of similarities CORR - correlation matrix DIST - matrix of distances If SIMI or DIST is specified, / PROC MEASURE (below) is not used.
/ PROCedure		Optional to select measure of similarity and clustering criteria (may be repeated). 452
MEASure = c.	ABSCORR.	Measure of similarity used to combine variables into clusters (one only). * ABSCORR - absolute value of correlation CORR - correlation between variables ANG - arccosine of correlation (i.e., angle between two variables) ABSANG - acute angle corresponding to arccosine of absolute value of correlation
LINKage = c.	SINGLE.	Criterion used to combine (amalgamate) clusters (one only). * SINGLE - maximum similarity (minimum distance), single linkage AVE - average similarity (distance), linkage COMP. - minimum similarity (maximum distance), complete linkage
VARiable = v list.	all	Names or subscripts of variables used in the analysis. *
/ PRINT		Optional to request printed output. 453
CORRelation.	no	Correlation matrix. *
SHADE.	yes	Graphical display with the size of a correlation (or distance measure) represented by a shaded symbol. The rows of the matrix are ordered by the clustering tree. The shading is done by overprinting at 5 or 8 levels (see NCUT below). *
NCUT = 5, 8 or 11.	8.	If overprinting is not available, (e.g., on a terminal), specify both SHADE and NCUT = 5 for shading. The first digit of each correlation is printed when 11 is specified. *
TREE.	yes	Cluster tree. *
EXPLain.	yes	Detailed explanation of the cluster tree. *
LINEsize = #.	132.	Number of columns permitted for printing (shaded) correlation or (shaded) distance matrix on narrow page size.
/ SAVE		Matrices to be saved in BMDP File. 454
CONTent = c list.	DATA.	One or more of DATA -- data; CORR -- correlation matrix.

Key:

/	-indicates paragraph
.	-period ends a sentence
●	-required
v	-variable (name or subscript)
g	-group (name or subscript)
#	-number
'c'	-characters (name or parameter) may omit apostrophes if contiguous letters only

*	-assigned value remains the same for additional problems
VT	-number of variables after transformations
list	-more than one item, often one per var.

Capitalized letters-paragraph or sentence names recognized by BMDP

Page numbers following refer to this Manual

P2M

17.2 Cluster Analysis of Cases

Laszlo Engelman

ABSTRACT

P2M forms clusters of cases (observations) based on one of four distance measures: the Euclidean distance (the square root of the sum of squares of the differences between the values of the variables for two cases); the distance calculated using the sum of the pth power of the absolute difference; the chi-square statistic and phi-square (the last two measure the difference of frequencies in two cases and are used when the data are counts). (See also program PKM.) Initially each case is considered a separate cluster. P2M joins cases and/or clusters of cases in a stepwise process until all cases are combined into one cluster. The algorithm uses the distance between centroid clusters or the kth nearest neighbor density estimator as a criterion for joining (amalgamating) clusters. Single linkage is a special case of the kth nearest neighbor density estimator. Output includes a tree diagram describing the sequence of cluster formation, a table that lists the amalgamation distance and the mean for each variable as each new cluster is formed. A matrix of distances between cases is printed in shaded form.

WHERE TO FIND IT

Example 2M.1 Basic Setup for Clustering Cases

In our first example we use preassigned options only: the PROBLEM, INPUT and VARIABLE paragraphs are common to all programs and are explained in Chapter 5. The preassigned distance measure is the Euclidean distance using standardized data. Clusters are formed using the single linkage algorithm.

The data used in our examples are health indicators for 11 countries, Table 17.2. The names of the countries are read as two A-format variables and are used as labels of the cases in the output. The instructions for clustering the countries are:

```
-------------------------------------
/ PROBLEM     TITLE IS 'HEALTH INDICATOR DATA'.
/ INPUT       VARIABLES ARE 9.
              FORMAT IS '(2A4, 4F6.2, 3F3.0)'.
/ VARIABLE    NAMES ARE COUNTRY1, COUNTRY2, DOCDNT,
                 PHARM, NURSES, HOSPBEDS,
                 ANIMAL, STARCH, LIFEEXP.
              LABELS ARE COUNTRY1, COUNTRY2.

/ END
-------------------------------------
```

(See end of this P2M section for organization of systems information, BMDP instructions and data.)

Table 17.2   Health indicators (Harbison et al., 1970, Appendix 1, p. 8)

	DOCDNT	PHARM	NURSES	HOSPBED	ANIMAL	STARCH	LIFEEXP
ALGERIA	129	023	350	3392	21	57	35
IRAN	329	107	290	1113	24	60	51
IRAQ	241	081	235	1898	28	57	54
JORDAN	284	096	241	1712	25	49	52
LEBANON	933	192	564	4071	35	50	60
LIBYA	338	041	612	3215	24	55	57
MOROCCO	094	026	233	1516	21	57	53
SYRIA	254	070	140	1163	13	69	52
TUNISIA	114	039	248	2967	21	57	53
TURKEY	412	057	306	1738	16	71	55
U.A.R.	483	131	454	2225	15	73	54

The health indicators measured are the relative number of doctors and dentists (DOCDNT), of pharmacists (PHARM), of NURSES and of hospital beds (HOSPBEDS), the percent of ANIMAL fat and STARCH in the diet and life expectancy (LIFEEXP). The name of country is recorded in columns 1-8, DOCDNT in 12-14, PHARM in 18-20, NURSES in 14-26, HOSPBED in 29-32, ANIMAL in 34-35, STARCH in 37-38 and LIFEEXP in 40-41; for DOCDNT, PHARM, NURSES and HOSPBED the numbers are recorded to two decimal points. The data are read using the format (2A4, 4F6.2, 3F3.0)

The results of the analysis are presented in Output 2M.1. Circled numbers below correspond to those in the output.

(1) The number of cases read. P2M uses only complete cases in all computations; that is, if a case has a missing value or a value out of range, the entire case is omitted. If there is a USE statement (Section 5.4), only variables in the USE statement are checked for acceptable values.

(2) Interpretations of the BMDP instructions specific to P2M. Since none are stated in Example 2M.1, preassigned values (options) are printed.

(3) A tree diagram of the clusters. Names and numbers of the cases (countries) are printed above the diagram; the cases are sorted to permit a tree to be drawn. The numbers to the left of the tree are amalgamation distances. Each horizontal line in the tree corresponds to a cluster formed in the amalgamation process. Iraq and Jordan are joined at the first step.

(4) The initial distances between each pair of cases are ordered according to the tree diagram and are printed in a shaded form.

Output 2M.1 Using health indicators to cluster countries. Circled numbers correspond to those in the text

---

```
NUMBER OF CASES READ. . . . . . . . . . . . . .    11    (1)
  PRINT DISTANCE MATRIX . . . . . . . . . . . .    NO
  TYPE OF TREE PRINTED. . . . . . . . . . . . .    VERTICAL
  CALCULATING PROCEDURE . . . . . . . . . . . .    SUM-SQR
  STANDARDIZATION OF INPUT DATA . . . . . . . .    YES      (2)
  AMALGAMATION RULE . . . . . . . . . . . . . .    SINGLE
  NUMBER OF NEIGHBORS USED FOR DISTANCE CALC. . .  1
```

```
       C N
       O        1 1
       A .  1 6 8 0 1 7 9 3 4 2 5

       S L  A L S T U M T I J I L
       A L  L I Y U . O U R O R E
       E B  G B R R A R N A R A B         (3)
       E    E Y I K . O I Q D N A
       L    R A A E R C S   A   N
            I     Y . C I   N   O
            A       O A       N

  AMALG.
  DISTANCE
            * * * * * * * * * * *
    1.213   I I I I I I I -+- I I
    1.394   I I I I I I I  -+-- I
    1.497   I I I I I -+-  I   I
    1.619   I I -+- I I    I   I
    1.726   I I  I I  --+--     I
    1.880   I I -+--     I      I
    2.323   I I  -----+---      I
    2.767   I --------+-        I
    2.988   ---------+--        I
    4.439           -+----------
```

DISTANCES BETWEEN CASES REPRESENTED IN SHADED FORM.
HEAVY SHADING INDICATES SMALL DISTANCES.

```
CASE   CASE
NO.    LABEL

  1    ALGERIA     ▨          (4)
  6    LIBYA       .▨
  8    SYRIA       . ▨
 10    TURKEY      .-▨▨▨
 11    U.A.R.      -X▨▨
  7    MOROCCO     -+▨▨.▨
  9    TUNISIA     X▨X▨-▨▨
  3    IRAQ        .XXX-▨▨▨
  4    JORDAN      .+++.▨▨▨▨
  2    IRAN        .+▨▨X▨X▨▨▨▨
  5    LEBANON                ▨
```

THE DISTANCES HAVE BEEN REPRESENTED ABOVE IN SHADED
FORM ACCORDING TO THE FOLLOWING SCHEME

▨			LESS THAN	1.846
▨	FROM	1.846	TO	2.366
▨	FROM	2.366	TO	2.792
X	FROM	2.792	TO	3.123
+	FROM	3.123	TO	3.502
-	FROM	3.502	TO	3.810
.	FROM	3.810	TO	4.401
			GREATER THAN	4.401

Output 2M.2 Using the average linkage rule to amalgamate clusters

----

DETAILS OF THE AMALGAMATION (CLUSTERING) PROCESS ⑤

FOR EACH AMALGAMATION, THE FOLLOWING ARE PRINTED

-- THE DISTANCE BETWEEN THE TWO CLUSTERS JOINED

-- THE CASE NUMBERS FOR THE 'BOUNDARIES' OF THE NEWLY
   FORMED CLUSTER AS GIVEN IN THE CLUSTER TREE WHICH
   FOLLOWS THESE DETAILS

-- THE NUMBER OF CASES IN THE CLUSTER (SUM OF THE
   CASE WEIGHTS FOR THE CLUSTER IF CASE WEIGHT
   VARIABLE IS SPECIFIED)

-- THE (WEIGHTED) AVERAGES OF THE VARIABLES FOR THE CLUSTER
   (DIFFERENCES BETWEEN CLUSTERS CAN BE DESCRIBED IN
   TERMS OF THOSE VARIABLES WHOSE MEANS DIFFER MOST
   BETWEEN THE CLUSTERS)

⑥

| AMALGAMATION | | | SUM OF | 3 | 4 | 5 | 6 | 7 | 8 | 9 |
ORDER	DISTANCE	CASES	CS. WTS.	DOCDNT	PHARM	NURSES	HOSPBEDS	ANIMAL	STARCH	LIFEEXP
1	1.213	4 3	2.000	-0.280	0.197	-0.645	-0.475	0.705	-0.811	0.101
2	1.356	3 2	3.000	-0.186	0.317	-0.528	-0.708	0.572	-0.522	-0.005
3	1.497	9 7	2.000	-0.954	-0.900	-0.628	-0.033	-0.174	-0.316	0.101
4	1.619	10 8	2.000	0.020	-0.293	-0.746	-0.834	-1.214	1.296	0.180
5	1.775	7 2	5.000	-0.493	-0.169	-0.568	-0.438	0.273	-0.440	0.038
6	2.309	11 8	3.000	0.233	0.148	-0.228	-0.572	-1.187	1.420	0.207
7	2.526	8 2	8.000	-0.221	-0.050	-0.441	-0.488	-0.274	0.258	0.101
8	3.060	6 2	9.000	-0.192	-0.126	-0.184	-0.328	-0.210	0.167	0.172
9	3.519	2 1	10.000	-0.257	-0.222	-0.155	-0.182	-0.206	0.118	-0.121
10	5.434	5 1	11.000	0.000	0.000	0.000	0.000	0.000	0.000	0.000

```
C N
O        1 1
A . 1 6 8 0 1 7 9 3 4 2 5

S L  A L S T U M T I J I L
A    L I Y U . O U R O R E
E B  G B R R A R N A R A B
E    E Y I K . O I Q D N A           ⑦
L    R A A E R C S   A   N
     I     Y . C I   N   O
     A       O A         N

AMALG.
DISTANCE
         * * * * * * * * * *
  1.213  I I I I I I I -+- I I
  1.356  I I I I I I I  -+-- I
  1.497  I I I I I -+-   I    I
  1.619  I I -+- I  I    I    I
  1.775  I I  I I  --+--      I
  2.309  I I -+--      I      I
  2.526  I I  ----+---        I
  3.060  I --------+-         I
  3.519  ---------+-          I
  5.434           -+----------
```

--- ④ in Output 2M.1 appears here ---

Example 2M.2 Using Centroid Linkage to Form Clusters

There are two methods available in P2M for amalgamating (linking) cases into clusters: one is the pseudo-nearest-neighbor algorithm and the other is the centroid linkage method.

In this example we request that clusters be formed using the centroid linkage method. We insert the following PROCEDURE paragraph in the BMDP instructions of Example 2M.1 before the END paragraph.

```
-------------------------------------
/ PROCEDURE    LINK IS CENTROID.
-------------------------------------
```

The results are presented in Output 2M.2.

⑤ Explanation of the table in ⑥.

⑥ A table that lists the step-by-step amalgamation (combination) of cases into clusters.

In the first step case 4 is combined with case 3. The amalgamation distance is the distance between the cases in the cluster; the distance is defined below. When weights are not specified for the cases, the sum of case weights is the number of cases in the cluster. The mean of the cluster formed at this step is computed and printed for each variable. Therefore, in the first line the values are the means of the variables for cases 4 and 3. In the second line case 2 is added to the cluster containing cases 4 and 3; the means of the variables for the three cases are given.

⑦ The cluster tree. Compare this tree with that in Output 2M.1.

Algorithms for joining clusters. The SINGLE linkage algorithm (and the pseudo-nearest-neighbor algorithm) begins by computing and storing a matrix of distances between each pair of cases. You can visualize that the distance between point i (a case plotted in the space of the variables) and point j is computed by placing the center of a tiny disk on each point and allowing the radius of each disk to expand until the intersection of the disks touches or covers another point (or the intersection of the two disks covers k points for the pseudo-nearest-neighbor algorithm). The distance is the length of the radius. In Example 2M.3 we discuss four metrics for measuring this distance. The matrix of these pseudo-distances is then stored. The two cases with the smallest distance are joined first. During the amalgamating process (a case with another case, a case with an already formed cluster or a cluster with another cluster), distances are always read from the initial distance matrix. Thus cases are assigned to clusters that have members closest to the case.

The pseudo-nearest-neighbor algorithm is an extension of the single linkage method. The value of k may be 1 (single) up to 10 and is specified using the LINK instruction. For example, for k = 10, the distance between case i and case j is the length of the radius of the disks whose intersection covers 10 points. We recommend that the data be standardized for this procedure (see Example 2M.3 for definition).

The CENTROID linkage algorithm also begins by computing the distance between each pair of cases. However, the complete pairwise distance matrix is not stored. For each case, the case number of the closest case and its distance are stored. After two cases are joined, a new pseudo-point (centroid) is formed by averaging the coordinates of each variable. Distances are measured from this centroid to candidates for membership (a case or the centroid of another cluster). Thus the number of cases (or pseudo-cases) is reduced by one at each step. A tally is kept of the number of cases in each cluster; the tally is used as a weight in the clustering.

For large data sets, the single linkage algorithm will require more memory space than that for the centroid linkage algorithm, but the computation time for the single linkage procedure should be less.

```
PROCedure ─────────────────────────────
  LINK = (one only) #,              # = 1 or
         SINGle, CENtroid.           SINGLE/prev.
  The number (#) of k nearest neighbors for the
  linkage algorithm; # must be positive and less
  than or equal to 11. SINGLE is the same as k =
  1 and CENTROID is the same as k = 11.
```

Example 2M.3 Distance Measures and Standardization of Data

Two types of criteria to join clusters are available. One is appropriate when the data are measurements; the other is appropriate when the data are frequency counts. They are specified in the PROCEDURE paragraph. When the data are measurements, the Euclidean distance SUMOFSQ between two cases or clusters (j and k) is defined

$$d_{jk} = [\Sigma_i (x_{ij} - x_{ik})^2]^{\frac{1}{2}} \qquad (1)$$

where x_{ij} is the value of the ith variable in the jth case. More generally the distance SUMOFP can be defined as

$$d_{jk} = [\Sigma_i (x_{ij} - x_{ik})^p]^{1/p} \qquad (2)$$

For SUMOFSQ or SUMOFP, the data values are standardized (to z-scores) before the computation of the distance unless you specify otherwise. Standardization is usually preferable when the variables are measured in different units; otherwise the distance between cases will give greater weight to variables with larger standard deviations than is given to variables with small standard deviations.

When the data are frequency counts, the distance between two cases or clusters is defined as the chi-square (CHISQ) test of equality of the two sets of frequencies.

$$d_{jk} = \left[\Sigma_i \left\{ \frac{(x_{ij} - e_{ijk})^2}{e_{ijk}} + \frac{(x_{ik} - e_{ikj})^2}{e_{ikj}} \right\} \right]^{\frac{1}{2}} \qquad (3)$$

where

$$e_{ijk} = (x_{ij} + x_{ik})\ \Sigma_i x_{ij}/N_{jk}$$

$$e_{ikj} = (x_{ij} + x_{ik})\ \Sigma_i x_{ik}/N_{jk}$$

$$N_{jk} = \Sigma_i (x_{ij} + x_{ik})\ .$$

The chi-square measure in (3) can be normalized so its magnitude does not depend on the sample size N_{jk}. The normalized statistic PHISQ is expresssion (3) divided by $\sqrt{N_{jk}}$.

Initially each case is placed in a cluster by itself. At each step the two clusters with the shortest distance between them are combined (amalgamated) into one cluster. The values of the variables for a cluster are either weighted averages of the cases in the cluster (when SUMOFSQ or SUMOFP is used) or the sum of the values of the cases (when CHISQ or PHISQ is used). The weight of the new cluster is the sum of the weights of the two clusters or the number of cases in the new cluster - unless the user has supplied a weight for each case using values stored in a WEIGHT variable (i.e., the weight of each case is one when no WEIGHT variable is specified). This algorithm continues, using the shortest distance each time, until all the cases are in one cluster.

In this example we reanalyze the data of Example 2M.1 using the sum of absolute differences on the unstandardized data as a distance measure; this is the distance between cases measured along the axes (grid distance). (Since these data are measured in very different units, we show how to request the unstandardized data only to illustrate the mechanics of the program.) We insert a PROCEDURE paragraph in the instructions of Example 2M.1 before the END paragraph.

```
------------------------------------
/ PROCEDURE     SUMOFP IS 1.
                NO STANDARDIZE.
------------------------------------
```

The results of this analysis are presented in Output 2M.3. The order of amalgamation of cases is changed, and the tree diagram differs from that of Output 2M.1.

PROCedure

(one only)	SUMOFSQ.	yes/prev.
	SUMOFP = #.	2/prev.
	CHISQ.	no/prev.
	PHISQ.	no/prev.

The criteria to combine cases and clusters are defined above. For measurements, SUMOFSQ is the distance measure and SUMOFP is the sum of powers measure with p to be specified. For frequency counts CHISQ or PHISQ is the criterion.

STANDardize. — STANDardize/prev.

The data are standardized to z-scores when the distance criterion is SUMOFSQ or SUMOFP unless you specify NO STANDARDIZE. This option is ignored if the distance criterion is CHISQ or PHISQ.

WEIGHT = v. — no case weights/prev.

Name or subscript of the variable that contains case weights. If WEIGHT is not stated or is set to zero, there are no case weights and each case is assigned unit weight.

Output 2M.3 Cluster analysis using grid distance

```
---------------------------------------------------

     C N
       O                   1 1
     A .   1 6 3 7 9 4 2 0 1 8 5

     S L   A L I M T J I T U S L
       A   L I R O U O R U . Y E
     E B   G B A R N R A R A R B
       E   E Y Q O I D N K . I A
       L   R A   C S A   E R A N
           I     C I N   Y .   O
           A     O A           N

 AMALG.
DISTANCE
           * * * * * * * * * * *
  11.800   I I I I I I I -+- I I
  13.860   I I -+- I I I  I  I I
  14.990   I I  -+-- I I  I  I I
  15.500   I I   -+--- I  I  I I
  15.760   I I    -+----  I  I I
  17.120   I I     I       -+-- I
  17.380   I -----+-        I   I
  23.580   ------+-         I   I
  24.120         ---+-------    I
  35.500            -+----------


DISTANCES BETWEEN CASES REPRESENTED IN SHADED FORM.
HEAVY SHADING INDICATES SMALL DISTANCES.

CASE  CASE
 NO.  LABEL

  1 ALGERIA   █
  6 LIBYA     X█
  3 IRAQ      .N█
  7 MOROCCO   -X██
  9 TUNISIA   ⊠█⊠██
  4 JORDAN    .X█⊠N█
  2 IRAN      .+⊠█N⊠█
 10 TURKEY     .XN++X█
 11 U.A.R.     .-++.-██
  8 SYRIA       -N--N█N█
  5 LEBANON    X        █


THE DISTANCES HAVE BEEN REPRESENTED ABOVE IN SHADED
FORM ACCORDING TO THE FOLLOWING SCHEME

   █                      LESS THAN      17.464
   ⊠    FROM     17.464      TO          24.088
   N    FROM     24.088      TO          29.809
   X    FROM     29.809      TO          35.530
   +    FROM     35.530      TO          37.336
   -    FROM     37.336      TO          43.659
   .    FROM     43.659      TO          51.789
                          GREATER THAN   51.789

---------------------------------------------------
```

Output 2M.4 Optional results printed by P2M

STANDARDIZED INPUT DATA

CASE		DOCDNT	PHARM	NURSES	HOSPBEDS	ANIMAL	STARCH	LIFEEXP	WEIGHT
NO.	LABEL	3	4	5	6	7	8	9	0
1	ALGERIA	-0.848	-1.085	0.108	1.133	-0.174	-0.316	-2.757	1.000
2	IRAN	0.003	0.559	-0.295	-1.176	0.305	0.056	-0.217	1.000
3	IRAQ	-0.371	0.050	-0.665	-0.380	0.945	-0.316	0.260	1.000
4	JORDAN	-0.188	0.343	-0.625	-0.569	0.465	-1.307	-0.058	1.000
5	LEBANON	2.573	2.223	1.547	1.820	2.065	-1.183	1.213	1.000
6	LIBYA	0.041	-0.733	1.870	0.953	0.305	-0.563	0.736	1.000
7	MOROCCO	-0.997	-1.027	-0.678	-0.767	-0.174	-0.316	0.101	1.000
8	SYRIA	-0.316	-0.165	-1.304	-1.125	-1.454	1.172	-0.058	1.000
9	TUNISIA	-0.912	-0.772	-0.578	0.702	-0.174	-0.316	0.101	1.000
10	TURKEY	0.356	-0.420	-0.188	-0.542	-0.974	1.420	0.419	1.000
11	U.A.R.	0.658	1.029	0.807	-0.049	-1.134	1.668	0.260	1.000

CASE		ORDER OF
NO.	LABEL	AMALGAMATION
1	ALGERIA	******------------
6	LIBYA	8.--------//
8	SYRIA	7.-------//
10	TURKEY	4.// //
11	U.A.R.	6./ //
7	MOROCCO	5.----//
9	TUNISIA	3./ //
3	IRAQ	2.--//
4	JORDAN	1.///
2	IRAN	9.//
5	LEBANON	10./

DISTANCES BETWEEN CASES REPRESENTED IN SHADED FORM.
HEAVY SHADING INDICATES SMALL DISTANCES.

CASE	CASE
NO.	LABEL
1	ALGERIA ▓
2	LIBYA .▓
3	SYRIA .▓▓
4	TURKEY .▓▓▓
5	U.A.R. ▓
6	MOROCCO .+X+ ▓
7	TUNISIA -▓▓▓ +▓
8	IRAQ .XX+ X▓
9	JORDAN X▓▓▓ N▓X▓
10	IRAN .▓X+ -N▓X▓+
11	LEBANON X-. -.X-▓▓

THE DISTANCES HAVE BEEN REPRESENTED ABOVE IN SHADED
FORM ACCORDING TO THE FOLLOWING SCHEME

▓			LESS THAN	1.846
▓	FROM	1.846	TO	2.366
X	FROM	2.366	TO	2.792
X	FROM	2.792	TO	3.123
+	FROM	3.123	TO	3.502
−	FROM	3.502	TO	3.810
.	FROM	3.810	TO	4.401
			GREATER THAN	4.401

INITIAL DISTANCES BETWEEN CASES

CASE NUMBER	1	2	3	4	5	6	7	8	9	10	11
1	0.0	3.97	3.84	3.82	6.83	4.07	3.52	4.40	2.99	4.30	4.75
2	3.97	0.0	1.39	1.57	5.33	3.49	2.07	2.45	2.59	2.32	2.83
3	3.84	1.39	0.0	1.21	5.10	3.11	1.73	3.01	1.85	2.78	3.54
4	3.82	1.57	1.21	0.0	5.08	3.31	2.00	3.30	2.19	3.29	3.88
5	6.83	5.33	5.10	5.08	0.0	4.44	6.48	7.10	5.82	6.09	5.33
6	4.07	3.49	3.11	3.31	4.44	0.0	3.36	4.65	2.77	3.51	3.59
7	3.52	2.07	1.73	2.00	6.48	3.36	0.0	2.37	1.50	2.50	3.82
8	4.40	2.45	3.01	3.30	7.10	4.65	2.37	0.0	2.91	1.62	2.90
9	2.99	2.59	1.85	2.19	5.82	2.77	1.50	2.91	0.0	2.68	3.62
10	4.30	2.32	2.78	3.29	6.09	3.51	2.50	1.62	2.68	0.0	1.88
11	4.75	2.83	3.54	3.88	5.33	3.59	3.82	2.90	3.62	1.88	0.0

Example 2M.4 Printing Data, Cluster Trees and Matrices of Distances and Shaded Distances

The tree diagram can be printed VERTICALLY, as it appears in ③ in Output 2M.1, or HORIZONTALLY as it appears in Output 2M.4. Note that the vertical tree contains the amalgamation distances and the horizontal tree takes notably less space for a large number of cases.

The initial distances between each pair of cases can be printed; they can also be printed in a histogram or in a shaded form after the cases are ordered according to the tree diagram. The user can suppress the sort, specify that blanks be printed for distances larger than a specified maximum limit, control the width of the displays in the output and request that five symbols be used in the shaded display when overprinting is not available.

The data (standardized or unstandardized) that are used in the computations can be printed.

When the amalgamation method LINK IS CENTROID is used it is possible to suppress the printing of the table of distances and weighted averages of the variables (⑥ in Output 2M.2).

We request several of these options by inserting a PRINT paragraph in the Control Language of Example 2M.1 before the END paragraph.

```
-----------------------------------
  / PRINT     DATA.
             HORIZONTAL.
             NO SORT.
             DISTANCES.
-----------------------------------
```

The results are presented in Output 2M.4.

```
PRINT ─────────────────────────────
  DATA.                              no/prev.
    Print the data used in the computation. If the
    data are standardized, the standardized data
    are printed.
  DISTances.                         no/prev.
    Print the initial distances between the cases.
    If the data are standardized, the distances are
    in terms of the standardized data.
  VERTical. or HORIZontal.      VERTical/prev.
    The tree diagram is printed VERTICALLY unless
    you specify HORIZONTAL. If neither is desired,
    state NO VERT. and NO HORIZ.
  AMALGamate.               AMALGamate/prev.
    The table of distances, case weights, and
    averages of the variables at each step is
    printed unless you specify NO AMALGAMATE.
  HIST.                              no/prev.
    Requests a histogram of the distances.
```

```
  SHADE.                          SHADE/prev.
    Print the distance matrix in shaded form after
    reordering the cases to correspond with the
    tree diagram. The printed codes are formed by
    overprinting (printing the same line more than
    once); this may not be possible at some
    facilities. Shading intervals are selected so
    that each shading interval is used for
    approximately the same number of cases.
  SORT.                           SORT./prev.
    To have the shaded distance matrix printed
    without having the cases sorted according to
    the clustering process, state NO SORT.
  LIMIT = #.                         no limit
    All distances greater than this # limit are
    represented by blanks.
  NCUT = 8 or 5.                     8/prev.
    The number of levels for shading. If your
    printer does not allow overprinting (or you are
    at a terminal) state NCUT = 5.
```

SIZE OF PROBLEM

When LINK is not equal to CENTROID, the distance matrix between cases and the data matrix are both stored in memory, hence core requirement is

$$(VU + CU) * VU.$$

When LINK is equal to CENTROID, only the data are in memory, so the maximum size of a problem that can be analyzed on medium-sized computer systems is a function of the number of variables and number of cases. The following table provides a guide to the maximum number of cases that can be analyzed.

number of variables	5	10	20
maximum number of cases when			
distance matrix is printed	500	400	300
distance matrix is not printed	630	520	370

COMPUTATIONAL METHOD

Means and standard deviations are computed in single precision by the method of provisional means (Appendix A.2).

The method of shading the distance matrix is similar to that of Ling (1973).

The clustering method is described on p. 693.

ACKNOWLEDGEMENT

P2M was designed by Laszlo Engelman and programmed by Laszlo Engelman and Sandra Fu. Later additions were made by James Frane and Albyn Jones.

SUMMARY

Order of Input Cards

```
// (job card)
// EXEC BIMED,PROG=BMDP2M        (see Appendix E)
//SYSIN DD *
/ PROBLEM
/ INPUT
/ VARIABLE
/ TRANSFORM
/ SAVE
/ PROCEDURE
/ PRINT
/ END
    (data if on cards)
// (system card)
```

Full sets of BMDP paragraphs (and data if on cards)
can be repeated for additional problems; see section
5.8.

instructions specific to P2M

Paragraph Statement	Preassigned	Comment and Manual Reference
/ PROCedure		Optional to specify the distance measure for combining cases and clusters. 460
LINK = (one only) #,SINGle, CENtroid.	1 or SINGle	See page 459. *
SUMOFSQ.	yes	Euclidean distance for measurement data. *
SUMOFPower = #.	2	Distance measure similar to SUMOFSQ, where "#" is the exponent (can be other than 2) for the measure. *
CHISQ.	no	Data are frequency counts; distance is test of equality of proportions for frequencies of two cases. *
PHISQ.	no	Distance measure same as CHISQ but normalized so magnitude does not depend on sample size. *
STANDardize.	yes	Standardize data to z-scores when distance is SUMOFSQ or SUMOFP, but not distances CHISQ or PHISQ. *
WEIGHT = v.	none	Name or subscript of variable containing case weights. *
/ PRINT		Optional to direct printing. If omitted, VERT and AMAL are printed. 462
DATA.	no	Print the data. If / PROC STAND. is specified, the standardized data are printed. *
DISTances.	no	Print initial distances between the cases. *
VERT. or HORIZ.	VERT.	Print the tree diagram vertically or horizontally. If neither is desired, state NO VERT. and NO HORIZ. *
AMALGamate.	yes	At each step in the clustering process print the mean of each variable in the cluster just formed, a table of the amalgamation distance and the sum of the case weights and averages. *
SHADE.	yes	Print the distance matrix in shaded form. Overprinting is used to produce the shaded symbols (see NCUT below). *
NCUT = 5 or 8.	8.	If overprinting is not available (e.g., on a terminal), specify both SHADE. and NCUT = 5. for shading. *
LINEsize = #.	132.	Number of columns permitted for printing (shaded) correlation or (shaded) distance matrix on narrow page size.
LIMIT = #.	no limit	Upper limit to intervals for shading.
SORT.	SORT.	Print sorted and shaded distances. *
HIST.	no	Print histogram of distances. *

Key:

/	–indicates paragraph	*	–assigned value remains the same for additional problems
.	–period ends a sentence		
●	–required	VT	–number of variables after transformations
v	–variable (name or subscript)	list	–more than one item, often one per var.
g	–group (name or subscript)		
#	–number	Capitalized letters–paragraph or sentence names recognized by BMDP	
'c'	–characters (name or parameter) may omit apostrophes if contiguous letters only	Page numbers following refer to this Manual	

PKM

17.3 K-Means Clustering

Laszlo Engelman
J. A. Hartigan

ABSTRACT

PKM partitions a set of cases (observations) into clusters. At the completion of the run each case belongs to the cluster whose center is closest to the case. The Euclidean distance is used to measure the distance between each case and the center of each cluster (mean of cases in the cluster). The data can be standardized four ways or left in original form -- making five distance measures available. The program begins with user-specified clusters or with all the data in one cluster and splits one cluster into two clusters at each step. When the requested number of clusters is reached, cases are iteratively reallocated into the cluster whose center is closest. You may specify initial cluster centers or use an indicator variable to identify initial cluster membership. More than one number can be specified for k (the number of clusters) so that results are obtained for several values of k. Cases can be classified whether or not they are used in the cluster computations (i.e., they have WEIGHT = 0 in the analysis). An indicator variable that identifies the final clusters can be saved with the data in a BMDP File. Output includes a description of each variable for each cluster -- the mean, minimum, maximum and variance; the distance of the cluster center to each case, and histograms displaying the distances for cases in a cluster and cases not in a cluster; a scatter plot of the orthogonal projection of cases into the plane defined by the centers of the three most populous clusters; for each variable a summary of the cluster means and standard deviations and an analysis of variance with descriptive F-ratio that compares the between-cluster mean square to the within-cluster square; and a cluster profile -- a graphical display for each cluster that shows the mean of each variable relative to the overall mean, and marks the center plus or minus one standard deviation.

Example KM.1 Basic Setup for K-Means Clustering

The data in this example are health indicators for 11 countries (see Table 17.2): the relative number of doctors and dentists, pharmacists, nurses, and hospital beds per unit of population, the percent of animal fat and starch in the diet, and the life expectancy in each country.

The instructions in the PROBLEM, INPUT and VARIABLE paragraphs are common to all programs and are explained in Chapter 5. Note that the names of the countries are input as two A format variables for use as labels for the cases in the output. In the CLUSTER paragraph we request three clusters. This instruction is not required; if omitted, the program would classify the 11 countries into 5 clusters. Because the data are recorded in different scales (e.g., number of pharmacists and percent of starch) we divide each variable by its standard deviation (STANDARDIZE IS VAR.). If this instruction is omitted, the data are not standardized. Our instructions are:

```
/ PROBLEM     TITLE IS 'HEALTH INDICATORS'.
/ INPUT       VARIABLES ARE 9.
              FORMAT IS '(2A4, 4F6.2, 3F3.0)'.
/ VARIABLE    NAMES ARE COUNTRY1, COUNTRY2, DOCDEN,
                  PHARM, NURSE, HOSPBEDS,
                  ANIMAL, STARCH, LIFEEXP.
              LABELS ARE COUNTRY1, COUNTRY2.

/ CLUSTER     NUMBER IS 3.
              STANDARDIZE IS VAR.

/ PLOT        SIZE IS 40, 25.

/ END
```

(See end of this PKM section for organization of systems information, BMDP instructions and data.)

The results are shown in Output KM.1. Circled numbers below correspond to those in the output. The results printed in ①, ② and ③ are printed for each cluster for each value of k. The remaining results are printed for the largest value of k.

① For each cluster two histograms display the distance from the cluster center to each case: a) for cases in the cluster, and, b) for cases not in the cluster. The digits in the display indicate the cluster assignment for each case. The scale for each pair of histograms is set to cover the maximum distance from that cluster center.

② The cases in cluster 1 are listed with their weight and distance from the center of cluster 1. When case labels are not used, the case number is printed. The average distance for cases in cluster 1 is also printed.

③ The program computes univariate statistics using the standardized data from the three countries in cluster 1: the center (mean), standard deviation and minimum and maximum values.

Output KM.1 K-means cluster analysis of health indicators. Circled numbers correspond to those in the text

----

--- the BMDP instructions are printed and interpreted ---

CLUSTER 1 OF 3 CONTAINS   3 CASES
===================================== ①
    STATISTICS ARE COMPUTED FROM THE STANDARDIZED DATA

            1   1 1   (a)
DISTANCE +.........+.........+.........+.........+.........+.........+.........+.........+.........+.........+
FROM CENTER TO CASES IN THIS CLUSTER   3.5000   7.0000

                             2   (b)
                 2   2 2   2   2   3   2
DISTANCE +.........+.........+.........+.........+.........+.........+.........+.........+.........+.........+
FROM CENTER TO CASES IN OTHER CLUSTERS   3.5000   7.0000

C A S E   WEIGHT DISTANCE   I   VARIABLE   MINIMUM   CENTER   MAXIMUM   ST.DEV.
-------------------------   I --
SYRIA   1.0000   1.5064   I   3 DOCDNT   1.1331   1.7085   2.1546   0.5229
TURKEY   1.0000   0.6877   I   4 PHARM   1.1697   1.7648   2.6882   0.8108
U.A.R.   1.0000   1.6138   I   5 NURSES   0.9868   2.1145   3.2000   1.1072
     ②   I   6 HOSPBEDS 1.2349   1.8143   2.3626   0.5645
                               I   7 ANIMAL   2.1799   2.4593   2.6829   0.2561   ③
                               I   8 STARCH   8.9675   9.2275   9.4874   0.2599
                               I   9 LIFEEXP   8.6573   8.9348   9.1567   0.2543

AVERAGE DISTANCE   1.2693

CLUSTER 2 OF 3 CONTAINS   7 CASES
=====================================
    STATISTICS ARE COMPUTED FROM THE STANDARDIZED DATA

             2   2   2 2   2   2   2
DISTANCE +.........+.........+.........+.........+.........+.........+.........+.........+.........+.........+
FROM CENTER TO CASES IN THIS CLUSTER   2.5000   5.0000

                               1   1 1   3
DISTANCE +.........+.........+.........+.........+.........+.........+.........+.........+.........+.........+
FROM CENTER TO CASES IN OTHER CLUSTERS   2.5000   5.0000

C A S E   WEIGHT DISTANCE   I   VARIABLE   MINIMUM   CENTER   MAXIMUM   ST.DEV.
-------------------------   I --
IRAN   1.0000   1.7081   I   3 DOCDNT   0.4193   1.4867   4.1620   1.2564
IRAQ   1.0000   1.1302   I   4 PHARM   0.5335   1.7062   3.9400   1.1722
JORDAN   1.0000   1.3758   I   5 NURSES   1.6423   2.4397   4.3136   1.1764
LEBANON   1.0000   4.6609   I   6 HOSPBEDS 1.1818   2.5017   4.3227   1.1410
LIBYA   1.0000   2.3137   I   7 ANIMAL   3.5213   4.2639   5.8689   0.8149
MOROCCO   1.0000   2.1473   I   8 STARCH   6.3683   7.1480   7.7979   0.5252
TUNISIA   1.0000   1.8280   I   9 LIFEEXP   8.4908   9.0378   9.9892   0.5240

AVERAGE DISTANCE   2.1663

(output continued)

465

Output KM.1 (continued)

```
    CLUSTER  3 OF  3 CONTAINS    1 CASES
    ====================================
      STATISTICS ARE COMPUTED FROM THE STANDARDIZED DATA


           3
DISTANCE +........+........+........+........+........+........+........+........+........+........+........+
FROM CENTER TO CASES IN THIS CLUSTER                  4.0000                                        8.0000


                                                  2
                                     2    2  22 2  11    1                          2
DISTANCE +........+........+........+........+........+........+........+........+........+........+........+
FROM CENTER TO CASES IN OTHER CLUSTERS                4.0000                                        8.0000


  C A S E     WEIGHT  DISTANCE   I   VARIABLE   MINIMUM   CENTER   MAXIMUM   ST.DEV.
-----------------------------    I  -------------------------------------------------
  ALGERIA     1.0000    -0.0     I   3 DOCDNT    0.5755   0.5755   0.5755    0.0
                                 I   4 PHARM     0.4720   0.4720   0.4720    0.0
                                 I   5 NURSES    2.4669   2.4669   2.4669    0.0
                                 I   6 HOSPBEDS  3.6017   3.6017   3.6017    0.0
                                 I   7 ANIMAL    3.5213   3.5213   3.5213    0.0
                                 I   8 STARCH    7.4080   7.4080   7.4080    0.0
                                 I   9 LIFEEXP   5.8270   5.8270   5.8270    0.0


-----------------------------
  AVERAGE DISTANCE     0.0
```

④ A scatter plot of the orthogonal projection of cases into the plane defined by the centers of the three most populous clusters.

⑤ Cluster means (centers), and within-cluster standard deviations, computed from data in the original scale.

⑥ Analysis of variance of each variable, comparing the between-cluster mean square to the within-cluster mean square. The F-ratios should be used to describe differences between the variable rather than to test significance: that is, the groups are obtained empirically.

⑦ Cluster profile plots: for each cluster the mean for each variable is marked by a numeral (e.g., 2 for cluster 2) and ±1 standard deviation by dashed lines. Vertical lines connecting the asterisks above and below each cluster display indicate the location of the grand mean.

⑧ Pooled within-cluster covariance and correlation matrices.

Specifying the number of clusters. The NUMBER instruction in the CLUSTER paragraph is used to specify the number of clusters (k). The number of specified clusters is obtained by splitting a cluster into two clusters at each step and iteratively reallocating cases followed by recomputing the statistics and standardizations until k clusters are formed. If NUMBER is not specified, five clusters are formed. If more than one value is given for NUMBER, results are printed for each value. For example, if

            NUMB = 4, 7, 8.

is specified, the clustering results are printed for k = 4, 7 and 8 when the number of initial clusters is less than or equal to 4. (Methods for specifying

REPORT ON CASES WITH POSITIVE WEIGHT

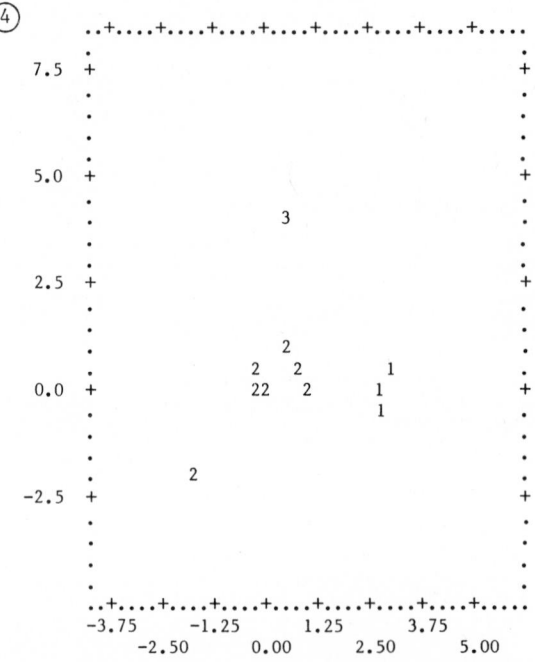

PROJECTION INTO PLANE THROUGH THE CENTERS O

(output continued)

```
CLUSTER   MEANS
--------------
              DOCDNT    PHARM    NURSES   HOSPBEDS   ANIMAL    STARCH    LIFEEXP

   1          3.8300    0.8600   3.0000   17.0867   14.6667   71.0000   53.6667      (5)
   2          3.3329    0.8314   3.4614   23.5600   25.4285   55.0000   54.2857
   3          1.2900    0.2300   3.5000   33.9200   21.0000   57.0000   35.0000

GRAND MEAN    3.2827    0.7845   3.3391   22.7363   22.0909   59.5454   52.3636


CLUSTER   STANDARD DEVIATIONS
-----------------------------
              DOCDNT    PHARM    NURSES   HOSPBEDS   ANIMAL    STARCH    LIFEEXP

   1          0.9571    0.3226   1.2826    4.3406    1.2472    1.6330    1.2472       (6)
   2          2.6076    0.5289   1.5452    9.9481    4.4994    3.7417    2.9137
   3          0.0       0.0      0.0       0.0       0.0       0.0       0.0

MEAN SQUARES
  BETWEEN     2.4435    0.1700   0.2378  112.7889  122.2632  272.3643  166.2253
  WITHIN      6.2934    0.2838   2.7061   93.6598   18.2976   13.2500    8.0119

  D.F.-S      2,  8     2,  8    2,  8     2,  8     2,  8     2,  8     2,  8

  F-RATIO     0.388     0.599    0.088     1.204     6.682    20.556    20.747

  P-VALUE     0.765     0.633    0.965     0.369     0.014     0.000     0.000


CLUSTER PROFILES - VARIABLES ARE ORDERED BY F-RATIO SIZE      (7)
--------------------------------------------------------

                         *                        *                        *
LIFEEXP                 -1                       -2-                     3
STARCH                    1-                    —2—                    3
ANIMAL             1-                            ÷-2--                    3
HOSPBEDS            --1—                    ------2-----             3
PHARM               ---÷1-----             --------2--------         3
DOCDNT               -÷-1----              ---------2--------       3
NURSES     ----------------1------------      -------------------2--------------------        3
                         *                        *                        *
```

EACH COLUMN DESCRIBES A CLUSTER .
THE CLUSTER NUMBER IS PRINTED AT THE MEAN OF EACH VARIABLE
DASHES INDICATE ONE STANDARD DEVIATION ABOVE AND BELOW

```
POOLED WITHIN CLUSTER COVARIANCES
---------------------------------
              DOCDNT    PHARM    NURSES   HOSPBEDS   ANIMAL    STARCH    LIFEEXP        (8)
                 3        4        5         6          7         8         9

DOCDNT     3    6.29
PHARM      4    1.17     0.28
NURSES     5    2.90     0.38     2.71
HOSPBEDS   6   16.27     2.07    12.41     93.66
ANIMAL     7    9.80     1.89     3.51     22.75      18.30
STARCH     8   -4.21    -0.73    -0.95    -12.72      -7.63     13.25
LIFEEXP    9    5.59     0.67     3.78     24.04       8.98     -4.12      8.01


POOLED WITHIN CLUSTER CORRELATIONS
----------------------------------
              DOCDNT    PHARM    NURSES   HOSPBEDS   ANIMAL    STARCH    LIFEEXP
                 3        4        5         6          7         8         9

DOCDNT     3    1.0000
PHARM      4    0.8757   1.0000
NURSES     5    0.7039   0.4304   1.0000
HOSPBEDS   6    0.6702   0.4017   0.7793    1.0000
ANIMAL     7    0.9134   0.8276   0.4986    0.5495     1.0000
STARCH     8   -0.4610  -0.3784  -0.1578   -0.3611    -0.4897    1.0000
LIFEEXP    9    0.7868   0.4425   0.8109    0.8777     0.7414   -0.4004    1.0000
```

initial clusters are explained below.) If there are 5, 6 or 7 clusters initially, results are printed for k = 7 and 8. If there are 8 clusters initially, reports are not given for k = 4 and 7. The final report (④ through ⑧) is printed for only the largest k.

The NUMBER instruction also controls the reallocation of cases. In the first example above the cases would be reallocated to the closest center when k = 4, 7 or 8. Using NUMB = 8, reallocation occurs only when k = 8. The instructions NUMB = 4, 7, 8. and NUMB = 8. may produce different cluster results. You may want to request reallocation for each value of k by stating NUMB = 2 to 8; however, this can be expensive since reallocation is an iterative computation.

```
CLUSTer ─────────────────────────────────────────
  NUMBer = # list.                                5
    Report results and reallocate cases for the
    number of clusters indicated by (#). Final
    report is also printed for largest cluster
    number.
 ──────────────────────────────────────────────────
```

Standardizing the data (selecting the distance measure). Cluster centers and distances can be computed from the raw data or from standardized data. The effect of standardization is to change the definition of the distance measure. Each variable can be standardized univariately by using its standard deviation (computed for the complete sample or within each cluster); or the data can be transformed using the covariance matrix (computed from the complete sample or the pooled within-cluster covariance matrix.) These last two are forms of the Mahalanobis distance measure. More specifically, the distance squared d_{ij}^2 of case i and cluster j is

$$d_{ij}^2 = \frac{1}{p}(x_i - c_j) M^{-1} (x_i - c_j)'$$

where

$x_i = (x_{i1}, x_{i2}, \ldots, x_{ip})$ designates case i

$c_j = (c_{j1}, c_{j2}, \ldots, c_{jp})$ designates the center of cluster j.

The five distance measures are

NONE   M is the identity matrix with ones on the diagonal and zeroes elsewhere. This is the Euclidean distance

VAR   M is a diagonal matrix with variances along the diagonal: each variable is divided by its standard deviation

WVAR   M is a diagonal matrix with pooled within-cluster variances: each variable is divided by its pooled within-cluster standard deviation

COV   M is the covariance matrix

WCOV   M is the pooled within-cluster covariance matrix

The WVAR and WCOV methods are similar to VAR and COV

respectively, except the standardization changes at each stage of the clustering.

```
CLUSTer ─────────────────────────────────────────
  STANDard = (one only)                   NONE/prev.
        NONE, VAR, COV, WVAR, WCOV.
    Standardization of data. The data can be
    standardized to

    NONE -- no standardization
    VAR  -- unit variance
    COV  -- unit covariance
    WVAR -- unit within-cluster variance
    WCOV -- unit within-cluster covariance
 ──────────────────────────────────────────────────
```

Example KM.2 Suppressing Cluster Descriptions and Requesting Distances and PLOTS

We add the following statements to the BMDP instructions of Example KM.1 before the END paragraph:

```
----------------------------------------
  / PRINT  NO MEMBERS.
           DISTANCES.

  / PLOT   SIZE IS 40,25.
           XVAR IS LIFEEXP.
           YVAR IS STARCH.
----------------------------------------
```

The results are shown in Output KM.2.

⑨ The list of cluster members and the within-cluster statistics are not printed. The histograms of the distances from cluster centers are printed.

⑩ The matrix of distances between cluster centers (means) is printed.

⑪ In the scatter plot of STARCH vs. LIFEEXP, numbers indicate the cluster membership for each point. We select these two variables because the p-values in ⑥ indicate that they have large between-cluster differences.

Print control. The PRINT paragraph is used to specify additional results. You can specify the number of input CASES for printing and the DISTANCES between cluster centers. The distance between cluster i and j is

$$\sqrt{(c_i - c_j) M^{-1} (c_i - c_j)'}$$

where c and M are defined above (the Data Standardization section).

The list of cluster members and within-cluster statistics (② and ③) can be suppressed by stating NO MEMBER. This is useful when the sample size is large.

If you suspect that final cluster membership is summarized by a variable with 10 or fewer categories, you can request PKM to verify this by CROSSTABULATING the variable (or variables) with the final cluster membership. The CROSSTAB variables may be different from those used to determine the cluster.

Output KM.2   Printing distances between cluster centers and plots that identify cluster membership

----

```
CLUSTER  1 OF  3 CONTAINS    3 CASES            ⑨
=====================================
   STATISTICS ARE COMPUTED FROM THE STANDARDIZED DATA

                 1          1 1
DISTANCE +.........+.........+.........+.........+.........+.........+.........+.........+.........+.........+
FROM CENTER TO CASES IN THIS CLUSTER                    3.5000                                  7.0000

                                                 2
                                 2       2 2     2       2       3                           2
DISTANCE +.........+.........+.........+.........+.........+.........+.........+.........+.........+.........+
FROM CENTER TO CASES IN OTHER CLUSTERS                  3.5000                                  7.0000
```

```
CLUSTER  2 OF  3 CONTAINS    7 CASES
=====================================
   STATISTICS ARE COMPUTED FROM THE STANDARDIZED DATA

                         2    2    2 2    2   2                                       2
DISTANCE +.........+.........+.........+.........+.........+.........+.........+.........+.........+.........+
FROM CENTER TO CASES IN THIS CLUSTER                    2.5000                                  5.0000

                                                 1        1   1        3
DISTANCE +.........+.........+.........+.........+.........+.........+.........+.........+.........+.........+
FROM CENTER TO CASES IN OTHER CLUSTERS                  2.5000                                  5.0000
```

```
CLUSTER  3 OF  3 CONTAINS    1 CASES
=====================================
   STATISTICS ARE COMPUTED FROM THE STANDARDIZED DATA

       3
DISTANCE +.........+.........+.........+.........+.........+.........+.........+.........+.........+.........+
FROM CENTER TO CASES IN THIS CLUSTER                    4.0000                                  8.0000

                                                 2
                                 2       2 22 2  11    1                              2
DISTANCE +.........+.........+.........+.........+.........+.........+.........+.........+.........+.........+
FROM CENTER TO CASES IN OTHER CLUSTERS                  4.0000                                  8.0000
```

```
          DISTANCES BETWEEN CLUSTER CENTERS

               1         2                    ⑩
     2      2.86740
     3      4.51338    3.80694
```

(output continued)

Output KM.2 (continued)

REPORT ON CASES WITH POSITIVE WEIGHT

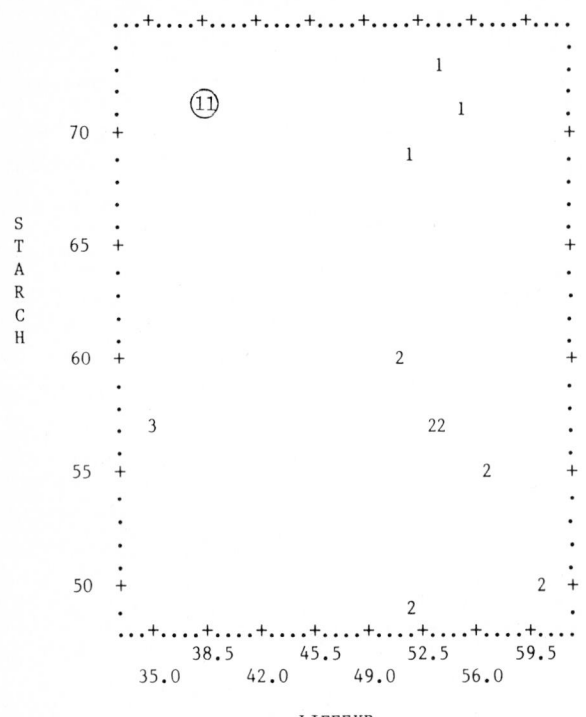

LIFEEXP

--- ⑤ to ⑧ in Output KM.1 appear here ---

PRINT ────────────────────────────────────
CASES = #.   10
  The number of cases for which data (after
  transformation) are printed.
MEMBer.   yes
  Stating NO MEMB. suppresses the printing of the
  within-cluster statistics and the list of
  cluster members.
DISTance.   no
  Requests printing of the distance matrix
  between cluster centers.
CROSStabulate = list.   none
  Names or indices of variables against which the
  final cluster membership is crosstabulated. The
  variable(s) can have no more than 10 distinct
  values and need not be one of the variables
  used for clustering.

PLOTS. Numbers indicating final cluster
membership can be plotted for each case in a
bivariate scatter plot. The user specifies a
variable for the x-axis (XVAR) and for the y-axis
(YVAR). This feature allows verification that the
greatest cluster separation occurs for a pair of
variables (we selected those with the smallest
p-values in ⑥).

The preassigned plot is one formed by projecting
the cases onto a plane through the centers of the
three largest clusters. This plot can be suppressed
by stating NO CLUSTER. The user also has control
over the SIZE of this plot.

PLOT ─────────────────────────────────────
XVAR = v.   none
  Name or index of the variable to plot on the
  horizontal axis. This variable need not be in
  the VAR USE list.
YVAR = v.   none
  Name or index of the variable to plot on the
  vertical axis. This variable need not be in the
  VAR USE list.

Note: Both XVAR and YVAR must be stated in order
to use variables as axes.

CLUSTer.   yes
  The scatter plot is printed unless NO CLUSTER
  is specified.
SIZE = #, #.   100,45
  The first number is the width (characters) and
  the second number is the height (lines). When
  comparable scales on the horizontal and
  vertical axes are desired, both the range of
  each variable and the printer spacings should
  be considered (on many printers there are 10
  characters/inch horizontally and 6 or 8
  lines/inch vertically).

Three Ways to Specify Initial Clusters

The preassigned starting point for PKM is to
assign all cases to the first cluster and to assume
that the number of initial clusters is 1. However,
if you know some information about the clusters, you
can speed up the algorithm by telling the program.
Three methods are available to do this:

MEMBER   A variable in the data file contains a
         code for each case indicating initial
         membership.
CENTER   Case numbers are listed for cases that
         define the initial cluster centers.
SEED   Coordinates in the variable space are
         specified for each cluster center. (The
         instruction is repeated with a list of
         coordinates for each center.)

When the MEMBERSHIP method is used, the initial
number of clusters is the largest value of the
variable. When the NUMBER of clusters is specified,
the MEMBERSHIP variable should not contain codes
larger than the maximum k. Cases with negative codes
or zero and cases with codes greater than the
largest k are initially placed in the first cluster.
If CENTERS are stated, cases are allocated to the
closest center and the number of initial clusters is
the number of centers stated.
The SEED method is useful when you know
approximately where each cluster center is located.
List the approximate value of the within-cluster
mean for each variable in the same order as the
variables. SEED = 3, 5, 4. and SEED = 1, 1, 1.
specify two centers in a 3-variable space. That is,

470

for the first cluster center, the first variable has a mean of 3; the second variable, a mean of 5; and the third variable, a mean of 4. In the second cluster, all three variables have mean 1.

```
CLUSter ─────────────────────────────────────
   SEED = # list.                        none
     Value or coordinate of each variable that
     specifies one cluster's initial center. Repeat
     for each cluster.
   CENTer = # list.                      none
     Cases (case numbers) that are used as initial
     cluster centers. These cases may not be
     deleted.
   MEMBer = v.                           none
     Name or index of the initial cluster
     membership-indicator variable. If this variable
     is less than one or greater than the number of
     clusters to be produced, or is missing, the
     corresponding case is initially placed in
     cluster number 1. If an initial cluster
     membership-indicator variable is not given, all
     cases are initially placed in cluster number 1.
```

Incomplete Data

PKM, unlike most multivariate procedures, allows cases with incomplete data when standardization options NONE, VAR or WVAR are used. Cluster centers, variances and distances are computed using all values that are present. Thus the mean and standard deviation for one variable in a cluster may be computed using a different number of values than those used for another variable. The contribution of a missing value to the square of the distance is the average of the contributions of the nonmissing values.

The maximum number of missing values allowed per case can be controlled using the MMV statement in the VARIABLE paragraph. The count of missing values includes cases with values listed under MISS and outside the MIN and MAX limits stated in the VARIABLE paragraph (values outside acceptable range limits are considered missing). The preassigned limit for missing values per case is one-half the number of variables used. When COV and WCOV standardizations are requested, MMV is set to zero, i.e., only complete cases are used.

```
VARiable ────────────────────────────────────
   MMV = #.              (number of variables used)/2
     Maximum number of missing values or values out
     of range. MMV is set to zero for STAND = COV or
     WCOV. Cases exceeding the MMV limit are not
     used in the analysis.
```

Case Weights and Automatic Zero Weights in Large Samples

The computations assume a weight of one for each case, unless a WEIGHT variable is specified in the VARIABLE paragraph (i.e., a variable in the data file contains a weight for each case). If a case weight is specified, only cases with positive weight

are used in the cluster center computations. Cases with zero weight are assigned to the final cluster centers. The cases with positive weight are plotted as in ④ of Output KM.1. The cases with zero weight are then plotted in a separate frame with the same scale.

During the cluster computations, cases with positive weight are stored in computer memory. When the number of cases with positive weight exceeds the available space, the remaining cases (after the memory is filled) are assigned zero weight. To increase the available memory space see Appendix B.

A random subsample (see Chapter 6) is also useful for a large file: transformations are used to randomly assign a weight of one to some cases and a weight of zero to others.

```
VARiable ────────────────────────────────────
   WEIGHT = v.                           none
     Index of the variable containing weights for
     each case. This variable is not used in the
     distance calculations.
```

Saving a Final Cluster Membership Indicator in a BMDP File

A variable containing the final cluster membership is added to the data for each case when a BMDP File is made. The variable named CLUSTER is added after the last input variable (or variable created through transformation). Cases with zero weight will also be included in the file with their cluster membership code. See Chapter 7 for information on BMDP Files.

```
SAVE ─────────────────────────────────────────
   CONTENT = DATA.                       DATA.
     The cluster membership variable is stored as a
     new variable after the data for each case. The
     new variable is named CLUSTER.
```

SIZE OF PROBLEM

PKM stores the data in computer memory. On medium-sized computer systems, with 10 variables the program can process approximately 450 cases into 10 clusters in 15,000 storage words. A more exact formula is given in Appendix B.

COMPUTATIONAL METHOD

The computational procedure is described in Appendix A.

ACKNOWLEDGEMENT

PKM was designed by John Hartigan and Laszlo Engelman, and programmed by William Eddy and Laszlo Engelman. Supported in part by NSF Contract MCS-7906218, Yale University.

SUMMARY

Order of Input Cards

```
// (job card)
// EXEC BIMED,PROG=BMDPKM          (see Appendix E)
//SYSIN DD *
/ PROBLEM
/ INPUT
/ VARIABLE
/ TRANSFORM
/ SAVE
/ CLUSTER
/ PRINT
/ END
     (data, if on cards)
// (system card)
```

Full sets of BMDP paragraphs (and data, if on cards) can be repeated for additional problems; see Section 5.8.

instructions specific to PKM

Paragraph Statement	Preassigned	Comment and Manual Reference
/ VARiable		Additional options specified. 471
WEIGHT = v.	none	Name or subscript of variable containing a weight for each case. Cases with zero weight are not used in the computations, but they are classified.
MMV = #.	(var. used)/2	Maximum number of missing values or values out of range. 471
/ CLUSTer		Optional to direct clustering. Begins with all the data in cluster 1 unless you specify initial cluster centers using SEED, CENTER or MEMB.
NUMBer = # list.	5.	Results are reported for each number in list. Final report is also printed for largest cluster number. 468
SEED = # list.	none	Values of the variables (coordinates) that are used for initial centers. Repeat SEED for each cluster. List value for each variable in the same order given in FORMAT (or USE) statement. 471
CENTER = # list.	none	Variable values for the cases that define initial cluster centers. Values for the first listed case define the first cluster, etc. 471
MEMBer = v.	none	Name or index of initial-cluster membership indicator variable. If the value of this variable is missing or outside the range 1 to k, the case is initially placed in cluster 1. 471
STANDard = c.	NONE	Method for standardizing the data; affects how the distance is measured. If the variables are measured in units that differ greatly the user should consider standardizing the data. WCOV yields the Mahalanobis distance, COV is similar, but uses the overall matrix instead of the pooled-within-covariance matrix (one only). * 468 NONE - no standardization VAR - unit variance (the value for each variable divided by the standard deviation of the variable) COV - unit covariance matrix WVAR - unit within-cluster variance WCOV - unit within-cluster covariance
/ PRINT		Optional to direct printing. 470
CASES = #.	none	The number of cases to be printed after transformation. *
DISTance.	no	Print the distances between cluster centers. Note: the method of standardizing affects distances. *
CROSStab = v list.	none	Names or subscripts of variables crosstabulated against final cluster membership for each case. The values of the CROSS variables should be categorical with up to 10 distinct values. (CUTP cannot be used to split variables into categories.) *
MEMBer.	yes	Cluster membership and within cluster statistics. To negate state NO MEMBER.

(continued)

(continued)

Paragraph Statement	Preassigned	Comment and Manual Reference
/ PLOT		See p. 470.
CLUSTer	yes	**Prints scatter plot. To negate, state NO CLUSTER.**
SIZE = #,#.	100,45	The width and height of the scatter plot.
XVAR = v.	none	Variable to be used as x-axis.
YVAR = v.	none	Variable to be used as y-axis.
/ SAVE		Additional paragraph required only if a BMDP File is created. The cluster membership variable is stored as a new variable after the data for each case. The new variable is named CLUSTER. 471

Key:

/	-indicates paragraph	*	-assigned value remains the same for additional problems
.	-period ends a sentence		
●	-required	VT	-number of variables after transformations
v	-variable (name or subscript)	list	-more than one item, often one per var.
g	-group (name or subscript)		
#	-number	Capitalized letters-paragraph or sentence names recognized by BMDP
'c'	-characters (name or parameter) may omit apostrophes if contiguous letters only		
		Page numbers following refer to this Manual

P3M

17.4 Block Clustering

John Hartigan
Laszlo Engelman

ABSTRACT

P3M constructs block clusters for categorical data. Each block is defined by a cluster of cases and a cluster of variables such that each variable in the block is constant over the cases in the block, except for cases that also belong to other blocks. (Blocks may overlap.) The constant value taken by a variable in a block is called the <u>modal value</u> for that block. The goal of the program is succinct representation of the data by a few large blocks with corresponding block modal values, together with residual single blocks consisting of single values deviating from the appropriate block modal value. The data matrix is printed in a block symbol matrix with each block identified by a different symbol, and the single blocks identified by a code for the corresponding value. The rows and columns are reordered so that each block is as nearly contiguous as possible. Given this output and a table of block modal values, all values in the data matrix may be recovered.

Blocks are evaluated by the block count, computed as the count of block modal values in the block (different for each variable), less the number of variables in the block. In a successful block clustering, the total block count should be a high proportion of the total number of data values.

Note: This program has been available as Q3M. In the 1983 release, it replaces the previous version of P3M (as described in the 1981 BMDP Statistical Software Manual). If you are using a version of P3M dated before 1983, use the description in the 1981 manual, or write to BMDP and request a copy of this previous description.

WHERE TO FIND IT

Example 3M.1 Basic Setup for Block Clustering

Consider the dentition of North American mammals (Hartigan, 1976). We can expect clusters of mammals (rabbit, gopher, and mouse) and clusters of teeth types (number of top and bottom canines), so block clustering may be effective.

The variables are

TINC	Number of top incisors
BINC	Number of bottom incisors
TCAN	Number of top canines
BCAN	Number of bottom canines
TPRM	Number of top premolars
BPRM	Number of bottom premolars
TMOL	Number of top molars
BMOL	Number of bottom molars

The PROBLEM, INPUT, and VARIABLE paragraphs are common to all programs and are explained in Chapter 5. The names of the mammals are read as the variable ANIMAL, which is specified as a label variable. (Eight-character names may be accommodated, using two label variables.)

Table 17.4 Mammal dentition

Number of teeth of various types

OPOS	5	4	1	1	3	3	4	4
SHRW	3	1	1	1	3	1	3	3
GSHW	3	2	1	0	1	1	3	3
MSHW	3	3	1	1	2	2	3	3
MOLE	3	3	1	1	4	4	3	3
LBAT	2	2	1	1	2	3	3	3
TBAT	2	0	1	1	2	3	3	3
MBAT	2	3	1	1	3	3	3	3
SBAT	2	3	1	1	2	3	3	3
PBAT	2	3	1	1	2	2	3	3
BBAT	2	3	1	1	1	2	3	3
RBAT	1	3	1	1	2	2	3	3
ABAT	1	2	1	1	1	2	3	3
PBAT	1	2	1	1	2	2	3	3
RABT	2	1	0	0	3	2	3	3
SQRL	1	1	0	0	2	1	3	3
GPHR	1	1	0	0	1	1	3	3
MOVS	1	1	0	0	0	0	3	3
JMOV	1	1	0	0	1	0	3	3
WOLF	3	3	1	1	4	4	2	3
RACC	3	3	1	1	4	4	2	2
MART	3	3	1	1	4	4	1	2
MINK	3	3	1	1	3	3	1	2
ROTT	3	3	1	1	4	3	1	2
SOTT	3	2	1	1	3	3	1	2
LION	3	3	1	1	3	2	1	1
LYNX	3	3	1	1	2	2	1	1
FSEL	3	2	1	1	4	4	2	1
SLIN	3	2	1	1	4	4	1	1
ELK	0	3	1	1	3	3	3	3
DEER	0	3	0	1	3	3	3	3
GOAT	0	3	0	1	3	4	3	3

```
/ PROBLEM     TITLE = 'MAMMAL DENTITION'.

/ INPUT       VAR = 9.
              FORMAT = '(A4, 8F1.0)'.

/ VARIABLE    NAME = ANIMAL, TINC, BINC, TCAN, BCAN,
              TPRM, BPRM, TMOL, BMOL.
              LABEL = 1.

/ BLOCK       NUMBER = 10.

/ END
```

The results of the block clustering are presented in Output 3M.1.

① Number of cases read.

② Code for each variable. The program operates on categorical data. Each variable may have at most ten distinct values. (Interval scale variables may be converted into categorical variables using a number of operators. See Example 3M.2.) The values taken by each variable are recoded into the range 0, 1, 2, ..., 9; if more than ten different values are taken by all variables together, each variable is recoded separately. Here all variables take values 0, 1, 2, 3, 4, 5 and no recoding is necessary.

③ The minimum number of rows in a block is 2. To alter this preassigned value, use ROWMIN option in the BLOCK paragraph of the setup (e.g., "ROWMIN = 3.").

④ The minimum number of columns in a block is 2. To alter this preassigned value, state, e.g., "COLMIN = 3." in the BLOCK paragraph of the setup.

⑤ NUMBER, the maximum number of blocks to appear in the output, is 10. Less than this number might appear because no more blocks can be found that satisfy the ROWMIN and COLMIN constraints.

⑥ If "REFINE." is stated in the BLOCK paragraph, then the blocks are readjusted after each new block is constructed. Use this for the final product, after exploratory studies are done. It produces slightly better blocks at some cost in computation.

⑦ Code frequencies give the frequency distribution for each recoded variable.

⑧ The block matrix identifies the blocks by block symbols. The preassigned block symbols are '.', '-', '+', '=', 'A', 'B', etc. The largest block is set blank so that the remaining blocks may be easily seen. Each single block is identified by the code for the values that define it. For example, the shrew (SHRW) deviates from the modal values for the standard cluster for mammals ( ) for only two variables: BINC and BPRM. Since no other case shares this pattern, it defines a single block.

⑨ Block counts and values. The block count for a particular block is the number of block symbols minus the number of variables in the block. For example, the block symbol (+) appears in the block matrix ten times, and there are two variables in the block (TCAN and BCAN). Hence, the block count for (+) is eight. The block count indicates the size of the block. A good clustering is one where the total block count is a substantial fraction of the total number of data values.

The modal values for each block permit recovery of the original data. Consider, for example, the cluster of carnivores (-). The modal values are 442 for premolars top and bottom, and for the top molar. Thus, the carnivores are characterized by these deviations from the standard 333 pattern for mammals ( ). Similarly, the rodent (+) cluster is characterized by absence of canines.

In general, the larger clusters are stable, appearing for almost all choices of the block formation parameters, and the smaller clusters are less stable, varying with the block parameters. The B cluster here should probably be ignored.

Example 3M.2 Interval Scale Variables

This example uses data on health indicators for 11 countries (see Table 17.2). The following variables are used:

DOCDNT	number of doctors per 100,000
PHARM	number of pharmacists per 100,000
NURSES	number of nurses per 100,000
HOSPBED	number of hospital beds per 100,000
ANIMAL	percent animal fat in diet
STARCH	percent starch in diet
LIFEEXP	life expectancy in years

```
/ PROBLEM     TITLE IS 'HEALTH INDICATORS'.

/ INPUT       VAR = 9.
              FORMAT = '(2A4, 4F6.0, 3F3.0)'.

/ VARIABLE    NAME = COUNTRY1, COUNTRY2, DOCDNT,
              PHARM, NURSE, HOSPBED, ANIMAL,
              STARCH, LIFEEXP.
              LABEL = COUNTRY1, COUNTRY2.

/ CATEGORY    CUTPT(1) =    200,400.
              CUTPT(2) =     50,100.
              CUTPT(3) =    250,500.
              CUTPT(4) =  1500,3000.
              CUTPT(5) =     20,25
              CUTPT(6) =     55,65.

/ BLOCK       START = 2.

/ END
```

Output 3M.1 Block clustering. Circled numbers correspond to those in the text

----

NUMBER OF CASES READ.   32   ①

```
        C O D E   F O R   E A C H   V A R I A B L E                              ②
                    0       1       2       3       4       5
TINC    REAL      0.0    1.00    2.00    3.00    4.00    5.00
BINC    REAL      0.0    1.00    2.00    3.00    4.00    5.00
TCAN    REAL      0.0    1.00    2.00    3.00    4.00    5.00
BCAN    REAL      0.0    1.00    2.00    3.00    4.00    5.00
TPRM    REAL      0.0    1.00    2.00    3.00    4.00    5.00
BPRM    REAL      0.0    1.00    2.00    3.00    4.00    5.00
TMOL    REAL      0.0    1.00    2.00    3.00    4.00    5.00
BMOL    REAL      0.0    1.00    2.00    3.00    4.00    5.00
```

NO BLOCKS WITH LESS THAN   2 ROWS WILL BE OUTPUTTED   ③

NO BLOCKS WITH LESS THAN   2 COLUMNS WILL BE OUTPUTTED   ④

THE MAX NO. OF BLOCKS THAT MAY BE OUTPUTTED IS   20   ⑤

THE BLOCKS ARE NOT REFINED   ⑥

```
    C O D E   F R E Q U E N C I E S                                 ⑦
    -------   ---------------------

VARIABLE MISSING    0    1    2    3    4    5
TINC                0    3    7    7   14    0    1
BINC                0    1    6    7   17    1    0
TCAN                0    7   25    0    0    0    0
BCAN                0    6   26    0    0    0    0
TPRM                0    1    5    9   10    7    0
BPRM                0    2    4    9   10    7    0
TMOL                0    0    7    3   21    1    0
BMOL                0    0    4    5   22    1    0
```

THE CLUSTERED MATRIX IS:

```
                TCAN
                 BCAN
                  TINC
                   BINC
                    BPRM
                     TPRM
                      TMOL
                       BMOL                      ⑧
                +....+....
OPOS      .  54  44. OPOS
SHRW      .  11   . SHRW
GSHW      . O 211 . GSHW
MSHW      .   22  . MSHW
MBAT      +  2    + MBAT
ELK       .  O    . ELK
DEER      .O O    . DEER
GOAT      .O O 4  . GOAT
MOLE      .   --3 . MOLE
WOLF      +   --- + WOLF
RACC      .   ---2. RACC
MART      .   --AA. MART
```

```
SLIN     .   B--AB. SLIN
FSEL     .   B---B. FSEL
MINK     +     AA+ MINK
ROTT     .    4AA. ROTT
SOTT     .   2  AA. SOTT
LION     .   2 A1. LION
LYNX     .   22A1. LYNX
LBAT     +  =2 =  + LBAT
TBAT     .  =O =  . TBAT
SBAT     .  =   =  . SBAT
PBAT     .  = 2=  . PBAT
BBAT     .  = 21  . BBAT
RBAT     +  .3.2  + RBAT
ABAT     .  .2.1  . ABAT
FBAT     .  .2.2  . FBAT
RABT     .++2..   . RABT
SQRL     .++..32  . SQRL
GPHR     +++..3   + GPHR
MOUS     .++..OO  . MOUS
JMOU     .++..O   . JMOU
         +....+....
```

```
BLK COUNT   VALUES                          ⑨
        137 11333333
    .    13 ..112...
    -    12 ....442.
    +     8 OO......
    =     7 ..2..2..
    A     9 ......12
    B     2 ...2...1
NO. OF SINGLETONS     46
```

THE CLUSTERED MATRIX IS: ⑩

```
                DOCDEN
                 PHARM
                  NURSE
                   HOSPBED
                    LIFEEXP
                     STARCH
                      ANIMAL
                +....+...
ALGERIA   .11 31 . ALGERIA
IRAN      . 3 1  . IRAN
IRAQ      .      3. IRAQ
JORDAN    .      1. JORDAN
LEBANON   +33....3+ LEBANON
LIBYA     . .... . LIBYA
MOROCCO   .1     . MOROCCO
TUNISIA   .1     . TUNISIA
SYRIA     .  11 --. SYRIA
TURKEY    +3   --+ TURKEY
U.A.R.    .33   --. U.A.R.
                +....+...
```

```
BLK COUNT   VALUES
        38 2222222
    .    4 ..3331.
    -    4 ....31
NO. OF SINGLETONS     18
```

Since P3M operates on categorical data, interval scale data must be converted to categorical scale. Here each variable is classified into three categories by two cutpoints. Another method would use INTERVAL(3) = 4 in the VARIABLE paragraph; this converts variable 3 to 4 categories by dividing its range into 4 equal intervals. Here START has been set equal to 2 to encourage clusters with small numbers of cases.

⑩ All variables have been converted to categories 1, 2, and 3. There are two clusters deviating from the modal values, which by choice of cutpoints, are always middle values of the variables. Lebanon and Libya are high on nurses, hospital beds, and life expectancy, and low on starch. Syria, Turkey, and the U.A.R. are high on starch and low on animal fat.

START specifies the minimum number of rows in an initial block. ROMIN + 2 is preassigned for START.

As a general procedure, we suggest that you use the quantiles as cutpoints. This will ensure that the modal values in the large block will be median values, and extremes will appear in the blocks.

COMPUTATIONAL METHOD

The first block is constructed by finding the minimum value for each variable that is modal (occurs with maximum frequency), and replacing each such value by the first block symbol.

Later blocks are obtained by an algorithm modified from Hartigan (1976). A seed case is first selected by scoring each case according to the sum of truncated frequencies of each value taken by the case, summed over all variables. The truncated frequency of a value is zero if the value is a block symbol or occurs with frequency less than START; otherwise it is the number of times the value appears in all variables. The seed case is the case with the maximum score.

Variables are also scored by summing over cases. Variables with positive truncated frequency are seed variables for the block.

Cases are added or deleted from the block according to whether they increase the total block count, or do not decrease it. Variables are then added or deleted according to the same criterion. This procedure continues until no further changes increase the block count.

If an entry in the matrix belongs to several blocks, it is always coded according to the most recently constructed block. After the maximum number of blocks have been constructed, all blocks with numbers of rows less than ROWMIN, or numbers of columns less than COLMIN, are deleted. Each block is then reevaluated by checking to see if the total block count may be increased by adding or deleting rows or columns. Output of the blocked matrix follows.

ACKNOWLEDGEMENT

P3M was designed by John Hartigan and programmed by Dan Barry, Albyn Jones, and Laszlo Engelman. It was supported in part by NSF contract no. MCS-7906218, Yale University.

SUMMARY

```
Order of Input Cards

   // (job card)
   // EXEC BIMED,PROG=BMDP3M          (see Appendix E)
   //SYSIN DD *
   / PROBLEM
   / INPUT
   / VARIABLE
   / TRANSFORM
   / SAVE
   / CATEGORY
   / BLOCK
   / PRINT
   / END
        (data, if on cards)
   // (system card)

   Full sets of BMDP paragraphs (and data, if on cards)
   can be repeated for additional problems; see Section
   5.8.
```

instructions specific to P3M

Paragraph Statement	Preassigned	Comment and Manual Reference
/ VARIABLE		
INTERvals = # list.		One number for each variable specifies the number of equal length intervals into which the variable is categorized. See ②, p. 475.
/ CATEGORY		
CUTP(#) = # list.		Categorizes variables into intervals. See ②, p. 475.
CODES(#) = # list.		Recodes variables, changes values and sets other values to missing.
/ BLOCK		
NUMBER = #.	20	Maximum number of blocks to create.
ROWMIN = #.	2	Minimum number of rows per block.
COLMIN = #.	2	Minimum number of columns per block.
START = #.	ROWMIN + 2	Minimum number of rows when initializing a block.
REFINE.	no	Rechecks all blocks after each new block is constructed.
SYMBOL = 'c' list.	'.',',','+','=', 'A', 'B'...	Characters identifying blocks.
/ PRINT		
REORDER.	no	Prints unreordered or reordered data matrix with original data values.

Key:

/	-indicates paragraph
.	-period ends a sentence
●	-required
v	-variable (name or subscript)
g	-group (name or subscript)
#	-number
'c'	-characters (name or parameter) may omit apostrophes if contiguous letters only

*	-assigned value remains the same for additional problems
VT	-number of variables after transformations
list	-more than one item, often one per var.

Capitalized letters-paragraph or sentence names recognized by BMDP
Page numbers following refer to this Manual

18
MULTIVARIATE ANALYSIS

The term "multivariate analysis" encompasses a variety of statistical procedures. In this chapter we discuss six BMDP programs used for multivariate analysis.

P4M performs a factor analysis of a correlation or covariance matrix. Initial factor extraction is by principal components, maximum likelihood, Kaiser's Second Generation Little Jiffy, or iterated principal factor analysis. Several methods of rotation are available, including varimax and direct quartimin. Factor scores are computed for each case. Mahalanobis distances are computed from the centroid of all cases for the factor scores, original data, and the residuals of the original data regressed on the factor scores. Input to P4M can be data, a correlation or covariance matrix, factor loadings, or factor score coefficients.

P6M performs a canonical correlation analysis between two sets of variables. It computes and prints the canonical correlations, coefficients for the canonical variables, canonical variable scores, and correlations of the original variables with the canonical variables (loadings). It also prints the eigenvalues associated with each pair of canonical variables and Bartlett's test for the significance of the remaining eigenvalues.

P6R computes the partial correlations of a set of variables after removing the linear effects of a second set of variables. The computation of the partial correlations includes the computations of the regression coefficients for predicting one set of variables from another set of variables (multivariate regression). P6R prints the partial correlations, regression coefficients and their standard errors, squared multiple correlations and residuals.

P7M performs a discriminant analysis between two or more groups. The variables used in computing the linear classification functions are chosen in a stepwise manner. Both forward and backward selection of variables are possible; at each step the variable that adds most to the separation of the groups is entered into (or the variable that adds the least is removed from) the discriminant function. The important group differences can be specified as contrasts: these contrasts guide the selection of the variables. Group classifications are evaluated and a classification table is printed. A jackknife-validation procedure may be requested to reduce the bias in the group classifications.

Multivariate methods are also available in other BMDP programs: The equality of the means of several variables in two groups is tested in P3D (Section 9.1). Cluster analysis (Chapter 17) provides methods of looking for data patterns, the similarity of cases and the similarity of variables. Multiway frequency tables are analyzed by P4F (Chapter 11).

Multivariate methods are sensitive to the assumptions of the analysis. P4M and P7M compute the Mahalanobis distance from each case to the overall mean (P4M) or to its group mean (P7M); the Mahalanobis distance can be used to examine the data for outliers or extreme values. Before a multivariate analysis is performed, the data should be screened for errors and checked for distributional assumptions by the methods described in Chapters 8 and 9. The pattern of missing values in the data can be examined with PAM (Section 12.2); PAM can also replace the missing values by estimates based on the acceptable values.

Boolean (binary) factor analysis, (P8M), is performed in BMDP8M. It has proved to be an effective tool for dealing with tissue typing problems for transplants, for example.

Linear Scores for Preference Pairs, (P9M), makes use of a set of preference judgments between pairs of cases provided by "experts" and a set of objective measures. These are used to create a linear function of the objective measures that reproduces as closely as possible the expert preferences between pairs of cases. This linear rating scale can then be applied to other cases. It has been used, for example, to develop a computer billing function and to develop an index of dental health.

P4M

18.1 Factor Analysis

James Frane
Robert Jennrich
Paul Sampson

ABSTRACT

P4M provides four methods of initial factor extraction from a correlation or covariance matrix, and several methods of rotation. Input can be data, a correlation or covariance matrix, factor loadings or factor score coefficients. Output includes rotated and unrotated factor loadings and their plots; display of sorted rotated factor loadings; factor score coefficients, scores for each case, and factor score plots; Mahalanobis distances from each case to the centroid of all cases for original data, factor scores and their differences; correlation matrix, squared multiple correlation of each variable with all others, eigenvalues; optional display of the correlation matrix in sorted and shaded form; and optional listing of data or standard scores, covariance matrix, inverse of correlation or covariance matrix, partial correlations, residual correlations, double precision computations.

Frane and Hill (1974, 1976) describe the use and interpretation of results of analyses by P4M.

WHERE TO FIND IT

Example 4M.1 Basic Setup for Factor Analysis

The Jarvik smoking questionnaire data (Table 17.1) are used to illustrate a factor analysis by P4M. We specify only Control Language instructions that describe the data and variables (these instructions are discussed in Chapter 5). For all options specific to P4M we use preassigned values: this includes principal components extraction, orthogonal rotation, plots of rotated factor loadings, factor scores and Mahalanobis distances for each case.

```
------------------------------------
/ PROBLEM    TITLE IS 'JARVIK SMOKING DATA'.
/ INPUT      VARIABLES ARE 12.
            FORMAT IS '(12F2.0)'.
/ VARIABLE   NAMES ARE CONCENTR, ANNOY, SMOKING1,
            SMOKING2, TENSE, SMOKING3,
            ALERT, IRRITABL, TIRED,
            CONTENT, SMOKING4.

/ END
------------------------------------
```

(See end of this P4M section for organization of systems information, BMDP instructions and data)

The results of the analysis are presented in Output 4M.1. Circled numbers below correspond to those in the output.

(1) Interpretation of the Control Language instructions specific to P4M. Since no instructions are stated in Example 4M.1, preassigned values or options are printed.

(2) Data for the first five cases are printed. The number of cases printed can be specified.

(3) Number of cases read. P4M uses only complete cases in all computations. That is, if the value of any variable in a case is missing or out of range, the case is omitted from all computations. If a USE statement is specified in the VARIABLE paragraph, only the values of variables in the USE statement are checked for missing value codes and values out of range.

④ Univariate summary statistics

- mean
- standard deviation
- coefficient of variation
- smallest observed value (not out of range)
- smallest standard score

- first case at which smallest observed value
  occurs
- largest observed value (not out of range)
- largest standard score
- first case at which largest observed value occurs

If case weights are specified, weighted means and
standard deviations are computed.

Output 4M.1 Factor analysis. Circled numbers correspond to those in the text

----

--- the BMDP instructions read by P4M are printed and interpreted ---

```
WEIGHT VARIABLE . . . . . . . . . . . . . .
UNROTATED FACTORS ARE PRINCIPAL COMPONENTS.
NUMBER OF FACTORS IS LIMITED TO THE NUMBER OF EIGENVALUES      ①
     GREATER THAN      1.000
TOLERANCE LIMIT FOR MATRIX INVERSION. . . . .    0.00010
VARIMAX ROTATION IS PERFORMED.
GAMMA . . . . . . . . . . . . . . . .           1.0000
MAXIMUM NUMBER OF ITERATIONS FOR ROTATION . . .    50
CONVERGENCE CRITERION FOR ROTATION. . . . . . 0.0000100
KAISER'S NORMALIZATION. . . . . . . . . . . .    YES
```

DATA AFTER TRANSFORMATIONS FOR FIRST   5 CASES.   ②
CASES WITH ZERO WEIGHTS AND MISSING DATA NOT INCLUDED.

C A S E NO. LABEL	1 CONCENTR 11 CONTENT	2 ANNOY 12 SMOKING4	3 SMOKING1	4 SLEEPY	5 SMOKING2	6 TENSE	7 SMOKING3	8 ALERT	9 IRRITABL	10 TIRED
---- -------	---------	---------	---------	---------	----------	----------	----------	----------	----------	----------
BASED ON INPUT FORMAT SUPPLIED		1 RECORDS READ PER CASE.								
1	3 3	2 2	1	3	2	2	1	3	2	2
2	4 4	2 5	5	3	5	4	5	4	3	4
3	5 3	3 4	4	4	5	5	4	5	3	4
4	4 3	2 5	4	3	5	4	4	4	3	4
5	4 3	2 4	4	3	4	2	4	4	2	4

NUMBER OF CASES READ.   110   ③

STATISTICS FOR EACH VARIABLE   ④

VARIABLE	MEAN	STANDARD DEVIATION	COEFFICIENT OF VARIATION	SMALLEST VALUE	SMALLEST STANDARD SCORE	FIRST CASE FOR SMALLEST	LARGEST VALUE	LARGEST STANDARD SCORE	FIRST CASE FOR LARGEST
1 CONCENTR	2.69091	1.07298	0.398744	1.0000	-1.58	12	5.0000	2.15	3
2 ANNOY	2.11818	0.97427	0.459957	1.0000	-1.15	12	5.0000	2.96	11
3 SMOKING1	3.36364	1.13111	0.336275	1.0000	-2.09	1	5.0000	1.45	2
4 SLEEPY	2.60909	1.02353	0.392295	1.0000	-1.57	6	5.0000	2.34	60
5 SMOKING2	3.58182	1.06126	0.296291	1.0000	-2.43	11	5.0000	1.34	2
6 TENSE	2.44545	0.99158	0.405480	1.0000	-1.46	33	5.0000	2.58	3
7 SMOKING3	3.42727	1.16098	0.338747	1.0000	-2.09	1	5.0000	1.35	2
8 ALERT	2.80909	1.01814	0.362445	1.0000	-1.78	73	5.0000	2.15	3
9 IRRITABL	2.21818	0.78263	0.352825	1.0000	-1.56	12	4.0000	2.28	11
10 TIRED	3.09091	0.95346	0.308473	1.0000	-2.19	23	5.0000	2.00	11
11 CONTENT	2.45455	0.84198	0.343027	1.0000	-1.73	12	5.0000	3.02	11
12 SMOKING4	3.50000	1.27610	0.364601	1.0000	-1.96	11	5.0000	1.18	2

CASE NUMBERS ABOVE REFER TO DATA MATRIX BEFORE ANY CASES
HAVE BEEN DELETED DUE TO MISSING DATA.
CASES WITH ZERO WEIGHTS ARE NOT INCLUDED.

(output continued)

⑤ Correlation matrix.

⑥ Squared multiple correlation (SMC) of each variable with all other variables. The condition number is the ratio of the largest eigenvalue to the smallest eigenvalue and is of interest to see how nearly singular the correlation matrix might be. The condition number 0.4920D02 is read as 49.2.

⑦, ⑧ The eigenvalues of the factors in ⑧ are all listed (under the heading "Variance Explained"). The preassigned criterion for the number of factors is the number of factors with eigenvalues greater than one (see third line of ①). Therefore, in ⑦ communalities are obtained for three factors (those with eigenvalues greater than one). The communality of a variable is its squared multiple correlation with the factors extracted.

The cumulative proportion of total variance in ⑧ is the sum of the variance explained (eigenvalues) up to and including the factor divided by the sum of all the eigenvalues. A successful factor analysis explains a large proportion of variance with a very few factors.

Output 4M.1 (continued)

CORRELATION MATRIX ⑤

		CONCENTR	ANNOY	SMOKING1	SLEEPY	SMOKING2	TENSE	SMOKING3	ALERT	IRRITABL	TIRED	CONTENT	SMOKING4
		1	2	3	4	5	6	7	8	9	10	11	12
CONCENTR	1	1.000											
ANNOY	2	0.562	1.000										
SMOKING1	3	0.086	0.144	1.000									
SLEEPY	4	•0.457	0.360	0.140	1.000								
SMOKING2	5	0.200	0.119	0.785	0.211	1.000							
TENSE	6	0.579	0.705	0.222	0.273	0.301	1.000						
SMOKING3	7	0.041	0.060	0.810	0.126	0.816	0.120	1.000					
ALERT	8	0.802	0.578	0.101	0.606	0.223	0.594	0.039	1.000				
IRRITABL	9	0.595	0.796	0.189	0.337	0.221	0.725	0.108	0.605	1.000			
TIRED	10	0.512	0.413	0.199	0.798	0.274	0.364	0.139	0.698	0.428	1.000		
CONTENT	11	0.492	0.739	0.239	0.240	0.235	0.711	0.100	0.605	0.697	0.394	1.000	
SMOKING4	12	0.228	0.122	0.775	0.277	0.813	0.214	0.845	0.201	0.156	0.271	0.171	1.000

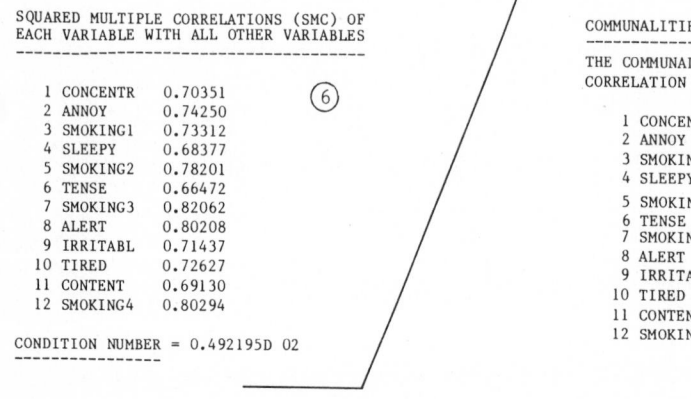

SQUARED MULTIPLE CORRELATIONS (SMC) OF
EACH VARIABLE WITH ALL OTHER VARIABLES

1	CONCENTR	0.70351
2	ANNOY	0.74250
3	SMOKING1	0.73312
4	SLEEPY	0.68377
5	SMOKING2	0.78201
6	TENSE	0.66472
7	SMOKING3	0.82062
8	ALERT	0.80208
9	IRRITABL	0.71437
10	TIRED	0.72627
11	CONTENT	0.69130
12	SMOKING4	0.80294

⑥

CONDITION NUMBER = 0.492195D 02

COMMUNALITIES OBTAINED FROM 3 FACTORS AFTER 1 ITERATIONS.

THE COMMUNALITY OF A VARIABLE IS ITS SQUARED MULTIPLE
CORRELATION (OR COVARIANCE) WITH THE FACTORS.

1	CONCENTR	0.6601
2	ANNOY	0.7956
3	SMOKING1	0.8391
4	SLEEPY	0.8474
5	SMOKING2	0.8561
6	TENSE	0.7804
7	SMOKING3	0.8941
8	ALERT	0.8258
9	IRRITABL	0.7978
10	TIRED	0.8453
11	CONTENT	0.7715
12	SMOKING4	0.8698

⑦

FACTOR	VARIANCE EXPLAINED	CUMULATIVE PROPORTION OF TOTAL VARIANCE
1	5.425688	0.452141
2	2.996636	0.701860
3	1.360520	0.815237
4	0.560300	0.861929
5	0.363261	0.892200
6	0.302254	0.917388
7	0.240804	0.937455
8	0.199752	0.954101
9	0.158162	0.967281
10	0.145653	0.979419
11	0.136736	0.990814
12	0.110235	1.000000

⑧

THE VARIANCE EXPLAINED BY EACH FACTOR IS THE EIGENVALUE FOR THAT FACTOR.

TOTAL VARIANCE IS DEFINED AS THE SUM OF THE DIAGONAL ELEMENTS OF THE
CORRELATION (COVARIANCE) MATRIX.

⑨ Unrotated factor loadings (pattern) for principal components. These loadings are the eigenvectors of the correlation matrix multiplied by the square roots of the corresponding eigenvalues. They are the correlations of the principal components with the original variables. The eigenvalues (VP) are printed at the bottom of each column.

⑩ Orthogonal rotation is performed. Gamma is preassigned to 1 because varimax rotation is performed. At each iteration the simplicity criterion G (p. 488) is printed.

⑪ Rotated factor loadings (pattern) -- coefficients of the factors after rotation. The sum of squares of the coefficients are printed below each column (VP). When the rotation is orthogonal, as in this example, VP is the variance explained by the factor and the rotated loadings are the correlations of the variables with the factors.

⑫ Plots of the rotated factor loadings. The loadings for one factor are plotted against those of another factor.

```
UNROTATED FACTOR LOADINGS (PATTERN)
------------------------------------
FOR PRINCIPAL COMPONENTS

                     FACTOR     FACTOR     FACTOR      ⑨
                       1          2          3

CONCENTR    1        0.742      -0.309      0.117
ANNOY       2        0.755      -0.361     -0.309
SMOKING1    3        0.491       0.763     -0.124
SLEEPY      4        0.611      -0.117      0.679
SMOKING2    5        0.561       0.735     -0.030
TENSE       6        0.770      -0.232     -0.366
SMOKING3    7        0.417       0.847     -0.055
ALERT       8        0.808      -0.337      0.244
IRRITABL    9        0.783      -0.302     -0.306
TIRED      10        0.702      -0.138      0.577
CONTENT    11        0.748      -0.256     -0.382
SMOKING4   12        0.540       0.757      0.070
            VP       5.426       2.997      1.361
```

THE VP FOR EACH FACTOR IS THE SUM OF THE SQUARES OF THE ELEMENTS OF THE COLUMN OF THE FACTOR LOADING MATRIX CORRESPONDING TO THAT FACTOR. THE VP IS THE VARIANCE EXPLAINED BY THE FACTOR.

```
ORTHOGONAL ROTATION, GAMMA =      1.0000

ITERATION    SIMPLICITY
             CRITERION
    0        -1.900373         ⑩
    1        -6.017688
    2        -6.019553
    3        -6.019557
```

```
ROTATED FACTOR LOADINGS (PATTERN)
---------------------------------
                                                          ⑪
                     FACTOR     FACTOR     FACTOR
                       1          2          3

CONCENTR    1        0.601      0.034      0.546
ANNOY       2        0.867      0.021      0.209
SMOKING1    3        0.131      0.907      0.007
SLEEPY      4        0.117      0.116      0.906
SMOKING2    5        0.141      0.905      0.128
TENSE       6        0.859      0.147      0.144
SMOKING3    7        0.005      0.945      0.010
ALERT       8        0.590      0.030      0.691
IRRITABL    9        0.863      0.085      0.214
TIRED      10        0.249      0.143      0.873
CONTENT    11        0.862      0.117      0.125
SMOKING4   12        0.061      0.910      0.195

            VP       3.802      3.443      2.538
```

THE VP FOR EACH FACTOR IS THE SUM OF THE SQUARES OF THE ELEMENTS OF THE COLUMN OF THE FACTOR PATTERN MATRIX CORRESPONDING TO THAT FACTOR. WHEN THE ROTATION IS ORTHOGONAL, THE VP IS THE VARIANCE EXPLAINED BY THE FACTOR.

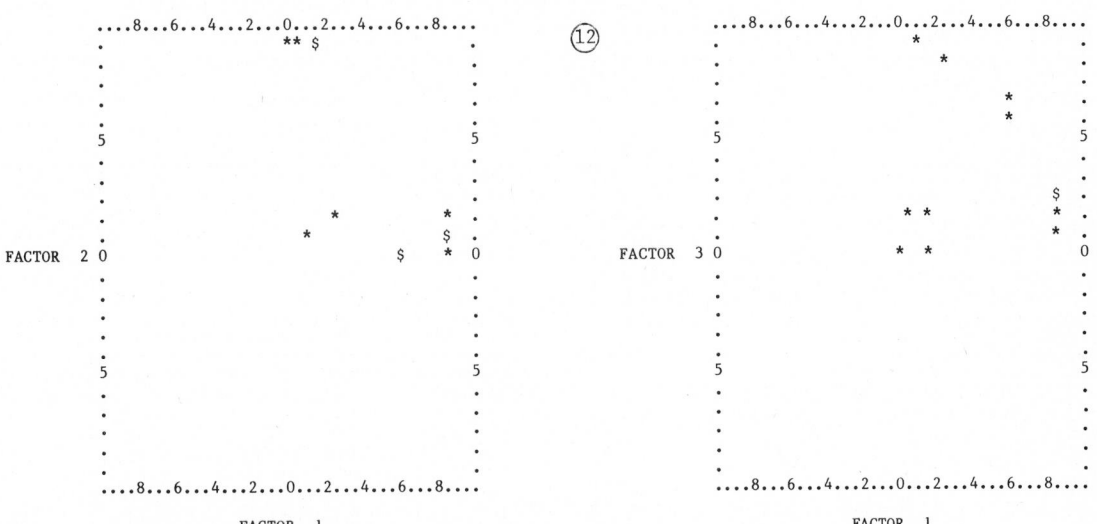

ROTATED FACTOR LOADINGS

OVERLAP IS INDICATED BY A DOLLAR SIGN. SCALE IS FROM -1 TO +1.

--- we omit the plot of factor 3 versus factor 2 ---   (output continued)

⑬ Sorted rotated factor loadings. The variables are reordered so the rotated factor loadings for each factor are grouped. Loadings less than 0.25 are set to zero. If a variable has two loadings greater than 0.5, it is ordered according to the larger of the two. This sorted presentation shows that CONCENTR and ALERT are in two factors; the other variables are each primarily in a single factor. The three factors appear to be "mood," "smoking" and "fatigue." The factors are sorted according to VP, the sum of the squared loadings for each factor.

⑭ Correlations in shaded form. The variables are reordered according to the sorted rotated factor loadings. The values of the correlations are replaced by the codes listed in the output and the shaded correlation matrix is printed.

⑮ Factor score covariances. The factor structure matrix is multiplied by the factor score coefficients to obtain the covariances of the factor scores. When the method of initial factor extraction is principal components (no communality estimates and only one iteration, as in our example), the factor score covariance matrix is the same as the factor correlation matrix. Otherwise, the diagonal of this covariance matrix contains the squared multiple correlations of each factor with the variables. This matrix is the identity matrix in our example because the initial extraction is by principal components and the rotation is orthogonal.

⑯ Estimated factor scores and Mahalanobis distances. Factor scores are obtained by multiplying the standard scores for the original variables by the factor score coefficients. The three factor scores are listed in the last three columns.
   The three columns labelled CHISQ/DF are Mahalanobis distances divided by degrees of freedom. The first column contains the Mahalanobis distance of the case to the mean of all cases, which is computed using the inverse of the correlation (or covariance) matrix and the standard scores. Its degrees of freedom is the number of variables (12). The second column contains the Mahalanobis distance of the factor scores for each case, which is computed using the factor scores and the inverse of the factor score covariance matrix. The difference between these two Mahalanobis D^2's (before dividing by the degrees of freedom) is the Mahalanobis D^2 for the residual space; i.e., the subspace of the original variables that is orthogonal to the factor scores. The third column contains this Mahalanobis D^2 divided by the appropriate degrees of freedom.
   For large samples from a multivariate normal distribution, these three distances divided by their degrees of freedom are distributed approximately as chi-square divided by degrees of freedom. Large distances indicate multivariate outliers. For a discussion of detecting outliers in multivariate data, see Hawkins (1974).

⑰ The factor score covariance matrix. This is recomputed using the factor scores, and serves as a check for numerical accuracy.

⑱ Plots of the factor scores; one factor against the other.

Output 4M.1 (continued)

SORTED ROTATED FACTOR LOADINGS (PATTERN)   ⑬

		FACTOR 1	FACTOR 2	FACTOR 3
ANNOY	2	0.867	0.0	0.0
IRRITABL	9	0.863	0.0	0.0
CONTENT	11	0.862	0.0	0.0
TENSE	6	0.859	0.0	0.0
CONCENTR	1	0.601	0.0	0.546
SMOKING3	7	0.0	0.945	0.0
SMOKING4	12	0.0	0.910	0.0
SMOKING1	3	0.0	0.907	0.0
SMOKING2	5	0.0	0.905	0.0
SLEEPY	4	0.0	0.0	0.906
TIRED	10	0.0	0.0	0.873
ALERT	8	0.590	0.0	0.691
VP		3.802	3.443	2.538

THE ABOVE FACTOR LOADING MATRIX HAS BEEN REARRANGED SO THAT THE COLUMNS APPEAR IN DECREASING ORDER OF VARIANCE EXPLAINED BY FACTORS. THE ROWS HAVE BEEN REARRANGED SO THAT FOR EACH SUCCESSIVE FACTOR, LOADINGS GREATER THAN 0.5000 APPEAR FIRST. LOADINGS LESS THAN 0.2500 HAVE BEEN REPLACED BY ZERO.

ABSOLUTE VALUES OF CORRELATIONS IN SORTED AND SHADED FORM

```
     2 ANNOY     ▆
     9 IRRITABL  ▆▆
    11 CONTENT   ▆▆▆                    ⑭
     6 TENSE     ▆▆▆▆
     1 CONCENTR  �써써X▆
     7 SMOKING3  . . ▆
    12 SMOKING4  ...--▆▆
     3 SMOKING1  ..-- ▆▆▆
     5 SMOKING2  .---.▆▆▆▆
     4 SLEEPY    ++--X.-..▆
    10 TIRED     +X++X.-.-▆▆
     8 ALERT     써써써▆ . -써▆▆
```

THE ABSOLUTE VALUES OF
THE MATRIX ENTRIES HAVE BEEN PRINTED ABOVE IN SHADED FORM
ACCORDING TO THE FOLLOWING SCHEME

	LESS THAN OR EQUAL TO	0.106
.	0.106 TO AND INCLUDING	0.211
-	0.211 TO AND INCLUDING	0.317
+	0.317 TO AND INCLUDING	0.423
X	0.423 TO AND INCLUDING	0.528
써	0.528 TO AND INCLUDING	0.634
▆	0.634 TO AND INCLUDING	0.740
▆	GREATER THAN	0.740

FACTOR SCORE COVARIANCE (COMPUTED FROM FACTOR   ⑮
STRUCTURE AND FACTOR SCORE COEFFICIENTS)

THE DIAGONAL OF THE MATRIX BELOW CONTAINS THE SQUARED
MULTIPLE CORRELATIONS OF EACH FACTOR WITH THE VARIABLES.

		FACTOR 1	FACTOR 2	FACTOR 3
FACTOR	1	1.000		
FACTOR	2	-0.000	1.000	
FACTOR	3	0.000	0.000	1.000

ESTIMATED FACTOR SCORES AND MAHALANOBIS DISTANCES (CHI-SQUARE S) FROM
EACH CASE TO THE CENTROID OF ALL CASES FOR THE ORIGINAL DATA
(12 D.F.) FACTOR SCORES (3 D.F.) AND THEIR DIFFERENCE (9 D.F.).
EACH CHI-SQUARE HAS BEEN DIVIDED BY ITS DEGREES OF FREEDOM.

CASE LABEL	NO.	CHISQ/DF 12	CHISQ/DF 3	CHISQ/DF 9	FACTOR 1	FACTOR 2	FACTOR 3
	1	1.432	1.212	1.505	0.167	-1.899	0.014
	2	1.113	1.063	1.130	1.114	1.341	0.389
	3	1.333	1.238	1.365	1.357	0.511	1.269
	4	0.715	0.593	0.755	0.781	0.848	0.670

⑯

--- similar statistics for cases 5 to 104 ---

	105	1.026	0.813	1.097	-0.354	-0.231	-1.504
	106	0.423	0.783	0.303	-0.388	0.652	-1.331
	107	0.451	0.288	0.505	-0.288	0.106	-0.878
	108	1.459	2.926	0.970	-1.067	-1.752	2.138
	109	0.530	0.199	0.640	-0.337	-0.295	0.629
	110	2.035	0.488	2.550	-0.066	-0.765	-0.935

FACTOR SCORE COVARIANCE (COMPUTED FROM FACTOR SCORES)

		FACTOR 1	FACTOR 2	FACTOR 3
FACTOR	1	1.000		
FACTOR	2	0.000	1.000	
FACTOR	3	-0.000	-0.000	1.000

⑰

⑱

FACTOR SCORES

X-AXIS IS FACTOR 1, Y-AXIS IS FACTOR 2 ... X-AXIS IS FACTOR 1, Y-AXIS IS FACTOR 3

OVERLAP IS INDICATED BY A DOLLAR SIGN. SCALE IS FROM -3 TO +3.
FACTOR SCORES GREATER THAN 3 ARE PLOTTED AS 3.
FACTOR SCORES LESS THAN -3 ARE PLOTTED AS -3.

Example 4M.2 Initial Factor Extraction (Maximum Likelihood)

Four methods of initial factor extraction are available: principal components (PCA) and iterated principal factor analysis (PFA), discussed in Harman (1967); maximum likelihood factor analysis (MLFA), discussed by Lawley and Maxwell (1971); and Kaiser's (1970) Second Generation Little Jiffy (LJIFFY).

Principal components analysis (PCA) is recommended for a first analysis or when the common factor model is not appropriate for the data. Maximum likelihood factor analysis (MLFA) is recommended when the common factor model is known to be appropriate, when the number of variables is 60 or less, and when the correlation matrix is nonsingular. Kaiser's Second Generation Little Jiffy also requires a nonsingular correlation matrix; it consists of image analysis followed by orthoblique rotation. Principal factor analysis (PFA) is appropriate for data known to follow the common factor model and can also be used with a singular correlation matrix; however, it is generally considered inferior to MLFA and LJIFFY.

If a method is not specified, PCA is used (see Example P4M.1).

When MLFA or PFA is specified, the maximum number of iterations can be specified (ITERATE). In addition, the convergence criterion (EPS) for PFA can be changed.

In Example 4M.2 we specify that the initial factor extraction is by maximum likelihood by introducing the FACTOR paragraph before the END paragraph in Example 4M.1.

```
------------------------------------
    / FACTOR      METHOD IS MLFA.
------------------------------------
```

The additional results are presented in Output 4M.2. Circled numbers below correspond to those in the output.

(19) The preassigned value for the communality estimates is SMCS when the METHOD of initial factor extraction is MLFA.

(20) The eigenvalues are computed from the original correlation matrix. These are the eigenvalues of the correlation matrix (without communalities substituted for the diagonal elements).

(21) The algorithm for maximum likelihood factor extraction is described in Appendix A.21.

(22) Interpretations for the remaining results are similar to those for the results in Output 4M.1 (from (7) to the end). The results differ slightly from Output 4M.1 because of the different method of initial factor extraction. Some of the remaining results are not presented.

```
FACTOR ────────────────────────────────
  METHod = (one only)              PCA/prev.
              PCA,MLFA,LJIFFY,PFA.
    The method of initial factor extraction.
    PCA:    principal component analysis
    MLFA:   maximum likelihood factor analysis
    LJIFFY: Kaiser's Second Generation Little
            Jiffy
    PFA:    principal factor analysis
  ITERate = #.   PFA or MLFA only     25/prev.
    Maximum number of iterations performed.
  EPS = #.       PFA only          0.001/prev.
    Convergence criterion for iteration on
    communalities. The iteration continues to the
    number of times specified for ITERATE, or until
    the estimated communalities from two successive
    iterations differ by EPS or less.
```

Output 4M.2 Maximum likelihood factor analysis

```
--------------------------------------------------------------------------------

WEIGHT VARIABLE . . . . . . . . . . . . . .
INITIAL COMMUNALITIES ARE SQUARED MULTIPLE CORRELATIONS
     OR COVARIANCES.
MAXIMUM LIKELIHOOD FACTOR ANALYSIS IS PERFORMED.
NUMBER OF ITERATIONS FOR INITIAL FACTOR EXTRACTION    25
NUMBER OF FACTORS IS LIMITED TO THE NUMBER OF EIGENVALUES
     GREATER THAN    1.000
TOLERANCE LIMIT FOR MATRIX INVERSION. . . . . .  0.00010
VARIMAX ROTATION IS PERFORMED.
GAMMA . . . . . . . . . . . . . . . . . . . .    1.0000
MAXIMUM NUMBER OF ITERATIONS FOR ROTATION : : :      50
CONVERGENCE CRITERION FOR ROTATION. . . . . . . 0.0000100
KAISER'S NORMALIZATION. . . . . . . . . . . .     YES


  --- (2) to (6) from Output 4M.1 appear here ---


COMMUNALITY ESTIMATES ARE SQUARED MULTIPLE CORRELATIONS (COVARIANCES).   (19)

CONDITION NUMBER = 0.492195D 02



EIGENVALUES OF UNALTERED CORRELATION MATRIX       (20)
-----------------------------------------------
    5.425688    2.996636    1.360520    0.560300    0.363261    0.302254    0.240804    0.199752    0.158162    0.145653
    0.136736    0.110235
```

ITERATION FOR MAXIMUM LIKELIHOOD

ITERATION	MAXIMUM CHANGE IN SQRT(UNIQUENESS)	LIKELIHOOD CRITERION TO BE MINIMIZED	STEP HALVINGS
		0.969191	
1	0.120209	0.900708	2
2	0.061833	0.836862	0
3	0.012304	0.834094	0
4	0.000609	0.834089	0
5	0.000002		

AN ASTERISK (IF ANY) AFTER THE ITERATION NUMBER INDICATES
THAT APPROXIMATE DERIVATIVES WERE USED.

CANONICAL CORRELATIONS

        0.9790
        0.9668
        0.9082

COMMUNALITIES OBTAINED FROM 3 FACTORS AFTER   5 ITERATIONS.

THE COMMUNALITY OF A VARIABLE IS ITS SQUARED MULTIPLE
CORRELATION (OR COVARIANCE) WITH THE FACTORS.

    1 CONCENTR   0.5753
    2 ANNOY   0.7457
    3 SMOKING1   0.7630
    4 SLEEPY   0.7596
    5 SMOKING2   0.8011
    6 TENSE   0.7110
    7 SMOKING3   0.8784
    8 ALERT   0.7561
    9 IRRITABL   0.7551
   10 TIRED   0.8043
   11 CONTENT   0.6993
   12 SMOKING4   0.8352

FACTOR	VARIANCE EXPLAINED	CUMULATIVE PROPORTION OF TOTAL VARIANCE
1	4.793273	0.399439
2	3.162091	0.662947
3	1.128832	0.757016

TOTAL VARIANCE IS DEFINED AS THE SUM OF THE DIAGONAL ELEMENTS OF THE
CORRELATION (COVARIANCE) MATRIX.

UNROTATED FACTOR LOADINGS (PATTERN)

FOR MAXIMUM LIKELIHOOD CANONICAL FACTORS

		FACTOR 1	FACTOR 2	FACTOR 3
CONCENTR	1	0.529	0.543	0.027
ANNOY	2	0.527	0.599	-0.329
SMOKING1	3	0.732	-0.466	-0.097
SLEEPY	4	0.518	0.389	0.583
SMOKING2	5	0.790	-0.419	-0.023
TENSE	6	0.579	0.490	-0.369
SMOKING3	7	0.722	-0.596	-0.040
ALERT	8	0.587	0.622	0.157
IRRITABL	9	0.574	0.562	-0.332
TIRED	10	0.590	0.448	0.506
CONTENT	11	0.552	0.507	-0.370
SMOKING4	12	0.789	-0.456	0.066
VP		4.793	3.162	1.129

THE VP FOR EACH FACTOR IS THE SUM OF THE SQUARES OF THE
ELEMENTS OF THE COLUMN OF THE FACTOR LOADING MATRIX
CORRESPONDING TO THAT FACTOR. THE VP IS THE VARIANCE
EXPLAINED BY THE FACTOR.

ORTHOGONAL ROTATION, GAMMA =   1.0000

ITERATION	SIMPLICITY CRITERION
0	-0.611441
1	-5.852844
2	-5.864646
3	-5.864750
4	-5.864750

ROTATED FACTOR LOADINGS (PATTERN)

		FACTOR 1	FACTOR 2	FACTOR 3
CONCENTR	1	0.595	0.051	0.468
ANNOY	2	0.839	0.030	0.204
SMOKING1	3	0.128	0.864	0.023
SLEEPY	4	0.164	0.116	0.848
SMOKING2	5	0.144	0.874	0.127
TENSE	6	0.818	0.142	0.146
SMOKING3	7	0.007	0.937	0.011
ALERT	8	0.597	0.039	0.631
IRRITABL	9	0.840	0.090	0.204
TIRED	10	0.283	0.137	0.840
CONTENT	11	0.817	0.111	0.142
SMOKING4	12	0.068	0.893	0.183
VP		3.604	3.264	2.216

THE VP FOR EACH FACTOR IS THE SUM OF THE SQUARES OF THE
ELEMENTS OF THE COLUMN OF THE FACTOR PATTERN MATRIX
CORRESPONDING TO THAT FACTOR. WHEN THE ROTATION IS
ORTHOGONAL, THE VP IS THE VARIANCE EXPLAINED BY THE FACTOR.

--- the remainder of the results is analogous to (12) to (18) in Output 4M.1 ---

Example 4M.3 Oblique Rotation

P4M allows both orthogonal and oblique rotation (the factors may be correlated). When principal component analysis is used, rotation is sometimes not necessary. The option to omit rotation is

METHOD = NONE.

in the ROTATE paragraph.

In this example we demonstrate the results of DQUART, the method of oblique rotation that we recommend.

To obtain the oblique rotation we insert a ROTATE paragraph before the END paragraph in the Control Language of Example 4M.1:

```
-----------------------------------------
/ ROTATE        METHOD IS DQUART.
-----------------------------------------
```

Some of the results are presented in Output 4M.3. Circled numbers correspond to the notes below.

㉓ Direct oblimin rotation is performed. The simplicity criterion is described on p.

㉔ Rotated factor loadings (pattern). The results differ from ⑪ in Output 4M.1. Since the rotation is <u>not</u> orthogonal, VP is <u>not</u> the variance explained by the factor, but large values of VP still indicate important factors and small values indicate unimportant factors.

㉕ Factor correlations for rotated factors. These are the correlations between the factors. When the rotation is orthogonal this matrix is the identity matrix and is not printed.

㉖ Sorted rotated factor loadings (pattern). See ⑬ (p. 484) for a description of sorted rotated factor loadings.

<u>More on rotation</u>. Rotations are performed to minimize the simplicity criterion G (Harman, 1967, Chapters 14 and 15).

$$G = \sum_{i \neq j} \left[\sum_{k=1}^{p} a_{ki}^2 a_{kj}^2 - \frac{\Gamma}{p} \left(\sum_{k=1}^{p} a_{ki}^2 \right) \left(\sum_{k=1}^{p} a_{kj}^2 \right) \right]$$

where

i, j	= 1,...,m
m	= number of factors
p	= number of variables
(a_{ij})	= is the matrix of factor loadings for orthogonal and direct oblimin rotation and is the factor structure for indirect oblimin

Although GAMMA=0 (the preassigned value) is almost always desirable, the value of gamma can be specified (GAMMA). For orthogonal rotation, low values of gamma (e.g., GAMMA=0) emphasize "simplifying" the rows of a loadings matrix, and large values (e.g., GAMMA=1) emphasize simplifying the columns (Harman, 1967, p. 304). For direct oblimin, increasing gamma causes factors to be <u>more</u>

highly correlated (more oblique), but positive values for gamma may result in convergence problems (Jennrich, 1978). Commonly used names of methods of rotation are given in the following table:

gamma	Type of Rotation	
	Orthogonal	Oblique
Γ		direct oblimin
	quartimax	direct quartimin (simple loadings)
1	varimax	
m/2	equamax	

More details concerning methods of rotation are found in Jennrich and Sampson (1966), Harman (1967), Kaiser (1970), and Jennrich (1978). Kaiser also includes the orthoblique method.

The rotation terminates when the maximum number of iterations is reached (MAXIT) or when the relative change in the value of G (defined above) between two successive iterations is less than CONSTANT.

<u>Kaiser's normalization</u> (Harman, 1967, p. 306) is performed unless

NO NORMAL.

is specified.

```
ROTATE ─────────────────────────────────────────
  METHod = one only of          VMAX unless
           list below           LJIFFY is
                                 specified/prev.
    The method of rotation
    VMAX:    varimax
    DQUART:  direct quartimin rotation for simple
             loadings (Jennrich and Sampson, 1966;
             this is the recommended method for
             oblique rotation)
    QRMAX:   quartimax
    EQMAX:   equamax
    ORTHOG:  orthogonal with gamma (see below)
    DOBLI:   direct oblimin with gamma (see below)
    ORTHOB:  orthoblique (this is the preassigned
             value for LJIFFY (Kaiser, 1970) and
             is available only with LJIFFY)
    NONE:    no rotation
  GAMMA = #.   only for ORTHOG      1.0 for ORTHOG
              and DOBLI            0.0 for DOBLI
    Value of gamma.
  MAXIT = #.                        50/prev.
    Maximum number of iterations for rotation.
  CONSTant = #.                     0.00001/prev.
    Convergence criterion for rotation. The
    convergence criterion is satisfied when the
    relative change in G between two successive
    iterations is less than CONSTANT.
  NORMal.                           NORMAL/prev.
    Kaiser's normalization is performed unless NO
    NORMAL is specified.
─────────────────────────────────────────────────
```

Output 4M.3   Factor analysis results using an oblique rotation

---

```
WEIGHT VARIABLE . . . . . . . . . . . . . . .
UNROTATED FACTORS ARE PRINCIPAL COMPONENTS.
NUMBER OF FACTORS IS LIMITED TO THE NUMBER OF EIGENVALUES
    GREATER THAN    1.000
TOLERANCE LIMIT FOR MATRIX INVERSION. . . . . .   0.00010
DIRECT QUARTIMIN ROTATION FOR SIMPLE LOADINGS IS PERFORMED.
GAMMA . . . . . . . . . . . . . . . . . . . . .   0.0
MAXIMUM NUMBER OF ITERATIONS FOR ROTATION . . .    50
CONVERGENCE CRITERION FOR ROTATION. . . . . . . 0.0000100
KAISER'S NORMALIZATION. . . . . . . . . . . .     YES
```

--- ② to ⑨ from Output 4M.1 appear here ---

DIRECT OBLIMIN ROTATION, GAMMA =   0.0

ITERATION	SIMPLICITY CRITERION	
0	4.970519	㉓
1	2.951623	
2	1.207235	
3	0.730899	
4	0.708151	
5	0.707762	
6	0.707759	

ROTATED FACTOR LOADINGS (PATTERN)

		FACTOR 1	FACTOR 2	FACTOR 3	
CONCENTR	1	0.506	-0.046	0.459	㉔
ANNOY	2	0.887	-0.054	0.028	
SMOKING1	3	0.083	0.912	-0.080	
SLEEPY	4	-0.123	0.044	0.961	
SMOKING2	5	0.062	0.901	0.050	
TENSE	6	0.887	0.080	-0.049	
SMOKING3	7	-0.057	0.960	-0.050	
ALERT	8	0.455	-0.061	0.621	
IRRITABL	9	0.877	0.012	0.031	
TIRED	10	0.028	0.065	0.893	
CONTENT	11	0.897	0.050	-0.069	
SMOKING4	12	-0.044	0.907	0.142	
VP		3.643	3.411	2.356	

THE VP FOR EACH FACTOR IS THE SUM OF THE SQUARES OF THE
ELEMENTS OF THE COLUMN OF THE FACTOR PATTERN MATRIX
CORRESPONDING TO THAT FACTOR. WHEN THE ROTATION IS
ORTHOGONAL, THE VP IS THE VARIANCE EXPLAINED BY THE FACTOR.

FACTOR CORRELATIONS FOR ROTATED FACTORS

		FACTOR 1	FACTOR 2	FACTOR 3	
FACTOR	1	1.000			㉕
FACTOR	2	0.170	1.000		
FACTOR	3	0.446	0.174	1.000	

SORTED ROTATED FACTOR LOADINGS (PATTERN)

		FACTOR 1	FACTOR 2	FACTOR 3	
CONTENT	11	0.897	0.0	0.0	㉖
TENSE	6	0.887	0.0	0.0	
ANNOY	2	0.887	0.0	0.0	
IRRITABL	9	0.877	0.0	0.0	
CONCENTR	1	0.506	0.0	0.459	
SMOKING3	7	0.0	0.960	0.0	
SMOKING1	3	0.0	0.912	0.0	
SMOKING4	12	0.0	0.907	0.0	
SMOKING2	5	0.0	0.901	0.0	
SLEEPY	4	0.0	0.0	0.961	
TIRED	10	0.0	0.0	0.893	
ALERT	8	0.455	0.0	0.621	
VP		3.643	3.411	2.356	

THE ABOVE FACTOR LOADING MATRIX HAS BEEN REARRANGED SO
THAT THE COLUMNS APPEAR IN DECREASING ORDER OF VARIANCE
EXPLAINED BY FACTORS. THE ROWS HAVE BEEN REARRANGED
SO THAT FOR EACH SUCCESSIVE FACTOR, LOADINGS GREATER
THAN 0.5000 APPEAR FIRST. LOADINGS LESS THAN 0.2500
HAVE BEEN REPLACED BY ZERO.

--- the remainder of the results is analogous
    to ⑭ to ⑱ in Output 4M.1 ---

Example 4M.4 Printed Results: Standardized Scores, the Factor Score Coefficients, Partial Correlations and Residual Correlations

The PRINT paragraph is used to specify the results to be printed. You can also specify the number of cases to be printed from the original data matrix (five is the preassigned number).

In addition, you can request STANDARD scores, COVARIANCE matrix, INVERSE of the correlation (or covariance) matrix, PARTIAL correlations of each pair of variables removing the effects of all other variables, factor structure matrix (FSTR) when oblique rotation is performed, and RESIDUAL correlation matrix. The correlation matrix can be printed in SHADED form after sorting the variables according to the factors.

Rotated factor loadings are printed twice (see ⑪ and ⑬ in Output 4M.1). At the second printing loadings less than LOLEV in absolute value are replaced by zero and the variables are sorted according to the levels of loadings greater than HILEV. Since HILEV affects the sorting of the variables according to the factor loadings, it also affects the SHADED correlation matrix. The SHADED correlation matrix can be printed without sorting the variables if you specify HILEV=10 or some other large value.

Two other instructions are available for controlling the printing of the shaded correlation matrix. The first, NCUT, is used when overprinting is not available (e.g., on a terminal); it substitutes five symbols of varying density for the overprinted symbols. The width of this display (as well as much of the other output) is controlled by the instruction LINESIZE.

For this example we expand the Control Language of Example 4M.1 requesting several of the options. We insert this PRINT paragraph before the END paragraph.

```
------------------------------------
 / PRINT      STANDARD.
             FSCF.
             PARTIAL.
             RESIDUAL.
------------------------------------
```

In Output 4M.4 we reproduce results that are not printed in Output 4M.1. Circled numbers below correspond to those in Output 4M.4.

(27) Standard scores. For each value, $z_{ij} = (x_{ij} - \bar{x}_j)/s_i$ is computed and printed, where x_{ij} is the value of the ith variable in the jth case.

(28) Partial correlations. These are the correlations between each pair of variables after removing the linear effects of all the other variables. This matrix is equivalent (except for the signs of the off-diagonal elements) to the "anti-image" correlation matrix.

(29) Residual correlations. The residual correlations are R-AA', where $\underset{\sim}{R}$ is the original correlation matrix, $\underset{\sim}{\tilde{A}}$ the initial loadings matrix and $\underset{\sim}{A}'$ is the transpose of $\underset{\sim}{A}$.

(30) Factor score coefficients. The rotated factor loadings are multiplied by the factor correlations to obtain the factor structure (identical to factor loadings in the orthogonal case). The factor structure matrix contains the correlations of the factors with the variables. The factor structure is multiplied by the inverse of the correlation (or covariance) matrix of the original variables to obtain the factor score coefficients. These factor score coefficients are for the standardized variables.

Output 4M.4 Standardized scores, factor score coefficients, partial correlations and residual correlations are printed

---

--- (1) to (4) from Output 4M.1 are printed here ---

```
STANDARD SCORES          VARIABLE INDICES
-----------------------------------------------
LABEL    NO.   WEIGHT   1    2    3    4    5    6    7    8    9   10   11   12
          1    1.000   0.3 -0.1 -2.1  0.4 -1.5 -0.4 -2.1  0.2 -0.3 -1.1  0.6 -1.2
          2    1.000   1.2 -0.1  1.4  0.4  1.3  1.6  1.4  1.2  1.0  1.0  1.8  1.2    (27)
          3    1.000   2.2  0.9  0.6  1.4  1.3  2.6  0.5  2.2  1.0  1.0  0.6  0.4
          4    1.000   1.2 -0.1  0.6  0.4  1.3  1.6  0.5  1.2  1.0  1.0  0.6  1.2
          5    1.000   1.2 -0.1  0.6  0.4  0.4 -0.4  0.5  1.2 -0.3  1.0  0.6  0.4
```

--- similar standard scores for cases 6 to 105 ---

```
        106    1.000  -0.6 -1.1  0.6 -1.6  0.4 -0.4  0.5 -0.8 -0.3 -1.1 -0.5  0.4
        107    1.000  -0.6 -0.1 -0.3 -0.6 -0.5 -0.4  0.5 -0.8 -0.3 -1.1 -0.5  0.4
        108    1.000   1.2 -1.1 -2.1  1.4 -1.5 -1.5 -1.2  1.2 -0.3  1.0 -0.5 -1.2
        109    1.000   1.2 -0.1 -0.3  0.4 -0.5 -0.4 -0.4  0.2 -0.3 -0.1 -0.5  0.4
        110    1.000  -0.6 -0.1 -0.3 -1.6  0.4 -0.4 -1.2 -0.8 -0.3 -0.1 -0.5 -2.0
```

--- (5) and (6) from Output 4M.1 are printed ---

```
PARTIAL CORRELATIONS
--------------------

              CONCENTR ANNOY   SMOKING1 SLEEPY   SMOKING2 TENSE   SMOKING3 ALERT   IRRITABL TIRED   CONTENT SMOKING4
                 1       2        3       4        5       6        7       8        9      10       11      12

CONCENTR  1    1.000
ANNOY     2    0.118   1.000
SMOKING1  3   -0.066   0.019   1.000
SLEEPY    4   -0.056   0.174  -0.055   1.000
SMOKING2  5   -0.008  -0.242   0.250  -0.053   1.000                                              (28)
TENSE     6    0.106   0.201  -0.006  -0.031   0.230   1.000
SMOKING3  7   -0.133   0.123   0.299  -0.036   0.350  -0.134   1.000
ALERT     8    0.606  -0.090  -0.097   0.168   0.074   0.068  -0.011   1.000
IRRITABL  9    0.145   0.448   0.023  -0.018   0.068   0.231   0.075   0.016   1.000
TIRED    10   -0.075  -0.029   0.086   0.641   0.087  -0.079  -0.048   0.305   0.052   1.000
CONTENT  11   -0.199   0.375   0.159  -0.241   0.030   0.239  -0.104   0.315   0.098   0.081   1.000
SMOKING4 12    0.241  -0.006   0.207   0.180   0.250   0.017   0.476  -0.048  -0.142  -0.041   0.015   1.000
```

THE ELEMENTS OF THIS MATRIX ARE THE PARTIAL CORRELATIONS OF EACH PAIR OF VARIABLES, PARTIALED ON ALL OTHER VARIABLES (I.E., HOLDING ALL OTHER VARIABLES FIXED). CONDITION NUMBER = 0.492195D 02

--- (7) to (9) from Output 4M.1 are printed ---

RESIDUAL CORRELATIONS

		CONCENTR 1	ANNOY 2	SMOKING1 3	SLEEPY 4	SMOKING2 5	TENSE 6	SMOKING3 7	ALERT 8	IRRITABL 9	TIRED 10
CONCENTR	1	0.340									
ANNOY	2	−0.074	0.204								
SMOKING1	3	−0.028	0.010	0.161							
SLEEPY	4	−0.112	0.066	0.013	0.153						
SMOKING2	5	0.014	−0.049	−0.055	−0.026	0.144					
TENSE	6	−0.021	−0.073	−0.024	0.024	0.028	0.220				
SMOKING3	7	−0.000	0.034	−0.048	0.008	−0.042	−0.025	0.106			
ALERT	8	0.070	−0.078	−0.008	−0.093	0.024	−0.017	0.001	0.174		
IRRITABL	9	−0.044	0.002	−0.002	0.031	−0.005	−0.060	0.021	−0.054	0.202	
TIRED	10	−0.120	0.011	0.030	−0.038	−0.002	0.003	−0.006	−0.056	0.013	0.155
CONTENT	11	−0.098	−0.036	0.020	0.012	−0.008	−0.064	−0.016	0.007	−0.083	0.053
SMOKING4	12	0.054	0.009	−0.059	−0.011	−0.045	−0.000	−0.017	0.004	−0.016	−0.043

(29)

		CONTENT 11	SMOKING4 12
CONTENT	11	0.228	
SMOKING4	12	−0.012	0.130

ORTHOGONAL ROTATION, GAMMA =   1.0000

ITERATION	SIMPLICITY CRITERION
0	−1.900373
1	−6.017688
2	−6.019553
3	−6.019557

--- (11) to (14) from Output 4M.1 are printed ---

FACTOR SCORE COEFFICIENTS

THESE COEFFICIENTS ARE FOR THE STANDARDIZED VARIABLES,
MEAN ZERO AND STANDARD DEVIATION ONE.

		FACTOR 1	FACTOR 2	FACTOR 3
CONCENTR	1	0.09301	−0.03935	0.16307
ANNOY	2	0.27541	−0.03385	−0.09242
SMOKING1	3	0.01728	0.27403	−0.07719
SLEEPY	4	−0.17902	−0.01809	0.48035
SMOKING2	5	−0.00784	0.26672	−0.01128
TENSE	6	0.28382	0.00873	−0.13400
SMOKING3	7	−0.03190	0.29001	−0.04754
ALERT	8	0.05389	−0.04844	0.24844
IRRITABL	9	0.27036	−0.01415	−0.09178
TIRED	10	−0.12227	−0.01241	0.42845
CONTENT	11	0.29053	0.00039	−0.14409
SMOKING4	12	−0.05440	0.26711	0.04592

(30)

--- (15) to (18) from Output 4M.1 are printed ---

PRINT ─────
CASE = #.   5/prev.
  Number of cases for which data are printed.
FSCORE = #.   all factors
  Number of factors for which factor scores are
  printed. If no factor scores are desired,
  specify FSCORE=0.
STANdard.   no/prev.
  The standard scores are printed.
COVAriance.   no/prev.
  The covariance matrix is printed.
CORRelation.   CORRelation/prev.
  The correlation matrix is printed unless NO
  CORRELATION is specified.
INVerse.   no/prev.
  The inverse of the correlation (or covariance)
  matrix is printed.
PARTial.   no/prev.
  The partial correlations of each pair of
  variables are printed after removing the linear
  effects of all other variables. These partial
  correlations are the negatives of the
  "anti-image correlations."
FSTR.   no/prev.
  The factor structure matrix is printed when
  oblique rotation is performed.
FSCF.   no/prev.
  The factor score coefficients are printed.
RESIdual.   no/prev.
  Residual correlations are printed. The residual
  correlations are R−AA', where R is the
  correlation matrix, A the initial loadings
  matrix and A' the transpose of A.
SHADE.   yes/prev.
  The correlation matrix is printed in shaded
  form after the variables are sorted according
  to the factor loadings.
HILEV = #.   0.5/prev.
  Value considered as a high factor loading.
  Variables are sorted for each factor according
  to loadings greater than HILEV.
LOLEV = #.   0.25/prev.
  Value considered as a low factor loading.
  Values less than LOLEV are replaced by zero in
  the second printing of the rotated factor
  loadings.
NCUT = 5, 8 or 11.   8/prev.
  If overprinting is not available (e.g., on a
  terminal), specify both SHADE and NCUT = 5 for
  shading. NCUT = 11 means to use the first digit
  of the correlation.
LINESIZE = #.   132
  Number of columns permitted for printing
  (affects some but not all results).

Example 4M.5 Saving Factor Scores, Factor Loadings and Factor Score Coefficients for Later Analyses

Many of the results computed by P4M can be stored in a BMDP File for input to subsequent analyses. The results that can be saved include

DATA: the data and factor scores (both the data and the factor scores for each case are written into the BMDP File -- first the data and then the factor scores, which are named FACTOR1, FACTOR2, etc.)

COVA: the covariance matrix, variances, means, sample size and sum of weights (this is equivalent to saving a correlation matrix; the correlation matrix can be used in an analysis that reads the covariance matrix as input and vice versa)

UFLD: unrotated factor loadings

RFLD: rotated factor loadings

FCOR: factor correlations

FSCF: factor score coefficients

This example illustrates the order in which the BMDP Files are formed. To save results in a BMDP File insert the following SAVE paragraph before the END paragraph in the Control Language of Example 4M.1.

```
-------------------------------------
/ SAVE    UNIT IS 11.
          NEW.
          CODE IS JARVIK.
          CONTENT IS DATA, COVA, UFLD, RFLD, FCOR,
                     FSCF.
-------------------------------------
```

Note: the System information that precedes the Control Language must contain a card describing where to store the BMDP File (Section 7.3). In addition, space must be allocated for the System File.

The messages verifying that the BMDP Files are written in Output 4M.5. Note that the data and factor scores (DATA) are in the last BMDP File formed. The message that this File is completed appears after the estimated factor scores and Mahalanobis distances are printed.

```
SAVE ───────────────────────────────────
   CONTent = one or more                      DATA
              of list below
     COVA:  covariance matrix
     UFLD:  unrotated factor loadings
     RFLD:  rotated factor loadings
     FCOR:  factor correlations
     FSCF:  factor score coefficients
   The data or matrices to be saved in a BMDP
   File. DATA includes both data and factor
   scores. The factor scores appear after the data
   in each case and are named FACTOR1, FACTOR2,
   etc.
```

Output 4M.5 Saving factor analysis results in BMDP Files

```
--------------------------------------------------------------------------------------------------------




                    REQUESTED OUTPUT BMDP FILE
                    UNIT    =    11
                    CODE    = JARVIK
                    LABEL   =
                    CONTENT =
                             DATA (INPUT DATA MATRIX AND FACTOR SCORES)
                             COVA (COVARIANCE MATRIX)
                             UFLD (UNROTATED FACTOR LOADINGS)
                             RFLD (ROTATED FACTOR LOADINGS)
                             FCOR (FACTOR CORRELATION MATRIX)
                             FSCF (FACTOR SCORE COEFFICIENTS)


                        ---  (2)  from Output 4M.1 is printed ---


                    NUMBER OF CASES READ. . . . . . . . . . . .    110




                    BMDP FILE IS BEING WRITTEN ON UNIT        11
                    CODE. . . IS      JARVIK
                    CONTENT . IS      COVA
                    LABEL . . IS

                    VARIABLES ARE
                        1 CONCENTR    2 ANNOY      3 SMOKING1   4 SLEEPY    5 SMOKING2
                        6 TENSE       7 SMOKING3   8 ALERT      9 IRRITABL  10 TIRED
                       11 CONTENT    12 SMOKING4


                    BMDP   FILE ON UNIT 11 HAS BEEN COMPLETED.

                        ---  (3)  to  (9)  from Output 4M.1 are printed ---
```

```
BMDP FILE IS BEING WRITTEN ON UNIT        11
CODE. . . IS      JARVIK
CONTENT . IS      UFLD
LABEL . . IS

VARIABLES ARE
      1 CONCENTR    2 ANNOY      3 SMOKING1   4 SLEEPY     5 SMOKING2
      6 TENSE       7 SMOKING3   8 ALERT      9 IRRITABL  10 TIRED
     11 CONTENT    12 SMOKING4

BMDP    FILE ON UNIT 11 HAS BEEN COMPLETED.
```

--- ⑩ to ⑬ from Output 4M.1 are printed ---

```
BMDP FILE IS BEING WRITTEN ON UNIT        11
CODE. . . IS      JARVIK
CONTENT . IS      RFLD
LABEL . . IS

VARIABLES ARE
      1 CONCENTR    2 ANNOY      3 SMOKING1   4 SLEEPY     5 SMOKING2
      6 TENSE       7 SMOKING3   8 ALERT      9 IRRITABL  10 TIRED
     11 CONTENT    12 SMOKING4

BMDP    FILE ON UNIT 11 HAS BEEN COMPLETED.
```

```
BMDP FILE IS BEING WRITTEN ON UNIT         4
CODE. . . IS      JARVIK
CONTENT . IS      FCOR
LABEL . . IS

VARIABLES ARE
      1 FACTOR1     2 FACTOR2    3 FACTOR3

BMDP    FILE ON UNIT  4 HAS BEEN COMPLETED.
```

--- ⑭ from Output 4M.1 is printed ---

```
BMDP FILE IS BEING WRITTEN ON UNIT        11
CODE. . . IS      JARVIK
CONTENT . IS      FSCF
LABEL . . IS

VARIABLES ARE
      1 CONCENTR    2 ANNOY      3 SMOKING1   4 SLEEPY     5 SMOKING2
      6 TENSE       7 SMOKING3   8 ALERT      9 IRRITABL  10 TIRED
     11 CONTENT    12 SMOKING4

BMDP    FILE ON UNIT 11 HAS BEEN COMPLETED.
```

--- ⑮ from Output 4M.1 is printed ---

```
BMDP FILE IS BEING WRITTEN ON UNIT        11
CODE. . . IS      JARVIK
CONTENT . IS      DATA
LABEL . . IS

VARIABLES ARE
      1 CONCENTR    2 ANNOY      3 SMOKING1   4 SLEEPY     5 SMOKING2
      6 TENSE       7 SMOKING3   8 ALERT      9 IRRITABL  10 TIRED
     11 CONTENT    12 SMOKING4  13 FACTOR1   14 FACTOR2   15 FACTOR3
```

```
ESTIMATED FACTOR SCORES AND MAHALANOBIS DISTANCES (CHI-SQUARE S) FROM
EACH CASE TO THE CENTROID OF ALL CASES FOR THE ORIGINAL DATA
( 12 D.F.) FACTOR SCORES ( 3 D.F.) AND THEIR DIFFERENCE ( 9 D.F.).
EACH CHI-SQUARE HAS BEEN DIVIDED BY ITS DEGREES OF FREEDOM.
      CASE     CHISQ/DF CHISQ/DF CHISQ/DF  FACTOR    FACTOR    FACTOR
LABEL  NO.        12       3        9        1         2         3
        1       1.432    1.212    1.505    0.167    -1.899    0.014
        2       1.113    1.063    1.130    1.114     1.341    0.389
        3       1.333    1.238    1.365    1.357     0.511    1.269


       --- similar statistics for cases 4 to 107 ---


      108       1.459    2.926    0.970   -1.067    -1.752    2.138
      109       0.530    0.199    0.640   -0.337    -0.295    0.629
      110       2.035    0.488    2.550   -0.066    -0.765   -0.935

BMDP    FILE ON UNIT 11 HAS BEEN COMPLETED.
```

--- ⑰ and ⑱ from Output 4M.1 are printed ---

Example 4M.6 Further Analysis of Factor Scores in P7D (input only)

A frequent use of factor analysis is to combine many variables into a small number of factors as summary variables. The factor scores may then be used as input to some other analysis, e.g., analysis of variance, regression, or cluster analysis of cases. Suppose you have a file with one grouping variable and many dependent variables, say from a psychological questionnaire or test, the basic setup to use BMDP4M would be similar to that given below:

```
/ PROBLEM
/ INPUT    ...
/ VAR      USE = list of variables, excluding
                   grouping variable
/ SAVE     NEW UNIT = 9. CODE = YOURNAME.
/ END
```

Control Language for analysis of variance with BMDP7D would be similar to that given below:

```
/ PROBLEM
/ INPUT    UNIT = 9. CODE = YOURNAME.
/ HIST     GROUPING = ...
           VAR = list of variables containing
                  factor scores
/ END
```

Example 4M.7 Input Forms: Using a Correlation Matrix (on Cards) as Input

P4M can start an analysis from data, from a covariance or correlation matrix, or from orthogonal factor loadings or factor score coefficients.

If your input is data, you can skip the following discussion. If your input is not data, you must specify the TYPE of input unless it is from a BMDP File and the CONTENT of the BMDP File corresponds to one of the permissible TYPES defined below.

When the input is *not* from a BMDP File and TYPE is CORR or COVA, either a square matrix or a lower triangular matrix can be read as input. A lower triangular matrix has one element (the diagonal) in the first row, two elements in the second, etc. Even when a square matrix is read as input, only the lower half is used; the values in the matrix above the diagonal do not affect the analysis.

The deck setup below illustrates how to input a correlation matrix from cards (these correlations are the lower triangle of a 6x6 matrix).

```
/ PROBLEM
/ INPUT     VARIABLES ARE 6.
            TYPE IS CORR.
            SHAPE IS LOWER.
            FORMAT IS '(4F4.0)'.
/ END
1.00                      (1st row of corr. matrix)
 .85  1.00                (2nd row)
 .72   .63  1.00          (3rd row)
 .56   .42   .64  1.00    (4th row)
 .01   .09  -.11   .24    (5th row)
1.00                      (completion of 5th row)
 .21   .17   .06   .31    (6th row)
 .90  1.00                (completion of 6th row)
```

In the input the first four rows of the correlation matrix require only one card each since the SHAPE is LOWER; the last two rows require two cards each because the format allows only four variables per card. We do not show the output for this example.

When the input is *not* from a BMDP File and TYPE is LOAD or FSCF, the factors are read one at a time; that is, a factor in LOAD or FSCF corresponds to a case in DATA. The number of factors must be specified in the FACTOR statement of the INPUT paragraph.

```
INPut ─────────────────────────────────────────
  CONTent = c.    used only when input        DATA
                    is from a BMDP File
    If the input is not DATA, CONTENT must be
    specified. It must be identical to the CONTENT
    stated in the SAVE paragraph when the BMDP File
    was created.
  TYPE = (one only)            determined by CONTENT
         DATA,CORR,              if input is from a
         COVA,LOAD,              BMDP File; DATA
         FSCF                    otherwise
    Type of input. TYPE need not be specified when
    the input is data or when the input is from a
    BMDP File whose CONTENT corresponds to one of
    the names listed above. If input is factor
    loadings (LOAD), the factors are assumed to be
    orthogonal.
  SHAPE = (one only)                   SQUARE/prev.
          SQUARE,LOWER.
    Shape of the matrix when the input TYPE is CORR
    or COVA and is not read from a BMDP File. Each
    row of the matrix must begin in a new record.
    The format describes the longest row.
  FACTOR = #.                                  none
    Number of factors when the input TYPE is LOAD
    or FSCF and input is not read from a BMDP File.
    If TYPE is LOAD, the factors are assumed to
    orthogonal.
```

Example 4M.8 Computing Factor Scores when Alternate Input Forms Are Used: BMDP File Covariance Matrix Input

When input is a correlation or covariance matrix from a BMDP File, you can obtain factor scores if the data are on the same BMDP File as the matrix with the same BMDP File code. To match up variables from the data with the variables in the correlation or covariance matrix, the SCORE statement must be given. This option avoids recomputing the covariance or correlation matrix without losing the ability to obtain factor scores when you are using several methods of factoring.

When factor loadings or factor score coefficients are input from a BMDP File, factor scores can be obtained if the data and covariance matrix are in the same system file with the same code. This allows you to try several methods of rotation and to obtain factor scores without recomputing the covariance matrix or initial loadings. Moreover, by using this option, scores for one set of subjects can be obtained using factor score coefficients computed from another set of subjects. Factor scores can also be obtained for one set of variables using the factor score coefficients computed from another set of variables; e.g., factor scores for posttreatment variables can be obtained using factor score coefficients from a pretreatment factor analysis of the same variables. To match variables from the covariance matrix with variables from the loadings or coefficients, the USE statement can be used. To match variables from the data with variables in the loadings or coefficients matrix, the SCORE statement must be given. (Note that the covariance matrix is needed when SCORE is used since the means and standard deviations required for computing standard scores for the factor scores are stored with the covariance matrix.)

To demonstrate the use of the SCORE statement, a COVARIANCE matrix stored in a BMDP File in Example 4M.5 is read as input. The CODE for both the covariance matrix and the data is JARVIK, and both matrices are in the same system file on UNIT number 11. The full set of BMDP instructions for this example are:

```
-------------------------------------
/ PROBLEM     TITLE IS 'JARVIK SMOKING DATA'.
/ INPUT       UNIT IS 11.
             CODE IS JARVIK.
             CONTENT IS COVA.

/ VARIABLE    SCORES ARE 1 TO 12.

/ END
-------------------------------------
```

Note: The System Cards that precede the Control Language must contain a card describing where to find the BMDP File (Section 7.3).

The results are presented in Output 4M.8; they are identical to those in Output 4M.1 except that the panel of univariate statistics is not printed.

Output 4M.8   Starting a factor analysis from a covariance matrix and computing factor scores

----

```
INPUT BMDP FILE
CODE. . . IS     JARVIK
CONTENT . IS     COVA
LABEL . . IS

VARIABLES
    1 CONCENTR    2 ANNOY      3 SMOKING1   4 SLEEPY     5 SMOKING2
    6 TENSE       7 SMOKING3   8 ALERT      9 IRRITABL  10 TIRED
   11 CONTENT    12 SMOKING4


VARIABLES TO BE USED
    1 CONCENTR    2 ANNOY      3 SMOKING1   4 SLEEPY     5 SMOKING2
    6 TENSE       7 SMOKING3   8 ALERT      9 IRRITABL  10 TIRED
   11 CONTENT    12 SMOKING4

NUMBER OF VARIABLES TO BE USED. . . . . . . .    12



WEIGHT VARIABLE . . . . . . . . . . . . . . .
UNROTATED FACTORS ARE PRINCIPAL COMPONENTS.
NUMBER OF FACTORS IS LIMITED TO THE NUMBER OF EIGENVALUES
     GREATER THAN      1.000
TOLERANCE LIMIT FOR MATRIX INVERSION. . . . .    0.00010
VARIMAX ROTATION IS PERFORMED.
GAMMA . . . . . . . . . . . . . . . . . . . .    1.0000
MAXIMUM NUMBER OF ITERATIONS FOR ROTATION . . .   50
CONVERGENCE CRITERION FOR ROTATION. . . . . . 0.0000100
KAISER'S NORMALIZATION. . . . . . . . . . . .    YES
TOTAL DEGREES OF FREEDOM TO BE USED IN COMPUTATIONS    110


THE FOLLOWING VARIABLES WILL BE USED FOR COMPUTING FACTOR SCORES.

    1 CONCENTR
    2 ANNOY
    3 SMOKING1
    4 SLEEPY
    5 SMOKING2
    6 TENSE
    7 SMOKING3
    8 ALERT
    9 IRRITABL
   10 TIRED
   11 CONTENT
   12 SMOKING4



   --- the remainder of the results are the same as those in Output 4M.1 ---
```

```
VARiable ─────────────────────────────────────────
  SCORE = v list.                                none
    Names or subscripts of variables used for
    factor scores. This is used only when input is
    from a BMDP File and the data are not read as
    input. The SCORE statement signals P4M that
    factor scores are to be computed and that the
    data are in a BMDP File in the same system file
    with the same CODE as the covariance matrix,
    factor loadings or factor score coefficients
    read as input.
```

The Choice of Matrix to be Factored

You may choose to factor the correlation matrix, covariance matrix, the correlation matrix about the origin (i.e., assuming variable means are zero) or the covariance matrix about the origin. If a choice is not specified, the correlation matrix is factored. Note that the FORM statement in the FACTOR paragraph differs from the INPUT TYPE statement (p. 494) where you can input a covariance matrix and request the factor analysis to be performed on the correlation matrix.

```
FACTOR ───────────────────────────────────────────
  FORM = one only of list below        CORR/prev.
    The matrix to be factored.
    CORR:    the correlation matrix
    COVA:    the covariance matrix
    OCORR:   the correlation matrix about the
             origin
    OCOVA:   the covariance matrix about the
             origin
```

The Initial Communality Estimates

Communality estimates can be specified as one of three Control Language options or as a list of values, one for each variable. The three Control Language options are

UNALT: the diagonal of the correlation (or covariance) matrix remains unaltered
SMCS: the diagonal of the correlation (or covariance) matrix is replaced by the squared multiple correlations of each variable with the remaining variables (if the covariance matrix is factored, the squared multiple correlations are multiplied by the corresponding variances)
MAXROW: the diagonal elements of the correlation (or covariance) matrix are replaced by the maximum absolute row values of the correlation matrix (if the covariance matrix is factored, these values are multiplied by the corresponding variances)

```
FACTOR ───────────────────────────────────────────
  COMMunality = (one only)         UNALT for PCA;
                UNALT,SMCS,         SMCS otherwise
                MAXROW.
  or
  COMMunality = # list.
    The initial estimates of the communalities

    UNALT:    unaltered
    SMCS:     squared multiple correlation
    MAXROW:   maximum value in row

    Or you may specify a list of values, one number
    for each variable used, as the estimates. If
    USE is specified in the VARIABLE paragraph, the
    first value is for the first variable in the
    USE list, etc.
```

The Number of Factors

A maximum NUMBER of factors can be specified. In addition, the number of factors can be limited by requiring that the eigenvalues be greater than a CONSTANT.

```
FACTOR ───────────────────────────────────────────
  NUMBer = #.                       no. of variables
    The maximum number of factors obtained.
  CONSTant = #.                            1.0/prev.
    The factors obtained are restricted to those
    with eigenvalues greater than CONSTANT (to be
    included, a factor must satisfy both criteria;
    e.g., if you state NUMBER=10. and CONSTANT=2.,
    but only 8 eigenvalues are greater than 2, only
    8 factors are used). When the covariance matrix
    is factored, the limit is applied to the
    CONSTANT times the average variance of the
    variables.
    The number of factors for PCA, MLFA and LJIFFY
    is determined from the eigenvalues of the
    unaltered correlation matrix; for PFA from the
    eigenvalues of the correlation matrix after the
    substitution of communality estimates at each
    iteration.
```

The PLOT Paragraph

Two kinds of plots printed by P4M are illustrated in Output 4M.1.
- plots of the rotated factor loadings ⑫
- plots of the factor scores ⑱
You can also request plots of the unrotated factor loadings.

```
PLOT ─────────────────────────────────────────────
  INITial = #.                                    0
    Number of unrotated factors for which factor
    loadings are plotted. For each pair of factors
    the loadings of one factor are plotted against
    those of the other.
  FINAL = #.                                       4
    Number of rotated factors for which factor
    loadings are plotted. For each pair of factors
    the loadings of one factor are plotted against
    those of the other. If no plots are desired,
    state FINAL = 0.
  FSCORE = #.                                      3
    Number of factors for which factor scores are
    plotted. For each pair of factors the scores of
    one factor are plotted against those of the
    other. If no plots are desired state FSCORE=0.
```

Case Weights

The data in each case can be weighted by the values of a WEIGHT variable. Weights are used when the variance is not homogeneous over all cases (the weight is the inverse of the variance), or to represent the frequencies of cases that are repeated in the data (the weight is the frequency of the case), or to remove the influence of some cases (with weight zero) while still obtaining their factor scores and Mahalanobis distances.

The variable containing the case WEIGHT is specified in the VARIABLE paragraph. Case weights affect the computations of the means, variances and covariances (see Section 2.1).

```
VARiable ──────────────────────────────────────────
  WEIGHT = v.                    no weight var./prev.
    Name or subscript of the variable containing
    the case weights. Values of the case weight
    should be zero or positive (but never
    negative). If WEIGHT is not specified or is set
    to zero, there are no case weights.
```

TOLERANCE

The inverse of the correlation or covariance matrix is computed by stepwise pivoting. The TOLERANCE limit is used to determine whether to pivot on a variable. If the TOLERANCE limit is not met for any variable, the computations continue when METHOD is PCA or PFA but terminate when METHOD is MLFA or LJIFFY.

```
FACTOR ────────────────────────────────────────────
  TOLerance = #.                          .0001/prev.
    Tolerance limit. If the squared multiple cor-
    relation of any variable exceeds 1.0 minus
    TOLERANCE, that variable is considered a linear
    combination of the other variables and pivoting
    is not performed for that variable. When METHOD
    is MLFA or LJIFFY, the program terminates if
    any variable does not pass the tolerance limit.
    Note that if a zero intercept model is used,
    then the R² is estimated under the assumption
    that all variables have zero means.
```

SIZE OF PROBLEM

On medium-sized computer systems P4M can analyze up to 100 variables with 10 factors unless maximum likelihood factor analysis is requested, in which case only 60 variables can be analyzed. Appendix B describes how to increase the capacity of the program.

COMPUTATIONAL METHOD

Single precision is used for reading data and performing transformations. All other computations are performed in double precision. Means, standard deviations and covariances are computed by the method of provisional means (Appendix A.2). When case weights are used, the statistics are adjusted so that the average nonzero weight is one.

The description of many of the formulas is given in the program descriptions. Appendix A.21 describes the method of maximum likelihood factor analysis.

The inverse of the correlation or covariance matrix is computed by stepwise pivoting (Appendix A.11). Eigenvalues and eigenvectors are computed using routines from EISPACK (Garbow et al, 1977 and Smith et al, 1974).

The method of shading the correlation matrix is similar to that of Ling (1973).

ACKNOWLEDGEMENT

P4M was designed by James Frane with major contributions from Robert Jennrich and Paul Sampson. It was programmed by James Frane with major contributions from Paul Sampson.

SUMMARY

Order of Input Cards

```
// (job card)
// EXEC BIMED,PROG=BMDP4M        (see Appendix E)
//SYSIN DD *
/ PROBLEM
/ INPUT
/ VARIABLE
/ TRANSFORM
/ SAVE
/ FACTOR
/ ROTATE
/ PRINT
/ PLOT
/ END
    (data, if on cards)
// (system card)
```

Full sets of BMDP paragraphs (and data, if on cards) can be repeated for additional problems; see Section 5.8.

Paragraph Statement	Preassigned	Comment and Manual Reference
/ INPut		Additional options for special input. 494

Special input form from a BMDP File

CONTent = c.	DATA.	If input is not DATA, CONT must be specified and must be identical to that stated when the BMDP File was created (one only).

DATA - data and factor scores   UFLD - unrotated factor loadings
CORR - correlation matrix   RFLD - orthogonally rotated
COVA - covariance matrix   factor loadings
FCOR - factor correlation   FSCF - factor score coefficient

Special input NOT from a BMDP File

TYPE = c.	DATA.	DATA, CORR, COVA, LOAD or FSCF (one only). Use to specify input that is not DATA and is not from a BMDP File. If input is factor loadings, the factors are assumed to be orthogonal.
SHAPE = c.	SQUARE.	SQUARE or LOWER. When TYPE = CORR or COVA, SHAPE describes the input matrix. Each row of the matrix must begin in a new record. FORMAT describes the longest row.
FACTOR = #.	none	Use when TYPE = LOAD or FSCF to specify the number of factors.

/ VARiable		Additional options to specify case weights and factor scores.
WEIGHT = v.	none	Name or subscript of variable containing weight for each case. If a case has zero weight it is not used in computing loadings or factor score coefficients, but scores and distances are computed for it. * 497
SCOREs = v list.	none	Signals the program to compute factor scores when the input is a BMDP File covariance, correlation or loadings matrix and the data are stored in the same system file with the same CODE. Use names or subscripts of variables to match variables from the data with variables in the correlation or covariance matrix. 496

/ FACTOR		Optional to direct the initial factor extraction.
METHOD = c.	PCA.	Method used for initial factor extraction (one only). * 486

PCA   - principal component analysis
MLFA   - maximum likelihood factor
LJIFFY - Kaiser's Second Generation Little Jiffy
PFA   - principal factor analysis

FORM = c.	CORR.	Matrix to be factored (one only). * 496

CORR   - correlation matrix
COVA   - covariance matrix
OCORR - correlation matrix about the origin
OCOVA - covariance matrix about the origin

NUMBer = #.	VT.	The maximum number of factors obtained. If omitted, see CONST. (below)
CONSTant = #.	1.	Restrict the factors obtained to those with eigenvalues greater than CONST. * 496
COMMunality = c. or COMMunality = # list.	(see comment)	UNALT, SMCS or MAXROW (one only): the initial estimates of the communalities. The diagonal of the correlation (or covariance) matrix remains unaltered (UNALT), if replaced by squared multiple correlations of each variable with the remaining variables (SMCS.), or is replaced by the maximum in each row (MAXROW.) For COMM = # list specify one number for each variable used as the communality estimate. The first number is for the first variable in the USE list (if specified), the second number for the second variable, etc. If omitted, UNALT is assumed for METHOD = PCA; SMCS is assumed for other methods. * 496
ITERations = #.	25.	Maximum number of iterations performed for factor extraction. Applies only to MLFA or PFA. * 486
EPS = #.	.001.	Convergence criterion for iteration on communalities when METHOD = PFA. Iteration continues until communalities differ from those of the last iteration by EPS or less. * 486
TOLerance = #.	.0001.	TOLERANCE limit. If squared multiple correlation of any variable exceeds (1 - TOL) pivoting is not performed, the variable is considered a linear combination of the others. A form of generalized inverse is used for computing SMCS and factor scores. * 497

(continued)

(continued)

Paragraph Statement	Preassigned	Comment and Manual Reference
/ ROTATE		Optional to direct factor rotation. 488
METHod = c.	(see comment)	Factor rotation method (one only). If omitted, VMAX is used unless / FACTOR METHOD = LJIFFY, then ORTHOB is used. *
		VMAX. - varimax
		DQUART. - direct quartimin rotation for simple loadings (this method is recommended for oblique rotation)
		QRMAX. - quartimax
		EQMAX. - equamax
		ORTHOG. - othogonal with gamma (see below)
		ORTHOB. - orthoblique (only available with LJIFFY)
		NONE - no rotation
GAMMA = #.	(see comment)	Number is value of gamma used in simplicity criterion G for ORTHOG and DOBLI rotations. If omitted, 1.0 is preassigned for ORTHOG, 0.0 for DOBLI.
MAXITerate = #.	50.	Maximum number of iterations for rotation. *
CONSTant = #.	.00001.	Convergence criterion for rotation. *
NORMal.	yes	Perform Kaiser's normalization. *
/ PRINT		Optional to control printing of cases and matrices. 491
CASE = #.	5.	Number of cases for which original transformed data are printed. *
FSCORE = #.	all	Number of factors for which factor scores are printed.
STANDard.	no	Standard scores for each case. *
COVAriance.	no	Covariance matrix. *
CORRelation.	yes	Correlation matrix. *
INVerse.	no	Inverse of the correlation or covariance matrix. *
PARTial.	no	Partial correlations (negative of "anti-image" correlations). *
FSTR.	no	Factor structure matrix (oblique rotation performed). *
FSCF.	no	Factor score coefficients. *
RESI.	no	Residual correlations. *
SHADE.	yes	Display reordered correlations with symbols of different shading. *
NCUT = 5, 8 or 11.	8.	If overprinting is not available (e.g. on a terminal) specify both SHADE. and NCUT = 5., for overprinting state 8, for first digit only if correlations state 11.
HILEV = #.	.5.	Sort variables for displays according to loadings greater than HILEV. *
LOLEV = #.	.25.	Replace loadings less than LOLEV by zero in the sorted rotated factor loading display. *
LINEsize = #.	132.	Number of columns permitted for printing. (Affects only some results).
/ PLOT		Optional to control the number of factors displayed in plots. 497
INITial = #.	0.	Number of unrotated factor loadings.
FINAL = #.	4.	Number of rotated factor loadings.
FSCORE = #.	3.	Number of factor scores.
/ SAVE		Additional options required only if a BMDP File is to be created.
CONTent = c list.	DATA.	Specifies data or matrices to be saved in a BMDP File (one or more). 492
		DATA - data and factor scores
		COVA - covariance matrix, means, standard deviation, sample size and sum of weights
		UFLD - unrotated factor loadings
		RFLD - rotated factor loadings
		FCOR - factor correlations
		FSCF - factor score coefficients

Key:

/	-indicates paragraph	*	-assigned value remains the same for additional problems
.	-period ends a sentence		
•	-required	VT	-number of variables after transformations
v	-variable (name or subscript)	list	-more than one item, often one per var.
g	-group (name or subscript)		
#	-number		Capitalized letters-paragraph or sentence names recognized by BMDP
'c'	-characters (name or parameter) may omit apostrophes if contiguous letters only		Page numbers following refer to this Manual

```
-------------------------------------
/ PROBLEM    TITLE IS 'JARVIK SMOKING DATA'.
/ INPUT      VARIABLES ARE 12.
            FORMAT IS '(12F2.0)'.
/ VARIABLE   NAMES ARE CONCENTR, ANNOY, SMOKING1,
               SLEEPY, SMOKING2, TENSE,
               SMOKING3, ALERT, IRRITABL,
               TIRED, CONTENT, SMOKING4.

/ CANONICAL  FIRST ARE SMOKING1, SMOKING2,
               SMOKING3, SMOKING4.
            SECOND ARE CONCENTR, ANNOY, SLEEPY,
               TENSE, ALERT, IRRITABL,
               TIRED, CONTENT.

/ END
-------------------------------------
```

(See end of this P6M section for organization of systems information, BMDP instructions and data)

The results of the analysis by P6M are presented in Output 6M.1. Circled numbers below correspond to those in the output.

① Interpretation of BMDP instructions specific to P6M. Except for specifying the two sets of variables, all options are preassigned.

② Data for the first five cases. The number of cases printed can be specified; five is the preassigned number.

③ Number of cases read. Cases included in the computations are those that contain acceptable values for all the variables used in the analysis; cases are omitted from all computations when the value of any variable used in the analysis is missing or out of range.

④ Univariate statistics
- mean
- standard deviation
- coefficient of variation
- smallest observed value (not out of range)
- largest observed value (not out of range)
- smallest standard score
- largest standard score
- skewness
- kurtosis

In Section 2.1 these univariate statistics are defined and the effect of case weights on their computation is described.

⑤ Correlation matrix.

⑥ Squared multiple correlations (R^2) of each variable in the second set with all other variables in the second set.

⑦ Squared multiple correlations (R^2) of each variable in the first set with all other variables in the first set.

⑧ Eigenvalues are found for the canonical correlation problem (for the matrix $R_{xx}^{-\frac{1}{2}} R_{xy} R_{yy}^{-1} R_{yx} R_{xx}^{-\frac{1}{2}}$ defined in Appendix A.22). Anderson (1958), Cooley and Lohnes (1971) and Morrison (1967) discuss canonical correlation analysis.
- The eigenvalues are printed.
- The canonical correlations are the square roots of the eigenvalues.

P6M

18.2 Canonical Correlation Analysis

James Frane

ABSTRACT

P6M computes a canonical correlation analysis for two sets of variables and Bartlett's test for the significance of the remaining eigenvalues. Input can be data, a covariance matrix or a correlation matrix. Output includes canonical correlations with their associated eigenvalues and canonical variable loadings. P6M prints optional canonical variable scores and coefficients, covariance matrix, and bivariate plots of any other variable or canonical variable. The computations are done in double precision.

Example 6M.1 Basic Setup for Canonical Correlation Analysis

The Jarvik smoking questionnaire data (Table 17.1) are used in a canonical analysis by P6M. We specify the two sets of variables between which the canonical correlations are computed. The remaining BMDP instructions are common to all BMDP programs and are discussed in Chapter 5.

Output 6M.1 Canonical correlation analysis. Circled numbers correspond to those in the text
----

--- the BMDP instructions read by P6M are printed and interpreted ---

FIRST SET OF VARIABLES
  3 SMOKING1   5 SMOKING2   7 SMOKING3   12 SMOKING4   ①

SECOND SET OF VARIABLES
  1 CONCENTR   2 ANNOY   4 SLEEPY   6 TENSE   8 ALERT
  9 IRRITABL   10 TIRED   11 CONTENT

NUMBER OF VARIABLES IN FIRST SET.   4
NUMBER OF VARIABLES IN SECOND SET   8
TOTAL NUMBER OF VARIABLES USED.   12
MAXIMUM NUMBER OF CANONICAL VARIABLES   4
MINIMUM CANONICAL CORRELATION TO BE USED. . . .   0.0
WEIGHT VARIABLE . . . .
PRECISION . . . . DOUBLE
TOLERANCE FOR MATRIX INVERSION. 0.0001000
EIGENVALUE LIMIT. 0.0
APPROX. NUMBER OF VARIABLES WHICH CAN BE ANALYZED   144

DATA AFTER TRANSFORMATIONS FOR FIRST   5 CASES   ②
CASES WITH ZERO WEIGHTS AND MISSING DATA NOT INCLUDED.

C A S E NO. LABEL	3 SMOKING1 10 TIRED	5 SMOKING2 11 CONTENT	7 SMOKING3	12 SMOKING4	1 CONCENTR	2 ANNOY	4 SLEEPY	6 TENSE	8 ALERT	9 IRRITABL
1	1 2	2 3	1	2	3	2	3	2	3	2
2	5 4	5 4	5	5	4	2	3	4	4	3
3	4 4	5 3	4	4	5	3	4	5	5	3
4	4 4	5 3	4	5	4	2	3	4	4	3
5	4 4	4 3	4	4	4	2	3	2	4	2

NUMBER OF CASES READ.   110   ③

UNIVARIATE SUMMARY STATISTICS   ④

VARIABLE	MEAN	STANDARD DEVIATION	COEFFICIENT OF VARIATION	SMALLEST VALUE	LARGEST VALUE	SMALLEST STANDARD SCORE	LARGEST STANDARD SCORE	SKEWNESS	KURTOSIS
			J36275	1.00000	5.00000	-2.09	1.45	-0.36	-0.57
5 SMOKING2	3.58182	1.06126	0.296291	1.00000	5.00000	-2.43	1.34	-0.40	-0.63
7 SMOKING3	3.42727	1.16098	0.338747	1.00000	5.00000	-2.09	1.35	-0.42	-0.63
12 SMOKING4	3.50000	1.27610	0.364601	1.00000	5.00000	-1.96	1.18	-0.54	-0.79
1 CONCENTR	2.69091	1.07298	0.398744	1.00000	5.00000	-1.58	2.15	0.10	-0.81
2 ANNOY	2.11818	0.97427	0.459957	1.00000	5.00000	-1.15	2.96	0.89	0.33
4 SLEEPY	2.60909	1.02353	0.392295	1.00000	5.00000	-1.57	2.34	0.01	-0.80
6 TENSE	2.44545	0.99158	0.405480	1.00000	5.00000	-1.46	2.58	0.26	-0.79
8 ALERT	2.80909	1.01814	0.362445	1.00000	5.00000	-1.78	2.15	0.02	-0.48
9 IRRITABL	2.21818	0.78263	0.352825	1.00000	4.00000	-1.56	2.28	0.06	-0.63
10 TIRED	3.09091	0.95346	0.308473	1.00000	5.00000	-2.19	2.00	-0.31	-0.25
11 CONTENT	2.45455	0.84198	0.343027	1.00000	5.00000	-1.73	3.02	0.19	-0.16

VALUES FOR KURTOSIS GREATER THAN ZERO INDICATE DISTRIBUTIONS
WITH HEAVIER TAILS THAN THE NORMAL DISTRIBUTION.

(output continued)

Output 6M.1 (continued)

CORRELATIONS

		SMOKING1 3	SMOKING2 5	SMOKING3 7	SMOKING4 12	CONCENTR 1	ANNOY 2	SLEEPY 4	TENSE 6	ALERT 8	IRRITABL 9	TIRED 10	CONTENT 11
SMOKING1	3	1.000											
SMOKING2	5	0.785	1.000										
SMOKING3	7	0.810	0.816	1.000									
SMOKING4	12	0.775	0.813	0.845	1.000								
CONCENTR	1	0.086	0.200	0.041	0.228	1.000							
ANNOY	2	0.144	0.119	0.060	0.122	0.562	1.000						
SLEEPY	4	0.140	0.211	0.126	0.277	0.457	0.360	1.000					
TENSE	6	0.222	0.301	0.120	0.214	0.579	0.705	0.273	1.000				
ALERT	8	0.101	0.223	0.039	0.201	0.802	0.578	0.606	0.594	1.000			
IRRITABL	9	0.189	0.221	0.108	0.156	0.595	0.796	0.337	0.725	0.605	1.000		
TIRED	10	0.199	0.274	0.139	0.271	0.512	0.413	0.798	0.364	0.698	0.428	1.000	
CONTENT	11	0.239	0.235	0.100	0.171	0.492	0.739	0.240	0.711	0.605	0.697	0.394	1.000

(5)

--- shaded correlation matrix appears here ---

SQUARED MULTIPLE CORRELATIONS OF EACH VARIABLE IN
SECOND SET WITH ALL OTHER VARIABLES IN SECOND SET

VARIABLE		
NUMBER	NAME	R-SQUARED
1	CONCENTR	0.68425
2	ANNOY	0.72147
4	SLEEPY	0.67121
6	TENSE	0.63869
8	ALERT	0.79529
9	IRRITABL	0.70704
10	TIRED	0.71877
11	CONTENT	0.67799

(6)

SQUARED MULTIPLE CORRELATIONS OF EACH VARIABLE IN
FIRST SET WITH ALL OTHER VARIABLES IN FIRST SET

VARIABLE		
NUMBER	NAME	R-SQUARED
3	SMOKING1	0.71036
5	SMOKING2	0.74227
7	SMOKING3	0.79150
12	SMOKING4	0.76658

(7)

EIGENVALUE		CANONICAL CORRELATION
0.27278		0.52229
0.14128	(8)	0.37588
0.05779		0.24040
0.01882		0.13719

NUMBER OF EIGENVALUES	BARTLETT'S TEST FOR REMAINING EIGENVALUES		
	CHI-SQUARE	D.F.	SIGNIFICANCE
0	56.31	32	0.00502
1	23.66	21	0.30975
2	8.05	12	0.78129
3	1.95	5	0.85637

BARTLETT'S TEST ABOVE INDICATES THE NUMBER OF CANONICAL
VARIABLES NECESSARY TO EXPRESS THE DEPENDENCY BETWEEN THE
TWO SETS OF VARIABLES. THE NECESSARY NUMBER OF CANONICAL
VARIABLES IS THE SMALLEST NUMBER OF EIGENVALUES SUCH THAT
THE TEST OF THE REMAINING EIGENVALUES IS NON-SIGNIFICANT.
FOR EXAMPLE, IF A TEST AT THE .01 LEVEL WERE DESIRED,
THEN   1 VARIABLES WOULD BE CONSIDERED NECESSARY.
HOWEVER, THE NUMBER OF CANONICAL VARIABLES OF PRACTICAL
VALUE IS LIKELY TO BE SMALLER.

CANONICAL VARIABLE LOADINGS (CORRELATIONS OF CANONICAL VARIABLES WITH ORIGINAL VARIABLES)

(9)

		CNVRF1 1	CNVRF2 2	CNVRF3 3	CNVRF4 4
SMOKING1	3	-0.445	-0.534	-0.659	0.286
SMOKING2	5	-0.728	-0.384	-0.151	0.548
SMOKING3	7	-0.289	-0.270	-0.473	0.787
SMOKING4	12	-0.639	0.056	-0.565	0.518

		CNVRS1 1	CNVRS2 2	CNVRS3 3	CNVRS4 4
CONCENTR	1	-0.721	0.356	-0.013	-0.311
ANNOY	2	-0.303	-0.141	-0.384	-0.401
SLEEPY	4	-0.600	0.347	-0.377	0.260
TENSE	6	-0.700	-0.333	0.001	-0.178
ALERT	8	-0.730	0.156	0.149	-0.361
IRRITABL	9	-0.457	-0.337	-0.115	-0.072
TIRED	10	-0.691	0.027	-0.256	0.072
CONTENT	11	-0.532	-0.440	-0.308	-0.558

- Bartlett's (1947) test for the significance of the k smallest eigenvalues is printed, where k can be 1, 2, etc. The uppermost line (chi-square = 56.31) tests whether the eigenvalues differ significantly from zero; this is a test that the correlations between the two sets of variables are zero. A significant chi-square indicates that the two sets of variables are not independent. The next line (chi-square = 23.66) tests whether all eigenvalues but the largest differ significantly from zero; this is a test of whether the first canonical variable is sufficient to describe the dependence between the two sets of variables. The number of canonical variables of practical value is less than or equal to the smallest number of eigenvalues for which Bartlett's test for the remaining eigenvalues is nonsignificant.

⑨ Canonical variable loadings. These are the correlations of the canonical variables with the original variables. CNVRF1 is the name assigned by P6M to the 1st canonical variable in the first set; CNVRF2 to the 2nd, etc. CNVRS1 is the name assigned to the 1st canonical variable in the second set, etc. These correlations are analogous to unrotated factor loadings.

The canonical paragraph. The variables included in each set of variables must be specified in the CANONICAL paragraph. Each set should contain at least two variables; otherwise a regression program (Chapter 13) should be used.

The number of canonical variables to be obtained can be stated explicitly (NUMBER). If not stated the number is determined by the program as being all canonical variables whose correlations are greater than CONSTANT. (CONSTANT is preset to zero.)

In addition, you can specify the tolerance for matrix inversion and whether covariances and correlations are computed about the mean or about the origin.

```
CANONical ─────────────────────────────────────────
  FIRST = v list.      required              none
    Names or subscripts of variables in the first
    set of variables. At least two variables must
    be specified.
  SECOND = v list.     required              none
    Names or subscripts of variables in the second
    set of variables. At least two variables must
    be specified.
  NUMBer = #.              # of vars. in smaller set
    Maximum number of canonical variables to be
    obtained.
  CONSTant = #.                         0.0/prev.
    Canonical variables obtained must have a
    canonical correlation that exceeds CONSTANT.
  TOLerance = #.     between          0.0001/prev.
                     0.0 & 1.0
    Tolerance for matrix inversion. Inversion is
    performed by stepwise pivoting. A variable is
    not pivoted if its squared multiple correlation
    with already pivoted variables exceeds 1 minus
    TOLERANCE, or if pivoting causes an already
    pivoted variable to have a squared multiple
    correlation with other pivoted variables that
    exceeds 1 minus TOLERANCE. Note that if a zero
    intercept model is used, then the R² is estima-
    ted under the assumption that all variables
    have zero means.
  ZERO.
    Covariances and correlations are computed about
    the origin and not about the mean. This is a
    rarely used option.
```

Example 6M.2 Printing the Coefficients of the Canonical Variables and the Canonical Variable Scores

In addition to the correlation matrix and the canonical variable loadings printed in 6M.1, P6M can print the covariance matrix, the canonical variables and the regression coefficients for the canonical variables. The number of cases for which the data

---

Output 6M.2 Scores and coefficients of the canonical variables

----

--- ② to ⑧ in Output 6M.1 are printed ---

COEFFICIENTS FOR CANONICAL VARIABLES FOR FIRST SET OF VARIABLES

		CNVRF1	CNVRF2	CNVRF3	CNVRF4	⑩
		1	2	3	4	
SMOKING1	3	0.378543D-01	-0.976451D 00	-0.965493D 00	-0.900841D 00	
SMOKING2	5	-0.109322D 01	-0.646536D 00	0.134105D 00	0.182999D 00	
SMOKING3	7	0.119115D 01	-0.173899D 00	-0.333693D-01	0.145194D 01	
SMOKING4	12	-0.704060D 00	0.128569D 01	-0.660196D 00	-0.214955D 00	

STANDARDIZED COEFFICIENTS FOR CANONICAL VARIABLES FOR FIRST SET OF VARIABLES
(THESE ARE THE COEFFICIENTS FOR THE STANDARDIZED VARIABLES - MEAN ZERO, STANDARD DEVIATION ONE.)

		CNVRF1	CNVRF2	CNVRF3	CNVRF4
		1	2	3	4
SMOKING1	3	0.043	-1.104	-1.092	-1.019
SMOKING2	5	-1.160	-0.686	1.423	0.194
SMOKING3	7	1.383	-0.202	-0.039	1.686
SMOKING4	12	-0.898	1.641	-0.842	-0.274

(output continued)

Output 6M.2 (continued)

<u>COEFFICIENTS</u> FOR CANONICAL VARIABLES FOR SECOND SET OF VARIABLES

		CNVRS1 1	CNVRS2 2	CNVRS3 3	CNVRS4 4
CONCENTR	1	-0.441692D 00	0.745510D 00	-0.470381D 00	-0.163811D 00
ANNOY	2	0.801410D 00	0.461495D 00	-0.605503D 00	-0.739549D 00
SLEEPY	4	-0.250790D 00	0.581216D 00	-0.685988D 00	0.615867D 00
TENSE	6	-0.692552D 00	-0.380734D 00	0.421877D 00	0.448775D 00
ALERT	8	0.140028D 00	0.204741D 00	0.150159D 01	-0.685341D 00
IRRITABL	9	0.900002D-01	-0.795294D 00	0.425982D 00	0.113746D 01
TIRED	10	-0.327905D 00	-0.616257D 00	-0.246355D 00	0.172116D 00
CONTENT	11	-0.402041D 00	-0.595032D 00	-0.971468D 00	-0.795208D 00

<u>STANDARDIZED COEFFICIENTS</u> FOR CANONICAL VARIABLES FOR SECOND SET OF VARIABLES
(THESE ARE THE COEFFICIENTS FOR THE STANDARDIZED VARIABLES - MEAN ZERO, STANDARD DEVIATION ONE.)

		CNVRS1 1	CNVRS2 2	CNVRS3 3	CNVRS4 4
CONCENTR	1	-0.474	0.800	-0.505	-0.176
ANNOY	2	0.781	0.450	-0.590	-0.721
SLEEPY	4	-0.257	0.595	-0.702	0.630
TENSE	6	-0.687	-0.378	0.418	0.445
ALERT	8	0.143	0.208	1.529	-0.698
IRRITABL	9	0.070	-0.622	0.333	0.890
TIRED	10	-0.313	-0.588	-0.235	0.164
CONTENT	11	-0.339	-0.501	-0.818	-0.670

CANONICAL VARIABLES (CASE NUMBERS REFER TO DATA BEFORE DELETION OF CASES)

LABEL	CASE NO.	WEIGHT	CNVRF1	CNVRF2	CNVRF3	CNVRF4	CNVRS1	CNVRS2	CNVRS3	CNVRS4
	1	1.0000	-0.1954	1.8242	1.2321	-1.3620	0.1247	1.1330	-0.5973	-0.9229
	2	1.0000	-0.6712	-0.8597	-0.7208	0.7465	-2.5299	-1.3010	0.2394	-0.1880
⑪	3	1.0000	-1.1961	-0.9950	0.9382	0.4104	-2.5714	0.9062	1.3725	0.0831
	4	1.0000	-1.9002	0.2907	0.2780	0.1954	-2.1278	-0.7060	1.2109	0.6072
	5	1.0000	-0.1029	-0.3485	-0.4028	0.2274	-0.8327	0.8508	-0.0588	-1.4278

--- canonical variables for cases 6 to 105 ---

	106	1.0000	-0.1029	-0.3485	-0.4028	0.2274	0.5286	-0.8461	1.3204	0.2293
	107	1.0000	0.9525	1.2745	-0.7784	0.9452	1.0792	0.1966	0.0289	0.1056
	108	1.0000	0.9958	1.6503	1.1987	0.0899	-0.7903	1.9462	0.4103	0.2740
	109	1.0000	-0.2387	1.4484	-0.7450	-0.5067	-0.2428	1.8573	-0.3426	-0.1194
	110	1.0000	-0.4109	-2.8813	2.6100	-1.1308	1.0021	-1.0009	0.4685	-0.3382

NUMERICAL CONSISTENCY CHECK

THE FOLLOWING VARIANCES OF CANONICAL VARIABLES SHOULD ALL BE EQUAL TO ONE

CANONICAL VARIABLE	VARIANCE	RELATIVE ERROR
CNVRF1	0.100000D 01	0.187350D-14
CNVRF2	0.100000D 01	0.301148D-14
CNVRF3	0.100000D 01	0.213718D-14
CNVRF4	0.100000D 01	0.337230D-14
CNVRS1	0.100000D 01	-0.155431D-14
CNVRS2	0.100000D 01	0.141553D-14
CNVRS3	0.100000D 01	0.366374D-14
CNVRS4	0.100000D 01	0.327516D-14

⑫

--- ⑨ in Output 6M.1 is printed ---

are printed can also be specified (CASE=). To get
the coefficients and scores we add a PRINT paragraph
to the BMDP instructions of Example 6M.1 before the
END paragraph

```
    ---------------------------------------
  / PRINT    MATRICES ARE CORR, CANV, COEF, LOAD.
    ---------------------------------------
```

The correlation and loading matrices are printed
in Output 6M.1. Circled numbers below correspond to
those in the Output 6M.2.

(10) Coefficients of the canonical variables for
the first set of variables. The second panel
contains the standardized coefficients; i.e.,
coefficients for the standardized variables (with
mean zero and standard deviation one). The two
panels are then repeated for the second set of
variables.

(11) Values of the canonical variables for each
case.

(12) A numerical consistency check.

```
PRINT ───────────────────────────────────────────
  CASE = #.                                        5/prev.
    Number of cases for which data are printed.
  MATRices = one or more of            CORR,LOAD
               the list below.
    Matrices to be printed.
    CORR: correlations
    COVA: covariances
    COEF: coefficients of the canonical variables
    CANV: values of the canonical variables
    LOAD: canonical variable loadings.
    When any matrix is specified, only the
    specified matrices are printed.
  NCUT = 5, 8 or 11.                               8/prev.
    If overprinting is not available (e.g., on a
    terminal), specify both SHADE and NCUT = 5 for
    shading. NCUT = 11 means to use the first digit
    of the correlation.
  SHADE.                                          yes/prev.
    The correlation matrix is printed in shaded
    form.
```

Output 6M.3 Plots of the canonical variable scores

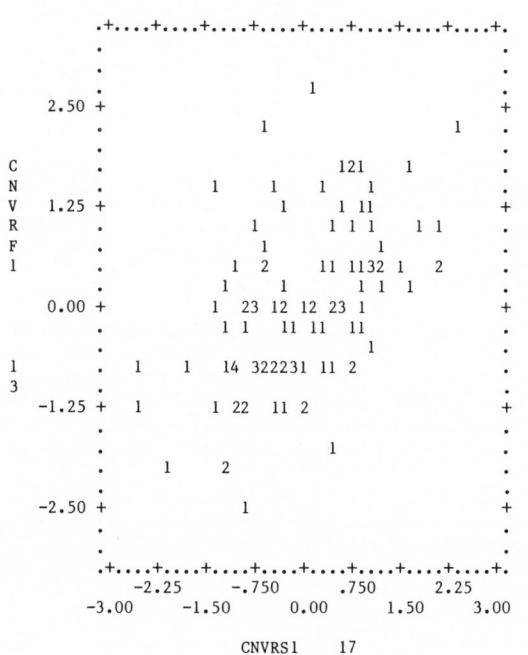

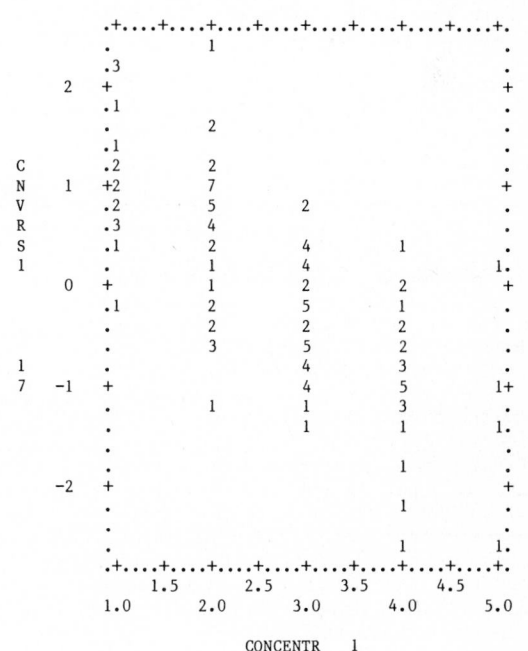

Example 6M.3 Plotting the Canonical Variable Scores

Any variable or canonical variable can be plotted against any other variable or canonical variable. The canonical variables are named
CNVRF1, CNVRF2, etc. for variables in the first set
and
CNVRS1, CNVRS2, etc. for variables in the second set.

To illustrate these plots we add a PLOT paragraph to the BMDP instructions of Example 6M.1 before the END paragraph

```
------------------------------------------
/ PLOT    XVARS ARE CNVRS1, CONCENTR.
         YVARS ARE CNVRF1, CNVRS1.
         SIZE IS 40, 25.
------------------------------------------
```

In the first frame the scores for the first canonical variable are plotted versus the scores for the second canonical variable. In the next frame scores for the second canonical variable are plotted against the values of the variable CONCENTR. We request that the plot size be smaller than the assumed size.

```
PLOT ─────────────────────────────────────
  YVARiable = v list.                        none
    Names or subscripts of variables to be plotted
    vertically (along the Y-axis).
  XVARiable = v list.                        none
    Names or subscripts of variables to be plotted
    horizontally (along the X-axis).

  Note: Both original and canonical variables can
  be specified. The first YVARiable is plotted
  against the first XVARiable, the second against
  the second, etc.

  SIZE = #,#.                          50,35/prev.
    The first number is the number of characters
    (width) in the horizontal axis and the second
    number is the number of lines (height) in the
    vertical axis.
```

Using a Covariance or a Correlation Matrix as Input

P6M can start an analysis from data or from a covariance or correlation matrix.

If your input is data, you can skip the following discussion. If your input is not data, you must specify the TYPE of input unless it is from a BMDP File and the CONTENT of the BMDP File corresponds to one of the permissible TYPES defined below.

When the input is not from a BMDP File and TYPE is CORR or COVA, either a square matrix or a lower triangular matrix can be read as input (SHAPE). A lower triangular matrix has one element (the diagonal) in the first row, two elements in the second, etc. The Control Language setup for this is given in the Example 4M.7.

```
INPut ─────────────────────────────────────
  CONTent = c.    used only when input          DATA
                  is from a BMDP File
    If the input is not DATA, CONTENT must be
    specified. It must be identical to the CONTENT
    stated in the SAVE paragraph when the BMDP File
    was created.
  TYPE = (one only)              determined by CONTENT
         DATA,COVA,              if input is from a
         CORR.                   BMDP File; DATA
                                 otherwise
    Type of input. TYPE need not be specified when
    the input is data or when the input is a
    covariance or correlation matrix from a BMDP
    File.
  SHAPE = (one only)                     SQUARE/prev.
          SQUARE,LOWER.
    Shape of the matrix when the input TYPE is CORR
    or COVA and is not read from a BMDP File. Each
    row of the matrix must begin in a new record.
    The format describes the longest row.
```

Saving Canonical Variable Scores and the Covariance Matrix for Later Analyses

Both the data (including canonical variables) and the covariance matrix can be saved in a BMDP File and used as input to subsequent analyses.

```
SAVE ──────────────────────────────────────
  CONTent = (one or both)                      DATA
            DATA, COVA.
    The data (including canonical variables) or the
    covariance matrix or both can be saved in a
    BMDP File. If DATA is specified, each case
    contains the variables, followed by the first
    set of canonical variables and then the second
    set of canonical variables; the variables in
    the first set are named CNVRF1, CNVRF2, etc.
    and those in the second set CNVRS1, CNVRS2,
    etc.
    Note: If a BMDP File is being created, an extra
    System Card is necessary (Section 7.1)
```

Case Weights

The data in each case can be weighted by the values of a WEIGHT variable. Weights are used when the variance is not homogeneous over all cases (the weight is the inverse of the variance), or to represent the frequencies of cases that are repeated in the data (the weight is the frequency of the case), or to remove the influence of some cases (with weight zero) from the computations of the canonical correlations while still allowing computation of their canonical variable scores.

The variable containing the case WEIGHT is specified in the VARIABLE paragraph. The effect of case weights on the computations of the means, variances and covariances is described in Section 2.1.

VARiable ──────────────────────────────────
| WEIGHT = v.   no weight var./prev.
| Name or subscript of the variable containing
| the case weights. Values of the case weight
| should be zero or positive (but never
| negative). If WEIGHT is not specified or is set
| to zero, there are no case weights.
└───

SIZE OF PROBLEM

On medium-sized computer systems P6M can analyze approximately 80 variables. Appendix B describes how to increase the capacity of the program.

COMPUTATIONAL METHOD

Single precision is used for reading data and performing transformations. All other computations are performed in double precision. Means, standard deviations, skewness and kurtosis are computed by the method of provisional means (Appendix A.2). When weights are used, the statistics are adjusted so that the average nonzero weight is one.

The computational procedure for the canonical analysis is described in Appendix A.22.

ACKNOWLEDGEMENT

P6M was designed and programmed by James Frane with assistance from Paul Sampson.

SUMMARY

Order of Input Cards

```
// (job card)
// EXEC BIMED,PROG=BMDP6M        (see Appendix E)
//SYSIN DD *
/ PROBLEM
/ INPUT
/ VARIABLE
/ TRANSFORM
/ SAVE
/ CANONICAL
/ PRINT
/ PLOT
/ END
    (data if on cards)
// (system card)
```

Full sets of BMDP paragraphs (and data, if on cards) can be repeated for additional problems; see Section 5.8.

Paragraph Statement	Preassigned	Comment and Manual Reference
/ INPut		Additional input options. 506
CONTent = c.	DATA.	Use when DATA, COVA or CORR is read from a BMDP File. If input is not DATA, CONT must be specified, and must be the same as that stated when the BMDP File was created.
TYPE = c.	(see comment)	DATA, COVA or CORR (one only). Specifies COVA or CORR matrix input not from a BMDP File. Also see SHAPE. If omitted, input is DATA, or is determined by CONT of input from a BMDP File.
SHAPE = c.	SQUARE.	SQUARE or LOWER (one only), shape of matrix. Use with TYPE = CORR or COVA to describe matrix. Each row of the matrix must begin a new record. FORMAT describes the longest row; only FORTRAN FORMAT is permitted.
/ VARiable		Additional option to specify case weight.
WEIGHT = v.	none	Name or subscript of variable containing weight for each case. * 507
/●CANONical		Required to direct the analysis. 503
● FIRST = v list.	none	Names or subscripts of variables in the first set of variables. At least two must be specified.
● SECOND = v list.	none	Names or subscripts of variables in the second set of variables. At least two must be specified.
NUMBER = #.	(see comment)	Maximum number of canonical variables. If omitted, number in smaller set is used.
CONSTant = #.	0.0.	Canonical variables are obtained only if they have a canonical correlation greater than CONST. *
TOLerance = #.	0.0001.	Tolerance for matrix inversion. *
ZERO.	no	Compute covariances and correlations about the origin, not about the mean. *
/ PRINT		Optional to direct printing. 505
CASE = #.	5.	Number of cases for which data are printed. *
MATRices = c list.	CORR,LOAD.	Matrices to be printed (one or more): CORR -correlations COEF -coefficients of the canonical variables COVA -covariances CANV -canonical variable scores LOAD -canonical variable loadings.
NCUT = 5, 8 or 11.	8.	If overprinting is not available (e.g., on a terminal), specify both SHADE and NCUT = 5 for shading. NCUT = 11 means to use the first digit of the correlation. *
SHADE.	yes	The correlation matrix is printed in shaded form. *
/ PLOT		Optional to specify variables and/or canonical variable scores to be plotted. 506
XVAR = v list. YVAR = v list.	none	Names or subscripts of variables to be plotted horizontally (XVAR) or vertically (YVAR). The names of the canonical variables in the First set are CNVRFj; in the Second set they are CNVRSj (see /SAVE).
SIZE = #, #.	50, 35.	Width of x-axis (characters); height of y-axis (lines). *
/ SAVE		Additional option required only to create a BMDP File. 506
CONTent = c list.	DATA.	The data (including the canonical variables), or the covariance matrix, or both, can be saved. For each case the saved data are the original data, then the canonical variables for the first set (named CNVRF1, CNVRF2, ...) and finally the canonical variables for the second set (CNVRS1, CNVRS2, ...).

Key:

/	-indicates paragraph	*	-assigned value remains the same for additional problems
.	-period ends a sentence		
●	-required	VT	-number of variables after transformations
v	-variable (name or subscript)	list	-more than one item, often one per var.
g	-group (name or subscript)		
#	-number	Capitalized letters-paragraph or sentence names recognized by BMDP
'c'	-characters (name or parameter) may omit apostrophes if contiguous letters only	Page numbers following refer to this Manual

P6R

18.3 Partial Correlation and Multivariate Regression

James Frane

ABSTRACT

P6R computes the partial correlations of a set of variables after removing the linear effects of a second set of variables. The program can also be used for regression, especially if several dependent variables are to be predicted with the same set of variables (multivariate regression). Computations are performed in double precision. The analysis can be started using data, the covariance matrix or the correlation matrix. Case weights can be specified. P6R prints the partial correlations, regression coefficients and their standard errors, squared multiple correlations, and residuals.

WHERE TO FIND IT

Example 6R.1 Basic Setup for Multivariate Regression and Partial Correlation

The Werner blood chemistry data (Table 5.1) are used to illustrate the results from P6R. The four blood chemistry measurements (CHOLSTRL, ALBUMIN, CALCIUM, URICACID) are specified as the DEPENDENT variables and the three physical measurements (AGE, HEIGHT and WEIGHT) as the INDEPENDENT variables. The remaining Control Language instructions are described in Chapter 5.

```
/ PROBLEM    TITLE IS 'WERNER BLOOD CHEMISTRY DATA'.
/ INPUT      VARIABLES ARE 9.
            FORMAT IS '(A4,5F4.0, 3F4.1)'.
/ VARIABLE   NAMES ARE ID, AGE, HEIGHT, WEIGHT,
                BRTHPILL  CHOLSTRL, ALBUMIN,
                CALCIUM, URICACID.
            MAXIMUM IS (6)400.
            MINIMUM IS (6)150.
            BLANKS ARE MISSING.
            LABEL IS ID.

/ REGRESS    DEPENDENT ARE CHOLSTRL, ALBUMIN,
                CALCIUM, URICACID.
            INDEPENDENT ARE AGE, HEIGHT, WEIGHT.

/ END
```

(See end of this P6R section for organization of systems information, BMDP instructions and data.)

The results of the analysis are presented in Output 6R.1. Circled numbers below correspond to those in the output.

① Interpretation of the Control Language instructions specific to P6R. Some of the listed options are preassigned.

② Data for the first five cases are printed. The number of cases printed can be specified.

③ Number of cases read. Cases included in the computations are those that contain acceptable values for all the variables used in the analysis; cases are omitted from all computations when the value of any variable used in the analysis is missing or out of range.

④ Univariate statistics
- mean
- standard deviation
- coefficient of variation
- smallest observed value (not out of range)
- largest observed value (not out of range)
- smallest standard score
- largest standard score
- skewness
- kurtosis

In Section 2.1 the univariate statistics are defined and the effect of a case weight on their computations is described.

⑤ Correlation matrix. The matrix is also printed in shaded form.

⑥ Squared multiple correlations (SMC or R^2) of each independent variable with all other independent variables. This is a measure of the multi-collinearity of the independent (predictor) variables (for a discussion see Gunst and Mason, 1977). The SMC is transformed to an F statistic that has $(I-1)$ and $(N-1)$ degrees of freedom, where I is the number of independent variables and N is the number of cases analyzed. The SMC is one minus the tolerance reported in other BMDP programs. The F statistic is a test of the significance of the regression of each independent variable on all the other independent variables and may not be appropriate in some circumstances.

⑦ Squared multiple correlations (SMC) of each dependent variable with the independent variables. The SMC is transformed to an F statistic with I and (N-I-1) degrees of freedom. These are tests of significance of the regression of each dependent variable on the independent variables.

⑧ Partial correlations between the dependent variables after removing the linear effects of the independent variables. In this example, these partial correlations do not differ greatly from the original correlations in ⑤ due to the relatively low correlations of the dependent variables with the independent variables.

Specifying the regression. The REGRESS paragraph is required. It is used to specify the DEPENDENT and INDEPENDENT variables. If the problem has only one DEPENDENT variable you should use one of the regression programs in Chapter 13.

REGRess ────────
  DEPENDent = v list.   required   none
    Names or subscripts of the dependent variables.
  INDEPendent = v list.   required   none
    Names or subscripts of the independent variables.

Note: The partial correlations of the variables in the DEPENDENT statement are computed, removing the linear effects of the variables in the INDEPENDENT statement.

Exception: If either the DEPENDENT or INDEPENDENT statement is not present, the correlation and covariance matrices will be produced for the variables indicated in whichever statement is present. If neither statement is present, the correlation and covariance matrices will be produced for all variables in the USE statement of the VARIABLE paragraph.

Output 6R.1 Partial correlation analysis. Circled numbers correspond to those in the text

----

--- the BMDP instructions read by P6R are printed and interpreted ---

```
INDEPENDENT VARIABLES ARE
    2 AGE          3 HEIGHT      4 WEIGHT

DEPENDENT VARIABLES ARE
    6 CHOLSTRL     7 ALBUMIN     8 CALCIUM      9 URICACID

NUMBER OF INDEPENDENT VARIABLES . . . . . . . .    3      ①
NUMBER OF DEPENDENT VARIABLES . . . . . . . . .    4
TOTAL NUMBER OF VARIABLES USED. . . . . . . .      7
WEIGHT VARIABLE . . . . . . . . . . . . . .
PRECISION . . . . . . . . . . . . . . . . . . .  DOUBLE
TOLERANCE FOR MATRIX INVERSION. . . . . . . 0.0001000
```

C A S E NO. LABEL	2 AGE	3 HEIGHT	4 WEIGHT	6 CHOLSTRL	7 ALBUMIN	8 CALCIUM	9 URICACID	
1 2381	22	67	144	200	4.300	9.800	5.400	
3 1610	25	62	128	243	4.100	10.400	3.300	②
5 561	19	64	125	158	4.100	9.900	4.700	
6 2519	19	67	130	255	4.500	10.500	8.300	
7 225	20	64	118	210	3.900	9.500	4	

```
NUMBER OF CASES READ. . . . . . . . . . . . . .    188
  CASES WITH DATA MISSING OR BEYOND LIMITS . .      8      ③
    REMAINING NUMBER OF CASES . . . . . . . .       180
```

UNIVARIATE SUMMARY STATISTICS   ④

VARIABLE	MEAN	STANDARD DEVIATION	COEFFICIENT OF VARIATION	SMALLEST VALUE	LARGEST VALUE	SMALLEST STANDARD SCORE	LARGEST STANDARD SCORE	SKEWNESS	KURTOSIS
2 AGE	33.53889	9.89801	0.295120	19.00000	55.00000	-1.47	2.17	0.40	-0.99
3 HEIGHT	64.46667	2.48211	0.385023D-01	57.00000	71.00000	-3.01	2.63	-0.12	-0.04
4 WEIGHT	131.09444	20.49982	0.156374	94.00000	215.00000	-1.81	4.09	1.06	1.94
6 CHOLSTRL	235.83889	42.74377	0.181241	155.00000	390.00000	-1.89	3.61	0.46	0.06
7 ALBUMIN	4.12056	0.35872	0.870566D-01	3.20000	5.00000	-2.57	2.45	-0.07	-0.36
8 CALCIUM	9.96778	0.47280	0.474325D-01	8.80000	11.10000	-2.47	2.39	-0.03	-0.58
9 URICACID	4.75556	1.12111	0.235748	2.20000	9.90000	-2.28	4.59	1.18	2.92

VALUES FOR KURTOSIS GREATER THAN ZERO INDICATE DISTRIBUTIONS WITH HEAVIER TAILS THAN THE NORMAL DISTRIBUTION.

CORRELATIONS

		AGE 2	HEIGHT 3	WEIGHT 4	CHOLSTRL 6	ALBUMIN 7	CALCIUM 8	URICACID 9
AGE	2	1.000						
HEIGHT	3	0.089	1.000					
WEIGHT	4	0.255	0.473	1.000				
CHOLSTRL	6	0.365	0.011	0.146	1.000			
ALBUMIN	7	-0.079	-0.006	-0.235	0.057	1.000		
CALCIUM	8	-0.009	0.143	0.065	0.255	0.453	1.000	
URICACID	9	0.209	0.125	0.304	0.274	0.030	0.166	1.000

(5)

ABSOLUTE VALUES OF CORRELATIONS IN SHADED FORM.

```
    2 AGE        ▊
    3 HEIGHT    .▊
    4 WEIGHT    X▊▊
    6 CHOLSTRL  ▊ -▊
    7 ALBUMIN   . +▊
    8 CALCIUM     -.X▊▊
    9 URICACID  +-▊X -▊
```

THE ABSOLUTE VALUES OF
THE MATRIX ENTRIES HAVE BEEN PRINTED ABOVE IN SHADED FORM
ACCORDING TO THE FOLLOWING SCHEME

		LESS THAN OR EQUAL TO	0.059
.	0.059	TO AND INCLUDING	0.118
-	0.118	TO AND INCLUDING	0.178
+	0.178	TO AND INCLUDING	0.237
X	0.237	TO AND INCLUDING	0.296
N	0.296	TO AND INCLUDING	0.355
▊	0.355	TO AND INCLUDING	0.414
▊		GREATER THAN	0.414

SQUARED MULTIPLE CORRELATION OF EACH INDEPENDENT
VARIABLE WITH ALL OTHER INDEPENDENT VARIABLES (MEASURES
OF MULTICOLLINEARITY OF PREDICTOR VARIABLES)
AND TESTS OF SIGNIFICANCE OF MULTIPLE REGRESSION
DEGREES OF FREEDOM FOR F-STATISTICS ARE   2 AND   177

VARIABLE NO. NAME	SQUARED MULTIPLE CORRELATION	MULTIPLE CORRELATION	F-STATISTIC	SIGNIFICANCE (P LESS THAN)
2 AGE	0.06645	0.25779	6.30	0.00228
3 HEIGHT	0.22522	0.47457	25.73	0.00000
4 WEIGHT	0.26991	0.51953	32.72	0.00000

(6)

SQUARED MULTIPLE CORRELATION OF EACH DEPENDENT VARIABLE
WITH THE INDEPENDENT VARIABLES
AND TESTS OF SIGNIFICANCE OF MULTIPLE REGRESSION
DEGREES OF FREEDOM FOR F-STATISTICS ARE   3 AND   176

VARIABLE NO. NAME	SQUARED MULTIPLE CORRELATION	MULTIPLE CORRELATION	F-STATISTIC	SIGNIFICANCE (P LESS THAN)
6 CHOLSTRL	0.13920	0.37310	9.49	0.00001
7 ALBUMIN	0.06957	0.26376	4.39	0.00527
8 CALCIUM	0.02087	0.14447	1.25	0.29301
9 URICACID	0.11080	0.33287	7.31	0.00012

(7)

PARTIAL CORRELATIONS OF DEPENDENT VARIABLES REMOVING
LINEAR EFFECTS OF INDEPENDENT VARIABLES

		CHOLSTRL 6	ALBUMIN 7	CALCIUM 8	URICACID 9
CHOLSTRL	6	1.000			
ALBUMIN	7	0.117	1.000		
CALCIUM	8	0.284	0.474	1.000	
URICACID	9	0.209	0.116	0.163	1.000

(8)

Example 6R.2 Partial Covariances, Standardized Regression Coefficients and Residuals

In this example we request all the available print options except for a printout of the covariance matrix and the data. You can specify the number of cases for which the data are listed; the data for five cases are listed if the number is not stated. The following PRINT paragraph is added to the Control Language of Example 6R.1 before the END paragraph.

```
------------------------------------
/ PRINT    MATRICES ARE CORR, PART, COVAPART,
                CREG, RREG, COEF,
                STANC, TTEST, RESI.
------------------------------------
```

The results are presented in Output 6R.2. The matrices that are not printed in Output 6R.1 are described below. Circled numbers below correspond to those in Output 6R.2.

⑨ Partial covariances of the dependent variables after removing the linear effects of the independent variables. The diagonal of the matrix contains the residual mean squares (RMS) for the regression of the dependent variable on the independent variables. The partial covariance is related to the partial correlation by $COV_{ik} = CORR_{ik} \cdot \sqrt{RMS_i \, RMS_k}$ where i and k are variable subscripts.

⑩ The covariances of the estimates of the regression coefficients are proportional to the inverse of the matrix of cross products of deviations for the independent variables. This inverse is printed in ⑩. It must be multiplied by the residual mean square of each dependent variable to obtain the covariances of the estimates for the dependent variable. The residual mean square can be obtained from the diagonal of the partial covariance matrix in ⑨.

⑪ Correlations of the estimates of the regression coefficients.

⑫ Regression coefficients for predicting the dependent variables from the independent variables. Each column in the output contains the coefficients for a dependent variable. The standard errors of the regression coefficients are printed in the second panel.

⑬ Standardized regression coefficients. These regression coefficients are for the standardized variables (mean zero and standard deviation one). The standardized regression coefficients are the ordinary coefficients divided by the standard deviations of the dependent variables and multiplied by the standard deviations of the independent variables.

⑭ t statistics for the regression coefficients. These are the ratios of the estimates of the regression coefficients to their standard errors. Two-tail significance levels for the t statistics are printed in the second panel.

⑮ Residuals. The values of the residuals for each dependent variable for each case are printed. P6R generates names for the residuals. Each name consists of the letter R followed by the first seven

Output 6R.2 Optional results: partial covariances, standardized regression coefficients, t statistics for regression coefficients and residuals

----

--- ① to ⑧ appear here ---

PARTIAL COVARIANCES OF DEPENDENT VARIABLES REMOVING LINEAR EFFECTS OF INDEPENDENT VARIABLES. (DIAGONAL CONTAINS RESIDUAL MEAN SQUARES).

		CHOLSTRL 6	ALBUMIN 7	CALCIUM 8	URICACID 9
CHOLSTRL	6	1599.51			
ALBUMIN	7	1.63423	0.121770		
CALCIUM	8	5.36129	0.780566D-01	0.222602	
URICACID	9	8.90839	0.432441D-01	0.820099D-01	1.13668

⑨

COVARIANCES FOR ESTIMATES OF REGRESSION COEFFICIENTS.

FOR EACH DEPENDENT VARIABLE, THE COVARIANCES OF THE REGRESSION COEFFICIENTS ARE OBTAINED BY MULTIPLYING THE MATRIX BELOW BY THE RESIDUAL MEAN SQUARE FOR THAT DEPENDENT VARIABLE. THE RESIDUAL MEAN SQUARE IS OBTAINED FROM THE DIAGONAL OF THE PARTIAL COVARIANCE MATRIX.

⑩		AGE	HEIGHT 3	WEIGHT 4
AGE	2	0.610824D-04		
HEIGHT	3	0.997340D-05	0.117038D-02	
WEIGHT	4	-0.809975D-05	-0.683191D-04	0.182083D-04

CORRELATIONS FOR ESTIMATES OF REGRESSION COEFFICIENTS

⑪		AGE 2	HEIGHT 3	WEIGHT 4
AGE	2	1.000		
HEIGHT	3	0.037	1.000	
WEIGHT	4	-0.243	-0.468	1.000

REGRESSION COEFFICIENTS FOR PREDICTING DEPENDENT VARIABLES (COLUMNS)
FROM INDEPENDENT VARIABLES (ROWS)

⑫

		CHOLSTRL 6	ALBUMIN 7	CALCIUM 8	URICACID 9
AGE	2	1.50586	-0.573597D-03	-0.105425D-02	0.158066D-01
HEIGHT	3	-1.03747	0.195152D-01	0.273779D-01	-0.813286D-02
WEIGHT	4	0.178744	-0.515375D-02	0.527286D-04	0.151227D-01
INTERCEPT		0.228784D 03	0.355734D 01	0.823126D 01	0.276721D 01

STANDARD ERRORS FOR REGRESSION COEFFICIENTS

		CHOLSTRL 6	ALBUMIN 7	CALCIUM 8	URICACID 9
AGE	2	0.313	0.273D-02	0.369D-02	0.833D-02
HEIGHT	3	1.37	0.119D-01	0.161D-01	0.365D-01
WEIGHT	4	0.171	0.149D-02	0.201D-02	0.455D-02
INTERCEPT		0.807D 02	0.704D 00	0.952D 00	0.215D 01

STANDARDIZED REGRESSION COEFFICIENTS FOR PREDICTING COLUMN VARIABLES
FROM ROW VARIABLES. (THESE ARE THE COEFFICIENTS FOR THE STANDARDIZED
VARIABLES - STANDARD DEVIATION ONE.)

⑬

		CHOLSTRL 6	ALBUMIN 7	CALCIUM 8	URICACID 9
AGE	2	0.349	-0.016	-0.022	0.140
HEIGHT	3	-0.060	0.135	0.144	-0.018
WEIGHT	4	0.086	-0.295	0.002	0.277
INTERCEPT		5.352	9.917	17.410	2.468

T-STATISTICS FOR REGRESSION COEFFICIENTS   DEGREES OF FREEDOM =   176

FOR EACH DEPENDENT VARIABLE, THE T-STATISTIC FOR EACH
INDEPENDENT VARIABLE IS FOR THE SIGNIFICANCE OF THAT
INDEPENDENT VARIABLE GIVEN THE OTHER INDEPENDENT VARIABLES.

⑭

		CHOLSTRL 6	ALBUMIN 7	CALCIUM 8	URICACID 9
AGE	2	4.82	-0.21	-0.29	1.90
HEIGHT	3	-0.76	1.63	1.70	-0.22
WEIGHT	4	1.05	-3.46	0.03	3.32
INTERCEPT		2.84	5.05	8.65	1.29

SIGNIFICANCE LEVELS (TWO-TAIL) FOR T-STATISTICS

		CHOLSTRL 6	ALBUMIN 7	CALCIUM 8	URICACID 9
AGE	2	0.000	0.834	0.775	0.059
HEIGHT	3	0.449	0.104	0.092	0.824
WEIGHT	4	0.296	0.001	0.979	0.001
INTERCEPT		0.005	0.000	0.000	0.200

(output continued)

Output 6R.2 (continued)

NAMES FOR RESIDUALS ARE CREATED BY THE PROGRAM USING R FOLLOWED
BY THE FIRST SEVEN CHARACTERS OF THE CORRESPONDING VARIABLE NAME.

RESIDUALS (CASE NUMBERS REFER TO DATA BEFORE DELETION OF CASES)

	CASE					
LABEL	NO.	WEIGHT	RCHOLSTR 10	RALBUMIN 11	RCALCIUM 12	RURICACI 13
2381	1	1.000	-18.1414	0.1899	-0.2500	0.6523
1610	3	1.000	18.0135	0.0067	0.4909	-1.2938
561	5	1.000	-55.3401	-0.0512	-0.0700	0.2626
2519	6	1.000	43.8786	0.3160	0.4476	3.8114
225	7	1.000	-3.5948	-0.2867	-0.4686	-0.3473

(15)

--- residuals for cases 8 to 182 ---

1250	183	1.000	-13.3523	0.1185	-0.3460	0.5955
1789	184	1.000	3.1088	0.4140	0.5205	1.6969
575	186	1.000	-46.1832	-0.0739	0.7377	-0.5935
2271	187	1.000	35.1310	0.1999	0.3104	-0.6734
39	188	1.000	-58.2387	-0.3211	-1.0260	0.5963

NUMERICAL CONSISTENCY CHECK

RESIDUAL MEAN SQUARES ARE COMPUTED FROM BOTH COVARIANCE
MATRIX AND RESIDUALS, AND RELATIVE DIFFERENCE (DIFFERENCE
DIVIDED BY SMALLER OF TWO ESTIMATES) IS COMPUTED.

RESIDUAL MEAN SQUARES COMPUTED FROM

	COVARIANCE MATRIX	RESIDUALS	RELATIVE DIFFERENCE
RCHOLSTR	0.159951D 04	0.159951D 04	0.106614D-15
RALBUMIN	0.121770D 00	0.121770D 00	0.136761D-14
RCALCIUM	0.222602D 00	0.222602D 00	0.498747D-15
RURICACI	0.113668D 01	0.113668D 01	-0.390690D-15

----

letters of the name of the dependent variable. For example, RCHOLSTR is the name assigned to the residual for CHOLSTRL.

PRINT ————
  CASE = #.   5/prev.
    Number of cases for which data are listed.
  MATRices = one or more of   CORR, PART
             the list below
    The matrices to be printed.

  CORR: correlations ((5) in Output 6R.1)
  COVA: covariances
  PART: partial correlations ((8) in Output 6R.1)
  COVAPART: partial covariances ((9) in Output 6R.2)
  CREG: covariances of the regression coefficients ((10) in Output 6R.2)
  RREG: correlations of the regression coefficients ((11) in Output 6R.2)
  COEF: regression coefficients and their standard errors ((12) in Output 6R.2)
  STANC: standardized regression coefficients ((13) in Output 6R.2)
  TTEST: t tests for regression coefficients ((14) in Output 6R.2)
  RESI: residuals for each dependent variable ((15) in Output 6R.2)

If any matrix is specified, only those matrices specified are printed.

SHADE.   yes/prev.
  The correlation matrix is printed in shaded form after the variables are sorted according to the factor loadings.
NCUT = 5, 8 or 11.   8/prev.
  If overprinting is not available (e.g., on a terminal), specify both SHADE and NCUT = 5 for shading. NCUT = 11 means to use the first digit of the correlation.

Example 6R.3 Plotting Variables and Residuals

Any variable or residual can be plotted against any other variable or residual. The residuals can also be plotted in a normal probability plot. In the set of residuals for each dependent variable the residuals are named R followed by the first seven letters of the variable name. We illustrate the use of the residual names by plotting the residuals of CHOLSTRL (named RCHOLSTR) against the residuals of ALBUMIN (named RALBUMIN) and the values of CHOLSTRL against values of ALBUMIN. The following PLOT paragraph is added to the Control Language of Example 6R.1 before the END paragraph:

/ PLOT   XVAR = RCHOLSTR, CHOLSTRL.
          YVAR = RALBUMIN, ALBUMIN.
          SIZE IS 40, 25.

The two plots are presented in Output 6R.3.

```
┌ PLOT ──────────────────────────────────────┐
│  XVAR = v list.                        none │
│    Names or subscripts of the variables or  │
│    residuals to be plotted horizontally (along the │
│    X-axis).                                 │
│  YVAR = v list.                        none │
│    Names or subscripts of the variables or  │
│    residuals to be plotted vertically (along the │
│    Y-axis).                                 │
│    Note: Each variable or residual in XVAR is │
│    plotted against the corresponding variable or │
│    residual in YVAR. The names of the residuals │
│    are R followed by the first seven letters of │
│    the name of the dependent variable.      │
│  SIZE = #,#.                      50,35/prev. │
│    The first number is the number of characters │
│    (width) in the horizontal axis and the second │
│    number is the number of lines (height) in the │
│    vertical axis.                           │
│  NORMal.                           no/prev. │
│    Print a normal probability plot of the   │
│    residuals.                               │
└─────────────────────────────────────────────┘
```

Example 6R.4 Saving Residuals, Partial Covariances and Correlations

The data (including residuals), covariance matrix and partial covariance matrix can be saved in a BMDP File for input to subsequent analyses. We illustrate saving the data and the partial covariance matrix in Example 6R.4 by adding the following SAVE paragraph to the Control Language of Example 6R.1 before the END paragraph:

```
----------------------------------------
/ SAVE      UNIT IS 9.
           NEW.
           CODE IS WERNER.
           CONTENT IS DATA, COVAPART.
----------------------------------------
```

Note: The System Cards that precede the Control Language must contain a card describing where to store the BMDP File (Section 7.1). The messages verifying that the BMDP Files are written are shown in Output 6R.4. In the BMDP File containing the data (DATA), each case consists of the data for the case followed by the residuals.

Output 6R.3 Plots of variables and residuals

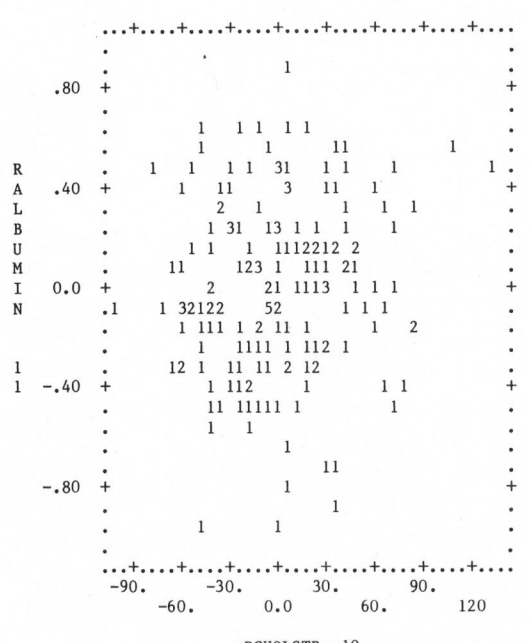

RCHOLSTR   10

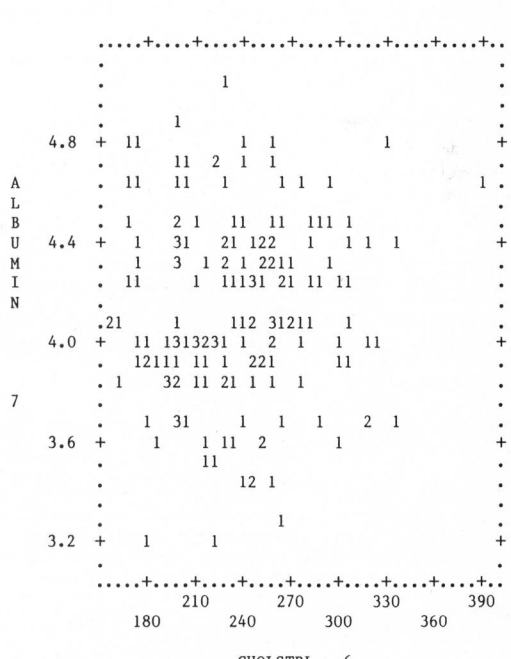

CHOLSTRL   6

SAVE ────────────────────────────────

| CONTent = (one or more)   DATA |
| DATA,COVA,COVAPART. |
| The data (including residuals), the covariance |
| matrix or the partial covariance matrix can be |
| saved in a BMDP File. If DATA is specified, |
| each case contains the data followed by the |
| residuals; the residuals are named R followed |
| by the first seven letters of the name of the |
| dependent variable. |

Alternate Input

   P6R can start an analysis from data or from a
covariance or correlation matrix. If your input is
data, you can skip the following discussion. If your
input is not data, you must specify the TYPE of
input unless it is from a BMDP File and the CONTENT
of the BMDP File corresponds to one of the
permissible TYPES defined below.

Output 6R.4   Saving partial covariances and residuals in BMDP Files

----

```
                        REQUESTED OUTPUT BMDP FILE
                           UNIT    =       9
                           CODE    = WERNER
                           LABEL   =
                           CONTENT =
                                    DATA
                                    COVAPART


                    --- results of the analysis are printed ---



            PARTIAL CORRELATIONS OF DEPENDENT VARIABLES REMOVING
            LINEAR EFFECTS OF INDEPENDENT VARIABLES

                         CHOLSTRL ALBUMIN  CALCIUM  URICACID
                             6        7        8        9


            CHOLSTRL  6    1.000
            ALBUMIN   7    0.117    1.000
            CALCIUM   8    0.284    0.474    1.000
            URICACID  9    0.209    0.116    0.163    1.000




            --------------------------------------------
            BMDP FILE IS BEING WRITTEN ON UNIT        9
            CODE. . . IS       WERNER
            CONTENT . IS       COVAPART
            LABEL . . IS

            VARIABLES ARE
                 10 RCHOLSTR    11 RALBUMIN    12 RCALCIUM    13 RURICACI

            BMDP   FILE ON UNIT  9 HAS BEEN COMPLETED.
            --------------------------------------------



            NAMES FOR RESIDUALS ARE CREATED BY THE PROGRAM USING R FOLLOWED
            BY THE FIRST SEVEN CHARACTERS OF THE CORRESPONDING VARIABLE  NAME.

            --------------------------------------------
            BMDP FILE IS BEING WRITTEN ON UNIT        9
            CODE. . . IS       WERNER
            CONTENT . IS       DATA
            LABEL . . IS

            VARIABLES ARE
                  1 ID           2 AGE        3 HEIGHT      4 WEIGHT      5 BRTHPILL
                  6 CHOLSTRL     7 ALBUMIN    8 CALCIUM     9 URICACID   10 RCHOLSTR
                 11 RALBUMIN    12 RCALCIUM   13 RURICACI


            BMDP   FILE ON UNIT  9 HAS BEEN COMPLETED.
            --------------------------------------------
            NUMBER OF CASES WRITTEN TO FILE      188
```

When the input is <u>not</u> from a BMDP File and TYPE is CORR or COVA, either a square matrix or a lower triangular matrix can be read as input. A lower triangular matrix has one element (the diagonal) in the first row, two elements in the second, etc.

Refer to Example 4M.7.

```
INPut ─────────────────────────────────────────
  CONTent = c.    used only when input      DATA
                  is from a BMDP File
    If the input is not DATA, CONTENT must be
    specified. It must be identical to the CONTENT
    stated in the SAVE paragraph when the BMDP File
    was created.
  TYPE = (one only)      determined by CONTENT
        DATA,COVA,     if input is from a BMDP
        CORR.          File; DATA otherwise
    Type or input. TYPE need not be specified when
    the input is data or when the input is a
    covariance or correlation matrix from a BMDP
    File.
  SHAPE = (one only)              SQUARE/prev.
        SQUARE,LOWER.
    Shape of the matrix when the input TYPE is CORR
    or COVA and is not read from a BMDP File. Each
    row of the matrix must begin in a new record.
    The format describes the longest row.
```

Covariances or Correlations Computed about the Origin

Usually covariances and correlations are computed around the mean. You may want to compute them about the origin (i.e., as if the means were known to be zero). If so, indicate ZERO in the REGRESS paragraph.

```
REGRess ───────────────────────────────────────
  ZERO.                           not ZERO/prev.
    If ZERO is specified, the covariances and
    correlations are computed about the origin.
    Note: This is a rarely used option.
```

TOLERANCE

Computations are done in double PRECISION. A TOLERANCE limit is used in the matrix inversion to guard against singularity.

```
REGRess ───────────────────────────────────────
  TOLerance = #.   between 0.0     0.0001/prev.
                   and 1.0
    Tolerance limit for matrix inversion. Inversion
    is performed by stepwise pivoting. A variable
    is not pivoted if its squared multiple correla-
    tion with already pivoted variables exceeds 1.0
    minus TOLERANCE or if pivoting it will cause
    the R² of any variable already pivoted with the
    remaining pivoted variables to exceed 1.0 minus
    TOLERANCE. Note that if a zero intercept model
    is used, then the R² is estimated under the
    assumption that all variables have zero means.
```

Case Weights

The data in each case can be weighted by a value supplied by the user. Weights are used when the variance is not homogeneous over all cases (the weight is the inverse of the variance), to represent the frequencies of cases that are repeated in the data (the weight is the frequency of the case), or to remove the influence of some cases (with zero weights) while still computing their residuals.

The variable containing the value of weight for each case is specified in the VARIABLE paragraph. The effect of case weights on the computations of the means, variances and covariances is described in Section 2.1.

```
VARiable ──────────────────────────────────────
  WEIGHT = v.              no weight var./prev.
    Name or subscript of the variable containing
    the case weights. Values of the case weight
    should be zero or positive (but never
    negative). If WEIGHT is not specified or is set
    to zero, there are no case weights.
```

SIZE OF PROBLEM

A maximum of 100 variables can be analyzed on medium-sized computer systems. Appendix B describes how to increase the capacity of the program.

COMPUTATIONAL METHOD

The data are read and transformations are made in single precision. All computations are performed in double precision. Means, standard deviations, and the covariance matrix are computed by the method of provisional means (Appendix A.2).

The computations performed by P6R are described in Appendix A.11, except that P6R can have more than one specified dependent variable.

ACKNOWLEDGEMENT

P6R was designed and programmed by James Frane.

SUMMARY

Order of Input Cards

```
// (job card)
// EXEC BIMED,PROG=BMDP6R        (see Appendix E)
//SYSIN DD *
/ PROBLEM
/ INPUT
/ VARIABLE
/ TRANSFORM
/ SAVE
/ REGRESS
/ PRINT
/ PLOT
/ END
    (data, if on cards)
// (system card)
```

Full sets of BMDP paragraphs (and data, if on cards) can be repeated for additional problems; see Section 5.8.

Paragraph Statement	Preassigned	Comment and Manual Reference
/ INPut		Additional input options. 517
TYPE = c.	DATA.	DATA, COVA or CORR (one only). Used to specify input that is not from a BMDP File.
SHAPE = c.	SQUARE.	SQUARE or LOWER (one only). Shape of matrix when TYPE is CORR or COVA and <u>not</u> read from a BMDP File. Each row of the matrix must begin a new record. FORMAT describes the longest row; only FORTRAN FORMAT is permitted. *
/ VARiable		Additional options to specify case weights. 517
WEIGHT = v.	none	Name or subscript of variable containing a case weight. *
/●REGRess		Required to direct regressions.
●DEPENDent = v list.	none	Names or subscripts of the dependent variables. Partial correlations of the variables in DEPEND are computed, removing the linear effects of the variables in INDEP. 510
●INDEP = v list.	none	Names or subscripts of the independent variables. 510
TOLerance = #.	.0001.	Value between 0.01 and 1.0 to prevent numerically redundant variables from being included in equation. * 517
ZERO.	no	Compute covariances and correlations about the origin (zero). This option is rarely used. * 517
/ PRINT		Optional to specify results to be printed. If MATR is specified, only matrices specified are printed; if omitted, CORR and PART are printed and data for the first 5 cases are listed. 514
CASE = #.	5.	Number of cases for which data are listed. *
MATRices = c list.	CORR,PART.	Print one or more of the following matrices: CORR - correlations COVA - covariances PART - partial correlations COVAPART - partial covariances CREG - covariances of the regression coefficients RREG - correlations of the regression coefficients COEF - regression coefficients and their standard errors STANC - standardized regression coefficients TTEST - t tests for regression coefficients RESI - residuals for each dependent variable
SHADE.	yes	The correlation matrix is printed in shaded form after the variables are sorted according to the factor loadings. *
NCUT = 5, 8 or 11.	8.	If overprinting is not available (e.g., on a terminal), specify both SHADE and NCUT = 5 for shading. NCUT = 11 means to use the first digit of the correlation. *
/ PLOT		Optional to request plots. No plots are printed unless requested. 515
XVAR = v list. YVAR = v list.	none	Names or subscripts of the variables or residuals to be plotted horizontally (along the x-axis) and vertically (along the y-axis). Residuals are named R followed by the first seven letters of the dependent variable name. Each variable or residual in the XVAR list is plotted against the corresponding variable or residual in the YVAR list.
NORMal.	no	Normal probability plot of the residuals. *
SIZE = #,#.	50,35.	Width of x-axis (characters); height of y-axis (lines). *
/ SAVE		Additional option required only if a BMDP File is to be created. 516
CONTent = c list.	DATA.	DATA, COVA, COVAPART (one or more). The DATA (including residuals), COVA (the covariance matrix) or COVAPART (the partial covariance matrix) can be saved in a BMDP File. Residuals follow the data for each case and are named R followed by the first seven letters of the name of the dependent variable.

Key:

/	–indicates paragraph
.	–period ends a sentence
●	–required
v	–variable (name or subscript)
g	–group (name or subscript)
#	–number
'c'	–characters (name or parameter) may omit apostrophes if contiguous letters only

*	–assigned value remains the same for additional problems
VT	–number of variables after transformations
list	–more than one item, often one per var.

Capitalized letters–paragraph or sentence names recognized by BMDP

Page numbers following refer to this Manual

P7M

18.4 Stepwise Discriminant Analysis

Robert Jennrich
Paul Sampson

ABSTRACT

P7M performs a discriminant analysis between two or more groups. The variables used in computing the linear classification functions are chosen in a stepwise manner. Both forward and backward selection of variables are possible; at each step the variable that adds the most to the separation of the groups is entered into (or the variable that adds the least is removed from) the discriminant function. Important group differences can be specified as contrasts; these contrasts guide the selection of the variables. Group classifications are evaluated and presented in a classification table. A jackknife-validation procedure may be requested to reduce the bias in the group classifications. (For only two groups Stepwise Logistic Regression (PLR) and All Possible Subsets Regression (P9R) can also be used if your grouping variable is coded as zero or one.) Cases can be classified even if they are not used in the computations. See Appendix A.23 for multivariate analysis of variance with P7M.

Output includes, at each step, F statistics for entering variables, Wilks' lambda or U statistics (with an approximate F statistic), Mahalanobis D^2 for group means; classification functions, classification matrix, jackknifed classification and percent correct classification; posterior probabilities and Mahalanobis distances for each case being assigned to each group; canonical discriminant function coefficients and eigenvalues and canonical scores for each case; and a plot of the first two canonical variables.

WHERE TO FIND IT

Example 7M.1 Basic Setup for Stepwise Discriminant Analysis

The Fisher iris data (Table 18.1) are used to illustrate the stepwise discriminant analysis by P7M. The data and variables are described in BMDP instructions and IRISTYPE is specified as the variable that identifies in which group each flower belongs -- Setosa, Versicolor or Virginica.

The following instructions are common to all BMDP programs and are described in Chapter 5: no instructions specific to P7M are used in this first run. If data editing or transformations are needed see the methods in Chapter 6.

```
-------------------------------------
/ PROBLEM    TITLE IS 'FISHER IRIS DATA'.
/ INPUT      VARIABLES ARE 5.
            FORMAT IS '(4F3.1, F3.0)'.
/ VARIABLE   NAMES ARE SEPALLEN, SEPALWID, PETALLEN,
                PETALWID, IRISTYPE.
            GROUPING IS IRISTYPE.

/ GROUP      CODES(5) ARE 1 TO 3.
            NAMES(5) ARE SETOSA, VERSICOL,
                VIRGINIC.

/ END
-------------------------------------
```

(See end of this P7M section for organization of systems information, BMDP instructions and data)

The results are presented in Output 7M.1. Circled numbers below correspond to those in the output.

(1) Interpretation of options specific to P7M. Many of the options in this example are preassigned. The GROUPING variable (IRISTYPE, the fifth variable) is specified in Example 7M.1.

(2) Number of cases read. P7M uses complete cases only in all computations. That is, if the value of any variable in a case is missing or out of range, the case is omitted from all computations. If a USE statement is specified in the VARIABLE paragraph, only the values of variables in the USE statement are checked for missing value codes and values out of range. When CODES are specified for the GROUPING variables, only cases with a specified code are used.

③ Means, standard deviations and coefficients of variation for each variable in each group and for all groups.

The pooled (within-groups) standard deviation is

$$\left\{ \Sigma (N_k - 1) s_k^2 / \Sigma (N_k - 1) \right\}^{\frac{1}{2}}$$

where s_k^2 is the variance and N_k is the sample size of the k-th group.

④ Step 0 is the step before any variable is entered into the discriminant function. P7M prints the F-to-enter for each variable. At step 0 the F-to-enter for a variable corresponds to the F statistic computed from a one-way analysis of variance (ANOVA) on the variable for the groups used in the analysis. The degrees of freedom correspond to those of the one-way ANOVA; i.e., (g-1) and $\Sigma(N_k - 1)$ where g is the number of groups.

The force level is discussed on p. 533 and tolerance on p. 535.

⑤ The variable with the highest F-to-enter at step 0 (PETALLEN) is entered into the discriminant functions; this is the variable that discriminates the best between groups. At step 1 the following are computed:

- F-to-remove for the variable in the equation (this is equal to the F-to-enter at step 0)
- F-to-enter for each variable not in the equation (this is equal to the F statistic corresponding to the one-way ANOVA on the residuals of the variable; i.e., at each step the F-to-enter is computed from a one-way analysis of covariance where the covariates are the previously entered variables)
- Wilks' lambda or U statistic (this is a multivariate analysis of variance statistic that tests the equality of group means for the variable(s) in the discriminant function)
- Approximate F statistic (this is a transformation of Wilks' lambda that can be compared with the F distribution; at step 1 the F statistic is the one-way ANOVA between the group means for the variable entered)
- F matrix (this contains F values computed from the Mahalanobis D^2 statistics that test the equality of group means for each pair of groups; the test is for only the variables in the discriminant functions)
- Classification functions (the classification function can be used to classify cases into groups; the case is assigned to the group with the largest value of the classification function - see Appendix A.26 for how you can use the classification functions to classify cases that may be observed in the future).

⑥ At the last step, in addition to the results printed at each step, P7M prints the

- classification matrix (each case is classified into a group according to the classification functions; the number classified into each group and the percent of correct classifications are printed)
- jackknifed classification matrix (each case is classified into a group according to the classification functions computed from all the data except the case being classified; see Lachenbruch and Mickey, 1968).

Table 18.1 Fisher iris data (Fisher, 1936). Length and width of sepals (SEPALLEN and SEPALWID) and petals (PETALLEN and PETALWID) on 50 flowers from each of three types of iris (IRISTYPE).

1	2	3	4	5
50	33	14	02	1
64	28	56	22	3
65	28	46	15	2
67	31	56	24	3
63	28	51	15	3
46	34	14	03	1
69	31	51	23	3
62	22	45	15	2
59	32	48	18	2
46	36	10	02	1
61	30	46	14	2
60	27	51	16	2
65	30	52	20	3
56	25	39	11	2
65	30	55	18	3
58	27	51	19	3
68	32	59	23	3
51	33	17	05	1
57	28	45	13	2
62	34	54	23	3
77	38	67	22	3
63	33	47	16	2
67	33	57	25	3
76	30	66	21	3
49	25	45	17	3
55	35	13	02	1
67	30	52	23	3
70	32	47	14	2
64	32	45	15	2
61	28	40	13	2
48	31	16	02	1
59	30	51	18	3
55	24	38	11	2
63	25	50	19	3
64	32	53	23	3
52	34	14	02	1
49	36	14	01	1
54	30	45	15	2
79	38	64	20	3
44	32	13	02	1
67	33	57	21	3
50	35	16	06	1
58	26	40	12	2
44	30	13	02	1
77	28	67	20	3
63	27	49	18	3
47	32	16	02	1
55	26	44	12	2
72	32	60	18	3
48	30	14	03	1
51	38	16	02	1
61	30	49	18	3
48	34	19	02	1
50	30	16	02	1
50	32	12	02	1
61	26	56	14	3
64	28	56	21	3
43	30	11	01	1
58	40	12	02	1
51	38	19	04	1
67	31	44	14	2
62	28	48	18	3
49	30	14	02	1
51	35	14	02	1
56	30	45	15	2
58	27	41	10	2
50	34	16	04	1
46	32	14	02	1
60	29	45	15	2
57	26	35	10	2
57	44	15	04	1
50	36	14	02	1
77	30	61	23	3
63	34	56	24	3
58	27	51	19	3
57	29	42	13	2
72	30	58	16	3
54	34	15	04	1
52	41	15	01	1
71	30	59	21	3
64	31	55	18	3
60	30	48	18	3
63	29	56	18	3
49	24	33	10	2
56	27	42	13	2
57	30	42	12	2
55	42	14	02	1
49	31	15	02	1
77	26	69	23	3
60	22	50	15	3
54	39	17	04	1
66	29	46	13	2
52	27	39	14	2
60	34	45	16	2
50	34	15	02	1
44	29	14	02	1
50	20	35	10	2
55	24	37	10	2
58	27	39	12	2
47	32	13	02	1
46	31	15	02	1
69	32	57	23	3
62	29	43	13	2
74	28	61	19	3
59	30	42	15	2
51	34	15	02	1
50	35	13	03	1
56	28	49	20	3
60	22	40	10	2
73	29	63	18	3
67	25	58	18	3
49	31	15	01	1
67	31	47	15	2
63	23	44	13	2
54	37	15	02	1
56	30	41	13	2
63	25	49	15	2
61	28	47	12	2
64	29	43	13	2
51	25	30	11	2
57	28	41	13	2
65	30	58	22	3
69	31	54	21	3
54	39	13	04	1
51	35	14	03	1
72	36	61	25	3
65	32	51	20	3
61	29	47	14	2
56	29	36	13	2
69	31	49	15	2
64	27	53	19	3
68	30	55	21	3
55	25	40	13	2
48	34	16	02	1
48	30	14	01	1
45	23	13	03	1
57	25	50	20	3
57	38	17	03	1
51	38	15	03	1
55	23	40	13	2
66	30	44	14	2
68	28	48	14	2
54	34	17	02	1
51	37	15	04	1
52	35	15	02	1
58	28	51	24	3
67	30	50	17	2
63	33	60	25	3
53	37	15	02	1

Key: 1 - SEPALLEN, 2 - SEPALWID, 3 - PETALLEN, 4 - PETALWID, 5 - IRISTYPE

The three groups of iris (IRISTYPE) are Setosa, Versicolor and Virginica. All variables but IRISTYPE are recorded to 1/10 of a centimeter. The data are recorded in columns 2-3, 5-6, 8-9, 11-12 and 15.

Output 7M.1 Stepwise discriminant analysis. Circled numbers correspond to those in the text
----

--- the BMDP instructions read by P7M are printed and interpreted ---

```
TOLERANCE. . . . . . . . .    0.010
F-TO-ENTER . . . . . . . .    4.000    4.000
F-TO-REMOVE. . . . . . . .    3.996    3.996
METHOD . . . . . . . . . .        1                    ①
MAXIMUM FORCED LEVEL . . .        0
MAXIMUM NUMBER OF STEPS. .       10
GROUPING VARIABLE. . . . .        5
NUMBER OF GROUPS . . . . .        3
PRIOR PROBABILITIES. . . .    0.33333  0.33333  0.33333
```

```
                 BEFORE TRANSFORMATION                            INTERVAL RANGE
VARIABLE      MINIMUM   MAXIMUM   MISSING   CATEGORY  CATEGORY   GREATER    LESS THAN
NO. NAME      LIMIT     LIMIT     CODE      CODE      NAME       THAN       OR EQUAL TO

 5   IRISTYPE                               1.00000   SETOSA
                                            2.00000   VERSICOL
                                            3.00000   VIRGINIC
```

NUMBER OF CASES READ.   150   ②

```
    MEANS

        GROUP =   SETOSA     VERSICOL    VIRGINIC    ALL GPS.      ③
VARIABLE
  1 SEPALLEN     5.00600     5.93600     6.58800     5.84333
  2 SEPALWID     3.42800     2.77000     2.97400     3.05733
  3 PETALLEN     1.46200     4.26000     5.55200     3.75800        --- standard deviations and coefficients of
  4 PETALWID     0.24600     1.32600     2.02600     1.19933            variation are printed in separate panels ---
  5 IRISTYPE     1.00000     2.00000     3.00000     2.00000

COUNTS            50.         50.         50.        150.
```

****

STEP NUMBER   0

```
VARIABLE     F TO   FORCE  TOLERANCE  *    VARIABLE        F TO   FORCE  TOLERANCE
           REMOVE   LEVEL             *                  ENTER   LEVEL
        DF=  2  148                   *              DF=  2  147                        ④
                                      *  1 SEPALLEN    119.264    1     1.000000
                                      *  2 SEPALWID     49.160    1     1.000000
                                      *  3 PETALLEN   1180.160    1     1.000000
                                      *  4 PETALWID    960.007    1     1.000000
```

STEP NUMBER   1
VARIABLE ENTERED   3 PETALLEN

```
VARIABLE     F TO   FORCE  TOLERANCE  *    VARIABLE        F TO   FORCE  TOLERANCE
           REMOVE   LEVEL             *                  ENTER   LEVEL
        DF=  2  147                   *              DF=  2  146                        ⑤
 3 PETALLEN  1180.161   1   1.000000  *  1 SEPALLEN     34.323    1     0.428216
                                      *  2 SEPALWID     43.035    1     0.857180
                                      *  4 PETALWID     24.766    1     0.765300
```

```
U-STATISTIC OR WILKS' LAMBDA   0.0586283   DEGREES OF FREEDOM   1   2      147
APPROXIMATE F-STATISTIC          1180.161   DEGREES OF FREEDOM      2.00   147.00
```

```
F - MATRIX        DEGREES OF FREEDOM =    1   147

           SETOSA    VERSICOL
VERSICOL  1056.87
VIRGINIC  2258.26     225.34
```

CLASSIFICATION FUNCTIONS

```
        GROUP =   SETOSA     VERSICOL    VIRGINIC
VARIABLE
  3 PETALLEN     7.89469    23.00368    29.98038

CONSTANT        -6.86962   -50.09642   -84.32411
```

****
(output continued)

⑦ Summary table. This contains a one line summary of each step including the F-to-enter (or remove) for the variable entered (or removed), the Wilks' lambda U statistic and the approximate F statistic.

⑧ Classification of each case. For each case Mahalanobis D is computed to each group mean. The posterior probability for the distance of a case from a group is the ratio of $exp(D^2)$ for the group over the sum of $exp(D^2)$ for all groups. Prior probabilities, if assigned, affect these computations (see Appendix A.23, step 4). Outliers can be identified as cases with large D^2 from their group means. For large samples from a multivariate normal distribution, the D^2 from a case to its group mean is approximately distributed as a chi-square with degrees of freedom equal to the number of variables selected.

Each case incorrectly classified is noted in the output (cases 5, 9 and 12).

Output 7M.1 (continued)

--- results for steps 2 and 3 ---

STEP NUMBER   4
VARIABLE ENTERED   1 SEPALLEN

VARIABLE	F TO REMOVE	FORCE LEVEL	TOLERANCE	*	VARIABLE	F TO ENTER	FORCE LEVEL	TOLERANCE
	DF= 2 144			*		DF= 2 143		
1 SEPALLEN	4.721	1	0.347993	*				
2 SEPALWID	21.936	1	0.608860	*				
3 PETALLEN	35.590	1	0.365126	*				
4 PETALWID	24.904	1	0.649314	*				

U-STATISTIC OR WILKS' LAMBDA	0.0234386	DEGREES OF FREEDOM	4 2 147
APPROXIMATE F-STATISTIC	199.145	DEGREES OF FREEDOM	8.00 288.00

F - MATRIX   DEGREES OF FREEDOM =   4 144

	SETOSA	VERSICOL
VERSICOL	550.19	
VIRGINIC	1098.27	105.31

CLASSIFICATION FUNCTIONS

GROUP = VARIABLE	SETOSA	VERSICOL	VIRGINIC	
1 SEPALLEN	23.54416	15.69820	12.44584	⑥
2 SEPALWID	23.58786	7.07252	3.68529	
3 PETALLEN	-16.43063	5.21145	12.76655	
4 PETALWID	-17.39839	6.43422	21.07909	
CONSTANT	-86.30843	-72.85257	-104.36826	

CLASSIFICATION MATRIX

GROUP	PERCENT CORRECT	NUMBER OF CASES CLASSIFIED INTO GROUP - SETOSA	VERSICOL	VIRGINIC
SETOSA	100.0	50	0	0
VERSICOL	96.0	0	48	2
VIRGINIC	98.0	0	1	49
TOTAL	98.0	50	49	51

JACKKNIFED CLASSIFICATION

GROUP	PERCENT CORRECT	NUMBER OF CASES CLASSIFIED INTO GROUP - SETOSA	VERSICOL	VIRGINIC
SETOSA	100.0	50	0	0
VERSICOL	96.0	0	48	2
VIRGINIC	98.0	0	1	49
TOTAL	98.0	50	49	51

SUMMARY TABLE   ⑦

STEP NUMBER	VARIABLE ENTERED	REMOVED	F VALUE TO ENTER OR REMOVE	NUMBER OF VARIABLES INCLUDED	U-STATISTIC	APPROXIMATE F-STATISTIC	DEGREES OF FREEDOM
1	3 PETALLEN		1180.1597	1	0.0586	1180.161	2.00 147.00
2	2 SEPALWID		43.0353	2	0.0369	307.104	4.00 292.00
3	4 PETALWID		34.5686	3	0.0250	257.503	6.00 290.00
4	1 SEPALLEN		4.7211	4	0.0234	199.145	8.00 288.00

⑨ Eigenvalues of the matrix $\underset{\sim}{W}{}^{-\frac{1}{2}}\underset{\sim}{B}\underset{\sim}{W}{}^{-\frac{1}{2}}$ are computed where $\underset{\sim}{B}$ is the between-groups sums of cross products and $\underset{\sim}{W}$ is the pooled (within-groups) sum of squares (see Appendix A.23 for a more precise definition). The eigenvalues, canonical correlations between the variables entered and dummy variables representing the groups, and the coefficients for the canonical variables are printed. The first canonical variable is the linear combination of variables entered that best discriminates among the groups (largest one-way ANOVA F statistic), the second canonical variable is the next best linear combination orthogonal to the first one, etc. The canonical variables are adjusted so that the (pooled) within-group variances are one and their overall mean is zero. The canonical variables are evaluated at the group means.

⑩ The group means only are plotted in a scatter plot. The axes are the first two canonical variables. (This plot is not reproduced in Output 7M.1).

	INCORRECT CLASSIFICATIONS	MAHALANOBIS D-SQUARE FROM AND POSTERIOR PROBABILITY FOR GROUP -		
GROUP SETOSA		SETOSA	VERSICOL	VIRGINIC
CASE				
1		0.2 1.000	90.7 0.000	181.6 0.000
6		1.3 1.000	84.0 0.000	170.1 0.000	⑧
10		2.3 1.000	113.7 0.000	210.0 0.0
18		2.8 1.000	67.5 0.000	145.7 0.000
26		4.0 1.000	113.2 0.000	210.2 0.0

--- similar statistics for the remaining SETOSA cases ---

GROUP VERSICOL		SETOSA	VERSICOL	VIRGINIC
CASE				
3		105.3 0.000	2.2 0.996	13.1 0.004
8		131.7 0.000	8.4 0.960	14.8 0.040
9	VIRGINIC	130.9 0.000	8.7 0.253	6.5 0.747
11		99.2 0.000	1.3 0.998	13.8 0.002
12	VIRGINIC	149.0 0.000	8.4 0.143	4.9 0.857

--- similar statistics for the remaining VERSICOL cases ---

GROUP VIRGINIC		SETOSA	VERSICOL	VIRGINIC
CASE				
2		208.6 0.0	27.3 0.000	1.9 1.000
4		207.9 0.0	31.7 0.000	4.5 1.000
5	VERSICOL	133.1 0.000	5.3 0.729	7.2 0.271
7		173.2 0.000	26.6 0.000	11.0 1.000
13		159.0 0.000	12.8 0.003	1.2 0.997

--- similar statistics for the remaining VIRGINIC cases ---

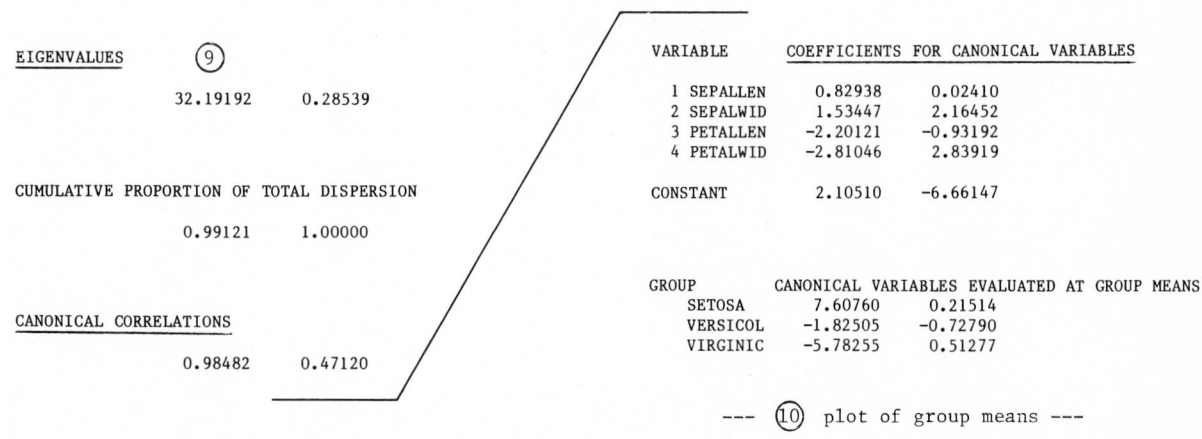

EIGENVALUES ⑨

     32.19192   0.28539

CUMULATIVE PROPORTION OF TOTAL DISPERSION

     0.99121   1.00000

CANONICAL CORRELATIONS

     0.98482   0.47120

VARIABLE	COEFFICIENTS FOR CANONICAL VARIABLES	
1 SEPALLEN	0.82938	0.02410
2 SEPALWID	1.53447	2.16452
3 PETALLEN	-2.20121	-0.93192
4 PETALWID	-2.81046	2.83919
CONSTANT	2.10510	-6.66147

GROUP	CANONICAL VARIABLES EVALUATED AT GROUP MEANS	
SETOSA	7.60760	0.21514
VERSICOL	-1.82505	-0.72790
VIRGINIC	-5.78255	0.51277

--- ⑩ plot of group means ---

(output continued)

⑪ The group means and all cases are plotted in a scatter plot. The axes are the first two canonical variables. In this plot group A (SETOSA) is well differentiated from the other two groups. Group B (VERSICOL) slightly overlaps group C (VIRGINIC).
Note: If there is only one canonical variable a histogram is plotted.

A discriminant analysis can be severely affected by the presence of an outlier. Such an outlier can sometimes be identified in this plot.

Identifying initial group membership. In Example 7M.1, the fifth variable IRISTYPE, contains a code for each case (flower) to identify the flower type. You must specify the variable that contains this GROUPING identification in the VARIABLE paragraph. (The specification of the group NAMES and identifying CODES or CUTPOINTS is given in the GROUP paragraph). If the GROUP paragraph is not used the number of groups analyzed must be stated in the INPUT paragraph. Note that the data need not be ordered by group.

Output 7M.1 (continued)

POINTS TO BE PLOTTED

GROUP	MEAN COORDINATES		SYMBOL FOR CASES	SYMBOL FOR MEAN
SETOSA	7.61	0.22	A	1
VERSICOL	-1.83	-0.73	B	2
VIRGINIC	-5.78	0.51	C	3

GROUP SETOSA

CASE	X	Y	CASE	X	Y	CASE	X	Y	CASE	X	Y	CASE	X	Y
1	7.67	-0.13	44	6.93	-0.71	64	7.13	-0.79	92	7.70	1.46	126	7.78	0.58
6	7.21	0.36	47	6.83	-0.54	65	8.06	0.30	96	7.61	-0.01	135	7.22	-0.11
10	8.68	0.88	51	6.76	-0.51	68	6.82	0.46	97	6.56	-1.02	136	7.33	-1.07
18	6.25	0.44	52	8.08	0.76	69	7.19	-0.36	101	7.49	-0.27	137	5.66	-1.93
26	8.61	0.40	54	6.56	-0.39	72	9.16	2.74	102	6.81	-0.67	139	8.08	0.97
31	6.76	-0.76	55	6.77	-0.97	73	8.13	0.51	107	7.69	-0.01	140	8.02	1.14
36	7.99	0.09	56	7.96	-0.16	79	7.37	0.57	108	7.92	0.68	144	7.50	-0.19
37	8.33	0.23	59	7.57	-0.81	80	9.13	1.22	113	7.34	-0.95	145	7.59	1.21
40	7.24	-0.27	60	9.85	1.59	88	9.47	1.83	116	8.40	0.65	146	7.92	0.21
42	6.41	1.25	61	6.86	1.05	89	7.06	-0.66	125	8.58	1.83	150	8.31	0.64

GROUP VERSICOL

CASE	X	Y	CASE	X	Y	CASE	X	Y	CASE	X	Y	CASE	X	Y
3	-2.55	-0.47	30	-1.00	-0.49	71	0.31	-1.32	100	-0.90	-0.90	121	0.48	-0.80
8	-3.50	-1.68	33	-1.11	-1.75	77	-1.62	-0.47	104	-1.42	-0.55	122	-1.55	-0.59
9	-3.72	1.04	38	-2.93	0.03	85	-0.22	-1.58	106	-1.86	0.32	129	-2.67	-0.64
11	-2.29	-0.33	43	-1.27	-1.21	86	-2.01	-0.91	110	-1.16	-2.64	130	-0.38	0.09
12	-4.50	-0.88	48	-2.40	-1.59	87	-1.18	-0.54	114	-2.14	0.09	131	-2.42	-0.09
14	-1.09	-1.63	49	-0.29	-1.80	93	-1.75	-0.82	115	-2.48	-1.94	134	-1.96	-1.15
19	-2.43	-0.97	62	-1.20	0.08	94	-1.96	-0.35	117	-1.33	-0.16	141	-2.26	-1.59
22	-2.45	0.80	66	-2.77	0.03	95	-2.10	1.19	118	-3.84	-1.41	142	-1.44	-0.13
28	-1.46	0.03	67	-0.78	-1.66	98	-1.19	-2.63	119	-2.26	-1.43	143	-2.46	-0.94
29	-1.80	0.48	70	-2.59	-0.17	99	-0.61	-1.94	120	-1.26	-0.55	148	-3.52	0.16

GROUP VIRGINIC

CASE	X	Y	CASE	X	Y	CASE	X	Y	CASE	X	Y	CASE	X	Y
2	-6.80	0.58	23	-6.85	2.43	46	-4.37	-0.12	81	-6.29	0.47	112	-6.33	-1.38
4	-6.65	1.81	24	-7.42	-0.17	50	-5.28	-0.04	82	-5.00	0.19	123	-6.85	0.83
5	-3.82	-0.94	25	-4.68	-0.50	53	-4.08	0.52	83	-3.94	0.61	124	-5.20	1.14
7	-5.11	1.99	27	-5.65	1.68	57	-5.11	-2.13	84	-5.61	-0.34	127	-6.85	2.72
13	-4.97	0.82	32	-4.68	0.33	58	-6.52	0.30	90	-9.17	-0.75	128	-4.44	1.35
15	-5.07	-0.03	34	-5.18	-0.36	63	-4.08	0.19	91	-4.76	-2.16	132	-5.45	-0.21
16	-5.51	-0.04	35	-5.81	2.01	74	-6.80	0.86	103	-6.27	1.65	133	-5.66	0.83
17	-6.80	1.46	39	-5.22	1.47	75	-6.52	2.45	105	-6.23	-0.71	138	-5.96	-0.09
20	-5.89	2.35	41	-5.72	1.29	76	-5.51	-0.04	109	-5.36	0.65	147	-6.76	1.60
21	-6.61	1.75	45	-7.58	-0.98	78	-4.58	-0.86	111	-6.32	-0.97	149	-7.84	2.14

VARiable ─────────────────────
  GROUPing = v.   required   no grouping
                                         var./prev.
    The name or subscript of the variable used to
    classify cases into groups. To make the printed
    results easier to read, we suggest that you
    specify group NAMES in the GROUP paragraph
    (Section 5.5).

    Note: P7M requires either a GROUP paragraph or
    that the number of groups be specified in the
    INPUT paragraph. A GROUP paragraph is required
    when each value (code) of the GROUPING variable
    does not designate a distinct group.

INPut ─────────────────────
  GROUP = #.   none/prev.
    Number of groups to be formed. This
    specification is required if neither CODES nor
    CUTPOINTS are specified for the GROUPING
    variable.

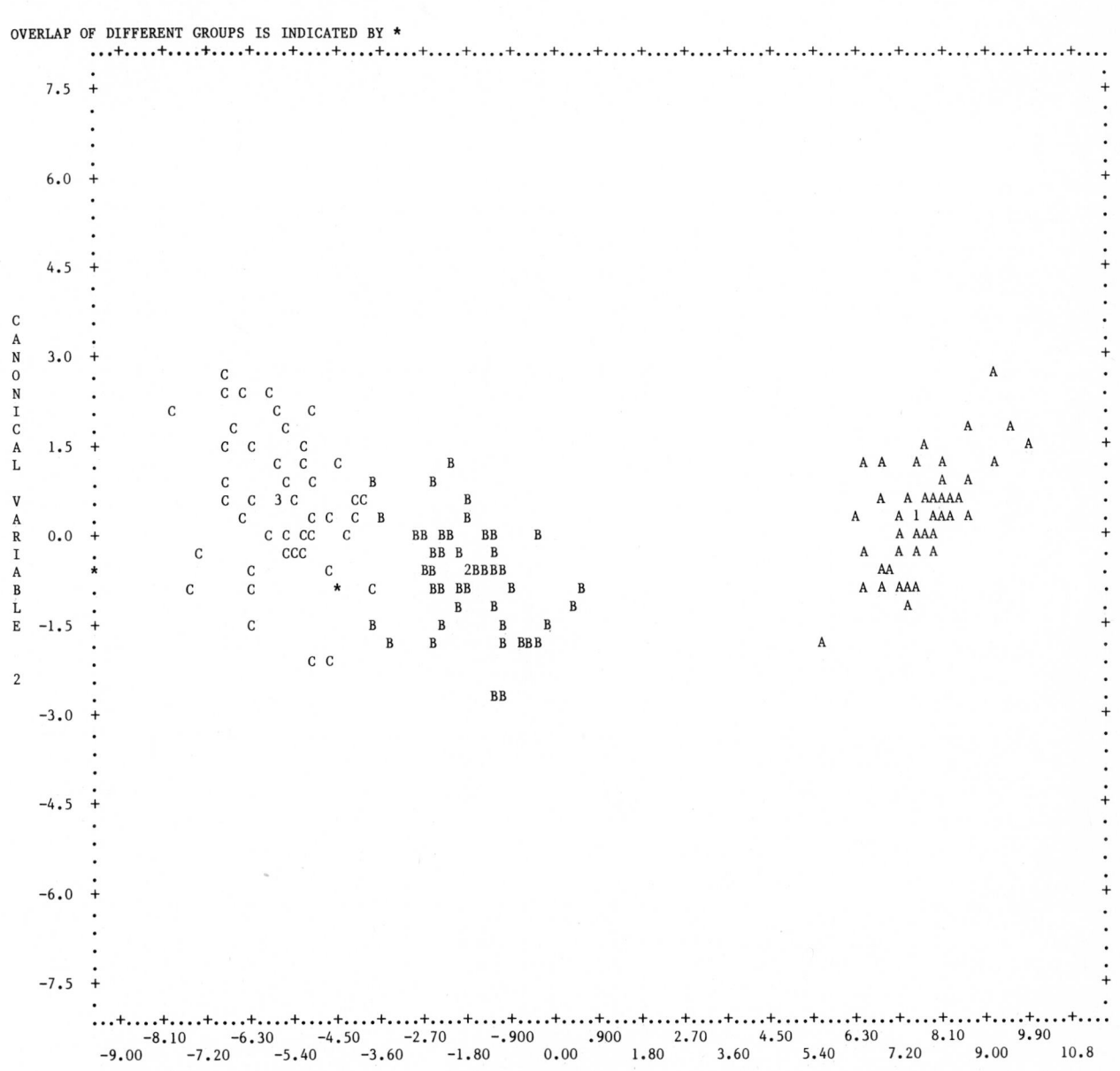

OVERLAP OF DIFFERENT GROUPS IS INDICATED BY *

CANONICAL VARIABLE 1

Example 7M.2 Cross Validation with Random Subsamples and Classifying New Cases

You can request that classification functions be computed for a subset of the groups. The program then uses these functions to classify the data in the remaining group or groups. Thus, a new set of data can be classified using functions derived for the original groups. This feature also allows cross validation -- you can randomly subdivide the cases in each group into two separate groups; the first group is then used to estimate the classification function and the second group is classified according to the function. By observing the proportion of correct classification for the second group, you have an empirical measure for the success of the discrimination.

In Example 7M.2 we demonstrate how random subsamples can be selected from each group to form subgroups that are not used to estimate the discriminant function. The subgroups are then used to validate the classification function. The groups to be analyzed are specified in a USE statement in the GROUP paragraph. Groups not included in the USE statement are classified into groups according to the classification function, but are not used in estimating the classification function. To do this we replace the GROUP paragraph in Example 7M.1 and add a TRANSFORM paragraph to create a new grouping variable with six codes.

The GROUPING variable is IRISTYPE. In the TRANSFORM paragraph, three is added to IRISTYPE for approximately 20% of the cases. For each case a uniform random number is generated and, when it is less than 0.2, IRISTYPE is set to IRISTYPE + 3 (group 1 becomes group 4, etc.).

In the GROUP paragraph we specify that <u>six</u> (not three) codes are possible and name the new groups formed: NEWSET (from SETOSA), NEWVERS (from VERSICOL) and NEWVIRG (from VIRGINIC).

```
-------------------------------------
/ TRANSFORM      IF(RNDU(783217) LE .2)
                 THEN IRISTYPE = IRISTYPE + 3.

/ GROUP          CODES(5) ARE 1 TO 6.
                 NAMES(5) ARE SETOSA, VERSICOL,
                              VIRGINIC, NEWSET,
                              NEWVERS, NEWVIRG.
                 USE = 1 TO 3.
-------------------------------------
```

In Output 7M.2 we present the classification functions and classification matrix. Only three groups (USE = 1 TO 3 in the GROUP paragraph) are used to estimate the classification function. But the cases in all six groups are classified according to the function. All the cases in NEWSET are correctly classified into SETOSA, 12 of the 13 cases in NEWVIRG are classified correctly, and all 10 cases in NEWVERS are correctly classified.

```
GROUP ─────────────────────────────
  USE = g list.                        all groups/prev.
    Names or subscripts of groups used in
    estimating the classification functions. Cases
    with acceptable values for the GROUPING
    variable but that are not in these groups will
    be classified by the function but will not be
    used in computing the cross-products matrix nor
    in estimating the classification function.
```

Output 7M.2   Cross validation of a discriminant function

		BEFORE TRANSFORMATION					INTERVAL RANGE	
VARIABLE	MINIMUM	MAXIMUM	MISSING	CATEGORY	CATEGORY	GREATER	LESS THAN
NO. NAME	LIMIT	LIMIT	CODE	CODE	NAME	THAN	OR EQUAL TO
5 IRISTYPE				1.00000	SETOSA		
				2.00000	VERSICOL		
				3.00000	VIRGINIC		
				4.00000	NEWSET		
				5.00000	NEWVERS		
				6.00000	NEWVIRG		

NUMBER OF CASES READ.   150

MEANS

GROUP =	SETOSA	VERSICOL	VIRGINIC	NEWSET	NEWVERS	NEWVIRG	GPS.USED
VARIABLE							
1 SEPALLEN	5.02143	5.87750	6.62703	4.92500	6.17000	6.47692	5.80840
2 SEPALWID	3.43571	2.76500	3.00811	3.38750	2.79000	2.87692	3.07731
3 PETALLEN	1.46428	4.24750	5.57297	1.45000	4.31000	5.49231	3.67731
4 PETALWID	0.23810	1.33500	2.02432	0.28750	1.29000	2.03077	1.16218
5 IRISTYPE	1.00000	2.00000	3.00000	4.00000	5.00000	6.00000	1.95798
COUNTS	42.	40.	37.	8.	10.	13.	119.

--- standard deviations and coefficients of variation for the six groups appear here ---

--- results for steps 0, 1 and 2 are printed ---

STEP NUMBER   3
VARIABLE ENTERED   4 PETALWID

VARIABLE	F TO REMOVE	FORCE LEVEL	TOLERANCE	*	VARIABLE	F TO ENTER	FORCE LEVEL	TOLERANCE
	DF= 2 114			*		DF= 2 113		
2 SEPALWID	47.072	1	0.758357	*	1 SEPALLEN	3.792	1	0.329800
3 PETALLEN	25.680	1	0.695746	*				
4 PETALWID	27.866	1	0.669123	*				

U-STATISTIC OR WILKS' LAMBDA   0.0236785   DEGREES OF FREEDOM   3   2   116
APPROXIMATE F-STATISTIC   208.948   DEGREES OF FREEDOM   6.00   228.00

F - MATRIX   DEGREES OF FREEDOM =   3   114

	SETOSA	VERSICOL	VIRGINIC	NEWSET	NEWVERS
VERSICOL	576.34				
VIRGINIC	1103.31	104.85			
NEWSET	0.36	178.30	355.55		
NEWVERS	222.91	0.43	46.42	116.94	
NEWVIRG	570.49	56.35	0.67	274.03	35.44

CLASSIFICATION FUNCTIONS

VARIABLE	GROUP = SETOSA	VERSICOL	VIRGINIC
2 SEPALWID	33.15436	12.92362	8.41314
3 PETALLEN	2.05212	16.62949	21.19389
4 PETALWID	-22.56166	6.36792	23.33980
CONSTANT	-56.86957	-58.53294	-96.43256

CLASSIFICATION MATRIX

GROUP	PERCENT CORRECT	NUMBER OF CASES CLASSIFIED INTO GROUP -		
		SETOSA	VERSICOL	VIRGINIC
SETOSA	100.0	42	0	0
VERSICOL	92.5	0	37	3
VIRGINIC	97.3	0	1	36
NEWSET	0.0	8	0	0
NEWVERS	0.0	0	10	0
NEWVIRG	0.0	0	1	12
TOTAL	96.6	50	49	51

JACKKNIFED CLASSIFICATION

GROUP	PERCENT CORRECT	NUMBER OF CASES CLASSIFIED INTO GROUP -		
		SETOSA	VERSICOL	VIRGINIC
SETOSA	100.0	42	0	0
VERSICOL	92.5	0	37	3
VIRGINIC	94.6	0	2	35
NEWSET	0.0	8	0	0
NEWVERS	0.0	0	10	0
NEWVIRG	0.0	0	1	12
TOTAL	95.8	50	50	50

SUMMARY TABLE

STEP NUMBER	VARIABLE ENTERED	REMOVED	F VALUE TO ENTER OR REMOVE	NUMBER OF VARIABLES INCLUDED	U-STATISTIC	APPROXIMATE F-STATISTIC	DEGREES OF FREEDOM	
1	3 PETALLEN		920.8586	1	0.0593	920.859	2.00	116.00
2	2 SEPALWID		39.1414	2	0.0353	248.740	4.00	230.00
3	4 PETALWID		27.8658	3	0.0237	208.948	6.00	228.00

(output continued)

Output 7M.2 (continued)

	INCORRECT CLASSIFICATIONS		MAHALANOBIS D-SQUARE FROM AND POSTERIOR PROBABILITY FOR GROUP -		
GROUP SETOSA			SETOSA	VERSICOL	VIRGINIC
CASE					
1			0.2 1.000	84.6 0.000	170.6 0.000
6			0.3 1.000	83.0 0.000	166.5 0.000
10			2.1 1.000	110.4 0.000	202.7 0.0
18			3.1 1.000	61.5 0.000	134.5 0.000
26			0.3 1.000	95.8 0.000	184.5 0.000

--- results for other cases in the SETOSA, VERSICOL and VIRGINIC groups ---

			SETOSA	VERSICOL	VIRGINIC
124			167.7 0.000	17.5 0.000	0.7 1.000
128			143.8 0.000	12.2 0.007	2.4 0.993
133			176.1 0.000	19.0 0.000	0.4 1.000
147			208.9 0.000	37.9 0.000	11.0 1.000
149			223.1 0.0	40.4 0.000	6.3 1.000

GROUP NEWSET			SETOSA	VERSICOL	VIRGINIC
CASE					
42	SETOSA		4.5 1.000	68.0 0.000	140.4 0.000
64	SETOSA		1.8 1.000	74.1 0.000	157.4 0.000
65	SETOSA		0.1 1.000	92.7 0.000	180.5 0.000
69	SETOSA		0.5 1.000	80.9 0.000	166.0 0.000
73	SETOSA		0.5 1.000	97.1 0.000	185.8 0.000
92	SETOSA		1.9 1.000	90.3 0.000	172.2 0.000
97	SETOSA		2.8 1.000	71.1 0.000	153.5 0.000
108	SETOSA		0.5 1.000	90.2 0.000	175.5 0.000

GROUP NEWVERS			SETOSA	VERSICOL	VIRGINIC
CASE					
14	VERSICOL		74.4 0.000	1.6 1.000	27.0 0.000
30	VERSICOL		75.7 0.000	0.5 1.000	20.9 0.000
62	VERSICOL		81.5 0.000	0.9 1.000	17.0 0.000
70	VERSICOL		98.1 0.000	0.8 0.993	10.7 0.007
71	VERSICOL		55.6 0.000	4.3 1.000	37.6 0.000
93	VERSICOL		89.9 0.000	1.2 1.000	17.1 0.000
104	VERSICOL		80.2 0.000	0.3 1.000	18.9 0.000
118	VERSICOL		130.0 0.000	4.8 0.795	7.5 0.205
119	VERSICOL		93.0 0.000	3.2 1.000	20.6 0.000
120	VERSICOL		80.2 0.000	0.3 1.000	18.9 0.000

GROUP NEWVIRG			SETOSA	VERSICOL	VIRGINIC
CASE					
4	VIRGINIC		207.4 0.0	34.0 0.000	5.2 1.000
7	VIRGINIC		180.4 0.000	27.4 0.000	6.6 1.000
15	VIRGINIC		150.1 0.000	10.3 0.014	1.8 0.986
20	VIRGINIC		175.1 0.000	25.5 0.000	4.6 1.000
27	VIRGINIC		188.3 0.000	28.3 0.000	5.6 1.000
57	VERSICOL		149.8 0.000	14.1 0.576	14.7 0.424
76	VIRGINIC		158.4 0.000	12.3 0.004	1.4 0.996
84	VIRGINIC		159.0 0.000	12.2 0.006	2.0 0.994
90	VIRGINIC		284.2 0.0	58.5 0.000	16.7 1.000
91	VIRGINIC		150.3 0.000	10.1 0.388	9.2 0.612
127	VIRGINIC		212.4 0.0	38.9 0.000	6.7 1.000
132	VIRGINIC		165.5 0.000	13.6 0.002	0.9 0.998
138	VIRGINIC		175.9 0.000	18.9 0.001	3.7 0.999

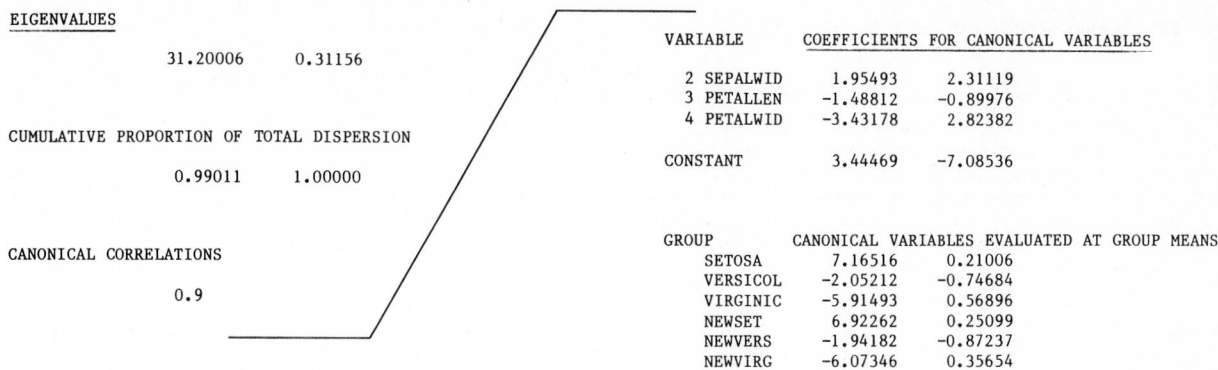

EIGENVALUES

      31.20006   0.31156

CUMULATIVE PROPORTION OF TOTAL DISPERSION

      0.99011   1.00000

CANONICAL CORRELATIONS

      0.9

VARIABLE	COEFFICIENTS FOR CANONICAL VARIABLES	
2 SEPALWID	1.95493	2.31119
3 PETALLEN	-1.48812	-0.89976
4 PETALWID	-3.43178	2.82382
CONSTANT	3.44469	-7.08536

GROUP	CANONICAL VARIABLES EVALUATED AT GROUP MEANS	
SETOSA	7.16516	0.21006
VERSICOL	-2.05212	-0.74684
VIRGINIC	-5.91493	0.56896
NEWSET	6.92262	0.25099
NEWVERS	-1.94182	-0.87237
NEWVIRG	-6.07346	0.35654

--- plot of the group means and coordinates of the points to be plotted appear here ---

OVERLAP OF DIFFERENT GROUPS IS INDICATED BY *

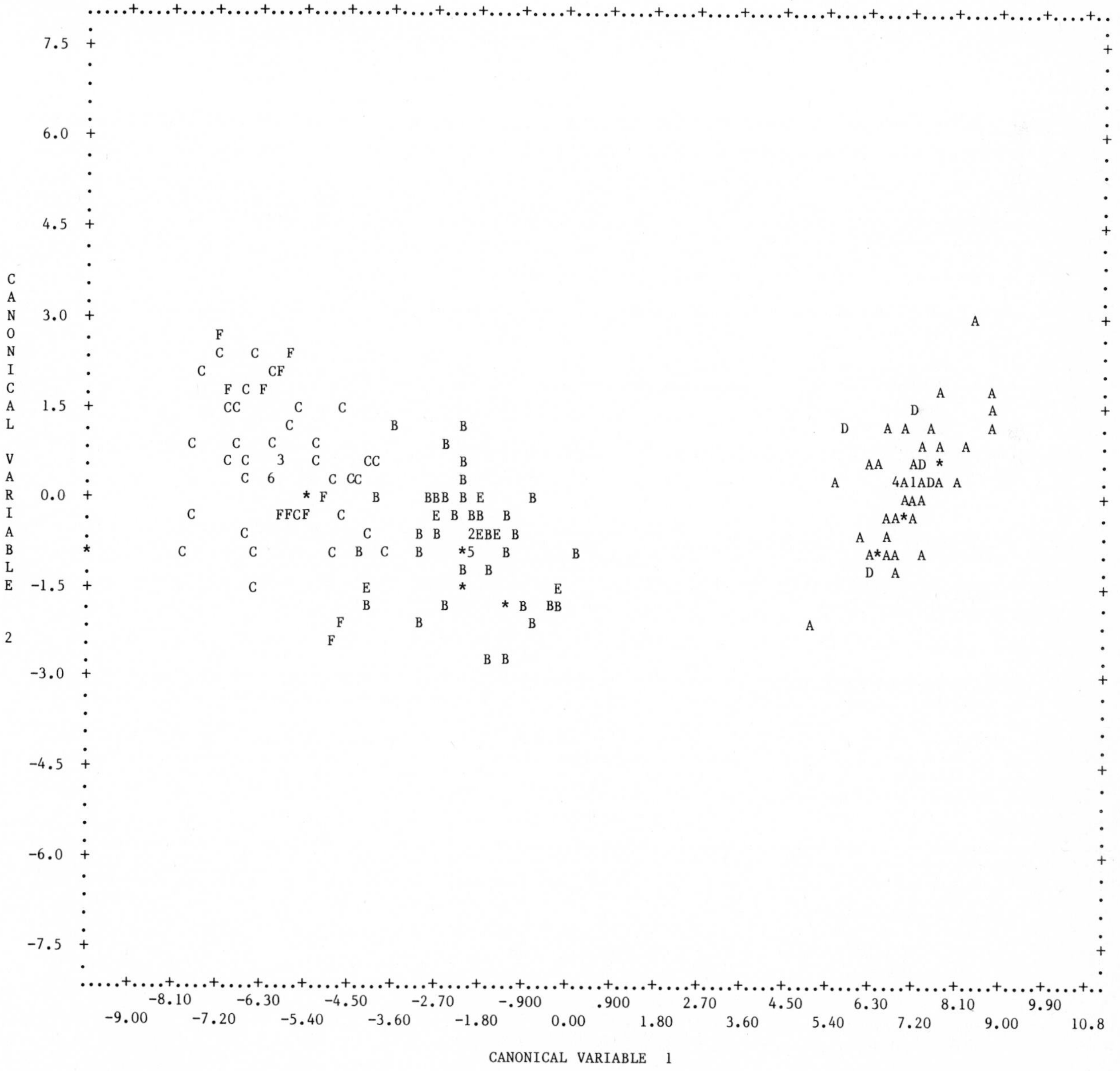

```
      .....+....+....+....+....+....+....+....+....+....+....+....+....+....+....+....+....+....+....+....+....+..
      .                                                                                                        .
 7.5 +                                                                                                          +
      .                                                                                                        .
      .                                                                                                        .
      .                                                                                                        .
 6.0 +                                                                                                          +
      .                                                                                                        .
      .                                                                                                        .
      .                                                                                                        .
 4.5 +                                                                                                          +
C     .                                                                                                        .
A     .                                                                                                        .
N 3.0 .                                                                A                                        +
O     .            F                                                                                           .
N     .          C   C  F                                                                                      .
I     .        C       CF                                                                            A     A   .
C     .         F C F                                                                        D          A     .
A 1.5 +        CC          C       C                                                    D  A A  A             +
L     .           C              B        B                                                A A  A            .
      .    C   C  C   C                B                                             AA    AD  *             .
V     .    C C   3  C       CC         B                                        A    4A1ADA A               .
A     .      C  6     C CC             B                                              AAA                   .
R 0.0 +         *  F     B    BBB  B E     B                                          AA*A                   +
I     .   C        FFCF  C           E B BB  B                                        AA  A                 .
A     .      C       C          B B   2EBE B                                         A*AA  A              .
B     *   C     C       C B C  B     *5   B        B                                  D  A                .
L     .                              B B                                                                  .
E -1.5 +         C            E          *            E                                                     +
      .              B       B   B    * B  BB                                                             .
2     .           F      F   B         B                               A                                 .
      .           F                                                                                      .
 -3.0 +                      B B                                                                           +
      .                                                                                                  .
      .                                                                                                  .
      .                                                                                                  .
 -4.5 +                                                                                                   +
      .                                                                                                  .
      .                                                                                                  .
      .                                                                                                  .
 -6.0 +                                                                                                   +
      .                                                                                                  .
      .                                                                                                  .
      .                                                                                                  .
 -7.5 +                                                                                                   +
      .                                                                                                  .
      .....+....+....+....+....+....+....+....+....+....+....+....+....+....+....+....+....+....+....+....+....+..
        -8.10     -6.30     -4.50     -2.70     -.900      .900      2.70      4.50      6.30      8.10      9.90
      -9.00     -7.20     -5.40     -3.60     -1.80      0.00      1.80      3.60      5.40      7.20      9.00     10.8

                                       CANONICAL VARIABLE  1
```

Example 7M.3 Using Contrasts to Direct the Stepping

You can specify one or more contrasts to direct the stepping. The F-to-enter limits are the F statistics for the tests for which the contrast(s) is zero. (This is described in greater detail in Appendix A.23.) You may use as many contrasts as the number of groups minus one. In Example 7M.1 the second and third groups (B and C in the plot) are much closer to each other than either is to the first group. In order to select variables that will maximize the difference between the second and third groups we specify the contrast on the groups as

CONTRAST IS 0, 1, -1.

(Note that these coefficients sum to one).

Output 7M.3 Stepwise discriminant analysis directed by a contrast

----

```
STEP NUMBER   0

   VARIABLE        F TO   FORCE  TOLERANCE  *    VARIABLE        F TO    FORCE   TOLERANCE
                 REMOVE  LEVEL              *                   ENTER   LEVEL
               DF=  1  148                 *                DF=  1  147
                                           *    1 SEPALLEN    40.103     1      1.000000
                                           *    2 SEPALWID     9.016     1      1.000000
                                           *    3 PETALLEN   225.347     1      1.000000
                                           *    4 PETALWID   292.490     1      1.000000
```

--- results for steps 1 to 3 ---

```
STEP NUMBER   4
VARIABLE ENTERED   2 SEPALWID

   VARIABLE        F TO   FORCE  TOLERANCE  *    VARIABLE        F TO    FORCE   TOLERANCE
                 REMOVE  LEVEL              *                   ENTER   LEVEL
               DF=  1  144                 *                DF=  1  143
   1 SEPALLEN    6.355    1     0.347993    *
   2 SEPALWID    5.211    1     0.608860    *
   3 PETALLEN   28.914    1     0.365126    *
   4 PETALWID   48.692    1     0.649314    *
```

```
U-STATISTIC OR WILKS' LAMBDA      0.2547542    DEGREES OF FREEDOM     4    1      147
APPROXIMATE F-STATISTIC            105.313     DEGREES OF FREEDOM      4.00   144.00
```

```
   F - MATRIX        DEGREES OF FREEDOM =    4  144

             SETOSA    VERSICOL
VERSICOL    550.19
VIRGINIC   1098.27     105.31
```

```
CLASSIFICATION FUNCTIONS

         GROUP =   SETOSA      VERSICOL     VIRGINIC
VARIABLE
   1 SEPALLEN     23.54416     15.69820     12.44584
   2 SEPALWID     23.58786      7.07252      3.68529
   3 PETALLEN    -16.43063      5.21145     12.76655
   4 PETALWID    -17.39839      6.43422     21.07909

CONSTANT        -86.30843    -72.85257   -104.36826
```

```
CLASSIFICATION MATRIX

GROUP      PERCENT    NUMBER OF CASES CLASSIFIED INTO GROUP -
           CORRECT
                      SETOSA   VERSICOL  VIRGINIC
SETOSA     100.0       50         0         0
VERSICOL    96.0        0        48         2
VIRGINIC    98.0        0         1        49

TOTAL       98.0       50        49        51
```

We do this by adding the following DISCRIMINANT and PLOT paragraphs before the END paragraph of Example 7M.1

```
-------------------------------------
/ DISCRIMINANT    CONTRAST IS 0, 1, -1.

/ PLOT            CONTRAST.
-------------------------------------
```

CONTRAST is stated in the PLOT paragraph to obtain a plot of the canonical variables based on the specified contrasts. Since only one contrast is specified for this example, only one canonical variable is estimated. Instead of a bivariate canonical plot, a histogram of the canonical variable is plotted.

Results are presented in Output 7M.3. The use of the contrast affects the entry order of the variables: petal width is the third variable to

JACKKNIFED CLASSIFICATION

GROUP	PERCENT CORRECT	NUMBER OF CASES CLASSIFIED INTO GROUP -		
		SETOSA	VERSICOL	VIRGINIC
SETOSA	100.0	50	0	0
VERSICOL	96.0	0	48	2
VIRGINIC	98.0	0	1	49
TOTAL	98.0	50	49	51

SUMMARY TABLE

STEP NUMBER	VARIABLE ENTERED	REMOVED	F VALUE TO ENTER OR REMOVE	NUMBER OF VARIABLES INCLUDED	U-STATISTIC	APPROXIMATE F-STATISTIC	DEGREES OF FREEDOM	
1	4 PETALWID		292.4905	1	0.3345	292.490	1.00	147.00
2	3 PETALLEN		19.6385	2	0.2948	174.607	2.00	146.00
3	1 SEPALLEN		16.9447	3	0.2640	134.766	3.00	145.00
4	2 SEPALWID		5.2108	4	0.2548	105.313	4.00	144.00

EIGENVALUES

2.92535

CUMULATIVE PROPORTION OF TOTAL DISPERSION

1.00000

CANONICAL CORRELATIONS

0.86328

VARIABLE	COEFFICIENTS FOR CANONICAL VARIABLES
1 SEPALLEN	0.78419
2 SEPALWID	0.81671
3 PETALLEN	-1.82164
4 PETALWID	-3.53109
CONSTANT	4.00143

GROUP	CANONICAL VARIABLES EVALUATED AT GROUP MEANS
SETOSA	7.19488
VERSICOL	-1.52373
VIRGINIC	-5.67115

(output continued)

enter in Example 7M.1; it is first here. The final set of four variables remains the same so the final classification functions are also the same. The means for each group are marked on the histogram scale by a '1', '2' and '3'.

DISCriminant ─────────────────────────────────────

| CONTRast = # list. | may be repeated | none/prev. |

Coefficients of a contrast used to direct the stepping. The first number is the coefficient for the first group, the second number for the second group, etc. (according to the CODES, CUTPOINTS or order of input -- not according to the order in the GROUP USE statement). The coefficients usually sum to zero. CONTRAST = may be repeated to specify additional contrasts. If more than one contrast is specified, all the specified contrasts are used to direct the stepping. If CONTRASTS are not specified, they are generated to test the equality of all group means. When any CONTRAST

is specified, the CONTRASTS specified in a previous DISCRIMINANT paragraph are cancelled. When CONTRASTS are specified, the computation of the F-to-enter, F-to-remove and Wilks' lambda are affected; the coefficients of the classification functions, the classification matrix and Mahalanobis distances are not directly affected; they depend only on the set of variables selected and <u>not</u> on the values of the contrasts.

The effect of specifying CONTRASTS is described in Appendix A.23.

PLOT ───

| CONTRast. | no/prev. |

When contrasts are specified in the DISCRIMINANT paragraph and CONTRAST in the PLOT paragraph, the canonical variables and the plot of the canonical variables use the contrasts specified in the DISCRIMINANT paragraph. Otherwise, the coefficients for the canonical variables are obtained from the matrix $W^{-\frac{1}{2}}BW^{-\frac{1}{2}}$.

Output 7M.3 (continued)

POINTS TO BE PLOTTED

GROUP	MEAN COORDINATES		SYMBOL FOR CASES	SYMBOL FOR MEAN
SETOSA	7.19	0.0	A	1
VERSICOL	-1.52	0.0	B	2
VIRGINIC	-5.67	0.0	C	3

GROUP SETOSA

CASE	CAN.V	CASE	CAN.V	CASE	CAN.V	CASE	CAN.V	CASE	CAN.V
1	7.36	44	6.83	64	7.04	92	6.91	126	7.25
6	6.78	47	6.68	65	7.60	96	7.26	135	6.92
10	8.02	51	6.61	68	6.37	97	6.56	136	7.31
18	5.83	52	7.48	69	6.97	101	7.23	137	5.98
26	8.10	54	6.38	72	7.92	102	6.70	139	7.42
31	6.68	55	6.75	73	7.61	107	7.34	140	7.31
36	7.60	56	7.64	79	6.87	108	7.35	144	7.21
37	7.88	59	7.47	80	8.34	113	7.29	145	6.88
40	6.99	60	8.92	88	8.49	116	7.82	146	7.50
42	5.75	61	6.23	89	6.94	125	7.64	150	7.74

GROUP VERSICOL

CASE	CAN.V	CASE	CAN.V	CASE	CAN.V	CASE	CAN.V	CASE	CAN.V
3	-2.29	30	-0.81	71	0.69	100	-0.59	121	0.69
8	-2.83	33	-0.53	77	-1.40	104	-1.19	122	-1.30
9	-3.86	38	-2.81	85	0.26	106	-1.87	129	-2.35
11	-2.09	43	-0.85	86	-1.64	110	-0.31	130	-0.39
12	-4.03	48	-1.81	87	-0.97	114	-2.07	131	-2.28
14	-0.55	49	0.26	93	-1.42	115	-1.79	134	-1.52
19	-2.03	62	-1.17	94	-1.76	117	-1.22	141	-1.68
22	-2.57	66	-2.65	95	-2.36	118	-3.24	142	-1.33
28	-1.40	67	-0.24	98	-0.35	119	-1.73	143	-2.07
29	-1.86	70	-2.42	99	0.00	120	-1.03	148	-3.41

GROUP VIRGINIC

CASE	CAN.V	CASE	CAN.V	CASE	CAN.V	CASE	CAN.V	CASE	CAN.V
2	-6.66	23	-7.26	46	-4.14	81	-6.14	112	-5.62
4	-6.89	24	-7.03	50	-5.02	82	-4.82	123	-6.79
5	-3.36	25	-4.31	53	-4.05	83	-3.94	124	-5.31
7	-5.47	27	-5.89	57	-4.24	84	-5.25	127	-7.35
13	-4.99	32	-4.57	58	-6.31	90	-8.53	128	-4.64
15	-4.83	34	-4.83	63	-3.95	91	-3.90	132	-5.14
16	-5.24	35	-6.14	74	-6.74	103	-6.48	133	-5.65
17	-6.92	39	-5.42	75	-6.96	105	-5.73	138	-5.66
20	-6.32	41	-5.85	76	-5.24	109	-5.31	147	-6.93
21	-6.83	45	-6.94	78	-4.12	111	-5.74	149	-8.12

HISTOGRAM OF CANONICAL VARIABLE

```
                                                              A
                    C                        B              A  AA
              C     C     C            B  B  B              A  AA
              C     C     C            B  B BB              A  AA
              CC         CC C C    C      B  B BB    BB      A AAAAAA
            CCC CC CCCCCC    CCC  C B  BBBBBBB B BB  B  B   A A AAAAAAAA
  C C   CCCCCCCCCCCCCCCCCCCCCCBB BB BBBBBBBBBBBBBBBBBB  B   AA AAAAAAAAAAAA  A
  ..+....+....+..3.+....+....+....+....+....+2.+....+....+....+....+....+....1...+....+....+..
 -8.1     -6.3     -4.5     -2.7     -.90      .90     2.7      4.5      6.3      8.1      9.9
     -7.2     -5.4     -3.6     -1.8      0.0      1.8      3.6      5.4      7.2      9.0
```

Variable Selection Features

In addition to the contrasts illustrated in Example 7M.3, there are other features useful in fine tuning your model:

Forward and backward stepping (ENTER and REMOVE). The discriminant analysis begins with no variables in the classification function. Variables are entered or removed one at a time according to the criterion used (see METHOD). After all variables are entered that can be entered, they can be removed from the classification function according to a second set of F-to-enter and F-to-remove limits. An example of forward and backward stepping is given for P2R (Example 2R.2); it is done in the same way for P7M using ENTER and REMOVE in the DISCRIMINANT paragraph.

Controlling the order that variables (or subsets of variables) enter the model (LEVEL and FORCE). The LEVEL statement in the DISCRIMINANT paragraph can be used to specify a complete or partial ordering, which divides the variables into groups containing one (complete ordering) or more (partial ordering) variables. The use of the FORCE statement with the LEVEL statement can insure that a variable(s) remains in the classification regardless of the influence of other variables.

In the LEVEL statement you assign positive numbers (integers) or zero to the variables. Variables assigned zero are excluded from the analysis. The first number is the level assigned to the first variable read as input, the second to the second variable read as input, etc. For example, if the grouping variable is the first variable, and we want the second variable entered first, the third second, etc., we would state

LEVEL = 0, 1, 2, ...

Variables assigned a positive value are entered into the equation -- variables with smaller values are entered before variables with larger values. Variables with the same value compete for entry according to the METHOD specified. P7M begins stepping with the lowest positive value of LEVEL and enters all possible variables with the LEVEL (provided they pass the F-to-enter and tolerance limit) before considering variables at the next higher level. Variables not assigned any value for LEVEL are set to a value greater than the maximum value assigned (one if no LEVEL statement is present). Variables with a LEVEL less than or equal to FORCE are forced into the classification function without regard to the F-to-enter limit and are not removed.

When variables are eliminated by setting LEVEL = 0, the F-to-enter statistic is printed for these variables at each step. When variables are eliminated from the analysis by omitting them from the USE statement in the VARIABLE paragraph, not even their F-to-enter is computed and printed.

Removing variables from the classification function (METHOD). Either of two criteria can be used to remove variables from the classification function:

– a variable is removed if its F-to-remove is less than the F-to-remove limit (METHOD = 1.)

– a variable is removed to obtain a smaller Wilks' lambda than was previously obtained at an earlier step with the same number of variables in the function (METHOD = 2.)

Limiting the number of steps (STEPS). It is possible to specify a maximum number of steps; stepping ends when this number is reached even though F-to-enter and remove limits may indicate an extended analysis.

DISCriminant ─────

ENTER = #,#.   4.0,4.0/prev.
F-to-enter limits. The first number is used when entering variables into the classification function until no more variables can be entered. The second number (if it is larger than the first) is then used for backward stepping to remove variables. If only one number is specified, the second number is set equal to the first by the program.

REMOVE = #,#.   3.996,3.996/prev.
F-to-remove limits. The first number is used when entering variables into the classification function until no more variables can be entered. The second number (if it is larger than the first) is then used for backward stepping to remove the variables. REMOVE must be less than ENTER, or a variable could be continuously entered and removed at alternate steps. If only one number is specified, the second number is set equal to the first by the program.

LEVEL = # list.   one per   highest level
                         variable   specified + 1
The first number is the level assigned to the first variable read as input, the second to the second variable read as input, etc. If LEVEL is not stated, all variables except the grouping variable are assigned a level of one. LEVEL determines the order of entering variables into the classification function (see above). If LEVEL is stated for some variables but not all of them, the remaining variables are assigned to the next level greater than the maximum assigned.

FORCE = #.   0/prev.
If FORCE is greater than zero, variables with LEVEL less than or equal to FORCE are entered into the classification function without regard to the F-to-enter limit, and cannot be removed from the function once entered.

METHod = 1. or 2.   1/prev.
Method of removing variables from the classification: 1, by an F-to-remove limit; 2, to obtain a smaller Wilks' lambda than was previously obtained at an earlier step with the same number of variables.

STEP = #.   2(no. of var.)/prev.
Maximum number of steps in the analysis.

Prior Probabilities

Unless stated otherwise, a case is assumed a priori to have equal probability of being in any group. If prior probabilities are stated, they affect only the constant term of the classification function and the computation of the posterior probabilities.

```
GROUP
  PRIOR = # list.            equal prior prob./prev.
    Prior probabilities for each group. The first
    number is the prior probability for the first
    group, the second for the second group, etc.
    This is according to the order specified in
    CODES, CUTPOINTS or to the order of input (not
    according to the order in the USE statement of
    the GROUP paragraph).
    The prior probabilities of the groups USED in
    the analysis should add to unity. Unequal prior
    probabilities affect the computation of the
    constant term in the classification function
    and of the posterior probabilities (see
    Appendix A.23); they do not affect the F
    statistic, Wilks' lambda or the selection of
    variables.
    When the number of groups differs between two
    problems, the preassigned value for the second
    problem is "equal prior probabilities" and not
    previous problem (prev.).
```

Using Jackknifing to Compute Mahalanobis D^2 and Posterior Probabilities

Mahalanobis D^2 and the posterior probabilities are computed for each case after the final step of the discriminant analysis. D^2 is the distance from each case to each group mean. Both the group mean and the cross-products matrices use the case in the computation of the cross products.

When JACKKNIFE is specified in the DISCRIMINANT paragraph each case is eliminated in turn from the computation of the group means and cross products; D and the posterior probability are computed for the distance from the case to the groups formed by the remaining cases (Lachenbruch and Mickey, 1968). In the output the distances and posterior probabilities are labelled "jackknifed distances and posterior probabilities."

```
DISCriminant
  JACKknife.                                   no/prev.
    When JACKKNIFE is specified, Mahalanobis
    distances and the posterior probabilities for
    each case are computed without using the case
    in the computation of the group mean and pooled
    within-group covariance matrix.
```

Plots

The canonical variable plot (Example 7M.1) is automatically plotted except when

- there is only one canonical variable
- only one variable enters the classification function
- a single contrast is supplied
- only two groups are analyzed

A histogram is plotted for these situations. Either display may be repressed by using the NO CANONICAL statement in the PLOT paragraph.

When group memberships overlap extensively you can limit the groups displayed in each frame by using a GROUP statement (e.g., for six groups, one

GROUP statement could request the first three groups, another GROUP statement the last three groups).

The use of CONTRASTS in the canonical variable plot is illustrated in Example 7M.3.

```
PLOT
  CANONical.                                   yes/prev.
    A plot of the canonical variables is printed
    unless NO CANONICAL is specified. The canonical
    variables plotted are determined by whether or
    not CONTRAST is specified in the PLOT
    paragraph. If there is only one canonical
    variable, a histogram is printed.
  GROUP = g list.   may be           all groups/prev.
                    repeated
    Groups to be plotted in the canonical variable
    plot. Each GROUP = statement describes a
    separate plot. g list lists the NAMES or
    subscripts of the groups.
```

Controlling the Printed Results

The PRINT paragraph is used to request that additional results be printed -- or that selected results not be printed.

```
PRINT
  CORRelation.                                 no/prev.
    The within-groups correlation matrix is
    printed.
  WITHin.                                      no/prev.
    The within-groups covariance matrix is printed.
  STEP.                                        yes/prev.
    If NO STEP is specified, the results are not
    printed at every step; they are printed at only
    step 0 and the last step.
  CLASSification = # list.                    none/prev.
    Steps at which the classification matrix and
    the jackknifed classification matrix are
    printed. They are printed automatically after
    the last step.
  POSTerior.                                   yes/prev.
    Mahalanobis $D^2$ and posterior probabilities are
    printed at the last step unless NO POSTERIOR is
    specified.
  POINT.                                       yes/prev.
    The values of the canonical variables used in
    the plot are printed unless NO POINT is
    specified.
```

Saving the Canonical Variable Scores and an Indicator of Predicted Group Membership

When a BMDP File is created, the data, the canonical variables, and the index of the group into which each case is classified are saved. The canonical variables are named CNVR1, CNVR2, etc. and placed immediately after the data for each case. The index of the group into which the case is classified comes last and is named PREDICTD.

The BMDP File can then be read as input to other BMDP programs. (See the discussion of CODE, UNIT and NEW in Chapter 7).

SAVE ────────────────────────────────

> NCAN = #.   see below
>
> The number of canonical variables to be saved in a BMDP File. If not specified, the number of canonical variables saved is equal to the number of CONTRASTS specified in the DISCRIMINANT paragraph, or is one less than the number of groups used in the analysis if no CONTRASTS are specified (but not more than the number of variables selected). If NCAN is greater than the number of contrasts, the first set of canonical variable(s) contains the canonical variables evaluated for the contrasts ordered by the size of the eigenvalues, and the remaining set contains the residual variables (variables orthogonal to those corresponding to the set of contrasts).
>
> A variable named PREDICTD is added to the BMDP File to indicate the group in which each case is classified.

TOLERANCE

Variables are <u>not</u> entered into the classification function unless they can pass the TOLERANCE limit.

DISCriminant ────────────────────────

> TOLerance = #.   between 0.001   0.01/prev.
>   and 1.0
>
> Tolerance limit. No variable is entered into the classification function whose squared multiple correlation (R^2) with already entered variables exceeds 1 minus TOLERANCE, or whose entry will cause the tolerance of an already entered variable with the other variables to exceed 1 minus TOLERANCE.

SIZE OF PROBLEM

The maximum size of a problem that P7M can analyze is a complicated function of the number of variables (V), the number of groups (G) and the number of cases (C). We indicate the maximum number of cases (C) for various combinations of G and V for medium-sized computers.

G	2	2	3	5	10
V	10	50	50	50	50
C	1800	1350	1150	859	450

Appendix B describes how to increase the capacity of the program.

COMPUTATIONAL METHOD

The data are read in single precision. All computations are performed in double precision.

The computational procedure is described in Appendix A.23. See also Jennrich (1977b).

ACKNOWLEDGEMENT

P7M was designed by Robert Jennrich and Paul Sampson and programmed by Paul Sampson.

SUMMARY

Order of Input Cards

```
// (job card)
// EXEC BIMED,PROG=BMDP7M        (see Appendix E)
//SYSIN DD *
/ PROBLEM
/ INPUT
/ VARIABLE
/ GROUP
/ TRANSFORM
/ SAVE
/ DISCRIMINANT
/ PRINT
/ PLOT
/ END
    (data if on cards)
// (system card)
```

Full sets of BMDP paragraphs (and data, if on cards) can be repeated for additional problems; see Section 5.8.

Paragraph Statement	Preassigned	Comment and Manual Reference
/ INPut		Additional input option.
○GROUP = #.	none	Number of groups to be formed. Needed only when neither / GROUP, CODE nor CUTP is specified. * 525
/●VARiable		Required option to classify cases into groups.
●GROUPing = #.	none	Required; name or subscript of variable that defines group membership (see also / GROUP). * 525
/ GROUP		Additional option to name groups and give prior probabilities for groups used in analysis.
USE = g list.	all	Names or subscripts of groups used in estimating the classification functions. * 526
PRIOR = # list.	equal	The prior probabilities for groups used in analysis. * 534
/ DISCriminant		Optional to influence the stepping (number and order of variables entering the classification functions). If omitted, variables enter in a forward manner using F = 4.0 for entering, F =3.996 for removal.
ENTER = #, #. REMOVE = #, #.	4, 4. 3.996, 3.996	F-to-enter and F-to-remove limits. The first number of each is used for forward stepping to control the entry or removal of variables. Entering variables must have F's > ENTER limit. (For removal, F < REMOVE limit.) The second number of each is used for backward stepping. * 533
JACKknife.	no	Exclude case in question when computing posterior probabilities and Mahalanobis' D^2. * 534
METHod = #.	1.	Method for removing variables from the classification (1 or 2): 1 removes variables using the F-to-remove limit; 2 uses Wilks' lambda. *
LEVEL = # list.	highest + 1	Modifies the automatic order of entry and removal of variables. Specify LEVEL as a nonnegative integer for each variable. F-to-enter is computed and printed for zero level variables, but they are not entered into the equation. Variables at the same level compete for entry according to METHOD. Stepping begins at lowest positive LEVEL and enters all possible variables (those that pass the F-to-enter and TOL criteria) at that level before considering variables at the next higher level. * 533
FORCE = #.	0.	Variables with LEVEL # $\leq$ FORCE(if FORCE is greater than zero) enter and are not removed (ENTER and REMOVE limits are ignored when FORCE is specified). * 533
CONTrast = # list.	none	Coefficients of a contrast used to direct stepping, (one number for each group; should sum to zero) according to CODE or CUTP order - not USE in the / GROUP paragraph (may be repeated). Used in F-to-enter and Wilks' lambda computations. * 532
STEP = #.	2(VT)	Maximum number of steps in analysis. * 533
TOLerance = #.	.01.	Tolerance limit. No variable enters whose R^2 with already entered variables exceed (1 - TOL) or whose entry causes the TOL of already entered variables to be unacceptable. * 535
/ PRINT		Optional to direct printing. 534
CORR.	no	Pooled within group correlation matrix. *
WITHin.	no	Within-groups covariance matrix. *
STEP.	yes	Results are printed at all steps. If NO STEP is specified, results printed only at Step 0 and last step. *
CLASS = # list.	after last	Steps at which the classification matrix and jackknifed classification matrix are printed.
POSTerior.	yes	Mahalanobis' D^2 and posterior probabilities for each case at the last step. *
POINT.	yes	Values of the canonical variables used in the plot. *

(continued)

(continued)

Paragraph Statement	Preassigned	Comment and Manual Reference
/ PLOT		Optional to control plots.
CONTRast.	no	Use CONT specified in / DISC to compute the canonical variables for the plots. * 532
CANONical.	yes	Plot the first two canonical variables. If there is only one, print a histogram. * 534
GROUPs = g list.	all	Groups to be plotted on a single page (may be repeated for additional plots). * 534
/ SAVE		Additional option only if a BMDP File is to be created. 535
NCAN = #.	groups − 1	The number of canonical variables for which scores are saved in a BMDP File. For each case the data saved are the values of the original variables followed by the scores for the canonical variables. * A variable is added to the BMDP File to indicate classification of each case into a group.

Key:

/   −indicates paragraph
.   −period ends a sentence
●   −required   O   −may be required
v   −variable (name or subscript)
g   −group (name or subscript)
−number
'c'   −characters (name or parameter) may omit apostrophes if contiguous letters only

*   −assigned value remains the same for additional problems
VT   −number of variables after transformations
list   −more than one item, often one per var.

Capitalized letters−paragraph or sentence names recognized by BMDP
Page numbers following refer to this Manual

P8M

18.5 Boolean Factor Analysis

M. R. Mickey
Peter Mundle
Laszlo Engelman

ABSTRACT

P8M performs a factor analysis of dichotomous (binary) data. The analysis in this program differs from that of classical factor analysis (see P4M) based on binary data even though the goal and model (symbolically) appear similar. The goal is to express p variables $X = (x_1, x_2, \ldots, x_p)$ by m factors $F = (f_1, f_2, \ldots, f_m)$, where m is considerably smaller than p. The model can be written as $X = F \odot A$, where A is the matrix of factor loadings. For n observations (cases), the data, factor score and loading matrices may be pictured as

$$
\begin{matrix}
\text{n cases} \\
\text{(subjects)}
\end{matrix}
\begin{bmatrix} & \\ & \text{data} \\ & (x_{ij}) \\ & \end{bmatrix}
=
\begin{bmatrix} & \\ & \text{factor} \\ & \text{scores} \\ & (F) \\ & \end{bmatrix}
\odot
\begin{bmatrix} \text{factor} \\ \text{loadings} \\ (A) \end{bmatrix}
\begin{matrix} \uparrow \\ m \\ \downarrow \end{matrix}
$$

$$
\begin{matrix} \text{p variables} & \text{m factors} \\ \text{(tests)} \end{matrix}
\qquad \leftarrow p \rightarrow
$$

where x_{ij} has the value zero or one.

Boolean factor analysis differs from the classical analysis in that the arithmetic used in the matrix multiplication is Boolean, so the scores and loadings are binary. For example, in classical factor analysis, the result of multiplying the following two vectors is two:

$$
(1,1,0,1) \begin{pmatrix} 1 \\ 1 \\ 0 \\ 0 \end{pmatrix} = 1 \otimes 1 + 1 \otimes 1 + 0 \otimes 0 + 1 \otimes 0
$$

while in Boolean arithmetic the result is one.

In classical factor analysis the score for each case (for a particular factor) is a linear combination of all the variables: the variables with large loadings all contribute to the score. In Boolean factor analysis, a case has a score of one if it has a positive response for any of the variables dominant in the factor (those not having zero loadings) and zero otherwise. Also in classical factor analysis, it is desirable to have each variable associated with one factor (a variable should not have sizable loadings for several factors). In Boolean analysis, a variable may have a loading of one for several factors.

In Boolean factor analysis the success of the technique is measured by comparing the observed binary responses with those estimated by multiplying the loadings times the scores. We count both the positive and negative discrepancies where the positive discrepancy is the number of times the observed score is one and the analysis estimates it to be zero and the negative discrepancy is the number of times the observed score is zero and the estimated value is one. A useful measure of agreement between the original data x_{ij} and the estimated values $\hat{x}_{ij}$ is the total number of discrepancies

$$
d = \sum_{i=1}^{n} \sum_{j=1}^{p} |\hat{x}_{ij} - x_{ij}| \ .
$$

As an example we consider a serological problem where p tests are performed on the blood of each subject (p reagents are added). The outcome is described as positive (a value of one is assigned for the test in the data matrix) or negative (a zero is assigned); or there is no outcome because there is a technical failure or the result is missing. The scores might be interpreted as antigens (for each subject) and the loadings as antibodies (for each test reagent).

The user can supply initial estimates of the loading matrix (or the initial estimates for the loadings may be computed by the program). First, the estimates of the loadings (columns of F) are held fixed and estimates are made of the scores (rows of A'). Next the scores are taken as fixed and new estimates are calculated for the loadings. This cyclic process is repeated until there are no further changes in assignment or until three cycles have been completed. The column with the largest number of discrepancies is then altered for the next iteration step by the introduction of an additional factor. The resulting scores, loadings and summary of discrepancies may be printed at each iteration.

WHERE TO FIND IT

Example 8M.1 Basic Setup for Boolean Factor Analysis

The data for this example come from a study of lymphocyte blood cells for 50 subjects tested with a panel of 20 reagent antisera. The data are displayed in Table 18.2. The underlying assumption is that the cell surface has features that can be recognized by constituents in the reagents. A reagent will cause a reaction if the cell tested has any one of the features associated with the reagent. Cells from a given person are assumed to have a few of these distinct surface features.

Table 18.2   Data from a study of lymphocyte blood cells

```
1111181111 1111110281      1111111111 1111111111
8811111111 1111112821      8811111111 1811881811
8811111118 1818881811      1111111110 1111111111
1111181181 8111118181      1111111111 1111111111
6481811118 1118811611      1111111111 1111118111
1111111888 8118118111      1181811111 1111118111
8081801101 1811801801      1281611111 1111111111
1111111111 1181111111      1111111111 1111111111
1111111888 8118111111      1681811118 1118111811
8811111111 1101111011      8811111118 1818881811
8181811888 8118111811      1111111111 1811821216
1101111118 1118118111      1181812888 8118211111
1111111111 1111111111      1111111111 1111111111
1111111888 8118111211      8811111118 1118111811
1111111118 1818881111      1111111888 8818881111
8818118111 1814881811      1111181118 1118118111
1111111118 1118111111      1111111111 1111118118
1111111118 1888881111      1111111181 8141118111
1111111118 1188111111      1111112888 8168111621
1111111111 1811886118      6181811188 8118111211
1118118111 1111111111      1111111111 1816881111
1111111881 8111118111      1111101888 8118111111
1118118881 8111118111      6881811111 1111111811
1111111111 1111111111      8681811111 1811881811
1118118118 1118111118      1111112118 1118111111
```

The BMDP instructions below in the INPUT paragraph are used for all BMDP programs and are described in Chapter 5. The instructions in the VARIABLE paragraph are specific to P8M and state that a reaction (a RESPONSE) is coded as 6 or 8 and that no reaction (NONRESPONSE) is coded as 1 or 2. Any other value in the data (e.g., 0) is then considered to be an unknown reaction.

```
------------------------------------
/ PROBLEM    TITLE IS 'NOMINAL SPECIFICITIES OF SOME
             HL-A ANTISERA.'.
/ INPUT      VARIABLES ARE 20.
             FORMAT IS '(10F1.0, 1X, 10F1.0)'.

/ VARIABLE   RESPONSES ARE 6, 8.
             NONRESPONSES ARE 1, 2.

/ END
------------------------------------
```

(See end of this P8M section for organization of systems information, BMDP instructions and data.)

The results of the analysis are presented in 8M.1. Circled numbers below correspond to those in the output.

① Preassigned values for P8M options are printed. The number of cases read and the numbers of responses, nonresponses and their total are reported. Codes not identified as RESPONSES or NONRESPONSES are omitted from the analysis. P8M also checks for missing value codes (MISS) and range limits for acceptable values (MINIMUM and MAXIMUM) when they are specified in the VARIABLE paragraph. In this example the data matrix has 20 x 50 = 1000 entries but only 986 are used.

② The initial estimates of the loadings are computed (without iterating) for three factors. The

Output 8M.1   Boolean factor analysis results. Circled numbers correspond to those in the text

---

```
COST OF PREDICTING RESPONSE FOR NONRESPONSE. .  1.00000
RESPONSE CODES . . . . . . . . . . . . . . . .  6.00  8.00
NONRESPONSE CODES. . . . . . . . . . . . . . .  1.00  2.00
FACTORS PRINTED AT ITERATIONS. . . . . . . . .  1  2  3  5


FACTOR TITLE . . . . . .  NOMINAL SPECIFICITIES OF SOME HL-A ANTISERA.

NUMBER OF FACTORS TO READ IN . . . . . . . . .      0
INITIAL NUMBER OF FACTORS. . . . . . . . . . .      3
MAXIMUM NUMBER OF FACTORS. . . . . . . . . . .      5
MAXIMUM NUMBER OF ITERATIONS . . . . . . . . .      5
STOP ITERATIONS WHEN DIFFERERENCE EQUALS . . .  0.0
PRINT INPUT DATA . . . . . . . . . . . . . . .     NO
PRINT LOADINGS . . . . . . . . . . . . . . . .    YES      ①
PRINT FACTOR SCORES. . . . . . . . . . . . . .     NO
PRINT DISCREPANCY MATRIX . . . . . . . . . . .     NO

NUMBER OF CASES READ . . . . . . . . . . . . .     50

NUMBER OF RESPONSES. . . . . . . . . . . . . .    204
NUMBER OF NORESPONSES. . . . . . . . . . . . .    782
                          TOTAL. . . . . . . .    986
```

STEP 0 FACTOR LOADINGS

```
(THE LOADINGS ARE              N
LISTED AT THE RIGHT            F  O
BELOW THE LABELS)              A  .  123
                              C
                               T  L  FFF     ②
                               O  A  CCC
                               R  B  TTT
                               E     123
                               L
```

| VARIABLE | | NUMBER OF | | PCT | |
NO.	LABEL	NONRESP	RESP	RESP	
1	X(1)	37	13	26	100
2	X(2)	38	10	21	100
3	X(3)	39	10	20	010
4	X(4)	46	4	8	001
5	X(5)	40	10	20	010
6	X(6)	45	3	6	000
7	X(7)	46	4	8	001
8	X(8)	40	10	20	000
9	X(9)	36	13	27	000
10	X(10)	27	22	45	000
11	X(11)	37	13	26	000
12	X(12)	38	12	24	000
13	X(13)	44	4	8	000
14	X(14)	26	23	47	000
15	X(15)	38	12	24	000
16	X(16)	39	10	20	000
17	X(17)	38	11	22	000
18	X(18)	36	13	27	100
19	X(19)	46	3	6	000
20	X(20)	46	4	8	000

(output continued)

number of responses RESP, nonresponses NONRESP and the percent of responses is reported for each variable. The number of factors extracted initially depends on how many can be computed without iterating. The preassigned total number of factors is five; the preassigned number of initial factors is three, or two less than the total number. The user can control these values using INITIAL and NUMBER in the FACTOR paragraph. The program builds up to the total number of factors in a stepwise fashion.

③ At the second step the program has four factors. For two steps the program increases the number of factors by one and then at the following step deletes an earlier factor. This pattern repeats (increase two, decrease one) until the total number of factors has been computed twice. For example, if the analysis begins with three factors and six factors are planned, the number of factors in consecutive steps is 3, 4, 5, 4, 5, 6, 5, 6. At each step, the program performs up to three cycles in search of the factors. In each cycle the factor scores are computed from the data and the current loadings, then the loadings are computed from the data and the new scores. At each half-cycle the number of discrepancies (positive, negative and total) is reported. The variables with the most positive and negative discrepancies are also identified.

④ At step 5, the last step, there are five factors (the number of factors in consecutive steps beginning at step 1 is 3, 4, 5, 4, and 5). For each variable, the program now prints the loadings for the five factors (at the right), the number of observed responses and nonresponses with the percent of responses. Using the differences between the observed and estimated values the program counts the positive and negative discrepancies and also reports the percent of positive discrepancies. This report is printed at the first, third, last minus two and the last steps unless the user specifies otherwise in the STEP statement in the PRINT paragraph.

From this report we can see which variables are similar: variables 1, 2, and 18 have the same loadings with a total of four discrepancies. That is, for these three variables and 50 subjects we have 150 observed responses -- by estimating responses using the loading and scores matrix we make four mistakes. Using the loadings and scores for the five factors we compute 50 x 20 estimates with 36 observed as zero now estimated as one and 6 observed as one now estimated as zero.

Output 8M.1 (continued)

③ STEP NUMBER 2   NUMBER OF FACTORS = 4

NO. FACTORS	CYCLE	TOTAL POS DISC.	TOTAL NEG DISC.	TOTAL DISC.
4	1	119	2	121

NO. FACTORS	CYCLE	TOTAL POS DISC.	TOTAL NEG DISC.	TOTAL DISC.
4	1	97	3	100

NO. FACTORS	CYCLE	TOTAL POS DISC.	TOTAL NEG DISC.	TOTAL DISC.
4	2	98	2	100

MAX POS DISC.	VARIABLE LABEL	NO.	MAX NEG DISC.	VARIABLE LABEL	NO.
13	X(9)	9	1	X(1)	1

--- the results for steps 3 to 5 appear here ---

STEP 5 FACTOR LOADINGS

(THE LOADINGS ARE LISTED AT THE RIGHT BELOW THE LABELS)   ④

```
                        N
                        F O
                        A .    12345
                        C
                        T L    FFFFF
                        O A    CCCCC
                        R B    TTTTT
                          E    12453
                          L
```

VARIABLE NO.	LABEL	NUMBER OF NONRESP	RESP	PCT RESP	DISCREP NEG	POS	PCT POS DISC	12345
1	X(1)	37	13	26	1	1	8	10000
2	X(2)	38	10	21	1	0	0	10000
3	X(3)	39	10	20	0	0	0	01000
4	X(4)	46	4	8	0	4	100	00000
5	X(5)	40	10	20	0	0	0	01000
6	X(6)	45	3	6	0	3	100	00000
7	X(7)	46	4	8	0	4	100	00000
8	X(8)	40	10	20	3	0	0	00010
9	X(9)	36	13	27	0	0	0	00010
10	X(10)	27	22	45	0	0	0	00100
11	X(11)	37	13	26	0	0	0	00010
12	X(12)	38	12	24	0	0	0	00001
13	X(13)	44	4	8	0	4	100	00000
14	X(14)	26	23	47	0	1	4	00100
15	X(15)	38	12	24	0	0	0	00001
16	X(16)	39	10	20	1	0	0	00001
17	X(17)	38	11	22	0	11	100	00000
18	X(18)	36	13	27	0	1	8	10000
19	X(19)	46	3	6	0	3	100	00000
20	X(20)	46	4	8	0	4	100	00000

```
VARiable
  RESponse = # list.                              1/prev.
    Values that represent a response in the data.
    If omitted, one is assumed to be a response.
  NONresponse = # list.                           0/prev.
    Values that represent a nonresponse in the
    data. If omitted zero is assumed as a
    nonresponse. Some researchers may want to
    consider the "nonresponse" as a "negative"
    response.

    Note: Each value in the list may contain no
    more than 10 values.

    Note: Values not listed in RES or NON
    statements are assumed to be unknown responses
    and are omitted from the computations.
```

Example 8M.2 Specifying the Number of Factors and the Cost of Negative Discrepancies

In the previous example we had 36 positive and 6 negative discrepancies. It may be possible to reduce the number of discrepancies by

a) reducing the number of initial factors. The procedure will then go through the iterative process for more factors, or
b) increasing the total number of factors.

The number of initial factors (INITIAL) and the total number of factors (NUMBER) are specified in the FACTOR paragraph.

One type of mistake may be considered more harmful than another. For example, we may be most concerned about negative discrepancies -- i.e., we do not want to predict a reaction when there is none. We can use the COST option in the VARIABLE paragraph to increase the cost of the negative discrepancies -- we will get fewer negative discrepancies but may get more positive discrepancies (likewise if we decrease the cost of

negative discrepancies we are apt to get more negative but fewer positive discrepancies). The COST parameter always refers to the cost of negative discrepancies. If omitted, the cost is assumed to be 1.0.

The following BMDP instructions are added to the Control Language of Example 8M.1 before the END paragraph (The COST statement is in the VARIABLE paragraph).

```
              COST IS  2.0.
  / FACTOR    INITIAL IS 4.
              NUMBER  IS 7.
```

The results are shown in Output 8M.2.

⑤ With INITIAL = 4. and NUMBER = 7., the number of factors in each consecutive step is: 4, 5, 6, 5, 6, 7, 6, 7 (resulting in 7 factors at step 8). At step 8, with 7 factors, there are 29 positive discrepancies and zero negative discrepancies. Note that in cycle 1 of this last step the total number of discrepancies is less (23 positive and 3 negative discrepancies). Because of the COST specification, the program settled with 29 positive and zero negative discrepancies.

```
VARiable
  COST = #.                                       1/prev.
    The cost of mispredicting nonresponses
    (negative discrepancies), i.e., predicting a
    response where none was observed.
```

```
FACTor
  TITLE = 'text'.        < 160 char.   PROB TITLE.
    Text to label the output for this analysis.
  NUMBer = #.                                     5/prev.
    Total number of factors.
  INITial = #.                                    NUMBER-2.
    Initial number of factors.
```

Output 8M.2 Increasing the cost of negative discrepancies and controlling the number of factors

STEP NUMBER 8   NUMBER OF FACTORS = 7   ⑤

NO. FACTORS	CYCLE	TOTAL POS DISC.	TOTAL NEG DISC.	TOTAL DISC.		MAX POS DISC.	VARIABLE LABEL	NO.		MAX NEG DISC.	VARIABLE LABEL	NO.
7	1	46	0	46								
7	1	23	3	26		4	X(13)	13		3	X(8)	8
7	2	29	0	29								
7	2	29	0	29		4	X(13)	13		0	X(1)	1

--- the loadings for the seven factor solution appear here ---

Example 8M.3 Printing Data, Loadings, Scores

At each step the program prints summary reports like ⑤ above; and at selected steps, the factor loadings and/or factor scores can be printed. The STEP instruction in the PRINT paragraph controls the summary reports, and if omitted, the reports are printed at the first, third, last and two steps before the last step. The loadings, ④ in Output 8M.1, are printed unless NO LOAD is specified in the PRINT paragraph. The factor scores are not printed unless SCORES. is requested in the PRINT paragraph.

Compact displays of the data and the discrepancies (residuals) can be printed after the last step by stating DATA and DISC in the PRINT

paragraph. The symbols in the discrepancy matrix are

+	a positive discrepancy
-	a negative discrepancy
blank	no discrepancy
0	the missing value, for unknown reponses, or values outside MIN-MAX range

We illustrate these options by adding the following PRINT paragraph before the END paragraph of Example 8M.2:

```
----------------------------------------
  / PRINT   SCORES.
           DATA.
           DISCREPANCIES.
----------------------------------------
```

Output 8M.3 Printing the data in a compact display, the factor scores and a matrix of discrepancies

----

C A S E NO. LABEL	1 X(1) 11 X(11)	2 X(2) 12 X(12)	3 X(3) 13 X(13)	4 X(4) 14 X(14)	5 X(5) 15 X(15)	6 X(6) 16 X(16)	7 X(7) 17 X(17)	8 X(8) 18 X(18)	9 X(9) 19 X(19)	10 X(10) 20 X(20)

BASED ON INPUT FORMAT SUPPLIED   1 RECORDS READ PER CASE.

CASE	X1	X2	X3	X4	X5	X6	X7	X8	X9	X10
1	1	1	1	1	1	8	1	1	1	1
	1	1	1	1	1	1	0	2	8	1
2	8	8	1	1	1	1	1	1	1	1
	1	1	1	1	1	1	2	8	2	1
3	8	8	1	1	1	1	1	1	1	8
	1	8	1	8	8	8	1	8	1	1
4	1	1	1	1	1	8	1	1	8	1
	8	1	1	1	1	1	8	1	8	1
5	6	4	8	1	8	1	1	1	1	8
	1	1	1	8	1	1	1	6	1	1
6	1	1	1	1	1	1	1	8	8	8
	8	1	1	8	1	1	8	1	1	1
7	8	0	8	1	8	0	1	1	0	1
	1	8	1	1	8	0	1	8	0	1
8	1	1	1	1	1	1	1	1	1	1
	1	1	8	1	1	1	1	1	1	1
9	1	1	1	1	1	1	1	8	8	8
	8	1	1	8	1	1	1	1	1	1
10	8	8	1	1	1	1	1	1	1	1
	1	1	0	1	1	1	1	0	1	1

(⑦a)

NUMBER OF CASES READ.   50

NUMBER OF RESPONSES.   204
NUMBER OF NORESPONSES.   782
                              TOTAL.   986

STEP NUMBER 8   NUMBER OF FACTORS = 7

NO. FACTORS	CYCLE	TOTAL POS DISC.	TOTAL NEG DISC.	TOTAL DISC.	MAX POS DISC.	VARIABLE LABEL	NO.	MAX NEG DISC.	VARIABLE LABEL	NO.
7	1	46	0	46						
7	1	23	3	26	4	X(13)	13	3	X(8)	8
7	2	29	0	29						
7	2	29	0	29	4	X(13)	13	0	X(1)	1

The results are presented in Output 8M.3.

(6) For each case the factor scores, the counts and percents of responses and discrepancies are printed. From this output we can identify the subjects whose pattern of reaction to the panel of 20 reagents is similar: for example, cases 2 and 10 and cases 3 and 35.

(7) The results of the DATA instruction in the PRINT paragraph are

a) the data for the first 10 cases are printed as entered,
b) the data are recoded into response, no response and unknown and printed in a compact display. The number of discrepancies for each case is printed to the left of the display.

(8) The matrix of discrepancies (residuals) is printed in the same format as the compact data display. These matrices may be overlaid on a light-table to study the location or pattern of the discrepancies.

Output 8M.3 (continued)

STEP 8 FACTOR SCORES

(THE SCORES ARE LISTED AT THE RIGHT BELOW THE LABELS) (6)

```
        N
        F O
        A .  12345  67
        C
        T L  FFFFF  FF      DATA MATRIX (7b)
        O A  CCCCC  CC      -----------
        R B  TTTTT  TT      +  MEANS  RESPONSE
        E    12357  46      -  MEANS  NORESPONSE
        L                   0  MEANS  UNKNOWN
```

MATRIX OF DISCREPANCIES (8)

```
+  MEANS  RESPONSE OBSERVED,
                   NORESPONSE PREDICTED
-  MEANS  NORESPONSE OBSERVED,
                   RESPONSE PREDICTED
0  MEANS  OBSERVED = UNKNOWN
BLANK MEANS  OBSERVED = PREDICTED
```

CASE NO.	LABEL	NUMBER OF NONRESP	NUMBER OF RESP	PCT RESP	DISCREP NEG	DISCREP POS	PCT POS DISC	12345	67
1		17	2	11	0	2	100	00000	00
2		17	3	15	0	0	0	10000	00
3		12	8	40	0	0	0	10011	00
4		15	5	25	0	4	80	00000	10
5		13	6	32	0	0	0	11010	00
6		14	6	30	0	0	0	00010	11
7		9	6	40	0	0	0	11001	00
8		19	1	5	0	1	100	00000	00
9		15	5	25	0	0	0	00010	01
10		16	2	11	0	0	0	10000	00
11		11	9	45	0	2	22	01010	01
12		16	3	16	0	0	0	00010	10
13		20	0	0	0	0	0	00000	00
14		15	5	25	0	0	0	00010	01
15		15	5	25	0	0	0	00011	00
16		11	8	42	0	0	0	10101	00
17		18	2	10	0	0	0	00010	00
18		14	6	30	0	1	17	00011	00
19		17	3	15	0	1	33	00010	00
20		15	5	25	0	1	20	00001	10
21		18	2	10	0	0	0	00100	00
22		16	4	20	0	0	0	00000	11
23		14	6	30	0	0	0	00100	11
24		20	0	0	0	0	0	00000	00
25		15	5	25	0	1	20	00110	00
26		20	0	0	0	0	0	00000	00
27		14	6	30	0	0	0	10001	00
28		19	0	0	0	0	0	00000	00
29		20	0	0	0	0	0	00000	00
30		19	1	5	0	0	0	00000	00
31		17	3	15	0	0	0	01000	10
32		18	2	10	0	0	0	01000	00
33		20	0	0	0	0	0	00000	00
34		14	6	30	0	2	33	01010	00
35		12	8	40	0	0	0	10011	00
36		17	3	15	0	3	100	00000	00
37		13	7	35	0	0	0	01010	01
38		20	0	0	0	0	0	00000	00
39		15	5	25	0	0	0	10010	00
40		12	8	40	0	0	0	00011	01
41		15	5	25	0	2	40	00010	10
42		18	2	10	0	1	50	00000	10
43		16	3	16	0	2	67	00010	10
44		13	7	35	0	2	29	00010	01
45		13	7	35	0	3	43	01010	00
46		16	4	20	0	1	25	00001	00
47		14	5	26	0	0	0	00010	01
48		15	5	25	0	0	0	11000	00
49		12	8	40	0	0	0	11001	00
50		18	2	10	0	0	0	00010	00

DATA MATRIX (7b)

NO. DISC	ROW	12345	67890	1 12345	11111 67890	11112
2	1	-----	+----	-----	-0-+-	
0	2	++---	-----	-----	--+--	
0	3	++---	----+	-+-++	+-+--	
4	4	-----	+--+-	+----	-+-+-	
0	5	+0+-+	----+	---+-	---+-	
0	6	-----	--+++	+--+-	-+---	
0	7	+0+-+	0--0-	-+--+	0-+0-	
1	8	-----	-----	--+--	-----	
0	9	-----	--+++	+--+-	-----	
0	10	++---	-----	--0--	--0--	
2	11	+-+-+	--+++	+--+-	--+--	
0	12	--0--	----+	---+-	-+---	
0	13	-----	-----	-----	-----	
0	14	-----	--+++	+--+-	-----	
0	15	-----	----+	-+-++	+----	
0	16	++-+-	-+---	-+-0+	+-+--	
0	17	-----	----+	---+-	-----	
1	18	-----	----+	-++++	+----	
1	19	-----	-----	--++-	-----	
1	20	-----	-----	-+--+	++--+	
0	21	---+-	-+---	-----	-----	
0	22	-----	--++-	+----	-+---	
0	23	---+-	-+++-	+----	-+---	
0	24	-----	-----	-----	-----	
1	25	---+-	-+--+	---+-	----+	
0	26	-----	-----	-----	-----	
0	27	++---	-----	-+--+	+-+--	
0	28	-----	----0	-----	-----	
0	29	-----	-----	-----	-----	
0	30	-----	-----	-----	-+---	
31	0	--+-+	-----	-----	-+---	
32	0	--+-+	-----	-----	-----	
33	0	-----	-----	-----	-----	
34	2	-++-+	----+	-----	--+--	
35	0	++---	----+	-+-++	+-+--	
36	3	-----	-----	-+--+	----+	
37	0	---+-	--+++	+--+-	-----	
38	0	-----	-----	-----	-----	
39	0	++---	----+	---+-	--+--	
40	0	-----	--+++	++-++	+----	
41	2	-----	+---+	---+-	-+-+-	
42	1	-----	----+	---+-	-+--+	
43	2	-----	----+-	+-0--	-+---	
44	2	-----	--+++	+-++-	--+--	
45	3	+-+-+	--++	+--+-	-----	
46	1	-----	-----	-+-++	+----	
47	0	-----	0-+++	+--+-	-----	
48	0	+++-+	-----	-----	--+--	
49	0	+++-+	-----	-+--+	+-+--	
50	0	-----	----+	---+-	-----	

MATRIX OF DISCREPANCIES (8)

NO. ROW	DISC	12345	67890	1 12345	11111 67890	11112
1	2		+		0 +	
2	0					
3	0					
4	4		+ +	+		+
5	0	0				
6	0					
7	0	0		0 0	+	0 0
8	1			+		
9	0					
10	0				0	0
11	2	+				+
12	0	0				
13	0					
14	0					
15	0					
16	0				0	
17	0					
18	1				+	
19	1				+	
20	1					+
21	0					
22	0					
23	0					
24	0					
25	1					+
26	0					
27	0					
28	0			0		
29	0					
30	0					
31	0					
32	0					
33	0					
34	2	+				+
35	0					
36	3			+ +		+
37	0					
38	0					
39	0					
40	0					
41	2		+			+
42	1					+
43	2		+	+ 0		
44	2				+	+
45	3	+		+ +		
46	1				+	
47	0	0				
48	0					
49	0					
50	0					

```
PRINT ─────────────────────────────────────────────────
   STEP = # list.                          1,2,last-2,last
      Steps at which loadings and/or scores are to be
      printed. If the number of initial factors is i
      and the total number of factors is n > i, then
      last = 3*(n-i)-1.
   LOAD.                                          LOAD/prev.
      The factor loadings are printed. To negate
      state NO LOAD.
   SCORE.                                    NO SCORE/prev.
      The factor scores are not printed unless SCORE
      is specified.
   DATA.                                      NO DATA/prev.
      The first ten cases, and the compact data
      display are not printed, unless DATA is
      specified.
   DISC.                                      NO DISC/prev.
      The discrepancies are not printed unless DISC
      is specified.
```

Storing Results in a BMDP File

The final factor loadings, scores, discrepancies, predicted values and data may be saved in a BMDP File. When SCORES is requested, the scores for each case are listed after the data. When DISCREPACNCIES is specified, the residuals described in Example 8M.3 are inserted for each case in the original data matrix - thus the values of variables not used in the Boolean analysis remain unaltered and the dichotomous variables used are replaced by their residuals. A request for PREDICTED values works in the same way - the original data values are replaced by the predicted values.

```
SAVE ──────────────────────────────────────────────────
   CONTent = DATA, LOAD, SCORE, PRED, DISC.        DATA
      The data or matrices saved in a BMDP File

      DATA    the data are saved
      SCORE   the data and factor scores are saved:
              the scores are listed after the data
              and are named FACTOR1, FACTOR2, etc.
      LOAD    factor loadings
      DISC    the data matrix is saved with the
              discrepancies (residuals) for variable
              i replacing the data for variable i
      PRED    the predicted values are saved in
              place of the original data

   Note: Both DISC and PRED cannot be saved in the
   same run.
```

Using Loadings as Input

Instead of extracting the initial factors from the data, P8M can read a matrix of loadings. The loadings are read in addition to the data. (The rows of the loadings matrix must match the columns of the data.) The loadings may be read from a BMDP File or from a formatted file.

The presence of a LOAD paragraph in the BMDP instructions is a signal to P8M that the loadings will be read. If the data and the loadings are read from the same formatted file (i.e., cards) the loadings must precede the data.

If the input loadings contain more factors than wanted, you can select initial factors with the USE statement in the FACTOR paragraph.

As an illustration, if we want to begin an analysis using the loadings saved in a BMDP File in an earlier run and decide to omit the sixth factor, our instructions are:

```
/ PROBLEM    TITLE IS 'BEGINNING THE ANALYSIS WITH A
                       USER SUPPLIED LOADING MATRIX'.

/ INPUT      VARIABLES ARE 20.
             FORMAT IS '(10F1.0, 1X, 10F1.0)'.

/ LOAD       UNIT IS 10.
             CODE IS ANTISERA.

/ VARIABLE   RESPONSES ARE 6, 8.
             NONRESPONSES ARE 1, 2.

/ FACTOR     USE = 1 TO 5, 7.
             NUMBER = 8.

/ END
```

The analysis begins with six initial factors (factors 1 to 5 and 7) and will finish with 8 factors. We do not show the output for this example.

```
LOAD ──────────────────────────────────────────────────
   UNIT = #.                                       5/prev.
      Unit number from which the factor loadings are
      read. If the loadings are read from a BMDP
      File, the unit number must not be 5.
   FORMat = 'c'.                               none/prev.
      Input format for the loading matrix. The format
      must specify one row of the loading matrix (the
      row must have as many values as there are
      factors).
   NUMBer = #.                               INITIAL/prev.
      Number of factors in the loading input matrix.
      If NUMBER is specified, it also becomes the
      number of initial factors, overriding the
      INITIAL statement of the FACTOR paragraph.
   CODE = 'c'.                                        none
      Signals that the loading matrix is read from a
      BMDP File.
   CONTent = 'c'.
      Content of the BMDP File input to read as
      loadings. If not specified, the first BMDP File
      with matching CODE is used.
   LABEL = 'c'.
      A label of up to 40 characters specified when
      the File was written. It is printed in the
      output when the file is used.
```

COMPUTATIONAL METHOD

In the computations, Boolean arithmetic is used on bits. Two machine specific subroutines are employed. They are

NWBITS — count the number of one bits in a
         sequence of N machine words,

NWAND — takes the bit-wise AND of two
         sequences of N machine words.

The computational method is further detailed in Appendix A.34.

SIZE OF PROBLEM

This program keeps the data matrix, loadings and scores in memory. Two bits are used to store elements of the data matrix and one bit is used to store an element of the loadings and scores matrices.

The formula to compute the core requirement is in Appendix B.

The following table can be used to approximate the core requirements:

number of cases	Number of variables		
	10	20	30
50	1100		
100	1350	1760	2180
150	1580		

ACKNOWLEDGEMENT

P8M is based on research done by M. R. Mickey. P8M was designed by M. R. Mickey with contributions from L. Engelman. P8M was programmed by Peter Mundle and Laszlo Engelman.

SUMMARY

Order of Input Cards

```
// (job card)
// EXEC BIMED,PROG=BMDP8M        (see Appendix E)
//SYSIN DD *
/ PROBLEM
/ INPUT
/ LOAD
/ VARIABLE
/ TRANSFORM
/ SAVE
/ GROUP
/ FACTOR
/ PRINT
/ END
    (data, if on cards)
// (system card)
```

Full sets of BMDP paragraphs (and data, if on cards) can be repeated for additional problems; see Section 5.8.

Paragraph Statement	Preassigned	Comment and Manual Reference
/ VARiable		Optional to code responses. 541
RESponse = # list.	1.	Values that represent a response in the data (at most 10). If omitted, one is assumed. *
NONResponse = # list.	0.	Values that represent a nonresponse in the data (at most 10). If omitted, zero is assumed. *
COST = #.	1.	The cost of mispredicting nonresponses (negative discrepancies), i.e., predicting a response where none was observed. *
/ FACTor		Optional to read the initial factor scores. 541
TITLE = 'text'.	PROB TITLE.	Text to label the output for this analysis. *
NUMBer = #.	5	Total number of factors. *
INITial = #.	NUMBER -2.	Initial number of factors. *
/ PRINT		Optional to control printing the discrepancies (residuals) data, loadings and scores. 544
STEP = # list.	1,2, last-2,last	Steps at which loadings are to be printed. If the number of initial factors is i and the total number of factors is n i, then last = 3*(n-i) - 1. *
LOAD.	LOAD.	The factor loadings are printed. To negate state NO LOAD. *
SCORE.	NO SCORE.	The factor scores are not printed unless SCORES is specified. *
DATA.	NO DATA.	The first ten cases and the compact data display are not printed unless DATA. is specified. *
DISC.	NO DISC.	The discrepancies are not printed unless DISC. is specified. *
/ LOAD		Optional to read the initial loadings. 544
UNIT = #.	5.	Unit number from which the factor loadings are read. If the loadings are read from a BMDP File, the unit numbers must not be 5. *
FORMat = 'c'.	none	Input format for the loading matrix. The format must specify are row of the loading matrix (the row must have as many values as there are factors). *
NUMBer = #.	INITIAL.	Number of factors in the loading input matrix. If NUMBER is specified, it also becomes the number of initial factors, overriding the INITIAL statement of the FACTOR paragraph. *
CODE = 'c'.	none	Signals that the loading matrix is read from a BMDP File.
CONTent = 'c'.		Content of the BMDP File input to read as loadings. If not specified, the first BMDP File with matching CODE is used.
LABEL = 'c'.		A label of up to 40 characters specified when the File was written. Printed in the output when the file is used.
/ SAVE		Additional option to save final factor loadings, discrepancies, predicted values. 544
CONTent = c.	DATA.	The data or matrices saved in a BMDP File. DATA - data to be saved SCORE - factor scores to be saved, named FACTOR1, FACTOR2, etc. LOAD - factor loadings to be saved DISC - data matrix to be saved with the discrepancies (residuals) for variable i replacing the data for variable i. PRED - the predicted values are saved in place of the original data (cannot choose both DISC and PRED) <u>Note</u>: Both DISC and PRED cannot be saved in the same run.

Key:

/	–indicates paragraph		*	–assigned value remains the same for additional problems
.	–period ends a sentence		VT	–number of variables after transformations
●	–required		list	–more than one item, often one per var.
v	–variable (name or subscript)			
g	–group (name or subscript)			
#	–number			Capitalized letters-paragraph or sentence names recognized by BMDP
'c'	–characters (name or parameter) may omit apostrophes if contiguous letters only			Page numbers following refer to this Manual

P9M

18.6 Scoring Based on Preference Pairs

Ray Mickey
Laszlo Engelman
Pat Britt

ABSTRACT

P9M constructs for each case a score that is a linear combination of the variables:

$$\text{score} = \beta_1 x_1 + \beta_2 x_2 + \ldots + \beta_p x_p$$

where the coefficients are based on the judgments (preferences) of experts. The expert compares cases two at a time, stating which of the pair he prefers. The preference may reflect a more costly item, or a better student, etc. The analysis weights the observed variables to best replicate the preference of the judge (whatever subjective or objective information he may use). The expert need not judge all possible pairs of cases. Since P9M computes a score for each case in the data matrix, the resulting scoring system obtained from his preferences can be used for all the items.

The linear function used in constructing the score is determined in a stepwise manner. This procedure weights variables by their importance to the expert. Preferences from more than one expert can be analyzed in the same run.

The input consists of a preference matrix and a data matrix. For each pair of cases that are compared, the preference matrix contains the case numbers and the judgments of one or more experts. For example, if case number 5 is preferred over case number 3, a row in the preference matrix is 5 3 1. The '1' indicates that the first case (number 5) is preferred. '5 3 -1' would indicate that the second case (number 3) is preferred. When there is no preference, a zero is recorded. A judgment may also indicate the strength of the preference; for example, a judgment of 2 is considered twice as preferable as a judgment of 1. If we compare case 5 with both case 3 and case 8 and consider case 5 much better than case 8 and slightly better than case 3, the entries in the preference matrix might read

5 3 1
5 8 4

Example 9M.1 Basic Setup for Deriving Scores

In this example the data matrix contains 14 grades on tests and projects for students in a college class; and the preference matrix contains the instructor's (Adams) judgment on overall performance for 16 pairs of students. The goal is to obtain one score for each student – the score will be a linear combination of the grades. The 14 grades are on six homework assignments, seven data analysis projects, plus the final exam score. The instructor decided that a grade of zero should be assigned for missing projects or homework.

The BMDP instructions below in the PROBLEM, INPUT and VARIABLE paragraphs are common to all programs and are described in Chapter 5. The instructions in the PREFERENCE paragraph are specific to P9M and are used to describe the preference matrix. Each row (record) in the preference matrix contains three entries (the FORMAT states that three entries are read in F2.0 format). The JUDGMENT instruction identifies the position of the preference in the row. In this example the preference follows the case numbers for each pair of subjects: it is the third entry (JUDGMENT IS 3). We indicate that comparisons are made for 16 pairs of students (PAIRS ARE 16). Note that the data records for the 16 comparisons precede the data matrix containing the grades for the 17 students. The program expects 16 records in the preference matrix (PAIRS ARE 16) followed by 17 records in the data matrix (CASES ARE 17). Note the blank fields in the data matrix: the BLANKS ARE ZERO statement causes them to be analyzed as zeros.

```
--------------------------------------
/ PROBLEM     TITLE IS 'STUDENT EVALUATION --
                 BASIC SETUP.'.

/ INPUT       VARIABLES ARE 16.
             FORMAT IS '(14F3.0, 2A4)'.
             CASES ARE 17.

/ VARIABLE    LABELS ARE ID1, ID2.
             NAMES ARE HOMEWRK1, HOMEWRK2,
                  HOMEWRK3, HOMEWRK4,
                  HOMEWRK5, HOMEWRK6,
                  ANNOTATE, ORTHOG, CHOLES,
                  CONSULT, OBESITY1, OBESITY2,
                  FACTOR, FINAL, ID1, ID2.
             BLANKS ARE ZEROS.

/ PREFERENCE  FORMAT IS '(3F2.0)'.
             JUDGMENT IS 3.
             PAIRS ARE 16.
             NAME IS ADAMS.

/ END
```

(continued)

```
10 9 1
117-1
 5 2-1
16 8 1                (data for Example 9M.1)
315 1
 8 3-1
 6 1 1
 9 7-1
1311-1
1215 1
 311-1
1217 1
17 6 1
17 7-1
11 6 1
 1 8-1
26 22 15 16  8 15 24  7  6 20  9 14  6 69JIM
30 24 19 18 12 14 25 10  8 18  8 18  8 87BETSY
24 23 17 17 12 10 24 10  7 16  8 16  9 86WILL
29 17 15 16 10  8 23     8 20    20  8 82AMY
25 22 15 17 11 12 23  8  7 14  7 12  8 84SARA
30 24 18 18 13 15 26 10  8 20  8 12  7 81LYDA
29 22 16 17 13 14 26  9 10 20 10 16  8101ALLEN
25 22 16 18 10 11 21  9  7 16  5 12  6 73PETER
23 15 12    10        5 20  8 10  6 57DAVE
31 23 17 18 15 14 27 10  8 14  8 18  8 59SUSAN
28 24 18 18 11 15 27  9  8 16  8 17  8 88ROBERT
30 23 18 16 13 15 28  9  8 14  5 18  8100KRAIG
30 22 19 18 13 15 27  9  9 16  9 17  8 83JEFFREY
                  8    18  7 20  6 70LINDA
26 21 16 17 10 10 24  9  5 16  8 14  7 69DONALD
31 24 17 18 14 15 25 10 10 20 10 18  8101HERMAN
30 24 19 18 14 15 26 10  8 16  9 16  9 91CHUCK
```

When both the preference matrix and the data matrix are read from cards as in this example (UNIT = 5.), the preference matrix must precede the data matrix. (See end of this P9M section for organization of systems information, BMDP instructions and data.)

The results are presented in Output 9M.1. Circled numbers below correspond to those in the output.

(1) The first 10 cases are reported. If more or less are desired, use the CASES = #. statement in the PRINT paragraph.

(2) Number of cases read. Only complete cases are used in the analysis, i.e., cases that have no missing values or values out of range. All variables are checked unless a USE statement is specified in the VARIABLE paragraph. When a USE statement is specified the variables in the USE statement are checked.

(3) For each step the program reports the estimated coefficients ($\hat{\beta}_i$'s) of the variables, the t-values of the coefficients, the multiple correlation and its square for a regression model:
judgment = $\Sigma \beta_i z_i + \varepsilon$

where
$$Z = \begin{pmatrix} x_{i1} - x_{j1} \\ x_{i2} - x_{j2} \\ x_{i3} - x_{j3} \\ . \\ . \\ . \\ x_{ip} - x_{jp} \end{pmatrix}$$

where i and j are the subscripts for each pair of cases compared in the preference matrix.

(4) For each pair of cases in the preference matrix, the judgment, prediction and the error = judgment minus predictions are printed.
The judgment prediction for comparing case j and k is: $\Sigma(x_{ji} - \bar{x}_{ki})\beta_i$.

(5) The scores for each case are computed from an estimate of the last step, $\hat{\beta}$'s. For case j the score is: $\Sigma x_{ji}\hat{\beta}_i$.

Output 9M.1 Deriving scores based on preferences of experts. Circled numbers correspond to those in the text
----

--- the BMDP instructions read by P5M are printed and interpreted ---

CASE NO.	LABEL	1 HOMEWRK1 / 11 OBESITY1	2 HOMEWRK2 / 12 OBESITY2	3 HOMEWRK3 / 13 FACTOR	4 HOMEWRK4 / 14 FINAL	5 HOMEWRK5	6 HOMEWRK6	7 ANNOTATE	8 ORTHOG	9 CHOLES	10 CONSULT
1	JIM	26	22	15	16	8	15	24	7	6	20
		9	14	6	69						
2	BETSY	30	24	19	18	12	14	25	10	8	18
		8	18	8	87						
3	WILL	24	23	17	17	12	10	24	10	7	16
		8	16	9	86						
4	AMY	29	17	15	16	10	8	23	0	8	20
		0	20	8	82						
5	SARA	25	22	15	17	11	12	23	8	7	14
		7	12	8	84						
6	LYDA	30	24	18	18	13	15	26	10	8	20
		8	12	7	81						
7	ALLEN	29	22	16	17	13	14	26	9	10	20
		10	16	8	101						
8	PETER	25	22	16	18	10	11	21	9	7	16
		5	12	6	73						
9	DAVE	23	15	12	0	10	0	0	0	5	20
		8	10	6	57						
10	SUSAN	31	23	17	18	15	14	27	10	8	14
		8	18	8	59						

NUMBER OF CASES READ. 17 (2)

COEFFICIENTS OF LINEAR FUNCTIONS OF VARIABLES.

PREFERENCE NAME= ADAMS

	STEP NUMBER 1	
	COEFF	T-VAL
HOMEWRK1	0.0	0.0
HOMEWRK2	0.0	0.0
HOMEWRK3	0.0	0.0
HOMEWRK4	0.0	0.0
HOMEWRK5	0.0	0.0
HOMEWRK6	0.0	0.0
ANNOTATE	0.0	0.0
ORTHOG	0.0	0.0
CHOLES	0.0	0.0
CONSULT	0.0	0.0
OBESITY1	0.0	0.0
OBESITY2	0.0	0.0
FACTOR	0.0	0.0
FINAL	0.04248	4.565

③

MULTIPLE R	R-SQUARED
0.76255	0.581

--- the stepping stops after entering the final
exam score because the t-values for the
remaining variables to enter are less than 2.0
(see Example 9M.3) ---

PREDICTIONS ARE DIFFERENCE SCORES OF CASES COMPARED.

CASES COMPARED		ADAMS JUDGMENT	PREDICTION	ERROR
10	9	1.00000	0.08497	0.91503
1	17	-1.00000	-0.93463	-0.06537
5	2	-1.00000	-0.12745	-0.87255
16	8	1.00000	1.18952	-0.18952
3	15	1.00000	0.72221	0.27779
8	3	-1.00000	-0.55228	-0.44772
6	1	1.00000	0.50980	0.49020
9	7	-1.00000	-1.86925	0.86925
13	11	-1.00000	-0.21242	-0.78758
12	15	1.00000	1.31697	-0.31697
3	11	-1.00000	-0.08497	-0.91503
12	17	1.00000	0.38235	0.61765
17	6	1.00000	0.42483	0.57517
17	7	-1.00000	-0.42483	-0.57517
11	6	1.00000	0.29738	0.70262
1	8	-1.00000	-0.16993	-0.83007

④

SCORES BASED ON JUDGMENTS EVALUATED FOR EACH CASE.

CASE NUMBER	CASE LABEL	ADAMS
1	JIM	2.93133
2	BETSY	3.69602
3	WILL	3.65354
4	AMY	3.48361
5	SARA	3.56857
6	LYDA	3.44112
7	ALLEN	4.29078
8	PETER	3.10126
9	DAVE	2.42153
10	SUSAN	2.50650
11	ROBERT	3.73851
12	KRAIG	4.24830
13	JEFFREY	3.52609
14	LINDA	2.97381
15	DONALD	2.93133
16	HERMAN	4.29078
17	CHUCK	3.86595

⑤

Example 9M.2 Comparing Two Judges

When there is only one judge for each pair of
cases, a comparison can be determined by the order
of the case numbers in the preference matrix.
However, when there is more than one judge for each
pair of cases, or when preferences are not simple
selections but are weighted, the location of the
preferences in the preference matrix must be
explicitly stated.

In this example we have two instructors (Adams
and Brown) so we change the JUDGMENT and NAME
statements in the PREFERENCE paragraph of Example
9M.1 to read:

       JUDGMENTS ARE 3, 4.
       NAMES   ARE ADAMS, BROWN.

We also add the judgments of Brown to the preference
matrix in the fourth column and change the FORMAT in
the PREFERENCE paragraph to read:

       FORMAT IS '(4F2.0)'.

Output 9M.2. contains:

- two stepwise reports, one for each judgment (not
shown),
- two sets of predictions of judgments and their
errors, one for each judgment (not shown).

⑥ Two sets of scores for each case, and

⑦ the matrix of the correlation between the
scores.

Output 9M.2 The preferences of two judges are compared

--- the scores based on Adams' preferences only
   use information from the final exam.
   Those for Brown use information from HOMEWRK1,
   a project named OBESITY2 and the final exam ---

SCORES BASED ON JUDGMENTS EVALUATED FOR EACH CASE.

CASE NUMBER	CASE LABEL	ADAMS	BROWN
1	JIM	2.93133	11.92774
2	BETSY	3.69602	14.72361
3	WILL	3.65354	13.67140
4	AMY	3.48361	14.26127
5	SARA	3.56857	13.19881
6	LYDA	3.44112	13.50850
7	ALLEN	4.29078	15.88871
8	PETER	3.10126	12.03305
9	DAVE	2.42153	9.89326
10	SUSAN	2.50650	11.88173
11	ROBERT	3.73851	14.48200
12	KRAIG	4.24830	16.10132
13	JEFFREY	3.52609	14.20315
14	LINDA	2.97381	9.34928
15	DONALD	2.93133	11.92774
16	HERMAN	4.29078	16.33282
17	CHUCK	3.86595	14.95445

⑥

CORRELATIONS BETWEEN SCORES

		ADAMS 1	BROWN 2
ADAMS	1	1.0000	
BROWN	2	0.9159	1.0000

⑦

The PREFERENCE paragraph: specifying the preference matrix. Selected pairs of cases are compared in the PREFERENCE paragraph. For each pair of cases one or more judgments are recorded. You specify the number of pairs of cases compared in the PAIRS = #. statement and the format of a row of the preference matrix in the FORMAT = c. statement. If the judgment is merely a selection of the preferred member, the order of case numbers may be used to indicate the preference: the preferred case has its number in the first column of the preference matrix; the next preferred case in the second column. If judgments are weighted or if there are multiple judgments for each selected pair of cases, the location(s) of judgment(s) (column numbers) in the preference matrix is stated in the JUDGMENT statement.

Column numbers that contain pairs of case numbers being compared in the preference matrix are assumed to be 1 and 2, unless specified otherwise in the CASENO statement.

PREFerence ─────────────────────────────
```
PAIRS = #.    required              none/prev.
   The number of pairs of cases in the preference
   matrix.
FORMat = 'c'.  required                 none
   The format of one row of the preference matrix.
   Each row of the preference matrix is read with
   a separate Fortran READ statement.
UNIT = #.                             5/prev.
   The unit number from which the preference
   matrix is read. If both the preference matrix
   and the data matrix are read from the same
   unit, the preference matrix must be placed in
   front of the data matrix.
CASEno = #, #.                       1,2./prev.
   The columns of the preference matrix containing
   the case numbers being compared.
JUDGment = # list.                      none
   The columns of the preference matrix containing
   the preference(s). If the JUDGMENT statement is
   not included, the case whose number is in the
   first column is assumed preferred to that in
   the second column.
NAMEs = c list.            JUDGE1, JUDGE2, ...
   The names of judges or experts. Used for
   labeling output. May also be used in plot
   requests.
```

Example 9M.3 Controlling the Stepwise Process

Variables are entered into the model one at a time. Which variable is entered at a step is based on the correlation or partial correlation of variables with the quantity we wish to predict. The absolute value of the correlation or partial

correlation is a monotonic function of the absolute value of a t value. P9M provides a way of controlling the stepwise process via the TENTER and TREMOVE statements of the PREFERENCE paragraph. A variable may only enter if the t value of its coefficient is larger than the limit set in the TENTER = #. statement. After more than two variables have entered, the t value of a coefficient may drop below the TREMOVE limit, and the corresponding variable is removed.

The preassigned value for these options is 2.0. We may want to see which candidate variable(s) is close to entering so we lower the entry criterion by adding the statements

```
------------------------------------------
           TENTER = 1.5.
           TREMOVE = 1.5.
------------------------------------------
```

to the PREFERENCE paragraph of Example 9M.2.

Output 9M.3 contains:

⑧ The stepwise output for the judgment based on Adams' preferences.

⑨ The stepwise output for the judgment based on Brown's preferences. It appears that Adams' assessments are predictable from the final test grade and on the grades on the OBESITY1 and OBESITY2 projects, while Brown's assessments appear to be related to the grades on the first, second, and fourth homework assignments, a consulting project, a project on obesity, and the final exam.

The stepwise process can also be limited by specifying the maximum number of steps in the STEP = #. statement of the PREFERENCE paragraph.

PREFerence ─────────────────────────────
```
STEP = #.      2* (no. of variables used)/prev.
   The maximum number of steps in which a variable
   is entered or removed.
TENTer = #.                           2.0/prev.
   The lower limit of the t value of a
   coefficient. A variable cannot enter if the t
   value of a coefficient is below this limit.
TREMove = #.                          2.0/prev.
   The t value limit for removing a variable. If
   the t value of the coefficient of a variable
   becomes less than this limit, the variable is
   removed.
TOLerance = #.                       .0001/prev.
   Controls the amount of numerical accuracy by
   not including variables that are numerically
   redundant.
```

Output 9M.3 Adjusting the limits for entering and removing variables

----

COEFFICIENTS OF LINEAR FUNCTIONS OF VARIABLES.   PREFERENCE NAME= ADAMS

	STEP NUMBER 1		STEP NUMBER 2		STEP NUMBER 3		
	COEFF	T-VAL	COEFF	T-VAL	COEFF	T-VAL	
HOMEWRK1	0.0	0.0	0.0	0.0	0.0	0.0	⑧
HOMEWRK2	0.0	0.0	0.0	0.0	0.0	0.0	
HOMEWRK3	0.0	0.0	0.0	0.0	0.0	0.0	
HOMEWRK4	0.0	0.0	0.0	0.0	0.0	0.0	
HOMEWRK5	0.0	0.0	0.0	0.0	0.0	0.0	
HOMEWRK6	0.0	0.0	0.0	0.0	0.0	0.0	
ANNOTATE	0.0	0.0	0.0	0.0	0.0	0.0	
ORTHOG	0.0	0.0	0.0	0.0	0.0	0.0	
CHOLES	0.0	0.0	0.0	0.0	0.0	0.0	
CONSULT	0.0	0.0	0.0	0.0	0.0	0.0	
OBESITY1	0.0	0.0	0.0	0.0	-0.11596	1.659	
OBESITY2	0.0	0.0	0.08660	1.661	0.11385	2.198	
FACTOR	0.0	0.0	0.0	0.0	0.0	0.0	
FINAL	0.04248	4.565	0.02933	2.477	0.02807	2.509	

MULTIPLE R	R-SQUARED	MULTIPLE R	R-SQUARED	MULTIPLE R	R-SQUARED
0.76255	0.581	0.80648	0.650	0.84351	0.712

COEFFICIENTS OF LINEAR FUNCTIONS OF VARIABLES.   PREFERENCE NAME= BROWN   ⑨

	STEP NUMBER 1		STEP NUMBER 2		STEP NUMBER 3		STEP NUMBER 4		STEP NUMBER 5	
	COEFF	T-VAL	COEFF	T-VAL	COEFF	T-VAL	COEFF	T-VAL	COEFF	T-VAL
HOMEWRK1	0.0	0.0	0.16915	4.970	0.12553	4.098	0.09359	2.675	0.09310	3.007
HOMEWRK2	0.0	0.0	0.0	0.0	0.0	0.0	0.07876	1.617	0.20703	2.752
HOMEWRK3	0.0	0.0	0.0	0.0	0.0	0.0	0.0	0.0	0.0	0.0
HOMEWRK4	0.0	0.0	0.0	0.0	0.0	0.0	0.0	0.0	-0.05769	2.080
HOMEWRK5	0.0	0.0	0.0	0.0	0.0	0.0	0.0	0.0	0.0	0.0
HOMEWRK6	0.0	0.0	0.0	0.0	0.0	0.0	0.0	0.0	0.0	0.0
ANNOTATE	0.0	0.0	0.0	0.0	0.0	0.0	0.0	0.0	0.0	0.0
ORTHOG	0.0	0.0	0.0	0.0	0.0	0.0	0.0	0.0	0.0	0.0
CHOLES	0.0	0.0	0.0	0.0	0.0	0.0	0.0	0.0	0.0	0.0
CONSULT	0.0	0.0	0.0	0.0	0.0	0.0	0.0	0.0	0.0	0.0
OBESITY1	0.0	0.0	0.0	0.0	0.0	0.0	0.0	0.0	0.0	0.0
OBESITY2	0.0	0.0	0.0	0.0	0.09654	3.031	0.07891	2.469	0.07073	2.477
FACTOR	0.0	0.0	0.0	0.0	0.0	0.0	0.0	0.0	0.0	0.0
FINAL	0.13637	14.202	0.11517	15.683	0.10598	16.117	0.10432	16.594	0.10091	17.401

MULTIPLE R	R-SQUARED	MULTIPLE R	R-SQUARED	MULTIPLE R	R-SQUARED	MULTIPLE R	R-SQUARED	MULTIPLE R	R-SQUARED
0.96477	0.931	0.98740	0.975	0.99264	0.985	0.99396	0.988	0.99567	0.991

	STEP NUMBER 6	
	COEFF	T-VAL
HOMEWRK1	0.07969	2.673
HOMEWRK2	0.21694	3.098
HOMEWRK3	0.0	0.0
HOMEWRK4	-0.05025	1.925
HOMEWRK5	0.0	0.0
HOMEWRK6	0.0	0.0
ANNOTATE	0.0	0.0
ORTHOG	0.0	0.0
CHOLES	0.0	0.0
CONSULT	0.03973	1.671
OBESITY1	0.0	0.0
OBESITY2	0.07607	2.852
FACTOR	0.0	0.0
FINAL	0.10035	18.627

MULTIPLE R	R-SQUARED
0.99661	0.993

Example 9M.4 Plotting the Results

You may request that a scatter plot be printed, plotting any variables or desired scores. The scores are added to the data matrix as additional variables. In our example, the data matrix has been augmented by two variables named ADAMS and BROWN (17 and 18).

We add the following paragraph to Example 9M.3:

```
-------------------------------------
/ PLOT      XVAR(17) = 18.
           XVAR(14) = ADAMS, BROWN.
           SIZE = 40, 25.
-------------------------------------
```

The resultant plots are shown in Output 9M.4:

⑩ The 17th variable (on the x-axis) is plotted against the 18th variable; the scores named ADAMS are plotted against the scores named BROWN. Note the lone 'A' in the bottom of the plot. This student did not turn in homework assignments: homework was used as a predictor in Brown's but not in Adams' scoring scheme.

⑪ The 14th variable, FINAL (on the x-axis) is plotted against ADAMS and BROWN (variables 17 and 18).

The size of the scatter plot may be controlled via the SIZE = #, #. sentence in the PLOT paragraph.

```
PLOT ──────────────────────────────────────
  XVAR(#) = v list.                       none
    The numbered variables are plotted on the
    x-axis against the v list variables on the
    y-axis. Each XVAR statement yields one frame.
    The XVAR statement may be repeated within a
    PLOT paragraph.
  SIZE = #, #.                      50,35/prev.
    Controls the size of the scatter plot. The
    first number is the width of the scatter plot
    in characters, the second number is the height
    of the scatter plot in lines.
──────────────────────────────────────────────
```

The number of cases to be printed can be **specified.**

```
PRINT ─────────────────────────────────────
  CASE = #.                           10/prev.
    The number of cases for which data are printed.
──────────────────────────────────────────────
```

Output 9M.4 A plot comparing the scores from two judges and a plot of the judges' scores versus the final exam score

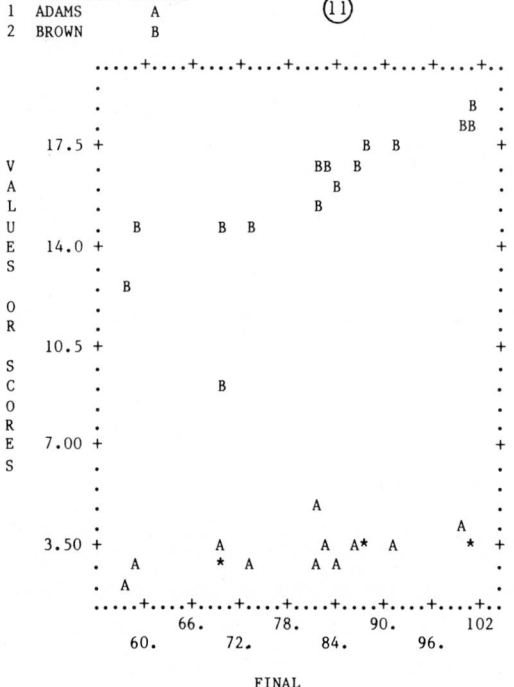

```
THE FOLLOWING VARIABLES ARE PLOTTED AGAINST  ADAMS

  VARIABLE  SYMBOL
1 BROWN       A              ⑩

        .....+....+....+....+....+..X.+....+....+..
        .                          A            .
        .                    A        A     Y   .
   18 + .                                        +
 V      .                      A A              .
 A      .                      A                .
 L      .                                       .
 U      .             A    AA                   .
 E   16 + .             A                        +
 S      .                                 A .
        .
 O      .          A   A                        .
 R      .          A  A                         .
   14 + .                                        +
 S      .                                       .
 C      . Y                                     .
 O      .                                       .
 R      . .A                                    .
 E   12 + .                                       +
 S      .                                       .
        .                                       .
        .                                       .
   10 + .                                        +
        .                                       .
        .                   A                   .
        .....+..X.+....+....+....+....+....+....+..
            2.45    3.15    3.85    4.55
          2.10    2.80    3.50    4.20
 N=  17
 COR= .465                   ADAMS

       MEAN    ST.DEV.   REGRESSION LINE    RES.MS.
  X   3.2087   .66803   X= .12696*Y+ 1.1954  .37327
  Y   15.858   2.4446   Y= 1.7002*X+ 10.402  4.9986
```

```
THE FOLLOWING VARIABLES ARE PLOTTED AGAINST  FINAL

  VARIABLE  SYMBOL
1 ADAMS       A              ⑪
2 BROWN       B

        .....+....+....+....+....+....+....+....+..
        .                                B     .
        .                               BB     .
 17.5 + .                      B   B            +
 V      .                   BB  B              .
 A      .                        B            .
 L      .                        B            .
 U      . B         B  B                      .
 E 14.0 + .                                     +
 S      . B
        .
 O      .
 R      .
 10.5 + .                                        +
 S      .                                       .
 C      .          B                            .
 O      .                                       .
 R      .                                       .
 E 7.00 + .                                       +
 S      .                                       .
        .                   A                   .
        .                                    A  .
 3.50 + .          A         A  A*  A     *  +
        . A      *  A      A  A                  .
        . A                                      .
        .....+....+....+....+....+....+....+....+..
               66.     78.     90.     102
             60.    72.    84.    96.
                         FINAL
```

SIZE OF PROBLEM

The amount of storage space required is approximately

$$400 + 2VM + 8VT + VU(VU/2 + J + 2S + 2PL + 8.5)$$
$$+ 2P + J(10 + P + CU)$$

where

    VM = maximum number of variables before or after transformation, whichever is larger
    VT = total number of variables after transformation
    VU = number of variables used
    P = number of comparisons
    J = number of judgments
    PL = number of plots
    CU = number of cases used
    S = maximum number of steps in regression computation

COMPUTATIONAL METHOD

All computations are in single precision. Means and cross products of deviations are computed by the provisional means method (Appendix A.2). The computations performed by P9M are described in Appendix A.35.

SUMMARY

Order of Input Cards

```
// (job card)
// EXEC BIMED,PROG=BMDP9M        (see Appendix E)
//SYSIN DD *
/ PROBLEM
/ INPUT
/ VARIABLE
/ TRANSFORM
/ SAVE
/ PREFERENCE
/ PLOT
/ PRINT
/ END
    (preference matrix)
    (data matrix)
// (system card)
```

Full sets of BMDP paragraphs (and data, if on cards) can be repeated for additional problems; see Section 5.8.

instructions specific to P9M

Paragraph Statement	Preassigned	Comment and Manual Reference
/●PREFerence		Required for the first problem only. 550
UNIT = #.	5	The number of the preference matrix input unit. *
●FORMat = 'c'.	none	The row format (up to 160 characters) of the preference matrix.
●PAIRS = #.	none	The number of pairs of cases to be compared. *
CASEno = #, #.	1, 2.	The first number is the first case number, the second the second case number in the comparison. *
JUDGment = # list.	none	The first number is the first preference, the second is the second preference, etc.
NAME = c list.	JUDGE1,JUDGE2..	The names of the judges (up to 8 characters).
STEP = #.	2*VU	The maximum number of steps in the analysis. *
TOLerance = #.	.0001	Tolerance limit. *
TENTer = #.	2.0	The minimum t-value to enter the analysis. *
TREMove = #.	2.0	The maximum t-value to be removed. *
/ PLOT		Optional to control plots. 552
SIZE = #, #.	50,35.	Width of x-axis (characters); height of y-axis (lines).
XVAR(#) = v list.	none	The names or subscripts of variables and/or judgment scores plotted against the variable X(i).
/ PRINT		Optional to request printed output. 552
CASE = #.	10.	Number of cases for which data are printed.

Key:

  /   -indicates paragraph
  .   -period ends a sentence
  ●   -required
  v   -variable (name or subscript)
  g   -group (name or subscript)
  #   -number
  'c' -characters (name or parameter) may omit apostrophes if contiguous letters only

  *   -assigned value remains the same for additional problems
  VT -number of variables after transformations
  list -more than one item, often one per var.

Capitalized letters-paragraph or sentence names recognized by BMDP
Page numbers following refer to this Manual

19

SURVIVAL ANALYSIS

The techniques described in this section are appropriate when measuring the time to occurrence of some event or response; for example, survival time (i.e., the response is death), or time to recurrence of a disease. Because many of the techniques were originally motivated by survival studies, we use the language of such problems in this chapter. Many other types of studies with a time-to-response outcome (e.g., time to conception, time on a job, time to failure) may be treated similarly.

The ability to use data from cases for which the response has not yet occurred distinguishes the techniques discussed in this chapter from other statistical methodology. Such data are called incomplete or censored, and may arise from loss to follow-up (that is, the patient may have moved away, or refused to participate in the study), death from causes other than the one under study, or no response before the end of the study (withdrawn alive).

A typical problem is assessment of the effect of an experimental drug on animal survival in a laboratory study. A fixed number of animals are treated at the start of the experiment; length of time from treatment to death is recorded for each animal. Frequently the study ends after a specified proportion of animals die, or after a certain time period has elapsed. The observations from animals that survive to the end of the study are censored at a common time. By contrast, in clinical studies patients usually enter the study at different times; therefore the lengths of follow-up time differ among patients.

Special techniques are required to analyze data with censored observations. The methods presented here assume that censored observations are not related to the individuals' true time-to-response. This assumption appears reasonable when entries and losses to followup occur randomly. If patients are lost as a consequence of treatment (e.g., harmful side effects), the censored observations and the true death times may be correlated. A major advantage of the techniques in this chapter is the use of all patient followup information (although unequal) in estimating survival probabilities.

In this chapter we describe two programs for handling censored survival data.

P1L - Life Tables and Survival Functions   p.557
P2L - Regression with Incomplete Survival Data p.576

P1L may be used to describe the distribution of survival times for a homogeneous group of subjects. Two methods are provided for estimating the survival (time-to-response) distribution of patients who have been observed over varying periods of time. Survival curves can be reported for all patients or for subsets of the patients, and the equality of curves between groups can be tested. Output includes estimates of the survival distribution by either the product-limit (Kaplan-Meier 1958), or the actuarial life table (Cutler-Ederer 1958) methods, and the Mantel-Cox and Breslow statistics for testing the equality of survival curves (optional). When each interval contains only one observation, the two estimates are identical. Graphical output is the cumulative survival function and the following optional plots: the log of the survival function, hazard function, cumulative hazard function, and the death density function. The survival curves can be reported for all the patients, or separately for subsets of the patients. For example, separate estimates may be desired for patients in different treatment groups. The equality of the survival distributions for the patient groups can be tested by two nonparametric rank tests.

Frequently it is desirable to compare two or more treatment regimens while accounting for extraneous variables known to be related to survival. For example, white blood cell count is known to influence the prognosis for leukemia patients. When comparing remission times among two groups of leukemia patients, it is important to know whether any differences are attributable to treatment alterations or to a difference in distribution of white blood cell counts. It may also be desirable to quantify the treatment effect. Analyses of this type are most conveniently handled with P2L.

P2L analyzes survival data for which the time-to-response is influenced by other measured variables. The goal of the analysis is to quantify the relationship between survival and a set of explanatory variables. These variables, often called prognostic factors or covariates, usually represent either measures of inherent differences among the subjects or constitute a set of one or more indicator variables representing different treatment groups. The covariates may also describe changes in a patient's prognostic status as a function of time.

Regression models are fit using the Cox proportional hazards model. The regression model is formulated in terms of the effects of covariates upon death (hazard) rates rather than times to death. No parametric assumptions about the shape of survival curve are made. The model is defined in terms of $h(t;z)$, the hazard rate for an individual with covariate vector z. The proportional hazards model is given by

$$h(t;z) = h_o(t) \exp(\underset{\sim}{\beta}'\underset{\sim}{z})$$

or

$$ln\,[\,h(t;z)/h_o(t)\,] = \underset{\sim}{\beta}'\underset{\sim}{z}$$

where β is a vector of unknown regression coefficients and $h_o(t)$ is an unknown nonnegative hazard rate for an individual with covariate vector $\underset{\sim}{z} = 0$. Estimation of regression coefficients is accomplished using a technique similar to maximum likelihood.

P2L output contains estimates of the regression coefficients, their estimated asymptotic standard errors and a global test of significance of the regression coefficients. A stepwise selection option facilitates identification of a subset of variables which are related to survival. Graphical output includes the cumulative survival function, the log minus log survival (log cumulative hazard) function and a goodness-of-fit plot. The data cases may be stratified into several groups allowing the survival function to be estimated separately for each stratum. Stratification is useful when subsets of the patients do not follow the proportional hazards

assumption. Hypothesis tests for the joint significance of subsets of regression coefficients may be specified easily.

Regression coefficients for parametric survival models with covariates could be estimated using maximum likelihood methods (Chapter 14.3). When there are no censored observations, you can analyze survival data by a variety of techniques such as regression (Chapter 13), analysis of variance (Chapter 15) or nonparametric statistics (Chapter 16). Basic references on survival analysis in the biomedical sciences are the books by Gross and Clark (1975), Kalbfleisch and Prentice (1980) and Lee (1980).

The BMDP instructions to describe the data and variables are common to all BMDP programs and are explained in Chapter 5: the PROBLEM, INPUT, VARIABLE and GROUP paragraphs are used in the survival analysis programs described in this chapter.

If data editing or transformations are necessary, the methods described in Chapter 6 can be used. Data can be read using free format, a FORMAT statement or from a BMDP File (Chapter 7). If a BMDP File is read as input and a new BMDP File is created in the same problem, the two Files must be in different system files and must have different UNIT numbers.

A summary of the BMDP instructions common to all BMDP programs is on the back cover; a summary of the BMDP instructions specific to each survival analysis program follows the program. These summaries can be used as an indexes to the program descriptions.

Each survival analysis program allows for flexible input of survival information. Survival times and their corresponding censoring status indicators may be input directly. If survival times are recorded as dates representing date of entry into the study and date of termination, the programs automatically convert these sets of dates to a time-on-study variable. The appropriate censoring status information is generated automatically. In addition, grouped data may be input to P1L for a life-table analysis.

P1L

19.1 Life Tables and Survival Functions

Jacqueline Benedetti
Karen Yuen
Larry Young

ABSTRACT

P1L may be used to describe the distribution of survival times for a homogeneous group of subjects. P1L provides two methods for estimating the survival (time-to-response) distribution of patients who have been observed over varying periods of time. Survival curves can be reported for all patients or for subsets of the patients. For example, separate estimates may be desired for patients in different treatment groups. The equality of the survival distributions for the patient groups can be tested by two nonparametric rank tests. Input can be data arranged as a life table, survival time or dates for individual patients. Output includes estimates of the survival distribution by either the product-limit (Kaplan-Meier 1958), or the actuarial life table (Cutler-Ederer 1958) methods, and the Mantel-Cox and Breslow statistics for testing the equality of survival curves (optional). When each interval contains only one observation, the two estimates are identical. Graphical output includes the cumulative survival function, log of the survival function and, with the actuarial method, plots of hazard function, cumulative hazard function and the death density function.

WHERE TO FIND IT

Example 1L.1 Life Table Analysis Using Time of Survival as Input

A life table is a method of summarizing the results of a study by grouping the times to response into time intervals. For each time interval the table records the number of subjects who are still in the study at the start of the interval, the number responding during the interval, and the number censored (lost to follow-up or withdrawn). From these numbers the probability of a response in an interval is estimated.

For example, suppose that the times to response are grouped into yearly intervals. A subject who showed a response (died) in his sixth year in the study would be counted as entering and leaving each of the first five years, but counted as entering the sixth year and showing a response in it; he would not appear in any computation for the seventh year and later. Similarly if a subject terminates participation in the study (either the study ends or he discontinues the follow-up) in the sixth year, he is counted as entering and leaving each of the first five years, but counted as entering the sixth year and then as withdrawn or lost (depending on the cause).

Two types of probabilities may be of interest. One is the conditional probability of showing no response in an interval (surviving) given that a subject has entered the interval. The second is the probability of showing no response (surviving) from the start of the study to any given interval. The latter is known as the survival distribution. These probabilities serve much the same purpose as a histogram or cumulative distribution function in describing data.

This example illustrates the life table technique applied to lung cancer data analyzed by Prentice (1973) and presented in Table 19.1.

Table 19.1 Survival in days of lung cancer patients (Prentice, 1973)

Survival	State	Treatment	Cell Type													
72	1	1	1		112	1	0	1		3	1	1	2
411	1	1	1		999	1	0	1		95	1	1	2
228	1	1	1		11	1	1	1		24	1	0	2
231	0	0	1		25	0	1	1		18	1	0	2
242	1	0	1		144	1	1	1		83	0	1	2
991	1	0	1		8	1	1	1		31	1	0	2
111	1	0	1		42	1	1	1		51	1	0	2
1	1	0	1		100	0	1	1		90	1	0	2
587	1	0	1		314	1	1	1		52	1	0	2
389	1	0	1		110	1	1	1		73	1	0	2
33	1	0	1		82	1	1	1		8	1	0	2
25	1	0	1		10	1	1	1		36	1	0	2
357	1	0	1		118	1	1	1		48	1	0	2
467	1	0	1		126	1	1	1		7	1	0	2
201	1	0	1		8	1	1	2		140	1	0	2
1	1	0	1		92	1	1	2		186	1	0	2
30	1	0	1		35	1	1	2		84	1	0	2
44	1	0	1		117	1	1	2		19	1	0	2
283	1	0	1		132	1	1	2		45	1	0	2
15	1	0	1		12	1	1	2		80	1	0	2
87	0	0	1		162	1	1	2					

Key: survival time, state (1=dead, 0=censored), treatment (1=standard, 0=test), cell type (1=squamous, 2=adeno). The time of survival is recorded in columns 1-3; the other variables are recorded in columns 6, 9 and 12.

The data represent survival times and patient characteristics from subjects enrolled in a lung cancer study. The survival information is provided by two variables. The first is patient's time on study (SURVIVAL), the second is a categorical variable called STATE that indicates whether the time represents a death (coded 1), or a censored observation (coded 0). That is, patients coded as 0 were alive when last observed. The information recorded for treatment and cell type is used in later examples.

P1L uses the PROBLEM, INPUT, VARIABLE and GROUP paragraphs to describe the data and variables. These instructions are common to all BMDP programs and are explained in Chapter 5. In addition, P1L requires a FORM paragraph that indicates the input structure of the survival time variables (survival time or dates for individual patients, or data arranged as a life table). In this example, SURVIVAL provides the patient's total time on study and STATE provides the STATUS of the patient, that is, whether the patient is a loss to follow-up, etc. RESPONSE indicates which values of the STATUS variable represent true responses. More than one code may be possible. For example, different causes of death may be individually coded, yet all represent the response under study (i.e., death). All other valid codes are treated as censored. The instructions for this example are:

```
-------------------------------------
/ PROBLEM    TITLE IS 'PRENTICE DATA'.
/ INPUT      VARIABLES ARE 4.
            FORMAT IS '(4F3.0)'.
/ VARIABLE   NAMES ARE SURVIVAL, STATE, TREAT, CELL.

/ FORM       TIME IS SURVIVAL.
            STATUS IS STATE.
            RESPONSE IS 1.

/ END
            -------------------------------------
```

(See end of this P1L section for organization of systems information, BMDP instructions and data.)

The results appear in Output 1L.1. Circled numbers below correspond to those in the output.

① Number of cases read. Cases that contain acceptable values for all variables specified in FORM and ESTIMATE paragraphs are used in the analysis. A case is omitted from all computations when the value of any variable used in the analysis is missing or is out of range. If CODES are specified for a GROUPING variable (as in Example 1L.3), a case is included only if the value of the GROUPING variable is equal to one of the specified codes.

② Time intervals. The range of survival times is divided into ten equally spaced intervals. Therefore, as in this example, intervals may not be whole numbers. The number or width of intervals can be specified (p. 573). The survival experience of the patients is summarized by interval. All 62 patients began the study, and hence entered the first interval, 0 - 99.9. Three patients were censored in that interval (i.e., were alive, but were on the study for less than 99.9 days at the time of analysis). Thirty-four patients died within 99.9 days of entry into the study. Hence 62-3-34 = 25 patients enter the next interval; that is, have survival times greater than 99.9 days.

③ Number of patients exposed to the risk of dying during the interval. This is estimated by

$$r_i = n_i - \frac{1}{2}c_i$$

where

n_i = number of patients entering the interval
c_i = number censored in the interval (due to patients that are either lost to follow-up, or withdrawn)

It is assumed that censored observations occur randomly (from a uniform distribution) in the interval. Hence, patients who are censored are considered to be at risk for half the interval. Based on the number of patients at risk, the conditional probability of dying in the interval is calculated. This is estimated by

$$q_i = d_i / r_i$$

where d_i = the number dying in the interval. q_i is the probability that an individual will die in the interval, given that he enters the interval. Implicit in this calculation is the assumption that the risk of dying is constant over the entire interval. The conditional probability of surviving is given by $p_i = 1 - q_i$.

④ The cumulative survival function: This is the estimate, P_i, of the cumulative proportion, surviving to the beginning of the ith interval, and defined as

$$P_i = p_{i-1}P_{i-1} ,$$

where $P_1 = 1$.

This estimate is based on the fact that survival to the ith interval requires that one survive to the (i-1)st. This is the usual life table estimate. Its approximate standard error, obtained from Greenwood's (1926) formula, is defined as

$$\text{s.e. } (P_i) \stackrel{\sim}{=} P_i \left\{ \sum_{j=1}^{i-1} (q_j / r_j p_j) \right\}^{\frac{1}{2}} .$$

This estimate may considerably underestimate the variance when the amount of censoring is high (Gross and Clark, 1975).

⑤ The hazard function (also called the failure rate, the instantaneous death rate, or the force of mortality) is estimated at the midpoint of each interval; i.e.,

$$\lambda_i = \frac{2q_i}{h_i(1+p_i)}$$

with approximate standard error

$$\text{s.e.}(\lambda_i) \stackrel{\sim}{=} \lambda_i \left(\frac{1-(h_i \lambda_i /2)^2}{r_i q_i} \right)^{\frac{1}{2}}$$

This estimate may considerably underestimate the variance when the amount of censoring is high (Gross and Clark, 1975).

Output 1L.1   Life table analysis using the actuarial life table method. Circled numbers correspond to those in the text

----

--- the BMDP instructions read by P1L are printed and interpreted ---

NUMBER OF CASES READ.   62

RESPONSE CODES	1	DEAD	①
CENSORED CODES	0	CENSORED	

LIFE TABLE AND SURVIVAL ANALYSIS

TIME VARIABLE IS SURVIVAL

INTERVAL ②	ENTERED	WITHDRAWN	LOST	DEAD	EXPOSED	PROPORTION DEAD ③	PROPORTION SURVIVING	CUMULATIVE SURVIVAL ④	HAZARD (S.E.) ⑤	DENSITY (S.E.)
0.0 - 99.90	62	3	0	34	60.5	0.5620	0.4380	1.0000 0.0	0.0078 0.0012	0.0056 0.0006
99.90 - 199.80	25	1	0	11	24.5	0.4490	0.5510	0.4380 0.0638	0.0058 0.0017	0.0020 0.0005
199.80 - 299.70	13	1	0	4	12.5	0.3200	0.6800	0.2414 0.0563	0.0038 0.0019	0.0008 0.0004
299.70 - 399.60	8	0	0	3	8.0	0.3750	0.6250	0.1641 0.0498	0.0046 0.0026	0.0006 0.0003
399.60 - 499.50	5	0	0	2	5.0	0.4000	0.6000	0.1026 0.0419	0.0050 0.0034	0.0004 0.0003
499.50 - 599.40	3	0	0	1	3.0	0.3333	0.6667	0.0615 0.0337	0.0040 0.0039	0.0002 0.0002
599.40 - 699.30	2	0	0	0	2.0	0.0	1.0000	0.0410 0.0280	0.0 0.0	0.0 0.0
699.30 - 799.20	2	0	0	0	2.0	0.0	1.0000	0.0410 0.0280	0.0 0.0	0.0 0.0
799.20 - 899.10	2	0	0	0	2.0	0.0	1.0000	0.0410 0.0280	0.0 0.0	0.0 0.0
899.10 - 999.00	2	0	0	2	2.0	1.0000	0.0	0.0410 0.0280	0.0200 0.0000	0.0004 0.0003

QUANTILE	ESTIMATE	STANDARD ERROR	
75TH	44.44	11.43	⑥
MEDIAN (50TH)	88.88	11.43	
25TH	195.41	51.31	

SUMMARY TABLE

TOTAL	DEAD	CENSORED	PERCENT CENSORED	
62	57	5	0.0806	⑦

(output continued)

Output 1L.1 (continued)

PATTERN OF CENSORED DATA

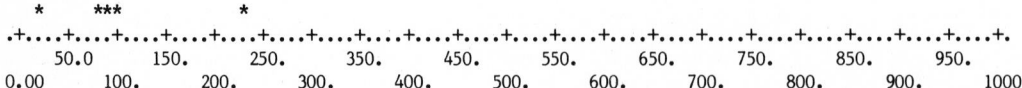

```
      *       ***              *
.+....+....+....+....+....+....+....+....+....+....+....+....+....+....+....+....+....+....+....+....+.
      50.0        150.        250.        350.        450.        550.        650.        750.        850.        950.
0.00        100.        200.        300.        400.        500.        600.        700.        800.        900.        1000
```

⑧

PATTERN OF TRUE RESPONSE TIMES

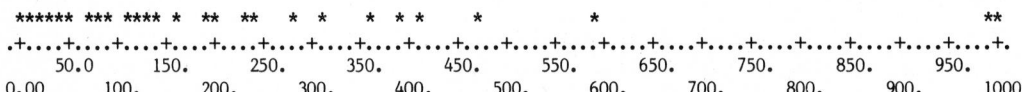

```
   ****** *** **** *  **  **   *  *   *  * *      *            *                                    **
.+....+....+....+....+....+....+....+....+....+....+....+....+....+....+....+....+....+....+....+....+.
      50.0        150.        250.        350.        450.        550.        650.        750.        850.        950.
0.00        100.        200.        300.        400.        500.        600.        700.        800.        900.        1000
```

CUMULATIVE PROPORTION SURVIVING

⑨

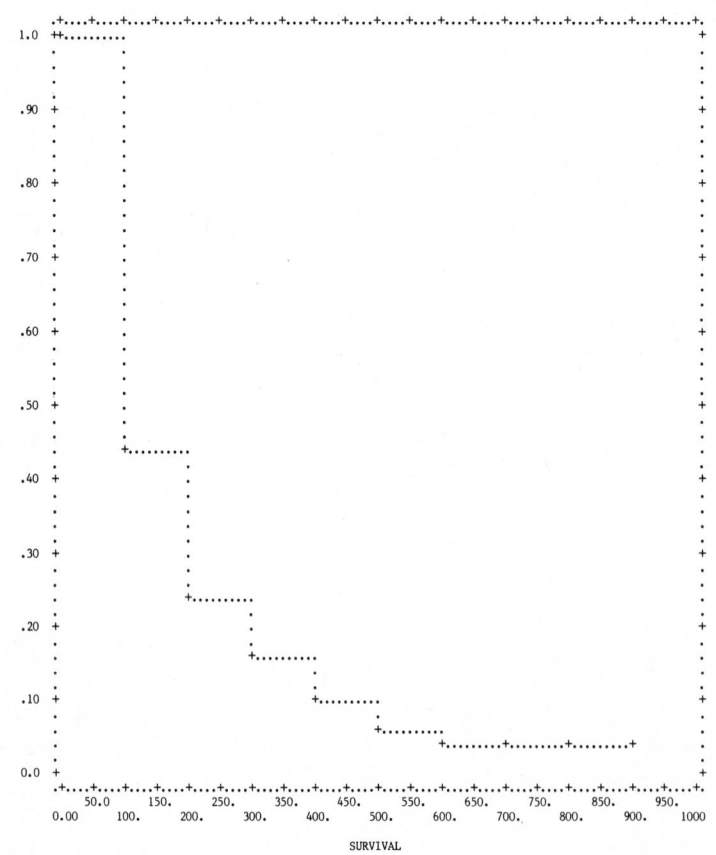

SURVIVAL

The <u>death density function</u> (probability of death per unit time) estimated at the midpoint of each interval i is given by

$$f_i = \frac{P_i - P_{i+1}}{h_i} = \frac{P_i q_i}{h_i}$$

where h_i is the width of the ith interval. The approximate standard error of the estimate is

$$s.e.(f_i) = \frac{P_i q_i}{h_i} \left(\sum_{j=1}^{i-1} \frac{q_j}{r_j p_j} + \frac{P_i}{r_i q_i} \right)^{\frac{1}{2}}.$$

The above two functions are alternate ways of describing survival data. These estimates are most useful for detecting patterns suggestive of parametric models that may describe the data. For example, a constant estimate of the hazard function over each interval is suggestive of an exponential distribution. Other forms of the hazard, and their interpretation are discussed in books such as Gross and Clark (1975).

(6) Estimates of the quantiles of the survival function. That is, the estimated times at which 75%, 50%, (median survival) and 25% of the patients are still alive. To estimate median survival, for example, let $[t_i, t_{i+1}]$ be the interval for which $P_i \geq \frac{1}{2}$ and $P_{i+1} < \frac{1}{2}$. Then the estimate of median survival (the 50% quantile) is given by

$$Q_{50} = (t_i - t_o) + \frac{(P_i - \frac{1}{2})}{f_i}$$

where t_o is the time at which the first interval begins (usually zero). The approximate standard error is

$$s.e. (Q_{50}) \cong 1/(2 f_i r_i^{\frac{1}{2}}).$$

(7) A summary of the total number of patients dying, and the number and percentage of censored observations.

(8) Plots of the individual censoring times and times of response. These are useful for comparing censoring patterns between groups, or for examining patterns of censoring within a group. For example, a treatment with numerous early losses may indicate lack of patient acceptance of the particular therapy.

(9) A plot of the estimated cumulative survival function. This is a step function that decreases at times corresponding to the <u>beginning</u> of each interval. The size of the plot can be specified. Note that the scale used in this plot is the same as that used for the plots of the individual response times and the pattern of censored data above. We suggest that you view these three plots together.

<u>How to use the patient's time on the study as input</u>. The FORM paragraph is required by P1L to describe the structure of the survival time variables. The form of such data may occur in many ways including survival time or dates for individual patients or data arranged as a life table. Examples 1L.1 - 1L.6 illustrate survival time for individual patients; 1L.7 uses dates and 1L.8, life table input. Data occurring in other forms may be transformed (Chapter 6) to one of these structures.

For <u>survival time input</u>, one variable contains the TIME that the subject is observed (to the response or until he is withdrawn or lost to follow-up), while a second variable, STATUS, contains codes, one (or more) to indicate the occurrence of a response and up to nine types of censored observations. A third variable, RESPONSE, is used to indicate which codes in the variable STATUS may be treated as responses (deaths). All eligible codes (i.e., not equal to the missing value code or out of range) not listed in RESPONSE are assumed to be censored. Censoring commonly is due to loss to follow-up (e.g., the patient has moved or dropped out of the study) and withdrawals (the patient is still alive at the end of the study or at the time of analysis). Separate codes may exist for different causes of death. These may be treated as responses (deaths), or as censored observations. All censored values are treated identically in the analysis.

If NAMES are given to the CODES of the STATUS variable in the GROUP paragraph, the names are used to label the results. Otherwise, if multiple codes are specified in RESPONSE, the names DEAD1, DEAD2, ... appear in the summary tables, and in the output of the product-limit estimate. Multiple censored observations are named CENSRD1, CENSRD2, ..., where CENSRD1 corresponds to the smallest code encountered in the data which is not specified in RESPONSE, CENSRD2 is the second, etc. The correspondence between names and codes is given in the summary table.

You may also identify values of the codes representing censored observations that are LOSSES. This is frequently useful in understanding the data, but in no way influences the analysis. All eligible codes not listed in either RESPONSE or LOSS are censored. When names are not specified for the values of STATUS in the GROUP paragraph, default names for values in LOSS are LOST1, LOST2, ...

See Example 1L.7 for survival date input and Example 1L.8 for life table input.

FORM
```
TIME = v.                                    none
  Name or subscript of the variable that contains
  the survival times.
STATus = v.                                  none
  Name or subscript of the variable that contains
  the status of the patient in the study. The
  variable can have at most ten values (the total
  of deaths, losses, and other censored
  observations).
RESPonse = # list.              first code of
                                STATUS variable
  Numbers specifying which values of the STATUS
  variable are to be treated as deaths
  (RESPONSES).
LOSS = # list.                               none
  Numbers specifying which values of the STATUS
  variable are to be treated as losses.
```

Output 1L.2   The product-limit (Kaplan-Meier) estimate of the cumulative survival curve

----

PRODUCT-LIMIT SURVIVAL ANALYSIS ⑪ TIME VARIABLE IS SURVIVAL

CASE LABEL	CASE NUMBER	TIME	STATUS	CUMULATIVE SURVIVAL	STANDARD ERROR	CUM DEATHS	CUM LOST	REMAIN AT RISK
	16	1.00	DEAD			1	0	61
	8 ⑩	1.00	DEAD	0.9677	0.0224	2	0	60
	43	3.00	DEAD	0.9516	0.0273	3	0	59
	56	7.00	DEAD	0.9355	0.0312	4	0	58
	27	8.00	DEAD			5	0	57
	36	8.00	DEAD			6	0	56
	53	8.00	DEAD	0.8871	0.0402	7	0	55
	33	10.00	DEAD	0.8710	0.0426	8	0	54
	24	11.00	DEAD	0.8548	0.0447	9	0	53
	41	12.00	DEAD	0.8387	0.0467	10	0	52
	20	15.00	DEAD	0.8226	0.0485	11	0	51
	46	18.00	DEAD	0.8065	0.0502	12	0	50
	60	19.00	DEAD	0.7903	0.0517	13	0	49
	45	24.00	DEAD	0.7742	0.0531	14	0	48
	12	25.00	DEAD	0.7581	0.0544	15	0	47
	25	25.00	CENSORED			15	0	46
	17	30.00	DEAD	0.7416	0.0556	16	0	45
	48	31.00	DEAD	0.7251	0.0568	17	0	44
	11	33.00	DEAD	0.7086	0.0578	18	0	43
	38	35.00	DEAD	0.6921	0.0588	19	0	42
	54	36.00	DEAD	0.6757	0.0597	20	0	41
	28	42.00	DEAD	0.6592	0.0604	21	0	40
	18	44.00	DEAD	0.6427	0.0611	22	0	39
	61	45.00	DEAD	0.6262	0.0618	23	0	38
	55	48.00	DEAD	0.6097	0.0623	24	0	37
	49	51.00	DEAD	0.5933	0.0627	25	0	36
	51	52.00	DEAD	0.5768	0.0631	26	0	35
	1	72.00	DEAD	0.5603	0.0634	27	0	34
	52	73.00	DEAD	0.5438	0.0637	28	0	33
	62	80.00	DEAD	0.5273	0.0638	29	0	32
	32	82.00	DEAD	0.5109	0.0639	30	0	31
	47	83.00	CENSORED			30	0	30
	59	84.00	DEAD	0.4938	0.0640	31	0	29
	21	87.00	CENSORED			31	0	28
	50	90.00	DEAD	0.4762	0.0641	32	0	27
	37	92.00	DEAD	0.4586	0.0641	33	0	26
	44	95.00	DEAD	0.4409	0.0641	34	0	25
	29	100.00	CENSORED			34	0	24
	31	110.00	DEAD	0.4226	0.0640	35	0	23
	7	111.00	DEAD	0.4042	0.0638	36	0	22
	22	112.00	DEAD	0.3858	0.0635	37	0	21
	39	117.00	DEAD	0.3674	0.0630	38	0	20
	34	118.00	DEAD	0.3491	0.0625	39	0	19
	35	126.00	DEAD	0.3307	0.0619	40	0	18
	40	132.00	DEAD	0.3123	0.0611	41	0	17
	57	140.00	DEAD	0.2939	0.0602	42	0	16
	26	144.00	DEAD	0.2756	0.0592	43	0	15
	42	162.00	DEAD	0.2572	0.0580	44	0	14
	58	186.00	DEAD	0.2388	0.0567	45	0	13
	15	201.00	DEAD	0.2205	0.0552	46	0	12
	3	228.00	DEAD	0.2021	0.0536	47	0	11
	4	231.00	CENSORED			47	0	10
	5	242.00	DEAD	0.1819	0.0519	48	0	9
	19	283.00	DEAD	0.1617	0.0499	49	0	8
	30	314.00	DEAD	0.1415	0.0476	50	0	7
	13	357.00	DEAD	0.1213	0.0449	51	0	6
	10	389.00	DEAD	0.1010	0.0417	52	0	5
	2	411.00	DEAD	0.0808	0.0379	53	0	4
	14	467.00	DEAD	0.0606	0.0334	54	0	3
	9	587.00	DEAD	0.0404	0.0277	55	0	2
	6	991.00	DEAD	0.0202	0.0199	56	0	1
	23	999.00	DEAD	0.0	0.0	57	0	0

MEAN SURVIVAL TIME =   158.00   S.E. = 29.467

	QUANTILE	ESTIMATE
⑫	75TH	30.00
	MEDIAN (50TH)	84.00
	25TH	186.00

Example 1L.2 The Product-Limit Estimate of the Cumulative Survival Curve

In Example 1L.1, the actuarial life table method was used to estimate the survival curve. Here we illustrate a second estimate of the cumulative survival distribution using the product-limit (Kaplan-Meier) estimate. When there is no censoring the product-limit estimate is the same as cumulative histogram (empirical distribution function). The product-limit and life table estimates are identical when the intervals of the life table contain at most one observation each. The product-limit estimate has the advantage of giving results that are independent of the choice of intervals. All instructions are the same as for Example 1L.1 except for the added ESTIMATE paragraph inserted before the END paragraph:

```
---------------------------------------
/ FORM        TIME IS SURVIVAL.
             STATUS IS STATE.
             RESPONSE IS 1.

/ ESTIMATE   METHOD IS PRODUCT.
---------------------------------------
```

The results of this example are presented in Output 1L.2. Circled numbers below correspond to those in the output.

(10) The N observed survival times are ordered $(t_1 \leq t_2 \leq \ldots \leq t_n)$ and printed. If names are assigned to the status codes in the GROUP paragraph, the appropriate name is printed for each response time; otherwise, the assumed codes are DEAD and CENSRD.

(11) The estimate of the survival curve is printed at each unique time of death. It is estimated as

$$P(t) = \prod_{t_i < t} \frac{N-i+1-\delta_i}{N-i+1}$$

where $\hat{\delta}_i = \begin{cases} 1 \text{ if } t_i \text{ represents a death (true response)} \\ 0 \text{ if } t_i \text{ is a censored observation.} \end{cases}$

Thus, $P(t)$ is a step function that changes at each distinct time of death. If tied observations occur, deaths are assumed to occur slightly before censored observations.

$$\text{s.e. } (P(t)) \cong P(t) \left(\sum_{t_i < t} \frac{\delta_i}{(N-i)(N-i+1)} \right)^{\frac{1}{2}}.$$

(12) Estimates of the mean and quantiles of the distribution. The estimated mean is

$$\hat{\mu} = \sum_{i=1}^{N} P(t_{i-1})(t_i - t_{i-1})$$

where the summation is over all times of death. When the patient who is longest on the study is a censored observation, $\hat{\mu}$ underestimates the true mean, and a warning is printed in the output. An estimate of the variance of $\hat{\mu}$ is also printed. See Appendix A.30 for its formula. Formulas for the quantiles of the distribution are also given in Appendix A.30.

Specifying the survival curves - the ESTIMATE paragraph. The ESTIMATE paragraph is used in P1L to specify the method of the analysis that is desired, and the statistics and plots to be printed. The ESTIMATE paragraph may be repeated for additional analyses of the same data. Examples 1L.1 and 1L.2 demonstrate the Control Language instructions necessary to compute the survival curves using two methods: the actuarial life table and the product-limit estimate. These are specified by the METHOD parameter.

```
ESTimate ───────────────────────────
  METHod = (one only) LIFE, PROD.      LIFE/prev.
    When PROD is specified, the survival
    distribution is estimated by the product-limit
    estimate. Otherwise, the life table method is
    used.
```

Example 1L.3 Variables Associated with the Product-Limit Survival Estimate

It is often desirable to associate individual observations with values of possible prognostic variables. For example, you may want to know whether

Output 1L.3 Printing an additional variable with the product-limit estimate

PRODUCT-LIMIT SURVIVAL ANALYSIS

TIME VARIABLE IS SURVIVAL

CASE LABEL	CASE NUMBER	TIME	STATUS	CUMULATIVE SURVIVAL	STANDARD ERROR	CUM DEATHS	CUM LOST	REMAIN AT RISK	CELL
	16	1.00	DEAD			1	0	61	SQUAMOUS
	8	1.00	DEAD	0.9677	0.0224	2	0	60	SQUAMOUS
	43	3.00	DEAD	0.9516	0.0273	3	0	59	ADENOCA
	56	7.00	DEAD	0.9355	0.0312	4	0	58	ADENOCA
	27	8.00	DEAD			5	0	57	SQUAMOUS
	36	8.00	DEAD			6	0	56	ADENOCA
	53	8.00	DEAD	0.8871	0.0402	7	0	55	ADENOCA
	33	10.00	DEAD	0.8710	0.0426	8	0	54	SQUAMOUS

--- similar results for the remaining cases ---

all early deaths were among elderly patients or among patients with a particular cell type. Since the product-limit estimate prints a separate line for each case, you can request that the values of certain variables also be printed.

If the values of these variables are codes and the CODES are specified and NAMED in the GROUP paragraph the appropriate code name will be printed in the output beside the survival information. We identify the VARIABLE with the patient's cell type (recorded in the input as the fourth variable, CELL) in the ESTIMATE paragraph and specify the NAMES and CODES in the GROUP paragraph. These instructions are inserted in those of Example 1L.1 before the END paragraph:

```
  ------------------------------------
  / FORM        TIME IS SURVIVAL.
               STATUS IS STATE.
               RESPONSE IS 1.

  / ESTIMATE    METHOD IS PRODUCT.
               VARIABLE IS CELL.

  / GROUP       CODES(4) ARE       1,      2.
               NAMES(4) ARE SQUAMOUS, ADENOCA.
  ------------------------------------
```

The results of this example are shown in Output 1L.3. The last column lists the values of CELLTYPE for individual cases. An examination of these variables may provide valuable information about their possible relationship to survival time.

```
ESTimate ─────────────────────────────────
  VARiable = v list.                      none
    Names or subscripts of variables to be printed
    when the product-limit estimate is specified. A
    maximum of 4 variables may be printed. If CODES
    (or CUTPOINTS) and NAMES are specified in a
    GROUP paragraph (Section 5.5) for one or more
    of these variables, the specified NAMES are
    printed in the output and not the values of the
    variable(s).
```

Example 1L.4 Plots of the Survival Curves, Log-survival, Cumulative Hazard, Hazard and Death Density Functions

In Example 1L.1, we illustrate a plot of the cumulative proportion surviving computed by the actuarial life-table method. The survival curve may

Output 1L.4   Plots of the hazard and cumulative hazard functions

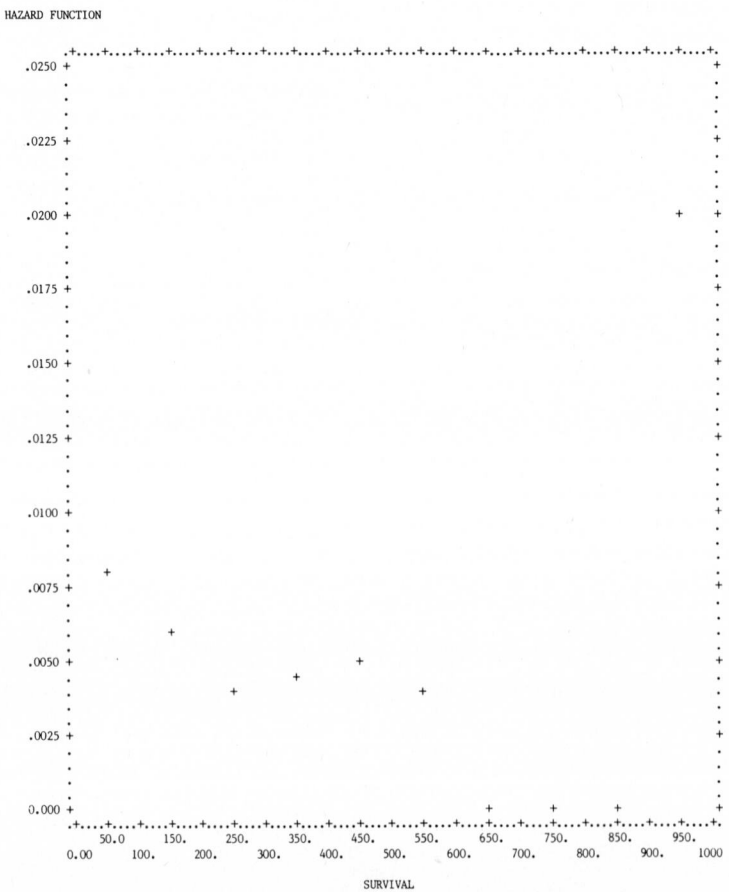

also be plotted for the product-limit method, and log-survival function may also be plotted for either method. This plot is useful for suggesting possible parametric models for the survival function. When the life-table estimate is used, the <u>hazard</u>, <u>cumulative hazard</u>, and <u>death density functions</u> can also be used to suggest parametric models.

In this example we illustrate plots for the hazard and the cumulative hazard functions by requesting them in the ESTIMATE paragraph which is inserted in the instructions of Example 1L.1 before the END paragraph.

```
-------------------------------------
/ FORM       TIME IS SURVIVAL.
            STATUS IS STATE.
            RESPONSE IS 1.

/ ESTIMATE   PLOTS ARE HAZ, CUM.
-------------------------------------
```

Since no METHOD is specified in the ESTIMATE paragraph, the life table analysis is performed. Output 1L.4 presents the plots requested.

The hazard function is often used to detect possible parametric descriptions of the data. Because the hazard rate often appears irregular, the cumulative hazard, $-\ln P(t)$, is often preferred. A discussion of the interpretation of such plots may be found, for example, in Gross and Clark (1975) and Nelson (1972). When a parametric model seems appropriate for your data, you can also analyze the data using P3R or PAR (Chapter 14).

ESTimate
PLOT = (one or more)   SURV
       SURV, LOG, CUM, HAZ, DEN.
    Plot one or more of the following:
    SURV -- the cumulative survival function P(t) estimated by either the life table or product-limit method
    LOG -- the natural logarithm of the survival function $\ln P(t)$
    CUM -- the cumulative hazard function $(-\ln P(t))$
    HAZ -- the hazard function if METHOD = LIFE
    DEN -- the death density function if METHOD = LIFE
            SIZE = etc.
    If any plots are specified, only those specified are printed.

CUMULATIVE HAZARD FUNCTION

Example 1L.5 A Separate Estimate of Survival for Each Group

If the data input is any form other than Life-Table input, then estimates of the survival curve may be obtained separately for different groups of patients. For example, in the Prentice data, you might wish to estimate survival separately by treatment, or by cell type.

This example illustrates the analysis obtained when the patients are divided by treatment group. The third variable in the input file contains a code for each patient that identifies his membership in a standard treatment group or a new "test" group. We specify the CODES and their NAMES in the GROUP paragraph and state that TREAT (treatment) is the variable with this grouping information in the ESTIMATE paragraph. These instructions are inserted before the END paragraph of Example 1L.1:

```
-------------------------------------
/ FORM          TIME IS SURVIVAL.
                STATUS IS STATE.
                RESPONSE IS 1.

/ ESTIMATE      METHOD IS PRODUCT.
                GROUP IS TREAT.
                PLOT = SURV.

/ GROUP         CODES(3) ARE    0,        1.
                NAMES(3) ARE TEST, STANDARD.
-------------------------------------
```

Output 1L.5 Product-limit analysis for two groups

PRODUCT-LIMIT SURVIVAL ANALYSIS   GROUPING VARIABLE IS TREAT   LEVEL IS TEST

TIME VARIABLE IS SURVIVAL

CASE LABEL	CASE NUMBER	TIME	STATUS	CUMULATIVE SURVIVAL	STANDARD ERROR	CUM DEATHS	CUM LOST	REMAIN AT RISK
	16	1.00	DEAD			1	0	37
	8	1.00	DEAD	0.9474	0.0362	2	0	36
	56	7.00	DEAD	0.9211	0.0437	3	0	35
	53	8.00	DEAD	0.8947	0.0498	4	0	34
	20	15.00	DEAD	0.8684	0.0548	5	0	33
	46	18.00	DEAD	0.8421	0.0592	6	0	32
	60	19.00	DEAD	0.8158	0.0629	7	0	31
	45	24.00	DEAD	0.7895	0.0661	8	0	30
	12	25.00	DEAD	0.7632	0.0690	9	0	29
	17	30.00	DEAD	0.7368	0.0714	10	0	28
	48	31.00	DEAD	0.7105	0.0736	11	0	27
	11	33.00	DEAD	0.6842	0.0754	12	0	26
	54	36.00	DEAD	0.6579	0.0770	13	0	25
	18	44.00	DEAD	0.6316	0.0783	14	0	24
	61	45.00	DEAD	0.6053	0.0793	15	0	23
	55	48.00	DEAD	0.5789	0.0801	16	0	22
	49	51.00	DEAD	0.5526	0.0807	17	0	21
	51	52.00	DEAD	0.5263	0.0810	18	0	20
	52	73.00	DEAD	0.5000	0.0811	19	0	19
	62	80.00	DEAD	0.4737	0.0810	20	0	18
	47	83.00	CENSORED			20	0	17
	59	84.00	DEAD	0.4458	0.0809	21	0	16
	21	87.00	CENSORED			21	0	15
	50	90.00	DEAD	0.4161	0.0808	22	0	14
	7	111.00	DEAD	0.3864	0.0803	23	0	13
	22	112.00	DEAD	0.3567	0.0794	24	0	12
	57	140.00	DEAD	0.3269	0.0782	25	0	11
	58	186.00	DEAD	0.2972	0.0765	26	0	10
	15	201.00	DEAD	0.2675	0.0744	27	0	9
	4	231.00	CENSORED			27	0	8
	5	242.00	DEAD	0.2341	0.0722	28	0	7
	19	283.00	DEAD	0.2006	0.0692	29	0	6
	13	357.00	DEAD	0.1672	0.0653	30	0	5
	10	389.00	DEAD	0.1337	0.0602	31	0	4
	14	467.00	DEAD	0.1003	0.0536	32	0	3
	9	587.00	DEAD	0.0669	0.0450	33	0	2
	6	991.00	DEAD	0.0334	0.0326	34	0	1
	23	999.00	DEAD	0.0	0.0	35	0	0

MEAN SURVIVAL TIME =   188.45   S.E. = 45.476

QUANTILE	ESTIMATE
75TH	30.00
MEDIAN (50TH)	80.00
25TH	242.00

PRODUCT–LIMIT SURVIVAL ANALYSIS   GROUPING VARIABLE IS TREAT   LEVEL IS STANDARD

TIME VARIABLE IS SURVIVAL

CASE LABEL	CASE NUMBER	TIME	STATUS	CUMULATIVE SURVIVAL	STANDARD ERROR	CUM DEATHS	CUM LOST	REMAIN AT RISK
	43	3.00	DEAD	0.9583	0.0408	1	0	23
	27	8.00	DEAD			2	0	22
	36	8.00	DEAD	0.8750	0.0675	3	0	21
	33	10.00	DEAD	0.8333	0.0761	4	0	20
	24	11.00	DEAD	0.7917	0.0829	5	0	19
	41	12.00	DEAD	0.7500	0.0884	6	0	18
	25	25.00	CENSORED			6	0	17
	38	35.00	DEAD	0.7059	0.0936	7	0	16
	28	42.00	DEAD	0.6618	0.0976	8	0	15
	1	72.00	DEAD	0.6176	0.1005	9	0	14
	32	82.00	DEAD	0.5735	0.1026	10	0	13
	37	92.00	DEAD	0.5294	0.1037	11	0	12
	44	95.00	DEAD	0.4853	0.1041	12	0	11
	29	100.00	CENSORED			12	0	10
	31	110.00	DEAD	0.4368	0.1044	13	0	9
	39	117.00	DEAD	0.3882	0.1034	14	0	8
	34	118.00	DEAD	0.3397	0.1012	15	0	7
	35	126.00	DEAD	0.2912	0.0977	16	0	6
	40	132.00	DEAD	0.2426	0.0927	17	0	5
	26	144.00	DEAD	0.1941	0.0859	18	0	4
	42	162.00	DEAD	0.1456	0.0769	19	0	3
	3	228.00	DEAD	0.0971	0.0648	20	0	2
	30	314.00	DEAD	0.0485	0.0472	21	0	1
	2	411.00	DEAD	0.0	0.0	22	0	0

MEAN SURVIVAL TIME =   110.97   S.E. =   22.259

QUANTILE	ESTIMATE
75TH	35.00
MEDIAN (50TH)	95.00
25TH	132.00

SUMMARY TABLE

	TOTAL	DEAD	CENSORED	PERCENT CENSORED
TEST	38	35	3	0.0789
STANDARD	24	22	2	0.0833
TOTALS	62	57	5	

PATTERN OF CENSORED DATA

```
TEST             **            *

STANDARD   *       *
         .+....+....+....+....+....+....+....+....+....+....+....+....+....+....+....+....+....+....+....+....+.
             50.0      150.     250.     350.     450.     550.     650.     750.     850.     950.
         0.00      100.     200.     300.     400.     500.     600.     700.     800.     900.     1000
```

PATTERN OF TRUE RESPONSE TIMES

```
TEST     ****** *** * *    **  *   *      * *      *         *                                    **

STANDARD ** ** *** **** *     *      *      *
         .+....+....+....+....+....+....+....+....+....+....+....+....+....+....+....+....+....+....+....+.
             50.0      150.     250.     350.     450.     550.     650.     750.     850.     950.
         0.00      100.     200.     300.     400.     500.     600.     700.     800.     900.     1000
```

(output continued)

Output 1L.5 (continued)

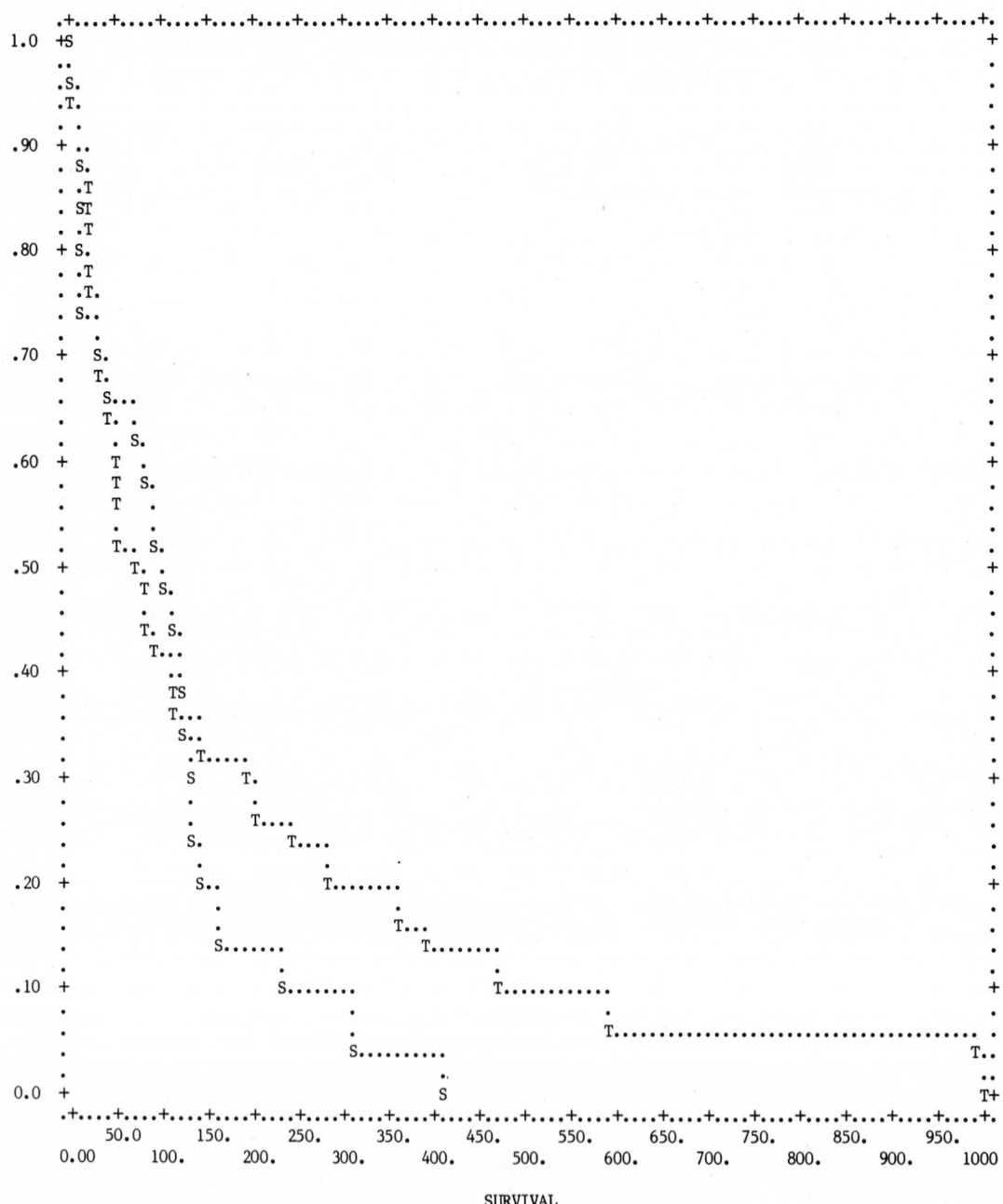

CUMULATIVE PROPORTION SURVIVING   T = TEST   S = STANDARD

SURVIVAL

The results of this example are presented in Output 1L.5. For each level of the grouping variable a separate estimate of the survival distribution is printed. The summary table presents individual entries for each group as well as for overall patient information. Plots of censoring times and death times are given for individual groups. This is particularly useful for monitoring the patterns of censoring between groups. The plot for each category of the grouping variable appears in the same plot frame. The character used for plotting is the first letter of the code name (if specified) in the GROUP paragraph. Otherwise, the letters A, B, C, ... are used.

ESTimate ───────

GROUPing = v.   no grouping

Name or subscript of variable to be used to classify cases into groups. A separate analysis is performed for each level of the grouping variable. If GROUPING is not specified or is set to zero, all data are in one group. If the GROUPING variable takes on more than 10 distinct values, you must specify CODES or CUTPOINTS for it in a GROUP paragraph.

Note: grouping of cases is not available with Life-table input.

Example 1L.6 Testing the Equality of Survival Distributions for Different Groups

You may want to test whether the survival curves obtained for the groups defined by the GROUPING variable are equal. Two such statistics appropriate for censored data can be requested; they are analogues of nonparametric rank tests. These statistics, along with the GROUPING parameter, are not available with Life-table input.

The first test was proposed by Mantel (1966). When there are no censored observations it is essentially an exponential scores test (or Savage statistic); that is, it uses scores based on the exponential distribution. The second statistic, which is analogous to the Kruskal-Wallis (or generalized Wilcoxon) test, was proposed by Breslow (1970).

The Mantel-Cox and Breslow tests differ in the way the observations are weighted. The Breslow test gives greater weight to early observations and is less sensitive to late events which occur when few patients on the study remain alive. Both tests are valid in large samples whether the censoring patterns are equal or unequal. Small sample sizes and the degree and pattern of censoring may affect the distribution of the tests. Small sample properties are still being studied (e.g., Tarone and Ware, 1977, or Lee, Desu and Gehan 1975). When there is unequal censoring you should assess the reasons for the censored observations. For example, disproportionate loss-to-followup in one treatment group could be related to the treatment under study (e.g., due to toxic reactions) and needs to be considered in making conclusions about treatment differences.

In this example we make one addition to the instructions in Example 1L.5 - we request both tests by including a STATISTICS instruction in the ESTIMATE paragraph. That is, the instructions we insert in the basic setup of Example 1L.1 are now:

```
/ FORM       TIME IS SURVIVAL.
             STATUS IS STATE.
             RESPONSE IS 1.

/ ESTIMATE   METHOD IS PRODUCT.
             GROUP IS TREAT.
             PLOT = SURV.
             STATISTICS ARE BRESLOW, MANTEL.

/ GROUP      CODES(3) ARE    0,      1.
             NAMES(3) ARE TEST, STANDARD.
```

The results are given in Output 1L.6. The individual survival times are used in the calculation of these statistics (see Appendix A.30).

ESTimate ───────

STATistics = (one or both)   none/prev.
             MANTEL, BRESLOW.

MANTEL specifies that the generalized Savage (Mantel-Cox) test is computed to test the equality of survival curves defined by GROUP. BRESLOW specifies that Breslow's version of the generalized Wilcoxon statistic be computed. These statistics are not available with life table input.

Output 1L.6 Comparing survival distributions for two groups. Only the test statistics are shown.

TEST STATISTICS

	STATISTIC	D.F.	P-VALUE
GENERALIZED WILCOXON (BRESLOW)	0.009	1	0.9229
GENERALIZED SAVAGE (MANTEL-COX)	0.770	1	0.3803

Example 1L.7 Using Dates for Time-on-study as Input

This form of input is similar to the time-status input shown in Examples 1L.1–1L.6. Instead of a time-on-study variable, the data are presented as two sets of dates; one set providing the month, day and year of ENTRY onto the study, the second set providing the date of TERMINATION. P1L automatically converts these two sets of dates into a time-on-study variable, which is assumed to be in months, unless otherwise specified.

For this example, we have changed the survival times of the 24 patients in the standard treatment group in Table 19.1 to entry and termination dates: these data are shown in Table 19.2.

Note: We use six variables to record the two dates: the first patient enters the study on the fifteenth day of the seventh month of 1976 and leaves the study on the eighteenth day of the same month and year. We use the FORM paragraph to specify the month, day and year for both the entry and the termination dates. The specification of the STATUS and RESPONSE variables remains the same as that shown in Examples 1L.1–1L.6.

Table 19.2 Artificial dates giving rise to the survival times in Table 19.1

Month	Day	Year	MonthT	DayT	YearT	State
7	15	76	7	18	76	1
6	1	75	6	9	75	1
12	10	75	12	18	75	1
1	1	74	1	11	74	1
6	1	75	6	12	75	1
4	3	75	4	15	75	1
5	1	74	5	26	74	0
10	1	75	11	5	75	1
1	1	76	2	12	76	1
7	1	73	9	11	73	1
7	1	73	9	21	73	1
1	1	72	4	2	72	1
1	1	72	4	5	72	1
12	1	73	3	11	74	0
12	1	73	3	21	74	1
12	1	73	3	28	74	1
12	1	73	3	29	74	1
4	15	75	8	19	75	1
4	15	75	8	25	75	1
3	1	74	7	23	74	1
3	1	74	8	10	74	1
1	1	72	8	16	72	1
9	15	73	7	26	74	1
6	1	75	7	16	76	1

Key: Date of entry is recorded as the first three variables. Date of termination is recorded as variables 4 to 6. The seventh variable is state (0 censored, 1 dead). The data are recorded in columns 3-4, 7-8, 11-12, etc.

The preassigned UNIT of time is month; for illustrative purposes in this example we change the time unit to days. Compare these instructions with those in Example 1L.1:

```
------------------------------------
/ PROBLEM     TITLE IS 'DATE-STATUS INPUT - PRENTICE
                  DATA'.
/ INPUT       VARIABLES ARE 7.
              FORMAT IS '(7F4.0)'.
/ VARIABLE    NAMES ARE ENTMONTH, ENTDAY, ENTYEAR,
                  TERMONTH, TERDAY, TERYEAR,
                  STATE.
/ ESTIMATE    METHOD IS PRODUCT.
/ FORM        ENTRY IS ENTMONTH, ENTDAY, ENTYEAR.
              TERMINATION IS TERMONTH, TERDAY,
                      TERYEAR.
              STATUS IS STATE.
              RESPONSE IS 1.
              UNIT IS DAY.
/ END
    7   15   76    7   18   76    1
    6    1   75    6    9   75    1
   12   10   75   12   18   75    1
    1    1   74    1   11   74    1
    6    1   75    6   12   75    1
    4    3   75    4   15   75    1
    5    1   74    5   26   74    0
   10    1   75   11    5   75    1
    1    1   76    2   12   76    1
    7    1   73    9   11   73    1
    7    1   73    9   21   73    1
    1    1   72    4    2   72    1
    1    1   72    4    5   72    1
   12    1   73    3   11   74    0
   12    1   73    3   21   74    1
   12    1   73    3   28   74    1
   12    1   73    3   29   74    1
    4   15   75    8   19   75    1
    4   15   75    8   25   75    1
    3    1   74    7   23   74    1
    3    1   74    8   10   74    1
    1    1   72    8   16   72    1
    9   15   73    7   26   74    1
    6    1   75    7   16   76    1
------------------------------------
```

The results from this example (Output 1L.7) are identical to the results obtained for the standard group in Output 1L.5.

How to use study entry and termination dates as input. Six variables are used to record the patients' month, day and year of entry onto the study and his month, day and year of termination. For example, if your date of ENTRY is recorded in variables 4 (month), 5 (day) and 6 (year) and date of TERMINATION is recorded in variables 7 (month), 8 (day) and 9 (year), you would specify

```
        ENTRY = 4, 5, 6.
        TERMINATION = 7, 8, 9.
```

in the FORM paragraph. P1L can also analyze the data if you record only two date variables, such as month and year. For example, if your date of ENTRY is recorded in variables 5 (month) and 6 (year), you would specify

ENTRY = 5, (3)6.

and TERMINATION would be similarly specified. Note that if both the year of entry and termination are in the 1900's, only the last two digits need be present (e.g., 77 instead of 1977). If one date is earlier than 1900, both years must be given in their entirety.

Frequently, TERMINATION is only present when a patient dies or is lost to follow-up, and no date is punched for a patient still alive at the end of the study or the time of analysis. You may specify a cut-off, or analysis date which will be treated as the date of CENSORING for patients still on-study. The appropriate status code for those individuals will be generated by P1L.

STATUS, RESPONSE and LOSS specifications are as in the time input form (Example 1L.1).

FORM ─────────────

ENTRY = v_1, v_2, v_3.   none
    Names or subscripts of the variables representing month, day and year of patient entry into the study. Note the <u>order is required</u>. You can specify one, two or three variables; for example, month and year is specified as ENTRY = v_1, (3)v_3.
TERMination = v_1, v_2, v_3.   none
    Names or subscripts of variables representing month, day and year of termination. Note the <u>order is required</u>.
CENSOR = #, #, #.   none
    Numbers indicating the date (month, day and year) when the study terminates or the date for the analysis. This is used only with date-status input and is necessary only when there is no date of TERMINATION for some of the censored observations.

Output 1L.7   An analysis beginning with entry and termination dates

----

PRODUCT-LIMIT SURVIVAL ANALYSIS

CASE LABEL	CASE NUMBER	TIME DAY	STATUS	CUMULATIVE SURVIVAL	STANDARD ERROR	CUM DEATHS	CUM LOST	REMAIN AT RISK
	1	3.00	DEAD	0.9583	0.0408	1	0	23
	3	8.00	DEAD			2	0	22
	2	8.00	DEAD	0.8750	0.0675	3	0	21
	4	10.00	DEAD	0.8333	0.0761	4	0	20
	5	11.00	DEAD	0.7917	0.0829	5	0	19
	6	12.00	DEAD	0.7500	0.0884	6	0	18
	7	25.00	CENSORED			6	0	17
	8	35.00	DEAD	0.7059	0.0936	7	0	16
	9	42.00	DEAD	0.6618	0.0976	8	0	15
	10	72.00	DEAD	0.6176	0.1005	9	0	14
	11	82.00	DEAD	0.5735	0.1026	10	0	13
	12	92.00	DEAD	0.5294	0.1037	11	0	12
	13	95.00	DEAD	0.4853	0.1041	12	0	11
	14	100.00	CENSORED			12	0	10
	15	110.00	DEAD	0.4368	0.1044	13	0	9
	16	117.00	DEAD	0.3882	0.1034	14	0	8
	17	118.00	DEAD	0.3397	0.1012	15	0	7
	18	126.00	DEAD	0.2912	0.0977	16	0	6
	19	132.00	DEAD	0.2426	0.0927	17	0	5
	20	144.00	DEAD	0.1941	0.0859	18	0	4
	21	162.00	DEAD	0.1456	0.0769	19	0	3
	22	228.00	DEAD	0.0971	0.0648	20	0	2
	23	314.00	DEAD	0.0485	0.0472	21	0	1
	24	411.00	DEAD	0.0	0.0	22	0	0

MEAN SURVIVAL TIME =   110.97   S.E. = 22.259

QUANTILE	ESTIMATE
75TH	35.00
MEDIAN (50TH)	95.00
25TH	132.00

Changing the units of the time measurement. You may want to specify the unit of time that you would like printed in the output. Or, if your data are in the form of dates (Example 1L.7), you may want to choose the appropriate scale for the calculation of the survival curve. P1L automatically converts the two sets of dates into a time-on-study variable. For example, if the response is recorded in minutes (or seconds), you specify only the first variable for ENTRY and the first for TERMINATION. Then, if you specify UNIT = MINUTE., all the statistics will be computed correctly and the time differences in the output will be labelled MINUTE.

```
FORM ─────────────────────────────────────
  │ UNIT = (one only)            MONTH/prev.
  │       DAY, WEEK, MONTH, YEAR.
  │ or UNIT = c.
  │   Unit for labelling the time scale in the
  │   output. If DAY, WEEK, MONTH, or YEAR are
  │   specified, and the data are in the form of
  │   dates, the specified UNIT will be used in the
  │   calculations.
  └─────────────────────────────────────────
```

Example 1L.8 Using a Life Table as Input

Survival data are frequently grouped for presentation in reports. Such grouped data may be input to P1L, but only the life table analysis will be computed. Suppose, for example, that the data in Table 19.1 had been summarized as in Table 19.3.

Table 19.3   Life table from Output 1L.1

ENTER	LOST	WITHDRAWN	DEAD
62	3	0	34
25	1	0	11
13	1	0	4
8	0	0	3
5	0	0	2
3	0	0	1
2	0	0	0
2	0	0	0
2	0	0	0
2	0	0	2

Key: ENTER   -- number entering interval
       LOST   -- number lost to follow-up during interval
       WITHDRAWN -- number withdrawn during interval
       DEAD   -- number dying during interval

The data are recorded in columns 3-4, 8, 12, and 15-16.

─────────────

Each case represents one line of the life table from Output 1L.1; that is, each case summarizes survival experience for a single interval. The first variable represents the number of individuals entering the interval, the second the number of losses, the third the number of withdrawals, and the final variable the number of deaths. The input of these data to P1L is illustrated here.

```
────────────────────────────────────────
/ PROB       TITLE IS 'PRENTICE DATA'.
/ INPUT      VARIABLES ARE 4.
            FORMAT IS '(4F4.0)'.
/ VARIABLE   NAMES ARE ENTER, LOST, WITHDRAW, DEAD.

/ FORM       NENTER IS ENTER.
            NLOST IS LOST.
            NWITH IS WITHDRAW.
            NDEAD IS DEAD.

/ END
     62   3   0   34
     25   1   0   11
     13   1   0    4
      8   0   0    3
      5   0   0    2
      3   0   0    1
      2   0   0    0
      2   0   0    0
      2   0   0    0
      2   0   0    2
────────────────────────────────────────
```

The results are identical to those in Output 1L.1 with one exception. In Example 1L.8 the intervals are labelled 0-1, 1-2, etc. If you have a variable that contains the lower limit for each interval, it may also be input.

How to use life tables as input. The FORM paragraph specifies which variables contain the number of patients entering an interval (NENTER) and the numbers lost (NLOST), withdrawn (NWITH), and dying during the interval (NDEAD). For these data NWITH could have been omitted since the variable contains only zeros. If NENTER is omitted, P1L assumes that the initial number of individuals in the study is the total number of patients in variables NDEAD, NLOST and NWITH.

An additional variable may be used to record the lower limit for each interval. When omitted, as in Example 1L.8, the integers 0, 1, 2, ... are used. Note that GROUPING parameter and STATISTICS are not available with this form of input.

Survival-type data may occur in many other forms. You can use the TRANSFORMATION paragraph or FORTRAN transformations via the BIMEDT procedure to put the data into one of the above forms for analysis (Chapter 6).

```
FORM ─────────────────────────────────────
  │ NENTer = v.              see discussion above
  │   Name or subscript of variable that contains the
  │   number of patients who entered each interval.
  │ NDEAD = v.                            none
  │   Name or subscript of variable that contains the
  │   number of patients who died in each interval.
  │ NLOST = v.                            none
  │   Name or subscript of variable that contains the
  │   number of patients who were lost in each
  │   interval.
  │ NWITH = v.                            none
  │   Name or subscript of variable that contains the
  │   number of patients who were withdrawn in each
  │   interval.
  │ INTERval = v.                      see above
  │   Name or subscript of variable that contains the
  │   lower limit for each interval. If INTERVAL is
  │   not stated, the integers 0, 1, 2, ... are
  │   assigned.
  │ Note: The GROUPING variable is not available with
  │ this type of input.
  └─────────────────────────────────────────
```

Suppressing the Printout of the Survival Estimates

The product-limit estimate is calculated at individual survival times, whereas the life table utilizes the data grouped into intervals. When the number of observations is large, the output from the product-limit estimate may be excessive. You may omit printing either estimate by stating

NO PRINT.

This is especially useful if you are mainly interested in obtaining plots (Example 1L.4) or test statistics (Example 1L.6).

ESTimate ──
    PRINT.   PRINT/prev.
      The survival distribution estimate is printed
    unless NO PRINT is stated.

Specifying the Intervals for the Life Table Survival Distribution

Analysis by the life table technique (METHOD = LIFE) groups observations into intervals of time. When no further specifications are made, the range of observed survival times is divided into 10 equally spaced intervals. A more suitable choice of interval may be obtained in one of three ways: you may specify the number of intervals desired by the PERIOD statement -- this divides the data into the requested number of equally spaced intervals; you may choose to define the width of the interval; or you may specify exact intervals, particularly if you wish to have them of unequal width. The use of too few intervals is discouraged (< 10), since the larger the interval the less likely it is that the force of mortality is the same throughout the interval.

ESTimate ──
              ⎧ PERIOD = #.   PERIOD = 10/prev.
(one only)   ⎨ WIDTH = #.
              ⎩ CUTPoint = # list.
    When the METHOD is LIFE, specify one of the
    following:
    PERIOD = #.
      Number of intervals desired; the range of
      observations is divided into intervals of
      equal width.
    WIDTH = #.
      The range of observations is divided into as
      many intervals as are needed with a given
      width.
    CUTPoints = # list.
      Cutpoints for dividing the range for time
      into intervals. Each cutpoint represents the
      upper limit of a time interval. The last
      interval contains all times greater than the
      last cutpoint.

    When METHOD is PROD, the above are ignored.

SIZE OF PROBLEM

The number of cases that can be handled by P1L is dependent on the amount of dynamic storage space supplied to the program. On large computers P1L can obtain a life table estimate for approximately 2500 cases when there are 20 intervals in the life table and 10 groups are being simultaneously analyzed. It can obtain the product-limit estimate for approximately 1850 cases if there is no censoring and approximately 3000 cases if there is extensive censoring. Appendix B gives formulas for estimating the amount of space needed and describes how to increase the storage capacity.

COMPUTATIONAL METHOD

All computations are performed in single precision. The formulas for the standard errors and the test statistics are in Appendix A.30.

ACKNOWLEDGEMENT

P1L was designed by Jacqueline Benedetti and Karen Yuen with major contributions from Virginia Clark, Robert Elashoff and Ray Mickey. It was programmed by Larry Young.

SUMMARY

Order of Input Cards

```
// (job card)
// EXEC BIMED,PROG=BMDP1L        (see Appendix E)
//SYSIN DD *
/ PROBLEM
/ INPUT
/ VARIABLE
/ TRANSFORM
/ SAVE
/ ESTIMATE          may be repeated
/ GROUP
/ FORM
/ END
    (data, if on cards)
// (system card)
```

Full sets of BMDP paragraphs (and data, if on cards) can be repeated for additional problems; see Section 5.8.

Paragraph Statement	Preassigned	Comment and Manual Reference
/ FORM		Required to describe the survival variables. There are three forms of input: (1) Time Status, (2) Date-Status, (3) Life Table.
UNIT = c.	MONTH	Units of time measurement. Can be any word, but if DAY, WEEK, MONTH or YEAR is used, the program calculates the appropriate information from the dates to express results in your selected unit. * 572
Time-status input		Time on study is recorded for each patient. 561
TIME = v.	none	Name or subscript of variable that contains the survival time for each patient. *
STATus = v.	none	Name or subscript of variable that contains codes to define a patient's status. Use with RESP and LOSS (below). Codes not listed in either RESP or LOSS are censored. NAMES can be given to CODES in / GROUP.
RESPonse = # list.	lowest	Codes of STAT variable that indicate response (e.g., death). If omitted, the lowest code of the STAT variable is considered a response.
LOSS = # list.	none	Codes of the STAT variable that represent censored observations that are lost to follow up. *
Date-status input		Entry and termination dates are given for each patient. Dates are given as three variables: month, day, year. If you skip a variable, use the tab feature (p. 29).
ENTRY = v,v,v.	none	Names or subscripts of three variables containing month, day and year of patient entry. Order is required. * 571
TERMination = v,v,v.	none	Names or subscripts of three variables containing month, day and year of patient termination. Order is required. If termination date is missing, a user-supplied CENSOR date is substituted. * 571
STATus = v.	none	Name or subscript of variable containing CODES to define a patient's status. NAMES can be given to CODES in the / GROUP paragraph. * 561
RESPonse = # list.	lowest	Codes of STAT variable that indicate response (e.g., death). If omitted, the lowest code of the STAT variable is considered a response. * 561
LOSS = # list.	none	Codes of the STAT variable that represent censored observations that are lost to follow up. * 561
CENSOR = #,#,#.	none	Three numbers indicating month, day and year study ended or analysis was made. Necessary only when no termination date for censored observations is available. 571
Life table input		Each case summarizes the events in a time interval – cases must be ordered by time. Each parameter below identifies the variable that contains the number of patients of each type. 572
NENTer = v.	none	Number entered in that interval; if omitted, the total number dead, withdrawn, and lost at and beyond the interval in question is used.
NDEAD = v.	none	Name or subscript for the number died in that interval.
NLOST = v.	none	Name or subscript for the number lost in that interval.
NWITHdrawn = v.	none	Name or subscript for the number withdrawn in that interval.
INTERval = v.	0,1,2,...	Name or subscript of variable that contains the lower limit for each interval; equal intervals are not required. *

- -

(continued)

(continued)

Paragraph Statement	Preassigned	Comment and Manual Reference
/ ESTimate		Optional to specify method of analysis, statistics and plots (may be repeated).
METHod = c.	LIFE.	LIFE table computation or PROD (product-limit) estimate. * 563
For METHOD = LIFE (one only)		
PERIOD = #.	10.	Number of equal intervals. * 573
WIDTH = #.	none	Number of time units in each equal interval. * 573
CUTPoint = # list.	none	CUTPOINTS for dividing time into intervals (equal intervals not required). * 573
For METHOD = PROD		
VARiables = v list.	none	Names or subscripts of variables to be printed with product-limit estimate. 564
PRINT.	yes	Print the survival distribution estimates. * 573
PLOT = c list.	SURV.	Print the following plots (one or more): * 565 SURV - cumulative survival CUM - cumulative hazard function LOG - natural logarithm of HAZ - hazard function the survival function DEN - death density function } if METHOD = LIFE
SIZE = #,#.	100,40	Width of x-axis (characters); height of y-axis (lines). * 565
GROUPing = v.	none	Name or subscript of variable used to classify cases into groups (see / GROUP). 569
STATistic = (one or both) MANTEL, BRESLOW	none	Optional to request test statistics (one or both). MANTEL specifies the generalized (Mantel-Cox) equality of survival curves test; BRESLOW, a generalized version of the Wilcoxon statistic. Also specify GROUP above. 569

Key:

/	—indicates paragraph	*	—assigned value remains the same for additional problems
.	—period ends a sentence		
●	—required	VT	—number of variables after transformations
v	—variable (name or subscript)	list	—more than one item, often one per var.
g	—group (name or subscript)		
#	—number		Capitalized letters-paragraph or sentence names recognized by BMDP
'c'	—characters (name or parameter) may omit apostrophes if contiguous letters only		Page numbers following refer to this Manual

P2L

19.2 Survival Analysis with Covariates—Cox Models

Alan Hopkins

ABSTRACT

P2L analyzes survival data for which the time-to-response is influenced by other measured variables. These explanatory variables, often called prognostic factors or covariates, usually represent either inherent differences among the study subjects (age, sex, etc.) or constitute a set of one or more indicator variables representing different treatment groups. The covariates may also describe changes in a patient's prognostic status as a function of time. The analysis is based upon the Cox proportional hazards regression model. This technique presumes death rates may be modelled as log-linear functions of the covariates.

One goal of the analysis is to quantify the relationship between survival and a set of explanatory variables. A set of regression coefficients is estimated which relates the effect of each covariate to the survival function. In other applications the proportional hazards regression model is used to test the significance of treatment effects while simultaneously accounting for baseline patient characteristics. The program may also be used in an exploratory manner to identify subsets of variables associated with survival.

P2L output contains estimates of the regression coefficients, their estimated asymptotic standard errors and a global test of significance of the regression coefficients. A stepwise selection option facilitates identification of a subset of variables which are related to survival. Graphical output includes the cumulative survival function, the log minus log survival (log cumulative hazard) function and a goodness-of-fit plot. The data cases may be stratified into several groups. With this option the survival function is estimated separately for each stratum. Stratification is useful when combined subsets of the patients do not follow the proportional hazards assumption. Hypothesis tests for the joint significance of subsets of regression coefficients may be specified easily.

WHERE TO FIND IT

Example 2L.1 Basic Setup for Proportional Hazards Regression Analysis

The Stanford heart transplant data reported and analyzed by Crowley and Hu (1977) is used to illustrate the basic results computed by P2L. A subset of these data is listed in Table 19.4. Briefly, the data consist of survival information and covariates for 65 patients who received heart transplants. The covariates are age at transplant (AGE) and two measures of donor-patient tissue incompatibility (ANTIGEN and MISMATCH). The endpoint used in the analysis is death by rejection. Persons who died from other causes are treated as censored.

In addition to the Control Language instructions common to all programs (Chapter 5), P2L requires a FORM paragraph that indicates the structure of the survival time variables and a REGRESSION paragraph that specifies the covariates. In this example, ENTRY1, ENTRY2 and ENTRY3 provide the month, day and year when the survival time measurement began (the date of transplantation) and TERM1, TERM2 and TERM3 provide the month, day and year that each patient died or was last observed. The program automatically converts these dates to a time-on-study variable. The variable REJECT provides the STATUS of the patient, that is, whether the observation is complete or incomplete. RESPONSE indicates which values of the STATUS variable represent complete responses. Multiple response codes may be specified when appropriate. All other valid STATUS codes are treated as censored. The REGRESSION paragraph specifies that AGE, ANTIGEN and MISMATCH are to be used as covariates in this analysis. The instructions for this example are:

```
-------------------------------------
/ PROBLEM      TITLE IS 'STANFORD HEART TRANSPLANT
                DATA'.
/ INPUT        VARIABLES ARE 10.
              FORMAT IS FREE.
/ VARIABLE     NAMES ARE ENTRY1, ENTRY2, ENTRY3,
                TERM1,  TERM2,  TERM3,
                REJECT, AGE,     ANTIGEN,
                MISMATCH.
/ FORM         ENTRY = ENTRY1, ENTRY2, ENTRY3.
              TERMINATION = TERM1, TERM2, TERM3.
              STATUS = REJECT.  RESPONSE = 1.
/ REGRESSION COVARIATES = AGE, ANTIGEN, MISMATCH.
/ END
-------------------------------------
```

(See end of this P2L section for organization of systems information, BMDP instructions and data.)

Before discussing the results we describe the Cox (1972) proportional hazards regression model. The model is formulated in terms of the effects of the covariates upon death (hazard) rates rather than upon times to death. Suppose $h(t;\underset{\sim}{z})$ is the hazard rate for an individual with covariate vector $\underset{\sim}{z}$. The proportional hazards model is given by

$$h(t;\underset{\sim}{z}) = h_0(t)\exp(\underset{\sim}{\beta}'\underset{\sim}{z})$$

or

$$\ln\,[h(t;\underset{\sim}{z})/h_0(t)] = \underset{\sim}{\beta}'\underset{\sim}{z}$$

where β is a vector of unknown regression coefficients and $h_0(t)$ is an unknown hazard function for an individual with covariate vector $\underset{\sim}{z} = \underset{\sim}{0}$. Notice that no parametric model is assumed for the underlying survival function; it is completely arbitrary. The model implicitly contains two assumptions. The first assumption is the multiplicative relationship between the underlying hazard function and the log-linear function of the covariates (the proportionality assumption). Thus the ratio of the hazard functions for two individuals with different sets of covariates does not depend upon time. (We discuss models where the covariates themselves are functions of time later.) The second assumption of the model is the log-linear effect of the covariates upon the hazard function.

Table 19.4   Heart transplant data from Crowley and Hu (1973)

ENTRY1	ENTRY2	ENTRY3	TERM1	TERM2	TERM3	REJECT	AGE	ANTIGEN	MISMATCH
1	6	68	1	21	68	0	54	0	1.11
5	2	68	5	5	68	0	40	0	1.66
8	31	68	5	17	70	1	51	0	1.32
8	22	68	10	7	68	1	42	0	0.61
9	9	68	1	14	69	0	48	0	0.36
10	5	68	12	8	68	1	54	0	1.89
10	26	68	7	7	72	1	54	0	0.87
11	22	68	8	29	69	1	49	0	1.12
11	20	68	12	13	68	0	56	0	2.05
2	15	69	2	25	69	1	55	1	2.76
2	8	69	11	29	71	1	43	0	1.13
3	29	69	5	7	69	1	42	0	1.38
4	13	69	4	13	71	1	58	0	0.96
7	16	69	11	29	69	1	52	1	1.62
5	22	69	4	1	74	0	33	0	1.06
8	16	69	8	17	69	0	54	0	0.47
9	3	69	12	18	71	1	44	0	1.58
9	14	69	11	13	69	1	64	0	0.69
1	16	70	4	1	74	0	49	0	0.91
1	3	70	4	1	74	0	40	0	0.38
5	19	70	7	12	70	1	49	0	2.09
5	13	70	6	29	70	1	61	1	0.87
5	9	70	5	9	70	0	41	0	0.87
7	4	70	4	1	74	0	48	0	0.75
10	15	70	4	1	74	0	45	0	0.98
1	5	71	2	18	71	0	36	0	0.0
1	11	71	10	1	73	1	48	0	0.81
2	22	71	4	14	71	1	47	0	1.38
3	22	71	4	1	74	0	36	0	1.35
4	24	71	1	2	72	1	48	1	1.08
8	18	71	10	8	71	1	52	0	1.51
11	8	71	4	1	74	0	38	0	0.98
10	13	71	8	30	72	1	48	1	1.82
12	15	71	4	1	74	0	41	0	0.19
11	20	71	1	9	72	1	49	0	0.66
1	7	72	4	1	74	0	32	1	1.93
3	4	72	9	6	73	0	48	0	0.12
3	17	72	5	22	72	1	51	0	1.12
5	18	72	1	1	73	0	19	0	1.02
4	9	72	6	13	72	1	45	1	1.68
6	10	72	4	1	74	0	48	0	1.20
6	21	72	7	16	72	1	53	1	1.68
8	20	72	4	1	74	0	47	0	0.97
8	17	72	4	1	74	0	26	1	1.46
10	7	72	12	9	72	1	56	1	2.16
9	22	72	10	4	72	0	29	0	0.61
11	18	72	4	1	74	0	52	1	1.70
5	31	73	4	1	74	0	49	0	0.81
2	4	73	3	5	73	1	54	0	1.08
12	31	72	4	1	74	0	46	0	1.41
1	17	73	4	1	74	0	52	1	1.94
2	24	73	4	13	73	0	53	0	3.05
3	7	73	12	29	73	1	42	0	0.60
3	8	73	4	1	74	0	48	1	1.44
5	19	73	7	8	73	1	46	0	2.25
4	27	73	4	1	74	0	54	0	0.68
8	21	73	10	28	73	1	51	1	1.33
9	12	73	10	8	73	0	52	0	0.82
3	2	74	4	1	74	0	45	0	0.16
8	7	73	4	1	74	0	47	0	0.33
9	17	73	2	25	74	1	43	0	1.20
10	16	73	4	1	74	0	26	0	0.46
12	12	73	4	1	74	0	23	1	1.78
3	19	74	4	1	74	0	28	1	0.77
3	31	74	4	1	74	0	35	0	0.67

Key:

ENTRY1	
ENTRY2	Month, day, and year of transplant
ENTRY3	
TERM1	
TERM2	Month, day, and year of last
TERM3	observation
REJECT	Censoring status (0 = incomplete, 1 = complete)
AGE	Age at transplant
ANTIGEN	Antigen mismatch
MISMATCH	Tissue mismatch scores

Estimates of the regression parameters are obtained in the following way. Let $t_1 < t_2 < \ldots < t_k$ represent k distinct times to death among n observed survival times. The conditional probability that an individual with covariate vector z_i dies at time t_i given that a single death occurs at t_i and given the set R_i (indices of individuals at risk just prior to t_i) is the ratio of the hazards:

$$\exp(\underset{\sim}{\beta}'\underset{\sim}{z_i})\, / \sum_{j \in R_i} \exp(\underset{\sim}{\beta}'\underset{\sim}{z_j}) \; .$$

Multiplying these probabilities together for each of the k death times gives the partial likelihood function (Cox, 1975):

$$L(\beta) = \prod_{i=1}^{k} \left(\exp(\underset{\sim}{\beta}'\underset{\sim}{z_i}) \, / \sum_{j \in R_i} \exp(\underset{\sim}{\beta}'\underset{\sim}{z_j}) \right) \; .$$

Maximization of the partial likelihood function yields estimators of $\underset{\sim}{\beta}$ with properties similar to those of usual maximum likelihood estimators such as asymptotic normality. When there are ties among the death times P2L maximizes the likelihood proposed by Breslow (1974):

$$L(\underset{\sim}{\beta}) = \prod_{i=1}^{k} \left\{ \exp(\underset{\sim}{\beta}'\underset{\sim}{s_i}) \, / [\sum_{j \in R_i} \exp(\underset{\sim}{\beta}'\underset{\sim}{z_j})]^{m_i} \right\} \; .$$

Here m_i is the number of deaths at t_i and s_i is the vector sum of the covariates of the m_i individuals.

The results from Example 2L.1 are presented in Output 2L.1. Circled numbers below correspond to those in the output.

① Interpretation of the REGRESSION paragraph. All values listed have been preassigned.

② The first ten input data cases are listed. Optionally, the number of cases to be printed may be controlled by the user (p. 591).

③ Number of cases read. Cases that contain acceptable values for all variables specified in FORM and REGRESSION paragraphs are used in the analysis. A case is omitted from all computations when the value of any variable used in the analysis is missing or is out of range. If CODES are specified for a GROUPING variable, a case is included only if the value of the GROUPING variable is equal to one of the specified codes.

④ Status code information. If names are assigned to the status codes in the GROUP paragraph, the appropriate name is printed for each response time; otherwise the assumed names are DEAD and CENSORED.

⑤ The minimum, maximum, mean, standard deviation, skewness and kurtosis are reported for all covariates specified in the COVARIATE sentence.

⑥ A summary of the total number of patients dying and the number and percentage of censored observations.

⑦ The logarithm of the maximized partial likelihood function and the global chi-square statistic (and its p-value) are printed. The global chi-square statistic tests the hypothesis that all regression coefficients are identically zero. This statistic is defined as follows:

$$\underset{\sim}{U}'(0)\,\underset{\sim}{I}^{-1}(0)\,\underset{\sim}{U}(0)$$

where

$\underset{\sim}{U}(0)$ represents the vector of first derivatives of the partial likelihood function evaluated at $\underset{\sim}{\beta} = 0$

and

$$\underset{\sim}{I}(0) \left(\underset{\sim}{I}(0) = - \left. \frac{\partial^2 L(\underset{\sim}{\beta})}{\partial \underset{\sim}{\beta}^2} \right|_{\underset{\sim}{\beta}=0} \right) \text{denotes the observed}$$

information matrix (the negative of the matrix of second order partial derivatives) evaluated at $\underset{\sim}{\beta} = 0$.

The global chi-square has asymptotic chi-square distribution with degrees of freedom equal to the number of covariates in the model.

⑧ For each covariate, the computed parameter estimates, their asymptotic standard errors, the standardized parameters, and a conversion factor relating the effect of each covariate on the hazard function are given. No intercept parameter is estimated; the parameter estimates are translation invariant.

The regression coefficient indicates the relationship between the covariate and the hazard function. A positive coefficient increases the value of the hazard function and therefore indicates a negative relationship with survival. A negative coefficient has the reverse interpretation.

The REGRESSION Paragraph — Specification of Non-Time-dependent Covariates

The REGRESSION paragraph is used to specify the analysis to be performed. The paragraph is required and may be repeated for additional analyses of the same data (see p. 592). The covariate statement is used to specify covariates that do not vary with time.

REGRESsion ──────────────────────
  COVariates = v list.   none
    Names or subscripts of variables to be used as
    covariates.

Output 2L.1 Analysis of the Stanford heart transplant data by P2L. Circled numbers correspond to those in the text

```
TOLERANCE . . . . . . . . . . . . . . . . . . .  0.0000100
CONVERGENCE CRITERION . . . . . . . . . . . . .  0.0000100
MAXIMUM NUMBER OF ITERATIONS. . . . . . . . . .       15
STRATIFICATION VARIABLE . . . . . . . . . . . .     NONE        ①
PRINT SORTED DATA . . . . . . . . . . . . . .       NO
PLOT SURVIVAL FUNCTION. . . . . . . . . . . . .     NO
PLOT LOG MINUS LOG SURVIVAL FUNCTION. . . . . .     NO
PLOT CUMULATIVE HAZARD FOR ERROR. . . . . . . .     NO


NUMBER OF CASES TO BE PRINTED . . . . .    10
```

C A S E NO. LABEL	1 ENTRY1	2 ENTRY2	3 ENTRY3	4 TERM1	5 TERM2	6 TERM3	7 REJECT	8 AGE	9 ANTIGEN	10 MISMATCH
1	1	6	68	1	21	68	0	54	0	1.110
2	5	2	68	5	5	68	0	40	0	1.660
3	8	31	68	5	17	70	1	51	0	1.320
4	8	22	68	10	7	68	1	42	0	.610
5	9	9	68	1	14	69	0	48	0	.360
6	10	5	68	12	8	68	1	54	0	1.890
7	10	26	68	7	7	72	1	54	0	.870
8	11	22	68	8	29	69	1	49	0	1.120
9	11	20	68	12	13	68	0	56	0	2.050
10	2	15	69	2	25	69	1	55	1	2.760

② (circled beside cases)

```
NUMBER OF CASES READ. . . . . . . . . . . . . .    65  ③


              RESPONSE CODES . . . . . . . .    1    DEAD          ④

              CENSORED CODES . . . . . . . .    0    CENSORED
```

```
DESCRIPTIVE STATISTICS OF INDEPENDENT VARIABLES        ⑤
-------------------------------------------------
```

VARIABLE NO. N A M E	MINIMUM	MAXIMUM	MEAN	STANDARD DEVIATION	SKEWNESS	KURTOSIS
8 AGE	19.0000	64.0000	45.6769	9.1857	-0.87	3.48
9 ANTIGEN	0.0	1.0000	0.2615	0.4429	1.06	2.11
10 MISMATCH	0.0	3.0500	1.1646	0.6233	0.56	3.25

```
        STATUS CODE FREQUENCIES
                          PERCENT
    TOTAL    DEAD    CENSORED  CENSORED        ⑥
      65      29        36      0.5538
```

```
INDEPENDENT VARIABLES
    8 AGE        9 ANTIGEN    10 MISMATCH


    LOG LIKELIHOOD =    -87.8674                    ⑦
    GLOBAL CHI-SQUARE =     19.85  D.F.=   3  P-VALUE =0.0002
```

VARIABLE	COEFFICIENT	STANDARD ERROR	COEFF./S.E.	EXP(COEFF.)	
8 AGE	0.1091	0.0333	3.2769	1.1153	⑧
9 ANTIGEN	-0.0488	0.4716	-0.1034	0.9524	
10 MISMATCH	1.0638	0.3946	2.6959	2.8973	

Example 2L.2 Stratification — Accommodating Nonproportional Hazards

P2L provides an option to perform a stratified analysis. The proportionality assumption requires that the ratio of hazard rates for different levels of an independent variable must be constant. When this assumption is violated, Kalbfleisch and Prentice (1980) suggest stratifying the data so that cases within each strata conform to the proportional hazards model. The model is modified as follows:

$$h_j(t;\underset{\sim}{z}) = h_{oj}(t)\exp(\underset{\sim}{\beta}'\underset{\sim}{z})$$

where j represents one of s different strata. Under this model the arbitrary hazard function $h_{oj}(t)$ is allowed to be different for each stratum while the regression coefficients are the same across strata. With the stratified model, the likelihood maximized is the product of the individual stratum specific likelihoods. Use of the stratified model for graphically checking the proportionality assumption is described with the plot options.

Suppose we want to stratify the heart transplant data of Example 2L.1 into two age groups and perform a stratified analysis. We must designate how the data will be split in a GROUP paragraph and the

STRATIFICATION variable must be assigned in the REGRESSION paragraph. The analysis Control Language from Example 2L.1 would be modified as follows.

```
--------------------------------------
/ GROUP       CUTPOINT(8) = 45.
             NAMES(8)    = '45ORLESS', OVER45.
/ FORM        ENTRY = ENTRY1, ENTRY2, ENTRY3.
             TERMINATION = TERM1, TERM2, TERM3.
             STATUS = REJECT.  RESPONSE = 1.
/ REGRESSION COVARIATES = ANTIGEN, MISMATCH.
             STRATA = AGE.
--------------------------------------
```

The results of this example are presented in Output 2L.2. The parameter estimates and global chi-square statistic have been computed from the stratified model.

How to Request a Stratified Analysis

If a stratified analysis is desired, the variable containing codes for the stratification must be specified in the REGRESSION paragraph. If there are more than 10 codes or if cutpoints are used to specify the strata, the GROUP paragraph must be used to specify CODES or CUTPOINTS. The stratification variable is designated in a STRATA statement.

Output 2L.2   Results of a stratified analysis of the Stanford heart transplant data

----

VARIABLE NO. NAME	MINIMUM LIMIT	MAXIMUM LIMIT	MISSING CODE	CATEGORY CODE	CATEGORY NAME	INTERVAL RANGE GREATER THAN	LESS THAN OR = TO
8 AGE							
					45ORLESS		45.0000
					OVER45	45.0000	

STATUS CODE FREQUENCIES

	TOTAL	DEAD	CENSORED	PERCENT CENSORED
45ORLESS	25	7	18	0.7200
OVER45	40	22	18	0.4500
	----	----	----	
TOTALS	65	29	36	

INDEPENDENT VARIABLES
    9 ANTIGEN   10 MISMATCH

LOG LIKELIHOOD =   -77.5072
GLOBAL CHI-SQUARE =   8.79 D.F.= 2 P-VALUE =0.0124

VARIABLE	COEFFICIENT	STANDARD ERROR	COEFF./S.E.	EXP(COEFF.)
9 ANTIGEN	-0.1095	0.4804	-0.2280	0.8963
10 MISMATCH	1.1700	0.4299	2.7217	3.2221

REGRession ────────────────────────────────
  STRATA = v.   optional   no grouping
    Name or subscript of variable used for
    stratification. The baseline hazard rate
    function is estimated separately for each
    stratum. If STRATA is not specified or is set
    to zero, all data are treated as one group.

The PLOT Paragraph

You may request plots of the survival function, the log minus log survival function and a "residual" plot. The latter two plots may be used to check the proportionality assumption and goodness-of-fit. When STRATA are specified, the functions are estimated separately for each stratum. The following functions may be plotted:

a) Survival function, $\hat{S}(t;\underset{\sim}{z})$. Given a pattern of covariate values $\underset{\sim}{z}$, the estimated survival function is given by

$$\hat{S}(t;\underset{\sim}{z}) = [\hat{S}_o(t)]^{\exp(\hat{\underset{\sim}{\beta}}'\underset{\sim}{z})}\ .$$

where $\hat{S}_o(t)$ is the baseline survival function corresponding to survival at $\underset{\sim}{z} = \underset{\sim}{0}$.

b) Log minus log survival function, $\ln[-\ln \hat{S}(t;\bar{\underset{\sim}{z}})]$ where $\bar{\underset{\sim}{z}}$ is the mean of the covariates. The log minus log plot may be used to check the proportionality assumption. Specify strata based upon independent variables suspected of having a nonproportional effect upon the hazard rate function. The plot should exhibit constant differences between strata if the proportionality assumption holds (Kalbfleisch and Prentice, 1980).

c) Cumulative baseline hazard function for residuals. The residual for the i-th individual is defined by the following relationship:

$$e_i = -\ln \hat{S}(t_i, \underset{\sim}{z}_i) \qquad i=1,\ldots,n$$

P2L plots the cumulative hazard (unadjusted for covariates) of the residuals against the residual itself (see Appendix A.31). If the model fits the data, the e_i's should behave as a random sample of censored unit exponential variates, and the resulting plot should be a straight line of unit slope. Deviations from the unit slope line indicate lack-of-fit (Kay, 1977).

PLOT ────────────────────────────────
  TYPE = (one or more) SURV, LOG, FIT.   none
    Plot one or more of the following:
    SURV -- the cumulative survival function
            $\hat{S}(t;\underset{\sim}{z})$; the covariate vector $\underset{\sim}{z}$ must be
            specified in a PATTERN statement.
    LOG -- log minus log plot ($\ln(-\ln \hat{S}(t;\bar{\underset{\sim}{z}}))$)
    FIT -- goodness-of-fit plot based upon
            residuals.

When plots of the survival function are requested, the covariate vector defining survival must be specified in a PATTERN statement. The survival function may be plotted for different sets of covariates by repeating the PATTERN statement.

PLOT ────────────────────────────────
  PATTERN = # list.   may be repeated   none
    Covariate values which define the survival
    function. A value must be stated for each
    covariate in the regression.

You can specify the size of the plots to be printed in the following manner.

PLOT ────────────────────────────────
  SIZE = #, #.   100,50/prev.
    The first number is the number of characters
    (width) in the horizontal axis and the second
    number is the number of lines (height) in the
    vertical axis.

Example 2L.3 Plots of the Survival Curve, the Cumulative Hazard Function and Residuals

To illustrate the various plots, we simply add a PLOT paragraph to the Control Language of Example 2L.2. The additional specification is:

```
------------------------------------------
/ PLOT     TYPE = SURV, LOG, FIT.
          PATTERN = 0, 2.
          SIZE = 40, 25.
------------------------------------------
```

The PLOT paragraph requests a plot of the survival function, a log minus log survival plot,

Output 2L.3 Plots printed by P2L after the results in Output 2L.2

──

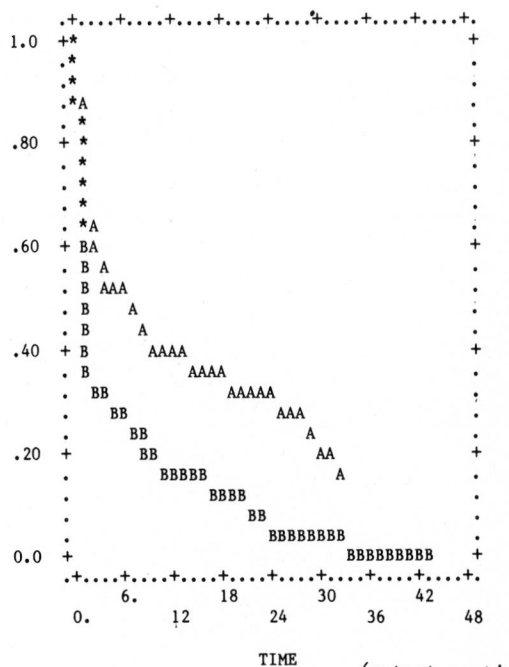

ESTIMATED SURVIVAL FUNCTION

(output continued)

and a residual plot. The survival function is estimated at covariate values of ANTIGEN = 0 and MISMATCH = 2. The resulting function plots are shown in Output 2L.3. In these plots the character 'A' represents the stratum corresponding to age 45 years or less and 'B' corresponds to age over 45 years.

Output 2L.3 (continued)

LOG MINUS LOG SURVIVAL FUNCTION

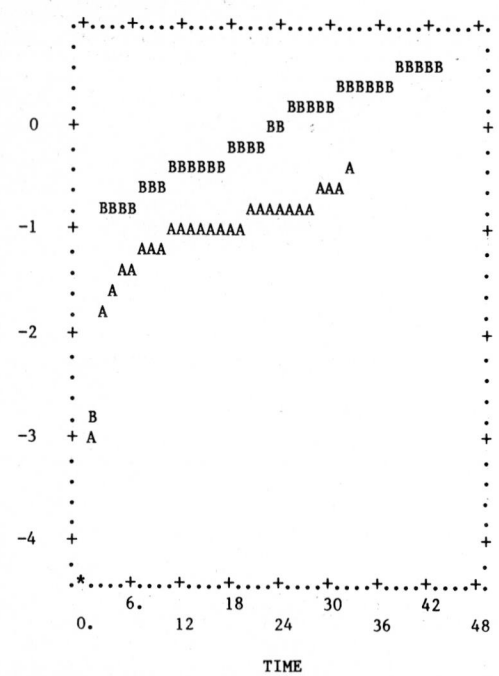

TIME

CUMULATIVE HAZARD FUNCTION OF RESIDUALS

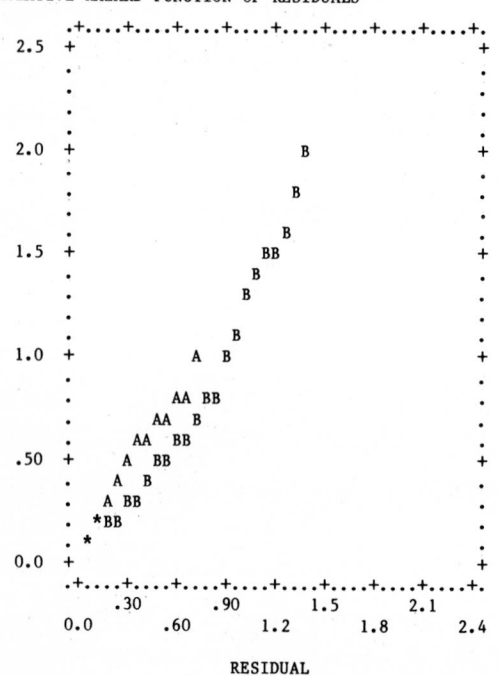

RESIDUAL

Example 2L.4 Time-dependent Covariates — Testing the Proportionality Assumption

Regression coefficients for models which include covariates expressible as simple functions of survival time may be computed with P2L. Models with time-dependent terms require additional Control Language to specify a function which defines the value of each time-dependent covariate in terms of the survival time variable. In this example, extracted from Kalbfleisch & Prentice (1980), a time-dependent covariate is used for testing the proportionality assumption. The data (Table 19.5) originally from Pike (1966) consist of survival times for two groups of rats that had been exposed to a carcinogen. We wish to fit the following conditional hazard function to the data:

$$h_o(t)\exp(\beta_1 z_1 + \beta_2 z_2(t))$$

where z_1 is an indicator variable denoting group and $z_2(t) = z_1(\ln t - 5.4)$. Notice that if the ratio of the hazards for the two groups is nearly constant for any value of time, then $\hat{\beta}_2$ should be close to zero.

Table 19.5 Survival times for two groups of rats (Pike, 1966)

SURVIVAL	FOLLOWUP	GROUP		SURVIVAL	FOLLOWUP	GROUP
143	1	0		156	1	1
164	1	0		163	1	1
188	1	0		198	1	1
188	1	0		205	1	1
190	1	0		232	1	1
192	1	0		232	1	1
206	1	0		233	1	1
209	1	0		233	1	1
213	1	0		233	1	1
216	1	0		233	1	1
220	1	0		239	1	1
227	1	0		240	1	1
230	1	0		261	1	1
234	1	0		280	1	1
246	1	0		280	1	1
265	1	0		296	1	1
304	1	0		296	1	1
216	0	0		323	1	1
244	0	0		204	0	1
142	1	1		344	0	1

Key:

SURVIVAL	Survival time (in days)
FOLLOWUP	Censoring status (0 = incomplete, 1 = complete)
GROUP	Group membership indicator

The Control Language for this example is given below.

```
------------------------------------
/ PROBLEM    TITLE IS 'CHECKING THE PROPORTIONALITY
                       ASSUMPTION'.
/ INPUT      VARIABLES ARE 3.    FORMAT IS FREE.
/ VARIABLE   NAMES ARE SURVIVAL, FOLLOWUP, GROUP.
/ FORM       TIME = SURVIVAL.   STATUS = FOLLOWUP.
            RESPONSE = 1.
/ PRINT      COVARIANCE.
/ REGRESS    COVARIATE = GROUP.   ADD = Z2.
/ FUNCTION   Z2 = GROUP*(LN(TIME) - 5.4).
/ END
------------------------------------
```

The PROBLEM, INPUT, and VARIABLE paragraphs describe the input data. The FORM paragraph indicates the variable SURVIVAL contains the time-to-response. The PRINT paragraph requests that the estimated asymptotic covariance matrix of the parameters be printed. One fixed covariate (GROUP) is specified in the REGRESSION paragraph as usual. The ADD sentence signifies that one time-dependent covariate called Z2 will be defined in the FUNCTION paragraph which follows. A name must be given for each time-dependent covariate to be added to the model.

Time-dependent covariates are defined in the FUNCTION paragraph using statements of the sort acceptable in the TRANSFORMATION paragraph. The time-dependent covariate is defined by appearing on the left hand side of an assignment statement. The word TIME is a reserved name which represents the value of the survival time variable.

The results for this example are shown in Output 2L.4. The usual statistics and the estimated asymptotic covariance matrix of the parameter estimates are given. The magnitude of the regression coefficient for the time-dependent term Z2 relative to its standard error (−.1258) does not suggest the proportional hazards model with the single fixed covariate GROUP is inappropriate.

Control Language for Time-dependent Covariates

When one or more covariates in a proportional hazards regression model is a function of survival time, additional Control Language is required. The names of time-dependent covariates in a model must be specified with an ADD statement in the REGRESSION paragraph. Fixed covariates are listed in the COVARIATE sentence as usual. When variables other than the covariates themselves must be used to define time-dependent covariates, they should be specified in a list of AUXILIARY variables.

```
REGRession ─────────────────────────────
   ADD = name list.                        none
      Names of time-dependent covariates defined in
      the FUNCTION paragraph.
   AUXiliary = v list. (optional)          none
      These variables are used to define
      time-dependent covariates.
```

Time-dependent covariates are defined in the FUNCTION paragraph.

The following rules apply to the FUNCTION paragraph.

- Syntax rules applicable to the transformation paragraph (Chapter 6) apply in the FUNCTION paragraph.
- Each time-dependent covariate must be assigned a value.
- Only variable names specified in the COVARIATE, ADD, or AUXILIARY sentences of the REGRESSION

Output 2L.4   Results for a model with a time-dependent covariate

```
-------------------------------------------------------------------------------------------------


                   INDEPENDENT VARIABLES
                     3 GROUP      4 Z2



          LOG LIKELIHOOD =   -100.7113
          GLOBAL CHI-SQUARE =      3.05  D.F.=   2  P-VALUE =0.2176

                                      STANDARD
              VARIABLE    COEFFICIENT   ERROR     COEFF./S.E.   EXP(COEFF.)
              --------    -----------  --------   -----------   -----------
              3 GROUP       -0.5998     0.3484     -1.7216        0.5489
              4 Z2          -0.2295     1.8249     -0.1258        0.7949




          ESTIMATED ASYMPTOTIC COVARIANCE MATRIX
          --------------------------------------

                            GROUP         Z2
                              3            4

              GROUP    3     0.1214
              Z2       4     0.0563       3.3302
```

paragraph may be used in the FUNCTION paragraph. Temporary names are allowed just as in the TRANSFORMATION paragraph.

- The word TIME is a reserved name which represents the current value of the survival time variable. Reserved words allowed in the TRANSFORMATION paragraph associated with data reading and case selection have no meaning in the context of the FUNCTION paragraph and are ignored. These words are NONB, KASE, USE, DELETE, TOOBIG, and TOOSMALL. XMIS may be used to detect missing values for auxiliary variables.

- The FUNCTION paragraph does not default between subproblems. Whenever time-dependent covariates are included in a regression model they must be stated explicitly.

Plots are not available for models with time-dependent covariates. Models with time-dependent covariates should be used with caution. Computation time necessary to obtain parameter estimates is much longer than the time required for models with only fixed covariates.

Defining Time-dependent Covariates with FORTRAN Statements

If time-dependent covariates cannot be defined conveniently using the constructs available in the FUNCTION paragraph, they may be defined using FORTRAN statements. Execution time may also be faster when FORTRAN statements are used. A user-supplied FORTRAN subroutine which calculates the value of time-dependent covariates temporarily becomes part of the P2L program by replacing a dummy subroutine. You may use both FORTRAN statements and FUNCTION Control Language statements to define the time-dependent covariates though this is not recommended. FORTRAN calculations are performed before any Control Language FUNCTION calculations.

The FORTRAN subroutine is called once for each case at risk at each distinct failure time. The first two statements of the subroutine are:

```
SUBROUTINE P2LFUN (Z, ZT, AUX, TIME, NFXCOV, NADD,
*                  NAUX, ISUBPR)
DIMENSION Z(1), ZT(1), AUX(1)
```

The following should not be changed

Z   - vector of fixed covariates corresponding to variables specified in the COVARIATE sentence of the REGRESSION paragraph

AUX   - vector of auxiliary variables corresponding to variables specified in the AUXILIARY sentence of the REGRESSION paragraph.

NFXCOV   - number of fixed covariates

NADD   - number of time-dependent covariates

NAUX   - number of auxiliary variables

ISUBPR   - subproblem number

The following must be evaluated in the subroutine: ZT(1), ZT(2), ..., ZT(NADD). These are the values of the time-dependent covariates evaluated at t=TIME.

The rules of FORTRAN apply in the subroutine (and not the rules of the Control Language). Any FORTRAN statements and functions are allowed. Notice however that the real variable arguments of P2LFUN are single precision. The time-dependent covariate in

Example 2L.4 would be specified in the FORTRAN subroutine as follows:

$$ZT(1) = Z(1)* (ALOG(TIME) - 5.4)$$

Example 2L.5 Time-dependent Covariates — Changes in Prognostic Status

Sometimes a patient's prognosis may change as a result of some event during the course of treatment. This example demonstrates how an event possibly altering prognosis may be included in a regression model as a time-dependent covariate. We return to the Stanford heart transplant study discussed in Example 2L.1. Patients were accepted in the transplant program and then waited until a suitable donor could be found. Some patients received hearts and some did not. (Example 2L.1 used data only on patients who had received transplants.) Table 19.6 contains data for 99 patients accepted into the transplant program. The variables are survival time (in days), censoring status, waiting time to transplant, age at transplant and mismatch score. Notice that not all information is available on nontransplanted patients.

In this example three prognostic variables will be defined which depend upon the transplantation time. The first covariate, transplant status, is an indicator variable equal to zero before transplantation and equal to one afterwards. Similarly, two other covariates, age at transplant and mismatch score, are zero before transplant and assume their measured value after transplant.

The Control Language for this example is given below. The FORM paragraph specifies the variable SURVIVAL contains the time-to-response. The REGRESSION paragraph indicates that the three time-dependent covariates are to be called XPLANT, XPLNTAGE and SCORE. The three AUXILIARY variables, waiting time to transplant (WAITTIME), age at transplant (AGE) and mismatch score (MISMATCH), are used in the FUNCTION paragraph to define the time-dependent covariates.

```
----------------------------------------
/ PROBLEM   TITLE IS 'HEART TRANSPLANT DATA WITH
                     TIME-DEPENDENT COVARIATES'.
/ INPUT     VARIABLES ARE 6.
            FORMAT IS '(2(F3.0, F5.0), F3.0, F5.2)'.
/ VARIABLE  NAMES ARE ID, SURVIVAL, FOLLOWUP,
                      WAITTIME, AGE, MISMATCH.
            BLANKS ARE MISSING.
/ FORM      TIME IS SURVIVAL.  STATUS IS FOLLOWUP.
            RESPONSE IS 1.
/ REGRESS   ADD IS XPLANT, XPLNTAGE, SCORE.
            AUXILIARY = WAITTIME, AGE, MISMATCH.
/ FUNCTION  XPLANT = 0.0.
            XPLNTAGE = 0.0.
            SCORE = 0.0.
            IF (TIME GE WAITTIME) THEN XPLANT = 1.0.
            IF (TIME GE WAITTIME) THEN XPLNTAGE=AGE.
            IF (TIME GE WAITTIME)
                THEN SCORE = MISMATCH.
/ PRINT     CASES ARE 10.  COVARIANCE.
/ END
----------------------------------------
```

The results of this example are given in Output 2L.5.

Table 19.6 Heart transplant data for 103 patients from Crowley and Hu (1973)

ID	SURVIVAL	FOLLOWUP	WAITTIME	AGE	MISMATCH
1	49	1			
2	5	1			
3	15	1	0	54	1.11
4	38	1	35	40	1.66
5	17	1			
6	2	1			
7	674	1	50	51	1.32
8	39	1			
9	84	1			
10	57	1	11	42	0.61
11	152	1	25	48	0.36
12	7	1			
13	80	1	16	54	1.89
14	1386	1	36	54	0.87
15	0	1			
16	307	1	27	49	1.12
17	35	1			
18	42	1	19	56	2.05
19	36	1			
20	27	1	17	55	2.76
21	1031	1	7	43	1.13
22	50	1	11	42	1.38
23	732	1	2	58	0.96
24	218	1	82	52	1.62
25	1799	0	24	33	1.06
26	1400	0			
27	262	1			
28	71	1	70	54	0.47
29	34	1			
30	851	1	15	44	1.58
31	15	1			
32	76	1	16	64	0.69
33	1586	0	50	49	0.91
34	1571	0	22	40	0.38
35	11	1			
36	99	1	45	49	2.09
37	65	1	18	61	0.87
38	4	1	4	41	0.87
40	1407	0	40	48	0.75
41	1321	0	57	45	0.98
42	2	1			
43	1	1			
44	39	1			
45	44	1	0	36	0.0
46	995	1	1	48	0.81
47	71	1	20	47	1.38
48	8	1			
49	1141	0	35	36	1.35
51	284	1	31	48	1.08
52	101	1			
54	2	1			
55	60	1	9	52	1.51
56	941	0	66	38	0.98
57	148	1			
58	342	1	20	48	1.82
59	915	0	77	41	0.19
60	52	1	2	49	0.66
61	1	1			
62	68	1			
63	841	0	26	32	1.93
64	583	1	32	48	0.12
65	77	1	11	51	1.12
66	31	1			
67	284	1	56	19	1.02
68	67	1	2	45	1.68
69	669	0	9	48	1.20
70	29	1	4	53	1.68
71	619	0	30	47	0.97
72	595	0	3	26	1.46
73	89	1	26	56	2.16
74	16	1	4	29	0.61
75	1	1			
76	544	0	45	52	1.70
77	20	1			
78	514	0	209	49	0.81
79	95	1	66	54	1.08
80	481	0	25	46	1.41
81	444	0	5	52	1.94
82	427	0			
83	79	1	31	53	3.05
84	333	1	36	42	0.60
85	4	1			
86	396	0	7	48	1.44
87	109	1	59	46	2.25
88	369	0	30	54	0.68
89	206	1	138	51	1.33
90	185	1	159	52	0.82
91	339	1			
92	339	0	309	45	0.16
93	264	0	27	47	0.33
94	164	1	3	43	1.20
96	179	0	12	26	0.46
97	130	0	20	23	1.78
98	108	0	95	28	0.77
99	20	1			
100	38	0	37	35	0.67
101	30	0			
102	10	0			
103	5	1			

Key:

ID	Patient identification	WAITTIME	Waiting time to transplant
SURVIVAL	Survival time	AGE	Age at transplant
FOLLOWUP	Censoring status (0 = incomplete, 1 = complete)	MISMATCH	Tissue mismatch score

---

Output 2L.5 Results for the Stanford heart transplant data using time-dependent covariates

```
-----------------------------------------------------------------------------------------------

                  INDEPENDENT VARIABLES
                     7 XPLANT        8 XPLNTAGE      9 SCORE


             LOG LIKELIHOOD =   -275.9557
             GLOBAL CHI-SQUARE =      9.01  D.F.=   3  P-VALUE =0.0291

                                              STANDARD
                    VARIABLE     COEFFICIENT     ERROR    COEFF./S.E.   EXP(COEFF.)
                    --------     -----------   --------   -----------   -----------
                  7 XPLANT         -3.1780       1.1861     -2.6793        0.0417
                  8 XPLNTAGE        0.0552       0.0226      2.4423        1.0567
                  9 SCORE           0.4442       0.2803      1.5851        1.5593


             ESTIMATED ASYMPTOTIC COVARIANCE MATRIX
             ---------------------------------------

                               XPLANT       XPLNTAGE       SCORE
                                  7             8             9

             XPLANT      7       1.4069
             XPLNTAGE    8      -0.0246        0.0005
             SCORE       9      -0.0870       -0.0003       0.0785

-----------------------------------------------------------------------------------------------
```

Table 19.7 Multiple myeloma data from Krall, Uthoff and Harley (1975)

KASEID	SURVIVAL	FOLLOWUP	LOGBUN	HGB	PLATELET	INFEC	AGE	SEX	LOGWBC	FRAC	LOGPBM	PLYMPH	PMYELOID	PROTEIN	BJP	TSP	SGLOBIN	SCALC
1	1.25	1	2.2175	9.4	1	0	67	1	3.6628	1	1.9542	0	0	12	2	11	7	10
2	1.25	1	1.9395	12.0	1	1	38	1	3.9868	1	1.9542	0	0	20	1	6	3	18
3	2.00	1	1.5185	9.8	1	1	81	1	3.8751	1	2.0000	0	0	2	1	11	8	15
4	2.00	1	1.7482	11.3	0	0	75	1	3.8062	1	1.2553	13	52	0	2	9	6	12
5	2.00	1	1.3010	5.1	0	0	57	1	3.7243	1	2.0000	0	0	3	1	10	6	9
6	3.00	1	1.5441	6.7	1	1	46	2	4.4757	0	1.9345	3	5	12	2	9	3	10
7	5.00	1	2.2355	10.1	1	0	50	2	4.9542	1	1.6628	8	27	4	1	6	4	9
8	6.00	1	1.6812	6.5	1	0	74	1	3.7324	0	1.7324	1	25	5	2	10	7	9
9	6.00	1	1.3617	9.0	1	1	77	1	3.5441	1	1.4624	7	51	1	2	7	5	8
10	6.00	1	2.1139	10.2	0	0	70	2	3.5441	1	1.3617	6	68	1	2	9	7	8
11	6.00	1	1.1139	9.7	1	0	60	1	3.5185	1	1.3979	11	30	0	2	11	7	10
12	6.00	1	1.4150	10.4	1	0	67	2	3.9294	1	1.6902	10	33	0	2	10	6	8
13	7.00	1	1.9777	9.5	1	0	48	1	3.3617	1	1.5682	9	41	5	2	9	3	10
14	7.00	1	1.0414	5.1	0	0	61	2	3.7324	1	2.0000	0	0	1	2	8	4	10
15	7.00	1	1.1761	11.4	1	0	53	1	3.7243	1	1.5185	13	42	1	1	9	6	13
16	9.00	1	1.7243	8.2	1	0	55	1	3.7993	1	1.7404	4	31	0	2	9	6	12
17	11.00	1	1.1139	14.0	1	0	61	1	3.8808	1	1.2788	8	49	0	2	9	5	10
18	11.00	1	1.2304	12.0	1	0	43	1	3.7709	1	1.1761	7	48	1	1	12	8	9
19	11.00	1	1.3010	13.2	1	0	65	1	3.7993	1	1.8195	4	21	1	2	8	4	10
20	11.00	1	1.5682	7.5	1	0	70	1	3.8865	0	1.6721	5	35	0	2	7	5	12
21	11.00	1	1.0792	9.6	1	0	51	2	3.5051	1	1.9031	5	10	0	2	7	3	9
22	13.00	1	0.7782	5.5	0	1	60	2	3.5798	1	1.3979	12	55	2	2	10	8	10
23	14.00	1	1.3979	14.6	1	1	66	1	3.7243	1	1.2553	7	51	2	1	9	4	10
24	15.00	1	1.6021	10.6	1	0	70	1	3.6902	1	1.4314	16	46	0	2	9	5	11
25	16.00	1	1.3424	9.0	1	0	48	1	3.9345	1	2.0000	0	0	0	2	8	4	10
26	16.00	1	1.3222	8.8	1	0	62	2	3.6990	1	0.6990	5	41	17	2	8	4	10
27	17.00	1	1.2304	10.0	1	0	53	1	3.8808	1	1.4472	9	50	4	2	10	7	9
28	17.00	1	1.5911	11.2	1	1	68	1	3.4314	1	1.6128	1	46	1	2	9	6	10
29	18.00	1	1.4472	7.5	1	0	65	2	3.5682	0	0.9031	17	46	7	2	6	4	8
30	19.00	1	1.0792	14.4	1	0	51	1	3.9191	1	2.0000	0	0	6	2	13	7	15
31	19.00	1	1.2553	7.5	0	0	60	2	3.7924	1	1.9294	2	10	5	1	6	3	9
32	24.00	1	1.3010	14.6	1	0	56	2	4.0899	1	0.4771	12	52	0	2	4	3	9
33	25.00	1	1.0000	12.4	1	0	67	1	3.8195	1	1.6435	3	23	0	2	7	3	10
34	26.00	1	1.2304	11.2	1	0	49	2	3.6201	1	2.0000	0	0	27	1	6	3	11
35	32.00	1	1.3222	10.6	1	0	46	1	3.6990	1	1.6335	6	32	1	2	12	8	9
36	35.00	1	1.1139	7.0	0	0	48	1	3.6532	1	1.1761	16	42	4	1	12	9	10
37	37.00	1	1.6021	11.0	1	0	63	1	3.9542	0	1.2041	10	53	7	1	7	4	9
38	41.00	1	1.0000	10.2	1	0	69	1	3.4771	1	1.4771	5	30	6	1	10	6	10
39	41.00	1	1.4161	5.0	1	0	70	2	3.5185	1	1.3424	18	53	0	2	7	4	9
40	51.00	1	1.5682	7.7	0	0	74	1	3.4150	1	1.0414	10	50	4	1	12	8	13
41	52.00	1	1.0000	10.1	1	0	60	2	3.8573	1	1.6532	1	27	4	1	10	7	10
42	54.00	1	1.2553	9.0	1	0	49	1	3.7243	1	1.6990	8	37	2	1	8	3	10
43	58.00	1	1.2041	12.1	1	0	42	2	3.6990	1	1.5798	9	35	33	1	7	4	10
44	66.00	1	1.4472	6.6	1	0	59	1	3.7853	1	1.8195	4	22	0	2	5	3	9
45	67.00	1	1.3222	12.8	1	0	52	1	3.6453	1	1.0414	24	54	1	1	11	7	10
56	88.00	1	1.1761	10.6	1	0	47	2	3.5563	0	1.7559	22	17	21	1	6	3	9
47	89.00	1	1.3222	14.0	1	1	63	1	3.6532	1	1.6232	7	38	1	1	9	7	9
48	92.00	1	1.4314	11.0	1	0	58	2	4.0755	1	1.4150	12	36	4	1	9	6	11
49	4.00	0	1.9542	10.2	1	0	59	1	4.0453	0	0.7782	21	51	12	1	7	3	10
50	4.00	0	1.9243	10.0	1	1	49	2	3.9590	0	1.6232	21	24	0	2	17	12	13
51	7.00	0	1.1139	12.4	1	0	48	2	3.7993	1	1.8593	1	11	0	2	6	3	10
52	7.00	0	1.5315	10.2	1	1	81	1	3.5911	0	1.8808	1	16	0	2	12	10	11
53	8.00	0	1.0792	9.9	1	0	57	2	3.8325	1	1.6532	1	40	0	2	8	4	8
54	12.00	0	1.1461	11.0	1	0	46	2	3.6435	0	1.1461	7	47	0	2	7	3	7
55	11.00	0	1.6128	14.0	1	0	60	1	3.7324	1	1.8451	0	0	3	1	6	2	9
56	12.00	0	1.3979	8.8	1	0	66	2	3.8388	1	1.3617	8	50	0	2	9	5	9
57	13.00	0	1.6628	4.9	0	0	71	2	3.6435	1	1.7924	2	21	0	2	10	11	9
58	16.00	0	1.1461	13.0	1	0	55	1	3.8573	0	0.9031	13	53	0	2	9	5	9
59	19.00	0	1.3222	10.0	1	0	59	2	3.7709	1	2.0000	0	0	1	2	8	4	10
60	19.00	0	1.3222	10.8	0	0	69	2	3.8808	1	1.5185	0	0	0	2	10	7	10
61	28.00	0	1.2304	7.3	1	1	82	2	3.7482	1	1.6721	7	40	0	2	7	4	9
62	41.00	0	1.7559	12.8	1	0	72	1	3.7243	1	1.4472	2	56	1	1	7	3	9
63	53.00	0	1.1139	12.0	1	0	66	1	3.6128	1	2.0000	0	0	1	2	6	3	11
64	57.00	0	1.2553	12.5	1	0	66	1	3.9685	0	1.9542	0	0	0	2	8	4	11
65	77.00	0	1.0792	14.0	1	0	60	1	3.6812	0	0.9542	4	50	0	2	6	3	12

Key:

KASEID	Case identification
SURVIVAL	Survival time
FOLLOWUP	Censoring status (0 = incomplete, 1 = complete)
LOGBUN	Log blood urea nitrogen
HGB	Hemoglobin
PLATELET	Platelets (0 = abnormal, 1 = normal)
INFEC	Infections (0 = none, 1 = present)
AGE	Age at diagnosis
SEX	Sex (1 = male, 2 = female)
LOGWBC	Log white blood cell count
FRAC	Fractures (0 = no, 1 = yes)
LOGPBM	Log percent plasma cells in bone marrow
PLYMPH	Percent lymphocytes in peripheral blood
PMYELOID	percent myeloid cells in peripheral blood
PROTEIN	Proteinuria at diagnosis
BJP	Bence Jones protein in urine
TSP	Total serum protein
SGLOBIN	Serum globin
SCALC	Serum calcium

Example 2L.6 Stepwise Regression

This example illustrates use of the stepwise option using data reported by Krall, Uthoff and Harley (1975) and given in Table 19.7. The data consist of survival times on 65 multiple myeloma patients with 16 concomitant variables. Forty-eight of the observations represent deaths and 17 are incomplete.

The BMDP instructions for this example are shown below.

```
-----------------------------------------
/ PROBLEM      TITLE IS 'MULTIPLE MYELOMA DATA'.
/ INPUT        VARIABLES ARE 19.    FORMAT IS FREE.
/ VARIABLE     NAMES ARE KASEID, SURVIVAL, FOLLOWUP,
                         LOGBUN, HGB, PLATELET, INFEC,
                         AGE, SEX, LOGWBC, FRAC,
                         LOGPBM, PLYMPH, PMYELOID,
                         PROTEIN, BJP, TSP, SGLOBIN,
                         SCALC.
/ FORM         TIME IS SURVIVAL.   STATUS IS FOLLOWUP.
               RESPONSE IS 1.
/ REGRESSION   COVARIATES ARE 4 TO 19.
               STEPWISE IS MPLR.
/ END
-----------------------------------------
```

The statement

STEPWISE = MPLR.

invokes stepwise selection using the MPLR (maximum partial likelihood ratio) method. With the MPLR method covariates are entered or removed on the basis of significance probabilities calculated from a large sample partial likelihood ratio test. (Another method, faster in computational time, is also available.) The assumed limit for significance to enter a term is 0.10, and the limit to remove a term is 0.15.

At each step, the stepwise algorithm prints the following statistics (circled numbers correspond to those in Output 2L.6):

⑨ the log of the maximized partial likelihood function, a chi-square statistic that measures the change in the log likelihood value from the previous step, and the global chi-square value (and their p-values).

⑩ for each variable in the model, the computed parameter estimates, their asymptotic standard errors, the standardized parameters, and the factor

Output 2L.6 Results of the stepwise algorithm using the multiple myeloma data. Circled numbers refer to those in the output

---

```
         STEP NUMBER  1            LOGBUN   IS ENTERED
         ---------------

                    LOG LIKELIHOOD = -151.0161
         IMPROVEMENT CHI-SQUARE  ( 2*(LN(MPLR) ) =     7.68  D.F.=  1  P-VALUE =0.0056    ⑨
                    GLOBAL CHI-SQUARE =     8.36  D.F.=  1  P-VALUE =0.0038

                                    STANDARD
            VARIABLE    COEFFICIENT    ERROR   COEFF./S.E.    EXP(COEFF.)     ⑩
            --------    -----------   --------  -----------   -----------
         4 LOGBUN         1.7556       0.6125     2.8663        5.7870
```

```
         STATISTICS TO ENTER OR REMOVE VARIABLES
         ----------------------------------------
                         APPROX.      APPROX.
               VARIABLE  CHI-SQ.      CHI-SQ.                      LOG
         NO. N A M E     ENTER        REMOVE    P-VALUE       LIKELIHOOD      ⑪

          4 LOGBUN                     7.68      0.0056       -154.8580
          5 HGB           3.41                   0.0650       -149.3131
          6 PLATELET      1.84                   0.1754       -150.0980
          7 INFEC         0.74                   0.3900       -150.6466
          8 AGE           0.86                   0.3539       -150.5864
          9 SEX           0.09                   0.7614       -150.9700
         10 LOGWBC        0.11                   0.7382       -150.9602
         11 FRAC          1.03                   0.3095       -150.4998
         12 LOGPBM        1.16                   0.2814       -150.4360
         13 PLYMPH        0.76                   0.3820       -150.6340
         14 PMYELOID      1.37                   0.2410       -150.3288
         15 PROTEIN       0.33                   0.5636       -150.8493
         16 BJP           2.83                   0.0925       -149.6009
         17 TSP           1.72                   0.1901       -150.1577
         18 SGLOBIN       0.53                   0.4652       -150.7494
         19 SCALC         1.44                   0.2297       -150.2947
```

```
         SUMMARY OF STEPWISE RESULTS
         ---------------------------
         STEP  VARIABLE              VARIABLE        LOG     IMPROVEMENT           GLOBAL
         NO    ENTERED      DF       REMOVED     LIKELIHOOD  CHI-SQUARE P-VALUE  CHI-SQUARE P-VALUE
         ---   -------      --       --------    ----------  ---------- -------  ---------- -------
          0                                       -154.858
          1    4 LOGBUN      1                     -151.016     7.684    0.006      8.361    0.004
          2    5 HGB         2                     -149.313     3.406    0.065     11.793    0.003
```

---

relating the effect of the variable on the hazard function. If requested in the PRINT paragraph, the asymptotic covariance and correlation matrix of the estimated parameters is given when there is more than one variable in the model.

(11) for each variable eligible to be moved in or out of the model, the approximate chi-square to enter or remove, the p-value and the log likelihood if the variable is moved.

(12) When no variables pass the entry or removal limits a summary table is printed. The table lists the variables entered or removed at each step, the value of the log likelihood function, the chi-square and associated p-value for measuring the change in the log likelihood from the previous step, and the global chi-square.

Selection of Prognostic Variables Using Stepwise Regression

After preliminary checks of the proportionality assumption, a large number of independent variables may be candidates for inclusion in a model. The P2L stepwise selection option allows automatic identification of a subset of independent variables which are significantly related to survival. At each step a variable is entered (or removed) from the regression equation on the basis of a computed significance probability.

The stepwise option allows significance probabilities to be estimated in either of two ways:

- The MPLR method computes the significance probabilities on the basis of a large sample partial likelihood ratio test using the chi-square value calculated from the log of the ratio of the maximized partial likelihood functions:

$$MPLR = 2 \left| \log(L(\hat{\beta}_{current})/L(\hat{\beta}_{candidate})) \right| .$$

- The PHH method computes significance probabilities to enter a variable using the statistic proposed by Peduzzi, Hardy and Holford (1980). The statistic is calculated as follows:

For candidate variable j, the vector of first derivatives of the partial likelihood function $U(\hat{\beta})$ and the observed information matrix $I(\hat{\beta})$ is calculated using current parameter estimates for those variables already in the model and zero for the candidate variable. The tail probability of $U_j^2(\hat{\beta})I_{jj}^{-1}(\hat{\beta})$ is calculated from the chi-square distribution with one degree of freedom. Here $U_j(\hat{\beta})$ represents the j-th component of $U(\hat{\beta})$ corresponding to the candidate variable and $I_{jj}(\hat{\beta})$ is the j-th diagonal element of $I(\hat{\beta})$. The distribution of the statistic is unknown, but is assumed to have an asymptotic chi-square distribution with one degree of freedom. For this reason, p-values computed should be used for descriptive purposes only.

The criterion for removal of a variable using the PHH option is based upon the asymptotic normality of the maximized partial likelihood estimates. The j-th variable is removed if the significance probability of $\hat{\beta}_j^2/Var(\hat{\beta}_j)$ exceeds the limit for removing a variable when compared to the chi-square distribution with one degree of freedom.

The PHH option is provided as an alternative to the MPLR method because computing partial likelihood ratio tests for each variable at each step may require considerable computer time for a large data set. There is no guarantee that both of these methods will select the same subset of variables for any given problem. We suggest using the PHH method to eliminate variables with little or no relationship to survival and then continuing with the MPLR method.

After the chi-square statistics and their corresponding p-values have been computed, the variable with the largest p-value is removed if it is larger than the REMOVE limit. If no variable has a p-value larger than the REMOVE limit, the term with the smallest p-value is entered if it is less than the ENTER limit.

```
REGRession ─────────────────────────────────
  STEPwise = (one only) MPLR, PHH.         none
    The method used for assessing the significance
    probability of each variable to be entered or
    removed.
    MPLR (maximum partial likelihood ratio test)
    PHH (Peduzzi-Hardy-Holford statistic)
  REMOVE = #.                           0.15/prev.
    Value used as limits of p-value to remove
    terms.
  ENTER = #.                            0.10/prev.
    Value used as limits of p-value to enter terms.
```

Controlling the Stepwise Process

This section describes how to influence which variables are entered or removed from the regression equation by the stepwise procedure. All covariates, whether fixed or time-dependent, are normally eligible to be used. For each covariate you may specify whether the variable should be forced into the model at the first step and the number of times each covariate is allowed to move in or out of the model.

Suppose the regression specification in Example 2L.6 was

COVARIATES = LOGWBC, LOGBUN, PLATELET.

For each covariate listed in the COVARIATE sentence (plus time-dependent covariates, if any) you can state whether the variable should be included at the beginning of the stepwise process with a START sentence. For example, the statement

START = IN, OUT, OUT.

used with the COVARIATE sentence above causes LOGWBC (the logarithm of white blood cell count) to be IN the regression equation at the first step and LOGBUN (the logarithm of blood urea nitrogen) and PLATELET to be OUT of the equation at step 1. Backward elimination results when all covariates are forced into the regression at the first step.

You may specify the number of times each covariate is allowed to move in or out of the regression equation. The statement

$$MOVE = 0, 2, 2.$$

used together with the statements above allows LOGBUN and PLATELET to move twice while LOGWBC is not allowed to move. The combination of forcing a variable into the regression equation (LOGWBC in our example) and then not allowing it to be removed in subsequent steps guarantees that the variable will be in the final regression model. This technique is useful when certain variables are known to be related to survival prior to analysis and must be included in any meaningful model. The MOVE limit also prevents possible cycling of a variable in and out of the model.

```
REGRession
  START = IN or OUT (or 1 or 2).    OUT, ..., OUT
    Indicates whether a covariate is in or out of
    the regression equation at the first step. When
    time-dependent covariates are used, their
    starting information follows the starting
    specification for the fixed covariates in the
    list.
  MOVE = # list.                      2, ..., 2
    The maximum number of times the corresponding
    covariates can be moved in or out of the
    regression equation. The number of moves for
    time-dependent covariates follows those for
    fixed covariates in the list. Each term is
    allowed to move twice unless otherwise
    specified.
```

Control of the Newton-Raphson Algorithm

The partial likelihood function is maximized using the iterative Newton-Raphson algorithm. The initial values for the parameter estimates are assumed to be zero unless otherwise specified in an INITIAL sentence. Zero starting values indicate the covariates have no effect upon survival. The algorithm terminates when the relative improvement in the partial likelihood function is less than the value of the CONVERGENCE criterion or when the maximum number of ITERATIONS has been reached.

When there is no improvement in the partial likelihood function between successive iterations, the computed parameter correction vector is halved and the partial likelihood function is recomputed. The halving process is repeated until the partial likelihood function is greater than in the previous iteration, or until the maximum number of HALVINGS has been reached. If the maximum number of HALVINGS is reached before increase in partial likelihood, computations terminate. When this occurs, you should reevaluate the suitability of your data and model.

If only plots are desired and you have parameter estimates from a past analysis, the Newton-Raphson algorithm may be bypassed to save the cost of recomputing the parameter estimates. Specify ITERATIONS = 0. to bypass it. When no iterations are specified, the parameter estimates to be used in plot calculations must be given in the INITIAL sentence.

The tolerance for inversion of the information matrix (the negative of the matrix of second order partial derivatives of the partial likelihood

function) is controlled by the TOLERANCE limit. A parameter estimate is not changed at an iteration if it fails the tolerance test. The tolerance check is described in Appendix A.11.

```
REGRession
  CONVergence = #.                    0.00001/prev.
    A number used as the convergence criterion of
    the partial likelihood function. A solution is
    reached when the relative improvement of the
    partial likelihood function is less than the
    value of the CONVERGENCE criterion.
  ITERation = #.                            15/prev.
    The maximum number of iterations allowed to
    maximize the partial likelihood function.
  HALving = #.                               5/prev.
    The maximum number of step halvings allowed.
  TOLerance = #.                      0.00001/prev.
    The value used as the tolerance limit in the
    inversion of the information matrix. The
    inverse and all partial derivatives are
    calculated in double precision.
  INITial = # list.                   0.0,...,0.0/prev.
    Initial values for parameter estimates
    corresponding in sequence and number to
    variables listed in the COVARIATE sentence.
```

Hypothesis Testing

Tests of the joint significance of subsets of regression coefficients which have been fit according to the REGRESSION paragraph may be requested by including a TEST paragraph in the Control Language. For example, you may wish to test for treatment effects while adjusting for baseline patient characteristics. This may be accomplished by indicating names of variables corresponding to the effects to be tested in the ELIMINATE sentence of the TEST paragraph. Multiple hypotheses may be tested by repeating the ELIMINATE sentence with different variable names. The p-values printed have not been adjusted for multiple significance tests. The TEST paragraph is ignored when the program is run in stepwise mode.

Three different large sample significance tests may be computed (see Rao, 1973):

(1) The likelihood ratio test is constructed by calculating the difference of log likelihoods under the full model (all covariates) and the restricted model (maximization restricted to variables not eliminated)

$$LRATIO = 2[\ln L(\hat{\beta}_{Full}) - \ln L(\hat{\beta}_{Restricted})] .$$

(2) The Wald test is based upon the asymptotic normality property of maximum likelihood estimates. Let $\hat{\beta}*$ represent the subset of MLE's obtained under the full model corresponding to the effects to be eliminated. Then,

$$WALD = \hat{\beta}*[\hat{COV}(\hat{\beta}*)]^{-1}\hat{\beta}* .$$

(3) The Score function test is based upon the derivatives of the partial likelihood function. Let $U(\beta_0)$ and $I(\beta_0)$ represent the vector of first derivatives and the observed information matrix.

These functions are evaluated using parameter estimates calculated under the restricted model with coefficients ELIMINATED constrained to zero.

$$SCORE = U'(\underset{\sim}{\beta}_o)I^{-1}(\underset{\sim}{\beta}_o)U(\underset{\sim}{\beta}_o)$$

All three statistics are compared with the chi-square distribution with degrees of freedom equal to the number of effects eliminated. Liu and Crowley (1978) give conditions under which the MLE's obtained from the partial likelihood function have an asymptotic multivariate normal distribution. To date, the asymptotic distribution of the likelihood ratio and the score function tests based upon the partial likelihood function have not been proved to be chi-square.

```
TEST
   ELIMinate = v list.   may be            optional
                         repeated
      Names or subscripts of covariates for which
      corresponding regression coefficients are to be
      tested for significance. This option is ignored
      if stepwise selection is requested.
   STATistics = (one or more)           WALD/prev.
                WALD, LRATIO, SCORE.
      Calculate one or more of the following
      statistics:
      WALD   - test based upon the asymptotic
               normality of the MLE's
      LRATIO - likelihood ratio test
      SCORE  - test based upon derivatives of the
               partial likelihood function
```

Describing the Survival Time Variable — the FORM Paragraph

The FORM paragraph is required by P2L to describe the structure of the survival time variable. The form of such data may occur in many ways. Commonly used structures may be directly input to the program. Data occurring in other forms may be transformed (Chapter 6) to one of these structures.

How to Use the Patient's Survival Time as Input

For survival time input (Examples 2L.4–2L.6) one variable contains the TIME that the subject is observed (to the response or until withdrawn or lost to follow-up), while a second variable, STATUS, contains codes, one (or more) to indicate the occurrence of a response and up to nine types of censored observations. A third variable, RESPONSE, is used to indicate which codes in the variable STATUS may be treated as responses (deaths). All eligible codes (i.e., not equal to the missing value code or out of range) not listed in RESPONSE are assumed to be censored. Censoring commonly is due to loss to follow-up (e.g., the patient has moved or dropped out of the study) and withdrawals (the patient is still alive at the end of the study or at the time of analysis). Separate codes may exist for different causes of death. These may be treated as responses (deaths), or as censored observations. All censored values are treated identically in the analysis.

If NAMES are given to the CODES of the STATUS variable in the GROUP paragraph, the names are used to label the results. Otherwise, if multiple codes are specified in RESPONSE, the names DEAD1, DEAD2, ..., appear in the summary tables. Multiple censored observations are named CENSRD1, CENSRD2, ..., where CENSRD1 corresponds to the smallest code encountered in the data which is not specified in RESPONSE, CENSRD2 is the second, etc. The correspondence between names and codes is printed in the output.

You may also identify values of the codes representing censored observations that are losses. This is frequently useful in understanding the data, but in no way influences the analysis. All eligible codes not listed in either RESPONSE or LOSS are censored. When names are not specified for the values of STATUS in the GROUP paragraph, default names for values in LOSS are LOST1, LOST2, ...

```
FORM
   TIME = v.                                    none
      Name or subscript of the variable that contains
      the survival times.
   STATus = v.                                  none
      Name or subscript of the variable that contains
      the status of the patient in the study. The
      variable can have at most ten distinct values
      (the total of deaths, losses, and other
      censored observations).
   RESPonse = # list.            first code of
                                  STATUS variable
      Numbers specifying which values of the STATUS
      variable are to be treated as deaths
      (RESPONSES).
   LOSS = # list.                               none
      Numbers specifying which values of the STATUS
      variable are to be treated as losses.
```

How to Use Study Entry and Termination Dates as Input

This form of input, illustrated in Example 2L.1, is similar to the time-status input. Instead of a time-on-study variable, the data are presented as two sets of dates; one set providing the month, day and year of ENTRY onto the study, the second set providing the date of TERMINATION. P2L automatically converts these two sets of dates into a time-on-study variable, which is assumed to be in months, unless otherwise specified.

In Example 2L.1, the date of ENTRY is recorded in variables ENTRY1 (month), ENTRY2 (day) and ENTRY3 (year) and date of TERMINATION is recorded in variables TERM1 (month), TERM2 (day) and TERM3 (year). The statements

```
        ENTRY = ENTRY1, ENTRY2, ENTRY3.
        TERMINATION = TERM1, TERM2, TERM3.
```

in the FORM paragraph define the survival time variable. P2L can also analyze the data if you record only two date variables, such as month and year. For example, if your date of ENTRY is recorded in variables 2 (month) and 3 (year), you would specify

$$ENTRY = 2, (3)3.$$

and TERMINATION would be similarly specified. (The (3) is the tab indication specifying that values are given for the third parameter, but not the second.) Note that if both the year of entry and termination occur after 1900, only the last two digits need be present (e.g., 77 instead of 1977). If one date is earlier than 1900, both years must be given in their entirety.

Frequently, TERMINATION is only present when a patient dies or is lost to follow-up, and no date is punched for a patient still alive at the end of the study or the time of analysis. You may specify a cut-off, or analysis date which will be treated as the date of CENSORING for patients still on study. The appropriate status code for those individuals will be generated by P2L.

STATUS, RESPONSE and LOSS specifications are as in the time input form (Examples 2L.4 - 2L.6).

FORM

ENTRY = v_1, v_2, v_3.   none
Names or subscripts of the variables representing month, day and year of patient entry into the study. Note the <u>order is required</u>. You can specify one, two or three variables; for example, month and year is specified as ENTRY = v_1, (3)v_3.

TERMination = v_1, v_2, v_3.   none
Names or subscripts of variables representing month, day and year of termination. Note the <u>order is required.</u>

CENSOR = #,#,#.   none
Numbers indicating the date (month, day and year) when the study terminates or the date for the analysis. This is used only with date-status input and is necessary only when there is no date of TERMINATION for some of the censored observations.

Changing the Units of Time Measurement

You may want to specify the unit of time that you would like printed in the output. Or, if your data are in the form of dates, you may wish to choose the appropriate scale for the calculation of the survival curve.

FORM

UNIT = (one only)   MONTH/prev.
    DAY, WEEK, MONTH, YEAR.
or UNIT = c.
Unit for labeling the time scale in the output. If DAY, WEEK, MONTH, or YEAR are specified, and the data are in the form of dates, the specified UNIT will be used in the calculations.

Specification for Optional Output

Several options are available which control the amount of printed output.

PRINT

CASES = #.   10/prev.
Number of raw input data cases to be printed.

ITERations.   no/prev.
Print log likelihood and parameter estimates at each Newton-Raphson step.

CORRelation.   no/prev.
Print estimated asymptotic correlation matrix.

COVAriance.   no/prev.
Print estimated asymptotic covariance matrix.

SURVIVAL.   no/prev.
Print sorted survival times, Kaplan-Meier survival function, hazard, cumulative hazard and survival functions under the proportional hazards model, and residuals (p. 581). If a stratification variable is specified, results are printed for each stratum separately. This option is not available with time-dependent covariates.

Multiple Analyses (Subproblems)

It is possible to request more than one analysis of the data defined in the INPUT paragraph within each PROBLEM. Each separate analysis specification is called a subproblem. Subproblems may be used to

(1) perform several analyses of the same survival time variable using different sets of covariates or options or
(2) redefine the survival time variable or censoring information.

The REGRESSION paragraph must appear in every subproblem. Optionally the GROUP, PRINT, FORM, FUNCTION, TEST and PLOT paragraphs may be redefined. If not, preassigned values from the previous subproblem are used. The FUNCTION paragraph must be respecified for every subproblem with time-dependent covariates. Each batch of subproblem paragraphs must terminate with an END paragraph. Subproblems are placed at the very end of a problem after the data cards, if any (see Summary, p. 592).

COMPUTATIONAL METHOD

The data are read and transformations performed in single precision. All subsequent computations are performed in double precision. Cases with missing values or data outside limits are excluded from the analysis. Mean covariate values across all cases are subtracted from each fixed covariate.

The computational procedure is described in detail in Appendix A.31.

SIZE OF PROBLEM

The number of cases that can be handled by P2L is dependent on the amount of storage space supplied to the program. Appendix B gives formulas for estimating the amount of space needed and describes how to increase storage capacity.

ACKNOWLEDGEMENT

P2L was designed and programmed by Alan Hopkins. Contributions to the design were made by Nancy Flournoy, Jacqueline Benedetti, and Michael Tarter. Assistance in developing the program was obtained from James Frane, Jerry Toporek, Larry Young and Laszlo Engelman.

SUMMARY

Order of Input Cards

A. Function Specified in Control Language
```
// (job card)
// EXEC BIMED,PROG=BMDP2L        (see Appendix E)
//SYSIN DD *
/ PROBLEM
/ INPUT
/ VARIABLE
/ TRANSFORM
/ SAVE
/ GROUP
/ PRINT
/ FORM
/ REGRESS
/ FUNCTION
/ TEST
/ PLOT
/ END
    (data, if on cards)
/ GROUP
/ PRINT
/ FORM           Analysis specification for
/ REGRESS        additional subproblems.
/ FUNCTION       May be repeated for additional
/ TEST           analyses of the same data.
/ PLOT
/ END
// (system card)
```

B. Function Specified in Fortran Statements
```
// (job card)
// EXEC BIMEDT,PROG=BMDP2L
//FUN DD *
      FORTRAN statements - for IBM OS, do not
      include SUBROUTINE and DIMENSION statements
      at the beginning and RETURN and END at the
      end.
//GO.SYSIN DD *
/ PROBLEM
/ INPUT
/ VARIABLE
/ TRANSFORM
/ SAVE
/ GROUP
/ PRINT
/ FORM
/ REGRESS
/ TEST
/ PLOT
/ END
    (data, if on cards)
/ GROUP
/ PRINT
/ FORM           Analysis specification for
/ REGRESS        additional subproblems.
/ TEST           May be repeated for additional
/ PLOT           analyses of the same data.
/ END
// (system card)
```

Full sets of BMDP paragraphs and data can be repeated for additional problems.

Paragraph Statement	Preassigned	Comment and Manual Reference
/ PRINT		Optional to control printed output. 591
CASES = #.	10.	Number of data cases to be printed after transformations. *
ITERations.	no	Print values of the log-likelihood and parameter estimates for intermediate iterations. *
CORRelation.	no	Estimated asymptotic correlation matrix of parameters. *
COVAriance.	no	Estimated asymptotic covariance matrix of parameters. *
SURVIVAL.	no	Print sorted data table. (not available with time-dependent covariates) *

/ FORM		Required to describe the survival variables. There are two forms of input: (1) Survival time input, (2) Dates as input.
UNIT = c.	MONTH	Units of time measurement. Can be any word, but if DAY, WEEK, MONTH or YEAR is used, the program calculates the appropriate information from the dates to express results in your selected unit. * 591
<u>Survival time input</u>		Time on study is recorded for each patient. 590
TIME = v.	none	Name or subscript of variable that contains the survival time for each patient. *
STATus = v.	none	Name or subscript of variable that contains codes to define a patient's status. Use with RESP and LOSS (below). Codes not listed in either RESP or LOSS are censored. NAMES can be given to CODES in / GROUP.
RESPonse = # list.	lowest	Codes of STAT variable that indicate response (e.g., death). If omitted, the lowest code of the STAT variable is considered a response.
LOSS = # list.	none	Codes of the STAT variable that represent censored observations that are lost to follow up. *
<u>Dates as input</u>		Entry and termination dates are given for each patient. Dates are given as three variables: month, day, year. If you skip a variable, use the tab feature (p. 29).
ENTRY = v,v,v.	none	Names or subscripts of three variables containing month, day and year of patient entry. Order is required. * 591
TERMination = v,v,v.	none	Names or subscripts of three variables containing month, day and year of patient termination. Order is required. If termination date is missing, a user-supplied CENSOR date is substituted. * 591
STATus = v.	none	Name or subscript of variable containing CODES to define a patient's status. NAMES can be given to CODES in / GROUP paragraph. * 590
RESPonse = # list.	lowest	Codes of STAT variable that indicate response (e.g., death). If omitted, the lowest code of the STAT variable is considered a response. * 590
LOSS = # list.	none	Codes of the STAT variable that represent censored observations that are lost to follow up. * 590
CENSOR = #,#,#.	none	Three numbers indicating month, day and year study ended or analysis was observations is available. * 591

(continued)

(continued)

Paragraph Statement	Preassigned	Comment and Manual Reference
/ REGRession		Required to describe regression model.
COVAriates = v list.		Names or subscripts of fixed covariates. 578
STRATA = v.	none	Name or subscript used to define strata membership. 581
Stepwise Options		
STEPwise = (one only) MPLR, PHH.	none	Stepwise selection method. 588
REMOVE = #.	0.15	Value used as limits of p-values to remove variables with stepwise regression option. * 588
ENTER = #.	0.10	Value used as limit of p-values to enter variables with stepwise regression option. * 588
START = (one for each variable) IN, OUT.	OUT,...,OUT	One for each covariate specified. 589
MOVE = # list.	2, ..., 2	Maximum number of times a covariate may be moved. 589
Newton-Raphson Options		See p. 589.
CONVergence = #.	.00001	Convergence criterion. *
ITERations = #.	15.	Maximum number of iterations. *
HALVings = #.	5.	Maximum number of step halvings. *
TOLerance = #.	.00001	Tolerance limit for matrix inversion. *
INITial = # list.	0.0,0.0,...	Initial values of parameters estimates. *
Time-Dependent Covariates		See p. 583.
ADD = name list.	none	Names of time-dependent covariates. A name must be given for each time-dependent covariate.
AUXiliary = v list.		Variables used to define the time-dependent covariates.
/ FUNction		Required with time-dependent covariates. User-supplied functions specify time-dependent covariates. 583
		Syntax rules applicable to the TRANSFORMATION paragraph apply. The variable TIME is a reserved name representing the current value of the survival time variable.
/ TEST		Optional. May be used to specify significance tests. 590
ELIMinate = v list.	none	Subset of covariates analyzed for which a joint test of significance is desired. May be repeated.
STATistics = c list.	WALD.	Print the following test statistics (one or more): *
		WALD - test based upon asymptotic normality of MLE's
		LRATIO - likelihood ratio test
		SCORE - test based upon derivatives of the log likelihood
/ PLOT		Optional. 581
TYPE = c list.	none	Print the following plots (one or more):
		SURV - survival function
		LOG - log minus log survival function
		FIT - goodness of fit plot using residuals
PATtern = # list.	none	Pattern of covariates defining the survival function. May be repeated for multiple plots. Must be stated if a plot of the survival function is requested.
SIZE = #, #.	100, 50.	Width of the x-axis (characters); height of the y-axis (lines).

Key:

/	–indicates paragraph		*	–assigned value remains the same for additional problems or subproblems
.	–period ends a sentence			
●	–required		VT	–number of variables after transformations
v	–variable (name or subscript)		list	–more than one item, often one per var.
g	–group (name or subscript)			
#	–number			Capitalized letters-paragraph or sentence names recognized by BMDP
'c'	–characters (name or parameter) may omit apostrophes if contiguous letters only			Page numbers following refer to this Manual

20
TIME SERIES ANALYSIS

A time series is a sequence of measurements made at regular time intervals, such as yearly gross national product (GNP), monthly unemployment, or daily temperatures. The goals of an analysis of one or more time series vary from one application to the next. We may initially seek descriptive statistics and simple graphical displays to gain a better appreciation of the data. For example, we might plot daily temperatures over time, or, if the data are extensive, we might average the daily temperatures within each month and then plot these monthly averages over time. Such results are useful in themselves by revealing various features of the data. They can also help us formulate further questions about the data.

Another possible goal in time series analysis is to build and verify a model for the series. We might, for example, model the GNP for each year as dependent on the GNP in previous years. A more ambitious model might relate the GNP to the annual balance of trade.

Modeling can be regarded as a refined description of how a single time series or system of time series works. Modeling may also be viewed as an important step toward another goal in time series analysis: to predict or control a time series. For example, the government uses a model to predict unemployment in future months and may also take actions based on the model to reduce the level of unemployment. Time series methods have also been applied to the control of certain operations in a paper mill, the automatic pilot in a ship, and many other mechanized processes.

Researchers have developed two approaches to time series analysis, a frequency domain (or spectral) approach, and a time domain (or finite parameter or Box-Jenkins) approach. The frequency domain and time domain approaches are embodied in programs P1T and P2T respectively. We describe these two programs in detail on the following pages :

P1T -- Univariate and Bivariate Spectral   p. 604
       Analysis
P2T -- Box-Jenkins Analysis   p. 639

In the remainder of this section we discuss the two programs in more general terms.

A Frequency Domain Approach: Spectral Analysis

One example of a time series is the annual number of Canadian lynx trappings for the years 1821–1934 shown in Figure 20.1 below.

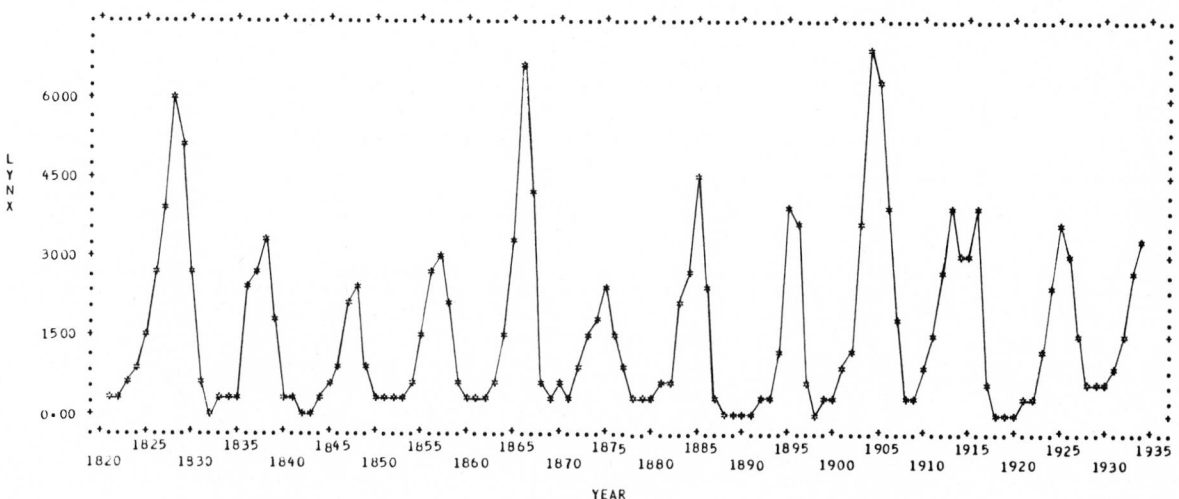

Figure 20.1   Lynx trappings 1821–1934 from Campbell and Walker (1977)

These data display an oscillatory behavior common to many time series. Noting the approximate 10-year cycle, we might try fitting a sine wave to the data of the same period. The result is shown in Figure 20.2. In Figure 20.3, a single point represents the amplitude and frequency (approximately one-tenth of a cycle per year) of the sine wave.

While the sine wave in Figure 20.2 matches the location of the peaks in the data, no single sine wave can mimic the irregular peak heights. A somewhat better fit is obtained by using a sum of sine waves, shown in Figure 20.4. The sum consists of seven sine waves with periods ranging from $7\frac{1}{2}$ to

$12\frac{1}{2}$ years. The corresponding frequencies thus fall in a band centered about .1 cycles per year. Figure 20.5 represents the frequency and amplitude of the individual sine waves forming the sum.

In Figure 20.6 the sine wave sum extends over not one but five frequency bands, further improving the approximation to the data. The frequencies and amplitudes of the individual terms are represented in Figure 20.7. Of course, we can perfectly fit the data if we use a sufficient number of terms, i.e., frequencies, in the approximating sine wave sum. The frequency representation of a perfectly fitting sine wave sum is shown in Figure 20.8.

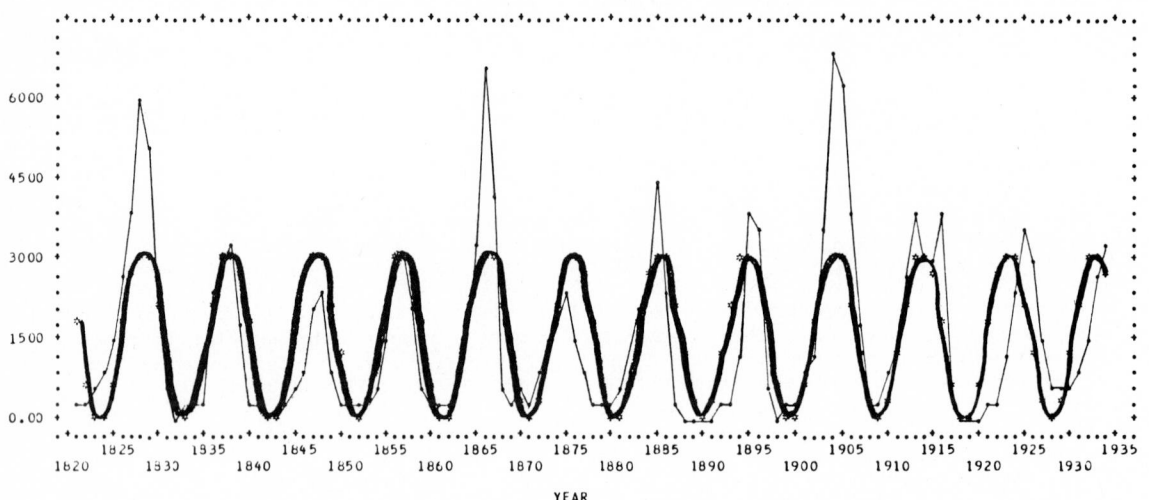

Figure 20.2   A sine wave fit by least squares to the lynx data

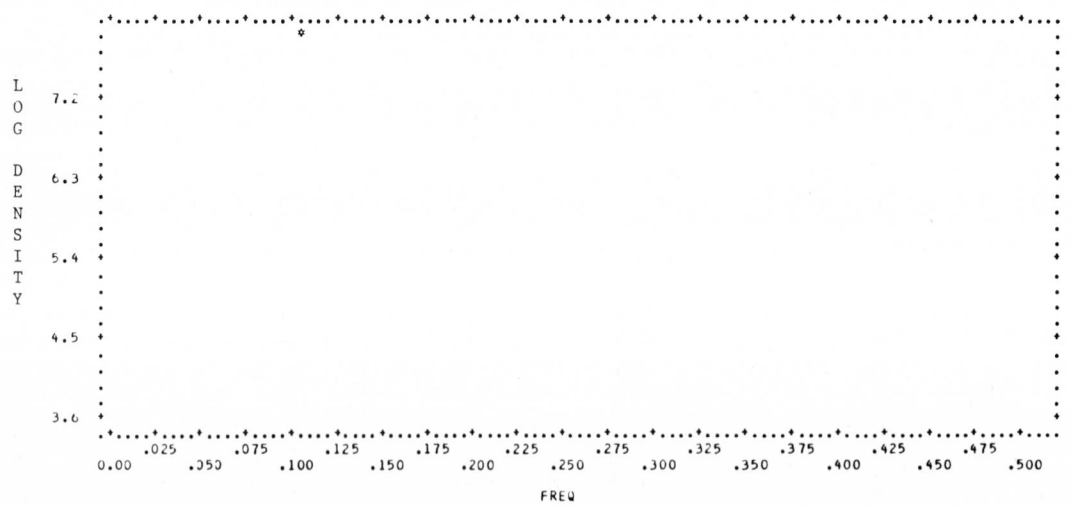

Figure 20.3   Frequency domain representation of the sine waves in Figure 20.2[1]

---

[1] Each plotted point represents the amplitude and frequency of an individual sine wave being summed. We have squared the amplitude, divided it by the width of the frequency interval it represents, and then taken the logarithm base 10 to be compatible with the spectrum plotted in Figure 20.9. Values in Figures 20.3, 20.5, and 20.7 are thus taken from the log periodogram in Figure 20.8.

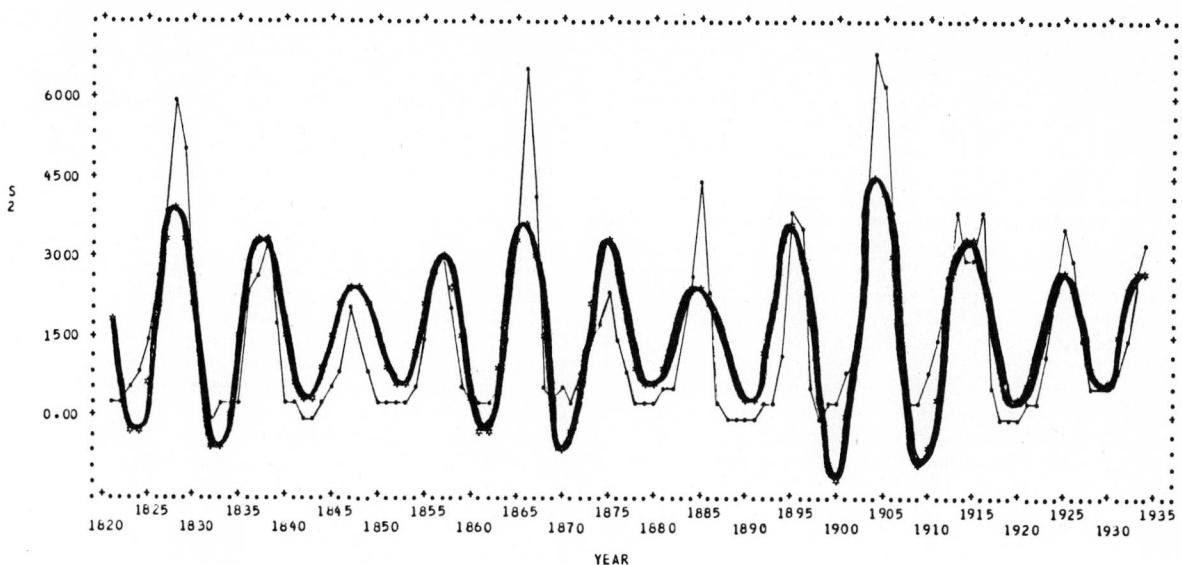

Figure 20.4   A sum of sine waves fit to the lynx data in one frequency band

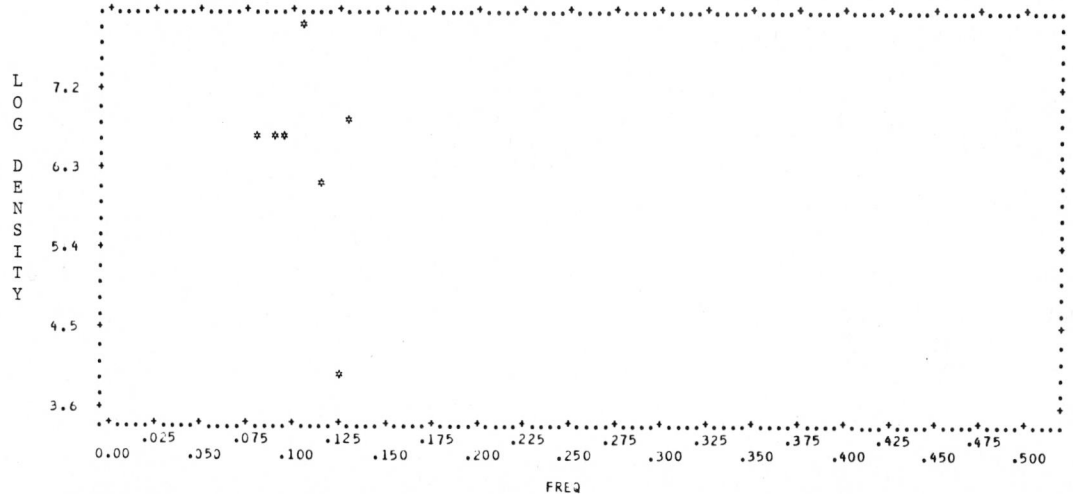

Figure 20.5   Frequency domain representation of the sum of sine waves in Figure 20.4[1]

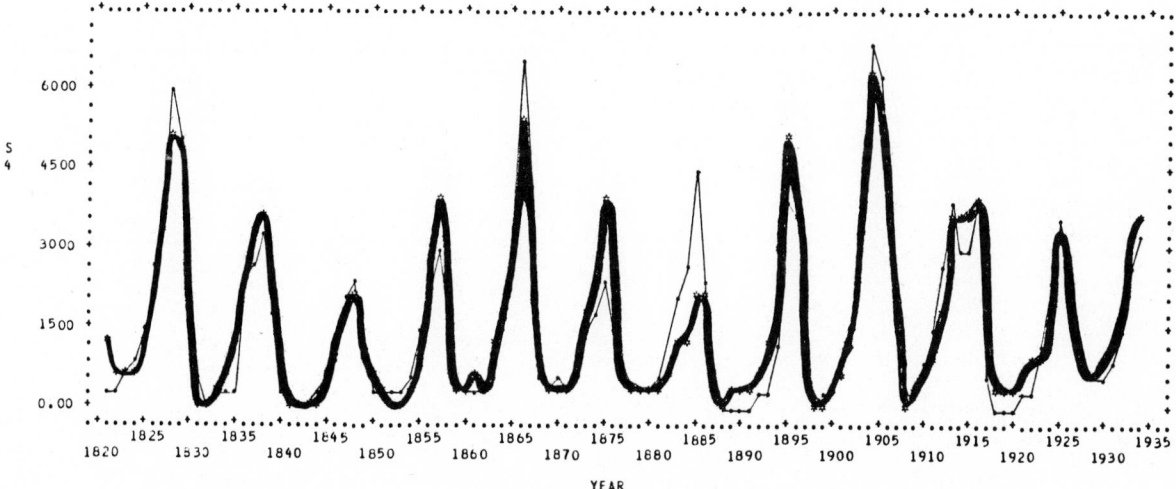

Figure 20.6   A sum of sine waves fit to the lynx data in five frequency bands

The method we have illustrated above is that of harmonic analysis. It consists of ascribing the variation in the data to a fixed set of sine waves at different frequencies, or periods. This method has met with some success in accurately predicting tides and other quite regular phenomena. But most time series, like the lynx trappings depicted above, require a great many frequencies, or periods, before an adequate fit is achieved. In fact, the number of needed frequencies is usually a substantial fraction of the number of observed data points so that very little statistical reliability can be attached to the final result.

Around the turn of the century, A. Shuster initiated a transition from harmonic analysis to present day frequency domain analysis by studying the periodogram of various time series. This is a frequency domain representation similar to those shown in Figures 20.3, 20.5, and 20.7, but based on a complete set of sine waves whose sum perfectly matches the observed time series. The periodogram of the lynx data is plotted on a log scale in Figure 20.8. Shuster and others looked for peaks in the periodogram that would reveal hidden periods, or frequencies, that would explain the variation in the data. The largest value shown in Figure 20.8 corresponds to the sine wave plotted in Figure 20.2. This method of analyzing periodograms was a more systematic way of analyzing time series, but seldom provided more insight than a plot of the data over time. Shuster's periodogram analyses did, however, serve as a catalyst for further developments.

The problems besetting harmonic analysis led to its generalization in the 1930's and 40's, most notably by A.N. Kolmogorov in the Soviet Union and by Norbert Wiener in the United States. These and

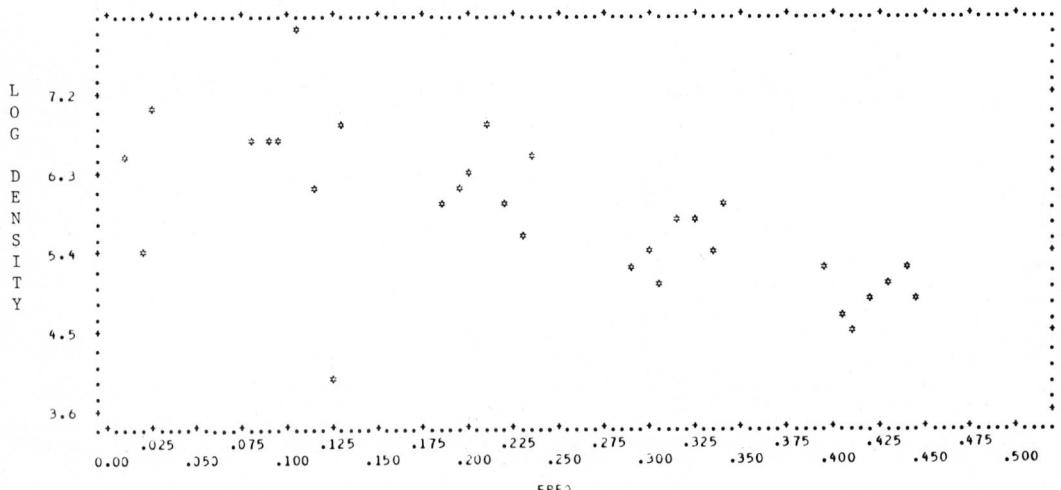

Figure 20.7   Frequency domain representation of the sum of sine waves in Figure 20.6[1]

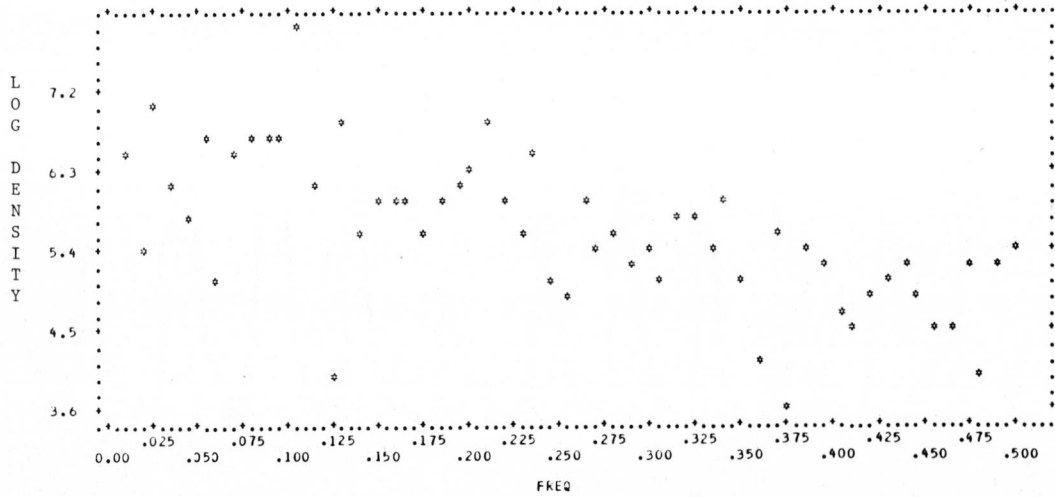

Figure 20.8   Frequency domain representation of a sine wave sum perfectly fitting the lynx data[1]

other scientists laid the foundations for present day spectral analysis, also known as frequency domain analysis.

In the frequency domain approach to time series analysis, we assume that each frequency (period) within a given continuous range, contributes to some extent to the variation of the data over time. The aim of spectral analysis is to assess how much of the variation in the data arises from various frequency bands, such as the frequency band containing the $7\frac{1}{2}$ to $12\frac{1}{2}$-year periods mentioned above. The spectral density function gives the distribution of the variance of the data over different frequency bands. An estimate of the spectral density function for the lynx data is shown on a log scale in Figure 20.9. It is essentially a smoothed version of Figure 20.8. The large peak near frequency 0.1 corresponds to the roughly 10-year

periodic character of the lynx data. The breadth of this peak indicates that the data are not so sharply periodic as the sine wave in Figure 20.2. The estimated spectral density thus provides a means for us to gauge the relative contribution of a given frequency band to the total variation of the data.

Pairs of variables may be similarly analyzed. The prime concern is often to see in which frequency bands the two variables have high coherence, a measure of linear association analogous to squared correlation. We can also estimate a linear regression of one variable upon another in a succession of frequency bands. This frequency domain bivariate analysis is illustrated in the P1T program description.

In practical time series analysis, the data often vary from one point to the next in an irregular fashion that we can conveniently smooth out before

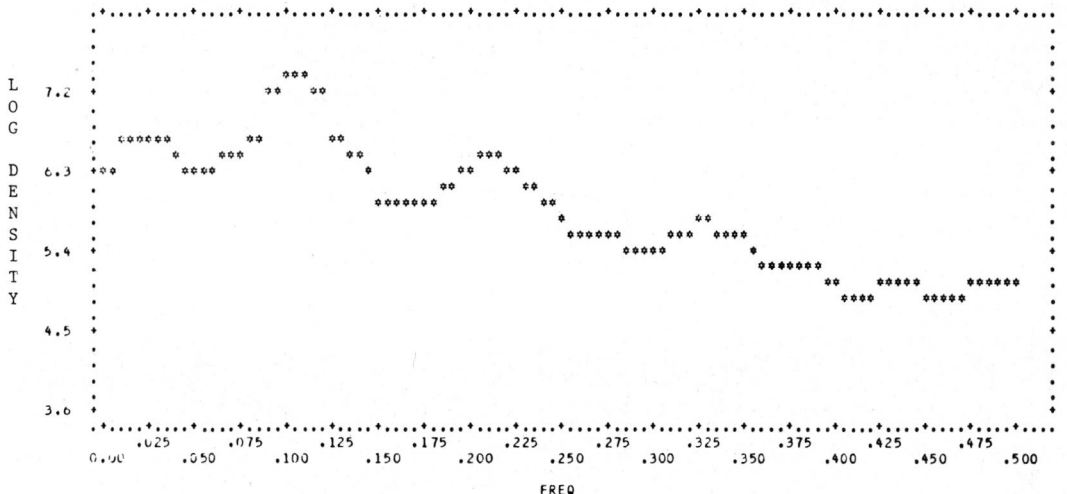

Figure 20.9   An estimate of the spectral density of the lynx trappings

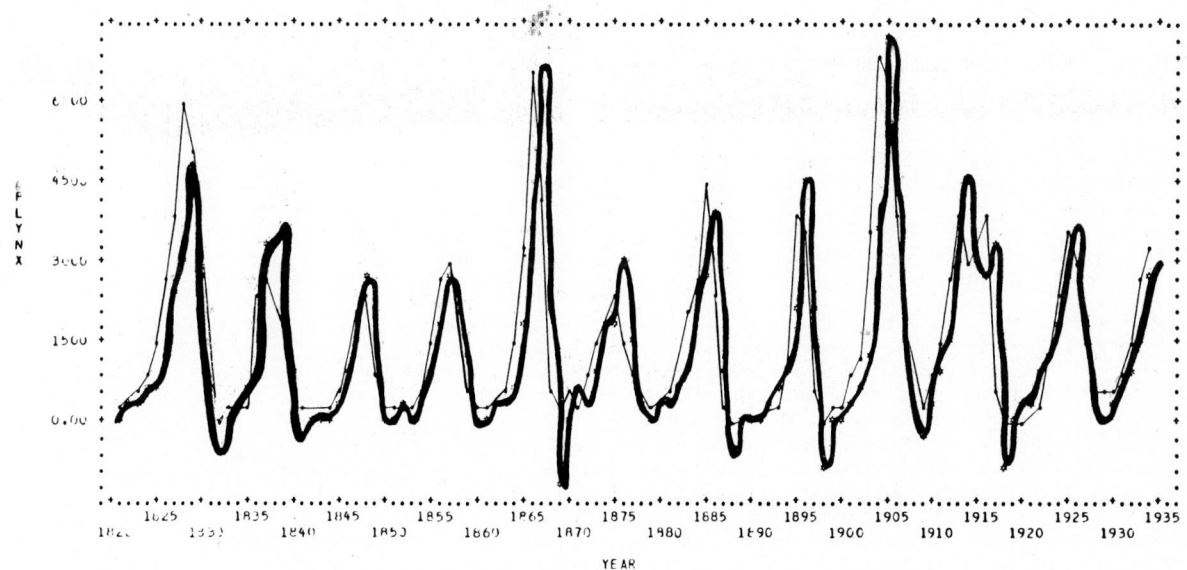

Figure 20.10   Observed and predicted annual lynx trappings

we attempt to analyze the data. For example, the Austrian meteorologist Julius von Hann would apply the numerical operation

$$Z(t) = \tfrac{1}{4}Y(t+1) + \tfrac{1}{2}Y(t) + \tfrac{1}{4}Y(t-1)$$

where $Y(t)$ might be a series of pressures or temperatures and where $Z(t)$ would be a smoothed version of $Y(t)$. This application of a fixed linear combination to an input series $Y(t)$, thereby producing an output series $Z(t)$, is called linear filtering. The operation is also simply referred to as a linear filter.

A linear filter can be characterized by its effect upon pure sine waves of different frequencies. The filter above preserves the slowly varying low frequency components of $Y(t)$ and attenuates the rapidly varying high frequency components. This causes $Z(t)$ to be a smoother sequence than $Y(t)$, so that the von Hann filter is an example of a lowpass or smoothing linear filter.

There are many types of linear filters and many uses for them. They are further discussed and illustrated in the program descriptions.

Just as von Hann smoothed his data, we may want to perform other operations on the data prior to analysis. For example, the yearly GNP has an upward trend that needs to be removed in some way as preparation to further analysis of this series. Similarly, average monthly temperatures have a predominant yearly cycle. A simple method of removing this effect is to subtract the average January temperature from each of the individual January temperatures, and to do the same for the remaining months of the year. The idea here is to remove some obvious effects in the data to allow the more subtle features to emerge. To this end, P1T will detrend or seasonally adjust the data upon request.

Other uses of the program include convenient viewing of the data, the detection of outliers, the replacement of missing values, and the estimation of autocovariance or autoregression coefficients. The primary function, however, is to perform a spectral analysis of any individual time series or of any pair of time series.

A Time Domain Approach: Box-Jenkins Analysis

In contrast to the frequency domain approach to time series analysis, the time domain approach is based on an explicit parametric model. For the lynx data of Figure 20.1, we might consider the model

$$\tilde{y}(t) = \phi_1\tilde{y}(t-1) + \phi_2\tilde{y}(t-2) + \phi_3\tilde{y}(t-10) + a(t)$$

where $\tilde{y}(t) = Y(t) - \mu_y$ is a mean-corrected version of $Y(t)$, the annual lynx trappings, where ϕ_1, ϕ_2, and ϕ_3 are regression coefficients whose values are to be estimated from the data, and where the random variables $a(t)$ are independently and normally distributed with mean zero and common variance.

A model of this type represents a linear regression of $Y(t)$ upon its past, and is called an autoregressive or AR model. The model implies that the lynx trappings can be predicted by using the data from the previous two years and from ten years previous. The ten year lag is included because the plot of the data in Figure 20.1 and the estimated

spectral density in Figure 20.9 reveal an approximate ten year period.

In Figure 20.10 we have the one step ahead forecast plotted over the original data. Note that this AR model serves merely as an illustration and is not intended as a definitive analysis of the lynx data. In particular, some of the forecasts are negative. This can be avoided by appropriately transforming the data, e.g., taking a log transformation. We refrained from data transformation to maintain a simple exposition.

Another type of model fundamental to time domain analysis is the moving average. We can imagine a data set that requires the entire past for adequate prediction or description, such as

$$\tilde{y}(t) = \phi_1\tilde{y}(t-1) + \phi_2\tilde{y}(t-2) + \cdots + \phi_k\tilde{y}(t-k) + \cdots + a(t) .$$

Of course, if we have an unlimited number of coefficients ϕ in the model, we cannot hope to estimate them all from a finite set of data. The problem however becomes tractable when the ϕ's themselves are given by a few parameters, as for example in the model

$$\tilde{y}(t) + \theta\tilde{y}(t-1) + \theta^2\tilde{y}(t-2) + \ldots = a(t)$$

Rewriting, we have

$$a(t) \quad = \tilde{y}(t) + \theta\tilde{y}(t-1) + \theta^2\tilde{y}(t-2) + \ldots$$
$$\theta a(t-1) = \qquad \theta\tilde{y}(t-1) + \theta^2\tilde{y}(t-2) + \ldots$$

or

$$\tilde{y}(t) \quad = a(t) - \theta a(t-1) .$$

The above model is an example of a moving average or MA model, so called because $\tilde{y}(\cdot)$ is a weighted average of the uncorrelated sequence $a(\cdot)$, the average being taken at successive points in time.

The autoregressive (AR) and moving average (MA) models can be combined in a simple fashion to produce a class of mixed autoregressive-moving average or ARMA models. As an illustration, we could model the lynx trappings as

$$\tilde{y}(t) = \phi_1\tilde{y}(t-1) + \phi_2\tilde{y}(t-2) + \phi_3\tilde{y}(t-10) + e(t)$$

where the sequence of random errors $e(\cdot)$ is not assumed to be uncorrelated but rather to follow the autoregressive scheme

$$e(t) = a(t) - \theta a(t-1)$$

where a is as before. This ARMA model may therefore be expressed as

$$\tilde{y}(t) = \phi_1\tilde{y}(t-1) + \phi_2\tilde{y}(t-2) + \phi_3\tilde{y}(t-10)$$
$$+ a(t) - \theta a(t-1) .$$

The great advantage of ARMA Models is that they require a minimal number of parameters to be estimated from the data, yet they can be used to describe a wide variety of time series. An important limitation, however, to the appropriateness of ARMA models is that the data should not exhibit strong upward or downward trends over time, or other types of nonstationary behavior.

In fact, many time series of interest do exhibit such trends. In particular, economic series often show a strong upward trend over time, due to inflation, increased population, and so on. An example shown in Figure 20.11 is the logarithm of monthly totals of international airline passengers for the years 1949 to 1960.

Note that within each year the maximum number of passengers occurs during the summer. One method of reducing this month-of-the-year effect is to form a new series of values by taking the difference between January values for successive years, between February values for successive years, and so on for the remaining months of the year. This is called seasonal differencing. The result is shown in Figure 20.12.

Because points still cluster together more tightly than is expected for an ARMA process, we might also take simple differences between successive months. The result is shown in Figure 20.13.

Because we have eliminated any sizable trends in the data, we can now represent the data of Figure 20.13 by an ARMA Model.

The differencing operation above may be written as

$$\tilde{y}(t) = Y(t) - Y(t-d)$$

and can be regarded as bringing the data closer to a suitable ARMA representation. As shown in our

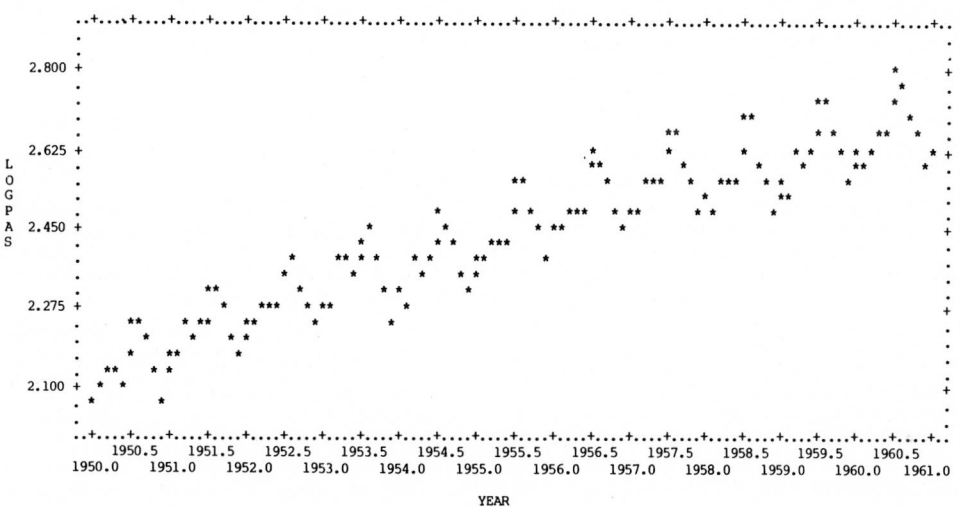

Figure 20.11   Logarithm of monthly total airline passengers from Box and Jenkins, (1976)

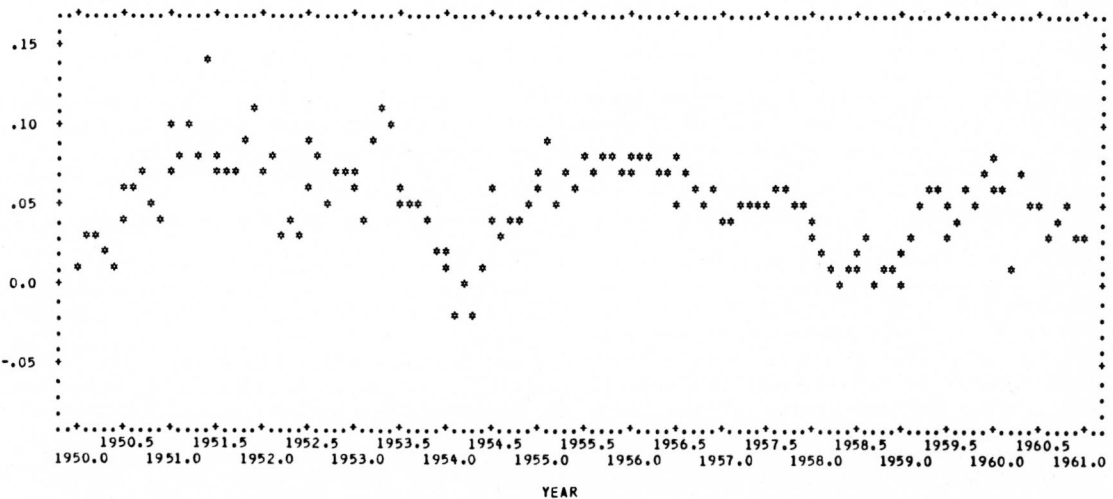

Figure 20.12   Seasonally adjusted differenced airline data

601

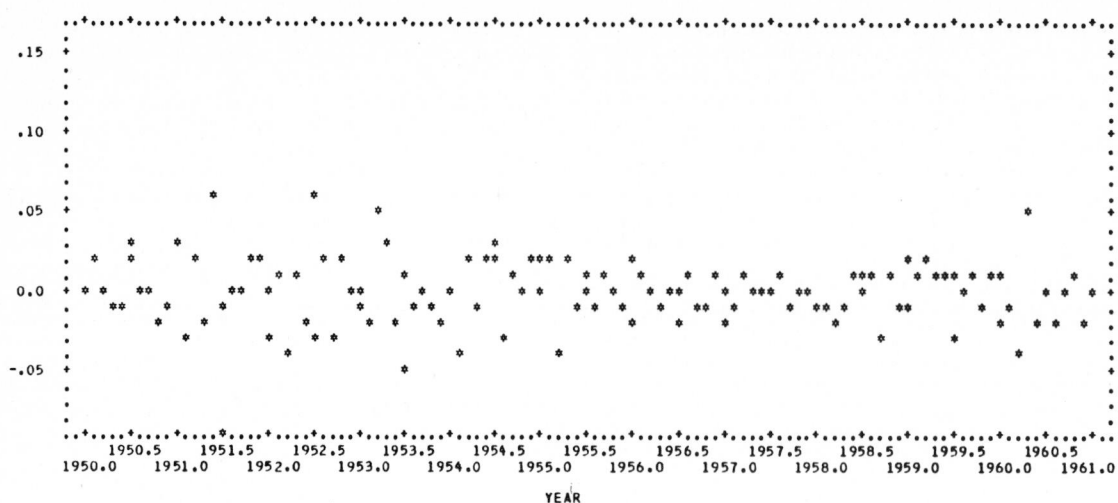

Figure 20.13   Further simple differencing of airline data

example above, we may difference the data more than once, possibly with distinct difference orders d, before we are satisfied that major trends or local trends in the data have been satisfactorily reduced.

Because $\tilde{y}(\cdot)$ is a differenced version of $Y(\cdot)$, we call $Y(\cdot)$ an integrated version of $\tilde{y}(\cdot)$. If $\tilde{y}(\cdot)$ is represented by an autoregressive-moving average, or ARMA schema, we say that Y follows an autoregressive-integrated-moving average or <u>ARIMA model</u>. We note in passing that the components of an ARIMA model are linear filters applied either to the data $Y(\cdot)$ or to the uncorrelated disturbances $a(\cdot)$.

ARIMA models are heavily used, particularly for economic and related series. They afford great flexibility in parametrically describing the behavior of a univariate series $Y(\cdot)$. In many applications, however, we are interested in several time series. We would often like to find a relationship between a dependent variable $Y(\cdot)$ and one or more independent variables $X(\cdot)$. We now briefly discuss two classes of model for this purpose. The first class is that of intervention models, which we introduce by means of an example.

We imagine an announced government policy to stimulate the lynx population by punishing further lynx trappings. We construct an <u>intervention model</u> by letting Y(t) denote the number of lynx trapped during the t-th year, and letting X(t) be equal to zero prior to the announced policy and equal to unity thereafter. We may evaluate the effects of the policy by investigating the relationship between Y(t) and X(t).

The class of intervention models can represent many relationships between the observed Y(t) and the intervention variable or variables X(t). Usually X(t) is an indicator variable assuming only the values zero and unity, however it is useful to allow the values of X(t) to be unrestricted. The class of intervention models includes the familiar linear regression model as a simple case. More generally, Y(t) may correspond not simply to X at time t, but to a function of X(t), X(t-1), X(t-2), ... Thus Y(t) and X(t) may have a dynamic rather than static relationship.

In the above discussion, we regard X(t), marking the advent of a new government policy, as a nonrandom quantity. In many situations, however, the dependent variable may be related to one or more independent variables that are themselves random. For example, we may want to examine the effects of the annual population of the snowshoe rabbit, the primary lynx prey, upon annual lynx trappings.

When we consider not only the dependent variable Y(t) but also the independent variable(s) X(t) to be random, the relationship between Y(t) and X(t) may be described by a <u>transfer function model</u>. We call Y(t) the output series and X(t) the input series. The precision of forecasts for the output series can be substantially improved if we are able to build an appropriate transfer function model relating the output and input series.

P2T facilitates the four stages of time domain analysis -- model identification, parameter estimation, diagnostic checking, and forecasting -- and offers a wide variety of ARIMA, intervention, and transfer function models.

SUMMARY

P1T and P2T offer complementary and partially overlapping approaches to time series analysis. For example, both programs can estimate autoregressive coefficients.

Spectral analysis is often used as an exploratory tool that can yield pertinent information about the data without determining, or requiring, a highly specified model. In contrast, time domain methods seek a parametric model that may be used to forecast future values. Spectral methods tend to work best on lengthy sequences of data from a stationary process, i.e., a process whose statistical nature remains the same regardless of the time origin chosen. This kind of data seems to be most common in the natural sciences. Current time domain methods, on the other hand, have been tailored to the analysis of data arising in economics and other social sciences, where short sequences of data and trends over time are more likely.

These comments are meant only as a guide to program usage, and should not be interpreted too strictly. To point out that both approaches may be considered in any time series analysis, we note that Yule (1927) and more recently Morris (1977) apply time domain methods to the analysis of annual numbers of sunspots, and that Fishman (1969), for example, analyzes economic data in the frequency domain.

The primary reference for P1T is Brillinger (1975) while that for P2T is Box and Jenkins (1976). Valuable introductory and illustrative accounts are also given by Bloomfield (1976), Chatfield (1975), Jenkins (1979), and Kendall (1973). An excellent survey of time series analysis is given in a sequence of articles by Bingham, Whittle, Wold, and Shishkin (1978).

Control Language

The Control Language instructions to describe the data and variables are common to all BMDP programs and are explained in Chapter 5. The PROBLEM, INPUT, and VARIABLE paragraphs are used by the time series programs.

If data editing or transformations are necessary, the methods described in Chapter 6 can be used. Data can be read from a BMDP File (Chapter 7) or in a number of other ways (Chapter 5).

The time series programs, along with P4V, introduce an interactive capability to the BMDP package. These programs execute the user supplied Control Language in three phases: data definition, data reading, and analysis. The distinctive feature of these programs is that the analysis paragraphs are executed in an interpretive fashion, that is, results are computed and printed immediately after each analysis paragraph.

When the programs are run interactively, the interpretive execution of analysis paragraphs allows the user to select further paragraphs and options based on currently obtained results. The user may supply these paragraphs in any order and with repetitions. Program execution proceeds in the same way when the user submits a batch job, e.g., when the problem is submitted on cards.

There are two notes worth mentioning here concerning these new programs. The first point is that the END paragraph serves as a switch, telling the program that one of the three phases - data definition, data reading, or analysis - is ending and a new phase may be beginning. In the time series programs, the END of the analysis paragraphs signals the end of the problem.

The other point to be made is that the slash used to separate paragraphs should be placed at the end of each interpretively executed paragraph, not at the beginning. Once the program begins reading the interpretively executed paragraphs, it ignores anything written to the right of a slash.

A summary of the Control Language instructions common to all BMDP programs is given on p. 48; a summary of Control Language instructions specific to each time series program follows the program description. These summaries can be used as indexes to the program descriptions.

P1T

20.1 *Univariate and Bivariate Spectral Analysis*

Tony Thrall
Laszlo Engelman

ABSTRACT

The chief purpose of P1T is to provide graphical displays and descriptive statistics for any single time series or for any pair of time series. This is accomplished in several ways, ranging from plotting the data over time, to estimating the spectral density. The data screening and analytical methods in P1T are applicable to a wide variety of time series data. This is illustrated in the examples below in the treatment of annual lynx trappings, monthly temperatures, monthly sunspots, monthly numbers of airlines passengers, and electrical potentials at a brain site.

Because spectral estimation is the focal point of P1T, we describe here what is being sought and how it is of use.

The underlying concept of spectral analysis is that each variable, thought of as a time series, or function over time, can be meaningfully represented by pure sine waves summed over different frequencies, with a different amplitude and phase at each frequency. Spectral analysis proceeds by Fourier transforming the data to obtain the coefficients of the sinusoids at a discrete set of frequencies, grouping neighboring frequencies into frequency bands, and estimating various quantities from the Fourier transformed data in one frequency band at a time. Frequencies are grouped together in bands to enhance the statistical stability of the estimates.

As an example, the spectral density of a variable is estimated by computing the average squared amplitude of the sinusoids within a frequency band. This estimated spectral density is then plotted as a function of frequency (more precisely thought of as a function of frequency band center and frequency band width). The spectral density indicates how the variation exhibited by the data is distributed over the different frequency bands. This is illustrated in Example 1T.1 below.

Frequency domain analysis has proved to be a powerful tool in many scientific investigations. An impressive example is given by Hays et al. (1976) who provide strong evidence, based on a comparison of estimated spectral densities, that long term variations in the earth's climate, e.g., ice ages, are linked to variations in the earth's orbit.

The spectral analysis of individual variables can be usefully extended to pairs of variables. One of the most important frequency domain quantities here is the coherence of two variables. Plotted as a function of frequency, the estimated coherence depicts the degree of linear association between two variables in different frequency bands. A demonstration of bivariate spectral analysis is given in Example 1T.2.

The utility of the estimated coherence is illustrated in a study of the response of different brain sites to verbal and nonverbal stimuli. A suprisingly large coherence between sites was noted at high frequencies. Further reflection led to the conclusion that a very weak signal had been imposed across all channels in the recording process. This artifact was masked at lower frequencies where the brain's response dominated the spectral estimates.

There are many other examples of how a frequency based analysis of the data can uncover subtle anomalies and, occasionally, new phenomena. P1T facilitates such an analysis by estimating spectral densities, coherences, and related quantities. This can be done by either of two alternative methods in paragraphs SPECTRA and COVARIANCE. (COVARIANCE is not available in the 1982 version of P1T.)

While spectral analysis plays a central role in P1T, the program can also be used to inspect time series data. This may be done through a variety of plots. Paragraph SNAPSHOT gives the user a condensed view of each variable over time, allowing assessment of possible trends or gross outliers. TPLOT produces detailed plots of one or more variables over time. LSCATTER forms lagged scatter plots, each plot consisting of two variables (or possibly the same variable) removed in time by a specified lag. Paragraph DEMODULATE traces a frequency band component of a variable over time, using complex demodulation. These plots are displayed in Example 1T.3.

In many situations, the data need to be prepared prior to spectral analysis. An obvious example is the replacement of missing values, which can be done in paragraph REPLACE (note however that alternative missing value procedures are available in paragraphs SPECTRA and COVARIANCE). Another common practice prior to spectral estimation is to estimate and remove seasonal means or a linear trend. This can be done in paragraph ADJUST. These features are used in Example 1T.4.

An advantage to representing a time series as a sum of sinusoidal functions is that sinusoids respond in a simple fashion to linear filtering operations. Linear filters play a key role in our understanding and examination of natural processes. The filtering of solar radiation by the earth's atmosphere, and the vocal tract's shaping of sounds produced in the larynx, are examples of filtering operations occurring in nature.

We also build filters, such as the mechanical filters used to transform coastal waves into electrical energy, or such as the numerical filter

$$Z(t) = \tfrac{1}{4}Y(t+1) + \tfrac{1}{2}Y(t) + \tfrac{1}{4}Y(t-1)$$

employed by von Hann to smooth out erratic effects in meteorological data. All of these filtering operations have similar mathematical descriptions. Those offered by P1T are, like the von Hann filter, linear combinations applied to the data at successive time points. Such filters are available in paragraphs

BANDPASS, FILTER, and AR (autoregression).

In the BANDPASS paragraph, the program constructs a linear filter to augment or reduce the effect of a user-designated frequency band. By specifying a band centered about frequency zero, a smoothing or lowpass filter can be obtained. When the data have been electronically recorded, the user may need to screen out anomalous ripples caused by a 60 cycle per second alternating current. This is another possible use of the BANDPASS paragraph.

In the FILTER paragraph the user can supply a linear combination of his own design. This can be useful in extracting a trend from the data, when the trend is of some special known form.

In the AR paragraph, the program estimates an autoregressive filter from the data. Here, the user may seek to reverse a natural filtering operation believed to have already occurred.

The filtering paragraphs BANDPASS, FILTER, and AR are featured in Example 1T.5.

The user may invoke the above paragraphs in any order and with repetitions. For example, he may plot the original data, apply a smoothing filter, and then plot the smoothed data. He may similarly evaluate the effects upon the estimated spectral density of removing a linear trend, and so on.

Computational details of the program are presented in Appendix A and in Thrall (1982).

WHERE TO FIND IT

BASIC SPECTRAL ANALYSIS: ONE VARIABLE AND TWO VARIABLES

Example 1T.1 Basic Setup for Univariate Spectral Analysis: Lynx Trappings, 1821-1934

We use P1T to analyze the annual series of Canadian lynx trappings for the years 1821-1934. We include year as a labelling variable, although this is not required by the program. Only the SPECTRA paragraph is specific to P1T. The remaining Control Language instructions are common to all BMDP programs and are described in Chapter 5. If data editing or transformations are needed, see the methods in Chapter 6. We use the following instructions:

```
--------------------------------------
/ PROBLEM    TITLE IS 'LYNX TRAPPINGS 1821-1934'.
/ INPUT      VARIABLES ARE 2.
            FORMAT IS '(F4,F5)'.
/ VARIABLE   NAMES ARE YEAR, LYNX.
            TIME IS YEAR
/ TFAXIS     TNAME IS YEAR.
            FNAME IS 'CYCLE/YR'.
/ END
```

1821	269	1860	299	1899	153
1822	321	1861	236	1900	387
1823	585	1862	245	1901	758
1824	871	1863	552	1902	1307
1825	1475	1864	1623	1903	3465
1826	2821	1865	3311	1904	6991
1827	3928	1866	6721	1905	6313
1828	5943	1867	4254	1906	3794
1829	4950	1868	687	1907	1836
1830	2577	1869	255	1908	345
1831	523	1870	473	1909	382
1832	98	1871	358	1910	808
1833	184	1872	784	1911	1388
1834	279	1873	1594	1912	2713
1835	409	1874	1676	1913	3800
1836	2285	1875	2251	1914	3091
1837	2685	1876	1426	1915	2985
1838	3409	1877	756	1916	3790
1839	1824	1878	299	1917	674
1840	409	1879	201	1918	81
1841	151	1880	229	1919	80
1842	45	1881	469	1920	108
1843	68	1882	736	1921	229
1844	213	1883	2042	1922	399
1845	546	1884	2811	1923	1132
1846	1033	1885	4431	1924	2432
1847	2129	1886	2511	1925	3574
1848	2536	1887	389	1926	2935
1849	957	1888	73	1927	1537
1850	361	1889	39	1928	529
1851	377	1890	49	1929	485
1852	225	1891	59	1930	662
1853	360	1892	188	1931	1000
1854	731	1893	377	1932	1590
1855	1638	1894	1292	1933	2657
1856	2725	1895	4031	1934	3396
1857	2871	1896	3495	/ END	
1858	2119	1897	587	SPECTRA VARIABLE IS LYNX.	
1859	684	1898	105	PERIOD.	

```
                                     PRINT.
                                     PLOT./
              END /
--------------------------------------
```

(An example of the complete setup with system cards,

BMDP instructions, and data is shown at the end of the P1T section.) Note that SPECTRA and the final END paragraph are terminated rather than preceded by slashes, as descussed in the Control Language section of the Chapter 20 Introduction.

The results of the above analysis are presented in Output 1T.1. Circled numbers below correspond to those in the output.

(1) The program reports on the reading of data and then prints the first five cases to provide an initial check that the format specification, the user-supplied data file, and the entry of the data into the program are as they should be.

(2) Univariate summary statistics are printed based upon all acceptable values. The number of acceptable values for each variable is given in the column titled COUNT. The slope indicates the degree of linear trend in each variable over time, where the units of time may be specified by the user (see the TFAXIS description on p. 628). In this example, the user has accepted the program default of letting time be identically equal to case number.

(3) The results printed pertain to the plot immediately below. The frequencies here refer to cycles per year. The spectral density at low frequencies (near 0.0) displays the contribution of slow sinusoidal variation of long periods to the overall variation in the data. The spectral density at high frequencies (near 0.5) shows contributions from fast sinusoidal variation, i.e., relatively short periods.

In this example the period is just the reciprocal of frequency. The lowest frequency (0.0) corresponds to an infinitely long period while the highest frequency (0.5) corresponds to a period of two years.

(4) The plot of $\log_{10}$ (spectrum). The peak in the estimated spectral density function near frequency 0.1 corresponds to the cyclic nature of the lynx trappings, with a periodicity of roughly ten years. A higher, narrower peak would reflect a more rigid ten year periodicity in the data.

The bandwidth, a value chosen by the program in this example, gives the width of the interval of frequencies in which periodograms have been averaged in calculating the estimate. In the absence of user-specified bandwidths, the program produces 3 sets of estimates ranging from narrow-band to wide-band. The user can use these estimates as a basis for future specifications. Bandwidths are discussed further on p. 629.

(5) The spectral density is estimated again using a larger bandwidth. That is, periodograms are here averaged in a wider interval of frequencies to form the estimated spectral density. This enhances the statistical stability of the estimate, i.e., it reduces the variance of the estimate, but it also gives less detail than the previous narrow-band estimate. So the narrow-band pictures provide greater, sometimes telling, detail while the wide-band estimates smooth out some detail, but may provide a more reliable portrayal of the observed time series. The user may specify several bandwidths to be used. Otherwise the program calculates two bandwidths for short data sequences (64 cases or less) and three bandwidths for longer data sequences.

Output 1T.1 Basic setup for univariate spectral analysis: lynx trappings 1821-1935

```
        LYNX TRAPPINGS, 1821-1935

  I N P U T   V A R I A B L E S . . . . .
       VARIABLE     RECORD   COLUMNS      FIELD   TYPE
   INDEX   NAME      NO.    BEGIN  END    WIDTH
   -----  --------   ----   -----  -----  -----   ----
      1 YEAR          1       1     4       4      F
      2 LYNX          1       5     9       5      F

  BASED ON INPUT FORMAT SUPPLIED    1 RECORDS READ PER CASE.

  DATA AFTER TRANSFORMATIONS FOR THE FIRST  5 CASES

   C A S E            1        2
   NO. LABEL        YEAR     LYNX
   ----- --------  --------- ---------
      1              1821      269
      2              1822      321
      3              1823      585
      4              1824      871
      5              1825     1475

  NUMBER OF CASES READ. . . . . . . . . . . .    114
```

①

                        UNIVARIATE SUMMARY STATISTICS
②   BASED ON CASES OCCURRING IN THE INTERVAL
          YEAR = 1821. THROUGH YEAR = 1935.

VARIABLE	COUNT	MEAN	SLOPE	STANDARD DEVIATION	MINIMUM VALUE	(FIRST OCCURRENCE) CASE NO.	YEAR	MAXIMUM VALUE	(FIRST OCCURRENCE) CASE NO.	YEAR
1 YEAR	114	1878.	1.0	33.	1821.	1	1821.	1934.	114	1934.
2 LYNX	114	1538.	3.3	1586.	39.	69	1889.	6991.	84	1904.

BAND WIDTH = 0.0439   SHAPE = COSINE

③

CYCLE/YR	VARIABLE LYNX	CYCLE/YR	LYNX
0.0	1.410E 06	0.2544	3.756E 05
0.0088	1.634E 06	0.2632	4.344E 05
0.0175	3.606E 06	0.2719	4.368E 05
0.0263	4.766E 06	0.2807	3.134E 05
0.0351	3.698E 06	0.2895	2.524E 05
0.0439	2.403E 06	0.2982	2.162E 05
0.0526	2.451E 06	0.3070	2.859E 05
0.0614	2.385E 06	0.3158	4.374E 05
0.0702	2.760E 06	0.3246	5.144E 05
0.0789	3.778E 06	0.3333	5.058E 05
0.0877	6.742E 06	0.3421	4.207E 05
0.0965	2.221E 07	0.3509	2.659E 05
0.1053	3.114E 07	0.3596	1.779E 05
0.1140	2.035E 07	0.3684	1.996E 05
0.1228	5.051E 06	0.3772	2.023E 05
0.1316	2.979E 06	0.3860	1.759E 05
0.1404	2.258E 06	0.3947	1.501E 05
0.1491	1.048E 06	0.4035	8.153E 04
0.1579	9.554E 05	0.4123	5.869E 04
0.1667	8.326E 05	0.4211	8.203E 04
0.1754	6.985E 05	0.4298	1.144E 05
0.1842	8.212E 05	0.4386	1.163E 05
0.1930	1.359E 06	0.4474	8.528E 04
0.2018	2.603E 06	0.4561	5.473E 04
0.2105	3.103E 06	0.4649	6.415E 04
0.2193	2.144E 06	0.4737	7.721E 04
0.2281	1.245E 06	0.4825	1.004E 05
0.2368	1.166E 06	0.4912	1.455E 05
0.2456	7.710E 05	0.5000	1.832E 05

(output continued)

Output 1T.1 (continued)

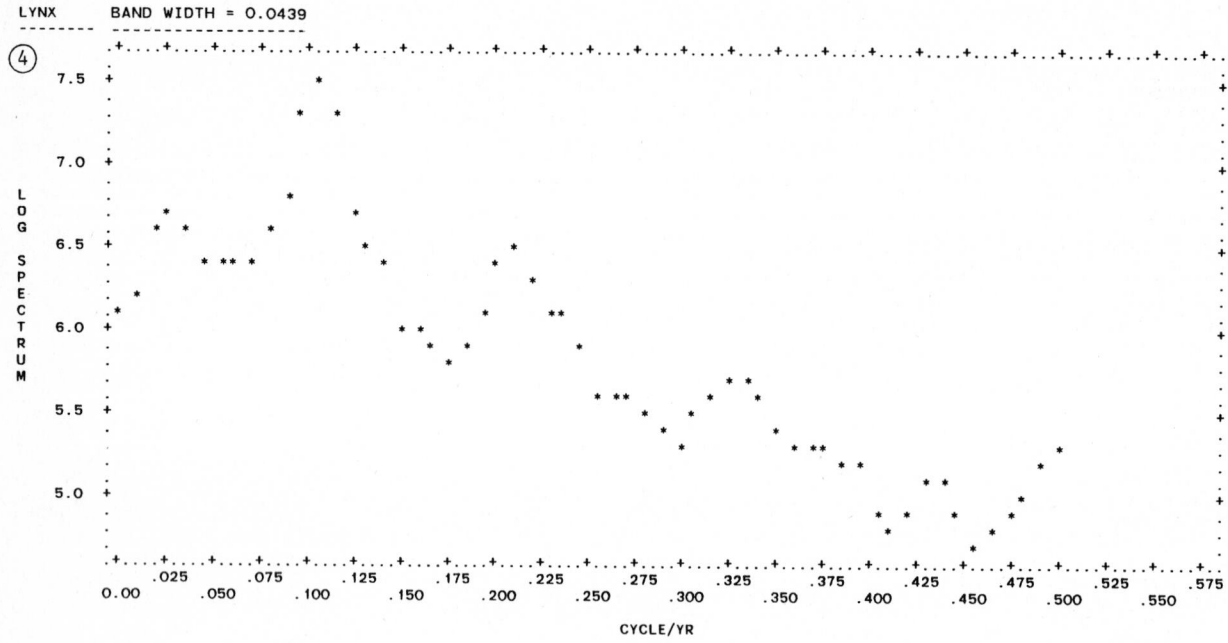

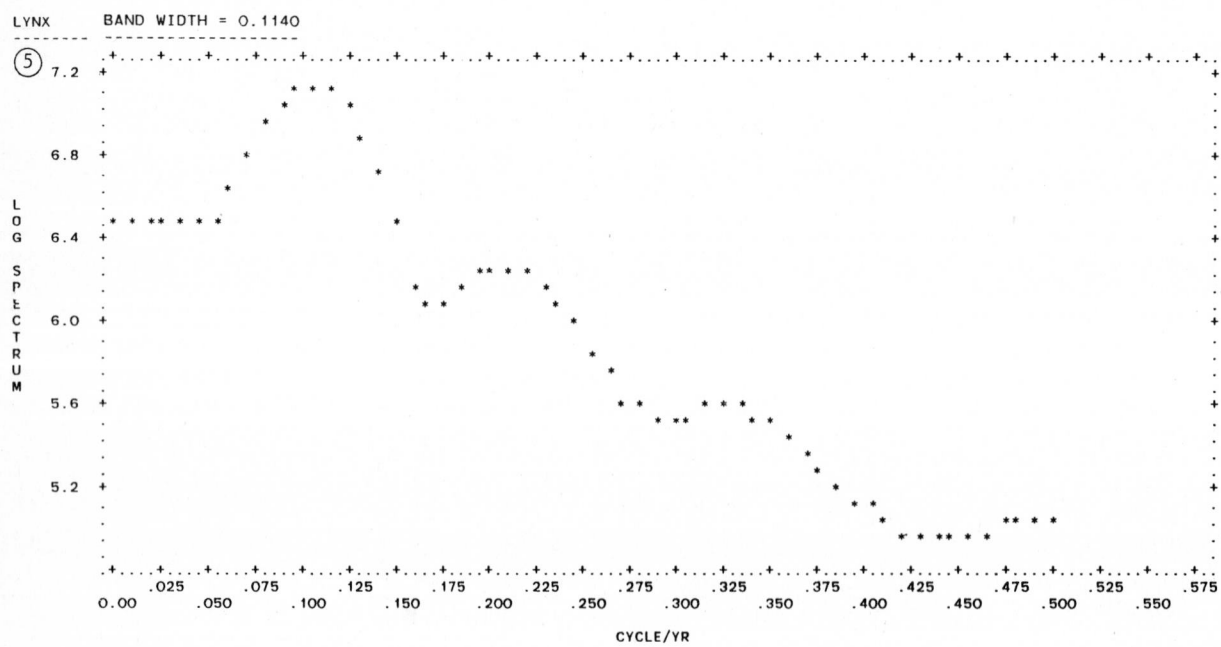

Example 1T.2 Bivariate Spectra: Monthly Temperatures for Berlin and Vienna, 1776–1950[1].

The data in our second example consist of average monthly temperatures (degrees centigrade) for Berlin and Vienna (see Smithsonian 1927, 1934, 1947). Each pair of temperatures is identified by month and year, serving as case labelling variables. In this example, we analyze Berlin and Vienna temperatures jointly, and we also perform a frequency domain regression of Berlin temperatures on Vienna temperatures.

The Control Language instructions are as follows:

```
/ PROBLEM    TITLE IS 'BERLIN-VIENNA TEMPERATURES'.
/ INPUT      VARIABLES ARE 4. UNIT = 20.
             FORMAT IS '(A4,4X,A4,8X,F8.1,32X,F8.1)'.
/ VARIABLE   NAMES ARE MONTH, YEAR, BERLIN, VIENNA.
             LABELS ARE MONTH, YEAR.
/ END
SPECTRA XVAR IS VIENNA.
        YVAR IS BERLIN.
        COVARIANCE.
        DEPENDENT IS YVAR./
END/
```

****
[1]To facilitate the illustration of SPECTRA, this bivariate series has had means subtracted out for each month of the year. This can be done using the ADJUST paragraph as shown on p. 618.

Output 1T.2 Bivariate spectra: monthly temperatures for Berlin and Vienna, 1776–1950

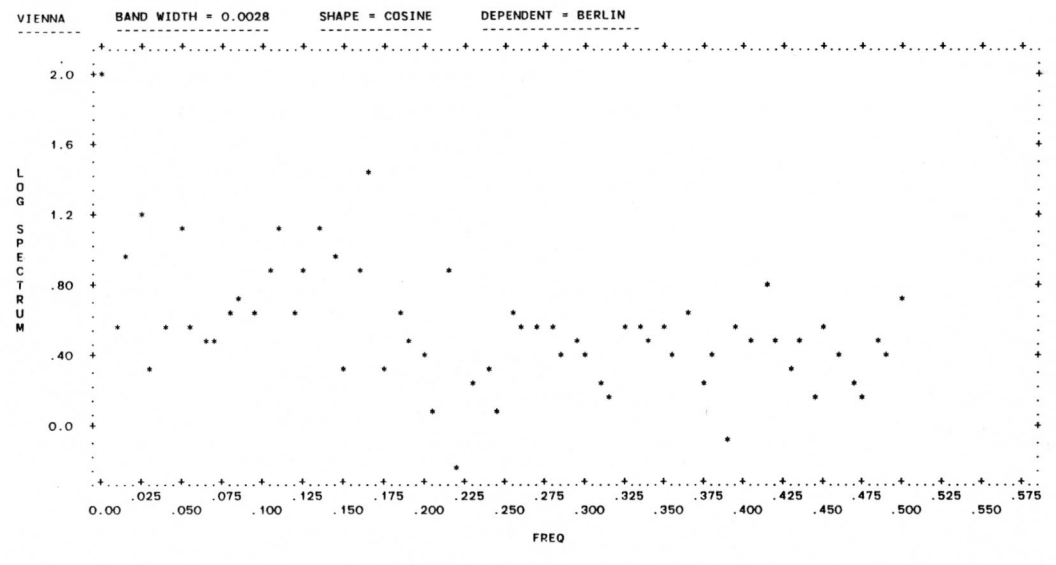

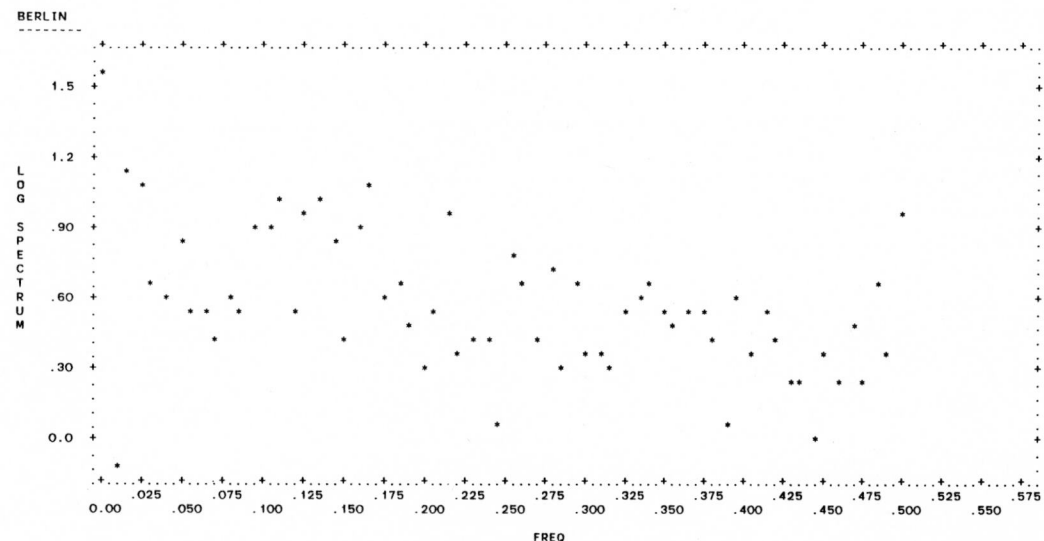

(output continued)

The results are presented in Output 1T.2. Circled numbers below correspond to those in the output.

(6) We see that the coherence between Berlin and Vienna is fairly high and constant at all frequencies.

(7) The plotted phase shows how the linear filter for fitting Berlin temperatures by Vienna temperatures shifts the phase of sinewaves at different frequencies. We see that the phase shift is near zero at all frequencies.

(8) The gain of the filter for fitting Berlin temperatures by Vienna temperatures is nearly constant at all frequencies. This fact, coupled with the zero phase shift of the filter, suggests that the linear association between Berlin and Vienna monthly temperatures is almost immediate, i.e., within one month, rather than being spread over several months.

(9) Cross covariances between Berlin and Vienna temperatures have been estimated and plotted. Note that all the covariances are small, except for the covariance at lag zero. This agrees with the indication of an instantaneous relationship between monthly temperatures in the two cities seen previously in the plots of the phase and gain.

Output 1T.2 (continued)

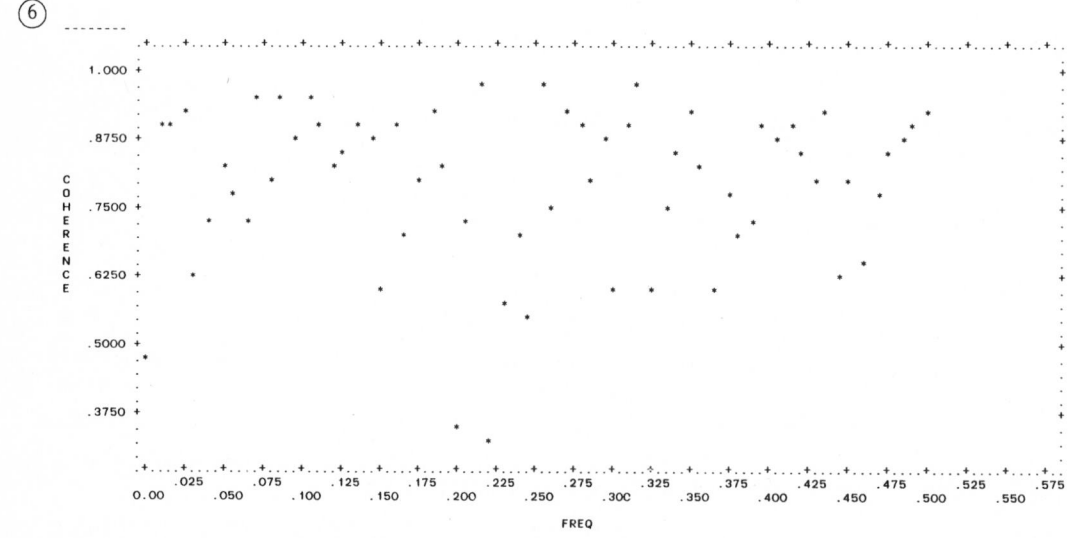

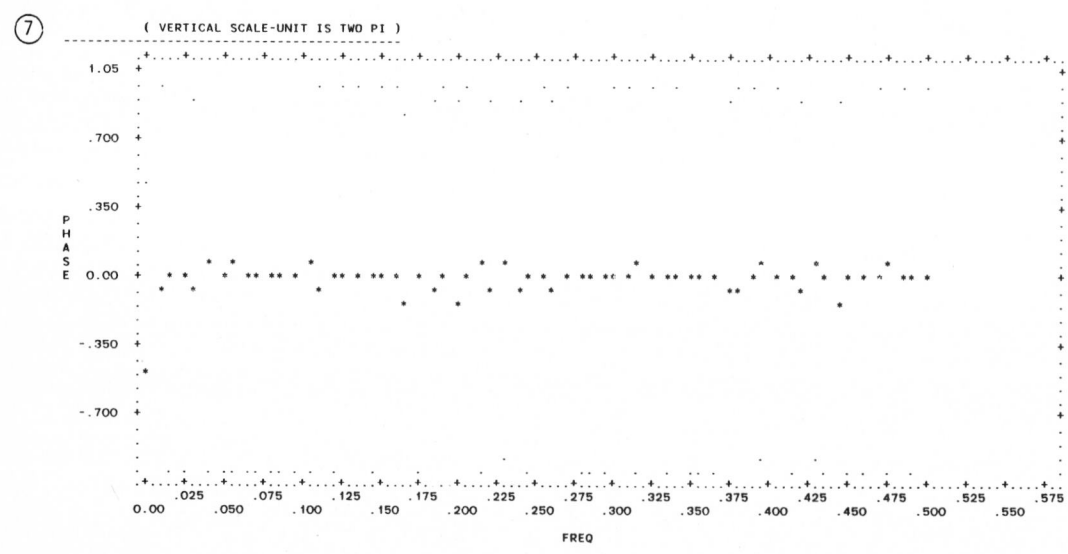

(output continued)

Specifying the spectral analysis in paragraph SPECTRA. Paragraph SPECTRA provides one method for estimating spectral densities and related frequency domain quantities. Each time series, or variable, is represented as a sum of sine waves at a discrete set of equispaced frequencies. The frequencies range from zero to the highest frequency discernible in the data, which is determined by the time interval between successive cases of data. The spacing between frequencies is determined by the length of the series, i.e., by the number of cases of data.

At each frequency, the amplitude (height) and phase (origin shift) of the sine wave best fitting the data is determined. This is done simultaneously at all frequencies by Fourier transforming the time series. The rescaled amplitude squared is called the periodogram of the series.

The periodogram may be regarded as a crude estimate of the spectral density. Its principal failing is its high variability (each periodogram ordinate is approximately proportional to a chi-square variable with two degrees of freedom). Because periodograms in a neighborhood of frequencies are nearly statistically independent and estimate the spectral density at nearly the same frequency, an improved spectral density estimate can be formed by averaging periodograms in a neighborhood, or band, of frequencies. This is the approach taken here.

Pairs of variables may also be analyzed in paragraph SPECTRA. The bivariate analysis consists of estimates of the coherence and phase between two

Output 1T.2 (continued)

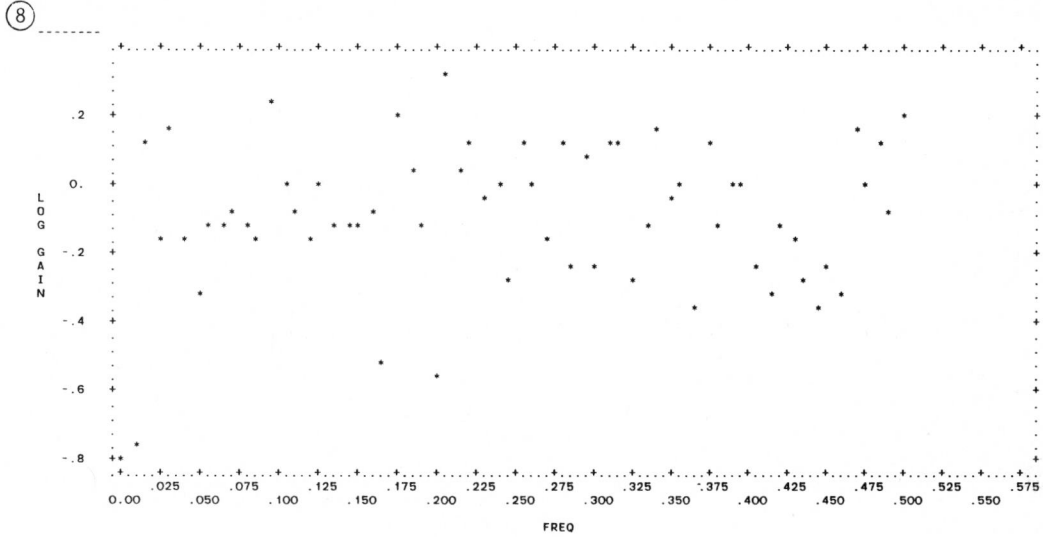

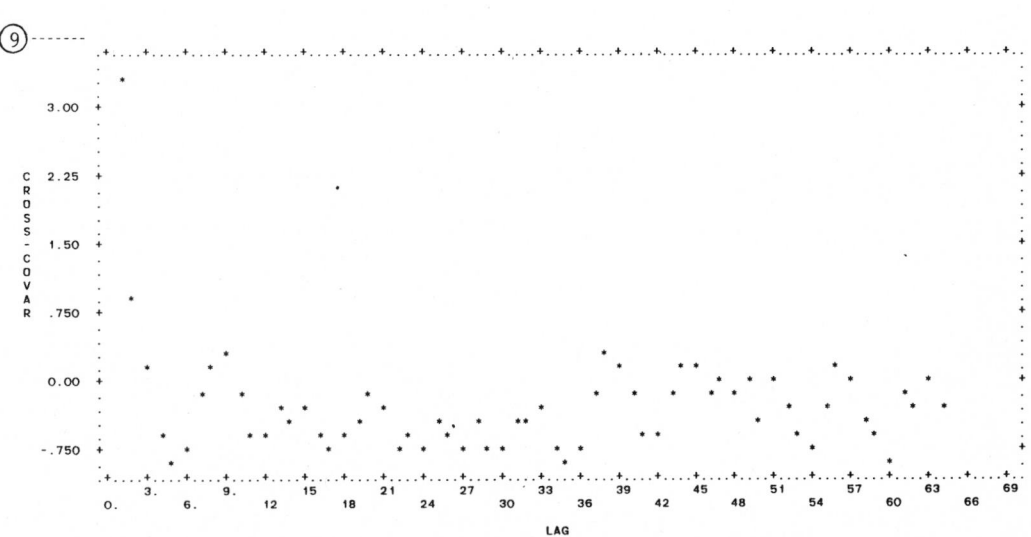

variables in successive frequency bands. When we restrict our attention to a single frequency band, the analysis resembles the usual analysis of two variables, only here adjacent frequencies take the place of independent observations. Coherence is a measure of linear association between the two variables similar to squared correlation. The phase, or phase difference, between the two variables indicates the direction of the linear association and is analogous to the sign of the correlation coefficient.

To obtain the coherence and phase between variables, the user must specify both X and Y variables in the XVAR, YVAR statements. If the user specifies CROSS, the program will match X and Y variables in all distinct combinations (redundancies are automatically avoided). Otherwise the program assumes that X and Y variables are to be PAIRED, i.e., that the first X variable is to be paired only with the first Y variable, the second X variable with the second Y variable, and so on. This requires that the number of listed X variables be the same as the number of listed Y variables.

The bivariate analysis may be extended to a regression analysis, with one variable DEPENDENT and the other independent. The magnitude of the regression coefficient in each frequency band is called the gain of the dependent variable over the independent variable. Frequency domain regression corresponds in the time domain to fitting the dependent variable by a linear filtered version of the independent variable. The output from the frequency domain regression consists of estimates of the gain and the filter coefficients.

Having given an overview of the methods and results available in paragraph SPECTRA, we present below a summary of the primary Control Language instructions for this paragraph. Further technical details may be found in Appendix A.

SPECtra

    XVAR = v list.   required   none
    1st set of variables for bivariate spectra.
    YVAR = v list.   none
    2nd set of variables for bivariate spectra.
    PAIR. or CROSs.   PAIR
    Method of matching X and Y variables. This requests the estimation of the coherence and phase between X and Y variables.
    DEPend = XVAR, YVAR.   none
    Requests frequency domain regression and indicates which variable within each pair is to be regarded as dependent. Output consists of estimates of the gain and the filter coefficients. Applicable only if both XVAR and YVAR have been specified.
    PLOT.   yes
    Plot results.
    PRINt.   yes
    Print results.

DATA SCREENING, MISSING VALUE REPLACEMENT, TREND REMOVAL, AND SEASONAL ADJUSTMENT

Example 1T.3 Viewing the Data Through a Variety of Plots: Monthly Sunspots, 1750-1965

We use monthly mean sunspot numbers, noted for their 11 year cyclic behavior, to illustrate several types of plotting available in P1T. The Control Language instructions are as follows

```
-------------------------------------
/ PROBLEM    TITLE IS 'MONTHLY SUNSPOTS, 1750-1965'.
/ INPUT      VARIABLE IS 1.
            FORMAT IS STREAM. UNIT = 20.
/ VARIABLE   NAME IS SUNSPOTS.
            LABEL IS O.
/ TFAXIS     TNAME=MONTH.
/ END
  SNAPSHOT   VARIABLE IS SUNSPOTS.
            TRIM IS 0./
  TPLOT      VARIABLE IS SUNSPOTS.
            SIZE IS 30.
            TIME IS 1, 50./
  LSCATTER   XVAR IS SUNSPOTS.
            YVAR IS SUNSPOTS.
            YLAG IS 132.
            TIME IS 1, 2592.
            STATISTICS.
            SIZE IS 70, 42.
  SPECTRA    VAR=SUNSPOTS./
  SPECTRA    VAR=SUNSPOTS.
            FREQ = 0.0, 0.05./
  DEMOD      VARIABLE IS SUNSPOTS.
            FREQUENCY IS 0.0075.
            TIME IS 133, 2460.
            SIZE IS 100./
  END/
-------------------------------------
```

The results are printed in Output 1T.3, with circled numbers corresponding to those in the comments below.

(10) The user has requested a SNAPSHOT of the data. In this example the data span over 2500 cases (months), so this graphical condensation of the data is a convenient way to look for major trends over time and for gross outliers. We have connected successive points in the plot to highlight the cyclic nature of this series. The program has used consecutive time intervals of 45 months, one interval overlapping the next by 22 months, to obtain the minimum number of sunspots within each time interval, the maximum number, and the trimmed mean. The time coordinate given to these three values is the midpoint time.

(11) The TPLOT output provides a more detailed view of the sunspot series. The user's instructions limit the plot to 50 months (cases). This is not enough to make the 11-year sunspot cycle evident. Nevertheless, the plot gives us an idea of the kind of local variability in the series.

(12) The user has formed a scatter plot of the sunspot series with itself lagged in time by 132 months, or 11 years. The scatter diagram shows high, but not perfect, correlation. Also evident from the plot is the absence of outlying points that can

Output 1T.3   Viewing the data through a variety of plots: monthly sunspots, 1750–1965

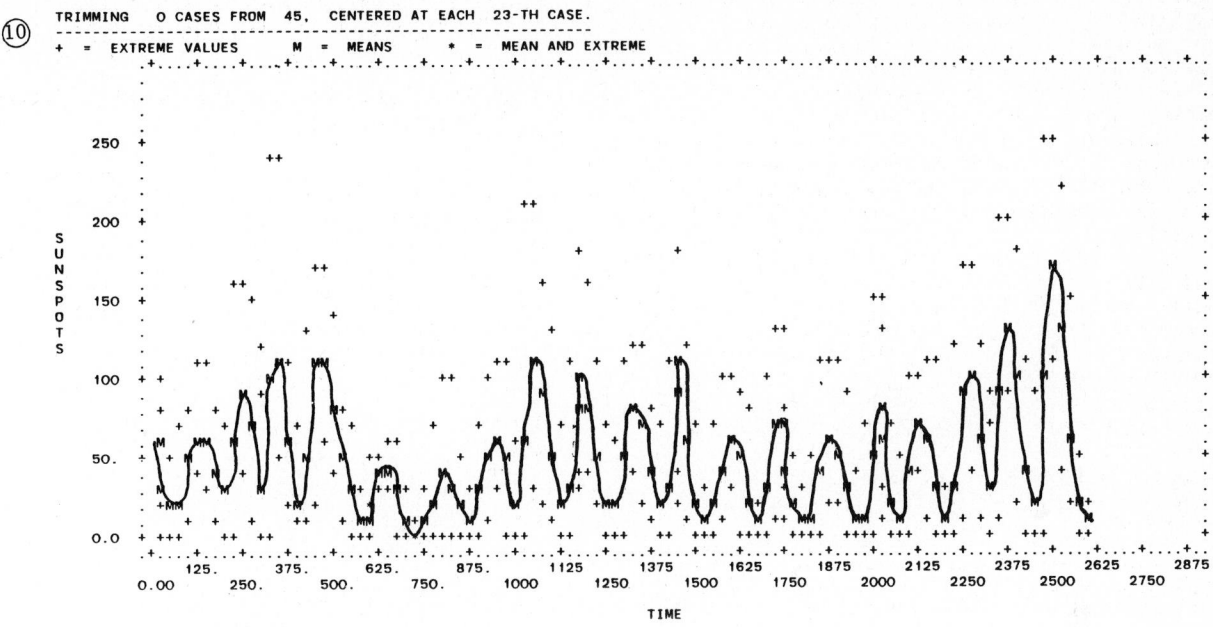

⑪   A   SUNSPOTS

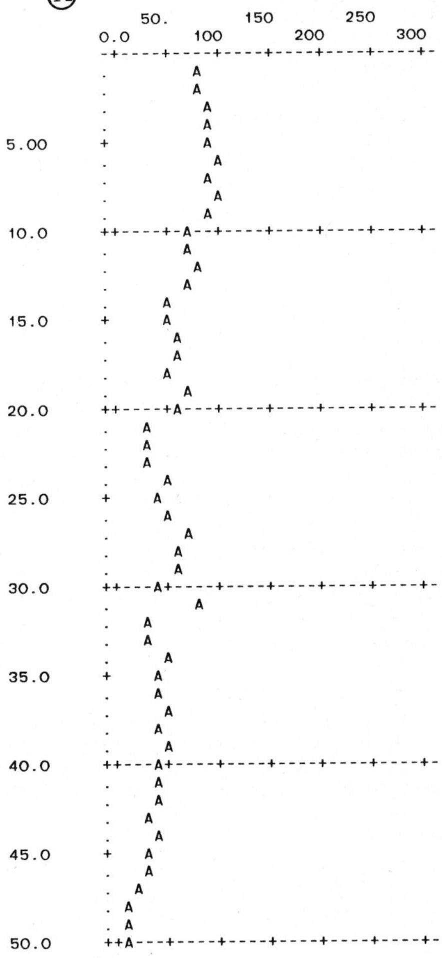

⑫   SUNSPOTS IS LAGGED   132.0000 MONTH

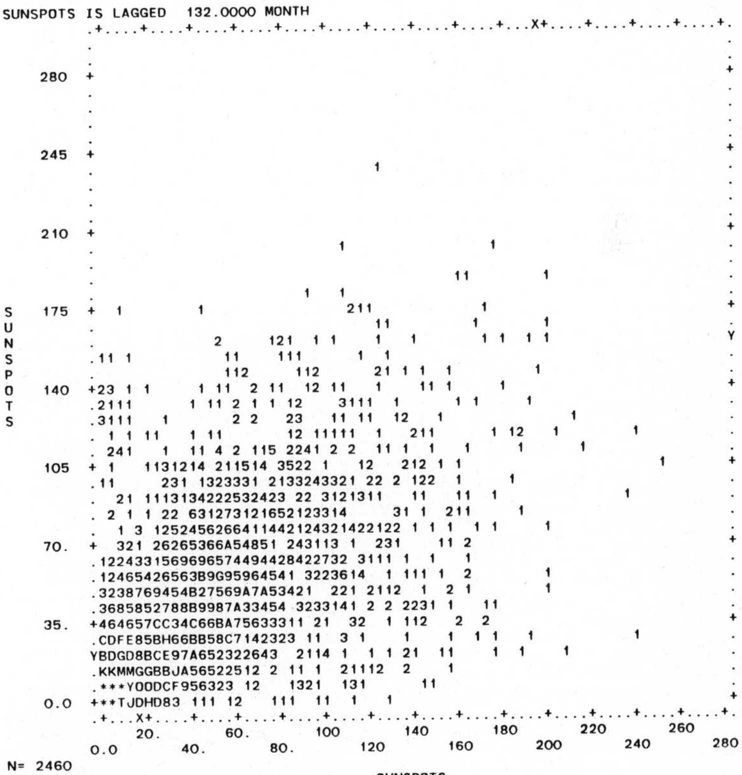

N= 2460
COR= .5298   SUNSPOTS

	MEAN	ST.DEV.	REGRESSION LINE	RES.MS.
X	49.172	42.906	X= .58221*Y+ 22.053	1324.7
Y	46.580	39.046	Y= .48218*X+ 22.870	1097.1

(output continued)

Output 1T.3 (continued)

⑬

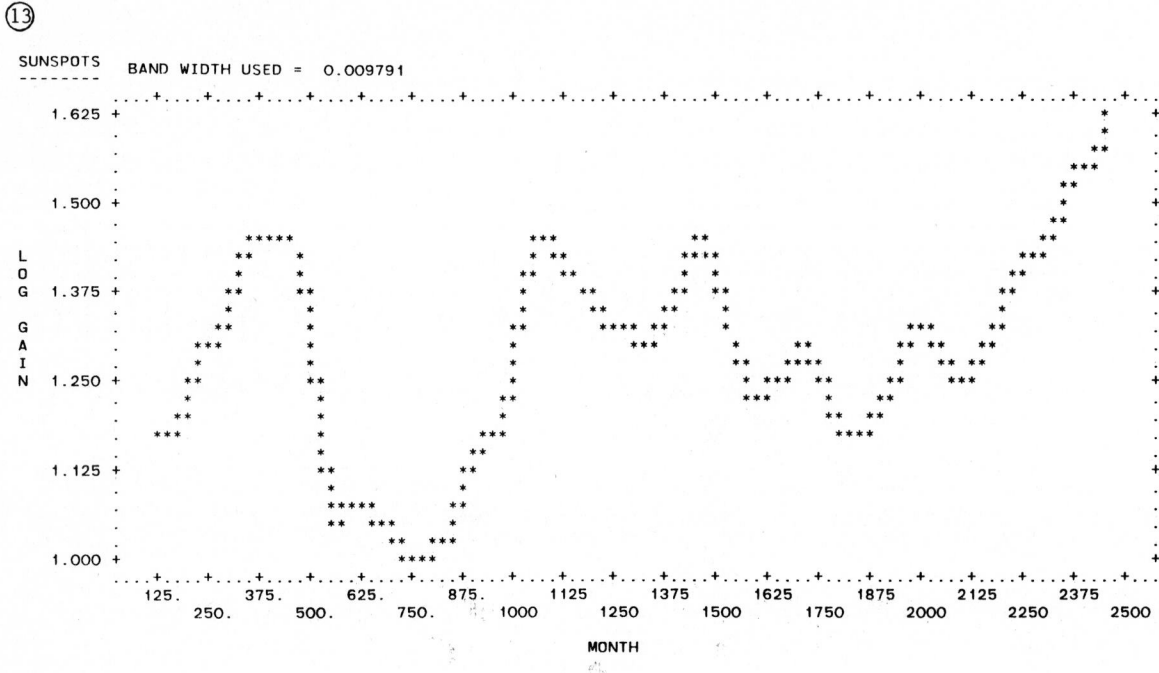

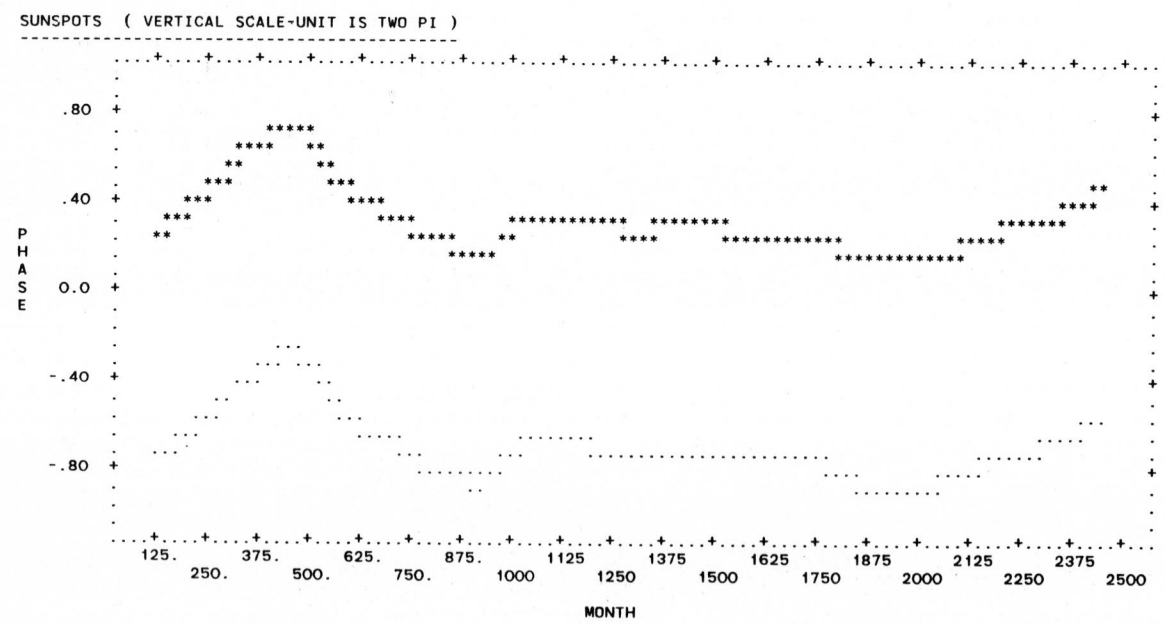

enhance or reduce the correlation. The detection of such outliers is important for the validity of further analyses of the time series.

(13) Complex demodulation is a technique for examining separate frequency band components of a series over successive time intervals. Here we are viewing the amplitude and phase of the sunspots' 11-year (132-month) cycle. The frequency given is approximately 1/132. We can use complex demodulation to check whether a peak in the estimated spectral density is due, as it seems to be here, to a strong component persisting throughout the time course. More generally, we can use complex demodulation to detect changes in the harmonic nature of a series over time. Complex demodulation is further discussed in Bloomfield (1976).

A plotted snapshot of each series may be obtained in paragraph SNAPSHOT. The program constructs a sequence of time intervals. Within each time interval, the minimum value, maximum value, and trimmed mean are calculated. These are plotted against the interval's midpoint time. Depending upon user specifications, intervals may overlap or may have gaps between them. The default is to construct intervals which overlap by about 50 percent and cover the entire range of cases. The default for the midpoint times is such that the entire snapshot fits on a single page, with time plotted horizontally across the page.

```
SNAPshot ─────────────────────────────────
  VARiable = v list.    required           none
    Name or subscript of variables to be plotted.
  TIME = #₁, #₂, #₃.                    see above
    The midpoint times of successive intervals in
    terms of starting time (#₁), final time (#₂),
    and time increment (#₃).
  SPAN = #.                      adjusts to page size
    The span of each time interval, i.e., the
    number of consecutive cases used for each
    computed minimum, maximum, and trimmed mean.
  TRIM = #.                         5% of span
    The number of smallest values and the number of
    largest values to be excluded from the
    calculation of the mean.
  PRINT.                                     no
    Print the minimum, maximum and trimmed mean
    calculated in each time interval.
```

Detailed plots of one or more variables over time are available in paragraph TPLOT. Here, individual values for each variable are plotted versus time, with time running vertically down the page.

The program default is to plot all cases. The user may want to limit the number of pages consumed by the plot by requesting that only a subset of cases be plotted. This can be done in the TIME statement. Note that time is identically equal to case number unless the user has established a different time axis. (See the description of paragraph TFAXIS on p. 627.) When the user specifies more than one variable in the TPLOT paragraph, he may request that the variables be plotted in a COMMON plot frame, or in separate individual plot frames side by side (the latter option is the

default). The user should take care not to request too many variables in one TPLOT paragraph, as this may result in a common frame too dense with variables or in individual frames so narrow that useful details are lost.

The user may specify the minimum and maximum values to be plotted for each variable, as well as specifying a plot symbol for each variable. This is done in the MIN, MAX, and SYMBOL statements. Note that when a common plot frame has been requested, distinct plot symbols are necessary to distinguish the variables in the plot.

In the MARK statement, the user may specify the spacing between tick marks along the vertical time axis. When the time axis runs down several pages, the user may want to have the horizontal axis reproduced every so often for reference. This can be done in the HLINE statement. The SIZE statement determines the width of the horizontal axis in the case of one plot frame, or the widths of the horizontal axes in the case of several adjacent plot frames. The default is to make the horizontal axis (axes) as wide as possible. In the case of several plot frames, the default is to have equal widths for the horizontal axes.

The user may also request that plotted values are subsequently printed. The default is not to print values.

```
TPLOT (time plots) ──────────────────────────
  VARiable = v list.    required            none
    Name or subscript of variables to be plotted.
  TIME = #₁, #₂, #₃.                    all cases
    Times to be plotted in terms of starting time
    (#₁), final time (#₂), and time increment (#₃).
  COMMon.                                     no
    Specifies that all variables are to be plotted
    in a common plot frame.
  MINimum = # list.                         none
    Minimum values to be plotted for the respective
    variables.
  MAXimum = # list.                         none
    Maximum values to be plotted for the respective
    variables.
  SYMBol = character list.             A,B,C,...
  LABEL.                                      no
    Print case labels, if any, down the left
    margin.
  MARK = #.                                    5
    Spacing between tick marks along the vertical
    time axis.
  HLine = #.                                  10
    The horizontal axis is reproduced for reference
    every # of lines.
  SIZE = # list.                  adjust to page size
    Width(s) of the horizontal axis (axes).
  PRINT.                                      no
    After the plot has been produced, print the
    plotted values.
```

Lagged scatter plots may be requested in paragraph LSCATTER. Each plotted point is of the form X(t), Y(t−u) where X and Y may refer to the same variable or to distinct variables, where u is a specified lag, and values of t range over time.

The number of points in each plot may be restricted in two ways. The user may restrict the range of values used in the plot by stating MINIMUM and

MAXIMUM values for each variable. To avoid confusion, the MIN and MAX lists refer to all variables in the order they were read in at the beginning of the problem. The user may find the tab feature described in Chapter 4 to be convenient here.

Another way to limit the number of plotted points is by stating a restricted range of TIME values.

The user can check the homogeneity of the data over time by repeating the LSCATTER paragraph with different TIME specifications. By default, the correspondence between units of time and case number is that time is identically equal to case number. The user may define a different time axis in paragraph TFAXIS, described on p. 627.

For each pair of X and Y variables formed, the program produces a plot with Y lagging behind X an integer number of time units given in the YLAG statement. A separate plot is produced for each pair of variables at the specified lag.

The user may request X and Y plot dimensions in the SIZE statement. He may also request that certain STATISTICS be computed and printed with each plot, and that plotted values be subsequently PRINTED.

LSCatter (lagged scatter plots) ─────────

XVAR = v list. required	none
Names or subscripts of X variables.	
YVAR = v list. required	none
Names or subscripts of Y variables.	
PAIR. or CROSs.	PAIR
Method of matching X and Y variables.	
MINimum = # list.	none
Minimum values to be plotted for respective variables.	
MAXimum = # list.	none
Maximum values to be plotted for respective variables.	
YLAG = #.	none
Integer number of time increment that Y lags behind X. (One time increment is the difference in time between one case and the next.)	
TIME = $\#_1$, $\#_2$.	all cases
Range of time values used in each plot. Includes starting time ($\#_1$) and final time ($\#_2$).	
SIZE = $\#_1$, $\#_2$.	fills one page
Number of characters for horizontal axis ($\#_1$) and number of lines for the vertical axis ($\#_2$).	
STATistics.	no
Requests mean and standard deviation of X and Y to be printed below plot, along with the X-Y correlation and the # of points in the plot.	
PRINT.	no
Requests that X-Y values be printed below plot.	

Tracing a frequency band component over time in paragraph DEMODULATE. DEMODULATE plots the amplitude (magnitude) and phase (origin shift) corresponding to components of a time series within a given frequency band. The user must state the band's central FREQUENCY; it should be between zero and the highest frequency seen in the data (0.5, unless the user has redefined units in the TFAXIS paragraph). The user may also specify the bandwidth (BW), or alternatively, the maximum number of filter coefficients (MAXLAG) to be used. Appendix A has further details.

The amplitude and phase are computed in each of a succession of time intervals. The midpoints of these time intervals may be specified in the TIME statement. The default is to plot time horizontally across one page, from the first available time to the last available time (results are not available

at the very first and last times corresponding to the first and last cases of data). Time refers to case number unless the user has redefined the time axis in paragraph TFAXIS. The user may specify the dimensions of the plot in the SIZE statement.

Results of the plot may be subsequently PRINTED, although this is not done by default.

DEModulate ─────────

VARiable = v list. required	none
Names or subscripts of variables to be plotted.	
FREQuency = #. required	none
Center of the desired frequency band.	
BW = #.	based on MAXLAG
Width of the desired frequency band.	
MAXLAG = #.	5% of no. of cases
Largest integer lag allowed for filter coefficients. Must be a positive integer less than half the number of cases.	
TIME = $\#_1$, $\#_2$, $\#_3$.	
Times at which results are evaluated and plotted, in terms of starting time ($\#_1$), final time ($\#_2$), and time increment ($\#_3$).	
SIZE = $\#_1$, $\#_2$.	fills one page
Number of characters for the horizontal axis ($\#_1$) and the number of lines for the vertical axis ($\#_2$).	
PRINT.	no
Print results after they have been plotted.	

Output 1T.4 Missing value replacement and mean adjustment: airline data

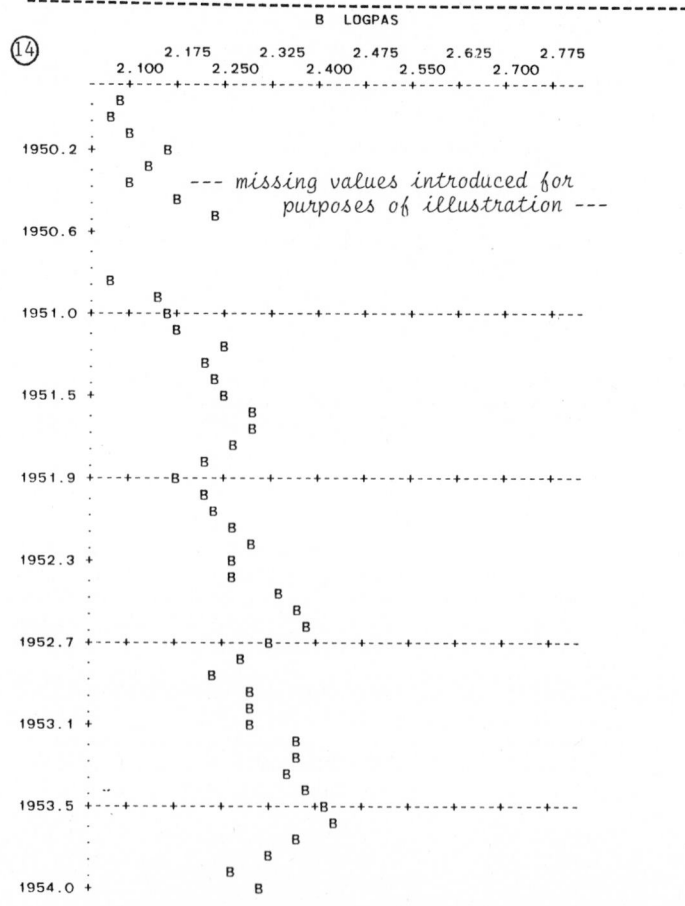

Example 1T.4 Mean Adjustments and Missing Value Replacement: Airline Data

We have taken data from Box and Jenkins (1976, p. 304) on the monthly numbers of international airline passengers during 1949-1960 and introduced a short stretch of missing values for purposes of illustration. We have followed Box and Jenkins in taking the logarithm base 10 of the actual number of passengers. The BMDP instructions for this problem are:

```
------------------------------------
/ PROBLEM    TITLE IS 'THE AIRLINE DATA'.
/ INPUT      VARIABLE IS 2.
            FORMAT IS '(F6,14X,F10)'. UNIT = 20.
/ VARIABLE   NAMES ARE DATE, LOGPAS.
            TIME IS DATE.
/ TRANSF IF(KASE GT 8 AND KASE LT 12) THEN X(2)=XMIS.
        DATE = DATE + (((KASE+10) MOD 12)+ .5)/12.
/ END
TPLOT     VARIABLE IS LOGPAS.
          SIZE IS 50./
REPLACE VARIABLE IS LOGPAS./
TPLOT     VARIABLE IS LOGPAS.
          SIZE IS 50./
------------------------------------
```

```
ADJUST    VARIABLE IS LOGPAS.
          DETREND.
          DESEASON = 12./
TPLOT     VARIABLE IS LOGPAS.
          SIZE IS 50./
END/
```

----

⑭ The transformed input data are plotted, with time on the vertical axis. Note that the 9th, 10th, and 11th data points are set to missing for the purpose of illustration.

⑮ The user has replaced missing values by the default method of linear interpolation. He then plots the result.

⑯ A linear trend has been removed from the data followed by the removal of monthly means, i.e., the average January value has been subtracted from each of the individual January values and so on for the remaining eleven months of the year. The user has then plotted the result.

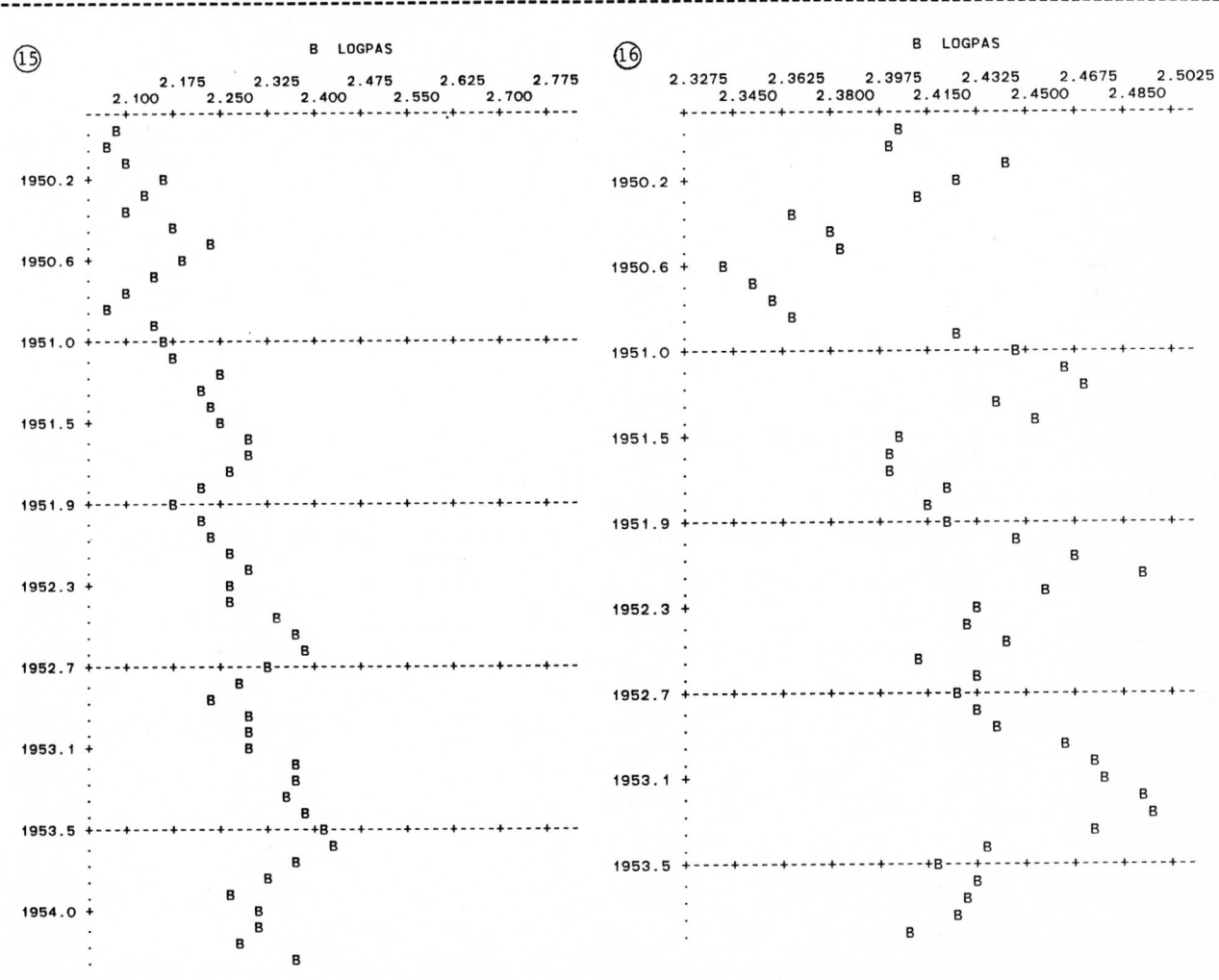

Saving the Data at Various Points in the Program

The SAVE paragraph is common to all BMDP programs and is described in Chapter 7. In P1T the SAVE paragraph can be used to initially store the data into a BMDP File, or to save an altered form of the data after execution of one of the paragraphs REPLACE, ADJUST, BANDPASS, FILTER, or AR (autoregression). Additional options (e.g., the saving of SPECTRA) are in preparation. To obtain further details add '/ PRINT NEWS.' after the first PROBLEM paragraph.

Replacing Missing Values

The user may replace missing values in paragraph REPLACE by one of three METHODS: linear interpolation (LINT), MEDIAN replacement, or MEAN replacement. When either of the latter two methods is requested, the user may specify the SPAN of surrounding observed values to be used in the calculation of the median or mean. Because the program uses the same number of observed values on either side of the missing value, the total SPAN should be an even number. The default procedure in paragraph REPLACE is to linearly interpolate missing values.

Missing value replacement can be a convenient method of proceeding with an analysis that would otherwise be difficult or impossible. Replacement is most appropriate when the number of missing values is small, and when the data do not exhibit erratic (high-frequency) fluctuations. Even under other circumstances, replacement can provide a convenient first look at the data, but the user is cautioned to regard the ensuing analysis with a healthy degree of skepticism in this case. P1T offers alternative treatments of missing values as described on p. 633.

```
REPlace (missing value replacement) ────────
  VARiable = v list.    required            none
    Names  or subscripts of variables whose missing
    values are to be replaced.
  METHod = (one only)                       LINT
         LINT, MEDian, MEAN.
    Method of  replacement - linear interpolation,
    local median, or local mean.
  SPAN = #.                                    4
    Number  of  adjacent  observed  values  used to
    calculate the local median or mean.
```

Trend Removal and Seasonal Adjustment in Paragraph ADJUST

Many economic series, for example the consumer price index, display an upward trend over time. A different, cyclic type of pattern is apparent in both economic and meteorological data. For example, both unemployment and temperatures tend to be higher during summer months than during other months of the year. We often wish to remove the effect of these trends or patterns by fitting a simple parametric model and then examining the residuals from the fit. The residual analysis can help us to evaluate and modify the original model, and it can also reveal subtle features not initially apparent.

Paragraph ADJUST allows the user to CENTER each variable about its sample mean (i.e., to subtract the sample mean from the data), to DETREND the data (i.e., to fit and remove a linear trend over time for each variable), and to adjust for seasonal periodicity in the data in the DESEAS statement. For example, the average January temperature would be subtracted from each of the individual January temperatures, and the same done for the remaining eleven months of the year by the statement DESEAS = 12. When both DETREND and DESEAS are requested, detrending is done first.

Implicit in the use of paragraph ADJUST is that the mean level of the time series changes with time in a simple way summarized by a few parameters, e.g., by a slope and intercept for a linear trend, or by seasonal means. (More complicated parametric trends may be fit and removed by using one of the regression programs, with one or more functions of time specified as independent variables.) When a parametric trend does not seem appropriate, the user may want to employ some alternative technique, such as highpass filtering (p. 625), for removing longterm movements in the series.

```
ADJust (for trend and season) ────────
  VARiable = v list.   required             none
    Names  or  subscripts  of  variables to be
    mean-adjusted.
  CENTer.                                     no
    Subtract the sample mean from each variable.
  DETRend.                                    no
    Fit  and  remove  a  linear trend over time for
    each variable.
  DESeas = #.                               none
    Subtract  the sample seasonal means, where # is
    the  number  of  distinct seasons, e.g., 12 for
    monthly                                   data.
  PRINT.                                      no
    Print data after adjustment.
```

FILTERING

Example 1T.5 Three Forms of Filtering an Averaged Evoked Potential

The data constitute an average of visually evoked electrical potentials recorded at a particular site of the brain. Successive time points are separated by an interval of four thousandths of a second. The duration of the time series is two seconds, with the first half-second preceding the stimulus and the remaining one-and-a-half seconds following the stimulus. The user has given these specifications to the program in paragraph TFAXIS as shown below.

The user wishes to examine a plot of the post-stimulus data in their initial form and of the corresponding spectrum. He then filters the data in three different ways, noting each time the effect of the filtering upon the time series and its spectrum. The Control Language instructions are as follows:

```
----------------------------------------
/ PROBLEM    TITLE IS 'AVERAGE EVOKED POTENTIAL'.
/ INPUT      VARIABLE IS 1.
            FORMAT IS STREAM. UNIT = 20.
/ VARIABLE   NAME IS AEP.
/ TFAXIS     START IS -500.
            DELTA IS    4.
            TNAME IS MILLISEC.
            FNAME IS HERTZ.
/ END
TPLOT       VARIABLE IS AEP.
            SIZE IS 100.
            TIME IS 0, 400./
SPECTRA     VARIABLE IS AEP.
            TIME IS 0, 1496./
BANDPASS    VARIABLE IS AEP.
            TYPE IS NOTCH.
            FREQUENCY IS .060.
            BWIDTH IS .010.  NO RECOLORING.
            PLOT./
TPLOT       VARIABLE IS AEP.
            SIZE IS 100.
            TIME IS 0, 400./
SPECTRA     VARIABLE IS AEP.
            TIME IS 0, 1496./
FILTER      VARIABLE IS AEP.
            PLOT.
            LAG IS 1.
            COEFFICIENTS ARE .23, .54, .23./
TPLOT       VARIABLE IS AEP.
            SIZE IS 100.
            TIME IS 0, 400./
SPECTRA     VARIABLE IS AEP.
            TIME IS 0, 1496./
AR          VARIABLE IS AEP.
            PLOT.
            MAXLAG IS 1.  NO RECOLOR./
TPLOT       VARIABLE IS AEP.
            SIZE IS 100.
            TIME IS 0, 400./
SPECTRA     VARIABLE IS AEP.
            TIME IS 0, 1496./
END/
----------------------------------------
```

(17) The plotted data display ripples that correspond to the small bump at 60 CPS (cycles per second) in the plotted spectrum. This is most likely due to the 60 CPS electrical power source, the standard frequency used in most of North America. To eliminate this artifact, the user has instructed the program to construct a notch filter at 60 CPS, and to apply this filter to the data. Because the 60 CPS ripple is not regarded as part of the brain's response, the user has requested that subsequent plots of the spectrum not be readjusted for the present notch filtering in the statement NO RECOLORING. The constructed filter coefficients are printed.

(18) Filtering the data effectively multiplies the spectrum by another function of frequency, the modulus square of the filter's frequency response function. The modulus, or magnitude, of the frequency reponse function is referred to as the gain of the filter, which is here plotted on a log scale. From the plotted spectrum below, we see that the 60 CPS component has been reduced by the filtering operation.

(19) The user has supplied the program with filter coefficients. Here the program prints its interpretation of the user's instructions. The particular coefficients provided by the user constitute a smoothing filter, which will further reduce erratic fluctuations in the average evoked potential.

(20) The plotted gain shows that the user's filter allows slowly varying low frequency components to pass while it damps out high frequency components. The filter is thus a lowpass or smoothing filter.

(21) The plot of the sequence after the user-supplied filtering.

(22) Having smoothed the data, the user now fits an autoregressive scheme, possibly to evaluate the scheme as a model for the evoked electrical potential of the brain. The estimated autoregressive coefficients are printed.

(23) The residuals of the fitted autoregressive scheme may be regarded as a filtered version of the data. The frequency responses of this filter are plotted here. We see that the model accounts for the low frequency components in the data, leaving the high frequency components to the residuals.

The residuals and their spectrum are then plotted over time, and their spectral density estimated to study the nature of the residuals, i.e., to see what the AR model may have missed and to evaluate the adequacy of and possible modifications to the AR model. Because the user is interested in the residuals, he has requested NO RECOLORING of the autoregressive filtering operation in subsequent spectral estimates. See p. 633 for further comments on recoloring.

Output 1T.5   Three forms of filtering an averaged evoked potential
----

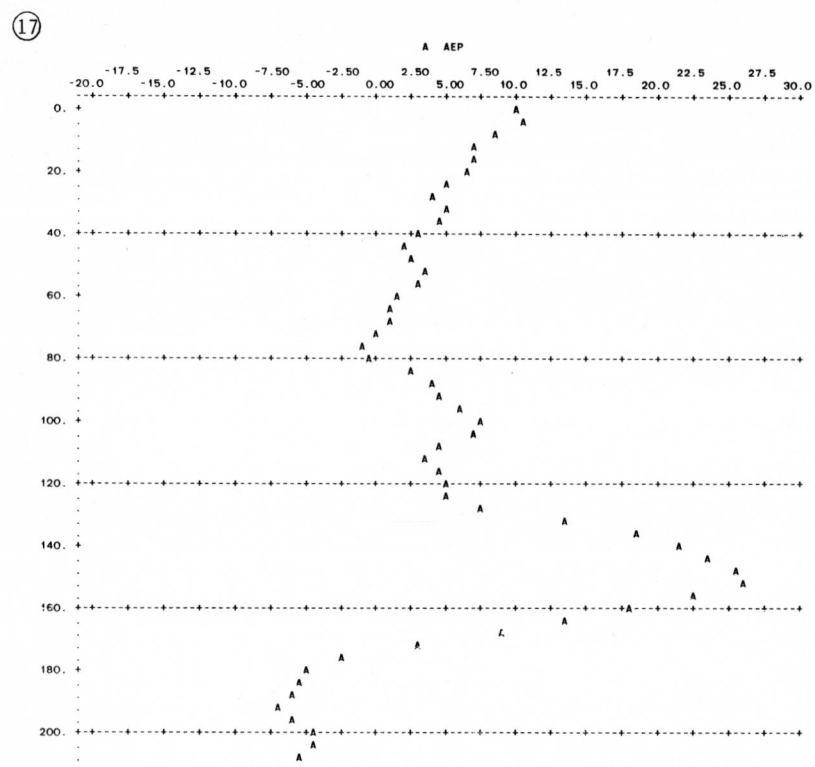

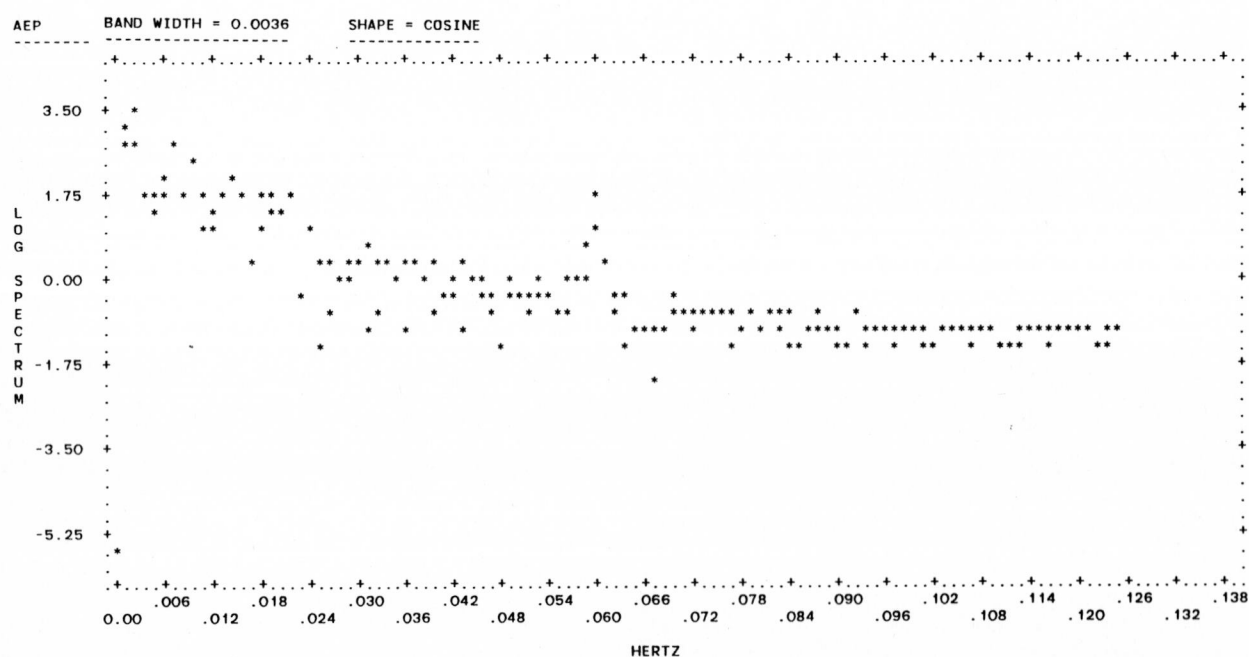

```
NOTCH    FILTER COEFFICIENTS FOR LAGS 31 THROUGH   0.
         (COEFFICIENTS AT NEGATIVE LAGS ARE OBTAINED BY SYMMETRY.)
FILTER      COEFFICIENT      LAG
------      -----------      ---
             0.0044         31           0.0137     23           0.0273     15           0.0223      7
            -0.0015         30           0.0030     22           0.0232     14           0.0503      6
            -0.0054         29          -0.0177     21          -0.0285     13          -0.0171      5
             0.0012         28          -0.0064     20          -0.0303     12          -0.0549      4
             0.0073         27           0.0215     19           0.0281     11           0.0108      3
            -0.0005         26           0.0110     18           0.0376     10           0.0578      2
(18)        -0.0102         25          -0.0249     17          -0.0260      9          -0.0037      1
            -0.0007         24          -0.0166     16          -0.0444      8           0.9412      0
```

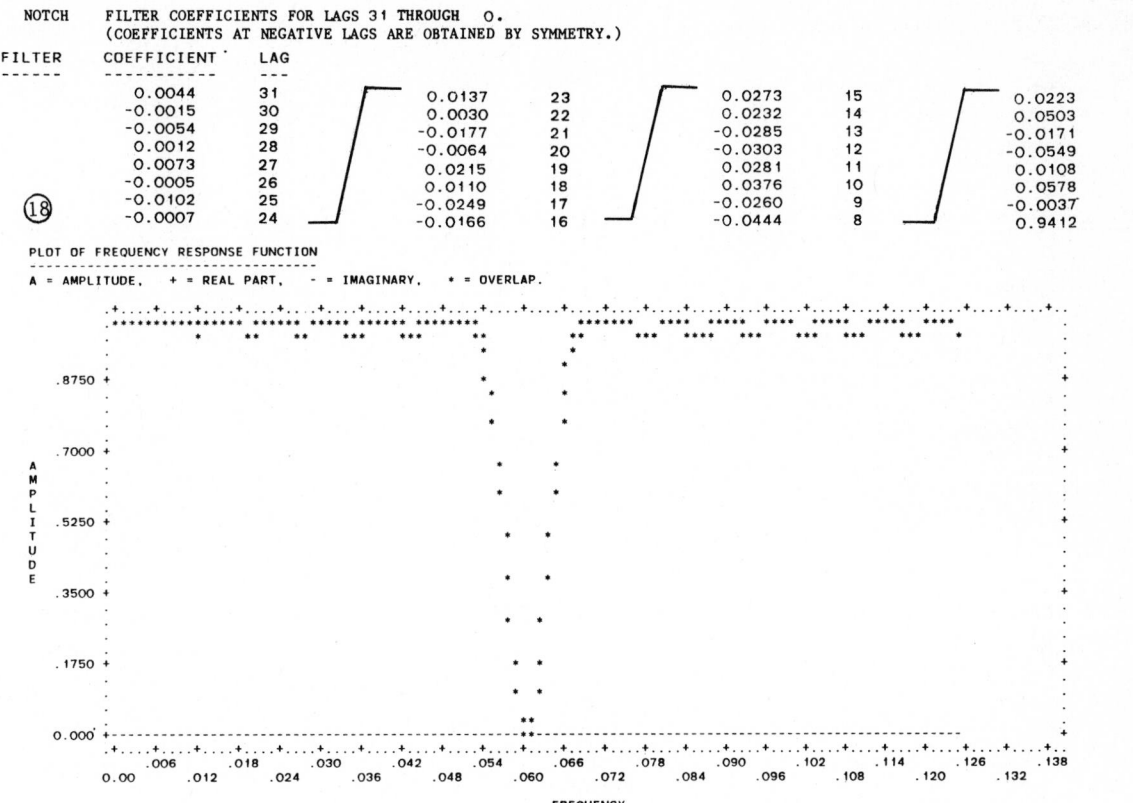

```
PLOT OF FREQUENCY RESPONSE FUNCTION
-----------------------------------
A = AMPLITUDE,   + = REAL PART,   - = IMAGINARY,   * = OVERLAP.
```

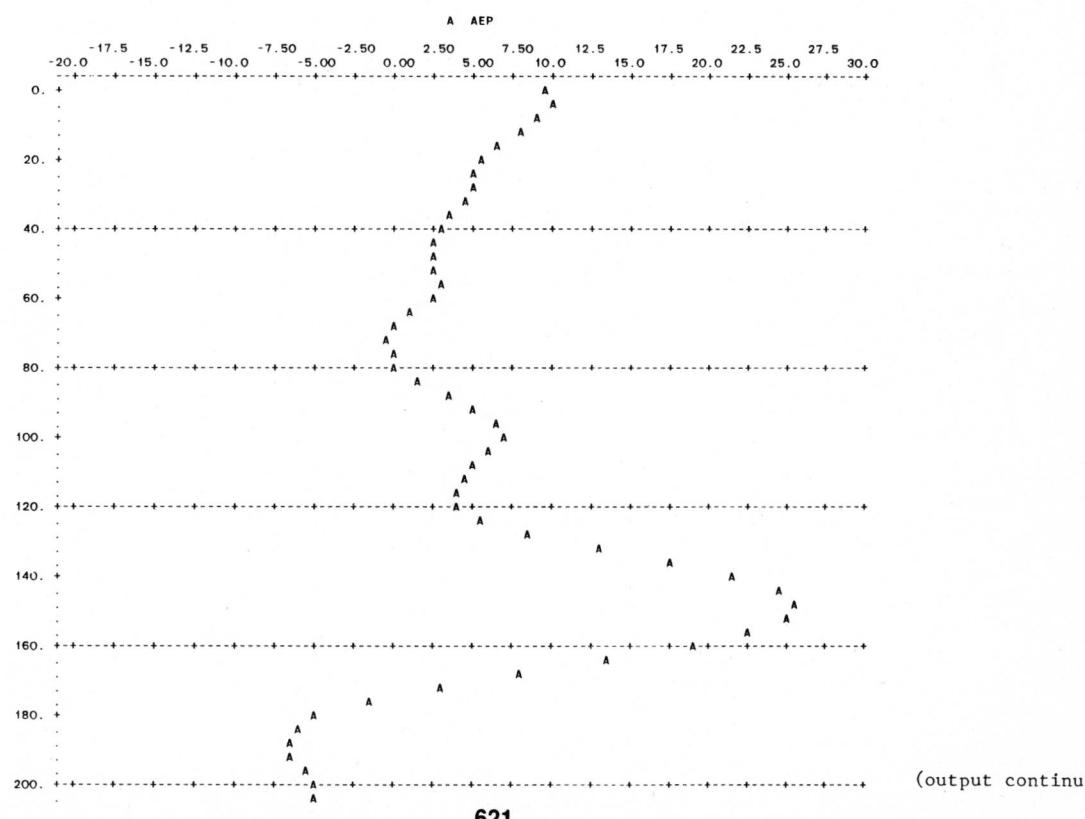

A AEP

(output continued)

Output 1T.5 (continued)

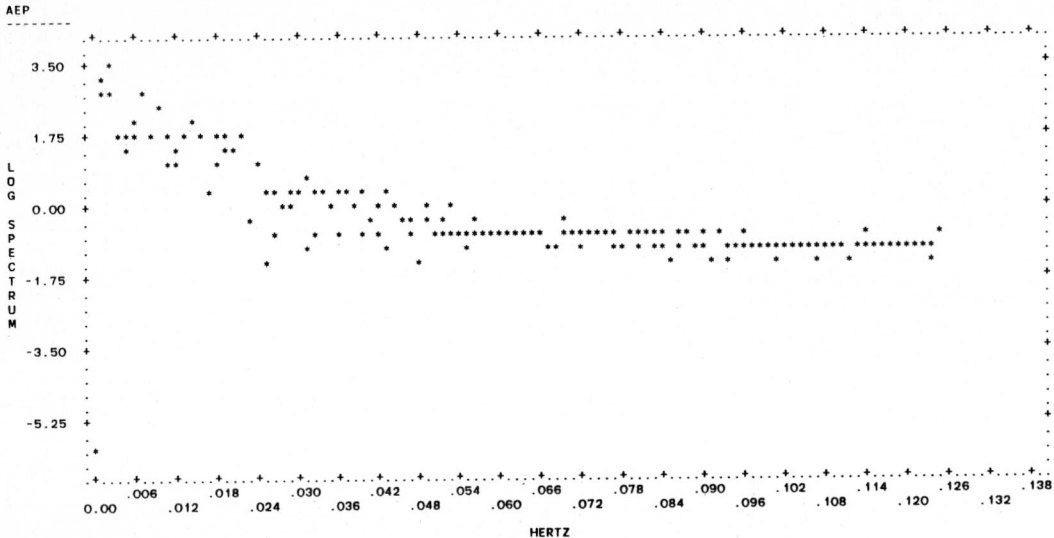

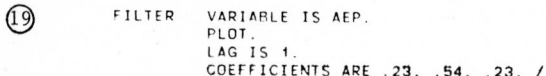

⑲   FILTER   VARIABLE IS AEP.
                     PLOT.
                     LAG IS 1.
                     COEFFICIENTS ARE .23, .54, .23. /

PLOT OF FREQUENCY RESPONSE FUNCTION

A = AMPLITUDE,   + = REAL PART,   - = IMAGINARY,   * = OVERLAP.

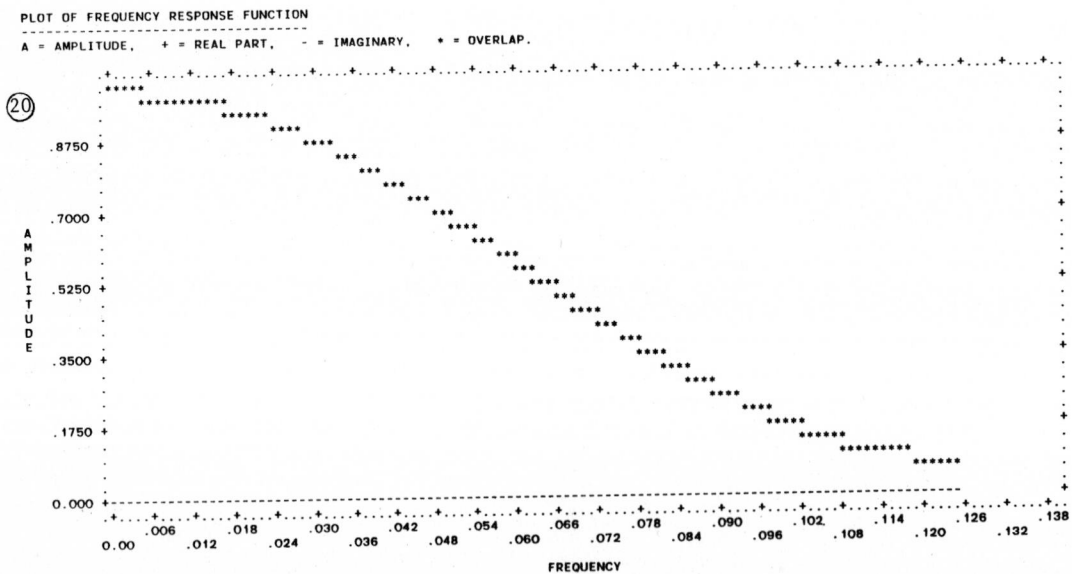

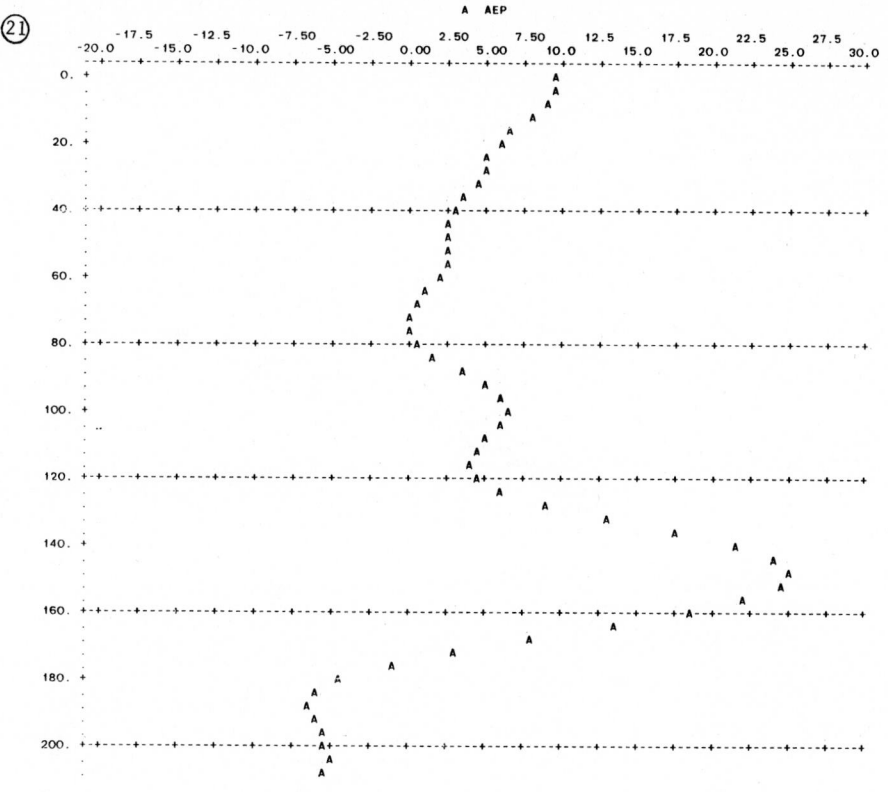

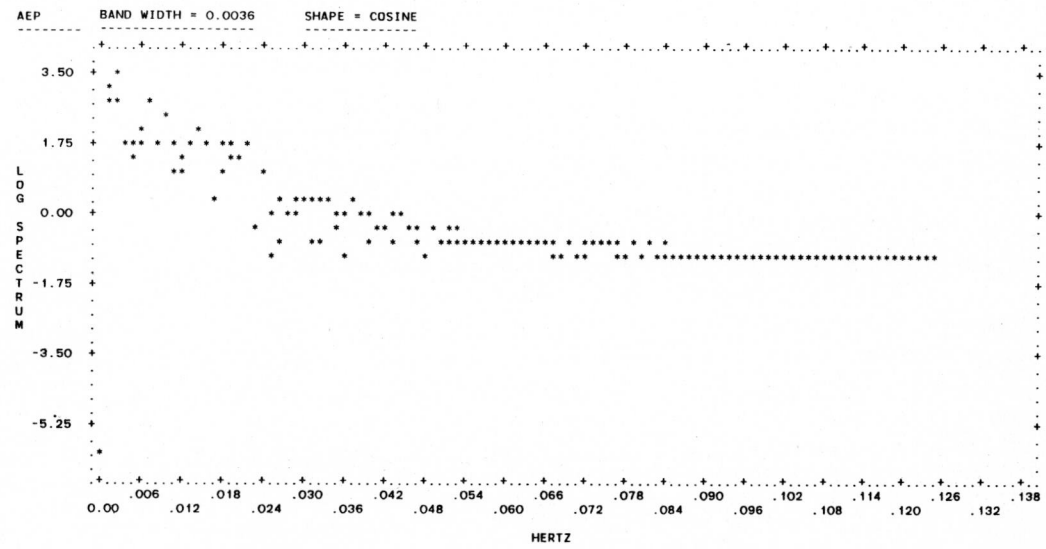

(output continued)

Output 1T.5 (continued)

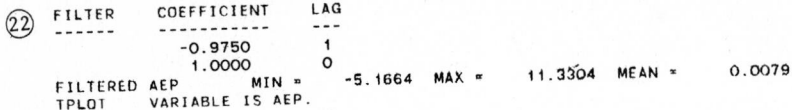

(22) FILTER   COEFFICIENT   LAG
      ------   -----------   ---
                    -0.9750   1
                     1.0000   0
      FILTERED AEP   MIN =   -5.1664   MAX =   11.3304   MEAN =   0.0079
      TPLOT   VARIABLE IS AEP.

PLOT OF FREQUENCY RESPONSE FUNCTION
----
(23) A = AMPLITUDE,   + = REAL PART,   - = IMAGINARY,   * = OVERLAP.

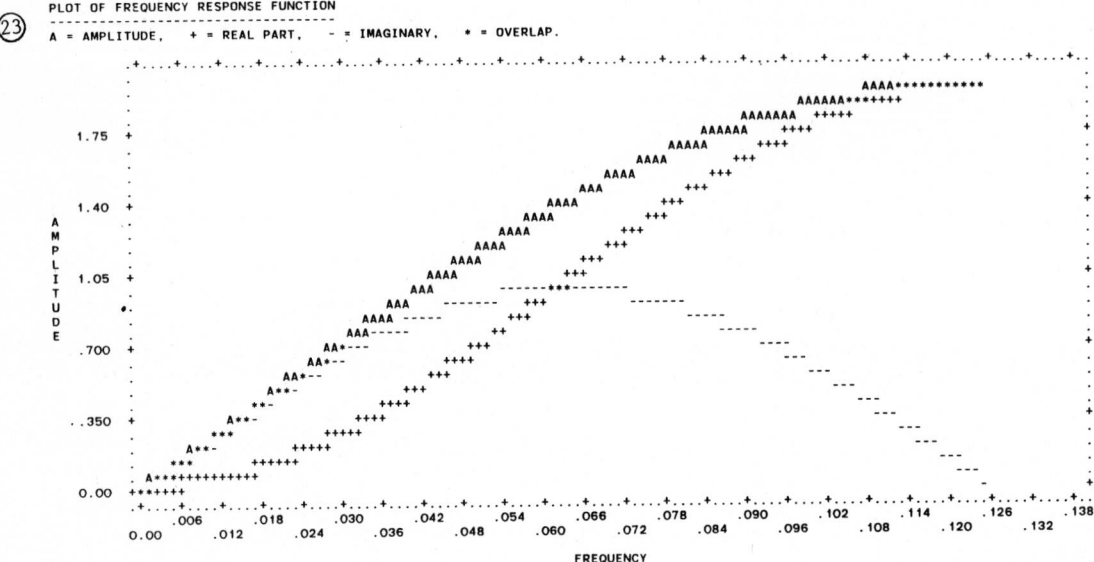

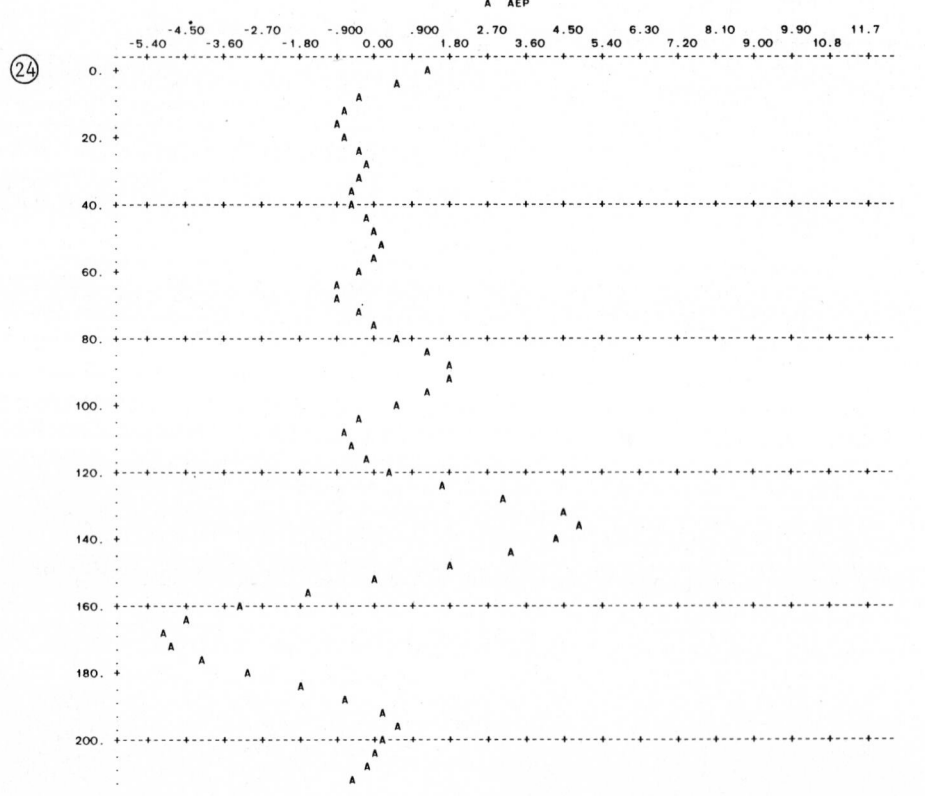

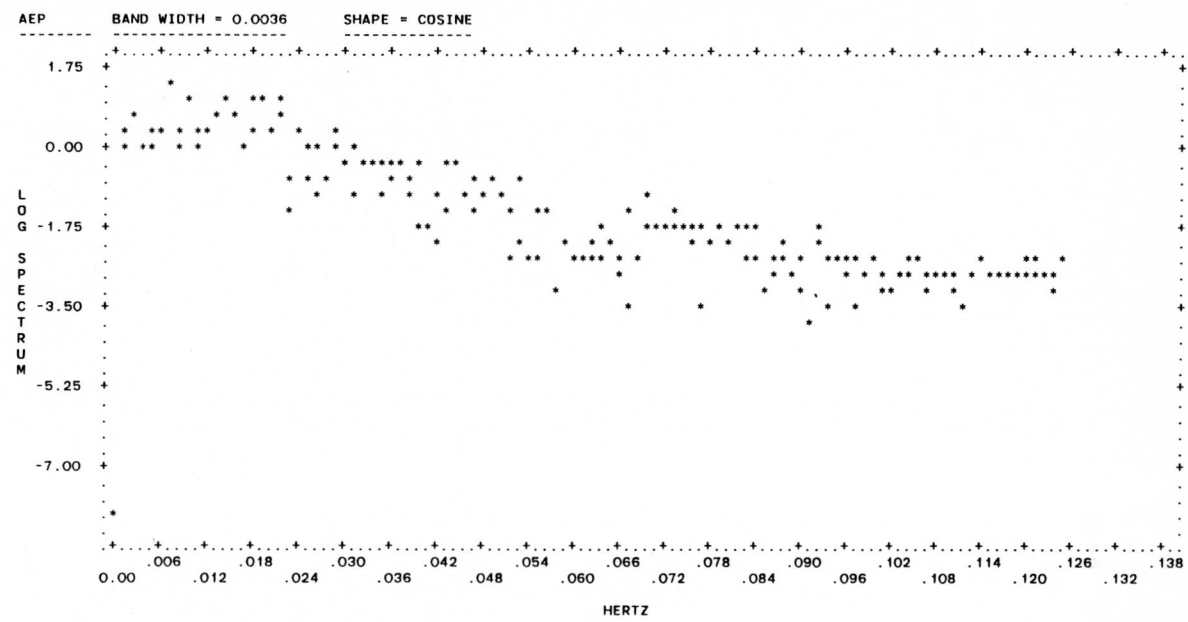

㉔ The final TPLOT paragraph shows relatively large residuals near the original peak response at 0.14 seconds. These large residuals correspond to the low frequency power in the plotted SPECTRUM. Thus the simple autoregressive filter reduces the overall variability in the data, but does not produce uncorrelated residuals.

BANDPASS and Related Types of Filtering

In paragraph BANDPASS, the user may alter a series by filtering out, or attenuating, all the components except those in a given frequency band, thus the name 'bandpass'. This operation is useful when a particular frequency band is of interest, for example, the alpha band of a subject's recorded EEG. The alpha component can be extracted from the EEG and viewed as it changes over time. Complex demodulation can also be recommended for this purpose.

If the bandpass version of a series is subtracted from the original series, all components are passed except those in the given frequency band. This is called band rejection filtering, or notch filtering (the frequency response of this operation is near unity except for a 'notch' at the given frequency band). In Example 1T.5 we saw notch filtering reduce a 60 CPS ripple that was not of intrinsic interest.

When the designated band of frequencies to be passed is centered about frequency zero, we have a lowpass filter (low frequencies are passed, high frequencies rejected). Lowpass filtering is one means of extracting a longterm trend in the data

without specifying a parametric model. Conversely, when low frequencies are rejected we have a highpass filter. Highpass filtering gives the residuals from a trend that has been obtained by lowpass filtering.

The user may specify one of these 4 kinds of filtering operation in the TYPE statement. If BAND or NOTCH has been specified, the center of the desired frequency band must be given in the FREQUENCY statement. The user may also request a certain bandwidth (BW). The program default is to assume that the desired type of filtering is BANDPASS and to use as narrow a bandwidth as is feasible. The MAXLAG specification places an upper limit on the largest allowable integer lag used in the construction of filter coefficients. This also limits the number of data points at the beginning and end of the time series that will be lost, i.e., set equal to missing values, as a result of the filtering operation.

Filtering operations essentially multiply spectra by a function of frequency (for a single variable the spectrum is multiplied by the modulus square of the filter's frequency response function). The program automatically compensates for this effect by RECOLORING spectra. If this is not desired, e.g., if a notch filter has been requested to remove some artifact from the data that is not of interest, the user may specify NO RECOLORING. The program assumes that once the filter coefficients have been calculated, they are to be used in filtering the time series, with the filtered output becoming the program's reference copy of the time series. If the user wishes only to examine filter characteristics without applying the filter, he may tell the program to RETAIN the original, unfiltered time series, in which case the RECOLORING option has no effect.

The user may limit the output produced by paragraph BANDPASS. P1T automatically prints the computed filter coefficients, and plots and prints the filter's frequency response function (factor by which a sine wave at a given frequency is multiplied). Curtail this output by stating NO PRINT or NO PLOT.

```
BANDpass (filtering) ─────────────────────
  VARiable = v list.   required              none
   Names  or  subscripts  of  variables  to  be
   filtered.
  TYPE = (one only)                          BAND
        BAND, NOTch, LOW, HIGH.
   Type of filtering operation desired.
  FREQUENCY = #.   required unless            none
              TYPE = LOW or
              TYPE = HIGH specified
   Center of the frequency  band  to  be passed or
   rejected.
  BW = #.                     narrow as feasible
   Width  of  the  frequency  band to be passed or
   rejected.
  MAXLag = #.             5% of no. of cases
   Largest  integer  lag  allowed  for  filter
   coefficients.  Must  be a positive integer less
   than half the number of cases.
  REColor.                                    yes
   Allow for the filtering operation in subsequent
   spectral analyses by recoloring the spectrum.
  RETAIN.                                     no
   Retain the original  time  series  as  the pro-
   gram's reference copy of the data, i.e., do not
   carry out the filtering operation. If RETAIN is
   specified, the RECOLORING option has no effect.
  PRINT.                                      yes
   Print the filter's frequency response function.
  PLOT.                                       yes
   Plot  the filter's frequency response function.
```

<u>User-constructed filtering in paragraph FILTER.</u> Occasionally, a user may want to apply a particular filter to the data rather than leave the construction of a filter to the program. This can be done in paragraph FILTER. For each listed variable or time series, say Y(t), P1T will compute a filtered version of the series, call it Z(t), using the relation

$$Z(t) = c_1 Y(t-u_1) + c_2 Y(t-u_2) + \ldots + c_L Y(t-u_L)$$

where the user has supplied the COEFFICIENTS c_1, c_2, ..., c_L and the corresonding LAGS u_1, u_2, ..., u_L.

One illustration of the FILTER paragraph is the smoothing filter used in Example 1T.5. As another example, suppose the user wishes to reduce seasonal effects in monthly temperatures (which we will call MOTEMPS) by taking twelfth differences. He may state

```
FILTER
   VARIABLE IS MOTEMPS.
   LAGS ARE 0, 12.
   COEFFICIENTS ARE 1, -1./
```

This forms a new series composed of the differences between monthly temperatures recorded 1 year apart.

As in the BANDPASS paragraph, the program automatically RECOLORS subsequent spectral estimates to allow for the filtering operation. This may be negated by stating NO RECOLORING. Similarly, P1T automatically applies the filter to the data unless the user tells P1T to RETAIN the unfiltered data.

The program PRINTS filter coefficients and PLOTS and PRINTS the filter's frequency response function in terms of gain (the factor by which the amplitude of a sine wave at a given frequency is multiplied) and phase (the phase or origin shift produced by the filter in a sine wave at a given frequency). Limit this output by requesting NO PRINT or NO PLOT.

```
FILter (by user) ─────────────────────
  VARiable = v list.   required              none
   Names  or  subscripts  of  variables  to  be
   filtered.
  LAG = # list.   required                    none
   Lags,  expressed  in  integer  numbers of time
   increments,  at  which  corresponding  filter co-
   efficients are to be applied.
  COEFficient = # list.  required             none
   Filter coefficients at specified lags.
  REColor.                                    yes
   Compensate  for  this  filtering  operation  in
   subsequent estimates of spectra.
  RETAIN.                                     no
   Retain the original  time  series  as  the pro-
   gram's reference copy of the data, i.e., do not
   carry out the filtering operation. If RETAIN is
   specified, the RECOLORING option has no effect.
  PRINT.                                      yes
   Print the filter's gain and phase.
  PLOT.                                       yes
   Plot the gain and phase of the filter.
  SIZE = #_1, #_2.               fills one page
   No. of  characters  for  horizontal axis (#_1) and
   number of lines for the vertical axis (#_2).
```

<u>The calculation of autoregressive coefficients and autoregressive filtering in paragraph AR.</u> In paragraph AR the user requests the program to find autoregressive coefficients ϕ_1, ..., ϕ_L minimizing the sum of squared residuals (t) given by

$$(t) = Y(t) - \phi_1 Y(t-1) - \ldots - \phi_L Y(t-L).$$

The user makes this request by specifying the maximum lag (MAXLAG) L to be used.

The program automatically produces the sequence $\varepsilon(t)$ of residuals, which are a filtered version of the input variable. Thereafter the residuals $\varepsilon(t)$ replace the input variable $Y(t)$ as the program's internal reference copy of the variable. The user may request that this not be done by telling the program to RETAIN the unfiltered input variable.

The RECOLOR, PRINT, and PLOT options operate as in the FILTER paragraph.

Autoregressive models give a parametric representation for the variation exhibited by the data. Alternatively, autoregression may be used as a prefiltering of the data to enhance subsequent spectral estimates. See p. 633.

AR (autoregression)

VARiable = v list. required none
 Names or subscripts of variables for which autoregressive coefficients are to be estimated.
MAXLag = #. required none
 Maximum lag to be used, expressed in terms of an integer number of time increments.
RETAIN. no
 Retain the original time series as the program's reference copy of the data, i.e., do not carry out the filtering operation. If RETAIN is specified, the RECOLORING option has no effect.
REColor. yes
 Compensate for the filtering operation in subsequent spectral estimates.
PRINT. yes
 Print the gain and phase of the autoregressive filter.
PLOT. yes
 Plot the gain and phase of the autoregressive filter.

Use of the TYPE statement in paragraph FILTER. If the user requests a filter of TYPE = BANDPASS, NOTCH, LOWPASS, or HIGHPASS, the program interprets the filter paragraph exactly as it does the BANDPASS paragraph. Similarly, if the user requests a filter of TYPE = AR, the program interprets the paragraph as it does the AR paragraph. When TYPE is stated, the program ignores user-specified filter coefficients. The TYPE statement is thus a convenience feature that allows all filtering to be accomplished in the FILTER paragraph.

FILTER
 TYPE = (one only) none
  BAND, NOTch, LOW, HIGH, AR.
 Desired type of program-constructed filter. If TYPE is stated, user-specified filter coefficients are ignored.

Defining the Time or Frequency axes in paragraph TFAXIS. In Example 1T.5, the unit of time is one second, although the time increment between data points (cases) is four thousandths of a second (0.004 sec). The user has specified the name of·the unit of time and the time increment from one case to the next by writing

    TFAXIS
      TNAME = SECOND.
      DELTA = 0.004.

He would also like the name of the unit of frequency to be CPS (cycles per second). He requests this by stating

    FNAME = CPS.

In this example, the relation between the unit of time and the unit of frequency is simple: a sine wave at frequency one CPS goes through exactly one cycle per unit of time (SECOND).

There are other possible relations between the unit of frequency and the unit of time. Suppose, for example, that a subject's ability to hear high pitch (high frequency) sounds is being tested. It may still be most convenient to measure time in seconds, but the audio signals being tried on the subject may be more conveniently labelled in kilohertz, abbreviated KHZ, which is thousands of cycles per second. (The highest detectable frequency for humans is roughly 20,000 cycles per second, i.e., 20 KHZ.) Thus a sine wave at one KHZ goes through 1000 cycles per unit of time (SECOND). The number of Cycles Per Unit of Time of a sine wave at one unit of frequency is given in the CPUT statement. In our second example the user would specify

    TFAXIS
      TNAME = SECOND.
      FNAME = KHZ.
      CPUT = 1000.

In the first example the CPUT specification was not needed because the default value (CPUT = 1.) was appropriate.

The user may also define the time axis for the problem, i.e., he may establish the correspondence between time and case number. This is done by stating START = #, the time value corresponding to the first case of data, and DELTA = #, the time increment from one case to the next.

In the absence of user specifications, output from the program has time and frequency measured in the dimensionless units TIME, FREQUENCY. The fastest sine wave that the program can analyze goes through one complete cycle in the course of two consecutive cases of data. Thus the range of frequencies used by the program is, under default values, zero to one-half. Generally, the frequency range is from zero to $1/(2*CPUT*DELTA)$. Subsequent frequency domain specifications, for example bandwidth, are assumed by the program to be expressed in units established in the TFAXIS paragraph, either by default or by the user.

```
TFAXIS (axes for time and frequency)
    TNAME = c.                              TIME
      Name of the unit of time.
    FNAME = c.                              FREQ
      Name of the unit of frequency.
    CPUT = #.                               1.0
      Cycles  per  unit time. A sine wave at one unit
      of  frequency  goes  through # of cycles during
      one unit of time.
    START = #.                              1.0
      Time  value  corresponding to the first case of
      data.
    DELTA = #.                              1.0
      Time increment from one case to the next.
```

FINE TUNING AND ALTERNATIVE METHODS FOR SPECTRAL ANALYSIS

Covariance-based Spectral Estimation in Paragraph COVARIANCE

Paragraph COVARIANCE is an alternative to paragraph SPECTRA (COVARIANCE is not available in the 1982 version of P1T). The Control Language and output for the 2 paragraphs differ in only a few details. The fundamental difference in the 2 approaches is the kind of smoothing used to produce spectral estimates. In paragraph SPECTRA, adjacent periodograms are averaged, while in COVARIANCE, a weighted sample covariance function is Fourier-transformed.

The spectral estimates produced by the two approaches are in substantial agreement for long time series (when a large number of cases of data are used in the analysis). For short time series, paragraph COVARIANCE tends to produce smoother results than SPECTRA, and can be recommended on this basis.

In general, paragraph COVARIANCE requires somewhat more computational time and produces somewhat smoother estimates than paragraph SPECTRA. The user, however, is given a range of options in both paragraphs enabling him to adjust the amount and kind of smoothing.

The basic specifications for paragraph COVARIANCE listed below are the same as those for paragraph SPECTRA. The output from the two paragraphs is also the same, except that covariances are automatically included as part of the results in paragraph COVARIANCE, whereas they must be explicitly requested in paragraph SPECTRA.

```
COVAriance (spectra) ─────────────────────────
  XVAR = v list.  required                      none
    Names or subscripts of X variables.
  YVAR = v list.                                none
    Names or subscripts of Y variables.
  PAIR. or CROSS.                               PAIR
    Method of matching X and Y variables. This
    requests the estimation of the coherence and
    phase between X and Y variables.
  DEPend = XVAR, YVAR.                          none
    Requests frequency domain regression and
    indicates which variable within each pair is to
    be regarded as dependent. Output consists of
    estimates of the gain and the filter
    coefficients. Applicable only if both XVAR and
    YVAR have been specified.
  PLOT.                                         yes
    Plot results.
  PRINT.                                        yes
    Print results.
```

Tapering and Padding the Data Prior to Spectral Estimation

The user may request that the data be TAPERED prior to the formation of periodograms in paragraph SPECTRA or the formation of covariances in paragraph COVARIANCE. This can enhance subsequent spectral estimates.

The technique is to TAPER off values near the beginning and ending portions of the data. This helps to reduce the influence of estimates

calculated in one frequency band upon those in another frequency band.

Another technique, PADDING, can be used in paragraph SPECTRA to obtain a finer mesh of frequencies by appending zeros to the end of the data. This is particularly useful when the original data length (number of cases) is small, and the original mesh of frequencies consequently coarse. We recommend that substantial padding of the data be accompanied by some tapering. Of note here is that paragraph COVARIANCE automatically pads the data prior to computing sample covariances. Further details are given in Appendix A.

There are two ways in which the user may specify the amount of padding. If the user states NPAD = n, the program will append exactly n zeros to the data. If the user states PAD = p, the program will extend the data with a number of zeros, the number being approximately p times the length of the original data sequence. If both NPAD and PAD are specified, the program uses the NPAD specification. The default specification is PAD = 0.0. Because the formation of periodograms requires the overall sequence length to be factored into smaller numbers, the user should check the sequence length prior to an NPAD specification.

We also note here that while we have discussed tapering and padding 'the data', the program actually operates on an extra copy of the data. The program's internal reference copy of the data is unaltered.

The tapering statement for paragraphs SPECTRA and COVARIANCE and the padding statements for paragraph SPECTRA are summarized below.

```
SPECtra (tapering and padding) ────────────────
  TAPer = #_1, #_2.                             zero
    Taper the first #_1 and the last #_2 portion of
    the data. TAPER = p is interpreted as TAPER =
    p, p.
  PAD = #.                                      zero
    Pad the end of the data with # proportion of
    zeros.
  NPAD = #.                                     see above
    Pad the end of the data with exactly # zeros.
```

```
COVAriance (tapering) ─────────────────────────
  TAPer = #_1, #_2.                             zero
    Taper the first #_1 and the last #_2 portion of
    the data. TAPER = p is interpreted as TAPER =
    p, p.
```

How Much Spectral Smoothing: Bandwidths and Alternative Specifications

In the Chapter 20 Introduction, we showed how the sinusoidal approximation to the lynx data improved as we broadened the band of frequencies used. One of the basic aims of spectral analysis is to answer the question, 'How much variation in the data is accounted for by different frequency bands of sine waves?' The computed spectral density is an estimate of the variance per unit of frequency. This estimated density is analogous to an estimate of a probability density by a histogram - the interval width, in our case the frequency bandwidth, is a key parameter in determining the smoothness of the resulting estimate (unlike most histograms, our spectral estimates are typically based upon overlapping rather than disjoint intervals).

In paragraph SPECTRA, the bandwidth specification is directly used to determine the breadth of the frequency interval (band), and hence the number of adjacent periodograms to average for the estimated spectral density in each frequency band. An alternative determination is obtained from the specified degrees of freedom for the spectral estimates. When the data have not been padded (see the discussion of tapering and padding), each periodogram averaged contributes two degrees of freedom to the spectral estimate. If the user specifies both bandwidth and degrees of freedom, the program uses the latter specification. The default is to form spectral estimates having 8 and 16 degrees of freedom for data sequences of length 64 or less, and to use 8, $3N^{1/3}$, and $N^{2/3}$ degrees of freedom when the data length N (number of cases) exceeds 64.

Appropriate bandwidths for spectral estimation depend on the objectives of the analysis and upon the characteristics of the data being analyzed. The default bandwidths should help the user decide what bandwidths, i.e., how much periodogram smoothing, will be best suited for further spectral analyses. More technical details are given in Appendix A.

The two ways of specifying the frequency bandwidth in paragraph SPECTRA are shown below.

SPECtra (bandwidths) ─────────────────
| DF = # list.
| Degrees of freedom used for spectral estimates.
| This is an alternative means of specifying
| bandwidth.
| BW = # list.   from DF
| Bandwidths used for spectral estimates.

In paragraph COVARIANCE, a different approach to spectral estimation is taken. First a sequence of covariances is computed, the elements of the sequence being the estimated covariance of a variable with itself (autocovariance) or with another variable (crosscovariance) at consecutive time lags. This sequence is then weighted and Fourier transformed to produce the spectral estimate. The smoothness of the estimate derives from the number of lags used, or more generally, allowing some weights to be zero, the nature of the weights applied to the covariance sequence. (The spectral estimate produced by COVARIANCE is a cosine polynomial, the degree of the polynomial determined by the largest lag having nonzero weight.) Fewer lags produce smoother estimates, so that a small number of lags corresponds to a large bandwidth.

As shown in Appendix A, it is possible to calculate an equivalent bandwidth and equivalent degrees of freedom for covariance-based spectral estimates. Thus the program can interpret a user statement of BW = # list, or DF = # list, in paragraph COVARIANCE to produce spectral estimates equivalent to those produced in paragraph SPECTRA.

Alternatively, the user may provide a list of the maximum lags (receiving nonzero weight) to be used by paragraph COVARIANCE in forming estimates at corresponding bandwidths. This is done by stating MAXLAG = # list. If the user supplies more than one of these three alternative smoothness

specifications, the program uses only one of the three, giving priority first to DF, then to MAXLAG, and last to BW. Program defaults are based on degrees of freedom, as described above for paragraph SPECTRA. The alternative smoothness specifications are summarized below.

COVAriance (bandwidths) ─────────────────
| DF = # list.
| Degrees of freedom used for spectral estimates.
| This is an alternative means of specifying
| bandwidth.
| MAXLag = # list.   from DF
| Largest lag (integer number of time increments)
| to be used in forming the spectral density
| estimate.
| BW = # list.   from DF
| Bandwidths used for spectral estimates.

Lagging Y with Respect to X for Bivariate Spectral Analysis

It occasionally happens that the correlation between two variables is greatest at one particular lag, and that the correlation at other lags is close to zero. In this situation, the bivariate spectral analysis can be improved by realigning the two series, i.e., by analyzing

$$X(t), \; Y(t-u_0)$$

where u_0 is the lag of high correlation. The user may request this in either paragraph SPECTRA or COVARIANCE. The program proceeds to analyze the realigned series, and then relabels the spectral output in terms of the original variables $X(t)$, $Y(t)$.

This technique can be particularly beneficial in estimating the coherence and phase between X and Y, and in estimating the filter coefficients for fitting one of the variables by a filtered version of the other.

Some of the data are not used by this method, i.e., the first u_0 points of X and the last u_0 points of Y when u_0 is positive. Care should be taken not to request too large a value for u_0 – the magnitude of u_0 should be less than half the number of cases. (Also note that in paragraph COVARIANCE, the highest possible MAXLAG specification is reduced by twice the magnitude of u_0.) We recommend that the original variables $X(t)$, $Y(t)$ be analyzed before $Y(t)$ is realigned.

The statement for realigning $Y(t)$ in either paragraph SPECTRA or in paragraph COVARIANCE is given below.

SPECtra or COVAriance (lagging) ─────────────────
| YLAG = #.   none
| Lag each Y variable a given integer number of
| time increments with respect to each X variable
| in the bivariate spectral analysis. Applicable
| only if both XVAR and YVAR have been specified.

The Shape of the Spectral Smoother: Weights for Covariances or Periodograms

If we were forced to restrict ourselves to only one adjustable parameter in spectral estimation, the best choice for that parameter would probably be the bandwidth used, or related parameters (degrees of freedom, or in paragraph COVARIANCE, the maximum lag used) from which the bandwidth can be derived. The bandwidth is simple in concept, and can be effectively used to control the degree of smoothness in the estimated spectra. Occasionally, the user will wish to control not only the degree of smoothing, but also the way in which the smoothing is done. One such option has already been presented - the user may either smooth periodograms in paragraph SPECTRA, or he may weight covariances in paragraph COVARIANCE. A more refined control is obtained by choosing the shape of the periodogram or covariance weighting functions. In paragraph SPECTRA the estimated spectral density is a weighted average of periodograms. The weights used fall along the curve of either a RECTANGULAR function producing uniform weights or a raised COSINE function (1+cos(x))/2, the latter being the program default. The PSHAPE (P for periodogram) statement controls this option, and is summarized here.

```
SPECtra (shape) ─────────────────────────────────
   PSHape = (one only)                    COSINE
         COSine, RECTangular, TRIAngular.
      Shape of the periodogram weighting function --
      rectangular or cosinusoidal.
```

Similarly in paragraph COVARIANCE, the user may use the CSHAPE (C for covariance) statement to select the form of the weights applied to the covariance function. The weighted covariance function is Fourier transformed to produce the spectral estimate. The shapes have been named according to an author who proposed their use. Thus DELP signifies de la Valle-Poussin (E. Parzen's name

is also associated with this choice), HAM signifies R.W. Hamming, and HAN signifies Julius von Hann. The formulas corresponding to these three choices are given in Appendix A. The CSHAPE statement is as follows.

```
COVAriance (shape) ──────────────────────────────
   CSHAPE = (one only)DELP, HAM, HAN          HAM
      Shape of the covariance weighting function.
```

Restricting the Spectral Analysis to a Subset of Time Points

In both paragraphs SPECTRA and COVARIANCE, the user may request that the analysis be restricted to a particular time interval, e.g., only the post-stimulus portion of an EEG record, or to a particular sequence of times, e.g., only January temperatures and not those for other months of the year. By exercising this option, the user may see how the spectra for different time intervals or time sequences vary. This is one way to check the homogeneity of the data. The request is made in the TIME statement shown below.

```
SPECtra or COVAriance (time subsets) ────────────
   TIME = #_1, #_2, #_3.                   all cases
      The spectral analysis may be restricted to a
      subset of time points (cases) given by the
      starting time (#_1), the final time (#_2), and
      the time increment (#_3).
```

Specifying the Frequency Range of Interest

In Example 1T.3 we presented several views of monthly sunspots recorded over a 200 year period. Another aspect of this data can be seen from the estimated spectral density shown in Figure 20.14. We see a low-frequency peak corresponding to the 11 year sunspot cycle, followed by a rather flat spectrum of relatively small magnitude. Once we have

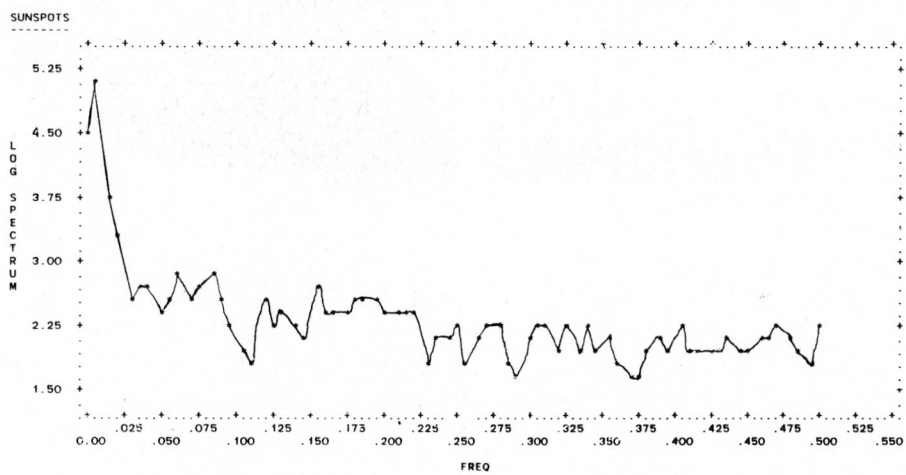

Figure 20.14 Spectrum of monthly sunspots

this initial picture of the sunspot spectrum, we may want to get a more detailed view of the low-frequency portion of the plot. We can request that the plotted spectrum be restricted to a certain frequency range by supplying a FREQUENCY statement either to paragraph SPECTRA or to paragraph COVARIANCE. This statement is summarized below. The default is to devote the width of one page to the entire frequency range. (Note that the user may define the units of frequency in paragraph TFAXIS.)

```
SPECtra or COVAriance (frequency range) ─────────
  FREQuency = #₁, #₂, #₃.                    see above
     Spectral estimates are to be plotted from
     frequency #₁ to frequency #₂, incremented by
     frequency #₃.
```

Plotting Confidence Bands about the Estimated Spectral Density

The estimated spectral density of each time series is normally plotted within 95 percent confidence bands to give a graphical indication of the estimate's sampling variability. The user may delete the confidence bands from the plot, or he may plot the confidence limits about a smooth (large bandwidth) estimate of the spectrum. Results of the latter option are shown in Figure 20.15 for the sunspot data discussed in Example 1T.3.

This form of plot highlights the difference between the smooth estimate and the narrower band estimate being plotted. The above figure thus represents a two-in-one plot of the estimated spectral density. This double-view of the underlying spectral density also reminds us that our choice of bandwidth constitutes a compromise. The wide band estimate represents a more reliable estimate of a smoothed version of the underlying spectrum, while the narrow band estimate gives us a detailed picture of the spectrum more vulnerable to sampling variability.

Another point to remember is that we can expect about 5 out of every 100 of the plotted confidence intervals to fail to cover the true underlying spectral density. (Under regularity conditions the plotted estimates are nearly independent for lengthy time series.)

The CONFIDENCE statement may be used in either paragraph SPECTRA or paragraph COVARIANCE to delete confidence bands or to place them about a smoother estimate than that being plotted. The default is to plot the bands about the plotted ESTIMATE. The SMOOTH estimate is the estimate corresponding to the largest bandwidth used in the paragraph.

```
SPECtra or COVAriance (confidence bands) ─────────
  CONFidence = EStimate,                     EStimate
               SMooth, NONE.
     Confidence bands may be plotted about the
     estimate, about a smoother estimate, or they
     may be omitted.
```

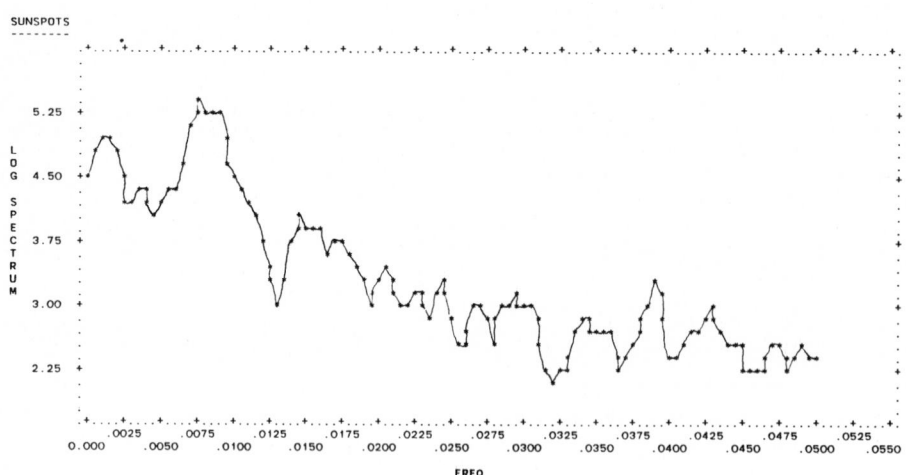

Figure 20.15   An expanded view of the low-frequency portion of the sunspot spectrum (a two-in-one plot)

Alternative Treatments of Missing Values

When only a few values are missing from a lengthy time series, it is probably satisfactory to fill in these values in paragraph REPLACE, keeping in mind that the interpretation of the subsequent analysis merits an extra degree of skepticism.

Alternatively, the user may proceed directly to one of the spectral analysis paragraphs, SPECTRA or COVARIANCE, and accept the default procedure, which effectively replaces missing values by the overall average of the variable.

When there are more than a few (e.g., more than 10) values missing for one variable, analysis of that variable deserves special care.

Paragraphs SPECTRA and COVARIANCE offer two different methods for the spectral analysis of variables with a substantial number of missing values. The method employed by paragraph SPECTRA is suitable when the sequence of missing values has a special structure. The missing value method in COVARIANCE applies to a broader class of missing value problems.

A serious drawback to the special missing value methods in paragraphs SPECTRA and COVARIANCE is that estimated spectral densities may be negative at some frequencies. The accuracy of computed standard errors of estimate is also adversely affected by missing values, regardless of the method employed. We recommend that, when possible, data containing a substantial number of missing values be analyzed using several different approaches. In addition to the strategies mentioned above, the user may be able to isolate for analysis a reasonably lengthy subset of the data with no missing values.

Paragraph SPECTRA treats incomplete data when the sequence of missing values is quasi-periodic. As an illustration, suppose that someone records the data on a daily basis and that there tend to be fewer recorded values on weekends than during the week. We might model this phenomenon by assigning to each day of the week a probability that the data for that day will be recorded. Under some simplifying assumptions we can recover an estimate of the spectral density even when a large percentage (e.g., 40 percent) of the data is missing. In the above example, the periodicity in our model of quasi-periodic missing values, is seven, corresponding to the seven days of the week. The simplest model is obtained by taking the period to be one. Then each value of the data is regarded as having the same chance of being recorded. In paragraph SPECTRA, the user requests this treatment of missing values by supplying the period of the model in the MISSING PERIOD (MPER) statement, as described below.

```
SPECtra (missing values)─────────────────────
│ MPER = #.                                none
│    The period, expressed as an integer number of
│    time units, to be used in the quasi-periodic
│    missing value model.
```

The special missing value procedure in paragraph COVARIANCE is requested by stating MISSING. The program then computes lagged products of a zero-one sequence indicating the absence or presence of a value in the data. The program adjusts the covariance sequence using this sequence of lagged products. This method is used when missing values occur in a regular fashion, e.g., when data are recorded every weekday and are missing every weekend, or when the zero-one sequence indicating the missing values is itself regarded as a stationary, random time series. The latter situation may apply, for example, when data are missing due to sporadic failures in the recording equipment. This feature is called as follows:

```
COVAriance (missing values) ─────────────────────
│ MISSing.                                     no
│    Adjust covariances to take account of the
│    missing values.
```

Improving Spectral Analysis Estimates by Prefiltering and Recoloring

In paragraph SPECTRA, the spectral density of a time series is estimated by averaging adjacent periodograms in an interval centered about the frequency of interest. The periodograms being averaged are crude measures of the underlying spectral density at slightly different frequencies. When the underlying spectral density varies considerably over the interval (frequency band), the periodogram average reflects an averaged spectral density, rather than the spectral density at one frequency. So there is necessarily some loss in precision (and a gain in stability) when we average periodograms in an interval of frequencies.

An exception to the loss in precision occurs when the underlying spectrum is constant. Then a smoothed version of the true spectrum is identical to the true spectrum. A constant, i.e., flat, spectrum corresponds to a time series whose values are uncorrelated. Such a time series is called a white noise series. Although rare in practice, it is an important concept.

An effective method for regaining some of the lost precision incurred by spectral smoothing is to prefilter the data, i.e., to apply a linear filter to the data prior to spectral estimation, so that the filtered results approximate an uncorrelated data sequence. Then the underlying spectrum of the filtered time series will be closer to a constant over the intervals in which periodograms are averaged. The final estimate of the original time series is obtained by adjusting the computed spectrum of the filtered data to allow for the filtering operation.

The prefiltering operation is also called prewhitening, and the adjustment to the computed spectrum is called RECOLORING. These names derive from the fact that white light exhibits a nearly flat spectrum as opposed, say, to red light having a spectrum concentrated at low frequencies.

Program P1T offers 3 kinds of filters in paragraphs BANDPASS, FILTER, and AR (autoregression), described in the filtering section above. In all 3 paragraphs, P1T automatically records the filtering operation being performed on each variable, so that subsequent spectral estimates may be RECOLORED. This may not always be desirable, as we saw in Example 1T.5 where a 60 cycle per second ripple was removed from the data in the BANDPASS paragraph and, because the ripple was an artifact not of intrinsic interest, NO RECOLORING was requested. The user may request that NO RECOLORING be performed in each of the filter paragraphs. When the user requests RECOLORING in the SPECTRA or COVARIANCE paragraph,

P1T produces recolored spectral estimates. If you do not wish the filtering operation to be recorded for subsequent spectral recoloring, state NO RECOLOR.

When the prefiltering and recoloring technique is desired, the best initial choice for the prefilter will usually be paragraph AR. The user may also have a special filter for this purpose. The filter can be supplied to the program in paragraph FILTER.

Note that some filters effectively set the spectrum equal to zero at a few isolated frequencies. This can happen, for example, in paragraph BANDPASS or when differencing filters are supplied to paragraph FILTER. RECOLORING at these frequencies is then not possible and causes missing values in the recolored spectrum. This does not prevent the recolored spectrum from being printed and plotted. The recolored spectrum may be requested as follows:

SPECtra or COVAriance (recoloring) ─────────
```
RECOLOR                                     no
   Use recorded filtering operations to recolor
   spectral estimates.
```

Additional Output: Covariances and Periodograms

Periodograms are computed in both paragraphs SPECTRA and COVARIANCE. In paragraph SPECTRA, periodograms are averaged, producing the spectral estimates. In COVARIANCE, periodograms are (inverse Fourier) transformed to produce covariances.

Paragraph SPECTRA includes neither periodograms nor covariances in the results normally printed and plotted. Users may request them in the PDGRAM (periodogram) and COVARIANCE statement as shown below.

Covariances are automatically included in the results plotted and printed by paragraph COVARIANCE. Defaults for the program are to exclude periodograms from these results but to include the same spectral estimates as are produced by paragraph SPECTRA. The defaults may be changed, as indicated below, by stating PDGRAM and NO SPECTRA in COVARIANCE.

The periodograms calculated by the two paragraphs may differ somewhat due to the automatic padding of the data by COVARIANCE (see the tapering and padding discussion). The covariances produced by the 2 paragraphs will typically differ to a greater degree. This is because paragraph SPECTRA calculates covariances from smooth spectral estimates rather than from periodograms, the number of covariances produced corresponding to the number of frequencies at which spectra are estimated.

We now summarize these features.

SPECtra ────────────────────────────────
```
PERIODOGram.                                no
   Include periodograms in the plotted and printed
   results.
COVA.                                       no
   Calculate covariances from spectral estimates.
   Include the covariances in the plotted and
   printed results.
```

COVAriance ──────────────────────────────
```
PDGram.                                     no
   Includes periodograms in the plotted and
   printed results.
SPECtra.                                    yes
   Fourier transform weighted covariances to form
   spectral estimates. Include spectral estimates
   in plotted and printed results.
```

SIZE OF PROBLEM

The spectral analysis is performed most efficiently by P1T when both the data and the Fourier transforms are held in core memory. Normally, BMDP programs have a capacity of at least 15,000 words of core memory (this number may be increased as discussed in Appendix B). Under these circumstances, the maximum number of cases is limited by the number of variables (time series) analyzed, as shown below.

	number of variables				
	1	2	5	10	20
maximum number of cases	5,000	2,500	1,363	681	357

P1T analyzes larger problems by using scratch files for temporary storage.

COMPUTATIONAL METHOD

P1T uses the fast Fourier transform algorithm to compute periodograms. The periodograms are averaged in paragraph SPECTRA to produce estimated spectra, and the periodograms are inverse Fourier transformed in paragraph COVARIANCE to produce sample covariance functions. These and most other computations are done in single precision. Sample means and slopes are computed in double precision. A more detailed technical discussion of P1T is given in Appendix A.

ACKNOWLEDGEMENT

Peter Bloomfield, David Brillinger, Bert Davis, and John Tukey generously gave of their time in commenting on the design of P1T. David Brillinger also provided a set of subroutines used in the pilot version of P1T. Gordon Sande contributed subroutines for the fast Fourier transform. Tony Thrall bears the responsibility for the basic design and initial coding of P1T. Laszlo Engelman is maintaining and extending the program.

SUMMARY

Order of Input Cards

```
// (job card)
// EXEC BIMED,PROG=BMDP1T
//SYSIN DD *
/ PROBLEM
/ INPUT
/ VARIABLE
/ TRANSFORM
/ SAVE
/ PRINT
/ TFAXIS
/ END

    (data, if on cards)

/ END
```

Note that each paragraph following the data
is terminated rather than preceded by a slash.

```
SNAPSHOT...... /
TPLOT......... /      data inspection
DEMODULATE.... /
LSCATTER...... /

REPLACE....... /      missing replacement

ADJUST........ /      trend removal

BANDPASS...... /
FILTER........ /      filtering
AR............ /

SPECTRA....... /      spectral analysis
COVARIANCE.... /

SAVE.......... /      save data

END/
```

may be repeat-
ed and placed
in any order

instructions specific to P1T

Paragraph Statement	Preassigned	Comment and Manual Reference
/ VARiable		Additional option to specify time variable.
Time = v.	none	Name or subscript of variable containing the time value. If not stated, time is implied by the order of cases, i.e., time is the case number.
/ TFAXis		Label the time and frequency axes. 627
TName = c.	TIME	Name for the unit of time.
FName = c.	FREQ	Name for the unit of frequency.
CPut = #.	1.0	Cycles per unit of time. Establishes relationship between FNAME and TNAME.
STart = #.	1.0	Time value corresponding to the first case of data.
DELta = #.	1.0	Time increment from one case to the next.
/ END		

Note: Paragraph TFAXIS is P1T's only addition to the data definition paragraphs. Note that the data definition paragraphs are terminated by an END paragraph, that the data may optionally follow, and that the analysis paragraphs are placed last. Also note that each analysis paragraph is terminated, rather than preceded, by a slash.

- -

/ VARiable		
TIME = v.	none	Name or index of the variable that records time.

- -

SNAPshot		Plot a snapshot of each series. 615
VAR = v list.	none	Required. Names or subscripts of variables.
SPAN = #.		The span of each time interval, i.e., the number of adjacent cases used for each trimmed mean.
TRIM = #.	5% SPAN	The number of smallest values and the number of largest values to be excluded from each trimmed mean.
TIME = $\#_1$, $\#_2$, $\#_3$.		Gives the midpoint times of successive intervals in terms of starting time ($\#_1$), final time ($\#_2$), and time increment ($\#_3$). The defaults for SPAN and TIME are such that adjacent intervals overlap by 50% and the end snapshot can be plotted on the upper or lower half of a page, with time running horizontally across the page.
PRINt.	no	For each interval print the minimum value, maximum value, and trimmed mean.
/		

- -

TPLot		Plot each series down the page. 615
VAR = v list.	none	Required. Names or subscripts of variables.
TIME = $\#_1$, $\#_2$, $\#_3$.	all cases	Times to be plotted in terms of starting time ($\#_1$), final time ($\#_2$), and time increment ($\#_3$).
COMmon.	no	Specifies that all variables are to be plotted in a common plot frame.
SYMBol = 'c' list.	A,B,C,...	Characters to be used as plotting symbols for the respective variables.
MINImum = # list.	none	See comment in LSCatter paragraph.
MAXimum = # list.	none	
LABEL	no	Print case labels, if any, on the left margin.

(continued)

(continued)

Paragraph Statement	Preassigned	Comment and Manual Reference
MARK = #.	5	Determines how often the vertical time axis is to be marked, i.e., labelled, with the time of the value being plotted.
HLine = #.	10	Determines how often a horizontal reference axis is to be printed.
SIZE = # list.		Character width(s) of the horizontal axis (axes) of the plot frame(s). The default is to use the largest horizontal axis (axes) possible, with one size for all axes.
PRINt. /	no	After all values have been plotted, print them.
LSCatter		Lagged scatter plots, i.e., plot points of the form (X(t+u), Y(t)) for a fixed lag u and for a range of t-values. 615
XVAR = v list.	none	Required. Names or subscripts of X-variables.
YVAR = v list.	none	Required. Names or subscripts of Y-variables.
PAIR. or CROSS.	PAIR	Method for matching X and Y variables.
MINimum = # list.	none	Minimum values to be used for the respective variables in the order the variables were read in by the program.
MAXimum = # list.	none	Maximum values to be plotted for the respective variables in the order the variables were read in by the program.
YLAG = #.	none	Integer number of time increments that Y lags behind X.
TIME = $\#_1$, $\#_2$.	all cases	Range of time values used for each plot in terms of starting time ($\#_1$) and final time ($\#_2$).
SIZE = $\#_1$, $\#_2$.		The character width ($\#_1$) and the number of lines ($\#_2$) used by the plot. The default is to use one entire page per plot.
STATistics.	no	Summary statistics printed with plot.
PRINt. /	no	Requests that X-Y values be printed below the plot.
DEModulate		Plot the amplitude and phase of complex demodulates. 616
VAR = v list.	none	Required. Names or subscripts of variables.
FREQ = #.	none	Required. Frequency of complex demodulation.
BW = #.		Band width used. The default is to take the smallest bandwidth possible using a number of filter coefficients not exceeding 10 percent of the number of cases.
MAXLAG = #.	5% no. of cases	Largest integer lag allowed for filter coefficients. Must be a positive integer less than half the number of cases.
TIME = $\#_1$, $\#_2$, $\#_3$.		Range of time values plotted in terms of starting time ($\#_1$), final time ($\#_2$), and time increment ($\#_3$). The default for time is such that the entire time series is represented on a single page, with time running horizontally across the page.
SIZE = $\#_1$, $\#_2$.		The character width ($\#_1$) and the number of lines ($\#_2$) used by the plot. The default is to use one entire page per plot.
PRINt. /	no	Print the amplitude and phase of the complex demodulates
REPlace		Replace missing values. 618
VAR = v list.	none	Required. Names or subscripts of variables.
METHod = (one only).	LINT	Method for missing value replacement -- linear interpolation, local median, or local mean. LINT, MEDian, MEAN.
SPAN = #. /	4	Number of adjacent cases (observed values) be used for MEDIAN or MEAN replacement.
ADJust		Mean-adjust the series. 618
VAR = v list.	none	Required. Names or subscripts of variables.
CENTer.	no	Subtract the sample mean.
DETRend.	no	Subtract the sample linear trend.
DESeas = #.	none	Subtract the sample seasonal means where # is the number of distinct seasons, e.g., 12 for monthly data.
PRINt. /	no	Print data after adjustment.
BANDpass		Apply bandpass or bandreject filter. 625
VAR = v list.	none	Required. Names or subscripts of variables.
TYPE = (one only).	BAND	Type of filter desired. LOW, HIGH, BAND, NOTCH.
FREQ = #.	none	Center of the desired frequency band. Applicable and required only when TYPE = BAND or NOTCH.
BW = #.		Band width used. Defaults are precisely stated in Appendix A. The overriding constraint is that the number of filter coefficients not exceed 10 percent of the number of cases.

(continued)

(continued)

Paragraph Statement	Preassigned	Comment and Manual Reference
MAXLag = #.	5% no. of cases	Largest integer lag allowed for filter coefficients. Must be a positive integer less than half the number of cases.
REColor.	yes	Compensate for the filtering in subsequent spectral estimates.
RETAIN.	no	Retain the unfiltered time series as the program's reference copy, i.e., do not carry out the filtering operation.
PLOT.	yes	Plot the frequency response of the filter.
PRINt.	yes	Print the frequency response of the filter.
/		
FILter		Apply user-specified filter coefficients. 626
VAR = v list.	none	Required. Names or subscripts of variables.
LAG = # list.	none	Required. Lags, expressed as integer numbers of time increments, at which the given coefficients are applied.
COEF = # list.	none	Required. Filter coefficients at specified lags.
REColor.	yes	Compensate for the filtering in subsequent spectral estimates.
RETAIN.	no	Retain the unfiltered time series as the program's reference copy, i.e., do not carry out the filtering operation.
PLOT.	yes	Plot the frequency response of the filter -- both the gain and phase.
SIZE = $\#_1$, $\#_2$.		The character width ($\#_1$) and the number of lines ($\#_2$) used by the plot. The default is to use one entire page per plot.
PRINt.	yes	Print the frequency response of the filter.
TYPE =(one only)	none	Desired type of program-constructed filter (one only). LOW, HIGH, BAND, NOTCH, AR.
/		
AR		Autoregressive filtering. 626
VAR = v list.	none	Required. Names or subscripts of variables.
MAXLag = #.	none	Required. Largest integer lag to be used for autoregressive filter coefficients.
REColor.	yes	Compensate for the filtering in subsequent spectral estimates.
RETAIN.	no	Retain the unfiltered time series as the program's reference copy, i.e., do not carry out the filtering operation.
PLOT.	yes	Plot the frequency response of the filter -- both the gain and phase.
PRINt.	yes	Print the frequency response of the filter.
/		
COVA †		Covariance-based spectral estimation.
PLOT.	yes	Plot covariance functions and spectral estimates. 629
PRINt.	yes	Print covariance functions and spectral estimates. 629
XVAR = v list.	none	Required. List of X-variables. 629
YVAR = v list.	none	List of Y-variables. 629
PAIR. or CROSS.	PAIR	Method for matching X and Y variables. 629
DEPend = XVAR, YVAR.	none	Indicates which variable in each pair is to be regarded as dependent. Applicable only if both XVAR and YVAR are specified. 629
SPEC.	yes	Fourier transform weighted covariances to form spectral estimates. 634
PERIODOGram.	no	Include periodograms in the plotted and printed results. 634
TAPer = $\#_1$, $\#_2$.	0, 0	Taper the first $\#_1$ and the last $\#_2$ portion of the data. TAPER = p is interpreted as TAPER = p, p. See p. 629
DF = # list.		Degrees of freedom used for spectral estimates. The default is 8, 3*M, and M**2, where M is the cubed root of the number of cases. 630
MAXLag = # list.	based on DF	Largest integer lag to be used in forming the spectral density mate.
BW = # list.	based on DF	Bandwidth used for spectral estimates. 630
YLAG = #.	none	Lag each Y variable a given integer number of time units with respect to each X variable in the bivariate spectral analysis. Applicable only if both XVAR and YVAR have been specified. 630
CSHape = (one only) DELP, HAM, HAN.	DELP	Shape of the covariance weighting function. 631
TIME = $\#_1$, $\#_2$, $\#_3$.	all cases	A subset of times (cases) may be used for the spectral analysis. $\#_1$ is the starting time, $\#_2$ is the final time, and $\#_3$ is the time increment. 631
FREQ = $\#_1$, $\#_2$, $\#_3$.		Spectral estimates are to be plotted from frequency $\#_1$ to frequency $\#_2$, incremented by frequency $\#_3$. The default is to plot the entire frequency range on one page, with frequency on the horizontal axis.
CONF = SMooth, ESTimate, NONE.	ESTimate	Confidence bands may be formed about spectral estimates, or about wideband (smooth) estimates. 632
MISS.	no	Adjust covariance estimates to allow for missing values. 633

(continued)

(continued)

Paragraph Statement	Preassigned	Comment and Manual Reference
RECOLOR	no	Use recorded filtering operations to produce recolored spectral estimates. 634
/		
SPEC		Estimate spectra by smoothing periodograms.
PLOT.	yes	Plot spectral estimates. 612
PRINt.	yes	Print spectral estimates. 612
XVAR = v list.	none	Required. List of X-variables. 612
YVAR = v list.	none	List of Y-variables. 612
PAIR. or CROSS.	PAIR	Method for matching X and Y variables. 612
DEPend = XVAR, YVAR.	none	Indicates which variable in each pair is to be regarded as dependent. Applicable only if both XVAR and YVAR are specified. 612
COVA.	no	Compute covariances by inverse Fourier transforming spectra. Include covariances in the plotted and printed results. 634
PERIODOGram.	no	Include periodograms in the plotted and printed results. 634
TAPer = $\#_1$, $\#_2$.	0.0	Taper the first $\#_1$ and the last $\#_2$ portion of the data. TAPER = p is interpreted as TAPER = p, p. See p. 629.
PAD = #.	0.0	Pad the end of the data with # proportion of zeros. 629
NPAD = # .	none	Pad the end of the data with exactly # of zeros. 629
DF = # list.		Degrees of freedom used for spectral estimates. The default is 8, 3*M, and M**2, where M is the cubed root of the number of cases. 630
BW = # list.	based on DF	Bandwidth used for spectral estimates. 630
YLAG = #.	none	Lag each Y variable a given integer number of time units with respect to each X variable in the bivariate spectral analysis. Applicable only if both XVAR and YVAR have been specified. 630
PSHape = (one only) COSine, RECTangular, TRIAngular.	COS	Shape of the periodogram weighting function. 631
TIME = $\#_1$, $\#_2$, $\#_3$.	all cases	A subset of times (cases) may be used for the spectral analysis. $\#_1$ is the starting time, $\#_2$ is the final time, and $\#_3$ is the time increment. 631
FREQ = $\#_1$, $\#_2$, $\#_3$.		Spectral estimates are to be plotted from frequency $\#_1$ to frequency $\#_2$, incremented by frequency $\#_3$. The default is to plot the entire frequency range on one page, with frequency on the horizontal axis. 632
†CONF = SMooth, ESTimate, NONE.	ESTimate	Confidence bands may be formed about spectral estimates, or about wideband (smooth) estimates. 632
†MPER = #.	none	Adjust spectral estimates for quasi-periodic missing values, where # is the periodicity. 633
RECOLOR.	no	Use recorded filtering operations to produce redolored spectral estimates. 634.
/		
SAVE		Save data. Additional option required only if BMDP File is to be created.
UNIT = #.	none	Required. Unit number for BMDP File. 68
CODE = c.	none	Required. Code for BMDP File.
LABEL = c.	none	Label for BMDP File.
NEW.	not NEW	When a BMDP File is not NEW, the program checks that new data are not being written over old data.
/		

Key:

/	–indicates paragraph	*	–assigned value remains the same for additional problems
.	–period ends a sentence		
●	–required	VT	–number of variables after transformations
v	–variable (name or subscript)	list	–more than one item, often one per var.
g	–group (name or subscript)		
#	–number		Capitalized letters–paragraph or sentence names recognized by BMDP
'c'	–characters (name or parameter) may omit apostrophes if contiguous letters only		Page numbers following refer to this Manual
†	–option not available at time of print; state /PRINT NEWS. to check on availability		

P2T

20.2 Box-Jenkins Time Series Analysis

Lon-Mu Liu

ABSTRACT

P2T allows a user to build a parametric time domain model for time series data. The derivation of a suitable time series model for a particular set of data can frequently be an involved task. As in the case of most statistical model-building, the model is developed iteratively. Following Box and Jenkins (1976), an iteration in the search for a time series model can be conveniently broken down into three stages: identification, estimation, and diagnostic checking, i.e., the selection of a tentative model; estimation of the model parameters; and testing for adequacy of fit (residual analysis). Once a suitable model has been obtained, the user may wish to proceed to the forecasting of future observations. Thus forecasting represents a fourth stage of Box-Jenkins analysis. This program provides convenient tools for these four stages of time series analysis.

P2T deals with a very general class of univariate time domain models, such as ARIMA (Autoregressive-Integrated Moving Average), regression, intervention and transfer function models. In univariate time series analysis, we may describe the present value of a time series as a linear function of past data and random errors. This class of models is referred to as ARIMA models. Frequently, a time series may be subjected to exogenous influences that make an ARIMA model inadequate. To remedy this inadequacy, the effect of the exogenous disturbances may be combined with the ARIMA model. If an exogenous variable is itself a random time series, we refer to that part of the model as a transfer function component. If an exogenous variable is a nonrandom process such as a nonrandom binary variable (i.e., a variable consisting of zeros and ones), we refer to it as an intervention component in the model. A time series model may be a combination of ARIMA, intervention and transfer function components. The regression model is a special type of parameteric time series model. When there are missing values in the series 2T analyzes only the series from the first nonmissing data value up to and not including the next missing value. No warning is given, however.

Technical details for this section can be found in Box and Jenkins (1976), the primary reference for 2T, or in Appendix A.33. We follow notational conventions used in Box and Jenkins. For example, "B" is used as the backshift operator, i.e., $BY(t) = Y(t-1)$, and $B^d Y(t) = Y(t-d)$.

Analyses using P1T can be found in Liu (1979a,b).

Example 2T.1 Identification of ARIMA Models

In our first example we use P2T to analyze the ozone data from a study in downtown Los Angeles (Box and Tiao, 1975). The data are the monthly averages of hourly readings of ozone (pphm) from January 1955 to December 1972 as shown in Table 20.1. This series was subject to major interventions in 1960 and 1966. In 1960, two events occurred which might have reduced the ozone pollution level in downtown Los Angeles: (1) traffic was diverted when the Golden State Freeway was opened, and (2) a new law (Rule 63) came into effect that reduced the allowable proportion of reactive hydrocarbons in the gasoline sold locally. In 1966, regulations were adopted requiring engine design changes that were expected to reduce the production of ozone in new cars. In this example our main interest is to determine whether ozone levels were reduced by the interventions in 1960 and 1966, and if so, the magnitude of the reduction. We treat this subject more fully in the example for intervention analysis. In this example, we ignore the interventions and only build an ARIMA model for the series; then we forecast the future ozone level.

The ARIMA class of models embraces many different kinds of time series. In practice, we can only choose a few of these models to try on the data. This is the process of model identification. The sample autocorrelation function and sample partial autocorrelation function are most frequently used in identifying an ARIMA model. The sample autocorrelations provide useful information for determining AR (autoregressive) polynomials and sample partial autocorrelations for MA (moving average) polynomials. Details are discussed in Box and Jenkins (1976). In addition to sample autocorrelations and sample partial autocorrelations, the plotting of data is also useful in identifying the time series model.

Model identification is an exploratory process and the analyses to be performed are usually based upon previous results. Therefore the exact sequence of paragraphs and selection of options usually cannot be predetermined. The Control Language presented below should be viewed as the result of interactive usage, i.e., the selection of each paragraph was made interactively after viewing the results at a computer terminal. This point of view applies to the whole P2T section. In the following example, TPLOT, ACF, and PACF are specific to P2T. The remaining Control Language instructions are common to all BMDP programs and are described in Chapter 5. Data editing and transformations are explained in Chapter 6. In the INPUT paragraph, FORMAT IS STREAM is used to facilitate reading data across a record. This option is useful when there is only one variable to be analyzed. This type of format is further discussed in Chapter 5.

The basic setup of the Control Language for model identification is shown below.

```
--------------------------------------
/ PROBLEM     TITLE IS 'LOS ANGELES OZONE DATA'.
/ INPUT       VARIABLE IS 1.
             FORMAT IS STREAM.
/ VARIABLE    NAME IS OZONE.
/ END
   data
/ END
   TPLOT      VARIABLE IS OZONE.
             SYMBOLS ARE A, B, C, D, E, F, G, H, I,
                         J, K, L.
             SIZE IS 60./

   ACF        VARIABLE IS OZONE./

   ACF        VARIABLE IS OZONE.
             DFORDER IS 12.
             MAXLAG IS 24./

   PACF       VARIABLE IS OZONE.
             DFORDER IS 12.
             MAXLAG IS 24./

   END/
--------------------------------------
```

Note that the TPLOT, ACF, PACF, and the final END paragraphs are terminated rather than preceded by a slash, as discussed in the Control Language section of the Chapter 20 Introduction.

The results of the above analysis are presented in Output 2T.1. Circled numbers below correspond to those in the output.

(1) The program reports on the reading of data and then prints summary information to provide an initial check that the format specification, the user-supplied data file, and the entry of the data into the program are as they should be.

(2) The TPLOT paragraph provides a graphical display of the data. The plot gives us a general idea of the series, enabling us to detect the presence of a long-term trend, seasonal fluctuations, or gross outliers in the series. The symbols in the plots are used to specify the month for each observation. "A" represents January, "B" February, etc. In this example, we find that the series completes an up-and-down cycle every 12 months. A series displaying this kind of pattern is said to be seasonal. In our example, the period of seasonality is 12 months.

(3) The ACF paragraph first prints a brief summary of the series which includes the number of observations, the mean of the series, and the standard error and t-value of the mean. This mean is a valid measurement only when it is computed from a stationary series. As can be seen from the plot of the data, this series is nonstationary. This conclusion is further supported by a cyclic pattern and slow decay in the sample autocorrelation function. Therefore the mean here is not a valid measurement. The nonstationarity is due to the 12-month seasonality.

Table 20.1 Monthly Averages of Hourly Readings of Ozone (pphm) in Downtown
Los Angeles (1955 - 1972)

	Jan.	Feb.	Mar.	Apr.	May	June	July	Aug.	Sept.	Oct.	Nov.	Dec.
1955	2.7	2.0	3.6	5.0	6.5	6.1	5.9	5.0	6.4	7.4	8.2	3.9
1956	4.1	4.5	5.5	3.8	4.8	5.6	6.3	5.9	8.7	5.3	5.7	5.7
1957	3.0	3.4	4.9	4.5	4.0	5.7	6.3	7.1	8.0	5.2	5.0	4.7
1958	3.7	3.1	2.5	4.0	4.1	4.6	4.4	4.2	5.1	4.6	4.4	4.0
1959	2.9	2.4	4.7	5.1	4.0	7.5	7.7	6.3	5.7	4.8	2.7	2.7
1960	1.7	2.0	3.4	4.0	4.3	5.0	5.5	5.0	5.4	3.8	2.4	2.0
1961	2.2	2.5	2.6	3.3	2.9	4.3	4.2	4.2	3.9	3.9	2.5	2.2
1962	2.4	1.9	2.1	4.5	3.3	3.4	4.1	5.7	4.8	5.0	2.8	2.9
1963	1.7	3.2	2.7	3.0	3.4	3.8	5.0	4.8	4.9	3.5	2.5	2.4
1964	1.6	2.3	2.5	3.1	3.5	4.5	5.7	5.0	4.6	4.8	2.1	1.4
1965	2.1	2.9	2.7	4.2	3.9	4.1	4.6	5.8	4.4	6.1	3.5	1.9
1966	1.8	1.9	3.7	4.4	3.8	5.6	5.7	5.1	5.6	4.8	2.5	1.5
1967	1.8	2.5	2.6	1.8	3.7	3.7	4.9	5.1	3.7	5.4	3.0	1.8
1968	2.1	2.6	2.8	3.2	3.5	3.5	4.9	4.2	4.7	3.7	3.2	1.8
1969	2.0	1.7	2.8	3.2	4.4	3.4	3.9	5.5	3.8	3.2	2.3	2.2
1970	1.3	2.3	2.7	3.3	3.7	3.0	3.8	4.7	4.6	2.9	1.7	1.3
1971	1.8	2.0	2.2	3.0	2.4	3.5	3.5	3.3	2.7	2.5	1.6	1.2
1972	1.5	2.0	3.1	3.0	3.5	3.4	4.0	3.8	3.1	2.1	1.6	1.3

Output 2T.1 Identification of ARIMA models for the ozone data. Circled numbers correspond to those in the text

----

```
PROBLEM TITLE IS   LOS ANGELES OZONE DATA

NUMBER OF VARIABLES TO READ IN. . . . . . . .     1
NUMBER OF VARIABLES ADDED BY TRANSFORMATIONS. .   0        ①
TOTAL NUMBER OF VARIABLES . . . . . . . . . .     1
NUMBER OF CASES TO READ IN. . . . . . . . . . TO END
CASE LABELING VARIABLES . . . . . . . . . . .
MISSING VALUES CHECKED BEFORE OR AFTER TRANS. . NEITHER
BLANKS ARE. . . . . . . . . . . . . . . . . .  ZEROS
INPUT UNIT NUMBER . . . . . . . . . . . . . .     9
REWIND INPUT UNIT PRIOR TO READING. . DATA. . .   NO
NUMBER OF WORDS OF DYNAMIC STORAGE. . . . . . 10000

VARIABLES TO BE USED   1 OZONE

INPUT FORMAT IS  STREAM

MAXIMUM LENGTH DATA RECORD IS   72 CHARACTERS.

NUMBER OF CASES READ. . . . . . . . . . . . .    216
```

```
TPLOT  VARIABLE IS OZONE. SIZE IS 60.
       SYMBOLS ARE A, B, C, D, E, F, G, H, I, J, K, L./
                                                              ②
       OZONE
```

```
ACF    VARIABLE IS OZONE./
                                          ③

NUMBER OF OBSERVATIONS        =        216
MEAN OF THE (DIFFERENCED) SERIES =     3.7726
STANDARD ERROR OF THE MEAN    =        0.1015
T-VALUE OF MEAN (AGAINST ZERO) =      37.1718

AUTOCORRELATIONS   ④

 1- 12    .73  .50  .28  .08 -.09 -.12 -.12  .01  .23  .46  .61  .67
 ST.E.    .07  .10  .11  .11  .11  .11  .11  .11  .11  .12  .12  .14

13- 24    .57  .37  .14 -.04 -.18 -.20 -.15 -.03  .19  .41  .52  .57
 ST.E.    .15  .16  .16  .17  .17  .17  .17  .17  .17  .17  .17  .18

25- 36    .44  .26  .08 -.13 -.25 -.24 -.19 -.08  .14  .32  .43  .48
 ST.E.    .19  .19  .20  .20  .20  .20  .20  .20  .20  .20  .20  .21

PLOT OF SERIAL CORRELATION

        -1.0 -0.8 -0.6 -0.4 -0.2 0.0 0.2 0.4 0.6 0.8 1.0
LAG  CORR.
  1  0.729
  2  0.495
  3  0.276
  4  0.076
  5 -0.088
  6 -0.121
  7 -0.116
  8  0.013
  9  0.233
 10  0.462
 11  0.607
 12  0.668
 13  0.567
 14  0.372
 15  0.145
 16 -0.043
 17 -0.180
 18 -0.201
 19 -0.148
 20 -0.032
 21  0.190
 22  0.409
 23  0.523
 24  0.567
 25  0.443
 26  0.262
 27  0.076
 28 -0.127
 29 -0.254
 30 -0.241
 31 -0.189
 32 -0.078
 33  0.136
 34  0.322
 35  0.427
 36  0.479
```

⑤

(output continued)

641

④ The ACF paragraph prints the sample autocorrelations of the series and their standard errors. This part of the output can be suppressed by using the command NO PRINT.

⑤ The ACF paragraph also plots the sample autocorrelations and their 95% confidence intervals, which are denoted by the "+" symbol on both sides of the vertical axis. The autocorrelation values are printed to the left of the plot. This part of the output can be suppressed by the NO PLOT command.

From the output in ④ and ⑤, we find the sample autocorrelation function of the original series has large values repeated every 12 periods. The slow decay of these values suggests that the series is seasonal and that a twelve-month difference must be taken in order to make the series stationary.

⑥ We now compute the sample autocorrelations of the twelve-month differenced series. The sample autocorrelations of the differenced series are much smaller, with significant values only at lags 1 and 12. This suggests that the differenced series is stationary and may follow a multiplicative MA (moving average) model with coefficients at lags 1 and 12. Since the mean of the differenced series is not very significant, it may not be necessary to include a constant term in the model. We are thus led to the model

$$y(t) = a(t) - \theta_2 a(t-12) - \theta_1(a(t-1) - \theta_2 a(t-13))$$

where $y(t) = Y(t) - Y(t-12)$ and $a(t)$'s are independent random errors with constant variance. Here $Y(t)$ is the original ozone variable and $y(t)$ is the twelve-month differenced ozone variable. This model may be written more compactly as

$$(1-B^{12})Y(t) = (1-\theta_1 B)(1-\theta_2 B^{12})a(t)$$

where B is the backshift operator, i.e.,

$$B^d Y(t) = Y(t-d).$$

⑦ We use the PACF paragraph to compute the sample partial autocorrelations of the twelve-month differenced series. The sample partial autocorrelations are informative if the series follows an AR model. Although we have already identified an MA model for the differenced ozone series as a candidate for our final model, we can use the PACF paragraph to check whether an AR model might be better. The output of the PACF paragraph shows several large sample partial autocorrelations, implying that any AR model for this series would require several parameters. The previously derived MA model is thus more parsimonious (requires fewer parameters) than an AR model.

⑧ A brief summary of the series (same as ③).

⑨ The PACF paragraph prints the sample partial autocorrelations and their standard errors. This part of the output can be suppressed by the NO PRINT command.

Output 2T.1 (continued)

ACF   VARIABLE IS OZONE. DFORDER IS 12. MAXLAG IS 24./ ⑥

```
NUMBER OF OBSERVATIONS            =          204
MEAN OF THE (DIFFERENCED) SERIES  =       -0.1485
STANDARD ERROR OF THE MEAN        =        0.0737
T-VALUE OF MEAN (AGAINST ZERO)    =       -2.0160
```

AUTOCORRELATIONS

```
 1- 12   .29  .10  .17  .18  .10  .08 -.03 -.10 -.08 -.09 -.11 -.41
 ST.E.   .07  .08  .08  .08  .08  .08  .08  .08  .08  .08  .08  .08

13- 24  -.06 -.05 -.17 -.05  0.0 -.04  .03  .01 -.02  .08  .02 -.03
 ST.E.   .09  .09  .09  .09  .09  .09  .09  .09  .09  .09  .10  .10
```

PLOT OF SERIAL CORRELATION

```
          -1.0 -0.8 -0.6 -0.4 -0.2  0.0  0.2  0.4  0.6  0.8  1.0
LAG  CORR. +---+---+---+---+---+---+---+---+---+---+---+
                                     I
  1  0.292                           +   IXX+XXXX
  2  0.104                           +   IXXX+
  3  0.175                           +   IXXXX
  4  0.180                           +   IXXXX
  5  0.098                           +   IXX +
  6  0.078                           +   IXX +
  7 -0.035                           +  XI  +
  8 -0.104                           +XXXI  +
  9 -0.083                           + XXI  +
 10 -0.086                           + XXI  +
 11 -0.106                           +XXXI  +
 12 -0.407                       XXXXX+XXXI  +
 13 -0.063                           + XXI   +
 14 -0.054                           + XI    +
 15 -0.167                           +XXXXI   +
 16 -0.053                           + XI    +
 17 -0.002                           + I     +
 18 -0.036                           + XI    +
 19  0.028                           + IX    +
 20  0.008                           + I     +
 21 -0.017                           + I     +
 22  0.077                           + IXX   +
 23  0.024                           + IX    +
 24 -0.031                           + XI    +
```

PACF   VARIABLE IS OZONE. DFORDER IS 12. MAXLAG IS 24./ ⑦

```
NUMBER OF OBSERVATIONS            =          204
MEAN OF THE (DIFFERENCED) SERIES  =       -0.1485
STANDARD ERROR OF THE MEAN        =        0.0737   ⑧
T-VALUE OF MEAN (AGAINST ZERO)    =       -2.0160
```

PARTIAL AUTOCORRELATIONS ⑨

```
 1- 12   .29  .02  .15  .10  .01  .02 -.11 -.11 -.06 -.05 -.03 -.37
 ST.E.   .07  .07  .07  .07  .07  .07  .07  .07  .07  .07  .07  .07

13- 24   .23 -.06 -.05  .12 -.02  .04 -.01 -.09 -.01  .02 -.04 -.24
 ST.E.   .07  .07  .07  .07  .07  .07  .07  .07  .07  .07  .07  .07
```

PLOT OF SERIAL CORRELATION ⑩

```
          -1.0 -0.8 -0.6 -0.4 -0.2  0.0  0.2  0.4  0.6  0.8  1.0
LAG  CORR. +---+---+---+---+---+---+---+---+---+---+---+
                                     I
  1  0.292                           +   IXX+XXXX
  2  0.020                           + I  +
  3  0.152                           +   IXX+X
  4  0.099                           +   IXX+
  5  0.013                           + I    +
  6  0.023                           + IX   +
  7 -0.112                          XXXI   +
  8 -0.114                          XXXI   +
  9 -0.058                           + XI  +
 10 -0.051                           + XI  +
 11 -0.032                           + XI  +
 12 -0.372                       XXXXX+XXI  +
 13  0.229                           +   IXX+XXX
 14 -0.062                           +XXI  +
 15 -0.046                           + XI  +
 16  0.124                           +   IXXX
 17 -0.016                           + I   +
 18  0.044                           + IX  +
 19 -0.014                           + I   +
 20 -0.087                           +XXI  +
 21 -0.008                           + I   +
 22  0.020                           + IX  +
 23 -0.037                           + XI  +
 24 -0.244                       XXX+XXI  +
```

----

⑩ The PACF paragraph plots the sample partial autocorrelations and their 95% confidence intervals. The sample partial autocorrelations are also printed to the left of the plot. This plot can be omitted by stating NO PLOT.

Plotting a Time Series -- The TPLOT Paragraph. The TPLOT paragraph plots multiple series either in one common frame, requested by stating COMMON, or in separate individual frames side by side. The latter mode is the program default. The SYMBOL sentence is used to display the periodicity of the series in this situation. If COMMON is specified, the SYMBOL sentence specifies the plotting symbol for each series.

```
TPLOt ──────────────────────────────────────────
   VARiable = v list.   required                    none
      Names of the series (variable) to be plotted.
   CASEs = # list.                              all cases
      Cases to be printed.
   MARK = #.                                            5
      The interval between time points where tick
      marks are printed.
   MINImum = # list.
      Lower bounds for the variables to be plotted
      one for each variable. The minimum of each
      series is used if it is not specified.
   MAXImum = # list.
      Upper bounds for the variables to be plotted
      one for each variable. The maximum of each
      series is used if it is not specified.
```

The specifications of plotting SYMBOLS and plot SIZES are interpreted in two different ways. When the command COMMON is specified, SIZE and SYMBOL sentences are used as follows:

```
TPLOt (if COMMON is specified) ─────────────────
   SIZE = #.                                           45
      Width in characters of the horizontal axis.
   SYMBols = character list.                      A,B,...
      Symbols used to distinguish different series.
      If the SYMBOL sentence is not specified, A is
      used to represent the first series, B the
      second, etc.
```

For the NO COMMON situation, SIZE and SYMBOL sentences are used as follows:

```
TPLOt (if NO COMMON is specified) ──────────────
   SIZE = # list.
      Width in characters for each horizontal axis.
      If omitted, P2T supplies one appropriate SIZE
      for each horizontal axis.
   SYMBols = character list.    optional              X
      The sequence of symbols repeated in the plot,
      displaying the periodic nature of the data.
```

The ACF paragraph computes, prints and plots the sample autocorrelations of a time series. The printing and plotting can be omitted by stating NO PRINT or NO PLOT. Prior to the formation of the sample autocorrelation function; a series may be differenced, i.e., the program can perform the operation

$$y(t) = Y(t) - Y(t-d).$$

In Example 2T.1 the difference order d (DFORDER) is 12, but it could be any positive integer. Sample autocorrelations are computed at lags 1, 2, ..., up to some maximum lag (MAXLAG).

```
ACF ────────────────────────────────────────────
   VARiable = v.   required                         none
      Name of the series (variable) for which the
      sample autocorrelations are to be computed.
   DFORders = # list.                               none
      Orders of differences to be made on the series
      before computing the sample autocorrelations.
   MAXLag = #.                                        36
      The maximum lag of sample autocorrelations to
      be computed.
   PLOT. or NO PLOT.                                PLOT
      This command specifies whether the sample
      autocorrelations are to be plotted.
   PRINt. or NO PRINt.                            PRINT
      This command specifies whether the sample
      autocorrelations are to be printed.
```

The PACF paragraph computes, prints and plots the sample partial autocorrelations of a time series. The printing and plotting of the sample partial autocorrelations can be turned off by stating NO PRINT or NO PLOT. The partial autocorrelation of a series at lag k may be thought of as the correlation at lag k with the effect of lags 1, 2, ..., k-1 removed, or 'partialed out'. A technical description is given in Appendix A.33.

```
PACF ────────────────────────────────────────────
   VARiable = v.   required                         none
      Name of the series (variable) for which the
      sample partial autocorrelations are to be
      computed.
   DFORders = # list.                               none
      Orders of differences to be made on the series
      before computing the sample partial
      autocorrelations.
   MAXLag = #.                                        36
      The maximum number of sample partial
      autocorrelations to be computed.
   PLOT. or NO PLOT.                                PLOT
      Specifies whether the sample partial
      autocorrelations are to be plotted.
   PRINt. or NO PRINt.                             PRINT
      Specifies whether the sample partial
      autocorrelations are to be printed.
```

Example 2T.2 Estimation and Diagnostic Checking of an ARIMA Model

After a tentative ARIMA model has been reached, we then estimate the parameters in the tentative model. P2T uses the ARIMA paragraph to specify an ARIMA model for a time series, and the ESTIMATION paragraph to perform model estimation.

The functional form of AR and MA polynomials can be characterized by the order of the parameters. Thus, in representing AR and MA polynomials, we simply drop all notation inside the parentheses except the order of the parameters. For example, the MA polynomial for the ozone data $(1-\theta_1 B)(1-\theta_2 B^{12})$ can be denoted by '(1),(12)'. Note that the orders must be enclosed in apostrophes.

In the ARIMA paragraph, we use ARORDER, MAORDER, and DFORDER as sentence names to specify the parameter orders in AR, MA, and difference polynomials respectively. The VARIABLE sentence is used to specify the series (variable) associated with the model.

P2T provides two methods of parameter estimation: one is by conditional least squares; the other by unconditional least squares, also known as the backcasting method (Box & Jenkins 1976).

This program performs conditional least squares estimation first, and then continues by the backcasting method, using the conditional least squares estimates as initial values. The parameter estimates from the backcasting method are more precise, but are also more costly to obtain.

When a model is correctly specified and estimated, the residuals should have independent and identical normal distributions. Therefore none of the sample autocorrelations or sample partial autocorrelations of the residuals should be significant. Thus ACF and PACF paragraphs can be used in the diagnostic checking of a model. Plotting of the residuals is also useful in detecting the

Output 2T.2 Model estimation and diagnostic checking for the ozone data

---

```
ARIMA  VARIABLE IS OZONE. DFORDER IS 12. MAORDER = '(1),(12)'./   ⑪

THE COMPONENT HAS BEEN ADDED TO THE MODEL

THE CURRENT MODEL HAS
OUTPUT VARIABLE = OZONE
INPUT  VARIABLE = NOISE


ESTIMATION RESIDUALS = ROZONE./   ⑫


ESTIMATION BY CONDITIONAL LEAST SQUARES METHOD

RELATIVE CHANGE IN RESIDUAL SUM OF SQUARES LESS THAN 0.1000E-04


SUMMARY OF THE MODEL

OUTPUT VARIABLE -- OZONE
INPUT VARIABLES -- NOISE
```

VARIABLE	VAR. TYPE	MEAN	TIME	DIFFERENCES
OZONE	RANDOM		1- 216	$(1-B^{12})$

PARAMETER	VARIABLE	TYPE	FACTOR	ORDER	ESTIMATE	ST. ERR.	T-RATIO
1	OZONE	MA	1	1	-0.3625	0.0658	-5.51
2	OZONE	MA	2	12	0.4882	0.0623	7.83

```
RESIDUAL SUM OF SQUARES  =     166.391937
DEGREES OF FREEDOM       =         202
RESIDUAL MEAN SQUARE     =       0.823722


ESTIMATION BY BACKCASTING METHOD   ⑬

RELATIVE CHANGE IN RESIDUAL SUM OF SQUARES LESS THAN 0.1000E-04


SUMMARY OF THE MODEL

OUTPUT VARIABLE -- OZONE
INPUT VARIABLES -- NOISE
```

VARIABLE	VAR. TYPE	MEAN	TIME	DIFFERENCES
OZONE	RANDOM		1- 216	$(1-B^{12})$

PARAMETER	VARIABLE	TYPE	FACTOR	ORDER	ESTIMATE	ST. ERR.	T-RATIO
1	OZONE	MA	1	1	-0.3675	0.0638	-5.76
2	OZONE	MA	2	12	0.5827	0.0519	11.23

```
RESIDUAL SUM OF SQUARES  =     150.014404 (BACKCASTS EXCLUDED)
DEGREES OF FREEDOM       =         202
RESIDUAL MEAN SQUARE     =       0.742646


ACF    VARIABLE IS ROZONE. MAXLAG IS 24./   ⑭


NUMBER OF OBSERVATIONS           =          216
MEAN OF THE (DIFFERENCED) SERIES =      -0.2180
STANDARD ERROR OF THE MEAN       =       0.0563
T-VALUE OF MEAN (AGAINST ZERO)   =      -3.8716


AUTOCORRELATIONS

 1- 12   0.0  .14  .11  .20  .03  .13  0.0  .01  .04  .05  .07 -.12
 ST.E.   .07  .07  .07  .07  .07  .07  .07  .07  .07  .07  .07  .07

13- 24   .08  .04 -.06  .07  0.0  0.0  .05 -.01 -.02  .12  0.0 -.04
 ST.E.   .08  .08  .08  .08  .08  .08  .08  .08  .08  .08  .08  .08


PLOT OF SERIAL CORRELATION

           -1.0 -0.8 -0.6 -0.4 -0.2  0.0  0.2  0.4  0.6  0.8  1.0
LAG   CORR. +---+---+---+---+---+---+---+---+---+---+---+
                                          I
  1  -0.001                            +  I  +
  2   0.140                            +  IXX+X
  3   0.106                            +  IXXX
  4   0.203                            +  IXX+XX
  5   0.035                            +  IX  +
  6   0.130                            +  IXXX+
  7  -0.001                            +  I  +
  8   0.008                            +  I  +
  9   0.038                            +  IX  +
 10   0.048                            +  IX  +
 11   0.071                            +  IXX +
 12  -0.122                            +XXXI +
 13   0.084                            +  IXX +
 14   0.041                            +  IX  +
 15  -0.065                            + XXI  +
 16   0.066                            +  IXX +
 17  -0.002                            +  I  +
 18   0.000                            +  I  +
 19   0.049                            +  IX  +
 20  -0.013                            +  I  +
 21  -0.016                            +  I  +
 22   0.122                            +  IXXX+
 23  -0.002                            +  I  +
 24  -0.040                            + XI  +
```

---

unusual behavior of the residuals, such as outliers, changing variance, etc.

Below, we use the ozone data to illustrate the ARIMA and ESTIMATION paragraphs, and also diagnostic checking of the model.

```
    ------------------------------------
ARIMA       VARIABLE IS OZONE.
            DFORDERS ARE 12.
            MAORDERS ARE '(1), (12)'./

ESTIMATION RESIDUAL = ROZONE./

ACF         VARIABLE IS ROZONE.  MAXLAG = 24./
    ------------------------------------
```

The results of the above analysis are presented in Output 2T.2. Circled numbers below correspond to those in the output.

(11) The ARIMA paragraph specifies the model for the ozone series. P2T prints out the names of the output and input series. In ARIMA models, the input series is always a white noise (random error) series.

(12) The ESTIMATION paragraph first prints the results of conditional least squares estimation. It includes the stopping condition of the nonlinear estimation and a summary table for the model estimated. This table includes

- names of the input and output series
- difference polynomials and time periods in which the analysis is made
- parameter estimates, their standard errors and t values
- residual sum of squares, degrees of freedom, and residual mean square

(13) The ESTIMATION paragraph continues to perform model estimation by the backcasting method using the parameter estimates under the conditional least squares method as initial estimates. The output is similar to that produced under the conditional least squares method. The residual mean square of the backcasting method is much smaller than that of the conditional least squares method which suggests the estimates arrived at by the backcasting method are more precise. From the results of the ESTIMATION paragraph, we obtain the following model for the ozone data

$$(1-B^{12})Y(t) = (1 + 0.3675B)(1 - 0.5827B^{12})a(t) .$$

The residuals produced by backcasting estimation are stored in the variable ROZONE for checking adequacy of the model.

(14) The ACF paragraph is used to compute the sample autocorrelations of the residuals obtained from the ESTIMATION paragraph. We find that the mean of the residuals is significant and there are still significant values at lags 2 and 4, although they are not very large. This may be due to the interventions mentioned in Example 2T.1. Therefore the model obtained so far is still not adequate. Further analyses of these data will be continued in Example 2T.4.

In the specification of the ARIMA models, it may be necessary to specify the initial values or the values of parameters. We use an ARVALUE sentence for the AR polynomials and an MAVALUE for the MA polynomials. The CONSTANT sentence is used to indicate the existence of the mean or trend of a series and its value.

```
ARIMa ─────────────────────────────────────────
  VARiable = v.   required.                    none
    Name of the series (variable) to be analyzed.
  DFORders = # list.                           none
    Orders of differences in the difference
    polynomial.
  ARORders = '(#, ..., #),...,(#, ..., #)'.    none
    Parameter orders in the AR polynomial.
  ARVAlues = # list.                           .1
    Values or initial values of the parameters in
    the AR polynomial. If not specified, a
    preassigned value .1 is assumed for each
    parameter. The number of arguments in this
    sentence must be the same as the number of
    orders in the ARORDER sentence.
  MAORders = '(#, ..., #),...,(#, ..., #)'.    none
    Parameter orders in the MA polynomial.
  MAVAlues = # list.                           .1
    Values or initial values of the parameters in
    the MA polynomial. If not specified, a
    preassigned value .1 is assumed for each
    parameter. The number of arguments in this
    sentence must be the same as the number of
    orders in the MAORDER sentence.
  CONStant = #. or CONStant.                   none
    Mean or trend of the series. If the value is
    not specified, P2T provides an estimated value
    which is usually very close to the final
    estimate.
───────────────────────────────────────────────
```

Model estimation. In some situations, the backcasting estimation does not significantly improve the precision of the estimates over the conditional least squares estimation (see the discussion in Appendix A) or the accuracy of the estimates may not be important. Thus only the conditional least squares estimation is necessary. The METHOD sentence is used to facilitate this option. When the METHOD sentence is not specified, both conditional least squares and backcasting estimation will be performed. If METHOD IS CLS is stated, only the conditional least squares estimation will be performed. Similarly, only the backcasting estimation will be performed if METHOD IS BACKCASTING is stated.

```
ESTImation ─────────────────────────────────────
  RESIduals = v.                               none
    Variable storing residuals of the output
    series. Note that the variable can be a
    previously defined variable or a new variable.
  METHod = (one only) CLS, BACKcasting
    Method of model estimation. The CLS option is
    to use the conditional least squares method
    only, the BACKCASTING option is to use the
    backcasting method only. If this sentence is
    omitted, the program will perform conditional
    least squares and backcasting estimation.
───────────────────────────────────────────────
```

Example 2T.3 Forecasting Under An ARIMA Model

Once a suitable time series model has been obtained, we may use the model for various purposes. A major application of a time series model is forecasting. To forecast 24 steps ahead at time period 205 of the ozone series we state

```
------------------------------------

        FORECAST  CASES = 24.
                  START = 205./

------------------------------------
```

The results of the above analysis are presented in Output 2T.3. Circled numbers below correspond to those in the output.

(15) The MMSE (minimum mean square error) forecast at each period. The MMSE forecast of $Y(T+\ell)$ at time T, denoted by $\hat{Y}(T,\ell)$, minimizes the quantity $E(Y(T+\ell) - \tilde{Y}(T,\ell))^2$, where $\tilde{Y}(T,\ell)$ is a linear function of current and previous $Y(t)$'s and $a(t)$'s.

(16) The standard error of each forecast.

(17) The actual value of the series is printed if it is available.

(18) The standard error used in computing the standard error of forecasts. This standard error is computed without backcasting the series.

Output 2T.3   Forecasts for the ozone data under an ARIMA model

```
-------------------------------------------------------

    FORECAST CASES = 24. START IS 205./


    FORECAST ON VARIABLE OZONE    FROM TIME PERIOD   205
```

	(15)	(16)	(17)
PERIOD	FORECASTS	ST. ERR.	ACTUAL
205	1.62302	0.93744	1.50000
206	2.12734	0.99875	2.00000
207	2.53592	0.99875	3.10000
208	3.12887	0.99875	3.00000
209	3.24157	0.99875	3.50000
210	3.46072	0.99875	3.40000
211	3.93131	0.99875	4.00000
212	4.24385	0.99875	3.80000
213	3.68756	0.99875	3.10000
214	3.10252	0.99875	2.10000
215	2.00092	0.99875	1.60000
216	1.48487	0.99875	1.30000
217	1.69041	1.07263	
218	2.12734	1.08223	
219	2.53592	1.08223	
220	3.12887	1.08223	
221	3.24157	1.08223	
222	3.46072	1.08223	
223	3.93131	1.08223	
224	4.24385	1.08223	
225	3.68756	1.08223	
226	3.10252	1.08223	
227	2.00092	1.08223	
228	1.48487	1.08223	

(18) STANDARD ERROR = 0.937443   (BY CONDITIONAL METHOD)

```
-------------------------------------------------------
```

A description of the FORECAST paragraph is shown below.

```
 FOREcast ─────────────────────────────────────
   CASEs = #.                                36
     Number of forecasts to be made.
   STARt = #.
     Time period where forecasting starts. If not
     specified, the last time period of the series
     plus one is taken as the starting period.
```

Example 2T.4 Intervention Analysis of the Ozone Data

By plotting the residuals and examining the sample autocorrelations of the residuals, we find that the ARIMA model derived in Example 2T.2 does not fit the ozone data well. It may be necessary to include an intervention in the ARIMA model to describe the series more closely. Below, we refer to an intervention in 1961 as I1, and that in 1966 as I2.

We can try various techniques to identify an intervention component in the model. In many cases, we may have some knowledge of how the intervention affects the outcome of the series. This information may help us choose a tentative model. Residual plotting of a fitted model may also reveal the functional form of the intervention effect. We can also compare the actual series with its forecasts (with a forecasting origin immediately prior to the intervention) during the intervention periods and choose an appropriate model to compensate for the difference.

For the ozone data, Box and Tiao (1975) argue that I1 might be expected to produce a step change in the ozone level at the beginning of 1960, since opening the freeway and the new law might affect the ozone level immediately and the effect might stay at the same level indefinitely. For the intervention in 1966 (I2), we could represent the possible intervention effect as a constant change from year to year, reflecting the increased proportion of newly designed vehicles in the car population. Because of the summer-winter differential in the atmospheric temperature inversion, and the difference in the density of sunlight, the net effect of reducing ozone by engine changes would differ from winter, when oxidant pollution is low, to summer, when it is high. Thus we tentatively obtain the following model:

$$Y(t) = U_{10}X1(t) + \frac{U_{20}}{1-B^{12}} X2(t) + \frac{U_{30}}{1-B^{12}} X3(t)$$

$$+ \frac{(1-\theta_1 B)(1-\theta_2 B^{12})}{1-B^{12}} a(t)$$

or

$$(1-B^{12})Y(t) = U_{10}(1-B^{12})X1(t) + U_{20}X2(t) + U_{30}X3(t)$$

$$+ (1-\theta_1 B)(1-\theta_2 B^{12})a(t)$$

where

$$X1(t) = \begin{cases} 0, & t < \text{January, } 1960 \\ 1, & t \geq \text{January, } 1960 \end{cases}$$

$$X2(t) = \begin{cases} 1, & \text{"Summer" months June-October} \\ & \text{beginning } 1966 \\ 0, & \text{Otherwise} \end{cases}$$

$$X3(t) = \begin{cases} 1, & \text{"Winter" months November-May} \\ & \text{beginning } 1966 \\ 0, & \text{Otherwise} \end{cases}$$

This model allows for a step change in the level of ozone beginning in 1960 of size U_{10} associated with I1 and for progressive yearly increments in the ozone level beginning in 1966 of U_{20} and U_{30} units, respectively, for the summer and the winter months. This representation may be improved as more data become available.

In general, the effect of an intervention component can be expressed as $U(B)D(B)/S(B)$ where $U(B)$ is referred to as the U-polynomial, $D(B)$ the difference polynomial and $S(B)$ the S-polynomial. The difference polynomial has the same form as shown in the ARIMA section, the S-polynomial has a form similar to the AR polynomial, and the U-polynomial can be written as, for example,

$$U(B) = U_0 + U_1 B + U_2 B^2 + \ldots + U_r B^r .$$

A detailed discussion of intervention models is given in Appendix A.33.

P2T uses an INDEPENDENT (INDEP) paragraph to specify a model for an intervention. As the specification of ARIMA models, we use UPORDER, SPORDER, and DFORDER to specify the orders of the U, S and difference polynomials, and UPVALUE and SPVALUE to specify the values (or initial values) of the corresponding parameters. If the values are not specified, the value 0.1 is assigned for those parameters. To indicate that the independent variable is a binary variable, TYPE IS BINARY must be specified. As an example, the first intervention component of the above model can be stated as

```
INDEP   VARIABLE IS X1.
        DFORDER  IS 12.
        UPORDER  IS '(0)'.
        TYPE IS BINARY./
```

This component has only a U-polynomial which has order 0, therefore only the UPORDER sentence is specified.

P2T also uses the ESTIMATION paragraph to perform parameter estimation for an intervention model. The ACF, PACF, and TPLOT paragraphs can also be used for diagnostic checking and the FORECAST paragraph for forecasting in intervention analysis.

The Control Language for an intervention analysis of the ozone data is shown below.

```
-------------------------------------
/ PROBLEM     TITLE IS 'INTERVENTION ANALYSIS OF
                       OZONE DATA'.
/ INPUT       VARIABLES ARE 4.
              FORMAT IS '(1X, 4F6.1)'.
/ VARIABLE    NAMES ARE OZONE, X1, X2, X3.
              MISSING = 99.

/ END
  data
/ END

  ARIMA       VARIABLE IS OZONE.
              MAORDERS ARE '(1),(12)'.
              DFORDER IS 12./

  INDEP       VARIABLE IS X1.

              UPORDER IS '(0)'.
              DFORDER IS 12.
              TYPE IS BINARY./

  INDEP       VARIABLE IS X2.
              UPORDER IS '(0)'.
              TYPE IS BINARY./

  INDEP       VARIABLE IS X3.
              UPORDER IS '(0)'.
              TYPE IS BINARY./

  CHECK       MODEL./

  ESTIMATION RESIDUAL IS ROZONE.
              TIME IS 1,216./

  ACF         VARIABLE IS ROZONE./

  FORECAST    CASE IS 24.  START IS 205./
-------------------------------------
```

The results of the above analysis are presented in Output 2T.4. Circled numbers below correspond to those in the output.

(19) We first erase the space for storing the model from the first part of our analysis to ensure that the component is added to the model correctly. If we had no previous model, there would be no need to erase. See summary p. 660.

(20) The ARIMA paragraph specifies the ARIMA component of the intervention model.

(21) This INDEPENDENT paragraph specifies the model for the intervention variable X1(t).

(22) This INDEPENDENT paragraph specifies the model for the intervention variable X2(t).

(23) This INDEPENDENT paragraph specifies the model for the intervention variable X3(t).

(24) The model is checked before estimation. This step is useful when P2T is used interactively. If any error is found in the model, it can be corrected by respecifying the model using the REPLACE option in the INDEPENDENT paragraph. Since there is only

one ARIMA component in a time series model, the ARIMA component is automatically replaced when it is respecified. See summary p. 660.

(25) The results produced by conditional least squares estimation are printed. Details of the output are similar to those in (12).

(26) The results produced by backcasting estimation are printed. We find that these results are substantially different from those produced by conditional least squares estimation, especially the second MA parameter estimate and the residual mean square. In this situation, the backcasting estimation provides much better results than the

Output 2T.4 Intervention analysis for the ozone data

```
ERASE  MODEL./   (19)


UNIVARIATE TIME SERIES MODEL ERASED


ARIMA  VARIABLE IS OZONE. DFORDER IS 12. MAORDER = '(1),(12)'./   (20)


THE COMPONENT HAS BEEN ADDED TO THE MODEL

THE CURRENT MODEL HAS
OUTPUT VARIABLE = OZONE
INPUT  VARIABLE = NOISE


INDEP  VARIABLE IS X1. DFORDER IS 12. UPORDER = '(0)'. TYPE = BINARY./   (21)


THE COMPONENT HAS BEEN ADDED TO THE MODEL

THE CURRENT MODEL HAS
OUTPUT VARIABLE = OZONE
INPUT  VARIABLE = NOISE    X1


INDEP  VARIABLE IS X2. UPORDER = '(0)'. TYPE IS BINARY./   (22)


THE COMPONENT HAS BEEN ADDED TO THE MODEL

THE CURRENT MODEL HAS
OUTPUT VARIABLE = OZONE
INPUT  VARIABLE = NOISE    X1     X2


INDEP  VARIABLE IS X3. UPORDER = '(0)'. TYPE IS BINARY./   (23)


THE COMPONENT HAS BEEN ADDED TO THE MODEL

THE CURRENT MODEL HAS
OUTPUT VARIABLE = OZONE
INPUT  VARIABLE = NOISE    X1     X2     X3


CHECK  MODEL./   (24)


SUMMARY OF THE MODEL

OUTPUT VARIABLE -- OZONE
INPUT VARIABLES -- NOISE    X1     X2     X3
```

VARIABLE	VAR. TYPE	MEAN	TIME	DIFFERENCES
OZONE	RANDOM		1- 228	$(1-B)^{12}$
X1	BINARY		1- 228	$(1-B)^{12}$
X2	BINARY		1- 228	
X3	BINARY		1- 228	

PARAMETER	VARIABLE	TYPE	FACTOR	ORDER	ESTIMATE	ST. ERR.	T-RATIO
1	OZONE	MA	1	1	0.1000		
2	OZONE	MA	2	12	0.1000		
3	X1	UP	1	0	0.1000		
4	X2	UP	1	0	0.1000		
5	X3	UP	1	0	0.1000		

```
ESTIMATION RESIDUAL = ROZONE. MAXIT IS 15. TIME = 1,216./
```

```
ESTIMATION BY CONDITIONAL LEAST SQUARES METHOD   (25)

RELATIVE CHANGE IN RESIDUAL SUM OF SQUARES LESS THAN 0.1000E-04


SUMMARY OF THE MODEL

OUTPUT VARIABLE -- OZONE
INPUT VARIABLES -- NOISE    X1     X2     X3
```

VARIABLE	VAR. TYPE	MEAN	TIME	DIFFERENCES
OZONE	RANDOM		1- 228	$(1-B)^{12}$
X1	BINARY		1- 228	$(1-B)^{12}$
X2	BINARY		1- 228	
X3	BINARY		1- 228	

PARAMETER	VARIABLE	TYPE	FACTOR	ORDER	ESTIMATE	ST. ERR.	T-RATIO
1	OZONE	MA	1	1	-0.2999	0.0677	-4.43
2	OZONE	MA	2	12	0.5934	0.0580	10.24
3	X1	UP	1	0	-1.2640	0.2583	-4.89
4	X2	UP	1	0	-0.2620	0.0885	-2.96
5	X3	UP	1	0	-0.0931	0.0815	-1.14

```
RESIDUAL SUM OF SQUARES  =      145.784073
DEGREES OF FREEDOM       =          199
RESIDUAL MEAN SQUARE     =        0.732583


ESTIMATION BY BACKCASTING METHOD   (26)

RELATIVE CHANGE IN RESIDUAL SUM OF SQUARES LESS THAN 0.1000E-04


SUMMARY OF THE MODEL

OUTPUT VARIABLE -- OZONE
INPUT VARIABLES -- NOISE    X1     X2     X3
```

VARIABLE	VAR. TYPE	MEAN	TIME	DIFFERENCES
OZONE	RANDOM		1- 228	$(1-B)^{12}$
X1	BINARY		1- 228	$(1-B)^{12}$
X2	BINARY		1- 228	
X3	BINARY		1- 228	

PARAMETER	VARIABLE	TYPE	FACTOR	ORDER	ESTIMATE	ST. ERR.	T-RATIO
1	OZONE	MA	1	1	-0.2568	0.0626	-4.10
2	OZONE	MA	2	12	0.9274	0.0156	59.38
3	X1	UP	1	0	-1.3535	0.1487	-9.10
4	X2	UP	1	0	-0.2131	0.0397	-5.37
5	X3	UP	1	0	-0.1039	0.0379	-2.74

```
RESIDUAL SUM OF SQUARES  =      102.163956 (BACKCASTS EXCLUDED)
DEGREES OF FREEDOM       =          199
RESIDUAL MEAN SQUARE     =        0.513387
```

```
ACF    VARIABLE IS ROZONE./   27
```

```
NUMBER OF OBSERVATIONS         =        216
MEAN OF THE (DIFFERENCED) SERIES =     -0.0105
STANDARD ERROR OF THE MEAN     =        0.0514
T-VALUE OF MEAN (AGAINST ZERO) =       -0.2040
```

```
AUTOCORRELATIONS

 1- 12   .02  .08  .06  .11 -.05  .07 -.07 -.07 -.02  .08 -.03  .04
 ST.E.   .07  .07  .07  .07  .07  .07  .07  .07  .07  .07  .07  .07

13- 24   .03  .03 -.06  .02 -.06 -.02 -.01 -.08 -.03  .07 -.08 -.01
 ST.E.   .07  .07  .07  .07  .07  .07  .07  .07  .07  .07  .07  .07

25- 36  -.09 -.03  .05 -.06 -.11  .05  .04 -.09  0.0  0.0 -.09  .02
 ST.E.   .07  .07  .07  .07  .07  .07  .08  .08  .08  .08  .08  .08
```

```
PLOT OF SERIAL CORRELATION

          -1.0 -0.8 -0.6 -0.4 -0.2  0.0  0.2  0.4  0.6  0.8  1.0
LAG  CORR. +----+----+----+----+----+----+----+----+----+----+
                                   I
 1   0.020                        + I +
 2   0.083                        + IXX+
 3   0.057                        + IX +
 4   0.107                        + IXXX
 5  -0.055                        + XI +
 6   0.075                        + IXX+
 7  -0.073                        +XXI +
 8  -0.068                        +XXI +
 9  -0.018                        + I +
10   0.075                        + IXX+
11  -0.027                        + XI +
12   0.038                        + IX +
13   0.026                        + IX +
14   0.032                        + IX +
15  -0.059                        + XI +
16   0.016                        +  I +
17  -0.065                        + XXI +
18  -0.025                        + XI +
19  -0.007                        +  I +
20  -0.083                        + XXI +
21  -0.026                        + XI +
22   0.074                        +  IXX +
23  -0.075                        + XXI +
24  -0.008                        +  I +
25  -0.091                        + XXI +
26  -0.028                        + XI +
27   0.054                        +  IX +
28  -0.058                        + XI +
29  -0.113                        +XXXI +
30   0.051                        + IX +
31   0.039                        + IX +
32  -0.089                        + XXI +
33  -0.002                        +  I +
34   0.004                        +  I +
35  -0.092                        + XXI +
36   0.016                        +  I +
```

```
FORECAST CASE IS 24. START IS 205. RMS = 0.5134./   28
```

```
FORECAST ON VARIABLE OZONE    FROM TIME PERIOD   205

PERIOD      FORECASTS      ST. ERR.      ACTUAL
 205         1.18618       0.71652       1.50000
 206         1.24064       0.73976       2.00000
 207         2.08367       0.73976       3.10000
 208         2.88232       0.73976       3.00000
 209         3.43129       0.73976       3.50000
 210         3.00852       0.73976       3.40000
 211         3.37658       0.73976       4.00000
 212         3.21824       0.73976       3.80000
 213         3.43465       0.73976       3.10000
 214         3.39701       0.73976       2.10000
 215         3.30223       0.73976       1.60000
 216         1.54984       0.73976       1.30000
 217         1.09443       0.74159
 218         1.13671       0.74171
 219         1.97974       0.74171
 220         2.77839       0.74171
 221         3.32737       0.74171
 222         2.79540       0.74171
 223         3.16345       0.74171
 224         3.00511       0.74171
 225         3.22152       0.74171
 226         3.18388       0.74171
 227         3.19831       0.74171
 228         1.44591       0.74171
```

```
STANDARD ERROR = 0.716519    (BY CONDITIONAL METHOD  )
```

conditional least squares estimation. The residuals of the backcasting estimation are stored in the variable ROZONE.

The estimation results reveal that there is a step change associated with I1 and a progressive reduction in ozone associated with I2 over the period studied. For the I2 intervention, the reduction of ozone in summer months is more substantial than that in winter months.

27 The ACF paragraph computes the sample autocorrelations of the ROZONE variable. Since all the sample autocorrelations are very small, the model is acceptable. Note that the mean of the residuals is insignificant.

28 The FORECAST paragraph is used to forecast 24 months ahead at the time period 205. Comparing the results with the Example 2T.3, we find that the forecasts under the intervention model are more precise (smaller standard error) and the forecast ozone levels are lower. Note that in order to forecast the ozone level between period 217 and 228, the values of X1, X2, and X3 must be provided for the corresponding period. These values are read by the INPUT paragraph in this problem.

The syntax of the INDEPENDENT paragraph is similar to that of the ARIMA paragraph. Details of the INDEPENDENT paragraph are described below.

```
INDEpendent ------------------------------------------
  VARiable = v.   required                       none
    Name of the intervention variable.
  DFORders = # list.                             none
    Orders of differences in the difference
    polynomial.
  SPORders = '(#,...,#), ..., (#,...,#)'.         none
    Parameter orders in S-polynomial.
  SPVAlues = # list.                               .1
    Values (or initial values) of the parameters in
    the S-polynomial. If not specified, a
    preassigned value .1 is used for each
    parameter. The number of arguments in this
    sentence must be the same as the number of
    order in the SPORDER sentence.
  UPORders = '(#,...,#), ..., (#,...,#)'.         none
    Parameter orders in the U-polynomial.
  UPVAlues = # list.                               .1
    Values (or initial values) of the parameters in
    the U-polynomial. If not specified, a
    preassigned value .1 is used for each
    parameter. The number of arguments in this
    sentence must be the same as the number of
    orders in the UPORDER sentence.
  TYPE = c.   required                           none
    Type of the independent variable. c may be
    BINARY for a binary variable and NONRANDOM for
    other nonstochastic variables or RANDOM for
    stochastic variables.
  REPLace.                               NO REPLACE
    The component with the same variable name is
    replaced by this model.
```

Example 2T.5 Identification of Transfer Function Models

When an independent variable in a time series model is also a time series, it is referred to as a transfer function component of the model. As an example Box and Jenkins (1976) study adaptive optimization of a gas furnace system in which air and methane are combined to form a mixture of gases containing carbon dioxide (CO_2). We first want to determine the relationship between the gas feedrate (the input series) and the carbon dioxide concentration (the output series).

Identification of a transfer function component is usually more involved than that of an ARIMA model. For a one-input situation, we may follow a procedure suggested in Box and Jenkins (1976). The application of that procedure on the gas furnace example is summarized below:

(1) Build an ARIMA model for the input series (gas feedrate), and obtain the prewhitened input series (i.e., residuals), say, $R_x(t)$.

(2) Filter the output series (carbon dioxide concentration) by the ARIMA model for the input series; denote the filtered output series as $R_y(t)$.

(3) Cross correlate $R_x(t)$ and $R_y(t)$. From the sample cross correlation function, we can identify the functional form of the transfer function component. The initial values of each parameter can be obtained from the estimated transfer function weights which in turn are based on the sample cross correlations. Under the tentative assumption that the errors are white noise, the model can then be estimated.

(4) Identify an ARIMA model for the residuals obtained at step (3). If the ARIMA component is not white noise, we combine the ARIMA component with the transfer function component and obtain a new tentative model.

In P2T, the FILTER paragraph is used to filter a time series and the CCF paragraph to compute sample cross correlations between two series.

The transfer function identification procedure described above works very well with a single input, but does not work for multiple inputs. For more general situations, we may use the procedure proposed by Liu and Hanssens (1980) using P2T.

The Control Language setup for transfer function identification is shown below:

```
/ PROBLEM      TITLE IS 'GAS FURNACE DATA'.
/ INPUT        VARIABLES ARE 2.
              FORMAT IS FREE.
/ VARIABLE     NAME IS GASRATE, CO2.
/ END
    data
/ END
   ACF         VARIABLE IS GASRATE.  MAXLAG IS 24./

   PACF        VARIABLE IS GASRATE.  MAXLAG IS 12./

   ARIMA       VARIABLE IS GASRATE.
              ARORDERS ARE '(1,2,3)'.
              CENTERED./

   ESTIMATION  RESIDUALS = RX.  METHOD IS CLS./

   FILTER      VARIABLE IS CO2.  RESIDUALS = RY./

   CCF         VARIABLE ARE RX, RY. MAXLAG IS 10./
```

Output 2T.5   Identification of transfer function models for the gas furnace data

---

```
ACF   VARIABLE IS GASRATE. MAXLAG IS 24./

NUMBER OF OBSERVATIONS          =            296
MEAN OF THE (DIFFERENCED) SERIES =        -0.0568
STANDARD ERROR OF THE MEAN      =         0.0624
T-VALUE OF MEAN (AGAINST ZERO)  =        -0.9116
```

AUTOCORRELATIONS (29)

```
 1- 12   .95 .83 .68 .53 .41 .32 .26 .23 .21 .21 .20 .19
 ST.E.   .06 .10 .12 .13 .14 .14 .15 .15 .15 .15 .15 .15

13- 24   .17 .14 .10 .08 .05 .04 .03 .04 .06 .07 .08 .08
 ST.E.   .15 .15 .15 .15 .15 .15 .15 .15 .15 .15 .15 .15
```

PLOT OF SERIAL CORRELATION

```
        -1.0 -0.8 -0.6 -0.4 -0.2  0.0  0.2  0.4  0.6  0.8  1.0
LAG  CORR. +----+----+----+----+----+----+----+----+----+----+
                                      I
 1   0.952                           +  IXX+XXXXXXXXXXXXXXXXXXXX
 2   0.834                           +  IXXXX+XXXXXXXXXXXXXXXX
 3   0.682                        +     IXXXXX+XXXXXXXXXX
 4   0.531                        +     IXXXXX+XXXXXXX
 5   0.408                     +        IXXXXXX+XXX
 6   0.318                     +        IXXXXXX+X
 7   0.260                     +        IXXXXXXX
 8   0.228                     +        IXXXXXX+
 9   0.213                     +        IXXXXX +
10   0.208                     +        IXXXXX +
11   0.203                     +        IXXXXX +
12   0.189                     +        IXXXXX +
13   0.167                     +        IXXXX  +
14   0.138                     +        IXXX   +
15   0.105                     +        IXXX   +
16   0.075                     +        IXX    +
17   0.052                     +        IX     +
18   0.037                  +           IX     +
19   0.034                  +           IX     +
20   0.042                  +           IX     +
21   0.056                  +           IX     +
22   0.069                  +           IXX    +
23   0.077                  +           IXX    +
24   0.076                  +           IXX    +
```

```
PACF   VARIABLE IS GASRATE. MAXLAG IS 12./

NUMBER OF OBSERVATIONS          =            296
MEAN OF THE (DIFFERENCED) SERIES =        -0.0568
STANDARD ERROR OF THE MEAN      =         0.0624
T-VALUE OF MEAN (AGAINST ZERO)  =        -0.9116
```

PARTIAL AUTOCORRELATIONS (30)

```
 1- 12   .95 -.79 .34 .12 .06 -.11 .05 .10 .02 -.07 -.09 .04
 ST.E.   .06  .06 .06 .06 .06  .06 .06 .06 .06  .06  .06 .06
```

PLOT OF SERIAL CORRELATION

```
        -1.0 -0.8 -0.6 -0.4 -0.2  0.0  0.2  0.4  0.6  0.8  1.0
LAG  CORR. +----+----+----+----+----+----+----+----+----+----+
                                      I
 1   0.952                           +  IXX+XXXXXXXXXXXXXXXXXXXX
 2  -0.788  XXXXXXXXXXXXXXX+XXI      +
 3   0.339                           +  IXX+XXXXX
 4   0.120                           +  IXXX
 5   0.061                           +  IXX+
 6  -0.112                        XXXI  +
 7   0.049                           +  IX +
 8   0.099                           +  IXX+
 9   0.016                           +  I  +
10  -0.070                         +XXI  +
11  -0.094                         +XXI  +
12   0.041                           +  IX +
```

```
ARIMA VARIABLE IS GASRATE. ARORDER = '(1,2,3)'. CENTERED./   (31)

THE COMPONENT HAS BEEN ADDED TO THE MODEL

THE CURRENT MODEL HAS
OUTPUT VARIABLE = GASRATE
INPUT  VARIABLE = NOISE
```

(output continued)

The results of the above analysis are presented in Output 2T.5. Circled numbers below correspond to those in the output.

㉙ The sample autocorrelations of the input series (GASRATE) are damped out. They suggest that the input series follow an AR model.

㉚ The sample partial autocorrelations of the input series have significant lags at 1, 2, 3. They suggest that the input series is an AR(3) model, i.e., $(1-\phi_1 B-\phi_2 B^2-\phi_3 B^3)x(t) = a(t)$.

㉛ Set up the model for the centered input series. This subtracts the mean from the series.

㉜ Estimate the model for the input series by the conditional least squares method. The residuals are stored in variable RX (i.e., $R_x(t)$).

㉝ Filter the output series (CO2) by the ARIMA model for the input series; store the filtered

series in RY (i.e., $R_y(t)$). The residual mean square of the filtered series is also printed.

㉞ Compute the sample cross correlations between the prewhitened input series and the filtered output series.

㉟ The sample cross correlations between two series are printed.

㊱ The standard errors of the sample cross correlations are printed. They are approximately equal to $1/\sqrt{n-k}$ if two series are uncorrelated, where n is the number of observations.

㊲ The transfer function weights between the two series are printed. The transfer weight at lag k is equal to the correlation between the input and output series multiplied by the standard error ratio of the output and input series.

㊳ The sample cross correlations and their 95%

Output 2T.5 (continued)

```
ESTIMATION RESIDUALS = RX. METHOD IS CLS./   ㉜


ESTIMATION BY CONDITIONAL LEAST SQUARES METHOD

RELATIVE CHANGE IN RESIDUAL SUM OF SQUARES LESS THAN 0.1000E-04


SUMMARY OF THE MODEL

OUTPUT VARIABLE -- GASRATE
INPUT VARIABLES -- NOISE

VARIABLE   VAR. TYPE   MEAN      TIME      DIFFERENCES

GASRATE    RANDOM    REMOVED   1- 296
```

PARAMETER	VARIABLE	TYPE	FACTOR	ORDER	ESTIMATE	ST. ERR.	T-RATIO
1	GASRATE	AR	1	1	1.9750	0.0551	35.82
2	GASRATE	AR	1	2	-1.3732	0.0999	-13.75
3	GASRATE	AR	1	3	0.3424	0.0551	6.21

```
RESIDUAL SUM OF SQUARES  =      10.434666
DEGREES OF FREEDOM       =            290
RESIDUAL MEAN SQUARE     =       0.035982


FILTER VARIABLE IS CO2. RESIDUALS = RY./   ㉝

RESIDUAL MEAN SQUARE     =       0.133077

VARIABLE CO2     IS FILTERED, RESULTS ARE STORED IN VARIABLE RY


CCF   VARIABLES ARE RX,RY. MAXLAG IS 10./   ㉞


EFFECTIVE NUMBER OF OBSERVATIONS = 293

CORRELATION      OF RX         AND RY        IS  -0.00

CROSS CORRELATIONS OF RX    (I) AND RY    (I+K)

1- 10    .05 -.03 -.28 -.33 -.46 -.27 -.17 -.03  .03 -.05   ㉟
ST.E.    .06  .06  .06  .06  .06  .06  .06  .06  .06  .06   ㊱

CROSS CORRELATIONS OF RY    (I) AND RX    (I+K)

1- 10   -.03  .01 -.05 -.02  0.0 -.12 -.03 -.09  0.0  .02
ST.E.    .06  .06  .06  .06  .06  .06  .06  .06  .06  .06
```

```
TRANSFER FUNCTION WEIGHTS        ㊲

        SCCF(X(I),Y(I+K))        SCCF(Y(I),X(I+K))
LAG     *SY/SX     *SX/SY        *SY/SX     *SX/SY

 0    -0.00375   -0.00101      -0.00375   -0.00101
 1     0.10333    0.02794      -0.05828   -0.01576
 2    -0.04845   -0.01310       0.01788    0.00483
 3    -0.54385   -0.14706      -0.09471   -0.02561
 4    -0.63660   -0.17213      -0.03075   -0.00832
 5    -0.87724   -0.23720      -0.00584   -0.00158
 6    -0.51577   -0.13946      -0.23129   -0.06254
 7    -0.32357   -0.08749      -0.05012   -0.01355
 8    -0.04866   -0.01316      -0.17166   -0.04642
 9     0.05984    0.01618       0.00163    0.00044
10    -0.10511   -0.02842       0.04184    0.01131

WHERE X(I) IS THE FIRST SERIES, Y(I) THE SECOND
SERIES, SX THE STANDARD ERROR OF X(I), AND SY
THE STANDARD ERROR OF Y(I)



PLOT OF SERIAL CORRELATION      ㊳

         -1.0 -0.8 -0.6 -0.4 -0.2  0.0  0.2  0.4  0.6  0.8  1.0
LAG  CORR. +---+---+---+---+---+---+---+---+---+---+
                                      I
-10  0.022                          +  IX +
 -9  0.001                          +   I +
 -8 -0.089                          +XXI  +
 -7 -0.026                          + XI  +
 -6 -0.120                          XXXI  +
 -5 -0.003                          +  I  +
 -4 -0.016                          +  I  +
 -3 -0.049                          + XI  +
 -2  0.009                          +  I  +
 -1 -0.030                          + XI  +
  0 -0.002                          +  I  +
  1  0.054                          + IX  +
  2 -0.025                          + XI  +
  3 -0.283                       XXXX+XXI  +
  4 -0.331                       XXXX+XXI  +
  5 -0.456                    XXXXXXX+XXI  +
  6 -0.268                       XXXX+XXI  +
  7 -0.168                          X+XXI  +
  8 -0.025                          + XI  +
  9  0.031                          + IX  +
 10 -0.055                          + XI  +
```

confidence limits are plotted against the lags.

From the sample cross correlations between the prewhitened input series and the filtered output series, we observe that the sample cross correlations at lags 3, 4, and 5 follow no fixed pattern and beginning at lag 5 they follow an exponential decay pattern. Thus the preliminary identification suggests a transfer function model

$$y(t) = \frac{U_1 B^3 + U_2 B^4 + U_3 B^5}{1 - S_1 B} x(t) + \varepsilon(t)$$

where $y(t)$ and $x(t)$ are the output and the input series deviated from their mean. The derivation of a transfer function model is described in detail by Box and Jenkins (1976).

Using the transfer function weights in the output of the CCF paragraph (i.e., the first column in ㊲) and the above tentative transfer function model, we obtain the initial estimates $U_1 = -.53$, $U_2 = -.33$, $U_3 = -.51$, and $S_1 = .57$. Thus we obtain a tentative transfer function model with a white noise ARIMA component.

The FILTER paragraph transforms a time series to another time series using the model specified in the ARIMA and INDEPENDENT paragraphs. The filtered series may be used to cross correlate with other filtered series. This is useful for transfer function identification. The coefficients of the filter are defined in the ARIMA and INDEPENDENT paragraphs.

```
FILTering ─────────────────────────────────────
  VARiable = v.                        name in ARIMA
    Name of the series to be filtered.
  RESIduals = v.   required                    none
    Variable where filtered series are stored.
```

The CCF paragraph prints and plots the sample cross correlations and transfer function weights between two series. The printing and plotting of the sample cross correlations can be turned off by stating NO PRINT or NO PLOT. The cross correlation between two series (say, $x(t)$, and $y(t)$ at lag k) represents the correlation between the series $x(t)$ and $y(t+k)$. A formal definition is given in Appendix A.33. Sample cross correlations are computed at lags 0, 1, 2, ..., up to some maximum lag (MAXLAG) in both directions.

```
CCF ─────────────────────────────────────────
  VARiable = v, v.   required                  none
    Names of the series for which sample cross
    correlations are computed. Note that the two
    series must have an equal number of
    observations.
  MAXLag = #.                                    36
    The maximum lag of sample cross correlations to
    be computed.
  PLOT. or NO PLOT.                            PLOT
    Specifies whether the sample cross correlations
    will be plotted.
  PRINt. or NO PRINt.                         PRINT
    Specifies whether the sample cross correlations
    will be printed.
```

Example 2T.6 Estimation and Diagnostic Checking of Transfer Function Models

In Example 2T.4, we use the INDEPENDENT paragraph to specify an intervention component in the model. We can also use the INDEPENDENT paragraph to specify a transfer function component. The syntax is the same as that for an intervention component except that the sentence TYPE IS RANDOM must be specified. The ESTIMATION paragraph is used to perform model estimation, and the ACF and PACF paragraphs are used for diagnostic checking.

The Control Language setup for estimation and diagnostic checking of a transfer function model is shown below.

```
─────────────────────────────────────────────
ARIMA        VARIABLE IS CO2.   CENTERED./

INDEP        VARIABLE IS GASRATE.
             SPORDERS = '(1)'.
             SPVALUES = .57.
             UPORDERS = '(3, 4, 5)'.
             UPVALUES = -.53, -.33, -.51./

ESTIMATION   RESIDUALS = RYX.   METHOD IS CLS./

ACF          VARIABLE IS RYX./

PACF         VARIABLE IS RYX./
─────────────────────────────────────────────
```

The results of the above analysis are presented in Output 2T.6. Circled numbers below correspond to those in the output.

㊴ Specify that the ARIMA component is a white noise.

㊵ Specify the model for the transfer function component.

㊶ Estimate the model by the conditional least squares method and store the residuals in the variable RYX. The CLS method is used since this estimation is only a stepping stone for model identification.

㊷ Compute the sample autocorrelations of the residuals. The decay of the sample autocorrelations suggests that the residuals follow an AR model.

㊸ Compute the sample partial autocorrelations of the residuals. The sample partial autocorrelations have significant values at lags 1 and 2 that suggest the residuals follow an AR(2) model.

From the above analysis, we find that the white noise model for the ARIMA component is inadequate and an AR(2) model must be used. Thus we obtain a revised model as

$$y(t) = \frac{U_1 B^3 + U_2 B^4 + U_3 B^5}{1 - S_1 B} x(t) + \frac{1}{1 - \phi_1 B - \phi_2 B^2} a(t).$$

To estimate the above model, we only need to revise the ARIMA component. The transfer function component defaults to the previous specification. The Control Language is shown below.

```
------------------------------------
ARIMA          VARIABLE IS CO2.  CENTERED.
               ARORDERS = '(1, 2)'./

ESTIMATION     RESIDUALS = RYX./

ACF            VARIABLE IS RYX.  MAXLAG = 24./
------------------------------------
```

The results of the above analysis are also presented in Output 2T.6. Circled numbers below correspond to those in the output.

(44) The ARIMA paragraph revises the ARIMA component of the model.

(45) The revised model is estimated by both conditional least squares and backcasting methods.

The residuals under backcasting estimation are stored in a variable RYX.

(46) The autocorrelations of RYX have no significant values, therefore the model may be adequate.

From the above analysis, we find that the estimates of the parameter and their standard errors are

$$U_1 = -0.5309$$
$$U_2 = -0.3800$$
$$U_3 = -0.5183$$
$$S_1 = -0.5491$$
$$\phi_1 = -1.5331$$
$$\phi_2 = -0.6339$$
$$\hat{\sigma}_\epsilon^2 = 0.058649$$

Output 2T.6   Estimation and diagnostic checking of transfer function models for the gas furnace data

----

```
ARIMA VARIABLE IS CO2. CENTERED./    (39)


THE COMPONENT HAS BEEN ADDED TO THE MODEL

THE CURRENT MODEL HAS
OUTPUT VARIABLE = CO2
INPUT  VARIABLE = NOISE

                                            (40)

INDEP VARIABLE IS GASRATE. SPORDER = '(1)'. SPVALUES ARE 0.57.
      UPORDER = '(3,4,5)'. UPVALUES ARE -0.53,-0.33,-.51.
      TYPE IS RANDOM. CENTERED./


THE COMPONENT HAS BEEN ADDED TO THE MODEL

THE CURRENT MODEL HAS
OUTPUT VARIABLE = CO2
INPUT  VARIABLE = NOISE      GASRATE




ESTIMATION RESIDUAL = RYX. METHOD IS CLS./   (41)



ESTIMATION BY CONDITIONAL LEAST SQUARES METHOD

RELATIVE CHANGE IN RESIDUAL SUM OF SQUARES LESS THAN 0.1000E-04


SUMMARY OF THE MODEL

OUTPUT VARIABLE -- CO2
INPUT VARIABLES -- NOISE     GASRATE

VARIABLE  VAR. TYPE  MEAN      TIME     DIFFERENCES

CO2       RANDOM    REMOVED  1- 296

GASRATE   RANDOM    REMOVED  1- 296


PARAMETER VARIABLE  TYPE  FACTOR  ORDER  ESTIMATE  ST. ERR.  T-RATIO
   1  GASRATE       UP      1       3    -0.5590    0.2234    -2.50
   2  GASRATE       UP      1       4    -0.4383    0.4629    -0.95
   3  GASRATE       UP      1       5    -0.2897    0.3516    -0.82
   4  GASRATE       SP      1       1     0.6017    0.0398    15.13

RESIDUAL SUM OF SQUARES  =      200.853607
DEGREES OF FREEDOM       =             287
RESIDUAL MEAN SQUARE     =        0.699838
```

```
ACF   VARIABLE IS RYX. MAXLAG IS 12./   (42)


NUMBER OF OBSERVATIONS          =          291
MEAN OF THE (DIFFERENCED) SERIES =      -0.0013
STANDARD ERROR OF THE MEAN      =        0.0488
T-VALUE OF MEAN (AGAINST ZERO)  =       -0.0261

AUTOCORRELATIONS

 1- 12   .89  .71  .50  .31  .17  .07  0.0  -.04  -.05  -.04  -.02  -.02
 ST.E.   .06  .09  .11  .12  .12  .12  .12  .12   .12   .12   .12   .12

PLOT OF SERIAL CORRELATION

        -1.0 -0.8 -0.6 -0.4 -0.2  0.0  0.2  0.4  0.6  0.8  1.0
LAG   CORR. +----+----+----+----+----+----+----+----+----+----+
                                      I
 1    0.893                         + IXX+XXXXXXXXXXXXXXXXX
 2    0.710                       +   IXXXX+XXXXXXXXXXXX
 3    0.502                       +   IXXXX+XXXXXXXX
 4    0.312                     +     IXXXXX+XX
 5    0.168                     +     IXXXX +
 6    0.066                     +     IXX   +
 7   -0.002                     +     I     +
 8   -0.039                     +     XI    +
 9   -0.054                     +     XI    +
10   -0.041                     +     XI    +
11   -0.022                     +     XI    +
12   -0.021                     +     XI    +
```

(output continued)

Output 2T.6 (continued)

PACF VARIABLE IS RYX. MAXLAG IS 12./

NUMBER OF OBSERVATIONS	=	291
MEAN OF THE (DIFFERENCED) SERIES =		-0.0013
STANDARD ERROR OF THE MEAN	=	0.0488
T-VALUE OF MEAN (AGAINST ZERO)	=	-0.0261

PARTIAL AUTOCORRELATIONS

```
  1- 12    .89 -.43 -.13  .02  .04 -.03 -.03  .02  0.0  .09 -.06 -.12
  ST.E.    .06  .06  .06  .06  .06  .06  .06  .06  .06  .06  .06  .06
```

PLOT OF SERIAL CORRELATION

```
          -1.0 -0.8 -0.6 -0.4 -0.2  0.0  0.2  0.4  0.6  0.8  1.0
LAG  CORR. +---+---+---+---+---+---+---+---+---+---+---+
                                    I
  1   0.893                         +  IXX+XXXXXXXXXXXXXXXXXXXX
  2  -0.431              XXXXXXXX+XXI  +
  3  -0.130                      XXXI  +
  4   0.023                         +  IX  +
  5   0.041                         +  IX  +
  6  -0.026                         + XI   +
  7  -0.025                         + XI   +
  8   0.020                         +  IX  +
  9  -0.000                         +  I   +
 10   0.088                         +  IXX+
 11  -0.061                        +XXI   +
 12  -0.115                      XXXI   +
```

ARIMA VARIABLES IS CO2. ARORDERS ARE '(1,2)'. CENTERED./

THE COMPONENT HAS BEEN ADDED TO THE MODEL

THE CURRENT MODEL HAS
OUTPUT VARIABLE = CO2
INPUT VARIABLE = NOISE   GASRATE

ESTIMATION RESIDUALS = RYX./ (45)

ESTIMATION BY CONDITIONAL LEAST SQUARES METHOD

RELATIVE CHANGE IN RESIDUAL SUM OF SQUARES LESS THAN 0.1000E-04

SUMMARY OF THE MODEL

OUTPUT VARIABLE -- CO2
INPUT VARIABLES -- NOISE   GASRATE

VARIABLE	VAR. TYPE	MEAN	TIME	DIFFERENCES
CO2	RANDOM	REMOVED	1- 296	
GASRATE	RANDOM	REMOVED	1- 296	

PARAMETER VARIABLE		TYPE	FACTOR	ORDER	ESTIMATE	ST. ERR.	T-RATIO
1	CO2	AR	1	1	1.5322	0.0475	32.29
2	CO2	AR	1	2	-0.6331	0.0499	-12.68
3	GASRATE	UP	1	3	-0.5298	0.0748	-7.08
4	GASRATE	UP	1	4	-0.3795	0.1028	-3.69
5	GASRATE	UP	1	5	-0.5189	0.1073	-4.84
6	GASRATE	SP	1	1	0.5491	0.0375	14.65

RESIDUAL SUM OF SQUARES	=	16.597580
DEGREES OF FREEDOM	=	283
RESIDUAL MEAN SQUARE	=	0.058649

ESTIMATION BY BACKCASTING METHOD

RELATIVE CHANGE IN RESIDUAL SUM OF SQUARES LESS THAN 0.1000E-04

SUMMARY OF THE MODEL

OUTPUT VARIABLE -- CO2
INPUT VARIABLES -- NOISE   GASRATE

VARIABLE	VAR. TYPE	MEAN	TIME	DIFFERENCES
CO2	RANDOM	REMOVED	1- 296	
GASRATE	RANDOM	REMOVED	1- 296	

PARAMETER VARIABLE		TYPE	FACTOR	ORDER	ESTIMATE	ST. ERR.	T-RATIO
1	CO2	AR	1	1	1.5331	0.0474	32.35
2	CO2	AR	1	2	-0.6339	0.0499	-12.72
3	GASRATE	UP	1	3	-0.5309	0.0748	-7.10
4	GASRATE	UP	1	4	-0.3800	0.1028	-3.70
5	GASRATE	UP	1	5	-0.5183	0.1073	-4.83
6	GASRATE	SP	1	1	0.5491	0.0375	14.65

RESIDUAL SUM OF SQUARES	=	16.597626 (BACKCASTS EXCLUDED)
DEGREES OF FREEDOM	=	283
RESIDUAL MEAN SQUARE	=	0.058649

ACF VARIABLE IS RYX. MAXLAG IS 12./

NUMBER OF OBSERVATIONS	=	296
MEAN OF THE (DIFFERENCED) SERIES =		0.0031
STANDARD ERROR OF THE MEAN	=	0.0138
T-VALUE OF MEAN (AGAINST ZERO)	=	0.2247

AUTOCORRELATIONS

```
  1- 12    .02  .06 -.07 -.05 -.06  .12  .03  .03 -.08  .05  .02  .10
  ST.E.    .06  .06  .06  .06  .06  .06  .06  .06  .06  .06  .06  .06
```

PLOT OF SERIAL CORRELATION

```
          -1.0 -0.8 -0.6 -0.4 -0.2  0.0  0.2  0.4  0.6  0.8  1.0
LAG  CORR. +---+---+---+---+---+---+---+---+---+---+---+
                                    I
  1   0.024                         +  IX  +
  2   0.056                         +  IX  +
  3  -0.072                        +XXI   +
  4  -0.055                         + XI   +
  5  -0.055                         + XI   +
  6   0.122                         +  IXXX
  7   0.030                         +  IX  +
  8   0.032                         +  IX  +
  9  -0.085                        +XXI   +
 10   0.050                         +  IX  +
 11   0.023                         +  IX  +
 12   0.102                         +  IXXX
```

Example 2T.7 Forecasting under Transfer Function Models

To forecast the output series (carbon dioxide), we need to provide forecasts of the input series (gas feedrate). In order to compute the standard errors for the forecasts of the output series, we must know the possible uncertainty for the forecasts of the input series. This information is contained in the psi-weights (Box and Jenkins, 1976, or see Appendix A) and the variance of the input series. P2T uses the PSIWEIGHT paragraph to compute the psi-weights and the variance of the input series. The setup for forecasting the output series CO2 is shown below:

```
-------------------------------------
ARIMA      VARIABLE IS GASRATE.
           ARORDERS = '(1, 2, 3)'.
           ARVALUES = 1.9750, -1.3732, .3424.
           CENTERED./

FORECAST   CASES ARE 24.  JOIN./

PSIWEIGHT  MAXPSI = 40./

ERASE      MODEL./

ARIMA      VARIABLE IS CO2.  ARORDERS = '(1, 2)'.
           ARVALUES = 1.5331, -0.6339.  CENTERED./

INDEP      VARIABLE IS GASRATE.
           UPORDERS = '(3, 4, 5)'.
           UPVALUES = -0.5322, -0.3653, -0.5041.
           SPORDERS = '(1)'.
           SPVALUES = 0.5765.
           CENTERED./

FORECAST   CASES = 40./
-------------------------------------
```

The results of the above analysis are presented in Output 2T.7. Circled numbers below correspond to those in the output.

(47) Specify the ARIMA model of the input series (gas feedrate).

(48) Forecast the input series 24 periods ahead and append the results to the data matrix. The information is used in forecasting the output series.

(49) Compute the psi-weights and the variance of the input series. This information is used in computing the standard error of the forecasts for the output series.

(50) Specify the ARIMA component for the model of output series.

(51) Specify the transfer function component for the model of the output series.

(52) Forecast the output series 40 periods ahead. Since we provide forecasts only 24 periods ahead for the input series, and the input series leads the output series by at least 3 periods, we can forecast at most 27 periods ahead for the output series.

Output 2T.7   Forecasts for the gas furnace data under a transfer function model

```
--------------------------------------------------------
```

```
ARIMA VARIABLE IS GASRATE. CENTERED.
      ARORDER = '(1,2,3)'. ARVALUES = 1.9750,-1.3732,0.3424./   (47)


THE COMPONENT HAS BEEN ADDED TO THE MODEL

THE CURRENT MODEL HAS
OUTPUT VARIABLE = GASRATE
INPUT  VARIABLE = NOISE


FORECAST CASES = 24. JOIN./   (48)
```

FORECAST ON VARIABLE GASRATE FROM TIME PERIOD   297

PERIOD	FORECASTS	ST. ERR.	ACTUAL
297	-0.26488	0.18969	
298	-0.22884	0.41992	
299	-0.18112	0.63732	
300	-0.13732	0.80842	
301	-0.10403	0.92631	
302	-0.08208	0.99908	
303	-0.06943	1.03992	
304	-0.06322	1.06106	
305	-0.06078	1.07136	
306	-0.06018	1.07620	
307	-0.06021	1.07849	
308	-0.06025	1.07961	
309	-0.06010	1.08020	
310	-0.05975	1.08054	
311	-0.05927	1.08075	
312	-0.05877	1.08089	
313	-0.05830	1.08097	
314	-0.05791	1.08103	
315	-0.05761	1.08107	
316	-0.05739	1.08109	
317	-0.05724	1.08110	
318	-0.05713	1.08111	
319	-0.05706	1.08111	
320	-0.05701	1.08111	

```
STANDARD ERROR = 0.189688    (BY CONDITIONAL METHOD  )



PSIWEIGHT MAXPSI = 40./   (49)

 33 PSI-WEIGHTS ARE STORED


ERASE MODEL./

UNIVARIATE TIME SERIES MODEL ERASED


ARIMA VARIABLE IS CO2. ARORDER = '(1,2)'. ARVALUES = 1.5331, -0.6339.
      CENTERED./
                                                              (50)
THE COMPONENT HAS BEEN ADDED TO THE MODEL

THE CURRENT MODEL HAS
OUTPUT VARIABLE = CO2
INPUT  VARIABLE = NOISE


INDEP VARIABLE IS GASRATE. CENTERED.
      SPORDER = '(1)'. SPVALUE = 0.5491.
      UPORDER = '(3,4,5)'. UPVALUES = -0.5309,-0.3800,-0.5183./   (51)

THE COMPONENT HAS BEEN ADDED TO THE MODEL

THE CURRENT MODEL HAS
OUTPUT VARIABLE = CO2
INPUT  VARIABLE = NOISE    GASRATE
```

(output continued)

Output 2T.7 (continued)

FORECAST CASES = 40./

FORECAST ON VARIABLE CO2		FROM TIME PERIOD	297
PERIOD	FORECASTS	ST. ERR.	ACTUAL
297	56.52968	0.24218	
298	56.05141	0.44328	
299	55.61597	0.60770	
300	55.23027	0.73553	
301	54.83199	0.87863	
302	54.43242	1.14412	
303	54.06631	1.54200	
304	53.76425	1.98002	
305	53.54196	2.37360	
306	53.39973	2.68169	
307	53.32675	2.89878	
308	53.30649	3.03913	
309	53.32132	3.12358	
310	53.35559	3.17156	
311	53.39719	3.19772	
312	53.43782	3.21167	
313	53.47263	3.21907	
314	53.49948	3.22307	
315	53.51813	3.22528	
316	53.52939	3.22655	
317	53.53471	3.22729	
318	53.53564	3.22774	
319	53.53368	3.22802	
320	53.53003	3.22819	
321	53.52565	3.22829	
322	53.52124	3.22835	
323	53.51721	3.22839	

BASED ON THE AVAILABLE DATA, ONLY   27 FORECASTS CAN BE MADE

STANDARD ERROR = 0.242175   (BY CONDITIONAL METHOD)

The PSIWEIGHT paragraph computes psi-weights and the variance of the time series specified in the ARIMA paragraph. The psi-weights and the variance are used in forecasting under a transfer function model.

```
PSIWeight
  MAXPsi = #.                                          200
    Maximum number of psi-weights to be computed.
```

Differencing a Time Series

The ACF, PACF, ARIMA, and INDEPENDENT paragraphs have options to specify a differencing polynomial for each series, therefore it is usually not necessary to difference a series before using these paragraphs, even if the series is nonstationary. However, in some situations, it may be more economical to store the differenced series. This can be achieved by using the DIFFERENCE paragraph. The DIFFERENCE paragraph may also be used in conjunction with the CCF paragraph since it does not have options to specify the difference polynomial for each series.

```
DIFFerence
  OLD = v.   required                                 none
    Name of the series to be differenced.
  NEW = c.   required                                 none
    Name to be given to the variable where the dif-
    ferenced series is to be stored.
  DFORder = # list.                                      1
    Orders of differences to be made on the old
    series.
```

Printing Variables

A user may wish to check if the data to be analyzed have been read appropriately, or whether some variables, such as residuals or filtered series, are computed as desired. To do so the user specifies the variables to be printed in the PRINT paragraph. All cases in the variables will be printed if the CASE sentence is not specified.

```
PRINt
  VARiables = v list.   required                      none
    Variables to be printed.
  CASEs = # list.                                 1, ..., N
    Cases to be printed.
```

Saving Variables at Various Points in Data Analysis

The SAVE paragraph is common to all BMDP programs and is described in Chapter 7. In P2T the SAVE paragraph can be used to store the original data in a BMDP File, or to save variables generated during the analyses.

```
SAVE
  KEEP = v list. required, at least one              none
    Variable to be saved to a BMDP File.
```

Other sentences UNIT, CODE, LABEL and NEW are described in Chapter 4.

Specification of Time Periods

Frequently we may want to analyze only a section of a series rather than the whole series. This need is facilitated by the specification of time periods in the TIME sentence. The ACF, PACF, CCF, FILTER, ESTIMATION, and PSIWEIGHT paragraphs contain the TIME sentence. The syntax for the TIME sentence is shown below

```
TIME = #, #.   optional                             1, N
  The first number specifies the beginning time
  period and the second the ending time period.
```

Other Options in the ESTIMATION Paragraph

In addition to the RESIDUAL, METHOD and TIME sentences, the ESTIMATION paragraph includes several other sentences for controlling the output and stopping criterion of nonlinear estimation. They are as follows:

```
ESTIMation ─────────────────────────────────
  ONEStep = v.                              none
    Variable storing one-step ahead forecasts of
    the output series.
  PCLS. or NO PCLS.                         PCLS
    The results under conditional least squares
    estimation are printed.
  PITEration. or NO PITE.                 NO PITE
    The parameter estimates at each iteration of
    nonlinear estimation are printed.
  PCOR. or NO PCOR.                       NO PCOR
    The correlation matrix of the parameter
    estimates is printed.
  MAXIt = #.                                  10
    The maximum number of iterations in the
    nonlinear estimation.
  SCRSs = #.                              .00001
    Stopping criterion for the nonlinear estimation
    in terms of residual sum of squares (RSS). The
    nonlinear estimation stops if
```
$$\left| (RSS^{(k)} - RSS^{(k-1)})/RSS^{(k)} \right| < \#, \quad \text{where } k$$
```
    denotes the cycle of iteration.
  SCEStimates = #.                          .0001
    Stopping criterion for the nonlinear estimation
    in terms of parameter estimates. The nonlinear
    estimation stops if
```
$$\operatorname*{MAX}_{j} \left| (\zeta_j^{(k)} - \zeta_j^{(k-1)})/\zeta_j^{(k)} \right| < \#, \quad \text{where } \zeta_j^{(k)}$$
```
    denotes an estimate of the j-th parameter at
    the k-th iteration.
  TOLerance = #.                           0.0001
    Tolerance limit for matrix inversion.
```

SIZE OF PROBLEM

P2T executes a paragraph as soon as it is read, thus there is no specific limitations for the number of variables or series as long as the data can be stored in core. Since P2T stores all data in core memory, the size of a problem depends on the total number of variables, and the number of cases. The estimation paragraph requires more storage than any other paragraph. The size of storage for an estimation paragraph also depends on the number of parameters in the model.

COMPUTATIONAL METHOD

P2T uses a Gauss-Marquardt method to perform the nonlinear least-squares estimation for a time series model. All computations are done in single precision.

ACKNOWLEDGEMENT

P2T is partially based on a time series program developed by David J. Pack (1977). The author wishes to thank Anthony D. Thrall for his assistance in preparing the description. Later improvements to this program were made by James Frane.

SUMMARY

Order of Input Cards

```
// (job card)
// EXEC BIMED,PROG=BMDP2T        (see Appendix E)
//SYSIN DD *
/ PROBLEM
/ INPUT
/ VARIABLE
/ TRANSFORM
/ SAVE
/ END
    (data, if on cards)
  PRINT ... /      ┐
  SAVE  ... /      │
  TPLOT ... /      │
  ACF   ... /      │
  PACF  ... /      │
  CCF   ... /      │
  DIFFERENCE ... / │  may be
  ARIMA ... /      │  repeated in
  INDEP ... /      │  any logical
  CHECK ... /      │  order
  ERASE ... /      │
  FILTER ... /     │
  ESTIMATION ... / │
  PSIWEIGHT  ... / │
  FORECAST  ... /  │
  END /            ┘
```

The PRINT, SAVE, TPLOT, ACF, PACF, CCF, DIFFERENCE, ARIMA, INDEP, CHECK, ERASE, FILTER, ESTIMATION, PSIWEIGHT, and FORECAST paragraphs can be repeated in any order before the END paragraph. Note that these paragraphs are executed one at a time and that the slash must come at the end of each of these paragraphs. The END paragraph signals the end of the current analysis.

Full sets of BMDP paragraphs (and data, if on cards) can be repeated for additional problems; see Section 5.8.

Paragraph Statement	Preassigned	Comment and Manual Reference
PRINt		Print data. 656
● VARiables = v list.	none	Variables to be printed. Required.
CASEs = # list.	1,...,N	Cases to be printed.
/		

SAVE — Save variables in a BMDP file. 656

KEEP = v list.	none	Variables to be saved to a BMDP File. Required.
/		

UNIT, CODE, LABEL, and NEW are described in the Common Control Language listed on the back cover.

TPLOt		Plot multiple series either in one common frame, or in separate individual frames side by side. 643
● VARiable = v list.	none	Names of the series (variable) to be plotted.
CASEs = # list.	all cases	Cases to be printed.
MARK = #.	5	The interval between time points where tick marks are printed.
MINImum = # list.		Lower bounds for the variables to be plotted.
MAXImum = # list.		Upper bounds for the variables to be plotted.

Plot in one common frame:		See p. 643.
COMMon		Plot the series in one common frame.
SIZE = #.	45	Number of characters for the horizontal data axis.
SYMBols = character list.	A,B,...	Symbols used to distinguish different series. If the SYMBOL sentence is not specified, A is used to represent the first series, B the second, etc.

Plot in separate frame:		See p. 643.
NO COMMon.		Plot the series in separate frames.
SIZE = # list.		Numbers of characters for each horizontal axis. If omitted, P2T supplies one appropriate SIZE used for each horizontal axis.
SYMBols = character list.	X .	A sequence of symbols repeated in the plot, displaying the periodic nature of the data.
/		

ACF		Compute, print and plot sample autocorrelations of a series. 643
● VARiable = v.	none	Name of the series (variable) for which the sample autocorrelations are to be computed.
DFORders = # list.	none	Orders of differences to be made on the series before computing the sample autocorrelations.
MAXLag = #.	36	The maximum lag of sample autocorrelations to be computed.
PLOT.	PLOT	Plot the sample autocorrelations.
PRINt.	PRINT	Print the sample autocorrelations.
CI.	CI	Plot the confidence interval of the sample autocorrelations
LBQ.	NO LBQ	Compute Ljung–Box Q statistic for a portmanteau lack of fit test.
TIME = #, #.	1, N	Range of time periods to be analyzed. 656
/		

PACF		Compute, print, and plot sample partial autocorrelations of a series. 643
● VARiable = v.	none	Name of the series (variable) for which the sample partial autocorrelation are to be computed.
DFORders = # list.	none	Orders of differences to be made on the series before computing the sample partial autocorrelations.
MAXLag = #.	36	The maximum lag of sample partial autocorrelations to be computed.
PLOT.	PLOT	Plot the sample partial autocorrelations.
PRINt.	PRINT	Print the sample partial autocorrelations.
CI.	CI	Plot the confidence interval of the sample partial autocorrelations.
TIME = #, #.	1, N	Range of time periods to be analyzed. 656
/		

(continued)

(continued)

Paragraph Statement	Preassigned	Comment and Manual Reference
CCF		Compute, print, and plot sample cross correlations between two series. 652
● VARiable = v, v.	none	Names of the series for which sample cross correlations are computed.
MAXLag = #.	36	The maximum lag of sample cross correlation to be computed.
PLOT.	PLOT	Plot the sample cross correlations.
PRINt.	PRINT	Print the sample cross correlations.
CI.	CI	Plot confidence intervals of the sample cross correlations.
TIME = #, #.	1, N	Range of time periods to be analyzed. 656
/		
DIFFerence		Difference a time series. 656
● OLD = v.		Name of the series to be differenced.
● NEW = 'c'.		Name (not index) for new variable where the differenced series is to be stored.
DFORder = # list.	0	Orders of differences to be made on the old series.
/		
FILTer		Filter a time series using the model specified in the ARIMA and INDEP paragraphs. 652
VARiable = v.	name in ARIMA	Name of the series to be filtered.
RESIduals = v.	none	Variable where filtered series are stored.
TIME = #, #.	1, N	Range of time for which the series is to be filtered.
/		
ARIMa		Specify the ARIMA component of a time series model. 645
● VARiable = v.	none	Name of the series (variable) to be analyzed.
DFORders = # list.	none	Orders of differences in the difference polynomial.
ARORders = '(#,...,#),...,(#,...,#)'.	none	Parameter orders in the AR polynomial.
ARVAlues = # list.	.1	Values or initial values of the parameters in the AR polynomial.
MAORders = '(#,...,#),...,(#,...,#)'.	none	Parameter orders in the MA polynomial.
MAVAlues = # list.	.1	Values or initial values of the parameters in the MA polynomial.
CONStant = #.	none	Mean or trend of the series.
CENTered.	not CENTERED	Remove the mean of the series. 651
/		
INDEpendent		Specify intervention or transfer function component of a time series model.
● VARiable = v.	none	Name of the intervention variable. 649
DFORders = # list.	none	Orders of differences in the difference polynomial.
SPORders = '(#,...,#),...,(#,...,#)'.	none	Parameter orders in S-polynomial.
SPVAlues = # list.	.1	Values (or initial values) of the parameters in the S-polynomial.
UPORders = '(#,...,#),...,(#,...,#)'.	none	Parameter orders in the U-polynomial.
UPVAlues = # list.	.1	Values (or initial values) of the parameters in the U-polynomial.
TYPE = c.	random	Type of the independent variable. c may be BINARY for binary variable, NONRANDOM for other nonstochastic variables, and RANDOM for stochastic variables.
REPLace.	NO REPLACE	The model for the component with the same variable name in the model is replaced by this model.
CENTered.	not CENTERED	Remove the mean of the series. 651
/		

(continued)

(continued)

Paragraph Statement	Preassigned	Comment and Manual Reference
ESTImation		Estimate the parameter of a time series model specified in the ARIMA and INDEP paragraph. Note that VARiable is inherited from ARIMA. 645, 657
RESIduals = v.	none	Variable storing residuals of the output series.
METHod =		Method of model estimation. The CLS option is to use the conditional
(one only)		least squares method only, the BACKCASTING option is to use the
CLS, BACKcasting.		backcasting method only. If this sentence is omitted, the program will perform conditional least squares estimation and backcasting estimation.
ONEStep = v.	none	Variable storing one-step ahead forecasts.
MAXIt = #.	10	The maximum number of iterations for the nonlinear estimation.
SCRSs = #.	.00001	Stopping criterion for the nonlinear estimation in terms of residual sum of squares (RSS).
SCEStimates = #.	.0001	Stopping criterion for the nonlinear estimation in terms of parameter estimates.
PCLS.	PCLS	Print the results under conditional least squares estimation.
PITEration.	NO PITE	Print the parameter estimates at each iteration of nonlinear estimation.
PCOR.	NO PCOR	Print the correlation matrix of the parameter estimates.
TOLerance = #.	.0001	Tolerance limit for matrix inversion.
TIME = #, #.	1, N	Time period in which the estimation is performed. In the 1982 release, if missing values are present, they can be excluded by means of this statement. 656
/		
PSIWeight		Compute psi-weights and variance of a time series specified in the ARIMA paragraph. 656
MAXPsi = #.	200	Maximum number of psi-weights to be computed.
TIME = #, #.	1, N	Time period in which the variance of a series is computed.
/		
FOREcast		Forecast future values of a time series.
CASEs = #.	36	Number of forecasts to be made. 646
STARt = #.		Time period where forecasting starts. If not specified, the last time period of the series plus one is taken as the starting period. 646
RMS = #.		RMS is the residual mean square of the series to be forecast. If not specified, the program will compute one by the conditional method.
JOIN.	NO JOIN	Store the forecast in the data matrix.
/		
CHECk		Print the specified time series model or computed psi-weights. 647
MODEl.		Print the specified time series model.
PSIWeight.		Print the computed psi-weight.
/		
ERASe		Erase the specified time series model or computed psi-weights. 647
MODEl.		Erase the specified time series model.
PSIWeight.		Erase the computed psi-weights.
/		

Key:

/	–indicates paragraph		*	–assigned value remains the same for additional problems
.	–period ends a sentence			
●	–required		VT	–number of variables after transformations
v	–variable (name or subscript)		list	–more than one item, often one per var.
g	–group (name or subscript)			
#	–number			Capitalized letters–paragraph or sentence names recognized by BMDP
'c'	–characters (name or parameter) may omit apostrophes if contiguous letters only			Page numbers following refer to this Manual

APPENDIX A

Contents

A.1 Random Numbers

You can generate both uniform and normal random numbers, either by Control Language instructions in the *TRANsform* paragraph or by FORTRAN statements in the FORTRAN transformation subroutine. Below we describe both random number generators and how to use them by FORTRAN statements. In Section 6.1 we describe how to use them by Control Language instructions.

UNIFORM RANDOM NUMBER GENERATOR

The FORTRAN code used in the uniform random number generator is

```
        FUNCTION RANDOM(I)
        M1=65539
        M2=4101
        M3=261
C          M1=2**16+3
C          M2=2**12+5
C          M3=2**8+5
        I=M3*I
        L=M1
        IF(I.LT.0)L=M2
        I=I*L
        IF(I.LT.0) I=I+2147483647+1
        RANDOM=FLOAT(I)*.4656613E-9
        RETURN
        END
```

Let I be a large odd integer. Then I is multiplied by (2^8+5) and again by either $(2^{12}+5)$ or $(2^{16}+3)$. This yields an integer (mod 2^{31}, still called I). This integer is now turned into a uniform random number (RANDOM) by dividing by 2^{31} (multiplying by 0.4656613×10^{-9}).

Therefore the integer that you specify in the Control Language instruction y=RNDU(i) is the initial value of I. To obtain each new random number I is multiplied as explained above and normalized to lie between zero and one.

To use FUNCTION RANDOM(I) in a FORTRAN subroutine you must specify an initial value for the random number generator in a data statement; e.g.,

        DATA IRAND/562345/

(IRAND should be odd) and then use RANDOM(IRAND); in your FORTRAN statements; i.e.,

        Y=RANDOM(IRAND)

stores the random number in Y. Y can be a subscripted variable, such as X(3) or it can be used in an expression to compute the value for a variable, such as

        X(2)=.7*RANDOM(IRAND)-.35

NORMAL RANDOM NUMBERS

Pairs of normal random numbers are generated from pairs of uniform random numbers by the Box and Muller (1958) method. That is, if r_1 and r_2 are two uniform random numbers, then

$$z_1 = (-2 \log_e r_1)^{1/2} \cos (2\pi r_2) \quad \text{and}$$
$$z_2 = (-2 \log_e r_1)^{1/2} \sin (2\pi r_2)$$

are a pair of statistically independent random numbers from a normal distribution with mean zero and variance one. The uniform random number generator described above is part of the normal random number generator subroutine.

The normal random number generator can be part of your FORTRAN transformation statements. Its calling sequence is

        CALL RANDG(N,Z,XBAR,SIGMA,IRAND)

where

N   is the number of normal random numbers that you want

Z   is a vector containing the random numbers

XBAR   is the mean of the normal population (i.e., 0.0 if random numbers from the standard normal distribution are wanted)

SIGMA   is the standard deviation of the normal population (i.e., 1.0 for the standard normal distribution)

IRAND   is a large odd integer used to start the generator

In Control Language instructions the i in RNDG(i) has the same role as in RNDU(i).

An example

In Section 6.2 we give an example of generating normal random numbers from the standard normal distribution with probability 0.7, and from the normal with mean zero and standard deviation 3 with probability 0.3. Using FORTRAN statements we could write

```
        DATA IRAND/567213/
        Y=RANDOM (IRAND)
        CALL RANDG (1, X(1), 0.0, 1.0, IRAND)
        1F(Y.GT.0.7) X(1)=3.0*X(1)
```

If you want to use either or both random number generators in FORTRAN statements for more than one problem (i.e., more than one *PROBlem* paragraph), you must initialize the first value of the random number generator as described below; otherwise you may get the same sequence of random numbers in each analysis. Use the following two FORTRAN statements.

```
COMMON/NUMBER/IRAND
IF(NPROB.EQ.1.AND.KASE.EQ.1)IRAND=572311
```

That is, the value of IRAND must be stored in a COMMON block (called NUMBER) and initialized at the first case of the first problem. Do not use a DATA statement for IRAND. (In many facilities overlays are used for BMDP programs. If overlays and a data statement are used IRAND is reset to its original value at each new *PROBlem* paragraph.)

A.2 Method of Provisional Means

Many BMDP programs compute the mean, variance or sum of squares, skewness, kurtosis and covariance. All but the mean require that deviation about the mean be used in the computations. If the data are kept in computer memory it is possible to first compute the mean and then compute each deviation. However, this restricts the number of cases that can be analyzed.

A provisional means algorithm is used to avoid keeping the data in memory or reading the data twice. This algorithm produces more accurate results than a formula such as $\Sigma \, x_i^2 - (\Sigma \, x_i)^2/N$ for the sum of squares.

MEANS AND VARIANCES

In the provisional means algorithm the mean $\bar{x}$ and sum of squares of deviations (S^2) for each variable are computed recursively as

$$d_j = w_j(x_j - \bar{x}_{j-1})$$

$$W_j = W_{j-1} + w_j$$

$$\bar{x}_j = \bar{x}_{j-1} + d_j/W_j$$

$$S_j^2 = S_{j-1}^2 + d_j(x_j - \bar{x}_j)$$

where

x_j is the jth observation

w_j is the weight for case j (if no case weight is specified, $w_j = 1$)

W_j is the sum of the weights for the first j cases

$\bar{x}_j$ is the mean of the first j cases

S_j^2 is the sum of squares of deviations for the first j cases

Only cases with acceptable data and a nonzero weight are used.

The mean is $\bar{x}_N$ and the variance $s^2 = S_N^2/[(N-1)W_N/N]$.

SKEWNESS AND KURTOSIS

Skewness (g_1) and kurtosis (g_2) are computed in a similar manner when no case weights are specified, or all case weights are either zero or one; Spicer (1972) describes a similar algorithm. When case weights are specified that are not zero or one, skewness and kurtosis are not computed.

COVARIANCES AND CORRELATIONS

All BMDP programs (except P8D and PAM) that compute the covariance between two variables use only cases for which both variables have acceptable values. Most programs are even more restrictive and use only cases that contain acceptable values for all the variables in the covariance matrix. We now describe how covariances are computed in all programs except P8D and PAM, which use a slightly modified algorithm.

The formula for the covariance between variable i and k is

$$cov_{ik} = \Sigma \, w_j(x_{ij}-\bar{x}_i)(x_{kj}-\bar{x}_k)/[(N-1)\Sigma \, w_j/N]$$

where

x_{ij} is the jth observation for variable i

$\bar{x}_i$ and $\bar{x}_k$ are the means of the variables computed from the cases used in the analysis

w_j is the weight of the jth case (1 if no case weights are specified)

N is the number of observations used in the computation with non-zero weight

The covariance is computed recursively as

$$d_{ij} = w_j(x_{ij}-\bar{x}_{i(j-1)}) \quad ; \quad d_{kj} = w_j(x_{kj}-\bar{x}_{k(j-1)})$$

$$W_j = W_{j-1} + w_j$$

$$\bar{x}_{ij} = \bar{x}_{i(j-1)} + d_{ij}/W_j \quad ; \quad \bar{x}_{kj} = \bar{x}_{k(j-1)} + d_{kj}/W_j$$

and

$$S_{ikj}^2 = S_{ik(j-1)}^2 + d_{ij}(x_{kj}-\bar{x}_{kj})$$

where

W_j is the sum of the weights for the first j cases

$\bar{x}_{ij}$ is the mean of the first j cases for variable i

S_{ikj}^2 is the sum of squares of cross-products for the first j cases

Then the covariance between variables i and k is

$$S_{ikN}^2/[(N-1)W_N/N],$$

the variance of variable i is

$$S_{iiN}^2/[(N-1)W_N/N] \, ,$$

and the correlation between variables i and k is

$$S_{ikN}^2/(S_{iiN}^2 \, S_{kkN}^2)^{\frac{1}{2}} \, .$$

Each program description specifies the cases that are used in the computations.

A.3 Hotelling's T^2 and Mahalanobis D^2 (P3D)

The pooled within-groups covariance between each pair of variables (say x and y) is computed using only cases for which both x and y are acceptable values; i.e., are not equal to the missing value codes and not out of range. If COMPLETE is specified in the *TEST* paragraph, only cases for which the values of all the variables are acceptable are used in the analysis.

Let (x_{ij},y_{ij}) be the values of x and y for the jth case in the ith group. Then

$$\bar{x}_i = \Sigma_j x_{ij}/n_i$$

is the mean of x in the ith group where n_i is the number of pairs of acceptable values (x_{ij},y_{ij}). When two groups are being compared, the pooled within-groups covariance is c_{xy} computed using data from only the two groups.

$$c_{xy} = \frac{\sum\limits_{i=1}^{2} \sum\limits_{j=1}^{n_i} (x_{ij}-\bar{x}_i)(y_{ij}-\bar{y}_i)}{\sum\limits_{i=1}^{2} (n_i-1)}$$

If there is only one group, the summation over i is omitted.

Let $C = (c_{k\ell})$ be the covariance matrix computed between all pairs of variables in the analysis and $C^{-1} = (c_{k\ell})^{-1}$ be the inverse of the covariance matrix.

Mahalanobis D^2 is computed only if the sample size n_i in each group is greater than 1. Let $\bar{X}_1$ represent a column vector of means for the first group and $\bar{X}_2$ for the second group. Then to compare two groups

$$D^2 = (\bar{X}_1 - \bar{X}_2)' \, C^{-1} \, (\bar{X}_1 - \bar{X}_2)$$

where the prime indicates matrix transposition

$$T^2 = D^2 / \left(\frac{1}{h_1} + \frac{1}{h_2} \right)$$

where h_1 and h_2 are the harmonic means of the sample sizes n_1 and n_2 respectively used in computing the covariance for each pair of variables. If COMPLETE is specified, n_1 and n_2 are constant for all pairings and $h_1=n_1$ and $h_2=n_2$. Otherwise

$$h_1 = \left[\sum_{\text{all pairings}} \frac{1}{n_1} \bigg/ \frac{v(v+1)}{2} \right]^{-1}$$

where v is the number of variables. h_2 is similarly defined. Lastly,

$$F = T^2 \frac{(h_1 + h_2 - v - 1)}{v(h_1 + h_2 - 2)}$$

When there is only one group

$$D^2 = \bar{X}_1' \, C^{-1} \, \bar{X}_1 \, , \quad T^2 = h_1 D^2$$

and

$$F = T^2 \frac{(N_1 - v)}{v(N_1 - 1)}$$

A.4 Bartlett's Statistic (P9D)

Bartlett's statistic for homogeneity of group variances is computed using only groups having nonzero variances. The formula is

$$M = (N-g) \; ln \; [\Sigma \; (n_i-1) \; s_i^2 \; / \; (N-g)] - \Sigma \; (n_i-1) \; ln \; (s_i^2)$$

where

g = the number of groups with nonzero variances

n_i = frequency of the ith group

$N = \Sigma n_i$

s_i^2 = variance of group i

The level of significance of Bartlett's statistic is computed by approximating M by an F statistic (Dixon and Massey, 1969, p. 308)

$$F = f_2 M/[f_1(b-M)]$$

where

$$f_1 = g-1 \quad , \quad f_2 = (g+1)/A^2 \quad ,$$

$$A = \frac{1}{3(g-1)} \left[\Sigma \; \frac{1}{n_i-1} - \frac{1}{N-g} \right] \quad \text{and} \quad b = f_2/(1 - A + 2/f_2) \; .$$

The F statistic is compared with the F distribution with f_1 and f_2 df.

A.5 Tests and Measures in the Two-way Frequency Table (P4F)

NOTATION

Let $(a_{ij}; \; i = 1,\ldots,R; \; j = 1,\ldots,C)$ be the frequency counts in the R x C two-way contingency table. Let

$$r_i = \Sigma_j \; a_{ij}, \quad c_j = \Sigma_i \; a_{ij} \quad \text{and} \quad N = \Sigma_i \Sigma_j \; a_{ij}$$

represent the row totals, column totals and table total respectively. Also let

$$A_{ij} = \Sigma_{k>i} \Sigma_{\ell>j} \; a_{k\ell} + \Sigma_{k<i} \Sigma_{\ell<j} \; a_{k\ell}$$

$$D_{ij} = \Sigma_{k>i} \Sigma_{\ell<j} \; a_{k\ell} + \Sigma_{k<i} \Sigma_{\ell>j} \; a_{k\ell}$$

$$P = \Sigma_i \Sigma_j \; a_{ij} \; A_{ij}$$

$$Q = \Sigma_i \Sigma_j \; a_{ij} \; D_{ij}$$

Therefore, A_{ij} is the sum of the frequencies in cells in which both indices are greater, or both indices are less than (i,j), and D_{ij} is the sum of frequencies in cells in which one index is greater and the other is less than (i,j). Hence P is twice the total number of agreements in the order of the subscripts between all pairs of observations, and Q is twice the total number of disagreements.

ASYMPTOTIC STANDARD ERRORS (ASEs)

Two ASEs are computed for each measure. One (labeled ASE1 in the output) is appropriate to use in setting confidence limits on the parameters. It is obtained by the method of Goodman and Kruskal (1972) based on multinomial sampling conditional on the total table frequency N (except for the Goodman and Kruskal τ and λ^* and the tetrachoric r_t). This ASE is denoted s_1 since it is the ASE derived by assuming the alternate hypothesis H_1 is true; i.e., the measure is not zero.

The second ASE, denoted s_0, is a modification by Brown and Benedetti (1977a) that is more appropriate to test the null hypothesis H_0 that the measure is zero. In the output, T-VALUE is the ratio of the statistic to this ASE (s_0).

The formulas to compute s_1 (ASE1) for Yule's Q and Y and ln(cross-product ratio) appear in Kendall and Stuart (1967); and for γ, Somer's D, λ, λ^*, τ appear in Goodman and Kruskal (1963, 1972). The formula for s_1 in the tetrachoric r_t is from Pearson (1913). The remaining ASEs, including all those under the null hypothesis, are derived according to Brown and Benedetti (1977a).

Guidelines to the use of these ASEs both to test if the measure is zero and to set confidence limits for the measure are given by Brown and Benedetti (1977a, 1976).

All but three ASEs are derived based on multinomial sampling conditional on the total table frequency. Two exceptions are the Goodman and Kruskal τ and λ^* whose ASEs are derived based on multinomial sampling conditional on the row or column totals. The third is the tetrachoric correlation.

The formulas for s_1 and s_0 follow the definition of the measure. Many measures can be written as a ratio v/w where v is the numerator and w the denominator. The notation v and w is used in the formulas for s_1 and s_0.

STATISTICS

Chi-Square (χ^2)

This is the classical chi-square test of independence between two categorical variables:

$$\chi^2 = \Sigma_i \Sigma_j \; [(a_{ij} - e_{ij})^2/e_{ij}] \; , \quad df = (R-1)(C-1)$$

where $e_{ij} = r_i c_j/N$. The significance level of χ^2 is also given.

Likelihood Ratio Chi-Square (G^2)

This is a test of independence between rows and columns based upon a likelihood ratio approach. In general the results are similar to that of the usual χ^2, but this one is computationally more expensive.

$$G^2 = 2 \; \Sigma_i \Sigma_j \; a_{ij} \; ln \; (a_{ij}/e_{ij}), \quad df = (R-1)(C-1)$$

where

$$e_{ij} = r_i c_j/N$$

The significance level of G^2 is also given.

Yates' Corrected Chi-Square (χ_y^2)

When the contingency table is 2x2, a chi-square that includes a correction for continuity is also computed

$$\chi_y^2 = \begin{cases} \dfrac{N(|a_{11}a_{22} - a_{12}a_{21}| - \frac{N}{2})^2}{r_1 r_2 c_1 c_2} & \text{if } |a_{11}a_{22} - a_{12}a_{21}| > \dfrac{N}{2} \\ 0 & \text{otherwise} \end{cases}$$

The significance level of χ_y^2 is also given.

Fisher's Exact Probability

For the 2x2 table, the exact probability of any configuration under the assumption of independence between rows and columns can easily be calculated.

$$Pr(a_{11},a_{12},a_{21},a_{22}) = \frac{r_1! r_2! c_1! c_2!}{N! a_{11}! a_{12}! a_{21}! a_{22}!}$$

conditioned on the row and column totals.

The <u>direction</u> of the 1-TAIL probability is chosen as follows:

If $a_{11}a_{22} \le a_{12}a_{21}$

choose the minimum of a_{11} and a_{22}; otherwise, choose the minimum of a_{12} and a_{21}. For example, let cell $(1,1)$ be the cell so chosen. Then the probability that a value of cell $(1,1)$ is equal to or less than a_{11} is

$$P_1 = \Sigma_{x=0}^{a_{11}} \; Pr(a_{11} - x, \; a_{12} + x, \; a_{21} + x, \; a_{22} - x)$$

Assuming that a_{11} was chosen, the other tail probability is computed as follows:

$$P_2 = \Sigma \; Pr(a_{11} + y, \; a_{12} - y, \; a_{21} - y, \; a_{22} + y)$$

where the sum is over y such that

$$Pr(a_{11},a_{12},a_{21},a_{22}) \ge Pr(a_{11} + y, \; a_{12} - y, \; a_{21} - y, \; a_{22} + y)$$

and y>0; i.e., over all terms in the second tail whose probability does not exceed that of the observed outcome $(a_{11},a_{12},a_{21},a_{22})$

$$PROB(1 - TAIL) = p_1$$

$$PROB(2 - TAIL) = p_1 + p_2$$

If a one-tail test is desired, you must check to see whether the tail chosen for PROB(1 - TAIL) corresponds to the tail appropriate for your test. If it does not, then the p-value for your test is ≥ 0.5, which is a nonsignificant result.

Phi (ϕ)

The value of χ^2 depends not only on the relative frequency in each cell but also on the total sample size N. A measure that is independent of N is

$$\phi = (\chi^2/N)^{\frac{1}{2}}$$

For a 2x2 table, ϕ may be positive or negative according to the formula

$$\phi = (a_{11}a_{22} - a_{12}a_{21})/(r_1 r_2 c_1 c_2)^{\frac{1}{2}}$$

The significance level of the test that $E(\phi) = 0$ may be obtained from the corresponding significance level for χ^2.

Maximum Value of Phi (ϕ_{max})

In a 2x2 table, the maximum possible absolute value of ϕ given the row and column totals is less than or equal to 1. This value is calculated.

If $a_{11}a_{22} < a_{12}a_{21}$, then $\phi_{max} = -[(r_1c_1)/(r_2c_2)]^{\frac{1}{2}}$ or $-[(r_2c_2)/(r_1c_1)]^{\frac{1}{2}}$

whichever is less than 1 in absolute value

otherwise $\phi_{max} = [(r_1c_2)/(r_2c_1)]^{\frac{1}{2}}$ or $[(r_2c_1)/(r_1c_2)]^{\frac{1}{2}}$

whichever is less than 1

Note that if $\phi < 0$, then ϕ_{max} is the lower bound; i.e., $\phi_{max} < 0$.

Contingency Coefficient (C)

Another transformation of χ^2 which does not depend on the sample size N is

$$C = [\chi^2/(N + \chi^2)]^{\frac{1}{2}} = [\phi^2/(1 + \phi^2)]^{\frac{1}{2}}$$

The significance level of the test for $E(C) = 0$ may be obtained from the significance level of χ^2.

Maximum Value of the Contingency Coefficient (C_{max})

C is always less than or equal to one. For the 2x2 table this maximum value is calculated

$$C_{max} = [\phi_{max}^2/(1 + \phi_{max}^2)]^{\frac{1}{2}}$$

Cramer's V

Another transformation of χ^2 (which reduces to ϕ for the 2x2 table) is

$$V = \left[\frac{\chi^2}{N(m-1)}\right]^{\frac{1}{2}} \qquad \text{where m = minimum (R,C)}$$

(See Bishop, Fienberg and Holland, 1975, p. 386.)

Yule's Q and Y

For a 2x2 table, Yule defined the measure of association Q

$$Q = \frac{a_{11}a_{22} - a_{12}a_{21}}{a_{11}a_{22} + a_{12}a_{21}}$$

The standard errors of Q are

$$s_1^2 = \frac{1}{4}(1-Q^2)^2\left[\frac{1}{a_{11}} + \frac{1}{a_{12}} + \frac{1}{a_{21}} + \frac{1}{a_{22}}\right]$$

$$s_0^2 = \frac{1}{4}\left[\frac{N^3}{(a_{11} + a_{12})(a_{11} + a_{21})(a_{12} + a_{22})(a_{21} + a_{22})}\right]$$

Yule also defined a measure of colligation y

$$Y = \frac{\sqrt{a_{11}a_{22}} - \sqrt{a_{12}a_{21}}}{\sqrt{a_{11}a_{22}} + \sqrt{a_{12}a_{21}}}$$

The standard errors of Y are

$$s_1^2 = \frac{1}{16}(1-Y^2)^2\left[\frac{1}{a_{11}} + \frac{1}{a_{12}} + \frac{1}{a_{21}} + \frac{1}{a_{22}}\right]$$

$$s_0^2 = \frac{1}{16}\left[\frac{N^3}{(a_{11} + a_{12})(a_{11} + a_{21})(a_{12} + a_{22})(a_{21} + a_{22})}\right]$$

Both Q and Y are -1 when a_{11} or a_{22} is equal to zero, 1 when a_{12} or a_{21} is equal to zero, and zero when $a_{11}a_{22} = a_{12}a_{21}$ (i.e., the cross-product ratio is one).

Cross-Product Ratio (α)

For a 2x2 table, the cross-product (or odds) ratio is defined as

$$\alpha = (a_{11}a_{22})/(a_{12}a_{21})$$

This is 1 when χ^2 is 0 and 0 or ∞ when one of the cells has zero frequency. Since its distribution is extremely asymmetric under the hypothesis of independence between rows and columns, but that of $ln(\alpha)$ is symmetric, the LN (CROSS-PRODUCT RATIO) is also given as well as its ASE.

The standard errors of $ln(\alpha)$ are

$$s_1^2 = \frac{1}{a_{11}} + \frac{1}{a_{12}} + \frac{1}{a_{21}} + \frac{1}{a_{22}}$$

$$s_0^2 = \frac{N^3}{(a_{11} + a_{12})(a_{11} + a_{21})(a_{12} + a_{22})(a_{21} + a_{22})}$$

Relative Risk and the Mantel-Haenszel Statistics

Suppose we have k two-by-two tables. Let a_{11i}, a_{12i}, a_{21i}, a_{22i} represent the four frequencies in the i-th table and let N_i be the total

frequency in the i-th table.

Then the Mantel-Haenszel statistic (Mantel and Haenszel, 1959) is defined as

$$R_{MH} = \frac{\Sigma_i(a_{11i}a_{22i}/N_i)}{\Sigma_i(a_{12i}a_{21i}/N_i)} \quad .$$

A test of the null hypothesis that the expected value of R_{MH} is one is provided by

$$\chi^2 = \frac{[\Sigma(a_{11i}a_{22i} - a_{12i}a_{21i})/N_i - 0.5]^2}{\Sigma r_{1i} r_{2i} c_{1i} c_{2i}/(N_i^2(N_i-1))}$$

where r_{1i}, r_{2i} are the row totals and c_{1i}, c_{2i} are the column totals. This statistic has approximately a chi-square distribution with one degree of freedom.

The weighted combination of $ln(risk)$ is defined as

$$ln\ R_W = \Sigma(w_i\ ln\ \alpha_i)/\Sigma w_i$$

where α_i is the cross-product for the i-th table and

$$1/w_i = 1/a_{11i} + 1/a_{12i} + 1/a_{21i} + 1/a_{22i} \quad .$$

When one of the cell frequencies in a table is zero, all cell frequencies in that table are incremented by 0.5 in the calculation of R_W and $1/w_i$.

The variance of $ln\ R_W$ is $1/\Sigma w_i$. Therefore approximate confidence limits for R_W are given as

$$\exp[ln(R_W) - 2(1/\Sigma w_i)^{\frac{1}{2}}] \quad \text{and} \quad \exp[ln(R_W) + 2(1/\Sigma w_i)^{\frac{1}{2}}] \quad .$$

The chi-square test for homogeneity is

$$\chi^2 = \Sigma w_i(ln\ \alpha_i)^2 - (\Sigma w_i)(ln\ R_W)^2 \quad .$$

This is distributed approximately as a chi-square with (k-1) degrees of freedom, where k is the number of tables.

Tetrachoric correlation (r_t)

The tetrachoric correlation is the correlation of a bivariate normal distribution that exactly duplicates the 4 cell probabilities in a 2x2 table. It is found by solving the following equations implicitly for r_t.

a	b
c	d

$$\Phi(z_1) = \frac{a + c}{N}$$

$$\Phi(z_2) = \frac{a + b}{N}$$

$$\int_{-\infty}^{z_2} \int_{-\infty}^{z_1} \phi(z_1, z_2, r_t)dz_2\,dz_2 = \frac{a}{N}$$

where $\Phi(z)$ is the Gaussian cdf with zero mean and unit variance and $\phi(z_1, z_2, r_t)$ is the bivariate normal with mean zero, variance one and correlation r_t.

The bivariate normal integral is approximated by an infinite series in r_t (Everitt, 1910) and r_t is found implicitly by iteration. When the infinite series does not converge within 100 terms ($|r_t| > 0.9$), Gaussian quadrature is used to evaluate the integral.

If a single cell is zero, the tetrachoric correlation can be defined as unity (or -1.0). We prefer to modify the cell to be $\frac{1}{2}$ and then solve for r_t. The tetrachoric correlation should then be considered as any value from the computed value up to unity. Our justification is that the pattern of frequencies is duplicated by the choice of r_t; yet since frequencies are ordinal, the underlying probability is estimated with uncertainty equal to $1/(2N)$ in each cell. Therefore, setting the zero cell to $\frac{1}{2}$ yields a lower bound for the estimate of the correlation (Brown and Benedetti, 1977b).

The formula for s_1^2 is from Pearson (1913).

$$s_1^2 = \frac{1}{N^3}\left(\frac{1}{\phi(z_1, z_2, r_t)}\right)^2 \left\{\frac{(a+d)(b+c)}{4} + (a+c)(b+d)\phi_2^2 + (a+b)(c+d)\phi_1^2\right.$$

$$\left. + 2(ad-bc)\phi_1\phi_2 - (ab-cd)\phi_2 - (ac-bd)\phi_1\right\}$$

$$s_0^2 = \left(\frac{1}{\phi(z_1, z_2, 0)}\right)^2 \frac{(a+b)(a+c)(b+d)(c+d)}{N^5}$$

where $\phi_1 = \Phi[(z_1 - r_t z_2)/(1 - r_t^2)^{\frac{1}{2}}] - 0.5$ and $\phi_2 = \Phi[(z_2 - r_t z_1)/(1 - r_t^2)^{\frac{1}{2}}] - 0.5$

and

$$\phi(z_1, z_2, r_t) = \frac{1}{2\pi(1-r_t^2)^{\frac{1}{2}}}\exp\left\{-\frac{z_1^2 - 2r_t z_1 z_2 + z_2^2}{2(1-r_t^2)}\right\}$$

Gamma (γ)

Gamma is a measure of the monotone relationship between two ordered variables (Goodman and Kruskal, 1954). It is estimated by

$$G = (P - Q)/(P + Q)$$

The standard errors of G are

$$s_1^2 = 16[\Sigma \Sigma \ a_{ij}(QA_{ij} - PD_{ij})^2]/(P+Q)^4$$

$$s_0^2 = 4[\Sigma \Sigma a_{ij}(A_{ij} - D_{ij})^2 - (P-Q)^2/N]/(P+Q)^2$$

Kendall's Tau-B (τ_b)

Kendall's τ_b is a correlation measure of the monotone relationship between two ordered variables that compares the number of agreements in the ordering of the indices between pairs of observations with the number of disagreements. Siegel (1956) gives the following estimate when many ties are expected.

$$t_b = \frac{(P - Q)}{\{[N(N-1) - \Sigma_i r_i(r_i-1)][N(N-1) - \Sigma_j c_j(c_{j-1})]\}^{\frac{1}{2}}} \equiv \frac{v}{w}$$

The standard errors of t_b are

$$s_1^2 = \{\Sigma \Sigma a_{ij}[2w(A_{ij}-D_{ij}) + t_b(r_i(N^2-\Sigma c_j^2) + c_j(N^2-\Sigma r_i^2))]^2$$
$$- Nt_b^2(2N^2-\Sigma r_i^2-\Sigma c_j^2)^2\}/w^4$$

$$s_0^2 = 4[\Sigma \Sigma a_{ij}(A_{ij}-D_{ij})^2 - \frac{(P-Q)^2}{N}]/w^2$$

where $w'_{ij} = -\frac{N}{w}[r_i(N^2-\Sigma c_j^2) + c_j(N^2-\Sigma r_i^2)]$

Stuart's Tau-C (τ_c)

A similar measure to τ_b, which uses a different denominator, is τ_c. It is estimated by

$$t_c = (P - Q)/N^2 \cdot [m/(m-1)]$$

where m = min(R,C).

The two standard errors of t_c are similar.

$$s_1^2 = s_0^2 = \frac{4}{N^4}(\frac{m}{m-1})^2 \Sigma \Sigma a_{ij}(A_{ij} - D_{ij})^2$$

Product Moment Correlation (r)

The ordinary correlation coefficient is computed using the cell entries as frequencies and cell indices as the observed values.

$$r = \frac{\Sigma_i\Sigma_j a_{ij}(i-\bar{i})(j-\bar{j})}{[\Sigma_i r_i(i-\bar{i})^2\Sigma_j c_j(j-\bar{j})^2]^{\frac{1}{2}}} \equiv \frac{v}{w}$$

where $\bar{i} = \Sigma_i ir_i/N$ and $\bar{j} = \Sigma_j jc_j/N$

The standard errors of r are

$$s_1^2 = \frac{1}{w^4} \Sigma \Sigma a_{ij} \{w(i-\bar{i})(j-\bar{j}) - \frac{v}{2w}[(i-\bar{i})^2\Sigma c_j(j-\bar{j})^2 + (j-\bar{j})^2\Sigma r_i(i-\bar{i})^2]\}^2$$

$$s_0^2 = \frac{1}{w^2}\{\Sigma \Sigma a_{ij}(i-\bar{i})^2(j-\bar{j})^2 - \frac{v^2}{N}\}$$

Spearman Rank Correlation Coefficient (r_S)

The Spearman rank correlation coefficient, r_S, is computed using the cell entries as frequencies and the cell indices to order the cells. The formula for ties (Siegel, 1956) has been rewritten in our notation.

$$r_S = \frac{\Sigma_i\Sigma_j a_{ij}[\Sigma_{k<i} r_k + \frac{r_i}{2} - \frac{N}{2}][\Sigma_{\ell<j} c_\ell + \frac{c_j}{2} - \frac{N}{2}]}{\frac{1}{12}[N^3 - N - \Sigma_i(r_i^3 - r_i)][N^3 - N - \Sigma_j(c_j^3 - c_j)]^{\frac{1}{2}}}$$

The standard errors of r_S are

$$s_1^2 = \frac{1}{N^2w^4} \Sigma \Sigma a_{ij}(wv'_{ij} - vw'_{ij} - \frac{w}{N}\Sigma\Sigma a_{ij}v'_{ij} + \frac{v}{N}\Sigma\Sigma a_{ij}w'_{ij})^2$$

$$s_0^2 = \frac{1}{N^2w^2} \Sigma\Sigma a_{ij}(v'_{ij} - \frac{1}{N}\Sigma\Sigma a_{ij}v'_{ij})^2$$

where $R(i) = 2\Sigma_{k<i} r_k + r_i - N$ $C(j) = 2\Sigma_{\ell<j} c_\ell + c_j - N$

$v = \frac{1}{4}\Sigma\Sigma a_{ij}R(i)C(j)$ and $w = \frac{1}{12}[(N^3 - \Sigma r_i^3)(N^3 - \Sigma c_j^3)]^{\frac{1}{2}}$

$$v'_{ij} = N[\frac{1}{4} R(i)C(j) + \frac{1}{4}\Sigma_{j'} a_{ij'}C(j') + \frac{1}{4}\Sigma_{i'} a_{i'j}R(i')$$
$$+ \frac{1}{2}\Sigma_{j'} \Sigma_{i'>i} a_{i'j'}C(j') + \frac{1}{2}\Sigma_{i'} \Sigma_{j'>j} a_{i'j'}R(i')]$$

$$w'_{ij} = - \frac{N}{96w}[(N^3 - \Sigma r_i^3)c_j^2 + (N^3 - \Sigma c_j^3)r_i^2]$$

Somers' D (d_{asym})

Somers' d is an asymmetric version of τ_b. It is appropriate when one ordered index is to be predicted from knowledge of the second ordered index.

$$d_{j|i} = (P - Q)/(N^2 - \Sigma_i r_i^2) \quad ; \quad d_{i|j} = (P - Q)/(N^2 - \Sigma_j c_j^2)$$

The standard errors of $d_{j|i}$ are

$$s_1^2 = \frac{4}{(N^2 - \Sigma r_i^2)^4} \Sigma\Sigma a_{ij}[(N^2 - \Sigma r_i^2)(A_{ij} - D_{ij}) - (N - r_i)(P - Q)]^2$$

$$s_0^2 = \frac{4}{(N^2 - \Sigma r_i^2)^2} \Sigma\Sigma a_{ij}(A_{ij} - D_{ij})^2$$

The ASEs of $d_{i|j}$ are obtained by permuting the indices.

Tau-Asymmetric (τ_{asym})

Goodman and Kruskal (1954) propose another measure of association in addition to λ. This measure, τ, compares random proportional prediction of an index with conditional proportional prediction based upon knowledge of the second index.

$$\tau_{j|i} = \frac{N \Sigma_i(a_{ij}^2/r_i) - \Sigma_j c_j^2}{N^2 - \Sigma_j c_j^2} \equiv \frac{v}{w} \quad ; \quad \tau_{i|j} = \frac{N \Sigma_i(a_{ij}^2/c_j) - \Sigma_i r_i^2}{N^2 - \Sigma_i r_i^2}$$

The ASE of $\tau_{j|i}$ (or $\tau_{i|j}$) are obtained by assuming multinomial sampling in each row (or column).

$$s_1^2 = \frac{4}{w^4}\left\{w^2N^2 \Sigma\Sigma\frac{a_{ij}^2}{r_i^2} + (v-w)^2\Sigma_j c_j^3 + 2 w(v-w)N \Sigma\Sigma\frac{a_{ij}^2 c_j}{r_i}\right.$$
$$- w^2N^2 \Sigma_i\frac{1}{r_i^3}(\Sigma_j a_{ij}^2)^2 - (v-w)^2\Sigma_i\frac{1}{r_i}(\Sigma_j a_{ij}c_j)^2$$
$$\left. + 2w(v-w)N\Sigma_i\frac{1}{r_i^2}(\Sigma_j a_{ij}^2)(\Sigma_j a_{ij}c_j)\right\}$$

The ASE of $\tau_{i|j}$ are obtained by permuting the indices.

Lambda-Asymmetric (λ_{asym})

Lambda is a measure of predictive association that measures the degree of success with which one index can be used to predict the second index (Goodman and Kruskal, 1954). No ordering of indices is assumed.

$$\lambda_{j|i} = \frac{\Sigma_i max_j a_{ij} - max_j c_j}{N - max_j c_j} \quad ; \quad \lambda_{i|j} = \frac{\Sigma_j max_i a_{ij} - max_i r_i}{N - max_i r_i}$$

The standard error of $\lambda_{j|i}$ is

$$s_1^2 = \frac{1}{(N-c_\ell)^2}\left\{\Sigma\Sigma a_{ij}[\delta_{ij}^{in} - \delta_j^\ell + \lambda \delta_j^\ell]^2 - N\lambda_{j|i}^2\right\}$$

where ℓ is the index of column such that c_ℓ is the maximum

$\delta_{ij}^{in} = 1$ if j = n and zero otherwise, $\delta_j^\ell = 1$ if $\ell = j$ and zero otherwise

The ASE for $\lambda_{i|j}$ are obtained by permuting the indices.

Lambda-Symmetric (λ)

This is a symmetric version of the previous statistics.

$$\lambda = \frac{\Sigma_i max_j a_{ij} + \Sigma_j max_i a_{ij} - max_j c_j - max_i r_i}{2N - max_j c_j - max_i r_i}$$

The standard error of λ is

$$s_1^2 = \frac{1}{(2N-c_\ell-r_k)}\left\{\Sigma\Sigma a_{ij}[(\delta_{ij}^{in} + \delta_{ij}^{mj} - \delta_j^\ell - \delta_i^k) + \lambda(\delta_j^\ell + \delta_i^k)]^2 - 4N\lambda^2\right\}$$

where, in addition to the notation for λ_{asym},

k is the index of row such that r_k is the maximum

$\delta_{ij}^{mj} = 1$ if i = m and zero otherwise

$\delta_i^k = 1$ if k = i and zero otherwise

Lambda-Star-Asymmetric (λ^*_{asym})

A modification of Lambda-Asymmetric that is not affected by differing row (or column) marginals is λ^* where

$$\lambda^*_{j|i} = \frac{\Sigma_i (\max_j a_{ij})/r_i - \max_j \Sigma_i (a_{ij}/r_i)}{R - \max_j \Sigma_i (a_{ij}/r_i)} \equiv \frac{v}{w}$$

$$\lambda^*_{i|j} = \frac{\Sigma_j (\max_i a_{ij})/c_j - \max_i \Sigma_j (a_{ij}/c_j)}{C - \max_i \Sigma_j (a_{ij}/c_j)}$$

The ASE for $\lambda^*_{j|i}$ (or $\lambda^*_{i|j}$) are derived based on multinomial sampling in each row (or column).

$$s_1^2 = \frac{1}{w^2} \quad \Sigma \; \Sigma \; \frac{a_{ij}}{r_i^2} [(\delta_{ij}^{in} - \delta_j^\ell) + \lambda^*_{j|i} \delta_j^\ell]^2 - \Sigma_i \frac{1}{r_i^2} [(a_{in} - a_{i\ell}) + \lambda^*_{j|i} a_{i\ell}]^2$$

where

  a_{in} is the maximum frequency in row i

  ℓ is the column j for which $\Sigma_j a_{ij}/r_i$ is a maximum

The ASE of $\lambda^*_{i|j}$ are obtained by permuting the indices.

Uncertainty Coefficient-Asymmetric

This is an asymmetric measure of association between two unordered variables based on an information theory approach that reflects the relative reduction of uncertainty about one factor when the second factor is known.

$$U_{j|i} = \frac{U_j + U_i - U_{ij}}{U_j} \equiv \frac{v}{w} \quad , \qquad U_{i|j} = \frac{U_j + U_i - U_{ij}}{U_i}$$

where

  $U_{ij} = - \Sigma_i \Sigma_j \frac{a_{ij}}{N} \log \frac{a_{ij}}{N}$, $U_j = -\Sigma_j \frac{c_j}{N} \log \frac{c_j}{N}$, $U_i = -\Sigma_i \frac{r_i}{N} \log \frac{r_i}{N}$

The standard error of $U_{j|i}$ is

$$s_1^2 = \frac{1}{N^2 w^4} \Sigma \Sigma a_{ij} [(U_i - U_{ij}) \log \frac{c_j}{N} + U_j (\log \frac{a_{ij}}{N} - \log \frac{r_i}{N})]^2$$

The ASE of $U_{i|j}$ are obtained by permuting the indices.

Uncertainty Coefficient-Symmetric

A symmetric measure related to the above asymmetric measures is

$$U = \frac{U_j + U_i - U_{ij}}{(U_j + U_i)/2}$$

This measure has been normalized so that U may range between zero and one. U is frequently defined without the 1/2 in the denominator (see Brown, 1975).

The ASE of U is

$$s_1^2 = \frac{4}{N^2 (U_j + U_i)^4} \Sigma \Sigma a_{ij} [U_{ij} (\log \frac{r_i}{N} + \log \frac{c_j}{N}) - (U_j + U_i) \log \frac{a_{ij}}{N}]^2$$

McNemar's Test of Symmetry (χ^2_{MC})

This is a test of symmetry which is calculated for square tables (R=C) only.

$$\chi^2_{MC} = \Sigma \; \Sigma_{i < j} \frac{(a_{ij} - a_{ji})^2}{a_{ij} + a_{ji}}$$

The significance level of χ^2_{MC} is also given. The degrees of freedom are $R(R-1)/2$.

Kappa

A test of reliability computed for square, two-way tables.

$$\kappa = (p_o - p_c)/(1 - p_c)$$

where $p_o = \sum_{i=1}^{K} x_{ii}/n_{..}$ (% observed agreement)

  $p_c = \sum_{i=1}^{K} n_{1i} n_{2i}/n_{..}^2$ (% expected agreement)

  $\sigma_\kappa = \sqrt{p_o(1-p_o)/n_{..}(1-p_c)^2}$

  $t = \kappa/\sigma_\kappa$

Test of Linear Regression

Let the frequency table be 2xk (2 rows and k columns) and a set of k coefficients (z_j) assigned, one to each column. The z_j's are either CODE values or when CUTPOINTS are assigned, the sequence 1, 2, ... The regression of a_{ij}/c_j, on z_j is performed and the following χ^2 test with 1 df is computed (Cochran, 1954).

$$\chi^2 = \frac{\left[\Sigma c_j \left(\frac{a_{ij}}{c_j} - \frac{r_1}{N} \right) (z_j - \tilde{z}) \right]^2}{\Sigma c_j (z_j - \tilde{z})^2} \cdot \frac{N^2}{r_1 r_2}$$

where $\tilde{z} = \frac{\Sigma c_j z_j}{N}$

A.6 The Log-linear Model (P4F)

Each log-linear model is fitted by the iterative proportional fitting algorithm starting from an initial fit matrix. The initial fit matrix is (a) entirely ones if EMPTY cells or INITIAL values are not specified for the table; (b) a table of zeros for the EMPTY cells and ones for the remaining cells; or (c) the set of INITIAL values specified by the user (ones for the cells that have no initial value specified).

The notation of P4F is used to describe a log-linear model. That is

$$\ell n \; F_{ijk\ell} = \theta + \lambda_i^A + \lambda_j^B + \lambda_k^C + \lambda_\ell^D + \lambda_{ij}^{AB} + \lambda_{ik}^{AC} + \lambda_{i\ell}^{AD} + \lambda_{jk}^{BC} + \lambda_{j\ell}^{BD}$$
$$+ \lambda_{k\ell}^{CD} + \lambda_{ijk}^{ABC} + \lambda_{ij\ell}^{ABD} + \lambda_{ik\ell}^{ACD} + \lambda_{jk\ell}^{BCD} + \lambda_{ijk\ell}^{ABCD}$$

where $f_{ijk\ell}$ and $F_{ijk\ell}$ are the observed and expected values of cell (i,j,k,ℓ) in an $I \times J \times K \times L$ contingency table. Also let

$$y_{ijk\ell} = \ell n \; F_{ijk\ell}$$

for all cells.

Computation of Degrees of Freedom

When fitting the models of full order (the SIMULTANEOUS option) or before fitting any other log-linear model, P4F computes the number of estimable parameters (EP) for each possible effect Z (Z can represent a main effect or interaction). The formula for degrees of freedom (df) is

  df = total number of cells - number of cells with expected values equal to zero $- \Sigma EP$

where the summation is over all effects in the model being fitted.

When there are no zeros in the marginal subtable corresponding to an effect Z, the number of estimable parameters for Z is

$$EP = (I-1)^{\delta^{ZA}} (J-1)^{\delta^{ZB}} (K-1)^{\delta^{ZC}} (L-1)^{\delta^{ZD}}$$

where $\delta^{ZA} = \begin{cases} 1 & \text{if the effect Z contains index A} \\ 0 & \text{otherwise} \end{cases}$

with similar definitions for δ^{ZB}, δ^{ZC}, and δ^{ZD}. The formula is the same as that used for effects in a balanced ANOVA.

When there are zeros in the marginal subtable corresponding to Z, the number of estimable parameters (EP') is

  EP' = EP - number of zeros in the marginal subtable corresponding to Z

    + number of zeros in all subtables formed by collapsing the marginal subtable over each index in Z (in turn)

    - number of zeros in all subtables formed by collapsing the marginal subtable over each pair of indices in Z (in turn)

    + ... - ...   (until there are no more zeros)

Note: The above formula for degrees of freedom is valid when the table is not separable with respect to the model analyzed; that is, the table cannot be separated into two or more parts -- each of which can be analyzed separately. If estimates of the parameters are requested and P4F obtains the estimates by Method 1 below, the degrees of freedom printed in the output for the model can be checked as follows: (a) if the number of pivots is printed, the number of degrees of freedom = number of cells - number of cells with expected value equal to zero - number of pivots. If this answer differs from that printed in the output, the table is separable; the answer obtained using the number of pivots should be used in place of the degrees of freedom in the output.

666

A.7 Parameter Estimates and Standard Errors for Log-linear Models (P4F)

<u>Computation of Parameter Estimates and Their Standard Errors</u>

The parameter estimates and their standard errors are obtained by one of two methods. The first method is used unless (a) the model is direct and there are no expected values equal to zero (and the variance-covariance matrix of the parameter estimates was not requested) or (b) there is insufficient space to form the variance-covariance matrix of the parameter estimates. When either of these two exceptions holds, the second method (the 'delta' method) will be used.

Method 1: Weighted least-squares

Form a design matrix X having p columns and n rows where p is the number of parameters to be estimated in the log-linear model (including the constant term) and n is the number of cells in the table that are not defined to be structural zeros. Each column in X consists of 1's, 0's and -1's; if there are no structural zeros, the sum of each column is zero except for the vector corresponding to the constant term.

Then the log-linear model can be written as

$$\underset{\sim}{Y} = X'\underset{\sim}{\lambda}$$

where $\underset{\sim}{\lambda}$ is a column vector of parameters, and $\underset{\sim}{Y}$ is column vector containing $\ell n\ F_{ijk\ell}$.

Let W be a diagonal matrix containing $1/F_{ijk\ell}$ on the diagonal; i.e., W is the asymptotic variance-covariance matrix of Y. The parameter estimates are obtained as

$$\hat{\underset{\sim}{\lambda}} = (X'WX)^{-1}\ X'WY$$

and the variance-covariance matrix of the parameter estimates is $(X'WX)^{-1}$. The standard errors of $\hat{\underset{\sim}{\lambda}}$ are the square roots of the diagonal elements of $(X'WX)^{-1}$.

The computations are performed by setting up the matrix

$$\begin{bmatrix} X'WX & X'WY \\ Y'WX & Y'WY \end{bmatrix}$$

and sweeping the matrix on X'WX (see Appendix A.11).

When not all parameters are estimable (one or more design vectors are aliased with other design vectors), P4F prints a message that not all pivots were performed and the number of pivots actually performed. This number can be used to validate the number of degrees of freedom (see above). P4F will either print a zero for each parameter that is not estimated or will omit printing the parameter entirely. When printing the variance-covariance matrix, nonestimable parameters are omitted entirely.

Method 2: The 'delta' method

The parameter estimates $\hat{\lambda}$ for each effect Z are obtained by applying the usual ANOVA formulas to $y_{ijk\ell} = \ell n\ F_{ijk\ell}$. For example, let Z represent the interaction ABC, then

$$\hat{\lambda}^{ABC}_{ijk} = y_{ijk\cdot} - y_{ij\cdot\cdot} - y_{i\cdot k\cdot} - y_{\cdot jk\cdot} + y_{i\cdot\cdot\cdot} + y_{\cdot j\cdot\cdot} + y_{\cdot\cdot k\cdot} - y_{\cdot\cdot\cdot\cdot}$$

where a dot represents the mean over the omitted index.

P4F computes the parameter estimates by using the following formula that is equivalent to the one above:

$$\hat{\lambda}^{ABC}_{ijk} = \frac{1}{IJKL}(IJKy_{ijk+} - IJy_{ij++} - IKy_{i+k+} - JKy_{+jk+} + Iy_{i+++} + JY_{+j++} + Ky_{++k+} - y_{++++})$$

where + signifies the total over the omitted index.

The asymptotic variance of Z (say ABC) in a saturated model can be written as

$$AV(\hat{\lambda}^{Z}_{i'j'k'\ell'}) = (\frac{1}{IJKL})^2 \sum_{ijk\ell} \frac{\left[(I-1)\delta^{ZA}_{ii'}(J-1)\delta^{ZB}_{jj'}(K-1)\delta^{ZC}_{kk'}(L-1)\delta^{ZD}_{\ell\ell'}\right]^2}{F_{ijk\ell}}$$

where $\delta^{ZA}_{ii'}$ is one if A is an index in Z and i=i'; otherwise it is zero.

Similar definitions are used for the other δ's.

P4F uses the following equivalent formula in order to compute the asymptotic variance of $\hat{\lambda}$ in a saturated model:

$$AV(\hat{\lambda}^{Z}_{i'j'k'}) = (\frac{1}{IJKL})^2 \left[I(I-2)J(J-2)K(K-2)w_{ijk+} + I(I-2)J(J-2)w_{ij++} \right.$$
$$+ I(I-2)K(K-2)w_{i+k+} + J(J-2)K(K-2)w_{+jk+}$$
$$+ I(I-2)w_{i+++} + J(J-2)w_{+j++} + K(K-2)_{++k+}$$
$$\left. + w_{++++} \right]$$

where $w_{ijk\ell} = 1/F_{ijk\ell}$ and + represents the sum over an index.

When the model is direct but not saturated, Lee (1977) describes how the asymptotic variance can be obtained as the sum and difference of asymptotic variances of the same term in a series of saturated models. P4F implements Lee's method whenever the model is direct.

When the model is not direct and there is not enough space to form the variance-covariance matrix, modifications of the 'delta' method are used although it is known that the answers are not exact. If the model is indirect, P4F finds a direct model that includes the indirect model as a subset and computes the asymptotic variances using the direct model; this provides an upper bound for the asymptotic variances. When there are zero expected values, P4F first estimates the expected values for cells with structural zeros from the model fitted to the data in all other cells. Then the parameters and standard errors are estimated using the 'completed' data; the resulting estimates of the variances are underestimates of the asymptotic variances. When there are zero expected values due to the model (and not as a result of declaring structural zeros), both the parameter estimates and their standard errors may be seriously affected.

A.8 Instructions for P1F, P2F, and P3F

P1F -- Two-way Frequency Tables -- Measures of Association

If your facility still does not have P4F, but does have P1F, the Control Language specific to P1F is:

Paragraph Statement	Preassigned	Comment and Manual Reference
INPut		Specify as part of INPUT paragraph.
TABLE = # list.	none	When input is a multiway frequency table, number of levels for each index (fastest moving index first). (same as P4F)
VARiable		Specify as part of VARIABLE paragraph.
DEFine(#) = v list.	none	Define new index by combining variables. (see STACK In P4F[1])
/ TABLE		Required, may be repeated.
ROW = v list.	none	Variables defining row categories. (same as P4F)
COLumn = v list.	none	Variables defining column categories. (same as P4F)
PAIR. or CROSS.	PAIR	Pair or cross ROW and COLUMN variables. (same as P4F)
CONDition = v list.	none	Tables formed for each level of each CONDITION variable. (same as P4F)
COUNT = v list.	none	Variables containing frequency counts when input is cell indices and frequency counts. (same as P4F)
DELTA = #.	0	Constant added to each cell frequency before calculating statistics. (same as P4F)
MINimum = #.	0	Adjacent rows or columns combined if minimum expected frequency is less than MINIMUM. (same as P4F[1])
/ CATEGory		Required if any ROW, COLUMN or CONDITION variable has more than 10 distinct values.
CODE(#) = # list.	10 smallest values	Codes for variable #, may be repeated. * (same as P4F)
CUTPoint(#) # list.	see CODE	Cutpoints to form intervals for variable #, may be repeated. * (same as P4F)
NAME(#) = c list.	CODES or CUTPOINTS	Code or interval names for variable #, may be repeated. * (same as P4F)
RESET.	not RESET	If RESET, all assignments in previous CATEGORY paragraph are reset to preassigned values. (same as P4F)
COEFficient(#) = # list.	none	Values assigned to categories when table is 2x2 or Rx2 to test for trend in probabilities. * (replaces LINEAR in P4F)
/ PRINT		Optional, tables to be printed.
OBServed.	OBS	Print table of observed frequencies. * (same as P4F)
EXPected.	no	Print table of expected values. * (same as P4F)
ROWPercent.	no	Print table of row percentages. * (replaces PERCENT in P4F)
COLPercent.	no	Print table of column percentages. * (replaces PERCENT in P4F)
TOTPercent.	no	Print table of percentages of total frequency. * (replaces PERCENT in P4F)
DIFference.	no	Print table of differences. * (same as P4F)
STANdardized.	no	Print table of standardized deviations. * (same as P4F)
ADJusted.	no	Print table of adjusted standardized deviations. * (same as P4F)
FREEMAN.	no	Print table of Freeman-Tukey deviates. * (same as P4F)
SMOOTHed.	no	Print table of smoothed values. * (not in P4F)
/ STATistics		Optional, tests and measures to be computed.
CHISQuare.	CHISQ.	χ^2 test and Yates' corrected χ^2 (2x2 table). * (same as P4F)
CONTingency	no	C, ϕ, Cramer's V and (for 2x2 table) α, Yule's Q and Y, C_{max}, ϕ_{max}. * (same as P4F)
LRCHI.	no	Likelihood ratio test G^2. * (same as P4F)
FISHer.	no	Fisher's exact probabilities. * (same as P4F)
TETRAchoric.	no	Tetrachoric correlation. * (same as P4F)
CORRelation.	no	Product-moment correlation. * (same as P4F)
SPEARman.	no	Spearman rank correlation. * (same as P4F)
GAMma.	no	Γ, Kendall's τ_b, Stuart's τ_c, Somers' D. * (same as P4F)
LAMBda.	no	λ. * (same as P4F)
LSTAR.	no	λ^*. * (see LAMBDA in P4F)
TAUS.	no	Goodman and Kruskal's τ. * (same as P4F)
UNCertainty.	no	Uncertainty coefficients. * (same as P4F)
MCNemar.	no	McNemar's test of symmetry. * (same as P4F)
/ END		Required. (same as P4F)

[1] This statement is in a different paragraph in P1F than in P4F.

P2F -- Two-way Frequency Tables -- Empty Cells and Departures from Independence

If your facility still does not have P4F, but does have P2F, the Control Language specific to P2F is:

Paragraph Statement	Preassigned	Comment and Manual Reference
/ INPut		Specify as part of INPUT paragraph.
TABLE = # list.	none	When input is a multiway frequency table, number of levels for each index (fastest moving index first). (same as P4F)
VARiable		Specify as part of VARIABLE paragraph.
DEFine(#) = v list.	none	Define new index by combining variables. (see STACK in P4F[1])
/ TABLE		Required, may be repeated.
ROW = v list.	none	Variables defining row categories. (same as P4F)
COLumn = v list.	none	Variables defining column categories. (same as P4F)
PAIR. or CROSS.	PAIR.	Pair or cross ROW and COLUMN variables. (same as P4F)
CONDition = v list.	none	Tables formed for each level of each CONDITION variable. (same as P4F)
COUNT = v list.	none	Variables containing frequency counts when input is cell indices and frequency counts. (same as P4F)
OBServed.	OBS.	Print table of observed frequencies. (same as P4F[1])
FITted.	no	Print table of fitted (expected) values. (same as P4F[1])
DELTA = #.	0	Value added to cell frequencies before analysis. (same as P4F)
EMPTY(#) = # list.	none	Cell indices to be excluded. (same as P4F)
CONVergence = #.	0.05	Convergence criterion for iteration. (same as P4F[1])
ITERation = #.	20	Maximum number of iterations. (same as P4F[1])
/ STEP		Optional, may be repeated, applies to preceding TABLE paragraph.
CRITerion = (one or more) CHISQ,LRCHI,DIF,STAN, ADJ,QUSTAN,QUADJ.	none	Required, criterion for cell elimination. (see CELL in P4F[1])
MAXSTep = #.	(R-1)(C-1)	Maximum number of steps. (see STEP In P4F[1])
ALPHA = #.	0.05	Stepping stops when χ^2 test nonsignificant at ALPHA level. (see PROB in P4F[1])
ELIMinate = #.	2.0	Lower limit of criterion to eliminate a cell. (not in P4F)
REENter = #.	1.0	Upper limit of criterion to reenter a cell. (same as P4F[1])
PRINT = # list, or ALL.	none	Steps at which tables below are printed. (same as P4F[1])
FITted.	no	Table of fitted (expected) values. (same as P4F[1])
CHISQuare.	no	Table of χ^2 values when each cell in turn is eliminated. (same as P4F[1])
LRCHI.	no	Table of G^2 values when each cell in turn is eliminated. (same as P4F[1])
DIFference.	no	Table of differences (observed-fitted). (same as P4F[1])
STANdardized.	no	Table of standardized residuals. (same as P4F[1])
ADJusted.	no	Table of adjusted standardized residuals. (same as P4F[1])
QUSTAN.	no	Table of quasi-standardized residuals when each cell in turn is eliminated. (not in P4F)
QUADJ.	no	Table of quasi-adjusted standardized residuals when each cell in turn is eliminated. (not in P4F)
/ CATEGory		Required if any ROW, COLUMN or CONDITION variable has more than 10 distinct values.
CODE(#) = # list.	10 smallest values	Codes for variable #, may be repeated. * (same as P4F)
CUTPoint(#) = # list.	see CODE.	Cutpoints to form intervals for variable #, may be repeated. * (same as P4F)
NAME(#) = c list.	CODEs or CUTPoints.	Code or interval names for variable #, may be repeated. (same as P4F)
RESET.	not RESET	If RESET, all assignments in prev. CATEGORY paragraph are reset to preassigned values. (same as P4F)
/ END		Required.

[1] These statements are in a different paragraph in P4F than in P2F.

P3F -- Multiway Frequency Tables -- the Log-linear Model

If your facility still does not have P4F, but does have P3F, the Control Language specific to P3F is:

Paragraph Statement	Preassigned	Comment and Manual Reference
INPut		Specify as part of INPUT paragraph.
TABLE = # list.	none	When input is a multiway frequency table, number of levels for each index (fastest moving first). (same as P4F)
VARiable		Specify as part of VARiable paragraph.
DEFine(#) = v list.	none	Define new index by combining variables. (see STACK in P4F[1])
/ TABLE		Required, may be repeated.
INDex = v list.	none	Required, variables used as indices for table, $\leq$ 7 variables. (same as P4F)
SYMBol = c list.	none	Required, symbols to denote INDEX variables in analysis, 1 character. (same as P4F)
CONDition = v list.	none	Tables formed for each level of each CONDITIONING variable. (same as P4F)
COUNT = v list.	none	Variables containing frequency counts when input is cell indices and frequency counts. (same as P4F)
OBServed.	OBS.	Print table of observed frequencies. * (same as P4F[1])
MARGinal = #.	0	Print all marginal subtables up to order #. * (same as P4F[1])
DELTA = #.	0.0	Added to each frequency before analysis. * (same as P4F)
SIMULtaneous.	SIMUL.	Tests-of-fit of models of full order. * (same as P4F[1])
ASSOCiation.	no	Tests of marginal and partial association. * (similar to P4F[1])
ALL.	no	All models in 2- or 3-way table. * (same as P4F[1])
CONVergence = #.	0.1	Criterion for convergence of model-fitting algorithm. (same as P4F[1])
ITERation = #.	20	Maximum number of iterations. * (same as P4F[1])
/ FIT		Optional, may be repeated, applies to preceding TABLE paragraph.
MODEL = c list.	none	Required, hierarchical model to be fitted, may be repeated. (same as P4F)
EXPected.	no	Table of fitted (expected) values. * (same as P4F[1])
STANdardized.	no	Table of standardized residuals. * (same as P4F[1])
FREEMAN.	no	Table of Freeman-Tukey deviates. * (same as P4F[1])
LAMBda.	no	Estimate log-linear parameters of MODEL. * (same as P4F[1])
BETA.	no	Estimate multiplicative parameters of MODEL. * (same as P4F[1])
ORTHogonal = c list.	no	Fit orthogonal contrast to LAMBDA for SYMBOLS specified. (not in P4F)
PROBability = #.	.05	LABMDA, BETA, ORTHOGONAL printed only if test-of-fit of MODEL exceeds PROBABILITY (is nonsignificant). (same as P4F)
ADD.	no	Form models containing MODEL as subset. (similar to P4F)
DELETE.	no	Form models contained by MODEL. (similar to P4F)
/ CATEGory		Required if any ROW, COLUMN or CONDITION variable has more than 10 distinct values.
CODE(#) = # list.	10 smallest values	Codes for variable #, may be repeated. * (same as P4F)
CUTPoint(#) = # list.	see CODE.	Cutpoints to form intervals for variable #, may be repeated. * (same as P4F)
NAME(#) = c list.	CODEs or CUTPoints	Code or interval names for variable #, may be repeated. * (same as P4F)
RESET.	no RESET	If RESET, all assignments in prev. CATEGORY paragraph are reset to preassigned values. (same as P4F)
/ END		Required.

[1] These statements are in a different paragraph in P4F than in P3F.

A.9 Estimating (Smoothing) the Missing Value Correlation Matrix (PAM)

After the covariance matrix is computed, it is converted to a correlation matrix. The eigenvalues of this correlation matrix are computed if the ALLVALUE option is selected or if the eigenvalues are requested in the *PRINT* paragraph. Some of these eigenvalues may be negative if the ALLVALUE option is selected. If any eigenvalues are negative, the correlation matrix is reestimated using the positive eigenvalues and their corresponding eigenvectors: First the matrix

$$A = V'EV$$

is computed where V is the matrix of eigenvectors of the positive eigenvalues and E is the diagonal matrix of positive eigenvalues. Then the reestimated correlation matrix B is computed from A by the usual method of converting a covariance matrix to a correlation matrix. The reestimated covariance matrix is obtained from B by multiplying the rows and columns of B by the original standard deviations.

Eigenvalues and eigenvectors are computed using routines from the EISPACK system (Garbow et al, 1977 and Smith et al, 1974).

A.10 Replacing Missing Values (PAM)

To substitute means for missing values, the data are read from a temporary unit and missing values are replaced by means.

If the simple linear regression method is used, the vector of maximum correlations and indices of variables of maximum correlations are computed. Then the data are read and estimates are made using simple linear regression of each missing variable on the variable with which it is most highly correlated. If the variable of maximum correlation is also missing, the available variable that has the highest correlation is found and used. If a grouping variable is specified, the standard deviations computed from the pooled within-groups covariance matrix and the appropriate group means are used in the regression.

When either SINGLE, TWOSTEP or STEP is specified, variables are chosen on the basis of the highest partial correlation or F-to-enter, as in P2R (there is no F-to-remove, so once variables are entered they remain). Tolerance is checked (Appendix A.11). If TWOSTEP is specified, or if only one step of STEP is needed, the correlation matrix is not altered. If more than three predictors are chosen pivoting is performed on the correlation matrix, as in P2R. To prevent accumulated round-off error a fresh copy of the correlation matrix is used after pivoting rather than using reverse pivots. If a grouping variable is specified the appropriate group means are used in the regressions.

When the multiple regression method is used, the correlation matrix is inverted in a stepwise manner under control of a tolerance such that pivoting is not performed for any variable whose squared multiple correlation with previously pivoted variables exceeds 1-tolerance. The data are then read from a scratch file one case at a time. A copy of the inverse is reverse pivoted for any variables that are missing and for which pivoting was previously performed. Pivoting will also be performed for any variables that are available for that case and for which pivoting was not previously performed due to tolerance, but can now be pivoted. Mahalanobis distances are computed from the case to the center of all cases in its group (as in P7M) using the variables that were originally available. If a grouping variable is specified, the appropriate group means are used in the regression.

When a grouping variable is specified and its value is missing for a case, the grouping variable is estimated using the classification functions from a standard discriminant analysis (similar to P7M) based on the available variables for that case. If other variables are missing, they are estimated using the means of the group into which the case has been classified. Estimation for a missing grouping variable is available only for the regression method.

A.11 Linear Regression—Estimating the Coefficients (P1R or P2R)

A multiple linear regression equation can be written as

$$E(y_j - \bar{y}) = \beta_1(x_{1j} - \bar{x}_1) + \ldots + \beta_p(x_{pj} - \bar{x}_p)$$

In matrix notation this can be written as

$$E(Y') = X'\beta'$$

where

$Y = (y_j - \bar{y})$ is a row vector of length N

$X = (x_{ij} - \bar{x}_i)$ is a pxN matrix

$\beta = (\beta_i)$ is a row vector of length p

Then the estimate b of β is

$$b' = (XX')^{-1}XY' .$$

In this section we explain how b is obtained numerically by "sweeping" the matrix XX' of cross products of deviations. Sweeping is a method of inverting the matrix of cross products of deviations so that at each step (as each variable is entered into the regression equation), the coefficients b, the partial correlations, the multiple correlation and tolerance, and the residual sum of squares are computed as part of the matrix inversion (see also Jennrich, 1977a).

SWEEPING AND ESTIMATES OF THE COEFFICIENTS

In BMDP programs, regression equations are usually computed by sweeping a matrix C of sums of cross-products of deviations:

$$C = \sum_1^N (x_j - \bar{x})'(x_j - \bar{x})$$

where x_j denotes the data for case j, $\bar{x}$ denotes the vector of sample means and N is the sample size. If case weights are used C is the weighted sum of cross-products. If a ZERO intercept is used, C is the sum of products $\sum x_j x_j'$.

The same results (except for minor differences in round-off error) are obtained whether a covariance or correlation matrix or the matrix of cross-products of deviations is used.

A basic reference for sweeping is Dempster (1969, p. 62). In BMDP, sweeping is used both to obtain regression equations and to do matrix inversion. Sweeping is most easily described in the context of stepwise regression (P2R).

Suppose we have p independent variables so that C is a p+1 x p+1 matrix with dependent variable as variable p+1. At step one of stepwise regression, an independent variable is chosen, say variable k. The matrix C is swept on variable k to produce a matrix $C*$, where

$$C^*_{ij} = C_{ij} - C_{ik}C_{kj}/C_{kk} \qquad \text{for } i \neq k, j \neq k$$

$$C^*_{kj} = C_{kj}/C_{kk}$$

$$C^*_{ik} = C_{ik}/C_{kk}$$

$$C^*_{kk} = -1/C_{kk}$$

Note that $C*$ is symmetric.

At this point, $C^*_{p+1,k}$ is the <u>regression coefficient</u> for predicting the dependent variable p+1 from variable k. (The intercept is computed separately.) Also, $C^*_{p+1,p+1}$ is the <u>residual sum of squares</u> from regressing the dependent variable (p+1) on variable k. The <u>partial correlation</u> of a pair of variables i and j for $i \neq k$ and $j \neq k$ can be computed as

$$r_{ij \cdot k} = \frac{C^*_{ij}}{\sqrt{C^*_{ii}C^*_{jj}}}$$

The estimate of the variance of the regression coefficient is proportional to $C^*_{p+1,p+1}C^*_{kk}$. In the computer, C^*_{ij} is stored in the same place that C_{ij} was stored so C is overwritten as $C*$ is computed. If we let C represent the computer FORTRAN array rather than the mathematical array, we define sweeping on variable k algorithmically as

$$C_{ij} = C_{ij} - C_{ik}C_{kj}/C_{kk} \qquad \text{for } i \neq k, j \neq k$$

$$C_{kj} = C_{ij}/C_{kk}$$

$$C_{ik} = C_{ik}/C_{kk}$$

$$C_{kk} = -1/C_{kk}$$

At step two, we choose another variable, say ℓ and sweep as we did for variable k. At this point $C_{p+1,p+1}$ contains the residual sum of squares for regressing the dependent variable p+1 on variables k and ℓ; $C_{p+1,k}$ and $C_{p+1,\ell}$ are the regression coefficients; the partial correlation of variables i and j (i and $j \neq k$ or ℓ) is

$$\frac{C_{ij}}{\sqrt{C_{ii}C_{jj}}}$$

The estimated covariance matrix of the regression coefficients (assuming an intercept) is

$$\frac{-C_{p+1,p+1}}{n-3} \begin{pmatrix} C_{kk} & C_{k\ell} \\ C_{\ell k} & C_{\ell\ell} \end{pmatrix}$$

where -3 is replaced by -2 if there is no intercept. The standard errors of the regression coefficient are obtained by taking square roots of the diagonal elements of the covariance matrix of the regression coefficients.

At an arbitrary step, suppose that sweeping has been performed for variables 1 to k. Let

$$C = \begin{pmatrix} -A_{kk} & B'_{kq} \\ B_{qk} & D_{qq} \end{pmatrix}$$

where q = p-k+1. A is the inverse of the cross product of deviations for the variables that have been swept (entered into the equation). B contains the <u>regression coefficients</u> for predicting variables k+1 to p+1 from variables 1 to k. The estimate of the <u>covariance matrix of the regression coefficients</u> for predicting variable i ($k < i \leq p+1$) is

$$\frac{C_{ii}}{N-k-1} A$$

where the term -1 is dropped if there is no intercept. D is the sum of cross-products of the residuals of the variables that have not been swept regressed on the variables that have been swept; the diagonal of D contains the residual sum of squares for each nonswept variable. The <u>partial correlations</u> for variables k+1 to p+1 adjusting for the linear effects of variables 1 to k are obtained by converting D to a correlation matrix. Thus the variables for which sweeping has been performed can be considered as independent variables and the remaining variables are dependent variables. Sweeping a variable changes a variable from being dependent to independent. Sweeping is also reversible.

If a reverse sweep is performed, a variable changes its status from independent to dependent.

The inverse of a matrix is obtained by sweeping all variables. More precisely, the inverse is equal to the negative of the result of sweeping all variables.

TOLERANCE

Sometimes the matrix $\underset{\sim}{C}$ is singular or nearly singular. In this case C cannot be inverted or cannot be inverted with satisfactory numerical accuracy. A deeper problem, say in the context of regression, is that the regression coefficients have poor statistical properties whenever the covariance matrix of the independent variables is nearly singular since the estimated variance of the regression coefficient for a particular independent variable is inversely proportional to one minus the squared multiple correlation of that independent variable with all other independent variables. One minus this squared multiple correlation is called the tolerance for that variable. The reciprocal of the tolerance is called the variance inflation factor. In practice, if one independent variable has a high squared multiple correlation with the other independent variables, it is extremely unlikely that the independent variable in question contributes significantly to the prediction equation. For these reasons, BMDP programs always perform regression analysis (and matrix inversion) in a stepwise manner in such a way that at any step no variable is added to the list of independent variables if either

- its squared multiple correlation with already included independent variables exceeds one minus the tolerance limit

- including the variable would cause the squared multiple correlation for an already included variable to exceed one minus the tolerance limit (see Frane, 1977)

Variables that do not pass the tolerance test are considered redundant. When the solution of an ill-conditioned problem is necessary, a program like P9R (with METHOD=NONE.) that uses double precision should be used.

A.12 Residual Analysis in P9R

Residuals for each case are computed as

$$(y-\bar{y}) - b_1(x_1-\bar{x}_1) - \ldots - b_p(x_p-\bar{x}_p)$$

where

y = dependent variable

b_i = regression coefficient for the ith independent variable x_i

The standard error of a residual for a case with positive weight is computed as the square root of

$$\left[\frac{1}{w} - \frac{1}{N} - (\underset{\sim}{x}-\underset{\sim}{\bar{x}})\underset{\sim}{C}^{-1}(\underset{\sim}{x}-\underset{\sim}{\bar{x}})'\right] RMS$$

where

$\underset{\sim}{C}^{-1}$ is the inverse of the matrix of cross products of deviations of the independent variables ($\underset{\sim}{A}$ in Appendix A.11)

N is the number of cases with nonzero weight

w is the case weight

RMS is the residual mean square

and the terms 1/N and $\bar{x}$ are dropped if there is no intercept.

The standard error of a residual with zero weight is computed as the square root of

$$\left[1 + \frac{1}{N} + (\underset{\sim}{x}-\underset{\sim}{\bar{x}})\underset{\sim}{C}^{-1}(\underset{\sim}{x}-\underset{\sim}{\bar{x}})'\right] RMS$$

Standardized residuals are obtained by dividing each residual by its standard error.

The Mahalanobis distance from the case to the centroid of all cases in the space defined by the independent variables is

$$w(N-1)(\underset{\sim}{x}-\underset{\sim}{\bar{x}})\underset{\sim}{C}^{-1}(\underset{\sim}{x}-\underset{\sim}{\bar{x}})'$$

where the terms -1 and $\bar{x}$ are dropped if there is a ZERO intercept.

Weighted residuals are computed by multiplying the residual by the square root of the weight for cases with positive weights and are the same as the ordinary residual for cases with zero weights.

For cases with positive weight, the deleted residual is obtained by dividing the ordinary residual by

$$1 - \frac{w}{N} - w(\underset{\sim}{x}-\underset{\sim}{\bar{x}})\underset{\sim}{C}^{-1}(\underset{\sim}{x}-\underset{\sim}{\bar{x}})'$$

where the terms w/N and $\bar{x}$ are dropped if there is no intercept. The deleted residual is the residual which would have been obtained had the case been given a zero case weight. For cases with zero weights, the deleted residual is the same as the ordinary residual. The adjusted (PRESS) predicted value is obtained by subtracting the deleted residual from the dependent variable.

Cook's (1977) distance is defined for cases with positive case weight as

$$\frac{r^{*2}vw}{(p+1)RMS}$$

where r* denotes the deleted residual; where the term +1 is dropped if the intercept is zero, and

$$v = \frac{w}{N} + d$$

where the term 1/N is dropped if there is a ZERO intercept and where d is the Mahalanobis distance divided by N-1 (or by N if there is a zero intercept). For a case with a zero case weight, Cook's distance is defined as the value that would have been computed had the case been given a case weight of one.

The standard error of the predicted value for a case is the square root of

$$RMS\left(\frac{1}{N} + (\underset{\sim}{x}-\underset{\sim}{\bar{x}})\underset{\sim}{C}^{-1}(\underset{\sim}{x}-\underset{\sim}{\bar{x}})'\right) .$$

The standard error of a residual for a case with positive weight is computed

Standardized residuals are obtained by dividing each residual by its standard

Durbin-Watson statistics are computed from the residuals r_i:

$$DW = \frac{\sum_{i=2}^{N}(r_i-r_{i-1})}{\sum_{i=1}^{N} r_i}$$

The serial correlation is computed as

$$= \frac{\sum_{i=2}^{N} r_i\, r_{i-1}}{\sum_{i=1}^{N} r_i}$$

Note the close relation between the Durbin-Watson statistics and the serial correlation.

$$DW = \frac{\sum_{i=2}^{N} r_i}{\sum_{i=1}^{N} r_i} + \frac{\sum_{i=2}^{N} r_{i-1}}{\sum_{i=1}^{N} r_i} - 2 \qquad\text{or approximately}\qquad DW \approx 2\frac{N-1}{N} - 2$$

A.13 Regression on Principal Components (P4R)

The eigenvalues (λ_k) and eigenvectors (a_{ki}) of the covariance or correlation matrix (C) of the independent variables are computed using the Jacobi method, and the principal component scores (z_{kj}) are obtained as

$$z_{kj} = \sum_i a_{ki}(x_{ij} - \bar{x}_i) \qquad j=1,\ldots,N;\ k=1,\ldots,p$$

where N is the number of cases and p is the number of independent variables, or

$$z_{kj} = \sum_i a_{ki}\left(\frac{x_{ij}-\bar{x}_i}{s_i}\right) , \text{ if standardization is requested.}$$

The regression coefficients (β_k) of the components, and the correlations ($r_{z_k y}$) of the principal component scores (z_k) with the dependent variable ($y=x_d$) are computed as

$$\beta_k = \frac{\sum_i a_{ki}C_{id}}{\lambda_k}$$

where C_{id} is the covariance of variable i with $y = x_d$, or

$$\beta_k = (\sum_i a_{ki}R_{id})\frac{s_d}{\lambda_k} , \text{ if standardization is requested}$$

where R_{id} is the correlation of variable i with $y = x_d$, and then

$$r_{z_k y} = \beta_k \cdot \frac{\sqrt{\lambda_k}}{s_y}$$

The regression coefficients of the variables (b_i) are computed.

$$b_i = \sum_k a_{ki}\beta_k$$

or

$$b_i = \frac{\sum_k a_{ki}\beta_k}{s_i} , \text{ if standardization is requested.}$$

The residual sum of squares, total F and F for the component are computed.

$$RSS_d = \sum_j (y_j-\bar{y})^2$$

$$RSS_k = RSS_{k-1} - (N-1)\beta^2_k\lambda_k$$

$$FTOT_k = \frac{(RSS_d - RSS_k)/k}{RSS_k/(N-1-k)}$$

$$F_k = \frac{(RSS_{k-1} - RSS_k)}{RSS_k/(N-1-k)}$$

A.14 Polynomial Regression (P5R)

Let w_j, x_j and y_j denote the weight, independent variable value and dependent variable value for the jth case where $j=1,\ldots,N$. For any two N-vectors $\underline{u}$, $\underline{v}$, let

$$[\underline{u},\underline{v}] = \sum_{j=1}^{N} w_j u_j v_j \qquad \text{(the weighted inner product of } \underline{u} \text{ and } \underline{v}\text{)}$$

Orthogonal polynomial values (P_s) for degrees $s=1,\ldots,r$ are computed recursively by the Forsythe (1957) method normalized so that the (weighted) sum of squares for each is one. The computation of the P_s is described later.

The regression coefficients for the fitted orthogonal polynomials are given by

$$\hat{\gamma}_s = [P_s, \underline{y}] ; \qquad s=0,\ldots,r$$

Those for the fitted polynomial in x of degree s are given by

$$\hat{\beta}_t = \sum_{q=0}^{s} b_{tq} \hat{\gamma}_q ; \qquad t=0,\ldots,s$$

The residual values of the dependent variable after fitting a polynomial of degree $s=0,\ldots,r$ are

$$\hat{\underline{e}}_s = \underline{y} - \hat{\gamma}_0 \underline{P}_0 - \hat{\gamma}_1 \underline{P}_1 - \cdots - \hat{\gamma}_s \underline{P}_s$$

The residual sum of squares and mean square are

$$RSS_s = [\hat{\underline{e}}_s, \hat{\underline{e}}_s] \quad \text{and}$$

$$RMS_s = RSS_s/(N-s-1)$$

The standard errors and covariances for polynomials of degree s are estimated by

$$s.e.(\hat{\gamma}_p) = RMS_s^{\frac{1}{2}} ; \qquad p=0,\ldots,s$$

$$\hat{cov}(\hat{\beta}_p, \hat{\beta}_q) = \sum_{t=0}^{s} b_{pt} b_{qt} RMS_s; \qquad p,q=0,\ldots,s$$

$$s.e.(\hat{\beta}_p) = [\hat{cov}(\hat{\beta}_p, \hat{\beta}_p)]^{\frac{1}{2}}; \qquad p=0,\ldots,s$$

An analysis of variance table is computed in the form

Degree	df	Mean Square	F
0	1	MS_0	MS_0/RMS_s
1	1	MS_1	MS_1/RMS_s
$\vdots$	$\vdots$	$\vdots$	$\vdots$
s	1	MS_s	MS_s/RMS_s
Residual	N-s-1	RMS_s	

where

$$MS_t = \hat{\gamma}_t^2 ; \qquad t=0,\ldots,s$$

The goodness-of-fit estimates

$$F_s = \frac{(RSS_s - RSS_r)/(r-s)}{RSS_r/(N-r-1)}$$

with r-s and N-r-1 degrees of freedom computed for each degree $s=0,\ldots,r-1$.

COMPUTATION OF ORTHOGONAL POLYNOMIAL VALUES (FORSYTHE, 1957)

Let $q_{0,j} = 1$ and $q_{1,j} = x_j - \bar{x}$ where x_j is the observed value of the independent variable for case j and

$$\bar{x} = \Sigma\, w_j x_j / \Sigma\, w_j$$

is the weighted mean. The orthogonal polynomials are computed recursively using the relation

$$q_{s+1,j} = q_{1,j} P_{s,j} - \alpha_{1s} P_{s,j} - \alpha_{2s} P_{s-1,j} \qquad s=1,2,\ldots,r-1$$

where

$$|q_s| = (\Sigma\, w_j q_{s,j}^2)^{\frac{1}{2}}$$

$$P_{s,j} = q_{s,j}/|q_s| \qquad \text{(normalized values)} \quad \text{where } P_{0,j} = N^{-\frac{1}{2}}$$

$$\alpha_{1s} = \Sigma\, w_j (x_j - \bar{x}) P_{s,j}^2$$

$$\alpha_{2s} = \Sigma\, w_j (x_j - \bar{x}) P_{s-1,j} P_{s,j}$$

$$r = \text{maximum degree of polynomial}$$

Let $b_{0s},\ldots,b_{ss}$ denote the coefficients for the expansion of the sth degree orthogonal polynomial in powers of x. The coefficients of the (s+1)th degree orthogonal polynomial are computed by letting

$$b_{00} = 1/|q_0|, \quad b_{01} = -\bar{x}/|q_1|, \quad b_{11} = 1/|q_1|$$

and then

$$b_{i,s+1} = (b_{i-1,s} - \bar{x}b_{is} - \alpha_{1s}b_{is} - \alpha_{2s}b_{i,s-1})/|q_{s+1}| ; \quad i=0,\ldots,s+1$$

where

$$b_{h,j} = 0 \quad \text{for } h < 0 \text{ or } h > j$$

A.15 Nonlinear Least Squares (P3R)

P3R minimizes the weighted residual sum of squares

$$RSS = \Sigma\, w[y-f(\underline{x},\underline{p})]^2$$

where the summation is over the N complete cases subject to linear constraints, if any are specified, of the form

$$\Sigma_i\, b_{\ell i} p_i = c_\ell$$

For each case

$\underline{x}$ is the vector of values of the independent variables

y is the value of the dependent variable

w is the case weight

$f(\underline{x},\underline{p})$ is the value of the function evaluated using the values of the parameters $\underline{p} = (p_1, p_2, \ldots, p_m)$

If prior knowledge of the parameters is used, the function minimized is

$$RSS + \Sigma\, r_i (P_i - \bar{P}_i)$$

where the summation is over the number of parameters, r_i represents the ridge values, and P_i represents the prior estimates of the parameters.

Initially the system of linear constraints (if specified) is solved in terms of a subset of the parameters. Let m be the number of parameters in the subset and m' the original number (m'=m when there are no linear constraints). To simplify the notation we let the m parameters be $p_1, p_2, \ldots p_m$. Therefore

$$p_\ell = \sum_{i=1}^{m} b_{\ell i} p_i + c_\ell \qquad m+1 \le \ell \le m'$$

Minimizing the residual sum of squares

The vector p that minimizes the RSS is obtained through iteration (Jennrich and Sampson, 1968). At each iteration the function is approximated by a first order Taylor series expansion; i.e.,

$$y = f(\underline{x}, \underline{p}^{(0)}) + \Sigma\, z_i (p_i - p_i^{(0)})$$

where the superscript (0) specifies the current value of the parameters and $z_i = \partial f(\underline{x}, \underline{p}^{(0)})/p_i$, $i=1,2,\ldots,m$ are the partial derivatives. (When there are linear equality constraints, more linear terms are necessary.) Then for any $\underline{p}^{(0)}$ the above can be written as a linear equation in the z_i, and the coefficient of z_i can be found as in linear regression. The new estimate of p_i is $p_i^{(0)}$ plus the estimated coefficient of z_i.

The following are computed for each case

$$z_i = \partial f(\underline{x},\underline{p})/\partial p_i \qquad i=1,2,\ldots,m$$

$$e = y - f(\underline{x},\underline{p})$$

or, if there are any linear equality constraints,

$$z_i = \frac{\partial f(\underline{x},\underline{p})}{p_i} + \sum_{\ell=m+1}^{m'} b_{\ell i} \frac{\partial f(\underline{x},\underline{p})}{\partial p_\ell} \qquad i=1,2,\ldots,m$$

and

$$e = y - f(\underline{x},\underline{p}) + \sum_{\ell=m+1}^{m'} \frac{\partial f(\underline{x},\underline{p})}{\partial p_\ell} [p_\ell - \Sigma\, b_{\ell i} p_i - c_\ell]$$

P3R then forms the matrix ($\underline{A}$) of weighted sums of cross products of $z_1, z_2, \ldots, z_m, e$; i.e., $A=(a_{ij})$ where $z_{m+1}=e$ and $a_{ij}=\Sigma\, wz_i z_j$.

Using the Gauss-Jordan algorithm for matrix inversion, the matrix $\underline{A}$ is swept on its diagonal elements (except $a_{m+1,m+1}$) in a stepwise manner. At each step the index of the pivoting element is the r which maximizes $a_{m+1,r}/a_{rr}$ such that the TOLERANCE limit is not violated (Appendix A.11). If any of the first m diagonal elements of $\underline{A}$ are left unpivoted because they fail the TOLERANCE test, corresponding elements of the last row of $\underline{A}$ are set to zero.

Let $\hat{p}_i$ be the provisionally estimated value; i.e., $\hat{p}_i = p_i^{(0)} + a'_{i(m+1)}$ where a'_{ij} is the value of a_{ij} after pivoting the matrix $\underline{A}$. The updated values are then chosen as

$$p_i = \hat{p}_i + d\,(\hat{p}_i - p_i^{(0)})$$

where $0 < d \leq 1$ and d is chosen so that the p_i's satisfy their upper and lower limits if specified (if $d <$ a small constant, one or more parameters are left unchanged from previous values). If there are linear constraints

$$p_\ell = \Sigma\, b_{\ell i} p_i + c_\ell \qquad m + 1 \leq \ell \leq m'.$$

Upper and lower limits for these parameters may be violated; these violations can be found by inspecting the parameter estimates.

A new value of RSS is computed. If the new RSS is greater than the previous RSS, d is halved and new values of the p_i are obtained. Increment halving continues until the new RSS is not larger than the previous RSS or the maximum number of HALVINGS is reached. If the maximum number of HALVINGS is reached, P3R continues using the values at the last halving.

Iterations are performed until the CONVERGENCE criterion is satisfied or the maximum number of ITERATIONS is reached.

Asymptotic standard deviations

The asymptotic covariance of p_i and p_j is $s^2 a'_{ij}$ where a'_{ij} is the pivoted value of a_{ij} and $s^2 = RSS/(N-m)$ where m'' is the number of independent (pivoted) parameter estimates ($m'' \leq m$). a'_{ij} is zero if either a_{ii} or a_{jj} is unpivoted. If a value is specified for MEANSQUARE, then s^2 is the specified value; otherwise s^2 is computed using the smallest RSS if CONVERGENCE is positive or the last RSS if CONVERGENCE is negative.

If there are linear constraints the asymptotic variances and covariances of the remaining parameters are obtained from those of the subset of m parameters.

The standard error of the predicted value for a case is

$$s\,\{\,\Sigma\,\Sigma\,z_i a'_{ij} z_j\,\}^{\frac{1}{2}}$$

A.16   Derivative-free Nonlinear Regression (PAR)

PAR finds the minimum of the function

$$Q(\underline{p}) = \Sigma w (y - f(\underline{x},\underline{p}))^2$$

(where the summation is over all cases) subject to constraints each of which can be written as

$$\underline{b}_\ell ' \underline{p} \geq c_\ell$$

Such constraints include MINIMUMS and MAXIMUMS on the parameters as well as the additional CONSTRAINTS and corresponding LIMITS, all of which are specified in the *PARAMeter* paragraph.

For each case

$$
\begin{array}{ll}
x & \text{is the vector of values of the independent variables} \\
y & \text{is the value of the dependent variable} \\
w & \text{is the case weight} \\
f(\underline{x},\underline{p}) & \text{is the value of the function evaluated using the values of} \\
& \text{the parameters } \underline{p} = (p_1, p_2, \ldots, p_m)
\end{array}
$$

If prior knowledge of the parameters is used, the function minimized is

$$Q(P) + \sum r_i (P_i - \bar{P}_i)$$

where the summation is over the number of parameters, r_i represents the ridge values, and P_i represents the prior estimates of the parameters.

Overview of the procedure

If there are no boundary constraints each iteration consists of approximating $f(\underline{x},\underline{p})$ by a linear function of $\underline{p}$ and solving the resulting linear regression problem to get a new estimate of $\hat{p}$. The linear function $\ell(\underline{x},\underline{p})$ equal to $f(\underline{x},\underline{p})$ at $\underline{p}^{(1)}, \ldots, \underline{p}^{(m'+1)}$ (estimates of $\hat{\underline{p}}$ computed in previous $m'+1$ iterations, where m' is the number of parameters to be estimated) is used to approximate $f(\underline{x},\underline{p})$. The $\underline{p}$ which minimizes

$$Q^*(\underline{p}) = \Sigma\, w (y - \ell(\underline{x},\underline{p}))^2$$

is found and used to replace the oldest member of the set $\underline{p}^{(1)}, \ldots, \underline{p}^{(m'+1)}$ and the revised set of parameter vectors is passed to the next iteration.

If there are boundary constraints on the parameters, the procedure described above is modified so that in each iteration an attempt is made to find a new estimate that satisfies all of the boundary constraints and decreases the value of Q^*. Unlike the unconstrained case, if $f(\underline{x},\underline{p})$ happens to be a linear function of $\underline{p}$, the constrained minimum may not be located in one iteration. Within each iteration the boundary constraints are divided into two sets -- the active constraints (those for which $\underline{b}_\ell ' \underline{p}^{(m+1)} = c_\ell$) and the inactive constraints ($\underline{b}_\ell ' \underline{p}^{(m+1)} \geq c_\ell$). The direction of the new estimate is constrained to be along boundaries formed by some of the active constraints if not doing so would lead to the violation of some of the active constraints. Then if necessary, the step length is shortened so that all of the inactive constraints are satisfied by the new estimate. LaGrange multipliers are used to compute the constrained minimum of Q^*.

Generating the starting values

The $m+1$ starting parameter vectors needed by the algorithm are generated from the INITIAL and DELTA parameters in the *PARAMeter* paragraph as follows:

$$p_i^{(k)} = INIT(i) + \delta_{ik} DELTA(i)$$

where δ_{ik} is the Kronecker delta.

If any parameters are designated as FIXED in the *PARAMeter* paragraph only $m'+1$ starting values are computed where m' is the number of parameters to be estimated. If any of the $p^{(k)}$ violate a boundary constraint the magnitude of DELTA(k) is decreased so that $\underline{p}^{(k)}$ lies halfway between $\underline{p}^{(m'+1)}$ and the nearest boundary.

The regression function is evaluated for each starting vector. Then the starting vectors are renumbered so that

$$Q(\underline{p}^{(k)}) \geq Q(\underline{p}^{(k+1)}) \text{ for } k=1,\ldots,m'$$

Description of one iteration when there are no boundary constraints

Let

$$
\begin{array}{ll}
\underline{y} & = \text{n component vector of values of the dependent variable} \\
\underline{f}(\underline{p}) & = \text{n component vector valued function of values of the regression} \\
& \quad \text{function for each case} \\
\Delta P & = m' \times m' \text{ matrix with columns } \underline{p}^{(k)} - \underline{p}^{(m'+1)} \\
\Delta F & = n \times m' \text{ matrix whose columns are } \underline{f}(\underline{p}^{(k)}) - \underline{f}(\underline{p}^{(m'+1)}) \\
W & = n \times n \text{ diagonal matrix of case weights}
\end{array}
$$

Step 1

Form the $(m'+1) \times (m'+1)$ matrix

$$\underline{A} = \begin{pmatrix} \Delta F' W \Delta F & \Delta F' W [\underline{y} - \underline{f}(\underline{p}^{(m'+1)})] \\ [\underline{y} - \underline{f}(\underline{p}^{(m'+1)})]' W \Delta F & 0 \end{pmatrix}$$

Step 2

A stepwise regression modification of the Gauss-Jordan algorithm for matrix inversion is used to pivot on the first m' diagonal elements of $\underline{A}$. At each step the index of the pivoting element is the r which maximizes $a_{m'+1,r}^2 / a_{rr}$ among all of the unpivoted a_{rr} such that the TOLERANCE limit is not violated.

Step 3

Let $\underline{\alpha}$ denote the vector containing the first m' elements of the $(m'+1)$th column of A. If any of the first m' diagonal elements of A were not used as pivots the corresponding elements of $\underline{\alpha}$ are set equal to zero. $\underline{\delta}$ is computed from $\underline{\delta} = \Delta P \underline{\alpha}$. Then $\underline{p}^{(m'+2)} = \underline{p}^{(m'+1)} + \underline{\delta}$ and $\underline{f}(\underline{p}^{(m'+2)})$ are computed.

Step 4

An attempt is made to find a point that decreases $Q(\underline{p})$. If $Q(\underline{p}^{(m'+2)}) > Q(\underline{p}^{(m'+1)})$, Q is evaluated at a sequence of points (up to step HALVING) in which the step length is successively halved and the direction alternates between $\underline{\delta}$ and $-\underline{\delta}$.

The set of parameter vectors to be passed to the next iteration is determined as follows:

Let r be the first subscript such that $|\alpha_r| > .00005$. Then for $k=r,\ldots,m'+1$ let

$$\underline{p}_{new}^{(k)} = \underline{p}_{old}^{(k+1)}$$

and if $r>1$ for $k=1,\ldots,r-1$

$$\underline{p}_{new}^{(k)} = (\underline{p}_{old}^{(k)} + \underline{p}_{old}^{(m'+2)}) / 2$$

This completes one iteration. Iterations are repeated until the convergence criterion is satisfied, or the maximum number of iterations is reached.

Boundary constraints

For each constraint a "tolerance" is computed as

$$t_\ell = \sum_{i=1}^{m} |\,b_{\ell i} DELTA(i)\,| \cdot TOLERANCE$$

A constraint will be considered satisfied as an equality (i.e., active) if

$$|\underline{b}_\ell ' \underline{p} - c_\ell| \leq t_\ell$$

An inequality constraint will be considered satisfied by $\underline{p}$ if

$$\underline{b}_\ell ' \underline{p} - t_\ell \geq c_\ell$$

At each iteration the constraints are divided into active and inactive constraints. Let s denote the number of active constraints at the current iteration.

For each active constraint, $\underline{A}$ (in Step 1 above) is augmented with a row and column whose first m' elements are the components of the vector $\underline{b}_\ell ' \Delta P$ and remaining elements are zero. Pivoting as described in Step 2 is performed on this augmented matrix. Values of $\underline{b}_\ell ' \underline{\delta}$ are found among the last s elements of the $(m'+1)$th column of A. To constrain $\underline{\delta}$ so that $\underline{p}^{(m'+1)+\underline{\delta}}$ will satisfy the active inequality constraints pivoting is performed as follows:

a. For $r = m'+2,\dots,m'+s+1$ pivot on $a_{r,r}$ if

    - r has not been used as a pivot index and

    - $a_{m'+1,r} < -t_{(r-m'-1)}$

Repeat until no r satisfies the criteria used for pivoting.

b. If $a_{m'+1,m'+1}/D < TOL$, pivot on $a_{r,r}$ and return to part a, where r denotes the first integer, such that

    - r was used as a pivot index in part a

    - $-\dfrac{a_{m'+1,r}}{a_{rr}} > t_{(r-m'-1)}$

Compute $\underline{\delta}^* = \Delta P \underline{\alpha}$, and $\underline{\delta} = d\underline{\delta}^*$ where $0 < d \leq 1$ and d is the largest number such that $\underline{p}^{(m'+2)} = \underline{p}^{(m'+1)} + \underline{\delta}$ satisfies all of the inactive constraints. Then compute $\underline{f}(\underline{p}^{(m'+2)})$.

Step 4 is performed as described above except:

    - If δ points in a direction interior to any active boundary, the direction is not reversed.

    - The step length in the reverse direction is shortened if not doing so would violate an inactive constraint.

Asymptotic standard deviations and correlations

The asymptotic covariance matrix of $\underline{p}$ is estimated by

$$\hat{\Sigma} = s^2 \Delta P (\Delta F' \Delta F)^{-1} \Delta P'$$

where ΔF and ΔP are the values in the last iteration

$$s^2 = Q(\hat{\underline{p}})/(n'-m'')$$

where

    n' = number of cases with nonzero weight
    $\underline{m}''$ = number of independent (pivoted) parameter estimates
    $\hat{\underline{p}}$ = the vector that gives the smallest value of Q if this is one of the last $m'+1$ estimates or the final value.

or if MEANSQ is specified

$$s^2 = MEANSQ.$$

The standard deviation of the predicted value $\hat{f}(\underline{x},\underline{p})$ is estimated by

$$s(\underline{g}(\underline{x})'(\Delta F'\Delta F)^{-1}\underline{g}(\underline{x}))^{\frac{1}{2}}$$

where $g_k(\underline{x}) = f(\underline{x},\underline{p}^{(k)}) - f(\underline{x},\underline{p}^{(m'+1)})$

A.17 One-way Analysis of Variance and Covariance (PIV)

The model analyzed is

$$y_{ij} = \mu_i + \beta_1(x_{1ij} - \bar{x}_1) + \dots + \beta_p(x_{pij} - \bar{x}_p) + e_{ij}$$

where

    $i = 1,\dots,g$ (the group index)
    $j = 1,\dots,n_i$ (the case index in group i)
    x_{kij} = the value of the kth variable for case j in group i

Assume that all g groups are to be compared, the first p variables are the covariates, and the $(p+1)$st variable is the dependent variable. The grand means $(\bar{x}_k)$, the between group sum of cross products $(b_{k\ell})$, the pooled within group sum of cross products $(w_{k\ell})$, and the total sum of cross products $(a_{k\ell})$ are given by

$$\bar{x}_k = \frac{1}{N} \sum_{i=1}^{g} n_i \bar{x}_{ki} \qquad\qquad (N = \sum_{i=1}^{g} n_i)$$

$$b_{k\ell} = \sum_{i=1}^{g} n_i(\bar{x}_{ki} - \bar{x}_k)(\bar{x}_{\ell i} - \bar{x}_\ell)$$

$$w_{k\ell} = \sum_{i=1}^{g} \sum_{j=1}^{n_i} (x_{kij} - \bar{x}_{ki})(x_{\ell ij} - \bar{x}_{\ell i})$$

$$a_{k\ell} = b_{k\ell} + w_{k\ell}$$

The between, within and total covariance matrices are obtained by dividing

$$(b_{k\ell}), (w_{k\ell}), (a_{k\ell})$$

by their degrees of freedom, g-1, N-g and N-1 respectively.

The regression coefficients are estimated by

$$\hat{\beta}_{k\ell} = \sum_{\ell=1}^{p} w^{k\ell} w_{\ell,p+1} \qquad\qquad \text{for } k=1,\dots,p$$

where

    $(w^{k\ell})$ is the inverse of the p x p matrix $(w_{k\ell})$

The error variance is estimated by

$$\hat{\sigma}^2 = (w_{p+1,p+1} - \sum_{k=1}^{p} \hat{\beta}_k w_{k,p+1})/(N-g-p)$$

The correlation matrix of the $\hat{\beta}_k$ is given by

$$corr(\hat{\beta}_k, \hat{\beta}_\ell) = w^{k\ell}/(w^{kk} w^{\ell\ell})^{\frac{1}{2}}$$

The estimates of the standard deviations of the $\hat{\beta}_k$ are given by

$$\hat{s}.d. (\hat{\beta}_k) = \sqrt{w^{kk}}$$

and the corresponding t statistics by

$$t_k = \hat{\beta}_k/\hat{s}.d. (\hat{\beta}_k)$$

The estimates of the adjusted group means are given by

$$\hat{\mu}_i = \bar{y}_i + \sum_{k=1}^{p} \hat{\beta}_k(\bar{x}_k - \bar{x}_{ik})$$

Let δ be the Kronecker delta, h and i the indices of two groups and

$$d_{hi} = \frac{1}{n_h} \delta_{hi} + \sum_k \sum_\ell (\bar{x}_k - \bar{x}_{kh}) w^{k\ell} (\bar{x}_\ell - \bar{x}_{\ell i})$$

The correlations of the adjusted group means are given by

$$\hat{corr}(\hat{\mu}_h, \hat{\mu}_i) = d_{hi}/(d_{hh} d_{ii})^{\frac{1}{2}}$$

and the estimates of their standard deviations are given by

$$\hat{s}.d. (\hat{\mu}_i) = \hat{\sigma} \sqrt{d_{ii}}$$

Pairwise t statistics for equality of adjusted group means are given by

$$t_{hi} = (\hat{\mu}_h - \hat{\mu}_i)/\hat{\sigma} (d_{hh} + d_{ii} - 2d_{hi})^{\frac{1}{2}}$$

Let $c_1,\dots,c_g$ denote a set of t test contrast coefficients. An estimate of the corresponding contrast is given by

$$\hat{\gamma} = \sum_{i=1}^{g} c_i \hat{\mu}_i$$

An estimate of its standard deviation is given by

$$\hat{s}.d. (\hat{\gamma}) = \hat{\sigma} \left(\sum_{h=1}^{g} \sum_{i=1}^{g} c_h d_{hi} c_i \right)^{\frac{1}{2}}$$

Let $\tilde{w}_{p+1,p+1}$ denote the value of the $(p+1)$st diagonal element of the $(p+1)$ x $(p+1)$ matrix $(w_{k k})$ which results from performing Gauss-Jordan pivots on the first p diagonal elements. Define $\tilde{w}_{i,p+1,p+1}$ and $\tilde{a}_{p+1,p+1}$ in the same way. The analysis of variance table is

Source	df	Sum of Sq.	Mean Sq.	F-value
Eq. of adj. group means	df_1	SS_1	SS_1/df_1	MS_1/MS_3
Zero slopes	df_2	SS_2	SS_2/df_2	MS_2/MS_3
Error	df_3	SS_3	SS_3/df_3	
Eq. of slopes	df_4	SS_4	SS_4/df_4	MS_4/MS_5
Error	df_5	SS_5	SS_5/df_5	

where

$$df_1 = g-1 \qquad SS_1 = \tilde{a}_{p+1,p+1} - \tilde{w}_{p+1,p+1}$$

$$df_2 = p \qquad SS_2 = \sum_{k=1}^{p} \hat{\beta}_k w_{k,p+1}$$

$$df_3 = n-g-p \qquad SS_3 = \tilde{w}_{p+1,p+1}$$

$$df_4 = df_3 - df_5 \qquad SS_4 = \tilde{w}_{p+1,p+1} - \sum_i \tilde{w}_{i,p+1,p+1}$$

$$df_5 = \sum (n_i-p-1) \qquad SS_5 = \sum_i \tilde{w}_{i,p+1,p+1}$$

The analysis of variance table for one-way analysis of variance consists of the first and third lines of the above table. The equality of slopes test is not performed if the within cross product of deviations for covariates

$$[(w_{k\ell i}) \quad k,\ell=1,\dots,p]$$

for any group i, is singular.

A.18 Analysis of Variance and Covariance, Including Repeated Measures (P2V)

We consider the case of several group factors, $g_1,\ldots,g_a$, and several trial factors $t_1,\ldots,t_b$. Let y_{st} be the response of subject s to trial combination $t = (t_1,\ldots,t_b)$. Similarly let x_{stv} be the vth covariate value for subject s on trial combination t; and for ease of exposition, let

$$x_{s,t,p+1} = y_{st}$$

It is assumed that the response and the covariates have been measured for each subject on each trial combination, although the covariates may be constant across some or all trials. The outline below is explained in the steps that follow.

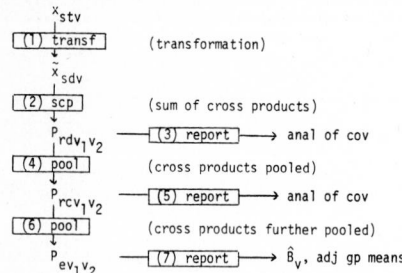

Step 1

For each subject s and variable v, the values x_{stv} across trials are transformed into orthogonal polynomial components $\tilde{x}_{sdv}$. Here, $d = (d_1,\ldots,d_b)$ denotes a degree combination. Specifically

$$\tilde{x}_{sdv} = \Sigma_{t_1} \cdots \Sigma_{t_b} \; \pi_{d_1 t_1} \cdots \pi_{d_b t_b} \; x_{stv}$$

where

$$\pi_{d_j t_j} = \text{the value of the orthogonal polynomial of degree } d_j \text{ at } t_j$$

Each trial factor t_j is assumed to range over equally spaced points unless otherwise specified by a POINT statement.

Step 2

For each degree combination d, an analysis of covariance is performed on the data $\tilde{x}_{sdv}$ producing a sum of cross products $P_{rdv_1v_2}$ for each pair of variables x_{v_1} and x_{v_2} and each analysis of variance component r defined by the group factors $g_1,\ldots,g_a$. This step and the next are described in greater detail below.

Step 3

The sums of cross products $P_{rdv_1v_2}$ are used to produce a standard analysis of covariance for each degree d.

Step 4

The cross products $P_{rdv_1v_2}$ are pooled over all degree combinations $d = (d_1,\ldots,d_b)$ that belong to the same analysis of variance component c defined by the trial factors $t_1,\ldots,t_b$. For this purpose, c may be represented by a list of zeros and ones so that

$$c = (0,1,0,1)$$

represents a $t_2 \times t_4$ interaction. With this convention

$$P_{rcv_1v_2} = \sum_{d\in c} P_{rdv_1v_2}$$

where $d\in c$ whenever $d = (d_1,\ldots,d_b)$ and $c = (c_1,\ldots,c_b)$ have exactly the same zeros.

Step 5

For each analysis of variance component c defined by the trial factors, the pooled cross products $P_{rcv_1v_2}$ are used to produce a standard analysis of covariance.

Step 6

Let e denote the error component defined by the group effects. The pooled cross products $P_{ecv_1v_2}$ are further pooled across the trial components c. This pooling is weighted by the reciprocals of the error mean squares MS_{ec} reported in the previous step. To be more specific, the pooled cross products are given by

$$P_{ev_1v_2} = \Sigma_c \; MS_{ec}^{-1} \; P_{ecv_1v_2}$$

Step 7

Let $\tilde{P}_{ev_1v_2}$ denote the result of performing pivots on the first p diagonal elements of $P_{ev_1v_2}$ (Jennrich and Sampson, 1968). Then

$$\hat{\beta}_v = \tilde{P}_{e,v,p+1}$$

are the pooled regression coefficient estimates that are used to compute the adjusted group means

$$\bar{y}^*_{gt} = \bar{y}_{gt} + \sum_{v=1}^{p} \hat{\beta}_v(\bar{x}_v - \bar{x}_{gtv})$$

for each group combination $g = (g_1,\ldots,g_a)$ and trial combination $t = (t_1,\ldots,t_b)$. Here $\bar{x}_{gtv}$ and $\bar{y}_{gt}$ denote the average of x_{stv} and y_{st} over all subjects s in group combination g; and $\bar{x}_v$ denotes the average of x_{stv} over all subjects s and trial combinations t.

Step 8

Using the regression coefficient estimates

$$\hat{\beta}_{cv} = P_{e,c,v,p+1}$$

obtained after pivoting in Step 5 and the analysis of variance component residuals x^*_{sdv} obtained by subtracting the group effects from the results $\tilde{x}_{sdv}$ of Step 1, the transformed residuals

$$\tilde{e}_{sd} = x^*_{s,d,p+1} - \sum_{v=1}^{p} x^*_{sdv}\hat{\beta}_{cv}$$

are computed for each subject s and degree combination d. Thus for each value of d, c is chosen so $d\in c$. The transformed fits are

$$\tilde{v}_{sd} = \tilde{y}_{sd} - \tilde{e}_{sd}$$

To obtain the untransformed fits and residuals, extend the definition of $\pi_{d_j t_j}$ so that it equals $\pi_{d_j 1}$ whenever $t_j=0$ and let

$$\pi_{dt} = \pi_{d_1 t_1} \; \pi_{d_2 t_2} \cdots \pi_{d_b t_b}.$$

Then the untransformed fits and residuals are given by

$$\hat{v}_{st} = \sum_{d\in t} \pi_{dt} \; \tilde{v}_{sd}$$

$$\hat{e}_{st} = \sum_{d\in t} \pi_{dt} \; \tilde{e}_{sd}$$

where $d\in t$ means that d has exactly the same zeros as t (as in Step 4).

COVARIANCE ANALYSIS

As indicated in the previous section, the core computations are covariance analyses; many of them are executed, and all of them are similar in form. Although the covariance analyses are applied to transformed data, there is no need to make that distinction here, nor do the trial indices need to appear, because the analyses are applied only across groups. Accordingly, let

$$g_1,\ldots,g_a, \; x_1,\ldots,x_p, \; x_{p+1}$$

denote the group factors and variables. As above, $y = x_{p+1}$ is the dependent variable. The fitted model form is

$$y = \mu_{r_1} +\ldots+ \mu_{r_q} + \beta_1 x_1 +\ldots+ \beta_p x_p + e$$

where $r_1,\ldots,r_q$ are all possible subsets of the factors $g_1,\ldots,g_a$ unless otherwise specified by an INCLUDE or EXCLUDE statement. A typical r_j has the form $r_j = (g_{i_1},\ldots,g_{i_k})$. For each factor g_i in r_j, the component

$$\mu_{r_j} = \mu_{g_{i_1}\cdots g_{i_k}}$$

is assumed to sum to zero over all values of g_i corresponding to fixed values of all the other g_i in r_j.

SUMS OF CROSS PRODUCTS (SCP)

This corresponds to Step 2 above. For each $v_1,v_2 = 1,\ldots,p+1$ and each $r = r_1,\ldots,r_q$, the residual cross products $P_{rv_1v_2}$ for the residuals in x_{v_1} and x_{v_2} after fitting all components $\mu_{r_1},\ldots,\mu_{r_q}$ except μ_r are obtained together with the residual cross products $P_{ev_1v_2}$ after fitting all components $\mu_{r_1},\ldots,\mu_{r_q}$. This is done by linear regression after generating the appropriate dummy variables to represent each component $\mu_{r_1},\ldots,\mu_{r_q}$. To simplify the analysis, it is assumed that the observed levels of the grouping factors are sufficient to uniquely define the components $\mu_{r_1},\ldots,\mu_{r_q}$. The computation proceeds by computing all cross products for all variables and dummy variables across all subjects. The residual cross products $P_{rv_1v_2}$ are obtained by means of pivots on the appropriate diagonal elements of this large cross product matrix.

Cross products are computed in single precision after means have been subtracted.

REPORT

This corresponds to Steps 3, 5 and 7 above. For each $r = r_1,\ldots,r_q$, view $P_{rv_1v_2}$ as a $(p+1) \times (p+1)$ matrix and let $\tilde{P}_{rv_1v_2}$ be the result of pivoting on the first p diagonal elements of $P_{rv_1v_2}$. If it is not possible to do this without encountering a diagonal zero (which can happen when the original covariates in the General Procedure are constant across trials) as many pivots as possible are performed. The pivoted cross products $\tilde{P}_{rv_1v_2}$ are used to report an analysis of covariance.

The error sums of squares

$$SS_e = \tilde{P}_{e,p+1,p+1}$$

has degrees of freedom

$$df_e = n - m - p'$$

where

n = total number of subjects times the number of orthogonal polynomials (degree combinations d) that are pooled for the covariance analysis
m = total number of dummy variables generated above
p' = number of covariates for which it was possible to perform the pivots in the previous paragraph

The sum of squares due to the analysis of variance component μ_r, $r = r_1,\ldots,r_q$, is

$$SS_r = \tilde{P}_{r,p+1,p+1} - SS_e$$

and has degrees of freedom df_r equal to the number of dummy variables required to represent μ_r. For each covariate x_v which was not eliminated because it corresponds to a diagonal zero, the sum of squares is

$$SS_{x_v} = \left(\tilde{P}_{e,v,p+1}\right)^2 / |P_{evv}|$$

and has one degree of freedom $df_{x_v} = 1$. Let $r = r_1,\ldots,r_q$, e, or any non-eliminated covariate $x_1,\ldots,x_p$. The mean square for the analysis of covariance component r is

$$MS_r = SS_r/df_r$$

and the F statistic for the corresponding hypothesis is

$$F_r = MS_r/MS_e$$

A.19 General Mixed Model Analysis of Variance (P3V)

The basic procedure is that described by Jennrich and Sampson (1976) although a slightly different parameterization is used here. Examples given in the text (Section 15.3) may help to clarify the points of major interest to the user.

The general model is the same as that treated by Hartley and Rao (1967), Rao (1972), Hemmerle and Hartley (1973) and Harville (1977).

$$y = X\alpha + U_1 b_1 + \ldots + U_c b_c + e$$

where

X   is an n by p matrix of known values
α is a p vector of unknown parameters
U_i is an n by q_i matrix of known values
b_i is a q_i vector of random values from $N(0,\sigma_i^2)$, and
e   is an n vector of random values from $N(0,\sigma^2)$.

The random vectors $b_1,\ldots,b_c$ and e are assumed independent. The parameters $\sigma_1^2,\ldots,\sigma_c^2,\sigma_e^2$ are called "variance components" and similarly the components $\alpha_1,\ldots,\alpha_p$ of α are called "mean components".

The first column of X is a one vector; the next columns of X are dummy variables, if any, generated according to the specified design; and the last columns are covariates provided explicitly by the user. If I is a grouping variable the specification

FIX = I.

in the *DESIGN* paragraph will generate $\ell-1$ dummy variables

$$x_i^{(r)} = \delta_{ir} - \delta_{i\ell}; \qquad r=1,\ldots,\ell-1.$$

where i denotes an arbitrary value (level) of I, ℓ is the total number of levels of I, and δ_{ir} denotes the Kroneker delta. If J is another grouping variable with m levels the specification

FIX = I,J.

will generate $(\ell-1)(m-1)$ dummy variables

$$x_{ij}^{(r,s)} = x_i^{(r)} x_j^{(s)}; \qquad r=1,\ldots,\ell-1; \qquad s=1,\ldots,m-1$$

where i and j denote arbitrary values of I and J. This provides a mechanism for parameterizing main effects and interactions for the fixed effects. A

third order interaction would take the form

FIX = I,J,K.

Similarly the columns of the matrices U_k are dummy variables generated under user specification. If I is a grouping variable the specification

RAND = I.

will generate ℓ dummy variables

$$\mu_i^{(r)} = \delta_{ir}; \qquad r=1,\ldots,\ell.$$

where ℓ is the number of levels of I. If J is another grouping variable with m levels, the specification

RAND = I,J.

will generate ℓm variables

$$\mu_{ij}^{(r,s)} = \delta_{ir}\delta_{js}; \qquad r=1,\ldots,\ell; \qquad s=1,\ldots,m.$$

Each specification RAND = "something" defines a matrix U_k and corresponding variance component σ_k^2. There need be no variance components other than σ^2. When this is the case the problem becomes a simple fixed effects general linear hypothesis problem.

Turning to the estimation procedure, let

$$\theta = (\alpha_1,\ldots,\alpha_p,\sigma_1^2,\ldots,\sigma_c^2,\sigma^2)$$

denote the complete parameter vector and let $\lambda(\theta)$ denote the corresponding log-likelihood of y. The estimation procedure is based on a combination Fisher-scoring and Newton-Raphson algorithm. The first step is a scoring step

$$\Delta\theta = -\mathcal{J}^{-1}(\theta)s(\theta).$$

Here $s(\theta) = d\lambda/d\theta$ is the Fisher score vector and $\mathcal{J}(\theta) = \text{cov}_\theta s(\theta)$ is the corresponding information matrix. Scoring steps are continued until $\Delta\lambda < 1$ at which point Newton-Raphson steps

$$\Delta\theta = -\left(\frac{d^2\lambda}{d\theta d\theta}\right)^{-1} s(\theta)$$

begin. Boundary constraints

$$\sigma_e^2 \geq 0; \quad \sigma_k^2 \geq 0; \qquad k=1,\ldots,c$$

and singularity problems are handled by partial sweeping strategies similar to those employed in P3R (Appendix A.15). The assumed initial values for the parameters are

$$\sigma_e^2 = s^2; \quad \alpha_k = \sigma_\ell^2 = 0; \quad k = 1,\ldots,p; \quad \ell = 1,\ldots,c$$

where s^2 is the sample variance of y. A considerable effort is devoted to making the number of computations required per iteration depend only on the number of levels of the fixed and random effects (except e) rather than on total sample size n (Hemmerle and Hartley, 1973).

Standard errors for the maximum likelihood estimates $\hat{\alpha}_1,\ldots,\hat{\alpha}_p,\hat{\sigma}_1^2,\ldots,\hat{\sigma}_c^2$, and $\hat{\sigma}^2$ are obtained from the appropriate diagonal elements of $\mathcal{J}^{-1}(\hat{\theta})$. Maximum likelihood estimates for the expected values $\mu_1,\ldots,\mu_n$ of the observations $y_1,\ldots,y_n$, namely

$$\hat{\mu} = X\hat{\alpha}$$

are computed together with the fitted residuals

$$\hat{e} = y - \hat{\mu}.$$

The standard errors for $\hat{\mu}_1,\ldots,\hat{\mu}_n$ are obtained from the appropriate diagonal elements of

$$\hat{\text{cov}} \, \hat{\mu} = X \, \hat{\text{cov}} \, \hat{\alpha} \, X'$$

where $\hat{\text{cov}} \, \hat{\alpha}$ is the appropriate submatrix of $\mathcal{J}^{-1}(\hat{\theta})$.

An estimate of the common standard deviation of the observations y_i is obtained from

$$\hat{\text{var}} \, y_i = \hat{\sigma}_1^2 + \ldots + \hat{\sigma}_c^2 + \hat{\sigma}^2.$$

Finally, estimates of the standard errors of the fitted residuals $\hat{e}_1,\ldots,\hat{e}_n$ are obtained from

$$\hat{\text{var}} \, \hat{e}_i = \hat{\text{var}} \, y_i - \hat{\text{var}} \, \mu_i$$

These estimates and standard errors are printed for each case together with the standardized residuals $\hat{e}_i/\text{std} \, \hat{e}_i$.

For each combination of values of the grouping variables, say I and J, a predicted (adjusted) cell mean

$$\mu_{ij}^* = x_{ij} \, \hat{\alpha}_1 + \bar{x} \, \hat{\alpha}_2$$

is computed. Here x_{ij} denotes the dummy variable values from X corresponding to any pair of values of I and J, $\bar{x}$ denotes the mean vector over all cases for all of the covariates in X, and $\hat{\alpha}_1$ and $\hat{\alpha}_2$ correspond to the fixed effects estimates and coefficients of the covariates respectively. Letting C denote the matrix with rows $(x_{ij},\bar{x})$, standard errors for the μ_{ij}^* are obtained from the appropriate diagonal elements of

$$\hat{\text{cov}} \, \mu^* = C \, \hat{\text{cov}} \, \hat{\alpha} \, C'.$$

The elements of this matrix are also used to construct pairwise tests

$$(\mu_{ij}^* - \mu_{i'j'}^*) / \text{std}(\mu_{ij}^* - \mu_{i'j'}^*)$$

for the equality of pairs of adjusted cell means.

Finally a specification such as

FIX = 2.

in an *HYPOThesis* paragraph will produce a likelihood ratio test of the hypothesis that the second set of fixed components specified in the *DESIGN* paragraph is zero. If, for example, the second specification in the *DESIGN* paragraph had been FIX = I,J a test for zero interaction would be obtained. A specification such as

RAND = 3.

in an *HYPOThesis* paragraph will give a likelihood ratio test for $\sigma_3^2 = 0$, where σ_3^2 is the third variance component defined in the *DESIGN* paragraph. These tests are obtained by fitting the appropriate restricted models and subtracting log-likelihoods. Degrees of freedom are differences of the numbers of parameters fitted.

RESTRICTED MAXIMUM LIKELIHOOD ESTIMATION (REML)

Restricted maximum likelihood estimates are computed in two stages. First the variance components $\gamma = (\sigma_1^2, \ldots, \sigma_e^2, \sigma_e^2)$ are estimated by maximizing the likelihood of the least squares residuals y.X obtained from the regression of y on X. This likelihood does not depend on the mean components α, which are estimated by maximizing the likelihhod of y with respect to α, holding the variance components γ fixed at the values $\hat{\gamma}$ obtained in the first stage. The required estimates of cov $\hat{\alpha}$ and cov $\hat{\gamma}$ are obtained from the inverses of the appropriate information matrices $\mathcal{J}(\hat{\alpha})$ and $\mathcal{J}(\hat{\gamma})$ evaluated at the REML estimates $\hat{\alpha}$ and $\hat{\gamma}$. All these are obtained by means of a minor modification of the unrestricted algorithm. Likelihood ratio χ^2 statistics are obtained by subtracting the log-likelihoods of y evaluated at the appropriate REML estimates.

A.20 General Univariate and Multivariate Analysis of Variance and Covariance (P4V)

There are three major segments of computations in BMDP4V. They are:

- reading and preliminary processing of the input data
- calculation of the D-matrices for the design in response to user or program generated design specifications
- calculation of parameter estimates and test statistics

We describe here some basic points of the computations. A detailed description of the computations for BMDP4V is in BMDP Technical Report #67. All computations are performed using double precision arithmetic.

Reading and Accumulation of Data

The data are read following specification of the between and within cell structure. The data is reduced to a vector of group sizes n_i, $i=1,\ldots,m$, and two matrices. The matrix $M(m \times \ell)$ contains means for the cells of the design with m groups and ℓ variables (cells of the within design). The matrix E $(\ell \times \ell)$ contains the within-groups sums of squares and cross products among the ℓ variables. The accumulation of M and E is performed using a provisional means method.

Eigenvalues and Eigenvectors of a Symmetric Matrix

Eigenvalues and eigenvectors are obtained using adapted versions of the EISPACK subroutines TRED3, TQL2 and TRBAK3. TRED3 reduces the matrix to tridiagonal form. TQL2 extracts the eigenvalues and TRBAK3 calculates the eigenvectors (when required). The reported rank is the number of eigenvalues non-zero to within numerical accuracy.

Inversion of a Symmetric Matrix

Inversion of a matrix is first attempted by sweeping the lower triangular matrix under control of complete tolerance checking (see Appendix A.11). If less than full rank is detected, the pseudoinverse $A^+ = P \Lambda^{-1} P'$ is computed, where Λ^{-1} is a diagonal matrix having the reciprocals of the non-zero eigenvalues on the diagonal and P is the corresponding eigenvector.

Orthogonalization

Given matrices X $(n \times k)$ and Y $(n \times \ell)$ and a vector W $(n \times 1)$ of weights we orthogonalize Y to X with respect to W by computing $Z = Y - X(X'WX)^{-} X'WY$, where W is a diagonal matrix with W on the diagonal.

Parameter Estimates and Test Statistics

Complete details of the computations for the analysis phase of BMDP4V are given in BMDP Technical Report #67.

Numerical Accuracy Monitoring

Virtually all computations in BMDP4V are accompanied by estimates of the degree of accuracy of the computations. This constant accuracy monitoring is important for two major reasons. First, at any point in the computations when a decision as to rank is required, the information necessary is readily available. Secondly, when numerical accuracy breaks down due to degeneracies in the problem as internally represented, the program is able to print messages accompanying any statistic any of whose printed digits are numerically in doubt. Complete details on accuracy monitoring can be found in Technical Report #67 and in Davidson (1979).

A.21 Maximum Likelihood Factor Analysis (P4M)

Maximum likelihood factor analysis is discussed by Lawley and Maxwell (1971). The algorithm used here was developed by R.I. Jennrich and P.F. Sampson at the Health Sciences Computing Facility, UCLA.

Let R be the sample correlation matrix. The normal theory maximum likelihood estimates are computed for the factor loading matrix Λ and the unique standard deviation matrix Ψ (square roots of one minus the communality for each variable) in the factor analytic decomposition

$$\Sigma = \Lambda \Lambda' + \Psi^2$$

where Σ is the population correlation matrix. (Maximum likelihood factor analysis is scale free so it does not matter whether the correlation or covariance matrix is used.) Here Ψ is diagonal and the loadings Λ are canonical (Rao, 1955).

The program uses a Newton-Raphson iteration

$$\Delta\Psi = -(f''_{ij})^{-1}(f'_i)$$

to minimize a function f of Ψ which is a negative slope affine transformation of the conditional maximum of the likelihood for the sample given Ψ (cf. Jennrich and Robinson, 1969; Clarke, 1970; Jöreskog and van Thillo, 1971).

In terms of the eigenvalues

$$\gamma_1 \leq \gamma_2 \leq \cdots \leq \gamma_p$$

and vectors

$$w_1, \ldots, w_p$$

of $\Psi R^{-1} \Psi$, the function

$$f = \sum_{m=k+1}^{p} (\log \gamma_m + \gamma_m^{-1} - 1)$$

where k is the number of factors and p the number of variables.

The required derivatives $f'_i = \partial f / \partial \Psi_i$ and $f''_{ij} = \partial^2 f / \partial \Psi_i \partial \Psi_j$ are given by

$$f'_i = \sum_{m=k+1}^{p} (1 - \gamma_m^{-1}) w_{im}^2$$

and

$$f''_{ij} = \sum_{m=k+1}^{p} \nu_{im} \nu_{jm} \sum_{n=1}^{k} \frac{\gamma_m + \gamma_n - 2}{\gamma_m - \gamma_n} w_{in} w_{jn} + \frac{1}{2} \delta_{ij} \sum_{m=k+1}^{p} (3\gamma_m^{-1} - 1) \nu_{im}^2$$

where

$$-\nu_m = 2\gamma_m^{-1} R^{-1} \Psi w_m$$

If, as frequently occurs during the initial steps, (f''_{ij}) is not positive definite, it is replaced by a matrix of approximate second order derivatives

$$f''_{ij} = (\sum_{m=k+1}^{p} \nu_{im} \nu_{jm})(\sum_{m=k+1}^{p} w_{im} w_{jm})$$

If the value of f is not decreased by the step $\Delta\Psi$, the step is halved (i.e., $\Delta\Psi$ is replaced by $\frac{1}{2} \Delta\Psi$) and halved again until the value of f decreases or ten halvings fail to produce a decrease. Stepping continues until all values of $\Delta\Psi_i$ are less than the convergence criterion or the number of steps equals its prescribed maximum.

Using the converged value of Ψ, the eigenvalue problem

$$\Psi^2 \nu_m = \gamma_m R^{-1} \nu_m, \qquad m = 1, \ldots, p$$

is solved and the estimated columns of Λ are computed using

$$u_m = \rho_m R^{-\frac{1}{2}} \nu_m, \qquad m = 1, \ldots, k$$

where $\rho_m = (1 - \gamma_m)^{\frac{1}{2}}$ is the estimated canonical correlation. The advantage of this parameterization is that it converges smoothly even in Heywood cases -- when some of the diagonal components of Ψ are zero.

Eigenvalues and eigenvectors are obtained using routines from the EISPACK system (Garbow et al, 1977, and Smith et al, 1974).

A.22 Canonical Analysis (P6M)

The covariance matrix is computed by the method of provisional means (Appendix A.2). If computations with means assumed to be zero are desired, the products of the means are added back into the covariance matrix and means are set to zero.

The covariance matrix is converted to a correlation matrix and all computations are then made in terms of standardized variables (mean zero, standard deviation one).

Denote the correlation matrix by

$$R = \begin{pmatrix} R_{XX} & R_{XY} \\ R_{YX} & R_{YY} \end{pmatrix}$$

where X denotes the smaller of the two sets of variables. R is stored as a triangular matrix (R is symmetric so only the lower half need be used).

The matrix

$$\begin{pmatrix} 0 & R_{XY} \\ R_{YX} & R_{YY} \end{pmatrix}$$

is pivoted on each of the Y variables to obtain

$$\begin{pmatrix} -R_{XY}R_{YY}^{-1}R_{YX} & R_{XY}R_{YY}^{-1} \\ R_{YY}^{-1}R_{YX} & -R_{YY}^{-1} \end{pmatrix}$$

Pivoting is performed in a stepwise manner such that no variable is pivoted whose squared multiple correlation with previously pivoted variables exceeds 1 - TOL, where TOL is specified in the *CANONical* paragraph. TOL thus determines the effective rank of the set of Y variables. Rows and columns corresponding to nonpivoted variables are set to zero.

The eigenvalue-eigenvector problem

$$R_{XY}R_{YY}^{-1}R_{YX}\beta = \lambda R_{XX}\beta$$

is then solved for the eigenvalues $\lambda_1 > \lambda_2 > \ldots > \lambda_m > 0$ where m is the smaller of the effective ranks of the two sets of variables; the corresponding eigenvectors are $\beta_1,\ldots,\beta_m$. This eigenvector-eigenvalue problem is solved in three stages. First, the problem is transformed to the problem

$$R_{XX}^{-\frac{1}{2}}R_{XY}R_{YY}^{-1}R_{YX}(R_{XX}^{-\frac{1}{2}})'\beta^* = \lambda \beta^*$$

$R_{XX}^{-\frac{1}{2}}$ is obtained by stepwise pivoting in such a way that no variable is pivoted whose squared multiple correlation with previously pivoted variables exceeds 1 - TOL. Rows and columns corresponding to nonpivoted variables are set equal to zero. Next, eigenvalues and eigenvectors are obtained for the transformed problem. Eigenvalues and eigenvectors are obtained using routines from the EISPACK system (Garbow et al, 1977, and Smith et al, 1974). The eigenvectors are normalized so that $\beta_i^{*'}\beta_i^{*} = 1$. Lastly, β is obtained as

$$\left(R_{XX}^{-\frac{1}{2}}\right)' \beta^* .$$

Canonical correlations are the square roots of the eigenvalues

$$\rho_i = \sqrt{\lambda_i} \qquad i = 1,\ldots,m$$

The coefficients for the canonical variables for the set of X variables are the eigenvectors β_i

$$B_X = (\beta_1,\ldots,\beta_m)$$

The coefficients for the canonical variables for the set of Y variables are obtained by dividing the eigenvectors by their corresponding canonical correlations and then multiplying by $R_{YY}^{-1}R_{YX}$

$$B_Y = R_{YY}^{-1}R_{YX}(\beta_1/\rho_1,\ldots,\beta_m/\rho_m)$$

Canonical variable scores for each case are obtained by multiplying the standard scores for the original variables by the canonical variable coefficients

$$\begin{pmatrix} v_X \\ v_Y \end{pmatrix} = \begin{pmatrix} B_X \\ B_Y \end{pmatrix} Z$$

where Z denotes the standard scores for the case.

Canonical variable loadings are the correlations of the original variables with the canonical variables. They are also the regression coefficients for predicting the standardized variables from the canonical variables. As such they may be of value in semantically interpreting the canonical variables. These loadings are analogous to unrotated factor loadings.

Loadings for X variables on canonical X variables are obtained by multiplying the canonical X variable coefficients by R_{XX}

$$A_{XX} = B_X R_{XX}$$

Loadings for Y variables on canonical Y variables are obtained by multiplying the canonical Y variable coefficients by R_{YY}

$$A_{YY} = B_Y R_{YY}$$

A.23 Stepwise Discriminant Analysis (P7M)

The following notations will be used:

p = number of variables available

q = number of variables entered at a given step

t = total number of groups

g = number of groups used to define the discriminant functions

n_i = number of cases in group i

n = total number of cases in the g defining groups

x_{ijr} = value of variable r in case j of group i

h = number of hypotheses (contrasts)

h_{ki} = coefficient for group i in hypothesis k

p_i = prior probability for group i

Assume for simplicity that the first g of the t groups are used to define the classification functions.

Step 1

The data are read and the method of provisional means (Appendix A.2) is used to compute the group means

$$\bar{x}_{ir} = \sum_{j=1}^{n_i} x_{ijr}/n_i \qquad \begin{matrix} i = 1,\ldots,t \\ r = 1,\ldots,p \end{matrix}$$

group standard deviations

$$s_{ir} = \left(\sum_{j=1}^{n_i} (x_{ijr} - \bar{x}_{ir})^2/(n_i-1) \right)^{\frac{1}{2}} \qquad \begin{matrix} i = 1,\ldots,t \\ r = 1,\ldots,p \end{matrix}$$

and pooled within groups sums of cross-product deviations

$$w_{rs} = \sum_{i=1}^{g} \sum_{j=1}^{n_i} (x_{ijr} - \bar{x}_{ir})(x_{ijs} - \bar{x}_{is}) \qquad \begin{matrix} r = 1,\ldots,p \\ s = 1,\ldots,p \end{matrix}$$

The latter are used to compute the within group correlations

$$r_{ij} = w_{ij}/(w_{ii}w_{jj})^{\frac{1}{2}} \qquad \begin{matrix} i = 1,\ldots,p \\ j = 1,\ldots,p \end{matrix}$$

Step 2

Let $H = (h_{ki})$ be the h by g matrix of hypothesis contrasts. If no contrasts are specified, h is set to g-1 and

$$h_{ki} = \begin{cases} 1 & i \le k \\ -k & i = k + 1 \\ 0 & \text{otherwise} \end{cases}$$

These contrasts test the equality of all g group means.

The stepwise procedure is defined in terms of the matrices

$$W = (w_{rs})$$

and

$$M = W + \bar{X}'H'(HN^{-1}H')^{-1}H\bar{X}$$

where $\bar{X} = (\bar{x}_{ir})$ is a g x p, and N is the diagonal matrix $\lceil n_1,\ldots,n_g \rfloor$ of group sizes. The entry and removal of variables is defined in terms of the results of sweeping on the diagonal elements of W and M (the computations themselves proceed somewhat more efficiently).

Assuming for simplicity that the first q variables have already been swept, write

$$W = \begin{bmatrix} W_{11} & W_{12} \\ W_{21} & W_{22} \end{bmatrix} \qquad M = \begin{bmatrix} M_{11} & M_{12} \\ M_{21} & M_{22} \end{bmatrix}$$

where W_{11} and M_{11} are q x q. At each step let

$$A = \begin{bmatrix} -W_{11}^{-1} & W_{11}^{-1}W_{12} \\ W_{21}W_{11}^{-1} & W_{22}-W_{21}W_{11}^{-1}W_{12} \end{bmatrix}$$

$$B = \begin{bmatrix} -M_{11}^{-1} & M_{11}^{-1}M_{12} \\ M_{21}M_{11}^{-1} & M_{22}-M_{21}M_{11}^{-1}M_{12} \end{bmatrix}$$

B is not actually computed, since only the diagonal elements are needed. These diagonal elements are computed from the matrix

$$\begin{bmatrix} A & T \\ T' & C \end{bmatrix}$$

which is defined at step zero to be

$$\begin{bmatrix} W & \overline{X} \\ \overline{X}' & 0 \end{bmatrix}$$

and is updated at each step by sweeping or reverse sweeping the diagonal elements of A. The diagonal elements of B are computed using the fact that

$$B = Q'Q + A$$

where

$$Q = (H(N^{-1} - C)H')^{-\frac{1}{2}} H'T'.$$

The following statistics are computed at each step

(a) F values for testing differences between each pair of groups:

$$F_{ij} = \frac{(n - g - q + 1)n_i n_j}{q(n_i + n_j)} \; D_{ij}^2/(n-g) \qquad\qquad i,j = 1,\dots,g$$

where

$$D_{ij}^2 = (n-g)(\overline{X}_i - \overline{X}_j)' \; W_{11}^{-1} \; (\overline{X}_i - \overline{X}_j)$$

is the (squared) Mahalanobis distance between groups i and j and where $\overline{X}_i$ is the vector of means for group i for the q variables that have been entered. D_{ij}^2 is computed as

$$(n-g)(2c_{ij} - c_{ii} - c_{jj})$$

(b) F values for each variable

If variable r has been entered

$$F_r = \frac{a_{rr} - b_{rr}}{b_{rr}} \cdot \frac{n - g - q + 1}{h}$$

with h and n - g - q + 1 degrees of freedom

If variable r has not been entered

$$F_r = \frac{b_{rr} - a_{rr}}{a_{rr}} \cdot \frac{n - g - q}{h}$$

with h and n - g - q degrees of freedom

(c) Wilks' Λ-statistic for the hypothesis defined by H

$$\Lambda = \det(W_{11})/\det(M_{11})$$

with (q, h, n - g) degrees of freedom. Λ is computed by initially setting it equal to one and updating it at each step by multiplying its previous value by a_{rr}/b_{rr} where r is the index of the variable entered or removed at the step.

(d) The F approximation to Λ (Rao, 1973, p. 556)

$$F = \frac{1 - \Lambda^{1/s}}{\Lambda^{1/s}} \cdot \frac{m*s + 1 - hq/2}{hq}$$

where
$$m* = n - g - \tfrac{1}{2}(q - h + 1)$$

$$s = \begin{cases} \left(\dfrac{h^2 q^2 - 4}{h^2 + q^2 - 5}\right)^{\frac{1}{2}} & h^2 + q^2 \neq 5 \\[2mm] 1 & h^2 + q^2 = 5 \end{cases}$$

The numbers of degrees of freedom for F are hq and (m*s+1 - hq/2). The approximation is exact if either h or q is 1 or 2.

(e) Tolerance values

$$t_r = a_{rr}/w_{rr} \qquad\qquad r = q + 1,\dots,p$$

Step 3

To move from one step to the next, a variable is removed or added according to the first of the following rules which applies.

Rule 1   If METHOD=1 is specified in the DISCriminant paragraph and one or more entered variables are available and have F values less than the F-to-remove threshold, the one with the smallest F value is removed.

Rule 2   If METHOD=2 is specified and one or more entered variables are available, the one with the smallest F value is removed if by its removal Wilks' Λ will be smaller than it was when the same number of variables were previously entered.

Rule 3   If one or more nonentered variables are available, with tolerance above the tolerance threshold and are either at a forced level or have F values above the F-to-enter threshold, the one with the highest F value is entered.

Variables in forced levels are available only if their level is equal to the working level, if they are not entered, and if they have tolerance above the tolerance threshold.

Variables in nonforced levels are considered available only if their level is less than or equal to the working level and, for nonentered variables, if their tolerance is above the tolerance threshold. (See Appendix A.11 for a discussion of tolerance.)

The working level begins at 1 and moves to the next level when none of the rules apply. If the specified maximum level has been reached, the specified maximum number of steps has been reached, or the specified maximum number of variables has been entered; the stepping terminates.

Step 4

When the stepping is complete, or when the number of variables entered is equal to one of the numbers indicated in the PRINT paragraph, the following are computed and printed except for (b) and (c) which are printed only when the stepping is complete:

(a) Group classification function coefficients, which are defined as

$$\hat{\beta}_i = (n - g) W_{11}^{-1} \overline{X}_i \qquad \text{(a q x 1 vector)} \qquad i = 1,\dots,g$$

and the corresponding constants

$$\hat{\alpha}_i = \log p_i - \tfrac{1}{2}(n - g) \overline{X}_i' W_{11}^{-1} \overline{X}_i \qquad\qquad i = 1,\dots,g$$

where

p_i is the prior probability for group i

Note that $W_{11}^{-1} \overline{X}_i$ is computed as a submatrix of T and $\overline{X}_i' W_{11}^{-1} \overline{X}_i = -c_{ii}$. (For additional discussion, see A.26, p. 840.)

(b) The squared Mahalanobis' distance of case j in group i from the mean of group k

$$D_{ijk}^2 = (n - g) \sum_{r=1}^{q} \sum_{s=1}^{q} (x_{ijr} - \overline{x}_{kr}) a_{rs} (x_{ijs} - \overline{x}_{ks}) \qquad \begin{array}{l} i = 1,\dots,t \\ j = 1,\dots,n_i \\ k = 1,\dots,g \end{array}$$

or if requested in the *PRINT* paragraph, the cross validation or jackknife distance, $*D_{ijk}^2$, obtained by withholding this case from all computations except the evaluation of the distance function.

The computing formulas are

$$D_{ijk}^2 = (n-g)e$$

$$*D_{ijk}^2 = (n - 1 - g)(e + a^2/b - \delta_{ik}/(n_i[n_i-1]))$$

where

$$e = f + 2(c_i - c_k) - c_{ii} + c_{kk}$$

$$a = \delta_{ik}/n_k + c_i - c_k - c_{ik} + c_{ii}$$

$$b = 1 - 1/n_i - f$$

δ_{ik} is the Kronecker delta

$c_k = X_{ij}' W_{11}^{-1} \overline{X}_k$ (where $W_{11}^{-1} \overline{X}_k$ has been computed as a submatrix of T)

$c_{ij} = -\overline{X}_i' W_{11}^{-1} \overline{X}_j$ (already computed in C)

$$f = \sum_{r=1}^{q} \sum_{s=1}^{q} (x_{ijr} - \overline{x}_{ir}) a_{rs} (x_{ijs} - \overline{x}_{is})$$

$$= (X_{ij} - \overline{X}_i)' W_{11}^{-1} (X_{ij} - \overline{X}_i)$$

$$X_{ij} = (x_{ij1},\dots,x_{ijq})'$$

(c) The posterior probability that case j from group i came from group k

$$p_{ijk} = p_k \exp(-\tfrac{1}{2}D_{ijk}^2) \Big/ \sum_{r=1}^{q} p_r \exp(-\tfrac{1}{2}D_{ijr}^2) \qquad \begin{array}{l} i = 1,\dots,t \\ j = 1,\dots,n_i \\ k = 1,\dots,g \end{array}$$

If *JACKKNIFE* is requested, the D's are replaced by *D's in the above formula. A classification matrix that gives the number of cases n_{ik} in group i whose posterior probability p_{ijk} was largest for group k is printed.

Step 5

The eigenvalue problem

$$H \overline{X} W_{11}^{-1} \overline{X}' H' u_i = H(-C)H' u_i = \lambda_i H N^{-1} H' u_i , \quad \text{where } \overline{X} \text{ is a g x q matrix of variable means for all groups}$$

680

is solved for eigenvalues $\lambda_1 \geq ... \geq \lambda_h$ and eigenvectors $u_1,...,u_h$ normalized so that

$$u_i' \, H \, N^{-1} H' u_i = 1$$

The coefficients $\hat{\gamma}_i$ of the ith canonical discriminant function defined by H are given by

$$\hat{\gamma}_i = W_{11}^{-1} \, \bar{x}' \, H' \, u_i \sqrt{\frac{n-q}{\lambda_i}} \qquad\qquad i = 1,...,h$$

If $h < q$ and if required, $q - h$ additional canonical functions will be computed corresponding to zero eigenvalues. For each $i = h+1,...,q$ in turn a random q-vector v_i is generated and orthogonalized by Gramm-Schmidt to $\hat{\gamma}_1,...,\hat{\gamma}_{i-1}$. Then

$$\hat{\gamma}_i = W_{11}^{-1} \, v_i / (v_i' \, W_{11}^{-1} \, v_i)^{\frac{1}{2}} \qquad\qquad i = h+1,...,q$$

The cumulative proportion of explained dispersion is computed as

$$v_i = \sum_{j=1}^{i} \lambda_j / \sum_{j=1}^{h} \lambda_j \qquad\qquad i = 1,...,h$$

The canonical variables (values of the canonical functions)

$$f_{ijr} = \sum_{s=1}^{q} \hat{\gamma}_{rs} (x_{ijs} - \bar{x}_s) \qquad\qquad \begin{array}{l} i = 1,...,t \\ j = 1,...,n_i \end{array}$$

for $r = 1,2$ are computed and plotted. All requested values of f_{ijr} are written on Save File.

The canonical correlations are computed from the eigenvalues as

$$\rho_i = \sqrt{\frac{\lambda_i}{1+\lambda_i}}$$

Eigenvalues and eigenvectors are computed using routines from the EISPACK system (Garbow et al, 1977, and Smith et al, 1974).

A.24   Using BMDP Programs from a Terminal

When Control Language instructions are submitted through a terminal, some systems automatically generate sequence numbers in columns 73-80 of each line of Control Language instructions. If there are digits in every column from column 73 through column 80, then columns 73 through 80 of all Control Language cards are ignored. Otherwise, sequence numbers can interfere with the interpretation of the instructions. If your BMDP programs are dated after August 1977, you can avoid this problem by stating the number of columns (characters) in each line that are to be read and interpreted. For example, if the sequence numbers begin in column 73, then state

/CONTROL   COLUMN=72.   /END

Both the CONTROL and END paragraphs should be stated in the first line and stated <u>before</u> any other Control Language instructions. Your other Control Language instructions (to describe the data, variables and analysis) begin in the next line.

```
CONTROL
  COLumn=#.                                              80/prev.
  Maximum number of characters per line that contain Control Language
  instructions.  Required only if the system automatically inserts a
  sequence number or other identification at the end of each line.

  The CONTROL paragraph followed by an END paragraph must be specified
  as the first line of Control Language instructions.
```

In addition, many (but not all) portions of the output can be adjusted in line width by specifying LINE = number of characters in the PRINT paragraph For additional information, see Section 4.4.

A.25   Missing Value Covariance Matrices (P8D)

The formulas for covariances and the correlations for CORPAIR, COVPAIR, and ALLVALUE are defined on page 211. The computing algorithm is quite different from the formulas and is given below.

Notation and definitions

x_{ij} - the value of the i-th variable at case j,

(Note: present = a value which is not missing and is inside stated range limits)

n_i - the number of values present for variable i,

$\sum^{n_i}$ - summation over cases where variable i is present,

$W_i = \sum^{n_i} w_j$

$\bar{x}_i = \sum^{n_i} w_j x_{ij} / W_i$

$V_i = \sum^{n_i} w_j (x_{ij} - \bar{x}_i)^2 \cdot (n_i / W_i) / (n_i - 1)$

n_{ik} - the number of cases where both variables i and k are present

$\sum^{n_{ik}}$ - summation over cases where variables i and k are both present

$W_{ik} = \sum^{n_{ik}} w_j$

$\bar{x}_{i(k)} = \sum^{n_{ik}} w_j x_{ij} / W_{ik}$

$V_{i(k)} = \sum^{n_{ik}} w_j (x_{ij} - \bar{x}_{i(k)})^2 \cdot (n_{ik} / W_{ik}) / (n_{ik} - 1)$

n - the number of cases without any missing values (complete cases)

$W = \sum^{n} w_j$

$\bar{x}_{i(complete)} = \sum^{n} w_j x_{ij} / W$

$V_{i(complete)} = \sum^{n} w_j (x_{ij} - \bar{x}_{i(complete)})^2 \cdot (n/w) / (n-1)$

$cov_{ik(complete)} = \sum^{n} w_j (x_{ij} - \bar{x}_{i(complete)})(x_{kj} - \bar{x}_{k(complete)}) \cdot (n/W) / (n-1)$

$cov_{ik(allvalue)} = \sum^{n_{ik}} w_j (x_{ij} - \bar{x}_i)(x_{kj} - \bar{x}_k) \cdot (n_{ik} / W_{ik}) / (n_{ik} - 1)$

$cov_{ik(covpair)} = \sum^{n_{ik}} w_j (x_{ij} - \bar{x}_{i(k)})(x_{kj} - \bar{x}_{k(i)}) \cdot (n_{ik} / W_{ik}) / (n_{ik} - 1)$

$cov_{ik(corpair)} = cov_{ij(covpair)} \left(\dfrac{V_{i(i)} \cdot V_{k(k)}}{V_{i(k)} \cdot V_{k(i)}} \right)^{\frac{1}{2}}$

$cor_{ik} = \dfrac{cov_{ik}}{(cov_{ii} \cdot cov_{jj})^{\frac{1}{2}}}$

Computational Steps

All computations are done in single precision arithmetic. The "two pass" algorithm is used in computing the cross product of deviation matrix. In pass 1 the mean and sum of squares of deviations of all existing values of each variable is computed. In pass 2 the cross products of deviations of all existing values are computed (the ALLVALUE method). The cross products of deviations are then adjusted to obtain covariance matrices.

Pass 1

(a) For each variable i the accumulators n_i, W_i, S_i and SS_i are initialized:

$$n_i = 0$$
$$W_i = 0$$
$$S_i = 0$$
$$SS_i = 0$$

(b) For each case j, if variable i exists then the following updates are made:

n_i is incremented by 1

W_i is incremented by w_j

S_i is incremented by $w_j \cdot x_{ij}$

SS_i is incremented by $(x_{ij}-S_i/W_i)w_j(x_{ij}-(S_i-w_jx_{ij})/(W_i-w_j))$

(c) After all the cases have been processed in step (b) the means $\overline{X}_i$ and variances V_i are computed:

$$\overline{X}_i = S_i/W_i$$

$$V_i = SS_i \cdot (n_i/W_i)/(n_i-1)$$

Pass 1 computations are done by subroutine P8DINP.

Pass 2A

This pass is used to compute the pairwise existing statistics if ALLVALUE, COVPAIR or CORPAIR covariance and/or correlation matrix are required.

(a) For each pair of variables i, k, the values n_{ik}, W_{ik}, $S_{i(k)}$, $SS_{i(k)}$ and C_{ik} are initialized:

$$n_{ik} = n_i$$

$$W_{ik} = W_i$$

$$S_{i(k)} = S_i$$

$$SS_{i(k)} = SS_i$$

$$C_{ik} = 0$$

(b) For each case j: if x_{ij} and x_{kj} exist then C_{ik} is incremented by $(x_{ij} - \overline{x}_i)w_j(x_{kj} - \overline{x}_k)$; if x_{ij} exists and x_{kj} is missing then

n_{ik} is decremented by 1

W_{ik} is decremented by w_j

$S_{i(k)}$ is decremented by w_jx_{ij}

$SS_{i(k)}$ is decremented by $w_j(x_{ij}-\overline{x}_i)^2$

(c) After all the cases have been processed in step (b) the means $\overline{X}_{i(k)}$ and variances $V_{i(k)}$ are computed:

$$\overline{X}_{i(k)} = S_{i(k)}/W_{ik}$$

$$V_{i(k)} = (SS_{i(k)} - W_{ik} \cdot (\overline{X}_{i(k)} - \overline{X}_i)^2) \cdot (n_{ik}/W_{ik})/(n_{ik}-1)$$

Pass 2A computations are done by subroutine WACRLM for lower triangular C_{ik} matrices, or by WACRRE for rectangular segments of C_{ik}.

Pass 2B

This pass is used if COMPLETE covariance and correlation matrices are required.

(a) The following accumulators are initialized:

$$n = 0$$

$$W = 0$$

$$SC_i = 0 \text{ for all values of } i$$

$$CC_{ik} = 0 \text{ for all values of } i \text{ and } k$$

(b) For each case j that contains no missing values the following updates are made:

n is incremented by 1
W is incremented by w_j
SC_i is incremented by w_jx_{ij} for all values of i
CC_{ik} is incremented by $(x_{ij} - \overline{x}_i)w_j(x_{kj} - \overline{x}_k)$ for all values of i and k

(c) After all cases have been processed by step (b) the means $\overline{X}_{i(complete)}$, $V_{i(complete)}$ and $COV_{ik(complete)}$ are computed:

$$\overline{X}_{i(complete)} = SC_i/W$$

$$V_{i(complete)} = (CC_{ii} - W(\overline{X}_{i(complete)} - \overline{X}_i)^2)(n/W)/(n-1)$$

$$COV_{ik(complete)} = (CC_{ik} - (\overline{X}_{i(complete)} - \overline{X}_i)W(\overline{X}_{k(complete)} - \overline{X}_k))(n/W)/(n-1)$$

Pass 2B computations are done by subroutine WCCALM for lower triangular $COV_{ik(complete)}$, or by WCCARE for rectangular segments of $COV_{ik(complete)}$.

T-test A

This part generates the t-test reports if ALLVALUE, COVPAIR, or CORPAIR type matrices, are requested. For each pair of variables i and k the following are printed:

(a) t-test (separate variance estimation)

$$\frac{\frac{S_i - S_{i(k)}}{W_i - W_{ik}} - \frac{S_{i(k)}}{W_{ik}}}{(SM + SE)^{\frac{1}{2}}}$$

where

$$SM = (SS_i - SS_{i(k)})/(W_i - W_{ik}) \cdot (n_i - n_{ik} - 1))$$

and

$$SE = SS_{i(k)}/(W_{ik} \cdot (n_{ik} - 1))$$

(b) Degree of freedom for t-test

$$\frac{1}{g^2/(n_i-n_{ik}-1) + (1-g^2)/(n_{ik}-1)}$$

where

$$g = SM/(SM+SE)$$

(c) F-ratio for variances:

$$SM/SE$$

(d) Number of times variable i exists and k does not and number of cases both variables exist:

$$(n_i - n_{ik}), \quad n_{ik}$$

T-test A computations are done by subroutine WMEFRE.

T-test B

This part generates the t-test reports if COMPLETE matrices are requested. For each variable i the following are printed:

(a) t-test (separate variance estimation):

$$\frac{\frac{S_i - SC_i}{W_i - W} - \frac{SC_i}{W}}{(SM + SE)^{\frac{1}{2}}}$$

where

$$SM = (SS_i - CC_{ii})/((W_i - W)(n_i - n - 1))$$

$$SE = CC_{ii}/(W \cdot (n-1))$$

(b) Degree of freedom for t-test:

$$\frac{1}{g^2/(n_i-n-1) + (1-g)^2/(n-1)}$$

where

$$g = SM/(SM+SE)$$

(c) F-ratio for variances:

$$SM/SE$$

(d) Number of times variable i exists but at least one other variable does not, and the number of complete cases:

$$(n_i - n), \quad n$$

T-test B computations are done by subroutine WCEFLM.

Covariance, Correlation

This part generates ALLVALUE, COVPAIR and CORPAIR type covariance and correlation matrices.

(a) ALLVALUE covariance matrix:

$$C_{ik} \cdot (n_{ik}/W_{ik})/(n_{ik} - 1)$$

(b) COVPAIR covariance matrix:

$$(C_{ik} - (\overline{X}_{i(k)} - \overline{X}_i)W_{ik}(\overline{X}_{k(i)} - \overline{X}_k))(n_{ik}/W_{ik})/(n_{ik} - 1)$$

(c) CORPAIR covariance matrix:

$$\left[(C_{ik} - (\overline{X}_{i(k)} - \overline{X}_i)W_{ik}(\overline{X}_{k(i)} - \overline{X}_k))(n_{ik}/W_{ik})/(n_{ik}-1) \right] \cdot \frac{V_{i(i)} \cdot V_{k(k)}}{V_{i(k)} \cdot V_{k(i)}}$$

These computations are done by subroutine WARCLM for lower triangular matrices, and by WARCRE for rectangular portions.

COMPLETE covariance and correlation matrices are computed by subroutine WCCALM or WCCARE. If COMPLETE and ALLVALUE or COVPAIR or CORPAIR type matrices are requested then both pass 2A and pass 2B and t-test A and t-test B are performed.

If all of the necessary matrices for pass 2A or pass 2B cannot fit in the available core space, the cross product matrix will be computed in several rectangular segments. Each of these segments consists of as many complete rows of the matrix as can fit in the available core space. If only the lower triangular portion is needed then "complete row" means as many as the row number of the last row.

Subroutine P8DCMP controls whether "lower triangular" or "rectangular" and "complete" or "allvalue" type computations are performed. Segmentation is also controlled by subroutine P8DCMP.

A.26 Classification Functions (P7M)

The classification functions from BMDP7M can be used to classify new cases into the groups used in the analysis. This can be done by means of defining a new group and rerunning the analysis specifying that only the original groups be used to define the classification functions (see p. 526).

Another method is to use the classification functions directly on new data (e.g., through transformations in BMDP1D, or your own computer program) as follows. For each case, compute the classification score for each group from the classification function coefficients (multiply the data by the coefficients and add the constant term). The case is classified into the group for which the classification score is highest.

You can also convert the classification scores to posterior probabilities: let q be the number of groups and s_{ij} be the classification score for the ith case for the jth group, then the posterior probability that case i belongs to group j is

$$p_{ij} = \frac{\exp(s_{ij})}{\sum_{k=1}^{q} \exp(s_{ij})}$$

A.27 General Mixed Model ANOVA—Empty Cells (P8V)

From the nesting relationships, a set of control words is generated to represent the analysis of variance components.

Let a_i = the ith analysis of variance index

B_i = the set of indices in which a_i is nested

n = the number of indices

First, all possible pairs (C,D) of sets of indices C and D such that

(i) $C \cap D = \emptyset$

(ii) $D = \bigcup_{a_i \in C} B_i$

are formed. This collection is then ordered by the number of indices in $C \cup D$. Let (C_k, D_k) denote the kth element in the ordered list. C_k contains the crossed indices and D_k the nested indices for the kth component. Let $E_k = C_k \cup D_k$. The list $\{E_k\}$ is used to generate the analysis of variance table by the following method:

Let ℓ_i = the number of levels of the ith index

$$m = \prod_{i=1}^{n} \ell_i$$

$$g_k = \prod_{a_i \in E_k} \ell_i$$

$$T_k = \frac{g_k}{m} \sum_{a_j \in E_k} \left(\sum_{a_i \not\in E_k} x_{a_1 a_2 \ldots a_n} \right)^2$$

where the sums are over all levels of the indicated indices.

The sums of squares S_k and degrees of freedom d_k are then formed recursively by the subtractive process:

$$S_k = T_k - \sum_{E_i \subset E_k} S_i$$

$$d_k = g_k - \sum_{E_i \subset E_k} d_i$$

The method is modified slightly so that the T_k are sums of deviations from the grand mean to eliminate roundoff error caused by subtracting the correction factor, T_0.

Let σ_ℓ^2 denote the population variance component corresponding to the ℓth term in the table (i.e., corresponding to (C_ℓ, D_ℓ)).

The expected value of S_k/d_k is given by

$$E_\ell \sum_{\ell \supseteq E_k} \alpha_{\ell,k} \sigma_\ell^2$$

where

$$\alpha_{\ell,k} = \prod_{i=1}^{n} \beta_{\ell,k,i}$$

$$\beta_{\ell,k,i} = \begin{cases} 1 - \frac{\ell_i}{p_i}, & \text{if } a_i \varepsilon C_\ell \cap E_k' \\ 1, & \text{if } a_i \varepsilon D_\ell \cup E_k \\ \ell_i, & \text{otherwise} \end{cases}$$

p_i = the population size for the ith index

If p_i is left blank on the index card, it is assumed infinite and ℓ_i/p_i is taken to be zero.

A.28 Logistic Regression (PLR)

Given p + 1 variables, y, x_1, x_2, ..., x_p, PLR estimates the parameters (β_i) of the linear logistic model

$$\Sigma(y) = \theta = \frac{\exp(\sum_{i \varepsilon I} \beta_i x_i)}{1 + \exp(\sum_{i \varepsilon I} \beta_i x_i)} \tag{1}$$

where $I = \{i_1, i_2, \ldots, i_q\} \subset \{1,2,\ldots,p,1*2,1*3,\ldots\}$ is determined by a stepwise selection process.

If x_i is a categoric variable, the notation "$\beta_i x_i$" in (1) means sum of products of coefficients and design variables; e.g., if x_i has 4 levels

$$\beta_i x_i \overset{D}{=} \beta_{i1} d_{i1} + \beta_{i2} d_{i2} + \beta_{i3} d_{i3}$$

where d_{i1} = 1, 0, 0, or -1

d_{i2} = 0, 1, 0, or -1

d_{i3} = 0, 0, 1, or -1

depending on the value of x_i.

If x_i is an interaction of categoric variables, then d_i is the product of its main effects' design variables.

In addition, let n denote the number of trials and s the number of successes.

The values $\hat{\beta}_i$ are estimated as the values that maximize the likelihood function

$$L_I(\beta) = \Pi \frac{\exp(y \sum_{i \varepsilon I} \beta_i x_i)}{1 + \exp(\sum_{i \varepsilon I} \beta_i x_i)}$$

via the method suggested by Jennrich and Moore (1975):

Let $$f_j = n_j \frac{\exp(\Sigma \beta_i x_i)}{1 + \exp(\Sigma \beta_i x_i)}$$

$$w_j = n_j / (f_j (n_j - f_j))$$

The β_i - s are estimated via an iteratively reweighted (weight$_j = w_j$) Gauss-Newton least square fit of f_j to s_j; i.e., minimizing

$$\sum_j \frac{n_j}{f_j(n_j-f_j)} (s_j - f_j)^2$$

Selection of a variable to enter or remove at each step is based on either the maximum likelihood ratio (MLR) computation or on the asymptotic covariance estimation (ACE).

The MLR method removes the variable k for which

$$x_k^2 = -2\ell n \frac{L_I(\beta)}{L_{I^-}(\beta)} \quad , \text{ where } I^- = I \cap \neg\{k\}$$

is the smallest if prob(x_k^2)>limit to remove, or

enters the variable k for which

$$\chi_k^2 = -2\ln \frac{L_{I^+}(\beta)}{L_I(\beta)} \quad , \text{ where } I^+ = I \cup \{k\}$$

is the largest if $prob(\chi_k^2)<$limit to enter.

The ACE method assumes that the effect of entering or removing a variable can be closely approximated by F-to-enter and F-to-remove computation, performed on the asymptotic covariance matrix, as described in P2R and Appendix A.11.

The standard error of residual j is computed as

$$\sqrt{\frac{\hat{\theta}_j(1-\hat{\theta}_j)}{n_j} - \sum_{i1,i2} \frac{\partial\theta}{\partial\beta_{i1}} \text{ cov}_{\beta_{i1,i2}} \frac{\partial\theta}{\partial\beta_{i2}}}$$

A.29   K-Means Clustering (PKM)

Cases to be used for determining the clusters are selected by
- removing all cases with non-positive weight,
- removing all cases with more missing values than allowed by the MMV parameter, and
- if COV or WCOV standardization is requested, removing all cases with any missing values for a variable that is to be used.

The computational steps are as follows:

1. Standardization of data by the overall variance or covariance, if so requested: obtain X_{new} such that

$$X_{new} \cdot M^{\frac{1}{2}} = X_{input}$$

where $M^{\frac{1}{2}}$ is the Cholesky decomposition of the matrix to standardize with.

2. Classify cases into clusters based on the SEED or CENTER parameters, if they have been stated.

3. If the desired number of clusters have been defined, then go to step 5, otherwise, split a cluster into two clusters via the following procedure:
a) for each variable i, in each cluster c, the variance, Var_{ic}, is estimated
b) the indices i* and c* are found, such that $Var_{i^*c^*} = \max(Var_{ic})$
c) cluster c* is split into two clusters, based on the value of variable i*, at the midpoint of the range of variable i* in cluster c*.

4. If the number of clusters is less than desired, repeat step 3.

5. Standardize the data by the within clusters variance or covariance matrix, if so requested, using a computation similar to that outlined in step 1.

6. Move each case to the cluster whose center is closest to the case.

7. Recompute centers of clusters (means) and repeat step 6 if any case was moved in step 6.

8. Repeat from step 5 if any case was moved since the last standardization.

9. Report clusters for the current number of clusters.

10. If a larger NUMBER of clusters has been requested, repeat from step 3.

11. Produce final report and save data, if requested.

A.30   Survival Functions (P1L)

Let the N observed times to response (survival times) or time on study (if the observation is censored) be ordered

$$t_1 \le t_2 \le \cdots \le t_N$$

Associated with each t_i is a δ_i such that

$$\delta_i = \begin{cases} 1 & \text{if } t_i \text{ is a response} \\ 0 & \text{if } t_i \text{ is a censored observation} \end{cases}$$

The product-limit estimate of the survival curve is given by

$$P(t) = \prod_{t_i < t} \frac{N-i+1-\delta_i}{N-i+1}$$

The corresponding estimate of the standard error is

$$\text{s.e. } (P(t)) = P(t) \left\{ \sum_{t_i < t} \frac{\delta_i}{(N-i)(N-i+1)} \right\}^{\frac{1}{2}}$$

Let the times corresponding to a response (i.e. $\delta_i = 1$) be represented by

$$T_1 \le \cdots \le T_D$$

where D is the total number of responses. Then the estimated mean survival time is

$$\hat{\mu} = \sum_{i=1}^{D} P(T_i)(T_i - T_{i-1})$$

where $P(T_i)$ is the product-limit estimate based on all the data at T_i. The estimated variance of $\hat{\mu}$ is

$$\hat{var} (\hat{\mu}) = \sum_j \frac{S_j^2}{(N-j)(N-j+1)}$$

where

$$S_j = \sum_{i=j}^{D} P(T_{i-1})(T_i - T_{i-1}) \quad .$$

An estimate of the 50th quantile (i.e., the median) is given by

$$P_{0.5} = \inf \{t: P(t) \ge 0.5\}$$

Estimates for other quantiles are obtained in a similar manner.

Comparing groups: The Mantel and Breslow statistics

Let k be the number of groups. The null hypothesis is that the groups have the same survival distribution.

At time T_i, let n_{ij} be the number of subjects in group j still in the study (that is, whose observation time t is greater than or equal to T_i). Let x_{ij} be the number of subjects responding at exactly time t_i in group j. (If there are no tied response times, x_{ij} is zero for all but one group; $x_{ij}=1$ for the group where the response occurs.)

Conditioned on the n_{ij} and the sum $x_{i+} = \Sigma x_{ij}$, the vector

$$\underline{x}_i = (x_{i1},\ldots,x_{ik})$$

has a k-1 dimensional hypergeometric distribution with mean vector

$$E(\underline{x}_i) = (E(x_{i1}),\ldots,E(x_{ik}))$$

where $E(x_{ij}) = n_{ij}x_{i+}/n_{i+}$

The covariance matrix $\underline{V}_i$ has elements

$$\text{cov}(x_{ij},x_{ij'}) = \frac{n_{ij}(\delta_{jj'} - n_{ij'}/n_{i+})x_{i+}(n_{i+} - x_{i+})}{n_{i+}(n_{i+} - 1)}$$

where

$$\delta_{jj'} = \begin{cases} 1 & \text{if } j=j' \\ 0 & \text{otherwise} \end{cases}$$

Let

$$\underline{E} = \Sigma E(\underline{x}_i)$$
$$\underline{O} = \Sigma \underline{x}_i$$
$$\underline{V} = \Sigma \underline{V}_i$$

The Mantel-Cox test (generalized Savage test) is

$$\chi_M^2 = (\underline{O}-\underline{E})' \ \underline{V}^{-1} \ (\underline{O}-\underline{E})$$

which is asymptotically distributed as χ^2 with k-1 df.

Now let

$$w_{ij} = n_{i+}x_{ij} - x_{i+}n_{ij} = n_{i+}(x_{ij} - x_{i+}n_{ij}/n_{i+}) \text{ , and } W_i = \sum_j w_{ij}$$

Hence the vector $\underline{W} = (W_1,\ldots W_{k-1})$ has mean zero and covariance

$$\underline{V}_W = \Sigma n_{i+}^2 \underline{V}_i$$

The statistic

$$\chi_B^2 = \underline{W}' \ \underline{V}_W^{-1} \ \underline{W}$$

is the Breslow (generalized Wilcoxon) statistic, which is asymptotically distributed as χ_{k-1}^2.

Note that χ_M^2 differs from χ_B^2 in the method of weighting the observations.

A.31   Regression with Incomplete Survival Data (P2L)

1. Estimation of Regression Coefficients

Let $t_1 < t_2 < \cdots < t_k$ represent k distinct times to death among the N survival times. Maximum likelihood estimates $\hat{\underline{\beta}}$ for the proportional hazards regression model are obtained by maximizing the log likelihood function:

$$\ln L(\underline{\beta}) = \sum_{i=1}^{k} \left\{ \sum_{j \in D_i} \ln r(\underline{\beta},\underline{z}_j(t_i)) - m_i \ln \left[\sum_{\ell \in R_i} r(\underline{\beta},\underline{z}_\ell(t_i)) \right] \right\}$$

where

D_i	= the set of individuals failing at time t_i
m_i	= number of deaths occurring at t_i
R_i	= the set of individuals alive and under observation just prior to t_i
$\underline{z}_\ell(t_i)$	= p-vector of covariates for the ℓ-th individual at time t_i

$$r(\underline{\beta},\underline{z}_\ell(t_i)) = \exp(\underline{\beta}'\underline{z}_\ell(t_i))$$

A Newton-Raphson algorithm is used to maximize the log likelihood function. The algorithm begins with initial estimates for β equal to zero unless otherwise specified in the REGRESSION paragraph. On subsequent iterations $\hat{\underline{\beta}}$ is changed by $\Delta\hat{\underline{\beta}}$ where

$$\Delta\hat{\underline{\beta}} = -I^{-1}(\hat{\underline{\beta}})U(\hat{\underline{\beta}}) \quad .$$

$U(\hat{\underline{\beta}})$ and $I(\hat{\underline{\beta}})$ represent the first derivatives and the negative of the matrix of second partials of the log likelihood function respectively.

Let $r(\hat{\underline{\beta}},\underline{z}_j(t_i)) = r_{ij}$ and $\frac{\partial r_{ij}}{\partial\beta_n} = r_{ij}'|n$.

The derivatives of the likelihood function are calculated according to the following equations:

$$U_\eta(\hat{\underset{\sim}{\beta}}) = \frac{\partial \ln L(\hat{\underset{\sim}{\beta}})}{\partial \hat{\beta}_\eta} = \sum_{i=1}^{k} \left[\sum_{j \in D_i} \frac{r'_{ij|\eta}}{r_{ij}} - m_i \frac{\sum_{j \in R_i} r'_{ij|\eta}}{\sum_{j \in R_i} r_{ij}} \right] \qquad \eta = 1, \dots, p$$

$$I_{\eta\zeta}(\hat{\underset{\sim}{\beta}}) = \frac{\partial^2 \ln L(\hat{\underset{\sim}{\beta}})}{\partial \hat{\beta}_\eta \partial \hat{\beta}_\zeta} = \sum_{i=1}^{k} m_i \, C_{\eta\zeta i} \qquad \eta, \zeta = 1, \dots, p$$

$$C_{\eta\zeta i} = \frac{\sum_{j \in R_i} r'_{ij|\eta} r'_{ij|\zeta}/r_{ij}}{\sum_{j \in R_i} r_{ij}} - \frac{\left[\sum_{j \in R_i} r'_{ij|\eta} \right]\left[\sum_{j \in R_i} r'_{ij|\zeta} \right]}{\left[\sum_{j \in R_i} r_{ij} \right]^2}$$

When a stratified analysis is requested, the likelihood function is simply the product of the likelihood calculated within each stratum. The derivatives of the log likelihood function are formed by summing derivatives across each stratum.

To calculate $\Delta\hat{\underset{\sim}{\beta}}$, P2L first augments the matrix of second partials $I(\hat{\underset{\sim}{\beta}})$ by putting the (p+1)-vector $(U(\hat{\underset{\sim}{\beta}}), 0)$ in the last row of the matrix. The new matrix is swept on the first p diagonal elements in the manner described in Appendix A.11. After sweeping, row p+1 contains $\Delta\hat{\underset{\sim}{\beta}}$ in the first p positions. If any diagonal element is not swept for failure of the tolerance test, the corresponding element in $\Delta\hat{\underset{\sim}{\beta}}$ is set to zero. The last element in row p+1 will contain $U(\hat{\underset{\sim}{\beta}})I^{-1}(\hat{\underset{\sim}{\beta}})U(\hat{\underset{\sim}{\beta}})$. When $\hat{\underset{\sim}{\beta}} = 0$, this is the global chi-square statistic.

At each iteration j, convergence is checked and the algorithm terminates if

$$\left| \frac{\ln L(\hat{\underset{\sim}{\beta}}^{(j)}) - \ln L(\hat{\underset{\sim}{\beta}}^{(j-1)})}{\ln L(\underset{\sim}{\beta}^{(j)})} \right| \leq c$$

where c is the CONVERGENCE criterion (default = .00001). At any iteration j, if $\ln L(\hat{\underset{\sim}{\beta}}^{(j)}) < \ln L(\hat{\underset{\sim}{\beta}}^{(j-1)})$, $\Delta\hat{\underset{\sim}{\beta}}$ is halved and new $\hat{\underset{\sim}{\beta}}$ are computed. The halving process continues until $\ln L(\hat{\underset{\sim}{\beta}}^{(j)}) > \ln L(\hat{\underset{\sim}{\beta}}^{(j-1)})$ or until the maximum number of halvings is reached. If this happens, the iterative procedure continues, using values at the last step halving. When convergence is reached, the asymptotic covariance matrix is calculated by inversion of the $I(\hat{\underset{\sim}{\beta}})$ matrix.

2. Stepwise Regression

For stepwise regression problems selection of a variable for entry or removal may be based on either the MPLR or SCORE method. Let M represent the set of indices of the covariates in the regression at any given step. The <u>MPLR method</u> removes the variable corresponding to index $j \in M$ for which

$$\chi_1^2 = -2\ln \frac{L_{M^-}(\hat{\underset{\sim}{\beta}})}{L_M(\hat{\underset{\sim}{\beta}})} \qquad M^- = M - \{j\}$$

is smallest if $\text{Prob}(\chi_1^2) > $ limit to remove, or enters the variable corresponding to index $j \notin M$ for which

$$\chi_1^2 = -2\ln \frac{L_{M^+}(\hat{\underset{\sim}{\beta}})}{L_M(\hat{\underset{\sim}{\beta}})} \qquad M^+ = M \cup \{j\}$$

is largest if $\text{Prob}(\chi_1^2) < $ limit to enter.

The <u>PHH method</u> uses the statistic proposed by Peduzzi, Hardy and Holford (1980). Let $\hat{\underset{\sim}{\beta}}$ represent the parameter estimates for covariate indices in M. First $U(\underset{\sim}{\beta}^*)$ and $I(\underset{\sim}{\beta}^*)$ are calculated where $\underset{\sim}{\beta}^*$ is a vector containing parameter estimates for variables in the model and zero for those not in the model. The matrix $I(\underset{\sim}{\beta}^*)$ is then swept on each element in M producing the matrix $I^*(\underset{\sim}{\beta}^*)$. $I^*(\hat{\underset{\sim}{\beta}}^*)$ contains the submatrix $I^{-1}(\hat{\underset{\sim}{\beta}})$, the variance-covariance matrix of the parameters in the model. For each covariate corresponding to index $j \in M$, the SCORE method removes the variable for which

$$\chi_1^2 = \hat{\beta}_j^2/\text{Var}(\hat{\beta}_j)$$

is smallest if $\text{Prob}(\chi^2) > $ limit to remove, or enters the variable corresponding to index $j \in M$ for which

$$\chi_1^2 = U_j^2(\underset{\sim}{\beta}^*)/I_{jj}^*(\underset{\sim}{\beta}^*)$$

is smallest if $\text{Prob}(\chi_1^2) < $ limit to enter. Here $U_j^2(\underset{\sim}{\beta}^*)$ is the j-th element of $U(\underset{\sim}{\beta}^*)$ and $I_{jj}^*(\underset{\sim}{\beta}^*)$ is the j-th diagonal element of $I^*(\underset{\sim}{\beta}^*)$.

3. Tests of Hypotheses

Hypotheses of the form $H_0: \underset{\sim}{\beta}^* = 0$ are tested where $\underset{\sim}{\beta}^*$ is a subset of $q \leq p$ elements of $\underset{\sim}{\beta}$. Let $\hat{\underset{\sim}{\beta}}^*$ represent the elements of $\hat{\underset{\sim}{\beta}}$ corresponding the effects eliminated and let $\hat{\underset{\sim}{\beta}}_R$ denote the MLE's calculated using the restricted model containing only $r = p-q$ elements not belonging to $\underset{\sim}{\beta}^*$. Tests are computed as follows:

$$\text{WALD} = \hat{\underset{\sim}{\beta}}^{*'}[\hat{\text{Cov}}(\hat{\underset{\sim}{\beta}}^*)]^{-1}\hat{\underset{\sim}{\beta}}^*$$

$$\text{LRATIO} = 2[\ln L(\hat{\underset{\sim}{\beta}}) - \ln L(\hat{\underset{\sim}{\beta}}_R)]$$

$$\text{SCORE} = U'(\underset{\sim}{\beta}_0)^{-1}(\underset{\sim}{\beta}_0)U(\underset{\sim}{\beta}_0) \qquad \text{where } \underset{\sim}{\beta}_0' = (\hat{\underset{\sim}{\beta}}_R, 0) .$$

All three statistics are compared with the chi-square distribution with q degrees of freedom.

4. Plots

All plots may be defined in terms of the estimated cumulative hazard function. This function, $\hat{H}(t,\underset{\sim}{z})$ is calculated using the method of Link (1979):

$$\hat{H}(t,\underset{\sim}{z}) = r(\hat{\underset{\sim}{\beta}},\underset{\sim}{z}) \int_0^t \hat{h}_0(u)du = r(\hat{\underset{\sim}{\beta}},\underset{\sim}{z})\left[\sum_{i=1}^\ell (t_i - t_{i-1})\hat{h}_{0i} + (t - t_\ell)\hat{h}_{0\ell+1} \right]$$

where

$$\hat{h}_{0i} = \frac{1}{t_i - t_{i-1}} \frac{m_i}{\sum_{j \in R_i} r(\hat{\underset{\sim}{\beta}}, \underset{\sim}{z}_j)} \qquad \text{and} \qquad t_\ell < t, \quad t_{\ell+1} \geq t, \quad t_0 \equiv 0 .$$

The baseline survival function ($\underset{\sim}{z} = 0$) is defined to be

$$\hat{S}_0(t) = \exp[-H(t,0)] .$$

The estimated survival function for covariate pattern $\underset{\sim}{x}$ is defined

$$\hat{S}(t,\underset{\sim}{x}) = [\hat{S}_0(t)]^{r(\hat{\underset{\sim}{\beta}}, \underset{\sim}{x})} .$$

The log minus log plot $\ln[-\ln \hat{S}(t,\bar{\underset{\sim}{z}})]$ is obtained by plotting the function $\ln \hat{H}(t,\bar{\underset{\sim}{z}})$ where $\bar{\underset{\sim}{z}}$ is the mean covariate vector. The goodness-of-fit (residual) plot is calculated in the following manner:

a) Residuals are calculated:

$$e_i = r(\hat{\underset{\sim}{\beta}}, \underset{\sim}{z}_i)H(t,0) \qquad i = 1, \dots, n$$

b) The e_i's are sorted and the cumulative hazard function for the residuals is calculated.

$$\hat{H}(e) = \sum_{j=1}^\ell \left(\frac{m_i}{\#R_j} \right) + (e - e_\ell)\frac{m_{\ell+1}}{\#R_{\ell+1}}$$

where $e_\ell < e$, $e_{\ell+1} \geq e$, $e_0 \equiv 0$, and $\#R_j$ denotes the number of cases in the risk set R_j.

c) The function $\hat{H}(e)$ is plotted.

5. Kaplan-Meier Estimate

With the SURVIVAL option on, the Kaplan-Meier product-limit estimate of the survival function is printed. It is estimated as

$$\hat{S}(t) = \prod_{t_i < t} \frac{N - i + 1 - \delta_i}{N - i + 1} \qquad i = 1, \dots, N$$

where

$$\delta_i = \begin{cases} 1 & \text{if } t_i \text{ represents a death} \\ 0 & \text{if } t_i \text{ is a censored observation} \end{cases}$$

A.32 Univariate and Bivariate Spectral Analysis (P1T)

Outline of topics covered:

Basic Spectral Calculations

The Fourier transform, periodograms, smoothing periodograms, covariance functions, covariance-based spectral estimates.

Plotted Results for Univariate and Bivariate Spectral Analysis

Log power spectra, coherence, phase, gain, filter coefficients, approximate degrees of freedom and bandwidth, approximate standard errors and confidence bounds.

Tapering and Padding

Techniques for producing less biased and more flexible spectral estimates.

Filtering

Lowpass filtering (a basic tool in P1T), bandpass and related filters, lowpass, highpass, bandpass, notch, autoregression.

Complex Demodulation

A plot of one frequency band component over time.

Missing Values

Procedures in paragraphs SPECTRA and COVARIANCE and quasi-periodically missing values in paragraph SPECTRA.

Basic Spectral Calculations

The Fourier transform. Given a time series $X(t)$, $t = 0,1,2,...,T-1$ the discrete Fourier transform $Z_X(\omega)$ at a given frequency ω is defined as

$$Z_X(\omega) = \sum_t X(t) \exp(-2\pi i \omega t) .$$

There are several algorithms, collectively known as the Fast Fourier Transform (FFT), for the rapid computation of $Z_X(\omega)$ at a discrete set of frequencies (the so-called Fourier frequencies)

$$\omega_k = k/T, \qquad k=0,1,2,...,T-1 .$$

Denoting the real and imaginary parts of Z by A and B, we write

$$A_X(\omega_k) = \sum_t X(t) \cos(2\pi\omega_k t)$$

$$B_X(\omega_k) = -\sum_t X(t) \sin(2\pi\omega_k t) .$$

Periodograms. Once we have the Fourier transform of $X(t)$ and $Y(t)$, we compute the periodogram of X, the periodogram of Y, and the cross-periodogram of Y with X. These are defined as

$$I_{XX}(\omega_k) = |Z_X(\omega_k)|^2/T = (A_X(\omega_k)^2 + B_X(\omega_k)^2)/T$$

$$I_{YY}(\omega_k) = |Z_Y(\omega_k)|^2/T = (A_Y(\omega_k)^2 + B_Y(\omega_k)^2)/T$$

$$I_{YX}(\omega_k) = (Z_Y(\omega_k) \overline{Z_X(\omega_k)})/T$$

$$= (A_Y(\omega_k)A_X(\omega_k) + B_Y(\omega_k)B_X(\omega_k))/T$$

$$+ i(A_Y(\omega_k)B_X(\omega_k) - B_Y(\omega_k)A_X(\omega_k))/T .$$

Both paragraphs SPECTRA and COVARIANCE use periodograms in the construction of spectral estimates.

Smoothing periodograms. In paragraph SPECTRA, periodograms are used directly to estimate the spectral density. Specifically, the spectral density estimate $s_{XX}(\alpha)$ at frequency α is formed from a weighted average of adjacent periodograms. Our estimates are formed not merely at one frequency, but at several frequencies α_j. We have

$$s_{XX}(\alpha_j) = \sum_k w_{jk} I_{XX}(\omega_k)$$

where the weights w_{jk} are constrained to sum to unity and follow the shape of a periodogram weighting function $W(\cdot)$. Also used in the calculation of the weights w_{jk} is a bandwidth parameter β determining the number of adjacent periodograms that are used for each spectral estimate. We have

$$w_{jk} = W\!\left(\frac{\alpha_j - \omega_k}{\beta}\right) \Big/ \sum_\ell W\!\left(\frac{\alpha_j - \omega_\ell}{\beta}\right) .$$

The spectrum of Y and the cross-spectrum of Y with X are similarly estimated.

$$s_{YY}(\alpha_j) = \sum_k w_{jk} I_{YY}(\omega_k)$$

$$s_{YX}(\alpha_j) = \sum_k w_{jk} I_{YX}(\omega_k)$$

The figure below shows how we are weighting periodogram values at adjacent Fourier frequencies ω_k in a band centered at α_j. the bandwidth β essentially determines how many periodogram values we use, while the weighting function $W(\cdot)$ determines the overall shape of the weights.

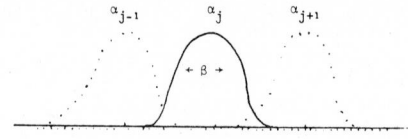

Fourier frequencies ω_k

The periodogram weighting function used in paragraph SPECTRA follows the above cosine shape. Alternatively, the user may request a rectangular shaped function by stating PSHAPE = RECTANGULAR.

There are a few technical points to be made here. The periodogram, as well as the underlying spectral density being estimated, is periodic and is symmetric about frequency zero. When the frequency band fails to lie entirely within the fundamental frequency range of zero to one-half, we may thus extend the periodogram to obtain the estimate $s_{XX}(\alpha_j)$. A way of achieving the same thing is to fold the weights back into the fundamental frequency interval. The other point to be made is that some periodogram ordinates are not appropriate for averaging into the spectral estimate. The periodogram at frequency zero reflects the sample average of $X(t)$ and not the spectral density, for example. Similarly, when a time series contains a strong seasonal component, e.g., monthly temperatures, the periodogram at seasonal frequencies reflects these seasonal means rather than the spectrum. See Thrall (1979).

Periodograms at frequency zero are not included in the average; i.e., their weight is set to zero.

Covariance functions. The sample autocovariance function $c_{XX}(\cdot)$ of $X(t)$ is defined as

$$c_{XX}(u) = \frac{1}{T} \sum_t (X(t+u) - c_X)(X(t) - c_X)$$

where u is the lag at which the sample autocovariance function is being evaluated, and where c_X is the sample mean of $X(t)$. The divisor T is used although there are only $T-(u)$ terms in the sum, so that $c_{XX}(u)$ will be a positive definite sequence. This is important for later estimates of spectra and of autoregressive coefficients.

We similarly define

$$c_{YY}(u) = \frac{1}{T} \sum_t (Y(t+u) - c_Y)(Y(t) - c_Y)$$

$$c_{YX}(u) = \frac{1}{T} \sum_t (Y(t+u) - c_Y)(X(t) - c_X)$$

the sample autocovariance function of Y, and the sample cross-covariance function of Y with X, respectively.

If we wish to evaluate a sample covariance function at a few (e.g., less than 30) lags, we may apply the above definitions directly. When the desired number of lags is larger, we may efficiently evaluate covariance functions as follows:

Let U be the maximum desired lag. (Note that greatest lag in the data is $T-1$.) We subtract the sample mean from X and Y and pad each with at least U zeros. Thus we form

$$x(t) = \begin{cases} X(t) - c_X, & t = 0, 1, 2,...,T-1 \\ 0, & t = T, ..., S-1 \end{cases}$$

$$y(t) = \begin{cases} Y(t) - c_Y, & t = 0, 1, 2, ..., T-1 \\ 0, & t = T, ..., S-1 \end{cases}$$

where S is $T+U$ or greater.

We then calculate the periodograms I_{xx}, I_{yy}, and I_{yx}. Finally we inverse Fourier transform the periodograms, producing the sample covariance functions

$$c_{XX}(u) = \frac{1}{S} \sum_k \exp(2\pi i \omega_k u) I_{xx}(\omega_k)$$

$$c_{YY}(u) = \frac{1}{S} \sum_k \exp(2\pi i \omega_k u) I_{yy}(\omega_k)$$

$$c_{YX}(u) = \frac{1}{S} \sum_k \exp(2\pi i \omega_k u) I_{yx}(\omega_k)$$

Note here that the Fourier frequencies ω_k are now of the form k/S rather than k/T.

Covariance-based spectral estimates. In paragraph COVARIANCE, spectral estimates are obtained by transforming weighted sample covariance functions. Specifically, we have

$$s_{XX}(\alpha_j) = \sum_u w(\beta u) c_{XX}(u) \exp(-2\pi i \alpha_j u)$$

where the u-summation extends from -U to U for some maximum lag U, and where the covariance weighting function w(x) has one of the following three shapes

DELP: $w(x) = 1 - 6x^2(1-|x|)$, $|x| \le \frac{1}{2}$

$w(x) = 2(1-|x|)^3$, $\frac{1}{2} \le |x| \le 1$

HAM: $w(x) = .54 + .46\cos(\pi x)$, $|x| \le 1$

HAN: $w(x) = \frac{1}{2}(1 + \cos(\pi x))$, $|x| \le 1$

Note that β is the numerical inverse of U, and corresponds to the bandwidth of the estimate, when standard units of frequency are used.

Plotted Results for Univariate and Bivariate Spectral Analysis

P1T uses the basic estimates $s_{XX}(\alpha)$, $s_{YY}(\alpha)$ of power spectra and $s_{YX}(\alpha)$ of cross-spectra to produce the plotted results

$$g_{XX}(\alpha) = \log_{10} s_{XX}(\alpha)$$

$$g_{YY}(\alpha) = \log_{10} s_{YY}(\alpha)$$

$$\text{coherence}(\alpha) = |s_{YX}(\alpha)|^2 / (s_{XX}(\alpha) s_{YY}(\alpha))$$

$$\text{phase}(\alpha) = \arg(s_{YX}(\alpha))/2\pi \ .$$

When a dependent variable, for example Y, has been specified, the program also computes the frequency domain regression coefficient

$$b_{yx}(\alpha) = s_{YX}(\alpha)/s_{XX}(\alpha) \ .$$

This is used to plot the log gain

$$g_{yx}(\alpha) = \log_{10} |b_{yx}(\alpha)|$$

and the filter coefficients

$$a_{yx}(u) = \frac{1}{n_\alpha} \sum_{j=0}^{n_\alpha - 1} b_{yx}(\alpha_j) \exp(2\pi i \alpha_j u)$$

where the frequencies $\alpha_j = j/n_\alpha$ are the band centers at which the spectral estimates are plotted. The distributions of these results are discussed in Chapter 8 of Brillinger (1975).

The statistical rationale for plotting log power spectra, rather than power spectra themselves, is that the logarithmic transformation provides approximate confidence bounds which are of uniform length for all frequencies α_j, i.e., the asymptotic standard error of $g_{XX}(\alpha_j)$ depends only on the length T of the time series, the bandwidth β, and the shape of the weights applied to periodograms or covariance functions. See Brillinger (1975), Sections 5.6 and 5.7.

Approximate degrees of freedom and bandwidth. A random variable having a chi-square distribution with K degrees of freedom can be represented as the sum of the squares of K independent standard normal variables. We may regard K as an index of statistical stability since the variable divided by K has a mean value of 1 and a variance inversely proportional to K. In spectral analysis, we assign approximate degrees of freedom to our estimates as an index of their stability, even when their distribution is not immediately related to the chi-square distribution.

Let us pursue this point by first taking a very simple example. Suppose that Y(t) consists of independent and identically distributed normal random variables. Then for any frequency ω in the interval $0 < \omega < 1/2$ we have that $A_Y(\omega)$ and $B_Y(\omega)$, the real and imaginary parts of the Fourier transform, are independent normal variables having mean zero and common variance. Thus the periodogram

$$I_{YY}(\omega) = (A_Y(\omega)^2 + B_Y(\omega)^2)/T$$

is proportional to a variable having a chi-square distribution with two degrees of freedom. Moreover, the entire set of $A_Y(\omega_k)$ and $B_Y(\omega_k)$ calculated at the Fourier frequencies ω_k, $0 < \omega_k < 1/2$, are independent normal variables having mean zero and common variance. If we estimate the power spectrum of Y(t) by taking a simple average of K adjacent periodograms, viz.

$$(1/K) \sum_k I_{YY}(\omega_k)$$

then our estimate is proportional to a chi-square variable having 2K degrees of freedom. In this simple case, our description of the power spectral estimate as having 2K degrees of freedom is in strict accordance with standard statistical terminology.

The above average of periodograms is an example of the use of uniform periodogram weights, i.e., the use of the rectangular spectral weighting function $W_R(x)$. Since the Fourier frequencies ω_k are spaced 1/T apart, and since the above average is over K adjacent Fourier frequencies, the bandwidth being used in standard units of frequency is $\beta = K/T$. Hence we have the relation

$$df = \text{degrees of freedom} = 2\beta T \ .$$

We take this as a definition of the 'degrees of freedom' of spectral estimates. From Brillinger p. 145 we can show that this terminology can be justified in much more general situations than the above simple example. In general, the 'degrees of freedom' refers to an approximating chi-square distribution. Since the purpose of the terminology is to provide a rough index of the statistical stability of the estimates, and because we wish to avoid undue emphasis by being over-precise, we will round $2\beta T$ to the nearest integer and label the result 'approximate degrees of freedom'.

Approximate standard errors and confidence bounds. P1T displays estimated log-power spectra with an associated standard error that is based on the asymptotic normality of the estimate (Brillinger 5.6.3, p. 149). From this estimated standard error, P1T constructs 95% confidence bounds around a wide-band estimate (the estimate having the largest bandwidth among the estimates within the SPEC paragraph).

The program also computes a 95% null-point for the coherence of X and Y based upon the asymptotic distribution of the coherence (Brillinger 8.9, p. 317). This null-point is the magnitude that would be exceeded only 5% of the time if the coherence between X and Y were zero.

Confidence bounds are also plotted about the estimated log gain $g_{YX}(\alpha)$ of the dependent variable over the independent variable. The length of the confidence interval is a frequency-dependent multiple of that for the log power spectra $g_{XX}(\alpha)$ and $g_{YY}(\alpha)$. The multiple at frequency α is

$$(1 - \text{coherence}(\alpha))/\text{coherence}(\alpha).$$

See equation (8.7.6) of Brillinger (1975).

Tapering and Padding

Tapering, a bias reduction technique in spectral estimation, consists of the following operation

$$\tilde{Y}(t) = h(t/(T+1)) \ Y(t)$$

for t=1,2,3,...,T. The Tapering function h(x) is subject to the constraints

$$h(x) = 0 \qquad \text{for } x < 0 \quad \text{or } x > 1$$

$$\int_0^1 h(x)^2 \, dx = 1$$

See Sections 3.3, 4.3, 5.6 and 5.8 of Brillinger (1975). In program P1T, we allow the user to taper the first p portion of the data and the last q portion of the data, for 0 < p, q < .5, by defining the tapering function h(x;p,q) as

$$h(x; p,q) = c \begin{cases} \frac{1}{2}[1 + \cos(\frac{\pi(x-p)}{p})] & 0 < x < p \\ 1 & p \le x \le 1-q \\ \frac{1}{2}[1 + \cos(\frac{\pi(x-1+q)}{q})] & 1-q < x < 1 \end{cases}$$

The constant $c = [1 - 5(p+q)/8]^{-\frac{1}{2}}$ is chosen to satisfy the second constraint. When tapering is requested, a weighted mean, using the set of tapering weights, is subtracted from each variable prior to Fourier transformation. See Section 5.3 and 7.7 of Brillinger (1975).

Padding consists of appending zeros to the data after any mean corrections and tapering have been performed and prior to Fourier transformation. Some of the reasons for padding are: (1) to provide a more convenient length of data for efficient Fourier transformation (Brillinger p. 66), (2) to obtain a finer mesh of Fourier frequencies, and (3) to ensure that the autocovariances obtained from the inverse Fourier transform of the periodogram are mathematically equivalent to those obtained from sums of lagged products (Brillinger 5.9).

Filtering

Basic concepts. We say that y(t) is a filtered version of Y(t) when the relation

$$y(t) = a(u_1) \ Y(t-u_1) + \ldots + a(u_k) \ Y(t-u_k)$$

holds for t=0, ±1, ±2, ... The filtering operation has the following effect on a complex-valued sine wave $Y_\omega(t) = \exp(2\pi i \omega t)$:

$$y(t) = a(u_1) \exp(2\pi i \omega(t-u_1)) + \ldots + a(u_k) \exp(2\pi i \omega(t-u_k))$$

$$= \{a(u_1) \exp(-2\pi i \omega u_1) + \ldots + a(u_k) \exp(-2\pi i \omega u_k)\} \exp(2\pi i \omega t)$$

$$= A(\omega) \ Y_\omega(t)$$

where $A(\omega)$ is the expression in brackets.

Thus the filtering operation multiplies the sine wave by a factor depending only on the frequency ω of the sine wave, and not the time value t. This multiplying factor $A(\omega)$ is called the frequency response of the filter.

The numbers $a(u_1),...,a(u_k)$ are called the filter coefficients.

The frequency response $A(\omega)$ is generally a complex valued quantity, and is usefully represented by the gain and the phase given by

$$\text{gain} = |A(\omega)|$$

$$\text{phase} = \arg(A(\omega)) .$$

The program plots the gain on a logarithmic (base ten) scale, and plots the phase modulo two pi.

As an example, the von Hann filter

$$y(t) = \frac{1}{4}Y(t-1) + \frac{1}{2}Y(t) + \frac{1}{4}Y(t+1)$$

has filter coefficients

$$a(u) = \begin{cases} 1/2, & u = 0 \\ 1/4, & u = \pm 1 \\ 0, & |u| > 1 \end{cases}$$

and has frequency response function

$$A(\omega) = \frac{1}{4}\exp(-2\pi i\omega) + \frac{1}{2} + \frac{1}{4}\exp(2\pi i\omega)$$

$$= \frac{1}{2} + \frac{1}{2}\cos(2\pi\omega) .$$

A sketch of the frequency response function is shown below.

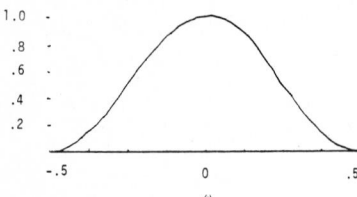

Because of the symmetry of the above frequency response function, we typically plot only the positive half of the frequency axis, thus

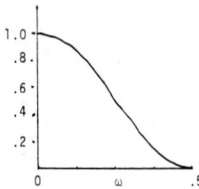

We see that the von Hann filter multiplies sine waves at low frequencies (near $\omega = 0$) by a factor of almost 1, while high frequency sine waves (with ω near $\frac{1}{2}$) are multiplied by a small factor.

The von Hann filter is an example of a _lowpass_ filter, that is, a filter that preserves low-frequency sine waves and attenuates high frequency sine waves.

One index of a filter's behavior is the bandwidth of the filter. A filter having the following rectangular frequency response function

$$A(\omega) = \begin{cases} 1, & |\omega| \leq \beta/2 \\ 0, & |\omega| > \beta/2 \end{cases}$$

has a bandwidth equal to β, the width of the frequency band in which sine waves are passed. More generally, we define the bandwidth of a symmetric filter to be

$$\beta_A = \left(\int_{-\frac{1}{2}}^{\frac{1}{2}} A(\omega)d\omega\right)^2 / \int_{-\frac{1}{2}}^{\frac{1}{2}} A^2(\omega)d\omega$$

This can be shown to equal

$$a(0)^2 / \sum_u a^2(u) .$$

Another indicator of the width of a low-pass filter is the frequency $\omega_{.01}$ at which the magnitude of the frequency response function falls below (and stays below) the value 0.01.

For the ideal rectangular filter above with bandwidth β we have $\omega_{.01} = \frac{1}{2}\beta$. When we construct a filter with a finite number of coefficients, the $\omega_{.01}/\beta$ ratio is typically larger, e.g., for the von Hann filter it is 0.7 rather than 0.5 .

Narrow bandwidths or sharp transitions of the frequency response from approximately unity to approximately zero generally require a large number K of filter coefficients $a(u_1)$, $a(u_2)$, ... , $a(u_k)$. Because we do not have data values $Y(t)$ extending indefinitely into the past or future, we can obtain filtered values $y(t)$ at only a finite number of points. In general, we have K-1 fewer filtered values than the original number of data points (number of cases). So we must find a compromise value for K that allows the filter to achieve desired effects without sacrificing too many data points.

Constructing highpass, bandpass, and notch filters from lowpass filters. If

$$y(t) = a(u_1)Y(t-u_1) + ... + a(u_k)Y(t-u_k)$$

represents a lowpass filtering operation, then

$$\tilde{y}(t) = Y(t) - y(t)$$

represents a highpass filter, with coefficients

$$\tilde{a}(u) = \begin{cases} 1 - a(0), & u = 0 \\ -a(u), & u \neq 0 \end{cases}$$

and frequency response function

$$\tilde{A}(\omega) = 1 - A(\omega)$$

We thus have a simple means of constructing highpass filters from lowpass filters. To construct a bandpass filter, with the passband centered at frequency θ, we use the following device

$$\hat{a}(u) = 2\cos(2\pi\theta u) a(u)$$

giving the frequency response

$$\hat{A}(\omega) = A(\omega + \theta) + A(\omega - \theta) .$$

Notch filters are obtained from bandpass filters just as highpass filters are obtained from lowpass filters:

$$\check{a}(u) = \begin{cases} 1 - \hat{a}(0), & u = 0 \\ -\hat{a}(u), & u \neq 0 \end{cases}$$

$$= \begin{cases} 1 - 2a(0), & u = 0 \\ -2\cos(2\pi\theta u)a(u), & u \neq 0 \end{cases}$$

$$\check{A}(\omega) = 1 - \hat{A}(\omega) = 1 - (A(\omega+\theta) + A(\omega-\theta)).$$

In paragraph BANDPASS, the bandwidth specification refers to the bandwidth of the lowpass filter employed. A narrow bandwidth is especially desirable for notch filtering, so that only a narrow frequency band component is removed from the time series.

Two families of lowpass filters. P1T uses lowpass filters to construct the four types of filters offered in paragraph BANDPASS: lowpass, highpass, bandpass, and notch. The program employs two distinct families of lowpass filters. Filters passing a wide band of low frequencies are taken from the incomplete beta function, as described in Chapter 7 of Hamming (1977). Filters having a narrower passband are obtained by sampling a raised cosine function (the Hamming window--see Chapter 5 of Hamming, 1977).

To be more specific, P1T uses wide band filters having a frequency response function

$$A_{pq}(\omega) = c_{pq} \int_{-1}^{\cos 2\pi\omega} (1+t)^{p-1}(t-t)^{q-1} dt, \quad |\omega| \leq \frac{1}{2},$$

with

$$c_{pq} = \left(\int_{-1}^{1} (1+t)^{p-1}(1-t)^{q-1} dt\right)^{-1}$$

$$= \left(\frac{1}{2}\right)^{p+q-1} \frac{(p+q-1)!}{(p-1)!(q-1)!}$$

where p and q are integers between 1 and 4, inclusive. When $(p,q) = (1,1)$, we have the von Hann filter with frequency response function $(1 + \cos 2\pi\omega)/2$ and coefficients $\frac{1}{4}$, $\frac{1}{2}$, $\frac{1}{4}$. In general, these filters are distinguished by their smoothly decreasing frequency response functions $A_{pq}(\omega)$ (for $0 \leq \omega \leq \frac{1}{2}$). When a narrower bandwidth is required, the program constructs the lowpass filter by sampling the Hamming raised cosine window, i.e., the program sets

$$a(u) \text{ proportional to } \begin{cases} .54 + .46 \cos(2\pi u/(2N+1)) & |u| \leq N \\ 0 & |u| > N \end{cases}$$

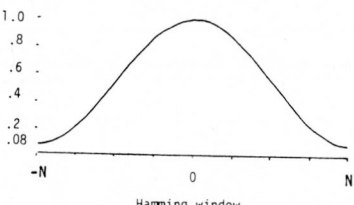

Hamming window

The coefficients a(u) are rescaled so that they sum to unity. These filters require fewer coefficients than do the beta filters to achieve a given narrow passband. They also avoid numerical problems (underflow) when applied to data, because the smallest coefficient is never less than 0.08 times the largest coefficient. The price paid for these advantages is that the frequency response function displays small ripples about the value 0.0 for the higher frequencies. They thus have more erratic frequency response functions than do the beta filters. However, this effect is usually quite tolerable for practical application.

Bandwidths of the computed lowpass filters. The bandwidth for each beta filter used by P1T is displayed in Table 1T.1 below. Given a bandwidth β and a maximum lag L, set by the user or by program default, the program first determines whether a beta filter can be used or whether a filter derived from the Hamming window is required. If a beta filter is to be used, the program obtains values for p and q by using the first pair of values (p,q) $q = m(-1)1$, $p = 1(1)m-q+1$, $m = \min(4,L)$, yielding a bandwidth less than or equal to β.

Table 1T.1

		q		
	1	2	3	4
1	.67	.75	.79	.81
2	.51	.61	.66	
p 3	.43	.53		
4	.38			

Beta Filter Bandwidths

Table 1T.2 gives, for each (p,q) cell, the frequency $\omega_{.01}$ at which the frequency response of the beta filter falls below the value 0.01.

Table 1T.2

		q		
	1	2	3	4
1	.47	.48	.48	.48
2	.40	.42	.43	
p 3	.35	.38		
4	.31			

Frequencies $\omega_{.01}$ of the beta filters

The bandwidths of the second family of filters, with coefficients proportional to the sampled Hamming window,

$$a(u) \propto .54 + .46 \cos(2\pi u/(2N+1)), \qquad |u| \leq N$$

depend on the sampling value N. The bandwidth β and frequency $\omega_{.01}$ are approximately given by

$$\beta \doteq \frac{6}{5} \frac{1}{N}$$

$$\omega_{.01} \doteq \frac{1}{N+1} .$$

Default filters. For lowpass and highpass filtering, the beta filter with $(p,q) = (2,2)$ is used unless the maximum allowable lag is less than 3. In that case the beta filter with $(p,q) = (1,1)$ is used, i.e., the von Hann filter.

When the user requests the program to construct a bandpass or notch filter centered about frequency θ, the default bandwidth β is given by

$$\beta = \min(\theta, \frac{1}{2} - \theta) .$$

Autoregressive prefiltering. An autocorrelation sequence is formed up to the specified maximum lag and is used in the algorithm described by Pagano (1972). That is, the Toeplitz matrix associated with the autocorrelation sequence is formed and subjected to a Cholesky decomposition in the solution of the Yule-Walker equations.

Complex Demodulation

A well-written account of the goals and methods of complex demodulation can be found in Chapter 6 of Bloomfield (1976). We confine ourselves here to the computation involved. Complex demodulation is related to bandpass filtering. Instead of constructing a bandpass filter about a specified frequency θ, we first form a complex valued series Z(t) from the input series x(t), viz.

$$Z(t) = \exp(-2\pi i\theta t)x(t)$$

and then lowpass filter Z(t). Finally, we plot the phase and gain of the filtered output. The construction of the lowpass filter is described in the filtering section above.

Missing Values

The default procedure in paragraphs SPECTRA and COVARIANCE. In paragraphs SPECTRA and COVARIANCE an extra copy of the time series is made and then Fourier transformed. Further results are obtained from the Fourier transform, as previously described.

Prior to Fourier transformation, observed values are tapered, if requested by the user, and a tapered mean is subtracted from each tapered observed value. Missing values are then set equal to zero. (Effectively, missing data values have been replaced by a tapered mean.) This series is then Fourier transformed.

Without special instructions as to the treatment of missing values, subsequent computations proceed exactly as in the case of a fully observed time series.

A missing value procedure in paragraph COVARIANCE. When the user specifies MISS in paragraph COVA, the program compensates for the bias of covariance estimates caused by missing values. This is done in the following simple fashion.

$$\hat{c}_{YY}(u) = \frac{n - |u|}{n} \sum_{j-k=u} (Y(j) - \bar{y})(Y(k) - \bar{y}) / \sum_{j-k=u} 1$$

where the indices j, k of summation are restricted by the conditions $j-k = u$ and Y(j) and Y(k) are observed values. Here n is the total number of cases.

These adjusted covariances are then used in subsequent spectral estimates. This procedure has been discussed by Jones (1962) and Parzen (1963) when missing values occur in a fixed pattern. Bloomfield (1970) derives essentially the same computational technique for the case in which the occurrence of missing values, denoted by a 0 - 1 sequence, is itself a stationary time series. This is a plausible model, for example, when missing values are caused by failures in the recording equipment.

Allowing for quasi-periodically missing values in paragraph SPECTRA. Daily stock market prices are recorded each weekday but not on weekends. This constitutes a sequence of strictly periodic missing values which could be handled by the general purpose missing value procedure in paragraph COVARIANCE.

We can also imagine a daily time series where weekend values are recorded, though less frequently than values during the week. We call such a series, where each day of the week carries its own probability of having an observation taken, a quasi-periodic missing sequence. An example is given by Thrall (1980). Here the periodicity is seven, corresponding to the seven days of the week.

Generally, the user informs the program to employ this model for missing values by specifying the missing periodicity, MPER, in paragraph SPEC.

The program calculates the probabilities of observation, divides each observed value by the estimate of the appropriate probability, seasonally adjusts the result and then proceeds with the usual series of computations, Fourier transformation, etc., leading to final spectral estimates.

Further computational details are given in Thrall (1980). Note that the final estimate of the spectral density may fail to be positive definite.

A.33 Box-Jenkins Time Series Analysis (P2T)

Sample Autocorrelation Function (SACF)

Let $Y(t)$, $t=1,2,...,n$ be the time series to be studied, the SACF of the series at lag k, r_k, is

$$r_k = c_k/c_0$$

where

$$c_k = \frac{1}{n} \sum_{t=1}^{n-k} (Y(t)-\bar{Y})(Y(t+k)-\bar{Y}), \qquad k=0,1,2,...$$

$$\bar{Y} = \frac{1}{n} \sum_{t=1}^{n} Y(t) .$$

The standard error of the SACF r_k is computed by

$$STE(r_k) = \left\{ \sum_{\ell=0}^{k-1} r_\ell^2 \right\}^{\frac{1}{2}} \bigg/ \sqrt{n} , \qquad k=1,2,...$$

and the portmanteau lack-of-fit test statistics Q at lag k, following Ljung and Box (1978), is computed by

$$Q(k) = n(n+2) \sum_{\ell=1}^{k} (n-\ell)^{-1} r_\ell$$

$Q(k)$ is approximately distributed in χ^2_{k-p} where p is the number of ARIMA parameters in the model.

Sample Partial Autocorrelation Function (SPACF)

The SPACF of a series at lag k, $\hat{\phi}_{kk}$, can be computed by the following recursive technique, where

$$\hat{\phi}_{kk} = \begin{cases} r_1 & k=1 \\ \dfrac{r_k - \sum_{j=1}^{k-1} \hat{\phi}_{k-1,j}\, r_{k-j}}{1 - \sum_{j=1}^{k-1} \hat{\phi}_{k-1,j}\, r_k} & k=2,3,... \end{cases}$$

and

$$\hat{\phi}_{kj} = \hat{\phi}_{k-1,j} - \hat{\phi}_{kk}\hat{\phi}_{k-1,k-j} , \qquad j=1,2,...,k-1$$

The standard error of $\hat{\phi}_{kk}$ is approximately equal to $1/\sqrt{n}$.

Sample Cross Correlation Function (SCCF)

Let $X(t)$, $Y(t)$, $t=1,2,...,n$ be the two time series to be analyzed, the SCCF between $\{X(t)\}$ and $\{Y(t)\}$ at lag k is

$$r_{xy}(k) = C_{xy}(k) \bigg/ \sqrt{C_{xx}(0)C_{yy}(0)}$$

where

$$C_{xy}(k) = \begin{cases} \dfrac{1}{n} \sum_{t=1}^{n-k} (X(t)-\bar{X})(Y(t+k)-\bar{Y}) & k=0,1,2,... \\[2mm] \dfrac{1}{n} \sum_{t=1}^{n+k} (Y(t)-\bar{Y})(X(t-k)-\bar{X}) & k=0,-1,-2,... \end{cases}$$

and

$$\bar{X} = \frac{1}{n} \sum_{t=1}^{n} X(t), \qquad \bar{Y} = \frac{1}{n} \sum_{t=1}^{n} Y(t) .$$

The standard error of $r_{xy}(k)$ is approximately equal to $1/\sqrt{n-k}$ if $X(t)$ and $Y(t)$ are independent and one is a white noise series.

Model Estimation

P2T uses a Gauss-Marquardt method (MACC, 1965) to perform nonlinear estimation of a time series model. This section describes the computation of the residuals $(a(t))$, which is the key computation in the model estimation.

Consider the following model

$$D(B)Y(t) = \sum_{k=1}^{m} \frac{U_k(B)D_k(B)}{S_k(B)} X_k(t) + \varepsilon(t) \qquad (1)$$

$$\varepsilon(t) = \frac{c}{\eta(B)} + \frac{\theta(B)}{\phi(B)} a(t) \qquad (2)$$

where

$$\eta(B) = 1 \text{ if } D(B)=1 \quad \text{and} \quad \eta(B) = \phi(B) \text{ if } D(B) \neq 1 .$$

In (1) and (2), $\{Y(t)\}$ is some appropriate transformation of the observed time series $\{Z(t)\}$ and $D(B)Y(t)$ is a stationary series; $U_k(B)D_k(B)/\delta_k(B)$ characterizes the effect of an exogenous variable $X_k(t)$ on $D(B)Y(t)$. $\{X_k(t)\}$ can be a stochastic or nonstochastic variable. $\{X_k(t)\}$ must be independent of $\{\varepsilon(t)\}$ and $D_k(B)X_k(t)$ must be stationary if it is a stochastic variable. $U_k(B)$, $S_k(B)$, $D_k(B)$ and $\eta(B)$ are products of a polynomial of B which is explained later; $\varepsilon(t)$ denotes stochastic variation not attributable to a known exogenous variable; $\{\varepsilon(t)\}$ follows an ARMA process. $\theta(B)$, $\phi(B)$ and $D(B)$ are also products of a polynomial of B that characterize the ARMA process; and c is a constant parameter.

The difference polynomial has an algebraic form as

$$\prod_{j=1}^{J} (1-B^{s_j}) \qquad \text{with } s_j \geq 1$$

where s_j is called "order of difference."

The MA, AR and S polynomials can be expressed as

$$\prod_{j=1}^{J} (1-\zeta_{j1}B^{d_{j1}} - \cdots - \zeta_{jr_j}B^{d_{jr_j}}) \qquad \text{with } d_{j\ell} \geq 1$$

where ζ represents θ, ϕ, or S.

The U polynomial can be written as

$$\prod_{j=1}^{J} (u_{j0} + u_{j1}B^{d_{j1}} + \cdots + u_{jr_j}B^{d_{jr_j}}) \qquad \text{with } d_{j\ell} \geq 1$$

The $d_{j\ell}$ is the power of B which will also be referred to as the order of the jk-th parameter.

The model in (1) can also be written as

$$y(t) = \sum_{k=1}^{m} \frac{U_k(B)}{S_k(B)} x_k(t) + \varepsilon_t \qquad (3)$$

with $y(t) = D(B)Y(t)$ and $x_k(t) = D_k(B)X_k(t)$.

To compute the residual $a(t)$'s, we need to obtain $\varepsilon(t)$'s first. The $\varepsilon(t)$'s can be computed as follows:

Let

$$\alpha_k(t) = \frac{U_k(B)}{S_k(B)} x_k(t) \qquad (4)$$

which implies

$$S_k(B)\alpha_k(t) = U_k(B)x_k(t) \qquad (5)$$

The $\alpha_k(t)$'s can be computed recursively by (5). The computation of the above difference equation is started from a value of t for which all previous $x_k(t)$'s are known (Box and Jenkins (1976) recommended a starting value of t for which all previous $x_k(t)$'s and $y(t)$'s are known). Thus $\alpha_k(t)$ in (5) is calculated from $t=v+1$ onwards, where v is the sum of the highest orders of the polynomials $S_k(B)$ and $D_k(B)$. For unknown $\alpha_k(t)$'s (with $t < v+1$), they are set to 0 if the input series is centered, and to $\bar{x}U_k(B)/S_k(B)$ if it is not centered ($\bar{x}$ is the sample mean of $x_k(t)$ series). Note that these starting values for $\alpha_k(t)$'s may not be appropriate if the series $x_k(t)$ is not a random variable with constant mean. When the input series $x_k(t)$ is a binary variable (i.e., a variable consists of zeros and ones), the unknown $\alpha_k(t)$'s are always set to zero.

After $\alpha_k(t)$'s, $k=1,...,m$ are computed, we can obtain $\varepsilon(t)$ by subtracting $\sum_{k=1}^{m} \alpha_k(t)$ from y_t; i.e.,

$$\varepsilon(t) = y_t - \sum_{k=1}^{m} \alpha_k(t) \qquad (6)$$

Once $\varepsilon(t)$'s are obtained, we can compute $a(t)$'s by (2). The model in (2) can also be expressed as

$$\phi(B)\tilde{\varepsilon}(t) = \theta(B)a(t) \qquad (7)$$

where $\tilde{\varepsilon}(t) = \varepsilon(t) - c/\eta(B)$.

To compute $a(t)$'s from (7), we may use either a conditional or backcasting method.

For the conditional method we set starting values for $a(t)$'s to zero and then proceed directly with the forward recursions to obtain $a(t)$'s. For the backcasting method, we first compute $\psi(B)$ with $\psi(B)$ satisfying $\phi(B)\psi(B) = \theta(B)$. From the results we decide the number of backcasts. After the starting values are backcast, we can proceed with forward recursions to obtain $a(t)$'s. The detailed computations and illustrated examples can be found in Box and Jenkins (1976). Note that all polynomials of B are expanded in each related computation.

Forecasting

For the time series model in (1) and (2), the minimum mean square error (MMSE) forecast of $Y(T+\ell)$ at time T, denoted by $\hat{Y}(T,\ell)$, can be obtained as follows:

(1) Compute $\alpha_k(t) = \dfrac{U_k(B)}{S_k(B)} x_k(t)$, $k=1,2,\ldots,m$, $t=1,2,\ldots,T,T+1,\ldots,T+m$,

where m is the number of forecasts to be made at time T. The computations at this stage are the same as those described in the previous section. Note that computing $\alpha_k(t)$ with $t > T$ may require $x_k(t)$'s, $t > T$. Therefore, the $x_k(t)$'s must be appropriately provided before this stage of computations. After $\alpha_k(t)$, $k=1,\ldots,m$, $t=1,2,\ldots,T$, are computed, the noise series $\varepsilon(t)$ can be obtained as below:

$$\varepsilon(t) = y_t - \sum_{k=1}^{m} \alpha_k(t) , \qquad t=1,2,\ldots,T$$

Using the conditional method for computing residuals, we can then obtain $a(t)$, $t=1,2,\ldots,T$.

(2) Using (2), the MMSE forecasts of $\varepsilon(T+\ell)$, also denoted by $\hat{\varepsilon}(T,\ell)$, can be obtained.

(3) The MMSE forecast of $y(T+\ell)$, denoted by $\hat{y}(T,\ell)$, can be expressed as $\sum_{k=1}^{m} \alpha_k(T+\ell) + \hat{\varepsilon}(T,\ell)$. Using the relation $y(t) = D(B)Y(t)$, the MMSE forecast of $Y(T+\ell)$ can be readily computed.

In the above three stages of computations, the first stage is the same as described in the previous section, and the third stage is straightforward. Below, we explain some details for the second stage of the computations.

The ARIMA model is (2) may be expressed as

$$\phi(B)\tilde{\varepsilon}(t) = \theta(B)a(t), \qquad \tilde{\varepsilon}(t) = \varepsilon(t) - c/\eta(B)$$

or

$$(1-\phi_1 B- \cdots - \phi_p B^p)\ \tilde{\varepsilon}(t) = (1-\theta_1 B- \cdots -\theta_q B^q)\ a(t)$$

where

$$1-\phi_1 B- \cdots -\phi_p B^p = \phi(B)$$

and

$$1-\theta_1 B- \cdots -\theta_q B^q = \theta(B)$$

The MMSE forecast of $\tilde{\varepsilon}(T+\ell)$, denoted by $\hat{\tilde{\varepsilon}}(T,\ell)$, can be expressed as

$$\hat{\tilde{\varepsilon}}(T,\ell) = \phi_1 E(\tilde{\varepsilon}(T+\ell-1)) + \cdots + \phi_p E(\tilde{\varepsilon}(T+\ell-p))$$
$$- \theta_1 E(a(T+\ell-1)) + \cdots + \theta_q E(a(T+\ell-q))$$

where

$$E\ \tilde{\varepsilon}(t) = \begin{cases} \tilde{\varepsilon}(t) & \text{if } t \leq T \\ \hat{\tilde{\varepsilon}}(T,t-T) & \text{if } t > T \end{cases}$$

and

$$E\ a(t) = \begin{cases} a(t) & \text{if } t \leq T \\ 0 & \text{if } t > T \end{cases}$$

Thus the MMSE forecast of $\varepsilon(T+\ell)$ is $\hat{\varepsilon}(T,\ell) = c/\eta(B) + \hat{\tilde{\varepsilon}}(T,\ell)$.

When the $X_k(t)$'s are all nonstochastic variables, the variance of $\hat{Y}(T,\ell)$ is

$$\text{Var}(\hat{Y}(T,\ell)) = \sigma_a^2 \{1 + \psi_1^2 + \psi_2^2 + \cdots + \psi_{\ell-1}^2 \}$$

where $\psi_1, \psi_2, \cdots$ are coefficients satisfying the following equation:

$$\phi(B)D(B)(1 + \psi_1 B + \psi_2 B^2 + \cdots) = \theta(B) .$$

When $X_k(t)$ is a stochastic variable and follows the ARIMA model.

$$D_x(B)X_k(t) = \frac{c_x}{\eta_x(B)} + \frac{\theta_x(B)}{\phi_x(B)} e_t , \qquad e_t \sim \text{iid } N(0,\sigma_e^2)$$

the variance of $\hat{Y}(T,\ell)$ will be increased by an amount of $\sigma_e^2 \{\nu_0 + \nu_1^2 + \nu_2^2 + \cdots + \nu_{\ell-1}^2 \}$ if we set $X_k(T+\ell) = \hat{X}_k(T,\ell)$ and if $X_k(t)$ is independent of other input variables. The coefficients $\nu_0, \nu_1, \cdots$ satisfy the following equation:

$$S_k(B)D(B)\phi_x(B)D_x(B)(\nu_0+\nu_1 B+\nu_2 B^2 + \cdots) = U_k(B)D_k(B)\theta_x(B)$$

or

$$S_k(B)D(B)(\nu_0+\nu_1 B+\nu_2 B^2 + \cdots) = U_k(B)D_k(B)(1+\psi_{x1} B+\psi_{x2} B^2 + \cdots)$$

where $\psi_{x1}, \psi_{x2}, \cdots$ satisfy $D_x(B)\phi_x(B)(1+\psi_{x1} B+\psi_{x2} B^2 + \cdots) = \theta_x(B)$.

Nonlinear Estimation

P2T uses the Gauss-Marquardt method to perform nonlinear estimation. This part of the program is partially based on a nonlinear estimation

subroutine, GAUSHAUS, developed at the Academic Computing Center of the University of Wisconsin, Madison. The algorithm of the nonlinear estimation is described below.

Consider the following nonlinear model:

$$Y(t) = f(\underline{\xi}(t), \underline{\beta}) + a(t) , \qquad t=1,2,\ldots,n \qquad (8)$$
$$a(t) \sim \text{iid } N(0, \sigma_a^2)$$

where $\underline{\beta} = [\beta_1,\beta_2,\cdots,\beta_p]'$ is a vector of parameters and $\underline{\xi}_t = [\xi_{t_1},\xi_{t_2},\cdots,\xi_{tk}]$ is a set of independent variables corresponding to the observation. Using the vector notations

$$\underline{Y} = [Y_1, Y_2, \cdots, Y_n]'$$

and

$$\underline{f}(\underline{\beta}) = [f(\underline{\xi}_1,\underline{\beta}), f(\underline{\xi}_2, \underline{\beta}), \cdots, f(\underline{\xi}_n, \underline{\beta})]' .$$

The main computation problem is to minimize

$$S(\underline{\beta}) = (\underline{Y} - \underline{f}(\underline{\beta}))'(\underline{Y} - \underline{f}(\underline{\beta})) \qquad (9)$$

as a function of $\underline{\beta}$. If $\underline{\beta}_0$ is an initial guess, the first order Taylor series expansion about $\underline{\beta}_0$ is

$$\underline{f}(\underline{\beta}) \doteq \underline{f}(\underline{\beta}_0) + X\underline{\delta} \qquad (10)$$

where $X = \{X_{tj}\}_{n \times p}$ with $X_{tj} = \dfrac{\partial f(\underline{\xi}_t, \underline{\beta})}{\partial \beta_j} \Big|_{\underline{\beta} = \underline{\beta}_0}$ $\begin{array}{l} t=1,2,\ldots,n \\ j=1,2,\ldots,p \end{array}$

and $\underline{\delta} = \underline{\beta} - \underline{\beta}_0$.

The sum of squares in (9) is then approximately equal to

$$\dot{S}(\underline{\beta}) \doteq (\underline{\gamma} - X\underline{\delta})'(\underline{\gamma} - X\underline{\delta}) \qquad (11)$$

where $\underline{\gamma} = \underline{Y} - \underline{f}(\underline{\beta}_0)$. Hence $\dot{S}(\underline{\beta})$ is minimized when

$$\underline{\delta} = (X'X)^{-1}X'\underline{\gamma} \qquad \text{if } (X'X)^{-1} \text{ exists.} \qquad (12)$$

Then, by definition of $\underline{\delta}$, the new guess is $\underline{\beta}_1 = \underline{\beta}_0 + \underline{\delta}$, and the next iteration can be started by expanding about $\underline{\beta}_1$. The method is originally due to Gauss (1821). Frequently the approximation (10) is not sufficiently accurate, making $\dot{S}(\underline{\beta})$ a poor approximation for $S(\underline{\beta})$. In fact, it may happen that $S(\underline{\beta}_1) > S(\underline{\beta}_0)$, which is contrary to the objective. Thus we need some way of systematically controlling the size of the region over which the linear approximation of $f(\underline{\xi}_t, \underline{\beta})$ is allowed to hold, and hence controlling the size of the correction vector $\underline{\delta}$. Marquardt's algorithm (1963) is very good in this respect and, with slight modifications, is used in this program. A short summary follows.

The correction vector $\underline{\delta}$ can be computed by the following formula

$$\underline{\delta}(\lambda) = (X'X + \lambda I)^{-1}X'\underline{\gamma} \qquad (13)$$

where λ is a nonnegative number. If γ is the angle between the correction vector $\Delta\underline{\beta}(\lambda)$ and the vector of "steepest descent" $\Delta\underline{\delta}_s$, then $\gamma \to 0$ monotonically as $\lambda \to \infty$, and $\underline{\delta}(\lambda)$ rotates toward $\underline{\delta}_s$. The correction vector $\underline{\delta}(\lambda)$ is effectively an interpolation between the vector produced by the Gauss method and that by the method of steepest descent. Since it is well known that the latter method is not scale invariant, it is necessary to scale the $\underline{\beta}$-space. Marquardt chooses to scale in units of the standard deviations of the $(\partial f/\partial \beta_j)$ that make up the matrix X. Suppose D is a $p \times p$ diagonal matrix whose ith diagonal element is the same as that of $X'X$. Then, after scaling, the equation that gives the correction vector is

$$\underline{\delta}(\lambda) = D^{-\frac{1}{2}}(D^{-\frac{1}{2}}X'XD^{-\frac{1}{2}} + \lambda I)^{-1} D^{-\frac{1}{2}}X'\underline{\gamma} \qquad (14)$$

The rationalization for the algorithm is as follows: the method of steepest descent often works will for the initial iterations, but the approach to the minimum grows progressively slower. On the other hand, the Gauss method works well when the minimum of $S(\underline{\beta})$ is near, but often gives trouble on the initial iterations. From (12) and (13), we see that these two extremes are represented by $\lambda \to \infty$ and $\lambda \to 0$ respectively. These results imply that initially a relatively large value of λ should be used, and decreased steadily as the iterations progress. Of course, λ should be decreased only if progress is satisfactory, i.e., only if the sum of squares, $S(\underline{\beta})$, at the new estimate is smaller than that at the old. Thus, at the i-th iteration, the basic strategy is as follows:

Let $\lambda_{(i-1)}$ be the value of λ from the previous iteration, $S_m(\lambda)$ the value of $S(\underline{\beta})$ obtained by using λ in (6), and $\nu > 1$.

(i) If $S_m(\lambda_{(i-1)}/\nu) \leq S(\underline{\beta}_{(i-1)})$, let $\lambda_{(i)} = \lambda_{(i-1)}/\nu$

(ii) If $S_m(\lambda_{(i-1)}/\nu) > S(\underline{\beta}_{(i-1)})$, and $S_m(\lambda_{(i-1)}) \leq S(\underline{\beta}_{(i-1)})$,

let $\lambda_{(i)} = \lambda_{(i-1)}$

(iii) Otherwise, increase λ by successive multiplication by ν until for some smallest w, $S_m(\lambda_{(i-1)}\nu^w) \leq S(\underline{\beta}_{(i-1)})$. Let $\lambda_{(i)} = \lambda_{(i-1)}\nu^w$.

This algorithm should share with the gradient, or steepest descent method, the ability to converge from a region far from the minimum, and like the Gauss method, should converge rapidly once the vicinity of the minimum is reached.

A.34 Boolean Factor Analysis (P8M)

This program computes Boolean factor loadings L and factor scores S of a data matrix X, such that $X = S \otimes L + E$, where E is the matrix of discrepancies.

The data consist of p binary valued variables observed on n cases: x_{ij}; i=1,2,..,n; j=1,2,...,p. The q, $q \le p$, factor scores are also binary valued: s_{ik}; i=1,2,...,n; k=1,2,...,q. The q by p loadings matrix has binary valued elements: ℓ_{jk}; j=1,2,...,p; k=1,2,...,q. The multiplication $\otimes$ indicates Boolean multiplication of rows and columns of the matrices S and L: (row i of S) $\otimes$ (col j of L) yields the value 1 if there exists at least one position k such that both s_{ik} and ℓ_{kj} are one; otherwise the result is zero.

Elements of the matrix E are either

positive - indicating a positive data matrix entry with zero prediction; i.e., false negative prediction, or
negative - indicating a zero data matrix entry with positive prediction; i.e., false positive prediction, or
zero - indicating correct prediction, or
missing - indicating a missing data matrix entry.

Computation is performed in two phases: first a set of r, r< q, initial factors are determined, then the remaining q-r factors are computed in a stepwise manner. To obtain the q-r factors, the program estimates r+1, then r+2 factors, then deletes the r-th factor, and reestimates r+1st factor. This pattern of increase by one twice then delete one is repeated until the desired number of factors is attained the second time. For example if r=2, q=5, the program computes 2, 3, 4, 3, 4, 5, 4, 5 factors.

The r initial factors are either read from a file by reading the factor loadings or extracted from the data by extracting a set of r factor loadings. The initial factor extraction is described in Section 1 below. This initial set of factors is refined by the iterative procedure described in Section 2 below.

The number of factors is increased by one as described in Section 4 below, then this increased number of factors is also refined by the iterative procedure (Section 2). The number of factors is decreased by one by dropping the r-th factor, then this set of one fewer factors is also refined by the procedure described in Section 2.

There may be missing data values. While the discrepency corresponding to a missing data matrix entry cannot be computed, an estimate exists. The corresponding entry of the discrepency matrix becomes zero when used for adding a factor (see Section 3).

1. Initial Factor Extraction

The idea underlying the initial factor extraction is illustrated by the following example

$$\begin{pmatrix} 1 & 0 & 1 \\ 1 & 0 & 1 \\ 0 & 1 & 1 \\ 0 & 1 & 1 \end{pmatrix}$$

The first colum of X is "included" in the third in that if $x_{j_1} = 1$ then $x_{i_3} = 1$. In general, the j-th column is said to be included in the k-th column if $x_{ij}x_{ik} = x_{ij}$, i=1,...,n. In the illustration the second column is also included in the third. The set of factors associated with the third column should include the factors associated with column 1 and also those associated with column 2. In this case one would associate a single factor with column 1, a single factor with column 2, and both factors with column 3. The loading matrix would be

$$\begin{pmatrix} 1 & 0 & 1 \\ 0 & 1 & 1 \end{pmatrix}$$

In general, the set of factors associated with a column should contain the set of factors for each included column.

The calculation starts by determining the inclusion relationships among the columns of X. In this calculation it is assumed that there may be errors, for whatever reasons, so that some exceptions to the criterion for inclusion are allowed. The computing routine then assigns factors to reflect the inclusion relationships. the number of factors required is consequent to the calculation, but the maximum number of such factors to be assigned can be entered.

The extraction of factors based on inclusions is a complex problem and the algorithm used here is provisional. It has been found useful in providing a starting point for stepwise adjustment.

2. Iterative Procedure to Refine Factors

The program estimates the columns of the loadings matrix from the data and current scores matrix, one column at a time, then estimates the rows of the scores matrix from the data and the current loadings matrix, one row at a time. This constitutes one cycle of the iteration. The cycle is repeated up to three times, or until no improvement is found in consecutive iterations.

The results are measured by (the number of correct positive predictions) less (cost) times (the number of false positive predictions) in a formula:

$$M = \sum_{ij} m_{ij} = \sum_{ij} [X_{ij} \sum_{k} (s_{ik}) \otimes (\ell_{kj}) - (cost) \cdot (1-X_{ij}) \sum_{k} (s_{ik}) \otimes (\ell_{kj})]$$

The cost, assumed to be 1.0, can be set to a larger or smaller value in the program control instructions. The larger the cost, the fewer false positives will be predicted, or equivalently, the more false negatives will be predicted.

The estimation of a column of the loadings matrix, or a row of the scores matrix is performed by a Boolean regression routine, solving one or the other of the following two regression models:

$$\begin{pmatrix} x_{1j} \\ x_{2j} \\ \cdot \\ \cdot \\ x_{nj} \end{pmatrix} = S \otimes \begin{pmatrix} \alpha_1 \\ \alpha_2 \\ \cdot \\ \cdot \\ \alpha_q \end{pmatrix} + \epsilon$$

$$(x_{i1}, x_{i2}, ..., x_{ip}) = (\beta_1, \beta_2, ..., \beta_q) \times L + \epsilon .$$

The vector α is the new estimate of column j of the loadings matrix, and the vector β is the new estimate of row i of the scores matrix. Each regression computation is guided by the appropriate portion, $\sum_{i} m_{ij}$ or $\sum_{j} m_{ij}$, of the measure M.

3. Boolean Regression

To estimate the coefficients $(\gamma_1, \gamma_2, ..., \gamma_t)$ of the Boolean regression model

$$\begin{pmatrix} y_1 \\ y_2 \\ \cdot \\ \cdot \\ y_u \end{pmatrix} = \begin{pmatrix} z_{11} & z_{12} & \cdots & z_{1t} \\ z_{21} & z_{22} & \cdots & z_{2t} \\ \cdot & \cdot & & \cdot \\ \cdot & \cdot & & \cdot \\ z_{u1} & z_{u2} & \cdots & z_{ut} \end{pmatrix} \begin{pmatrix} \gamma_1 \\ \gamma_2 \\ \cdot \\ \cdot \\ \gamma_t \end{pmatrix} + \epsilon .$$

the following steps are performed:

1) All γ_j's are set to zero.

2) For each column of the matrix Z the measure $m_j = \sum y_i z_{ij} - (cost) \cdot \sum (1-y_i) z_{ij}$ is evaluated.

3) The subscript k, for which $m_k = \max_j (m_j)$ is determined.

4) If m_k is positive γ_k is set to one, and all entries of rows of vector y and matrix Z, in which column k of Z contains a one, are set to zero.

Steps 2, 3, and 4 are repeated until the largest m_j is zero or negative. When the largest m_j is non-positive the Boolean regression is completed.

4. Adding a Factor

A column of the discrepancy matrix with negatives and missing values replaced by zeros is added to the scores matrix. The corresponding entries of the loadings matrix is set to zero, except for the column position from which the additional scores column is copied; this entry is set to one. The discrepancy matrix column selected for this operation is the one with the most positive values. After adding a factor, the scores and loadings are refined, as described in Section 2 above.

5. Dropping a Factor

Starting with r-th factor, two factors are added, the r-th factor is then dropped, two more factors are added and the r+1st factor is then dropped. This procedure is continued until the q-th (maximum number of factors) is computed twice. It is possible that a dropped factor may reenter the equation as one of the added factors produced by the refining process. After deletion of a factor, the scores and loadings are refined, as described in Section 2 above.

A.35 Linear Scores for Preference Pairs (P9M)

Step 1 Data Input

The data matrix is read one case (row) at a time. Cases are checked for maximum, minimum, and missing values and transformed as requested.

Cases identified in the preference matrix are kept in core; the complete data matrix is written onto scratch unit 1.

Step 2 Form the Differences

From the ℓ-th pair of cases $X_i = (X_{i1}, X_{i2}, ..., X_{iv})$ and $X_j = (X_{j1}, X_{j2}, ..., X_{jv})$ the v+1 vector

$$Z_\ell = \begin{pmatrix} X_{i1} - X_{j1} \\ X_{i2} - X_{j2} \\ \cdot & \cdot \\ \cdot & \cdot \\ X_{iv} - X_{jv} \\ D_\ell \end{pmatrix}$$

is formed resulting in judgment D_ℓ; v is the number of variables.

Step 3 Form the Cross Product Matrix

The cross products of deviations C of Z is computed using the provisional means algorithm

$$\bar{Z}_k^\ell = \bar{Z}_k^{(\ell-1)} + (Z_{\ell k} - \bar{Z}_k^{(\ell-1)})/(\ell-1) \quad ; \quad k=1,v$$

$$C_{kh}^\ell = C_{kh}^{(\ell-1)} + (Z_{\ell k} - \bar{Z}_k^\ell)(Z_{\ell h} - \bar{Z}_h^{(\ell-1)}) \quad ; \quad \begin{array}{l} h=1,v, \\ k=1,v \end{array}$$

$$\bar{Z}_k = \bar{Z}_k^p \quad ; \qquad\qquad C = (C_{kh}^p)$$

where p is the number of pairs of cases compared.

Step 4 Regression Computation

The parameters $\hat{\beta}_k$ from the model

$$D_\ell = Z_{\ell(v+1)} = \sum_{1 \leq k \leq v} \hat{\beta}_k Z_{\ell k} + e_\ell$$

are used in computing the scores

$$S_i = \Sigma \hat{\beta}_k X_{ik} \quad \text{and} \quad S_j = \Sigma \hat{\beta}_k X_{jk}$$

which should have the property that they reflect the expert's judgments:

$$\hat{D}_\ell = S_i - S_j .$$

The variables Z_k, k=1,....,v are considered for inclusion (or exclusion), provided they pass the tolerance test, in a stepwise manner:

1st step: the variable Z_k which most highly correlates with Z_{v+1} is entered

later steps: if a variable already entered has a t value (β/SE_β) less than TREM (stated in PREF paragraph) the variable is removed. If there are no variables to be removed, then the Z_k that has the largest t value among the variables not yet entered is stepped in, provided that its tolerance ($1 - R^2$ with those already entered) exceeds TOL (stated in PREF paragraph) and its t value exceeds TENT (stated in PREF paragraph).

Step 5

Steps 2, 3 and 4 are repeated for each judgment.

Step 6

The data are read from scratch unit 1; the scores $S = \Sigma \beta X$ are computed and reported for each case, and if requested, are plotted.

A.36 Robust Estimators (P2D)

Program 2D includes robust estimators. The psi-function for the biweight estimator is:

$$\psi(u) = u \cdot w(u)$$

where the weight function w(u) is

$$w(u) = \begin{cases} (1-u^2)^2 & \text{for } |u| \leq 1 \\ 0 & \text{elsewhere} \end{cases}$$

$$u = \left(\frac{x_i - \text{estimate}}{k * \text{MAD}} \right)$$

with k=6.0 and the scale estimate MAD is the median of the absolute deviations from the median.

The psi-function for the Hampel estimate is

$$\psi(u; a,b,c) = (\text{sign } u) \begin{cases} |u| , & 0 \leq |u| < a \\ a , & a \leq |u| < b \\ \frac{c-|u|}{c-b} a , & b \leq |u| < c \\ 0 , & c \leq |u| \end{cases}$$

with (a,b,c) = 1.7, 3.4, 8.5. (u = $(x_i - $estimate$)$/MAD)

A.37 Cluster Analysis of Cases (P2M)

Computational Procedure

P2M forms a hierarchical cluster tree (dendogram) of cases of a data matrix. The program uses only complete cases. Cases with any variable missing are deleted from the data matrix.

The cluster tree is formed by a leaf-to-stem algorithm. The algorithm starts by considering each case to be a cluster; each cluster contains only one case (the leaves). Then the two closest clusters are amalgamated into one cluster. The amalgamation of two closest clusters into one cluster is repeated until there is only one cluster (the stem). The recording of the repeated amalgamation is the cluster tree.

Based on a user-selected option the distance between two clusters is determined either by the k-th nearest neighbor's distance described in Section 1, or by the distance between the centroids, described in Section 2. The available measures of distances between pairs of cases or centroids are described in Section 3. The method of amalgamation, directly tied to the measure of distance selected, is described in Section 4.

1. k-th nearest neighbor distance

The k-th nearest neighbor distance, D_k, between two clusters is the minimum radius r of the disk which, when centered at one point of each of the clusters, covers k other points.

Formally:

Given two clusters: A = $\{a_1, a_2, ..., a_m\}$ and
                     B = $\{b_1, b_2, ..., b_n\}$.
The distance $D_k(A,B) = r$,
where r is the smallest value for which there
exist two subscripts i and j, and k points
$x_1, x_2, ..., x_k$ such that $d(a_i, x_\ell) \leq r$,
$d(b_j, x_\ell) \leq r$, $a_i \neq x_\ell$, and $b_j \neq x_\ell$, for $\ell=1,2,...,k$.

In the above definition $d(\cdot, \cdot)$ refers to the distance measure selected, one of the measures described in Section 3.

2. Centroid Distance

The centroid distance, D_C between two clusters is the distance between the centroids of the two clusters. Here by centroid we mean the result of the amalgamation, which is either the vector of averages of variables in a cluster, or the vector of sums of variables.

Note that
a) the distance between averages is not the same as the average of distances; the latter is known as average linkage.
b) the centroid is not necessarily the geometric center of points, it is the sum of coordinate values when the distance measure is chi-square or phi-square (see Section 3).

3. Measure of Distance

Given two points or two centroids: $x_1 = (x_{11}, x_{12}, ..., x_{1p})$ and
$x_2 = (x_{21}, x_{22}, ..., x_{2p})$ the distance between x_1 and x_2 can be the

Euclidean distance:

$$d_1(x_1, x_2) = \sqrt{\sum_\ell (x_{1\ell} - x_{2\ell})^2} \quad , \text{ or}$$

Minkowski or p-th power distance:

$$d_2(x_1, x_2) = \left(\sum_\ell (x_{1\ell} - x_{2\ell})^p \right)^{1/p}, \text{ or}$$

Chi-square distance:

$$d_3(x_1, x_2) = \sqrt{\sum_\ell \left(\frac{(x_{1\ell} - e_{1\ell})^2}{e_{1\ell}} + \frac{(x_{2\ell} - e_{2\ell})^2}{e_{2\ell}} \right)}$$

where

$$e_{i\ell} = \frac{\sum_k x_{ik} \cdot (x_{1\ell} + x_{2\ell})}{\sum_k (x_{1k} + x_{2k})} \quad , \text{ or}$$

Phi-square distance

$$d_4 = d_3 / \sqrt{\sum_k (x_{1k} + x_{2k})}$$

The measures d_1 and d_2 are appropriate when the variables are measured on interval scales. The measures d_3 and d_4 are appropriate when the data matrix consists of frequency counts. By adjusting the value p, d_2 can be made more or less sensitive to outlying coordinate values. The measure d_3 is sensitive to the magnitude of the frequencies, e.g., two cases will seem further apart if each frequency is inflated by the same constant multiplier larger than one. This sensitivity to magnitude is eliminated in d_4.

4. Amalgamation

Two cases are amalgamated into one pseudo-case, referred to as the centroid in Section 2 above. The amalgamation method depends on the distance used. For d_1 or d_2 distance the amalgamation produces the variable by variable averages. For d_3 and d_4 the corresponding variable values (frequencies) are added to created the new pseudo-case.

B.1 Increasing the Capacity of a BMDP Program

At the end of each program description, a section entitled SIZE OF PROBLEM gives example(s) of the maximum number of cases, variables, groups, etc. (whichever are relevant) that can be analyzed by the program. If your problem does not exceed the capacity of the program (and most problems do not), this Appendix can be omitted. If your data exceed the capacity of the program, you can either do the analysis in parts or increase the capacity of the program.

In this section we describe how to increase the capacity of the program. In the following section (Appendix B.2) we give formulas from which you can estimate the capacity needed. The amount of space for arrays that you have is reported shortly after your input BMDP instructions are printed.

For IBM OS and similar systems, additional array space is obtained by increasing the REGION parameter of the EXEC system card as described in Section 4.2 of Chapter 4. The amount of increase you need is approximately equal to four times the difference between the available array space as reported by the program and the amount specified below.

Additional documentation specific to your system may be available. Check with the BMDP coordinator at your location for any local documentation.

On many other systems, each program allots 15000 locations (real computer words) to store the matrices used in the analysis. The matrices used include the data (if the data are kept in memory), a vector of means, a covariance or correlation matrix or any vector or matrix computed during the analysis. Once you estimate the number of locations needed, you can modify the BMDP program to use more than 15000 locations by redefining the FORTRAN subroutine IBSIZE.

In each BMDP program there is a small subroutine similar to

```
SUBROUTINE IBSIZE
COMMON/MEMORY/B1,B2,IB(15000)
COMMON/MEMST1/N,LPAD(34)
N=15000
LPAD(2)=0
RETURN
END
```

In this subroutine N is the number of integer locations for the matrices (15000) and IB is the vector that contains N locations. To increase the capacity of the program, for example to integer 18000 words, you need to modify this subroutine to be

```
SUBROUTINE IBSIZE
COMMON/MEMORY/B1,B2,IB(18000)
COMMON/MEMST1/N,LPAD(34)
N=18000
LPAD(2)=0
RETURN
END
```

This subroutine must be compiled and the load (execution) module must be recreated. Estimates of the value of N are given in the following section. If your system has integer words that are half the size of real words, the value of N must be doubled.

B.2 Program Limitations

At the end of each program description we give an example of how many variables or combinations of variables and cases can be analyzed by the program. The exact formula for the maximum number of variables, cases, groups, etc. that can be analyzed by a program is very complex. The only time these formulas are of interest is when your problem exceeds the maximum size that can be analyzed. At times when your problem is too large, it can be analyzed in segments; otherwise, you may need to increase the capacity of the program as described in Appendix B.1.

In this appendix we give formulas that you can use to estimate the number of locations (computer words) necessary to store the vectors and matrices used in the analysis. To be sure that you have enough array space, you should increase the amount by ten percent.

First we describe the notation. Then one or two formulas are presented for each program; we present a simplified formula that is usually conservative (estimate too many locations) when the more detailed estimate is very complex. It is usually best to add a thousand or so words to the formulas if you increase computer memory as in Appendix B.1.

Notation

The following notation is used in many of the formulas

M - numer of locations needed to analyze the data (When $M \leq 15{,}000$, the data can be analyzed on most systems by the BMDP program without change; when $M > 15{,}000$, the capacity of the program must be increased as described in Appendix B.1.)

VI - number of variables read as input (specified in the INPUT paragraph or recorded in the BMDP File)

VT - number of variables after transformations (the sum of VI and the number of variables added by transformation, ADD in the VARIABLE paragraph)

VM - max (VI, VT)

VU - number of variables used in the analysis (specified by a USE statement in the VARIABLE paragraph or VT if no USE statement is present)

CI - number of cases read as input

CU - number of cases used in the analysis (such as number of complete cases if complete cases only are used or number of cases with USE set to one by case selection

GN - number of groups

NGV - number of grouping or category variables

NCAT - total number of categories in all grouping variables (the sum of the CODEs specified + the intervals specified by CUTPOINTS + 10 times the number of grouping or categorical variables for which CODEs or CUTPOINTS are not specified)

NT - number of Control Language transformation statements (each OMIT or DELETE statement generates the equivalent of a Control Language transformation for each case omitted or deleted)

NLCL - number of characters in the Control Language instructions after redundant blanks are eliminated

All programs allot the following number of locations for basic information (such as NAMEs of variables, transformations, etc.)

$$Q = 8 \cdot VM + 6 \cdot NT + 2*NLCL/4$$

and if there are grouping or categorical variables, they allot an additional

$$G = 2 \cdot VT + 6 \cdot NGV + 3 \cdot NCAT$$

In our conservative formulas Q is often replaced by $8 \cdot VM + 300$ and G by $2 \cdot VT + 700$, or both by $10 \cdot VM + 1000$.

Scatter plots and normal probability plots are printed by many programs; e.g., those that perform regression and multivariate analysis. In general, the plots reuse the same locations as the analysis, and as many plots are formed at one time as there are memory locations available. Each plot requires $(NH + 11)(NW + 15)/4$ locations where NH is the height (number of lines in the vertical axis) and NW is the width (number of characters in the horizontal axis). The data are reread as many times as necessary to form all the plots requested. (P3R and PAR keep the data in memory; therefore they form one or at most two plots at a time).

P1D The simple formula is

$$M = 30 \cdot VM + 1000$$

and the detailed formula is

$$M = Q + G + 15 \cdot VM + 5 \cdot VT + NCAT + 11 \cdot NGV + 40$$

P2D The simple formula is

$$M = 2 \text{ (number of distinct values in the data)} + 8 \cdot VM + 2000$$

In more detail the space required is:

To estimate the space you need, consider that storage is initially allocated for each selected variable sufficient to store 24 distinct values and their frequencies; for variables with more than 24 distinct values, additional storage is allocated in blocks sufficient to store 50 more values and their frequencies.

$$M = \text{space as described above} + Q$$

P3D The simple formula is

$$M = 10 \cdot VM + 26 \cdot VU \cdot GN + H + 1000$$

and the detailed formula is

$$M = Q + G + GN + 26 \cdot VU \cdot GN + H$$

where GN = number of groups (2 if there is no grouping variable)

$$H = \begin{cases} 0 & \text{if NO HOTEL and NO CORR} \\ VU^2 \cdot GN + \dfrac{(VU+1)^2 \cdot VU \cdot GN}{4} & \text{if HOTEL or CORR} \end{cases}$$

P4D The simple formula is

$$M = 76 \cdot VM + 300$$

and the detailed formula is

$$M = 65 \cdot VU \cdot VT + 9 \cdot VM + NLCL/4$$

__P5D__ P5D forms as many plots as possible at one time and reads the data as many times as necessary to form all plots. The following formulas assume that __all__ plots are formed simultaneously.

The simple formula is

$$M = 13 \cdot VM + \sum_i NCI + \sum_i 9 \cdot NPV \cdot NPT \cdot NPG + H + 2000$$

and the detailed formula is

$$M = Q + G + \max_i(2 \cdot VT, VM) + VT + \max_i NPV + 2 \max_i NPG + VM$$
$$+ \sum_i NCI + 2 \cdot GN \cdot NICAT + \sum_i 9 \cdot NPV \cdot NPT \cdot NPG + H$$

where

$\max_i$ and $\sum_i$ are the maximum and summation respectively over all *PLOT* paragraphs

and

NCI = number of categories (lines in the plots) summed over all variables specified to be plotted in a *PLOT* paragraph

NPV = number of variables specified to be plotted in a *PLOT* paragraph

NPT = number of types of plots specified to be plotted in a *PLOT* paragraph

NPG = total number of groups (in all GROUP statements) specified in a *PLOT* paragraph

$$H = \begin{cases} (NH+11) \cdot (NW+15)/4 + 30 & \text{if any of CUM, NORM, DNORM or HALFNORM is specified} \\ 0 & \text{otherwise} \end{cases}$$

NW = number of characters in horizontal axis (width)

NH = number of lines in vertical axis (height)

GN = number of groups (10, if there is a grouping variable but neither CODEs nor CUTPOINTS are specified)

NICAT = number of variables to be plotted for which CODEs and CUTPOINTS are not specified

__P6D__ P6D forms as many plots as possible at one time and rereads the data as many times as necessary to form all the plots. The following formulas are based on forming all plots simultaneously.

The simple formula is

$$M = 14 \cdot VM + \max_i(NH + 11)(NW + 15)/4 + \sum_i H + 2000$$

and the detailed formula is

$$M = Q + G + \max(VI, 2 \cdot VT) + VT + \max_i NPVX + \max_i NPVY + \max_i NPG$$
$$+ VM + \max_i 2 \cdot NG \cdot NPVM + \max_i (NH + 11) \cdot (NW + 15)/4$$
$$+ \sum_i H + 40$$

where

$\max_i$ and $\sum_i$ are the maximum and summation respectively over all *PLOT* paragraphs

and

NW = number of characters in the horizontal axis (width)

NH = number of lines in the vertical axis (height)

$$H = \begin{cases} 16 \cdot NPG \cdot \min(NPVX, NPVY) & \text{if PAIR} \\ 16 \cdot NPG \cdot NPVX \cdot NPVY & \text{if CROSS} \end{cases}$$

NPG = number of groups specified in GROUP statements in a *PLOT* paragraph

NPVX = number of XVARIABLES

NPVY = number of YVARIABLES

NPVM = max (NPVX,NPVY)

__P7D__ Space requirements:

NG = number of groups

VT = number of variables after transformation

CU = number of cases used

$$M = (VT + 1)(CU + 15) + (NG + 1)(82 + A)$$

where

$$A = \begin{cases} 2NG & \text{if a two-way table is requested} \\ 0 & \text{otherwise} \end{cases}$$

__P8D__ The simple formula is

$$M = 8 \cdot VM + H + 300$$

and the detailed formula is

$$M = Q + H + 300$$

where

$$H = \begin{cases} VU(\tfrac{1}{2} \cdot VU + 15) & \text{if TYPE is COMPLETE} \\ VU(4 \cdot VU + 8) & \text{if TYPE is CORPAIR} \\ VU(3 \cdot VU + 8) & \text{if TYPE is COVPAIR or ALLVALUE} \end{cases}$$

If ROW or COLUMN is specified, then

$$H = \begin{cases} NRC (NRC + 1)/2 & \text{if TYPE is COMPLETE} \\ 8 \cdot NR \cdot NC & \text{if TYPE is CORPAIR} \\ 6 \cdot NR \cdot NC & \text{if TYPE is COVPAIR or ALLVALUE} \end{cases}$$

where
NR is the number of rows selected
NC is the number of columns selected, and
NRC is the total number of distinct row and column variables

__P9D__ P9D analyzes up to 4 variables at a time and rereads the data as often as necessary to analyze all the variables.

The simple formula is

$$M = 14VM + NGV(50 + MG) + 12(NCAT + CL) + 1000$$

and the detailed formula is

$$M = P + Q + 4 \cdot VT + NGV(50 + MG) + 3i(NCAT + CL) + 300$$

where

MG = number of marginal specifications

CL = total number of cells (the product of the numbers of levels of the grouping variables)

i = 1, 2, 3 or 4 depending on the maximum number of variables that can be analyzed at one time

__P4F__ $M = Q + 2G + VI + 50 \cdot NTAB + O_3 + \max(O_1 + O_2 + 5 \cdot vt + \sum NCELL, 2NCELL + O_4 + O_5)$

where

NCAT = total number of categories (codes or intervals) for all variables used as indices; when no codes or cutpoints are assigned, 10 codes are assumed. NCAT is used in the computation of G above

NTAB = total number of tables requested

NCELL = number of cells in table: on input 10 levels are allocated for any index that has no codes or cutpoints assigned (including the index defined by a CONDITION statement); during the analysis any index preassigned to have 10 levels is reset to have the number of levels equal to the number of distinct observed values

$$O_1 = \begin{cases} NCELL & \text{if frequency table is read as input} \\ VI + 5 \cdot VT & \text{otherwise} \end{cases}$$

$$O_2 = \begin{cases} NTAB & \text{if PRINT LIST option is in effect} \\ 0 & \text{otherwise} \end{cases}$$

$$O_3 = \begin{cases} 25 \cdot NTAB & \text{if PRINT EXCLUDE option is in effect} \\ 0 & \text{otherwise} \end{cases}$$

$$O_4 = \begin{cases} NCELL & \text{if there are any structural zeros specified} \\ 0 & \text{otherwise} \end{cases}$$

$$O_5 = \begin{cases} 2^{DIM} + O_6 + \begin{pmatrix} DIM \\ DIM/2 \end{pmatrix}(3 + DIM + (STEP+4)) & \text{if table is more than two-way or contains struc-ture zeros} \\ 0 & \text{otherwise} \end{cases}$$

where

DIM = no. of indices in table

STEP = no. of STEPS specified in FIT paragraph

O_6 = no. of cells required for marginal subtables used in fitting log-linear models; if there are structural zeros the number of cells required is doubled

__P1L__ The simple formula is

$$M = 16 \cdot VM + 3 \cdot CU + H + 3000$$

and the detailed formula is

$$M = Q + G + 6 \cdot VM + 3 \cdot CU + 50 \cdot GN + H + 2500$$

where

$$H = \begin{cases} NPER \cdot (6 + 4 \cdot GN) + GN \cdot (10 + 2 \cdot GN) & \text{if LIFE table} \\ 2 \cdot NKM & \text{if PRODUCT-limit analysis} \end{cases}$$

and

NPER = number of intervals in life table

NKM = number of distinct uncensored survival times

__P2L__ Parameter estimates and plots for up to 1000 cases with 6 covariates may be obtained without increasing memory size.

A conservative formula for calculating necessary storage is:

$$CU \cdot (VU+4+NLAB) + \frac{3(VU)(VU+5)}{2} + 2VU + 3000$$

where

CU: number of cases used

VU: number of fixed covariates and auxiliary variables

NLAB: number of variable labels

695

<u>P1M</u> The simple formula is

$$M = 17 \cdot VM + VT(VT + 1)/2 + 300$$

and the detailed formula is

$$M = Q + 8 \cdot VT + VT(VT + 1)/2 + VM$$

<u>P2M</u> P2M keeps the distance matrix and the data in memory. The simple formula is

$$M = 8 \cdot VM + H + 500$$

and the detailed formula is

$$M = Q + H + 300$$

where
$$H = \begin{cases} CU(VU + CU + 21) & \text{if the distance matrix is printed} \\ CU(VU + CU + 14) & \text{otherwise} \end{cases}$$

If LINK = CENTROID, then delete CU from within the parentheses.

<u>P3M</u> P3M keeps the data in memory. The simple formula is

$$M = 50 \cdot VM + CI(7 + VU) + B + 300$$

and the detailed formula is

$$M = Q + P + 3 \cdot VT + 5 \cdot CU + VU(4 + CI + C) + VU^2 + \max(2 \cdot CU, VT) + B$$

where
B = number of blocks x 4 (B $\geq$ 8)
P = number of passes
C = maximum number of codes for any variable (C $\leq$ 35)

The maximum number of blocks B is nearly VU·CU/4. The number of blocks formed is reduced by specifying a fewer number of passes. P3M forms only as many blocks as there are locations available in memory.

<u>PKM</u> The detailed formula is

$$3 \cdot VM + 6 \cdot VT + VX + 8 \cdot VC + 7 \cdot VU + 2(VU)^2 + 3 \cdot VU \cdot VC + 2 \cdot CU + \max(6 \cdot VT, 3 \cdot CU)$$
$$+ \max((VU + VC + 4)CU, 10 \cdot VX(VC + 1) + 4000) + 500 \leq M.$$

where
VX is the number of CROSS variables
VC is the number of clusters

<u>P4M</u> The detailed formula is

$$M = 8 \cdot VM + 17 \cdot VU + 2 \cdot VU \cdot FN + 2 \cdot FN^2 + \max(VU^2 + VU, 9028)$$
$$+ \max(VU, FN^2 + FN) + 90$$

where FN = number of factors

<u>P6M</u> $$M = 14 \cdot VM + 15 \cdot VU + VU^2 + 2 \cdot VQ^2 + 100$$

where VQ is the number of variables in the smaller set

<u>P7M</u> A simple formula is

$$M = 56 \cdot VM + VU^2 + 7VU \cdot GN + 4 \cdot CU + 1500$$

and the detailed formula is

$$M = Q + G + VU^2 + 5VU \cdot GN + 2 \cdot VIN(GN-1) + 7 \cdot VT + 10 \cdot GN^2$$
$$+ 35 \cdot VU + 4 \cdot VM + 4 \cdot CU + 26 \cdot GN + H_1 + H_2$$

where
$$H_1 = \begin{cases} 2500 & \text{if the CANONICAL variables are plotted} \\ 0 & \text{otherwise} \end{cases}$$

$$H_2 = \begin{cases} GN \cdot CU & \text{if POSTERIOR probabilities are printed} \\ 0 & \text{otherwise} \end{cases}$$

VIN = number of variables in the discriminant function

<u>P8M</u> Approximate formula for core requirement

In addition to storage requirement common to all BMDP routines, this program requires approximately

$$\frac{800}{NCHW} + MAXIT + 34*NIRW + NFW*[\max(NCLU, NRWU)+1+NCLU+NRWU]$$
$$+ NF*(4+3*NIRW+2*NINW) + NRWU*(4+NIRW) + 4*NCLU + \frac{NIRW}{15} \cdot NCLU$$

integer words of storage;

where
NCHW = the number of characters per integer word
MAXIT = the maximum number of iterations
NIRW = the number of integers in a real word
NINW = the number of integers needed to store an 8-character name
NFW   = the number of integer words required to store NF bits
NCLU = the number of cases used
NRWU = the number of variables used
NF   = the number of factors

<u>P9M</u> In addition to space required to store information needed by any BMDP program, P9M needs to store

$$(NV+1)(NC+NV/2+NJ+2*NS+10) + (6+NP)*NJ$$

real values, 2*NP+NU integers, and NV names, where

NV = number of variables
NC = number of cases
NJ = number of judges
NS = number of steps
NP + number of pairs of cases judged

For example, 16 variables, 17 cases, 1 judge, 13 steps, and 16 pairs of cases compared requires 13300 words of memory.

<u>PAM</u> $$M = G + 14 \cdot VM + 19 \cdot VU + 4 \cdot GN + 10 \cdot VU \cdot GN + 2 \cdot VU^2 + 1000$$

<u>P1R</u> A simple formula is

$$M = 23 \cdot VM + VU(VU+1)/2 + 1000$$

and the detailed formula is

$$M = Q + G + VU(VU+1)/2 + 5 \cdot VT + 8 \cdot VU + 3 \cdot NP$$

where NP = number of plots

<u>P2R</u> A simple formula is

$$M = 18VM + VU(VU+1)/2 + 1000$$

and the detailed formula is

$$M = Q + 12 \cdot VU + VU(VU+1)/2 + 3 \cdot NP + H + 20$$

where
NP = number of plots
$$H = \begin{cases} 11 + VU & \text{if FLOAT is specified} \\ 0 & \text{otherwise} \end{cases}$$

<u>P3R</u> P3R keeps the data in memory. Before the analysis P3R prints how many cases can be used in the analysis (C). If the number of cases in your data (CI) exceeds C, you can estimate the number of locations required as $M = (CI/C) \cdot 15000$.

A simple formula is

$$M = 16 \cdot VM + CU(VT+5) + 1000$$

and a detailed formula is

$$M = Q + CU \cdot (VT+5) + 2 \cdot VM + 3 \cdot VT + \max(2 \cdot VT + 2, VI)$$
$$+ 12 \cdot NP + NP(NP+3)/2 + 48 + H_1 + H_2$$

where
NP = number of parameters
$$H_1 = \begin{cases} 3 \cdot NC + NC(NC+3)/2 + 2 \cdot NP \cdot NC & \text{if NC constraints are specified} \\ 0 & \text{if there are no constraints} \end{cases}$$
$$H_2 = \begin{cases} VT + 2 & \text{if BMDP File is created} \\ 0 & \text{otherwise} \end{cases}$$

<u>P4R</u> A simple formula is

$$M = 25VM + 3 \cdot VM^2 + 300$$

and the detailed formula is

$$M = Q + VM \cdot (3 \cdot VM + 17)$$

<u>P5R</u> A simple formula is

$$M = 8 \cdot VM + 10 \cdot CU + H_1 + 1200$$

and the detailed formula is

$$M = Q + 10 \cdot CU + 3 \cdot D^2 + H + 200$$

where
$$H_1 = \begin{cases} 2 \cdot CU & \text{if case weights are specified} \\ 0 & \text{otherwise} \end{cases}$$
D = degree of polynomial

<u>P6R</u> $$M = 13 \cdot VM + 15 \cdot VU + VU^2 + 300$$

<u>P9R</u> $$M = 14 \cdot VM + VU^2 + 10 \cdot VU + 300 \qquad \text{if METHOD=NONE}$$
$$M = 14 \cdot VM + VU(VU+1)(VU+2)/3 + 6VU^2 + 56VU + 300 \quad \text{otherwise}$$

<u>PAR</u> PAR keeps the data in memory. Before the analysis PAR prints how many cases can be used in the analysis (C). If the number of cases in your data (CI) exceeds C, you can estimate the number of locations required as $M = (CI/C) \cdot 15000$.

A simple formula is

$$M = 15 \cdot VM + CU(5+2PT+2VM) + 35PT + 8PT^2 + 300$$

and a detailed formula is

$$M = Q + CU \cdot (5+2PE+2VS) + 7 \cdot VT + 10PT + 24PE + 3PE^2 + 2PE \cdot CON$$
$$+ BE + 2 \cdot BE \cdot PE + BE^2 + 300$$

where

PT = total number of parameters

PE = number of parameters estimated

$VS = \begin{cases} \text{largest variable subscript in USE statement} \\ VT \quad \text{otherwise} \end{cases}$

CON = number of specified constraints

BE = maximum number of boundaries encountered during iteration

PLR The highest-order interaction in the model cannot be larger than 10.

$$13 \cdot VM + VT + NCAT + NPAT(VU+2) + VU + 11 \cdot VD + 3(VD+1)(VD+2)/2 + NMOD$$
$$+ 2 \cdot NCA + 1000 < M$$

where

NPAT = # of distinct covariate patterns

VD = # of variable and/or design variables used in the model

NMOD = # of variable names appearing in the MODEL statement

NCA = # of terms in the model.

P1S A simple formula is
$$M = 31\ VM + 500$$
and a detailed formula is
$$M = Q + 3 \cdot VM + 20 \cdot VT + 100$$

P3S P3S keeps the data in memory. The detailed formula is
$$M = Q + 2 \cdot VT + VU + (VT+2) \cdot CU + H_1 + H_2 + H_3 + H_4 + H_5 + 40$$

where

$H_1 = \begin{cases} 3(VU+1)VU/2 + VT & \text{if SIGN test} \\ 0 & \text{otherwise} \end{cases}$

$H_2 = \begin{cases} VU \cdot (VU+1)/2 + 2 \cdot CU + VT & \text{if KENDALL} \\ 0 & \text{otherwise} \end{cases}$

$H_3 = \begin{cases} VU(VU+1)/2 + 2 \cdot CU + VT & \text{if SPEARMAN} \\ 0 & \text{otherwise} \end{cases}$

$H_4 = \begin{cases} 3 \cdot (VU+1) \cdot VU/2 + \max(VT, 3 \cdot CU) & \text{if WILCOXON} \\ VT \cdot (CU+2) & \text{if FRIEDMAN} \\ \max(2 \cdot VT, 3 \cdot CU) + CU \cdot VT & \text{if both WILCOXON and FRIEDMAN} \\ 0 & \text{otherwise} \end{cases}$

$H_5 = \begin{cases} G + GN + CU & \text{if KRUSKAL-WALLIS} \\ 0 & \text{otherwise} \end{cases}$

P1V A simple formula
$$M = 19 \cdot VM + 12VU + 18GN + 8VU \cdot GN + VU^2 \cdot (GN+1) + 1000$$
and a detailed formula is
$$M = Q + G + 5 \cdot VM + 4 \cdot VT + 7 \cdot VU + 13 \cdot GN + 8 \cdot VU \cdot GN$$
$$+ VU^2 \cdot (GN + 1) + 5 \max(VU, GN) + 60$$

P2V

$$M = Q + G + NVV(NTP + 2) + NDV\left[NTP(NX+NY) + NDV/2\right]$$
$$+ NX \cdot NY(NTP + 2^{NT} + 1) + NY \cdot NTE + 2GN(NX + NY + NG)$$
$$+ NT \cdot NTP + (NX + NY)(7 \cdot NTP + 2) + NTSS + NTS + 3VM$$
$$+ 16GN + 3NDV + 3NTP + 9 \cdot NXY + NTS + 2^{NT+1} + GN$$
$$+ 14 \cdot NCM + NY$$

where

NX = number of covariates

NY = number of dependent variables (separate analyses on each)

NTP = number of repeated measures (product of number of levels of the trial factors)

NVS = number of variables saved

NTS = sum of number of levels of the trial factors

NDV = number of dummy variables generated for the grouping factors (GN if the INCLUDE or EXCLUDE options are not used)

NG = number of grouping variables

GN = number of groups defined by the grouping variables

NTSS = sum of squares of the number of levels of the trial factors

NVV = $(NX + NY)(NX + NY + 1)/2$

NTE = number of lines in the ANOVA table

NCM = number of components corresponding to each error term in the ANOVA table

NXY = NX + NY

NT = number of trial factors

P4V The program BMDP4V is significantly larger than the other programs in BMDP. To obtain a minimal amount of storage requires a correspondingly greater computer region. To obtain 15000 real words of memory for BMDP4V execution on IBM 370-like systems, a REGION request of 246K is required if the program is run overlaid and 630K if the program is not overlaid.

There is no precise formula for the number of words of storage required for a particular size problem. This is because the nature of the data and decisions made during interactive execution will determine the space required. We can provide some guidelines and an estimation equation which should be sufficient. P4V does not keep the data in storage, so the number of cases used has no impact. The space required will grow rapidly as the number of between and within cells gets large (over 25). The following formula can be used to estimate storage requirement (in real words). (Note that this is a prediction equation obtained from a regression analysis; hence the coefficients, particularly their signs, can be misleading under individual scrutiny.)

M, the program storage area, can be estimated by:

$$M = 3000 + 28*NV - 38*NBFAC - 1200*NWFAC - 500*NBC/NBFAC$$
$$+ 500*NWC/NWFAC + 12*NBC**2 + 5*NWC**2 + 24*NBC**NWC$$
$$- 7*NVU - 200*NRV + 1500*ESTM + 2200*FFAC$$

where

NV = number of variables input

NBFAC = number of between factors

NWFAC = number of within factors

NBC = number of between cells (= 1 if NBFAC = 0)

NWC = number of within cells (= 1 if NWFAC = 0)

NVU = number of variables used

NRV = number of dependent variates

$ESTM = \begin{cases} 1 & \text{if parameter estimates are requested} \\ 0 & \text{otherwise} \end{cases}$

$FFAC = \begin{cases} 1 & \text{if a procedure is requested in the ANALYSIS paragraph} \\ 0 & \text{otherwise} \end{cases}$

P3V

$$M = Q + G + NV^2 + NR^2 + GN^2 + GN \cdot NV + NP^2 + 25 \cdot NP + 12 \cdot VT$$
$$+ 18 \cdot NV + 9 \cdot GN + 11 \cdot NR + NN$$

where

NR = number of dummy variables generated by P3V in the random part of the model

NV = total number of variables including covariates and generated dummy variables

NP = number of parameters (one for each fixed dummy variable, covariate and variance component)

NN = $NH \cdot NC$ where NH is the number of hypotheses and NC is the number of components

GN = number of cells in the fixed part of the model

P8V An approximate formula is

$$M = (25 + 2 \cdot NINDEX + NDEP) \cdot NCOMP + NUMBAR + VT*10$$

where

NINDEX = number of analysis of variance indices

NDEP = number of dependent variables

NCOMP = number of components in ANOVA table

NUMBAR = the number of means that must be stored. The number of means stored is a function of which means are printed, the number of levels in the factors, the design, etc.

P1T The amount of computer memory needed is a complex function of the number of variables used, the number of cases used, and the options selected. The following formula is satisfactory for most applications.

$$M = 7500 + 4.5\ CU$$

P2T There is no precise formula for the number of words of storage required for a particular size problem in P2T. This is because the nature of the data and decisions made during execution will determine the space required. P2T keeps the data in storage. In addition to the storage for the data, the execution of each paragraph also requires some scratch storage. The ESTIMATION paragraph requires more storage than any other paragraph. The scratch storage for the ESTIMATION paragraph is approximately equal to:

$$M = NOB*(NP+4) + 3*NP*NP + 9*NP + 120$$

where

$NOB = \begin{cases} CU & \text{(if CLS estimation)} \\ CU + \text{number of backcasts (if BACKCAST estimation)} \end{cases}$

NP = number of parameters in the model

Note that the BACKCAST estimation requires more storage than the CLS estimation.

APPENDIX C

The BMDP Newsletter provides information on various releases of the programs, tutorials, etc. Short articles are also included on topics related to program use. We include here some of these articles of lasting interest.

Contents

```
// EXEC BIMEDT,PROG=BMDP2R
//TRANSF DD *
      DO 1 I=1,21
    1 X(I+2)=0.0
      X(KASE+2)=1.0
//GO.SYSIN  DD *
/ PROBLEM TITLE='DETECTING OUTLIERS
    WITH STEPWISE REGRESSION'.
/ INPUT VARIABLES=2.  FORMAT='(F2.0,F3.0)'.
    CASES=21.
/ VARIABLE ADD=21.  NAMES=AGE,GESELL.
/ REGRESS DEPENDENT=2.  LEVELS=1,0,21*2.
/ END
  1595        8104        12105
  2671        2094        10100
  1083        7113        12105
   991         996         4257
15102        1083        17121
  2087        1184         1186
  1893       11102        10100
11100       10100        FINISH/
                         //
```

The augmenting variables are entered stepwise at a level of forcing that prohibits them from entering until the original independent variable has been accounted for. The F-to-enter for the augmenting variables then supplies an indicator of the aberrancy of the cases relative to the regression structure. The entering of an augmenting variable is equivalent to deleting the corresponding case.

Further details are given in: Mickey, Dunn and Clark (1967). "Note on the use of stepwise regression in detecting outliers." <u>Computers and Biomedical Research</u>, 1, 105-111.

C.1 Detecting Outliers with Stepwise Regression (P2R)

M.R. Mickey
Department of Biomathematics, UCLA

Stepwise regression can be used for detecting outliers - cases for which the value of the dependent variable is relatively poorly accounted for by an appropriate regression equation. The residuals may not indicate an aberrant value if the case causes the fitted regression plane to lie reasonably close to the outlier point. One needs to consider the plane fitted with the case not included in the calculation. This case deletion is in effect readily accomplished by augmenting the set of independent variables by an additional set, one corresponding to each case. The values of the additional variables are zero with the exception that the value of the variable corresponding to a given case is 1 for that case. In effect one augments the X-matrix with an identity to produce (X,I) as the matrix of independent variables. A deck setup using BMDP2R is shown below.

C.2 It Wasn't an Accident (F-to-enter, F-to-remove)

A.B. Forsythe
Health Sciences Consulting Clinic, UCLA

Several users of the stepwise regression and discriminant function analysis programs have asked why we use the terms F-to-enter and F-to-remove throughout the writeup and output, rather than simply calling them F values. Some have suggested that we could ask the user for the level of significance (α) and have the program convert it to the appropriate F values. The computer programming to do this is simple enough but the statistics are difficult. Since the program is selecting the "best" variable, the usual F tables do not apply. The appropriate critical value is a function of the number of cases, the number of variables, and, unfortunately, the correlation structure of the predictor variables. This implies that the level of significance corresponding to an F-to-enter depends upon the particular set of data being used. For example, with several hundred cases and 50 potential predictors, an F-to-enter of 11, would roughly correspond to α = 5% if all 50 predictors were uncorrelated. The usual use of the F table would erroneously suggest a value of 4.

There is nothing wrong with the F table. It was constructed for testing the significance of a preselected variable and not the "best" variable out of many. However, the F-to-enter and F-to-remove are still useful values for guiding the regression program's variable selection, but the probability statements are tough.

References

Forsythe, A.B., P.R.A. May and L. Engelman (1970). Computing advantage scores by multiple regression. In Psychopharmacology and the Individual Patient. Wittenborn, Soloman, Goldberg and May, Eds. Raven Press, 116-123.

Forsythe, A.B., P.R.A. May and L. Engelman (1971). Prediction of multiple regression. Journal of Psychiatric Research 8, 119-126.

Forsythe, A.B., L. Engelman, R. Jennrich and P.R.A. May (1973). A stopping rule for variable selection in multiple regression. Journal of the American Statistical Association, 68, 75-77.

Anderson, R.L., D.M. Allen and F.B. Cady (1972). Selection of predictor variables in linear multiple regression. In Statistical Papers in Honor of George W. Snedecor, T.A. Bancroft, Ed. Ames, Iowa, University of Iowa Press.

C.3   Scaling for Minimum Interaction Using BMDP6M

Robert I. Jennrich
Department of Biomathematics, UCLA

At times one wishes to scale categorical responses in an otherwise classical analysis of variance in such a way that the resulting model is as additive (has as little interaction) as possible. For example, consider a pair of treatments used at three hospitals to inhibit postoperative infection resulting from colon surgery. The infection may be totally inhibited (A), mild (B), or severe (C). Assume that a total of 18 patients experience infections as recorded in the following table:

	H_1	H_2	H_3
T_1	A B C	A B B	C A B
T_2	C B A	A B A	C C A

We wish to assign values to A, B and C to minimize the size of the interaction relative to that of the main effects which is equivalent to

minimizing the

$$\text{relative interaction} = \frac{\text{interaction sum of squares}}{\text{total sum of squares}}$$

This is an eigenvalue problem that can be solved by means of canonical correlation. Let a_{ij}, b_{ij}, c_{ij} be the proportions of A's, B's and C's in the ij cell. Clearly, minimizing the relative interaction is equivalent to maximizing

$$\frac{\text{total main effect sum of squares}}{\text{total sum of squares}}$$

This is equivalent to finding a variable

$$y = Aa + Bb + Cc$$

which has maximum multiple correlation with an arbitrary basis x,y,z of the total main effect space - in other words the first canonical variable a,b,c relative to x,y,z. Since correlations are unaffected by additive constants we may assume that

$$x_{ij} = \delta_{ij}, \qquad y_{ij} = \delta_{1j}, \qquad z_{ij} = \delta_{2j}$$

where δ_{ij} is the Kronecker delta. For the same reason we may assume that A = 0 and perform a canonical analysis of x,y,z versus b,c. The coefficients B and C of b and c in the definition of the first canonical variable provide a set of values of A, B and C which minimize the relative interaction.

Larger tables, more letters and more dimensions may be treated in the same way. Cell frequencies need not be equal. For the table given above the input data could be

x	y	z	b	c
1	1	0	.333	.333
1	0	1	.667	.0
1	0	0	.333	.333
0	1	0	.333	.333
0	0	1	.333	.0
0	0	0	.0	.667

Using BMDP6M gives the optimum values

$$A = 0, \qquad B = 1.352, \qquad C = 2.981$$

and a squared canonical correlation

$$\rho^2 = 0.891$$

which means that 89% of the total variance is in main effects and 11% in the interaction. The optimized cell means are

.543	-.901	.543
.543	-.451	1.987

This table may be obtained from the first canonical variable values by appropriate translation and scaling. The required input is

```
/ PROBLEM TITLE='SCALING FOR MINIMUM RELATIVE
    INTERACTION'.
/ INPUT VARIABLES=5.  FORMAT='(5F5.0)'.
/ VARIABLE NAMES=R,C1,C2,'B(I,J)','C(I,J)'.
/ CANONICAL FIRST=R,C1,C2.  SECOND='B(I,J)',
    'C(I,J)'.
/ PRINT MATRIX=CANV,COEF.     / END
  1 1 0.3333.3333
  1 0 1.6667.0
  1 0 0.3333.3333
  0 1 0.3333.3333
  0 0 1.3333.0
  0 0 0.0   .6667
```

An alternative approach might have been to minimize the interaction sum of squares directly after setting A = 0 and C = 1 to eliminate zero solutions. The difficulty here is that the solution may have small main effects as well as small interaction which is not satisfactory.

C.4   Computing Predictions

Laszlo Engelman
BMDP Statistical Software, UCLA

The equations of a model may be evaluated on a set of cases other than those used to determine the parameters of the model. This is accomplished by assigning zero weight to cases you do not want to affect the computations of the regression coefficients.

Suppose for the first 100 cases the dependent variable is recorded and for the next 50 you wish to predict the dependent variable. Your input could be

```
/ PROBLEM    TITLE = 'PREDICTION'.
/ INPUT      VARIABLES = 5.
             FORMAT = '(5F7.0))'.
             CASES = 150.
/ VARIABLE   ADD = 1.
             WEIGHT = 6.
/ TRANSFORM  X(6) = KASE LE 100.
/ REGRES     ...
/ END
   .
   . (data matrix)
   .
```

The above example sets the weight variable (6th variable) equal to 1 for the first 100 cases and to 0 for the next 50 cases.

If knowledge of the outcome variable is coded in the data by some other scheme, appropriate coding can be devised to accommodate the scheme. For example, if X(1), the dependent variable, is zero only when it is not known, one can use the transformation.

$$X(6) = 1.0$$
$$IF(X(1) \text{ EQ } 0)THEN \ X(6) = 0.$$

to set the weight to zero or one.

C.5   Tolerance in Regression Analysis

Laszlo Engelman
BMDP Statistical Software, UCLA

Many BMD and BMDP program writeups refer to a concept called "tolerance" and ask the user to state a "limit for tolerance." The meaning of this concept is discussed below.

The concept is mentioned in programs that deal with the prediction of a dependent variable using several independent variables. Although the concept is relevant in nonstepwise procedures, we discuss its use in a stepwise regression program.

Suppose a regression computation proceeds in a stepwise manner: at each step one more independent variable is added to the set of variables to be used in the prediction of the dependent variable. Let's denote the dependent variable by y and the variables already selected to be predictors by $x_1, x_2, ..., x_q$. At the next step a new variable, x_{q+1} will be selected, but only if it passes a test -- if its tolerance is greater than the tolerance limit.

But what is the "tolerance of the new predictor x_{q+1}"? It is the proportion of the variability in x_{q+1} not explained by $x_1, x_2, ..., x_q$; it is one minus the squared multiple correlation of x_{q+1} with the previously accepted predictors. That is, the tolerance of x_{q+1} is

$$1 - R^2_{x_{q+1} \cdot x_1, x_2, ..., x_q}.$$

When the tolerance of x_{q+1} is small (e.g., < .001) the variable is unlikely to be of any significant help in the prediction and will cause the standard errors of the regression coefficients to be large. Furthermore, since a small tolerance means a large multiple correlation, which indicates that x_{q+1} is very close to being expressible as a linear combination of $x_1, x_2, ..., x_q$, admitting x_{q+1} as a predictor could cause serious computational accuracy problems. If computers were infinitely accurate, tolerance would still be useful to guard against results being overly dependent on the inaccuracy (truncation or rounding) in the recorded data.

C.6   Random Case Selection

Laszlo Engelman
BMDP Statistical Software, UCLA

Random sub-sampling, a frequently used analytical technique, can be accomplished with the BMDP programs. The example below randomly selects approximately 1/4 of the cases to be included in the computations.

```
/ PROBLEM    TITLE = 'RANDOM SAMPLES'.
/ INPUT      VARIABLES = 5.
             FORMAT = '(5F7.0)'.
/ TRANSFORM  USE = RNDU(152319) LT .25.
/ END

   .  (data matrix)
   .
```

The transformation generates a uniform (0-1) random value, and selects the case if the generated random value is less than .25.

C.7   Ridge Regression Using BMDP2R

MaryAnn Hill
BMDP Statistical Software, UCLA

In a regression analysis when the independent variables are highly correlated, the data are often said to be ill conditioned. The resulting regression coefficients may be quite unstable and not useful for future predictive purposes on a new sample. Ridge regression is a technique that is used to "tame" the estimates of regression coefficients, to portray sensitivity of the estimates to the particular set of data being used, and to obtain point estimates with smaller mean square error (although the estimates will be biased).

In the regression model $Y = Z\beta + e$, the ridge estimate of the coefficient vector β is

$$\hat{\beta} = (Z'Z + \lambda I)^{-1} Z'Y$$

where Z is the matrix (n cases by p variables) of the standardized independent variables and Y is the vector of the standardized dependent variable. The usual least squares estimate is obtained when $\lambda=0$.

Plotting the resulting coefficients for a number of values of λ gives an indication of the stability of the coefficients. You hope to find the value of λ where the coefficients begin to smooth out and no longer make sudden changes (e.g., switching signs). The estimates of the coefficients eventually approach zero as λ goes to infinity.

By adding "dummy" cases to the end of the standardized data file and using the zero intercept option (TYPE=0), you can try this technique with your own data using BMDP2R. The "dummy" cases determine the amount added to the diagonal of the Z'Z matrix. Add one "dummy" case for each of the p

independent variables with $\sqrt{(n-1)\lambda}$ as the value of the corresponding variable and zeros for the remaining variables. Note that the Z'Z matrix is (n-1) times the correlation matrix. It is useful to think of ridge regression in terms of the correlation matrix; the size of the value added to the diagonal elements of the correlation matrix is then comparable from problem to problem. In this context values of λ less than one are of most interest.

EXAMPLE: Hoerl (1962) discussed a ridge technique in an article dealing with the measurement of the performance of a chemical process. He specified a relationship between three highly correlated process variables and a response variable, added random noise to the response variable and then analyzed the data. Although the specified relationship had all positive coefficients, the usual least squares solution produced inflated coefficients -- one of which was negative. He then applied a ridge technique to these data showing the taming effect on the coefficients and producing solutions closer to the "true" values.

To see the effect of $\lambda = .16$ on the regression coefficients for the Hoerl data, we compute $\sqrt{(n-1)\lambda}$ = $\sqrt{9 \times .16}$ = 1.2 and submit the following cards for the HSCF system:

```
// EXEC BIMEDT,PROG=BMDP2R
//TRANSF DD *
   IF(KASE.GT.10)GO TO 1        Using the sample x̄
   X(1)=(X(1)-1.82)/.4022  ⎤    and s to standardize
   X(2)=(X(2)-1.86)/.4088  ⎥    the independent vari-
   X(3)=(X(3)-1.88)/.4492  ⎬    ables, X(1),X(2),X(3)
   X(4)=(X(4)-28.9)/4.0213 ⎦    and the dependent
 1 CONTINUE                     variable, X(4) for 10
/*                              cases.
//GO.SYSIN DD *
/ PROBLEM TITLE IS RIDGE.
/ INPUT VARIABLES ARE 4.
   FORMAT IS '(4F4.1)'.
/ REGRESSION DEPENDENT IS 4.
   ENTER IS .001.  REMOVE IS 0.
   TYPE IS ZERO.
/ END
   11 11 12 223 ⎤
   14 15 11 223 ⎥
   17 18 20 292 ⎥
   17 17 18 270 ⎥
   18 19 18 285 ⎬  10 cases of raw data
   18 18 19 304 ⎥
   19 18 20 311 ⎥
   20 21 21 314 ⎥
   23 24 25 328 ⎥
   25 25 24 340 ⎦
   12  0  0   0 ⎤
    0 12  0   0 ⎬  3 dummy cases
    0  0 12   0 ⎦
/*
//
```

Inserting different values of $\sqrt{(n-1)\lambda}$ and rerunning the program, we obtain and plot ridge estimates of the coefficient for each λ (see figure). (Note: A number of problems can be run together and the BIMEDT procedure can be used to change the values of the dummy cases in each problem.)

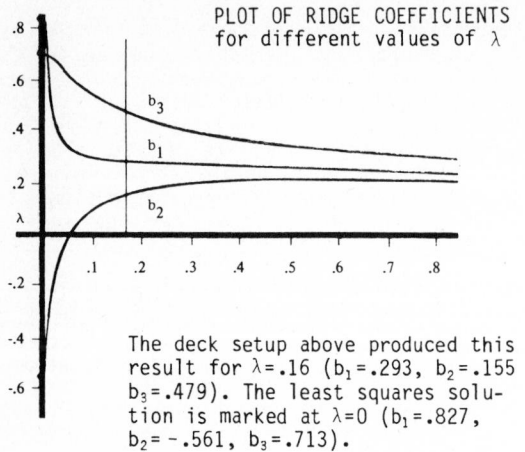

PLOT OF RIDGE COEFFICIENTS
for different values of λ

The deck setup above produced this result for λ=.16 (b₁=.293, b₂=.155 b₃=.479). The least squares solution is marked at λ=0 (b₁=.827, b₂=-.561, b₃=.713).

You will also want to plot the residual sum of squares versus λ. The most desirable coefficients hopefully will correspond to that value of λ where the residuals have not started to increase rapidly, but yet the values of the coefficients have settled down.

Technical Report No.32 discusses the problem of ridging.

References

Hoerl, A.E. (1962). Application of ridge analysis to regression problems. Chem. Eng. Prog. 58, 54-59.

Hoerl, A.E. and R.W. Kennard (1970). Ridge regression: biased estimation for nonorthogonal problems. Technometrics 12, 55-67.

Hoerl, A.E. and R.W. Kennard (1970). Ridge regression: applications to nonorthogonal problems. Technometrics 12, 69-82.

C.8   Analysis of Multivariate Change Scores

James W. Frane
BMDP Statistical Software, UCLA

Changes in subjects from pretreatment to posttreatment on a large number of variables may be analyzed in a number of ways using BMDP programs. The first way is by using P3D which includes t tests for each variable and Hotelling's T for all the variables simultaneously. Two other methods can also be used to gain insight into the changes.

Factor analysis: The large number of change scores may be reduced to a smaller number of factors by using the factor analysis program P4M. Data must be preprocessed, e.g., by P1S (Multipass Transformations). First change scores and their standard deviations are computed. Next, the change scores are divided by their standard deviations. Means should not be subtracted. These "standardized" data are used as input to P4M. In P4M, specify that the covariance matrix around the origin is to be factor analyzed. This is done by stating FORM IS OCOVAR in the FACTOR paragraph. Salient factors will be identified by variables whose changes are large and highly correlated.

Stepwise selection of variables: Whereas factor analysis summarizes a large number of variables by means of derived factors which involve all the variables, stepwise regression achieves a summary by means of an artful selection of variables. To analyze change scores using P2R, an additional variable is created which is identically equal to one. This added variable is the dependent variable in a regression with zero intercept and the change scores are the independent variables. At step zero, the F-to-enter values are equal to the squares of the t-statistics for testing zero change which would be obtained in P3D. At any step in P2R, the F statistic for regression is the same as the F statistic for Hotelling's T in P3D which would be obtained for the set of variables entered in the regression in P2R. Variables that are not entered are variables whose changes can be explained by the variables which have entered the regression. This procedure is also equivalent to a "one group discriminant analysis" in which a sample of change scores is compared to a theoretical group with zero mean.

C.9   Checking Order of Cards in a Data Deck

James W. Frane
BMDP Statistical Software, UCLA

When there are several cards per subject or experimental unit, the proper ordering of cards in a data deck is essential. Each card should include a case identification number and a card number. The order of cards in a deck can be checked and deviant cards flagged by using BMDP1D. Suppose that you have two cards per subject, that the case identification number appears as variables 1 and 21, and that the card number (1 or 2) is recorded as variables 2 and 22. The following deck setup can then be used:

```
/ PROBLEM   TITLE IS 'CHECK ORDER OF CARDS'.
/ INPUT     VARIABLES ARE 40.
            FORMAT IS '(20F4.0)'.
/ VARIABLE  MINIMUMS ARE (2)1,(21)0,2.
            MAXIMUMS ARE (2)1,(21)0,2.
            AFTERT.
/ TRANSF    X(21) IS X(21)-X(1).
/ PRINT     MAXIMUM.
            MINIMUM.
/ END
```

In the VARIABLE paragraph, we state that the minimum and maximum values for the second identification variable (variable 21) are precisely zero; i.e., before subtracting the first case identification variable, the second case identification variable was the same as the first. In order to be sure that the cards for a subject are in order, we specify that the minimum and maximum value of the card number variables (2 and 22) are precisely 1 and 2. We specify AFTERT because the limits must be checked after variable 21 is transformed. The effect of the PRINT paragraph is to print the data for any deviant cases.

C.10 Quick and Dirty Monte Carlo

James W. Frane
BMDP Statistical Software, UCLA

Sometimes it is desirable to get a quick idea of the sensitivity of a statistic to departures from the usual underlying assumptions. The following setup can be used in BMDP3D to assess the sensitivity of the ordinary two-sample t test to the assumption of equal variances. BMDP3D reports both the usual Student's t and a t test based on separate variances.

```
/ PROBLEM    TITLE IS 'MONTE CARLO'.
/ INPUT      VARIABLES ARE 0. CASES ARE 100.
/ VARIABLES  ADDED ARE 3.   GROUPING IS 1.
/ TRANSF     X(1) IS KASE GT 75.
            X(2) IS RNDG(1794831).
            X(3) IS RNDG(49819327).
            IF(X(1) EQ 1) THEN
            (X(2) = X(2)*2.
             X(3) = X(3)*2.).
/ END
```

In this example, data are generated randomly for two statistically independent variables (X(2) and X(3)) and two groups (N$_1$ = 75, N$_2$ = 25) with the variances in the second group four times those of the first group. The first variable is the grouping variable.

More complex Monte Carlo experiments can be made easily by using the BIMEDT procedure. In the following example, 100 statistically independent variables are generated for two groups. The p-values for the t tests obtained for these 100 variables should constitute a random sample from the uniform distribution. However, since the variances are unequal, the p-values will not have a uniform distribution.

```
// EXEC BIMEDT,PROG=BMDP3D
//TRANSF  DD  *
    DATA IST/19748217/
    X(1)=0.
    IF(KASE.GT.75) X(1)=1.
    SIGMA=1.
    IF(KASE.GT.75) SIGMA=2.
    CALL RANDG(100,X(2),0.,SIGMA,IST)
//GO.SYSIN DD  *
/ PROBLEM
/ INPUT      VARIABLES ARE 0.  CASES ARE 100.
/ VARIABLES  ADDED ARE 101.    GROUPING IS 1.
/ END
//
```

The same methods can be used in any of the BMDP programs. The random number generator invoked above is part of the BMDP package; you could also use any other random number generator in the BIMEDT procedure.

These methods are quick and dirty. They are not intended to be used for extensive Monte Carlo experiments since special purpose programs would be more efficient.

C.11 First Steps

W.J. Dixon
BMDP Statistical Software, UCLA

Students reading standard textbooks on statistics (including my own) or books on computers may easily gain the notion that a statistical analysis done on the computer is a fairly simple one-step operation -- one need only decide on the form of analysis, punch the data cards and submit the problem to the computer via a packaged program with specified control statements. However, real life is not so simple. An analysis of real data for a real problem is usually much more complex. Many things should be considered in the early stages of the analysis:

- The data will almost always contain missing values and erroneous entries that arise from keypunch errors or other transcribing errors: the pattern and extent of missing values should be studied and decisions should be made about what to do with them; erroneous entries should be found and procedures should be specified for dealing with them.

- Data distributions may not be as advertised -- often they are not normal, are probably not symmetric, have tails high enough to be uncomfortable for least squares procedures, and contain a few wandering values that defy correction but are not believable: transformations and/or trimming procedures may need to be considered to deal with these problems.

- It may not be possible to specify the most appropriate analysis until the data are examined in a variety of ways.

- The question of whether the data are a homogeneous group or need to be stratified should be resolved.

- A decision should be made as to whether the data sufficiently satisfy the assumptions of later analyses that are planned to follow.

So what should you do?

A general discussion in the absence of real data with real problems may not be very enlightening because problems with different data sets differ widely. It may help, however, to know what size the problem may be when planning a data analysis for a study with many variables (more than ten or twenty) and many cases (more than 200). An exploratory examination of the data dealing with the problems stated above can be expected to demand at least ten times more effort than an analysis of the main research hypothesis for which the study was launched. Larger data sets or those with many missing values are almost entirely exploratory; they can keep someone with a large responsive computer busy for weeks, or perhaps years. At each stage of the screening, analysis uncovers information that affects the subsequent steps in the analysis (for example, the need for stratification on age, sex, diagnosis, the need for transformation, etc.).

The BMDP Manual has a discussion of these problems (Chapter 2). A number of the examples associated with the D programs are included in the manual and illustrate the screening operations suggested above. See also TR.77. How other programs are used to serve screening or exploratory functions is also more fully explained in the manual. The P-programs are, in general, easy to use for screening since many of them are constructed to allow the designation of subgroups, which can be analyzed separately, and supply printer graphics that allow one to more easily examine differences in the subgroups. For example, programs P5D and P6D allow the graphical identification of subgroups with different alphabetic letters (see Examples 6D.3 and 6D.4). A paper by D.J. Finney discussing the importance of screening data has appeared in Biometrics 31, 1975, pp. 375-386. His title is: "Numbers and Data."

Which programs could be used in a sequence of analyses for screening data with 15 variables recorded for 400 cases?

- P4D needs no format and gives a column-by-column summary of the data. It lists all data in various forms (garbage included) so long as they are legal. This permits a simple first screening of the data file. Usually this program is run several times, once listing the data as they exist and then additional runs are made with certain types of values replaced with specific characters.

- P2D supplies basic frequency counts, uncovers more keypunch errors, identifies how many values fall outside acceptable minimum and maximum limits, and reveals various distributional anomalies for each variable in turn (errors that are evident from these distributions can then be corrected).

- P5D allows the pictorial visualization of each variable with histograms and plots for subgroups as well as for the entire group; probit plots allow an assessment of normality.

- P6D provides crossplots of two variables, which allows an examination of the interrelation of pairs of variables and may make further errors evident.

- P4F tabulates two-way contingency tables with a variety of descriptors of the relationship between two variables; such tables are frequently used in the screening phase of analysis to reveal the presence of impossible values in the data.

- P7D provides histograms of each variable for designated subgroups or strata from which you can observe the character of changes in the distributions from strata to strata, such as basic information for anticipated regression or other multivariate procedures.

- P3M provides multidimensional histograms, etc.

See article on P1D (below) for detailed examples of using that program for screening purposes.

C.12 Using P1D to Identify and List Cases Containing Special or Unacceptable Values

MaryAnn Hill
BMDP Statistical Software, UCLA

Even the most thorough univariate data screening may fail to reveal the presence of inconsistencies or incorrect values in the data; blunders or outliers in the data may be identified if one variable is examined with another variable. For example, an adult weighing 195 pounds is not too unusual until you notice that the corresponding height is five feet. Knowledge of the data structure and internal relations can be used to complete a better data screening. Scatter plots and two-way tables help identify problems. However, if the data file is large it is difficult to identify the extreme or illogical cases. Investigators want to locate such cases quickly and to be able to examine other variables for that case.

P1D can be used to print only the cases containing such problems. A listing of such cases is obtained by using transformations to create new variables that represent the problems of interest, stating minimum, maximum and/or missing values for the new variables, and then requesting that cases with extreme values be printed.

Two-way tables confirm the existence of inconsistencies, such as a male coded as a birth control pill user. Here such a two-way table (code values are indicated) might appear as

		Pill User	
		1 yes	2 no
SEX	1 Male	X	
	2 Female		

Counts found in the "male" - "pill yes" cell indicate a miscoding or recording error. In order to identify cases with this mistake, create a new variable, NEW1=10xSEX + PILL. The new variable now contains codes 11,12,21,22 corresponding to each cell; 11 is the code for the problem cell. Stating a minimum code of 12 makes the value 11 fall outside the acceptable range. P1D has the option to list cases outside stated limits.

A particular response to a survey question may limit the range of answers to another question or require that it be skipped. This type of inconsistency can also be detected with a two-way table:

		Type of Drug		
		not applicable 0	type A 1	type B 2
DRUG TAKEN	1 yes			
	2 no		X	X

Counts found in the marked cells are unacceptable. Here the transformation NEW2=10xDRUG + TYPE, results in a code for each cell: 10,11,12,20,21,22. Cases with codes 21 or 22 need to be examined. They can be listed by stating a maximum of 20 and requesting that cases with larger values be printed.

A scatter plot of systolic blood pressure versus diastolic blood pressure reveals such errors as a systolic reading less than a diastolic one. To locate this error we generate a new variable NEW3 = SYSTOLIC - DIASTOLIC and request that any case with a value of NEW3 less than zero be printed. At the same time we might be concerned about readings differing by more than 60 units so a maximum value of 60 can also be stated.

P1D program control instructions for listing the problem cases discussed above are

```
/ PROBLEM
/ INPUT     VARIABLES ARE 7.
            FORMAT IS '(A4,6F5.0)'.

/ VARIABLE NAMES ARE ID, SEX, PILL, DRUG, TYPE,
            SYSTOLIC, DIASTOLIC, NEW1, NEW2, NEW3.
            LABEL IS ID.  ADD = 3.  AFTERT.
            MIN = (8)12, (10)0.  MAX = (9)20, 60.

/ TRANSF    NEW1 = 10 * SEX + PILL
            NEW2 = 10 * DRUG + TYPE.
            NEW3 = SYSTOLIC-DIASTOLIC.

/ PRINT     MIN.  MAX.
/ END
```

NEW1, NEW2 and NEW3 are the three new variables ADDED through the TRANSFORM paragraph. AFTERT indicates that the check for extreme values should be made after the transformations are performed. Cases with the new codes falling outside the stated limits are listed with their ID number as a label, along with the data values for variables one through ten. The words TOOBIG, TOOSMALL or MISSING are printed instead of the actual value out of range. In the above example the unacceptable new codes were extremes. If a code of interest falls in the middle, the MISSING option can be used to print out such cases. The output example below lists only unusual cases.

CASE NO	LABEL	SEX	PILL	DRUG	TYP1	SYSTOLIC	DIASTOLIC	NEW1	NEW2	NEW3
3	368	1	2	2	0	90	135	12	20	TOO SMALL
25	403	1	1	1	2	150	120	TOO SMALL	12	30
53	1072	2	1	2	1	130	95	21	TOO LARGE	35

A listing of a subpopulation may be obtained in a similar manner. For example, the following transformations may be used to obtain female pill users who take Drug A and have a systolic blood pressure over 200.

```
      NEW4 = SEX EQ 2  AND PILL EQ 1 AND
             TYPE EQ 1 AND SYSTOLIC GT 200.
```

NEW4 is 1 (true) only if the four conditions are all true. Otherwise NEW4 is 0 (false). Declaring 1 to be a MISSING value for NEW4 and requesting PRINT MISSING will cause a listing of the desired subpopulation to be printed.

C.13 The Iterated Least Square Method of Estimating Mean and Variance Components Using P3R

R.L. Anderson and R.I. Jennrich, Department of Biomathematics, UCLA

Program P3R provides a convenient means of implementing R.L. Anderson's iterated least squares method. Consider a normal random vector y whose mean $\mu = \mu(\alpha)$ depends on a vector α of "mean components" and whose covariance matrix $\Sigma = \Sigma(\sigma^2)$ depends on a vector σ^2 of "variance components." We begin with a set of statistics $\bar{y}_1,\ldots,\bar{y}_p$ that are sufficient for α, and a second set $MS_1,\ldots,MS_q$ that are sufficient for σ^2. The general procedure is to fit both sets of statistics to their expectations using the inverses of their covariance matrices as weights. This will produce maximum likelihood estimates and information theory standard errors.

To illustrate the procedure, consider the unbalanced two-stage nested model developed by Anderson and Crump (1967) and further explored by Thompson and Anderson (1975). The sampling process involves k_1 classes with one sample per class and k_2 classes with two samples per class. The model is

$$y_{ij} = \alpha + a_i + b_{ij}; \quad i = 1,\ldots,k_1 + k_2$$

$$j = \begin{cases} 1; & i \leq k_1 \\ 1, 2; & i > k_1 \end{cases}$$

The a_i are NID(0, σ_a^2), and b_{ij} are NID(0, σ_b^2), and the a_i are independent of the b_{ij}. The means

$$\bar{y}_1 = \sum_{i \leq k_1} y_{i1}/k_1, \quad \bar{y}_2 = \sum_{i > k_1} \sum_j y_{ij}/2k_2$$

are sufficient for α and the following sums of squares are sufficient for σ_a^2 and σ_b^2:

$$SSM_1 = k_1(\bar{y}_1 - \alpha)^2, \quad SSM_2 = 2k_2(\bar{y}_2 - \alpha)^2$$

$$SSA_1 = \sum_{i \leq k} (y_{i1} - \bar{y}_1)^2, \quad SSA_2 = 2 \sum_{i > k_1} (\bar{y}_i. - \bar{y}_2)^2$$

$$SSB_2 = \sum_{i > k_1} \sum_j (y_{ij} - \bar{y}_i.)^2$$

where $\bar{y}_i. = \sum_{j=1}^{2} y_{ij}/2$, $i > k_1$. Note that SSM_1 and SSM_2 depend on α. We summarize these statistics as means and mean squares.

df	Mean or Mean Sq	Expectation	Variance
1	MSM_1	$\sigma_b^2 + \sigma_a^2$	$2EMS^2/df$
$k_1 - 1$	MSA_1	$\sigma_b^2 + \sigma_a^2$	$2EMS^2/df$
1	MSM_2	$\sigma_b^2 + 2\sigma_a^2$	$2EMS^2/df$
$k_2 - 1$	MSA_2	$\sigma_b^2 + 2\sigma_a^2$	$2EMS^2/df$
k_2	MSB_2	σ_b^2	$2EMS^2/df$
	$\bar{y}_1$	α	$\sigma_b^2/k_1 + \sigma_a^2/k_1$
	$\bar{y}_2$	α	$\sigma_b^2/2k_2 + \sigma_a^2/k_2$

The procedure is to fit the expectations in the third column to the mean squares and means in the second column using (since everything in sight is independent) the reciprocals of the variances in the fourth column as weights. Using P3R for this purpose and the data (Davies, 1954, p. 117)

```
851  863  854  863  869  875  845  869  857  869
                         869  857  869  857  881
```

where $k_1 = 5$ and $k_2 = 5$, the required P3R setup for the FUN routine is:

```
X(7)=X(2)
IF(X(5).NE.0.0) X((7)=X(5)*(X(2)-P(3))**2
F=P(1)*X(3)+P(2)*X(4)
DF(1)=X(3)
DF(2)=X(4)
DF(3)=0.0
X(6)=X(1)/(2*F**2)
IF(X(1).NE.0.0)GO TO 1
F=P(3)
DF(1)=0.0
DF(2)=0.0
DF(3)=1.0
X(6)=1.0/(P(1)/X(3)+P(2)/X(4))
1 CONTINUE
```

The required program control information is:

```
/ PROBLEM TITLE = 'ITERATED LEAST SQUARES'.
/ INPUT VARIABLE = 7. FORMAT = '(F2.0,F7.0,5F3.0)'.
/ REGRESSION DEPEND = 7. PARAM = 3. WEIGHT = 6.
        ITER = 10. HALV = 0. CONVER = -1.0.
        MEANSQ = 1.0.
/ PARAMETER INITIAL = 1.0,1.0,1.0.
/ END
```

And the required data are:

```
1 860.0  1 1   5 1
4  54.0  1 1     1
1 864.8  1 2  10 1
4 212.4  1 2     1
5  32.4  1 0     1
  860.0  5 5     1
  864.8 10 5     1
```

Here

$$\bar{y}_1 = 860.0 , \quad MSA_1 = 54.0$$

$$\bar{y}_2 = 864.8 , \quad MSA_2 = 212.4 , \quad MSB_2 = 32.4.$$

These were computed by hand but could have been obtained through using a program such as P7D. The program converged in 5 iterations from "arbitrary" starting values $\alpha = \sigma_a^2 = \sigma_b^2 = 1$ to give the results:

Component	Estimate	Standard Error
σ_b^2	30.23	18.9
σ_a^2	52.65	35.7
α	862.64	2.73

See the July 1975 BMD Communications for further comments on using P3R for iteratively reweighted least squares fitting.

References

Davies, O.L. (1954). The Design and Analysis of Industrial Experiments, New York, Hafner.

Anderson, R.L. and P.P. Crump (1967). Comparison of designs and estimation procedures for estimating parameters in a two-stage nested process. Technometrics 9, 499-516.

Thompson, W.O. and R.L. Anderson (1975). A comparison of designs and estimators for the two-stage nested random model. Technometrics 17, 37-44.

C.14 Lagged Variables Using Transformation Paragraph

Alan B. Forsythe
Department of Biomathematics, UCLA

We have been asked how to generate lagged variables without recreating the data set or using the FORTRAN transformation option in the BMDP programs. A lagged variable has as its value for case i the value of the variable at case i-1 (lag 1). For example, if we wish to estimate the weekly incidence of a disease as a linear function of the incidence the previous two weeks, we could have as our model

Incidence (week i) = $\alpha + \beta_1$ Incidence (week i-1) $+ \beta_2$ Incidence (week i-2) $+ \varepsilon$.

Our data could be one weekly incidence per card. We do not want to repunch the deck to put the previous two weeks data on the cards. Here is the program control information for a linear regression program:

```
/ PROBLEM      TITLE IS 'LAGGED REGRESSION'.
/ INPUT        VARIABLE IS 1.  FORMAT IS '(F3.2)'.
/ VARIABLE     NAMES ARE INCIDENC, LAG1, LAG2, TEMP.
               ADDED ARE 3.  RETAIN.
               USE ARE INCIDENC, LAG1, LAG2.
/ TRANSFORM    LAG2 = LAG1.      LAG1 = TEMP.
               TEMP = INCIDENC.  USE = KASE GT 2.
/ REGRESSION   DEPENDENT IS INCIDENC.
/ END
```

Notes: (1) The USE statement in VARIABLE paragraph discards the variable named TEMP.

(2) The TRANSFORM USE = KASE GT 2. discards the first two cases, since they do not have the data for both previous weeks

(3) RETAIN. is required in the VARIABLE paragraph to obtain lagged variables.

C.15   Cross Validation in BMDP9R

James W. Frane
BMDP Statistical Software, UCLA

The ultimate assessment of the merit of a regression equation is how well it fits new data. P9R allows easy evaluation of a regression equation by means of the case weight variable. The input data are divided into two groups: the training set from which the regression equation is computed and a cross validation set. Cases in the training set are given weight equal to one. Cases in the cross validation set are given weight zero. P9R computes the residual mean square for the cases with positive weight and the average squared residual for the cases with zero weight.

The case weights can be assigned randomly to divide a single sample into two parts. The following setup will divide a sample into two roughly equal parts.

```
/ PROBLEM      TITLE IS 'CROSS VALIDATION'.
/ INPUT        VARIABLES ARE 10.
               FORMAT IS '(10F4.0)'.
/ VARIABLE     ADD IS 1.
               WEIGHT IS 11.
/ REGRESS      DEPENDENT IS 1.
               INDEPENDENT ARE 2 TO 10.
/ PRINT        MATRICES ARE CORR, RESID.
/ TRANSFORM    X(11) = 0.
               IF(RNDU(5793171) LT .5)
                 THEN X(11) = 1.
/ END
```

The IF-THEN transformation statement uses the logical operator "less than" to set X(11) equal to one if the uniform random number (between zero and one) is less than one-half.

If the first fifty cases comprise the training set, and the remaining cases comprise the cross validation set, we could use the transformation statement

```
X(11) IS KASE LE 50.
```

C.16   Partial and Canonical Correlation

Mitchell Karpman
University of Maryland

Canonical correlation attempts to define underlying between sets covariation for two groups of variables (a,b). By removing a set of variables (c) from one or both sets (a,b), part or partial canonical correlation can be performed. You begin by regressing a set of variables on another set (a|c) using BMDP6R and saving the residuals by stating CONTENT=DATA in the SAVE paragraph. Then input the saved file into BMDP6M and use set b with the residuals (a|c) in the part canonical analysis. For partial canonical analysis, regress both a and b on c and use both residuals (a|c, b|c) in BMDP6M. For bipartial canonical analysis, it is necessary to save two different sets of residuals (a|c, b|d) by running BMDP6R Save file twice and using the two sets of residuals in BMDP6M.

In addition Cooley and Lohnes (1971) suggest using the pooled within groups correlation matrix in a canonical solution when encountered with a grouping variable. This can be accomplished by generating a dummy variable in BMDP6R in the TRANSFORM paragraph and regressing both sets of variables on the dummy variables and saving the residuals for analysis in BMDP6M. Similarly by creating appropriate dummy variables and product interaction terms, you can generate a pooled within groups correlation matrix for any factorial design.

References

Cooley W.W. & P. Lohnes. Multivariate Data Analysis. N.Y.: Wiley, 1971.
Timm, N.H. & J. Carlson. Part and Bipartial Canonical Correlation Analysis. Psychometrika, 1976, 41, 159-176.

APPENDIX D

How To:

Request Copies of the BMDP Programs
Report Difficulties and Suspected Errors
Learn About BMDP on a Microcomputer
Arrange a Visit by a BMDP Statistician
Find Out More About Our Short Courses
Obtain Additional Manuals
Obtain BMDP Communications and Pocket Guide
Obtain BMDP Technical Reports

Our Address

BMDP Statistical Software
1964 Westwood Blvd., Suite 202
Los Angeles, CA   90025
(213) 475-5700

Copies of the BMDP Programs

BMDP programs are written in FORTRAN (to maximize portability) and distributed on tape as FORTRAN card images. The BMDP programs are also distributed as load and object modules for IBM 360/370 computers.

Since there are some differences in FORTRAN from computer to computer, we have established redistribution centers for other computer systems.

Requests for copies of the IBM version of the BMDP programs must be made on one of our request forms. For our Tape Copy Request Brochure, call or write:

BMDP Program Librarian
1964 Westwood Blvd., Suite 202
Los Angeles, CA   90025
(213) 475-5700

Current addresses and telephone numbers of the redistribution centers for other computer systems are included in the Tape Copy Request Brochure. Note that versions obtained from redistribution centers may not be as recent as those obtained from us. As of 1982 there are redistribution centers for the following computer systems:

Burroughs
CDC 6000/CYBER
Data General MV 8000/MV 6000
DEC 10/20
Fujitsu Facom series
HP-3000
Hitachi Hitac Series
Honeywell
ICL System 4 and 2900 series
MODCOMP Classic
PDP-11
Perkin-Elmer (Interdata)
Prime
Siemens

Telefunken
Univac 70/90 series
Univac 1100 series
Vax
Xerox Sigma 7

We encourage users of other computer equipment to become redistribution centers and so avoid duplication of effort.

Difficulties and Suspected Errors

We are most anxious to improve the quality of the BMDP programs. To report an error, please send a complete listing of the input and output to

BMDP Statistical Software
1964 Westwood Blvd., Suite 202
Los Angeles, CA   90025

BMDP on a Microcomputer

The 1982 mainframe version of BMDP (with many of the new features introduced in the 1983 release) is available on a desktop computer system.

The microcomputer features a high-performance Motorola 68000 CPU (executing 1 million instructions per second), the UNIX™ System III operating system, and supports software development in FORTRAN, PASCAL, C, APL, and LISP.

The standard configuration is 256 kilobytes of memory and is expandable to 1.5 megabytes of memory. A wide variety of peripherals such as printers, plotters, color graphics terminals, magnetic tape drives, and an array processor can be easily added.

Numerous application software packages are available for our computer, including word processing, financial modeling, and relational data base management.

Human engineering plays an important role in the integration of BMDP with our desktop computer. An output manager supports interactive use of BMDP software. Entire session input and output may be viewed through horizontal and vertical scrolling on the screen. Data may easily be moved between this and other computer systems via serial communications or ETHERNET local area networks.

The desktop system is fully supported with on-site and depot maintenance worldwide. Lease/purchase financing can be arranged.

For further information, contact:

BMDP Statistical Software
1964 Westwood Blvd.
Suite 202
Los Angeles, CA   90025
(213) 475-5700

SPECIFICATIONS

Processor
 Motorola 68000 CPU (8 Mhz, 1 million
  instructions/second)
 IEEE 796 Multibus Architecture, 6 board slots,
  32-bit registers, 16-bit data bus, 24-bit
  address bus
 Memory management

Memory
 256 Kbytes RAM, expandable to 1.5 Mbytes
 16 Kbytes EPROM, expandable to 64 Kbytes

Peripherals
 CRT terminal (ANSI 3.64, VT-100 keyboard, P31)
 10 Mbyte Winchester disk (optional 21 Mbyte)
 600 Kbyte floppy disk
 2 RS-232C serial ports (50-19200 baud)
 16-bit parallel port (1 Mbyte/second)

System Software
 UNIX™ System III operating system, C, Assembler
 Languages: FORTRAN, PASCAL, LISP, APL, COBOL
 Screen editor and session manager
  (UNIX is a trademark of Bell Laboratories)

Electrical
 AC power - 110/220 VAC, 50/60 Hz
 240 watts power consumption

Physical
 Height - 16"   Depth - 18"
 Width - 19"   Weight - 55 lbs.

Environment
 FCC Part 15, Subpart J, Class A
 UL 478 and 114, CSA 154 and 143

On-Site Visits by BMDP Statisticians

Arrangements can be made to have BMDP statisticians stop by your facility to give seminars, short courses and consulting regarding your statistical design and analysis problems. Consulting fees are $500 per day plus travel and other expenses. Travel expenses can be reduced by coordinating a visit to your facility with other travel by our staff. Discounts are available for academic institutions.

European visits can be made as well. Our staff visits several sites in Western Europe each year. Contact us now to make arrangements for a BMDP statistician to visit you. Call or write

 Robert Hensley
 1964 Westwood Blvd., Suite 202
 Los Angeles, CA 90025
 (213) 475-5700

BMDP Short Courses

We also offer a number of introductory and intermediate short courses in the United States and Europe. For more information, call or write us at the above address.

BMDP Manuals

BMDP Manuals can be ordered from

 University of California Press
 2223 Fulton Street
 Berkeley, CA 94720
 (415) 642-6682
or
 University of California Press, Ltd.
 Ely House
 37 Dover St.
 London, W1X 4HQ
 ENGLAND
 Telephone: 01-499-4688 or
       01-493-5061
 Telex: 24224 ref 3545
 Cable: CCJ London W1

(We supply a copy of the manual with each Tape Copy.)

BMDP Communications

BMDP Communications is a newsletter that contains notices of updates to the BMDP programs and manual, and short articles that discuss the programs (see Appendix C). It is currently issued approximately three times a year at no charge. To be put on the mailing list, please send a letter to the Editor,

 BMDP Statistical Software
 1964 Westwood Blvd., Suite 202
 Los Angeles, CA 90025

Other BMDP Documentation

Available from us here at BMDP are the following:

BMDP User's Digest - a 157-page condensed guide to the BMDP programs. Coat pocket-size, with spiral wire binding.

BMDP Reference Card - a shirt pocket-size, quick reference list of BMDP Control Language instructions.

BMDP Technical Reports

We publish a series of technical reports, some of which discuss uses of the programs. Published versions of many of the reports are available from the books or journals where they were published. The following reports are available for a nominal handling and mailing fee. Send orders to the address above.

Technical Reports Currently Available
(Recent reports are listed with a
brief abstract)

2. Novel Uses of BMD Programs: Canonical Correlation Analysis of Contingency Tables (1970) - Ray Mickey, 6 pp., $1.

8. Annotated Computer Output for Factor Analysis Using Professor Jarvik's Smoking Questionnaire (1974) - James Frane and Mary Ann Hill, 46 pp., $4.

D

9. Maximum Likelihood Estimation by Means of Nonlinear Least Squares (1975) - Robert I. Jennrich and Roger H. Moore, 9 pp., $1.

11. Newton-Raphson and Related Algorithms for Maximum Likelihood Variance Component Estimation (1975) - R.I. Jennrich, 27 pp., $3.

15. Chi-Square Probabilities for 2x2 Tables (1975) - D. Goyette and M. Mickey, 133 pp., $7.

19. Experimental Data Sets (1975) - Alan Forsythe, Editor, 293 pp., $20.

28. Randomization or Minimization in the Treatment Assignment of Patient Trials: Validity and Power (1977) - A.B. Forsythe and F.W. Stitt, 9 pp., $1.

30. Robustness in Real Life (1978). MaryAnn Hill and W.J. Dixon, 52 pp., $5.

32. Ridge Regression, Bayes Estimation, Variance Components and the General Mixed Model (1977) - R.I. Jennrich, 19 pp., $2.

34. Letting BMDP8V Tell Us Something About Randomized Blocks, Repeated Measures and Split Plots (1977) - R.I. Jennrich, 17 pp., $2.

41. BMDP and BMDP Approaches to Unbalanced Data (1978) - James W. Frane, 11 pp., $1.

42. Sample Program to Write a Data Matrix on a BMDP File (1978) - James W. Frane, 6 pp., $1.

44. Detecting and Describing Statistical and Numerical Ill-Conditioning (1978) - James W. Frane, 42 pp., $3.

45. Missing Data and BMDP: Some Pragmatic Approaches (1978) - James W. Frane, 12 pp., $2.

46. Fitting Nonlinear Models to Data (1978) - R.I. Jennrich and M.L. Ralston, 80 pp., $6.

48. Annotated Computer Output for Regression Analysis: A Supplement to Writeups for Computer Programs BMDP2R and BMDP9R (1979) - MaryAnn Hill, 78 pp., $6.

Two multiple linear regression programs, BMDP2R (Stepwise Regression) and BMDP9R (All Possible Subset Regression) are exemplified with detailed comments directly inserted on the computer printouts. The data set is typical in that it discloses many of the common problems found in the real world of regression analysis.

49. Analysis of the Time Series with Calendar Effects (1979) - Lon-Mu Liu, 16 pp., $2.

This article presents a comprehensive way to identify and estimate a time series model that is subject to calendar intervention. A theoretical study is presented, followed by the analysis of an actual series.

50. A Bayesian Approach to Generalized Kalman Filter Models (1979) - Lon-Mu Liu, 23 pp., $3.

This paper discusses a Bayesian approach to regression models with time-varying parameters, usually referred to as the Kalman filter models. Unlike most other Kalman filter models, the models presented here (called generalized Kalman filter models) assume that more than one data point can be obtained at each time period. The problems of parameter inferences and prediction are discussed, illustrated by an actual example.

51. A Spectral Analysis of a Time Series in which Probabilities of Observation are Periodic (1979) - Anthony Thrall, 32 pp., $3.

Time series containing more than a few missing values challenge current methods of analysis. This paper offers an approach when missing values occur independently of one another and with periodic probabilities. An entomological time series of this nature is discussed.

52. Some Computing Methods for Unbalanced Analysis of Variance and Covariance (1979) - James W. Frane, 17 pp., $2.

Many computing algorithms are used for analysis of variance and covariance. Choice of an ideal algorithm is dependent on many factors, including balance, type of model (fixed, random, or mixed), number of dependent variables, covariates, sample size, required auxiliary output, numerical conditioning, and the statistical hypotheses to be tested. Attention is focused on the general linear hypothesis (general linear model), repeated measures, and efficient computation for multiple observations per cell. Discussion is directed toward testing fixed effects.

54. Parameter Estimation in Dynamic Models (1979) - Lon-Mu Liu, 16 pp., $2.

We study the parameter estimation of a first-order dynamic model for intervention and transfer function analysis. We propose a new parameterization to avoid the "overshoot" problem in nonlinear estimation in a frequently used parameterization (Box and Tiao, 1975).

55. BMDP Programmer's Guide (1981) - J.W. Frane, about 500 pp., $30.

Use of this Programmer's Guide assumes basic familiarity with the BMDP programs, especially the Control Language and BMDP Files as described in the BMDP User's Manual. The Programmer's Guide contains three major sections: writeups for approximately 200 subroutines and common blocks used extensively in the BMDP programs; a fully-operational prototype, or shell, BMDP program with overlay control cards; and the main body of the Guide, which discusses commonly used BMDP subroutines and common blocks in the context of the prototype program. The Guide is written to be used by BMDP programmers at UCLA, by people who want to make enhancements to BMDP programs, and by people who want to write a BMDP-style program by expanding the prototype program.

56. Annotated Output for BMDQ4V (URWAS) (1979)
    - Jerome Toporek, 37 pp., $3.

This report contains a series of annotated output from analysis of variance problems run on BMDQ4V, URWAS (University of Rochester Weighted ANOVA System). Most of the common aspects of the input and output for this program are highlighted. Several less common features are also used and described.

58. Fitting Pharmacokinetic Models with BMDPAR
    (1979) - M.L. Ralston and R.I. Jennrich, P.F. Sampson, F.K. Uno, 37 pp., $3.

Fitting pharmacokinetic models to observed data is an important application of nonlinear regression. It is natural to describe such models in terms of compartmental analysis schematics or as a system of differential equations. At times, the system of differential equations can be easily solved explicitly for the regression function to be fitted, but this is not always the case. The more general approach adopted here uses numerical integration to solve the system of differential equations for specific values of the parameters. It then uses the results to evaluate the regression function being fitted.

This report provides a set of subroutines that perform numerical integration, and describes how to use them with BMDPAR to fit pharmacokinetic models.

59. ANOVA with General Cell Weights (1979) - M.L. Davidson and Jerome D. Toporek, 29 pp., $3.

This report discusses the role of cell weights in ANOVA, presents methods for conducting an ANOVA for any given weights, and introduces a new program, URWAS (University of Rochester Weighted ANOVA System), in which these methods have been implemented. Among the program's capabilities are between-group and within-observation designs; factorial, nested, and incomplete designs; and multivariate analysis of variance and covariance. (In the 1981 version of BMDP, URWAS appears as BMDP4V).

60. Spectral Estimation Following Simple Seasonal Adjustment (1979) - A.D. Thrall, 11 pp., $1.

In economics, meteorology, and other areas, we often construct a time series model consisting of seasonal means plus a stationary component. A simple treatment of such a model is to estimate and remove the seasonal means, leaving a residual series for spectral analysis. This paper recommends a slight modification of a standard method of spectral estimation to avoid the "overadjusted" appearance of the resulting spectra.

61. Test Problems from the Pharmacokinetic Literature Requiring Fitting Models Defined by Differential Equations (1979) - Frederic K. Uno, Mary L. Ralston, Robert I. Jennrich and and Paul F. Sampson, 13 pp., $1.

This report provides test problems in a readily accessible form for researchers interested in fitting pharmacokinetic models, and more generally, for those interested in fitting models defined by differential equations. The models and data we describe were taken from papers reporting actual pharmacokinetic experiments. The parameter estimates (and their standard deviations) reported here were computed with BMDPAR, using the numerical integration routines described in BMDP Technical Report No. 58.

62. A Bayesian Approach to Random Coefficient Regression Models (1979) - Lon-Mu Liu, 17 pp.,$2.

Linear regression models with coefficients across individual units regarded as random samples from some population are studied in this article from a Bayesian viewpoint. A prior distribution of the secondary parameters, and the predictive distribution of the future value are then examined. Data from a performance test on pigs is analyzed and discussed. We also discuss the difficulties involved in using a Lindley and Smith (1972) prior in this problem.

64. Random Coefeicient First Order Autoregressive Models (1979) - Lon-Mu Liu and G.C. Tiao, 27 pp., $2.

This paper discusses the random coefficient model applied to panel data in a time series context. Some of the basic issues involved in pooling problems are studied. An analysis of a first order autoregressive model, where the autoregressive coefficients across units are regarded as a random sample from a beta distribution, is presented and illustrated by an example using real data. Generalizations to higher-order models are discussed.

66. The BMDP Programmer's Guide, An Overview (1979) - James Frane, 7 pp., $1.

Please see abstract for Technical Report No. 55.

67. User's Manual for BMDP4V (URWAS): General Univariate and Multivariate Analysis of Variance (1981) - M. Davidson and J. Toporek, under revision.

This report is the complete reference manual for BMDP4V. It contains descriptions and discussion of advanced features not found in the 1981 BMDP Manual.

The Control Language for BMDP4V consists of two major parts: Input Control Language and Analysis Control Language. Both are described in this report. Input Control Language is divided into two parts, explaining those specifications used once for each problem, and those that may be changed for successive subproblems that are largely peculiar to P4V. Also presented are conventions for describing the data as classified into cells, possibly using both between-groups factors and within-cases (within-subjects, repeated measures) factors, the rules for specifying cell weights and a brief review of the meaning of these weights. The role of weights in the two-factor ANOVA with interaction and in the fitting of orthogonal polynomials are discussed as examples.

The topics covered in this report that are not discussed in detail in the BMDP Manual include use of DESIGN, ORTHO, and INTERACT paragraphs for model description, the STRUCTURE formula procedure, and treatment of unsaturated models.

D

68. Identification of Transfer Function Models Via Least Squares (1980) - Lon-Mu Liu and Dominique M. Hanssens, 19 pp., $2.

This report proposes a procedure for transfer function identification based on least-squares estimates of transfer function weights using the original or filtered series. Arguments are presented in favor of a common filter to all series. This common filter can be obtained from the autoregressive structure of the input variables. The method is illustrated using a simulated and an actual example; in both, it is shown how this straightforward approach outperforms other identification methods, such as Box and Jenkins' (1976) prewhitening and Haugh and Box's (1977) double prewhitening approaches.

69. The Univariate Approach to Repeated Measures - Foundation, Advantages, and Caveats (1980) - James W. Frane, under revision.

Repeated-measures and changeover designs are very common in the health and behavioral sciences. These designs lie in concept between fixed effects and mixed models and are similar to split-plot designs. This report presents a review of several issues, including a description of the general repeated measures design, a comparison with split-plot designs, testing special assumptions required by repeated measures, analysis of carryover effects, different kinds of predicted values and residuals, orthogonal polynomial decomposition, unbalanced designs, cell weights, missing values, and blocking. Examples are given using computer program BMDP2V.

70. Fitting Models Defined by Differential Equations (1980) - M.L. Ralston, R.I. Jennrich, P.F. Sampson, and F.K. Uno, 9 pp., $1.

A methodology for fitting models defined by systems of differential equations is investigated. We interface a nonlinear regression program, BMDPAR, with one of the better numerical integration codes evaluated by Shampine, Watts, and Davenport. Applications, primarily in pharmacology, are characterized and used to compare our approach to that of others. Fitting difficulties inherent in such applications are discussed, and issues arising in the design of a general-purpose program are considered.

71. Annotated Output for BMDPKM K-means Clustering - Laszlo Engelman, 47 pp., $4.

Clustering is the process of partitioning a set of subjects or items into subgroups, based on some measure of similarity of the items. The data items may be blood measurements taken from patients at a clinic, soil samples taken at different locations, scores for students at a high school, etc. Cluster analysis differs from other statistical techniques (e.g., analysis of variance, discriminant analysis) in that group membership is not known.

74. Stepwise Logistic Regression by Maximum Likelihood or Asymptotic Covariance - Laszlo Engelman, 5 pp., $1.

This report describes how maximized likelihood ratios or the asymptotic covariance matrix can be used for selection of the next term to be entered or removed from a logistic model.

75. The Multivariate Approach to Repeated Measures - Michael L. Davidson. (University of Rochester), 30 pp., $3.

If repeated measures are construed as elements of multivariate observations and are then permitted arbitrary covariance structure, there results a growth-curve or "profile" model that is naturally analyzed as a MANOVA on specified contrasts among the repeated observations. Where the assumptions of both are met, the multivariate approach is equivalent asymptotically, but inferior in small samples, to the univariate. Where the univariate approach has been adapted to arbitrary covariance structure, the analysis may be much more, or much less, powerful and precise than the multivariate analysis. A number of so far unsolved technical problems emerge from the multivariate approach to some topics, such as the repeated measures analysis of covariance.

76. An Efficient Algorithm for Computing Covariance from Data with Missing Values - Laszlo Engelman 9 pp., $1.

An algorithm for computing covariance and correlation matrices from data with missing values is presented. In terms of the number of operations performed (hence CPU time used), this algorithm is more efficient than that used by most statistical computing packages. CPU time efficiency is attained without undue increase in the number of input/output operations or memory space requirements.

77. Annotated Computer Output for Data Screening - MaryAnn Hill, 92 pp., $8.

A step-by-step guide is presented for screening data and preparing them for analysis. Eight BMDP computer programs are exemplified with the author's detailed comments written on the output; the comments describe the screening process and interpret the techniques and options available in the programs. The data set is typical in that it discloses many of the common problems found in clinical studies. An emphasis is placed on the need for careful screening and for close collaboration between the investigator, the statistician, and the computer support staff.

78. IBM MVS/TSO CLISTS for Running BMDP Interactively (1981) - Jerome D. Toporek and James W. Frane, 13 pp., $2.

In this report, the authors present two CLISTS for running BMDP interactively. The first list corresponds to the usual BIMED batch procedures, the second to the batch BIMEDT procedure used to interface FORTRAN statements with BMDP.

APPENDIX E

IBM OS SYSTEM CARDS REQUIRED TO USE BMDP PROGRAMS

<u>IBM OS</u>   <u>Fill in those needed at your facility</u>

● STANDARD DECK ●

```
job card               //job card for your computer
program ID             //  EXEC  BIMED,PROG=BMDPxx
end of system cards    //SYSIN DD  *
```

```
                       ┌─────────────────────────┐
                       │ Control Language instructions │
                       │ and data (if on cards) are │
                       │ placed here -- see program │
                       │ description             │
                       └─────────────────────────┘
```

```
end of job             //
```

If you are using a tape or disk
(as for a BMDP File), insert

```
    //FTyyF001  DD  DSNAME=filename,DISP=OLD
```

before

```
    //SYSIN  DD  *
```

- -

● FORTRAN TRANSFORMATIONS ●

When transformations are specified by FORTRAN statements (Section 6.4)

```
job card               //job card for your computer
program ID             //  EXEC  BIMEDT,PROG=BMDPxx
FORTRAN statement      //TRANSF  DD  *
```

```
                       ┌─────────────────┐
                       │ FORTRAN statements │
                       └─────────────────┘
```

```
Control Language       //GO.SYSIN  DD  *
is next
```

```
                       ┌─────────────────────────┐
                       │ Control Language instructions │
                       │ and data (if on cards) are │
                       │ placed here -- see program │
                       │ description             │
                       └─────────────────────────┘
```

```
end of job             //
```

If you are using a tape or disk
(as for a BMDP File), insert

```
    //GO.FTyyF001  DD  DSNAME=filename,DISP=OLD
```

before

```
    //GO.SYSIN  DD  *
```

- -

● FUNCTIONS FOR PAR or P3R ●

When using PAR or P3R and specifying the function by FORTRAN statements

```
job card               //job card for your computer
program ID (note       //  EXEC  BIMEDT,PROG=BMDPxx
the T)
FORTRAN statement      //FUN  DD  *
```

```
                       ┌─────────────────┐
                       │ FORTRAN statements │
                       └─────────────────┘
```

```
Control Language       //GO.SYSIN  DD  *
is next
```

```
                       ┌─────────────────────────┐
                       │ Control Language instructions │
                       │ and data (if on cards) are │
                       │ placed here -- see program │
                       │ description             │
                       └─────────────────────────┘
```

```
end of job             //
```

If you are using a tape or disk
(as for a BMDP File), insert

```
    //GO.FTyyF001  DD  DSNAME=filename,DISP=OLD
```

before

```
    //GO.SYSIN  DD  *
```

APPENDIX F

NEW FEATURES, EXAMPLES, AND AMPLIFICATIONS.

Contents

F.1   The FOR notation — Further Examples

The use of the FOR % notation to generate multiple versions of an instruction, a paragraph, or a problem is described in Chapter 4, Section 4.1. Examples illustrating some common uses of the feature follow. General rules for using it appear at the end of this section (see Format).

EXAMPLES

Multiple Versions of an Instruction. If you want a separate plot for each subject's response over time, the required instructions for 6D would be:

```
/ PLOT    XVAR IS TIME. YVAR IS RESPONSE.

         GROUP IS 1.
         GROUP IS 2.
              .
              .
              .
         GROUP IS 30.
```

Instead of writing all of the GROUP statements, you can specify:

```
/ PLOT    XVAR IS TIME. YVAR IS RESPONSE.

         FOR J = 1 TO 30.
         % GROUP IS J. %
```

Note that the name (J) may be more than one character. We could write:

```
FOR SUBJECT = 1 TO 30. % GROUP IS SUBJECT. %
```

You may find it easier to read the BMDP instructions when a single letter is used, however.

Multiple Versions of a Paragraph. A majority of the BMDP programs have paragraphs that may be repeated within one problem (e.g., the HISTOGRAM paragraph in 7D). If you want to repeat the 2R REGRESSION paragraph for different dependent variables, as below,

```
/REGRESS    DEPEND IS Y1.   INDEP ARE AGE,BP.
/REGRESS    DEPEND IS Y2.   INDEP ARE AGE,BP.
/REGRESS    DEPEND IS Y3.   INDEP ARE AGE,BP.
```

specify

```
          FOR    Z=Y1,Y2,Y3.
% / REGRESS DEP IS Z.  INDEP ARE AGE,BP. %
```

The complete text between the % signs is repeated three times, first for Y1, then for Y2 and Y3. Use of this notation is not limited to generation instructions involving one name (as with "Z" above). For example, to obtain the regression setup shown on the left, specify the instructions on the right.

```
/REGR DEP=A. IND=E.        FOR U=A,B,C,D.
/REGR DEP=B. IND=F.            V=E,F,G,H.
/REGR DEP=C. IND=G.        % /REGR DEP=U.IND=V. %
/REGR DEP=D. IND=H.
```

Also, one generation instruction may be nested within another. For example,

```
/REGR DEP=A. IND=C.        FOR U=A,B.
/REGR DEP=A. IND=D.        %    FOR V=C,D,E.
/REGR DEP=A. IND=E.        % /REGR DEP=U. IND=V. % %
/REGR DEP=B. IND=C.
/REGR DEP=B. IND=D.
/REGR DEP=B. IND=E.
```

Multiple Problems. In the following setup, two runs of 2D are made: the first for males, the second for females. The data are read from a BMDP File in which the variable named SEX has the value 1 or 2.

```
FOR K=1,2.
%    / INPUT      UNIT IS 9.  CODE IS MYDATA.
     / TRANSFORM  USE=SEX EQ K.
     / END
```

Note that the / END replaces the final % sign here and no % sign should follow the / END. Nesting, as shown in the regression example above, is NOT allowed for multiple problems.

Generating Names. In this example we want to generate the names for 30 scores. The generated names will be listed within a longer list of names,

```
NAMES ARE AGE, SEX, SCORE1, SCORE2,...,
            SCORE29, SCORE30, TOTAL.
```

Using the new notation, we specify:

```
NAMES ARE AGE, SEX
    FOR J=1 TO 30. % , SCORE|J %
                        , TOTAL.
```

Note that the vertical bar character | is a symbol that tells the BMDP program to link the value of J to the text (e.g., SCORE|2 becomes SCORE2). On some printers the symbol "|" may appear as a caret mark or a copyright symbol instead.

A Caution About Trailing Commas. The list of names must end with a period. Thus, when the generated names are the last (or only) ones in the list, a period must follow the ending percent sign. For example, the instructions to provide grade-in-school labels for frequency table categories might be

```
CODES(GRADE) = 1 TO 12.
NAMES(GRADE) = GRADE_1, GRADE_2, ...,
            GRADE_12.
```

The appropriate shorthand notation to generate the names is

```
NAMES(GRADE) =
    FOR K=1 TO 12. % GRADE_|K , %.
```

The period following the second percent sign tells BMDP to change the trailing comma to a period.

Combining the INCLUDE Feature with the Generation Instruction. (The INCLUDE feature is also described in Section 4.1 of Chapter 4.) In the following set-up, two runs of 3D, the two-sample t test program, are made: in the first, variables are screened for sex differences and in the second, for differences between people who own or rent their home. The grouping information, stored in the INCLUDE file on Fortran unit 22, has the following records:

```
SEX             GROUPING IS SEX.
SEX     / GROUP CODES(SEX) = 1,2.
SEX             NAMES(SEX) = MALE,FEMALE.
HOME            GROUPING IS HOME.
HOME    / GROUP CODES(HOME) = 1,2.
HOME            NAMES(HOME) = OWN,RENT.
```

The 3D instructions that read the data from a BMDP File on unit 11 and the INCLUDE file from unit 22 are:

```
    / CONTROL MACUNIT IS 22. / END
FOR   A = SEX,HOME.
%   / INPUT UNIT IS 11.  CODE IS MYDATA.
    / VARIABLE
        FOR % INCLUDE A %
    / TEST  VAR = 3 TO 18.
    / END
```

The SEX grouping information is incorporated in the first run, the HOME information in the second. Note that the statements GROUPING IS SEX. and GROUPING IS HOME. are the last statements in the two resulting VARIABLE paragraphs. The same INCLUDE file also could be used with other programs (1D,5D, 6D,7M,AM,1R,1V) that require the GROUPING variable to be identified in the VARIABLE paragraph.

An Application Using Transformations. The FOR notation can be used to do more complex tasks, such as summing the scores for 30 questions (variables 3 to 32) and reporting the total when, say, at least 27 of the items are present (i.e., if four or more values are missing, we want the total to be missing.)

```
            / TRANSFORM  TOTAL = 0.  N = 0.
    FOR I=3 TO 32.
    % IF (X(I) NE XMIS)
                THEN (TOTAL = TOTAL + X(I).
                        N = N + 1.).      %
        IF (N LT 27)    THEN TOTAL = XMIS.
```

The BMDP transformation processor checks the values for the 30 questions, one case at a time. For each question, N is increased if the value is not missing. Note that the last line ·of the transformations is not within the % signs. This line is executed after all 30 questions have been checked; it will set the TOTAL to missing when too many values are missing.

Note that the SUM transformation could also be used for summing the scores (see Table 6.1).

Format. The basic form of the instruction-generating notation is:

$$\text{FOR } a_i = b_i. \ \% \ c \ \%$$
or
$$\text{FOR } a_i = b_i. \ \cdots \ a_n = b_n. \ . \% \ c \ \%$$

where:
- a_i is a name (or letter) to be replaced in text c.

- b_i is a list of the form $d_1,...,d_n$ where each d_i is a number, a name, or another list of the form $\#_1$ TO $\#_2$ BY $\#_3$ (see p. 30). The number of elements represented in list b_i determines the number of times c is repeated. When more than one replacement is specified, the a_i are replaced simultaneously in c, and the b_i must all be the same length. Note that the form "number TO number" is acceptable, but "name TO name" is not.

- c is the text (character string) that is repeated; for each copy, one element of list b_i replaces name a_i.

If c contains the /END paragraph, then the last % sign is not stated:

```
        FOR a=b. %... /END
```

Only one "FOR...%" may include the /END paragraph.

FOR instructions may be nested to any desired depth. When nested, the innermost "FOR....%" is resolved first.

FOR a_1 = b_1. % FOR a_2 = b_2. % c % %

If the replaced text should become a part of a word, as in "SCORE1, SCORE2, SCORE3," use the concatenation symbol "|", as in:

FOR J=1,2,3 % SCORE|J, %.

If the text generated is a list terminated with a period, such as "A,B,C,D.", then the notation

FOR X=A,B,C,D. % X, %.

may be used; the last comma will be replaced by a period when a period is inserted after the last % sign.

F.2   BMDP Transformations – Further Examples of the Use of Summary Statistics and Date Functions

See Chapter 6, Section 6.1 for rules for using summary statistics and date functions. Table 6.1 (pp. 51-52) lists all available functions.

A COMPLETE EXAMPLE USING SUMMARY STATISTICS

Suppose the investigator analyzing the success of a weight loss program wants to study different measures of weight change as follows:

CHANGE   - each subject's weight the first week minus his weight the last week

'REL CHANGE'   - the weight change divided by the subject's weight at the first week

SLOPE   - the slope of a line through the points (1, WT1), (2, WT2) ..., (6, WT6)

For the first computer run, the investigator wants to print these change measures, insert a note when a subject made fewer than four visits, and save the new measures, the number of visits, and the original data in a BMDP File.

The data look like this (asterisks indicate missed visits)

```
BOB     155   151   152   153   148   146
TIM     259   255   260   261   263    *
SARA    109    *    102   105    *     *
JOE     173    *     *    167    *     *
SAM     247   243   239   238   235   233
```

and are stored in a system file on UNIT 12.

The BMDP instructions for deriving the weight measures, printing them, and saving the derived measures along with the original data are:

```
/ INPUT       VARIABLES ARE 7.  UNIT IS 12.
              FORMAT IS FREE.
```

```
/ VARIABLE    NAMES ARE ID, WT1, WT2, WT3, WT4,
                   WT5, WT6, VISITS, CHANGE,
                   'REL CHANGE', SLOPE.
              ADD  IS 4.
              LABEL IS ID.
/ TRANSFORM

              VISITS = N(WT1, WT2, WT3,
                   WT4, WT5, WT6).
              IF (VISITS LT 4)
                 THEN (USE=0.
                    TEXT ('TOO FEW VISITS').).

              CHANGE = WT1 - LVAL(WT1, WT2, WT3,
                   WT4, WT5, WT6).
        'REL CHANGE' = CHANGE/WT1.
              SLOPE = TRND(WT1, WT2, WT3,
                   WT4, WT5, WT6).

              SHOW (VISITS, CHANGE, 'REL CHANGE',
                   SLOPE).

/ SAVE        UNIT IS 10.   NEW.   CODE IS WTSTUDY.
/ END
```

In the VARIABLE paragraph, we add the names of the measures to be derived and specify that we are ADDING four variables to the input data. The new measures are generated in the TRANSFORM paragraph. To compute the number of VISITS for each subject, the function N counts the number of VISITS for values present (the third case made only three visits). The IF THEN statement sets the value of USE to zero for a case when the number of VISITS is less than four and also requests that a note be printed. The functions LVAL and TRND are used to compute the CHANGE and SLOPE measures. The SHOW function requests that the transformation results be printed.

The information requested by the TEXT and SHOW commands is printed near the beginning of the output and will look like this.

		(VISITS)	(CHANGE)	('REL CHANGE')	(SLOPE)
1	BOB	6	9.0	.058	-1.51
2	TIM	5	-4.0	-.015	1.40
3	SARA	TOO FEW VALUES			
3	SARA	3	4.0	.037	-1.64
4	JOE	TOO FEW VALUES			
4	JOE	2	6.0	.035	-2.00
5	SAM	6	14.0	.057	-2.71

Note that the lines are printed in the same order as the requests are specified; thus, the TEXT message precedes that of the SHOW command.

MORE EXAMPLES

For each example listed below, the first line contains the function as a user might specify it, the second line, values for a sample case that is processed.

Trend

TRND(WT1, WT2, WT3, WT4)
data (98, missing, 102, 107)

The trend is the slope of a line through the points

(1, 98), (2, missing), (3, 102), and (4, 107)

The value computed by the function is 2.857.

Order of the last usable value and its value

LIND(X(5), X(6), X(7), X(8))
LVAL(X(5), X(6), X(7), X(8))
data (98, 102, 107, missing)

The last usable value in the sequence of the four variables named is 107. The result of the LIND function is 3 because 107 is the third argument in the list.

INDX function -- to identify a variable with a specific value

INDX(2, WK1, WK2, WK3, WK4)
data (2, 1, 1, 2, 2)

Suppose you record a patient's weekly infection status (code 1 indicates an infection; code 2, no infection). We use the INDX function to find the first week (variable in the list) for which the value is 2. For these data, the result of INDX is 3. The value "2" is first found for the third variable in the list (WK3). If no variable in the list contains the value 2, the result of the INDX function is zero. If you want the result to be missing when 2 is not found, use the REC function.

Recoding data

REC(OCCUP, 11,1, 25,1, 33,2, 64,2, 71,3)
data (64)
data (12)

We illustrate data for two cases. The occupation code for the first is 64, for the second, 12. Following the occupation code are pairs of numbers. The first member of each pair is an original occupation code, the second is the new code to be assigned. From these pairs we see that codes 11 and 25 should become 1, codes 33 and 64 should become 2, and code 71 should be a 3. The function tries to match the actual code with the first number in each pair. When a match occurs, the second number in the pair replaces the original code. Thus, the case with code 64 has its occupation value recoded to 2. The result for the case with code 12 is a missing value because there is no 12 among the first entries of each pair.

F.3 FORTRAN Transformations — Further Examples

The use of FORTRAN transformations is described in Section 6.2. Further examples follow.

Examples Comparing FORTRAN Transformations with the BMDP TRANSFORM Paragraph Statements. We use some of the examples given in Section 6.1 for the TRANSFORM paragraph to illustrate how the same variable transformations and case selection can be done with FORTRAN statements.

The first example (p. 53) creates a new variable RATIO (the 10th variable) from the ratio of WEIGHT (the 4th variable) to HEIGHT (the 3rd variable). If you know that both WEIGHT and HEIGHT are always recorded, in FORTRAN you can specify

X(10) = X(4)/X(3)

However, if either WEIGHT or HEIGHT can be missing or out of range, you must first check whether the value is present by specifying

X(10) = XMIS
IF(ABS(X(3)).LT.XMIS .AND. ABS(X(4)).LT.XMIS)
*X(10) = X(4)/X(3)

(We insert an asterisk in column 6 to indicate a continuation from the previous line.) The first statement specifies that X(10), RATIO, is missing unless reset by the second statement. Before computing the value of X(10), you first check that both X(3) and X(4) are not missing and not out of range. It is necessary to compare the absolute values of the variables against XMIS, since values out of range are set to internal codes more extreme than XMIS and can be positive (if greater than the upper bound) or negative (if less than the lower bound).

The second example converts FEET and INCHES to height. Suppose FEET is variable 4, X(4), and INCHES is variable 5, X(5). You can specify

IF(ABS(X(4)).LT.XMIS .AND. ABS(X(5)).LT.XMIS)
*X(4) = X(4) + X(5)/12.

(The asterisk in column 6 indicates a continuation from the previous line.) The alternative specification in the TRANSFORM paragraph is

FEET = FEET + INCHES/12.

A third example will show transforms with COUNT data. Suppose COUNT is X(2) and ANSWER is X(3). Your statement is

X(3) = XMIS
IF(ABS(X(2)).LT.XMIS)
*X(3) = SQRT(X(2)) + SQRT(X(2) + 1.0)

(The asterisk in column 6 is the same as above.) The alternative specification in the TRANSFORM paragraph is

ANSWER = SQRT(COUNT) + SQRT(COUNT + 1)

You can recode data to the missing value code. For example, if STATUS (p. 53) is X(4), then

IF(X(4).EQ.4.0 .OR. X(4).EQ.8.0) X(4) = XMIS

transforms STATUS to the missing value code if it is either 7 or 8. The equivalent statement in the TRANSFORM paragraph is

IF(STATUS EQ 7 OR STATUS EQ 8) THEN STATUS = XMIS.

Recoding Nonnumeric Data. Nonnumeric data can also be recoded using FORTRAN statements. To illustrate how the data are recoded, let SEX be one of the variables, coded M, F; and MONTH be a second variable, coded 1, 2, 3, 4, 5, 6, 7, 8, 9, 0, A, B. (Many old data sets code November as "-" and

December as "+". The same method can be used to recode these symbols.) If SEX is variable 5 and MONTH variable 7, they can be recoded by the following FORTRAN statements. (Explanations appear below.)

```
        DIMENSION AMONTH(12),ASEX(2)
 (a) [  DATA AMONTH/1H1,1H2,1H3,1H4,1H5,1H6
     *            1H7,1H8,1H9,1H0,1HA,1HB/
 (b) [  DATA ASEX/1HM,1HF/
     ┌  DO 1 I=1,2
     │     IF(X(5).NE.ASEX(I)) GO TO 1
 (c) │     X(5)=I
     └     GO TO 2
      1 CONTINUE
 (d) [    X(5)=XMIS
     ┌2 DO 3 I=1,12
     │     IF(X(7).NE.AMONTH(I)) GO TO 3
 (e) │     X(7) = I
     │     GO TO 4
     └3 CONTINUE
 (f) [    X(7)=XMIS
      4 CONTINUE
```

(a) AMONTH are the valid codes for MONTH (1, 2, ..., A, B)

(b) ASEX are valid codes for SEX

(c) Check for code: M replaced by 1, F replaced by 2

(d) Neither M nor F was found; a missing value indicator is assigned

(e) Check for code: 0 replaced by 10, A replaced by 11, B replaced by 12

(f) No valid code was found; a missing value indicator is assigned

The two variables, SEX and MONTH, must each be read with format specification A1. In addition, you must specify

AFTER.

in the VARIABLE paragraph so the data in SEX and MONTH will not be checked for MISSING value codes or MIN and MAX limits until they are transformed to legitimate values. The above FORTRAN statements must be used with the System Cards described in chapter 6 (the BIMEDT procedure).

F.4 Stepwise Regression Analysis with Sets of Variables Specified in the Independent Variables: A New Feature in 2R

The independent variables in stepwise regression analysis can now be grouped so that all variables in a set are entered into or removed from the regression equation in the same step. The word SETs in the REGRess paragraph is used to list the set names. Each set of variables is defined by a list of variable names or subscripts. The set names can then be referred to in the list for the independent variables.

Variables in a set are allowed to enter the equation only if they pass a tolerance test. In order to pass the tolerance test, two conditions must be met: a variable must have a tolerance value larger than a preassigned limit, and its entrance into the equation must not cause the tolerance value of any previously entered variable to be reduced below the limit. The variable whose entrance will cause the greatest reduction in the residual sum of squares is entered first. This permits the tolerance value of each variable to be computed in a reasonable way. A variable in a set that was not entered because it failed the tolerance test may subsequently pass the test and be allowed to enter after some variables are removed from the equation.

Since the degrees of freedom for each set of variables can be different, we use smallest P-values[*] from F distributions instead of largest F ratios as entry criteria. The set of variables in the equation having the largest P-value-to-remove is removed from the equation, provided the value is larger than the limit for P-value-to-remove. If no set of variables is to be removed, then the set of variables not in the equation having the smallest P-value-to-enter enters the equation, provided the value is smaller than the limit for P-value-to-enter. The stepping procedure is terminated when there are no longer any sets of variables to be entered. A user can use INPval and OUTPval to specify the limits for P-value-to-enter and P-value-to- remove, respectively (the defaults are 0.050 and 0.051).

When the levels for variables are specified, the level for a set is determined by the lowest level for variables in the set. A warning message will be printed if the levels for variables in a set are not consistent.

This new feature has led to the following changes in the computer printout. The P-values of larger F ratios are printed along with the F ratios. The partial correlation coefficient of a set of variables with the dependent variable is computed as the square root of the proportion of reduction in the current residual sum of squares that the set of variables can achieve. It can be obtained by computing $\sqrt{F/(C + F)}$, where F is the F ratio for the set of variables and C is the ratio of the degree of freedom for the residual to the degrees of freedom for the set of variables. Also, note that the tolerance value printed for each variable is computed as though the variable is entered or removed by itself. Hence, the actual tolerance value for a variable other than the first to be entered in a set is smaller than the value printed if the set is not in the equation. When removing a variable, the actual value is larger.

In addition to the above changes to 2R, a new option is available in the REGRess paragraph. By specifying SEQUential, variables or sets of variables are forced to enter in the same order as the list of the independent variables. If only variables or sets of variables having sufficiently small P-values-to-enter are to be allowed to enter, limits must be specified for entry and removal.

---

[*] Note that we avoid calling this a probability, since a probability would be appropriate only for a single, preselected variable and not one chosen by a variable-selection algorithm (see Appendix C.2).

F.5 New Options in the SAVE Paragraph

Several new features have been added to the SAVE paragraph, allowing structural changes to the data and the replacement or elimination of missing values.

The KEEP and DELETE options can be used to save a subset of input variables. Specifying KEEP, followed by a variable list, saves only those variables in the list. The order in which the variables are stored is determined by their order in the list. Specifying DELETE, followed by a list of variables, saves only those that are <u>not</u> in the list; their order is determined by their original sequence.

The COMPLETE option can be used to eliminate cases with values missing, too large, or too small. Specifying COMPLETE will save only cases with a full set of nonmissing values.

The MISSING statement may be used to specify replacement values for variables with values missing, too large, or too small. It may be used in conjunction with the COMPLETE statement to eliminate cases with missing values for a selected set of variables; any missing values for variables not in the set are replaced before tests for a complete set of nonmissing values are performed.

The APPEND option, with a variable list, may be used to generate multiple output cases from a single input case. The number of cases written on the output file is determined by the number of APPEND statements in the SAVE paragraph. Each output case generated consists of two parts: a common set of variables and an appended set of variables. The common variables are selected using KEEP or DELETE. The values for these variables will appear on all output cases generated from a single input case. The appended variables are specified using the APPEND statement.

The variable list in the first APPEND statement determines names for the appended set as well as values for the first case generated from a particular input case. Subsequent cases generated obtain their values for the appended variables from those listed in the corresponding APPEND statements. For example, consider a SAVE paragraph of the form

```
/SAVE   KEEP   = A,C,E.
        APPEND = B,G.
        APPEND = D,H.
        APPEND = F,I.
```

and some case, say Case Number i, containing these values for the nine original input variables

Variable name:
```
A    B    C    D    E    F    G    H    I
```
Value of the ith case:
```
1.0  2.0  3.0  4.0  5.0  6.0  7.0  8.0  9.0
```

The saved file will contain only five variables: three common variables, A, C, and E, and the two appended variables, B and G. However, the saved file will contain three cases for each case originally read. The three cases generated from Case i will appear as

```
            A    C    E    B    G
Case 3i-2 : 1.0  3.0  5.0  2.0  7.0
Case 3i-1 : 1.0  3.0  5.0  4.0  8.0
Case 3i   : 1.0  3.0  5.0  6.0  9.0
```

The APPEND statement can be used with other SAVE options as well. Specifying COMPLETE deletes cases generated that contain missing values. The replacement of missing values is organized by the original variable names. Not specifying a KEEP list will result in only appended variables being saved.

/SAVE KEEP = v list.	all variables	Optional. Used to save a subset of the variables.
DELETE = v list.	none	Optional. Used in lieu of KEEP.
MISSING = # list.	none	Optional. Replace missing values with numeric values in the list.
APPEND = v list.	none	Optional. Used to generate multiple output cases from a single input case.
COMPLETE.	none	Optional. Used to save only those cases with nonmissing values.

F.6 New Features in P4V

A number of new features have been added to make P4V easier to set up and interpret.

<u>Specification of the Design.</u> In the BETWEEN paragraph, specification of CODES or CUTPOINTS for each factor is no longer required. The program will allow up to 10 group code values for any factor for which grouping information is not supplied. For example, if cases are classified by AGE and SEX, where AGE is coded as 5, 7, and 9, all that is now required in the BETWEEN paragraph is:

/ BETWEEN FACTORS ARE AGE, SEX.

In the WITHIN paragraph, category information for the within factors was formerly required. This was unnecessarily confusing, since most within designs are completely crossed and the category values did not appear with the data. To specify the number of levels of the within factors in a completely crossed design, use the LEVELS sentence. For instance,

/ WITHIN   FACTORS ARE DAY, TEST.
           LEVELS ARE   5,   2.

describes a design where each subject receives two tests on each of five days.

For repeated measures designs with a single dependent variate, 4V previously guessed the name of the dependent variate by using the name of the input variable associated with the first measure. In most cases, the output showed a label for the dependent variate, such as TEMP1, which made it appear as though only the first measure was being analyzed. Currently in 4V, the name for the dependent variate in a univariate repeated measures design is specified by using the DEPVAR sentence in the WITHIN paragraph. For example,

```
/ WITHIN  FACTOR  IS  DAYS.
          LEVELS ARE    5.
          DEPVAR IS  TEMPRTUR.
```

If not supplied, the dependent variate is labelled DEP_VAR.

The ANOVA TABLE. The analysis of variance table generated by P4V accommodates a large number of possibilities, such as multivariate statistics, multivariate tests of repeated measures, reports of loss of numerical accuracy, etc. Although we consider presentation of all of these features essential, it is often desirable to have a briefer presentation of all tests for a single dependent variable. To obtain a summary table for each dependent variate in a classical ANOVA format (almost identical to P2V), state UNISUM in the ANALYSIS paragraph. For example, when doing an orthogonal decomposition of a repeated measures factor when there are multiple variates, the usual BMDP4V ANOVA table would present tests of all variates for each component of the decomposition. However, in this type of analysis, we are looking for a dominating component of the factor effect for a single variate, so we would like to see these components listed together in the output. This is the form of the table provided by requesting UNISUM.

Saving Marginal Statistics for Graphical Displays.
P4V now allows the user to request that all marginal statistics be saved in a BMDP file. This file of marginals contains sufficient information to make this file easy to use by the plotting programs, P5D and P6D. To obtain this file of marginals and cell statistics, the user supplies a standard BMDP SAVE paragraph with the specification CONTENT = CELLS. BMDP4V will produce a file with one record ("case") for each line of marginals printed. There will be NB + NW + 8 columns ("variables") in this file, where the first NB columns are the group numbers of the NB between (grouping) factors; the next NW columns are the level numbers for the NW within (repeated measures) factors; the next column, labelled INTLEVEL, is the interaction level (or number of factors involved in the interaction constituting this line of marginal statistics); and the last seven columns are the statistics and are labelled COUNT, MEAN, STDERROR, STD_DEV, WTD_MEAN, MAXIMUM, and MINIMUM.

References

Afifi, A.A., and S.P. Azen, (1972). Statistical Analysis: A Computer-Oriented Approach. New York, Academic Press.

Anderson, R.L., D.M. Allen, and F.B. Cady (1972). Selection of predictor variables in linear multiple regression. In Statistical Papers in Honor of George W. Snedecor, T.A. Bancroft, ed. Ames, Iowa, University of Iowa Press.

Anderson, R.L., and P.P. Crump (1967). Comparison of designs and estimation procedures for estimating parameters in a two-stage nested process. Technometrics 9, 499-516.

Anderson, T.W. (1958). An Introduction to Multivariate Statistical Analysis. New York, Wiley.

Andrews, D.F., P.J. Bickel, F.R. Hampel, P.J. Huber, W.H. Rogers, and J.W. Tukey (1972). Robust Estimates of Location: Survey and Advances. Princeton, Princeton University Press.

Armitage, P. (1971). Statistical Methods in Medical Research. Oxford, Blackwell Scientific Publications.

Bartlett, M.S. (1947). Multivariate analysis. J. Roy. Statist. Soc. 9, Series B, 176-197.

Beale, E.M.L., and R.J.A. Little (1975). Missing values in multivariate analysis. J. Roy. Statist. Soc. 37, Series B, 129-145.

Benedetti, J.K., and M.B. Brown (1976). Alternate methods of building log-linear models. Proceedings of the 9th International Biometric Conference 2, 209-227.

Benedetti, J.K., and M.B. Brown (1978). Strategies for the selection of log-linear models. Biometrics 34, 680-686.

Bingham, C., P. Whittle, H. Wold, and J. Shishkin (1978). Time series. In International Encyclopedia of Statistics, W.H. Kruskal and J.M.Tanur, eds., Macmillan.

Bishop, Y., S. Fienberg, and P. Holland (1975). Discrete Multivariate Analysis: Theory and Practice. Cambridge, Massachusetts, MIT Press.

Bloomfield, P. (1970). Spectral analysis with randomly missing observations. J. Roy. Statist. Soc. 32, Series B, 369-380.

Bloomfield, P. (1976). The Fourier Analysis of Time Series: An Introduction. New York, Wiley.

Bock, R.D. (1975). Multivariate Statistical Methods in Behavioral Research. New York, McGraw-Hill.

Bowker, A.H. (1948). A test for symmetry in contingency tables. J. Amer. Statist. Assoc. 43, 572-574.

Bowker, A.H., and G.J. Lieberman (1963). Engineering Statistics. Englewood Cliffs, New Jersey, Prentice-Hall.

Box, G.E.P., and G.M. Jenkins (1976). Time Series Analysis, Forecasting and Control (revised edition). San Francisco, Holden-Day.

Box, G.E.P., and M.A. Muller (1958). A note on the generation of random normal deviates. Ann. Math. Statist. 29, 610-613.

Box, G., and G. Tiao (1975). Intervention analysis with application to ecomomic and environmental problems. J. Amer. Statist. Assoc. 70, 70-79.

Breslow, N. (1970). A generalized Kruskal-Wallis test for comparing k samples subject to unequal patterns of censorship. Biometrika 57, 579-594.

Breslow, N. (1974). Covariance analysis of censored survival data. Biometrics 30, 89-99.

Brillinger, D.R. (1975). Time Series: Data Analysis and Theory. New York, Holt, Rinehart and Winston.

Brown, C.C. (1976). A generalization of the probit and logit methods for dose response curves. Biometrics 32, 761-768.

Brown, M.B. (1974). The identification of sources of significance in two-way contingency tables. Appl. Statist. 23, 405-413.

Brown, M.B. (1975). The asymptotic standard errors of some estimates of uncertainty in the two-way contingency table. Psychometrika 40, 291-296.

Brown, M.B. (1976). Screening effects in multidimensional contingency tables. Appl. Statist. 25, 37-46.

Brown, M.B., and J.K. Benedetti (1976). Asymptotic standard errors and their sampling behavior for measures of association and correlation in the two-way contingency table. I. Testing the null hypothesis; II. Power and confidence limits. BMDP Technical Report No. 23, BMDP Statistical Software.

Brown, M.B., and J.K. Benedetti (1977a). Sampling behavior of tests for correlation in two-way contingency tables. J. Amer. Statist. Assoc. 72, 309-315.

Brown, M.B., and J.K. Benedetti (1977b). On the mean and variance of the tetrachoric correlation coefficient. Psychometrika 42, 347-355.

Brown, M.B., M. Doron, and A. Laron (1974). Approximate confidence limits for the concentration of insulin in radioimmunoassays. *Diabetologia* 10, 23-25.

Brown, M.B., and A.B. Forsythe (1974a). The small sample behavior of some statistics which test the equality of several means. *Technometrics* 16, 129-132.

Brown, M.B., and A.B. Forsythe (1974b). Robust tests for the equality of variances. *J. Amer. Statist. Assoc.* 69, 364-367.

Brownlee, K.A. (1965). *Statistical Theory and Methodology in Science and Engineering*. New York, Wiley.

Campbell, M.J., and A.M. Walker (1977). A survey of statistical work on the Mackenzie River series of annual Canadian lynx trappings for the years 1821-1934 and a new analysis. *J. Roy. Statist. Soc.* 40, Series A, 411-468.

Chatfield, C. (1975). *The Analysis of Time Series: Theory and Practice*. London, Chapman and Hall (Halsted Press).

Church, J.D., and E.L. Wike (1976). The robustness of homogeneity of variance tests for asymmetric distributions: a Monte Carlo study. *Bulletin of the Psychometric Society* 7(5), 417-420.

Clarke, M.R.B. (1970). A rapidly converging method for maximum likelihood factor analysis. *Brit. J. Math. Statist. Psych.* 23, 43-52.

Cochran, W.G. (1954). Some methods for strengthening the common χ^2 tests. *Biometrics* 10, 417-441.

Cochran, W.G., and G.M. Cox (1957). *Experimental Designs*, 2nd ed. New York, Wiley.

Conover, W.J. (1971). *Practical Nonparametric Statistics*. New York, Wiley.

Cook, R.D. (1977). Detection of influential observations in linear regression. *Technometrics* 19, 15-18.

Cooley, W.W., and P.R. Lohnes (1971). *Multivariate Data Analysis*. New York, Wiley.

Corbeil, R.R., and S.R. Searle (1976). Restricted maximum likelihood (REML) estimation of variance components in the mixed model. *Technometrics* 18, 31-38.

Cornfield, J. and J.W Tukey (1956). Average values of mean squares in factorials. *Ann. Math. Statist.* 27, 907-49.

Cox, D.R. (1970). *The Analysis of Binary Data*. London, Methuen.

Cox, D.R. (1972). Regression models and life tables. *J. Roy. Statist. Soc.* 34, Series B, 187-220.

Cox, D.R. (1975). Partial likelihood. *Biometrika* 62, 269-276.

Cramer, H. (1946). *Mathematical Methods of Statistics*. Princeton, Princeton University Press.

Crowley, J., and M. Hu (1977). Covariance analysis of heart transplant survival data. *J. Amer. Statist. Assoc.* 72, 27-36.

Cutler, S.J., and F. Ederer (1958). Maximum utilization of the life-table method in analyzing survival. *J. Chron. Dis.* 8, 699-713.

Daniel, C. (1959). Use of half-normal plots in interpreting factorial two-level experiments. *Technometrics* 1, 311-341.

Daniel, C., and F.S. Wood (1971). *Fitting Equations to Data*. New York, Wiley.

Davidson, M.L. (1972). Univariate versus multivariate tests in repeated-measures experiments. *Psychological Bulletin* 77, 446-452.

Davidson, M.L. (1979a). Monitoring rounding errors in a large statistical program. In *Proceedings of Computer Science and Statistics: 12th Annual Symposium on the Interface*, Waterloo.

Davidson, M.L. (1980). The multivariate approach to repeated measures. BMDP Technical Report No. 75, BMDP Statistical Software.

Davidson, M.L., and J.D. Toporek (1979b). ANOVA with general cell weights. BMDP Technical Report No. 59, BMDP Statistical Software.

Davidson, M.L., and J.D. Toporek (1981). User's manual for BMDP4V (URWAS): general univariate and multivariate analysis of variance. BMDP Technical Report No. 67, BMDP Statistical Software.

Davies, O.L. (1954). *The Design and Analysis of Industrial Experiments*. New York, Hafner.

Dempster, A.P. (1969). *Elements of Continuous Multivariate Analysis*. San Francisco, Addison-Wesley.

Dixon, W.J., ed., (1975). *BMDP Biomedical Computer Programs*. Berkeley, Univ. of Calif. Press.

Dixon, W.J., ed., (1977). *BMDP Biomedical Computer Programs*. Berkeley, Univ. of Calif. Press.

Dixon, W.J., and F.J. Massey, Jr. (1969). *Introduction to Statistical Analysis*, 3rd ed. New York, McGraw-Hill.

Dixon, W.J., and J.W. Tukey (1968). Approximate behavior of the distribution of Winsorized t (Trimming/Winsorization 2). *Technometrics* 10, 83-98.

Everitt, P.F. (1910). Table of the tetrachoric functions for fourfold correlation tables. *Biometrika* 7, 437-451.

Fienberg, S.E. (1972). The analysis of incomplete multiway contingency tables. Biometrics 28, 177-202.

Fienberg, S.E. (1977). The Analysis of Cross-Classified Categorical Data. Cambridge, Massachusetts, MIT Press.

Fisher, R.A. (1936). The use of multiple measurements in taxonomic problems. Ann. Eugen. 7, 179-188.

Fishman, G.S. (1969). Spectral Methods in Econometrics. Harvard University Press.

Fleiss, J.L. (1973). Statistical Methods for Rates and Proportions. New York, Wiley.

Forsythe, A.B. (1977). Post hoc decision to use a covariate. J. Chron. Dis. 30, 61-64.

Forsythe, A.B., L. Engelman, R. Jennrich, and P.R.A. May (1973). A stopping rule for variable selection in multiple regression. J. Amer. Statist. Assoc. 68, 75-77.

Forsythe, A.B., P.R.A. May, and L. Engelman (1970). Computing advantage scores by multiple regression. In Psychopharmacology and the Individual Patient. J.R. Wittenborn, S.C. Goldberg, and P.R.A. May, eds. Raven Press, 116-123.

Forsythe, A.B., P.R.A. May, and L. Engelman (1971). Prediction of multiple regression. J. Psychiatric Res. 8, 119-126.

Forsythe, G.E. (1957). Generation and use of orthogonal polynomials for data fitting with a digital computer. J. Soc. Ind. Appl. Math. 5, 74-88.

Frane, J.W. (1976). Some simple procedures for handling missing data in multivariate analysis. Psychometrika 41, 409-415.

Frane, J.W., and M. Hill (1974). Annotated computer output for factor analysis using Professor Jarvik's smoking questionnaire. BMDP Technical Report No. 8, BMDP Statistical Software.

Frane, J.W., and M. Hill (1976). Factor analysis as a tool for data analysis. Commun. Statist. - Theor. Meth. A5, 487-506.

Frane, J.W. (1977). A note on checking tolerance in matrix inversion and regression, Technometrics 19, 513-514.

Frane, J. (1978a). Detecting and describing statistical and numerical ill-conditioning. BMDP Technical Report No. 44, BMDP Statistical Software.

Frane, J.W. (1978b). Missing data and BMDP: some pragmatic approaches. BMDP Technical Report No. 45, BMDP Statistical Software.

Frane, J.W. (1980). The univariate approach to repeated measures: foundation, advantages, and caveats. BMDP Technical Report No. 69, BMDP Statistical Software.

Frank, M., and C. Pfaffman (1969). Taste nerve fibers: A random distribution of sensitivities to four tastes. Science 164, 1183-1185.

Furnival, G.M., and R.W. Wilson (1974a). Regression by leaps and bounds. Technometrics 16, 499-511.

Furnival, G.M., and R.W. Wilson (1974b). Regression by Leaps and Bounds -- A Program for Finding the Best Subset Regressions (computer program). New Haven, Yale University and U.S. Forest Service, Nov. 11, 1974.

Geisser, S., and S. Greenhouse (1958). An extension of Box's results on the use of the F distribution in multivariate analysis. Ann. Math. Statist. 29, 885-891.

Geisser, S., and S.W. Greenhouse (1959). On methods in the analysis of profile data. Psychometrika 24, 95-112.

Goodman, L.A. (1968). The analysis of cross-classified data. J. Amer. Statist. Assoc. 63, 1091-1131.

Goodman, L.A., and W.H. Kruskal (1954). Measures of association for cross-classification. J. Amer. Statist. Assoc. 49, 732-764.

Goodman, L.A., and W.H. Kruskal (1963). Measures of association for cross-classification. III. Approximate sampling theory. J. Amer. Statist. Assoc. 58, 310-364.

Goodman, L.A., and W.H. Kruskal (1972). Measures of association for cross-classification. IV. Simplification of asymptotic variances. J. Amer. Statist. Assoc. 67, 415-421.

Greenwood, M. (1926). The natural duration of cancer. Reports on Public Health and Medical Subjects 33. H.M. Stationary Office, London.

Gross, A., and V. Clark (1975). Survival Distributions: Reliability Applications in the Biomedical Sciences. New York, Wiley.

Gunst, R.F., and R.L. Mason (1977). Advantages of examining multicollinearities in regression analysis. Biometrics 33, 249-260.

Haberman, S.J. (1972). Log-linear fit for contingency tables, algorithm AS 51. Appl. Statist. 21, 218-224.

Haberman, S.J. (1973). The analysis of residuals in cross-classified tables. Biometrics 29, 205-220.

Hajek, J. (1969). Nonparametric Statistics. San Francisco, Holden-Day.

Hamming, R. W. (1977). Digital Filters. Englewood Cliffs, N.J. Prentice-Hall.

Harbison, F.H., J. Maruhnic, and J.R. Resnick (1970). Quantitative Analysis of Modernization and Development. Princeton, Princeton University, Industrial Relations Section, Research Report Series No. 115, Appendix 1, p. 8.

723

Harman, H.H. (1967). _Modern Factor Analysis_, 2nd ed. Chicago, Univ. of Chicago Press.

Harris, R.J. (1975). _A Primer of Multivariate Statistics_. New York, Academic Press.

Hartigan, J.A. (1975). _Clustering Algorithms_. New York, Wiley.

Hartigan, J.A. (1976). Modal blocks in dentition of west coast mammals. _Syst. Zoology_ 25, 149-60.

Hartley, H.O., and J.H.K. Rao (1967). Maximum likelihood estimation for the mixed analysis of variance model. _Biometrika_ 54, 93-108.

Hartley, H.O., and W.K. Vaughn (1972). A computer program for the mixed analysis of variance model based on maximum likelihood. In _Statistical Papers in Honor of George W. Snedecor_. T.A. Bancroft, ed. Ames, Iowa State University Press.

Harville, D.A. (1977). Maximum likelihood approaches to variance component estimation and to related problems. _J. Amer. Statist. Assoc._ 72, 320-340.

Hawkins, D.M. (1974). The detection of errors in multivariate data using principal components. _J. Amer. Statist. Assoc._ 69, 340-344.

Hays, J.D., J. Imbrie, and N.J. Schackleton (1976). Variations in the Earth's orbit: pacemaker of the Ice Ages. _Science_ 194(4270), 1121-32.

Hemmerle, W.J., and H.O. Hartley (1973). Computing maximum likelihood estimates for the mixed A.O.V. model using the W transform. _Technometrics_ 15, 819-831.

Hill, M.A. (1979). Annotated computer output for regression analysis: a supplement to writeups for computer programs BMDP2R and BMDP9R. BMDP Technical Report No. 48, BMDP Statistical Software.

Hocking, R.R. (1972). Criteria for selection of a subset regression: which one should be used. _Technometrics_ 14, 967-970.

Hoerl, A.E. (1962). Application of ridge analysis to regression problems. _Chem. Eng. Prog._ 58, 54-59.

Hoerl, A.E., and R.W. Kennard (1970a). Ridge regression: biased estimation for nonorthogonal problems. _Technometrics_ 12, 55-67.

Hoerl, A.E., and R.W. Kennard (1970b). Ridge regression: application to nonorthogonal problems. _Technometrics_ 12, 69-82.

Hollander, M., and D.A. Wolfe (1973). _Nonparametric Statistical Methods_. New York, Wiley.

Hosmer, D., and S. Lemeshow (1980). Goodness-of-fit tests for the multiple logistic regression model. _Commun. Statist. - Part A Theor. Meth._ A9(10), 1043-1069.

Huynh, H., and L.S. Feldt (1976). Estimation of the Box Correction for degrees of freedom from sample data in the randomized block and split-plot designs. _J. Educ. Statist._ 1, 69-82.

Huynh, H., and L.S. Feldt (1970). Conditions under which mean square ratios in repeated-measurement designs have exact F-distributions. _J. Amer. Statist. Assoc._ 65, 1582-1589.

Huynh, H., and L.S. Feldt (1980). Performance of traditional F tests in repeated measures designs under covariance heterogeneity. _Commun. Statist. - Theor. Meth._ A9(1), 61-74.

Jenkins, G.M. (1979). _Practical Experience with Modeling and Forecasting Time Series_. Gwilym Jenkins and Partners.

Jennrich, R.I. (1977a). Stepwise regression. In _Statistical Methods for Digital Computers_, K. Enslein, A. Ralston, and H.S. Wilf, eds. New York, Wiley.

Jennrich, R.I. (1977b). Stepwise discriminant analysis. In _Statistical Methods for Digital Computers_, K. Enslein, A. Ralston, and H.S. Wilf, eds. New York, Wiley.

Jennrich, R.I. (1978). Admissible values of gamma in direct oblimin rotation. _Psychometrika_ 44, 173-7.

Jennrich, R.I., and P.B. Bright (1976). Fitting systems of linear differential equations using computer-generated exact derivatives. _Technometrics_ 18, 385-392.

Jennrich, R.I., and R.H. Moore (1975). Maximum likelihood estimation by means of nonlinear least squares. In _Proceedings of the Statistical Computing Section_, Amer. Statist. Assoc. 57-65.

Jennrich, R.I., and S.M. Robinson (1969). A Newton-Raphson algorithm for maximum likelihood factor analysis. _Psychometrika_ 34, 111-123.

Jennrich, R.I., and P.F. Sampson (1966). Rotation for simple loadings. _Psychometrika_ 31, 313-323.

Jennrich, R.I., and P.F. Sampson (1968). Application of stepwise regression to nonlinear least squares estimation. _Technometrics_ 10, 63-67.

Jennrich, R.I., and P.F. Sampson (1976). Newton-Raphson and related algorithms for maximum likelihood variance component estimation. _Technometrics_ 18, 11-17.

John, P.M. (1971). _Statistical Design and Analysis of Experiments_. New York, MacMillan.

Jones, R. H. (1962). Spectral analysis with regularly missed observations. _Ann. Math Statist._ 33, 455-61.

Jöreskog, K.G., and M. van Thillo (1971). New rapid algorithms for factor analysis by unweighted least squares, generalized least squares and maximum likelihood. _Research Memorandum, 71-S._ Princeton, Educational Testing Service.

Kaiser, H.F. (1970). A second-generation Little Jiffy. _Psychometrika_ 35, 401-415.

Kalbfleisch, J.D., and R.L. Prentice (1980). The Statistical Analysis of Failure Time Data. New York, Wiley.

Kaplan, E.L., and P. Meier (1958). Nonparametric estimation from incomplete observations. J. Amer. Statist. Assoc. 53, 457-481.

Kaplan, S., R. Weinfeld, C. Abruzzo, and M. Lewis (1972). Pharmacokinetic profile of sulfisoxazole following intravenous, intramuscular, and oral administration to man. J. Pharm. Sci. 61, 773-778.

Kasser, I., and R.A. Bruce (1969). Comparative effects of aging and coronary heart disease and submaximal and maximal exercise. Circulation 39, 759-774.

Kay, R. (1977). Proportional hazard regression models and the analysis of censored survival data. Applied Statistics, 26, 227-237.

Kendall, M.G. (1973). Time Series, 2nd ed. New York, Hafner.

Kendall, M.G., and A. Stuart (1967). The Advanced Theory of Statistics, Vol. 2, 2nd ed. New York, Hafner.

Krall, J.M., V.A. Uthoff, and J.B. Harley (1975). A step-up procedure for selecting variables associated with survival. Biometrics 31, 49-57.

Kronmal, R.A., and M. Tarter (1973). The use of density estimates based on orthogonal expansions. In Exploring Data Analysis -- The Computer Revolution in Statistics, W.J. Dixon and W.L. Nicholson, eds. Berkeley, Univ. of Calif. Press.

Kruskal, W.H., and W.A. Wallis (1952). Use of ranks in one-criterion variance analysis. J. Amer. Statist. Assoc. 47, 583-621.

Kutner, M.H. (1974). Hypothesis testing in linear models (Eisenhart Model I). Amer. Statist. 28, 98-100.

Lachenbruch, P., and R.M. Mickey (1968). Estimation of error rates in discriminant analysis. Technometrics 10, 1-11.

Landaw, E., P. Sampson, and J. Toporek (1982). Advanced nonlinear regression in BMDP: comparison to ad hoc dummy data procedures. In Proceedings of the Statistical Computing Section, Amer. Statist. Assoc.

Larsen, W.A., and S.J. McCleary (1972). The use of partial residual plots in regression analysis. Technometrics 14, 781-790.

Lawley, D.N., and A.E. Maxwell (1971). Factor Analysis as a Statistical Method, 2nd ed. New York, American Elsevier.

Lee, E.G., M.M. Desu, and E.H. Gehan (1975). A Monte Carlo study of the power of some two-sample tests. Biometrika 62, 425-432.

Lee, E.T. (1980). Statistical Methods for Survival Data Analysis. Belmont, Lifetime Learning Publications.

Lee, S.K. (1977). On the asymptotic variances of u-terms in log-linear models of multidimensional contingency tables. J. Amer. Statist. Assoc. 72, 412-419.

Lehmann, E.L. (1959). Testing Statistical Hypotheses. New York, Wiley.

Lehmann, E. L. (1975). Nonparametrics: Statistical Methods Based on Ranks. San Francisco, Holden-Day.

Levene, H. (1960). Robust tests for equality of variance. In Contributions to Probability and Statistics, I. Olkin, ed. Palo Alto, California, Stanford University Press, 278-292.

Ling, R.F. (1973). A computer-generated aid for cluster analysis. Communications of ACM 16, 355-361.

Link, C.L. (1979). Confidence intervals for the survival function using Cox's proportional hazard model with covariates. Technical Report No. 45, Division of Biostatistics, Stanford University.

Liu, L.M. (1979a). Analysis of time series with calender effects. BMDP Technical Report No. 49, BMDP Statistical Software.

Liu, L.M. (1979b). Parameter estimation in dynamic models. BMDP Technical Report No. 54, BMDP Statistical Software.

Liu, L.M., and D.M. Hanssens (1980). Identification of multiple-input transfer function models. BMDP Technical Report No. 68, BMDP Statistical Software.

Liu, P.Y., and John Crowley (1978). Large-sample theory of the MLE based on Cox's regression model for survival data. Technical Report No. 1, Wisconsin Clinical Cancer Center, University of Wisconsin, Madison.

Ljung, G., and G.E.P. Box (1978). On a measure of lack of fit in time series models. Biometrika 65, 297-304.

MACC (1965). GAUSHAUS - Nonlinear Least Squares MACC, University of Wisconsin, Madison.

Mantel, N. (1966). Evaluation of survival data and two new rank order statistics arising in its consideration. Cancer Chemotherapy Reports 50, 163-170.

Mantel, N., and W. Haenszel (1959). Statistical aspects of the analysis of data from retrospective studies of disease. J. Natl. Cancer Inst. 22, 719-748.

Marquardt, D.L. (1963). An algorithm for least squares estimation of nonlinear parameters. J. Soc. Ind. Appl. Math. 2, 431-441.

Mickey, M.R., and P.M. Britt (1974). Obtaining linear scores from preference pairs. Comm. Statist. 3, 501-511.

Mickey, M.R., O.J. Dunn, and V. Clark (1967). Note on the use of stepwise regression in detecting outliers. Comp. Biomed. Res. 1, 105-111.

Miller, R.G., Jr. (1966). Simultaneous Statistical Inference. New York, McGraw-Hill.

Morris, M.J. (1977). Forecasting the Sunspot Cycle. J. Roy. Statist. Soc. 140, Series A, 437-448.

Morrison, A.S., M.M. Black, C.R. Lowe, B. MacMahon, and S.Y. Yuasa (1973). Some international differences in histology and survival in breast cancer. Intl. J. Cancer 11, 261-267.

Morrison, D.F. (1967). Multivariate Statistical Methods. New York, McGraw-Hill.

Mosteller, F. (1968). Association and estimation of contingency tables. J. Amer. Statist. Assoc. 63, 1-28.

Nelson, W. (1972). Theory and applications of hazard plotting for censored failure data. Technometrics 14, 945-966.

Orchard and Woodbury (1972). A missing information principle: theory and applications. Proc. 6th Berkeley Symp. 1, 697-715.

Pack, D.J. (1977). A Computer Program for the Analysis of Time Series Models Using Box-Jenkins Philosophy. Hatboro, Pennsylvania, Automatic Forecasting System Inc.

Parzen, E. (1963). On spectral analysis with missing observations and amplitude modulation. Sankhya A 25, 180-9.

Pearson, E.S., and H.O. Hartley, eds. (1958). Biometrika Tables for Statisticians, Vol I. Cambridge, University Press.

Pearson, K. (1913). On the probable error of a coefficient of correlation as found from a fourfold table. Biometrika 9, 22-27.

Peduzzi, P., Hardy, R., and Holford, T. (1980). A stepwise variable selection procedure for nonlinear regression models. Biometrics 36, 511-516.

Pike, M.C. (1966). A method of analysis of certain class of experiments in carcinogenesis. Biometrics 22, 142-161.

Plackett (1974). The Analysis of Categorical Data, London, Griffin.

Pratt, J.W. (1964). Robustness of some procedures for the two-sample location problem. J. Amer. Statist. Assoc. 59, 665-680.

Prentice, R.L. (1973). Exponential survivals with censoring and explanatory variables. Biometrika 60, 279-288.

Prescott, P. (1975). An approximate test for outliers in linear regression. Technometrics 17, 129-132.

Ralston, M. and R. Jennrich (1977). Derivative-free nonlinear regression. In Proceedings of Computer Science and Statistics: Tenth Annual Symposium on the Interface. D. Hogben and D. Fife, eds. Washington, D.C., Bureau of Standards, 312-322.

Ralston, M.L., R.I. Jennrich, P.F. Sampson, and F.K. Uno (1979). Fitting pharmacokinetic models with BMDPAR. BMDP Technical Report No. 58, BMDP Statistical Software.

Rao, C. (1955). Estimation and tests of significance in factor analysis. Psychometrika 20, 93-111.

Rao, C.R. (1973). Linear Statistical Inference and its Application. 2nd ed. New York, Wiley.

Rao, C.R. (1972). Estimation of variance and covariance components in linear models. J. Amer. Statist. Assoc. 67, 112-115.

Reinsch, C.H. (1973). Algorithm 464. Eigenvalues of a real, symmetric, tridiagonal matrix. Communications of ACM 16, 689.

Scheffe, H. (1959). The Analysis of Variance. New York, Wiley.

Searle, S.R. (1971). Linear Models. New York, Wiley.

Siegel, S.S. (1956). Nonparametric Statistics for the Behavioral Sciences. New York, McGraw-Hill.

Snedecor, G.W., and W.G. Cochran (1967). Statistical Methods, 6th ed. Ames, Iowa State University Press.

Speed, F.M., and R.R. Hocking (1976). The use of R( )-notation with unbalanced data. Amer. Statist. 30, 30-33.

Spicer, C.C. (1972). Algorithm AS 52. Calculation of power sums of deviations about the mean. Appl. Statist. 21, 226-227.

Svalastoga, K. (1959). Prestige, Class and Mobility. London, Heineman.

Taljedal, I.B., and S. Wold (1970). Fit of some analytic functions to radio-immunoassay standard curves. Biochem. J. 119, 139-143.

Tarone, R.E., and J. Ware (1977). On distribution-free tests for equality of survival distributions. Biometrika 64, 1, 156-160.

Theil, H. (1971). Principles of Economics, New York, Wiley.

Thompson, W., and R. Anderson (1975). A comparison of designs and estimators for the two-stage nested random model. Technometrics 17, 37-44.

Thrall, A. D. (1979). Spectral estimation following simple seasonal adjustment. BMDP Technical Report No. 60, BMDP Statistical Software.

Thrall, A. D. (1980). A spectral analysis of a time series in which probabilities of observation are periodic. In Time Series, O. D. Anderson, ed., North-Holland.

Thrall, A. D. (1982). Computer programming of spectrum estimation. In Handbook of Statistics, 3, Time Series in the Frequency Domain, D. R. Brillinger and P. R. Krishnaiah, eds., North-Holland (in press).

Tiku, M.L. (1971). A note on the distribution of Hotelling's generalized T-zero squared statistic. Biometrika, 58, 237-241.

Toporek, J.D. (1979). Annotated computer output for BMDP4V (URWAS). BMDP Technical Report No. 56, BMDP Statistical Software.

Waldemeir, M. (1961). The Sunspot Activity in the Years 1610-1960. Zurich, Schulthess.

Weisberg, S. (1980). Applied Linear Regression. New York, Wiley.

Wermuth, N. (1976). Model search among multiplicative models. Biometrics 32, 253-264.

Werner, M., R. Tolls, J. Hultin, and J. Mellecker (1970). Sex and age dependence of serum calcium, inorganic phosphorus, total protein, and albumin in a large ambulatory population. In Fifth International Congress on Automation, Advances in Automated Analysis, Vol. 2, 59-65.

Winer, B.J. (1971). Statistical Principles in Experimental Design, 2nd ed. New York, McGraw-Hill.

Woolf, B. (1955). On estimating the relation between blood group and disease. Ann. Hum. Genet. 19, 251-253.

World Weather Records. Smithsonian Miscellaneous Collections, Vols. 79(1927), 90(1934), 105(1947). Washington, D.C., Smithsonian Institute.

Yates, F. (1934). The analysis of multiple classifications with unequal numbers in the different classes. J. Amer. Statist. Assoc. 29, 51-66.

Yuen, K., and W. Dixon (1973). The approximate behavior and performance of the two-sample trimmed T. Biometrika 61, 369-374.

Yuen, K. (1974). The two-sample trimmed T for unequal population variances. Biometrika 61, 165-170.

Index

Control Language Features

- Abbreviations can be used. Here the names are written in upper case letters to denote the letters checked by BMDP and completed with lower case letters to make the name easier to read.

- Variable and group names can be up to 8 characters long; if they contain blanks or special characters or do not begin with a letter they must be enclosed in apostrophes.

- An implied list uses TO and BY for easy specification of a list of equally spaced numbers. (YVAR = 4 TO 10 BY 2 refers to Y variables 4, 6, 8 and 10). Repetition of the same numerical values in a list can be specified by an asterisk (5,1,1,1,1,10,10 is the same as 5,4*1,2*10).

- You can tab directly to a selected item in a list (NAMES = AGE, SEX, (15) WEIGHT, (20) PULSE, PRESSURE gives the names for the 1st, 2nd, 15th, 20th and 21st variables).

- If the first 80-column record of input Control Language contains all digits in columns 73-80 (as generated by IBM TSO and other text editors) only the first 72 columns of subsequent records are interpreted. In general, / CONTROL   COL = #. / END signals the program to read the BMDP control information and any included free-format data input from columns 1 through #. This avoids interference from sequence numbered records. Place / CONTROL as first record.

Free Format Data Input

Type of input is specified in the FORMAT sentence in the / INPUT paragraph:

FORMAT = FREE.   Each case starts on a new record. More than one record can be used for each case, but each case must have the same number of records. (No excess data are allowed on a record).

FORMAT = STREAM   One record can contain more than one case. The only error checks are for bad data and the END-OF-DATA before all variables are read for the last case (see last item below).

FORMAT = SLASH.   One record can contain more than one case. Either a slash or the end of a record must follow the last variable for each case.

Common rules for all free-format modes are:

- Variables are separated by either a blank or a comma.

- Missing values are indicated by either a missing value symbol or multiple commas. The missing value symbol is assumed to be an asterisk, but may be user-defined by an MCHAR sentence in the / INPUT paragraph.

- If two case label variables are specified and appear together, up to eight non-blank characters can be used.

- Fields that have illegal symbols are set to missing. The count of errors is incremented only once for each case, regardless of the number of data errors for that case. The maximum error count is defined by an ERRMAX sentence in the / INPUT paragraph. If the count exceeds the number specified the program stops. The preassigned value for ERRMAX is 10.

- The length for data input records is ordinarily the same as for Control Language input (see / CONTROL.). If the data are read from a different unit than the Control Language, the preassigned record length for data is 80. The record length can be specified in a RECLEN sentence in the / INPUT paragraph.

- END-OF-DATA is indicated by either an END-OF-FILE condition while data are being read, or by an / END paragraph. The required position of / END varies according to the input mode. If END-OF-DATA is indicated by / END, additional Control Language for new problems and subproblems can be specified.